Introduction to
Jurisprudence and Legal Theory
Commentary and Materials

Introduction to

Jurisprudence and Legal Theory
Commentary and Materials

Edited by
James Penner, David Schiff and Richard Nobles

Written by

Anne Barron	*Lecturer in Law, LSE*
Hugh Collins	*Professor in Law, LSE*
Emily Jackson	*Senior Lecturer in Law, LSE*
Nicola Lacey	*Professor of Criminal Law,LSE*
Richard Nobles	*Reader in Law, LSE*
James Penner	*Senior Lecturer in Law,LSE*
Robert Reiner	*Professor of Criminology,LSE*
Hamish Ross	*Senior Lecturer in Law, Napier University, sometime Lecturer in Law, LSE*
David Schiff	*Reader in Law,LSE*
Gunther Teubner	*Professor of Private Law and Legal Socialogy, University of Frankfurt, Visiting Centennial Professor, LSE*

OXFORD
UNIVERSITY PRESS

OXFORD
UNIVERSITY PRESS

Great Clarendon Street, Oxford OX2 6DP

Oxford University Press is a department of the University of Oxford.
It furthers the University's objective of excellence in research, scholarship,
and education by publishing worldwide in

Oxford New York

Auckland Cape Town Dar es Salaam Hong Kong Karachi Kuala Lumpur
Madrid Melbourne Mexico City Nairobi New Delhi Shanghai Taipei Toronto

With offices in

Argentina Austria Brazil Chile Czech Republic France Greece
Guatemala Hungary Italy Japan South Korea Poland Portugal
Singapore Switzerland Thailand Turkey Ukraine Vietnam

Oxford is a registered trade mark of Oxford University Press
in the UK and in certain other countries

Published in the United States
by Oxford University Press Inc., New York

British Library Cataloguing in Publication Data
Data available

Library of Congress Cataloging in Publication Data
Data available

ISBN: 978-0-406-94678-2

5 7 9 10 8 6

Printed in Great Britain by
CPI Antony Rowe
Chippenham, Wilts.

Preface

It is no easy exercise to teach or study jurisprudence or legal theory today, which is perhaps indicated by the use of both 'jurisprudence' and 'legal theory' in the title to this book. Although at a very general level this subject can be characterised as the activity of producing theories about law, 'jurisprudence' now includes a large variety of such theories – many of them highly sophisticated, some with a long history of elaboration and refinement, and all to a greater or lesser extent at odds with each other. Moreover, the body of writings, which tend to be gathered together under the heading of jurisprudence, is related in complicated ways to other theoretical traditions that are not primarily concerned with the law at all, but with justice; morality or ethics; language; culture; the economy; power; or society in general. The readings offered to you in this book reflect that complexity.

This book is directed toward those who have been studying law for at least a year or two without exploring the interconnectedness between its various subject areas and these other traditions. The readings presented here will expose you to arguments and terminology that may bear little relationship to anything you will have read before. You should not however conclude that these materials are separated by such a large distance from everything else that you have studied so far on your degree course that jurisprudence is akin to a foreign language. Nor should you treat it as a subject which has no practical relevance whatsoever to learning the law, and one which you will never (you hope) need to consider again. Jurisprudence should not leave you with the general impression that jurisprudential or theoretical talk about law is attractively 'deep and meaningful', but impenetrable to all but the professional scholar, and ultimately irrelevant to the routine study and practice of law. However, the fact that some students are left with such negative impressions is at least partially a result of the available teaching materials which, we believe, could be made more accessible and coherent. Our response is this book.

Within an undergraduate degree, jurisprudence offers students an opportunity to consider what, other than an aggregation of discrete courses and laws, they have been studying. Properly understood, it can help to locate the nature of those courses (their content, materials, arguments, approaches, etc) within a larger map of intellectual interests. Properly taught, it is accessible.

Any attempt to represent the current range of important theories about law is bound to be complex, and there can be no excuse for making a demanding subject easier than it is. However, what we attempt in this book is to communicate jurisprudential insights in a way which *both* does justice to their complexity *and* renders them accessible to undergraduate students. Jurisprudence and legal theory is undoubtedly more difficult for some students than others, and having a good grasp of substantive law is no guarantee of success here: there are brilliant lawyers who are very poor theorists, and vice versa. Our concern about accessibility is not to try to make the issues easier than they are: our concern is to provide you with a way of grasping these difficult issues so that you can think about them critically for yourselves. With a bit of perseverance you will find yourself thinking thoughts and, even better, *assessing* thoughts, that are the painstaking results of the most committed efforts by serious and important intellectuals.

At present, faced with the inaccessibility of many texts of, or on, jurisprudence, many students take refuge in a simple summary, often of the 'nutshell' variety, which seeks to reduce the theories taught in most jurisprudence courses to a more digestible form. Such summaries, when well executed, can make a certain kind of knowledge about the subject reasonably accessible. With their help, students can teach themselves to recognise the broad features of different jurisprudential schools; list the main arguments characteristic of each of them and the major criticisms that could be made against these arguments; and repeat the examples used by each theorist and by leading critics to illustrate these arguments and criticisms. Yet these texts, helpful though they may seem to be, tend to reduce jurisprudence to a collection of propositions and ideas which students may claim, quite rightly, has no relevance to the rest of their studies. This is because students who have learned jurisprudence from nutshell texts will often see no link whatsoever between jurisprudence and their other law subjects: since it has only been absorbed as packaged nuggets of information about particular legal theories, jurisprudence can quite reasonably be seen as information that will never be used again. Texts which generate this impression of the subject cannot be said to succeed as jurisprudence texts.

On the other hand, that is no reason to make jurisprudence more difficult, and less accessible, than it needs to be – by assuming, for example, that the student is already 'au fait' with all the latest developments and controversies in the subject. If jurisprudence succeeds as a pedagogical project, then it does so by developing the capacity to engage meaningfully with, and reflect critically upon, theoretical discourses in which law is the main, or a major, focus. This book hopes to encourage you to find routes to, and achieve standards of, engagement and reflection. In particular, we seek to overcome two ways in which you may be left uneducated by jurisprudence.

First, while some (note *some*) nutshells may provide you with more or less sound summaries of jurisprudence, you will not feel that you have mastered the subject if the original materials remain impenetrable to you. Commentary should offer you a guide to the reading of these materials, a means to decipher them for yourselves, rather than serve as a substitute for such reading. Even the best nutshells can only operate as short cuts, which at the same time short-circuit the student's capacity to engage with theoretical arguments, follow their logic, spot their incoherence and develop alternatives. Second, as well as being able to summarise jurisprudence materials for yourselves, if you understand the subject you should be able to apply it. This can be likened to asking you to treat theories like different pairs of spectacles and to put them on to see how the world looks from a particular perspective. For example, you could be asked to look at the rest of your law subjects and to consider what the theory does when it is applied to them. One of the most obvious indicators that you have summarised a theory without understanding it is if you end up describing that theory using the same examples as those chosen by the theorists to illustrate their work. Students who write essays on HLA Hart, for example, typically refer to section 9 of the Wills Act 1837 as an example of what Hart calls a 'power conferring rule', and to the game of chess to illustrate what he means by 'social rules' and 'internal point of view'. Those writing on Dworkin typically refer to the Charles Dickens' novel *A Christmas Carol*, and the New York Court of Appeals decision, *Riggs v Palmer*, to illustrate what Dworkin means by 'interpretation', a 'hard case' and 'principles'. If you have really engaged with Hart and Dworkin, you should be able to use any novel or game, or any legal rule drawn from any area of law, to make the same points (*Animal Farm, Harry Potter and the Prisoner of Azkaban, Captain Corelli's Mandolin* or Monopoly, Table Tennis, Football). To draw an analogy with the process of learning substantive law, students who merely memorise rules do not understand their subject. To understand what the rule means one has to be able to apply it to a fresh situation.

There may be a number of reasons why you may fail to progress beyond memorising other people's summaries of legal theories. However, one of the major reasons, and the impetus for this book, is that the available texts that combine materials and commentary are insufficiently accessible for undergraduate law students. Many self-described 'undergraduate' texts, which began life as shorter books seeking to engage undergraduate law students, have grown into much larger books containing a sophisticated and dense commentary accompanying a selection of extremely difficult materials.

In the commentaries and materials that make up this book, we aim to offer you an opportunity to explore with us some (not all) important theories of law. The first part of the book introduces what we think are foundational theories. They are foundational in the sense that they loosely represent the historical development of jurisprudential thought. The second part of the book introduces current extensions and negations of these foundational theories. Each section aims to assist you in reaching a point where you can not only summarise the selected theories, or the criticisms that have been made of them, but can also begin to understand the implications of each perspective for the enterprise in which you are engaged: the study of law. You will see that some theories intend not only to explain but also to discredit the law as a legitimate practice. Give all of the theories their due. They would not be presented here if their intellectual merit, their power to compel assent (however hesitant), were so insubstantial that they could rightly be ignored. The purpose of this subject is not to make you happy, to give you a deeper sense of complacency that the world and all within it – in particular the legal system – is well. The essence of this kind of subject is to allow you to experience the power, perhaps even the joy, of flexing your brain cells with a view to revealing to yourself something significant about the world you cannot but live in. Our project is to enable you to reflect on many contemporary questions that circumscribe law, the legal system, and the enterprise that law seems to be involved in, in the modern world. It proceeds from our own involvement in teaching jurisprudence at a particular institution, the LSE.

One final caveat. Jurisprudence should not be viewed as a tournament in which the strongest or 'best' theory will beat all opponents and win the title. To remind you of the request to put on 'spectacles', what you are likely to end up with is a series of different views, none of which is complete, and all of which are flawed. The point is that you still see more, and better, than with your eyes closed.

Part I

There are 10 chapters. They are arranged as follows. First an introductory chapter. Then a chapter discussing and describing natural law theories. There follows three chapters on theories of legal positivism: early analytical positivism, the theory of HLA Hart and the theory of Hans Kelsen. Next come two chapters as examples of what can broadly be described as realist theories: one general, in the form of classical social theories and their understanding of the nature and function of law and the other more specific concentrating on modern American jurisprudence. The next two chapters deal with the writings of Ronald Dworkin and his critics, and chapter 10 looks at several current debates. These writings contain elements or at least insights from all of the main jurisprudential traditions: natural law, legal positivism and realism.

It is inevitable that there is a large amount of selectivity in deciding which writings by which theorist are explored in each chapter. As mentioned earlier, there is no attempt to be comprehensive – indeed, quite the opposite. None of the theories are explored in order to cover all that they have to say about law, or any part of it. None of them is criticised as fully as they are criticised by their critics. But you are given an opportunity to enter into the ways of thinking represented by these different traditions of scholarship, to be able to understand enough so that you could, if you wished, continue with your explorations and develop your thinking further.

Part II

Such further exploration and thinking will be engaged in, in the course of the second part of the book. During such engagement your background knowledge and understanding of jurisprudential theories will be tested. You will be asked to consider topics that represent examples of extensions or negations of the background theoretical traditions developed in Part I. Although we have included 10 chapters representing 10 topics, in Part II your jurisprudence teacher(s) may decide not to teach all of these topics, but to concentrate on a smaller number, perhaps even just one. The negations chapters are by no means easy and some part of the task of teaching them or studying them is taken up with learning how they say things, as much as what they have to say. There is a reason for this. At least four of the five negations chapters can be classified as anti-jurisprudence. In saying what they want to say, they are concerned to find a way to speak which, in confronting the paradigms of other theories, cannot complacently accept conventional forms of academic speech.

Parts I and II

The division between Parts I and II of the book represent our judgement about the best way to approach teaching and studying a course on jurisprudence and legal theory. Without an adequate background many of the fruitful debates engendered within the discipline are inadequately contextualised. These concerns are reflected in the division between the different parts of the book. Part I should provide enough breadth of coverage for adequate foundation and context, and Part II provides an opportunity for deeper analysis and thought.

A Health Warning on reading and further reading

You may ask, how much of each chapter do I need to read? Some are longer than others are. Some contain rather difficult extracts (difficult in a number of ways; for example, some were written many centuries ago). We should be explicit about what we have done. Our aim has been to include enough in the extracts to allow you to read for yourselves what the writer has to say, and what the theory is about. Our commentaries and questions are designed to try to help you with this. You need to read all of the commentary and materials. If this is not possible in a particular week, read all of the commentary and skim-read as much of the materials as possible, then go back later and complete the reading.

You may also wonder, what further reading should I undertake? Your teachers should guide you in this. However, subject to such advice, one of the most important 'further reading' to be done is to re-read the chapter, look at your class and lecture notes, and have an imaginary debate with the authors of the text. How would you explain, or criticise, their positions? How would other authors from this book criticise their positions? Unless you have reached this level of understanding, lists of further reading may represent a distraction ('I would like to read more rather than understand what is here') or a discouragement ('Oh my god, even if I understood all this, there is a further list of things that I ought to read').

Nevertheless, if you have understood the commentary and extracts, there is always more that can be read. Each chapter (after the first) will list a few extra works which ought to take your understanding of the issues a little further.

A Health Warning on other basic introductory texts

The commentary and extracts in this book are not easy to understand. There will be a temptation to turn to other introductory texts as an addition, or alternative, to struggling with this one. Be careful. If this book forms the basis of your course, familiarity with other books, which will often be presenting authors and theories in general, will not equal a successful understanding of the issues and materials which your teacher has selected for you to study. If you go to other introductions, make sure that you come back to this book. If your excursion makes this book more accessible to you, only then is it worthwhile.

The production of this book would have been impossible without the generosity of others who read and commented on drafts, helped in the location of sources, and gave guidance and assistance in other ways; the editors and writers would like to thank Julie Dickson, Ronald Dworkin, Timothy Endicott, Stephen Guest, Mike Redmayne, Stephanie Roberts, Declan Roche, Richard Samuels, Nicos Stavropoulos; finally, we would all express our immense gratitude to the 2001-2002 jurisprudence students at the LSE – on whom we tested the prototype of this book and whose responses and comments were invaluable.

James Penner

David Schiff

Richard Nobles

September 2002

Contents

Introducing Part II – Extensions and Negations   475

Acknowledgments

The publishers and authors wish to thank the following for permission to reprint material from the sources indicated The publishers would also be pleased to hear from those copyright holders from whom copyright permission has been sought but not yet received.

Aspen:

* Posner, R (1998) *Economic Analysis of Law* (5th ed, New York: Aspen).

Barron:

* A Barron: 'The Illusions on the "I": Citizenship and the Politics of Identity' in ' A Norrie (ed) *Closure or Critique: New Directions in Legal Theory*, Edinburgh: Edinburgh University Press, 1993. Reprinted by permission of the author.

Basic books:

* From *Justice, Gender and the Family* by Susan Moller Okin. Copyright © 1989 by Basic Books Inc. Reprinted by permission of Basic Books, a member of Perseus Books, LLC.

Blackwell:

* Nozick, R *Anarchy, State and Utopia* 1974. Copyright 1974 by Blackwell Publishers Ltd.

* Bentham J *Concluding footnote* to *An Introduction to the Principles of Morals and Legislation* 1789. Now set out in Bentham, Jeremy *A Fragment on Government and An Introduction to the Principles of Morals and Legislation* 1948. Copyright 1948 by Blackwell Publishers Ltd.

* Lacey, N, 'Theory into Practice: Pornography and the Public/Private Dichotomy' in Bottomley, A and Conaghan, J eds *Feminist Theory and Legal Strategy* 1993. Copyright 1993 by Blackwell Publishers Ltd.

- Aquinas, *Selected Political Writings* (translated by J G Dawson) 1959. Copyright 1959 by Blackwell Publishers Ltd.

- Conaghan, J, 'Reassessing the Feminist Theoretical Project in Law' 27 *Journal of Law and Society* 2000. Copyright 2000 by Blackwell Publishers Ltd.

- Luhmann, N, 'The Third Question: The Creative Use of Paradoxes in Law and Legal History' 15 *Journal of Law and Society* 1988. Copyright by Blackwell Publishers Ltd.

- Collins, H, 'The Decline of Privacy in Private Law' 14 *Journal of Law and Society* 1987. Copyright by Blackwell Publishers Ltd.

- Albrow, M, 'Legal Positivism and Bourgeois Materialism: Max Weber's View of the Sociology of Law' 2 *British Journal of Law and Society* 1975. Copyright by Blackwell Publishers Ltd.

- Unger, RM, 'Legal Analysis as Institutional Imagination' 59 *Modern Law Review* 1996. Copyright by Blackwell Publishers Ltd.

California Law Review:

- Raz, J (1986) 'Dworkin: A New Link in the Chain' 74 *California Law Review* (1986).

- Raz, J (1971) ' The Authority of Law: Essays on Law and Morality. *California Law Review* (1971)

Cambridge Law Journal:

- Simmonds '*Why Conventionalism Does Not Collapse Into Pragmatism*' 1990 49 *Cambridge Law Journal.* Reproduced by permission of the Cambridge Law Journal.

Cambridge University Press:

- James E G Zetzel, ed '*Circero, On the Commonwealth and On the Laws*' 1999. Reproduced by permission of Cambridge University Press.

- B. Reiner, ' Crime, Law and Deviance: The Durkheim Legacy' in S Fenton *Durkheim and Modern Sociology* 1984. Reproduced by permission of Cambridge University Press.

- Honneth, A 'The Other of Justice: Jurgen Habermas and the Ethical Challenge of Postmodernism' in SK White ed *The Cambridge Companion to Habermas* 1995. Reproduced by permission of Cambridge University Press.

Collins Publishers:

- Dworkin, R (1986) *Law's Empire.* © Copyright Collins publishers 1986.

Continuum:

- Irigaray: '*Thinking the Difference: For a Peaceful Revolution,* Athlone Press 1994. Reprinted by permission of Athlone Press.

Cotterell, Roger

- Roger Cotterell, '*The Sociology of Law*' Butterworths 1992. Reproduced by permission of the author.

- Roger Cotterell, *'The Politics of Jurisprudence: A Critical Introduction to Legal Philosophy'* Butterworths 1989. Reproduced by permission of the author.

Duckworth:

- Dworkin, R, 'Taking Rights Seriously' (1977) published by Gerald Duckworth and Company Ltd.

Dworkin:

- Dworkin, R (1980) 'Is Wealth a Value?' 9 *Journal of Legal Studies*. Reprinted by permission of the author.

Edward Arnold:

- MacCormick, N (1981) *HLA Hart* (London: Edward Arnold), 32-40.

Fuller:

- Fuller, LL (1940) *The Law In Quest Of Itself* (Boston: Beacon Press).

Georges Borchardt Inc:

- Foucault, M (1980) 'Two Lectures' in *Power/Knowledge* (ed C Gordon, London: Harvester). © Georges Bordchardt, Inc.

Hans Kelsen-Institut:

- Kelsen, H (1967) *Pure Theory of Law* (2nd ed, translated by M Knight, California: University of California Press). © Hans Kelsen-Instutut.

Harcourt:

- Olsen, F (1990) 'Feminism and Critical Legal Theory: An American Perspective' 18 *International Journal of the Sociology of Law* 199-201. Harcourt Inc.

HarperCollins:

- B A O Williams, 1985 *Ethics and the Limits of Philosophy*. Reprinted by permission of HarperCollins Publishers Ltd. © BAO Williams, 1985.

Hart:

- Emily Jackson: *Regulating Reproduction: Law, Technology and Autonomy* 2001. Reprinted by permission of Hart Publishing Ltd.

- Nicola Lacey: *Unspeakable Subjects* 1998. Reprinted by permission of Hart Publishing Ltd.

Harvard Law Review:

- Lon Fuller: *'The Case of the Speluncean Explorers'* Harvard Law Review 1949 vol 62. Copyright © 1949 by the Harvard Law Review Association.

- Polinsky AM *'Economic Analysis as a Potentially Defective Product: a Buyer's guide to Posner's Economic Analysis of Law'* 1974 Harvard Law Review vol 87. Copyright © 1974 by the Harvard Law Review Association.

- Frug, Gerald: 'The Ideology of Bureaucracy in American Law' (1984) 97 Harvard Law Review. Copyright © 1984 by the Harvard Law Review Association.

- Unger, Roberto Mangabeira: *'The Critical Legal Studies Movement'* (1983) 96 Harvard Law Review. Copyright © 1983 by the Harvard Law Review Association.

- Dworkin: *'Hard Cases'* (1975) 88 Harvard Law Review. Copyright © 1975 by the Harvard Law Review Association.

- Hart, HLA 'Positivism and the Separation of Law and Morals' 71 *Harvard Law Review* (1958). Copyright by the Harvard Law Review Association.

Harvard University Press:

- Mackinnon, Catherine *Toward a Feminist Theory of the State* 1989. Copyright 1989 by the Harvard University Press.

- Gilligan, Carol *In a Different Voice* 1982. Copyright 1982 by the Harvard University Press.

- Posner, R *The Problems of Jurisprudence* 1990. Copyright 1990 by the Harvard University Press.

- Williams, Patricia *The Alchemy of Race and Rights* 1991. Copyright 1991 by the Harvard University Press.

- Dworkin *A Matter of Principle* 1985. Copyright 1985 by the Harvard University Press.

Hutchinson:

- D'Entreves, AP (1970) *Natural Law: an introduction to legal philosophy* (2nd revised ed, London: Hutchinson).

Kluwer:

- JE Penner (1997), *Hohfeldian Use-Right in Property*, in Harris (ed) 1998 ' Property Problems: From Genes to Pension Funds, London Kluwer 1998. Reprinted with kind permission of Kluwer Law International.

Kluwer Academic Publishers:

- Finnis, J (1987) 'On Reason and Authority in Law's Empire' 6 *Law and Philosophy* 6, Kluwer Academic Publishers 1987. Reprinted with kind permission of Kluwer Academic Publishers.

Law Book Co Information Services:

- Davies, M (1994) *Asking The Law Question* © Law Book Co Information Services.

Lawrence and Wishart:

- K Marx, Preface to *'A Contribution to the Critique of Political Economy'* in *Marx and Engels Selected Works* 1968. Reprinted by permission of Lawrence & Wishart.

Little Brown:

- Polinsky, A (1989) *An Introduction to Law and Economics* (2nd ed, Boston: Little Brown).

Nigel Simmonds:

- Simmonds, *The Decline of Juridical Reason* (Manchester: Manchester University Press) 1984. Reproduced by permission of the author.

McGraw-Hill:

- Cleaver, E (1992 ed) *Soul on Ice,* McGraw-Hill Education.

The Monist:

- Raz, J: Ethics in the Public Domain: Essays in the Morality of Law and Politics 1994. Published by The Monist, 68/3 (1985)

Naffine, Ngaire:

- *'In Praise of Legal Feminism'* Legal Studies [2002] 1 New York Aspen

Northwestern University Law Review:

- Luhmann: *'Law as a Social System'* Northwestern University Law Review 1989 (83). Reprinted by permission of Northwestern University Law Review.

Notre Dame Press:

- From *The Treatise on Law,* by Thomas Aquinas, translated by R J Hente. Copyright 1993 by University of Notre Dame Press. Used by permission.

Nottingham Law Journal:

- Ross H (2001) *Social Power and the Hohfeldian Relation'* 10 (1) Nottingham Law Journal. Reprinted by permission of the Nottingham Law Journal.

Oxford University Press:

- © 1977, Christie: *'Conflicts as Property'* British Journal of Criminology (1977) Vol 17 pp1-13 reprinted by permission of Oxford University Press.

- © Copyright 1971 by the President and Fellows of Harvard College. Reprinted from *A Theory of Justice* by John Rawls (1972) by permission of Oxford University Press.

- © Hugh Collins 1982. Reprinted from *Marxism and Law* by Hugh Collins (1982) by permission of Oxford University Press.

- © John Finnis 1980. Reprinted from *Natural Law and Natural Rights* by John Finnis (1980) by permission of Oxford University Press.

- Reprinted from *Law, Society and Economy: Centenary Essays for the London School of Economics and Political Science 1895-1995* edited by Richard Rawlings (1997) by permission of Oxford University Press.

- © Joseph Raz 1979. Reprinted from *The Authority of Law: Essays on Law and Morality* by Joseph Raz (1979) by permission of Oxford University Press.

- © Jules L Coleman 2001. Reprinted from *The Practice of Principle: In Defence of a Pragmatist Approach to Legal Theory* by Jules L Coleman (2001) by permission of Oxford University Press.

Prospect:

- B Rodgers, 'John Rawls' *Prospect* Issue 42, June 1999, pp 50-55

Raz:

- Raz, J (1981) 'The Purity of the Pure Theory' 138 *Revue Internationale de Philosophie* 441: 442-453. Reproduced by permission of the author.

Routledge:

- Copyright 1991. From *Black Feminist Thought: Knowledge, Consciousness and the Politics of Empowerment* by Patricia Hill Collins. Reproduced by permission of Routledge Inc, part of the Taylor & Francis Group.

- Copyright 1990. H Thoreau *On the Duty of Civil disobediance,* from *Civil Disobediance in Focus* by H Bedau. Reproduced by permission of Routledge Inc, part of the Taylor & Francis Group.

- Copyright 1993. From *Transformations: Recollective Imagination and Sexual Difference* by Drucilla Cornell. Reproduced by permission of Routledge Inc, part of the Taylor & Francis Group.

- Copyright 1992. From *The Mythology of Modern Law* by P Fitzpatrick. Reproduced by permission of Routledge Inc, part of the Taylor & Francis Group.

- Copyright 1989. From *Feminism and the Power of Law* by Carol Smart. Reproduced by permission of Routledge Inc, part of the Taylor & Francis Group.

Sage Publications Inc:

- Sandel, M, 'The Procedural Republic and the Unencumbered Self' 12 *Political Theory* pp 81- 96, copyright © 1984 by Sage Publications. Reprinted by permission of Sage Publications, Inc.

Sage Publications Ltd:

- Kapur, R, 'A Love Song to Our Mongrel Selves: Hybridity, Sexuality and the Law', 1999, *Social and Legal Studies,* pp 357-358. © Sage Publications Ltd 1999. Reprinted by permission of Sage Publications Ltd.

- Harris, A, 'Building Theory, Building Community', 1999, *Social and Legal Studies,* copyright © Sage Publications Ltd 1999. Reprinted by permission of Sage Publications Ltd.

Stanford Law Review:

- Kelsen, H (1965) 'Professor Stone and the Pure Theory of Law' 17 *Stanford Law Review.*

- Kelman, M (1981) 'Interpretive Construction in the Substantive Criminal Law' 33 *Stanford Law Review.*

Sweet and Maxwell:

- Hart, HLA (1954) 'Definition and Theory in Jurisprudence' 70 *Law Quarterly Review* 37: 37-41, 45-48, 56-59. Reproduced by permission of Sweet and Maxwell.

Texas Law Review:

- Fish, S (1982) 'Working on the Chain Gang: Interpretation in Law and Literature' 60 *Texas Law Review*

Tulane Law Review:

- Honoré, AM (1960) 'Rights of Exclusion and Immunities against Divesting' 34 Tulane Law Review 453: 453-467. © 2002 by the Tulane Law Review Association

UCLA:

- HLA Hart, 'Kelsen Visited'. Originally published in 10 UCLA L Rev 709 (1963)

- Richard Wasserstrom, 'The Obligation to Obey the Law'. Originally published in 10 UCLA L Rev 780. Copyright 1963, The Regents of the University of California. All Rights Reserved

University of California Press:

- Max Weber, 'Economy and Society', Published by the University of California Press. Reproduced by permission of the University of California Press.

University of Chicago Press:

- Duff, RA (1996) 'Penal Communications: Recent Work in the Philosophy of Punishment' in M Tonry (ed) Crime and Justice: A Review of Criminal Research, Vol 20 (Chicago: University of Chicago Press), 1-97. © 1996 by The University of Chicago. All rights reserved Reproduced by permission of the University of Chicago Press.

- MacKinnon, C (1983) 'Feminism, Marxism, Method and the State: Towards Feminist Jurisprudence' 8 *Signs: Journal of Women in Culture and Society.* © 1983 by The University of Chicago. All rights reserved Reproduced be permission of the University of Chicago Press.

- Foucault, M (1991) 'Governmentality' in G. Burchell, C. Gordon and P. Miller (eds.) *The Foucault Effect.* © 1991 by The University of Chicago. Reproduced by permission of The University of Chicago Press.

University of Chicago Legal Forum:

- Crenshaw, K (1989) 'Demarginalizing the Intersection of Race and Sex: A Black Feminist Critique of Antidiscrimination Doctrine, Feminist Theory and Antiracist Politics'. The University of Chicago Press.

University of Chicago Law Review:

- West, R (1988) 'Jurisprudence and Gender' 55 *University of Chicago Law Review.*

University of Toronto:

- Trebilcock, M (1976) 'The doctrine of inequality of bargaining power: Post-Benthamite Economics in the House of Lords' 26 *University of Toronto Law Journal*

- Brudner, A (1980) 'Retribution and the Death Penalty' 30 *University of Toronto Law Journal*

University of Western Ontario:

- Joseph Raz, 'Ethics in the Public Domain: Essays in the Morality of Law and Politics', University of Western Ontario Law Review, 21 (1983). Reproduced with permission from the University of Western Ontario.

Virginia Law Review:

- Leff, A (1974) 'Economic Analysis of Law: Some Realism about Nominalism' 60 *Virginia Law Review* 451.

Yale Law Journal:

- Raz, J (1972) 'Legal Principles and the Limits of Law'. Reprinted by permission of The Yale Law Journal Company and William S Hein Company from The Yale Law Journal, Vol 81. Pages 823-854

- Smith, M (1973) 'Is There A Prima Facie Obligation To Obey The Law? Reprinted by permission of The Yale Law Journal Company and William S Hein Company from The Yale Law Journal, Vol 82, pp 950-976.

- Hohfeld, WN (1923) *Fundamental Legal Conceptions: as applied in judicial reasoning.* Reprinted by permission from The Yale Law Journal, and William S Hein Company from The Yale Law Journal, Vol 23 pp 25-31.

Yale University Press:

- Fuller, Lon L, (1969) *The Morality of Law* © 1964 by Yale University, Revised copyright edition © 1969 by Yale University, published by Yale University Press.

Yale Journal of Law and Feminism:

- Nedelsky, J (1989) 'Reconceiving Autonomy: Sources, Thoughts and Possibilities' *Yale Journal of Law and Feminism.*

Part I

1 Approaches to Jurisprudence, Legal Theory, and the Philosophy of Law

James Penner, David Schiff, Richard Nobles

Approaching Jurisprudence[1]

Whatever the title of this book or other books on jurisprudence, the subject matter and issues addressed here have fallen under different names, by far the most common being 'jurisprudence', 'legal theory', and 'the philosophy of law'. These names reflect different theoretical perspectives, different political orientations, and more generally, different interests giving rise to different sorts of questions that may be posed about law, or about matters related to law. While it is impossible to specify precisely the orientation of 'jurisprudence', or 'legal theory' and/or 'the philosophy of law', as a matter of rough representation we can say the following.

Jurisprudence is 'Law' with a capital 'L'. It is not the law of any particular subject area (contract, crime, property etc) or even, apparently, the law of any particular country. It attempts to analyse law at its most general level, to identify what is important and significant rather than what is mundane and inessential. Those who write jurisprudence do not give answers to questions about what particular laws, or laws on particular subjects, are. Rather, they explore what it might mean to say that a particular rule is the law of this or that particular legal system, for example, or they might try to explain what it is to have legal rights or legal duties or, to take a third example, might specify what

---

1   With the emphasis in this book on teaching the subject, it is worth noting the place of jurisprudence within the law curriculum. A leading theorist has recently made the following claim: 'Perhaps jurisprudence has a moderately secure place in undergraduate law curricula in the UK at present – after much controversy and many local skirmishes in university law departments. If this is so, it is because it is thought to offer something important that other law school courses cannot or do not offer. But the nature of this 'something' and how important it is are far from clear ... teachers of jurisprudence themselves give a wide variety of views about the purpose of the subject. Yet the vast majority consider that it "makes students think about the nature of law" or "gives a broader perspective" on law as "an important social activity". (Barnett 1995, 107) This suggests that jurisprudence presents material to inspire this radical thinking and provide this broadening of view.' (Cotterrell 2000, 179)

sort of reasoning judges and lawyers in any legal system engage in when they decide cases or advise clients.

In this way, jurisprudence explores what is *implicit* in a lawyer's understanding of law that forms the background assumptions or beliefs he or she has when 'doing law'. (And, as such, helps the lawyer to be in a better position to justify his or her practice. As Northrop (1959, 6) has stated: 'In Law, as in other things, we shall find that the only difference between a person "without a philosophy" and someone with a philosophy is that the latter knows what his philosophy is, and is, therefore, more able to make clear and justify the premises that are implicit in his statement of the facts of his experience and his judgment about those facts.') Jurisprudential questions, while 'theoretical', are the sorts of questions about 'the nature of law' to which any lawyer or judge might be expected to provide a reasonably intelligent answer, though not one which couldn't be challenged, especially by other lawyers. Lawyers have different views, for example, about whether the law really administers 'justice'. Laypersons, of course, can often provide intelligent answers as well, but the point is that knowledge of the law and how it works is an important source of ideas and critical assessment of the questions jurisprudence asks, and the more knowledge of, or perhaps, familiarity one has with the actual workings of the law, the better. If jurisprudence explores what it means to give answers to these sorts of questions, then it follows that all law students implicitly **do** jurisprudence. They do so in the sense that the materials that they have read and have had to deal with in the course of their degrees are informed by, or represent different positions within, the range of answers that might be given to these questions, answers which rival theories of jurisprudence might challenge or support. Usually, such positions are not formally articulated and their implications not fully explored until a jurisprudence course is undertaken. Jurisprudence aims to make the implicit explicit, and the unconscious self-conscious.

But making sense of how lawyers (including law students) think about law, is only part of the enterprise. Law cannot be reduced to the practices and knowledge of lawyers. Law is experienced and thought about by non-lawyers in quite different ways. 'The Law' as experienced by the socially excluded cannot be reduced to doctrines, cases and statutes; or rather to reduce it in this way is simply to edit out much of what others have experienced of law. Similar observations can be made with respect to other academic disciplines. Sociologists and political scientists have things to say about law, the nature of its authority and its role in society, but little of what they describe and analyse refers to law as it is learned and understood by lawyers. The traditional focus of jurisprudence, lawyers' understanding of law, what Stone calls 'the lawyer's extraversion' (1950, 25) can usefully be contrasted with 'legal theory'. The latter makes no such claim to reveal the underlying but implicit lawyer's knowledge of the law *as such*. Legal theory embraces, rather, theorising about law *as such*. It might properly be regarded as the most freewheeling perspective on the questions raised by this book, and many legal theorists intentionally seek to unseat the lawyer's self-understanding of the law. What unites legal theorists is that they take law, or indeed theorising about law, as a point of departure for exploring any and all types of issues, of many different kinds. Feminist, economic, Marxist, psychoanalytic perspectives are all here, as is treating law as a kind of literary enterprise, a social institution best understood from a shared language perspective, and so on.

Although some describe jurisprudence as the philosophy of law, the philosophy of law is not the whole of jurisprudence or legal theory, although it is often implicated in both of these enterprises. (The terms jurisprudence, legal theory and philosophy of law tend to be used interchangeably. Sometimes the philosophy of law is employed to convey a meaning that includes the 'narrower' concerns of jurisprudence and legal theory, such as the meaning presented by Roscoe Pound (1954). Sometimes legal theory is given priority (see Kelly, 1992). There is no magic in any particular use, only in the purpose to which that use is put.) The philosophy of law is grounded in the traditions of one branch of knowledge, that of philosophy. In the same way that philosophy departments have moral philosophers, political philosophers, philosophers of mathematics and philosophers of physics, so they might include philosophers of law. Philosophers of law pursue philosophically interesting issues that law raises, and share much of their turf with moral and political philosophers. The sort of things they worry about are often the principal concerns of these other kinds of philosophers: the nature of authority, the nature of obligation and consent, the nature of freedom and responsibility, the way rules work, and so on. Philosophers of law and jurisprudents may appear to resemble each other more than either of them resembles legal theorists. This is so because, as Simmonds (1986, v) points out, jurisprudence is philosophical: '... jurisprudence shares a basic characteristic with other philosophical inquiries: it is self-reflective, in that its questions include questions about its own nature and status as a subject.' However, there is a significant difference in perspective. Philosophers of law don't think the practice of philosophising about law has any necessary connection with legal practice, but jurisprudents often do. A philosopher of law doesn't necessarily think learning any legal philosophy will make you a better lawyer, any more than learning any philosophy of physics will make you a better physicist. The practice of law is one thing; exploring the philosophically interesting features of that practice is another. Of course, doing legal philosophy, or jurisprudence or legal theory for that matter, will require you to make and assess arguments. And getting better at that will undoubtedly make you more practically intelligent, and that should make you a better lawyer (and a better politician, parent, consumer, or anything else which requires practical intelligence), but only in this indirect way.

One of the questions posed for you, by the range of materials presented in this book, is whether you are best suited to taking a jurisprudential, legal theoretical, or legal philosophical perspective. Doing a jurisprudence course is an excellent way to measure your own intellectual personality – to what sorts of problems and issues are you particularly drawn, and perhaps more importantly, what sorts of problems and issues, for one reason or another, are you prone to downplay or discount, and why? It is important at least to consider whether these particular aspects of your thought are the result of insufficient education, inadequate sympathy, or rank prejudice.

Beginning to think about Jurisprudence

Although Part I of this book, as you will see, may reasonably be seen as incorporating jurisprudential, legal theoretical, and philosophical perspectives, to call Part I an exploration of 'jurisprudence' as characterised above, is probably a fair assessment. Part I principally addresses questions about the nature of law. In so doing it makes demands of you to think seriously about the understanding of law you have gleaned from doing a law degree so far, from learning what it is to think as a lawyer, as someone who might practice law.

That, you may be disheartened to learn, does not mean Part I lets you off the hook. Original thinking is required as much here as in Part II. Consider the following. A typical jurisprudence exam question asks you to: 'Distinguish (a) a Law (b) the Law (c) Law (d) Laws.' How, pray, do you think you will deal with that? The only basic advice to be offered (we will return to a closer analysis of this question immediately) is that you must not forswear what you have learned about the nature of law in your study of the subject so far. You've read cases. You've looked at statutes. You've written essays giving what, according to you, is 'the better view' of the law where it is currently unsettled. For heaven's sake, don't forget the mental effort you've already put into doing that now. You already have a much more refined sense of how lawyers, judges, and the law as an institution operates, than any layperson on the street. Take advantage of that knowledge, that understanding, as a kind of 'reality check' on the implications of various theorists' views as to 'What is a law, the law, law, or laws?' You might inwardly think that this 'most discerning' of questions is over-elaborate, and really boils down to one simple question: 'What is Law?'. But you would also be likely to expect that simply by asking the four-part question, it must be more complex than that.

To ask 'What is *a* Law?' implies certain contrasts. It is indirectly a question that asks you to think about particular laws. In order to articulate the basis of a particular law, rather than to describe a particular law, or even an area of law, you have to think about how particular laws become members of a larger system of laws. What makes a particular rule, norm, standard or principle part of the legal system? What would such a rule, etc amount to, if it was not part of such a system?

'What is *the* Law?' Is this a different question? Does adding the word 'the' make the term referred to into a collective term describing a collection of, or **the** collection of, laws? Is this a reference to a particular legal system to which any particular law must inevitably belong? Or does anything worthy of the description '*the* Law' imply justice? What are the essential elements of any entity that can be identified with the referent 'the Law'?

Then what is 'Law'? Perhaps, and quite simply, it is more than 'a Law' is. But how can 'Law' be distinguished from 'the Law'? Is the former a reference to things that might be common to all legal systems, suggesting a distinction between particular legal systems and something more general or absolute than any particular legal system? Perhaps 'the Law' does not imply justice, while 'Law' might. 'The Law' may be more descriptive of the given body of legal rules in a particular jurisdiction, while 'Law' seems more detached from that description, seeming to refer to some additional element.

So then what, if anything, is added by the word 'Laws'? Does this refer to the aggregate, the sum total of laws, within all jurisdictions? Or could it refer to the type of thing that each law, in order to be called a law, must correspond to? If the latter, are we back to where we started? To quote from T S Eliot's poem Little Gidding:

We shall not cease from exploration
And the end of all our exploring
Will be to arrive where we started
And know the place for the first time

This might seem to be a pointless exercise in semantics. But be patient and come back to this section in future. For example, when you have read Bentham's attempt to describe law, set out in an extract in Chapter 3, return to these questions and see whether you can make more of them than has been done here. You will find that much of the commentary and materials in this book requires you to go back and forth in this manner. For example, thinking of what makes a contract of employment part of the law of the United Kingdom. Then asking whether the manner in which it does so tells you anything about the manner in which rules of other legal systems become part of such systems. Then thinking about the qualities that make a particular rule belong to a *legal* system rather than some other aggregate that includes elements of morality. If, by the end of the book, you come to the conclusion that these distinctions really are pure semantics, you may well have reached, and be able to justify, a quite radical position: that there is nothing that objectively distinguishes particular laws from other social rules. But this is only one position. At each point in a jurisprudence course there is the possibility that some answers can be filled in as to the relationships between these different aspects of legal study: the most particular law, and the greater whole of which it does, or does not, form a part. Whatever the answers might be, they are the stuff of jurisprudence. They provide the possibility of discourses that prioritise particular views of law's essential nature or character. Such answers provide the mixture of the whole and the parts that make up law.

The first Part of this book should enable you to fill in some of the answers to the ever-increasing number of questions that the apparently simple 'distinguish (a) a Law (b) the Law (c) Law (d) Laws' has dissolved into. Those answers are developed in jurisprudential or legal theories, or philosophies of law. Some theories are likely to address more obviously one or other of the elements of the simple question. In other words, the question being addressed might predispose the answer that is given. Exploring the question of how particular laws come to be included within legal systems is a characteristic question of some theories known as theories of Legal Positivism. The question of whether all legal systems, or even all laws, partake of some more general moral qualities is characteristic of some theories known as Natural Law theories. The search for referents in the real world for particular laws is a characteristic question of some Realist theories (an approach which often makes the meaning of particular laws quite concrete, only to make the manner in which they could ever be related together in some greater whole quite problematic). And some hybrid theories (most notably that of Dworkin) suggest that the manner in which any and *every* particular law becomes part of a legal system can only be understood in terms of the enterprise of law at its most general level.

This analysis is by no means watertight and can easily be criticised. But, for our purposes it is a useful starting point. At the end of the first Part of this book you might be able to think through the differences between (a), (b), (c), and (d) and reach the conclusion that what distinguishes them is far from semantic. Rather it is the possibility of explicitly expressing substantially different claims about the nature of law.

A comment on the extracts that follow

In the materials that follow, we offer you two very different routes into the process of thinking about these questions. The first, 'The Case of the Speluncean Explorers', by Lon Fuller, is an old favourite of jurisprudence teachers. It draws students into jurisprudential questions by requiring them to think about a hypothetical case in which the appropriate reaction of different judges of a mythical Supreme Court depends on the particular jurisprudential theories they hold. The exercise resembles a cinema trailer – a taste of the delights to follow in the coming weeks. It also seeks to demonstrate some of the issues already described in this chapter: that lawyers (including students) can hold jurisprudential positions without knowing lots of theories of jurisprudence. And it is also only a partial introduction. It seeks to make students think about the lawyer's orientations to the question of what law is. Thus, for example, because the focus is on whether a judge should punish particular individuals according to the law, it entirely neglects sociological or historical accounts of the nature of law, or particular laws. Indeed, the decontextualised nature of the hypothetical suggests that meaningful answers can be provided as to the nature of law without reference to the particular circumstances of real societies, a claim that some legal theorists would stoutly resist.

In this mythical case, one finds the later judges criticising the positions of the earlier ones. Some of the difficulties of each judge's position are therefore revealed to you if you read on to the next judgment. The case and the positions adopted, and the criticisms of those positions illustrate some important questions.

1. Are laws, or any particular law understandable, or binding, without reference to ideas of purpose, and do those ideas of purpose include notions of fairness or justice?

2. Is it really possible to generate consensus on the purpose of law, or even particular laws? Is the authority and guidance provided by law actually a function of our ability to understand and be bound by it without reference to a consensus on its purpose(s)?

3. Is the interpretation of law different from its enactment? Is the range of permissible interpretations less than the range of permissible enactments? How do texts, enacted by a parliament, restrict what judges may do? Would interpretation by reference to a judge's view of the appropriate moral purpose of laws, or a particular law, facilitate or undermine the relationship between enactment and interpretation?

4. If there is no law on a subject, what does this leave for judges to do? Can their pronouncements be anything more than the personal beliefs of private individuals? If judges regularly pronounce on the appropriate action to be taken in such cases, would you assume that they have been implicitly authorised to decide the law,

where there is no law? (For a contemporary example that raises this question in similar terms to Fuller's hypothetical example, see *Re A* [2000] 4 All ER 961, the conjoined twins separation case.)

5.   What, if anything, has democracy, or public opinion, to do with the correct interpretation of law?

When you read the case, pause after the facts (set out in the first judgment by Chief Justice Truepenny) and think what you would do if you were a judge. You could sketch out your own judgment. Then read on to see how your views differ from those of Fuller's judges, and how your own sketch changes, if at all, in response.

Fuller (1949, 616–645)

THE CASE OF THE SPELUNCEAN EXPLORERS

IN THE SUPREME COURT OF NEWGARTH, 4300

The defendants, having been indicted for the crime of murder, were convicted and sentenced to be hanged by the Court of General Instances of the County of Stowfield. They bring a petition of error before this Court. The facts sufficiently appear in the opinion of the Chief Justice.

TRUEPENNY, C.J.

The four defendants are members of the Speluncean Society, an organization of amateurs interested in the exploration of caves. Early in May of 4299 they, in the company of Roger Whetmore, then also a member of the Society, penetrated into the interior of a limestone cavern of the type found in the Central Plateau of this Commonwealth. While they were in a position remote from the entrance to the cave, a landslide occurred. Heavy boulders fell in such a manner as to block completely the only known opening to the cave. When the men discovered their predicament, they settled themselves near the obstructed entrance to wait until a rescue party should remove the detritus that prevented them from leaving their underground prison. On the failure of Whetmore and the defendants to return to their homes, the Secretary of the Society was notified by their families. It appears that the explorers had left indications at the headquarters of the Society concerning the location of the cave they proposed to visit. A rescue party was promptly dispatched to the spot.

The task of rescue proved one of overwhelming difficulty. It was necessary to supplement the forces of the original party by repeated increments of men and machines, which had to be conveyed at great expense to the remote and isolated region in which the cave was located. A huge temporary camp of workmen, engineers, geologists, and other experts was established. The work of removing the obstruction was several times frustrated by fresh landslides. In one of these, ten of the workmen engaged in clearing the entrance were killed. The treasury of the Speluncean Society was soon exhausted in the rescue effort, and the sum of eight hundred thousand frelars, raised partly by popular subscription and partly by legislative grant, was expended before the imprisoned men were rescued. Success was finally achieved on the thirty-second day after the men entered the cave.

Since it was known that the explorers had carried with them only scant provisions, and since it was also known that there was no animal or vegetable matter within the cave on which they might subsist, anxiety was early felt that they might meet death by starvation before access to them could be obtained. On the twentieth day of their imprisonment it was learned for the first time that they had taken with them into the cave a portable wireless machine capable of both sending and receiving messages. A similar machine was promptly installed in the rescue camp and oral communication established with the unfortunate men within the mountain. They asked to be informed how long a time would be required to release them. The engineers in charge of the project answered that at least ten days would be required even if no new landslides occurred. The explorers then asked if any physicians were present, and were placed in communication with a committee of medical experts. The imprisoned men described their condition and the rations they had taken with them, and asked for a medical opinion whether they would be likely to live without food for ten days longer. The chairman of the committee of physicians told them that there was little possibility of this. The wireless machine within the cave then remained silent for eight hours. When communication was re-established, the men asked to speak again with the physicians. The chairman of the physicians' committee was placed before the apparatus, and Whetmore, speaking on behalf of himself and the defendants, asked whether they would be able to survive for ten days longer if they consumed the flesh of one of their number. The physicians' chairman reluctantly answered this question in the affirmative. Whetmore asked whether it would be advisable for them to cast lots to determine which of them should be eaten. None of the physicians present was willing to answer the question. Whetmore then asked if there were among the party a judge or other official of the government who would answer this question. None of those attached to the rescue camp was willing to assume the role of advisor in this matter. He then asked if any minister or priest would answer their question, and none was found who would do so. Thereafter no further messages were received from within the cave, and it was assumed (erroneously, it later appeared) that the electric batteries of the explorers' wireless machine had become exhausted. When the imprisoned men were finally released, it was learned that on the twenty-third day after their entrance into the cave Whetmore had been killed and eaten by his companions.

From the testimony of the defendants, which was accepted by the jury, it appears that it was Whetmore who first proposed that they might find the nutriment without which survival was impossible in the flesh of one of their own number. It was also Whetmore who first proposed the use of some method of casting lots, calling the attention of the defendants to a pair of dice he happened to have with him. The defendants were at first reluctant to adopt so desperate a procedure, but after the conversations by wireless related above, they finally agreed on the plan proposed by Whetmore. After much discussion of the mathematical problems involved, agreement was finally reached on a method of determining the issue by the use of the dice.

Before the dice were cast, however, Whetmore declared that he withdrew from the arrangement, as he had decided on reflection to wait for another week before embracing an expedient so frightful and odious. The others charged him with a breach of faith and proceeded to cast the dice. When it came Whetmore's turn, the dice were cast for him by one of the defendants, and he was asked to declare any objections he might have to the fairness of the throw. He stated that he had no such objections. The throw went against him, and he was then put to death and eaten by his companions.

After the rescue of the defendants, and after they had completed a stay in a hospital where they underwent a course of treatment for malnutrition and shock, they were indicted for the murder of Roger Whetmore. At the trial, after the testimony had been concluded, the foreman of the jury (a lawyer by profession) inquired of the court whether the jury might not find a special verdict, leaving it to the court to say whether on the facts as found the defendants were guilty. After some discussion, both the Prosecutor and counsel for the defendants indicated their acceptance of this Procedure, and it was adopted by the court. In a lengthy special verdict the jury found the facts as I have related them above, and found further that if on these facts the defendants were guilty of the crime charged against them, then they found the defendants guilty. On the basis of this verdict, the trial judge ruled that the defendants were guilty of murdering Roger Whetmore. The judge then sentenced them to be hanged, the law of our Commonwealth permitting him no discretion with respect to the penalty to be imposed. After the release of the jury, its members joined in communication to the Chief Executive asking that the sentence be commuted to an imprisonment of six months. The trial judge addressed a similar communication to the Chief Executive. As yet no action with respect to these pleas has been taken, as the Chief Executive is apparently awaiting our disposition of this petition of error.

It seems to me that in dealing with this extraordinary case the jury and the trial judge followed a course that was not only fair and wise, but the only course that was open to them under the law. The language of our statute is well known: 'Whoever shall wilfully take the life of another shall be punished by death' N.C.S.A. (N.S.) §12–A. This statute permits of no exception applicable to this case, however, our sympathies may incline us to make allowance for the tragic situation in which these men found themselves.

In a case like this the principle of executive clemency seems admirably suited to mitigate the rigors of the law, and I propose to my colleagues that we follow the example of the jury and the trial judge by joining in the communications they have addressed to the Chief Executive. There is every reason to believe that these requests for clemency will be heeded, coming as they do from those who have studied the case and had an opportunity to become thoroughly acquainted with all its circumstances. It is highly improbable that the Chief Executive would deny these requests unless he were himself to hold hearings at least as extensive as those involved in the trial below, which lasted for three months. The holding of such hearings (which would virtually amount to a retrial of the case) would scarcely be compatible with the function of the Executive as it is usually conceived. I think we may therefore assume that some form of clemency will be extended to these defendants. If this is done, then justice will be accomplished without impairing either the letter or spirit of our statutes and without offering any encouragement for the disregard of law.

FOSTER, J.

I am shocked that the Chief Justice, in an effort to escape the embarrassments of this tragic case, should have adopted, and should have proposed to his colleagues, an expedient at once so sordid and so obvious. I believe something more is on trial in this case than the fate of these unfortunate explorers; that is the law of our Commonwealth. If this Court declares that under our law these men have committed a crime, then our law is itself convicted in the tribunal of common sense, no matter what happens to the individuals involved in this petition of error. For us to assert that the law we uphold and expound compels us to a conclusion we are ashamed of, and from which we can only escape by appealing to a dispensation resting within the personal whim of the Executive, seems to me to amount to an admission that the law of this Commonwealth no longer pretends to incorporate justice. For myself, I do not believe that our law compels the monstrous conclusion that these men are murderers. I believe, on the contrary, that it declares them to be innocent of any crime. I rest this conclusion on two independent grounds, either of which is of itself sufficient to justify the acquittal of these defendants.

The first of these grounds rests on a premise that may arouse opposition until it has been examined candidly. I take the view that the enacted or positive law of this Commonwealth, including all of its statutes and precedents, is inapplicable to this case, and that the case is governed instead by what ancient writers in Europe and America called 'the law of nature'.

This conclusion rests on the proposition that our positive law is predicated on the possibility of men's coexistence in society. When a situation arises in which the coexistence of men becomes impossible, then a condition that underlies all of our precedents and statutes has ceased to exist. When that condition disappears, then it is my opinion that the force of our positive law disappears with it. We are not accustomed to applying the maxim *cessante ratione legis, cessat et ipsa lex* [where the reason for the law ceases, the law itself ceases] to the whole of our enacted law, but I believe that this is a case where the maxim should be so applied.

The proposition that all positive law is based on the possibility of men's coexistence has a strange sound, not because the truth it contains is strange, but simply because it is a truth so obvious and pervasive that we seldom have occasion to give words to it. Like the air we breathe, it so pervades our environment that we forget that it exists until we are suddenly deprived of it. Whatever particular objects may be sought by the various branches of our law, it is apparent on reflection that all of them are directed toward facilitating and improving men's coexistence and regulating with fairness and equity the relations of their life in common. When the assumption that men may live together loses its truth, as it obviously did in this extraordinary situation where life only became possible by the taking of life, then the basic premises underlying our whole legal order have lost their meaning and force.

Had the tragic events of this case taken place a mile beyond the territorial limits of our Commonwealth, no one would pretend that our law was applicable to them. We recognize that jurisdiction rests on a territorial basis. The grounds of this principle are by no means obvious and are seldom examined. I take it that this principle is supported by an assumption that it is feasible to impose a single legal order upon a group of men only if they live together within the confines of a given area of the earth's surface. The premise that men shall coexist in a group underlies, then, the territorial principle, as it does all of law. Now I contend that a case may be removed morally from the force of a legal order, as well as geographically. If we look to the purposes of law and government, and to the premises underlying our positive law, these men when they made their fateful decision were as remote from our legal order as if they had been a thousand miles beyond our boundaries. Even in a physical sense, their underground prison was separated from our courts and writ-servers by a solid curtain of rock that could be removed only after the most extraordinary expenditures of time and effort.

I conclude, therefore, that at the time Roger Whetmore's life was ended by these defendants, they were, to use the quaint language of nineteenth-century writers, not in a 'state of civil society' but in a 'state of nature'. This has the consequence that the law applicable to them is not the enacted and established law of this Commonwealth, but the law derived from those principles that were appropriate to their condition. I have no hesitancy in saying that under those principles they were guiltless of any crime.

What these men did was done in pursuance of an agreement accepted by all of them and first proposed by Whetmore himself. Since it was apparent that their extraordinary predicament made inapplicable the usual principles that regulate men's relations with one another, it was necessary for them to draw, as it were, a new charter of government appropriate to the situation in which they found themselves.

It has from antiquity been recognized that the most basic principle of law or government is to be found in the notion of contract or agreement. Ancient thinkers, especially during the period from 1600 to 1900, used to base government itself on a supposed original social compact. Sceptics pointed out that this theory contradicted the known facts of history, and that there was no scientific evidence to support the notion that any government was ever founded in the manner supposed by the theory. Moralists replied that, if the compact was a fiction from a historical point of view, the notion of compact or agreement furnished the only ethical justification on which the powers of government, which include that of taking life, could be rested. The powers of government can only be justified morally on the ground that these are powers that reasonable men would agree upon and accept if they were faced with the necessity of constructing a new social order to make their life in common possible.

Fortunately, our Commonwealth is not bothered by the perplexities that beset the ancients. We know as a matter of historical truth that our government was founded upon a contract or free accord of men. The archaeological proof is conclusive that in the first period following the Great Spiral the survivors of that holocaust voluntarily came together and drew up a charter of government. Sophistical writers have raised questions as to the power of those remote contractors to bind future generations, but the fact remains that our government traces itself back in an unbroken line to that original charter.

If, therefore, our hangmen have the power to end men's lives, if our sheriffs have the power to put delinquent tenants in the street, if our police have the power to incarcerate the inebriated reveller, these powers find their moral justification in that original compact of our forefathers. If we can find no higher source for our legal order, what higher source should we expect these starving unfortunates to find for the order they adopted for themselves?

I believe that the line of argument I have just expounded permits of no rational answer. I realize that it will probably be received with a certain discomfort by many who read this opinion, who will be inclined to suspect that some hidden sophistry must underlie a demonstration that leads to so many unfamiliar conclusions. The source of this discomfort is, however, easy to identify. The usual conditions of human existence incline us to think of human life as an absolute value, not to be sacrificed under any circumstances. There is much that is fictitious about this conception even when it is applied to the ordinary relations of society. We have an illustration of this truth in the very case before us. Ten workmen were killed in the process of removing the rocks from the opening to the cave. Did not the engineers and government officials who directed the rescue effort know that the operations they were undertaking were dangerous and involved a serious risk to the lives of the workmen executing them? If it was proper that these ten lives should be sacrificed to save the lives of five imprisoned explorers, why then are we told it was wrong for these explorers to carry out an arrangement which would save four lives at the cost of one?

Every highway, every tunnel, every building project involves a risk to human life. Taking these projects in the aggregate, we can calculate with some precision how many deaths the construction of them will require; statisticians can tell you the average cost in human lives of a thousand miles of a four-lane concrete highway. Yet we deliberately and knowingly incur and pay this cost on the assumption that the values obtained for those who survive outweigh the loss. If these things can be said of a society functioning above ground in a normal and ordinary manner, what shall we say of the supposed absolute value of human life in the desperate situation in which these defendants and their companion Whetmore found themselves?

This concludes the exposition of the first ground of my decision. My second ground proceeds by rejecting hypothetically all the premises on which I have so far proceeded. I concede for purposes of argument that I am wrong in saying that the situation of these men removed them from the effect of our positive law and I assume that the Consolidated Statutes have the power to penetrate 50 feet of rock and to impose themselves upon these starving men huddled in the underground prison.

Now it is, of course, perfectly clear that these men did an act that violates the literal wording of the statute which declares that he who 'shall wilfully take the life of another' is a murderer. But one of the most ancient bits of legal wisdom is the saying that a man may break the letter of the law without breaking the law itself. Every proposition of positive law, whether contained in a statute or a judicial precedent, is to be interpreted reasonably, in the light of its evident purpose. This is a truth so elementary that it is hardly necessary to expatiate on it. Illustrations of its application are numberless and are to be found in ever branch of law. In *Commonwealth v. Staymore* the defendant was convicted under statute making it a crime to leave one's car parked in certain areas for a period longer than two hours. The defendant had attempted to remove his car, but was prevented from doing so because the streets were obstructed by a political demonstration in which he took no part and which he had no reason to anticipate. His conviction was set aside by this Court, although his case fell squarely within the wording of the statute. Again, in *Fehler v. Neegas* there was before the Court for construction a statute, in which the word 'not' had plainly been transposed from its intended position in the final and most crucial section of the act. This transposition was contained in all the successive drafts of the act, where it was apparently overlooked by the draftsmen and sponsors of the legislation. No one was able to prove how the error came about, yet it was apparent that, taking account of the contents of the statute as a whole, an error had been made, since a literal reading of the final clause rendered it inconsistent with everything that had gone before and with the object of the enactment as stated in its preamble. This Court refused to accept a literal interpretation of the statute, and in effect rectified its language by reading the word 'not' into the place where it was evidently intended to go.

The statute before us for interpretation has never been applied literally. Centuries ago it was established that a killing in self-defense is excused. There is nothing in the wording of the statute that suggests this exception. Various attempts have been made to reconcile the legal treatment of self-defense with the words of the statute, but in my opinion these are all merely ingenious sophistries The truth is that the exception in favor of self-defense cannot be reconciled with the *words* of the statute, but only with its *purpose*.

The true reconciliation of the excuse of self-defense with the statute making it a crime to kill another is to be found in the following line of reasoning. One of the principal objects underlying any criminal legislation is that of deterring men from crime. Now it is apparent that if it were declared to be the law that a killing in self-defense is murder such a rule could not operate in a deterrent manner. A man whose life is threatened will repel his aggressor, whatever the law may say. Looking therefore to the broad purposes of criminal legislation, we may safely declare that this statute was not intended to apply to cases of self-defense. When the rationale of the excuse of self-defense is thus explained, it becomes apparent that precisely the same reasoning is applicable to the case at bar. If in the future any group of men ever find themselves in the tragic predicament of these defendants, we may be sure that their decision whether to live or die will not be controlled by the contents of our criminal code. Accordingly, if we read this statute intelligently, it is apparent that it does not apply to this case. The withdrawal of this situation from the effect of the statute is justified by precisely the same considerations that were applied by our predecessors in office centuries ago to the case of self-defense.

There are those who raise the cry of judicial usurpation whenever a court, after analyzing the purpose of a statute, gives to its words a meaning that is not at once apparent to the casual reader who has not studied the statute closely or examined the objectives it seeks to attain. Let me say emphatically that I accept without reservation the proposition that this Court is bound by the statutes of our Commonwealth and that it exercises its powers in subservience to the duly expressed will of the Chamber of Representatives. The line of reasoning I have applied above raises no question of fidelity to enacted law, though it may possibly raise a question of the distinction between intelligent and unintelligent fidelity No superior wants a servant who lacks the capacity to read between the lines. The stupidest housemaid knows that when she is told 'to peel the soup and skim the potatoes' her mistress does not mean what she says. She also knows that when her master tells her to 'drop everything and come running' he has over-looked the possibility that she is at the moment in the act of rescuing the baby from the rain barrel. Surely we have a right to expect the same modicum of intelligence from the judiciary. The correction of obvious legislative errors or oversights is not to supplant the legislative will, but to make that will effective.

I therefore conclude that on any aspect under which this case may be viewed these defendants are innocent of the crime of murdering Roger Whetmore, and that the conviction should be set aside.

TATTING, J.

In the discharge of my duties as a justice of this Court, I am usually able to dissociate the emotional and intellectual sides of my reactions, and to decide the case before me entirely on the basis of the latter. In pausing on this tragic case I find that my usual resources fail me. On the emotional side I find myself torn between sympathy for these men and a feeling of abhorrence and disgust at the monstrous act they committed. I had hoped that I would be able to put these contradictory emotions to one side as irrelevant, and to decide the case on the basis of a convincing and logical demonstration of the result demanded by our law. Unfortunately, this deliverance has not been vouchsafed me.

As I analyze the opinion just rendered by my brother Foster, I find that it is shot through with contradictions and fallacies. Let us begin with his first proposition: these men were not subject to our law because they were not in a 'state of civil society' but in a 'state of nature'. I am not clear why this is so, whether it is because of the thickness of the rock that imprisoned them, or because they were hungry, or because they had set up a 'new charter of government' by which the usual rules of law were to be supplanted by a throw of the dice. Other difficulties intrude themselves. If these men passed from the jurisdiction of our law to that of 'the law of nature', at what moment did this occur? Was it when the entrance to the cave was blocked, or when the threat of starvation reached a certain undefined degree of intensity, or when the agreement for the throwing of the dice was made? These uncertainties in the doctrine proposed by my brother are capable of producing real difficulties. Suppose, for example, one of these men had had his twenty-first birthday while he was imprisoned within the mountain. On what date would we have to consider that he had attained his majority – when he reached the age of twenty-one, at which time he was, by hypothesis, removed from the effects of our law, or only when he was released from the cave and became again subject to what my brother calls our 'positive law'? These difficulties may seem fanciful, yet they only serve to reveal the fanciful nature of the doctrine that is capable of giving rise to them.

But it is not necessary to explore these niceties further to demonstrate the absurdity of my brother's position. Mr Justice Foster and I are the appointed judges of a court of the Commonwealth of Newgarth, sworn and empowered to administer the laws of that Commonwealth. By what authority do we resolve ourselves into a Court of Nature? If these men were indeed under the law of nature, whence comes our authority to expound and apply that law? Certainly we are not in a state of nature.

Let us look at the contents of this code of nature that my brother proposes we adopt as our own and apply to this case. What a topsy-turvy and odious code it is! It is a code in which the law of contracts is more fundamental than the law of murder. It is a code under which a man may make a valid agreement empowering his fellows to eat his own body. Under the provisions of this code, furthermore, such an agreement once made is irrevocable, and if one of the parties attempts to withdraw, the others may take the law into their own hands and enforce the contract by violence – for though my brother passes over in convenient silence the effect of Whetmore's withdrawal, this is the necessary implication of his argument.

The principles my brother expounds contain other implications that cannot be tolerated. He argues that when the defendants set upon Whetmore and killed him (we know not how, perhaps by pounding him with stones) they were only exercising the rights conferred upon them by their bargain. Suppose, however, that Whetmore had had concealed upon his person a revolver, and that when he saw the defendants about to slaughter him he had shot them to death in order to save his own life. My brother's reasoning applied to these facts would make Whetmore out to be a murderer, since the excuse of self-defense would have to be denied to him. If his assailants were acting rightfully in seeking to bring about his death, then of course he could no more plead the excuse that he was defending his own life than could a condemned prisoner who struck down the executioner lawfully attempting to place the noose about his neck.

All of these considerations make it impossible for me to accept the first part of my brother's argument. I can neither accept his notion that these men were under a code of nature which this Court was bound to apply to them, nor can I accept the odious and perverted rules that he would read into that code. I come now to the second part of my brother's opinion, in which he seeks to show that the defendants did not violate the provisions of N.C.S.A. (N.S.) §12–A. Here the way, instead of being clear, becomes for me misty and ambiguous, though my brother seems unaware of the difficulties that inhere in his demonstrations.

The gist of my brother's argument may be stated in the following terms: No statute, whatever its language, should be applied in a way that contradicts its purpose. One of the purposes of any criminal statute is to deter. The application of the statute making it a crime to kill another to the peculiar facts of this case would contradict this purpose, for it is impossible to believe that the contents of the criminal code could operate in a deterrent manner on men faced with the alternative of life or death. The reasoning by which this exception is read into the statute is, my brother observes, the same as that which is applied in order to provide the excuse of self-defense.

On the face of things this demonstration seems very convincing indeed. My brother's interpretation of the rationale of the excuse of self-defense is in fact supported by a decision of this court, *Commonwealth v. Party*, a precedent I happened to encounter in my research on this case. Though *Commonwealth v. Party* seems generally to have been overlooked in the texts and subsequent decisions, it supports unambiguously the interpretation my brother has put upon the excuse of self-defense.

Now let me outline briefly, however, the perplexities that assail me when I examine my brother's demonstration more closely. It is true that a statute should be applied in the light of its purpose, and that *one* of the purposes of criminal legislation is recognized to be deterrence. The difficulty is that other purposes are also ascribed to the law of crimes. It has been said that one of its objects is to provide an orderly outlet for the instinctive human demand for retribution: *Commonwealth v. Scape*. It has also been said that its object is the rehabilitation of the wrongdoer: *Commonwealth v. Makeover*. Other theories have been propounded. Assuming that we must interpret a statute in the light of its purpose, what are we to do when it has many purposes or when its purposes are disputed?

A similar difficulty is presented by the fact that, although there is authority for my brother's interpretation of the excuse of self-defense, there is other authority which assigns to that excuse a different rationale. Indeed, until I happened on *Commonwealth v. Party* I had never heard of the explanation given by my brother. The taught doctrine of our law schools, memorized by generations of law students, runs in the following terms: The statute concerning murder requires a 'wilful' act. The man who acts to repel an aggressive threat to his own life does not act 'wilfully', but in response to an impulse deeply ingrained in human nature. I suspect that there is hardly a lawyer in this Commonwealth who is not familiar with this line of reasoning, especially since the point is a great favorite of the bar examiners.

Now the familiar explanation for the excuse of self-defense just expounded obviously cannot be applied by analogy to the facts of this case. These men acted not only 'wilfully' but with great deliberation and after hours of discussing what they should do. Again we encounter a forked path, with one line of reasoning leading us in one direction and another in a direction that is exactly the opposite. This perplexity is in this case compounded, as it were, for we have to set off one explanation, incorporated in a virtually unknown precedent of this Court, against another explanation, which forms a part of the taught legal tradition of our law schools, but which, so far as I know, has never been adopted in any judicial decision.

I recognize the relevance of the precedents cited by my brother concerning the displaced 'not' and the defendant who parked overtime. But what are we to do with one of the landmarks of our jurisprudence, which again my brother passes over in silence? This is *Commonwealth v. Valjean.* Though the case is somewhat obscurely reported, it appears that the defendant was indicted for the larceny of a loaf of bread, and offered as a defense that he was in a condition approaching starvation. The court refused to accept this defense. If hunger cannot justify the theft of wholesome and natural food, how can it justify the killing and eating of a man? Again, if we look at the thing in terms of deterrence, is it likely that a man will starve to death to avoid a jail sentence for the theft of a loaf of bread? My brother's demonstrations would compel us to overrule *Commonwealth v. Vajlean,* and many other precedents that have been built on that case.

Again, I have difficulty in saying that no deterrent effect whatever could be attributed to a decision that these men were guilty of murder. The stigma of the word 'murderer' is such that it is quite likely, I believe, that if these men had known that their act was deemed by the law to be murder they would have waited for a few days at least before carrying out their plan. During that time some unexpected relief might have come. I realize that this observation only reduces the distinction to a matter of degree, and does not destroy it altogether. It is certainly true that the element of deterrence would be less in this case than is normally involved in the application of the criminal law.

There is still a further difficulty in my brother Foster's proposal to read an exception into the statute to favor this case, though again a difficulty not even intimated in his opinion. What shall be the scope of this exception? Here the men cast lots and the victim was himself originally a party to the agreement. What would we have to decide if Whetmore had refused from the beginning to participate in the plan? Would a majority be permitted to overrule him? Or, suppose that no plan were adopted at all and the others simply conspired to bring about Whetmore's death, justifying their act by saying that he was in the weakest condition. Or again, that a plan of selection was followed but one based on a different justification than the one adopted here, as if the others were atheists and insisted that Whetmore should die because he was the only one who believed in an afterlife. These illustrations could be multiplied, but enough have been suggested to reveal what a quagmire of hidden difficulties my brother's reasoning contains.

Of course I realize on reflection that I may be concerning myself with a problem that will never arise, since it is unlikely that any group of men will ever again be brought to commit the dread act that was involved here. Yet, on still further reflection, even if we are certain that no similar case will arise again, do not the illustrations I have given show the lack of any coherent and rational principle in the rule my brother proposes? Should not the soundness of a principle be tested by the conclusions it entails, without reference to the accidents of later litigational history? Still, if this is so, why is it that we of this Court so often discuss the question whether we are likely to have later occasion to apply a principle urged for the solution of the case before us? Is this a situation where a line of reasoning not originally proper has become sanctioned by precedent, so that we are permitted to apply it and may even be under an obligation to do so?

The more I examine this case and think about it, the more deeply I become involved. My mind becomes entangled in the meshes of the very nets I throw out for my own rescue. I find that almost every consideration that bears on the decision of the case is counterbalanced by an opposing consideration leading in the opposite direction. My brother Foster has not furnished to me, nor can I discover for myself, any formula capable of resolving the equivocations that beset me on all sides.

I have given this case the best thought of which I am capable. I have scarcely slept since it was argued before us. When I feel myself inclined to accept the view of my brother Foster, I am repelled by a feeling that his arguments are intellectually unsound and approach mere rationalization. On the other hand, when I incline toward upholding the conviction, I am struck by the absurdity of directing that these men be put to death when their lives have been saved at the cost of the lives of ten heroic workmen. It is to me a matter of regret that the Prosecutor saw fit to ask for an indictment for murder. If we had a provision in our statutes making it a crime to eat human flesh, that would have been a more appropriate charge. If no other charge suited to the facts of this case could be brought against the defendants, it would have been wiser, I think, not to have indicted them at all. Unfortunately, however, the men have been indicted and tried, and we have therefore been drawn into this unfortunate affair.

Since I have been wholly unable to resolve the doubts that beset me about the law in this case, I am with regret announcing a step that is, I believe, unprecedented in the history of this tribunal. I declare my withdrawal from the decision of this case.

KEEN, J.

I should like to begin by setting to one side two questions which are not before this Court.

The first of these is whether executive clemency should be extended to these defendants if the conviction is affirmed. Under our system of government, that is a question for the Chief Executive, not for us. I therefore disapprove of that passage in the opinion of the Chief Justice in which he in effect gives instructions to the Chief Executive as to what he should do in this case and suggests that some impropriety will attach if these instructions are not heeded. This is a confusion of governmental functions – a confusion of which the judiciary should be the last to be guilty. I wish to state that if I were the Chief Executive I would go farther in the direction of clemency than the pleas addressed to him propose. I would pardon these men altogether, since I believe that they have already suffered enough to pay for any offence they may have committed. I want it to be understood that this remark is made in my capacity as a private citizen who by the accident of his office happens to have acquired an intimate acquaintance with the facts of this case. In the discharge of my duties as judge, it is neither my function to address directions to the Chief Executive, nor to take into account what he may or may not do, in reaching my own decision, which must be controlled entirely by the law of this Commonwealth.

The second question that I wish to put to one side is that of deciding whether what these men did was 'right' or 'wrong', 'wicked' or 'good'. That is also a question that is irrelevant to the discharge of my office as a judge sworn to apply, not my conceptions of morality, but the law of the land. In putting this question to one side I think I can also safely dismiss without comment the first and more poetic portion of my brother Foster's opinion. The element of fantasy contained in the arguments developed there has been sufficiently revealed in my brother Tatting's somewhat solemn attempt to take those arguments seriously.

The sole question before us for decision is whether these defendants did, within the meaning of N.C.S.A. (N.S.) §12–A, wilfully take the life of Roger Whetmore. The exact language of the statute is as follows: 'Whoever shall wilfully take the life of another shall be punished by death.' Now I should suppose that any candid observer, content to extract from these words their natural meaning, would concede at once that these defendants did 'wilfully take the life' of Roger Whetmore.

Whence arise all the difficulties of the case, then, and the necessity for so many pages of discussion about what ought to be so obvious? The difficulties, in whatever tortured form they may present themselves, all trace back to a single source, and that is a failure to distinguish the legal from the moral aspects of this case. To put it bluntly, my brothers do not like the fact that the written law requires the conviction of these defendants. Neither do I, but unlike my brothers I respect the obligations of an office that requires me to put my personal predilections out of my mind when I come to interpret and apply the law of this Commonwealth.

Now, of course, my brother Foster does not admit that he is actuated by a personal dislike of the written law. Instead he develops a familiar line of argument according to which the court may disregard the express language of a statute when something not contained in the statute itself, called its 'purpose', can be employed to justify the result the court considers proper. Because this is an old issue between myself and my colleague, I should like, before discussing his particular application of the argument to the facts of this case, to say something about the historical background of this issue and its implications for law and government generally.

There was a time in this Commonwealth when judges did in fact legislate very freely, and all of us know that during that period some of our statutes were rather thoroughly made over by the judiciary. That was a time when the accepted principles of political science did not designate with any certainty the rank and function of the various arms of the state. We all know the tragic issue of that uncertainty in the brief civil war that arose out of the conflicts between the judiciary, on the one hand, and the executive and the legislature, on the other. There is no need to recount here the factors that contributed to that unseemly struggle for power, though they included the unrepresentative character of the Chamber, resulting from a division of the country into election districts that no longer accorded with the actual distribution of the population, and the forceful personality and wide popular following of the then Chief Justice. It is enough to observe that those days are behind us, and that in place of the uncertainty that then reigned we now have a clear-cut principle, which is the supremacy of the legislative branch of our government. From that principle flows the obligation of the judiciary to enforce faithfully the written law, and to interpret that law in accordance with its plain meaning without reference to our personal desires or our individual conceptions of justice. I am not concerned with the question whether the principle that forbids the judicial revision of statutes is right or wrong, desirable or undesirable; I observe merely that this principle has become a tacit premise underlying the whole of the legal and governmental order I am sworn to administer.

Yet though the principle of the supremacy of the legislature has been accepted in theory for centuries, such is the tenacity of professional tradition and the force of fixed habits of thought that many of the judiciary have still not accommodated themselves to the restricted role which the new order imposes on them. My brother Foster is one of that group; his way of dealing with statutes is exactly that of a judge living in the 3900s.

We are all familiar with the process by which the judicial reform of disfavored legislative enactments is accomplished. Anyone who has followed the written opinions of Mr Justice Foster will have had an opportunity to see it at work in every branch of the law. I am personally so familiar with the process that in the event of my brother's incapacity I am sure I could write a satisfactory opinion for him without any prompting whatever, beyond being informed whether he liked the effect of the terms of the statute as applied to the case before him.

The process of judicial reform requires three steps. The first of these is to divine some single 'purpose' which the statute serves. This is done although not one statute in a hundred has any such single purpose, and although the objectives of nearly every statute are differently interpreted by the different classes of its sponsors. The second step is to discover that a mythical being called 'the legislator', in the pursuit of this imagined 'purpose', overlooked something or left some gap or imperfection in his work. Then comes the final and most refreshing part of the task, which is, of course, to fill in the blank thus created: *Quod eratfaciendum* [which was to be done].

My brother Foster's penchant for finding holes in statutes reminds one of the story told by an ancient author about the man who ate a pair of shoes. Asked how he liked them, he replied that the part he liked best was the holes. That is the way my brother feels about statutes; the more holes they have in them the better he likes them. In short, he doesn't like statutes.

One could not wish for a better case to illustrate the specious nature of this gap-filling process than the one before us. My brother thinks he knows exactly what was sought when men made murder a crime, and that was something he calls 'deterrence'. My brother Tatting has already shown how much is passed over in that interpretation. But I think the trouble goes deeper. I doubt very much whether our statute making murder a crime really has a 'purpose' in any ordinary sense of the term. Primarily, such a statute reflects a deeply felt human conviction that murder is wrong and that something should be done to the man who commits it. If we were forced to be more articulate about the matter, we would probably take refuge in the more sophisticated theories of the criminologists, which, of course, were certainly not in the minds of those who drafted our statute. We might also observe that men will do their own work more effectively and live happier lives if they are protected against the threat of violent assault. Bearing in mind that the victims of murders are often unpleasant people, we might add some suggestion that the matter of disposing of undesirables is not a function suited to private enterprise, but should be a state monopoly. All of which reminds me of the attorney who once argued before us that a statute licensing physicians was a good thing because it would lead to lower life insurance rates by lifting the level of general health. There is such a thing as over-explaining the obvious.

If we do not know the purpose of §12–A, how can we possibly say there is a 'gap' in it? How can we know what its draftsmen thought about the question of killing men in order to eat them? My brother Tatting has revealed an understandable, though perhaps slightly exaggerated, revulsion to cannibalism. How do we know that his remote ancestors did not feel the same revulsion to an even higher degree? Anthropologists say that the dread felt for a forbidden act may be increased by the fact that the conditions of a tribe's life create special temptations toward it, as incest is most severely condemned among those whose village relations make it most likely to occur. Certainly the period following the Great Spiral was one that had implicit in it temptations to anthropophagy. Perhaps it was for that very reason that our ancestors expressed their prohibition in so broad and unqualified a form. All of this is conjecture, of course, but it remains abundantly clear that neither I nor my brother Foster knows what the 'purpose' of §12–A is.

Considerations similar to those I have just outlined are also applicable to the exception in favor of self-defense, which plays so large a role in the reasoning of my brothers Foster and Tatting. It is of course true that in *Commonwealth v. Pany* an *obiter dictum* justified this exception on the assumption that the purpose of criminal legislation is to deter. It may well also be true that generations of law students have been taught that the true explanation of the exception lies in the fact that a man who acts in self-defense does not act 'wilfully', and that the same students have passed their bar examinations by repeating what their professors told them. These last observations I could dismiss, of course, as irrelevant for the simple reason that professors and bar examiners have not as yet any commission to make our laws for us. But again the real trouble lies deeper. As in dealing with the statute, so in dealing with the exception, the question is not the conjectural *purpose* of the rule, but its *scope*. Now the scope of the exception in favor of self-defense as it has been applied by this Court is plain: it applies to cases of resisting an aggressive threat to the party's own life. It is therefore too clear for argument that this case does not fall within the scope of the exception, since it is plain that Whetmore made no threat against the lives of these defendants.

The essential shabbiness of my brother Foster's attempt to cloak his remaking of the written law with an air of legitimacy comes tragically to the surface in my brother Tatting's opinion. In that opinion Justice Tatting struggles manfully to combine his colleague's loose moralisms with his own sense of fidelity to the written law. The issue of this struggle could only be that which occurred, a complete default in the discharge of the judicial function. You simply cannot apply a statute as it is written and remake it to meet your own wishes at the same time.

Now I know that the line of reasoning I have developed in this opinion will not be acceptable to those who look only to the immediate effects of a decision and ignore the long-run implications of an assumption by the judiciary of a power of dispensation. A hard decision is never a popular decision. Judges have been celebrated in literature for their sly prowess in devising some quibble by which a litigant could be deprived of his rights where the public thought it was wrong for him to assert those rights. But I believe that judicial dispensation does more harm in the long run than hard decisions. Hard cases may even have a certain moral value by bringing home to the people their own responsibilities toward the law that is ultimately their creation, and by reminding them that there is no principle of personal grace that can relieve the mistakes of their representatives.

Indeed, I will go farther and say that not only are the principles I have been expounding those which are soundest for our present conditions, but that we would have inherited a better legal system from our forefathers if those principles had been observed from the beginning. For example, with respect to the excuse of self-defense, if our courts had stood steadfast on the language of the statute the result would undoubtedly have been a legislative revision of it. Such a revision would have drawn on the assistance of natural philosophers and psychologists, and the resulting regulation of the matter would have had an understandable and rational basis, instead of the hodgepodge of verbalisms and metaphysical distinctions that have emerged from the judicial and professorial treatment.

These concluding remarks are, of course, beyond any duties that I have to discharge with relation to this case, but I include them here because I feel deeply that my colleagues are insufficiently aware of the dangers implicit in the conceptions of the judicial office advocated by my brother Foster.

I conclude that the conviction should be affirmed.

HANDY, J.

I have listened with amazement to the tortured ratiocinations to which this simple case has given rise. I never cease to wonder at my colleagues' ability to throw an obscuring curtain of legalisms about every issue presented to them for decision. We have heard this afternoon learned disquisitions on the distinction between positive law and the law of nature, the language of the statute and the purpose of the statute, judicial functions and executive functions, judicial legislation and legislative legislation. My only disappointment was that someone did not raise the question of the legal nature of the bargain struck in the cave – whether it was unilateral or bilateral, and whether Whetmore could not be considered as having revoked an offer prior to action taken thereunder.

What have all these things to do with the case? The problem before us is what we, as officers of the government, ought to do with these defendants. That is a question of practical wisdom, to be exercised in a context, not of abstract theory, but of human realities. When the case is approached in this light, it becomes, I think, one of the easiest to decide that has ever been argued before this Court.

Before stating my own conclusions about the merits of the case, I should like to discuss briefly some of the more fundamental issues involved – issues on which my colleagues and I have been divided ever since I have been on the bench.

I have never been able to make my brothers see that government is a human affair, and that men are ruled, not by words on paper or by abstract theories, but by other men. They are ruled well when their rulers understand the feelings and conceptions of the masses. They are ruled badly when that understanding is lacking. Of all branches of the government, the judiciary is the most likely to lose its contact with the common man. The reasons for this are, of course, fairly obvious. Where the masses react to a situation in terms of a few salient features, we pick into little pieces every situation presented to us. Lawyers are hired by both sides to analyze and dissect, judges and attorneys vie with one another to see who can discover the greatest number of difficulties and distinctions in a single set of facts. Each side tries to find cases, real or imagined, that will embarrass the demonstrations of the other side. To escape this embarrassment, still further distinctions are invented and imported into the situation. When a set of facts has been subjected to this kind of treatment for a sufficient time, all the life and juice have gone out of it and we have left a handful of dust.

Now I realize that wherever you have rules and abstract principles lawyers are going to be able to make distinctions. To some extent the sort of thing I have been describing is a necessary evil attaching to any formal regulation of human affairs. But I think that the area which really stands in need of such regulation is greatly overestimated. There are, of course, a few fundamental rules of the game that must be accepted if the game is to go on at all. I would include among these the rules relating to the conduct of elections, the appointment of public officials, and the term during which an office is held. Here some restraint on discretion and dispensation, some adherence to form, some scruple for what does and what does not fall within the rule, is, I concede, essential. Perhaps the area of basic principle should be expanded to include certain other rules, such as those designed to preserve the free civilmoign system.

But outside of these fields I believe that all government officials, including judges, will do their jobs best if they treat forms and abstract concepts as instruments. We should take as our model, I think, the good administrator, who accommodates procedures and principles to the case at hand, selecting from among the available forms those most suited to reach the proper result.

The most obvious advantage of this method of government is that it permits us to go about our daily tasks with efficiency and common sense. My adherence to this philosophy has, however, deeper roots. I believe that it is only with the insight this philosophy gives that we can preserve the flexibility essential if we are to keep our actions in reasonable accord with the sentiments of those subject to our rule. More governments have been wrecked, and more human misery caused, by the lack of this accord between ruler and ruled than by any other factor that can be discerned in history. Once drive a sufficient wedge between the mass of people and those who direct their legal, political, and economic life, and our society is ruined. Then neither Foster's law of nature nor Keen's fidelity to written law will avail us anything.

Now when these conceptions are applied to the case before us, its decision becomes, as I have said, perfectly easy. In order to demonstrate this I shall have to introduce certain realities that my brothers in their coy decorum have seen fit to pass over in silence, although they are just as acutely aware of them as I am.

The first of these is that this case has aroused an enormous public interest, both here and abroad. Almost every newspaper and magazine has carried articles about it; columnists have shared with their readers confidential information as to the next governmental move; hundreds of letters-to-the-editor have been printed. One of the great newspaper chains made a poll of public opinion on the question, 'What do you think the Supreme Court should do with the Speluncean explorers?' About ninety per cent expressed a belief that the defendants should be pardoned or let off with a kind of token punishment. It is perfectly clear, then, how the public feels about the case. We could have known this without the poll, of course, on the basis of common sense, or even by observing that on this Court there are apparently four-and-a-half men, or ninety per cent, who share the common opinion.

This makes it obvious, not only what we should do, but what we must do if we are to preserve between ourselves and public opinion a reasonable and decent accord. Declaring these men innocent need not involve us in any undignified quibble or trick. No principle of statutory construction is required that is not consistent with the past practices of this Court. Certainly no layman would think that in letting these men off we had stretched the statute any more than our ancestors did when they created the excuse of self-defense. If a more detailed demonstration of the method of reconciling our decision with the statute is required, I should be content to rest on the arguments developed in the second and less visionary part of my brother Foster's opinion.

Now I know that my brothers will be horrified by my suggestion that this Court should take account of public opinion. They will tell you that public opinion is emotional and capricious, that it is based on half-truths and listens to witnesses who are not subject to cross-examination. They will tell you that the law surrounds the trial of a case like this with elaborate safeguards, designed to insure that the truth will be known and that every rational consideration bearing on the issues of the case has been taken into account. They will warn you that all of these safeguards go for naught if a mass opinion formed outside this framework is allowed to have any influence on our decision.

But let us look candidly at some of the realities of the administration of our criminal law. When a man is accused of crime, there are, speaking generally, four ways in which he may escape punishment. One of these is a determination by a judge that under the applicable law he has committed no crime. This is, of course, a determination that takes place in a rather formal and abstract atmosphere. But look at the other three ways in which he may escape punishment. These are: (1) a decision by the Prosecutor not to ask for an indictment; (2) an acquittal by the jury; (3) a pardon or commutation of sentence by the executive. Can anyone pretend that these decisions are held within a rigid and formal framework of rules that prevents factual error, excludes emotional and personal factors, and guarantees that all the forms of the law will be observed?

In the case of the jury we do, to be sure, attempt to combine their deliberations within the area of the legally relevant, but there is no need to deceive ourselves into believing that this attempt is really successful. In the normal course of events the case now before us would have gone on all of its issues directly to the jury. Had this occurred we can be confident that there would have been an acquittal or at least a division that would have prevented a conviction. If the jury had been instructed that the men's hunger and their agreement were no defense to the charge of murder, their verdict would in all likelihood have ignored this instruction and would have involved a good deal more twisting of the letter of the law than any that is likely to tempt us. Of course the only reason that didn't occur in this case was the fortuitous circumstance that the foreman of the jury happened to be a lawyer. His learning enabled him to devise a form of words that would allow the jury to dodge its usual responsibilities.

My brother Tatting expresses annoyance that the Prosecutor did not, in effect, decide the case for him by not asking for an indictment. Strict as he is himself in complying with the demands of legal theory, he is quite content to have the fate of these men decided out of court by the Prosecutor on the basis of common sense. The Chief Justice, on the other hand, wants the application of common sense postponed to the very end, though, like Tatting, he wants no personal part in it.

This brings me to the concluding portion of my remarks, which has to do with executive clemency. Before discussing that topic directly, I want to make a related observation about the poll of public opinion. As I have said, ninety per cent of the people wanted the Supreme Court to let the men off entirely or with a more or less nominal punishment. The ten per cent constituted a very oddly assorted group, with the most curious and divergent opinions. One of our university experts has made a study of this group and has found that its members fall into certain patterns. Substantial portions of them are subscribers to 'crank' newspapers of limited circulation that gave their readers a distorted version of the facts of the case. Some thought that 'Speluncean' means 'cannibal' and that anthropophagy is a tenet of the Society. But the point I want to make, however, is this: although almost every conceivable variety and shade of opinion was represented in this group, there was, so far as I know, not one of them, nor a single member of the majority of ninety per cent, who said, 'I think it would be a fine thing to have the courts sentence these men to be hanged, and then to have another branch of the government come along and pardon them'. Yet this is a solution that has more or less dominated our discussions and which our Chief Justice proposes as a way by which we can avoid doing an injustice and at the same time preserve respect for law. He can be assured that if he is preserving anybody's morale, it is his own, and not the public's, which knows nothing of his distinctions. I mention this matter because I wish to emphasize once more the danger that we may get lost in the patterns of our own thought and forget that these patterns often cast not the slightest shadow on the outside world.

I come now to the most crucial fact in this case, a fact known to all of us on this Court, though one that my brothers have seen fit to keep under the cover of their judicial robes. This is the frightening likelihood that if the issue is left to him, the Chief Executive will refuse to pardon these men or commute their sentence. As we all know, our Chief Executive is a man now well advanced in years, of very stiff notions. Public clamor usually operates on him with the reverse of the effect intended. As I have told my brothers, it happens that my wife's niece is an intimate friend of his secretary. I have learned in this indirect, but, I think, wholly reliable way, that he is firmly determined not to commute the sentence if these men are found to have violated the law.

No one regrets more than I the necessity for relying in so important a matter on information that could be characterized as gossip. If I had my way this would not happen, for I would adopt the sensible course of sitting down with the Executive, going over the case with him, finding out what his views are, and perhaps working out with him a common program for handling the situation. But of course my brothers would never hear of such a thing.

Their scruple about acquiring accurate information directly does not prevent them from being very perturbed about what they have learned indirectly. Their acquaintance with the facts I have just related explains why the Chief Justice, ordinarily a model of decorum, saw fit in his opinion to flap his judicial robes in the face of the Executive and threaten him with excommunication if he failed to commute the sentence. It explains, I suspect, my brother Foster's feat of levitation by which a whole library of law books was lifted from the shoulders of these defendants. It explains also why even my legalistic brother Keen emulated Pooh-Bah in the ancient comedy by stepping to the other side of the stage to address a few remarks to the Executive 'in my capacity as a private citizen'. (I may remark, incidentally, that the advice of Private Citizen Keen will appear in the reports of this Court printed at taxpayers' expense.)

I must confess that as I grow older I become more and more perplexed at men's refusal to apply their common sense to problems of law and government, and this truly tragic case has deepened my sense of discouragement and dismay. I only wish that I could convince my brothers of the wisdom of the principles I have applied to the judicial office since I first assumed it. As a matter of fact, by a kind of sad rounding of the circle, I encountered issues like those involved here in the very first case I tried as judge of the Court of General Instances in Fanleigh County.

A religious sect had unfrocked a minister who, they said, had gone over to the views and practices of a rival sect. The minister circulated a handbill making charges against the authorities who had expelled him. Certain lay members of the church announced a public meeting at which they proposed to explain the position of the church. The minister attended this meeting. Some said he slipped in unobserved in a disguise; his own testimony was that he had walked in openly as a member of the public. At any rate, when the speeches began he interrupted with certain questions about the affairs of the church and made some statements in defense of his own views. He was set upon by members of the audience and given a pretty thorough pummelling, receiving among other injuries a broken jaw. He brought a suit for damages against the association that sponsored the meeting and against ten named individuals who he alleged were his assailants.

When we came to the trial, the case at first seemed very complicated to me. The attorneys raised a host of legal issues. There were nice questions on the admissibility of evidence, and, in connection with the suit against the association, some difficult problems turning on the question whether the minister was a trespasser or a licensee. As a novice on the bench I was eager to apply my law school learning and I began studying these questions closely, reading all the authorities and preparing well-documented rulings. As I studied the case I became more and more involved in its legal intricacies and I began to get into a state approaching that of my brother Tatting in this case. Suddenly, however, it dawned on me that all these perplexing issues really had nothing to do with the case, and I began examining it in the light of common sense. The case at once gained a new perspective, and I saw that the only thing for me to do was to direct a verdict for the defendants for lack of evidence.

I was led to this conclusion by the following considerations. The melee in which the plaintiff was injured had been a very confused affair, with some people trying to get to the center of the disturbance, while others were trying to get away from it; some striking at the plaintiff, while others were apparently trying to protect him. It would have taken weeks to find out the truth of the matter. I decided that nobody's broken jaw was worth that much to the Commonwealth. (The minister's injuries, incidentally, had meanwhile healed without disfigurement and without any impairment of normal faculties.) Furthermore, I felt very strongly that the plaintiff had to a large extent brought the thing on himself. He knew how inflamed passions were about the affair, and could easily have found another forum for the expression of his views. My decision was widely approved by the press and public opinion, neither of which could tolerate the views and practices that the expelled minister was attempting to defend. Now, thirty years later, thanks to an ambitious Prosecutor and a legalistic jury foreman, I am faced with a case that raises issues which are at bottom much like those involved in that case. The world does not seem to change much, except that this time it is not a question of a judgment for five or six hundred frelars, but of the life or death of four men who have already suffered more torment and humiliation than most of us would endure in a thousand years. I conclude that the defendants are innocent of the crime charged, and that the conviction and sentence should be set aside.

TATTING, J.

I have been asked by the Chief Justice whether, after listening to the two opinions just rendered, I desire to re-examine the position previously taken by me. I wish to state that after hearing these opinions I am greatly strengthened in my conviction that I ought not to participate in the decision of this case.

The Supreme Court being evenly divided, the conviction and sentence of the Court of General Instances is affirmed. It is ordered that the execution of the sentence shall occur at 6 a.m., Friday, April 2, 4300, at which time the Public Executioner is directed to proceed with all convenient dispatch to hang each of the defendants by the neck until he is dead.

POSTSCRIPT

Now that the court has spoken its judgment, the reader puzzled by the choice of date may wish to be reminded that the centuries which separate us from the year 4300 are roughly equal to those that have passed since the Age of Pericles. There is probably no need to observe that the *Speluncean case* itself is intended neither as a work of satire nor as a prediction in any ordinary sense of the term. As for the judges who make up Chief Justice Truepenny's court, they are, of course, as mythical as the facts and precedents with which they deal. The reader who refuses to accept this view, and who seeks to trace out contemporary resemblances where none is intended or contemplated, should be warned that he is engaged in a frolic of his own, which may possibly lead him to miss whatever modest truths are contained in the opinions delivered by the Supreme Court of Newgarth. The case was constructed for the sole purpose of bringing into a common focus certain divergent philosophies of law and government. These philosophies presented men with live questions of choice in the days of Plato and Aristotle. Perhaps they will continue to do so when our era has had its say about them. If there is any element of prediction in the case, it does not go beyond a suggestion that the questions involved are among the permanent problems of the human race.

The second extract is taken from Eldridge Cleaver's book, written in prison, *Soul on Ice*. Cleaver was a Black Panther, a group of radical black activists in the United States in the 1960s who advocated armed resistance to white oppression. The book was written in the aftermath of rioting in American cities. It celebrates the fact that blacks fought back with violence against their oppressors, and challenges any claim that the forces of 'Law and Order' have any greater legitimacy than do those who violently oppose them. This piece of legal theory questions some of the cosy assumptions of lawyers about the nature of law. As you read it, think about the following.

1.   What does this piece of writing say about the relationships between law and violence, law and morality, law and power?

2.   What is the connection between his perception of law and the deliberations of a Supreme Court?

Cleaver (1992, 121–129)

DOMESTIC LAW AND INTERNATIONAL ORDER

The police department and the armed forces are the two arms of the power structure, the muscles of control and enforcement. They have deadly weapons with which to inflict pain on the human body. They know how to bring about horrible deaths. They have clubs with which to beat the body and the head. They have bullets and guns with which to tear holes in the flesh, to smash bones, to disable and kill. They use force, to make you do what the deciders have decided you must do.

Every country on earth has these agencies of force. The people everywhere fear this terror and force. To them it is like a snarling wild beast which can put an end to one's dreams. They punish. They have cells and prisons to lock you up in. They pass out sentences. They won't let you go when you want to. You have to stay put until they give the word. If your mother is dying, you can't go to her bedside to say goodbye or to her graveside to see her lowered into the earth, to see her, for the last time, swallowed up by that black hole.

The techniques of the enforcers are many: firing squads, gas chambers, electric chairs, torture chambers, the garrotte, the guillotine, the tightening rope around your throat. It has been found that the death penalty is necessary to back up the law, to make it easier to enforce, to deter transgressions against the penal code. That everybody doesn't believe in the same laws is beside the point.

Which laws get enforced depends on who is in power. If the capitalists are in power, they enforce laws designed to protect their system, their way of life. They have a particular abhorrence for crimes against property, but are prepared to be liberal and show a modicum of compassion for crimes against the person – unless, of course, an instance of the latter is combined with an instance of the former. In such cases, nothing can stop them from throwing the whole book at the offender. For instance, armed robbery with violence, to a capitalist, is the very epitome of evil. Ask any banker what he thinks of it.

If Communists are in power, they enforce laws designed to protect their system, their way of life. To them, the horror of horrors is the speculator, that man of magic who has mastered the art of getting something with nothing and who in America would be a member in good standing of his local Chamber of Commerce.

'The people', however, are nowhere consulted, although everywhere everything is done always in their name and ostensibly for their betterment, while their real-life problems go unsolved. 'The people' are a rubber stamp for the crafty and sly. And no problem can be solved without taking the police department and the armed forces into account. Both kings and bookies understand this, as do first ladies and common prostitutes.

The police do on the domestic level what the armed forces do on the international level: protect the way of life for those in power. The police patrol the city, cordon off communities, blockade neighborhoods, invade homes, search for that which is hidden. The armed forces patrol the world, invade countries and continents, cordon off nations, blockade islands and whole peoples; they will also overrun villages, neighborhoods, enter homes, huts, caves, searching for that which is hidden. The policeman and the soldier will violate your person, smoke you out with various gases. Each will shoot you, beat your head and body with sticks and clubs, with rifle butts, run you through with bayonets, shoot holes in your flesh, kill you. They each have unlimited firepower. They will use all that is necessary to bring you to your knees. They won't take no for an answer. If you resist their sticks, they draw their guns. If you resist their guns, they call for reinforcements with bigger guns. Eventually they will come in tanks, in jets, in ships. They will not rest until you surrender or are killed. The policeman and the soldier will have the last word.

Both police and the armed forces follow orders. Orders. Orders flow from the top down. Up there, behind closed doors, in antechambers, in conference rooms, gavels bang on the tables, the tinkling of silver decanters can be heard as icewater is poured by well-fed, conservatively dressed men in hornrimmed glasses, fashionably dressed American widows with rejuvenated faces and tinted hair, the air permeated with the square humor of Bob Hope jokes. Here all the talking is done, all the thinking, all the deciding. Grey rabbits of men scurry forth from the conference room to spread the decisions throughout the city, as News. Carrying out orders is a job, a way of meeting the payments on the house, a way of providing for one's kiddies. In the armed forces it is also a duty, patriotism. Not to do so is treason.

Every city has its police department. No city would be complete without one. It would be sheer madness to try operating an American city without the heat, the fuzz, the man. Americans are too far gone, or else they haven't arrived yet; the center does not exist, only the extremes. Take away the cops and Americans would have a coast-to-coast free-for-all. There are, of course, a few citizens who carry their own private cops around with them, built into their souls. But there is robbery in the land, and larceny, murder, rape, burglary, theft, swindles, and brands of crime, profit, rent, interest – and these blasé descendants of Pilgrims are at each other's throats. To complicate matters, there are also rich people and poor people in America. There are Negroes and whites, Indians, Puerto Ricans, Mexicans, Jews, Chinese, Arabs, Japanese – all with equal rights but unequal possessions. Some are haves and some are have-nots. All have been taught to worship at the shrine of General Motors. The whites are on top in America and they want to stay there, up there. They are also on top in the world, on the international level, and they want to stay up there, too. Everywhere there are those who want to smash this precious toy clock of a system, they want ever so much to change it, to rearrange things, to pull the whites down off their high horse and make them equal. Everywhere the whites are fighting to prolong their status, to retard the erosion of their position. In America, when everything else fails, they call out the police. On the international level, when everything else fails, they call out the armed forces.

A strange thing happened in Watts, in 1965, August. The blacks, who in this land of private property have all private and no property, got excited into an uproar because they noticed a cop before he had a chance to wash the blood off his hands. Usually the police department can handle such flare-ups. But this time it was different. Things got out of hand. The blacks were running amok, burning, shooting, breaking. The police department was powerless to control them; the chief called for reinforcements. Out came the National Guard, that ambiguous hybrid from the twilight zone where the domestic army merges with the international; that hypocritical force poised within America and capable of action on either level, capable of backing up either the police or the armed forces. Unleashing their formidable firepower, they crushed the blacks. But things will never be the same again. Too many people saw that those who turned the other cheek in Watts got their whole head blown off. At the same time, heads were being blown off in Vietnam. America was embarrassed, not by the quality of her deeds but by the surplus of publicity focused upon her negative selling points, and a little frightened because of what all those dead bodies, on two fronts, implied. Those corpses spoke eloquently of potential allies and alliances. A community of interest began to emerge, dripping with blood, out of the ashes of Watts. The blacks in Watts and all over America could now see the Viet Cong's point: both were on the receiving end of what the armed forces were dishing out.

So now the blacks, stung by the new knowledge they have unearthed, cry out: 'POLICE BRUTALITY!' From one end of the country to the other, the new war cry is raised. The youth, those nodes of compulsive energy who are all fuel and muscle, race their motors, itch to do something. The Uncle Toms, no longer willing to get down on their knees to lick boots, do so from a squatting position. The black bourgeoisie call for Citizens' Review Boards, to assert civilian control over the activity of the police. In back rooms, in dark stinking corners of the ghettos, self-conscious black men curse their own cowardice and stare at their rifles and pistols and shotguns laid out on tables before them, trembling as they wish for a manly impulse to course through their bodies and send them screaming mad into the streets shooting from the hip. Black women look at their men as if they are bugs, curious growths of flesh playing an inscrutable waiting game. Violence becomes a homing pigeon floating through the ghettos seeking a black brain in which to roost for a season.

In their rage against the police, against police brutality, the blacks lose sight of the fundamental reality: that the police are only an instrument for the implementation of the policies of those who make the decisions. Police brutality is only one facet of the crystal of terror and oppression. Behind police brutality there is social brutality, economic brutality, and political brutality. From the perspective of the ghetto, this is not easy to discern: the TV newscaster and the radio announcer and the editorialists of the newspapers are wizards of the smoke screen and the snow job.

What is true on the international level is true also at home; except that the ace up the sleeve is easier to detect in the international arena. Who would maintain that American soldiers are in Vietnam on their own motion? They were conscripted into the armed forces and taught the wisdom of obeying orders. They were sent to Vietnam by orders of the generals in the Pentagon, who receive them from the Secretary of Defense, who receives them from the President, who is shrouded in mystery. The soldier in the field in Vietnam, the man who lies in the grass and squeezes the trigger when a little half-starved, trembling Vietnamese peasant crosses his sights, is only following orders, carrying out a policy and a plan. He hardly knows what it is all about. They have him wired-up tight with the slogans of TV and the World Series. All he knows is that he has been assigned to carry out a certain ritual of duties. He is well trained and does the best he can. He does a good job. He may want to please those above him with the quality of his performance. He may want to make sergeant, or better. This man is from some hicky farm in Shit Creek, Georgia. He only knew whom to kill after passing through boot camp. He could just as well come out ready to kill Swedes. He will kill a Swede dead if he is ordered to do so.

Same for the policeman in Watts. He is not there on his own. They have all been assigned. They have been told what to do and what not to do. They have also been told what they better not do. So when they continually do something, in every filthy ghetto in this shitty land, it means only that they are following orders.

It's no secret that in America the blacks are in total rebellion against the System. They want to get their nuts out of the sand. They don't like the way America is run, from top to bottom. In America, everything is owned. Everything is held as private property. Someone has a brand on everything. There is nothing left over. Until recently, the blacks themselves were counted as part of somebody's private property, along with the chickens and goats. The blacks have not forgotten this, principally because they are still treated as if they are part of someone's inventory of assets – or perhaps, in this day of rage against the costs of welfare, blacks are listed among the nation's liabilities. On any account, however, blacks are in no position to respect or help maintain the institution of private property. What they want is to figure out a way to get some of that property for themselves, to divert it to their own needs. This is what it is all about, and this is the real brutality involved. This is the source of all brutality.

The police are the armed guardians of the social order. The blacks are the chief domestic victims of the American social order. A conflict of interest exists, therefore, between the blacks and the police. It is not solely a matter of trigger-happy cops, of brutal cops who love to crack black heads. Mostly it's a job to them. It pays good. And there are numerous fringe benefits. The real problem is a trigger-happy social order.

The Utopians speak of a day when there will be no police. There will be nothing for them to do. Every man will do his duty, will respect the rights of his neighbor, will not disturb the peace. The needs of all will be taken care of. Everyone will have sympathy for his fellow man. There will be no such thing as crime. There will be, of course, no prisons. No electric chairs, no gas chambers. The hangman's rope will be the thing of the past. The entire earth will be a land of plenty. There will be no crimes against property, no speculation.

It is easy to see that we are not on the verge of entering Utopia: there are cops everywhere. North and South, the Negroes are the have-nots. They see property all around them, property that is owned by whites ... With many shackled by unemployment, hatred in black hearts for this system of private property increases daily. The sanctity surrounding property is being called into question. The mystique of the deed of ownership is melting away. In other parts of the world, peasants rise up and expropriate the land from the former owners. Blacks in America see that the deed is not eternal, that it is not signed by God, and that new deeds, making blacks the owners, can be drawn up.

The Black Muslims raised the cry, 'WE MUST HAVE SOME LAND! SOME LAND OF OUR OWN OR ELSE!' Blacks in America shrink from the colossus of General Motors. They can't see how to wade through that thicket of common stocks, preferred stocks, bonds and debentures. They only know that General Motors is huge, that it has billions of dollars under its control, that it owns land, that its subsidiaries are legion, that it is a repository of vast powers. The blacks want to crack the nut of General Motors. They are meditating on it. Meanwhile, they must learn that the police take orders from General Motors. And that the Bank of America has something to do with them even though they don't have a righteous penny in the bank. They have no bank accounts, only bills to pay. The only way they know of making withdrawals from the bank is at the point of a gun. The shiny fronts of skyscrapers intimidate them. They do not own them. They feel alienated from the very sidewalks on which they walk. This white man's country, this white man's world. Overflowing with men of color. An economy consecrated to the succor of the whites. Blacks are incidental. The war on poverty, that monstrous insult to the rippling muscles in a black man's arms, is an index of how men actually sit down and plot each other's deaths, actually sit down with slide rules and calculate how to hide bread from the hungry. And the black bourgeoisie greedily sopping up what crumbs are tossed into their dark corner.

There are 20,000,000 of these blacks in America, probably more. Today they repeat, in awe, this magic number to themselves: there are 20,000,000 of us! They shout this to each other in humiliated astonishment. No one need tell them that there is vast power latent in their mass. They know that 20,000,000 of anything is enough to get some recognition and consideration. They know also that they must harness their number and hone it into a sword with a sharp cutting edge. White General Motors also knows that the unity of these 20,000,000 ragamuffins will spell the death of the system of its being. At all costs, then, they will seek to keep these blacks from uniting, from becoming bold and revolutionary. These white property owners know that they must keep the blacks cowardly and intimidated. By a complex communications system of hints and signals, certain orders are given to the chief of police and the sheriff, who pass them on to their men, the footsoldiers in the trenches of the ghetto.

We experience this system of control as madness. So that Leonard Deadwyler, one of these 20,000,000 blacks, is rushing his pregnant wife to the hospital and is shot dead by a policeman. An accident. That the sun rises in the east and sets in the west is also an accident, by design. The blacks are up in arms. From one end of America to the other, blacks are outraged at this accident, this latest evidence of what an accident-prone people they are, of the cruelty and pain of their lives, these blacks at the mercy of trigger-happy Yankees and Rebs in coalition against their skin. They want the policeman's blood as a sign that the Viet Cong is not the only answer. A sign to save them from the deaths they must die, and inflict. The power structure, without so much as blinking an eye, wouldn't mind tossing Bova to the mob, to restore law and order, but it knows in the vaults of its strength that at all cost the blacks must be kept at bay, that it must uphold the police department, its guardian. Nothing must be allowed to threaten the set-up. Justice is secondary. Security is the byword.

Meanwhile, blacks are looking on and asking tactical questions. They are asked to die for the System in Vietnam. In Watts they are killed by it. Now – NOW! they are asking each other, in dead earnest: Why not die right here in Babylon fighting for a better life, like the Viet Cong? If those little cats can do it, what's wrong with big studs like us?

A mood sets in, spreads across America, across the face of Babylon, jells in black hearts everywhere.

The Speluncean explorers case (and, in a very different way, the extract from Cleaver) will have introduced you to some of the arguments and issues which fall within the tradition known as natural law. It should also have sensitised you to the fact that these issues arise within substantive law materials, where they usually appear without their jurisprudential labels. The next chapter is intended to initiate you in, and deepen your understanding of, natural law.

Question

(The arguments and materials in this chapter are introductory: they point forward to issues that you will tackle in more detail later. To reflect this, here is a question that you might like to tackle twice: today, to organise what you know thus far, and later, when these introductory materials can be used as examples within more complex arguments.)

'Jurisprudence informs the politics of law.' Discuss.

2 The Evolution of Natural Law

Richard Nobles and David Schiff

Introduction

'It ain't natural.' 'It's just part of the human condition.' Remarks like these point to an attempt to reason conclusions about the appropriateness of particular circumstances by reference to things which are universal, immutable, and otherwise generally experienced by all mankind. This kind of thinking, which used to be extended to understand regularities in nature such as the expected movement of the planets and the characteristics of chemicals (matters now covered by natural science) has been far more important than it is today. Collectively, such approaches can be subsumed under the title Natural Law. Within jurisprudence, the focus of this approach is on the arrangements appropriate for people to live together in society, and the roles played within this task by the establishment of laws. As a history of ideas, the development of Natural Law as a jurisprudence usually brings together a range of theories or theoretical insights from early Greek thinkers right up to the present day that are labelled as Natural Law theories. But the breadth of ideas represented by such theories goes beyond the narrow focus on law that is characteristic of jurisprudence writing. Selecting the legal aspects of such theories, and attempting to unify them under a single label, inevitably simplifies an extremely complex intellectual history. However, within jurisprudence this depiction of one tendency in the history of ideas about law serves some useful purposes. It encourages one to look for the unity to a range of ideas, to the basic tenets that are characteristic of the enterprise that many call Natural Law. And it provides a central benchmark for criticism. Apart from criticisms that are only aimed at the revision or improvement of such theories, if you are criticising the underlying approach of one of these theories then you are by implication taking an anti-Natural Law position. Such a position itself had become characterised during the nineteenth century, as one of Legal Positivism. Again, although the label Legal Positivism does not span the centuries like Natural Law, it does represent a large number of different theories. However, what unites those theories, rather than what different approaches they each take, is their anti-Natural Law position. Whether or not a particular Legal Positivist accepts that it is possible to recognise law as ethical (and they differ on this) they are united in asserting that ethical questions are different from and need not necessarily be implicated in an exploration of the background meaning to law. Natural Law theories within jurisprudence assert the opposite: to them the meaning of law is in some sense necessarily ethical. In other words, the subject matter of jurisprudence has incorporated, for most writers for well over a century, a clearly demarcated fundamental opposition. Jurisprudence theories are either Natural Law theories or theories of Legal Positivism. And even those theories that react to Legal Positivism (for example Realist theories, see Chapters 6 and 7, and economic analysis of law, see Chapter 17) often have as their starting assumption that Legal Positivism is right in its underlying anti-Natural Law stance.

By glancing at different theories that have been called theories of Natural Law, one is both looking at what each individual theory has to say, and exploring what the tenets of Natural Law theory are. Such an exploration involves questioning whether Natural Law theories are asking the right questions about law. Whether their questions are coherent questions, that permit the possibility of coherent answers, whether their questions are important, or enable important answers to be provided that are relevant to the conditions of our existence in the modern world etc. Without exploring these types of questions about the wide range of theories classified as Natural Law, much of jurisprudence seems ungrounded. Natural Law is the obvious starting point of jurisprudence, although it may be that this disguises much, or leads to many false trails. It is where most writers start. These theories in some form or other have always been with us and continue to be with us, despite all their faults. (For contemporary defences of Natural Law theory, see essays in George 1999, Part 1.)

The trouble with starting with Natural Law theory is that the range of ideas represented by it are so wide, and involve such wide-ranging arguments, that it tends to offer confusion rather than clarity. Indeed, as we will show, it is exactly this aspect of Natural Law theorising that primarily motivated those early writers who became known as Legal Positivists to develop their anti-Natural Law positions. Instead of starting with one theory or a set of theories about law that are sufficiently precise to allow for clear acceptance, rejection or revision, one finds large numbers of theories containing wide-ranging and differing ideas. Moreover, those ideas involve a knowledge base (their epistemology), political assumptions, emotional or psychological commitments that are so varied, that it is difficult to know what one would be accepting or rejecting. That said, the benchmark against which anti-Natural Law reasoning starts is the claim that all Natural Law theories, in some way or other, mistakenly assume that in order to understand what law is, it is necessary to involve oneself in an exploration and explanation of what law ought to be. To ask the evaluative question of what law ought to be is to ask about its legitimacy, the nature of its 'binding force' (why one has a duty to obey), about its intrinsic relationship to concepts such as justice, rights, reason, order etc. Such an exercise, valuable though it may be, is inherently faulty. It confuses description (law's actual existence) with prescription (the evaluation of law as good or bad, legitimate or illegitimate, in accord with reason or not, a part of not simply order but 'good' order). This principal criticism, and the point at which anti-Natural Law theory takes Natural Law theories as having a definite unity, is that they stray between the logically unconnected fields of meaning of 'is' (fact) and 'ought' (value), often called 'the naturalistic fallacy'. Why are those fields unconnected, because, according to the classic interpretation of Hume's law (the sceptical eighteenth century Scottish philosopher), you cannot derive a statement about what ought to be (one involving evaluation) from a statement about what is (one about fact), or an is statement from an ought statement. To try to do so is to talk incoherently and illogically: '... I am surprized to find, that instead of the usual copulations of propositions, *is*, and *is not*, I meet with no proposition that is not connected with an *ought*, or *ought not*. This change is imperceptible; but is, however, of the last consequence.' Hume explains that this often imperceptible slippage attempts to deduce some propositions from others, 'which are entirely different'. (1888/1740, Book III, Part I, Section I, 469. For a short explanation, see Hudson 1970, 250; for further discussion see Hudson 1969.) To given an example of the non sequitur involved in this kind of reasoning consider the now controversial argument that the fact that only women can bear children, points to the conclusion that they ought to be mothers. Whatever the rhetorical appeal of this argument, it is, and always has been, a logical non sequitur. (Many philosophers describe this form of incoherent reasoning in different terms, one evocative example being Moore's reference to it (1903, 13–14) as the 'naturalistic fallacy'.) If it is true that every theory called Natural Law has this fault line running through it, then that at least points to an aspect of unity to those theories labelled Natural Law. Whether that fault line exists, or whether it matters, is a question that you will gradually explore. It is a question that underpins the essential opposition in jurisprudence between Natural Law and Legal Positivist theories.

Why Natural Law?

As we have said, Natural Law theory is not a single theory of law. It is the application of ethical or political theories to the question of how legal orders can acquire, or have legitimacy. It is often presented as a history of such ethical and political ideas. The debates engendered within Natural Law theory are essentially ethical ones. Which of the ideas presented by the different theories best serves as a source for the legitimacy of law? Which are found within particular legal systems? What are the implications for themes such as justice, or claims that citizens ought to obey laws? These are important themes. If nothing else, those who use terms like 'justice' and 'democracy', who talk of a moral obligation to obey the law, or appeal to the need to uphold the constitution or the rule of law, should have some idea of the implications of their use of such terms.

Within jurisprudence, or at least modern jurisprudence, much of the importance and richness of Natural Law theory has been eroded by a focus on the relationship between Natural Law theories and those of Legal Positivism. That focus gives priority to the analytic question of the meaning of law, and how that meaning can be translated into legal practice. Thus, instead of asking what we mean by justice, or how a system of law could be understood as legitimate, the issue becomes what is the relationship between Natural Law theories and the everyday operations (legislation, adjudication, enforcement, the existence of legal duties and powers) of a legal system. In the modern world, this is a discussion in which Natural Law theory is unlikely to seem particularly important. Much of modern law (as opposed to earlier legal systems or modern religiously inspired ones) takes the form of detailed regulations whose content and form bears no **obvious** relation to any particular ethical theory. Thus, exploring the character of such theories and their import for law can seem to be peripheral to modern law. Ethical legitimacy hardly seems to arise, and if it does at all, only on the basis of some unproven claim that these regulations further the 'common good', or by reference to the legitimacy of their source (democratic, constitutional etc). Further, attempts to identify a necessary common element of ethics in all legal systems appear to founder on the difficulty of agreeing on a common set of ethical values, in the knowledge that coherent moral values are extremely difficult to articulate, let alone to prove. And the greater knowledge and tolerance towards different societies and cultures, leads to awareness that what 'we' think, or thought is good is not what 'they' think or thought is good. This position translates easily into awareness that legal systems have existed and will continue to exist that cannot easily be justified by reference to any universal set of ethical values.

While the difficulties of making ethical theories relevant to everyday life (let alone every legal order) seem obvious, the practice of imposing ethical values onto life and law does not abate. (As a modern example of such an attempt by a natural lawyer, see George 1993, Ch 1.) We have a new Human Rights Act, which introduces the European Convention on Human Rights into domestic law, and makes explicit the implicit importance of individual rights, as an ethical idea, to law. We have a new international war crimes tribunal in The Hague, seeking to enforce some fundamental human rights standards at an international level, as common standards that know of no national boundaries. And we continue to find examples of persons who defend their breaches of the law on 'conscientious' grounds. Some of these will argue that their actions, being moral, cannot amount to a breach of the law. Others, while accepting that they are breaking the law, nevertheless profess the need to justify their actions as moral (a position that still accepts that law **necessarily** involves some ethical value, whether in its nature or its practice).

In what follows we introduce you to some examples of Natural Law reasoning, and how the examples given offer foci for exploring the essential nature of law. Thus we look at some theories that try to explain what they believe makes legal orders exist, or at least exist as legitimate and 'valid'. We also consider an example of Natural Law in its debate with Positivist legal theories on the relevance of ethical theories to the practical operation (the fact and manner of their existence) of all laws and any legal system.

A Very Brief History of Natural Law

What is the reason for demanding a mina as a ransom for the prisoner, or that a goat and not two sheep should be sacrificed? (See Aristotle, *Nicomachean Ethics*, Book V, Ch 7. Or, as we might say today, is the appropriate fine £3,000 or £4,000, or the correct sentence 4 months or 3?)

This strange question sums up much of the origin and focus of Natural Law theory, and is the basis for the earliest distinctions between natural and positive law. The content of laws and the specific consequences that flow from them (the degree of punishment and the inability to deduce it logically from offences) is, to a certain extent, entirely arbitrary, in ancient as well as modern times. Laws are a matter of convention or convenience, political interest or local ideology. If not, what else could they be? Some of the first people to explore this question were the Greek philosophers. The issue arose at the time of the formation of the Greek city states, a development which brought together persons from different regions and families with different customs. Such a development posed the practical problem of how a 'common law' could be more than the consequence of which group had most power. The need for this 'common law' arose also in response to the background of a breakdown of belief in the Greek sense of *nomos*, originally understood as sacred custom. *Nomos* is an idea that makes sense of customs and conventions. The ritual and regular practices of a society are seen as legitimate and right through their association with the sacred. This conflation of what is right with what occurs ('ought' and 'is') is not the result of some idealistic view that everything is perfect. It is rather the ability to identify some practices as both normal and desirable and then to see them as a basis for identifying what are deviant and undesirable practices.

Bringing persons with different customs into contact with each other cannot easily be reconciled using the concept of *nomos*. Two Greek philosophers who attempted to find an alternative ethical basis for social life were Plato and Aristotle. A small digression into their ethical theories will be revealing. Plato saw the basis of ethics and other knowledge in absolute values to which things could approximate. And he saw evidence of this in language. Let's see how. He gives the example of an object, a vase. A vase could be beautiful, but it is not itself 'Beauty' (the value here is that of aesthetics). The elements of beauty found within the vase enable the description 'beautiful' to be used. Men know that value intuitively, although its content could be more fully identified through the application of reason. The absolute values identified by Plato include justice, which plays (and according to all Natural Law theories continues to play) an intrinsic relationship to law. Plato postulates that relationship in the following way:

> only such law can be considered right as aims like a good bowman always at that which has something of the externally beautiful and which neglects everything, be it wealth or something else of that kind, which is devoid of virtue. (*Laws* 705E–706A, quoted in Friedrich 1963, 19.)

Here we have two ideas that continue to have widespread application. Firstly, that justice is an absolute value at which law should aim, and second, that law which can be bought with wealth is not thereby just.

For Plato ideas such as justice, virtue and beauty were ideals, but they have greater ethical value than the customs of particular regions. The latter ('a goat and not two sheep') he described as 'conventions', denying that there was anything sacred about particular local practices. Rather he sought to locate ethics in universal values. The latter could transcend the particularity of local practices, and thus offer the prospect of a common ethics amongst different communities. As we shall see from the rest of this history, greater contacts between divers peoples is a common stimulus for Natural Law theorising.

Aristotle was also responding to problems arising out of the creation of city states and, like Plato, he sought to identify values through the use of reason. However, with Aristotle the source of those values is not absolute values, glimpsed within but lying in some way outside of this world. For him, the source of values lies in nature, and in particular, human nature. Nature, for Aristotle, had elements of both change and stability. The concept that unified this opposition was the *telos* or end of things. Things evolve towards their ends, or purpose: '… nature makes nothing without some end in view, nothing to no purpose …' (*Politics* Book 1, Ch 8). We still speak of nature in this way on occasions: acorns grow into oaks, calves into cows, human babies into adults. Our sense of what is wrong, or pathological, takes its meaning from what is healthy. So a doctor may talk of the purpose of the heart being to pump blood around the body. Aristotle applied this teleological form of reasoning to human development. Man, he observed, was a social animal, which meant that he needed social groups in order to flourish. This points to the necessity of the family. But man, for Aristotle, was also a political animal, one who could participate in politics: 'It follows that the state belongs to a class of objects which exist in nature, and that man is by nature a political animal; it is his nature to live in a state.' (*Politics* Book I, Ch 2) But politics (as conceived by Aristotle) was only possible within a city state, or *polis*. Only here could one find political debate. Thus, for Aristotle, the creation of the *polis* allowed man to fulfil a potential which remained unfulfilled whilst he lived only in small family groups. His conclusion was that the *polis* was not a threat to the *nomos*, but essential to the fulfilment of man's purpose. This reasoning also led him to conclusions about the law appropriate to a *polis*. For example, from man's nature as a social animal he concluded that there must be laws appropriate for the rearing and education of the young. Again, we still find this form of reasoning in modern popular speech. The actions of parents who grossly abuse their children may be called 'unnatural'.

As with Plato, we find in Aristotle one of the typical ways of seeking to construct ethical arguments: looking at human beings to find essential elements, which transcend particular customs. One can see this methodology still at work in attempts to articulate fundamental human rights. Aristotle's own conclusions also point to the difficulties of such approaches; he found no contradiction in speculating on human nature while seeing all non-Greeks as barbarians who could legitimately be owned as slaves.

Unfortunately for Aristotle, the development of human society did not stop at the Greek city state. Alexander the Great founded the Greek Empire. This brought Greeks and barbarians into contact in ways that went beyond the former making slaves of the latter. Attempts to make ethical sense of this experience led a group of philosophers known as the Stoics to talk of a community beyond the city state: the *cosmopolis*. Ethics, in the *cosmopolis*, were to be based on what wise men from any *polis* could identify. This philosophy represents the first attempt to identify sources of law that transcend particular states. Whilst not resulting in any concrete rules of international law in its time, one can see how this idea links with the legitimacy of international law as a legal order superior to local states. This relationship, between local laws and some more universal and higher legal order, forms the basis for the development of natural law from the time of the Stoics (see the extracts later in this chapter from Cicero, who interpreted Stoic philosophy for the Romans) right through to the eighteenth century. With the creation of the Roman Empire came the development of a common legal order for Roman Colonies and Rome itself, based on the customs common to them all, *jus gentium*. This notion started life as a second class legal system intended to facilitate trade. But when it became associated with Stoical ideas of the *cosmopolis*, and natural law, *jus naturale*, it began to operate as a superior law to that of the various colonies and cities, including that of Rome itself. This law operated both as a system of international law, and as a means of improving local laws (much like the relationship of equity to the common law).

The next important flourishing of Natural Law reasoning took place in the thirteenth century, in the work of St Thomas Aquinas. His writings were stimulated by developments that had taken place in Europe at that time, in particular the growth of city states whose authority seemed to challenge that of the Pope and the Holy Roman Empire. This period was also marked by the rediscovery of the works of Aristotle, whose philosophy included the celebration of city states (*polis*) as a completion of man's development. The authority of the Pope in dealing with such states was handicapped by the absence in Christian theology of any great concern with secular power. Augustine, the leading Christian theologian prior to this period, in keeping with Christ's instructions to 'Render therefore unto Ceasar, the things which are Caesar's' (The Bible, St Matthew, Ch 22, v 21) had written: 'What does it matter to a man, in this brief mortal life, under whose rule he lives, provided that the rulers do not force him to do evil' (*The City of God*, Book XIX). Aquinas developed the writings of Aristotle to reconcile the secular authority of princes with the theological authority of the church. Essentially, he treated the obvious fact that men in Europe were Christians (to be anything else ran all the risks of heresy) as part of man's purpose. Thus, for Aquinas Christianity was a stage of man's development that went beyond the developments open to the Greeks. Man was meant to live in a *polis*, but a Christian one.

> Just as the good life on this earth is directed, as to its end, to the blessed life which is promised us in heaven, so also all those particular benefits which men can procure for themselves, such as riches, or gain, or health, or skill, or learning, must be directed to the good of the community. But, as we have said, he who has charge of supreme ends must take precedence over those who are concerned with aims subordinate to these ends, and must guide them by his authority; it follows, therefore, that a king, though subject to that power and authority must, nevertheless, preside over all human activities, and direct them in virtue of his own power and authority. Now, whoever has a duty of completing this task, which is itself connected with some higher aim, must satisfy himself that his action is rightly directed towards that aim. Thus the smith forges a sword that is fit to fight with; and the builder must construct a house so that it is habitable. And because the aim of a good life on this earth is blessedness in heaven, it is the king's duty to promote the welfare of the community in such a way that it leads fittingly to the happiness of heaven; insisting upon the performance of all that leads thereto, and forbidding, as far as is possible, whatever is inconsistent with this end. (Aquinas 1959, 79)

Aquinas needed to tackle the same problems as the Greeks, the presence of different laws in different places. He achieved this by distinguishing natural law from human law. The former was based on reason, and could be understood by reflecting on the nature of man and God's purpose in creating him. Law is, according to Aquinas, 'a rational ordering of things which concern the common good; promulgated by whoever is charged with the care of the community' (1959, 113). To the extent that human law partook of natural law, it would 'oblige in conscience' (1959, 135). Note that, for Aquinas, a law that did not 'oblige in conscience' was not really a law at all. Human law partook of natural law to the extent that it was Christian, and to the extent that it served the common good rather than vested interests. The content of this 'common good' could be reasoned from man's nature: the need to preserve life, to raise and educate the young, and to establish a stable political order. Aquinas acknowledged a fact of medieval life that is even more apparent today: that the specific content of particular legal systems cannot be reasoned from general ethical principles. Thus for Aquinas, the rules of different principalities could still all be law, despite their differences, provided that they had as their aim the furtherance of the common good. Certain aspects of legal systems, most particularly sanctions, had only the most tangential relationship to natural law. The customs of punishment ('a goat and not two sheep') could not be deduced from natural law. The natural law precept 'do not kill' provides no basis in reason (although it may do so in particular schemes of moral thought) for a conclusion such as 'murderers shall be hung'. Human law goes beyond the natural law question 'What am I obliged to do by my conscience?'. It has to deal with sanctions, because any answer to the question 'What am I obliged to do by my conscience?' would not restrain 'evil' men.

The Reformation created new pressures. From a Catholic perspective Protestantism was a heresy. The laws of Protestant territories could command no respect. More importantly, given the need to form alliances and trade with persons of different religious faiths, what could be the basis of international obligations? In this development we see parallels with the conditions which generated the Roman *jus gentium*, and it was to this law that jurists turned to find a basis for international law. In his use of the *jus gentium*, Grotius (1583–1645) argued that a common universal law of nations did not require a Catholic or any other religious source for its obligatory force: 'natural law would retain its validity even if God did not exist' (*De Jure Belli ac Pacis*, 1925 edn, Vol 1, ss 10–17).

The history of Natural Law up to the end of the sixteenth century is often termed 'conservative' to distinguish it from the theories that followed. The label conservative refers to the concern of theorists to establish a basis for the legitimacy of existing legal orders. The theories that appeared from the seventeenth century are often termed 'revolutionary'. This does not mean that persons who desired to ferment rebellion wrote them all. Rather, it was that the focus of such writing turned from the issue of how legal orders could have legitimacy, to the limits of that legitimacy. The change in focus gave such theories the potential to promote and support revolutionary politics. These theories also have a different starting point. While the Greeks reasoned from the nature of man, they did not understand men as essentially equal as individuals. The Greek state was an obviously hierarchical community. The 'Man' whose purpose was politics in Aristotle's scheme of reasoning was not only not a barbarian, but also not a woman or a worker. Only the heads of important families debated politics in the forum. But from the middle of the seventeenth century the naturalness of hierarchical orders came under sustained attack. This is not the place to provide a historical account of the changes which gave individualism and individual rights an intuitive appeal, and made them both a source of, and inspiration for, natural law theorising. But with the rise of new classes whose status depended on wealth rather than birth, and trade rather than land, came the development of a new type of theory that saw legitimate rule as a contract between ruler and ruled. Sovereignty now becomes something which individuals surrendered, on conditions, to those who had authority over them.

These seventeenth and eighteenth century theories saw nature not as a universal order implicit in existing legal systems, but as something which operated prior to their creation: a state of nature which had, or would, operate in the absence of the current political and legal order. The question then became: on what conditions would persons in such a state of nature agree to surrender their freedom to those who ruled over them? Different theorists answered this question differently. Hobbes had such a pessimistic view of life in the state of nature: 'solitary, poor, nasty, brutish, and short' (*Leviathan* 1651, Pt 1, Ch 13), that isolated individuals would rationally contract with each other to hand over all of their sovereignty to a single sovereign. Such a handing over was, for Hobbes, virtually unconditional except possibly if the individual's life is threatened. Locke saw not only sovereignty but also natural rights present in the state of nature, including the right to hold property. Locke's sovereign would only retain legitimacy to the extent that he protected the individual's right to property: 'The great and chief end, therefore, of men's uniting into commonwealths, and putting themselves under government, is the preservation of their property' (*The Second Treatise of Civil Government* 1690, Ch 9, s 124). Rousseau saw sovereignty in the will of the people, which remained with them: 'Man was born free, and everywhere he is in chains' (*The Social Contract* 1762, Ch 1). It could not be the subject of a contract, but could only be loaned to representatives, and may be withdrawn. The ground that could be covered by such social contract reasoning gives legitimacy to widely different political orders. Hobbes argued for absolute monarchy, Rousseau for a continuously operating spontaneous popular democracy. Locke provided philosophical support for the American Constitution and, some would argue capitalism. These social contract theories continue to provide a philosophical basis for modern theories of justice and modern forms of government. Consider for example, the contract represented by the 'veil of ignorance' described by John Rawls in his book '*A Theory of Justice*' (discussed in Chapter 15).

Moving from these seventeenth and eighteenth century theories to the modern world, since the Second World War there is said to have been a revival in Natural Law thinking. During a large part of the nineteenth and early twentieth centuries Natural Law theory was thought to be unimportant. Positivists and natural lawyers agreed that the rules of a particular community were not necessarily just, but disagreed on whether this fact affected one's ability to describe these rules as law. This threatened to deteriorate into a terminological debate as to which group had to put inverted commas around their particular use of the word 'law': those seeking to describe the rules of particular communities, or those seeking to describe an ideal form of law which corresponded with justice. What also seemed to reduce this dispute to one of terminology, was the different tasks undertaken by those belonging to the different groups: positivists wanted to describe the laws of particular communities, natural lawyers wanted to consider how to construct just systems of law, or identify when existing systems ceased to be just. The claim about its revival specifically represents, among other things, the claim that Legal Positivism as an underlying philosophy was implicated in the way that law operated in Nazi Germany. German lawyers trained in a Legal Positivist tradition of

'Gesetz ist Gesetz' (the law is the law – see extract from D'Entreves below) were at fault in misunderstanding the nature of their subject, and misapplying it. In denying the connection between the practice of law and issues of ethics and justice, they impoverished the notion of law and abrogated their responsibility to resist the immorality of Nazi law. The causal link made in such a claim is contentious. But whether it is accurate or not, it has spurred modern natural lawyers into seeking to demonstrate the relevance of Natural Law theory to modern concerns, including legal practice. They deny that the issue is simply one of terminology, or that there can be a division of roles between those who describe or practice law, and those who seek to describe, or put into effect, just laws. While the impetus for much Legal Positivism is the desire to make an accurate general statement of law as an operating system, debating with this tradition leads to modern natural law theorists claiming that such descriptions are incomplete without including ethical elements. And to show this, Natural Law is forced to demonstrate its relevance to current legal practices.

Lon Fuller, a Harvard law professor, offered a procedural version of Natural Law theory. His writing has elements of social contract theories, seeing law as a special relationship between the rulers and the ruled, which allows the latter to show 'fidelity' to law. Fuller makes no claim for the substantive content of law. He concentrates instead on the conditions necessary for a citizenry to be capable of obeying law, of being subject to the 'governance of rules'. These conditions, which include the requirement for laws to be published, understandable, and prospective, provide one version of what is commonly described as the 'Rule of Law'. For Fuller, the quality of a legal system as law, as opposed to something less, is crucially linked to the idea of obedience. If there are procedural requirements for good law, then every law, even the most technical regulation, can be subjected to a critique in terms of its accessibility to citizens: their ability to obey it.

Writing in the late 1970s, the Oxford academic John Finnis offered a Natural Law theory that, despite the author's personal commitments, is not based on Christianity or any other theology. It involves what is essentially a liberal conception of the good. Rather than seeking to defend the particular practices of any society, Finnis seeks to identify the values that underlie all human activity, arguing that such activity affirms these values. The values he identifies are life, knowledge, play, aesthetic experience, friendship, religion (in the sense of a concern with things beyond the currently knowable), and practical reasonableness (a desire to pursue the former values in an intelligent and ordered fashion). Our common ability to experience these things gives meaning to our understanding of a common good. The task and responsibility of those involved in fashioning society, is to respect these values and seek to give effect to them in our practical arrangements, including law. Finnis does not claim that all systems of law have sought to acknowledge and respect the experiences and values common to all humans. But he claims that systems of law which genuinely engage in this enterprise are more complete examples of what constitutes law, than those that do not (all other things being equal). Finnis' aim is not simply to assert that one can have ethical theories about the proper role of the state, but to engage with Legal Positivism, and its presentation of legal practice. Finnis insists that all those involved in the administration of law, whether in legislation or adjudication, are parts of a system whose purpose must be, if it is to realise its 'proper' purpose, the achievement of the common good. Full participation in that enterprise requires one to apply the skills of practical reason to realise the common good.

The best known contemporary attempt to assert the relevance of moral reasoning to legal practice is found in the works of Ronald Dworkin. His theory seeks to demonstrate the inability of theories which deny the relevance of moral reasoning to account for the practices of legal officials, most importantly, the judiciary. He seeks to argue that adjudication cannot be separated from ethical reasoning, and to argue in turn for the importance of adjudication in establishing the content of any legal system (Dworkin's ideas are dealt with extensively in Chapters 8 and 9 and in other chapters in this book.)

What we have traced in this very brief history are the seeds of Natural Law theory that resonate down the centuries, as they continue to do with so many modern ideas. (For example, the modern ideas associated with fundamental human rights, which have earlier antecedents in ideas of natural rights.) Let us just state a few of these key ideas extracted from our brief history. Law is a value, and like all values, one can and should strive to achieve it. Not to do so is barely worthy of the title of this virtue, law. Law is implicated in the common good, and without satisfying that overall aim to some extent is anything but law, perhaps better described as a form of violence or terror. Law that can and does serve the common good is available to be known by our use of reason. Reason is both the means of knowledge of what serves the common good, and what is law, and the test for conformity between law and nature. In nature there is natural order and regularity, and equally a characteristic of human existence that conforms to the natural order is the use of human laws to achieve natural regularity, and peaceful coexistence. What commands us and has the value of law rather than terror, is that which 'obliges in conscience'. Law is concerned with the duty to obey, not merely with the achievement of obedience. Law involves an exercise of judgement of human behaviour. Judgement is inherently a moral exercise that will, over the long time span, achieve its natural purpose, which is the moral purpose, to do that which is right and good (see, for example, Beyleveld and Brownsword 1986).

Providing a history (albeit brief) of Natural Law theories should help you to appreciate how they, in their descriptions of the essential ingredients or nature of law, give answers to questions that address law's persistence over a long time span, rather than simply at any particular instance. They are concerned with the continuity of law. Such a focus is not surprising in the light of the broader philosophical tradition of Natural Law theory. It concerns itself with questions unlimited by time (thus less concerned with short-term questions) and even, to some extent, unlimited by space (thus not only concerned with the here and now). Thus, when modern ideas pick up the themes represented by the tradition of Natural Law, and try to attach those themes to modern conditions, one has a sense that one is talking about what is universal and enduring, holistic rather than overly particularised.

Extracts

We start with short extracts from the writings of the early Roman jurist, orator and statesman Cicero. These extracts illustrate the sort of eloquent and confident reasoning characteristic of much Natural Law writing, in which a broad understanding of 'nature' is thought to be available to all individuals through the use of reason, and to be expressive of God's law. Cicero is aware that different states have different laws, and that the rules of states produce 'legal documents and legal questions' which are the day-to-day business of lawyers. But this kind of law is only a small part of a more general form of law, based on reason, which transcends these particular rule systems.

A few questions may assist your reading of this text:

1. Is everything ratified by laws necessarily just? If not, does this mean that a local law can be unjust?

2. Is every law, which is democratically approved of, just?

3. How are we to know that a law is just?

4. Why should law created by legislation have the status of law 'more as a matter of courtesy than fact'?

5. If we found out that doctors had prescribed poison, would we cease to be able to describe this as 'medicine'? Does this analogy work for law? Do we today associate the word law with something as positive and good as medicine?

Cicero (*On the Commonwealth*, Book 3, 33)

True law is right reason, consonant with nature, spread through all people. It is constant and eternal; it summons to duty by its orders, it deters from crime by its prohibitions. Its orders and prohibitions to good people are never given in vain; but it does not move the wicked by these orders or prohibitions. It is wrong to pass laws obviating this law; it is not permitted to abrogate any of it; it cannot be totally repealed. We cannot be released from this law by the senate or the people, and it needs no exegete or interpreter like Sextus Aelius. There will not be one law at Rome and another at Athens, one now and another later; but all nations at all times will be bound by this one eternal and unchangeable law, and the god will be the one common master and general (so to speak) of all people. He is the author, expounder, and mover of this law; and the person who does not obey it will be in exile from himself. Insofar as he scorns his nature as a human being, by this very fact he will pay the greatest penalty, even if he escapes all the other things that are generally recognized as punishments.

Cicero (*On the Laws*, Book 1, 17–22)

MARCUS: The object of inquiry in this conversation, Atticus, is not how to write legal documents or how to answer legal questions. Granted, that is a great task, which used to be performed by many famous men and is now done by one man of the greatest authority and wisdom – but in this discussion we must embrace the whole subject of universal justice and law, so that what we call 'civil law' will be limited to a small and narrow area. We must explain the nature of law, and that needs to be looked for in human nature; we must consider the legislation through which states ought to be governed; and then we must deal with the laws and decrees of peoples as they are composed and written, in which the so-called civil laws of our people will not be left out.

QUINTUS: You are looking deep, and (as is right) to the source of what we seek; people who teach civil law differently are teaching not so much the way of justice as of the courtroom.

MARCUS: That isn't true, Quintus, and in fact ignorance of law leads to more lawsuits than knowledge of it. But that comes later; now we should consider the origins of law.

Philosophers have taken their starting point from law; and they are probably right to do so if, as these same people define it, law is the highest reason, rooted in nature, which commands things that must be done and prohibits the opposite. When this same reason is secured and established in the human mind, it is law. And therefore they think that law is judgment, the effect of which is such as to order people to behave rightly and forbid them to do wrong; they think that its name in Greek is derived from giving to each his own, while I think that in Latin it is derived from choosing. They put the essence of law in equity, and we place it in choice; both are attributes of law. I think that these ideas are generally right; and if so, then the beginning of justice is to be sought in law: law is a power of nature, it is the mind and reason of the prudent man, it distinguishes justice and injustice. But since all our speech is based on popular conceptions, we must sometimes speak in popular terms and call that a law (in the language of the common people) which prescribes in writing what it wants by ordering or forbidding. But in establishing the nature of justice, let us begin from that highest law, which was born aeons before any law was written or indeed before any state was established.

...

Then shall we go back to the beginning, to the source of justice itself? Once we have found it, there will be no doubt about how to judge what we are seeking.

...

This is its relevance: this animal — provident, perceptive, versatile, sharp, capable of memory, and filled with reason and judgment — which we call a human being, was endowed by the supreme god with a grand status at the time of its creation. It alone of all types and varieties of animate creatures has a share in reason and thought, which all the others lack. What is there, not just in humans, but in all heaven and earth, more divine than reason? When it has matured and come to perfection, it is properly named wisdom. And therefore, since there is nothing better than reason, and it is found both in humans and in god, reason forms the first bond between human and god. And those who share reason also share right reason; and since that is law, we humans must be considered to be closely allied to gods by law. Furthermore, those who share law also share the procedures of justice; and those who have these things in common must be considered members of the same state, all the more so if they obey the same commands and authorities. Moreover, they do obey this celestial order, the divine mind and the all-powerful god, so that this whole cosmos must be considered to be the common state of gods and humans. And as in states distinctions in the legal condition of individuals are made in accordance with family relationships (according to a kind of system with which I will deal at the proper time), it is all the more grand and glorious in nature at large that men should be a part of the family and race of gods.

Cicero (*On the Laws*, Book 1, 42–45)

The most stupid thing of all, moreover, is to consider all things just which have been ratified by a people's institutions or laws. What about the laws of tyrants?

...

There is only one justice, which constitutes the bond among humans, and which was established by the one law, which is right reason in commands and prohibitions. The person who does not know it is unjust, whether the law has been written anywhere or not. And if justice is obedience to the written law and institutions of a people, and if (as these same people say) everything is to be measured by utility, then whoever thinks that it will be advantageous to him will neglect the laws and will break them if he can. The result is that there is no justice at all if it is not by nature, and the justice set up on the basis of utility is uprooted by that same utility: if nature will not confirm justice, all the virtues will be eliminated.

...

If justice were determined by popular vote or by the decrees of princes or the decisions of judges, then it would be just to commit highway robbery or adultery or to forge wills if such things were approved by popular vote. If the opinions and the decrees of stupid people are powerful enough to overturn nature by their votes, why don't they ordain that what is evil and destructive should be considered good and helpful? If law can make justice out of injustice, why can't it make good from evil? But in fact we can divide good laws from bad by no other standard than that of nature. And it is not only justice and injustice that are distinguished naturally, but in general all honorable and disgraceful acts. For nature has given us shared conceptions and has so established them in our minds that honorable things are classed with virtue, disgraceful ones with vice. To think that these things are a matter of opinion, not fixed in nature, is the mark of a madman. What we call (and it is a misuse of the word) the virtue of a tree or of a horse is not a matter of opinion; it is natural. And if that is true, honorable and disgraceful can also be distinguished by nature.

Cicero (*On the Laws*, Book 2, 8–15)

MARCUS: Then before we get to particular laws, let us consider again the meaning and nature of law, so that – since everything else in our discussion rests on this – we don't slip from time to time in the misuse of language and make mistakes about the meaning of the [word] by which our laws are to be defined.

QUINTUS: Fair enough; that's the right course of instruction.

MARCUS: This has, I know, been the opinion of the wisest men: that law was not thought up by human minds; that it is not some piece of legislation by popular assemblies; but it is something eternal which rules the entire universe through the wisdom of its commands and prohibitions. Therefore, they said, that first and final law is the mind of the god who compels or forbids all things by reason. From that cause, the law which the gods have given to the human race has rightly been praised: it is the reason and mind of a wise being, suited to command and prohibition.

...

From the time we were small, Quintus, we were taught to call 'if there is a summons to court' and other things of that sort 'laws'. But in fact it should be understood that both this and other commands and prohibitions of peoples have a force for summoning to proper behavior and deterring from crime, a force which is not only older than the age of peoples and states but coeval with the god who protects and steers heaven and earth. It is not possible for there to be a divine mind without reason, nor does divine reason lack this force in sanctioning right and wrong. The fact that it was not written down anywhere that one man should stand on the bridge against all the forces of the enemy and order the bridge to be cut down behind him does not mean that we should not believe that the famous Horatius Cocles performed his great deed in accordance with the law and command of bravery; nor does the absence of a written law on sexual assault during the reign of Lucius Tarquinius mean that the violence which Sextus Tarquinius brought against Lucretia the daughter of Tricipitinus was not contrary to the eternal law. Reason existed, derived from nature, directing people to good conduct and away from crime; it did not begin to be a law only at that moment when it was written down, but when it came into being; and it came into being at the same time as the divine mind. And therefore that true and original law, suitable for commands and prohibitions, is the right reason of Jupiter, the supreme god.

QUINTUS: I agree, brother, that what is right and true is also eternal and neither rises nor falls with the texts in which legislation is written.

MARCUS: Therefore, just as that divine mind is the highest law, so too when in a human being it is brought to maturity, it resides in the mind of wise men. The legislation that has been written down for nations in different ways and for particular occasions has the name of law more as a matter of courtesy than as a fact; for they teach that every law that deserves that name is praiseworthy, using arguments such as these: it is generally agreed that laws were invented for the well-being of citizens, the safety of states, and the calm and happy life of humans; and that those who first ordained legislation of this sort demonstrated to their peoples that they would write and carry such legislation the adoption of which would make their lives honorable and happy; and that what was so composed and ordained they would call laws. From this it should be understood that those who wrote decrees that were destructive and unjust to their peoples, since they did the opposite of what they had promised and claimed, produced something utterly different from laws; so that it should be clear that in the interpretation of the word 'law' itself there is the significance and intention of choosing something just and right. So I ask you, Quintus, as they generally do: if the lack of something causes a state to be worthless, is that something to be considered a good thing?

QUINTUS: Among the very best.

MARCUS: Then should not a state lacking law be considered as nothing for that very reason?

QUINTUS: No other conclusion is possible.

MARCUS: Then it is necessary that law be considered one of the best things.

QUINTUS: I agree completely.

MARCUS: What of the fact that many things are approved by peoples that are damaging and destructive, which no more approach the name of law than whatever bandits have agreed upon among themselves? The instructions of doctors cannot truly be so called if in ignorance and inexperience they prescribe poisons in place of medicine; nor, even if the people approve of it, will something harmful in a nation be a law of any kind. Law, therefore, is the distinction between just and unjust things, produced in accordance with nature, the most ancient and first of all things, in accordance with which human laws are constructed which punish the wicked while defending and protecting the good.

QUINTUS: I understand entirely, and I now think that any other law should not only not be accepted, but should not even be given the name of law.

MARCUS: So you think that the laws of Titius and Appuleius are no laws at all?

QUINTUS: And not even the laws of Livius.

MARCUS: Rightly, since in a single moment they were removed by a single word from the senate. The law whose force I have explained, however, can be neither removed nor abrogated.

QUINTUS: So the laws that you will pass, I imagine, are never to be abrogated.

MARCUS: Certainly, so long as you two accept them. But I think that I must do as Plato did, the most learned of men and also the most serious of philosophers, who first wrote about the commonwealth and also wrote a separate work about its laws, namely to speak in praise of the law before I recite it. And I see that Zaleucus and Charondas did the same thing, not as a matter of intellectual enjoyment but in writing laws for their states for the sake of the commonwealth. In imitating them Plato appears to have thought that it was a function of law to persuade rather than to compel all things through force and threats.

Next, we have a longer extract from Aquinas. His words have been translated but not updated, which makes it difficult to understand some of his arguments. We have inserted questions to assist your understanding of each part of the extract. The extract bears careful reading. It is the classic exposition of a natural law position. Aquinas attempts to provide a systematic answer to the question of how law can have moral authority, so that obedience to law becomes a matter of conscience. The questions should alert you to the problems and difficulties of providing an answer to this question. Aquinas is anticipating all sorts of objections that can be made not only to his theory of natural law, but to any such theory.

Aquinas (1959, Selected Political Writings, 109–149)

3.   *VALUE AND SIGNIFICANCE OF THE POLITICAL ORDER*

THE SENSE IN WHICH THE STATE HAS THE VALUE OF AN END

Not all that a man has or is, is subject to political obligation: hence it is not necessary that all of his actions be considered worthy of praise or blame with respect to the political community. But all that a man is, and all that he has or can be, must bear a certain relationship to God. Hence every human act, be it good or bad, so far as it proceeds from reason is meritorious or demeritorious before God.

THE POLITICAL ORDER COMPARED WITH THE DIVINE AND NATURAL ORDER

There is a threefold order to be found in man. The first is that which derives from the rule of reason: in so far as all our actions and experiences should be commensurate with the guidance of reason. The second arises from comparison with the rule of divine law, which should be our guide in all things. And if man were actually a solitary animal, this double order would suffice: but because man is naturally a social and political animal, as is proved in I. *Politics*, chap. 2, it is necessary that there should be a third order, regulating the conduct of man to his fellows with whom he has to live.

Q. Why should one's political obligations (legal duties under the community's laws) cover less of one's actions than one's moral obligations?

Q. Why is it 'necessary' for man to develop rules regulating his conduct vis-á-vis his fellow man?

4.   LAW IN GENERAL

THE NATURE OF LAW

Law is a rule or measure of action in virtue of which one is led to perform certain actions and restrained from the performance of others. The term 'law' derives [etymologically] from 'binding', because by it one is bound to a certain course of action. But the rule and measure of human action is reason, which is the first principle of human action: this is clear from what we have said elsewhere. It is reason which directs action to its appropriate end; and this, according to the philosopher, is the first principle of all activity.

Q. How is a rule a 'measure of action'? Is this the same as saying that law provides a standard?

Q. Do humans work out how to achieve their ends through reason? Is so can they also work out how to achieve 'appropriate' ends through reason?

REASON AND WILL IN LAW

Reason has power to move to action from the will, as we have shown already: for reason enjoins all that is necessary to some end, in virtue of the fact that that end is desired. But will, if it is to have the authority of law, must be regulated by reason when it commands. It is in this sense that we should understand the saying that the will of the prince has the power of law. In any other sense the will of the prince becomes an evil rather than law.

Q. How does the will of a ruler get the authority of law?

THE OBJECT OF THE LAW IS THE COMMON GOOD

Since every part bears the same relation to its whole as the imperfect to the perfect, and since one man is a part of that perfect whole which is the community, it follows that the law must have as its proper object the well-being of the whole community. So the

Philosopher, in his definition of what pertains to law, makes mention both of happiness and of political union. He says (*Ethics* V, chap. 1): 'We call that legal and just which makes for and preserves the well-being of the community through common political action': and the perfect community is the city, as is shown in the first book of the *Politics* (chap. 1).

This section links to Aristotle's idea that man is a political animal fulfilled only by living in a political community (see the earlier commentary).

Q.   If it is man's purpose, to live in a political community, should the purpose of the laws of that community be the well-being of the community?

Q.   Is the well-being of the community what we commonly understand by 'the common good'?

WHO HAS THE RIGHT TO PROMULGATE LAW

Law, strictly understood, has as its first and principal object the ordering of the common good. But to order affairs to the common good is the task either of the whole community or of some one person who represents it. Thus the promulgation of law is the business either of the whole community or of that political person whose duty is the care of the common good. Here as in every other case it is the one who decrees the end who also decrees the means thereto.

A private person has no authority to compel right living. He may only advise; but if his advice is not accepted he has no power of compulsion. But law, to be effective in promoting right living must have such compelling force; as the Philosopher says (X *Ethics*, chap. 9). But the power of compulsion belongs either to the community as a whole, or to its official representative whose duty it is to inflict penalties, as we shall see later. He alone, therefore, has the right to make laws.

Just as one man is a member of a family, so a household forms part of a city: but a city is a perfect community, as is shown in the first book of the *Politics*. Similarly, as the well-being of one man is not a final end, but is subordinate to the common good, so also the well-being of any household must be subordinate to the interests of the city, which is a perfect community. So the head of a family may make certain rules and regulations, but not such as have, properly speaking, the force of law.

Q.   Why do things required by private individuals, or heads of families, not have the force of law?

DEFINITION OF LAW

From the foregoing we may gather the correct definition of law. It is nothing else than a rational ordering of things which concern the common good; promulgated by whoever is charged with the care of the community.

5. THE VARIOUS TYPES OF LAW

THE ETERNAL LAW

As we have said above, law is nothing else but a certain dictate of the practical reason 'in the prince' who rules a perfect community. It is clear, however, supposing the world to be governed by divine providence as we demonstrated in the First Part, that the whole community of the Universe is governed by the divine reason. Thus the rational guidance of created things on the part of God, as the Prince of the universe, has the quality of law … This we can call the eternal law.

THE NATURAL LAW

Since all things which are subject to divine providence are measured and regulated by the eternal law – as we have already shown – it is clear that all things participate to some degree in the eternal law; in so far as they derive from it certain inclinations to those actions and aims which are proper to them. But, of all others, rational creatures are subject to divine providence in a very special way; being themselves made participators in providence itself, in that they control their own actions and the actions of others. So they have a certain share in the divine reason itself, deriving therefrom a natural inclination to such actions and ends as are fitting. This participation in the eternal law by rational creatures is called the natural law. Thus when the Psalmist said (*Psalm* IV, 6): 'Offer up the sacrifice of justice', he added, as though being asked the question, what is the sacrifice of justice 'Many say, who sheweth us good things?', and then replied, saying: 'The light of Thy countenance, O Lord, is signed upon us'. As though the light of natural reason, by which we discern good from evil, and which is the natural law were nothing else than the impression of the divine light in us. So it is clear that natural law is nothing else than the participation of the eternal law in rational creatures.

Q. God's law is his rational ordering of the whole universe for all time. Why is man uniquely placed to identify the part of eternal law which applies to himself?

HUMAN LAW

Just as in speculative reason we proceed from indemonstrable principles, naturally known, to the conclusions of the various sciences, such conclusions not being innate but arrived at by the use of reason; so also the human reason has to proceed from the precepts of the natural law, as though from certain common and indemonstrable principles, to other more particular dispositions. And such particular dispositions, arrived at by an effort of reason, are called human laws: provided that the other conditions necessary to all law, which we have already noted, are observed. So Cicero says (*De Invent. Rhetor.* II, 53): 'Law springs in its first beginnings from nature: then such standards as are judged to be useful become established by custom: finally reverence and holiness add their sanction to what springs from nature and is established by custom.'

Q. Is the content of human law dictated by the principles of natural law?

Q. How can human laws differ, and yet still be commonly related to natural law?

THE NECESSITY FOR A DIVINE LAW

In addition to natural law and to human law there had of necessity to be also a divine law to direct human life: and this for four reasons. In the first place because it is by law that man is directed in his actions with respect to his final end. If therefore, man were destined to an end which was no more than proportionate to his natural faculties, there would be no need for him to have any directive on the side of reason above the natural law and humanly enacted law which is derived from it. But because man is destined to an end of eternal blessedness, and this exceeds what is proportionate to natural human faculties as we have already shown, it was necessary that he should be directed to this end not merely by natural and human law, but also by a divinely given law. – Secondly: because of the uncertainty of human judgement, particularly in matters that are contingent and specific, it is often the case that very differing judgements are passed by various people on human activities; and from these there proceed different, and even contrary, laws. In order, therefore, that man should know without any doubt what he is to do and what to avoid, it was necessary that his actions should be directed by a divinely given law, which is known to be incapable of error. – Thirdly: because laws are enacted in respect of what is capable of being judged. But the judgement of man cannot reach to the hidden interior actions of the soul, it can only be about external activities which are apparent. Nevertheless, the perfection of virtue requires that a man should be upright in both classes of actions. Human law being thus insufficient to order and regulate interior actions, it was necessary that for this purpose there should also be a divine law. – Fourthly: because, as Augustine says (I *De Lib. Arb.*), human law can neither punish nor even prohibit all that is evilly done. For in trying to prevent all that is evil it would render impossible also much that is good; and thus would impede much that is useful to the common welfare and therefore necessary to human intercourse. In order, therefore, that no evil should go unforbidden and unpunished it was necessary that there should be a divine law which would prohibit all manner of sin.

Q.   Divine law deals with those parts of eternal law that are directly revealed to man by divine revelation (through the bible, Pope etc). If man has reason, and can use this to work out his part in eternal law, why is there any need for Divine Law?

6.   THE EFFECTS OF LAW

THE MORAL OBJECT OF LAW

It is clear that the true object of law is to induce those subject to it to seek their own virtue. And since virtue is 'that which makes its possessor good', it follows that the proper effect of law is the welfare of those for whom it is promulgated: either absolutely or in some certain respect. If the intention of the law-giver is directed to that which is truly good, that is to the common good regulated by divine justice, it will follow that man will, by such a law, be made unconditionally good. If on the other hand the intention of the law-giver is directed, not to that which is absolutely good, but merely to what is useful – in that it is pleasurable to himself or contrary to divine justice – then such a law does not make men good unconditionally, but only in a certain respect; namely, in so far as it has reference to some particular political regime. In this sense good is to be found even in those things which are intrinsically evil: as when a man is termed a good thief, because he is expert in attaining the object he sets before himself.

The goodness of any part is to be considered with reference to the whole of which it forms a part: so Augustine says (III *Confess.*, 8): 'All parts are base which are not fittingly adapted to their whole'. So, all men being a part of the city, they cannot be truly good unless they adapt themselves to the common good. Nor can the whole be well constituted if its parts be not properly adapted to it. So it is impossible for the welfare of the community to be in a healthy state unless the citizens are virtuous: or at least such of them as are called to take up the direction of affairs. It would be sufficient for the common well-being if the rest were virtuous to the extent of obeying the commands of the ruler. So the Philosopher says (III *Polit.*, 2): 'A ruler must have the virtue of a truly upright man: but not every citizen is bound to reach a similar degree of uprightness.'

Tyrannical law, not being according to reason, is not law at all in the true and strict sense, but is rather a perversion of law. It does, however, assume the nature of law to the extent that it provides for the well-being of the citizens. Thus it bears relationship to law in so far as it is the dictate to his subjects of some one in authority; and to the extent that its object is the full obedience of those subjects to the law. For them such obedience is good, not unconditionally, but with respect to the particular regime under which they live.

Q. Can laws which further the well-being of part of the community, amount to a partial good? Can obedience to such laws, also represent a partial good? What aim must the laws serve in order for obedience to them to be wholly good?

7. THE ETERNAL LAW

ITS DERIVATION FROM THE DIVINE WISDOM

Just as in the mind of every artist there already exists the idea of what he will create by his art, so in the mind of every ruler there must already exist an ideal of order with respect to what shall be done by those subject to his rule. And just as the ideal of those things that have yet to be produced by any art is known as the exemplar, or actual art of the things so to be produced, the ideal in the mind of the ruler who governs the actions of those subject to him has the quality of law – provided that the conditions we have already mentioned above are also present. Now God, in His wisdom is the creator of all things, and may be compared to them as the artist is compared to the product of his art; as we have shown in Part I. Moreover he governs actions and movements of each individual creature, as we also pointed out. So, as the ideal of divine wisdom, in so far as all things are created by it, has the quality of an exemplar or art or idea, so also the ideal of divine wisdom considered as moving all things to their appropriate end has the quality of law. Accordingly, the eternal law is nothing other than the ideal of divine wisdom considered as directing all actions and movements.

ALL LAW DERIVES ULTIMATELY FROM THE ETERNAL LAW

In every case of ruling we see that the design of government is passed from the head of the government to his subordinate governors; just as the scheme of what shall be done in a city derives from the king to his subordinate ministers by statute; or again, in artistic construction, the plan of what is to be made is passed from the architect to the subordinate operators. Since, then, the eternal law is the plan of government in the supreme governor, all schemes of government, in those who direct as subordinates must derive from the eternal law. Consequently, all laws, so far as they accord with right reason, derive from the eternal law. For this reason Augustine says (I *De Lib. Arb.*): 'In human law nothing is just or legitimate if it has not been derived by men from the eternal law.'

Human law has the quality of law only in so far as it proceeds according to right reason: and in this respect it is clear that it derives from the eternal law. In so far as it deviates from reason it is called an unjust law, and has the quality not of law but of violence. Nevertheless, even an unjust law, to the extent that it retains the appearance of law through its relationship to the authority of the lawgiver, derives in this respect from the eternal law. 'For all power is from the Lord God' (*Rom.* XIII, 1).

Q.   What features of eternal law can human law still share even when it is unjust?

8.   *THE NATURAL LAW*

PRECEPTS OF THE NATURAL LAW

The order of the precepts of the natural law corresponds to the order of our natural inclinations. For there is in man a natural and initial inclination to good which he has in common with all substances; in so far as every substance seeks its own preservation according to its own nature. Corresponding to this inclination, the natural law contains all that makes for the preservation of human life, and all that is opposed to its dissolution. Secondly, there is to be found in man a further inclination to certain more specific ends, according to the nature which man shares with other animals. In virtue of this inclination there pertains to the natural law all those instincts 'which nature has taught all animals', such as sexual relationship, the rearing of offspring, and the like. Thirdly, there is in man a certain inclination to good, corresponding to his rational nature: and this inclination is proper to man alone. So man has a natural inclination to know the truth about God and to live in society. In this respect there come under the natural law, all actions connected with such inclinations: namely, that a man should avoid ignorance, that he must not give offence to others with whom he must associate and all actions of like nature.

Q.   What does it mean to claim that all men have a natural inclination to live in society?

Q.   Does man's reason allow him to understand that he has to find peaceful ways of co-existing with those with whom he must associate?

THE UNIVERSALITY OF THE NATURAL LAW

As we have just said, all those actions pertain to the natural law to which man has a natural inclination: and among such it is proper to man to seek to act according to reason. Reason, however, proceeds from general principles to matters of detail, as is proved in the *Physics* (Book I, 1). The practical and the speculative reason, however, go about this process in different ways. For the speculative reason is principally employed about necessary truths, which cannot be otherwise than they are; so that truth is to be found as surely in its particular conclusions as in general principles themselves. But practical reason is employed about contingent matters, into which human actions enter:

thus, though there is a certain necessity in its general principles, the further one departs from generality the more is the conclusion open to exception.

So it is clear that as far as the general principles of reason are concerned, whether speculative or practical there is one standard of truth or rightness for everybody, and that this is equally known by every one. With regard to the particular conclusions of speculative reason, again there is one standard of truth for all; but in this case it is not equally known to all: it is universally true, for instance, that the three interior angles of a triangle equal two right angles; but this conclusion is not known by everybody. When we come to the particular conclusions of the practical reason, however, there is neither the same standard of truth or rightness for every one, nor are these conclusions equally known to all. All people, indeed, realize that it is right and true to act according to reason. And from this principle we may deduce as an immediate conclusion that debts must be repaid. This conclusion holds in the majority of cases. But it could happen in some particular case that it would be injurious, and therefore irrational, to repay a debt if for instance, the money repaid were used to make war against one's own country. Such exceptions are all the more likely to occur the more we get down to particular cases: take, for instance, the question of repaying a debt together with a certain security, or in some specific way. The more specialized the conditions applied, the greater is the possibility of an exception arising which will make it right to make restitution or not.

So we must conclude that the law of nature, as far as general first principles are concerned, is the same for all as a norm of right conduct and is equally well known to all. But as to more particular cases which are conclusions from such general principles it remains the same for all only in the majority of cases, both as a norm and as to the extent to which it is known. Thus in particular instances it can admit of exceptions: both with regard to rightness, because of certain impediments, (just as in nature the generation and change of bodies is subject to accidents caused by some impediment), and with regard to its knowability. This can happen because reason is, in some persons, depraved by passion or by some evil habit of nature; as Caesar relates in *De Bello Callico* (VI, 23), of the Germans, that at one time they did not consider robbery to be wrong; though it is obviously against natural law.

Q. Aquinas is comparing natural law reasoning with mathematics. In the latter, particular conclusions are as certain as general principles. Why is it not so when one reasons from the general principles of natural law to the circumstances of a particular community?

THE IMMUTABILITY OF NATURAL LAW

There are two ways in which natural law may be understood to change. One, in that certain additions are made to it. And in this sense there is no reason why it should not change. Both the divine law and human laws do, in fact, add much to the natural law which is useful to human activity.

Or again the natural law would be understood to change by having something subtracted from it. If, for instance, something ceased to pertain to natural law which was formerly part of it. In this respect, and as far as first principles are concerned, it is wholly unchangeable. As to secondary precepts, which, as we have said, follow as immediate conclusions from first principles, the natural law again does not change; in the sense that it remains a general rule for the majority of cases that what the natural law prescribes is correct. It may, however, be said to change in some particular case, or in a limited number of examples; because of some special causes which make its observation impossible; as we have already pointed out.

Things may be said to pertain to the natural law for two reasons. First, if there is a natural inclination to them: as, for example, that it is wrong to do injury to one's neighbour. Secondly, if nature does not lead us to do what is contrary. So we might say that man has a natural right to go naked because, nature not having provided him with clothing he has had to fashion it for himself. In this sense the 'common possession of all things and the equal liberty of all' can be said to pertain to the natural law. For neither private possession nor servitude were imposed by nature: they are the adoptions of human reason in the interests of human life. And in these cases the natural law is not altered but is added to.

9.   HUMAN LAW

THE NECESSITY FOR HUMAN LAWS

From the foregoing it is clear that there is in man a natural aptitude to virtuous action. But men can achieve the perfection of such virtue only by the practice of a 'certain discipline'. – And men who are capable of such discipline without the aid of others are rare indeed. – So we must help one another to achieve that discipline which leads to a virtuous life. There are, indeed, some young men, readily inclined to a life of virtue through a good natural disposition or upbringing, or particularly because of divine help; and for such, paternal guidance and advice are sufficient. But there are others, of evil disposition and prone to vice, who are not easily moved by words. These it is necessary to restrain from wrongdoing by force and by fear. When they are thus prevented from doing evil, a quiet life is assured to the rest of the community; and they are themselves drawn eventually, by force of habit, to do voluntarily what once they did only out of fear, and so to practice virtue. Such discipline which compels under fear of penalty is the discipline of law. Thus the enactment of laws was necessary to the peaceful and virtuous life of men. And the Philosopher says (I *Politics*, 2): 'Man, when he reaches the perfection of virtue is the best of all animals: but if he goes his way without law and justice he becomes the worst of all brutes.' For man, unlike other animals, has the weapon of reason with which to exploit his base desires and cruelty.

Q.   Why do human laws need sanctions? Why can't one just rely on persons obeying natural law?

THE SUBORDINATION OF HUMAN LAWS TO THE NATURAL LAW

Saint Augustine says (I *De Lib. Arbitrio*, 5) 'There is no law unless it be just.' So the validity of law depends upon its justice. But in human affairs a thing is said to be just when it accords aright with the rule of reason: and, as we have already seen, the first rule of reason is the natural law. Thus all humanly enacted laws are in accord with reason to the extent that they derive from the natural law. And if a human law is at variance in any particular with the natural law, it is no longer legal, but rather a corruption of law.

But it should be noted that there are two ways in which anything may derive from natural law. First, as a conclusion from more general principles. Secondly, as a determination of certain general features. The former is similar to the method of the sciences in which demonstrative conclusions are drawn from first principles. The second way is like to that of the arts in which some common form is determined to a particular instance: as, for example, when an architect, starting from the general idea of a house, then goes on to design the particular plan of this or that house. So, therefore, some derivations are made from the natural law by way of formal conclusion: as the conclusion, 'Do no murder', derives from the precept, 'Do harm to no man'. Other conclusions are arrived at as determinations of particular cases. So the natural law establishes that whoever transgresses shall be punished. But that a man should be punished by a specific penalty is a particular determination of the natural law.

Both types of derivation are to be found in human law. But those which are arrived at in the first way are sanctioned not only by human law, but by the natural law also; while those arrived at by the second method have the validity of human law alone.

Q.   Why do some human laws fail to derive their force from natural law?

10.   THE POWERS OF HUMAN LAW

ITS GENERALITY

Whatever exists in virtue of some end must be proportionate to that end. But the end of law is the common welfare: for, as Isidore says (*Etym.* II, 10): 'Laws must be formulated, not in view of some particular interest, but for the general benefit of the citizens.' So human laws must be related to the common welfare. But the common wellbeing is made up of many different elements. It is, therefore, necessary that the law should take account of these diverse elements, both with respect to persons and to affairs, and with reference to different times. For the political community is composed of many persons; its welfare entails much varied provision; and such provision is not confined to any one period of time, but should continue through successive generations of citizens: as St. Augustine says in *De Civitate Dei* (XXII, 6).

ITS LIMITS

Laws when they are passed should take account of the condition of the men who will be subject to them; for, as Isidore says (*Etym.* II, 10): the law should be 'possible both with regard to nature and with regard to the custom of the country.' But capacity to act derives from habit, or interior disposition: not everything that is possible to a virtuous man is equally possible to one who lacks the habit of virtue; just as a child is incapable of doing all that a grown man can do. For this reason there is not the same law for children and for adults: there are many things permitted to children which are punished by the law, and even abhorred, in adults. Equally, it is possible to permit many things to those not far advanced in virtue which would not be tolerated in a virtuous man.

Now human law is enacted on behalf of the mass of men, the majority of whom are far from perfect in virtue. For this reason human law does not prohibit every vice from which virtuous men abstain; but only the graver vices from which the majority can abstain;

and particularly those vices which are damaging of others, and which, if they were not prohibited, would make it impossible for human society to endure: as murder, theft, and suchlike which are prohibited by human law.

The object of the different virtues may be considered either with respect to the private benefit of the individual person, or with respect to the general welfare of the community. So, for example, the virtue of fortitude may be exercised by a person either for the protection of the city or in defence of the rights of his friends: and similarly with respect to the other virtues. Law, however, as we have said, regards the common welfare. So there is no virtue whose practice may not be prescribed by law. At the same time not every act of all virtues is ordered by the law, but only those which may be directed towards the common welfare; either directly, when something is done explicitly for the common benefit; or indirectly, as when, for example the legislator enacts certain provisions relative to good discipline which accustom the citizens to respect the common need for justice and peace.

Q.   Does human law require all men to be moral, so that it has the same content as morality? If not, why not?

THE OBLIGATION OF HUMAN LAW

Laws enacted by men are either just or unjust. If just, they draw from the eternal law, from which they derive, the power to oblige in conscience; as is said in the book of *Proverbs* (VIII, 15): 'By me kings reign, and lawgivers decree just things.' Now laws can be considered just, either with respect to their object that is when they are directed to the common welfare or with respect to their author, that is when the law which is enacted does not exceed the powers of him who enacts it; or again with reference to their form, when the burdens they impose upon the citizens are distributed in such proportion as to promote the common welfare. For since every man is part of the community, all that any man is or has, has reference to the community: just as any part belongs, in that which it is, to the whole. For this reason nature is seen to sacrifice a part for the preservation of the whole. In the light of this principle, laws which observe due proportion in the distribution of burdens are just, and oblige in conscience; they are legitimate laws.

Contrariwise, laws may be unjust for two reasons. Firstly, when they are detrimental to human welfare, being contrary to the norms we have just established. Either with respect to their object, as when a ruler enacts laws which are burdensome to his subjects and which do not make for common prosperity, but are designed better to serve his own cupidity and vainglory. Or with respect to their author; if a legislator should enact laws which exceed the powers vested in him. Or, finally with respect to their form; if the burdens, even though they are concerned with the common welfare, are distributed in an inequitable manner throughout the community. Laws of this sort have more in common with violence than with legality: for, as St. Augustine says, in the *De Libro Arbitrio* (I, 5): 'A law which is not just cannot be called a law.' Such laws do not, in consequence, oblige in conscience, except, on occasion, to avoid scandal or disorder. For in this case a man may be bound even to give up his rights, as St. Matthew teaches (V, 40–41): 'Whosoever will force thee one mile, go with him other two: and if a man take away thy coat, let go thy cloak also unto him.'

Secondly, laws may be unjust through being contrary to divine goodness: such as tyrannical laws enforcing idolatry, or any other action against the divine law. Such laws may under no circumstances be obeyed: for, as it is said (*Acts* V, 29): 'We must obey God rather than man.'

Q.   Are you obliged by your conscience to obey an unjust law?

Q.   In what ways might a human law be unjust?

ITS POWERS OF COMPULSION

Law, as we see from what has been said, has two essential characteristics: the first, that of a rule directive of human action: the second, that of power to compel. So there are two ways in which a man may be subject to the law. Either as that which is ruled is subject to the rule. And, in this respect, all who are subject to a certain power are subject also to the laws which emanate from that power. There are two cases in which such subjection does not obtain. First, when a person is wholly absolved from such subjection. So the citizens of one city or realm are not bound by the laws of the ruler of another city or realm, just as they do not come under his dominion. Secondly, when persons are subject to a higher law. So, for instance, one who is subject to a proconsul must obey his command, but not in those matters in which he is dispensed by the emperor: for in these matters, being subject to higher commands, he is not bound by the orders of a subordinate. In such a case it happens that one who is subject to a certain law in principle, is in certain matters exempt from it, being subject in such matters to a higher law.

The second way in which a man may be said to be subject to the law is as one who is constrained to what constrains him. In this sense virtuous and just men are not subject to the law, but only the wicked. For whatever pertains to constraint and to violence is against the will. But the will of the good is at one with the law, whereas in the bad the will is opposed to the law. So, in this sense, the good are not under the law, but only the bad.

A ruler is said to be above the law with respect to its constraining force: for nobody can be constrained by himself; and law derives its power of constraint only from the power of the ruler. So it is said that the prince is above the law, because if he should act against the law nobody can bring a condemnatory judgement against him. So, commenting on the text of *Psalm* L (verse 6) 'To thee only have I sinned' etc., the Gloss explains that 'there is no man who can judge the actions of a king.' – But with respect to the directive power of law, a ruler is voluntarily subject to it, in conformity with what is laid down: 'Whoever enacts a law for another should apply the same law to himself. And we have it on the authority of the wise man that you should subject yourself to the same law which you promulgate.' And in the *Codex*, the Emperors, Theodosius and Valentinian, write to the Prefect Volusianus: 'It is a saying worthy of the majesty of a ruler, if the prince professes himself bound by the laws: for even our authority depends upon that of the law. And, in fact, the most important thing in government is that power should be subject to laws.' The Lord also reproves those who 'say and do not do'; and who 'bind heavy and insupportable burdens for others, but with a finger of their own they will not move them' (*Matthew*, XXIII, 3, 4). So, in the judgement of God, a ruler is not free from the directive power of the law; but should voluntarily and without constraint fulfil it. – A ruler is above the law also in the sense that he may, if it be expedient, change the law, or dispense from it according to time and to place.

Q.   In what ways may one be 'subject' to a law?

Q.   Are rulers subject to their own laws, or is this simply a matter of morality – 'do unto others', etc? (Note that this section deals with matters that concern Austin in the next chapter – natural lawyers share the concerns of positivists with the actual application of positive law).

THE INTERPRETATION OF HUMAN LAWS. EXCEPTIONAL CASES

As we have said above, all law is directed to the common well-being of men, and for this reason alone does it obtain the power and validity of law: so to the extent that it falls short of this object it has no power of obligation. So the Jurisconsult says that 'neither justice nor equity permit that what has been usefully established in the interests of men should be made harsh and damaging to the community through too rigid an interpretation.' Now it frequently happens that the observance of a certain rule, though generally useful to the community, is, in certain other cases extremely damaging. For the legislator, not being able to foresee all particular cases, frames the law to meet what is commonly the case, and with a view to its general usefulness. Consequently, if it should happen that the observance of such a law would be damaging to the general well-being, it should not be observed. So, for example in a city during a state of siege there might be a law ordering that all gates should be kept closed, and such a regulation would, in general, be useful to the common welfare. But if it should happen that the enemy were pursuing some of the citizens on whom the safety of the city depended, it would be a disaster for the city if the gates were not opened to them. In such a case the gates should obviously be opened, against the letter of the law, but for the sake of the common welfare which the legislator intended.

It must, however, be borne in mind, that if the decision on the letter of the law is not a matter of immediate danger which requires prompt action, it is not open to anybody to act as interpreter of what is and what is not in the public interest: such decision belongs rightly to rulers, and it is to meet such cases that they have authority to dispense from the law. When, however, danger is so imminent that there is no time to refer the matter to the authorities, necessity itself carries its own dispensation: for necessity knows no law.

Q.   Is this a natural law argument for subjecting the interpretation of all human laws to a moral override? Why should such overrides operate only exceptionally? Who should decide when such overrides apply?

II.   *THE MUTABILITY OF HUMAN LAW*

REASONS FOR SUCH MUTABILITY

As we have said above, human law is a certain dictate of reason by which human actions are regulated. From this point of view there can be two causes which justify a changing of human law. The first is on the part of reason: the second on the part of men whose actions are regulated by the law. On the part of reason because it would seem natural for human reason to proceed by stages from the imperfect to the more perfect. So we see in speculative science that those who first began to philosophize arrived at an incomplete system which their successors later elaborated into something more perfect. It is the same also in practical affairs. For those who first set themselves to consider what was useful to the common well-being of man, not being able to solve the entire problem themselves, established certain regulations which were imperfect and deficient in many respects; and these regulations were later modified by their successors to retain those which were the least defective from the point of view of the public interest.

On the part of men, whose actions are regulated by law, changes in law may be justified on account of altered circumstances: for according to the different circumstances in which men are found, different standards obtain. St. Augustine gives an example of this in (I *De Lib. Arbitrio, 6*): 'If a people is orderly, serious-minded and jealously observes the public interest, there is justification for a law which confers upon them the faculty of electing their own magistrates for the administration of public affairs. But if that people should gradually become dishonest, and the elections become corrupt, so that the government falls into the hands of dishonourable and vicious men, then it is right that the power of electing to office should be taken from them and that a return should be made to limited suffrage for the few and honest.'

Q.   If Human law, to the extent that it obliges in conscience, draws on eternal law, why should its content ever need to change?

THE LIMITS OF SUCH MUTABILITY

As has been said, change in human law is justified only to the extent that it benefits the general welfare. Now the very fact of change in the law is, in a certain sense, detrimental to the public welfare. This is because, in the observance of law, custom is of great importance: so much so, that any action which is opposed to general custom, even if itself of little importance, always seems more serious. So when law is changed its coercive power is diminished, to the extent that custom is set aside. Thus human law should never be changed unless the benefits which result to the public interest are such as to compensate for the harm done. This may be the case if the new statutes contain great and manifest advantages; or if there is urgent necessity due to the fact that the old law contains evident injustice, or its observance is excessively harmful. So the Jurisconsult says that 'in passing new constitutions their utility must be very evident before renouncing those laws which have long been regarded as equitable.'

Q.   Why would it be wrong to change human law too often, or too radically?

...

12.   THE DIFFERENCE BETWEEN LEGAL AND MORAL OBLIGATION

LAW AND THE PRACTICE OF VIRTUE

As we have shown above, a precept of law has power to compel: thus whatever is obliged by law may be said to fall directly under the precept of law. But the compulsion of law obtains through fear of penalty, as is shown in the tenth book of the *Ethics*; for those matters may be said to come strictly under the precept of law for which a legal penalty is inflicted. Hence divine law differs from human law in the imposition of its penalties. For a legal penalty is inflicted only for those matters about which the law-giver is competent to judge, since the law punishes in view of a judgement passed. Now man, the maker of human law, can pass judgement only upon external actions, because 'man seeth those things that appear', as we are told in the first book of *Kings*. God alone, the divine Law-giver, is able to judge the inner movements of the will, as the Psalmist says. 'The searcher of hearts and reins is God.'

In view of this we must conclude that the practice of virtue is in one respect subject both to human and to divine law, while in another respect it is subject to divine but not to human law. Again there is a third sense in which it is affected neither by divine nor by human law. Now the mode of the practice of virtue consists, according to Aristotle (II *Ethics*, 4), in three things. The first of these is that a person should act knowingly. And this is subject to judgement both by divine and by human law. For whatever a man does in ignorance he does accidentally, and in consequence both human and divine law must consider the question of ignorance in judging whether certain matters are punishable or pardonable.

The second point is that a man should act voluntarily, deliberately choosing a particular action for its own sake. This involves a twofold interior action of the will and of intention, and of these we have already spoken above. Divine law alone is competent to judge of these, but not human law. For human law does not punish the man who meditates murder but does not commit it, though divine law does punish him, as we are told by *St. Matthew* (V, 22): 'Whosoever is angry with his brother shall be in danger of the judgement.'

The third point is that a man should act upon a firm and unchanging principle; and such firmness proceeds strictly from habit, and obtains when a man acts from a rooted habit. In this sense the practice of virtue does not fall under the precept either of divine or of human law for no man is punished for breaking the law, either by God or by man, if he duly honours his parents, though lacking the habit of filial piety.

Q. If a precept of law has the power to compel, what gives divine law this power?

Q. Why should human law necessarily lack the power to compel everything that is virtuous?

Q. Why should all laws have regard to whether law breaking is deliberate?

Q. Why is law's power to compel (whether divine or human) irrelevant to the truly virtuous man?

In order to see how the modern Natural Law thinker Finnis applies Aquinas, it is important to understand the idea of self-evident knowledge of good and evil (practical reason) that Aquinas adopts. Here is a succinct statement from Aquinas (repeating and refining '8. The Natural Law' set out above).

... the precepts of Natural Law are related to Practical Reason, as the first principles of demonstrations are related to the speculative reason, for, both are self-evident principles.

Now, something can be said to be self-evident in two ways. First, in itself and secondly, with reference to us. Any proposition is said to be self-evident in itself, if the predicate is contained in the notion of the subject. It happens, however, that such a proposition will not be self-evident to one who does not know the definition of the subject ... Hence it is that, as Boethius says, 'Certain axioms or propositions are universally known to everyone.' And of this sort are those propositions the terms of which are known to all, as 'Every whole is greater than any one of its parts' and 'Things equal to one and the same thing are equal to each other.'

Some propositions, however, are known only to the wise who understand the meaning of the terms of the proposition, as to one who knows that an angel is not a body, it is self-evident that an angel is not circumscriptively in a place, but this is not manifest to the unlearned who cannot grasp it. (Aquinas 1993, 245–246)

Aquinas does not claim that moral knowledge is something that we learn empirically, by looking at things in nature to see what is 'good'. He thinks that it is like the axioms of mathematics or science. Learned men will understand these axioms. Ignorant men will adopt axioms without realising the conclusions that must follow from them, or apply knowledge built up from axioms without understanding their foundation. His own example is: if angels are not three-dimensional beings, how can they occupy a particular place?

In these things, however, which man comes to apprehend, a certain order is to be found. For, that which first comes into the understanding is 'being' which is included in the understanding of everything whatever. And, therefore, the first indemonstrable principle is that one cannot simultaneously affirm and deny something; this principle which is founded on the notion of being and non-being, and on this principle all the others are based ...

Now, just as being is the first thing that, without qualification, comes into man's apprehension, so good is the first thing that comes into the apprehension of the Practical Reason, which is ordered to action, for every agent acts for an end under the aspect of good. And, therefore, the first principle of the Practical Reason is based on the notion of good which is that which all desire. Therefore, the first principle of the Natural Law is this, that good should be done and sought and evil is to be avoided. And on this principle are based all the other precepts of the law of nature so that all the things that Practical Reason apprehends as human goods belong to the law of nature.

Now, since the good has the formality of the end and evil has the opposite formality, all those things to which man has a natural inclination are naturally apprehended by Practical Reason as good and, consequently, as to be actively pursued while their opposites are apprehended as evil and to be avoided. (Aquinas 1993, 247–250)

Aquinas claimed that all men know the difference between good and evil. At the most general level, he is correct. We all know that 'good' things are to be pursued and 'bad' things opposed. Moral reasoning assumes this opposition. Aquinas also pointed to the evidence for moral knowledge that is implicit in common speech. To call something a 'debt' is to acknowledge some kind of obligation to repay; to speak of something being 'wrong' is to confirm some basis for judging good and evil (and always confirms the opposition between the two). Aquinas was pointing to the difficulties of entirely rejecting ethics. Not only does everyone understand the opposition between good and evil but also our speech implies the existence of objective moral standards. A statement like 'killing me would be wrong' implies the existence of standards that forbid, at least in some circumstances, killing. And despite our sensitivity to the fact that different groups hold different opinions on what is right or wrong (ethical relativism) statements that something is 'wrong' cannot always be reduced to claims that 'given my upbringing it would be wrong if I did it', or 'given your culture it would be wrong if you did it'. It is actually incredibly difficult to go through life without using language that implies the existence of objective values. (Similarly, the next short extract from Finnis deals with the difficulty facing those who wish to deny the value of knowledge.) Those who wish to turn their back on ethics should consider the difficulties of never being able to pronounce something simply 'wrong'.

While the starting point of Aquinas' thought, the opposition of good and evil (what he calls the first precept of natural law) may be inescapable, carrying the reasoning any further and claiming one's conclusions as objective knowledge is very difficult. Starting from the 'ought' position represented by a refusal to reject all ethical values, one looks to facts (intuitions, nature, society) to see what the content of that ethics might be. Reason does not supply the answers, although it does impose some restrictions on our ability to hold too many incompatible positions simultaneously (Lyons 1984, Ch 1, 'Moral judgment and the law', is a particularly readable argument that supports this conclusion, against the challenge of ethical nihilism, social and individualistic relativism). Nevertheless, and even within the same system of Natural Law reasoning, different persons can reach diametrically opposite conclusions. Thus, for example, those who share a common commitment to the importance of human life can reach diametrically opposite views on the acceptability of abortion, or capital punishment, or military service. And attempts to reason from what seems to be 'natural' continues to be disturbed by new developments: what happens to the laws of procreation and the rearing of the young in the brave new world of bio-technological advances?

Q.   If we can all understand the opposition between good and evil (without necessarily knowing or agreeing what must be grouped under each label) can we look at what is pursued by human beings, given their natures, for evidence of what, in fact, constitutes the good? (To answer this question consider again the section by Aquinas on natural inclinations above, the description in the earlier commentary of how Finnis selects his seven basic values, and the extract which follows in which Finnis argues that all human societies affirm these values.)

While Finnis (applying Aquinas) sees the basic values as self-evidently affirmed in all cultures, he has a further basis for claiming that knowledge is a self-evident value: that there is something inconsistent in a person denying the value of knowledge.

Finnis (1980, 73–75)

111.6 SCEPTICISM ABOUT THIS BASIC VALUE IS INDEFENSIBLE

In the case of the basic values and practical principles to be identified in the next chapter, the discussion of their self-evidence and objectivity would have to rest at this point. But in the case of the basic value of knowledge we can go one step further. We can show that *any* argument raised by the sceptic is going to be self-defeating. To show this is not to show that the basic value of knowledge is self-evident or objective; it is only to show that counter-arguments are invalid. But to make even this limited defensive point, in relation to only one basic value, may help to undermine sceptical doubts about all and any of the basic principles of practical reasoning

Some propositions refute themselves either because they are directly self-contradictory or because they logically entail their contradictory: for example, 'I know that I know nothing'; 'It can be proved that nothing can be proved'; 'All propositions are false'.

Then again, there are some statements whose occurrence *happens* to refute their content. An example of this pragmatic self-refutation is afforded by someone singing 'I am not singing'. Here there is what we may call performative inconsistency, that is, inconsistency between what is asserted by a statement and facts that are given in and by the making of the statement.

Thirdly, there are propositions which cannot be coherently asserted, because they are *inevitably* falsified by any assertion of them. The proposition 'I am not singing' is not such a proposition, for it can be asserted in writing. But the proposition 'I do not exist' is inevitably falsified by an assertion of it. Another example of this operational self-refutation is 'No one can put words (or other symbols) together to form a sentence'. Operationally self-refuting propositions are not logically incoherent. Nor are they meaningless or empty or semantically paradoxical, as are 'This sentence is false' or 'This provision shall come into effect on 1st January' (where 'this sentence' or 'this provision' in each case is not a colloquial reference to some other sentence or norm but is self-referential and fails to establish any definite reference). Operationally self-refuting propositions have a quite definite reference and so can be (and inevitably are) false. They have a type of performative inconsistency; that is, they are inconsistent with the facts that are given in and by *any* assertion of them. An operationally self-refuting proposition cannot be coherently asserted, for it contradicts either the proposition that someone is asserting it or some proposition entailed by the proposition that someone is asserting it.

The sceptical assertion that knowledge is not a good is operationally self-refuting. For one who makes such an assertion, intending it as a serious contribution to rational discussion, is implicitly committed to the proposition that he believes his assertion is worth making, and worth making qua true; he thus is committed to the proposition that he believes that truth is a good worth pursuing or knowing. But the sense of his original assertion was precisely that truth is not a good worth pursuing or knowing. Thus he is implicitly committed to formally contradictory beliefs.

One can certainly toy with the notion that knowledge is not a good worth pursuing. But the fact that to *assert* this (whether to an audience, or as the judgment concluding one's own inner cogitations) would be operationally self-refuting should persuade the sceptic to cut short idle doubting. Self-defeating positions should be abandoned. The sceptic, on this as on other matters, can maintain coherence by *asserting* nothing; but coherence is not the only requirement of rationality.

A judgment or belief is objective if it is correct. A proposition is objective if one is warranted in asserting it, whether because there is sufficient evidence for it, or compelling grounds, or because (to one who has the experience and intelligence to understand the terms in which it is expressed) it is obvious or self-evidently correct. And if a proposition *seems* to be correct and could never be coherently denied, we are certainly justified in affirming it and in considering that what we are affirming is indeed objectively the case (in the relevant sense of 'what is the case'). But all this is true of the proposition we have been considering, viz. that knowledge is a good to be pursued. We do not thereby directly demonstrate that knowledge is a good to be pursued; that principle remains indemonstrable, self-evident. What we demonstrate is simply that it is presupposed in all demonstrations, indeed in all serious assertions, whatsoever, and has as much title to be called 'objective' as any other proposition whose contradictory is inevitably falsified by the act of asserting it.

The next extract from Finnis deals with his claim that a full statement of law must have regard to the common good. His argument may be likened to arguments about the definition of the game of football. Football may be played in a park on rough ground with piles of coats as goal posts, and with any number on each side. Where to draw the line at what may deserve the name of football may be a pointless exercise. But the sort of paradigm case which allows all of us to recognise even these practices (in a park on rough ground) as football is: an eleven a side match with 45 minutes each way, a referee, two goals each with posts and nets, played in a stadium (usually known as Wembley). That is the game that all can agree, **is** football.

John Finnis (1980, 276–81)

X.6   A DEFINITION OF LAW

Throughout this chapter, the term 'law' has been used with a focal meaning so as to refer primarily to rules made, in accordance with regulative legal rules, by a determinate and effective authority (itself identified and, standardly, constituted as an institution by legal rules) for a 'complete' community, and buttressed by sanctions in accordance with the rule-guided stipulations of adjudicative institutions, this ensemble of rules and institutions being directed to reasonably resolving any of the community's co-ordination problems (and to ratifying, tolerating, regulating, or overriding co-ordination solutions from any other institutions or sources of norms) for the common good of that community, according to a manner and form itself adapted to that common good by features of specificity, minimization of arbitrariness, and maintenance of a quality of reciprocity between the subjects of the law both amongst themselves and in their relations with the lawful authorities.

This multi-faceted conception of law has been reflectively constructed by tracing the implications of certain requirements of practical reason, given certain basic values and certain empirical features of persons and their communities. The intention has not been lexicographical; but the construction lies well within the boundaries of common use of 'law' and its equivalents in other languages. The intention has not been to describe existing social orders; but the construction corresponds closely to many existing social phenomena that typically are regarded as central cases of law, legal system, Rule of Law, etc. Above all, the meaning has been constructed as a *focal* meaning, not as an appropriation of the term 'law' in a univocal sense that would exclude from the reference of the term anything that failed to have all the characteristics (and to their full extent) of the central case. And, equally important, it has been fully recognized that each of the terms used to express the elements in the conception (e.g. 'making', 'determinate', 'effective', 'a community', 'sanctioned', 'rule-guided', 'reasonable', 'non-discriminatory', 'reciprocal', etc.) has itself a focal meaning and a primary reference, and therefore extends to analogous and secondary instances which lack something of the central instance. For example, custom is not *made* in the full sense of 'made' – for making is something that someone can set himself to do, but no one sets himself (themselves) to make a custom. Yet customs are 'made', in a sense that requirements of practical reason are not made but discovered. The way in which each of the other crucial terms is *more or less* instantiated is quite obvious. (If the term 'reasonable' arouses misgivings, see VI.1) Law, in the focal sense of the term, is fully instantiated only when each of these component terms is fully instantiated.

If one wishes to stress the empirical/historical importance, or the practical/rational desirability, of sanctions, one may say, dramatically, that an unsanctioned set of laws is 'not really law'. If one wishes to stress the empirical/historical importance, or the practical/rational desirability of determinate legislative and/or adjudicative institutions, one may say, dramatically, that a community without such institutions 'lacks a real legal system' or 'cannot really be said to have 'a legal system''. If one wishes to stress the empirical/historical importance, or the practical/rational desirability, of rules authorizing or regulating private or public change in the rules or their incidence, one may say, dramatically, that a set of rules which includes no such rules 'is not a legal system'. All these things have often been said, and can reasonably be said provided that one is seeking to draw attention to a feature of the central case of law and not to banish the other non-central cases to some other discipline.

I have by now sufficiently stressed that one would be simply misunderstanding my conception of the nature and purpose of explanatory definitions of theoretical concepts if one supposed that my definition 'ruled out as non-laws' laws which failed to meet, or meet fully, one or other of the elements of the definition. But I should add that it would also be a misunderstanding to condemn the definition because 'it fails to explain correctly our ordinary concept of law which does allow for the possibility of laws of [an] objectionable kind'. For not only does my definition 'allow for the possibility'; it also is not advanced with the intention of 'explaining correctly our [sc. the ordinary man's] ordinary concept of law'. For the truth is that the 'ordinary concept of law' (granting, but not admitting, that there is *one* such concept) is quite unfocused. It is a concept which allows 'us' to understand lawyers when they talk about sophisticated legal systems, and anthropologists when they talk about elementary legal systems, and tyrants and bandits when they talk about the orders and the customs of their Syndicate, and theologians and moralists ... There is no point in trying to explain a common-sense concept which takes its meanings from its very varied contexts and is well understood by everyone in those contexts. My purpose has not been to explain an unfocused 'ordinary concept' but to develop a concept for use in a theoretical explanation of a set of human actions, dispositions, interrelationships, and conceptions which (i) hang together as a set by virtue of their adaptation to a specifiable set of human needs considered in the light of empirical features of the human condition, and (ii) are accordingly found in very varying forms and with varying degrees of suitability for, and deliberate or unconscious divergence from, those needs as the fully reasonable person would assess them. To repeat: the intention has been not to explain a concept, but to develop a concept which would explain the various phenomena referred to (in an unfocused way) by 'ordinary' talk about law – and explain them by showing how they answer (fully or partially) to the standing requirements of practical reasonableness relevant to this broad area of human concern and interaction.

The lawyer is likely to become impatient when he hears that social arrangements can be *more or less* legal, that legal systems and the rule of law exist as a matter of degree … and so on. For the lawyer systematically strives to use language in such a way that from its use he can read off a definite solution to definite problems – in the final analysis, judgment for one party rather than the other in a litigable dispute. If cars are to be taxed at such and such a rate, one must be able, as a lawyer, to say (i.e. to rule) of every object that it simply is or is not a car: qualifications, 'in this respect … but in that respect', *secundum quids,* and the like are permissible in argument (and a good lawyer is well aware how open-textured and analogous in structure most terms and concepts are); but just as they do not appear in statutory formulae, so they cannot appear in the final pronouncement of law. And the lawyer, for the same good practical reasons, intrinsic to the enterprise of legal order as I have described it in this chapter, extends his technical use of language to the terms 'law', 'rule', 'legal', 'legal system' themselves. To make his point propositionally he will say that a purported law or rule is either valid or invalid. There are no intermediate categories (though there are intermediate states of affairs, e.g. voidable laws, which now are valid, or are treated as valid, or are deemed to be valid, but are liable to be rendered or treated as or deemed invalid). Equipped with this concept of validity, the lawyer aspires to be able to say of every rule that, being valid, it is a legal rule, or, being invalid, is not. The validity of a rule is identified with membership of the legal system (conceived as a set of valid rules), which thus can be considered legally as the set of all valid rules, including those rules which authorized the valid rule-originating acts of enactment and/or adjudication which are (in this conception) the necessary and sufficient conditions for the validity of the valid rules.

There is no need to question here the sufficiency of this set of concepts and postulates for the practical purposes of the lawyer – though questions could certainly be raised about the role of principles (which have no determinate origin and cannot without awkwardness be called valid) in legal argumentation. Rather it must be stressed that the set is a technical device for use within the framework of legal process, and in legal thought directed to arriving at solutions within that process. The device cannot be assumed to be applicable to the quite different problems of describing and explaining the role of legal process within the ordering of human life in society, and the place of legal thought in practical reason's effort to understand and effect real human good. It is a philosophical mistake to declare, in discourse of the latter kinds, that a social order or set of concepts must either be law or not be law, be legal or not legal.

For our purposes, physical, chemical, biological, and psychological laws are only metaphorically laws. To say this is not to question the legitimacy of the discourse of natural scientists, for whose purposes, conversely, what we call 'law strictly speaking' is only metaphorically a set of laws. The similarity between our central case and the laws of arts and crafts and applied sciences is greater; in each case we are considering the regulation of a performance by a self-regulating performer whose own notion of what he is up to affects the course of his performance. But the differences still are systematic and significant; as I said before (VII.7, X.1), ordering a society for the greater participation of its members in human values is not very like following a recipe for producing a definite product or a route to a definite goal. 'Natural law' – the set of principles of practical reasonableness in ordering human life and human community – is only analogically law, in relation to my present focal use of the term: that is why the term has been avoided in this chapter on Law, save in relation to past thinkers who used the term. These past thinkers, however, could, without loss of meaning, have spoken instead of 'natural right', 'intrinsic morality', 'natural reason, or right reason in action', etc. But no synonyms are available for 'law' in our focal sense.

The full implications of what Finnis is saying, of why he is arguing that it is 'a philosophical mistake to declare ... that a social order or set of concepts must either be law, or not be law, be legal or not legal' will become clear as you read the next three chapters on Positivist theories of law. His focal meaning of law allows him to incorporate a range of ideas within it, including those associated with 'the common good'.

Our next two extracts are from Fuller. His arguments represent an attempt to side-step the claim that Natural Law theories are invariably and unacceptably subjective: 'Like a harlot, natural law is at the disposal of everyone. The ideology does not exist that cannot be defended by an appeal to the law of nature.' (Ross 1974, 261) Fuller counters this criticism of Natural Law theory. In the short extract from one of his earlier writings, *The Law in Quest of Itself*, he denounces attempts by Legal Positivists to exclude ethical criteria from their background understanding of, or ability to give meaning to, law. Here he is asserting that Legal Positivism's critique of Natural Law (as a 'harlot') ends with unsatisfactory and unfinished theorising. In a longer extract from *The Morality of Law* you will see how Fuller's attempt to theorise about law avoids Legal Positivism's principal criticisms of it. In that attempt there are echoes of Platonic thought, particularly his idea of a 'morality of aspiration'. The ideal of law to Fuller is one of a system, which all citizens **could** obey. No system on earth achieves the ideal of total obedience. Nevertheless, for Fuller, the ideal remains as a value (or virtue) against which to assess the extent to which any real system is *legal*.

Fuller (1940, 5–11)

By legal positivism I mean that direction of legal thought which insists on drawing a sharp distinction between the law *that is* and the law *that ought to be.* Where this distinction is taken it is, of course, for the sake of the law *that is,* and is intended to purify it by purging it of what Kelsen calls 'wish-law'. Generally – though not invariably – the positivistic attitude is associated with a degree of ethical skepticism. Its unavowed basis will usually be found to rest in a conviction that while one may significantly describe the law *that is*, nothing that transcends personal predilection can be said about the law *that ought to be.*

Natural law, on the other hand, is the view which denies the possibility of a rigid separation of the *is* and the *ought*, and which tolerates a confusion of them in legal discussion. There are, of course, many 'systems' of natural law. Men have drawn their criteria of justice and of right law from many sources: from the nature of things, from the nature of man, from the nature of God. But what unites the various schools of natural law, and justifies bringing them under a common rubric, is the fact that in all of them a certain coalescence of the *is* and the *ought* will be found. Though the natural law philosopher may admit the authority of the state even to the extent of conceding the validity of enacted law which is obviously 'bad' according to his principles, it will be found in the end that he draws no hard and fast line between law and ethics, and that he considers that the 'goodness' of his natural law confers on it a kind of reality which may be temporarily eclipsed, but can never be wholly nullified, by the more immediately effective reality of enacted law. So far as the question of ultimate motives is concerned, it is fairly obvious that if the positivist insists on separating the *is* and the *ought* for the sake of the *is,* the natural-law philosopher is attempting to serve the *ought* when he refuses to draw a sharp distinction between it and the *is.*

As I have drawn the issue between these two directions of legal thought, it may seem that choice between them does not present the kind of problem I described at the outset, that of electing between competing ways of applying our energies in the law. If, as an American philosopher has asserted without apparent irony, there exists a 'clear distinction between what is in fact law and what on ethical grounds we think ought to be the law', then is it not our duty simply to acquiesce in that distinction? If we are presented with an alternative of obfuscation or clarity, how can we legitimately refer to the problem as one of choosing between alternative ways of applying ourselves to legal study? If, as the positivist asserts, there are two distinct routes for legal thought, one directed toward the *is* and the other directed toward the *ought*, what possible utility can there be in following the phantom route of natural law, which pretends to lead in both directions at once?

The answer to these doubts lies in the fact that nature does not, as the positivist so often assumes, present us with the *is* and the *ought* in neatly separated parcels. If there is to be a 'clear distinction' between them it will have to be brought about by the analytical efforts of the positivist. Such a distinction may serve as the legitimate end of his activities; it cannot serve as his starting point. A rather trivial illustration will suffice to show, I believe, how difficult it is to draw a sharp line between the *is* and the *ought* in any field touched by creative human energies.

If I attempt to retell a funny story which I have heard, the story as I tell it will be the product of two forces: (1) the story as I heard it, the story *as it is* at the time of its first telling; (2) my conception of the point of the story, in other words, my notion of the story *as it ought to be.* As I retell the story I make no attempt to estimate exactly the pressure of these two forces, though it is clear that their respective influences may vary. If the story as I heard it was, in my opinion, badly told, I am guided largely by my conception of the story as it ought to be, though through inertia or imperfect insight I shall probably repeat turns of phrase which have stuck in my memory from the former telling. On the other hand, if I had the story from a master raconteur, I may exert myself to reproduce his exact words, though my own conception of the way the story ought to be told will have to fill in the gaps left by faulty memory. These two forces, then, supplement one another in shaping the story as I tell it. It is a product of the *is* and the *ought* working together. There is no way of measuring the degree to which each contributes to the final result. The two are inextricably interwoven, to the point where we can say that 'the story' as an entity really embraces both of them. Indeed, if we look at the story across time, its reality becomes even more complex. The 'point' of the story, which furnishes its essential unity, may in the course of retelling be changed. As it is brought out more clearly through the skill of successive tellers it becomes a new point; at some indefinable juncture the story has been so improved that it has become a new story. In a sense, then, the thing we call 'the story' is not something that is, but something that becomes; it is not a hard chunk of reality, but a fluid process, which is as much directed by men's creative impulses, by their conception of the story as it ought to be, as it is by the original event which unlocked those impulses. The *ought* here is just as real, as a part of human experience, as the *is,* and the line between the two melts away in the common stream of telling and retelling into which they both flow.

Exactly the same thing may be said of a statute or a decision. It involves two things, a set of words, and an objective sought. This objective may or may not have been happily expressed in the words chosen by the legislator or judge. This objective, like the point of the anecdote, may be perceived dimly or clearly; it may be perceived more clearly by him who reads the statute than by him who drafted it. The statute or decision is not a segment of being, but, like the anecdote, a process of becoming. By being reinterpreted it becomes, by imperceptible degrees, something that it was not originally. The field of possible objectives is filled with overlapping figures, and the attempt to trace out distinctly one of these figures almost inevitably creates a new pattern. By becoming more clearly what it is, the rule of the case becomes what it was previously only trying to be. In this situation to distinguish sharply between the rule as it is, and the rule as it ought to be, is to resort to an abstraction foreign to the raw data which experience offers us.

It is well to be clear concerning the difficulties which confront positivism in its quest for some criterion of the law *that is,* for these difficulties are by no means apparent without reflection. Common sense tells us that there must be a distinction between *a law* and *a good law*, and at first glance positivism seems amply justified in resting its whole case on the self-evident quality of this distinction. But we must remember that those distinctions which seem too obvious to require analysis are often precisely those which will not stand analysis. Common sense tells me that there is a clear distinction between a thing's being a steam engine and its being a good steam engine. Yet if I have a dubious assemblage of wheels, gears, and pistons before me and I ask, 'Is this a steam engine?' it is clear that this inquiry overlaps mightily with the question: 'Is this a good steam engine?' In the field of purposive human activity, which includes both steam engines and the law, value and being are not two different things, but two aspects of an integral reality.

Fuller (1969, 33–42, 106, 145–151)

33–42

THE MORALITY THAT MAKES LAW POSSIBLE

[A] law which a man cannot obey, nor act according to it, is void and no law: and it is impossible to obey contradiction or act according to them. – Vaughan, C.J. in Thomas v. Sorrell, 1677

It is desired that our learned lawyers would answer these ensuing queries ... whether ever the Commonwealth, when they chose the Parliament, gave them a lawless unlimited power, and at their pleasure to walk contrary to their own laws and ordinances before they have repealed them? – Lilburne, England's Birth-Right Justified, 1645

This chapter will begin with a fairly lengthy allegory. It concerns the unhappy reign of a monarch who bore the convenient, but not very imaginative and not even very regal sounding name of Rex.

EIGHT WAYS TO FAIL TO MAKE LAW

Rex came to the throne filled with the zeal of a reformer. He considered that the greatest failure of his predecessors had been in the field of law. For generations the legal system had known nothing like a basic reform. Procedures of trial were cumbersome, the rules of law spoke in the archaic tongue of another age, justice was expensive, the judges were slovenly and sometimes corrupt. Rex was resolved to remedy all this and to make his name in history as a great lawgiver. It was his unhappy fate to fail in this ambition. Indeed, he failed spectacularly, since not only did he not succeed in introducing the needed reforms, but he never even succeeded in creating any law at all, good or bad.

His first official act was, however, dramatic and propitious. Since he needed a clean slate on which to write, he announced to his subjects the immediate repeal of all existing law, of whatever kind. He then set about drafting a new code. Unfortunately, trained as a lonely prince, his education had been very defective. In particular he found himself incapable of making even the simplest generalizations. Though not lacking in confidence when it came to deciding specific controversies, the effort to give articulate reasons for any conclusion strained his capacities to the breaking point.

Becoming aware of his limitations, Rex gave up the project of a code and announced to his subjects that henceforth he would act as a judge in any disputes that might arise among them. In this way under the stimulus of a variety of cases he hoped that his latent powers of generalization might develop and, proceeding case by case, he would gradually work out a system of rules that could be incorporated in a code. Unfortunately the defects in his education were more deep-seated than he had supposed. The venture failed completely. After he had handed down literally hundreds of decisions neither he nor his subjects could detect in those decisions any pattern whatsoever. Such tentatives toward generalization as were to be found in his opinions only compounded the confusion, for they gave false leads to his subjects and threw his own meager powers of judgment off balance in the decision of later cases.

After this fiasco Rex realized it was necessary to take a fresh start. His first move was to subscribe to a course of lessons in generalization. With his intellectual powers thus fortified, he resumed the project of a code and, after many hours of solitary labor, succeeded in preparing a fairly lengthy document. He was still not confident, however, that he had fully overcome his previous defects. Accordingly, he announced to his subjects that he had written out a code and would henceforth be governed by it in deciding cases, but that for an indefinite future the contents of the code would remain an official state secret, known only to him and his scrivener. To Rex's surprise this sensible plan was deeply resented by his subjects. They declared it was very unpleasant to have one's case decided by rules when there was no way of knowing what those rules were.

Stunned by this rejection Rex undertook an earnest inventory of his personal strengths and weaknesses. He decided that life had taught him one clear lesson, namely, that it is easier to decide things with the aid of hindsight than it is to attempt to foresee and control the future. Not only did hindsight make it easier to decide cases, but – and this was of supreme importance to Rex – it made it easier to give reasons. Deciding to capitalize on this insight, Rex hit on the following plan. At the beginning of each calendar year he would decide all the controversies that had arisen among his subjects during the preceding year. He would accompany his decisions with a full statement of reasons. Naturally, the reasons thus given would be understood as not controlling decisions in future years, for that would be to defeat the whole purpose of the new arrangement, which was to gain the advantages of hindsight. Rex confidently announced the new plan to his subjects, observing that he was going to publish the full text of his judgments with the rules applied by him, thus meeting the chief objection to the old plan. Rex's subjects received this announcement in silence, then quietly explained through their leaders that when they said they needed to know the rules, they meant they needed to know them *in advance* so they could act on them. Rex muttered something to the effect that they might have made that point a little clearer, but said he would see what could be done.

Rex now realized that there was no escape from a published code declaring the rules to be applied in future disputes. Continuing his lessons in generalization, Rex worked diligently on a revised code, and finally announced that it would shortly be published. This announcement was received with universal gratification. The dismay of Rex's subjects was all the more intense, therefore, when his code became available and it was discovered that it was truly a masterpiece of obscurity. Legal experts who studied it declared that there was not a single sentence in it that could be understood either by an ordinary citizen or by a trained lawyer. Indignation became general and soon a picket appeared before the royal palace carrying a sign that read, 'How can anybody follow a rule that nobody can understand?'

The code was quickly withdrawn. Recognizing for the first time that he needed assistance, Rex put a staff of experts to work on a revision. He instructed them to leave the substance untouched, but to clarify the expression throughout. The resulting code was a model of clarity, but as it was studied it became apparent that its new clarity had merely brought to light that it was honeycombed with contradictions. It was reliably reported that there was not a single provision in the code that was not nullified by another provision inconsistent with it. A picket again appeared before the royal residence carrying a sign that read, 'This time the king made himself clear – in both directions.'

Once again the code was withdrawn for revision. By now, however, Rex had lost his patience with his subjects and the negative attitude they seemed to adopt toward everything he tried to do for them. He decided to teach them a lesson and put an end to their carping. He instructed his experts to purge the code of contradictions, but at the same time to stiffen drastically every requirement contained in it and to add a long list of new crimes. Thus, where before the citizen summoned to the throne was given ten days in which to report, in the revision the time was cut to ten seconds. It was made a crime, punishable by ten years' imprisonment, to cough, sneeze, hiccough, faint or fall down in the presence of the king. It was made treason not to understand, believe in, and correctly profess the doctrine of evolutionary, democratic redemption.

When the new code was published a near revolution resulted. Leading citizens declared their intention to flout its provisions. Someone discovered in an ancient author a passage that seemed apt: 'To command what cannot be done is not to make law; it is to unmake law, for a command that cannot be obeyed serves no end but confusion, fear and chaos.' Soon this passage was being quoted in a hundred petitions to the king.

The code was again withdrawn and a staff of experts charged with the task of revision. Rex's instructions to the experts were that whenever they encountered a rule requiring an impossibility, it should be revised to make compliance possible. It turned out that to accomplish this result every provision in the code had to be substantially rewritten. The final result was, however, a triumph of draftsmanship. It was clear, consistent with itself, and demanded nothing of the subject that did not lie easily within his powers. It was printed and distributed free of charge on every street corner.

However, before the effective date for the new code had arrived, it was discovered that so much time had been spent in successive revisions of Rex's original draft, that the substance of the code had been seriously overtaken by events. Ever since Rex assumed the throne there had been a suspension of ordinary legal processes and this had brought about important economic and institutional changes within the country. Accommodation to these altered conditions required many changes of substance in the law. Accordingly as soon as the new code became legally effective, it was subjected to a daily stream of amendments. Again popular discontent mounted; an anonymous pamphlet appeared on the streets carrying scurrilous cartoons of the king and a leading article with the title: 'A law that changes every day is worse than no law at all.'

Within a short time this source of discontent began to cure itself as the pace of amendment gradually slackened. Before this had occurred to any noticeable degree, however, Rex announced an important decision. Reflecting on the misadventures of his reign, he concluded that much of the trouble lay in bad advice he had received from experts. He accordingly declared he was reassuming the judicial power in his own person. In this way he could directly control the application of the new code and insure his country against another crisis. He began to spend practically all of his time hearing and deciding cases arising under the new code.

As the king proceeded with this task, it seemed to bring to a belated blossoming his long dormant powers of generalization. His opinions began, indeed, to reveal a confident and almost exuberant virtuosity as he deftly distinguished his own previous decisions, exposed the principles on which he acted, and laid down guide lines for the disposition of future controversies. For Rex's subjects a new day seemed about to dawn when they could finally conform their conduct to a coherent body of rules.

This hope was, however, soon shattered. As the bound volumes of Rex's judgments became available and were subjected to closer study, his subjects were appalled to discover that there existed no discernible relation between those judgments and the code they purported to apply. Insofar as it found expression in the actual disposition of controversies, the new code might just as well not have existed at all. Yet in virtually every one of his decisions Rex declared and redeclared the code to be the basic law of his kingdom.

Leading citizens began to hold private meetings to discuss what measures, short of open revolt, could be taken to get the king away from the bench and back on the throne. While these discussions were going on Rex suddenly died, old before his time and deeply disillusioned with his subjects.

The first act of his successor, Rex II, was to announce that he was taking the powers of government away from the lawyers and placing them in the hands of psychiatrists and experts in public relations. This way, he explained, people could be made happy without rules.

THE CONSEQUENCES OF FAILURE

Rex's bungling career as legislator and judge illustrates that the attempt to create and maintain a system of legal rules may miscarry in at least eight ways; there are in this enterprise, if you will, eight distinct routes to disaster. The first and most obvious lies in a failure to achieve rules at all, so that every issue must be decided on an ad hoc basis. The other routes are: (2) a failure to publicize or at least to make available to the affected party, the rules he is expected to observe; (3) the abuse of retroactive legislation, which not only cannot itself guide action, but undercuts the integrity of rules prospective in effect, since it puts them under the threat of retrospective change; (4) a failure to make rules understandable; (5) the enactment of contradictory rules or (6) rules that require conduct beyond the powers of the affected party; (7) introducing such frequent changes in the rules that the subject cannot orient his action by them; and, finally, (8) a failure of congruence between the rules as announced and their actual administration.

A total failure in any one of these eight directions does not simply result in a bad system of law; it results in something that is not properly called a legal system at all, except perhaps in the Pickwickian sense in which a void contract can still be said to be one kind of contract. Certainly there can be no rational ground for asserting that a man can have a moral obligation to obey a legal rule that does not exist, or is kept secret from him, or that came into existence only after he had acted, or was unintelligible, or was contradicted by another rule of the same system, or commanded the impossible, or changed every minute. It may not be impossible for a man to obey a rule that is disregarded by those charged with its administration, but at some point obedience becomes futile – as futile, in fact, as casting a vote that will never be counted. As the sociologist Simmel has observed, there is a kind of reciprocity between government and the citizen with respect to the observance of rules. Government says to the citizen in effect, 'These are the rules we expect you to follow. If you follow them, you have our assurance that they are the rules that will be applied to your conduct.' When this bond of reciprocity is finally and completely ruptured by government, nothing is left on which to ground the citizen's duty to observe the rules.

The citizen's predicament becomes more difficult when, though there is no total failure in any direction, there is a general and drastic deterioration in legality, such as occurred in Germany under Hitler. A situation begins to develop, for example, in which though some laws are published, others, including the most important, are not. Though most laws are prospective in effect, so free a use is made of retrospective legislation that no law is immune to change ex post facto if it suits the convenience of those in power. For the trial of criminal cases concerned with loyalty to the regime, special military tribunals are established and these tribunals disregard, whenever it suits their convenience, the rules that are supposed to control their decisions. Increasingly the principal object of government seems to be, not that of giving the citizen rules by which to shape his conduct, but to frighten him into impotence. As such a situation develops, the problem faced by the citizen is not so simple as that of a voter who knows with certainty that his ballot will not be counted. It is more like that of the voter who knows that the odds are against his ballot being counted at all, and that if it is counted, there is a good chance that it will be counted for the side against which he actually voted. A citizen in this predicament has to decide for himself whether to stay with the system and cast his ballot as a kind of symbolic act expressing the hope of a better day. So it was with the German citizen under Hitler faced with deciding whether he had an obligation to obey such portions of the laws as the Nazi terror had left intact.

In situations like these there can be no simple principle by which to test the citizen's obligation of fidelity to law, any more than there can be such a principle for testing his right to engage in a general revolution. One thing is, however, clear. A mere respect for constituted authority must not be confused with law. Rex's subjects, for example, remained faithful to him as king throughout his long and inept reign. They were not faithful to his law, for he never made any.

THE ASPIRATION TOWARD PERFECTION IN LEGALITY

So far we have been concerned to trace out eight routes to failure in the enterprise of creating law. Corresponding to these are eight kinds of legal excellence toward which a system of rules may strive. What appear at the lowest level as indispensable conditions for the existence of law at all, become, as we ascend the scale of achievement, increasingly demanding challenges to human capacity. At the height of the ascent we are tempted to imagine a utopia of legality in which all rules are perfectly clear, consistent with one another, known to every citizen, and never retroactive. In this utopia the rules remain constant through time, demand only what is possible, and are scrupulously observed by courts, police, and everyone else charged with their administration. For reasons that I shall advance shortly, this utopia, in which all eight of the principles of legality are realized to perfection, is not actually a useful target for guiding the impulse toward legality; the goal of perfection is much more complex. Nevertheless it does suggest eight distinct standards by which excellence in legality may be tested in expounding in my first chapter the distinction between the morality of duty and that of aspiration, I spoke of an imaginary scale that starts at the bottom with the most obvious and essential moral duties and ascends upward to the highest achievements open to man. I also spoke of an invisible pointer as marking the dividing line where the pressure of duty leaves off and the challenge of excellence begins. The inner morality of law, it should now be clear, presents all of these aspects. It too embraces a morality of duty and a morality of aspiration. It too confronts us with the problem of knowing where to draw the boundary below which men will be condemned for failure, but can expect no praise for success, and above which they will be admired for success and at worst pitied for the lack of it.

In applying the analysis of the first chapter to our present subject, it becomes essential to consider certain distinctive qualities of the inner morality of law. In what may be called the basic morality of social life, duties that run toward other persons generally (as contrasted with those running toward specific individuals) normally require only forbearances, or as we say, are negative in nature: Do not kill, do not injure, do not deceive, do not defame, and the like. Such duties lend themselves with a minimum of difficulty to formalized definition. That is to say, whether we are concerned with legal or moral duties, we are able to develop standards which designate with some precision – though it is never complete – the kind of conduct that is to be avoided.

The demands of the inner morality of the law, however, though they concern a relationship with persons generally, demand more than forbearances; they are, as we loosely say, affirmative in nature: make the law known, make it coherent and clear, see that your decisions as an official are guided by it, etc. To meet these demands human energies must be directed toward specific kinds of achievement and not merely warned away from harmful acts.

106

LEGAL MORALITY AND THE CONCEPT OF POSITIVE LAW

Our next task is to bring the view of law implicit in these chapters into its proper relation with current definitions of positive law. The only formula that might be called a definition of law offered in these writings is by now thoroughly familiar: law is the enterprise of subjecting human conduct to the governance of rules. Unlike most modern theories of law, this view treats law as an activity and regards a legal system as the product of a sustained purposive effort. Let us compare the implications of such a view with others that might be opposed to it.

145–151

LAW AS A PURPOSEFUL ENTERPRISE AND LAW AS A MANIFESTED FACT OF SOCIAL POWER

The many different oppositions of viewpoint that have been examined in this chapter may be said to reflect in shifting contexts a single, underlying disagreement. The nature of this fundamental divergence may be expressed in these terms: I have insisted that law be viewed as a purposeful enterprise, dependent for its success on the energy, insight, intelligence, and conscientiousness of those who conduct it, and fated, because of this dependence, to fall always somewhat short of a full attainment of its goals. In opposition to this view it is insisted that law must be treated as a manifested fact of social authority or power, to be studied for what it is and does, and not for what it is trying to do or become.

In dealing with this fundamental opposition let me begin with a statement of the considerations that seem to me to have led to the view which I oppose. Since I have no authority to speak for the opposition, this statement will have to be hypothetical in form. I shall, however, try to phrase it as persuasively as I can.

Such a statement would begin with a concession that purpose has a proper role to play in the interpretation of individual legal enactments. A statute is obviously a purposive thing, serving some end or congeries of related ends. What is objected to is not the assignment of purposes to particular laws, but to law as a whole.

Any view that ascribes some purpose or end to a whole institutional complex has, it may be said, very unattractive antecedents in the history of philosophy. It calls to mind the excesses of German and British idealism. It suggests that if we start talking about the purpose of law we may end by talking about the Purpose of the State. Even if we dismiss as unreal the danger that the spirit of Hegel may ride again, the view under consideration has other affinities that are far from reassuring. It recalls, for example, the solemn discussions about the Purpose of Swamps that Thomas Jefferson conducted with his associates in the American Philosophical Society. A naive teleology, it may be said, has shown itself to be the worst enemy that the scientific pursuit of objective truth can have.

Even if its historic affinities were less disturbing, there is an intrinsic improbability about any theory that attempts to write purpose in a large hand over a whole institution. Institutions are constituted of a multitude of individual human actions. Many of these follow grooves of habit and can hardly be said to be purposive at all. Of those that are purposive, the objectives sought by the actors are of the most diverse nature. Even those who participate in the creation of institutions may have very different views of the purpose or function of the institutions they bring into being.

In answering these criticisms I shall begin by recalling that the purpose I have attributed to the institution of law is a modest and sober one, that of subjecting human conduct to the guidance and control of general rules. Such a purpose scarcely lends itself to Hegelian excesses. The ascription of it to law would, indeed, seem a harmless truism if its implications were not, as I believe I have shown in my second chapter, far from being either self-evident or unimportant.

Before denying ourselves the modest indulgence in teleology I have proposed, we should consider carefully the cost entailed in this denial. The most significant element of that cost lies in the fact that we lose wholly any standard for defining legality. If law is simply a manifested fact of authority or social power, then, though we can still talk about the substantive justice or injustice of particular enactments, we can no longer talk about the degree to which a legal system as a whole achieves the ideal of legality; if we are consistent with our premises we cannot, for example, assert that the legal system of Country X achieves a greater measure of legality than that of Country Y. We can talk about contradictions in the law, but we have no standard for defining what a contradiction is. We may bemoan some kinds of retroactive laws, but we cannot even explain what would be wrong with a system of laws that were wholly retroactive. If we observe that the power of law normally expresses itself in the application of general rules, we can think of no better explanation for this than to say that the supreme legal power can hardly afford to post a subordinate at every street corner to tell people what to do. In short, we can neither formulate nor answer the problems to which my second chapter was devoted.

It may be said that if in truth these problems cannot be formulated in a manner that enables us to answer them then we ought to face that fact courageously and not deceive ourselves with fictions. It is at this point that issue is most sharply joined. The question becomes, not which view is most comforting and reassuring, but which view is right, which view corresponds most faithfully to the reality with which we must deal. In the remainder of this chapter I shall seek to show that the view which pretends to abstract from the purpose of law and to treat law simply as a manifested fact of social power cannot be supported except through a falsification of the reality on which it purports to build.

The view I am criticizing sees the reality of law in the fact of an established lawmaking authority. What this authority determines to be law *is* law. There is in this determination no question of degree; one cannot apply to it the adjectives 'successful' or 'unsuccessful'. This, it seems to me, is the gist of the theory which opposes that underlying these chapters.

Now this theory can seem tenable, I submit, only if we systematically strike from view two elements in the reality it purports to describe. The first of these lies in the fact that the established authority which tells us what is law is itself the product of law. In modern society law is typically created by corporate action. Corporate action – by a parliament, for example – is possible only by adopting and following rules of procedure that will enable a body of men to speak legally with one voice. These rules of procedure may meet shipwreck in all of the eight ways open to any system of law. So when we assert that in the United Kingdom Parliament has the final say as to what law is, we are tacitly assuming some measure of success in at least one legal enterprise, that directed toward giving Parliament the corporate power to 'say' things. This assumption of success is normally quite justified in countries with a long parliamentary tradition. But if we are faithful to the reality we purport to describe, we shall recognize that a parliament's ability to enact law is itself an achievement of purposive effort, and not simply a datum of nature.

The second falsification of reality consists in ignoring the fact that a formal structure of authority is itself usually dependent on human effort that is not required by any law or command. Weber points out that all formal social structures – whether embodied in a tradition or a written constitution – are likely to have gaps that do not appear as such because they are filled by appropriate actions taken, often, without any awareness that an alternative is open. Men do not, in other words, generally do absurd things that would defeat the whole undertaking in which they are engaged, even though the formal directions under which they operate permit these absurdities.

A good example of a gap in formal structure is to be found in the Constitution of the United States. That laws should be promulgated is probably the most obvious demand of legality. It is also the demand that is most readily reduced to a formal constitutional requirement. Yet the Constitution says nothing about the publication of laws. Despite this lack I doubt if it has ever entered the mind of any Congressman that he might curry favor with the taxpayers through a promise to save them money by seeing to it that the laws were left unpublished. One can, of course, argue that a constitutional requirement of publication can be reached by interpretation, since otherwise the provisions against certain retrospective laws would make little sense. But the point is that no such interpretation was in fact engaged in by those who from the first assumed as a matter of course that laws ought to be published.

The scholar may refuse to see law as an enterprise and treat it simply as an emanation of social power. Those whose actions constitute that power, however, see themselves as engaged in an enterprise and they generally do the things essential for its success. To the extent that their actions must be guided by insight rather than by formal rule, degrees in the attainment of success are inevitable.

Hart's problem of 'the persistence of law' – how can the law made by Rex IV still be law when Rex V comes to the throne? – is another example of a gap in postulated formal structure that does not appear as such in practice. The need for continuity in law despite changes in government is so obvious that everyone normally assumes this continuity as a matter of course. It becomes a problem only when one attempts to define law as an emanation of formal authority and excludes from its operations the possible influence of human judgment and insight.

The heavy emphasis theory tends to place on an exact definition of the highest legal power expresses, no doubt, a concern that obscurity on this point may cause the legal system as a whole to disintegrate. Again, it is forgotten that no set of directions emanating from above can ever dispense with the need for intelligent action guided by a sense of purpose. Even the lowly justice of the peace, who cannot make head or tail of the language by which his jurisdiction is limited, will usually have the insight to see that his powers derive from an office forming part of a larger system. He will at least have the judgment to proceed cautiously. Coordination among the elements of a legal system is not something that can simply be imposed; it must be achieved. Fortunately, a proper sense of role, reinforced by a modicum of intelligence, will usually suffice to cure any defaults of the formal system.

There is, I think, a curious irony about any view that refuses to attribute to law as a whole any purpose, however modest or restricted. No school of thought has ever ventured to assert that it could understand reality without discerning in it structure, relatedness, or pattern. If we were surrounded by a formless rain of discrete and unrelated happenings, there would be nothing we could understand or talk about. When we treat law as a 'fact,' we must assume that it is a special kind of fact, possessing definable qualities that distinguish it from other facts. Indeed, all legal theorists are at great pains to tell us just what kind of fact it is – it is not 'the gunman situation writ large', it normally involves the application of general rules to human behavior, etc., etc.

This effort to discover and describe the characteristics that identify law usually meets with a measure of success. Why should this be? The reason is not at all mysterious. It lies in the fact that in nearly all societies men perceive the need for subjecting certain kinds of human conduct to the explicit control of rules. When they embark on the enterprise of accomplishing this subjection, they come to see that this enterprise contains a certain inner logic of its own, that it imposes demands that must be met (sometimes with considerable inconvenience) if its objectives are to be attained. It is because men generally in some measure perceive these demands and respect them, that legal systems display a certain likeness in societies otherwise quite diverse.

It is, then, precisely because law is a purposeful enterprise that it displays structural constancies which the legal theorist can discover and treat as uniformities in the factually given. If he realized on what he built his theory, he might be less inclined to conceive of himself as being like the scientist who discovers a uniformity of inanimate nature. But perhaps in the course of re-thinking his subject he might gain a new respect for his own species and come to see that it, too, and not merely the electron, can leave behind a discernible pattern.

The final extract in this chapter is taken from the Italian Natural Lawyer D'Entreves, from an Appendix to the second edition of his book *Natural Law*. We could sub-title this extract 'Natural Law's optimism'. According to D'Entreves, the slightest glimmer of recognition by an avowed Legal Positivist that some values are inherent to law's content, form, structure, reasoning etc is enough to provide proof of the importance of Natural Law, not only historically but also in the present day. This extract describes D'Entreves view of the 'minimum content of law' as set out by H L A Hart in his classic Positivist text *The Concept of Law*. Hart's theories are outlined in Chapter 4 where this concession is characterised as 'Hart's gesture to natural law'. D'Entreves sees it as more than a gesture. You may wish to read that chapter first. Here, the concluding extract to this chapter is D'Entreves account of one small part of Hart's analysis.

D'Entreves (1970, Essay C, 'A Core of Good Sense: Reflections on Hart's Theory of Natural Law', 185–203)

...

Mr N. Bobbio, who still maintained not long ago that the notion of natural law is meaningless and contradictory, has come to recognise more and more explicitly the 'historical function' of this superannuated concept in the defence of certain values against the organised force of those in power. He has done more. In a detailed analysis of the various meanings of the terms 'natural law' and 'legal positivism', he has brought out with surprising clarity the true dimensions of the difference between them and exposed the often crude misunderstandings which nurture that difference. Here I shall merely recall his three versions of legal positivism: as a method, as a theory, and as an ideology. As a method, or better, as a way of considering law, positivism is closely bound up with legal science and the work of jurists. As a theory it corresponds to the modern concept of the statist character of law. Finally, as an ideology, positivism implies the attribution of moral values to positive law. It is expressed in the phrase: *Gesetz ist Gesetz* (law is law), and its corollary is a rigid theory of obedience.

If these distinctions are accepted, the only kind of positivism which seems to me to have its papers in order is the first, for it is evident that whoever pursues the science and not the philosophy of law is required to limit himself to the facts, to the rules actually in force in the place and time in which he lives. Furthermore it is to its rigorous 'neutrality', its careful avoidance of value judgements, and its presentation of a faithful picture of the positive juridical order that the modern science of law is indebted for the success of which it is justly proud. As far as the second and third types of positivism are concerned, both seem to me to be open to criticism. As a reflection of a particular historical situation, the success of legal positivism as a theory is bound up with a contingent fact, the fact that the modern State has assumed a monopoly of law and the making of law. This concept also runs into serious difficulties when it tries to explain the juridical character of a law that is not from the State, such as canon law or international law. Finally, legal positivism as an ideology ends up as a simple inversion of natural law, if not as a theory of natural law in its own right. To affirm the moral duty of obeying laws is exactly what natural law theories have always proposed. The only difference between the two ideologies is the way in which they present the obligation of obedience. Those who oppose natural law to positive law see obedience as conditioned and limited, while those who conceive positive law as an end in itself find no such limits. One ideology deserves another. There will always be those who refuse to accept the maxim, Gesetz ist Gesetz, and who will prefer to obey God rather than men.

I find that Mr Bobbio's distinctions lead to two important results. On the one hand they show us the basis of positivist theory as a foundation and even as a condition of legal science. On the other hand they also – in the author's own opinion – make it possible to safeguard certain positions of natural law theory with respect to the criticism of positive law and to the problem of justice. It seems clear to me in any case that the principal argument of positivism against natural law is a speculative one: it is moral relativism, according to which natural law is only one ideology among others. In particular the theory of natural law would be but one way of justifying certain values (which may vary endlessly) through recourse to a supposed 'nature' of things or of men. It is indeed a fact, as I have pointed out elsewhere, that the majority of our positivists are also sceptics. But if they oppose the universal pretensions of natural law, they do not deny the need behind it.

...

Modern criticism of natural law – to summarise Hart – can all be brought back to the familiar distinction between 'descriptive' and 'prescriptive' propositions, between judgments of fact and judgments of value. The very expression, natural law, illustrates the difference in meaning which the word law can assume as a description of a factual condition and as a prescription of conduct or of order. In its prescriptive acceptation the idea of natural law is not necessarily linked to belief in a personal God who has 'ordered' the laws of nature. The very fact that its hold is independent of both divine and human authority ought to lead us to inquire if in spite of everything this idea does not contribute to a better understanding of both law and morality. There is certainly no question of reviving the whole teleological view of nature on which the classical doctrine of natural law was founded and which was used to transform into prescriptions what was in fact only a description of the normal development of things. But there is no need to postulate with Aristotle or St Thomas the existence of an end proper to man and constituting his 'good' in order to account for the fact that there is a sense in speaking, as one commonly does, of the proper end of all animate existence, namely, that of survival, perseverare in esse suo. Hobbes and Hume were satisfied with this 'very attenuated version' of natural law, and according to Hart it justifies natural law even today. (Concept of Law, 182–7) If we are concerned with societies organised for survival and not with a 'suicide club', we have a perfect right to ask, 'whether, among these social arrangements, there are some which may illuminatingly be ranked as natural laws discoverable by reason, and what their relation is to human law and morality. To raise this or any other question concerning *how* men should live together, we must assume that their aim, generally speaking, is to live. From this point the argument is a simple one. Reflection on some very obvious generalisations – indeed truisms – concerning human nature and the world in which men live, show that as long as these hold good, there are certain rules of conduct which any social organisation must contain if it is to be viable.' (Concept of Law, 188)

I have tried to give a faithful summary of Hart's reasoning, and I think I have shown how far he has gone along the path I spoke of at the beginning of this article. He speaks of 'universally recognised principles of conduct which have a basis in elementary truths concerning human beings, their natural environment, and aims'. These principles 'may be considered the *minimum content* of Natural Law, in contrast with the more grandiose and more challengeable constructions which have often been proffered under that name.' (Concept of Law, 189)

...

Hart therefore proposes a modernised version of Hobbes and Hume. He says as much, with a sincerity that does him credit, and the fact gives us a useful guide. I imagine the questions I am going to ask him differ little from questions proposed long ago to the two authors who inspired him. My first question is: what value does this natural law have as a normative proposition; what obligation does it carry with it? My second question is: How is this natural law related to positive law, and to what extent can positive law avoid taking its requirements into account? It is hardly necessary to add that these two questions are closely related.

To answer the first question I think we should make the most of a remark that Hart glides over casually but which is of capital importance; namely, that the relationship between the natural facts enumerated above and the 'content' of legal and moral regulations is a 'rational' one, not a relationship of causality. Psychology, sociology, and other sciences deal with the causes for which certain rules flow necessarily from a given social situation, but they do not treat the existence of these rules as depending on a choice, on a conscious resolve on the part of those who enact them. Only the 'truisms' of the natural law give us the reasons why, given the end of survival, 'law and morals should include a specific content'. (Concept of Law, 254) If I am not mistaken, this is how Hart seeks to bridge the gap between fact and value, to transform the natural law from a descriptive proposition to a normative one: 'The general form of the argument is simply that without such a content laws and morals could not forward the minimum purpose of survival which men have in associating with each other. In the absence of this content men, as they are, would have no reason for obeying voluntarily any rules; and without a minimum of co-operation given voluntarily by those who find that it is in their interest to submit to and maintain the rules, coercion of others who would not voluntarily conform would be impossible.' (Concept of Law, 189)

Is this a convincing reason? Has Hart really succeeded in bridging the gap between fact and value, between the is and the ought, a task deemed impossible by analytical philosophy following the celebrated judgment of Hume? ... Nevertheless if is not difficult – and Hart admits it himself – to see the value judgment implicit in what is at first presented as a simple observation of fact, namely in the proposition that the aim of all human association is survival. ... But in fact he interposes a value judgment between the observation and the prescription, the judgment that the conservation and defence of human life are a good thing.

...

A statement from Hume seems to summarise better than any commentary the thesis of Hart, to which I have no difficulty in subscribing: 'Tho' the rules of justice be *artificial*, they are not *arbitrary*. Nor is the expression improper to call them *Laws of Nature*; if by natural we understand what is common to any species, or even if we confine it to mean what is inseparable from the species.'

Let us now proceed to the obligations which flow from the natural law as a normative proposition. I have just cited Hart as saying that it is the specific content furnished by natural law which assures the voluntary obedience of men to positive law. Clearly then this voluntary obedience is an essential feature of law and the obligatory character of law is not derived exclusively from the coercive force which it possesses.

...

The reasons for voluntary obedience are complex. They constitute what Hart calls the accepted moralitv in a given society, and it can happen that the morality accepted by a dominant group implies the isolation or oppression of another group, as in slavery or racism. But it is none the less true, says Hart, that for a system of rules to be imposed by force on one group, there must be others in sufficient numbers who accept it voluntarily. 'Without their voluntary co-operation, thus creating *authority*, the coercive power of law and government cannot be established.' (Concept of Law, 196) 'Hence a society with law contains those who look upon its rules from the internal point of view as accepted standards of behaviour ... But it also comprises those upon whom, either because they are malefactors or mere helpless victims of the system, these legal standards have to be imposed by force or threat of force; they are concerned with the rules merely as a source of possible punishment. The balance between these two components will be determined by many different factors. If the system is fair and caters genuinely to the vital interests of all those from whom it demands obedience, it may gain and retain the allegiance of most for most of the time, and will accordingly be stable. On the other hand it may be a narrow and exclusive system run in the interests of the dominant group, and it may be made continually more repressive and unstable with the latent threat of upheaval. Between these two extremes various combinations of these attitudes to law are to be found, often in the same individual.' (Concept of Law, 197)

Let us notice the light which this relationship between law and morality throws on the political scene. We should like to know to what extent law and morality condition each other. On the one hand Hart seems to admit that positive law is closely linked to a specific content indicated by natural law. On the other hand he maintains, as we have seen, 'that it is in no sense a necessary truth that laws reproduce or satisfy certain demands of morality'. This is the fundamental dogma of legal positivism, and he accepts it. We must therefore look further into this point, my second question: what is the relationship between positive and natural law, and to what extent may the former ignore the latter?

To understand Hart we must again turn to other ideas on which the solution of our problem depends, the most important of which is the notion of validity. Hart treats it amply, and I shall recall here only what seems essential to our question. For Hart, if I understand him correctly, the notion of validity goes beyond the existential or factual judgment of the type: law is the system of rules which are in fact observed in a certain place and at a certain time. It is rather a 'normative' judgment which supposes a criterion or 'rule of recognition', which in turn allows us to declare that a particular rule corresponds to a given system of which it forms a part and that one can and ought to make use of it to qualify certain behaviour as relevant from the legal point of view.

...

He affirms very clearly that the problem of determining the criterion of validity of the legal order is an 'empirical, though complex, question of fact', not of hypothesis. What does this question of fact boil down to? Simply to the acceptance on the part of those who obey and apply the rules as 'valid': 'There are therefore two minimum conditions necessary and sufficient for the existence of a legal system. On the one hand those rules of behaviour which are valid according to the system's ultimate criteria of validity must be generally obeyed, and, on the other hand, its rules of recognition specifying the criteria of legal validity and its rules of change and adjudication must be effectively accepted as common public standards of official behaviour by its officials.' (Concept of Law, 113)

...

His notion of validity, as we have seen, implies two criteria and no others: the formal criterion of the legal qualification of one rule by another, and the criterion of fact, of the existence of an ultimate rule of recognition. It follows that the validity of a particular rule cannot depend in any way on its content, on its conformity to the principles of natural law or morality, a criterion exterior to the system. Hart realises that to accept the thesis of the subordination of positive law to natural law means to abandon or at least to constrict to the point of total transformation the notion of validity generally accepted by those who deal with positive law, a very broad notion which recognises the validity of any rule which satisfies the criteria established by the particular legal order under study.

Let us observe, however, that Hart appeals more to practical considerations than to logical argument in support of his thesis ... He merely asks the question: 'What then of the practical merits of the narrower concept of law in moral deliberation? In what way is it better, when faced with morally iniquitous demands, to think 'This is in no sense law' rather than 'This is law but too iniquitous to obey or apply'?' In Hart's eyes it is the merit of the positivists such as Austin, Gray and Kelsen to have seen clearly that the second proposition is the correct one.

...

I must nevertheless add that I fail to see this as the end of the story. It seems to me that in spite of the clarity of his treatment Hart may have unwittingly become bogged down on an impassable road. Is it perhaps because he has ventured too far along the way of the natural law? The first step is not always the one that costs the most. I see two difficulties in Hart's reasoning, and I shall close this long discussion by asking him to clarify them.

My first difficulty arises not from a disagreement with Hart but from a desire to determine the precise role and place of natural law as he conceives them with respect to law on the one hand and morality on the other. We have just learned that the validity of a legal norm does not depend in any way on its equity or iniquity, its moral value or lack of it. On the other hand Hart tells us that natural law constitutes a minimum content of any legal order, that it contains the elementary principles which men must respect as long as men are what they are and propose to set up a viable society. Are we to conclude that natural law is a central and privileged sphere of morality distinguished by its sacred and inviolable character? It may readily be admitted that a society founded on evil laws may lack that voluntary co-operation of which Hart speaks; but the system might still maintain itself, at least for a time, by force. Furthermore we know that the most viable of systems must be prepared to have recourse to force … Finally we know, and again it is Hart who says it, 'that neither the law nor the accepted morality of societies need extend their minimal protections and benefits to all within their scope, and often they have not done so.'

This last point perplexes me, even though I follow Hart's reasoning. What happens if the forced imposition of the so-called morality of a group which has seized power is in flagrant violation not only with the morality of the oppressed group but even with the minimal conditions imposed by the natural law for the very existence of a legal order; if, in other words, the contradiction reaches the point of violating the 'minimum protection for persons, property, and promises' which are, in Hart's own view, the 'indispensable features' of law and hence of the legal order? If a despot, for example, were to order the death of all his subjects, or the confiscation of all their goods, or their reduction to slavery, could we still maintain that while these laws are evil they are still laws? Or must we concede that natural law represents, so to speak, the borderline of evil, the frontier beyond which iniquity gains the upper hand and destroys law itself?

…

For those who like myself believe that the central problem of all legal philosophy is the problem of obligation, it is certainly gratifying to see this old problem restored to honour and placed at the very centre of recent debate. Hart tells us expressly that to accept the positivist thesis is not to deny that there is a problem concerning obedience. Specifically he says that the certification of the positive validity of a rule by no means constitutes a demand that it be obeyed. I shall only ask: to whom is the invitation addressed, the invitation to refuse obedience to a law recognised as juridically valid but morally iniquitous? I imagine that it could be addressed to the subjects of a State, to those who belong to a particular legal order, to the members of a social group whose acceptance, as we have seen, is the ultimate condition for the validity of the system. In that case it would be an appeal to resistance or insurrection, an invitation to act in such a way that the system will collapse. This would be the phenomenon which Hart describes under various aspects as pathology of the legal order. A system in which obedience begins to bend is a system in which the criterion of validity has become, or is about to become, blurred and useless.

But this invitation could also be extended – as the Englishman Hart is well aware – to the officials, the magistrates and judges who explain and interpret the law, who have the task of deciding case for case what the valid rule is. Hart likes to compare the declaration of the judge, 'It is the law', to that of the umpire who says 'Goal', or anyone who marks up a point when applying the rules of a game. What puzzles me is this: what does the judge do, and what would Hart have him do, in the case of an 'evil law'? I suppose he would have to say: I admit that this law is valid according to the established order, but I refuse to apply it in the name of a higher and holier cause. I suppose he could do even more: jam the machinery of the established order, offer his resignation, suffer for the cause. The judge can go farther than the simple citizen toward aggravating the pathology of the system and making it irreparable. What puzzles me is not that Hart asks the hypothetical judge to be a hero – we all knew real ones during the Resistance – but that he asks him to say that a law is valid when he clearly does not consider it so, since he refuses to apply it. I fail to see the distinction between his refusing to 'declare' the law and saying that it is not valid. In refusing is he not recurring to a criterion of validity that is above the system? This is precisely what the defenders of natural law have always done, and Hart has opened the door – perhaps imprudently – to one of their strongest arguments.

...

I fear, however, that in stirring up what had become the calm coexistence of positivism and natural law, Hart will draw fire from both sides. I strongly doubt that the Continental positivist, for whom positivism is closely bound up with moral relativism, will embrace without flinching Hart's restoration of natural law as a minimum of incontestable truth, modest as it is. On the other hand I do not believe that the logical proponent of natural law can be content with what Hart offers him. Not only will he reject the purely formal and nominalistic concept of reason of which I spoke, but he will have his foot in the door to make further demands. Why should natural law be limited to the question of survival? If the conservation of life is good, it is because there is a 'good life', the Aristotelian would say, or, the Thomist would add, because natural life is the means of assuring eternal life. The barriers are down, and all the values which have appealed in turn to natural law will find support once more, each with its exclusive pretensions.

I have already stated why I find Hart's interpretation of natural law completely plausible. As Hart reminds us, the wisdom of Hobbes and Hume was to 'have been willing to lower their sights', and this expression seems apt here also. The art of the happy medium is a difficult one, and it is perhaps this very English art which led Hart not only to find good common sense in natural law but also to put such a generous share of it into the composition of his book.

Further Reading

For a short statement by a modern natural lawyer on what natural law is and what its relation to positive law is: George 1996.

For a more extensive discussion of Fuller's version of natural law: Summers 1984.

For contemporary essays on, or in defence of natural law theory: George 1992, especially chapters by George, McCormick, Finnis, Waldron, Moore, Weinreb, Raz.

For an alternative example of modern natural law theory to that of John Finnis: Beyleveld and Brownsword 1986.

Questions

1. 'The difference between coercion and law is the difference between order, and good order.' Discuss.

2. 'The fact that all law aims at some level to ensure human survival, does not ensure that its content is moral in any meaningful way.' Discuss.

3. 'Even if laws have to be communicated in order to speak meaningfully of duties, this would still not guarantee that law had a minimum moral content.' Discuss.

4. 'Traditional natural law theory seeks to show why existing legal systems must necessarily be just. Modern natural law theories seek to identify what, within any given legal system, must be just.' Discuss.

5. Can natural law theorists escape the naturalistic fallacy (an illogical conflation of 'is' and 'ought')? Illustrate your answer by reference to the writings of at least two of the following: Aquinas, Fuller, Finnis.

3 Debating with Natural Law: the Emergence of Legal Positivism

Richard Nobles and David Schiff

Legal Positivism makes a deliberate break from Natural Law theorising, with theories representative of that label being offered as superior alternatives. It is important however to see exactly what is at stake in the choice. Theories of Legal Positivism are sometimes presented (and more often understood) as if they were able to present clearer statements of what law is. The implication of such a claim is that natural law theorists were and are confused. A classic example is Austin's bold claim that: 'The existence of law is one thing; its merit or demerit is another ... to say that human laws which conflict with the Divine law are not binding, that is to say, are not laws, is to talk stark nonsense' (1955/ 1832, Lecture V, 184–85). Justification for those kinds of remarks may be found in the quaintly paradoxical statement attributed to Aquinas that 'An unjust law is not a law: *lex injusta non est lex.*' However, as Finnis makes clear, such an attribution is wrong: 'Thus Aquinas carefully avoids saying flatly that "an unjust law is not a law ..." But in the end it would have mattered little had he said just that' (1980, 364). Indeed, a careful reading of Natural Law theories (such as that perhaps already undertaken by yourselves) points to the fact that its theorists had no problem recognising as law the kinds of systems that Legal Positivists would call law. Their focus was, and is, however more than simple recognition, but rather recognition that involves elements that are unashamedly ethical. Remember, Aquinas identified, as having the full quality of law, only those just human laws that 'oblige in conscience' (1959, 135). Just as Natural Law theorising is often misunderstood by being interpreted from a point of view that does not represent its principal focus, so equally an accurate reading of Legal Positivism will show that many of the claims made about their writings are false or overstated. (For example see how Morrison (1958, 212) sets out 'current misunderstanding of Austin's position'. For references to articles that dispute or reflect on those misunderstandings, see Morrison 1982, Appendix 1, 'Recent commentaries on Austin'.)

In moving from Natural Law theories to those of Legal Positivism, one has to be aware of the shift that is taking place. Legal Positivists, and there are many such theorists in many countries, are not a breed of persons who see things more clearly. They are persons who wish to focus on clear things. Such an attitude is reflective of many other

'Positivisms', whether philosophical, sociological, logical, scientific or legal. The overriding concern of Positivism is to concentrate on the real, observable world and its actual existence. Its basic method is descriptive: what exists, and how can what exists be best described. Legal Positivists seek to identify the essential elements of the legal systems set down, or posited, by men. But there is no one theory of Legal Positivism. Different Legal Positivists hold different views on what is essential. Indeed, they adopt different approaches to the problems of identifying what is essential. But the common elements of Legal Positivism, from the perspective of how they differ from Natural Law theories, is that Legal Positivists want the study of law to examine the nature of stable rule systems. It is on such an examination that they focus, rather than the question of how, and to what extent, such systems can be ethical, or why they might persist over time. Like Natural Law theories, their theories concern themselves with the general and universal rather than the particular and specific. But what they seek to generalise is the common features of all centralised rule-based systems that are stable, rather than the common features of all centralised rule-based systems that are legitimate. This chapter deals with one of the earliest examples of this tradition.

There developed during the nineteenth century a particular brand of Legal Positivism in England, which became known as analytical positivism. Its spiritual father is the utilitarian philosopher Jeremy Bentham who wrote extensively about law among his even more extensive writings about many other subjects. Its classic and many feel its clearest expression can be found in the writings of Bentham's follower, John Austin. The approach of analytical positivism starts from the premise that certain words have 'real' meaning, because they refer to real things. Such words can be distinguished from others, which refer to things that are not real, but only, for example, mystical or metaphysical. Knowledge is found by separating one from the other. (With reference to law, and reflecting back on the last chapter, you should be able to anticipate which side of this division most of the values that inform Natural Law are, in these legal positivists' views, likely to fall. However, you should be careful not to assume that such theorists found all ethical ideas or moral values to be mystical, metaphysical or meaningless. Bentham's moral philosophy of Utilitarianism (which Austin followed up to a point) saw moral values as expressing ideas with clear and definite referents. What is good, within Utilitarian philosophy, is that which produces pleasure and the avoidance of pain. Thus, good for the community is the calculation of that which produces 'the greatest happiness of the greatest number'. In the way that Bentham demonstrated how such a calculation could be made, he attempted to make it as objective and clear as possible.) As well as seeking to distinguish words that have real referents, from those that do not, the method of analytical positivism requires careful elaboration of the differences between words with overlapping meanings. With certain words, this is quite a simple exercise. If you can find words that refer to a group or genus of real things (eg mammals) you can clarify your understanding by identifying the different elements of such groups (eg a species such as elephants). But words such as law refer to a complex family of elements that cannot be reduced to a simple comparison of this kind. For Austin, to examine the elements of law requires a 'long, intricate and coherent' dissertation (1955/1863, 371).

Early Legal Positivism tried to expel what they saw as the lack of clarity associated with Natural Law theory, and some of the consequences of that lack of clarity. In particular they wanted to expel the speculations associated with nature and those associated with values that were implicated in Natural Law theories. In order to do so it was committed to defining or clearly elucidating the basic terms that make up its subject matter. Through such definitions, elucidation and classification, it was thought, not only could law be known, but also the discipline of law could be developed. To explain this we will, in this chapter, deal with what this brand of Legal Positivism included as within its subject matter, and with what it felt it was necessary to expel as beyond or outside its subject matter. And we will deal with the substantive definition of law that it developed.

In reading our examples of extracts from early Legal Positivists, you should find it useful to think about what is included and excluded from the definition of law. The theories are an opportunity, par excellence, for putting on a certain kind of spectacles and looking at the world through them. Much of the traditional criticism of these theories by later Legal Positivists (particularly Hart, see Chapter 4) is that their spectacles filter out too much that is important. Here are a few questions to help you think about this.

1. How do these theories exclude ethics from law? (Clue: how do they define obligation?)

2. How do they address constitutional law and international law?

3. How do they see or understand law as different from violence or terror?

4. Are the rules of the law of contract, according to their theories, really law at all?

What were the early Legal Positivists attacking?

Bentham, who had an enormous reform agenda, had many targets for his criticism. And his own theory of morality, Utilitarianism, with its focus on the consequences of actions rather than a priori reasoning, was a challenge to many of the ethical theories within Natural Law thinking. He wrote a scathing attack on the Social Contract theories which had inspired the French and American revolutions, calling natural rights 'simple nonsense': 'Natural rights is simple nonsense: natural and imprescriptible rights, rhetorical nonsense – nonsense upon stilts' (1843, 501). He did not believe that Natural Law theories provided any objective guide to what was moral or immoral. He felt that such theories either duplicated Utilitarianism in a clouded form, or were reducible to subjective (if culturally determined) likes and dislikes. But, as well as attacking the anarchical tendencies of revolutionary Natural Law theories, he also attacked the conservative use of natural law ideas within English society. Many of his writings on law were written in response to attempts by English lawyers to justify the then, existing legal system, and particularly common law, by reference to natural law. He chose to attack a powerful defence and exposition of English law written by the renowned English jurist of the eighteenth century, Sir William Blackstone, particularly the four volumes of his *Commentaries on the Laws of England* (1765–69). Claims that English law expressed natural law were considered by Bentham to be wrong for a number of reasons. Such claims obfuscated the nature of law. Not only was English law not an expression of natural law (Bentham saw it as badly in need of reform) but descriptions of law that made this claim blinded lawyers and the general public to the need for, and possibilities of, change. (See Harrison's Introduction to (xxvi–xxxii) and Bentham's Preface to *Fragment on Government*, 1948, 3–8.)

The new project

In place of works like Blackstone's *Commentaries*, which attempted to describe the particular features of a single legal system while at the same time claiming that they were an expression of natural law, Bentham attempted to describe the nature of law in general, while at the same time denying that the feature that linked different legal systems was any ethical value. John Austin, his disciple, in the extract that follows, made one of the clearest statements of this endeavour.

In reading this extract, try to consider the following questions:

1. Does Austin regard modern legal systems as more complete examples of positive law than primitive legal systems?

2. Is what way is the science of legislation distinguishable from the philosophy of positive law or general jurisprudence? Can the latter be done without the former? Does this suggest that practising lawyers have no need to understand ethics?

3. How are different kinds of law to be distinguished from one another?

4. What is Austin's understanding of unwritten (customary) law?

John Austin (1863/1955, 365–373)

The appropriate subject of Jurisprudence, in any of its different departments, is positive law: Meaning by positive law (or law emphatically so called), law established or 'positum', in an independent political community, by the express or tacit authority of its sovereign or supreme government.

Considered as a whole, and as implicated or connected with one another, the positive laws and rules of a particular or specified community, are a system or body of law. And as limited to any one of such systems, or to any of its component parts, jurisprudence is particular or national.

Though every system of law has its specific and characteristic differences, there are principles, notions, and distinctions common to various systems, and forming analogies or likenesses by which such systems are allied.

Many of these common principles are common to all systems; – to the scanty and crude systems of rude societies, and the ampler and maturer systems of refined communities. But the ampler and maturer systems of refined communities are allied by the numerous analogies which obtain between all systems and also by numerous analogies which obtain exclusively between themselves. Accordingly, the various principles common to maturer systems (or the various analogies obtaining between them), and are the subject of an extensive science: which science (as contra-distinguished to national or particular jurisprudence on one side, and, on another, to the science of legislation) has been named General (or comparative) Jurisprudence, or the philosophy (or general principles) of positive law.

As principles abstracted from positive systems are the subject of general jurisprudence, so it is the exposition of such principles its exclusive or appropriate object. With the goodness and the badness of laws, as tried by the test of utility (or by any of the various tests which divide the opinions of mankind), it has no immediate concern. If, in regard to some of the principles which form its appropriate subject, it adverts to considerations of utility, it adverts to such considerations for the purpose of explaining such principles, and not for the purpose of determining their worth. And this distinguishes the science in question from the science of legislation: which affects to determine the test or standard (together with the principles subordinate or consonant to such test) by which positive law ought to be made, or to which positive law ought to be adjusted.

If the possibility of such a science appear doubtful, it arises from this; that in each particular system, the principles and distinctions which it has in common with others, are complicated with its individual peculiarities, and are expressed in a technical language peculiar to itself.

It is not meant to be affirmed that these principles and distinctions are conceived with equal exactness and adequacy in every particular system. In this respect different systems differ. But, in all, they are to be found more or less nearly conceived; from the rude conceptions of barbarians, to the exact conceptions of the Roman lawyers or of enlightened modern jurists.

I mean, then, by General Jurisprudence, the science concerned with the exposition of the principles, notions, and distinctions which are common to systems of law: understanding by systems of law, the ampler and maturer systems which, by reason of their amplitude and maturity, are pre-eminently pregnant with instruction.

Of the principles, notions, and distinctions which are the subjects of general jurisprudence, some may be esteemed necessary. For we cannot imagine coherently a system of law (or a system of law as evolved in a refined community), without conceiving them as constituent parts of it.

Of these necessary principles, notions, and distinctions, I will suggest briefly a few examples.

1. The notions of Duty, Right, Liberty, Injury, Punishment, Redress; with their various relations to one another, and to Law, Sovereignty, and Independent Political Society:

2. The distinction between written or promulged, and unwritten or unpromulged law, in the juridical or improper senses attributed to the opposed expressions; in other words, between law proceeding immediately from a sovereign or supreme maker, and law proceeding immediately from a subject or subordinate maker (with the authority of a sovereign or supreme):

3.   The distinction of Rights, into rights availing against the world at large (as, for example, property or dominion), and rights availing exclusively against persons specifically determined (as, for example, rights from contracts):

4.   The distinction of rights availing against the world at large, into property or dominion, and the variously restricted rights which are carved out of property or dominion:

5.   The distinction of Obligations (or of duties corresponding to rights against persons specifically determined) into obligations which arise from contracts, obligations which arise from injuries, and obligations which arise from incidents that are neither contracts nor injuries, but which are styled analogically obligations 'quasi ex contractu':

6.   The distinction of Injuries or Delicts, into civil injuries (or private delicts) and crimes (or public delicts); with the distinction of civil injuries (or private delicts) into torts, or delicts (in the strict acceptation of the term), and breaches of obligations from contracts, or of obligations 'quasi ex contractu'.

It will, I believe, be found, on a little examination and reflection, that every system of law (or every system of law evolved in a refined community) implies the notions and distinctions which I now have cited as examples; together with a multitude of conclusions imported by those notions and distinctions, and drawn from them, by the builders of the system, through inferences nearly inevitable.

Of the principles, notions, and distinctions which are the subjects of General Jurisprudence, others are not necessary (in the sense which I have given to the expression). We may imagine coherently an expanded system of law, without conceiving them as constituent parts of it. But as they rest upon grounds of utility which extend through all communities, and which are palpable or obvious in all refined communities, they in fact occur very generally in matured systems of law; and therefore may be ranked properly with the general principles which are the subjects of general jurisprudence.

...

But it will be impossible, or useless, to attempt an exposition of these principles, notions and distinctions, until by careful analysis, we have accurately determined the meaning of certain leading terms which we must necessarily employ; terms which recur incessantly in every department of the science: which, whithersoever we turn ourselves, we are sure to encounter. Such, for instance, are the following: Law, Right, Obligation, Injury, Sanction: Person, Thing, Act, Forbearance. Unless the import of these are determined at the outset, the subsequent speculations will be a tissue of uncertain talk.

It is not unusual with writers who call and think themselves '*institutional*' to take for granted, that they know the meaning of these terms, and that the meaning must be known by those to whom they address themselves. Misled by a fallacious test, they fancy that the meaning is simple and certain, because the expressions are familiar. Not pausing to ask their import, not suspecting that their import can need inquiry, they cast them before the reader without an attempt at explanation, and then proceed (without ceremony) to talk about them.

These terms, nevertheless, are beset with numerous ambiguities: their meaning, instead of being simple, is extremely complex: and every discourse which embraces Law as a whole, should point distinctly at those ambiguities, and should sever that complex meaning into the simpler notions which compose it.

Many of those who have written upon Law, have defined these expressions. But most of their definitions are so constructed that, instead of shedding light upon the thing defined, they involve it in thicker obscurity. In most attempts to define the terms in question, there is all the pedantry without the reality of logic: the form and husk, without the substance. The pretended definitions are purely circular: turning upon the very expressions which they affect to elucidate, or upon expressions which are exactly equivalent.

In truth, some of these terms will not admit of definition in the formal or regular manner. And as to the rest, to define them in that manner is utterly useless. For the terms which enter into the abridged and concise definition, need as much elucidation as the very expression which is defined.

The import of the terms in question is extremely complex. They are short marks for long series of propositions. And, what aggravates the difficulty of explaining their meaning clearly, is the intimate and indissoluble connection which subsists between them. To state the signification of each, and to show the relation in which it stands to the others, is not a thing to be accomplished by short and disjointed definitions, but demands a dissertation, long, intricate and coherent.

For example: Of Laws or Rules there are various classes. Now these classes ought to be carefully distinguished. For the confusion of them under a common name, and the consequent tendency to confound Law and Morals, is one most prolific source of jargon, darkness, and perplexity. By a careful analysis of leading terms, law is detached from morals, and the attention of the student of jurisprudence is confined to the distinctions and divisions which relate to law exclusively.

But in order to distinguish the various classes of laws, it is necessary to proceed thus: – To exhibit, first, the resemblance between them, and, then, their specific differences: to state *why* they are ranked under a common expression, and then to explain the marks *by which* they are distinguished. Till this is accomplished, the appropriate subject of Jurisprudence is not discernible precisely. It does not stand out. It is not sufficiently detached from the resembling or analogous objects with which it is liable to be confounded.

Thus, for example, in order to establish the distinction between Written and Unwritten Law, we must scrutinise the nature of the latter: a question which is full of difficulty; and which has hardly been examined with the requisite exactness by most of the writers who have turned their attention to the subject. I find it much vituperated, and I find it as much extolled; but I scarcely find an endeavour to determine *what it is*. But if this humbler object were well investigated, most of the controversy about its merits would probably subside.

To compare generally, or in the abstract, the merits of the two species, would be found useless: and the expediency of the process which has been styled Codification, would resolve itself into a question of time, place, and circumstance.

The word jurisprudence itself is not free from ambiguity; it has been used to denote –

The knowledge of Law as a science, combined with the art or practical habit or skill of applying it; or, secondly,

Legislation; – the science of what *ought to be done* towards making good laws, combined with the art of doing it.

Inasmuch as the knowledge of what ought to be, supposes a knowledge of what is, legislation supposes jurisprudence, but jurisprudence does not suppose legislation. What laws have been and are, may be known without a knowledge of what they ought to be. Inasmuch as a knowledge of what ought to be, is bottomed on a knowledge of antecedents *cognato genere*, legislation supposes jurisprudence.

With us, Jurisprudence is the science of what is essential to law, combined with the science of what it ought to be. It is particular or universal. Particular Jurisprudence is the science of any actual system of law, or of any portion of it. The only practical jurisprudence is particular.

The proper subject of General or Universal Jurisprudence (as distinguished from Universal Legislation) is a description of such subjects and ends of Law as are common to all systems; and of those resemblances between different systems which are bottomed in the common nature of man, or correspond to the resembling points in their several positions.

And these resemblances will be found to be very close, and to cover a large part of the field. They are necessarily confined to the resemblances between the systems of a few nations; since it is only a few systems with which it is possible to become acquainted, even imperfectly. From these, however, the rest may be presumed. And it is only the systems of two or three nations which deserve attention: – the writings of the Roman Jurists; the decisions of English Judges in modern times; the provisions of French and Prussian Codes as to arrangement. Though the points are also few in which the laws of nations ought to be the same (i.e. precisely alike), yet there is much room for universal legislation: i.e. the circumstances not precisely alike may be treated of together, in respect of what they have in common; with remarks directed to their differences. Whether the principles unfolded deserve the name of Universal or not, is of no importance. Jurisprudence may be universal with respect to its subjects: Not less so than legislation.

While Bentham and Austin expounded their theories of law separately, using different methods, they were united in the view that law was essentially imperative in character (expressive of a desire that someone do or abstain from something) and coercive. While they recognised that most statements of law make no reference to sanctions, they felt that this omission obscured a connection that made law different from other expressions of desire or guides to behaviour. And the obvious example of laws that appear to make no reference to sanctions were the wealth of civil laws, such as contract and property laws. But for Bentham, the distinction between civil and criminal law was artificial. Stealing (dishonestly appropriating **property** belonging to another) brought a vast amount of civil law into criminal law. Conversely, stealing, by protecting possessions by the punishment of others, provided a large measure of what it meant to **own** property. For Bentham, statements of law that made no reference to sanctions were 'incomplete'.

Jeremy Bentham (1789/1948, Concluding Note, 429–435)

II.   What is a law? What the parts of a law? The subject of these questions, it is to be observed, is the *logical*, the *ideal*, the *intellectual* whole, not the *physical* one: the *law*, and not the *statute*. An enquiry, directed to the latter sort of object, could neither admit of difficulty nor afford instruction. In this sense whatever is given for law by the person or persons recognized as possessing the power of making laws, is *law*. The Metamorphoses of Ovid, if thus given, would be law. So much as was embraced by one and the same act of authentication, so much as received the touch of the sceptre at one stroke, is *one* law: a whole law, and nothing more. A statute of George II made to substitute an *or* instead of an *and* in a former statute is a complete law; a statute containing an entire body of laws, perfect in all its parts, would not be more so. By the word *law* then, as often as it occurs in the succeeding pages is meant that ideal object, of which the part, the whole, or the multiple, or an assemblage of parts, wholes, and multiples mixed together, is exhibited by a statute; not the statute which exhibits them.

III.   Every law, when complete, is either of a *coercive* or an *uncoercive* nature. A coercive law is a *command*. An uncoercive, or rather a *discoercive*, law is the *revocation*, in whole or in part, of a coercive law.

IV.   What has been termed a *declaratory* law, so far as it stands distinguished from either a coercive or a discoercive law, is not properly speaking a law. It is not the expression of an act of the will exercised at the time: it is a mere notification of the existence of a law, either of the coercive or the discoercive kind, as already subsisting: of the existence of some document expressive of some act of the will, exercised, not at the time, but at some former period. If it does any thing more than give information of this fact, viz. of the prior existence of a law of either the coercive or the discoercive kind, it ceases *pro tanto* to be what is meant by a declaratory law, and assumes either the coercive or the discoercive quality.

V.   Every coercive law creates an *offence*, that is, converts an act of some sort, or other into an offence. It is only by so doing that it can *impose obligation*, that it can *produce coercion*.

VI.   A law confining itself to the creation of an offence, and a law commanding a punishment to be administered in case of the commission of such an offence, are two distinct laws; not parts (as they seem to have been generally accounted hitherto) of one and the same law. The acts they command are altogether different; the persons they are addressed to are altogether different. Instance, *Let no man steal*; and, *Let the judge cause whoever is convicted of stealing to be hanged.*

They might be styled; the former, a *simply imperative* law; the other a *punitory*: but the punitory, if it commands the punishment to be inflicted, and does not merely permit it, is as truly *imperative* as the other: only it is punitory besides, which the other is not.

VII.   A law of the discoercive kind, considered in itself, can have no punitory law belonging to it: to receive the assistance and support of a punitory law, it must first receive that of a simply imperative or coercive law, and it is to this latter that the punitory law will attach itself, and not to the discoercive one. Example; discoercive law. *The sheriff has power to hang all such as the judge, proceeding in due course of law, shall order him to hang.* Example of a coercive law, made in support of the above discoercive one. *Let no man hinder the sheriff from hanging such as the judge, proceeding in due course of law, shall order him to hang.* Example of a punitory law, made in support of the above coercive one. Let *the judge cause to be imprisoned whosoever attempts to hinder the sheriff from hanging one, whom the judge, proceeding in due course of law, has ordered him to hang.*

VIII. But though a simply imperative law, and the punitory law attached to it, are so far distinct laws, that the former contains nothing of the latter, and the latter, in its direct tenor, contains nothing of the former; yet by *implication*, and that a necessary one, the punitory does involve and include the import of the simply imperative law to which it is appended. To say to the judge, *Cause to be hanged whoever in due form of law is convicted of stealing*, is, though not a direct, yet as intelligible a way of intimating to men in general that they must not steal, as to say to them directly, *Do not steal:* and one sees, how much more likely to be efficacious.

IX. It should seem then, that, wherever a simply imperative law is to have a punitory one appended to it the former might be spared altogether: in which case, saving the exception (which naturally should seem not likely to be a frequent one) of a law capable of answering its purpose without such an appendage, there should be no occasion in the whole body of the law for any other than punitory, or in other words than *penal*, laws. And this, perhaps, would be the case, were it not for the necessity of a large quantity of matter of the *expository* kind, of which we come now to speak.

X.   It will happen in the instance of many, probably of most, possibly of all commands endued with the force of a public law, that, in the expression given to such a command, it shall be necessary to have recourse to terms too complex in their signification to exhibit the requisite ideas without the assistance of a greater or less quantity of matter of an expository nature. Such terms like the symbols used in algebraical notation, are rather substitutes and indexes to the terms capable of themselves of exhibiting the ideas in question, than the real and immediate representatives of those ideas.

Take for instance the law, *Thou shalt not steal.* Such a command, were it to rest there, could never sufficiently answer the purpose of a law. A word of so vague and unexplicit a meaning can no otherwise perform this office than by giving a general intimation of a variety of propositions, each requiring, to convey it to the apprehension a more particular and ample assemblage of terms. Stealing, for example, (according to a definition not accurate enough for use, but sufficiently so for the present purpose), is *the taking of a thing which is another's, by one who has no* TITLE *so to do, and is conscious of his having none.* Even after this exposition, supposing it a correct one, can the law be regarded as completely expressed? Certainly not. For what is meant by *a man's having a* TITLE *to take a thing?* To be complete, the law must have exhibited, amongst a multitude of other things, two catalogues: the one of events to which it has given the quality of *conferring title* in such a case; the other of the events to which it has given the quality of *taking it away.* What follows? That for a man to have *stolen*, for a man to *have had no title to what he took*, either no one of the articles contained in the first of those lists must have happened in his favour, or if there has, some one of the number of those contained in the second must have happened to his prejudice.

XI. Such then is the nature of a general law, that while the imperative part of it, the *punctum saliens* as it may be termed, of this artificial body, shall not take up above two or three words, its expository appendage, without which that imperative part could not rightly perform its office, may occupy a considerable volume.

But this may equally be the case with a private order given in a family. Take for instance one from a bookseller to his foreman. *Remove, from this shop to my new one, my whole stock according to this printed catalogue. – Remove, from this shop to my new one, my whole stock*, is the imperative matter of this order; the catalogue referred to contains the expository appendage.

XII. The same mass of expository matter may serve in common for, may appertain in common to, many commands, many masses of imperative matter. Thus, amongst other things, the catalogue of *collative and ablative* events, with respect to *titles* above spoken of (see No. IX of this note), will belong in common to all or most of the laws constitutive of the various offences against property. Thus, in mathematical diagrams, one and the same base shall serve for a whole cluster of triangles.

XIII. Such expository matter, being of a complexion so different from the imperative it would be no wonder if the connection of the former with the latter should escape the observation: which, indeed, is perhaps pretty generally the case. And so long as any mass of legislative matter presents itself, which is not itself imperative or the contrary, or of which the connection with matter of one of those two descriptions is not apprehended, so long and so far the truth of the proposition, *That every law is a command or its opposite*, may remain unsuspected, or appear questionable; so long also may the incompleteness of the greater part of those masses of legislative matter, which wear the complexion of complete laws upon the face of them, also the method to be taken for rendering them really complete, remain undiscovered.

XIV. A circumstance, that will naturally contribute to increase the difficulty of the discovery, is the great variety of ways in which the imperation of a law may be conveyed – the great variety of forms which the imperative part of a law may indiscriminately assume: some more directly, some less directly expressive of the imperative quality. *Thou shalt not steal. Let no man steal. Whoso stealeth shall be punished so and so. If any man steal, he shall be punished so and so. Stealing is where a man does so and so; the punishment for stealing is so and so. To judges* so and so named, and so and so constituted, *belong the cognizance of such and such offences; viz. stealing* – and so on. These are but part of a multitude of forms of words, in any of which the command by which stealing is prohibited might equally be couched: and it is manifest to what a degree, in some of them, the imperative quality is clouded and concealed from ordinary apprehension.

XV. After this explanation, a general proposition or two, that may be laid down, may help to afford some little insight into the structure and contents of a complete body of laws. – So many different sorts of *offences* created, so many different laws of the *coercive* kind: so many *exceptions* taken out of the descriptions of those offences, so many laws of the *discoercive kind*.

To class offences, as hath been attempted to be done in the preceding chapter, is therefore to class *laws*: to exhibit a complete catalogue of all the offences created by law, including the whole mass of expository matter necessary for fixing and exhibiting the import of the terms contained in the several laws, by which those offences are respectively created, would be to exhibit a complete collection of the laws in force: in a word a complete body of law; a *pannomion*, if so it might be termed.

XVI. From the obscurity in which the limits of a *law*, and the distinction betwixt a law of the civil or simply imperative kind and a punitory law, are naturally involved, results in the obscurity of the limits betwixt a civil and a penal *code*, betwixt a civil branch of the law and the penal.

The question, *What parts of the total mass of legislative matter belong to the civil branch, and what to the penal?* supposes that divers political states, or at least that some one such state, are to be found, having as well a civil code as a penal code, each of them complete in its kind, and marked out by certain limits. But no *one* such state has ever yet existed.

To put a question to which a true answer can be given, we must substitute to the foregoing question some such a one as that which follows:

Suppose two masses of legislative matter to be drawn up at this time of day, the one under the name of a civil code, the other of a penal code, each meant to be complete in its kind – in what general way, is it natural to suppose, that the different sorts of matter, as above distinguished, would be distributed between them?

To this question the following answer seems likely to come as near as any other to the truth.

The *civil* code would not consist of a collection of civil laws, each complete in itself, as well as clear of all penal ones:

Neither would the *penal* code (since we have seen that it *could* not) consist of a collection of punitive laws, each not only complete in itself, but clear of all civil ones. But –

XVII. The civil code would consist chiefly of mere masses of expository matter. The imperative matter, to which those masses of expository matter respectively appertained, would be found – not in that same code – not in the civil code – nor in a pure state, free from all admixture of punitory laws; but in the penal code – in a state of combination – involved, in manner as above explained, in so many correspondent punitory laws.

XVIII. The penal code then would consist principally of punitive laws, involving the imperative matter of the whole number of civil laws: along with which would probably also be found various masses of expository matter, appertaining not to the civil, but to the punitory laws. The body of penal law, enacted by the Empress-Queen Maria Theresa, agrees pretty well with this account.

XIX.   The mass of legislative matter published in French as well as German, under the auspices of Frederic II of Prussia, by the name of Code Frederic, but never established with force of law, appears, for example, to be almost wholly composed of masses of expository matter, the relation of which to any imperative matter appears to have been but very imperfectly apprehended.

XX.   In that enormous mass of confusion and inconsistency, the ardent Roman, or, as it is termed by way of eminence, the *civil* law, the imperative matter, and even all traces of the imperative character, seem at last to have been smothered in the expository. *Esto* had been the language of primaeval simplicity: *esto* had been the language of the twelve tables. By the time of Justinian (so thick was the darkness raised by clouds of commentators) the penal law had been crammed into an odd corner of the civil – the whole catalogue of offences, and even of crimes, lay buried under a heap of *obligations* – *will* was hid in *opinion* – and the original *esto* had transformed itself into *videtur*, in the mouths even of the most despotic sovereigns.

XXI. Among the barbarous nations that grew up out of the ruins of the Roman Empire, Law, emerging from under the mountain of expository rubbish, reassumed for a while the language of command: and then she had simplicity at least, if nothing else, to recommend her.

XXII. Besides the civil and the penal, every complete body of law must contain a third branch, the *constitutional.*

The constitutional branch is chiefly employed in conferring, on particular classes of persons, *powers*, to be exercised for the good of the whole society, or of considerable parts of it, and prescribing *duties* to the persons invested with those powers.

The powers are principally constituted, in the first instance, by discoercive or permissive laws, operating as exceptions to certain laws of the coercive or imperative kind. Instance: *A tax-gatherer, as such, may, on such and such an occasion, take such and such things, without any other* TITLE.

The duties are created by imperative laws, addressed to the persons on whom the powers are conferred. Instance: *On such and such an occasion, such and such a tax-gatherer shall take such and such things. Such and such a judge shall, in such and such a case, cause persons so and so offending to be hanged.*

The parts which perform the function of indicating who the individuals are, who, in every case, shall be considered as belonging to those classes, have neither a permissive complexion, nor an imperative.

They are so many masses of expository matter, appertaining in common to all laws, into the texture of which, the names of those classes of persons have occasion to be inserted. Instance: imperative matter: – *Let the judge cause whoever, in due course of law, is convicted of stealing, to be hanged.* Nature of the expository matter:– Who is the person meant by the word *judge?* He who has been *invested* with that office in such a manner: and in respect of whom no *event* has happened of the number of those, to which the effect is given, of reducing him to the condition of one *divested* of that office.

XXIII. Thus it is, that one and the same law, one and the same command, will have its matter divided, not only between two great codes, or main branches of the whole body of the laws, the civil and the penal; but amongst three such branches, the civil, the penal, and the constitutional.

Austin, Bentham's disciple, took many of Bentham's observations and attempted to include them within a comprehensive definition of law. As such, his works appear clearer than Bentham's does (a single working through of a definition is easier to assimilate than a series of separate observations on different aspects of law). But they suffer from a particular weakness. By seeking to encompass law within a definition, Austin was forced to accept the logical consequences of his own definitions, and to accommodate all aspects of law within his definitions. While the method provides insights, it necessarily has its shortcomings. Some important aspects of legal systems, such as constitutional law, are as a result defined as non-law. And whilst Bentham argued for the essential interconnectedness of criminal and civil law, Austin appears to define the latter as not law 'properly so called' (1832, 1 – the phrase with which Austin starts and which he constantly deploys in his analysis of the meaning of law).

Or Austin seems to include much of civil law as law only if one regards the absence of legal validity (things such as voidness, nullity, ultra vires or judgements overturned on appeal) as a kind of sanction.

Austin and Bentham both define law as a species of coercion. It is the presence of coercion (rather than ethics) that makes it possible to talk meaningfully of law's obligation. As you can see from the extract that follows, law is a type of command, and a command is an intimation of will backed by sanctions in the event of disobedience. It is the presence of sanctions (the power to inflict evil in the event of disobedience) that makes particular expressions of will into obligations, or duties. According to Austin, the sanction need not be large. Any evil, no matter how small, can constitute a sanction. By using sanctions to identify 'proper' laws, these theories identify 'rights' not with ethical theories, but with legal powers. Thus, for Bentham: 'Right ... is the child of law: from real laws come real rights; but from imaginary laws, from laws of nature, fancied and invented by poets, rhetoricians, and dealers in moral and intellectual poisons, come imaginary rights, a bastard brood of monsters' (1843, 523). A right exists when someone is under a duty. The ability to create such duties (legal powers) may lie in the citizen or an official.

Identifying law as a *species* of command requires further definitions to identify those commands that are law as opposed to those which are not. For Austin, commands are law if they are general and if they issue from a Sovereign. This is a definite person or body of persons who is identified not by ethical theories, or even constitutional law (which he called 'positive morality') but through the behaviour of the populace. The Sovereign was the body to whom the populace owed a habit of obedience, provided that that body was not in the habit of obedience to any other body. This series of definitions drives one to reach certain conclusions that run directly contrary to what might result from Natural Law. How can obligation based solely on the presence of sanctions be an ethical concept? If law is the command of a Sovereign how can the legal powers of a Sovereign be limited by its obligations to another party, or to the population itself?

Attempts to identify the source of law by reference to some kind of brute social fact (the obedience of a population to a definite body) instead of an ethical theory offered the prospect of greater clarity and agreement as to what constituted positive (man-made) law. It also made sense in a world where the dominant form of law had become legislation, as opposed to that of customary or judge made law. Law is not found in the consensus of values held by the population, or its enlightened elites, but in government. But this approach creates numerous problems. Even if one can find a single ('common') body to which the population show obedience (as opposed to a number of legal institutions – judiciary – executive – legislative, or centres of power – Church – Unions – Mafia) can one track which commands emanate from this body and which do not. Are the interpretations of law by judges the commands of a sovereign? Are the instructions of an employer to his employees, legal commands? Later positivists sought to avoid these problems by seeking the source of law in particular kinds of law – constitutional law. But this suffers from its own weakness. Is it constitutional law that explains the location of law making authority across history? Or is a theory, one which seeks to locate law making authority in centralised power, an outcome of ideology, political loyalties and traditional beliefs (positive morality) rather than constitutional law, cynically realistic (see Cotterrell 1989, 78). Is it that, to adopt the words of Hobbes, as Austin does 'the Legislator is he, not by whose authority the law was first made, but by whose authority it continues to be a Law'?

We set out below a long extract from Austin's lectures, one, five and six. To help you read this extract first we set out Austin's classification of law in the form of a table, which you can use to aid your reading of the extract. Also, with an eye to the next chapter (which deals with H L A Hart, who used his criticisms of Austin as a springboard for his own version of Legal Positivism), consider the following questions while reading the extracts:

1. Does Austin say that people obey laws out of fear, or does he simply use sanctions to identify what is to count as law?

2. Does he say why people develop a habit of obedience or, again, is the presence of this habit, for whatever reason, simply the means for identifying the Sovereign?

3. What do you understand by a habit of obedience? Would a habit of obedience to general commands involve an understanding of what it means to follow a rule? Could one have a habit of obedience in the same manner as one might have a habit of drinking cocoa before going to bed – a regularity of behaviour without any understanding that one is involved in something normative? (If you find this word confusing see Chapter 5.)

4. Can one understand the overruling of judges by higher courts, with the implicit criticism this entails, as a sanction, making their duty to apply the law obligatory? Can one understand findings of fault against doctors, even when they are insured, as a sanction, making their duties towards patients obligatory? Can one understand declarations that official actions are ultra vires, as a sanction, making their acting only within the law obligatory? Can the power to contract, be seen as a power to subject other people to sanctions, making their behaviour obligatory?

The Austinian classification of law

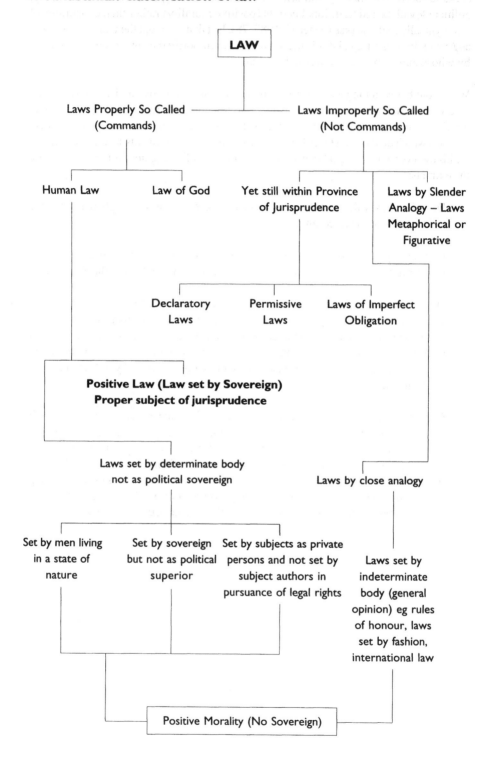

Austin (1832/1955, extracts from lectures one, five and six)

9–19

LECTURE I

The matter of jurisprudence is positive law: law, simply and strictly so called: or law set by political superiors to political inferiors. But positive law (or law, simply and strictly so called) is often confounded with objects to which it is related by *resemblance*, and with objects to which it is related in the way of *analogy*: with objects which are *also* signified, *properly and improperly*, by the large and vague expression *law*. To obviate the difficulties springing from that confusion, I begin my projected Course with determining the province of jurisprudence, or with distinguishing the matter of jurisprudence from those various related objects: trying to define the subject of which I intend to treat, before I endeavour to analyse its numerous and complicated parts.

A law, in the most general and comprehensive acceptation in which the term, in its literal meaning, is employed, may be said to be a rule laid down for the guidance of an intelligent being by an intelligent being having power over him. Under this definition are concluded, and without impropriety, several species. It is necessary to define accurately the line of demarcation which separates these species from one another, as much mistiness and intricacy has been infused into the science of jurisprudence by their being confounded or not clearly distinguished. In the comprehensive sense above indicated, or in the largest meaning which it has, without extension by metaphor or analogy, the term law embraces the following objects: – Laws set by God to his human creatures, and laws set by men to men.

The whole or a portion of the laws set by God to men is frequently styled the law of nature, or natural law: being, in truth, the only natural law of which it is possible to speak without a metaphor, or without a blending of objects which ought to be distinguished broadly. But, rejecting the appellation Law of Nature as ambiguous and misleading, I name those laws or rules, as considered collectively or in a mass, the *Divine law*, or the *law of God*.

Laws set by men to men are leading or principal classes: classes which are often blended, although they differ extremely; and which, for that reason, should be severed precisely, and opposed distinctly and conspicuously.

Of the laws or rules set by men to men, some are established by *political* superiors, sovereign and subject: by persons exercising supreme and subordinate *government*, in independent nations, or independent political societies. The aggregate of the rules thus established, or some aggregate forming a portion of that aggregate, is the appropriate matter of jurisprudence, general or particular. To the aggregate of the rules thus established, or to some aggregate forming a portion of that aggregate, the term *law*, as used simply and strictly, is exclusively applied. But, as contradistinguished to *natural* law, or to the law of nature (meaning, by those expressions, the law of God), the aggregate of the rules, established by political superiors, is frequently styled *positive* law, or law existing *by position*. As contradistinguished to the rules which I style *positive morality*, and on which I shall touch immediately, the aggregate of the rules, established by political superiors, may also be marked commodiously with the name of *positive law*. For the sake, then, of getting a name brief and distinctive at once, and agreeably to frequent usage, I style that aggregate of rules, or any portion of that aggregate, *positive law*: though rules, which are not established by political superiors, are also *positive,* or exist *by position,* if they be rules or laws in the proper signification of the term.

Though *some* of the laws or rules, which are set by men to men, are established by political superiors, *others* are *not* established by political superiors, or are *not* established by political superiors, in that capacity or character.

Closely analogous to human laws of this second class, are a set of objects frequently but *improperly* termed *laws*, being rules set and enforced by mere opinion, that is, by the opinions or sentiments held or felt by an indeterminate body of men in regard to human conduct. Instances of such a use of the term *law* are the expressions 'The law of honour'; 'The law set by fashion'; and rules of this species constitute much of what is usually termed 'International law'.

The aggregate of human laws properly so called belonging to the second of the classes above mentioned, the aggregate of objects *improperly* but by *close analogy* termed laws, I place together in a common class, and denote them by the term *positive morality*. The name *morality* severs them from *positive law*, while the epithet *positive* disjoins them from the *law of God*. And to the end of obviating confusion, it is necessary or expedient that they *should* be disjoined from the latter by that distinguishing epithet. For the name *morality (or morals)*, when standing unqualified or alone, denotes indifferently either of the following objects: namely, positive morality *as it is*, or without regard to its merits; and positive morality *as it would be*, if it conformed to the law of God, and were, therefore, deserving of *approbation*.

Besides the various sorts of rules which are included in the literal acceptation of the term law, and those which are by a close and striking analogy, though improperly, termed laws, there are numerous applications of the term law, which rest upon a slender analogy and are merely metaphorical or figurative. Such is the case when we talk of *laws* observed by the lower animals; of *laws* regulating growth or decay of vegetables; of *laws* determining the movements of inanimate bodies or masses. For where *intelligence* is not, or where it is too bounded to take the name of *reason* and, therefore, is too bounded to conceive the purpose of a law, there is not the *will* which law can work on, or which duty can incite or restrain. Yet through these misapplications of a *name*, flagrant as the metaphor is, has the field of jurisprudence and morals been deluged with muddy speculation.

Having suggested the *purpose* of my attempt to determine the province of jurisprudence: to distinguish positive law, the appropriate nature of jurisprudence, from the various objects to which it is related by resemblance, and to which it is related, nearly or remotely, by a strong or slender analogy: I shall now state the essentials of a *law* or *rule* (taken with the largest signification which can be given to the term *properly*).

Every law or rule or rule (taken with the largest signification which can be given to the term properly) is a *command*. Or, rather, laws or rules, properly so called, are a species of commands.

Now, since the term *command* comprises the term *law*, the first is the simpler as well as the larger of the two. But, simple as it is, it admits of explanation. And since it is the key to the sciences of jurisprudence and morals, its meaning should be analysed with precision.

Accordingly, I shall endeavour, in the first instance, to analyse the meaning of '*command*': an analysis which I fear, will task the patience of my hearers, but which they will bear with cheerfulness, or, at least, with resignation, if they consider the difficulty of performing it. The elements of a science are precisely the parts of it which are explained least easily. Terms that are the largest, and, therefore, the simplest of a series, are without equivalent expressions into which we can resolve them *concisely*. And when we endeavour to *define* them, or to translate them into terms which we suppose are better understood, we are forced upon awkward and tedious circumlocutions.

If you express or intimate a wish that I shall do or forbear from some act, and if you will visit me with an evil in case I comply not with your wish, the *expression* or *intimation* of your wish is a *command*. A command is distinguished from other significations of desire, not by the style in which the desire is signified, but by the power and the purpose of the party commanding to inflict an evil or pain in case the desire be disregarded. If you cannot or will not harm me in case I comply not with your wish, the expression of your wish is not a command, although you utter your wish in imperative phrase. If you are able and willing to harm me in case I comply not with your wish, the expression of your wish amounts to a command, although you are prompted by a spirit of courtesy to utter it in the shape of a request. '*Preces* errant, sed *quibus contradici non posset.*' Such is the language of Tacitus, when speaking of a petition by the soldiery to a son and lieutenant of Vespasian.

A command, then, is a signification of desire. But a command is distinguished from other significations of desire by this peculiarity: that the party to whom it is directed is liable to evil from the other, in case he comply not with the desire.

Being liable to evil from you if I comply not *with a wish which you signify, I am bound* or *obliged* by your command, or I lie under a *duty* to obey it. If, in spite of that evil in prospect, I comply not with the wish which you signify, I am said to disobey your command, or to violate the duty which it imposes.

Command and duty are, therefore, correlative terms: the meaning denoted by each being implied or supposed by the other. Or (changing the expression) wherever a duty lies, a command is signified, a duty is imposed.

Concisely expressed, the meaning of the correlative expressions is this. He who will inflict an evil in case his desire be disregarded, utters a command by expressing or intimating his desire: He who is liable to the evil in case he disregard the desire, is bound or obliged by the command.

The evil which will probably be incurred in case a command be disobeyed or (to use an equivalent expression) in case a duty be broken, is frequently called a *sanction,* or an *enforcement of obedience.* Or (varying the phrase) the command or the duty is said to be *sanctioned or enforced* by the chance of incurring the evil.

Considered as thus abstracted from the command and the duty which it enforces, the evil to be incurred by disobedience is frequently styled a *punishment.* But, as punishments, strictly so called, are only a *class of* sanctions, the term is too narrow to express the meaning adequately.

I observe that Dr Paley, in his analysis of the term *obligation,* lays much stress upon the *violence* of the motive to compliance. In so far as I can gather a meaning from his loose and inconsistent statement, his meaning appears to be this: that unless the motive to compliance be *violent or intense*, the expression or intimation of a wish is not a *command*, nor does the party to whom it is directed lie under a duty to regard it.

If he means, by a *violent* motive, a motive operating with certainty, his proposition is manifestly false. The greater the evil to be incurred in case the wish be disregarded, and the greater the chance of incurring it on that same event, the greater, no doubt, is the *chance* that the wish will *not* be disregarded. But no conceivable motive will *certainly* determine to compliance, or no conceivable motive will render obedience inevitable. If Paley's proposition be true, in the sense which I have now ascribed to it, commands and duties are simply impossible. Or, reducing his proposition to absurdity by a consequence as manifestly false, commands and duties are possible, but are never disobeyed or broken.

If he means by a *violent* motive, an evil which inspires fear, his meaning is simply this: that the party bound by a command is bound by the prospect of an evil. For that which is not feared is not apprehended as an evil: or (changing the shape of the expression) is not an evil in prospect.

The truth is, that the magnitude of the eventual evil, and the magnitude of the chance of incurring it, are foreign to the matter in question. The greater the eventual evil, and the greater the chance of incurring it, the greater is the efficacy of the command, and the greater is the strength of the obligation: Or (substituting expressions exactly equivalent), the greater is the *chance* that the command will be obeyed, and that the duty will not be broken. But where there is the smallest chance of incurring the smallest evil, the expression of a wish amounts to a command, and, therefore, imposes a duty. The sanction, if you will, is feeble or insufficient; but still there *is* a sanction, and, therefore, a duty and a command.

By some celebrated writers (by Locke, Bentham, and, I think, Paley), the term *sanction*, or *enforcement of obedience*, is applied to conditional goods as well as to conditional evil: to reward as well as to punishment. But, with all my habitual veneration for the names of Locke and Bentham, I think that this extension of the term is pregnant with confusion and perplexity.

Rewards are, indisputably, *motives* to comply with the wishes of others. But to talk of commands and duties as *sanctioned* or *enforced* by rewards, or to talk of rewards *as obliging* or *constraining* to obedience, is surely a wide departure from the established meaning of the terms.

If *you* expressed a desire that I should render a service, and if you proffered a reward as the motive or inducement to render it, *you* would scarcely be said to *command* the service, nor should I, in ordinary language, be *obliged* to render it. In ordinary language, *you* would *promise* me a reward, on condition of my rendering the service, whilst I might be *incited or persuaded* to render it by the hope of obtaining the reward.

Again: If a law hold out a *reward* as an inducement to do some act, an eventual *right* is conferred, and not an *obligation* imposed, upon those who shall act accordingly: The *imperative* part of the law being addressed or directed to the party whom it requires to *render* the reward.

In short, I am determined or inclined to comply with the wish of another, by the fear of disadvantage or evil. I am also determined or inclined to comply with the wish of another, by the hope of advantage or good. But it is only by the chance of incurring *evil*, that I am *bound or obliged* to compliance. It is only by conditional *evil*, that duties are *sanctioned or enforced*. It is the power and the purpose of inflicting eventual evil, and *not* the power and purpose of imparting eventual *good*, which gives to the expression of a wish the name of a *command*.

If we put *reward* into the import of the term *sanction*, we must engage in a toilsome struggle with the current of ordinary speech; and shall often slide unconsciously, notwithstanding our efforts to the contrary, into the narrower and customary meaning.

It appears, then, from what has been premised, that the ideas or notions comprehended by the term *command* are the following. 1. A wish or desire conceived by a rational being, that another rational being shall do or forbear. 2. An evil to proceed from the former, and to be incurred by the latter, in case the latter comply not with the wish. 3. An expression or intimation of the wish by words or other signs.

It also appears from what has been premised, that *command*, *duty*, and *sanction* are inseparably connected terms: that each embraces the same ideas as the others, though each denotes those ideas in a peculiar order or series.

'A wish conceived by one, and expressed or intimated to another, with an evil to be inflicted and incurred in case the wish be disregarded', are signified directly and indirectly by each of the three expressions. Each is the name of the same complex notion.

But when I am talking *directly* of the expression or intimation of the wish, I employ the term *command*: The expression or intimation of the wish being presented *prominently* to my hearer; whilst the evil to be incurred, with the chance of incurring it, are kept (if I may so express myself) in the background of my picture.

When I am talking *directly* of the chance of incurring the evil, or (changing the expression) of the liability or obnoxiousness to the evil, I employ the term *duty* or the term *obligation*: The liability or obnoxiousness to the evil being put foremost, and the rest of the complex notion being signified implicitly.

When I am talking *immediately* of the evil itself, I employ the term *sanction*, or a term of the like import: The evil to be incurred being signified directly; whilst the obnoxiousness to that evil, with the expression or intimation of the wish, are indicated indirectly or obliquely.

To those who are familiar with the language of logicians (language unrivalled for brevity, distinctness, and precision), I can express my meaning accurately in a breath: – Each of the three terms *signifies* the same notion; but each denotes a different part of that notion, and *connotes* the residue.

Commands are of two species. Some are *laws* or *rules*. The others have not acquired an appropriate name, nor does language afford an expression which will mark them briefly and precisely. I must, therefore, note them as well as I can by the ambiguous and inexpressive name of '*occasional* or *particular* commands'.

The term *laws* or *rules* being not unfrequently applied to occasional or particular commands, it is hardly possible to describe a line of separation which shall consist in every aspect with established forms of speech. But the distinction between laws and particular commands may, I think, be stated in the following manner.

By every command, the party to whom it is directed is obliged to do or to forbear.

Now where it obliges *generally* to acts or forebearances of a *class*, a command is a law or rule. But where it obliges to a *specific* act or forebearance, or to acts or forebearances which it determines *specifically* or *individually*, a command is occasional or particular. In other words, a class or description of acts is determined by a law or rule, and acts of that class or description are enjoined or forbidden generally. But where a command is occasional or particular, the act or acts, which the command enjoins or forbids, are assigned or determined by their specific or individual natures as well as by the class or description to which they belong.

133–144

LECTURE V

Now those essentials of a law proper, together with certain consequences which those essentials import, may be stated briefly in the following manner: – 1. Laws properly so called are a species of *commands*. But, being a *command,* every law properly so called flows from a *determinate* source, or emanates from a *determinate* author. In other words, the author from whom it proceeds is a *determinate* rational being, or a *determinate* body or aggregate of rational beings. For whenever a *command* is expressed or intimated, one party signifies a wish that another shall do or forbear: and the latter is obnoxious to an evil which the former intends to inflict in case the wish be disregarded. But every *signification* of a wish made by a single individual, or made by a body of individuals *as a body or collective whole,* supposes that the individual or body is *certain* or *determinate.* And every *intention or purpose* held by a single individual, or held by a body of individuals *as a body or collective whole,* involves the same supposition. 2. Every sanction properly so called is an eventual evil *annexed to a command.* Any eventual evil may operate as a *motive* to conduct: but, unless the conduct be commanded and the evil be annexed to the command purposely to enforce obedience, the evil is not a *sanction* in the proper acceptation of the term. 3. Every duty properly so called supposes a *command* by which it is created. For every sanction properly so called is an eventual evil *annexed to a command.* And duty properly so called is obnoxiousness to evils of the kind.

Now it follows from these premises, that the laws of God, and positive laws, are laws proper, or laws properly so called.

The laws of God are laws proper, inasmuch as they are *commands* express or tacit, and therefore emanate from a *certain* source.

Positive laws, or laws strictly so called, are established directly or immediately by authors of three kinds: – by monarchs, or sovereign bodies, as supreme political superiors: by men in a state of subjection, as subordinate political superiors: by subjects, as private persons, in pursuance of legal rights. But every positive law, or every law strictly so called, is a direct or circuitous command of a monarch or sovereign number in the character of political superior: that is to say, a direct or circuitous command of a monarch or sovereign number to a person or persons in a state of subjection to its author. And being a *command* (and therefore flowing from a *determinate* source), every positive law is a law proper, or a law properly so called.

Besides the human laws which I style positive law, there are human laws which I style positive morality, rules of positive morality, or positive moral rules.

The generic character of laws of the class may be stated briefly in the following negative manner: – No law belonging to the class is a direct or circuitous command of a monarch or sovereign number in the character of political superior. In other words, no law belonging to the class is a direct or circuitous command of a monarch or sovereign number to a person or persons in a state of subjection to its author.

But of positive moral rules, some are laws proper, or laws properly so called: others are laws improper, or laws improperly so called. Some have all the essentials of an *imperative* law or rule: others are deficient in some of those essentials, and are styled *laws or rules* by an analogical extension of the term.

The positive moral rules which are laws properly so called, are distinguished from other laws by the union of two marks: – 1. They are imperative laws or rules set by men to men. 2. They are not set by men as political superiors, nor are they set by men as private persons, in pursuance of legal rights.

Inasmuch as they bear the latter of these two marks, they are not commands of sovereigns in the character of political superiors. Consequently, they are not positive laws: they are not clothed with legal sanctions, nor do they oblige legally the persons to whom they are set. But being *commands* (and therefore being established *by determinate* individuals or bodies), they are laws properly so called: they are armed with sanctions, and impose duties, in the proper acceptation of the terms.

It will appear from the following distinctions, that positive moral rules which are laws properly so called may be reduced to three kinds.

Of positive moral rules which are laws properly so called, some are established by men who are not subjects, or are not in a state of subjection: Meaning by 'subjects', or by 'men in a state of subjection', men in a state of subjection to a monarch or sovereign number. – Of positive moral rules which are laws properly so called, and are not established by men in a state of subjection, some are established by men living in the negative state which is styled a state of nature or a state of anarchy: that is to say, by men who are *not* in the state which is styled a state of government, or are not members, sovereign or subject, of any political society. – Of positive moral rules which are laws properly so called, and are not established by men in a state of subjection, others are established by sovereign individuals or bodies, but are not established by sovereigns in the character of political superiors. Or a positive moral rule of this kind may be described in the following manner: It is set by a monarch or sovereign number, but not to a person or persons in a state of subjection to its author.

Of laws properly so called which are set by subjects, some are set by subjects as subordinate political superiors. But of laws properly so called which are set by subjects, others are set by subjects as private persons: Meaning by 'private persons', subjects not in the class of subordinate political superiors, or subordinate political superiors not considered as such. – Laws set by subjects as subordinate political superiors, are positive laws: they are clothed with legal sanctions, and impose legal duties. They are set by sovereigns or states in the character of political superiors, although they are set by sovereigns circuitously or remotely. Although they are made directly by subject or subordinate authors, they are made through legal rights granted by sovereigns or states, and held by those subject authors as mere trustees for the granters. – Of laws set by subjects as private persons, some are not established by sovereign or supreme authority. And these are rules of positive morality: they are not clothed with legal sanctions, nor do they oblige legally the parties to whom they are set. – But of laws set by subjects as private persons, others are set or established in pursuance of legal rights residing in the subject authors. And these are positive laws or laws strictly so called. Although they are made directly by subject authors, they are made in pursuance of rights granted or conferred by sovereigns in the character of political superiors: they legally oblige the parties to whom they are set, or are clothed with legal sanctions. They are commands of sovereigns as political superiors, although they are set by sovereigns circuitously or remotely.

It appears from the foregoing distinctions, that positive moral rules which are laws properly so called are of three kinds: – 1 Those which are set by men living in a state of nature. 2.Those which are set by sovereigns, but not by sovereigns as political superiors. 3. Those which are set by subjects as private persons, and are not set by the subject authors in pursuance of legal rights.

To cite an example of rules of the first kind were superfluous labour. A man living in a state of nature may impose an imperative law: though, since the man *is* in a state of nature, he cannot impose the law in the character of sovereign, and cannot impose the law in pursuance of a legal right. And the law being *imperative* (and therefore proceeding from a *determinate* source) is a law properly so called: though, for want of a sovereign author proximate or remote, it is not a positive law but a rule of positive morality.

An imperative law set by a sovereign to a sovereign, or by one supreme government to another supreme government, is an example of rules of the second kind. Since no supreme government is in a state of subjection to another, an imperative law set by a sovereign to a sovereign is not set by its author in the character of political superior. Nor is it set by its author in pursuance of a legal right: for every legal right is conferred by a supreme government, and is conferred on a person or persons in a state of subjection to the granter. Consequently, an imperative law set by a sovereign to a sovereign is not a positive law or a law strictly so called. But being *imperative* (and therefore proceeding from a *determinate* source), it amounts to a law in the proper signification of the term, although it is purely or simply a rule of positive morality.

If they be set by subjects as private persons, and be not set by their authors in pursuance of legal rights, the laws following are examples of rules of the third kind: namely, imperative laws set by parents to children; imperative laws set by masters to servants; imperative laws set by lenders to borrowers; imperative laws set by patrons to parasites. Being *imperative* (and therefore proceeding from *determinate* sources), the laws foregoing are laws properly so called: though, if they be set by subjects as private persons, and be not set by their authors in pursuance of legal rights, they are not positive laws but rules of positive morality.

Again: A club or society of men, signifying its collective pleasure by a vote of its assembled members, passes or makes a law to be kept by its members severally under pain of exclusion from its meetings. Now if it be made by subjects as private persons, and be not made by its authors in pursuance of a legal right, the law voted and passed by the assembled members of the club is a further example of rules of the third kind. If it be made by subjects as private persons, and be not made by its authors in pursuance of a legal right, it is not a positive law or a law strictly so called. But being *an imperative* law (and the body by which it is set being therefore *determinate*), it may be styled a *law* or rule with absolute precision or propriety, although it is purely or simply a rule of positive morality.

The positive moral rules which are laws improperly so called, are *laws set or imposed by general opinion*: that is to say, by the general opinion of any class or any society of persons. For example, Some are set or imposed by the general opinion of persons who are members of a profession or calling: others, by that of persons who inhabit a town or province: others, by that of a nation or independent political society: others, by that of a larger society formed of various nations.

A few species of the laws which are set by general opinion have gotten appropriate names. – For example, There are laws or rules imposed upon gentlemen by opinions current amongst gentlemen. And these are usually styled *the rules of honour*, or *the laws or law of honour.*– There are laws or rules imposed upon people of fashion by opinions current in the fashionable world. And these are usually styled *the law set by fashion.* – There are laws which regard the conduct of independent political societies in their various relations to one another: Or, rather, there are laws which regard the conduct of sovereigns or supreme governments in their various relations to one another. And laws or rules of this species, which are imposed upon nations or sovereigns by opinions current amongst nations, are usually styled *the law of nations* or *international law*.

Now a law set or imposed by general opinion is a law improperly so called. It is styled a law *or* rule by an analogical extension of the term. When we speak of a law set by general opinion, we denote, by that expression, the following fact: Some *indeterminate body* or *uncertain* aggregate of persons regards a kind of conduct with a sentiment of aversion or liking: Or (changing the expression) that indeterminate body opines unfavourably of a given kind of conduct. In *consequence* of that sentiment, or in *consequence of* that opinion, it is likely that they or some of them will be displeased with a party who shall pursue or not pursue conduct of that kind. And, in *consequence* of that displeasure, it is likely that *some party* (what party being undetermined) will visit the party provoking it with some evil or another.

The body by whose opinion the law is said to be set, does not *command*; expressly or tacitly, that conduct of the given kind shall be forborne or pursued. For, since it is not a body precisely determined or certain, it cannot, *as a body*, express or intimate a wish. As *a body*, it cannot *signify* a wish by oral or written words, or by positive or negative deportment. The so called law or rule which its opinion is said to impose, is merely the *sentiment* which it feels, or is merely the *opinion* which it holds, in regard to a kind of conduct.

A determinate member of the body, who opines or feels with the body, may doubtless be moved or impelled, by that very opinion or sentiment, to *command* that conduct of the kind shall be forborne or pursued. But the command expressed or intimated by that determinate party is not a law or rule imposed by general opinion. It is a law properly so called, set by a determinate author. – For example, The so called law of nations consists of opinions or sentiments current among nations generally. It therefore is not law properly so called. But one supreme government may doubtless *command* another to forbear from a kind of conduct which the law of nations condemns. And, though it is fashioned on law which is law improperly so called, this command is a law in the proper signification of the term. Speaking precisely, the command is a rule of positive morality set by a determinate author. For, as no supreme government is in a state of subjection to another, the government commanding does not command in its character of political superior. If the government receiving the command were in a state of subjection to the other, the command, though fashioned on the law of nations, would amount to a positive law.

The foregoing description of a law set by general opinion imports the following consequences: – that the party who will enforce it against any future transgressor is never determinate and assignable. The party who actually enforces it against an actual transgressor is, of necessity, certain. In other words, if an actual transgressor be harmed in consequence of the breach of the law, and in consequence of that displeasure which the breach of the law has provoked, he receives the harm from a party, who, of necessity, is certain. But that certain party is not the executor of a *command* proceeding from the uncertain body. He has not been authorised by that uncertain body to enforce that so called law which its opinion is said to establish. He is not in the position of a minister of justice appointed by the sovereign or state to execute commands which it issues. He harms the actual offender against the so called law or (to speak in analogical language) he applies the sanction annexed to it, of his own spontaneous movement. Consequently, though a party who actually enforces it is, of necessity, certain, the party who will enforce it against any future offender is never determinate and assignable.

It follows from the foregoing reasons, that a so called law set by general opinion is not a law in the proper signification of the term. It also follows from the same reasons, that it is not armed with a sanction, and does not impose a duty, in the proper acceptation of the expressions. For a sanction properly so called is an evil annexed to a command. And duty properly so called is an obnoxiousness to evils of the kind.

But a so called law set by general opinion is closely analogous to a law in the proper signification of the term. And, by consequence, the so called sanction with which the former is armed, and the so called duty which the former imposes, are closely analogous to a sanction and a duty in the proper acceptation of the expressions.

The analogy between a law in the proper signification of the term and a so called law set by general opinion, may be stated briefly in the following manner: – 1. In the case of a law properly so called, the determinate individual or body by whom the law is established wishes that conduct of a kind shall be forborne or pursued. In the case of a law imposed by general opinion, a wish that conduct of a kind shall be forborne or pursued is felt by the uncertain body whose general opinion imposes it. 2. If a party obliged by the law proper shall not comply with the wish of the determinate individual or body, he probably will suffer, in *consequence* of his not complying, the evil or inconvenience annexed to the law as a sanction. If a party obnoxious to their displeasure shall not comply with the wish of the uncertain body of persons, he probably will suffer, in *consequence* of his not complying, some evil or inconvenience from some party or another. 3. By the sanction annexed to the law proper, the parties obliged are inclined to act or forbear agreeably to its injunctions or prohibitions. By the evil which probably will follow the displeasure of the uncertain body, the parties obnoxious are inclined to act or forbear agreeably to the sentiment or opinion which is styled analogically a law. 4. In consequence of the law properly so called, the conduct of the parties obliged has a steadiness, constancy, or uniformity, which, without the existence of the law, their conduct would probably want. In consequence of the sentiment or opinion which is styled analogically a law, the conduct of the parties obnoxious has a steadiness, constancy, or uniformity which, without the existence of that sentiment in the uncertain body of persons, their conduct would hardly present. For they who are obnoxious to the sanction which arms the law proper, commonly do or forbear from the acts which the law enjoins or forbids; whilst they who are obnoxious to the evil which will probably follow the displeasure of the uncertain body of persons, commonly do or forbear from the acts which the body approves or dislikes. – Many of the applications of the term law which are merely metaphorical or figurative, were probably suggested (as I shall show hereafter) by that uniformity of conduct which is consequent on a law proper.

192–196

LECTURE VI

To distinguish positive laws from the objects now enumerated, is the purpose of the present attempt to determine the province of jurisprudence.

In pursuance of the purpose to which I have now adverted, I stated, in my first lecture, the essentials of a *law* or *rule* (taken with the largest signification which can be given to the term *properly*).

In my second, third, and fourth lectures, I stated the marks or characters by which the laws of God are distinguished from other laws. And, stating those marks or characters, I explained the nature of the index to his unrevealed laws, or I explained and examined the hypothesis which regard the nature of that index.

In my fifth lecture, I examined or discussed especially the following principal topics (and I touched upon other topics of secondary or subordinate importance). – I examined the distinguishing marks of those positive moral rules which are laws properly so called: I examined the distinguishing marks of those positive moral rules which are styled *laws or rules* by an analogical extension of the term: and I examined the distinguishing marks of the laws merely metaphorical, or laws merely figurative.

I shall finish, in the present lecture, the purpose mentioned above, by explaining the marks or characters which distinguish positive laws, or laws strictly so called. And, in order to [give] an explanation of the marks which distinguish positive laws, I shall analyze the expression *sovereignty,* the correlative expression *subjection,* and the inseparably connected expression *independent political society.* With the ends or final causes for which governments *ought* to exist, or with their different degrees of fitness to attain or approach those ends, I have no concern. I examine the notions of *sovereignty* and *independent political society,* in order that I may finish the purpose to which I have adverted above: in order that I may distinguish completely the appropriate province of jurisprudence from the regions which lie upon its confines, and by which it is encircled. It is necessary that I should examine those notions, in order that I may finish that purpose. For the essential difference of a positive law (or the difference that severs it from a law which is not a positive law) may be stated thus. Every positive law or every law simply and strictly so called, is set by a sovereign person, or a sovereign body of persons, to a member or members of the independent political society wherein that person or body is sovereign or supreme. Or (changing the expression) it is set by a monarch, or sovereign number, to a person or persons in a state of subjection to its author. Even though it sprung directly from another fountain or source, it *is* a positive law, or a law strictly so called, by the institution of that present sovereign in the character of political superior. Or (borrowing the language of Hobbes) 'the legislator is he, not by whose authority the law was first made, but by whose authority it continues to be a law'.

Having stated the topic or subject appropriate to my present discourse, I proceed to distinguish sovereignty from other superiority or might, and to distinguish society political and independent from society of other descriptions.

The superiority which is styled sovereignty, and the independent political society which sovereignty implies is distinguished from other superiority, and from other society, by the following marks or characters: – 1. The *bulk* of the given society are in a *habit* of obedience or submission to a *determinate* and *common* superior: let that common superior be a certain individual person, or a certain body or aggregate of individual persons. 2. That certain individual, or that certain body of individuals, is *not* in a habit of obedience to a determinate human superior. Laws (improperly so called) which opinion sets or imposes, may permanently affect the conduct of that certain individual or body. The express or tacit commands of other determinate parties, that certain individual or body may yield occasional submission. But there is no determinate person, or determinate aggregate of person, to whose commands, express or tacit, that certain individual or body renders habitual obedience.

Or the notions of sovereignty and independent political society may be expressed concisely thus. – If a *determinate* human superior, not in a habit of obedience to a like superior, receive *habitual* obedience from the *bulk* of a given society, that determinate superior is sovereign in that society; and the society (including the superior) is a society political and independent.

To that determinate superior, the other members of the society are *subject*: or on that determinate superior, the other members of the society are *dependent*. The position of its other members towards that determinate superior, is a *state of subjection*, or a *state of dependence*. The mutual relation which subsists between that superior and them, may be styled *the relation of sovereign and subject*, or *the relation of sovereignty and subjection*.

Hence it follows, that it is only through an ellipsis, or an abridged form of expression, that the *society is* styled *independent*. The party truly independent (independent, that is to say, of a determinate human superior), is not the society, but the sovereign portion of the society: that certain member of the society, or that certain body of its members, to whose commands, expressed or intimated, the generality or bulk of its members render habitual obedience. Upon that certain person, or certain body of persons, the other members of the society are *dependent*: or to that certain person, or certain body of persons, the other members of the society are *subject*. By 'an independent political society', or 'an independent and sovereign nation', we mean a political society consisting of a sovereign and subjects, as opposed to a political society which is merely subordinate: that is to say, which is merely a limb or member of another political society, and which therefore consists entirely of persons in a state of subjection.

In order that a given society may form a society political and independent, the two distinguishing marks which I have mentioned above must unite. The *generality* of the given society must be in the *habit of* obedience to a *determinate* and *common* superior: whilst that determinate person, or determinate body of persons must *not* be habitually obedient to a determinate person or body. It is the union of that positive, with this negative mark, which renders that certain superior sovereign or supreme, and which renders that given society (including that certain superior) a society political and independent.

To show that the union of those marks renders a given society a society political and independent, I call your attention to the following positions and examples.

1.   In order that a given society may form a society political, the generality or bulk of its members must be in a *habit* of obedience to a determinate and common superior.

In case the generality of its members obey a determinate superior, but the obedience be rare or transient and not habitual or permanent, the relation of sovereignty and subjection is not created thereby between that certain superior and the members of that given society. In other words, that determinate superior and the members of that given society do not become thereby an independent political society. Whether that given society be political and independent or not, it is not an independent political society whereof that certain superior is the sovereign portion.

For example: In 1815 the allied armies occupied France; and so long as the allied armies occupied France, the commands of the allied sovereigns were obeyed by the French government, and, through the French government, by the French people generally. But since the commands and the obedience were comparatively rare and transient, they were not sufficient to constitute the relation of sovereignty and subjection between the allied sovereigns and the members of the invaded nation. In spite of those commands, and in spite of that obedience, the French government was sovereign or independent. Or in spite of those commands, and in spite of that obedience, the French government and its subjects were an independent political society whereof the allied sovereigns were not the sovereign portion.

Now if the French nation, before the obedience to those sovereigns, had been an independent society in a state of nature or anarchy, it would not have been changed by the obedience into a society political. And it would not have been changed by the obedience into a society political, because the obedience was not habitual. For, inasmuch as the obedience was not habitual, it was not changed by the obedience from a society political and independent, into a society political but subordinate. – A given society, therefore, is not a society political, unless the generality of its members be in a *habit* of obedience to a determinate and common superior.

200–203

A natural society, a society in a state of nature, or a society independent but natural, is composed of persons who are connected by mutual intercourse, but are not members, sovereign or subject, of any society political. None of the persons who compose it lives in the positive state which is styled a state of subjection: or all the persons who compose it live in the negative state which is styled a state of independence.

Considered as entire communities, and considered in respect of one another, independent political societies live, it is commonly said, in a state of nature. And considered as entire communities, and as connected by mutual intercourse, independent political societies form, it is commonly said, a natural society. These expressions, however, are not perfectly apposite. Since all the members of each of the related societies are members of a society political, none of the related societies is strictly in a state of nature: nor can the larger society formed by their mutual intercourse be styled strictly a natural society. Speaking strictly, the several members of the several related societies are placed in the following positions. The sovereign and subject members of each of the related societies form a society political: but the sovereign portion of each of the related societies lives in the negative condition which is styled a state of independence.

Society formed by the intercourse of independent political societies, is the province of international law, or of the law obtaining between nations. For (adopting a current expression) international law, or the law obtaining between nations, is conversant about the conduct of independent political societies considered as entire communities: *circa negotia et causas gentium integrarum*. Speaking with greater precision, international law, or the law obtaining between nations, regards the conduct of sovereigns considered as related to one another.

And hence it inevitably follows, that the law obtaining between nations is not positive law: for every positive law is set by a given sovereign to a person or persons in a state of subjection to its author. As I have already intimated, the law obtaining between nations is law (improperly so called) set by general opinion. The duties which it imposes are enforced by moral sanctions: by fear on the part of nations, or by fear on the part of sovereigns, of provoking general hostility, and incurring its probable evils, in case they shall violate maxims generally received and respected.

A society political but subordinate is merely a limb or member of a society political and independent. All the persons who compose it, including the person or body which is its immediate chief, live in a state of subjection to one and the same sovereign.

Besides societies political and independent, societies independent but natural, society formed by the intercourse of independent political societies, and societies political but subordinate, there are societies which will not quadrate with any of those descriptions. Though, like a society political but subordinate, it forms a limb or member of a society political and independent, a society of the class in question is not a political society. Although it consists of members living in a state of subjection, it consists of subjects considered as private persons. – A society consisting of parents and children, living in a state of subjection, and considered in those characters, may serve as an example.

To distinguish societies political but subordinate from societies not political but consisting of subject members, is to distinguish the rights and duties of subordinate political superiors from the rights and duties of subjects considered as private persons. And before I can draw that distinction, I must analyze many expressions of large and intricate meaning which belong to the detail of jurisprudence. But an explanation of that distinction is not required by my present purpose. To the accomplishment of my present purpose, it is merely incumbent upon me to determine the notion of sovereignty, with the inseparably connected notion of independent political society. For every positive law, or every law simply and strictly so called, is set directly or circuitously by a monarch or sovereign number to a person or persons in a state of subjection to its author.

The definition of the abstract term *independent political society* (including the definition of the correlative term *sovereignty*) cannot be rendered in expressions of perfectly precise import, and is therefore a fallible test of specific or particular cases. The least imperfect definition which the abstract term will take, would hardly enable us to fix the class of every possible society. It would hardly enable us to determine of every *independent* society, whether it were *political or natural*. It would hardly enable us to determine of every *political* society, whether it were *independent or subordinate*.

In order that a given society may form a society political and independent, the positive and negative marks which I have mentioned above must unite. The *generality* or *bulk* of its members must be in a *habit of* obedience to a *certain and common* superior: whilst that certain person, or certain body of persons, must not be habitually obedient to a certain person or body.

But, in order that the *bulk* of its members may render obedience to a *common* superior, *how many* of its members, or *what proportion* of its members, must render obedience to *one and the same* superior? And, assuming that the bulk of its members render obedience to a common superior, *how often* must they render it, and *how long* must they render it, in order that that obedience be *habitual?* – Now since these questions cannot be answered precisely, the positive mark of sovereignty and independent political society is a fallible test of specific or particular cases. It would not enable us to determine of every *independent* society, whether it were *political* or *natural*.

253–87

From the various shapes which sovereignty may assume or from the various possible forms of supreme government, I proceed to the limits, real and imaginary, of sovereign or supreme power.

Subject to the slight correctives which I shall state at the close of my discourse, the essential difference of a positive law (or the difference that severs it from a law which is not a positive law) may be put in the following manner: – Every positive law, or every law simply and strictly so called is set directly or circuitously, by a sovereign person or body, to a member or members of the independent political society wherein that person or body is sovereign or supreme. Or (changing the expression) it is set, directly or circuitously, by a monarch or sovereign number, to a person or persons in a state of subjection to its author.

Now it follows from the essential difference of a positive law, and from the nature of sovereignty and independent political society, that the power of a monarch properly so called, or the power of a sovereign number in its collegiate and sovereign capacity, is incapable of legal limitation. A monarch or sovereign number bound by a legal duty, were subject to a higher or superior sovereign: that is to say, a monarch or sovereign number bound by a legal duty, were sovereign and not sovereign. Supreme power limited by positive law, is a flat contradiction in terms.

Nor would a political society escape from legal despotism, although the power of the sovereign were bounded by legal restraints. The power of the superior sovereign immediately imposing the restraints, or the power of some other sovereign superior to that superior, would still be absolutely free from the fetters of positive law. For unless the imagined restraints were ultimately imposed by a sovereign not in a state of subjection to a higher or superior sovereign, a series of sovereigns ascending to infinity would govern the imagined community. Which is impossible and absurd.

Monarchs and sovereign bodies have attempted to oblige themselves, or to oblige the successors to their sovereign powers. But in spite of the laws which sovereigns have imposed on themselves, or which they have imposed on the successors to their sovereign powers, the position that 'sovereign power is incapable of legal limitation' will hold universally or without exception.

The immediate author of a law of the kind, or any of the sovereign successors to that immediate author, may abrogate the law at pleasure. And though the law be not abrogated, the sovereign for the time being is not constrained to observe it by a legal or political sanction. For if the sovereign for the time being were legally bound to observe it, that present sovereign would be in a state of subjection to a higher or superior sovereign.

As it regards the successors to the sovereign or supreme powers, a law of the kind amounts, at the most, to a rule of positive morality. As it regards its immediate author, it is merely a law by a metaphor. For if we would speak with propriety, we cannot speak of a law set by a man to himself: though a man may adopt a principle as a guide to his own conduct, and may observe it as he would observe it if he were bound to observe it by a sanction.

The laws which sovereigns affect to impose upon themselves, or the laws which sovereigns affect to impose upon their followers, are merely principles or maxims which they adopt as guides, or which they commend as guides to their successors in sovereign power. A departure by a sovereign or state from a law of the kind in question, is not illegal. If a law which it sets to its subjects conflict with a law of the kind, the former is legally valid, or legally binding.

For example: The sovereign Roman people solemnly voted or resolved, that they would never pass, or even take into consideration, what I will venture to denominate a *bill of pains and penalties*. For though, at the period in question, the Roman people were barbarians, they keenly felt a truth which is often forgotten by legislators in nations boasting of refinement: namely, that punishment ought to be inflicted agreeably to prospective rules, and not in pursuance of particular and *ex post facto* commands. This solemn resolution or vote was passed with the forms of legislation, and was inserted in the twelve tables in the following imperative terms: *privilegia ne irroganto*. But although the resolution or vote was passed with the forms of legislation, although it was clothed with the expressions appropriate to a law, and although it was inserted as a law in a code or body of statutes, it scarcely was a law in the proper acceptation of the term, and certainly was not a law simply and strictly so called. By that resolution or vote, the sovereign people adopted, and commended to their successors in the sovereignty, an ethical principle or maxim. The present and future sovereign which the resolution affected to oblige, was not bound or estopped by it. Privileges enacted in spite of it by the sovereign Roman people, were not illegal. The Roman tribunals might not have treated them as legally invalid acts, although they conflicted with the maxim, wearing the guise of a law, *privilegia ne irroganto*.

Again: By the authors of the union between England and Scotland, an attempt was made to oblige the legislature, which, in consequence of that union, is sovereign in both countries. It is declared in the Articles and Acts, that the preservation of the Church of England, and of the Kirk of Scotland, is a fundamental condition of the union: or, in other words, that the Parliament of Great Britain shall not abolish those churches, or make an essential change in their structures or constitutions. Now, so long as the bulk of either nation shall regard its established church with love and respect, the abolition of the church by the British Parliament would be an *immoral* act; for it would violate positive morality which obtains with the bulk of the nation, or would shock opinions and sentiments which the bulk of the nation holds. Assuming that the church establishment is commended by the revealed law, the abolition would be *irreligious*: or, assuming that the continuance of the establishment were commended by general utility, the abolition, as generally pernicious, would also amount to a *sin*. But no man, talking with a meaning, would call a parliamentary abolition of either or both of the churches an *illegal* act. For if the parliament for the time being be sovereign in England and Scotland, it cannot be bound legally by that condition of the union which affects to confer immortality upon those ecclesiastical institutions. That condition of the union is not a positive law, but is counsel or advice offered by the authors of the union to future supreme legislatures.

By the two examples which I have now adduced, I am led to consider the meanings of the epithet, *unconstitutional*, as it is contradistinguished to the epithet *illegal*, and as it is applied to conduct of a monarch, or to conduct of a sovereign number in its collegiate and sovereign capacity. The epithet *unconstitutional*, as thus opposed and applied, is sometimes used with a meaning which is more general and vague, and is sometimes used with a meaning which is more special and definite. I will begin with the former.

1.   In every, or almost every, independent political society, there are principles or maxims which the sovereign habitually observes, and which the bulk of the society, or the bulk of its influential members, regard with feelings of approbation. Not unfrequently, such maxims are expressly adopted, as well as habitually observed, by the sovereign or state. More commonly, they are not expressly adopted by the sovereign or state, but are simply imposed upon it by opinions prevalent in the community. Whether they are expressly adopted by the sovereign or state, or are simply imposed upon it by opinions prevalent in the community, it is bound or constrained to observe them by merely moral sanctions. Or (changing the phrase) in case it ventured to deviate from a maxim of the kind in question, it would not and could not incur a legal pain or penalty, but it probably would incur censure, and might chance to meet with resistance from the generality or bulk of the governed.

Now, if a law or other act of a monarch or sovereign number conflict with a maxim of the kind to which I have adverted above, the law or other act may be called *unconstitutional* (in that more general meaning which is sometimes given to the epithet). For example:

The ex *post facto* statutes which are styled acts of attainder, may be called *unconstitutional*, though they cannot be called *illegal*. For they conflict with a principle of legislation which parliament has habitually observed, and which is regarded with approbation by the bulk of the British community.

In short, when we style an act of a sovereign an *unconstitutional* act (with that more general import which is sometimes given to the epithet), we mean, I believe, this: That the act is inconsistent with some given principle or maxim: that the given supreme government has expressly adopted the principle, or, at least, has habitually observed it: that the bulk of the given society, or the bulk of its influential members, regard the principle with approbation: and that, since the supreme government has habitually observed the principle, and since the bulk of the society regard it with approbation, the act in question must thwart the expectations of the latter, and must shock their opinions and sentiments. Unless we mean this, we merely mean that we deem the act in question generally pernicious: or that, without a definite reason for the disapprobation which we feel, we regard the act with dislike.

2.   The epithet *unconstitutional* as applied to conduct of a sovereign, and as used with the meaning which is more special and definite, imports that the conduct in question conflicts with *constitutional law*.

And here I would briefly remark, that I mean by the expression *constitutional law*, the positive morality, or the compound of positive morality and positive law, which fixes the constitution or structure of the given supreme government. I mean the positive morality, or the compound of positive morality and positive law, which determines the character of the person, or the respective characters of the persons, in whom, for the time being, the sovereignty shall reside: and, supposing the government in question an aristocracy or government of a number, which determines moreover the mode wherein the sovereign powers shall be shared by the constituent members of the sovereign number or body.

Now, against a monarch properly so called, or against a sovereign body in its collegiate and sovereign capacity, constitutional law is positive morality merely, or is enforced merely by moral sanctions: though, as I shall show hereafter, it may amount to positive law, or may be enforced by legal sanctions, against the members of the body considered severally. The sovereign for the time being, or the predecessors of the sovereign, may have expressly adopted, and expressly promised to observe it. But whether constitutional law has thus been expressly adopted, or simply consists of principles current in the political community, it is merely guarded, against the sovereign, by sentiments or feelings of the governed. Consequently, although an act of the sovereign which violates constitutional law, may be styled with propriety *unconstitutional*, it is not an infringement of law simply and strictly so called, and cannot be styled with propriety *illegal*.

For example: From the ministry of Cardinal Richelieu down to the great revolution, the king for the time being was virtually sovereign in France. But, in the same country, and during the same period, a traditional maxim cherished by the courts of justice, and rooted in the affections of the bulk of the people, determined the succession to the throne: It determined that the throne, on the demise of an actual occupant, should invariably be taken by the person who then might happen to be heir to it agreeably to the canon of inheritance which was named the Salic law. Now, in case an actual king, by a royal ordinance or law, had attempted to divert the throne to his only daughter and child, that royal ordinance or law might have been styled with perfect propriety an *unconstitutional* act. It would have conflicted with the traditional maxim which fixed the constitution of the monarchy, and which was guarded from infringement by sentiments prevalent in the nation. But *illegal* it could not have been called: for, inasmuch as the actual king was virtually sovereign, he was inevitably independent of legal obligation. Nay, if the governed had resisted the unconstitutional ordinance, their resistance would have been illegal or a breach of positive law, though consonant to the positive morality which is styled constitutional law, and perhaps to that principle of utility which is the test of positive rules.

Again: An act of the British parliament vesting the sovereignty in the king, or vesting the sovereignty in the king and the upper or lower house, would essentially alter the structure of our present supreme government, and might therefore be styled with propriety an *unconstitutional* law. In case the imagined statute were also generally pernicious, and in case it offended moreover the generality or bulk of the nation, it might be styled *irreligious and immoral* as well as *unconstitutional*. But to call it *illegal* were absurd: for if the parliament for the time being be sovereign in the united kingdom, it is the author, directly or circuitously, of all our positive law, and exclusively sets us the measure of legal justice and injustice.

But when I affirm that the power of a sovereign is incapable of legal limitation, I always mean by a 'sovereign', a monarch properly so called, or a sovereign number in its collegiate and sovereign capacity. Considered collectively, or considered in its corporate character, a sovereign number is sovereign and independent: but considered severally, the individuals and smaller aggregates composing that sovereign number are subject to the supreme body of which they are component parts. Consequently, though the body is inevitably independent of legal or political duty, any of the individuals or aggregates whereof the body is composed may be legally bound by laws of which the body is the author. For example: A member of the house of lords, or a member of the house of commons, may be legally bound by an act of parliament, which, as one of the sovereign legislature, he has concurred with others in making. Nay, he may be legally bound by statutes, or by rules made judicially, which have immediately proceeded from subject or subordinate legislatures: for a law which proceeds immediately from a subject or subordinate legislature is set by the authority of the supreme.

And hence an important difference between monarchies or governments of one, and aristocracies or governments of a number.

Against a monarch properly so called, or against a sovereign number in its collegiate and sovereign capacity, *constitutional law* (as I have remarked already) is enforced, or protected from infringement, by merely moral sanctions. Against a monarch properly so called, or against a sovereign number in its collegiate and sovereign capacity, constitutional law and the law of nations are nearly in the same predicament. Each is positive morality rather than positive law. The former is guarded by sentiments current in the given community, as the latter is guarded by sentiments current amongst nations generally.

But, considered severally, the members of a sovereign body, even as members of the body, may be legally bound by laws of which the body is the author, and which regard the constitution of the given supreme government. – In case it be clothed with a legal sanction, or the means of enforcing it judicially be provided by its author, a law set by the body to any of its own members is properly a positive law: It is properly a positive law, or a law strictly so called, although it be imposed upon the obliged party as a member of the body which sets it. If the means of enforcing it judicially be not provided by its author, it is rather a rule of positive morality than a rule of positive law. But it wants the essentials of a positive law, not through the character of the party to whom it is set or directed, but because it is not invested with a legal or political sanction, or is a law of imperfect obligation in the sense of the Roman jurists. – In case the law be invested with a legal or political sanction, and regard the constitution or structure of the given supreme government, a breach of the law, by the party to whom it is set, is not only *unconstitutional,* but is also *illegal.* The breach of the law is *unconstitutional,* inasmuch as the violated law regards the constitution of the state. The breach of the law is also illegal, inasmuch as the violated law may be enforced by judicial procedure.

For example: The king, as a limb of the parliament, might be punishable by act of parliament, in the event of his transgressing the limits which the constitution has set to his authority: in the event, for instance, of his pretending to give to a proclamation of his own the legal effect of a statute emanating from the sovereign legislature. Or the members of either house might be punishable by act of parliament, if, as forming a limb of the parliament, they exceeded their constitutional powers: if, for instance, they pretended to give that legal effect to an ordinance or resolution of their own body.

Where, then, the supreme government is a monarchy or government of one, constitutional law, as against that government, is inevitably nothing more than positive morality. Where the supreme government is an aristocracy or government of a number, constitutional law, as against the members of that government, may either consist of positive morality, or of a compound of positive morality and positive law. Against the sovereign body in its corporate and sovereign character, it is inevitably nothing more than positive morality. But against the members considered severally, be they individuals or be they aggregates of individuals, it may be guarded by legal or political, as well as by moral sanctions.

In fact or practice, the members considered severally, but considered as members of the body, are commonly free, wholly or partially, from legal or political restraints. For example: The king, as a limb of the parliament, is not responsible legally, or cannot commit a legal injury: and, as partaking in conduct of the assembly to which he immediately belongs, a member of the house of lords, or a member of the house of commons, is not amenable to positive law. But though this freedom from legal restraints may be highly useful or expedient, it is not necessary or inevitable. Considered severally, the members of a sovereign body, be they individuals or be they aggregates of individuals, may clearly be legally amenable, even as members of the body, to laws which the body imposes.

And here I may remark, that if a member considered severally, but considered as a member of the body, be wholly or partially free from legal or political obligation, that legally irresponsible aggregate, or that legally irresponsible individual, is restrained or debarred in two ways from an unconstitutional exercise of its legally unlimited power. I. Like the sovereign body of which it is a member, it is obliged or restrained morally: that is to say, it is controlled by opinions and sentiments current in the given community. 2. If it affected to issue a command which it is not empowered to issue by its constitutional share in the sovereignty, its unconstitutional command would not be legally binding, and disobedience to that command would therefore not be illegal. Nay, although it would not be responsible legally for thus exceeding its powers, those whom it commissioned to execute its unconstitutional command, would probably be amenable to positive law, if they tried to accomplish their mandate. For example: If the king or either of the houses, by way of proclamation or ordinance, affected to establish a law equivalent to an act of parliament, the pretended statute would not be legally binding, and disobedience to the pretended statute would therefore not be illegal. And although the king or the house would not be responsible legally for this supposed violation of constitutional law or morality, those whom the king or the house might order to enforce the statute, would be liable civilly or criminally, if they attempted to execute the order.

I have affirmed above, that, taken or considered severally, all the individuals and aggregates composing a sovereign number are subject to the supreme body of which they are component parts. By the matter contained in the last paragraph, I am led to clear the proposition to which I have now adverted, from a seeming difficulty.

Generally speaking, if a member of a sovereign body, taken or considered severally, be not amenable to positive law, it is merely as a member of the body that he is free from legal obligation. Generally speaking, he is bound, in his other characters, by legal restraints. But in some of the mixed aristocracies which are styled limited monarchies, the so called limited monarch is exempted or absolved completely from legal or political duty. For example: According to a maxim of the English law, the king is incapable of committing wrong: that is to say, he is not responsible legally for aught that he may please to do, or for any forbearance or omission.

But though he is absolved completely from legal or political duty, it cannot be thence inferred that the king is sovereign or supreme, or that he is not in a state of subjection to the sovereign or supreme parliament of which he is a constituent member.

Of the numerous proofs of this negative conclusion, which it were easy to produce, the following will amply suffice.– 1. Although he is free in fact from the fetters of positive law, he is not incapable of legal obligation. A law of the sovereign parliament, made with his own assent, might render himself and his successors legally responsible. But a monarch properly so called, or a sovereign number in its corporate and sovereign character, cannot be rendered, by any contrivance, amenable to positive law. – 2. If he affected to transgress the limits which the constitution has set to his authority, disobedience on the part of the governed to his unconstitutional commands, would not be illegal: whilst the ministers or instruments of his unconstitutional commands, would be legally amenable for their unconstitutional obedience, to laws of that sovereign body whereof he is merely a limb. But commands issued by sovereigns cannot be disobeyed by their subjects without an infringement of positive law: whilst the ministers or instruments of such a sovereign command, cannot be legally responsible to any portion of the community, excepting the author of their mandate. – 3. He habitually obeys the laws set by the sovereign body of which he is a constituent member. If he did not, he must speedily yield his office to a less refractory successor, or the British constitution must speedily expire. If he habitually broke the laws set by the sovereign body, the other members of the body would probably devise a remedy: though a prospective and definite remedy, fitted to meet the contingency, has not been provided by positive law, or even by constitutional morality. Consequently, he is bound by a cogent sanction to respect the laws of the body, although that cogent sanction is not predetermined and certain. A law which is set by the opinion of the upper and lower houses (besides a law which is set by the opinion of the community at large) constrains him to observe habitually the proper and positive laws which are set by the entire parliament. – But habitually obeying the laws of a determinate and sovereign body, he is not properly sovereign: for such habitual obedience consists not with that independence which is one of the essentials of sovereignty. And habitually obeying the laws of a certain and supreme body, he is really in a state of subjection to that certain and supreme body, though the other members of the body, together with the rest of the community, are commonly styled his subjects. It is mainly through the forms of procedure which obtain in the courts of justice, that he is commonly considered sovereign. He is clothed by the British constitution, or rather by the parliament of which he is a limb, with subordinate political powers of administering the law, or rather of supervising its administration. Infringements of the law are, therefore, in the style of procedure, offences against the king. In truth, they are not offences against the king, but against that sovereign body of king, lords, and commons, by which our positive law is directly or circuitously established. And to that sovereign body, and not to the king, the several members of the body, together with the rest of the community, are truly subject.

But if sovereign or supreme power be incapable of legal limitation, or if every supreme government be legally absolute, wherein (it may be asked) doth political liberty consist, and how do the supreme governments which are commonly deemed free, differ from the supreme governments which are commonly deemed despotic?

I answer, that political or civil liberty is the liberty from legal obligation, which is left or granted by a sovereign government to any of its own subjects: and that, since the power of the government is incapable of legal limitation, the government is legally free to abridge their political liberty, at its own pleasure or discretion. I say it is *legally* free to abridge their political liberty, at its own pleasure or discretion. For a government may be hindered by *positive morality* from abridging the political liberty which it leaves or grants to its subjects: and it is bound by the *law of God*, as known through the principle of utility, not to load them with legal duties which general utility condemns. – There are kinds of liberty from legal obligation, which will not quadrate with the foregoing description: for persons in a state of nature are independent of political duty, and independent of political duty is one of the essentials of sovereignty. But *political* or *civil* liberty supposes a political society, or supposes a … *civitas*: and it is the liberty from legal obligation which is left by a state to its subjects, rather than the liberty from legal obligation which is inherent in sovereign power.

Political or civil liberty has been erected into an idol, and extolled with extravagant praises by doting and fanatical worshippers. But political or civil liberty is not more worthy of eulogy than political or legal restraint. Political or civil liberty, like political or legal restraint, may be generally useful, or generally pernicious; and it is not as being liberty, but as conducing to the general good, that political or civil liberty is an object deserving applause.

To the ignorant and bawling fanatics who stun you with their pother about liberty, political or civil liberty seems to be the principal end for which government ought to exist. But the final cause or purpose for which government ought to exist, is the furtherance of the common weal to the greatest possible extent. And it must mainly attain the purpose for which it ought to exist, by two sets of means: *first*, by conferring such rights on its subjects as general utility commends, and by imposing such relative duties (or duties corresponding to the rights) as are necessary to the enjoyment of the former: *secondly*, by imposing such absolute duties (or by imposing such duties without corresponding rights) as tend to promote the good of the political community at large, although they promote not specially the interests of determinate parties. Now he who is clothed with a legal right, is also clothed with a political liberty: that is to say, he has the liberty from legal obligation, which is necessary to the enjoyment of the right. Consequently, in so far as it attains its appropriate purpose by conferring rights upon its subjects, government attains that purpose through the medium of political liberty. But since it must impose a duty wherever it confers a right, and should also impose duties which have no corresponding rights, it is less through the medium of political liberty, than through that of legal restraint, that government must attain the purpose for which it ought to exist. To say that political liberty ought to be its principal end, or to say that its principal end ought to be legal restraint, is to talk absurdly: for each is merely a means to that furtherance of the common weal, which is the only ultimate object of good or beneficent sovereignty. But though both propositions are absurd, the latter of the two absurdities is the least remote from the truth. – As I shall show hereafter, political or civil liberties rarely exist apart from corresponding legal restraints. Where persons in a state of subjection are free from legal duties, their liberties (generally speaking) would be nearly useless to themselves, unless they were protected in the enjoyment of their liberties, by legal duties on their fellows: that is to say, unless they had legal rights (importing such duties on their fellows) to those political liberties which are left them by the sovereign government. I am legally free, for example, to move from place to place, in so far as I can move from place to place consistently with my legal obligations: but this my political liberty would be but a sorry liberty unless my fellow-subjects were restrained by a political duty from assaulting and imprisoning my body. Through the ignorance or negligence of a sovereign government, some of the civil liberties which it leaves or grants to its subjects, may not be protected against their fellows by answering legal duties: and some of those civil liberties may perhaps be protected sufficiently by religious and moral obligations. But, speaking generally, a political or civil liberty is coupled with a legal right to it: and, consequently, political liberty is fostered by that very political restraint from which the devotees of the idol liberty are so fearfully and blindly averse.

From the nature of political or civil liberty, I turn to the supposed difference between free and despotic governments.

Every supreme government is *free* from legal restraints: or (what is the same proposition dressed in a different phrase) every supreme government is legally *despotic*. The distinction, therefore, of governments into *free and despotic*, can hardly mean that some of them are freer from restraints than others: or that the subjects of the governments which are denominated free, are protected against their governments by positive law.

Nor can it mean that the governments which are denominated free, leave or grant to their subjects more of political liberty than those which are styled despotic. For the epithet free importing praise, and the epithet *despotic* importing blame, they who distinguish governments into free and despotic, suppose that the first are better than the second. But inasmuch as political liberty may be generally useful or pernicious, we cannot infer that a government is better than another government, because the sum of the liberties which the former leaves to its subjects, exceeds the sum of the liberties which are left to its subjects by the latter. The excess in the sum of the liberties which the former leaves to its subjects, may be purely mischievous. It may consist of freedom from restraints which are required by the common weal; and which the government would lay upon its subjects, if it fulfilled its duties to the Deity. In consequence, for example, of that mischievous freedom, its subjects may be guarded inadequately against one another, or against attacks from external enemies.

They who distinguish governments into free and despotic, probably mean this:

The rights which a government confers, and the duties which it lays on its subjects, ought to be conferred and imposed for the advancement of the common weal, or with a view to the aggregate happiness of all the members of the society. But in every political society, the government deviates, more or less, from that ethical principle or maxim. In conferring rights and imposing duties, it more or less disregards the common or general weal, and looks, with partial affection, to the peculiar and narrower interests of a portion or portions of the community. – Now the governments which deviate less from that ethical principle or maxim, are better than the governments which deviate more. But, according to the opinion of those who make the distinction in question, the governments which deviate less from that ethical principle or maxim, are *popular* governments (in the largest sense of the expression): meaning by a popular government (in the largest sense of the expression), any aristocracy (limited monarchy or other) which consists of such a number of the given political community as bears a large proportion to the number of the whole society. For it is supposed by those who make the distinction in question, that, where the government is democratical or popular, the interests of the sovereign number, and the interests of the entire community, are nearly identical, or nearly coincide: but that, where the government is properly monarchical, or where the supreme powers reside in a comparatively few, the sovereign one or number has numerous sinister interests, or interests which are not consistent with the good or weal of the general. – According, therefore, to those who make the distinction in question the duties which a government of many lays upon its subjects, are more consonant to the general good than the duties which are laid upon its subjects by a government of one or a few. Consequently, though it leaves or grants not to its subjects, more of political liberty than is left or granted to its subjects by a government of one or a few, it leaves or grants to its subjects more of the political liberty *which conduces to the common weal*. But as leaving or granting to its subjects more of that *useful* liberty, a government of many may be styled *free*: whilst, as leaving or granting to its subjects less of that *useful* liberty, a government of one or a few may be styled *not free*, or may be styled *despotic* or *absolute*. Consequently, a *free* government, or a *good* government is a democratical or popular government (in the largest sense of the expression): whilst a *despotic* government, or a *bad* government, is either a monarchy properly so called, or any such narrow aristocracy (limited monarchy or other) as is deemed an oligarchy.

They who distinguish governments into free and despotic, are therefore lovers of democracy. By the epithet *free*, as applied to governments of many, they mean that governments of many are comparatively *good*: and by the epithet *despotic*, as applied to monarchies or oligarchies, they mean that monarchies or oligarchies are comparatively bad. The epithets *free* and *despotic* are rarely, I think, employed by the lovers of monarchy or oligarchy. If the lovers of monarchy or oligarchy did employ those epithets, they would apply the epithet free to governments of one or a few, and the epithet *despotic* to governments of many. For they think the former comparatively good, and the latter comparatively bad; or that monarchical or oligarchical governments are better adapted than popular, to, attain the ultimate purpose for which governments ought to exist. They deny that the latter are less misled than the former, by interests which are not consistent with the common or general weal: or, granting that excellence to governments of many, they think it greatly outweighed by numerous other excellences which they ascribe to governments of one or to governments of a few.

But with the respective merits or demerits of various forms of government, I have no direct concern. I have examined the current distinction between free and despotic governments, because it is expressed in terms which are extremely inappropriate and absurd, and which tend to obscure the independence of political or legal obligation, that is common to sovereign governments of all forms or kinds.

That the power of a sovereign is incapable of legal limitation, has been doubted, and even denied. But the difficulty, like thousands of others, probably arose from a verbal ambiguity. – The foremost individual member of a so called limited monarchy, is styled improperly *monarch or sovereign*. Now the power of a monarch or sovereign, thus improperly so styled, is not only capable of legal limitations, but is sometimes actually limited by positive law. But monarchs or sovereigns, thus improperly so styled, were confounded with monarchs, and other sovereigns, in the proper acceptation of the terms. And since the power of the former is capable of legal limitations, it was thought that the power of the latter might be bounded by similar restraints.

Whatever may be its origin, the error is remarkable. For the legal independence of monarchs in the proper acceptation of the term, and of sovereign bodies in their corporate and sovereign capacities, not only follows inevitably from the nature of sovereign power, but is also asserted expressly by renowned political writers of opposite parties or sects: by celebrated advocates of the governments which are decked with the epithet *free*, as by celebrated advocates of the governments which are branded with the epithet *despotic*.

> 'If it be objected (says Sidney) that I am a defender of arbitrary powers, I confess I cannot comprehend how any society can be established or subsist without them. The difference between good and ill governments is not, that those of one sort have an arbitrary power which the others have not; for they all have it; but that in those which are well constituted, this power is so placed as it may be beneficial to the people.'

> 'It appeareth plainly (says Hobbes) to my understanding, that the sovereign power whether placed in one man, as in monarchy, or in one assembly of men, as in popular and aristocraticall commonwealths, is as great as men can be imagined to make it. And though of so unlimited a power men may fancy many evill consequences, yet the consequence of the want of it, which is warre of every man against his neighbour, is much worse. The condition of man in this life shall

never be without inconveniences: but there happeneth in no commonwealth any great inconvenience, but what proceeds from the subjects' disobedience. And whosoever, thinking sovoraign power too great, will seek to make it lesse, must subject himselfe to a power which can limit it: that is to say, to a greater.' – 'One of the opinions (says the same writer) which are repugnant to the nature of a commonwealth, is this: that he who hath the sovoraign power is subject to the civill lawes. It is true that all sovoraigns are subject to the lawes of nature; because such lawes be Divine, and cannot by any man, or by any commonwealth, be abrogated. But to the civill lawes, or to the lawes which the sovoraign maketh, the sovoraign is not subject: for if he were subject to the civill lawes, he were subject to himselfe; which were not subjection, but freedom. The opinion now in question, because it setteth the civill lawes above the sovoraign, setteth also a judge above him, and a power to punish him: which is to make a new sovoraign; and, again, for the same reason, a third to punish the second; and so continually without end, to the confusion and dissolution of the commonwealth.' – 'The difference (says the same writer) between the kinds or forms of commonwealth, consisteth not in a difference between their powers, but in a difference between their aptitudes to produce the peace and security of the people: which is their end.'

Before I discuss the origin of political government and society, I will briefly examine a topic, allied to the liberty of sovereigns from political or legal restraints.

A sovereign government of one, or a sovereign government of a number of its collegiate and sovereign capacity, has no *legal rights* (in the proper acceptation of the term) *against its own subjects*.

Every legal right is the creature of a positive law: and it answers to a relative duty imposed by that positive law, and incumbent on a person or persons other than the person or persons in whom the right resides. To every legal right, there are therefore three parties: The sovereign government of one or a number which sets the positive law, and which through the positive law confers the legal right, and imposes the relative duty: the person or persons on whom the right is conferred: the person or persons on whom the duty is imposed, or to whom the positive law is set or directed. – As I shall show hereafter, the person or persons invested with the right, are not necessarily members of the independent political society wherein the author of the law is sovereign or supreme. The person or persons invested with the right, may be a member or members, sovereign or subject, of another society political and independent. But (taking the proposition with the slight correctives which I shall state hereafter) the person or persons on whom the duty is imposed, or to whom the law is set or directed, are necessarily members of the independent political society wherein the author of the law is sovereign or supreme. For unless the party burthened with the duty were subject to the author of the law, the party would not be obnoxious, to the legal or political sanction by which the duty and the right are respectively enforced and protected. A government can hardly impose legal duties or obligations upon members of foreign societies: although it can invest them with legal rights, by imposing relative duties upon members of its own community. A party bearing a legal right, is not necessarily burthened with a legal trust. Consequently, a party may bear and exercise a legal right, though the party cannot be touched by the might or power of its author. But unless the opposite party, or the party burthened with the relative duty, could be touched by the might of its author, the right and the relative duty, with the law which confers and imposes them, were merely nominal and illusory. And (taking the proposition with the slight correctives which I shall state hereafter) a person obnoxious to the sanction enforcing a positive law, is necessarily subject to the author of the law, or is necessarily a member of the society, wherein the author is sovereign.

It follows from the essentials of a legal right, that a sovereign government of one, or a sovereign government of a number in its collegiate and sovereign capacity, has no legal rights (in the proper acceptation of the term) against its own subjects.

To every legal right, there are three several parties: namely, a party bearing the right; a party burthened with the relative duty; and a sovereign government setting the law through which the right and the duty are respectively conferred and imposed. A sovereign government cannot acquire rights through laws set by itself to its own subjects. A man is no more able to confer a right on himself, than he is able to impose on himself a law or duty. Every party bearing a right (divine, legal or moral) has necessarily acquired the right through a law and a duty (proper or improper) laid by that other party on a further and distinct party. Consequently, if a sovereign government had legal rights against its own subjects, those rights were the creatures of positive laws set to its own subjects by a third person or body. And, as every positive law is laid by a sovereign government on a person or persons in a state of subjection to itself, that third person or body were sovereign in that community whose own sovereign government bore the legal rights: that is to say, the community were subject to its own sovereign, and were also subject to a sovereign conferring rights upon its own. Which is impossible and absurd.

But so far as they are bound by the law of God to obey their temporal sovereign, a sovereign government has *rights divine* against its own subjects: rights which are conferred upon itself, through duties which are laid upon its subjects, by laws of a common superior. And so far as the members of its own community are severally constrained to obey it by the opinion of the community at large, it has also *moral rights* (or rights arising from positive morality) against its own subjects severally considered: rights which are conferred upon itself by the opinion of the community at large, and which answer to relative duties laid upon its several subjects by the general or prevalent opinion of the same indeterminate body.

Austin's theory has been subjected to sustained attack, most notably from Hart, for failing to provide an adequate description of the essential elements of positive legal systems. These criticisms cover many aspects of Austin's theory (as demonstrated in the next chapter). However, one of the most damaging of these criticisms, is the claim that one cannot find a single body, a sovereign, which provides a single unifying source of law. If this is correct, much of Austin's extended definitions lose meaning, thus undermining his attempt to offer clarity. One of the best defences of this part of Austin's theory is the following extract from Cotterrell's *The Politics Of Jurisprudence*. Later, when you have read Hart's criticisms of Austin you might find it useful to come back to this section, to review it. At that time you may be able to assess more fully the following questions:

1. Does Cotterrell manage to save Austin from Hart's criticisms, especially those directed at his description of the sovereign?

2.   Is Austin/Cotterrell entitled to take the notion of an institution as representing some fact that exists in the real world? What is an institution?

Cotterrell (1989, 67–79)

SOVEREIGNTY

Consideration of other criticisms and possible defences of the command theory must wait until its most crucial component – the concept of the sovereign – has been discussed. If law is a type of command, the identity and character of the commanders and what enables them to issue legal commands must be established. If laws provide for sanctions, the authority to impose sanctions must be explained. The theory of sovereignty which Austin adapts from Hobbes' political philosophy and, to a lesser extent, from Bentham's commentaries on Blackstone is intended to serve these purposes.

What makes commands rules is the element of generality in them; what makes rules laws – in the sense of positive laws, the subject of Austin's jurisprudence – is the fact that they are direct or indirect commands of the *sovereign* of an independent political society. These commands are addressed to the members of that society, who are thus *subjects* of that sovereign. Austin writes of the sovereign as a person (for example, an absolute monarch) or a body of persons (for example the lawmakers or electorate of a democracy, or the members of an established ruling elite). It is essential, however, to note that he always means by the sovereign the *office* or *institution* which embodies supreme authority; never the individuals who happen to hold that office or embody that institution through their relationships at any given time. Austin's sovereign is an abstraction – the location of the ultimate power which allows the creation of law in a society. As will appear later, this point is of the greatest importance, since he has often been criticised for describing sovereignty, and the source of legal authority, in 'personal' terms.

Undoubtedly he felt no need to labour the matter for, in the tradition of political theory which he relies on, sovereignty is explicitly 'abstract'. Hobbes, writing in the context of Cromwellian England, describes sovereignty as the 'artificial soul' of 'an artificial man', the latter being the state or commonwealth. The sovereign is an office, not a particular person or particular people. In the seventeenth century, Hobbes transformed English discussion of the authority of the ruler by substituting for the power of the king the abstract notion of the state as expressed in the concept of sovereignty; although, eventually, faced with the difficulty of locating sovereignty in England, he found it (prudently, after the royal Restoration) in the institution of the monarch. No doubt it was Hobbes' image of sovereignty which predominantly shaped Austin's (his admiration for the earlier writer is very clear in the lectures). By contrast, Austin distances himself in important respects, as will appear, from Bentham's tentative and somewhat confusing discussion of sovereignty.

What is the sovereign of an independent political society? Hobbes had defined such a society as one which could defend itself, unaided, against any attacks from without. Austin realistically notes that few if any societies would qualify on this basis. Accordingly, it is the existence of sovereignty which defines independence, assuming the society is of a certain minimum size. Political independence and sovereignty are correlative terms.

Sovereignty exists when two conditions are satisfied: first, the bulk of the society are in a habit of obedience or submission to a determinate and common superior (whether an individual or a body of individuals) and, secondly, that individual or body is not, itself, in a habit of obedience to a determinate human superior. The idea of a habit of obedience introduces a factual, indeed sociological, criterion of the existence of sovereignty and, in this, Austin follows Bentham rather than Hobbes. Hobbes founded the existence of sovereignty in an assumed 'social contract' by which individuals could be thought of as joining together to form a society and entrusting the absolute power of government to a sovereign who would provide peace and physical protection for them. The 'war of all against all' which would exist without government would be replaced by the domination of the sovereign to whom all are subject. But this analysis presupposed that individuals have natural rights which, by the social contract, they agree to forego so as to institute a sovereign power over them. As has been seen earlier, neither Bentham nor Austin was prepared to accept ideas of natural rights, treating them as irrational dogma. Thus Bentham, and Austin following him, discard Hobbes' social contract basis of sovereignty and replace it with the idea of a factual basis of sovereignty in actual habitual obedience. One consequence of this is that while Hobbes' social contract gave the sovereign the right to rule, both Bentham and Austin deny that it makes any sense to talk of a right in this context. The existence of sovereignty is merely a political fact, not a matter of right and wrong.

On one view, the 'weak side of the 'Austinian analysis' is this transference of a legal conception to a sociological problem' and certainly the grounding of the ultimate authority to create law in a sociological consideration stores up problems for normative legal theory. Nevertheless, it is easy to see here the utilitarian attempt to be realistic, to avoid dogma and abstract talk about arbitrarily assumed natural rights, and to avoid sanctifying authority. Austin cannot resist speculating on *why* people might habitually obey but for the moment that matter can be left aside. Like the sociological question of how far state sanctions induce compliance with law, it is not important to the *analytical* issue of the location of sovereignty. All that is necessary for the latter is the fact that habitual obedience by the majority of the population exists. Where there is no such obedience there is either anarchy (no recognised sovereign at all) or revolution (the population is divided into groups rendering habitual obedience to different authorities).

SOME CHARACTERISTICS OF AUSTIN'S SOVEREIGN

Two important characteristics of the Austinian sovereign have already been noted. It must be common (that is, only one sovereign can exist in any single political society; the sovereign is, in that sense, indivisible although it can be made up of several components). And it must be determinate (that is, the composition of the sovereign body or the identity of the sovereign person must be clear). A further characteristic has produced more controversy than any other aspect of Austin's conception of sovereignty. This is that *the sovereign is illimitable by law*. This follows directly from Austin's definition of law. Every law is the direct or indirect command of the sovereign of an independent political society. But a sovereign cannot issue enforceable commands to itself – or at least, even if such an idea is conceivable, the sovereign can abrogate them at any time. And no laws other than the sovereign's own commands can exist to bind it. 'Supreme power limited by positive law, is a flat contradiction in terms ... Every supreme government is legally despotic'.

Many critics have considered that Austin's view of sovereignty conjures up the image of a despotic monarch – an archaic and wholly inappropriate way of thinking upon which to found an analysis of the authority of law in modern Western societies. But if we look more closely this is not necessarily so. First, Austin does not suggest the sovereign is free of limitations but only legal limitations. Thus positive morality (reflected in public opinion, widespread moral or political expectations, and ultimately the threat of rebellions) may provide important constraints. Secondly, most of Austin's discussions of sovereignty relate primarily to the conditions of representative democracies (especially Britain and the United States). Thirdly, Austin's concept of delegation by the sovereign, which will be considered below, is used by him to express the possibility (which has become a reality in most complex modern industrialised societies) of very extensive dispersion of legislative, adjudicative and administrative authority within the overall hierarchical framework of a centralised state.

Nevertheless, it is widely considered that Austin's conception of an indivisible and legally illimitable sovereign quickly runs into the most serious analytical difficulties. The problems seem to begin as soon as one seeks to identify the sovereign in particular societies. In orthodox British constitutional law the sovereign is said to be the Queen in Parliament: that is, the sovereign is made up of the monarch and the two houses of Parliament. Constitutional law supports the claim that such a sovereign is legally illimitable. Parliament cannot bind itself or its successors by legislation. Since the House of Commons is the representative of the electorate, however, Austin locates sovereignty in the monarch, the House of Lords and the electorate of the Commons.

Many critics have seen this as either problematic or utterly misleading. In particular, Austin has been seen as confusing legal and political sovereignty ... Popular sovereignty may well reside in the electorate, but for legal purposes surely Parliament is sovereign. In fact, there is no confusion. Austin does not write of *legal* sovereignty or treat sovereignty as supreme legal competence. As C A W Manning points out, Austin's sovereignty is not a legal but a pre-legal notion. It is 'the logical correlate of an assumed factual obedience'. In modern terms, we can say it is the loçus of legitimate ultimate political authority. It is not 'a specified organ or complex of organs, but ... that individual or collectivity at whose pleasure the constitution is changed or subsists intact'. But if this is so how can the electorate as subjects be in a state of habitual obedience to themselves as sovereign? The answer is that the members of an independent political society *as individuals* can be in a state of habitual obedience to a sovereign which is the abstract institution defined as monarch, Lords and *the collectivity* represented by the electorate of the Commons. The distinction between the subject population and the electorate forming part of the sovereign (and made up of essentially the same people) is a distinction between subject individuals and a sovereign collectivity. There is nothing incoherent in claiming that the individual is subject to the authority of the collectivity as an institution, or that the collectivity as a whole retains authority because the bulk of individuals continue to accept its authority.

What of the case of written constitutions and those where the distribution of governmental authority is especially complex; as, for example, in federal systems? Austin considers at some length the location of sovereignty in the United States to illustrate his approach. The sovereign must be a person or body of persons, but the ultimate authority of the American polity appears to be *a document* – the Constitution. Where then does sovereignty lie? Of course, in the Austinian analysis it must lie with that body of people that has ultimate authority to alter the Constitution. The Constitution itself provides in Article 5 that amendments to it must, to be valid, be ratified by the legislatures of (or conventions in) three quarters of the states. Again, in an Austinian analysis, where representatives are involved, it is the electors of these representatives who form the sovereign body.

Critics note that the Austinian sovereign in such a context is 'a despot hard to arouse', 'a monarch who slumbers and sleeps', since constitutional amendments are rare. But this situation matters only if we are seeking (as Austin is not) a legal sovereign – that is, an active, ultimately authoritative lawmaker. By contrast Austin is identifying only the location of ultimate authority underlying the constitutional order; the institution which is recognised as having authority to confirm or amend that order. Suppose that in a political society with a written constitution there is no such institution; no means of constitutional amendment. Sovereignty would then seem to lie in those governmental and legislative institutions which the constitution recognises as ultimately authoritative, since nothing capable of changing their authority stands behind them. In an Austinian view, however, sovereignty resides in these authorities not *because* of their designation by the constitution, but because the authorities so designated are themselves habitually accepted.

MUST THE SOVEREIGN BE LEGALLY ILLIMITABLE?

We have noted that Austin insists that by definition the sovereign cannot be subject to legal limitations. Blackstone had earlier claimed that in every legal system there is a supreme, absolute and unlimited legislative power. Bentham, however, thought differently. While claiming that there are no *a priori* theoretical limits on sovereign power, he nevertheless considered that legal limits on such power were practically possible. Like Austin, he grounds the existence of sovereignty in the fact of habitual obedience. Hence he sees the possibility of *conditional* habitual obedience; that is, obedience habitually rendered to sovereign acts *within certain limits*. The 'obedience of the governed is susceptible of every modification of which human conduct is susceptible: and the rules which mark it out, of every diversity which can be clearly described by words'.

This is plausible, but seems to run into problems when it is suggested that the limitations on sovereign power are *legal*. In *Of Laws in General* Bentham does suggest this by terming some of these limitations *leges in principem*. But where does their legal quality come from? He recognises that *leges in principem*, like all other laws, must derive from the sovereign but his explanations of how the sovereign can bind itself are far from satisfactory, relying on suggestions about the invocation of external pressures of popular opinion, religious or moral sanctions, or international relations. For Austin, of course, these kinds of sanctions are characteristic not of law but of positive morality. It is by no means apparent how Bentham's *leges in principem* acquire their legal character. His apparently inconclusive discussion seems motivated here primarily by the desire to recognise clearly the variety of constitutional structures which do indeed distribute authority within states in complex ways – for example, through federal arrangements, provision for judicial review of legislation, entrenched constitutional clauses, or the explicit separation of governmental powers.

Austin's simpler and clearer conception of legally unlimited sovereignty is not incapable of dealing with these complexities. It has been seen that for Austin the sovereign is always an institution – for example, the monarch, not the person who is king at any given time; the body which can change the constitution, not the particular individuals who may form that body. How is the institution defined or identified? It would seem that two kinds of rules may do this: rules of positive law and rules of positive morality (for example, public opinion expressed in customary, moral or other rules, conventions or expectations). Only positive morality can actually bind the sovereign so as to fix its institutional character. Positive law cannot do this since the sovereign can alter this law at will. But even if it does not bind the sovereign it can have the status of law if commanded by the sovereign and addressed to any *part* or agent of the sovereign body (for example, to the British parliament – perhaps defining its procedures; to judges – perhaps specifying jurisdiction; or to the monarch within a constitutional monarchy – perhaps defining the monarch's powers as well as the right of succession to the throne). Positive law can bind each part of such a sovereign body as 'the Queen in Parliament' since each part is not itself sovereign.

Nevertheless, the considerations which fix the nature of sovereignty in general in a particular political society must be founded in positive morality, not law. Sovereignty is, as has been seen, a pre-legal concept. In an Austinian view no law can confer or validate sovereignty. Austin asserted that much of constitutional 'law' must, in fact be merely positive morality for this reason. This is a much less unrealistic view than has often been claimed, once it is appreciated that, on the basis of the arguments above, laws directed to distinct parts of the sovereign body (or, perhaps more accurately, distinct institutions through which sovereignty is expressed) can certainly be accepted as laws in Austinian terms, even though they cannot bind the sovereign as a whole.

The acceptance of the sovereign as an institution seems to remove much of the difficulty which has been thought to exist for Austinian attempts to explain the persistence and continuity of laws. Laws can remain in force as long as the institutional sovereign remains, perhaps for centuries. Equally, the problem of succession to authority (for example, how one king succeeds another in a recognised line of succession) and the continuity of laws which accompanies it may be explained in Austinian terms by the existence of rules of positive morality or of positive law as described above. Where sovereignty appears to reside entirely in a single person such as an absolute monarch it would seem that that the rules governing succession to the throne can only be rules of positive morality. But Austin would consider this a wholly realistic view of the matter. Whatever may be written in 'legal' form (as statutes, for example), succession in such a situation depends on political loyalties, traditional beliefs, and ideological notions which only a most narrow-minded jurist could try to reduce to purely 'legal' determinants of succession.

This defence of Austin is far from claiming that law *must* be interpreted in something like his terms. He offers only a particular partial perspective which emphasises a certain relationship between law and the modern state, viewed in terms of sovereign power. Writers who have argued forcefully against his interpretation have usually wanted to see the legal system as being governed by rules, even in its highest regions of authority, rather than – as Austin's theory so starkly claims – governed by *people*, mere human decision-makers with all their frailties and potential for arbitrary or tyrannous exercise of power. As noted earlier, Austin's theory is not a theory of the Rule of Law – of government subject to law. It is a theory of the 'rule of men' – of government using law as an instrument of power. Such a view may be considered realistic or merely cynical. But it is, in its broad outlines, essentially coherent.

THE JUDGE AS DELEGATE OF THE SOVEREIGN

The concept of *delegation* of sovereign power is fundamental to Austin's thinking. It is obvious that the theory of sovereignty applied to modern conditions must entail such delegation among numerous agencies, empowered to transact the business of the state in one way or another. Indeed, the idea of delegation in this sense is the element necessary to complete the discussion of power-conferring rules which was begun earlier in this chapter. The sovereign, in Austinian terms, delegates legislative and administrative functions to many institutions – including, significantly, the judiciary. Equally, law-making power is delegated to private citizens who exercise it, for example, in the creation of contracts according to terms chosen by the contracting parties, but which the sovereign's institutions will enforce. Each dispersion of sovereign power in this way is a delegation, not a release of it. Each legitimate exercise of such power to create legal obligations (for example, when a court lays down a new rule in a case or when an official establishes a rule on the basis of statutory authority conferred on him) must be treated as an exercise of the sovereign's power of command. Hence, insofar as such an act is not revoked or invalidated by higher authority representing the sovereign, it can be considered a *tacit command* of the sovereign.

Many critics have claimed that this notion of tacit command – which is present also in the theory of Hobbes – is unrealistic as regards law-making through judicial decisions. Are not judges independent in such democracies as, for example, Britain and the United States? How can they be considered mere delegates of some other authority? The difficulty again arises from treating Austin's sovereign as a legal sovereign – an ultimate legislating institution. Thus, the legal doctrine of parliamentary sovereignty in Britain – which recognises Parliament as the highest law-creating authority – does not, of course, entail that judges are delegates of Parliament. Austin's theory does not, however, suggest that they are. It claims merely that they must act as representatives of the constitutional order of which they are a part. In Austinian terms that constitutional order is the consequence of the pre-legal sovereign authority embodied in monarch, Lords and the electorate of the Commons.

Logically, it would seem to follow that delegation of sovereign power, insofar as it is accomplished by law, must itself be accomplished by means of the sovereign's commands – whether as specific requirements for action or prohibitions imposing limits on action, whether addressed to holders of an office or to those people who are to be subject to the power of the office-holder, and whether express or tacit.

Many important consequences follow from Austin's way of looking at the distribution of political and legal authority in the state in this way. For example, his view of the judge as delegate of the sovereign entails a straightforward recognition that judges *legislate* no less than do legislatures. Judges make law insofar as their decisions embody what can be considered to be the sovereign's tacit commands. Austin's carefully expressed views on judicial law-making have often been misinterpreted and are certainly very different from Bentham's. Bentham sought a rational, codified legal system which would make not only judicial law-making but probably also judicial interpretation of law unnecessary and inappropriate. The role of the judge would be to decide cases not by appeal to legal precedent but by following the demands of utility in the particular case, and seeking to reconcile differences between the parties where possible. Judicial decision-making would thus be radically separated from the rational code structure of the law itself. Such a position follows from Bentham's conviction that rational law could only be constructed through purposive legislation, not by judicial pronouncements inspired only by the accidents of litigation. As Bentham's recent interpreter Gerald Postema admits, it is hard to construct a coherent theory of the place of the judiciary in the legal order from such ideas.

Austin is the model of cautious moderation beside Bentham's radicalism. But he does claim that judges 'of capacity, experience and weight' have generally been insufficiently active in developing the law. He argues against the idea that judicial law-making (or, as he calls it, 'judiciary law') is arbitrary or undemocratic, taking as his primary point that judiciary law is no different in this respect from any other form of subordinate legislation and, in all such situations, positive law and public opinion must provide the necessary safeguards. The most radical theme which emerges is that insofar as judges make law there is no reason to treat their law-making role as necessarily and essentially different from that of other delegates (officials, administrators, boards and committees) of the sovereign entrusted with rule-making functions. Thus, Austin's criticisms of judiciary law are entirely technical ones. It tends to be made in haste; it is inevitably established *ex post facto;* it 'exists nowhere in fixed or determinate expressions'; it tends to be vague and inconsistent; its rules are 'never or rarely comprehensive'; there is no clear test of its validity; its existence tends to make accompanying statute law 'imperfect, unsystematic, and bulky'. Hence code systems are, as Bentham had argued, better than common law systems. But, whereas Bentham rests the matter squarely on unshakeable assumptions about where perfect legal rationality resides and would, it seems, like to sweep away the law-making judge into the museum of archaic curiosities, Austin painstakingly weighs up the practical considerations and on balance confirms the purely technical virtues of codification and legislation.

AUSTIN'S THEORY OF THE CENTRALISED STATE

Austin's view of the judge as essentially just one variety of state functionary among many others leads us into a wider consideration of his image of the modern state. Austin's political and social theory is ignored in most jurisprudential discussions of his work, yet it provides the essential context in which his concept of delegation of sovereign power is given significance. In his early political writings he made clear his belief in the virtues of political centralisation. Austin's top-down image of law reflects a top-down image of the polity ... he was far from being a democrat. Austin viewed government as a matter of rational management to be guided by principles of utility. As such – and rather like Maine – he viewed it as a matter for experts ...

...

All this suggests that to see Austin's view of law (as commands supported by sanctions) as much like a view of mere orders backed by threats (such as those of a gunman pointing his gun at the person addressed) is misleading (cf. Hart, Concept of Law, ch 2). The relation between sovereign and subject is far more than one founded on coercion. The habit of obedience to the sovereign is, according to Austin, rooted in custom, prejudices and 'reason bottomed in the principle of utility' – that is, a recognition of the expediency of government. In a soundly educated people, reason would play a most important role. Equally, when we consider the significance of the sanctions attaching to law in actually securing obedience to law, Austin notes that fear of state (legal) sanctions is not likely to be more powerful as a deterrence against deviance than is 'the fear of public disapprobation, with its countless train of evils'. In forming moral character the latter is far more significant than the former.

Thus, Austin's image of the centralised state, making extensive use of coercion through law in the matter of government, is also an image of a state which can be based on reason; guided in governmental activity by utility, and securing the allegiance of subjects to the sovereign ideally through their rational understanding, not prejudice, fear or blind habit. Nevertheless, Austin considers that it must realistically be recognised that populations are kept largely unenlightened by their rulers. Hence much government, in fact, relies on irrational, habitual acquiescence by the population. Universal education is thus the Austinian prescription for a sound and enlightened polity.

A need for acquiescence in a centralised source of state authority in the sovereign goes along with the need for extensive delegation of sovereign powers, as has been seen. Austin praised the institutions of local government and recognised the appropriateness of judicial law-making and extensive rule-making in administrative contexts. Nevertheless, in his writings on the virtues of centralisation he insists that none of this delegation must be allowed to defeat the central co-ordination of government by which rational utilitarian policies can be consistently brought into effect.

...

... It should alert us only to the fact that his 'timeless' concepts of 'sovereign', 'command', 'sanction' and 'habitual obedience' are not formulated in isolation from specific political conditions. Like most elements of normative legal theory they are conceptual reflections of a particular time and place, transformed in a way that gives them the potential to speak to other generations in other legal conditions. In Austin's case, however, these concepts are formulated with a clear awareness of the sociological questions they entail. This dimension of his thought has been almost totally ignored by his critics in the field of normative legal theory.

In the next chapter, Hart's criticisms of Austin's theory (some of which are perhaps based on a convenient misstatement of Austin) are set out. They can create the misleading impression that early Legal Positivism has no contemporary significance. This is far from the truth. Positivist analytical jurisprudence, the attempt to understand law and legal concepts through the analysis of language, is still an important school of modern jurisprudence. (See, in Part II of this book, Chapter 13, Hohfeld and the Analysis of Rights.) Hart's theories themselves, set out in the next chapter, develop rather than demolish analytical jurisprudence, using an approach that differs significantly from that used by Austin, but which shares much in common with Bentham's more sophisticated methodology and writings. And to refer backwards as well as forwards, early legal positivism did not simply inspire further developments in positivism, but the counter attacks of modern natural law. Writers like Fuller and Finnis (see Chapter

2) and Dworkin (Chapters 8 and 9) take as their starting points the understandings of legal systems articulated by positivists, in order to identify the manner in which natural law continues to operate within legal systems. (And even some of the negations dealt with in Part II of this book are constructed in contrast to a view of law as centralised coercion, along the lines set out by Austin.) The modern debate between Legal Positivism and Natural Law theories centres on the degree to which law and morals can ever be completely separated. This debate lacks the grandeur and scope of traditional Natural Law theory. The issue now is not how rulers can claim legitimacy, but what, within the everyday practices of law (and lawyers), remains necessarily moral. This change of emphasis within Natural Law theorising reflects, amongst other things, the success of early positivist theories.

In the next two chapters you will be introduced to the leading twentieth century legal positivists: H L A Hart and Hans Kelsen. Both theorists were closely linked to contemporary developments in philosophy, and sought to apply the insights and methodologies of those contemporary developments to the study of law.

Further Reading

For a more extensive account of Austin and his jurisprudence: Morrison 1982.

For Hart's sustained critique of Austin, Hart 1961/1994, Chs 2–4.

For some classic essays on Bentham and the continuing importance of the jurisprudence he engendered: Hart 1982a, especially the first 5 essays.

For more background on Bentham's reaction to talk of natural law, nature, natural rights, see his attack: 'A Critical Examination of the Declaration of Rights' set out in Parekh 1973, Ch 20.

To help you think about where the positivism of Austin and Bentham leads: Twining, in Guest 1996, and other essays in that volume.

Questions

1. 'Law is the command of a sovereign backed by a sanction.' Is this a useful definition of law? Is it equally useful for the judge, the lawmaker and the citizen?

2. 'The legal theories of Austin and Bentham build on one essential truth, if there is no basis on which all lawmakers can claim a moral right to rule, then law must be a species of coercion.' Discuss.

3. 'Austin's theory cannot account for Constitutional law, International law, or the law of contract. As such, its weaknesses outweigh its strengths.' Discuss.

4 Modern Positivism: H L A Hart and Analytical Jurisprudence

Nicola Lacey

Introduction

H L A Hart was born in 1907, and graduated from New College, Oxford, where he read classics, ancient history and philosophy, in 1929. Over the next decade, he had a successful practice at the Chancery Bar. Following the outbreak of war, being unfit for military service, he took up a position at MI5. At the end of the war, he felt no enthusiasm for a return to the Bar: his practice had included a large proportion of tax work, which he had increasingly come to see as inconsistent with his social democratic politics. After considering a post in the civil service, he took up a fellowship in philosophy at New College.

On Hart's return to Oxford, he entered a philosophical world vastly different from that which he had left in 1929. The classical philosophy which had dominated his own education was being subjected to a radical challenge from the linguistic philosophy which was gradually emerging from Wittgenstein's work in Cambridge and from that of Gilbert Ryle and J L Austin in Oxford. His early years as a philosophy tutor in New College were marked by a deep immersion in the new work. Hart was quick to see that his legal experience produced a fund of examples on which the new linguistic philosophy could usefully be brought to bear. Though he was slow to publish his own work, his reputation in Oxford was such that in 1952 he was elected to the Chair of Jurisprudence recently vacated by the American jurist Arthur Goodhart.

Two papers which Hart published between 1949 and 1958 serve both to illustrate the intellectual context that informed his scholarship and to indicate the future direction of his thinking. In particular, 'Definition and Theory in Jurisprudence' (1953), his inaugural lecture as Professor of Jurisprudence, set out Hart's stall as a linguistic philosopher prepared both to bring the insights of linguistic philosophy to law, and to exploit his legal understanding to generate a fund of examples suitable for philosophical analysis. In this essay Hart argued that his jurisprudential predecessors, in seeking to define terms of legal art such as 'corporation' had been both asking the wrong question and using the wrong methods to answer it. (Although he discusses examples such as the meaning of 'corporation', the same criticisms can, and later were, applied to attempts to define the meaning of 'law'). Instead, Hart returned to Bentham's insight that such words can only be understood in the context of sentences in which they have meaning. Here, standard definition per genus et differentiam (for example, 'an elephant is a quadruped distinguished from other such creatures by the possession of a trunk') is unhelpful because we are confused not about marginal but about the very central cases of the term. His argument was that the distinctive task of explanation, therefore, is to elucidate the conditions under which statements including the term are true. In the case of a corporation, these conditions include a variety of legal rules and arrangements. In constructing this argument, Hart was laying some of the most basic foundations for his major jurisprudential work, *The Concept of Law*; he was also drawing on what were to remain two of his three main sources of inspiration: the legal philosophy of Jeremy Bentham and modern linguistic philosophy. The extracts from 'Definition and Theory in Jurisprudence' set out below should enable you to enter into Hart's overall project and understand something of what inspired it. While the extract discusses corporations, read it with the following question in mind: Is it more useful to ask 'what is law' or to ask 'what are the conditions which enable us to state, with some confidence and on at least some occasions, what the law is'?

Hart (1954, 37–41, 45–48, 56–59)

I

In law as elsewhere, we can know and yet not understand. Shadows often obscure our knowledge, which not only vary in intensity but are cast by different obstacles to light. These cannot all be removed by the same methods, and till the precise character of our perplexity is determined we cannot tell what tools we shall need.

The perplexities I propose to discuss are voiced in those questions of analytical jurisprudence which are usually characterized as requests for definitions: What is law? What is a State? What is a right? What is possession? I choose this topic because it seems to me that the common mode of definition is ill adapted to the law and has complicated its exposition; its use has, I think, led at certain points to a divorce between jurisprudence and the study of the law at work, and has helped to create the impression that there are certain fundamental concepts that the lawyer cannot hope to elucidate without entering a forbidding jungle of philosophical argument. I wish to suggest that this is not so; that legal notions however fundamental can be elucidated by methods properly adapted to their special character. Such methods were glimpsed by our predecessors but have only been fully understood and developed in our own day.

Questions such as those I have mentioned, 'What is a State?', 'What is law?', 'What is a right?', have great ambiguity. The same form of words may be used to demand a definition or the cause or the purpose or the justification or the origin of a legal or political institution. But if, in the effort to free them from this risk of confusion with other questions, we rephrase these requests for definitions as 'What is the meaning of the word 'State'?', 'What is the meaning of the word 'right'?', those who ask are apt to feel uneasy, as if this had trivialized their question. For what they want cannot be got out of a dictionary, and this transformation of their question suggests it can. This uneasiness is the expression of an instinct which deserves respect: it emphasizes the fact that those who ask these questions are not asking to be taught how to use these words in the correct way. This they know and yet are still puzzled. Hence it is no answer to this type of question merely to tender examples of what are correctly called rights, laws, or corporate bodies, and to tell the questioner if he is still puzzled that he is free to abandon the public convention and use words as he pleases. For the puzzle arises from the fact that though the common use of these words is known, it is not understood; and it is not understood because compared with most ordinary words these legal words are in different ways anomalous. Sometimes, as with the word 'law' itself, one anomaly is that the range of cases to which it is applied has a diversity which baffles the initial attempt to extract any principle behind the application, yet we have the conviction that even here there is some principle and not an arbitrary convention underlying the surface differences; so that whereas it would be patently absurd to ask for elucidation of the principle in accordance with which different men are called Tom, it is not felt absurd to ask why, within municipal law, the immense variety of different types of rules are called law, nor why municipal law and international law, in spite of striking differences, are so called.

But in this and other cases, we are puzzled by a different and more troubling anomaly. The first efforts to define words like 'corporation', 'right', or 'duty' reveal that these do not have the straightforward connection with counterparts in the world of fact which most ordinary words have and to which we appeal in our definition of ordinary words. There is nothing which simply 'corresponds' to these legal words, and when we try to define them we find that the expressions we tender in our definition specifying kinds of persons, things, qualities, events, and processes, material or psychological, are never precisely the equivalent of these legal words, though often connected with them in some way. This is most obvious in the case of expressions for corporate bodies, and is commonly put by saying that a corporation is not a series or aggregate of persons. But it is true of other legal words. Though one who has a right usually has some expectation or power, the expression 'a right' is not synonymous with words like 'expectation' or 'power' even if we add 'based on law' or 'guaranteed by law'. And so too, though we speak of men having duties to do or abstain from certain actions the word 'duty' does not stand for or describe anything as ordinary words do. It has an altogether different function which makes the stock form of definition, 'a duty is a ... ', seem quite inappropriate.

These are genuine difficulties and in part account for something remarkable: that out of these innocent requests for definitions of fundamental legal notions there should have arisen vast and irreconcilable theories, so that not merely whole books but whole schools of juristic thought may be characterized by the type of answer they give to questions like 'What is a right?', or 'What is a corporate body?' This alone, I think, suggests that something is wrong with the approach to definition; can we really not elucidate the meaning of words which every developed legal system handles smoothly and alike without assuming this incubus of theory? And the suspicion that something is amiss is confirmed by certain characteristics that many such theorists have. In the first place they fall disquietingly often into a familiar triad. Thus the American Realists [some of whose theories are discussed in Chapter 7] striving to give us an answer in terms of plain fact tell us that a right is a term by which we describe the prophecies we make of the probable behaviour of courts or officials; the Scandinavian jurists, after dealing the Realist theory blows that might well be thought fatal (if these matters were strictly judged), say that a right is nothing real at all but an ideal or fictitious or imaginary power, and then join with their opponents to denigrate the older type of theory that a right is an 'objective reality' – an invisible entity existing apart from the behaviour of men. These theories are in form similar to the three great theories of corporate personality, each of which has dealt deadly blows to the other. There too we have been told by turn that the name of a corporate body like a limited company or an organization like the State is really just a collective name or abbreviation for some complex but still plain facts about ordinary persons, or alternatively that it is the name of a fictitious person, or that on the contrary it is the name of a real person existing with a real will and life, but not a body of its own. And this same triad of theories has haunted the jurist even when concerned with relatively minor notions. Look for example at Austin's discussion of status and you will find that the choice lies for him between saying that it is a mere collective name for a set of special rights and duties, or that it is an 'ideal' or 'fictitious' basis for these rights and duties, or that it is an 'occult quality' in the person who has the status, distinguishable both from the rights and duties and from the facts engendering them.

Secondly, though these theories spring from the effort to define notions actually involved in the practice of a legal system, they rarely throw light on the precise work they do there. They seem to the lawyer to stand apart with their heads at least in the clouds; and hence it is that very often the use of such terms in a legal system is neutral between competing theories. For that use 'can be reconciled with any theory, but is authority for none'.

Thirdly, in many of these theories there is often an amalgam of issues that should be distinguished. It is of course clear that the assertion that corporate bodies are real persons and the counter-assertion that they are fictions of the law were often not the battle-cries of analytical jurists. They were ways of asserting or denying the claims of organized groups to recognition by the State. But such claims have always been confused with the baffling analytical question, 'What is a corporate body?', so that the classification of such theories as Fiction or Realist or Concessionist is a criss-cross between logical and political criteria. So too the American Realist theories have much to tell us of value about the judicial process and how small a part deduction from predetermined premises may play in it, but the lesson is blurred when it is presented as a matter of definition of 'law' or 'a right'; not only analytical jurisprudence but every sort of jurisprudence suffers by this confusion of aim.

Hence, though theory is to be welcomed, the growth of theory on the back of definition is not. Theories so grown, indeed, represent valuable efforts to account for many puzzling things in law; and among these is the great anomaly of legal language – our inability to define its crucial words in terms of ordinary factual counterparts. But here I think they largely fail because their method of attack commits them all, in spite of their mutual hostility, to a form of answer that can only distort the distinctive characteristics of legal language.

. . .

III

…

The fundamental point is that the primary function of these words ['right', 'duty' and 'corporation'] is not to stand for or describe anything but a distinct function; this makes it vital to attend to Bentham's warning that we should not, as does the traditional method of definition, abstract words like 'right' and 'duty', 'State', or 'corporation' from the sentences in which alone their full function can be seen, and then demand of them so abstracted their genus and differentia.

Let us see what the use of this traditional method of definition presupposes and what the limits of its efficacy are, and why it may be misleading. It is of course the simplest form of definition, and also a peculiarly satisfying form because it gives us a set of words which can always be substituted for the word defined whenever it is used; it gives us a comprehensible synonym or translation for the word which puzzles us. It is peculiarly appropriate where the words have the straightforward function of standing for some kind of thing, or quality, person, process, or event, for here we are not mystified or puzzled about the general characteristics of our subject-matter, but we ask for a definition simply to locate within this familiar general kind or class some special subordinate kind or class. Thus since we are not puzzled about the general notions of furniture or animals we can take a word like 'chair' or 'cat' and give the principle of its use by first specifying the general class to which what it is used to describe belongs, and then going on to define the specific differences that mark it off from other species of the same general kind. And of course if we are not puzzled about the general notion of a corporate body, but only wish to know how one species (say a college) differs from another (say a limited company), we can use this form of definition of single words perfectly well. But just because the method is appropriate at this level of inquiry, it cannot help us when our perplexities are deeper. For if our question arises, as it does with fundamental legal notions, because we are puzzled about the general category to which something belongs and how some general type of expression relates to fact, and not merely about the place within that category, then until the puzzle is cleared up this form of definition is at the best unilluminating and at the worst profoundly misleading. It is unilluminating because a mode of definition designed to locate some subordinate species within some familiar category cannot elucidate the characteristics of some anomalous category; and it is misleading because it will suggest that what is in fact an anomalous category is after all some species of the familiar. Hence if applied to legal words like 'right', 'duty', 'State', or 'corporation' the common mode of definition suggests that these words, like ordinary words, stand for or describe some thing, person, quality, process, or event; when the difficulty of finding these becomes apparent, different contrivances varying with tastes are used to explain or explain away the anomaly. Some say the difference is that the things for which these legal words stand are real but not sensory; others that they are fictitious entities; others that these words stand for plain fact but of a complex, future, or psychological variety. So this standard mode of definition forces our familiar triad of theories into existence as a confused way of accounting for the anomalous character of legal words.

How then shall we define such words? If definition is the provision of a synonym which will not equally puzzle us, these words cannot be defined. But I think there is a method of elucidation of quite general application and which we can call definition, if we wish.

Bentham and others practised it, though they did not preach it. But before applying it to the highly complex legal cases, I shall illustrate it from the simple case of a game. Take the notion of a trick in a game of cards. Somebody says 'What is a trick?', and you reply 'I will explain: when you have a game and among its rules is one providing that when each of our players has played a card then the player who has put down the highest card scores a point, in these circumstances that player is said to have 'taken a trick'.' This natural explanation has not taken the form of a definition of the single word 'trick': no synonym has been offered for it. Instead we have taken a sentence in which the word 'trick' plays its characteristic role and explained it first by specifying the conditions under which the whole sentence is true, and secondly by showing how it is used in drawing a conclusion from the rules in a particular case. Suppose now that after such an explanation your questioner presses on: 'That is all very well, that explains 'taking a trick'; but I still want to know what the word 'trick' means just by itself. I want a definition of 'trick'; I want something which can be substituted for it whenever it is used.' If we yield to this demand for a single-word definition we might reply: 'The trick is just a collective name for the four cards.' But someone may object: 'The trick is not just a name for the four cards because these four cards will not always constitute a trick. It must therefore be some entity to which the four cards belong.' A third might say: 'No, the trick is a fictitious entity which the players pretend exists and to which by a fiction which is part of the game they ascribe the cards.' But in so simple a case we would not tolerate these theories, fraught as they are with mystery and empty of any guidance as to the use made of the word within the game: we would stand by the original two-fold explanation; for this surely gave us all we needed when it explained the conditions under which the statement 'He has taken a trick' is true and showed us how it was used in drawing a conclusion from the rules in a particular case.

...

VI

If we put aside the question 'What is a corporation?', and ask instead 'Under what types of conditions does the law ascribe liabilities to corporations?', this is likely to clarify the actual working of a legal system and bring out the precise issues at stake when judges, who are supposed not to legislate, make some new extension to corporate bodies of rules worked out for individuals. Take for example the recent extension to corporations of liability for crimes involving knowledge and intention, or some other mental element which are such that a natural person would not be criminally responsible if his servant with the requisite knowledge and intention committed the *actus reus* in the course of his employment. There are two ways, one illuminating and the other misleading, of representing the issues at stake here: two ways, that is, of interpreting the word 'can' in the question 'can a limited company commit a crime involving knowledge and intention?' The illuminating way would be to exhibit the obstacle to such an extension as consisting in the type of analogy that has been followed in fitting corporate bodies into the general structure of our law. It is, of course, predominantly the analogy with the case of an individual held liable for what his servant does in the course of employment. It is by use of this analogy that the liabilities of corporations were extended from contract to ordinary torts and then to torts involving malice; and the whole vocabulary of the law of principal and agent has been adapted to the case of the limited companies. But for crimes of the type under consideration this analogy is useless and the fundamental question is: is this the only analogy available to the courts? Is the law closed on this matter, or are there other criteria for the application to companies of rules originally applied to individuals? In fact judges have felt that they were not restricted in this way, and of course it has often been pointed out that it is possible in English law to find authority for imputing to a company the actions and mental states of those who are substantially carrying on its work. How far this alternative source of analogy can or should be utilized is of course a debatable legal issue, but the important thing is to see that this legal issue, and not some logical issue, is the character of the question. Here then is the force of the word 'can' in 'can a company be liable for a crime involving intention to deceive?' By contrast, the confusing way of stating the issue is to bring in definitions of what a company is and to deduce from them answers to the question in hand. 'A company is a mere abstraction, a fiction, a metaphysical entity.' 'A company has no mind and therefore cannot intend.' These statements confuse the issue because they look like eternal truths about the nature of corporations given us by definitions; so it is made to appear that all legal statements about corporations *must* square with these if they are not to be logically inconsistent. It seems therefore that there is something over and above the analogies which are actually used in the legal system for the application to corporations of rules worked out for individuals, and that this limits or controls that application. And of course a Fiction theory taken seriously can impose irrelevant barriers just as much as a Realist theory: for just as a Realist theory appears to tell us that a company 'cannot' be bound by an agreement empowering another company to direct its business and appoint its personnel because this would be 'to degrade to the position of a tool' a person with a real will, so a Fiction theory appears to say that a company 'cannot' be guilty of certain crimes because it has no mind.

Indeed the *suggestio falsi* in the use of the notion of 'fiction' in the exposition of this branch of the law merits our consideration. Its peculiar vice is to conceal that when words used normally of individuals are applied to companies as well as the analogy involved, there is also involved a radical difference in the mode in which such expressions are now used and so a shift in meaning. Even in the simplest case of all when we say 'X is a servant of Y & Company' the facts which justify the use of the words 'X is a servant' are not *just* the same as the facts which support 'Smith is a servant of Brown'. Hence any ordinary words or phrases when conjoined with the names of corporations take on a special legal use, for the words are now correlated with the facts, not solely by the rules of ordinary English, but also by the rules of English law, much as when we extend words like 'take' or 'lose' by using them of tricks in a game they become correlated with facts by the rules of that game. Now if we talk here of 'fiction' we cannot do justice to this radical difference in use of ordinary expressions when conjoined with the names of corporations; we can only distort it. For when, for example, we say of a company that it resides in England even though its members and servants were killed last night by a bomb, the meaning of these words is to be found only by examining the legal rules which prescribe in what conditions such a statement is correct. But if we talk of 'fiction' we suggest that we are using words in their ordinary sense and are merely pretending that something exists to which they apply. In novels – real fiction – we do preserve the ordinary meanings of words and pretend that there are persons of whom they are true in their ordinary sense. This is just what we do not do when we talk of corporations in law. Yet one of the most curious pieces of logic that ever threatened to obstruct the path of legal development owes, I think, its origin to the confusion of such a shift in meaning with fiction. It was once said that a corporation has no real will but a fictitious will imputed by law, and that since such a will so imputed could effect only lawful ends, we cannot, if we are logically consistent, say that it could commit a crime, or even perhaps a tort. Of course this use of the fiction theory does conjure up an allegorical picture: Law breathing into the nostrils of a Limited Company a Will Fictitious but, like that of its Creator, Good. But the picture is more misleading than even an allegory should be, because it conceals the fact that the word 'will' shifts its meaning when we use it of a company: the sense in which a company has a will is not that it wants to do legal or illegal actions but that certain expressions used to describe the voluntary actions of individuals may be used of it under conditions prescribed by legal rules. And from the bare fact that the law does prescribe such conditions for a wide range of expressions (which is all that imputing a will to a company can mean) it cannot be deduced that these conditions do not include the commission of a criminal or tortious act. Analogy with a living person and shift of meaning are therefore of the essence of the mode of legal statement which refers to corporate bodies. But these are just what they are. Analogy is not identity, so though we can now (as lawyers) say that a company has intended to deceive, this has no theoretical consequences; and shift in meaning is not fiction, so the need for logical consistency with an irrelevant notion of a law-created pure Will need not have been added to the difficulties of judges who, in a case-law system, have to decide how far the analogies latent in the law permit them to extend to corporations rules worked out for individuals when justice seems to demand it.

...

Hart continued to lay foundations for *The Concept of Law* in his article 'Positivism and the Separation of Law and Morals', originally delivered as the Holmes Lecture at Harvard and published in 1958. In this paper, Hart mapped out his agenda as the intellectual successor to the legal positivism of Bentham and Austin. In particular, he defended their brand of analytical jurisprudence against the charges laid by the two groups of legal theorists who were to become his main antagonists in the development of his own theory. First, he rejected the charge, current in much American Realist jurisprudence (see Chapter 7) of the first half of the twentieth century, that legal positivism provides a mechanistic and formalistic vision of legal reasoning, with judges simply grinding out deductive conclusions from closed sets of premises. Secondly, as against the claim of modern natural lawyers, he defended the positivist insistence on the lack of any conceptual connection between law and morality, and he denied that this betrays an indifference to the moral status of laws. In resounding terms, Hart insisted on the propriety of Bentham's distinction between descriptive, 'expository' jurisprudence, and prescriptive, 'censorial' jurisprudence. Indeed, he claimed that there are moral advantages to making a clear separation between our understanding of how to determine what the law is on the one hand, and our criticisms or vision of what it ought to be on the other. Here are some extracts that, following from your reading of Chapter 3 should not prove difficult to follow, and should confirm (before delving into Hart's development of these ideas) your understanding of the opposition between Legal Positivism and Natural Law as developed in jurisprudence. (For the natural lawyer's response, see Fuller 1958.)

Hart 1958, 594–599

... jurisprudence trembles so uncertainly on the margin of many subjects that there will always be a need for someone, in Bentham's phrase, 'to pluck the mask of Mystery' from its face. This is true, to a pre-eminent degree, of the subject of this article. Contemporary voices tell us we must recognize something obscured by the legal 'positivists' whose day is now over: that there is a 'point of intersection between law and morals', or that what *is* and what *ought* to be are somehow indissolubly fused or inseparable, though the positivists denied it. What do these phrases mean? Or rather which of the many things that they could mean, do they mean? Which of them do 'positivists' deny and why is it wrong to do so?

I

I shall present the subject as part of the history of an idea. At the close of the eighteenth century and the beginning of the nineteenth the most earnest thinkers in England about legal and social problems and the architects of great reforms were the great Utilitarians. Two of them, Bentham and Austin, constantly insisted on the need to distinguish, firmly and with the maximum of clarity, law as it is from law as it ought to be. This theme haunts their work, and they condemned the natural law thinkers precisely because they had blurred this apparently simple but vital distinction. By contrast, at the present time in this country and to a lesser extent in England, this separation between law and morals is held to be superficial and wrong. Some critics have thought that it blinds men to the true nature of law and its roots in social life. Others have thought it not only intellectually misleading but corrupting in practice, at its worst apt to weaken resistance to a state of tyranny or absolutism, and at its best apt to bring law into disrespect. The now pejorative name 'Legal Positivism', like most terms which are used as missiles in intellectual battles, has come to stand for a baffling multitude of different sins. One of them is the sin, real or alleged, of insisting, as Austin and Bentham did, on the separation of law as it is and law as it ought to be.

How then has this reversal of the wheel come about? What are the theoretical errors in this distinction? Have the practical consequences of stressing the distinction, as Bentham and Austin did, been bad? Should we now reject it or keep it? In considering these questions we should recall the social philosophy which went along with the Utilitarians' insistence on this distinction. They stood firmly but on their own utilitarian ground for all the principles of liberalism in law and government. No one has ever combined, with such even-minded sanity as the Utilitarians, the passion for reform with respect for law together with due recognition of the need to control the abuse of power even when power is in the hands of reformers. One by one in Bentham's works you can identify the elements of the *Rechtsstaat* and all the principles for the defence of which the terminology of natural law has in our day been received. Here are liberty of speech, and of press, the right of association, the need that laws should be published and made widely known before they are enforced, the need to control administrative agencies, the insistence that there should be no criminal liability without fault, and the importance of the principle of legality, *nulla poena sine lege*. Some, I know, find the political and moral insight of the Utilitarians a very simple one, but we should not mistake this simplicity for superficiality, nor forget how favourably their simplicities compare with the profundities of other thinkers. Take only one example: Bentham on slavery. He says the question at issue is not whether those who are held as slaves can reason, but simply whether they suffer. Does this not compare well with the discussion of the question in terms of whether or not there are some men whom Nature has fitted only to be the living instruments of others? We owe it to Bentham more than anyone else that we have stopped discussing this and similar questions of social policy in that form.

So Bentham and Austin were not dry analysts fiddling with verbal distinctions while cities burned, but were the vanguard of a movement which laboured with passionate intensity and much success to bring about a better society and better laws. Why then did they insist on, the separation of law as it is and law as it ought to be? What did they mean? Let us first see what they said. Austin formulated the doctrine:

> The existence of law is one thing; its merit or demerit is another. Whether it be or be not is one enquiry; whether it be or be not conformable to an assumed standard, is a different enquiry. A law, which actually exists, is a law, though we happen to dislike it, or though it vary from the text, by which we regulate our approbation and disapprobation. This truth, when formally announced as an abstract proposition, is so simple and glaring that it seems idle to insist upon it. But simple and glaring as it is, when enunciated in abstract expressions the enumeration of the instances in which it has been forgotten would fill a volume.

> Sir William Blackstone, for example, says in his 'Commentaries', that the laws of God are superior in obligation to all other laws; that no human laws should be suffered to contradict them; that human laws are of no validity if contrary to them; and that all valid laws derive their force from that Divine original.

> Now, he *may* mean that all human laws ought to conform to the Divine laws. If this be his meaning, I assent to it without hesitation ... Perhaps, again, he means that human lawgivers are themselves obliged by the Divine laws to fashion the laws which they impose by that ultimate standard, because if they do not, God will punish them. To this also I entirely assent ...

> But the meaning of this passage of Blackstone, if it has a meaning, seems rather to be this: that no human law which conflicts with the Divine law is obligatory or binding; in other words, that no human law which conflicts with the Divine law *is a law* ...

Austin's protest against blurring the distinction between what law is and what it ought to be is quite general: it is a mistake, whatever our standard of what ought to be, whatever 'the text by which we regulate our approbation or disapprobation'. His examples, however, are always a confusion between law as it is and law as morality would require it to be. For him, it must be remembered, the fundamental principles of morality were God's commands, to which utility was an 'index': besides this there was the actual accepted morality of a social group or 'positive' morality.

Bentham insisted on this distinction without characterizing morality by reference to God but only, of course, by reference to the principles of utility. Both thinkers' prime reason for this insistence was to enable men to see steadily the precise issues posed by the existence of morally bad laws, and to understand the specific character of the authority of a legal order. Bentham's general recipe for life under the government of laws was simple: it was *'to obey punctually; to censure freely'*. But Bentham was especially aware, as an anxious spectator of the French revolution, that this was not enough: the time might come in any society when the law's commands were so evil that the question of resistance had to be faced, and it was then essential that the issues at stake at this point should neither be oversimplified nor obscured. Yet this was precisely what the confusion between law and morals had done, and Bentham found that the confusion had spread symmetrically in two different directions. On the one hand Bentham had in mind the anarchist who argues thus: 'This ought not to be the law, therefore it is not and I am free not merely to censure but to disregard it.' On the other hand he thought of the reactionary who argues: 'This is the law, therefore it is what it ought to be', and thus stifles criticism at its birth. Both errors, Bentham thought, were to be found in Blackstone: there was his incautious statement that human laws were invalid if contrary to the law of God, and 'that spirit of obsequious quietism that seems constitutional in our Author' which 'will scarce ever let him recognise a difference' between what is and what ought to be. This indeed was for Bentham the occupational disease of lawyers: '[I]n the eyes of lawyers – not to speak of their dupes – that is to say, as yet, the generality of non-lawyers – the *is* and the *ought to be* ... were one and indivisible.' There are therefore two dangers between which insistence on this distinction will help us to steer: the danger that law and its authority may be dissolved in man's conceptions of what law ought to be and the danger that the existing law may supplant morality as a final test of conduct and so escape criticism.

In view of later criticisms it is also important to distinguish several things that the Utilitarians did not mean by insisting on their separation of law and morals. They certainly accepted many of the things that might be called 'the intersection of law and morals'. First, they never denied that, as a matter of historical fact, the development of legal systems had been powerfully influenced by moral opinion, and, conversely, that moral standards had been profoundly influenced by law, so that the content of many legal rules mirrored moral rules or principles. It is not in fact always easy to trace this historical causal connection, but Bentham was certainly ready to admit its existence; so too Austin spoke of the 'frequent coincidence' of positive law and morality and attributed the confusion of what law is with what law ought to be to this very fact.

Secondly, neither Bentham nor his followers denied that by explicit legal provisions moral principles might at different points be brought into a legal system and form part of its rules, or that courts might be legally bound to decide in accordance with what they thought just or best. Bentham indeed recognized, as Austin did not, that even the supreme legislative power might be subjected to legal restraints by a constitution and would not have denied that moral principles, like those of the Fifth Amendment, might form the content of such legal constitutional restraints. Austin differed in thinking that restraints on the supreme legislative power could not have the force of law, but would remain merely political or moral checks; but of course he would have recognized that a statute, for example, might confer a delegated legislative power and restrict the area of its exercise by reference to moral principles.

What both Bentham and Austin were anxious to assert were the following two simple things: first, in the absence of an expressed constitutional or legal provision, it could not follow from the mere fact that a rule violated standards of morality that it was not a rule of law; and, conversely, it could not follow from the mere fact that a rule was morally desirable that it was a rule of law.

Hart's work can usefully be divided into three main groups, roughly corresponding to three periods of time. First, there is a body of work, notably including *The Concept of Law* and his book on *Causation in the Law* written with Tony Honoré, which applies the insights of linguistic philosophy to law and which develops a distinctive brand of analytical jurisprudence. However, as Hart himself observed in the introduction to his *Essays in Jurisprudence and Philosophy*, published in 1983, linguistic philosophy has limits as well as strengths as a framework for the analysis of jurisprudential questions. By the early 1960s, Hart was feeling these constraints and was feeling the need to branch out – with the self-confidence and public platform which the Oxford Chair had given him, and perhaps under the influence of the more politically engaged atmosphere of the United States' law schools which he visited in the late 1950s and early 1960s, where constitutional analysis took lawyers to the heart of policy debates – from a rigorous descriptive to a more critical and prescriptive genre of work. From this development there emerges, secondly, a body of work that combines the techniques of analytical philosophy with those of liberal political theory. In this period, Hart's work engages with the normative structure of particular areas of law – notably, in *Punishment and Responsibility*, criminal law – and with the moral and political framework which ought to inform the use of law as a tool of social regulation – in *Law, Liberty and Morality*, and in *The Morality of the Criminal Law*. These two bodies of work, mainly published during the 1960s, represent Hart's main original contribution to scholarship: this chapter deals with the first, while part of the second is examined in Chapter 12 and, to a lesser extent, in Chapter 15.

After his retirement from the Chair of Jurisprudence in 1968, Hart devoted himself to the analysis, critique and editing of the works of Jeremy Bentham, and his *Essays on Bentham* constitute the single most important part of a third identifiable body of work engaging with his intellectual ancestors and successors. Bentham was a figure for whom Hart had profound intellectual admiration, and whom he believed to have anticipated philosophical ideas not further developed until the early twentieth century, and still being developed today (see Hart 1973). Bentham – a curious eccentric with a mania for clarity, demystification, classification and rational argument, whose work was never fully appreciated in England in his lifetime and who felt himself to be something of an outsider – also undoubtedly held a personal fascination for Hart. Towards the end of Hart's writing career, Bentham's work provided a framework within which Hart could subtly develop some of the main themes from his own earlier work without either explicitly replying to his critics or writing a further self-standing monograph. However, Bentham was not the only object of this dialogic mode of scholarship which dominated Hart's work between his retirement and his death in 1992; others included Robert Nozick, John Rawls, Joseph Raz and, most importantly, his successor to the Oxford Chair, Ronald Dworkin. (See, for his critique of Dworkin and Raz, Hart 1982b, 147–161.) A further engagement with Dworkin was published, posthumously, in 1994 as a Postscript to the second edition of *The Concept of Law*.

1953–61: Law in the perspective of philosophy

This body of work, which forms the focus of this chapter, is dominated by two books: *Causation in the Law*, written with Tony Honoré and published in 1959, and *The*

Concept of Law, based on Hart's Oxford lectures, published in 1961. (Page references to *The Concept of Law* here will be to the 1994 edition. Although the text of the 1961 edition is unaltered, the pagination has been changed.)

Causation in the Law is a monumental analysis of the idea of causation in criminal law, the law of torts and the law of contract (for a brief statement of the project of this book and the use of linguistic philosophy in it, see pages 1–7). When A shoots B who later dies after having received negligent medical treatment from C, has A, or C, or have both, caused B's death? If E and F simultaneously aim and fire a potentially fatal shot at G, who later dies of her injuries, do both of them cause G's death? Or is neither of them the cause, given that G would have died even without either one's action? When a fire destroys a house, why do we tend to describe the causation in terms of the person who lit a match and poured petrol through the letter-box rather than focussing equally on the presence of inflammable material in the house, the presence of oxygen in the air and so on?

The book's argument is constructed in opposition to an influential school of thought which Hart and Honoré call 'causal minimalism'. Causal minimalism claims that there is no sui generis concept of causation deployed in law beyond the 'factual' idea of causation as a sine qua non – ie as all the conditions but for which an event would not have happened or a consequence would not have occurred. Beyond this 'but for' sense of causation, the minimalist claims, decisions about how to attribute causal liability are based on policy considerations such as efficiency or moral considerations such as fault. For example, we would treat both E and F as causes because both are equally at fault; we would treat A rather than C as the cause of B's death, unless C's negligence had been especially gross, because we don't want to discourage medics from intervening in emergencies.

As against this, Hart and Honoré insist that law does operate with a distinctive notion of causation richer than that of 'but for' causation. They argue, however, that most philosophical analyses of causation are inapposite to explain the legal uses of the term, because they focus on causation in the context of science, and hence seek to identify general laws of causation. No such invariant, general laws, however, can govern the identification of causes in the essentially particularistic legal context. In law, causation is a complex and many-faceted notion: it has to be traced not to one overarching principle but to many principles and sub-principles clustering around the centrally recognised bases for attributing causation. According to Hart and Honoré, voluntary human action is the centrally significant variable in the attribution of legal causal responsibility. The central case is that of action intentionally aimed towards a particular end which it produces, or done with foresight that that end will occur; secondary but important cases are those in which a person provides an opportunity for a result to be created (for example, leaving a house unlocked with the result that a burglary occurs) and in which a person incites or assists another person to produce a certain effect (for example, persuading or helping another person to kill a third person). Where, however, another voluntary human act intervenes between one human action and a consequence – particularly if that second act is 'abnormal' or unexpected; or where another abnormal event such as an 'act of God' like a storm or earthquake intervenes, the law will generally regard the causal chain as being 'broken'.

At the level of method, *Causation in the Law* represents a thoroughgoing application of the linguistic philosophical analysis to the law. For Hart and Honoré's approach is to seek to unearth the principles underlying judges' use of causal language – itself often metaphorical, as in the familiar idea of a 'chain of causation' being 'broken' – and moreover to explore the relationship between this judicial usage and more general, common sense understandings of causation embedded in linguistic usage in particular contexts. Hence they analyse hundreds of cases, drawing out common approaches to elicit general principles. *Causation in the Law* presents a spirited defence of the idea that causation in law is indeed a distinctive ground for the attribution of liability, and a persuasive critique of the causal minimalist position as collapsing questions of the ground of liability (causation) into questions about its scope or extent (policy factors affecting the extent of damages or the scope of the rule), and, in doing so, as blurring the proper division of labour between judge and jury, between law and fact. It is, however, a challenging book to read, because the method of eliciting general principles from hundreds of cases sometimes makes it difficult to see the wood for the trees. Nonetheless, the book had a deep impact in legal scholarship and was widely read and cited by judges both in the United Kingdom and beyond: a second, expanded edition was prepared (mainly by Honoré) and published in 1985.

Although *Causation in the Law* contains the most detailed use of linguistic philosophy by Hart, his worldwide reputation as the foremost analytic philosopher writing in English in the twentieth century rests primarily on *The Concept of Law*. (No extended extracts from *The Concept of Law* can be included in this Reader because of a general bar on its partial reproduction. For that reason, this introduction gives a relatively full outline of its main arguments.) To understand why this work had such an extraordinary impact, one needs to locate the book within the history of English legal philosophy canvassed in Chapter 3. As we have seen, from the late eighteenth to the mid-nineteenth centuries, the utilitarian philosophers Jeremy Bentham and John Austin had developed an influential version of legal positivism. Rejecting the older idea that law derives its authority from God, or from some metaphysical conception of nature or reason – so-called 'natural law' – Bentham and Austin argued that law is essentially man-made: it is a command issued by a political superior or sovereign, to whom the populace is in a habit of obedience.

This promising start to the development of a conception of law appropriate to modern, secular democracies, although influential and applied in much legal writing, had not as a theory been much developed since Austin's death. Reasons include Austin's and Bentham's rather uninviting literary styles; the fact that much of Bentham's work had never been published; the relatively unintellectual nature of English legal education, which only found a secure place in university departments well into the twentieth century (and which remained steadfastly vocational for a yet longer period); and the slow reception in the English-speaking world of the brilliant Austrian jurist Hans Kelsen's work (see Chapter 5), which developed a positivist 'pure' theory of law within a very different, continental philosophical tradition. In the decades preceding Hart's election to the Oxford Chair, such jurisprudence and legal philosophy as was taught in Britain tended to consist in a rather dry offshoot of technical legal analysis: writers dissected, minutely, legal concepts such as ownership, possession, or the corporation. There was no attempt either to link this analysis to any broader idea of the nature of law, or to consider how technical legal concepts assisted law to serve its various social functions. Prescriptive questions about what purposes law *ought* to pursue were left to the attention of moral and political philosophy – the latter itself a field that was relatively stagnant at this time.

Hart's approach to legal philosophy was at once disarmingly simple and breathtakingly ambitious. This first single-authored book, *The Concept of Law*, which stands as his most important work, claimed to provide – in the space of a mere 250 pages – a general, descriptive theory of law which was at once a contribution to 'analytical jurisprudence' and to 'descriptive sociology'. In other words, Hart sought to elucidate a concept of law that would be of relevance to all forms of law, wherever or whenever they arose. In pursuing this project, Hart returned to the insights of Austin and Bentham, but – in a crucial philosophical innovation – combined their methods with those of the new linguistic philosophy represented by the work of Gilbert Ryle, J L Austin and Ludwig Wittgenstein.

The nub of Hart's theory is the startlingly simple idea that law is a system of rules structurally similar to the rules of games such as chess or cricket. The rules themselves are of different kinds, with complementary functions. Some – 'primary rules' – directly govern behaviour; others – 'secondary rules' – provide for the identification, interpretation and alteration of the former. The most obvious example of primary rules would be criminal laws; examples of secondary rules range from constitutional laws to laws governing the creation of contracts, marriages or wills.

> ... of all the varieties of law, a criminal statute, forbidding or enjoining certain actions under penalty, most resembles orders backed by threats given by one person to others ... there are other varieties of law, notably those conferring legal powers to adjudicate or legislate (public powers) or to create or vary legal relations (private powers) which cannot, without absurdity, be construed as orders backed by threats. (CL 79)

Like his nineteenth century counterparts, Hart insisted that law was a social, human invention: though legal rules generate genuine obligations, they are not straightforwardly moral rules. Their authority derives not from their content but from their source, which lies in a distinctively institutionalised system of social recognition. For example, the rule that we should drive on the left is authoritative not because there is any intrinsic value to driving on the left. Rather, it is because the rule can be identified in accordance with an agreed set of criteria for recognition, such as parliamentary enactment or judicial precedent. Precisely the same is true, moreover, of legal rules that overlap with moral standards: the legal prohibition on murder is not the same as, and derives its validity in a different way from, the moral injunction against killing. Though law is certainly characterised by some distinctive values – such as the principle of formal justice, or treating like cases alike; and though all legal systems, because they are geared to the survival of a social group, will contain a 'minimum content of natural law' in the form of rules governing physical integrity, property, honesty and so on, neither of these grains of truth in the natural law tradition entails that valid laws are necessarily morally good. (See D'Entreves analysis of this aspect of Hart's theory in the final extract of Chapter 2.)

Hart's account of how legal rules are recognised as valid, and hence as generating 'real' obligations served, on the other hand, to distinguish law from a mere system of force, or 'orders backed by threats'. For, crucially, according to Hart, legal rules have not only an external but also an internal aspect: we know that a rule is in existence not only because it is regularly observed, but also because those subject to it use it as a reason or standard for behaviour, criticising themselves and/or others for breaches of the rules.

> This internal aspect of rules may be simply illustrated from the rules of any game. Chess players do not merely have similar habits of moving the Queen in the same way which an external observer, who knew nothing about their attitude to the moves which they make, could record. In addition they have a reflective critical attitude to this pattern of behaviour: they regard it as a standard for all who play the game. Each not only moves the Queen in a certain way himself but 'has views' about the propriety of all moving the Queen in that way. These views are manifested in the criticism of others and demands for conformity made upon others when deviation is actual or threatened, and in the acknowledgement of the legitimacy of such criticism and demands when received from others. For the expression of such criticisms, demands, and acknowledgements a wide range of 'normative' language is used. 'I (You) ought not to have moved the Queen like that', 'I (You) must do that', 'That is right', 'That is wrong'. (CL 56–57)

It is in this aspect of Hart's theory that linguistic philosophy becomes so important, for he builds up his argument by paying close attention to linguistic practices: quoting J L Austin, he seeks to use 'a sharpened awareness of words to sharpen our perception of the phenomena'. For example, he explores the distinction between habitual behaviour (going to the pub on Sunday lunch time) and rule-governed behaviour (within religious systems, avoiding work or attending worship on certain days and at certain times); between being obliged to do something (handing over money because someone threatens to kill you if you don't) and having an obligation to do it (paying your taxes).

By moving from the early 'positivist' notion of law as a sovereign command to the notion of law as a system of rules, Hart produced a theory which fitted far better the impersonal idea of authority embedded in modern democracies: his theory of law encapsulated the idea of 'the rule of law and not of men'. As such, it provided a powerful and remarkably widely applicable rationalisation of the nature of legal authority in a secular and pluralistic world. It offered not only a descriptive account of law's social power but also an account of legal validity which purported to explain the (limited) sense in which citizens have an obligation to obey the law. (How far such an account can take us is explored in Chapter 11.)

The Concept of Law has been translated into many languages and remains, forty years after its publication, the main point of reference in Britain for teaching analytical jurisprudence and, along with Kelsen's *Pure Theory of Law*, the starting point for jurisprudential research in the analytic tradition. Hart later modified some of its arguments (notably in the *Essays on Bentham*, in which he refined his concept of legal obligation and authority in terms of the existence of content-independent peremptory reasons). However, as the Postscript to the second edition shows, he stood firmly by both its overall approach and its main substantive claims. *The Concept of Law* has been widely read by senior judges and has had a distinctive impact on the development of judicial culture in Britain and beyond. It has also, of course, been subject to intense scrutiny and lively criticism. The most significant criticism has come from two very different directions. First, from the direction of the social sciences, it has been argued that although the techniques of analytic philosophy may establish that law is simply one form of social rule, the further question of just what is distinctive about legal as opposed to other social rules can only be understood in terms of historical and social facts in which Hart shows little interest. Furthermore, Hart's approach may be seen, from a social science point of view, as naive in failing to consider the relevance of power relations, of conflicts of interest or value that cannot be resolved by rational debate, and of the symbolic dimensions of law's authority. (The third extract from Fitzpatrick at the end of this chapter presents one version of this argument.) Secondly, from the direction of modern versions of 'natural law' theory, it has been argued that, ultimately, the reason why those subject to legal rules adopt an 'internal attitude' to them has to do with moral factors, and that consequently Hart's restricted sense of 'legal obligation', and with it his distinction between law and morality, collapses. (This is an important theme of Dworkin's critique of Hart, which is dealt with in Chapters 8 and 9. See particularly Dworkin 1986, 29–30 and 32–44 where he sets out why brands of positivist theories, which he designates as semantic theories, should be 'confronted'. A natural law critique of Hart and other positivists is set out in Finnis 1980, 6–18. You also have the opportunity to read some of Finnis' arguments in extracts in Chapter 2.)

Principal themes in *The Concept of Law*

Six main themes emerge from *The Concept of Law* (for reference purposes designated as CL, with page references to the 1994 edition). It will be useful to examine them in a little more detail.

1. Hart's method

Hart's book claims to be an exercise in both analytical jurisprudence and descriptive sociology; it also claims to present not 'a' concept of law but *the* concept of law. Each of these claims is highly significant. Hart set out to produce a descriptive, positivist legal theory: his approach is empiricist in the (restricted) sense that it seeks to respond directly and descriptively to features of the world. But the dominant methods are those not of the social sciences but of analytic philosophy, and the book has elements of what Cotterrell (1989, 85–87) has labelled 'conceptualism'. This involves explicating law as a system in terms of a number of concepts that are elaborated and refined and then in a sense imposed on the world, which is then interpreted in their terms. Hart seeks to answer the question 'what is law' – ie he purports to provide a general theory of law, rather than of laws: and he does so within a very particular theoretical tradition. This is revealed (as is often the case) by his criticisms of another jurist – Austin – whom he chooses to demolish as a prelude to the construction of his own theory. And, although many of his criticisms of Austin concern their descriptive inaccuracy, others are conceptual.

'... the elements out of which the theory [Austin's] was constructed, viz. the ideas of orders, obedience, habits and threats, do not include, and cannot by their combination yield, the idea of a rule, without which we cannot hope to elucidate even the most elementary forms of law.' (CL 80)

2.   Definition and theory: the central case technique

A further very important point to note about Hart is his deployment of what he calls the 'central case technique', along with a distinction between core, paradigm examples of a phenomenon and penumbral, non-central examples. Hart's book opens by observing that the question of a 'definition' of law is peculiar among the disciplines: no one asks, for example, what is chemistry or physics or maths. He also observes that, at least to lawyers, and perhaps to citizens, the question is peculiarly difficult to answer: it is like the old joke about the elephant – I can't define it, but I know one when I see it. He then points out that conventional modes of definition do not work well with law, and he suggests – most clearly in his inaugural lecture – that the clue to understanding law is, first, to see that legal concepts have to be understood in the context of the sentences and legal doctrines in which they arise – eg the idea of a corporation: and, second, that it is impossible to 'define' law in terms of a finite number of features of which, if any is missing, the phenomenon fails to qualify. This is one of the bases on which he rejects Austin's inflexible model of law as commands backed up by sanctions, with its view of international law as merely 'positive morality'. From Hart's point of view, the idea was not so much to define as to theorise law in terms of a number of core features – primary and secondary rules, internal and external aspects – and then to allow phenomena such as customary law or international law or judicial discretion to count as penumbral, non-central cases, rather than banishing them to another discipline.

> At various points in this book the reader will find discussions of the borderline cases where legal theorists have felt doubts about the application of the expression 'law' or 'legal system', but the suggested resolution of these doubts ... is only a secondary concern of the book. For its purpose is not to provide a definition of law, in the sense of a rule by reference to which the correctness of the use of the word can be tested; it is to advance legal theory by providing an improved analysis of the distinctive structure of a municipal legal system ... treated as the central elements in the concept of law and of prime importance in its elucidation. (CL 17)

(To help you think about this method, you might ask yourselves 'how does Hart's idea of the core meaning of law differ from the natural lawyer, Finnis' focal meaning, as set out in Chapter 2?')

3.   Hart's critique of Austin

The early chapters (2–4) of Hart's book progressively take apart Austin's imperative theory of law. They identify inadequacies both with the account of sovereignty and with the notion of laws as orders backed by threats. The method, in effect, is to construct his own theory out of the ashes of Austin's. It is therefore worth looking at his critique of Austin in some detail. (Remember that, in defence of Austin, Cotterrell has argued that some of these criticisms rely on an overly simplistic view of Austin's theory – see the extract from Cotterrell at the end of Chapter 3).

the problem of sovereignty

Hart argues that the theory of legal authority implicit in Austin's account of sovereignty is unrealistic, because legal authority has to be defined in terms of normative ideas and not merely persistent habits. He argues that it is nonsensical to regard sovereignty as necessarily illimitable and indivisible. And he points to the legal realities of federal systems, bicameral legislatures and entrenched bills of rights so as to represent Austin's theory of sovereignty as an unrealistic conceptual framework into which he shoves real legal phenomena. Closely related to this critique of sovereignty is his critique of Austin's failure to account for

the scope and persistence of laws

Austin is unable to explain the continuity of legal authority: how do we know when and where a new sovereign emerges when an existing one dies or is destroyed? Does his theory imply total discontinuity every time there is an election? How does the populace know that its habit of obedience should be shifted to one group rather than another? Moreover Austin cannot account for the persistence of laws set by one sovereign beyond the life of that sovereign. Why do laws enacted hundreds of years ago survive today, given successive changes in the identity of the sovereign? This is particularly problematic in the case of incomplete revolutions: eg in the new South Africa, certain laws – eg commercial and property laws – remained intact, notwithstanding a new political regime. And finally – returning to Austin's ideas of the sovereign as illimitable – how does he account for constitutional law – ie for laws that bind the sovereign himself?

> ... for the conception of the legally unlimited sovereign misrepresents the character of law in many modern states where no one would question that there is law. (CL 68)

the variety of laws

Hart argues that Austin's theory cannot explain the variety of different types of laws encompassed within a legal system – eg contract or family laws. Austin (and, in a different way, Kelsen) had argued that such laws can be accommodated within the concept of commands backed up by sanctions through the idea of nullity of contract as a form of sanction or the idea of property laws as fragments of laws. Hart rejected this first defence on conceptual grounds; the idea that all laws have to conform to the straitjacket of orders backed by threats is a conceptual distortion – eg criminal laws can be understood independently of sanction, whereas nullity is part of the concept of contract. The second defence (that all non-coercive laws are merely expository matter (see Bentham extract in Chapter 3)) fails to recognise the different social functions of different rules: power-conferring or facility-creating rules such as those of contract, property, wills or marriage serve different social functions from criminal law, creating facilities for citizens rather than aiming merely to impose duties or prevent certain kinds of behaviour.

> Rules conferring private powers must, if they are to be understood, be looked at from the point of view of those who exercise them. They appear then as an additional element introduced by the law into social life over and above that of coercive control. This is so because possession of these legal powers makes of the private citizen, who, if there were no rules, would be a mere duty-bearer, a private legislator. He is made competent to determine the course of the law within the sphere of his contracts, trusts, wills, and other structures of rights and duties which he is enabled to build. Why are rules which are used in this special way, and confer this huge and distinctive amenity, not be recognized as distinct from rules which impose duties, the incidence of which is indeed in part determined by the exercise of such powers? Such power-conferring rules are thought of, spoken of, and used in social life differently from rules which impose duties, and they are valued for different reasons. (CL 41)

law and coercion

Moreover Hart argues that even in the case of criminal laws, which most easily fit the notion of command, Austin overplays the notion of sanction in a way which obscures the distinction between predictive and normative statements about law. Austin's approach cannot distinguish between the idea of being obliged, in the sense of having to do something 'or else', and that of having an obligation – there being a standard which one recognises ought to be followed, independently of any expectations of bad consequences such as punishment for breach.

> The fundamental objection is that predictive interpretation obscures the fact that, where rules exist, deviations from them are not merely grounds for a prediction that hostile reactions will follow or that a court will apply sanctions to those who break them, but are also a reason or justification for such reaction and for applying the sanctions. (CL 84)

This brings us to the habit of obedience, which Hart criticises as a predictive rather than a normative, explanatory approach. On his view, we do not obey laws merely because of a habit of obedience to authority or merely because we are frightened of being punished, rather, we use laws themselves as reasons for action. Hart therefore sees a crucial distinction between a habit and a rule: dressing or behaving in certain ways in places of worship is, for many, an entirely different kind of social regularity from people taking their shoes off when they get home at night.

4.   Law as a system of rules

Out of this critique, Hart begins to identify (especially in Chapters 5 and 6 of *The Concept of Law*) the features that his own theory elaborates as those central to an explication of the nature of law. These include the idea of a rule, with its internal and external aspects; the differentiation among different kinds of rules; the depersonification of legal authority; the decentring of the notion of sanction.

internal and external aspects of rules

Pivotal to Hart's understanding of the nature of social rules is their internal aspect. While the external aspect of rule-governed behaviour consists in observable regularities of behaviour such as removal of hats, or stopping at red traffic lights, the internal aspect consists in adopting the rule as a standard for, guide to or – in Hart's later formulation – reason for action. This internal aspect therefore consists in a 'critical reflective attitude' which cannot merely be observed from outside: it is manifested in the account which people give of their own behaviour, and in their reactions to, and criticisms of, the actions of others. The crucial point about this internal aspect of rules is that it means that the notion of a rule can make sense without that of a regularly following sanction. One may adopt an internal attitude for a variety of reasons – prudential, conventional or moral.

> The internal aspect of rules is often misrepresented as a mere matter of 'feelings' in contrast to externally observable physical behaviour. No doubt, where rules are generally accepted by a social group and generally supported by social criticism and pressure for conformity, individuals may often have psychological experiences analogous to those of restriction or compulsion. But such feelings are neither necessary nor sufficient for the existence of 'binding' rules. There is no contradiction in saying that people accept certain rules but experience no such feelings of compulsion. (CL 57)

The internal aspect has been described by MacCormick as the 'hermeneutic' aspect of Hart's theory – ie his theory gives a theoretical centrality to the attitudes and interpretations of agents who are law's subjects. (See extract 1 at the end of this chapter. In this extract, MacCormick gives a clear account of the meaning and importance of an individual's attitude to rules, in understanding what law is.) In a sophisticated analysis of the internal aspect, MacCormick summarizes its importance in the following terms: 'There is a genuine distinction as drawn by Hart between "external" and "internal" points of view with reference to human activity. But the "internal" point of view as characterized by Hart contains essentially distinguishable components, which ought to be distinguished. There is a "cognitively internal" point of view, from which conduct is appreciated and understood in terms of the standards which are being used by the agent as guiding standards: that is sufficient for an understanding of norms and the normative. But it is parasitic on – because it presupposes – the "volitionally internal" point of view: the point of view of an agent, who in some degree and for reasons which seem good to him has a volitional commitment to observance of a given pattern of conduct as a standard for himself or for other people or for both: his attitude includes, but is not included by, the "cognitively internal" attitude.' (MacCormick 1978, 284–292 at 292)

To make sense of this, when reading MacCormick's analysis in extract 1 (towards the end of this chapter), you might like to keep in mind the following two questions.

1.   If you studied French civil law, would you have an internal or an external attitude to it?

2.   Do criminals who calculate the likelihood of suffering sanctions before committing their crimes have an external or an internal attitude to legal rules?

the union of primary and secondary rules as 'the key to the science of jurisprudence'

Hart insists that legal rules come in two irreducibly different forms. There are, in fact, two relevant distinctions buried in his differentiation of primary and secondary rules. First, Hart distinguishes between power-conferring rules such as rules about the formation of contracts, and duty-imposing rules such as criminal laws. This is a normative or conceptual distinction, and it is illustrated by the different structural role of sanction in contract and crime: while the content of a criminal law can be readily described without reference to its sanction, it is impossible to describe the law of contract without reference to the concept of validity (and hence, implicitly, to that of nullity). Second, Hart distinguishes between rules which directly govern behaviour, and rules about the creation, identification and interpretation of other rules. This is basically a functional distinction about the roles played by different sets of rules within a legal order. It is not co-terminous with the normative distinction elaborated above, although unfortunately Hart himself did not make the difference clear and often wrote as if the conceptual distinction mapped directly onto the crude functional distinction. (See the critical analysis by Raz in extract 2 at the end of this chapter.)

In terms of this second, functional distinction, Hart describes the 'public secondary rules' as emerging to 'cure the defects' of a system of primary rules; until their formation, such a system is static, uncertain, inefficient. Sometimes he speaks of their emergence as marking the transition from law to a legal system; sometimes from pre-law to law.

> The remedy for each of these three main defects in this simplest form of social structure consists in supplementing the *primary* rules of obligation with *secondary* rules which are rules of a different kind. The introduction of the remedy for each defect might, in itself, be considered a step from the pre-legal world into the legal world; since each remedy brings with it many elements that permeate law: certainly all three remedies together are enough to convert the regime of primary rules into what is indisputably a legal system. (CL 94)

In other words, for Hart, the 'central case' of law is a system which consists of interlocking primary and secondary rules. The 'public secondary rules' are rules of recognition (identifying other rules as valid and unifying and identifying the system); rules of adjudication (rules about the interpretation and application of rules); rules of change (rules about the creation of new rules and extinction of old ones). You could think of these public secondary rules as types or branches of constitutional law. Of particular importance is the rule of recognition in unifying, identifying and validating laws: what distinguishes legal from other social rules is their source, which in turn lies in their validation through a 'master-rule' or practice of recognition shared by the officials of the system.

> The rule of recognition providing the criteria by which the validity of other rules of the system is assessed is in an important sense ... an *ultimate* rule: and where, as is usual,

there are several criteria ranked in order of relative subordination and primacy one of them is *supreme.* (CL 105)

The rule of recognition, however is not itself a valid rule of the system; since there is no further rule in terms of which it can be validated, we must see it as merely a complex social fact about official attitudes and practices.

For whereas a subordinate rule of a system may be valid and in that sense 'exist' even if it is generally disregarded, the rule of recognition exists only as a complex, but normally concordant, practice of the courts, officials, and private persons in identifying the law by reference to certain criteria. Its existence is a matter of fact. (CL 110)

5. Hart's gesture towards natural law

While Hart's positivism is undoubtedly the hallmark of his approach, he does make certain gestures towards what he sees as the 'core of truth' in the natural law tradition. First, positive law deploys a distinctive concept of justice, consisting in principles such as equality before the law and treating like cases alike. Moreover, in an argument strongly reminiscent of the eighteenth century philosopher Thomas Hobbes, Hart argues that so long as law is oriented to the survival of human societies, all positive legal systems will contain a 'minimum content of natural law': given certain contingent but persistent facts about the nature of human beings and their world – our approximate equality, physical vulnerability and limited altruism, for example – any legal system will have to contain laws governing, for example, the protection of physical integrity and a regime of property entitlements. This appears to be a very weak concession to natural law, given that – as the history of human societies shows all too clearly – unfair or even brutal regimes of rules may serve the purpose of social survival perfectly well. (But, on whether this is such a weak concession, see D'Entrèves' critique of this element of Hart's analysis set out as the final extract of Chapter 2.)

A further, weak concession to natural law can be discerned in Hart's theory of adjudication – a concession which has been seized upon by natural lawyers such as Fuller to suggest that Hart cannot sustain the absolute separation between law and morality which he asserts. For Hart, it is inevitable that in some cases positive law 'runs out' in the sense either that there is a gap in the law or that there is uncertainty about how legal rules should be interpreted. In such cases, he asserts that judges must be guided by their conception of 'what the law ought to be'. This discretion, he claims, may be morally based; but this doesn't mean law collapses into morality: in the vast majority of cases, rules of positive law guide human or judicial conduct with relative determinacy. As against legal realists, conversely, Hart denies that the existence of gaps or uncertainties reduces law to a game of scorers' discretion in which the law is simply whatever the judge decides it to be: rules do genuinely constrain and set standards.

Here, at the fringe of these very fundamental things, we should welcome the rule-sceptic, as long as he does not forget that it is at the fringe that he is welcome; and does not blind us to the fact that what makes these striking developments by courts of the most fundamental rules is, in great measure, the prestige gathered by the courts from their unquestionably rule-governed operations over the vast, central areas of the law. (CL 154)

6. Officials and citizens in Hart's theory

Returning to the internal aspect of rules and the importance of the rule of recognition, we can see that the relative focus on the roles of officials and citizens raises some key questions about Hart's theory. On the one hand, Hart's is a very citizen-oriented theory – its interpretive focus is on the active citizen with the internal, critical reflective attitude. On the other hand, when Hart comes to speak of the conditions of existence of a legal system, he makes it clear that only the officials need have an internal attitude towards the system's rules.

There are therefore two minimum conditions necessary and sufficient for the existence of a legal system. On the one hand those rules of behaviour which are valid according to the system's ultimate criteria of validity must be generally obeyed, and, on the other hand, its rules of recognition specifying the criteria of legal validity and its rules of change and adjudication must be effectively accepted as common standards of official behaviour by its officials. (CL 116)

This entails that law can be a system of imposed authority as much as a democratic system – and this makes Hart's positivism a very broadly encompassing theory. The internal aspect allows him to tread a fine line between natural law and sanction-based positivism – a line whose integrity many critics have questioned, for example by pointing out that the criticism evoked by Hart's 'critical reflective attitude' might itself be regarded as a kind of sanction – albeit of a broader form than that envisaged by Austin.

Critical questions about *The Concept of Law*

In the vast critical literature which has grown up around *The Concept of Law*, a number of general issues recur:

the force of appeals to linguistic usage

Whose usage is being appealed to in the distinction between being obliged and having an obligation, following a rule and being in a habit? Is Hart's theory really tracking usage or imposing a certain usage onto the world in order to produce a coherent theory?

empiricism and conceptualism

There seems to be a general tension between empiricist and conceptualist approaches in Hart's theory, reflected in his dual – but uneasy – commitment to be doing both descriptive sociology and analytical jurisprudence. Where does the balance really lie? Is there any real sociology here, as a sociologist would understand it? Certainly, Hart's theory is less of a conceptual straitjacket into which the legal world is forced than is Austin's. But is it a difference of quality or only of degree?

The difference between conceptual and empirical approaches to legal theory is explained in the following extract from Cotterrell (1989, 85–86).

Cotterrell (1989, 85–86)

EMPIRICISM AND CONCEPTUALISM

... Quite apart from any particular merits or demerits Austin's jurisprudence has in clarifying the nature of modern Western law, it has apparently left a deep ambiguity at its core; one which continues to puzzle later writers. The ambiguity relates to Austin's aims and methods of analysis.

One view claims, in essence, that Austin's purpose was to produce in his general jurisprudence a systematic and orderly account of the key components of modern legal systems. Austin's concern was empirical in the sense that he wished to represent or describe in theoretical terms the reality of actually existing legal systems, identifying elements common to these modern systems of law and organising them into a body of scientific knowledge. Thus, Austin sought, in W. L. Morison's words, 'to represent law empirically, as something we can readily understand in terms of observable occurrences' – observable at least, for example, in the form of actual statutes, judicial decisions and instances of other official action, and the habitual behaviour of subjects. So Morison argues that 'all the evidence indicates that when Austin made general factual statements about independent political communities, he believed them to be universally true'. They could be tested for their truth against the circumstances of particular legal systems. The idea that theory is, in some such way, a direct representation of empirical reality, with its concepts derived from observation of and generalisation about that reality and so corresponding with it and testable for truth against it, will be called here *empiricism*.

There is, however, another view of theory which, in fact, has been more widely attributed to Austin by recent commentators on his work. It can be explained as follows. Empirical reality – the world of objects and experiences 'out there' – does not, in fact, present us with evidence which we can merely package together or generalise about to arrive at scientific truth. Concepts need to be formed in advance – *a priori* – in order to organise empirical evidence. The previously established concepts not only determine what is empirically relevant but also reflect a view of why it is relevant. Thus, theory aiming at a scientific explanation of any object of knowledge cannot take its concepts from observed experience but must deliberately *construct* concepts as a means of interpreting experience, of *imposing* order on it. A theory is not an attempted representation of observable reality but an intellectual construction – a logically worked out model – which can be used to organise the study of what can be observed in experience. This idea of the nature of theory will be termed here *conceptualism*.

Thus, Julius Stone, rejecting the view of Austin as an empiricist, argues that he should be understood as a conceptualist, 'presenting an apparatus for seeing as clearly as possible the aspect of a legal order with which his analytical system was concerned'; he 'sought the starting-points which would enable him to construct definitions and classifications on the basis of which he could, to a maximum extent, show the logical inter-relations of the various parts of the law to each other, and the subordination of the less general to the more general parts'. Whereas an empiricist view would say that a theory's truth can be tested in the light of experience, a conceptualist would claim that it is usefulness, not truth, which is the issue. Do the ideas of the theory make it possible to interpret and organise what we know about actual legal systems in a clearer and more illuminating fashion?

social fact theories and the normativity of law

Can a theory which defines law in terms of social facts, and which defines the criteria of legal validity in terms of the complex attitudes of officials, really account for the nature of law as a normative system – ie as a system which generates 'oughts'? Does the internal point of view allow this balance to be made? When you explore Kelsen's analysis in the next chapter, the contrast between his positivism and that of Hart should encourage you to explore this question.

the persistence of sanctions

Does Hart's theory of law as rule rather than command really escape the reliance on sanctions which he criticises in Austin? For example, the idea of the critical reflective attitude, or the strong social pressure, which he describes as backing up duty-imposing rules, could be seen as forms of sanction.

> Rules are conceived and spoken of as imposing obligations when the general demand for conformity is insistent and the social pressure brought to bear upon those who deviate or threaten to deviate is great. (CL 86)

Perhaps, like Bentham, he just has a more inclusive notion of sanction rather than dispensing with it entirely. But in which case, is his theory really normative rather than predictive?

history and universality

Can a theory which claims to engage in descriptive sociology really produce a general or universal theory of law? Does this enterprise make any sense, given the different forms which law takes in different societies at different times and in different places?

Internal and External Critique

Criticisms of Hart's theory of law fall into two groups: internal critiques, which accept the validity of Hart's project but find it inadequately developed when judged in its own terms, and external critiques, which challenge the very basis of Hart's project and method.

1. External critique: Dworkin on rules and principles

One telling external critique of Hart derives from Dworkin's argument about the distinction between rules and principles. (See Chapter 8 and, in particular, Dworkin 1977, 28–68.) As we have seen, Hart's central question is 'what is law': with his answer being given in terms of (albeit complex) social facts: law is a specific kind of social rule, whose existence is a complicated question of fact. According to Dworkin, the quest for a social fact theory of law is misplaced, because law is essentially an evaluative practice. This means it is one in which reasons are being weighed up and argued about in a way whose determinacy or pattern cannot be captured in terms of sources or pedigree. If, as Hart insists in his Postscript, the rule of recognition can include criteria which consist in values to which the act of recognition constitutes a commitment, how can these values then be 'fixed' in the transition to legal rules: what stops controversial questions about the interpretation of values (eg constitutional values such as equality or liberty) re-emerging in legal practice?

The way to see this, Dworkin argues, is to ask not 'what is law' but 'how is the law determined by judges in difficult cases?' In other words, Dworkin argues for a quite different starting point: as soon as we focus on hard cases, we see the weakness in Hart's account: if law is a system of rules, it simply runs out in cases where there are gaps (ie no relevant rules to be applied) and ambiguities (ie uncertainties about the meaning of rules or controversy about the values which underpin them, which require a process of evaluation and weighing). All Hart can say about such cases is that the decision is merely a product of judicial discretion – ie of the judge's conception of what the law ought to be. This is an admission which seems to undermine the very idea of the distinctiveness of law as inhering in its status as a system of rules: it militates, as natural lawyers like Fuller saw, against law's 'closure'. Once we see that judges in difficult cases in fact reason as if they were still bound by legal standards, we start to perceive that there are non-rule yet legally relevant standards in play. These are standards which have an added dimension of weight which cannot be explained by their pedigree, ie by facts about their origin in official recognising practices. On this view – though Dworkin didn't use the terminology in his early work – law is constructed as an interpretive process. Hart goes some way to admitting this (cf Finnis's internal critique at 3 below) in his accommodation of the internal attitude, but this is inconsistent with the very foundations of his positivist project, which will hence have to be abandoned. It is important to see that Dworkin's critique is external – ie about Hart's project – and not internal: principles can't just be added into the picture, because their authority cannot be captured by their source. One way of illustrating this is by looking at a famous example of Dworkin's: *Riggs v Palmer* (see Chapter 8). This couldn't have been a hard case on an internal critique – there was a clear rule which ostensibly applied to the facts: so unless the judge or critic was already open to looking beyond the positivist concept of law, they would not think of the case as a difficult one at all.

2. Internal Critique: MacCormick on rules and principles

Dworkin's argument can usefully be compared to an internal critique on similar terrain. In *Legal Reasoning and Legal Theory*, MacCormick takes off from Dworkin's external critique and rereads it as an internal critique which aims to rationalise Hart's theory so as to rescue his project. Essentially, the argument is that principles can be accommodated within the model of rules as simply general standards – Hart was only using 'rule' loosely to mean 'a standard with internal and external aspects'. Another example is MacCormick's treatment of the internal attitude. His argument distinguishes between cognitive and volitional aspects and hence reveals the spectrum within both internal and external; for example, for Hart, someone who recognises that a rule is in play without accepting it has an internal attitude just as much as someone who affirms the standard. MacCormick's account of the 'cognitive' and 'volitional' aspects of the internal attitude can be read as an internal 'gloss' which basically seeks to refine and rescue Hart's enterprise rather than undermine it. (See extract 1 set out below.)

3.   Internal critique leading to external critique: Finnis on the internal attitude

Although Finnis ultimately defends a natural law position, aspects of his approach are very sympathetic to Hart's positivist model of rules. His critique of Hart's account of the internal attitude is an interesting example of how a critique which starts out by reading a theorist on their own terms can then be used to undermine aspects of their project. Finnis acknowledges the importance of the internal attitude. But he points out that the fact that descriptive projects in legal theory are always interpretive – ie that Hart's whole 'hermeneutic' idea that the agent's point of view has to be privileged in producing an explanation of law as a social practice – entails a selection of factors to be prioritised in one's theory. This selection will be according to criteria of importance held by those agents themselves, and relative to an understanding of what the purpose/ point/function of law as a social institution is. Given, Finnis argues, that Hart sees law as essentially about maintaining social order (cf the argument from the minimum content of natural law), he must be concerned with law's stability. In which case, he is logically committed to applying the 'central case' technique to the internal attitude. (See Finnis 1980, 6–18) Hart resists this, arguing that someone who adopts the internal attitude out of conformity, to avoid sanctions or for other prudential reasons is just as much an exemplar as the person who accepts law for moral reasons. But Finnis argues that if law is definitionally tied to even a broad notion of order-maintenance, the central case or paradigm of the internal attitude would be that which best meets the conditions necessary for the maintenance of law's stability, and hence of its contribution to social order. This entails admitting that the attitude of the person who has a morally committed critical reflective attitude is the paradigm, whereas that of the person who adopts an internal attitude for prudential reasons is a 'penumbral' case – it is essentially pragmatic and will therefore shift with changing conditions and interests. Without at least a core of people (?officials) with a morally committed internal attitude, a legal system would be hopelessly unstable. There is a beautiful irony here: a natural lawyer hoists Hart on his own sociological petard.

4.   External critique: Fitzpatrick on neutrality and universalism

In Fitzpatrick's work (see extract 3 below) we find a yet clearer case of 'external critique'. Fitzpatrick is manifestly unsympathetic to the terms in which Hart frames his project, calling into question the very idea of seeking a universal concept of law. Hart's project is reconstructed as an enterprise in which the formulation of a mythic account of the origins and essence of western law is used to bolster the moral authority of the ideology of the rule of law. But Fitzpatrick's critique too has internal aspects. For example, like Finnis and Cotterrell (1989, 94), Fitzpatrick draws Hart along the 'sociological drift' which he himself has unleashed, and points out that a consistent commitment to a genuinely sociological approach would lead Hart in a very different direction. For example, if Hart is genuinely interested in 'descriptive sociology', why does he give no actual analysis of how language is used by different groups of people: why does he provide no anthropological evidence about 'primitive' societies and primary rules? This is a key failure for Fitzpatrick, because it symbolises the slippage in Hart's account between apparently empirical or historical claims and expositional devices, which consist in illustrative stories that have a mythic status. Fitzpatrick also asks questions about the point of view that is implicitly privileged in Hart's account. If the internal, critical attitude on the part of its subjects is the key to understanding the nature of law, as the critique of Austin would suggest, why does the second part of the book abandon the centrality of the citizen and make it clear that the ultimate precondition for the existence of law is merely that the officials of the system should have an internal attitude and that rules should by and large be obeyed?

But, unlike Finnis, Fitzpatrick is not making these points to pull Hart in a direction he might otherwise be unwilling to be drawn in. Rather, he is concerned to reveal that, all along, Hart's project is rather different from that which it announces itself to be. In other words, rather than merely being a descriptive theory of law (a project which is itself absurd given the variety of laws and legal systems across space and time), it is a mythic construction which locates western law within an evolutionary story in which the emergence of the rule of law (Hart's model of rules as the summit of depersonalised authority) is represented as a sublime cultural achievement, against which any other type of model is to be regarded as 'primitive' (understood as a political rather than a descriptive term). It is important to see that this is not a personal accusation of bad faith: it is a much broader point about the cultural meaning of a certain kind of theoretical project. Hence Fitzpatrick sees the positivist, law-as-a-neutral-tool-of-government theory which finds its clearest and most systematic expression in Hart's *The Concept of Law* as intimately related to the imperialism of the west – particularly in its obscuring of the basically authoritarian and hierarchical nature of legal authority.

Extract 1: MacCormick on the internal aspect of rules

MacCormick (1981, 32–40)

... Hart's attempt to highlight and focus on an 'internal aspect' of social rules as against mere habits and external regularities of behaviour seems to me to be correct in its essentials. To show why, I shall start by considering the force of the objection to taking the use of normative terminology as a sufficient identifier of the attitude Hart is trying to elucidate. What that objection shows is that attitudes matter, but that Hart has been insufficiently subtle in differentiating between relevant attitudes. What is the difference between somebody's holding that meat eating is wrong, and that same person's holding that crossing a red light is wrong, or that smoking before the Loyal Toast at formal dinners is wrong?

If there were no differences, the objection laid against Hart would lose force. If there are differences, and there are, how are we to capture them save by trying to understand the differences of judgment expressed in the three given instances of calling something 'wrong'? To capture that we must grasp what we would be doing if we were the person making these judgments, and making them seriously. That is to say that the explanation we seek must be sought not at the level of outward observation, experimentation, etc., but rather at the level of 'hermeneutic' inquiry. We have to interpret the meaning of such judgments from the point of view of being the person who passes judgment rather than from the point of view of one who scrutinizes behaviour from the outside. Hart's introduction of the idea of an 'internal aspect' into the discussion of rules was on this very account a decisive advance for analytical jurisprudence; as P. M. S. Hacker has said, it involved the introduction of the hermeneutic method to British jurisprudence. And that method, as will be argued, is the essentially appropriate one to the subject matter.

These considerations suggest that Hart's elucidation of rules is not radically mistaken, but is only incomplete. What it rightly does is direct us to the question: what are the attitudes to patterns of social acting which, together with some regularity in action (or 'behaviour'), must exist or be held by human beings for it to be true that for some group of human beings a rule exists? To answer that crucial question we must start from, but cannot finish with, the materials which Hart has furnished.

THE INTERNAL ASPECT OF RULES RECONSIDERED

A 'critical reflective attitude' can best be understood as comprehending an element of cognition, caught by the term 'reflective' and an element of or relating to volition or will, caught by the term 'critical'. The cognitive element covers the very notion of a 'pattern' of behaviour – a capacity to conceive in general terms some such abstract correlation of a certain act with certain circumstances as 'drivers stopping their cars when facing a red light', 'human beings refraining from eating animal flesh'. It further covers a capacity to appraise actual doings or contemplated doings against that abstract and general pattern, and to register instances conforming to, not conforming to, or irrelevant to, the pattern. Since the pattern is a generalized one of act-in-circumstances, whenever the circumstances exist an act is either a conforming or non-conforming one, and when they do not exist, the pattern is irrelevant.

The element of volition or will comprehends some wish or preference that the act, or abstention from acting, be done when the envisaged circumstances obtain. Such wish or preference need not be unconditional; commonly such a preference may be conditional upon the pattern in question being one for which there is and continues to be a shared preference among an at least broadly identifiable group of people – as in the case of my preference or wish that those who drive cars in the UK drive on the left-hand side of the road. This would be pointless if it ceased to be a common preference shared by all or most such drivers. Further, as the last example indicates, such a preference or wish need not be conceived as an ultimate wish, a wish for something as an end in itself. I have an ulterior reason for preferring that drivers keep left, namely that adherence to some conventional arrangement (either 'keep left' or 'keep right') will enhance my own and others' safety on the roads, and hence will conduce to the protection of life and limb.

(What distinguishes our imagined vegetarian is that he makes no assumption that the pattern of behaviour he favours, not eating meat, is a conventional one or one common to members of the groups in which he moves. He holds it to be a preferable pattern to the common one, and his volitional commitment to it is a commitment on a point of principle, hence not in any way conditional upon common or shared observance in a group. This explanation depends upon the account of principles and other standards (as distinct from rules) developed in the later parts of this, and in the next, chapter).

In so far as it is possible to distinguish between emotional elements and volitional elements in human attitudes, it seems correct to view the 'internal aspect of' or 'internal attitude to' rules as comprehending the volitional rather than the emotional. Hart stresses that the latter is not necessary to what he envisages:

> The internal aspect of rules is often misrepresented as a mere matter of 'feelings' in contrast to externally observable physical behaviour. No doubt, where rules are generally accepted by a social group and generally supported by social criticism and pressure for conformity, individuals may have psychological experiences analogous to those of restriction or compulsion. When they say they 'feel bound' to behave in certain ways they may indeed refer to these experiences. But such feelings are neither necessary nor sufficient for the existence of 'binding' rules. There is no contradiction in saying that people accept certain rules but experience no such feelings of compulsion. What is necessary is that there should be a critical reflective attitude to certain patterns of behaviour as a common standard ... (*C.L.* p.56)

This seems correct in what it says. But it is a deficiency of Hart's account in *Concept of Law* that he fails to elucidate what is denoted by rules being generally '*accepted*', '*supported*' by criticism, supported by '*pressure*' for conformity, and so on. As I have suggested, an elucidation of these features must be by reference to a volitional element: a wish or will that the pattern be upheld, a preference for conforming to non-conforming conduct in relevant circumstances. Such wishes or preferences may be, probably are normally, wishes or preferences for states of affairs which themselves are or conduce to some ultimate ends or values, as John Finnis has argued. But people do have affective or emotional attitudes to whatever they do hold as ultimate ends or values, as John Finnis has argued. So we ought not to make the mistake of supposing any entire disjunction between the volitional and the emotional, even while agreeing with Hart that 'feeling bound' in particular is not necessary to the 'internal aspect' of any rule.

SOME KEY TERMS REVIEWED

The foregoing account extends, but is consistent with, the theory expounded in *Concept of Law*. It enables us to assign clearer meanings to some crucial terms and ideas in Hart's discourse about rules.

The notion of an 'internal point of view' or 'internal attitude' is to be understood by reference to those who have and act upon a wish or preference for conduct in accordance with a given pattern, both in their own conduct and in relation to those others to whom they deem it applicable, as indicated *inter alia* by the criticisms they make and the pressures they exert.

'Acceptance' of a rule seems to cover two distinguishable attitudes. The stronger case, that of 'willing acceptance' is the same as the above, with an elaboration upon it. Not merely has one a preference for observance of the 'pattern', but one prefers it as constituting a rule which one supposes to be sustained by a shared or common preference among those to whom it is deemed applicable. The latter feature, for reasons which will appear, is essential to acceptance of a *rule* as such.

When some people have that attitude of acceptance – willing acceptance – a weaker case may also exist, namely the case of those who are aware that there are some such willing accepters, who are aware that the rule is held as applicable to themselves, and who therefore have reason (a) to conform to it and so avoid justified criticism of themselves and (b) to prefer that it be generally applied to all others to whom it is held applicable rather than that their own unenthusiastic conformity be taken advantage of. People in this position may be said 'merely to accept' or 'unenthusiastically or reluctantly to accept' or to 'accept without fully endorsing' the rules.

...

There is a related difficulty about how we are to understand the 'external point of view'. What Hart calls the 'extreme external point of view' is the case of a person who as an observer of human behaviour restricts himself to viewing it 'purely in terms of observable regularities of conduct, predictions, probabilities and signs' (*C.L.* p.87). Notice that there could be two cases in which one might hold this point of view. First, one might fail to understand or realize that some regularity in human behaviour is ascribable to rule-acceptance-and-observance as explained by Hart. For example, Kafka's novels abound with characters who observe others' behaviour, but wholly fail to understand it as being oriented to social rules and conventions. Secondly, one might adopt the standpoint of a natural scientist or behavioural scientist concerned to establish regularities of human behaviour to bodily conditions or movements without regard to supposed subjective grounds for acting held by the population subject to scrutiny. In this second case, the party who *acting as a scientist* 'keeps austerely to this extreme external point of view' may be one who *acting as a citizen* accepts the rules of the relevant community. Nor is his scientific observation necessarily a pointless enterprise. There are other dimensions of understanding than the hermeneutic and the methods of natural science, while not relevant to interpreting the orientation of actions to rules, may help us to amend partly at least some of our understanding of and attitudes to behaviour and hence our readiness to subject it to rules. A case to which Hart has drawn attention is the contribution scientists have made during this century to revolutionizing social attitudes to sexual behaviour.

In a sense this extreme external point of view is a chief or primary target for Hart's criticisms. For his argument in the earlier chapters of *Concept of Law* is aimed at showing why John Austin's mode of theorizing about law is necessarily inadequate. Austin's (and Bentham's) starting point is that of a 'habit of obedience' by a population to an individual or collectivity (the *sovereign*) who issues general commands to the members of that population, having the power and the purpose to inflict some evil by way of sanction upon those who disobey. But to speak only of 'habit' in such a context is in effect to confine oneself to viewing conduct 'purely in terms of observable regularities of conduct, predictions, probabilities and signs'; to confine oneself, in short, to the extreme external point of view and thus to commit oneself to a scheme of description or understanding which precludes an adequate representation of rules, including legal rules, as they function within the consciousness of people in society.

So the prime point of attention in relation to the 'extreme external point of view' is a methodological one. The method of observation of conduct from that point of view, however useful it might be for certain scientific purposes, including at least some varieties of sociological inquiry, is inadequate to capture those concepts of lawyers and of laymen which are bound up with rules and standards of conduct. We must have a different point of view. But what point of view?

It is an unsatisfactory feature of Hart's account that he passes too lightly over the other variant – the non-extreme variant, presumably – of the external point of view.

> Statements made from the external point of view may themselves be of different kinds. For the observer may, without accepting the rules himself, assert that the group accepts the rules, and thus may from outside refer to the way in which *they* are concerned with them from the internal point of view. [Alternatively], we can if we choose occupy the position of an observer who does not even refer in this way to the internal point of view of the group. (*C.L.* p.87)

If there is any point of view which seems to capture that which the Hartian legal theorist as such must hold, it is surely this non-extreme external point of view depicted by Hart. He does, after all, describe himself as a legal positivist, taking as his ground for that the proposition that understanding a law or a legal system in its character as such is a matter quite independent of one's own moral or other commitment to upholding that law or legal system, and of one's view as to the moral quality of the law or legal system in question. Hence, precisely what the legal theorist of Hart's school must do is take as his standpoint that of a person who understands and seeks to describe legal rules as they are held from the internal point of view regardless of any commitment he himself has for or against these rules in their internal aspect.

To be an 'outsider' in this sense is neither necessarily to be a member nor necessarily to be a non-member of the group governed by those legal rules (*or, mutatis mutandis,* some other set or system of social rules). It is simply to hold apart questions of one's own commitments, critical morality, group membership or non-membership, in order to attend strictly to the task of the descriptive legal or social theorist concerned to portray the rules for what they are in the eyes of those whose rules they are. This is no doubt easier to do if one is, for other purposes, an 'insider'. But that is contingent. This, surely, is the central methodological insight of Hart's analytical jurisprudence; the one which justifies our styling his approach a 'hermeneutic' one.

Further to elucidate this non-extreme external point of view, we must refer back to the clarification given earlier of what the internal point of view requires. We saw that it has two elements: a cognitive and a volitional. Now we may notice that the non-extreme external-point of view requires (a) full sharing in the cognitive element of the internal point of view – the understanding of the pattern or patterns of behaviour as such, and (b) full appreciation of, but no necessary sharing in, the volitional element, the will or preference for conformity to the pattern as a standard. Take a case: I, who am not a practising Christian but who have had much exposure in particular to the Scottish Presbyterian mode of Christian observance can give an account of the rules and articles of faith by which Presbyterians conduct themselves. I could doubtless do it better if I were or had for some time been a fully committed member of the Church. But my giving a fully adequate descriptive account of the rules and articles of faith would require understanding and appreciation of these as committed members understand them, not volitional commitment by me to them. Here of course one touches upon a range of subject-matter focal to one strand in the 'hermeneutic' tradition, that concerned with explanation and interpretation of religious texts and traditions. But there are, as here indicated, other strands. And for that reason, and to avoid the awkwardness of continuing to talk of a 'non-extreme external point of view', I shall henceforward dub that position the 'hermeneutic point of view', and foist this upon Hart in the hope of making clearer an essential but not fully elucidated fulcrum of his theory and methodology. His theory stands or falls upon the truth of the propositions that social rules can only be understood, analysed and described from this hermeneutic point of view, and that legal systems can only be understood, analysed and described as specialized systems of social rules.

A part of the grounding Hart gives for these propositions is the evidence of linguistic usage, in particular the use of the 'normative terminology of 'ought', 'must' and 'should', 'right' and 'wrong' '. What Hart has to tell us here is concerned with the presuppositions implicit in our use of such terminology. Those who speak of what one ought to or must do or not do, who discourse about what is right or wrong, reveal themselves as presupposing some standard of rightness or wrongness. That is, they disclose that their point of view is an 'internal' one with respect to such standards. Hence Hart chooses to call statements of the right and the wrong and such like 'internal statements'. That we are familiar with, and regularly make or hear, such statements is one way of drawing our attention to that very internal point of view which, upon consideration, we see them to presuppose. This, Hart claims, is the real pay-off of the 'linguistic' approach to philosophy.

> ... the suggestion that inquiries into the meanings of words merely throw light on words is false. Many important distinctions which are not immediately obvious, between types of social situation or relationships may best be brought to light by an examination of the standard uses of the relevant expressions and of the way in which these depend on a social context, itself often left unstated. In this field of study it is particularly true that we may use, as Professor J. L. Austin said, 'a sharpened awareness of words to sharpen our awareness of phenomena'. (*C.L.* p.vii)

The words just quoted are drawn from the point in the preface to *Concept of Law* where Hart made a claim (since hotly disputed) to be engaging in 'descriptive sociology' as well as conceptual analysis; and the words and the claim were uttered with reference to the asserted importance of the distinction between 'internal' and 'external' statements'.

There is, it is submitted, an important point and a sound claim to be made here. But the point and the claim are vitiated by the ambiguity earlier discovered in Hart's talk of the external point of view. We distinguished an 'internal', a 'hermeneutic' or 'non-extreme external' and an 'extreme external' point of view. If there are *three* distinct points of view, not a simple internal/external dichotomy, what is to become of the internal/external distinction in relation to statements?

The answer is that it is simply not true that all statements of 'ought', 'must', 'should', 'right', 'wrong', 'obligation', 'liability' or whatever, do presuppose an assumption *on the speaker's part* of the internal point of view or of committed acceptance of rules or other standards. Such statements do certainly presuppose some rule or standard to which reference is made. But it need not be a standard which the speaker accepts or adheres to from the internal point of view. Consider the difference between 'As a good Catholic, you ought to go to Mass today' (i) uttered by a parish priest to a member of his flock and (ii) uttered by a non-believer to a friend whom he supposes to be one of the faithful. There is a difference indeed – but the truth of the statement *conceived as a statement* (not an exhortation, or an implied reproach or criticism or whatever) is quite independent of the character or standing or viewpoint of the person who utters it.

Any such normative statement may be made *either* from the internal point of view or from the hermeneutic point of view, and the mere act of making such a statement is entirely ambiguous in its presuppositions as between the two. What is the case, however, is that the hermeneutic point of view is possible only if an actual or hypothetical internal point of view is postulated or presupposed. In this way it is true that what Hart perhaps misleadingly calls 'internal statements' (it would seem preferable to adopt the terminology of Joseph Raz, and to call these statements 'normative statements') do presuppose and thus draw attention to the actual or hypothetical existence of an 'internal point of view'. My ability to state, explain and interpret rules and other standards and their applicability to given cases (my ability to take on the hermeneutic point of view) does indeed depend upon the supposition that somebody or some people accept(s) such rule(s) or standard(s). But I need not be one of those people, nor does my making such a statement of itself disclose any volitional commitment of my own.

Hart's view of this matter is different. At page 99 of *C.L* he characterizes an 'internal statement' as one which 'manifests the internal point of view and is naturally used by one who, accepting the rule ... applies [it]'. The external statement by contrast is 'the natural language of an external observer ... who, without accepting [the] rule ... states the fact that others accept it'. But the error here is in supposing that those who are outsiders to a particular rule or rule system are restricted to stating facts *that* ... or facts *about* the rule. Not so. As a non-citizen of the USSR, and one who has little liking for its political and legal principles, I can nevertheless make true statements *of,* as well as true statements *about,* Soviet Law. When Hart (C.L. p.101) notes that the student of Roman Law may make his study of that subject more 'vivid' by speaking 'as if the system were still efficacious', and discussing 'the validity of particular rules', and solving problems 'in their terms', he effectively recognizes this. This rather demonstrates than alleviates the unsatisfactory quality of his earlier distinction between internal and external statements.

Extract 2: Raz on the rule of recognition

Raz (1979, 90–102, 177–79)

B.   THE DISTINCTION BETWEEN MAKING A NEW LAW AND APPLYING AN EXISTING
ONE

The statement that a law is part of a legal system only if it is recognized by the law-applying organs – the courts – of the system means only that it would have been acted on by the courts had they been presented with the appropriate problem. That a court would apply a law if faced with a case to which the law applies is an indication that either the law exists in the legal system or that the law will be made by the courts when they have an opportunity to do so. Recognition by the courts or other law-applying organs is not a complete criterion of identity because these organs often have power to make new laws, and often what law they are going to make can be determined in advance. As a first step towards completing the criterion, one must incorporate in it reference to the fact that the law would not only be recognized by the courts but would be recognized as a previously existing law. It is not a new law that they would make when faced with an appropriate case. For this reason the distinction between applying an existing law and creating and applying a new one is the second jurisprudential issue involved in the problem of identity. Of the major legal theorists Hart is the only one to face this problem, and a brief discussion of the relevant aspects of his theory will clarify the nature of the issue.

Hart argues that the distinction between the application of a new law and the application of a previously existing one turns on the existence or absence of a duty to apply the law. If and only if the court applies a law that it is under a duty to apply is it acting on a previously existing law; on the other hand, when it applies a rule that it has no duty to apply it is not acting on a previously existing law. This is a consequence of Hart's doctrine of the rule of recognition. In every legal system, he argues, there is of necessity a rule of recognition that identifies the laws of the system; the criterion of identity of legal systems can be formulated as follows: A legal system consists of a rule of recognition and all the laws identified by that rule. Hart's discussion of the rule of recognition falls short of the high standard of lucidity characterizing the rest of his book and requires interpretation, which will be limited to the doctrine's effects on the problem of identity.

A rule of recognition is 'a rule for conclusive identification of primary rules of behaviour'. Here, as occasionally elsewhere, Hart states that the rule identifies only primary rules. It is quite clear, however, that his rule of recognition is a rule for the identification of all the other rules of the system, and only them. It specifies 'some feature or features possession of which by a suggested rule is taken as a conclusive affirmative indication that it is a *rule of the group*. This means that the rule of recognition of a system constitutes its criterion of validity: 'To say that a given rule is valid is to recognize it as passing all the tests provided by the rule of recognition and so as a *rule of the system*'. The rule of recognition provides also the means for the resolution of conflicts between laws. This is conceived by Hart as an essential part of the rule's function in identifying the laws of the system, for it is a condition of the validity of a rule that it does not conflict with a superior rule.

How does the rule of recognition fulfil its function? The rule is unique among the rules of the legal system. It is a necessary rule in the sense that every legal system necessarily has one and only one rule of recognition and a set of rules which does not include a rule of recognition is not a legal system. Furthermore, all the other laws exist and are part of the legal system if they fulfil conditions laid down in the existence of the rule of recognition [which] itself cannot, of course, [be] ascertained in this manner. 'Its existence is a matter [of fact and] … must consist in an actual practice.' Hart offers a detailed analysis earlier in his book of what it means for a rule to exist as a matter of fact – as a social practice; this analysis is quite clearly meant to apply to the rule of recognition.

Whose practice constitutes the conditions for the existence of the rule of recognition? Hart's answer is far from clear. Often he refers to 'the practice of courts, legislatures, officials or private citizens'. On occasion, while including reference to the behaviour of private citizens, he attributes special importance to the practice of the courts. Finally, we are told – and this should be regarded as Hart's position – that the behaviour of the population is not part of the conditions for the existence of the rule of recognition. Its existence consists in the behaviour of the 'officials' of the system, by which he presumably means law-applying officials.

Hart holds that the conditions for the existence of social rules are practices of those people to whom the rules are addressed. It follows, then, that the rule of recognition is addressed to the officials of the legal system Furthermore, Hart's explanation of social rules is basically an explanation of duty-imposing rules. The only other type of rules Hart recognizes are power-conferring rules, but he does not consider what social practices constitute the existence of a customary power-conferring rule. Therefore, since the rule of recognition is a customary rule, it must be interpreted as duty-imposing. Besides, all the legal powers of officials are conferred on them by the rules of change and adjudication, authorizing them to make new laws and to settle disputes. To claim that the rule of recognition is a power-conferring rule is to confuse it with either rules of change or rules of adjudication.

The rule of recognition imposes an obligation on the law-applying officials to recognize and apply all and only those laws satisfying certain criteria of validity spelled out in the rule, which criteria include indications of how conflicts of laws are to be resolved. From Hart's examples it would seem that although he thinks that the criteria of validity most commonly refer to the mode of origin of the laws, this is not always the case.

The jurisprudential criterion of identity implied by this theory is: A legal system consists of a rule of recognition and all the laws that ought to be applied according to it. When the courts apply a rule that they were not obliged to apply they may make it thereby into a law (if there is in the system a rule of precedent that will oblige all courts henceforth to apply it), but they do not apply an existing law and the rule was not part of the system before its application.

Hart's rule of recognition is subject to criticism on a few points and requires some clarification. One should remember that clear conceptual distinctions do not entail the existence of clear instances of the concepts involved. Therefore, the absence of clear instances should not deter one from striving to formulate clear conceptual distinctions. The courts, in most cases brought before them, probably neither merely apply an existing law nor do they merely initiate a new law. They may be doing a little of both. But this does not detract from the ability of a clear distinction between applying existing law and creating a new one to shed light on legal processes.

The application of the rule of recognition to concrete cases may be beset by similar problems. Hart makes it quite clear that the rule of recognition, like any other rule, is necessarily open-textured and vague to some extent. It may also be incomplete, for it may not include an accepted answer to some legal questions such as the validity of rules of public international law within the municipal legal system. The existence of a rule of recognition does not entail that all the legal problems, the solution of which may depend on the nature of the criteria of validity, such as the problems mentioned above, have found their solution in the system. So long as the rule is incomplete some such problems will remain unanswered, but when the courts are faced with such unsolved problems and accept a certain solution they modify the rule of recognition. This should surprise no one. The rule of recognition, being a customary rule, is constantly open to change.

Asserting that there is in every legal system a rule of recognition does not involve one in the task of giving a systematic and reasonable account of the limits of a legal system based on accepted or proposed solutions to a whole host of legal problems, as described above. However, any attempt to articulate the details of the criteria of validity incorporated in any rule of recognition of any legal system means embarking on precisely this endeavour. Attempting to formulate criteria of validity based on complex court practices that are in a constant state of change and that are necessarily vague and almost certainly incomplete, involves not only legal perceptiveness and theoretical skill, it demands sound judgment and reasonable value-decisions as well. Hart's theory leads one to the point where the boundaries between analytic and critical jurisprudence, between general and particular jurisprudence, begin to blur. But he himself does not cross the boundary. Rather, he provides conceptual tools for dealing with particular and critical problems, but he does not deal with those problems himself.

There is no reason to suppose that the rule of recognition refers to all the criteria of validity of a legal system, and it is clearly wrong to think that it determines them all. A criterion of validity is a set of conditions set by law, satisfaction of which is sufficient for being a law of the system. All the laws of a legal system, except the rule of recognition the existence of which is a matter of social practice, are valid; they exist in the system because they satisfy some criterion of validity. Besides the rule of recognition, other laws can also set criteria of validity. All the laws conferring legislative powers, for example, determine criteria of validity; so also does a law stipulating conditions that a social custom must fulfil to be legally binding.

That the rule of recognition sets up some criteria of validity is clear. There must be in every system some criteria of validity that, although legally binding, are not legally valid, hence they must be set in the rule of recognition. There is, however, no reason to think that all the criteria must be stipulated in that rule. The fact that all the criteria of validity are determined in laws that, directly or indirectly, are valid according to criteria determined in the rule of recognition, guarantees that by imposing a duty to apply the laws satisfying its criteria of validity, the rule of recognition imposes a duty to apply all the laws of the system.

Furthermore, there is no reason to suppose that every legal system has just one rule of recognition. It may have more. Imagine a legal system in which no valid law makes custom or precedent a source of law, but in which, nevertheless, both custom and precedent are sources of law. It follows that the criteria for the validity of laws created by custom or precedent are determined by rules of recognition imposing obligations on the courts to apply such laws. But we should not assume that there is just one rule of recognition rather than two – one relating to each source of law – simply because the system must contain means of resolving conflicts between laws of the various sources. First, as was pointed out above, the rule of recognition, even if it is one rule, may be incomplete, which means that the system may not include any means of resolving conflicts. Perhaps the problem has never arisen and there is no generally accepted solution to it. Secondly, there may be two or more rules of recognition that provide methods of resolving conflicts; for example, the rule imposing an obligation to apply certain customs may indicate that it is supreme, whereas the rule relating to precedent may indicate that it is subordinate.

In most legal systems courts have authority to settle at least some of the disputes to which there is no clear solution in the laws of the system. Courts have a duty to apply the laws of the system when they are applicable and to exercise discretion in order to decide (partially) unregulated disputes – disputes to which the laws do not provide a clear answer or where the courts have power to change the law. By the rule of precedent this exercise of discretion often amounts to the creation of new laws. The courts' discretion to decide unregulated disputes may be absolute or guided. They may be guided by law as to the manner in which discretion should be exercised. The law may, for example, direct judges to act on the rule that they think best for such cases, or to render a decision that would be the best from the point of view of the parties to the present dispute, or direct the courts to consult their conscience or the writings of moralists. Such instructions may be given in a statute, but they may also exist only in the practice of the courts. Very often, however, they are not ordinary precedents, but may instead derive their force from the continuing practice of the courts. When this happens, the legal system concerned contains two types of ultimate laws: laws of one type directing the courts which laws to apply, those of the other type guiding their discretion in deciding (partly) unregulated disputes. Laws of the first type are laws of recognition, laws of the second type are ultimate laws of discretion, and both impose duties on the courts. But laws of recognition oblige the courts to apply certain laws, leaving them no choice which laws to apply. Laws of discretion, on the other hand, whether ultimate or not, merely guide the courts' discretion in the choice of laws to adopt and apply; they limit the courts' freedom of choice but do not deprive them of it.

Laws of recognition are thus deprived of part of their uniqueness. They are still the only ultimate laws that necessarily exist in every legal system, but they are not the only ultimate laws that can exist in a system. Moreover, the distinction between applying an existing law and applying a new one is seen to be more a difference of degree than of kind. This fact, together with the fact that in practice it is often difficult to decide whether in a particular case a new law was created or an old one applied, does not mean that the distinction cannot be drawn or that it is unimportant. Every legal system rests on its ultimate laws, which commonly means on a set of ultimate laws of recognition and discretion. The former provide the ultimate criteria of validity of the laws of the system, the latter guide the courts in the exercise of their powers to modify the system when deciding unregulated disputes and creating precedents for the future. The difference may be one of degree, but it is indispensable for the formulation of criteria of identity.

C.   THE RELATION OF LAW AND STATE

If the theory of the rule of recognition is substantially correct, as I think it is, it forms part of the answer to the problem of identity. Although it sets necessary conditions for membership in a legal system, it does not provide all the sufficient conditions. Nothing is part of a legal system unless either it is a rule of recognition of the system, or the courts ought to recognize and apply it. To be a rule of recognition is sufficient to be counted as a law of the system, but to be a law that the courts are obliged to apply is not. Quite often the courts have an obligation to apply laws of other legal systems, rules of private associations, and so on, although these were not and do not become part of the legal system. Therefore, the rule of recognition provides no complete answer to the problem of the scope of a legal system – the problem of the identity of momentary legal systems.

Nor does the rule of recognition solve the problem of the continuity of legal systems. That one legal system comes to an end and another takes its place manifests itself in a change of rule of recognition, for each legal system has a different rule of recognition. The rule of recognition, however, is a customary rule; hence it is constantly in a process of change. What changes are consistent with the continued existence of the same rule, and what changes compel the admission that a new rule has replaced the old one? It is easy to bring examples for either situation, as well as examples of borderline cases. However, it is not the existence of borderline cases, which are inevitable, that is disturbing. The disturbing fact is that Hart's theory provides no clue as to *how* to draw the conceptual distinction. Even more disturbing is that this is no mere oversight on the part of Hart that can be easily remedied. He did not provide the answer because he did not ask the question to which the distinction is an answer. His theory provides substantially complete answers (whether or not they are correct) to the problems with which he was concerned: the role of the courts in a legal system, the truth in rule scepticism, the variety of laws and their interrelation, the relation of efficacy and existence. If his theory fails to provide a complete solution to the problem of identity it is because he overlooked not only part of the answer but also a whole question: that of the relation of law and state.

The relation of law and state affects the two distinct aspects – scope and continuity – of the problem of identity. Every state – by which is meant a form of political system and not a juristic person – has one legal system that constitutes the law of that state, and every municipal legal system is the law of one state. Since, then, the identity of a legal system is bound up with that of the state the law of which it is, the relation between law and state necessarily affects the problem of scope. So too, since an end to the existence of a state is the end of its legal system, and since a law that is not a law of the state is not part of its legal system, the problem of continuity is similarly affected by the relation of state and law.

Two diametrically opposed views have on the relation of law and state have been expressed by legal philosophers. Kelsen claimed that the concept of the state can be explained only in legal terms. That is, the concept of a legal system must be explained first; from it naturally flows the explanation of the concept of a state, for a state is but a (municipal) legal system. No social facts, no social norms that are not relevant to the explanation of law have any relevance to the theory of the state. Bentham and Austin, on the other hand, held that law can only be explained after some theory of state has been established. First one must define the meaning of an 'independent political society' – 'a state'. On the basis of this definition 'law' can be defined. Bentham's and Austin's definitions of an 'independent political society' are purely sociological, making use of no legal concepts, and the same is true of their definitions of sovereign and subject that are part of it.

Bentham and Austin have the better of this controversy. Because Kelsen lacks the concept of the state as a political system, he fails to account for the identity of a legal system. He is driven to rely on constitutional continuity as a sole mark of identity, disregarding the fact that new states can be created and new legal systems established without any break in the constitutional continuity taking place. A theory of law must be based, at least partly, on a theory of state, and denying this has been one of Kelsen's gravest mistakes. A theory of state, however, is partly based on a theory of law – the two are intimately interrelated.

Since I am concerned with the nature of the problem of identity rather than its solution, there is no need to discuss the concept of a state beyond mentioning some truisms. A state is the political organization of a society, it is a political system that is a subsystem of a more comprehensive social system. The social system includes, of course, many other subsystems and the political system interacts with most if not all of them, as well as interacting with other political systems. These social and political systems are normative systems; in other words, at least part of the pattern of interrelations constituting the systems is norm governed.

The legal system is only part of the norms constituting the political system; most political systems include numerous non-legal norms. Some of these non-legal norms apply to society in general: however much the system is resented and hated, if it is viable at all, it is based, among other things, on some norms of respect for at least some of the laws and some authorities on the part of some important sections in the society. Some non-legal political norms are more limited, of which Dicey's conventions of the constitution can serve as an example.

It follows that since the continuity of a legal system is tied to the continuity of the political system, the former is affected by the fate of the non-legal norms that happen to form part of the political system concerned. However, emphasizing the importance of the fate of non-legal norms to the continuity of the legal system does not mean that these are the only factors affecting continuity. The substance of my contention is that whatever form one's ultimate account of continuity takes, it must, in view of the relation of law and state, be based on the following two points: first, that continuity depends on the interaction of legal and non-legal norms, and the extent and manner of their change; and secondly, that among the legal norms concerned some are more relevant than others. Since the continuity of the legal system is fundamentally a function of the continuity of the political system, political laws are more relevant than others. Constitutional and administrative laws are, therefore, more relevant than, for example, the law of contract or torts.

The problem of scope is similarly affected, and can be sub-divided into four sub-problems: first, that of the dividing line between political norms that are part of the legal system and those that are not; secondly, that of the dividing line between legal norms and social norms of the social system of which the political system is a subsystem; thirdly, that of the dividing line between the law and norms of other subsystems of the same society; and fourthly, that of the dividing line between one legal system and coexisting laws of other legal systems.

The first of these sub-problems of the problem of scope may be solved by insisting that the laws of a system are either the ultimate rules of its courts or the laws its courts ought to recognize and apply. Those political norms that are neither the courts' practice nor norms that the courts ought to apply are not part of the law of the state. The other three sub-problems, though each involving somewhat different considerations, have this much in common: sometimes the courts are under an obligation to apply norms because those norms belong to these other social or political systems. The courts ought to enforce private contracts, the rules of some private associations within the state, the laws of foreign countries, and so on. Some theorists have seen this as a reason for regarding those laws as part of the legal system, and Bentham maintained that all commands that are enforceable in law are laws of the sovereign. Hart maintained in *The Concept of Law* that all the rules that the courts have a duty to apply are laws of the system.

As indicated above, the backing of the state power is a defining characteristic of municipal law, but it is not the only one. Also characteristic of the state system is that one of its main functions is to maintain and support other forms of social grouping; it is, therefore, characteristic of the law that it upholds and enforces contracts, agreements, rules, and customs of private persons and associations. To obscure the distinction between norms recognized as part of the law and norms that, although not part of the law, are recognized and enforced because it is the function of the law to support various social groupings is to misunderstand the nature of the state and its relations to other social systems.

Admitting that not all the norms that the courts ought to apply are part of the law, where should one draw the line? This is not the place to attempt a solution. I wish, however, to conclude with one last remark bearing on the problem. That a norm is identified as one the courts ought to apply by the fact that it is a norm of a certain society, association, or state is no indication whether or not it is part of the system. Legislation by reference is a familiar technique; for example, a statute passed in one country adopting by reference the civil code of another country. No other formal distinction will succeed in drawing a reasonable dividing line. The reasons for enforcing the norm, and the attitude of the courts and the legislature to its enforcement, are the crucial factors. Formal distinctions may give some indication as to the nature of the reasons for enforcing, but are never in themselves conclusive. Ultimately the problem turns on an accumulation of evidence justifying a judgment whether the norm is enforced on the grounds that it is part of the law's function to support other social systems or because it is part of the law itself.

...

4. ON H. L. A. HART'S CLASSIFICATION OF LAWS

The classification of legal functions outlined above has not revealed any unknown functions of the law. It was not meant to do so. People have been thinking about the law long enough to have discovered all its main functions. But in discussing them they have often disregarded some and confused others. It has been my aim in this essay to attempt a comprehensive classification of the main legal functions, trying to distinguish between those functions which have often been confused and to separate various levels of analysis. Doing this is not solving the problems of the functions of laws, it is merely presenting them. In assessing the merits and failures of the proposed classification it may be useful to compare it with the ideas of other writers. I conclude this essay with some remarks (no complete analysis is intended) on the classifications suggested by H. L. A. Hart. Legal theorists of the positivist school, by concentrating on the criminal law, tended to emphasize the first primary function of prohibiting undesirable behaviour and to overlook the other functions. Bentham, for example, thought that in arranging the law:

> ... the penal code ought to precede the civil code and the constitutional code. In the first, the legislator exhibits himself to every individual, he permits, he commands, he prohibits, he traces for everyone the rules of his conduct ... In the other codes he has less to do with commandments than with regulations and explanations, which do not so clearly address themselves to everybody, and which are not generally interesting to those concerned ...

In *The Concept of Law* H. L. A. Hart has paid special attention to the second primary function, that of providing facilities for private arrangements, as well as to the secondary legal functions. The analysis proposed here is largely an elaboration of his ideas. Hart, however, did not clearly distinguish between normative types and social functions. Consequently, his theory suggests a simple relation between types of rules and social functions, according to which duty-imposing rules perform the first primary function whereas power-conferring rules perform the second primary function. In fact both rules have to do with each of these functions. Furthermore, this simplified picture of a one to one correlation between types of rules and types of functions obscures the fact that legal systems perform two more primary functions, those of providing services and settling unregulated disputes.

The confusion engendered by conflating normative types and social functions is increased when Hart turns to the examination of the secondary functions of the law. At this stage he again identifies types of rule with types of social function, but now with the distinction between primary and secondary functions. By doing this he obscures the distinction between the primary function of facilitating private arrangements and the secondary function of law-making. He also obscures the important role of duty-imposing laws in performing the secondary functions. Finally, the careless reader, who came to identify the distinction between primary and secondary rules with that between duty-imposing and power-conferring rules, may be misled into regarding the rule of recognition as power-conferring, whereas in fact it is a duty-imposing rule. All these confusions are caused by the fact that the classification of rules into primary and secondary is meant to serve two incompatible purposes. It is sometimes regarded as a distinction between normative types, sometimes as a distinction between social functions.

Extract 3: Fitzpatrick's external critique of Hart's 'Concept'

Fitzpatrick (1992, 3–6, 192–4, 197–8)

THE ASSUMPTION OF LAW

Seeing law as autonomous doctrine is supposedly the antithesis of social approaches to law. The doctrinal study of law – or, in cognate terms, black-letter law, formalism or legal positivism – takes legal rules and reports of cases as the universe. This approach remains predominant in legal education and legal research. Ostensibly, it renders law as distinct, unified and internally coherent. In its guise of analytical or positivist jurisprudence, it has assiduously protected law's autonomy. Numerous, seemingly devastating assaults on this position have failed fundamentally to alter it. The remorseless observation of its divergence from the practice of law has not undermined the standard perception of its place at the foundation of that practice.

The form which this approach has recently taken within jurisprudence has been that of the elevation of the heroic champion – the champion as both protector of true knowledge and the predominant figure in the field. The champion's conceptual defence of law's autonomy is promulgated and refined but eventually found wanting in some ways. The new champion's rise is effected by the discovery of ways which significantly qualify the old position and by the provision of some generally acceptable protection of law's autonomy to put in its place. The current champion remains H. L. A. Hart with his 'concept of law'. The leading challenger is Ronald Dworkin with his notion of 'law's empire'

...

Hart attacked the long dominant, and still influential, positivist conception of law provided by John Austin. Austin saw law as the command of a sovereign power which is generally obeyed by the populace: the relation between the sovereign and members of society is one of simple dependence. By paying some regard to sociolinguistic usage, Hart finds Austin's conception to be deficient on several grounds. Most significantly, it ignores the various social uses of legal rules. If we regard these, we find that people have an 'internal', participating approach to law in which they adopt a creative, reflective attitude to legal rules. We find them endowed with abilities to act on and evaluate legal standards of behaviour and to pursue the highly skilled enterprise of rule-following. This popular element proves, in Hart's analysis, to be essential for law's being. Having inserted this popular element into law so as to displace the current positivist champion, Hart proceeds to assume his mantle in a mystifying shift. Hart erases the element of the popular and reaffirms the positivist equation of law with official authority and with formal, pre-set meaning. The populace is thus excluded from law and relegated to a state of Austinian inertness. Hart achieves all this through forms of the mythic elevation of law and of the official voice as the source of law. The popular element is silenced in a fabulous story of law's primal origin ... In short, what counts as law becomes exclusively and comprehensively determined by officials, and the positivist enterprise is preserved.

...

The relation between law's autonomy and society in these accounts is thus somewhat paradoxical. With both Hart and Dworkin, law's social being serves to reveal the inadequacy of the reigning positivist conception of law. That conception is shown to be inextricably dependent on a social dimension. But when it came to purifying law and sustaining the positivist enterprise, the social dimension was arbitrarily excluded and law's dependence proved to be readily, if mysteriously, extricable. Law could thence occupy a transcendent position where it has no specific connection with society but nonetheless exercises a general domination over it. Positivist domination has to be constantly secured in the face of social challenges that would render law as something apart from what it is posited to be. Both Hart and Dworkin adopt their particular, limiting participants' perspective partly to counter 'external' or 'pragmatic' perspectives that would reduce law in terms of social factuality.

...

THE PRIMAL SCENE

... As we saw, a view of law bearing an uncertain relation to that of Austin was found to be deficient because it did not accommodate 'the idea of a rule, without which we cannot hope to elucidate even the most elementary forms of law'. Now the slippage occurs. From the conclusion that a conception of law must include the idea of a rule, Hart moves towards confining law to rules. Rules provide 'the elements of law' and the foundations of a legal system. The vaunted union of primary and secondary rules – the 'fresh start' which we consider shortly – is 'the heart of' or is 'at the centre of a legal system'. Such a 'union may be justly regarded as the 'essence' of law'. Those distancing quotes around 'essence' as well as the relating of law to rules in foundational and biological metaphors – common preludes to modern myth – do perhaps evidence a residual reluctance simply to equate law with rules. This reluctance is an attenuated tribute to Hart's previous reliance on linguistic philosophy. As a linguistic philosopher, Hart would not seek the essence of law. He would not seek out what it is since for linguistic philosophy and for Hart that was a misconceived quest, as we saw. But it is a quest on which Hart now embarks. He founds the quest on the arbitrary and continuous reduction of law to a matter of rules. And he simply asserts that for the existence of such rules we need only look to other rules, for it is 'a very familiar chain of reasoning' that '[i]f the question is raised whether some suggested rule is legally valid, we must in order to answer the question use a criterion of validity provided by some other rule'. This stunning familiarity and Hart's confining of 'law' to rules, controversial as they have proved in Western jurisprudence, would be spectacularly alien to other major legal systems. So much for the claimed universality of Hart's concept of law.

Nonetheless Hart confidently locates his fresh start for jurisprudence in a speculative-universal history of early humanity. There Hart is witness to a primal scene in which law as the union of primary and secondary rules is conceived. This is the mythic return to origins, to what gives law form and makes it real. Spurious 'historical' origins create and give way to law's validating, formal origins. The myth of origin begins with a type of 'simple tribal society', 'a small community closely knit by ties of kinship, common sentiment, and belief and placed in a stable environment'. The narration continues in a manner almost indistinguishable from Locke's account of law's creation ... The society is found to have only primary rules of obligation whereby 'human beings are required to do or abstain from certain actions, whether they wish to or not'. The primary rules are in Hart's view similar to custom. The imperative of social control means that they 'are in fact always found in primitive societies' where they have to be widely accepted in their internal aspect in order to be effective. Societies with only primary rules eventually appreciate the inadequacies of such an adamic simplicity and thus provide Hart with the components of his concept of law. In that state there would be no way of settling 'what the [primary] rules are or ... the precise scope of some given rule'. The resulting uncertainty is cured by a rule of recognition providing 'conclusive identification of primary rules' in some authoritative, written form. Again, 'there will be no means, in such a society, of deliberately adapting the rules to changing circumstances, either by eliminating old rules or introducing new ones'. The resulting 'static quality of the regime of primary rules' is cured by the introduction of 'rules of change' empowering 'an individual or body of persons to introduce new primary rules ... and to eliminate old rules'. Finally, there would be 'the *inefficiency* of the diffuse social pressures by which the rules are maintained' which would be cured by 'rules of adjudication ... identifying the individuals who are to adjudicate' and identifying 'the procedure to be followed.'

> [T]he remedy for each defect might, in itself, be considered a step from the pre-legal into the legal world; since each remedy brings with it many elements that permeate law: certainly all three remedies together are enough to convert the regime of primary rules into what is indisputably a legal system ... If we stand back and consider the structure which has resulted from the combination of primary rules of obligation with the secondary rules of recognition, change and adjudication, it is plain that we have here not only the heart of a legal system, but a most powerful tool for the analysis of much that has puzzled both the jurist and the political theorist.

Whatever else this antique story may be, it is not linguistic philosophy. It is for a start an elaboration of Hart's arbitrary and essentialist confining of law to rules. But Hart's retreat from linguistic philosophy goes much further. Like those whom he has castigated for doing so, Hart now looks explicitly for what law is, not to its use and context. The discovery of law as the civilized outgrowth of the primal scene provides its essence. The very history forming law's essence supersedes itself and nullifies any continuing influence it could have. The pure, mechanical essence of law stands solitarily and autonomously apart from the forces that created it and apart from any informing context. If we explore the sources of what Hart is looking to, if we explore the knowledge that enables Hart to present this 'step from the pre-legal into the legal world', we may more extensively grasp the mythic elevation of an essential law.

...

THE APOTHEOSIS OF THE OFFICIAL

These foundations of a legal system mark the triumph of one side of the duality – that is, the triumph of official determinations. The other side of the duality is reduced by Hart in terms of rules and their internal aspect. Hart effects the triumph of official determinations by making the internal aspect necessary only for them. Such a resolution is reached through an astonishing compression of contradictions. Having based both his criticism of previous ideas of law and the lineaments of his alternative on the necessity for rules to have an internal aspect, Hart proceeds to deny that necessity. Having said that the internal aspect cannot be envisaged in terms of individual mental states, he now proceeds to treat its presence and absence in terms of individual mental states.

And having thus subordinated the internal aspect to individual mentality, Hart posits the possibility of a society in which that mentality eliminates the internal aspect for 'the ordinary citizen'. This is a strange society. It is a society without social relations, a society which Hart bolsters with desperate metaphor rather than sociolinguistic or sociological observation. It is a society which lacks attributes which Hart elsewhere in *The Concept of Law* considers necessary for the existence of any society. And the contradictions multiply. Again myth is evoked to mediate them.

Further Reading

For copyright reasons we have not been able to utilise extracts from *The Concept of Law*. In the circumstances, for students who wish to get a real grip – or better purchase – on the issues presented here, we recommend that you read *The Concept of Law*, either the whole book, or at least the key Chapters 5 and 6.

While Hart continued to endorse the use of techniques borrowed from linguistic philosophy, following astute criticism he later repudiated claims (Hart 1968, v (preface), Hart 1983, 2) that legal terms were used in a special prescriptive, not descriptive, way, claims he presented in his 1948 'The Ascription of Responsibility and Rights' and in his 1954 'Definition and Theory in Jurisprudence'. For an accessible example of the criticism Hart came to accept, see Simpson 1964.

For a difficult but interesting argument that Hart's rule of recognition is unworkable, see Kramer 1988.

For a very clear argument that however well positivism, including Hart's version of it, characterises statute law, it fails absolutely to describe the common law, see Simpson 1987.

For an extended analysis of Hart, see MacCormick 1981.

Questions

1. Can the standards used by officials to identify laws be reduced to a single 'rule of recognition'?

2. Is the claimed existence of a rule of recognition in every legal system a fact, or a myth?

3. 'The critical reflective attitude that identifies the presence of law is more complex than the opposition between an internal and an external understanding of what it means to breach legal rules.' Discuss in relation to Hart's theory of law.

4. Assess Hart's claim that his 'The Concept of Law' is a contribution to both analytical jurisprudence and descriptive sociology.

5 Modern Positivism: Kelsen's Pure Theory of Law[1]

David Schiff

Hans Kelsen was an Austrian educated in Vienna at the beginning of the twentieth century. He left Europe when Hitler came to power, and for the last years of his prolific academic life was a professor at the University of California. He had a different target from both early analytical positivists and later Anglo-American legal positivists. Rather than principally debating with natural law theorists, his debate was also with other legal positivists and early sociologists that focused on law in the course of their analyses of society (see Chapter 6). His writings represent a different tradition of philosophy from that encountered in the last two chapters. Usually described as neo-Kantiansim (Paulson 1992), they offer a sophisticated and highly intellectual approach to the concerns of jurisprudence and legal theory. (On whether it is accurate to describe Kelsen's writings in this way, see Wilson 1986.) One of the problems for students of Kelsen's jurisprudence is that it is extremely difficult to extract and appreciate those parts of Kant's philosophy in which Kelsen's writings are grounded. There is no simple avenue to approach Kant's writings, and their radical unity makes piecemeal reference to them suspect. However, and you will have to take this on faith, unless you have the courage to try to read some Kant for yourselves, there can be no doubt that Kant's philosophy is the inspiration for Kelsen's theories. With Kant as his mentor, Kelsen's version of legal positivism, or 'theory of positive law' (PTL 1) is best understood as an unfinished search for the fundamental character of law, or at least those necessary features that allow us to perceive it. Such a search is not satisfied by a finding of what

1 All of Kelsen's major jurisprudential works (as opposed to other theoretical works on topics such as international law) are editions, enlargements or revisions of the original *Pure Theory of Law* published in German (*Reine Rechtslehre*) in 1934 (a translation entitled *Introduction to the Problems of Legal Theory* was published in English in 1992). This is partially rewritten as *General Theory of Law and State* published in English in 1945. Then comes the second edition of *Reine Rechtlehre* published in 1960, and in English in 1967. The collection of essays that can be read as further revisions of the *Pure Theory of Law* were published after Kelsen's death in 1973, in 1979, and published in English in 1991 under the title *General Theory of Norms*. References to the English edition of *Pure Theory of Law* 1967 in the text will be simply **PTL**.

law might be (its contingency) or ought to be, but rather what it is. The sense of what it is, its defining characteristics are the conditions 'for the possibility of experience' of it (Kant 1787/1964, 45). Although he believed that he went some way towards stating these conditions, the restatements of his theory during his life demonstrate that he did not himself believe that his work was finished. Indeed many statements in Kelsen's writings allude to the unfinished nature of his theory. 'As it is the task of natural science to describe its object-reality in one system of laws of nature, so it is the task of jurisprudence to comprehend all human law in one system of rules of law ... the Pure Theory of Law, imperfect and inaccurate though it may be in detail, has gone a measurable distance toward this accomplishment' (Kelsen 1957b, 287). Hartney (Introduction to Kelsen 1991a) makes it clear how misleading it is 'to think of Kelsen's Pure Theory of Law as an unchanging doctrine'. It is easy to confuse what some writers see as Kelsen's dogmatism, or perhaps arrogance, with the suggestion that he believed the pure theory of law to be finished.

Kelsen, despite the abstract nature of his theory of law had a considerable practical influence: for example he is credited with drafting the Austrian Constitution after the First World War and was a member of that country's Constitutional Court. He is probably the best known, worldwide and most influential legal theorist of the twentieth century. Even though Kelsen's major theoretical works were written before those of H L A Hart, it is useful to think of Kelsen as debating with all other legal positivists including those who developed their theories after him, but within other traditions of legal positivism. (For Hart's account of his actual debate with Kelsen in California in 1961, see Hart 1963b.) The starting point for this short introduction will however be with the sociological and psychological writings that he had learned about in his studies and intellectual environment in Vienna in the early half of the twentieth century. The social sciences had arrived, and their impact on other branches of knowledge, particularly those that might be grouped together as social philosophy, was profound. Speculation about human behaviour and human behaviour in society was giving way to new concrete disciplines: psychology, sociology, economics and political science. As those new disciplines were transforming speculation about human behaviour they offered the prospect of a better and more realistic understanding of the techniques of political authority and social control, such as law.

In the early Legal Positivist writings of Austin and Bentham (described in Chapter 3) the crucial ingredient of law is identified as coercive and imperative. Writing in 1912 in his book *Fundamental Principles of the Sociology of Law*, the Austrian writer Eugene Ehrlich criticises the idea of coercion or compulsion as that crucial ingredient, arguing that such a view is unrealistic. 'It is quite obvious that a man lives in innumerable legal relations, and that, with few exceptions, he quite voluntarily performs the duties incumbent upon him because of these relations ... The jurist ought to be the last person of all to overlook the fact that that which men do or leave undone as a legal duty ... is quite different from the rule that is obeyed because of compulsion.' He goes on, as many sociologists before and after him have done, to downplay the coercive character of law, and the real effects (law in action, or as he called it 'living law') of legal provisions (law in the books, that are not 'effective' in ordering human behaviour). From such a 'realist' understanding he argues: 'Three elements, therefore, must under all circumstances be excluded from the concept of law as a compulsory order maintained by the state … It is not an essential element of the concept of law that it be created by the state, nor that it constitute the basis for the decisions of the courts or other tribunals, nor that it be the basis of a legal compulsion consequent upon such a decision.' (Ehrlich 1912/1936, 21–24) In response to Ehrlich's arguments Kelsen writes: 'The result of Ehrlich's attempt to emancipate the definition of law from the element of coercion is the definition: the law is an ordering of human behavior. But this is a definition of society, not of law.' (Kelsen 1945/1961, 28) Not only does Kelsen criticise such sociologically inspired writing for confusing what society is with what law is, but also he, unlike Hart, puts coercion back into the centre stage of law.

Methodological Syncretism

Kelsen shares with many other legal positivists a concern to identify what is peculiarly legal in social life. His reason for doing so is not to deny the connection between law and other activities, such as politics or religion, in the sense that these different aspects of social life influence each other. But he reacted against a tendency which he found in many areas of legal study to incorporate writings from different disciplines without considering what made each of them different and how, if at all, they could be combined. He called this tendency by the pejorative term: syncretism. Kelsen did not deny that law has effects, or even that it can be assessed for its effectiveness. Nor did he deny that concepts of what was good or bad could influence the content of particular legal systems. But a focus on the political influences on say, legislation, should not lead to a conclusion that law was simply a continuation of politics. Nor should the discovery say, that policemen assault certain kinds of suspects, lead to a conclusion that such behaviour is legal in the same manner as statutes authorising arrests. Indeed (although this is not a point made by Kelsen) combinations such as 'Law and Medicine', 'Law and Poverty' etc, or attempts to study the effects *of law*, point to the existence of something legal. And that something has a relationship to, but is not the same as, the 'other' material, which is being considered. Kelsen, applying Kant, sought to identify law, as a particular kind of knowledge that is available to us. For example, that which distinguishes law from natural science is their different form as a body of knowledge. This is what makes scientific practice's understanding of natural science peculiarly scientific, as opposed to moral or legal. If one could identify carefully what this knowledge is, and how it is available to us, one could avoid confusion. One could study the relationships between law and natural science, or law and morality (as Kelsen does in PTL, Ch 2) without losing sight of what was different about these different fields of study.

One has to keep this concern in mind when dealing with Kelsen. If you ask which, as between Hart and Kelsen, provides the best descriptive account of a legal system, there will be no contest: Hart wins. However poor his 'descriptive sociology' may or may not be it is a fuller description than Kelsen's avowedly 'pure' theory that is solely directed toward describing 'its object' (PTL 1). But if you ask which theory, when dealing with such sociological aspects of law as crime statistics, impact studies etc, keeps one most focused on what is peculiarly legal, Kelsen's analysis is likely (even if you were to believe it to be wrong) to be far more useful. Let us consider the problem from the other side. Would one identify the nature of scientific knowledge by examining how lay persons, or even scientists, spoke about science, or would one first try to explore the nature of scientific knowledge in itself, what it is and how that knowledge is available to us?

Kelsen, apart from being a philosopher and legal theorist was also an international lawyer, and his approach has definite implications for the study of international law. Austin's theory, which attempts to identify law with the commands of a sovereign backed by sanctions, suggests that international law is 'not law properly so called' (Austin 1832/1955, Lecture V, 142). Hart, who seeks to identify a legal system with the union of primary and secondary rules, particularly a rule of recognition, which identifies what may count as law within that system, sees international law as analogous to custom, having developed secondary rules only to a limited extent. It does not exhibit in full all of the necessary features of his concept of a legal system, and so its classification as law remains in doubt. (Although he definitely accepts that the use of the word law in the context of international law is a common and acceptable use – see Hart 1961, Chapter 10.) Kelsen, who sees law as a particular kind of normative knowledge, has no problem in regarding international law as law (PTL, Ch 7). Indeed, he sees the absence of the features, which these other theorists identify with law, as a consequence of non-law (impure) reasoning. The identification of law with sovereign states, or legislatures and courts, is an ideological and unnecessary addition to what is necessary for something to be legal. By insisting that institutions associated with nation states are the only appropriate basis for law, one starts from a definition that denies, or at least undermines, the possibility that state actions can meaningfully be assessed for their legality. But if legality lies in a form of knowledge, and not in state action (whether at the national or international level) one is left with the possibility that the actions of state officials can, meaningfully, be declared illegal. Moreover, his theory leads to the possibility of exploring the potential for international law to develop consistently with national law, as a 'higher' form of law, or even subject to national law. In other words it offers a considerable opportunity for increasing our understanding of, and the potential development of, international law.

Kelsen's attempt to articulate a 'pure' theory of law has often been criticised as an arid exercise, or as Laski puts it 'an exercise in logic, not in life' (see Laski 1948, vi; Stewart 1986, 127). This view may have much to commend it, but it fails to value the enterprise in which Kelsen was engaged, or the insights that follow from it. To attempt to describe, in rigorous terms, the distinctive features of a particular body of knowledge and resultant social technique, is necessarily to be involved in reasoning that appears abstract. And an approach rooted in Kant inevitably leads to the introduction of concepts that have no 'existence in reality'. (For Kant, before we can know that things exist, we must explore what in our conceptual apparatus allows us to know objects that we experience as things: 'only by means of them can any object whatsoever of experience be thought' (Kant, 1787/1964, 126).) This is because one cannot organise any body of knowledge without already 'knowing' things, which things cannot be either directly experienced, or proved. Within Kelsen's theory this leads him to discuss law's logico-meaningful existence, and to locate its validity in a transcendental-logical presupposition which he calls the 'grundnorm' or basic norm. One can overcome the strangeness of these terms by focussing on what he is seeking to describe: what we (and that includes you) think when you describe something as valid or invalid, legal or illegal. And if, at the end of your consideration of his theory, you decide that there is **no** such thing as an objective, necessary meaning when something is said to be 'legal', or 'the law', then this is hardly a conclusion that is irrelevant to life. It means that **all** statements such as 'it is the law of England that ...' are subjective, indeterminate, hopelessly and endlessly contested. If, on the other hand, you reach the opposite conclusion, then treating Kelsen's jurisprudence as an unfinished attempt to overcome the subjective, indeterminate, endlessly contested meaning of law is, at least, a useful if exacting starting point.

The Elements of Legal Knowledge

Before we start exploring Kelsen's pure theory, it may be useful for you to think about an example that illustrates Kelsen's concerns and methods. This example can be used to think about the quote that follows, and may convince you that the problems he is seeking to analyse, and the kinds of thoughts that he is trying to describe, are not as unfamiliar as the language he uses might suggest.

An ordinary person visits a lawyer to complain that his flat has been broken into, and some of his property taken away. The lawyer asks who did it. If the answer is 'bailiffs', the lawyer would wish to know whether their actions were authorised or not. He would probably look for a court order. The order would be justified by a judgment, which he could scrutinise. The order might be valid, void, or voidable, statuses which he would try to establish by reference to other rules (the law of contract, rules of court procedure etc). If some of these rules were statutory instruments, he might check that they came within the scope of the authorising statute.

What kind of thinking is involved in this checking back and forth between different rules, and between those rules and facts? Does it matter if the lawyer were a communist, anarchist, or a committed supporter of the present political regime? Would this affect the answer given to the question of whether the goods were **lawfully** seized? If one can have an objective answer to this question, what kinds of thought-processes are involved? What does it mean to conclude, as the lawyer might conclude: 'Your door was broken down and your goods were lawfully seized in accordance with a valid order of the court'.

Now for Kelsen:

> It follows that a legal order may be characterized as a coercive order, even though not all its norms stipulate coercive acts; because norms that do not stipulate coercive acts (and hence do not command, but authorize the creation of norms or positively permit a definite behaviour) are dependent norms, valid only in connection with norms, that *do* stipulate coercive acts. (PTL 58)

As a description of the basic elements of legal knowledge, and thus of law (the aim of Kelsen's theory of positive law) the above statement needs to be understood. It can be restated as a definition of law: 'Law is the primary norm which stipulates the sanction' (Kelsen 1945/61, 63). But what is a norm, and what a primary norm, and what does stipulating a sanction involve? To answer these questions we must work through some of Kelsen's reasoning.

A norm functions as a 'measure of human action' and 'as a scheme of interpretation' (PTL 4). Others have used the same language, despite coming from very different intellectual traditions. (For example, Aquinas defines law as a 'measure of human action' – *Summa Theologica*, see extract in Chapter 2. It is often not the differences in language between legal theorists that are important, but the different uses to which the same language may be put.) Just as a metre ruler might be used to measure length, and the result of using that measure would be objective, in the sense that we would all reach the same conclusion about the length of a given object as long as we were using the same ruler. So a legal norm enables us to give an objective meaning to human action, to measure it. Human action will always have a subjective meaning, an intention, or mix of intentions. To kill someone might be willingly to end someone's life for whatever reason(s) one performs the act, malevolent or benevolent. It might be for the subjective reason to rid oneself of someone one dislikes, or to help someone to die with dignity, to kill someone in anger, or to execute (as a legal executioner) in cold blood. That subjective meaning can be explored as a question of psychology, or perhaps sociology (in terms of cultural patterns of killing, or behaviour in wars etc). But there is another meaning that can be attributed to such action, an objective meaning. If there is a norm saying that one ought not to kill, then measuring one's action against that norm produces the objective conclusion, that one has acted immorally, or illegally, that one has committed a sin or legal murder. Or, in other circumstances, one has acted morally or legally because such killing was associated with a just war, or legally authorised. If there is a norm then there is always the opportunity to find an objective meaning, but without a norm there is only subjective meaning(s). An objective meaning can be characterised as one that is de-psychologised. Not only is the subjective element (the intention behind the act) ignored, but also so is the will or intention (political will) behind the norm. Thus, for the purpose of determining the objective meaning of an act or act of will there is no need for individual or group psychology or psychological knowledge at all, avoiding syncretism.

Having said what a norm does (its function), the question remains what it is. Norms are ought propositions, that is statements in an 'ought' form (PTL 4). Such propositions can take a number of subsidiary forms: '"Norm" is the meaning of an act by which a certain behavior is commanded, permitted or authorized' (PTL 5), or what one should, may, or can do. The subjective meaning of actions can be explored by asking, in relation to our earlier example: 'why did someone wish to kill, what was their psychological state, and what caused it?' Subjective meaning, in other words, can be explored through forms of explanation or understanding, a typical one being the analysis of cause and effect. Killing, or willing to kill, is the effect of socio-psychological causes, which are the effects of underlying causes, and so on until infinity. The nature of such knowledge, all such 'scientific knowledge', at least according to Kant and Kelsen, is infinitely regressive, '... endless in both directions' (PTL 90). Because norms are not scientific in that way, they are not dependent on cause and effect analysis, their 'scientific' character is of a different kind. The basis for the explanation of norms does not lie in any 'facts' of our existence. Norms are not the objective effects of any causes in the natural world. (If you wish to follow up this statement and see how Kelsen attacks any other position, try reading his 'A "Dynamic" Theory of Natural Law' in Kelsen 1957c, 174–197.) Rather, a norm cannot exist independently of other norms. To say that one ought (objectively) not to kill begs the question why? A meaningful answer is dependent on finding another norm by which to measure and give objective meaning to this norm. That other norm could be that you ought to obey your parents or God or the law, and your parents and God and the law have told (commanded) you not to kill. Norms are related to other norms by 'imputation'. We can call this a chain in the line, not of causation, but validity. Kelsen understands the body of knowledge that makes up law to consist of norms related to other norms by the process of imputation: law then is a 'normative science'. 'By defining law as a norm (or, to be precise, as a system of norms or as a normative order) and by limiting the science of law to the cognition and description of legal norms and to the norm-constituted relations between the norm-determined facts, the law is delimited against nature, and the science of law as a science of norms is delimited against all other sciences that are directed toward causal cognition of actual happenings' (PTL 25).

Norms cannot exist objectively without reference to other norms. 'An isolated act of one individual cannot be regarded as a legal act, its meaning cannot be regarded as a legal norm, because law, as mentioned, is not a single norm, but a system of norms; and a particular norm may be regarded as a legal norm only as a part of such a system' (PTL 47). If this is so, then don't norms involve an infinite regression both forwards and backwards from norms to norms? Kelsen sees the 'concretisation' and individuation (working forwards) of norms, as imputing the application of primary norms. Imputation is a normative relation, 'if *a* is then *b* ought to be' (PTL 89–90). The causal relation is, of course, 'if *a* is, then *b* is (or will be)'. The most concrete norms that themselves do not command, permit or authorise any other norms, but still allow one to objectively measure human behaviour he calls primary norms. Primary norms can take different forms according to different normative orders. What is characteristic of the primary norms of a moral normative order is that they are commands that tell people what they ought and ought not to do, they describe duties and relate to 'internal behaviour' (PTL 60–62). They do not operate through authorising an official (external behaviour) to exercise coercion, which does not mean that they do not rely on coercion.

Kelsen believes that all norms rely on coercive power. But the kind of coercive power usually associated with a moral normative order is psychic or transcendental power rather than physical or socially imminent power. 'The fundamental difference between law and morals is: law is a coercive order, that is, a normative order that attempts to bring about a certain behavior by attaching to the opposite behavior a socially organized coercive act; whereas morals is a social order without such sanctions. The sanctions of the moral order are merely the approval of the norm-conforming and the disapproval of the norm-opposing behavior, and no coercive acts are prescribed as sanctions.' (PTL 62) On the other hand the kind of coercive power mainly associated with a legal normative order is physical power. Primary legal norms, the concretised norms of legal normative orders are commands, permissions or authorisations to officials to exercise coercion. They tell officials of different sorts what they should, can or may do in the way of depriving people of life, liberty, economic or other values. All legal norms are, in essence, in and of themselves, nothing more than normative directions to officials to coerce. The enforcement of that form of coercion might in the end require the sanction of a court official and the use of a state's monopoly of force, but those factors go beyond the implicit nature of legal knowledge. In and of itself the law designates the circumstances by which officials 'ought' objectively to coerce. Unlike moral norms that are duty imposing on people at large, that objectively validate individual duties, no such individual duties are intrinsic to law. There is no space for them within the bare relationships of legal normative orders. At its sparsest legal normative orders do not tell citizens what their duties are, in other words there is no meaningful concept of legal obligation in relation to citizens. Or rather, any such concept is secondary; it may be deduced from the primary norms, it may be proposed as a dependent norm, or it may be a condition for the application of those norms. If the concretised, primary legal norm authorises the prison officer to imprison the person convicted of a crime, or the bailiff to deprive the defendant of their goods for having acted contrary to the civil code, then it can be deduced that as preconditions the person convicted or found liable ought not to have done the particular acts in question. To have a duty not to do any particular act, or to have been adjudged, in law, to have done it, are preconditions to the operation of legal normative orders. 'The sanction is the consequence of the delict; the delict is the condition of the sanction.' (PTL 39) Here a delict does not refer to a wrong in itself, *mala in se*, but only a wrong prohibited, *mala prohibita* (PTL 112): 'The human behavior against which the coercive act is directed is to be considered as prohibited, illegal – as a delict.'(PTL 35) Beyond those preconditions lies law: legal normative orders are coercive orders in which law is the primary norm that stipulates the sanction.

Kelsen's juristic definition of 'delict' has been severely criticised. Here is Hart's criticism, which argues that Kelsen's definition fails crucially to distinguish between a fine and a tax. And, on the basis of this criticism, more extensive criticisms of the pure theory become apparent.

Hart (1963b, 299–300)

Sanctions may take the form of compulsory money payments, e.g. fines; but taxes also take this form. In both cases alike, to use Kelsen's terminology, certain behaviour of the subject is a condition under which an official or organ of the system ought to demand a money payment from the subject. So if we confine our attention to the contents of the law as represented in the canonical form 'If A, then B ought to be' it is impossible to distinguish a criminal law punishing behaviour with a fine from a revenue law taxing certain activities. Both when the individual is taxed and when he is fined the law's provisions when cast into the Kelsenian canonical form are identical. Both cases are therefore cases of delict unless we distinguish between them by reference to something that escapes the net of the canonical form, i.e. that the fine is the punishment for an activity officially condemned and the tax is not. It may perhaps be objected that a tax, though it consists of a compulsory money payment as some sanctions also do, is not a 'sanction' and that Kelsen's juristic definition of delict refers to a 'sanction'. But this does not really avoid the difficulty; it only defers it; for we shall have to step outside the limits of juristic definition in order to determine when a compulsory money payment is a sanction and when it is not. Presumably it is a sanction when it is intended as or assumed to be a punishment to discourage 'socially undesired behaviour' to which it is attached; but this is precisely the element which Kelsen considers to be excluded from the definition of delict.

It is plain that Kelsen himself is aware of these difficulties, because he concedes that the juristic definition only holds good on the presupposition that the behaviour, which is the condition of the sanction, is considered detrimental to society. But does not this concession show that the severely restricted juristic definition is useless as well as confusing? Here it is important to stress that many of the illuminating definitions of the Pure Theory are not or could not be *juristic* definitions in the severely restricted sense that Kelsen intends. Plainly for the reasons given above the definition of a sanction is not. It is even possible to doubt whether the definition of a legal norm (quite apart from its dependence on the definition of a sanction) conforms to the strict requirements of juristic definition. For Kelsen tells us that the norm 'is the expression of the idea that something ought to occur, especially that an individual ought to behave in a certain way'. But though a norm may *be* an expression of an idea it is not clear that 'an expression' or 'an idea' or 'an expression of an idea' are *contents* or *elements* of the norm or fit any other of the descriptions given by Kelsen of what may be used in a strictly juristic definition.

Elemental Knowledge

A Chain of Validity of Legal Norms

The Basic Norm (Grundnorm) – a Presupposition

The Historically First Constitution

The 'Reigning' Constitution

Acts of Parliament – Custom – Precedents

Statutory Instruments

Bye-laws

Primary (Concretised/Individuated) Norms

(eg Court Order Commanding, Permitting and Authorising Coercive Acts)

If the concretisation and individuation of legal norms can be found in primary coercive norms what, working backwards, about the most general or highest legal norm? If cause and effect analysis leads to an infinite regression, does the same apply to all forms of knowledge? Aren't moral norms traceable to *a priori* moral assumptions, which are unproven or unprovable and thus neither scientific nor objective? Part of the answer given by Kelsen (and Kant) is dependent on where you start. If we ought not to kill because it says so in the Bible, and if we ought to obey the Bible because it contains God's law, then why ought we to obey God? If you are able to find measures (normative propositions) that give an objective account for why one ought to obey God, then you must ask the next normative question in that regression until you come to an inability to do so. If not, then all you have is the normative statement, one ought to obey God or God's will (a subjective act of will, or your interpretation of it). But in what sense can it be said that the normative statement that you ought to obey God, or whatever other normative proposition you have reached, is an objective statement? How can it function to enable objective validity to be given to all the other measures within the normative order? Now, if you try to rely on a factual basis for your most general or highest normative proposition, you are liable to be criticised for being illogical, for determining what ought to be from what is, for deriving an evaluative proposition from a descriptive one. (Look back to the reference to 'is' and 'ought' and Hume's critique in Chapter 2.) Here is the Kant/Kelsen critique: 'For whereas, so far as nature is concerned, experience supplies the rules and is the source of truth, in respect of the moral law it is, alas, the mother of illusion! Nothing is more reprehensible than to derive the laws prescribing what *ought to be done* from what *is done*, or to impose upon them the limits by which the latter is circumscribed.' (Kant, quoted by Kelsen, in 'Is and Ought in Kant's Philosophy': Kelsen 1991b.) Even more, you can be accused of starting with something which itself is an effect of a cause and therefore itself liable to recede down the route of infinite regression. But if you simply state your highest normative proposition, then its objective validity is questioned, as it appears to be no more than an assumption, even if, as a matter of fact, everybody agreed with it. What everybody agrees with is a description of people's views and has little to tell us about whether those views are good or right, or have an objective meaning. (Translating what people think into what gives them pleasure would allow a utilitarian to argue that there is an objective basis for such moral reasoning, although such a position has numerous problems. For example, how would you react to an opinion poll that showed that 90% of the population thought killing babies that weighed over 4 kilos at birth was right – an eminent 'scientist' having linked antisocial behaviour to high birth-weight?)

Kelsen would try to help us to understand this differently. At a certain stage of generalisation rising up from the concretised primary norm, one reaches a point in one's knowledge where one can go no further. At this point one is left with a problem. The problem for a purely moral normative order, if such an order could exist, is capable of resolution if one takes the opportunity to address the question of what general norm is both consistent with and inductively determined by the norms that you have identified. To find such a norm you must assume only that all the norms that you have identified are non contradictory in the sense that they are all consistent with the content of the most general norm. Thus such norms must be non-contradictory and capable of deductive and inductive inference. (These qualities do not apply to legal norms, as will be illustrated.) Let's give one version of Kant's famous categorical imperative: 'Act only according to that maxim by which you can at the same time will that it should become a universal law.' (1788/1956, 80) From such a general maxim, particular maxims might follow deductively, as a matter of consistency. For example, perhaps it is implied that one ought to 'love thy neighbour as thyself'. Then as even more concrete examples of that maxim, one ought not to kill others or harm others, but befriend others and care for others (although, always, with exceptions). From the other end, one could work upwards. If [you ought to] 'love thy neighbour' is a norm in a moral system, what more general norm could in turn authorise it? Answer (inductive): act as if all your actions were a universal law, applicable to others as well as yourself. Working down from the top one is only committed to deductive consistency. Working up from the bottom is more problematic, because more than one general norm can validate what can be deduced from it (is God's will above 'love thy neighbour' or Kant's categorical imperative?). Despite this problem it is possible to claim that what objectively validates any group of norms that can be gathered together from the base or primary norms, through more general, dependent or secondary norms to the most general norm, is a presupposed most general norm. That general norm has a unity in its content with all the norms of the system. 'Love thy neighbour as thyself' might precipitate such unity.

Legal systems, and some moral orders, have a dynamic as well as a static quality. This depends on the ability of bodies to posit new norms. With static normative orders, reasoning deductively requires one to consider the content of the norm, and what can be derived logically from that content (love thy neighbour includes don't torture thy neighbour). 'The norms of the order of the first type [static] are valid on the strength of their content: because their validity can be traced back to a norm under whose content the content of the norms in question can be subsumed as the particular under the general.' (PTL 195) Although, in the example given, the lower norms flow from higher norms as deductions from their general content, such a description does not, for Kelsen, ground the validity of the general norm (see 'Logical Problems about Grounding the Validity of Norms': Kelsen 1991c). But, with a dynamic order the validity of a norm will depend not simply on content. For example, if a moral order is based on the duty to obey God, and God can issue new commands or commandments, then moral duties are not simply a question of the relationship between the new and old commands. That one ought to obey God validates whatever God commands (dynamic). That one ought 'to love thy neighbour as thyself' does not permit you to ignore your neighbour's cries for help (static), even though your God might permit you to do so.

The nature of dynamic normative orders is particularly relevant to legal orders. Here the most general normative proposition consistent with the system of norms is that one ought to obey the 'historically first constitution' (PTL 200). Such a proposition is consistent with a system that is characterised by authorising many officials to make, change, or determine what norms apply, and ultimately authorise coercive primary norms. Thus the grundnorm of legal normative orders is exactly that, a 'transcendental-logical presupposition' (PTL 201) giving objective meaning to the 'historically first constitution'. It proposes that one ought to obey the historically first constitution. That is its objective measure. Or, as Kelsen says: 'the subjective meaning of the acts by which legal norms are created can be interpreted as their objective meaning only if we presuppose in our juristic thinking, the norm: "One ought to obey the prescriptions of the historically first constitution."' (PTL 204) Transcending beyond legal norms lies the grundnorm, as a foundation for legal knowledge it is presupposed, as a matter of necessity, perhaps logical necessity, it **must** be presupposed. (The debate engendered by some of Kelsen's later writings about whether the grundnorm is a presupposition or a fiction need not concern us at this stage.) Because the grundnorm does not depend for its own normative validity on a higher norm, it must have a different character from all the other norms within the system of norms. The difference is that it is the meaning of an act of thinking, rather than, with other norms, the objective meaning of an act of will. And here, crucially, lies the difference between Kelsen's grundnorm and Hart's rule of recognition. The rule of recognition is, according to Hart, a fact, and one that is available to be described. The grundnorm, rather than having an existence in fact, is the meaning of an act of thinking, and one that is only available to be conceived.

While Kelsen's theory is positivistic, one can use it without abandoning natural law. A legal grundnorm has only a dynamic, and not a static quality: 'obey the historically first constitution'. As such, the question of whether legal systems can exist without natural law elements is an empirical question that the theory is incapable of answering. If, as a matter of fact, different persons would give different reasons why they might think it right to obey the constitution, including non-moral ones, the notion of a grundnorm captures the implications of this: legal thinking is possible without agreement on the basis of the normativity of the constitution. It only requires all persons involved in legal thinking to presuppose that the constitution is valid. This suggests that the theory describes an anti-natural law position. But if, as a matter of fact, constitutions would not be regarded as valid unless they contained natural law elements, then every grundnorm authorises a legal order with such elements. The theory does not tell one whether such elements are necessary or not. Such empirical questions lie outside what the theory recognises as legal knowledge, which is not to say that such preconditions do not exist.

A lot more could be said about this. Much of the debate about the importance of Kelsen's pure theory is focused on the nature, character and coherence of the grundnorm. (For a stringent account of the faults in Kelsen's account of the grundnorm, see Raz 1979b.)

Weighing the Elements

With the elements of the pure theory of law at his disposal Kelsen was able to grapple with a whole range of questions that others might pose in rather different ways. What will be illustrated is how theorisation about law as normative allows for the possibility of a systematic exploration of law and its related ideas. It gives some tools for clear, consistent thinking, which, for example, Hart's reliance on the everyday linguistic practices of officials and citizens does not. We might try to look at a few examples of these explorations. However, it needs to be appreciated that this kind of analysis leads to a deeper and more demanding understanding of Kelsen's theory/science of law; in other words, there is a lot more to be said and understood, and the greater the understanding the more sophisticated the basic analysis becomes. Before exploring such questions it is important that you are clear about what the 'purity' of the pure theory involves. In the extract below from Raz that is exactly what he clarifies. (In his article Raz also raises strong criticisms about aspects of Kelsen's reasoning, which are well worth considering. However, those criticisms have been edited out of this extract, which is only designed to increase your understanding of what Kelsen is actually proposing.)

Raz (1981, 442–453)

...

Kelsen's theory is, as is well known, doubly pure. It is free of sociological and psychological investigations and it separates law from morality. The first purity has attracted much criticism ... based on one or the other of two quite separate objections. First is the objection that the content of the law cannot be established without regard to the actions and intentions of legal institutions be they legislative or adjudicative. Second, there is the objection that the law and its significance cannot be appreciated unless one studies it in its social context, with an emphasis on its actual effects in practice. Both objections are familiar and I will not discuss them in detail. Let me, though, make a couple of observations about the second one.

It is beyond doubt part of the task of legal philosophy to explain the methods by which the existence and content of the law are ascertained. If it is true that they cannot be ascertained without regard to the practices and manifested attitudes of legal institutions, then the first objection is – as I believe it to be – an important valid objection to Kelsen's theory. It is less clear that the second objection is an objection at all. Kelsen did not deny the possibility of sociological jurisprudence. He was content to maintain four theses. First, that beside sociological jurisprudence there is also an independent enquiry, normative jurisprudence, whose subject is different. Normative jurisprudence is the study of legal norms, that is, the study of how people ought to behave according to law. It is not an enquiry into how they actually do behave. Second, normative jurisprudence is no less empirical than sociological jurisprudence, since it is concerned exclusively with *positive* law, that is, law as the product of the activity of social custom and of legislative and adjudicative institutions. Thirdly, normative jurisprudence enjoys in an important way a logical priority over sociological jurisprudence. The very definition of the subject-matter of sociological jurisprudence presupposes an understanding of law as provided by its normative study, since sociology of law is the study of those aspects of human behaviour which are related to the law. Here 'the law' must be normatively interpreted. Fourthly, normative jurisprudence is presupposed by sociology in another important way as well. The explanation of human behaviour related to law has to take account of the way people's beliefs about the law, normatively understood, affect their behaviour.

...

Kelsen's semantic anti-reductivism is of course intimately connected with the other purity of Kelsen's theory: its being free of moral elements. Here the antagonists were not the sociological theorists but the natural lawyers. The opposition to natural law was a major preoccupation of Kelsen's and he wrote extensively on the subject throughout his life. His views place him in the historical tradition of legal positivism.

Three major theses have been traditionally associated with legal positivism. First is the reductive semantic thesis which proposes a reductive analysis of legal statements according to which they are non-normative, descriptive statements of one kind or another. Second is the contingent connection thesis according to which there is no necessary connection between law and moral values. Third is the sources thesis which claims that the identification of the existence and content of law does not require resort to any moral argument.

The three theses are logically independent and one is free to accept any one of them while rejecting the others. They were, however, collectively endorsed by many leading positivists such as Bentham, Austin, Holmes, and Ross among others. Where does Kelsen stand on these issues? The question is of the utmost importance to the understanding of his theory of law. In many ways it is the most important set of problems that any philosophy of law has to face since it raises the problem of the double aspect of law, its being a social institution with a normative aspect. The supreme challenge for any theory of law is to do justice to both facets of the law.

Kelsen's solution is to reject the reductive semantic thesis and to embrace the contingent connection and the sources theses. Kelsen regards the law as positive law. It is based on social sources identifiable without any reference to moral argument. On this Kelsen never had any doubt. He never wavered in his endorsement of the two aspects of the thesis. The existence or non-existence of a legal system as a whole is a matter of social fact. It depends entirely on its efficacy in the society in question. Moreover, the test determining for every individual rule whether it belongs to a legal system in force in a certain country is equally a matter of social fact. It turns on whether or not it was posited in the appropriate way: whether or not it can be traced to an authorized social source.

Equally firm is Kelsen's belief in the contingent connection thesis. Kelsen insists that (1) to claim that there is a necessary connection between (the content of) law and morals either presupposes absolute moral values to which the law necessarily conforms or assumes that all the divers relativistic moralities have some values in common and that the law conforms to those. He further argues that (2) there are no absolute moral values and there is no content common to all the relativistic moralities. Hence he concludes that there is no necessary connection between law and morals.

Kelsen's departure from the traditional positivist view is in his rejection of the semantic reductive thesis. Reductive positivists have variously argued that legal statements are statements about commands, or predictions of the likelihood of sanctions or of courts' decisions, etc. Kelsen is adamant in rejecting all reductive analyses of legal statements. He holds that 'a norm ... is 'valid' means that it is binding – that an individual ought to behave in the manner determined by the norm'. Kelsen regards legal statements as fully normative statements. This view of his, as has been often noted, is difficult to reconcile with his acceptance of the sources and the contingent connection theses which leads him to say at the same time that 'juristic value judgments are judgments which can be tested objectively by facts'. It is in his handling of the tension between his non-reductive semantic views and the sources and the contingent connection theses that one finds his most original contribution to the general theory of law. It is this tension which leads directly to his best-known doctrine, that of the basic norm.

...

One would expect Kelsen to propound a view of legal statements rather like Hart's since Hart's account shares three of the most important features of Kelsen's doctrine of the law and of legal discourse. First, the existence of law can be objectively ascertained by reference to social facts. Hence Hart says, and one would expect Kelsen to agree, that legal statements are either true or false and that their truth conditions are their relations to complex social practices. Second, Hart, like Kelsen, regards legal statements as having a normative dimension which cannot be reduced to an assertion of any social facts. Third, Hart's account of the normative dimension in terms of the illocutionary and expressive force of legal statements avoids any reference to moral facts and does not presuppose the existence of moral values. Since Kelsen denies the existence of absolute moral values one might have expected him to provide an analysis of legal discourse along lines similar to Hart's.

Despite these similarities Kelsen's view of legal statements is radically different from Hart's, because Kelsen advances a cognitivist interpretation of all normative discourse. He rejects expressive explanations such as Hart's. For him a normative statement, be it legal, moral, or other, expresses a practical attitude only in that it expresses a belief in the existence of a valid norm, and a norm constitutes a value. Hence the normative aspect of legal statements is not to be explained by their illocutionary force nor by the fact, taken by itself, that they express an acceptance of a standard of behaviour. It has to be explained by the fact that such statements state or presuppose the existence of a value or a norm, that is, a normatively binding standard and not merely a social practice.

...

Legal statements are normative statements in the same sense and in the same way that moral statements are normative. This is as we saw the gist of Kelsen's semantic anti-reductivism. The implication of his persistent emphasis is that legal statements are 'ought' statements, not to be confused with 'is' statements. The threat that this view poses to the purity of one's theory of law is evident. If legal statements are as normative as ordinary moral ones, if they are moral statements, then the law and its existence and content, which is what legal statements state, seem to be essentially moral facts. But the study of moral facts and their identification cannot be free of moral considerations and arguments.

Kelsen's solution is threefold. First, he points out that the existence of law can be established and its content ascertained without the use of normative statements. The law can be described in sociological terms, be described as a power structure in a society, etc. Such a description is not synonymous with a normative description of the law. If it were then it would amount to a reductive analysis of the normative description. But such a description will convey all the social facts which form the factual basis of the law, all the social practices which Hart regards as constituting the existence of law. What will be left out is the claim that these social facts are 'objectively valid', that they give rise to rights and duties and to other normative consequences. Some people have the appropriate moral beliefs and they regard the law as a normative system and describe it using legal statements. Those who do not share these moral views deny that the law is normative. But they can acknowledge its existence as a social fact.

But this first answer to the problem is not enough. It shows the possibility of a pure study of law as a complex social fact but it does not by itself establish the possibility of a pure study of law as a *normative* system. Therefore, Kelsen reinforces the first move with a second one. People have many moral beliefs. It is likely that for any individual in a society some of his moral beliefs coincide with the law and some diverge from it. But imagine a man whose moral beliefs are identical with the law. He does not add nor detract one iota from it. Furthermore assume that his moral beliefs all derive from his belief in the moral authority of the ultimate lawmaking processes. For him, in other words, his belief in the validity of all and only the legal norms is not a haphazard result of chance but a logical consequence of one of his beliefs. Let us call this person the legal man. Legal science, says Kelsen, studies the law as a normative system but without committing itself to its normativity. Basically the legal statements of legal science are conditional legal statements: if the legal man is right, they say, then this is what you ought to do. 'The Pure Theory', he says, 'describes the positive law as an objectively valid normative order and states that this interpretation is possible only under the condition that a basic norm is presupposed according to which the subjective meaning of the law-creating acts is also their objective meaning. The Pure Theory thereby characterizes this interpretation as possible, not necessary, and presents the objective validity of positive law only as conditional – namely conditioned by the presupposed basic norm'. Therefore all the legal statements of legal science are hypothetical.

My legal man is one who endorses the basic norm and all that follows from it and nothing else. Scientific legal statements, being conditional statements of the form 'if the legal man is right then one ought to …' or 'if the basic norm is valid one ought to …' etc., are value-neutral. They are free of any moral presuppositions. By using them legal science can both be pure and describe the law as a normative system.

The problem with this second answer is that although it allows legal science to describe the law as a normative system it does not allow it to use categorical statements, for they state that the law is a system of valid norms. It merely enables legal science to state what the law is *if it is valid*. This may be all that legal scholars need do. But it is not all that legal practitioners, barristers and solicitors, do. They do not merely talk about the law. They use it to advise clients and to present arguments before courts. Kelsen does not distinguish between the scholar and the practitioner. His analysis of legal discourse is meant to apply to both. But the practitioner does not state what the law is if it is valid. He states that it is valid. Yet if legal theory is pure such statements cannot be moral statements. They cannot be full-blooded normative statements. Kelsen requires a value-neutral interpretation of categorical legal statements. He solves this problem by making his third move. Legal scientists, he says, do not merely describe what the law is if the basic norm is valid. They do actually presuppose the basic norm themselves. They assume its validity. '[T]he basic norm really exists in the juristic consciousness.'

Kelsen sometimes draws obscurely on a distinction between positing and presupposing the basic norm, to suggest that legal scientists (by which he refers to practitioners as well) presuppose but do not posit it as do people who actually believe in the moral validity of the law. This terminological distinction is not a happy one. His idea seems to be that not all scientific legal statements are hypotheticals of the type analysed above. Some or most are categorical statements based on a presupposition of the basic norm as a fiction. Categorical legal statements are therefore of two types, which I have called elsewhere committed and detached. Committed statements are those of ordinary people who use normative language when stating the law because they believe or purport to believe in its binding force. Detached statements are typical of legal science, which assumes the point of view of the legal man without being committed to it. It describes the law in normative statements, but this is a description from a point of view which is not necessarily accepted by the speaker. He talks as if he accepts the basic norm and this pretence is what Kelsen refers to as presupposing the basic norm as a fiction. Detached statements state the law as a valid normative system; they do not merely describe what would be valid if the basic norm is valid. But they do so from a point of view, that of the legal man, to which they are not committed. Therefore, legal science is pure, free of moral commitment despite its use of normative language.

...

1. Contradictory norms

Let us take the example of legal contradiction: legal rules that seem to contradict each other. Many theories of law have as their focus the analysis of contradiction and the mechanisms of legal reasoning that allow such contradiction to be reconciled. Kelsen approaches the subject from a definite starting point. Legal norms **can** contradict each other. He writes: 'It follows that within such a normative order the same behaviour may be – in this sense – commanded and forbidden at the same time, and that this situation may be described without logical contradiction.' (PTL 25) What he means by this is not that such norms can give rise to objective meaning at the level of the most individuated primary norms. If an official is both authorised and forbidden to apply sanctions one cannot say that the sanction is authorised, but one can recognise the normative quality of contradictory norms, which have been authorised by the same higher dynamic norm, they are both valid. (Parliament can pass contradictory laws.) Indeed, it is the fact that both norms can be valid if the higher norm is dynamic that makes it possible to speak meaningfully of contradictory norms. In norms authorised by a static higher norm, or a static normative order, one cannot have contradiction: where '"*a* ought to be" and "*a* ought not to be" exclude each other ... only one can be valid.' (PTL 25, and see earlier discussion of moral, static normative orders.) The problem with contradictory legal norms is not their validity but that they are 'politically unsatisfactory' (PTL 26). They are unlikely to achieve their purposes, not least because they cannot create objective fields of meaning as to the authority of sanctions applied by officials. Kelsen points out that legal orders will contain rules to deal with apparent contradiction, rules that prioritise one or other, such as later rather than earlier rules, statutes rather than common law, the decisions of higher courts rather than those of lower courts. Legal orders may also contain rules that allow rules under particular circumstances to lose their validity (desuetude), or rules of interpretation that permit narrowing and extending the meaning of the rules in question so as to avoid the apparent contradiction.

For Kelsen, the unity of a legal system lies not in the presence of non-contradictory norms, but in the relationships of validity. All norms within a single legal system are valid by reference to the same valid constitution. Why might this be important? Kelsen saw his theory as the basis of legal science. While his pure theory establishes the nature of relationships of validity, it allows one to make statements about law that go not just to their validity, but their truth (hence legal science). Take the statement 'the Theft Act 1968 is part of English law'. Such a statement has a meaning as a descriptive statement, a meaning dependent on the notions of truth or falsity, a meaning that excludes one or other of these notions: either such a statement is true or false. Legal science is full of such statements. But they are not statements of primary norms, 'coercive ought propositions', nor do they refer to higher authorising norms. Kelsen would claim that only when one identifies what it means for norms to be valid, can one go on to say whether a particular rule of a particular legal system exists at any particular time. For a statement of law to be true, there must be valid norms within a particular legal system, whose objective meaning can be described.

Consider the following short extract from Kelsen to see how he deals with these conflicts of norm questions, and how logical he is.

Kelsen (*Pure Theory of Law*, 205–208)

e) The Logical Unity of the Legal Order; Conflict of Norms

Since the basic norm is the reason for the validity of all norms belonging to the same legal order, the basic norm constitutes the unity of the multiplicity of these norms. This unity is expressed also by the fact that a legal order may be described in rules of law that do not contradict each other. To be sure, it is undeniable that legal organs may create conflicting norms – that they perform acts whose subjective meaning is an 'ought' and which may be in conflict with each other if their subjective meaning is interpreted as their objective meaning. Such a conflict of norms is present, if one norm prescribes a certain behavior, and another norm prescribes another behavior incompatible with the first. For example, if one norm prescribes that adultery ought to be punished, and another norm that it ought not to be punished; or if one norm prescribes that theft ought to be punished by death, and another by imprisonment. This conflict, however, as has been demonstrated earlier, is not a logical contradiction in the strict sense of the word, even though it is usually said that the two norms 'contradict' each other. For logical principles, especially the principle of the exclusion of contradictions, are applicable to assertions that can be true or false; if a logical contradiction exists between two assertions, only the one or the other assertion can be true; if one is true, the other must be false. But a norm is neither true nor false, but either valid or invalid. However, the assertion describing a normative order by saying that a certain norm is valid according to that order can be true or false; and particularly so the rule of law describing a legal order by saying that, according to that order, a certain coercive act ought to or ought not to be performed under certain conditions. Therefore, logical principles in general, and the Principle of the Exclusion of Contradictions in particular, are applicable to rules of law describing legal norms and therefore indirectly also to legal norms. Hence it is by no means absurd to say that two legal norms 'contradict' each other. And therefore only one of the two can be regarded as objectively valid. To say that *a* ought to be and at the same time ought not to be is just as meaningless as to say that *a* is and at the same time that it is not. A conflict of norms is just as meaningless as a logical contradiction.

But since the cognition of law, like any cognition, seeks to understand its subject as a meaningful whole and to describe it in noncontradictory statements, it starts from the assumption that conflicts of norms within the normative order which is the object of this cognition can and must be solved by interpretation. Since the structure of the legal order is a hierarchy of higher and lower norms, whereby the higher norm determines the creation of the lower one, the problem of norm conflicts within the same legal order presents itself in two forms, depending on whether the conflict is between two norms of the same level or between a higher and a lower norm.

To begin with, we shall consider conflicts between norms of the same level. If we have a conflict between general norms, created by the same organ at different times, then the validity of the later norm supersedes the validity of the earlier, contradictory, one according to the principle *lex posterior derogat priori*. Since the norm-creating organ – the king or the parliament – is normally authorized to prescribe changeable and therefore abolishable norms, the principle *lex posterior derogat priori* may be presumed to be included in the authorization. The principle also applies if the conflicting norms are prescribed by two different organs; for example, if the constitution authorizes the king and the parliament to regulate the same subject by general norms, or if legislature and custom are both established as law-creating facts. However, the conflicting norms may have been prescribed simultaneously, by the same act and by the same organ, so that the mentioned principle is not applicable, for example if contradictory clauses are contained in the same statute, such as: adultery is punishable and adultery is not punishable; or: everybody who committed a certain delict is punishable and persons of less than fourteen years of age are not punishable. Then the following possibilities for the solution of the conflict exist: Either the two norms can be understood to be subject to a choice by the law-applying organ, e.g., the judge; or if, as in the second example, the two norms are only partly contradictory, then the one norm can be understood to be limiting the validity of the other. The law-describing rule does not say: 'Adultery ought to be punished and ought not to be punished'; it says: 'He who commits adultery ought to be punished or he ought not to be punished.' Nor does the law-describing rule say: 'Everybody who commits a certain delict ought to be punished and persons below the age of fourteen ought not to be punished'; it says: 'Everybody who has committed a certain delict, with the exception of persons below the age of fourteen, ought to be punished.' If neither the one nor the other interpretation is possible, then the legislator creates something meaningless; we then have a meaningless act of norm creation and therefore no act at all whose subjective meaning can be interpreted as its objective meaning; no objectively valid legal norm is present, although the act has been posited according to the basic norm. The basic norm does not bestow the objective meaning of a valid norm upon every act, but only upon an act that has a meaning – the subjective meaning that individuals ought to behave in a certain way. The act must be meaningful in this normative sense. If the act has a different meaning (such as the meaning of an assertion, for example of a theory propounded in a statute) or no meaning at all (for example, if a statute contains nonsensical words or prescriptions incompatible with each other), then no subjective meaning is present that can be interpreted as objective meaning; no act is present whose subjective meaning is capable of being legitimized by the basic norm.

A conflict may also exist between two individual norms, such as two court decisions, particularly if the two norms have been created by different organs. A law might authorize two courts to decide the same case without giving the decision of the one court the authority to abolish the decision of the other. To be sure, this is a most inadequate legal technique, but it is not impossible and has happened. In that case it may well be that an accused person is condemned by one court and acquitted by another, that is, he ought to be punished according to the one norm and not punished according to the other; or it may be that one court may find for the plaintiff as claimed and another court may dismiss the action, which means that according to the one norm civil execution ought to be directed into the property of the defendant, but according to the other norm that civil execution ought not to be directed. The conflict is solved by giving the executive organ the choice between the two decisions. If civil execution is carried out as prescribed by the one norm, then the other norm remains permanently ineffective and therefore loses its validity; if execution is not carried out, it is the other way around. This interpretation is advanced according to the basic norm. For the basic norm prescribes: 'Force ought to be exerted under the conditions and in the manner prescribed by the by and large effective constitution and by the by and large effective general and effective individual norms created according to the constitution.' Effectiveness is stipulated as a condition for the validity by the basic norm. If a conflict is present within the same court decision (for example if the judge is insane), then the act is simply meaningless and therefore no objectively valid legal norm exists. In this way the basic norm makes it possible to interpret the material submitted to legal cognition as a meaningful whole, which means, to describe it in logically noncontradictory sentences.

No conflict is possible between a higher norm and a lower norm, that is, between one norm which determines the creation of another norm and this other norm, because the lower norm has the reason for its validity in the higher norm. If a lower norm is regarded as valid, it must be regarded as being valid according to a higher norm. How this is done will be discussed in the description of the hierarchy of the legal order.

The further consequences of such an analysis are large. Hart discusses these in his essay 'Kelsen's Doctrine of the Unity of Law'. He describes 'one of the most striking doctrines expounded by Kelsen' as follows. 'Its central positive contention is that all valid laws necessarily form a single system, and its central negative contention is that valid laws cannot conflict ... For Kelsen, this doctrine of the unity of law yields certain conclusions concerning the possible or actual relationships between international law and all systems of municipal law. On the strong version of his theory international law and systems of municipal law necessarily form one single system, and there can be no conflicts between the laws of international law and municipal law. On the weaker version it just is the case that all these laws form a single system and there are in fact no conflicts between them.' (Hart 1983, 309–310)

2. Validity and effectiveness

Our deep problem with apparently contradictory legal norms is related to their effects. Not only do contradictory norms appear to be politically unsatisfactory, or as Fuller would argue, fail to guide human behaviour, but how can they exist within the same scheme of objective meaning? In particular how can they be, or effectively be? What, in other words, does the pure theory have to say about the relationship between the validity of legal norms and their effectiveness? Kelsen was aware that he was steering a difficult course in trying to deal with this. Of course validity is not effectiveness, what one ought to do is not identical with what one does, in fact do. But 'A positivist legal theory is faced by the task to find the correct middle road between the two extremes which both are untenable. The one extreme is the thesis that there is no connection between validity as something that ought to be and effectiveness as something that is; that the validity of the law is entirely independent of its effectiveness. The other extreme is the thesis that validity and effectiveness are identical' (PTL 211). For you to follow Kelsen's arguments closely, the short section, that the above statement is taken from, is set out in full.

Kelsen (*Pure Theory of Law*, 211–214)

g) Validity and Effectiveness

This limitation reveals the repeatedly emphasized connection (so important for a theory of positive law) between the validity and the effectiveness of law. The correct determination of this relationship is one of the most important and at the same time most difficult problems of a positivistic legal theory. It is only a special case of the relationship between the 'ought' of the legal norm and the 'is' of natural reality. Because the act by which a positive legal norm is created, too, is an 'is-fact' (German: *Seinstatsache*) just as the effectiveness of the legal norm. A positivistic legal theory is faced by the task to find the correct middle road between two extremes which both are untenable. The one extreme is the thesis that there is no connection between validity as something that ought to be and effectiveness as something that is; that the validity of the law is entirely independent of its effectiveness. The other extreme is the thesis that validity and effectiveness are identical. An idealistic theory of law tends to the first solution of this problem, a realistic theory to the second. The first is wrong for it is undeniable that a legal order in its entirety, and an individual legal norm as well, lose their validity when they cease to be effective; and that a relation exists between the *ought* of the legal norm and the *is* of physical reality also insofar as the positive legal norm, to be valid, must be created by an act which exists in the reality of being. The second solution is wrong because it is equally undeniable that there are many cases – as has been shown before – in which legal norms are regarded as valid although they are not, or not yet, effective. The solution proposed by the Pure Theory of Law is this: Just as the norm (according to which something ought to be) as the meaning of an act is not identical with the act (which actually is), in the same way is the validity of a legal norm not identical with its effectiveness; the effectiveness of a legal order as a whole and the effectiveness of a single legal norm are – just as the norm-creating act – the condition for the validity; effectiveness is the condition in the sense that a legal order as a whole, and a single legal norm, can no longer be regarded as valid when they cease to be effective. Nor is the effectiveness of a legal order, any more than the fact of its creation, the reason for its validity. The reason for the validity – that is, the answer to the question why the norms of this legal order ought to be obeyed and applied – is the presupposed basic norm, according to which one ought to comply with an actually established, by and large effective, constitution, and therefore with the by and large effective norms, actually created in conformity with that constitution. In the basic norm the fact of creation and the effectiveness are made the condition of the validity – 'effectiveness' in the sense that it has to be added to the fact of creation, so that neither the legal order as a whole nor the individual legal norm shall lose their validity. A condition cannot be identical with that which it conditions. Thus, a man, in order to live, must have been born; but in order that he remain alive other conditions must also be fulfilled, for example, he must receive nutrition. If this condition is not fulfilled, he will lose his life. But life is neither identical with birth nor with being nourished.

In the normative syllogism leading to the foundation of the validity of a legal order, the major premise is the ought-sentence which states the basic norm: 'One ought to behave according to the actually established and effective constitution'; the minor premise is the is-sentence which states the facts: 'The constitution is actually established and effective'; and the conclusion is the ought-sentence: 'One ought to behave according to the legal order, that is, the legal order is valid.' The norms of a positive legal order are valid *because* the fundamental rule regulating their creation, that is, the basic norm, is presupposed to be valid, not because they are effective; but they are valid only *as long as* this legal order is effective. As soon as the constitution loses its effectiveness, that is, as soon as the legal order as a whole based on the constitution loses its effectiveness, the legal order and every single norm lose their validity.

However, a legal order does not lose its validity when a single legal norm loses its effectiveness. A legal order is regarded as valid, if its norms are by and large effective (that is, actually applied and obeyed). Nor does a single legal norm lose its validity if it is only exceptionally not effective in single cases. As mentioned in another connection, the possibility of an antagonism between that which is prescribed by a norm as something that ought to be and that which actually happens must exist; a norm, prescribing that something ought to be, which, as one knows beforehand must happen anyway according to a law of nature, is meaningless – such a norm would not be regarded as valid. On the other hand, a norm is not regarded as valid which is never obeyed or applied. In fact, a legal norm may lose its validity by never being applied or obeyed – by so-called *desuetude*. *Desuetudo* may be described as negative custom, and its essential function is to abolish the validity of an existing norm. If custom is a law-creating fact at all, then even the validity of statutory law can be abolished by customary law. If effectiveness in the developed sense is the condition for the validity not only of the legal order as a whole but also of a single legal norm, then the law-creating function of custom cannot be excluded by statutory law, at least not as far as the negative function *of desuetudo* is concerned.

The described relation between validity and effectiveness refers to general legal norms. But also individual legal norms (judicial decisions, administrative decrees) that prescribe an individual coercive act lose their validity if they are permanently unexecuted and therefore ineffective, as has been shown in the discussion of a conflict between two legal decisions.

Effectiveness is a condition for the validity – but it is not validity. This must be stressed because time and again the effort has been made to identify validity with effectiveness; and such identification is tempting because it seems to simplify the theoretical situation. Still, the effort is doomed to failure, not only because even a partly ineffective legal order or legal norm may be regarded as valid, and an absolutely effective norm which cannot be violated as invalid because not being regarded as a norm at all; but particularly for this reason: If the validity, that is, the specific existence of the law, is considered to be part of natural reality, one is unable to grasp the specific meaning in which the law addresses itself to reality and thereby juxtaposes itself to reality, which can be in conformity or in conflict with the law only if reality is not identical with the validity of the law. Just as it is impossible in determining validity to ignore its relation to reality, so it is like-wise impossible to identify validity and reality. If we replace the concept of reality (as effectiveness of the legal order) by the concept of power, then the problem of the relation between validity and effectiveness of the legal order coincides with the more familiar problem of the relationship between law and power or right and might. And then, the solution attempted here is merely the scientifically exact formulation of the old truism that right cannot exist without might and yet is not identical with might.

Right (the law), according to the theory here developed, is a certain order (or organization) of might.

Does the analogy between the conditions of validity and those of life being 'neither identical with birth nor with being nourished' help us, or is it confusing? According to Kelsen it seems to have been the latter to Professor Julius Stone. (Stone, a leading Australian writer of jurisprudence, is considered to be a disciple of Roscoe Pound one of the founders of sociological jurisprudence. The criticism that he levels at Kelsen's theories are set in his volume *Legal System and Lawyers' Reasonings*, 1964.) Consider the following extract from Kelsen in his reply to Stone. Although this extract does not do justice to Stone's critique, it gives an opportunity to hear Kelsen's defence against the sort of criticisms that the pure theory has regularly attracted.

Kelsen (1965, 1139–1151)

III. VALIDITY AND EFFICACY

Professor Stone maintains that according to my doctrine: 'For a norm to be valid two requirements must be fulfilled. First, that norm must be part of a system of norms. Second, the system of norms to which it belongs must be efficacious ...' This, too, is incorrect. In my *Reine Rechtslehre* I say: 'The efficacy of the legal order as a whole and the efficacy of a single legal norm are – just as the act by which the norms or the single norm are created – conditions of the validity ...' This means that the conditions of the validity of the legal order as a whole and of a single legal norm are: for the legal order as a whole, the acts by which the norms of the legal order are created; for the single norm, the act by which this norm is created; and, *in addition,* the fact that the legal order as a whole and the single legal norm are, respectively, effective.

My thesis that 'the reason of the validity of a norm can never be a fact' is – according to Professor Stone – incompatible with my view that a legal norm, in order to be valid, must be by and large effective. Professor Stone says: '[W]hen the efficaciousness of the system as a whole *is not given,* the validity of each offered norm also depends in part (even according to Kelsen's own account) on the question of fact whether men actually do behave in a certain manner towards the system of norms as a whole.' The problem in question is the relationship between validity and efficacy of legal norms. I deal with this delicate problem very carefully in my *Reine Rechtslehre.* A whole section, 'Geltung und Wirksamkeit', is devoted to this problem. The essence of my view of the relationship between validity and efficacy of legal norms is that 'the efficacy of the legal order is only the condition of validity, not the validity itself.' On page 219 I say that positing (*Setzung*) of the norms and efficacy (*Wirksamkeit*) of the norms are 'conditions of the validity'; efficacy in the sense that the established legal norms must be by and large obeyed and, if not obeyed, applied; otherwise the legal order as a whole, just as a single norm, would lose its validity. A condition is not identical with that which is conditioned. To illustrate this I continue: 'Thus a human being in order to live, must be born, and to remain alive also other conditions must be fulfilled, e.g., it must get nourishment. If these other conditions are not fulfilled it will lose its life. But life is not identical with being born or with being nourished.' The validity is conditioned by the efficacy in the sense that a legal order as a whole just as a single norm *loses* its validity if it does not become by and large effective. I call attention to the fact that a legal norm becomes valid *before* it can be effective. A court has to apply only a valid statute. Hence if a court applies a statute immediately after it has been enacted by the legislator it applies legal norms which are *not yet* effective, which become effective by their application. All this Professor Stone ignores in his presentation of my view of the relationship between validity and efficacy of legal norms.

In the same connection Professor Stone says: 'Kelsen has also given us no means of distinguishing the efficaciousness of the aggregate of single norms from that of the system of norms as a whole.' If Professor Stone understands by a 'system' of norms in contradistinction to an 'aggregate of single norms' a legal order constituting a unity in the plurality of legal norms, I refer to my *Reine Rechtslehre* where I say: 'A legal order does not lose its validity by the fact that a single legal norm loses its efficacy, that is to say that this legal norm is not at all or in some particular cases not applied. A legal order is considered to be valid if its norms are *by and large* effective, that is, actually obeyed and applied.'

IV. THE BASIC NORM

One of the main objects of Professor Stone's criticism is my theory of the *basic norm*. Professor Stone says with respect to this concept that it conceals

> an ambiguity, swinging between, on the one hand, a norm that is at the top of the pyramid of norms of each legal order, and on the other, some other norm which remains outside this pyramid, and is thus wholly meta-legal, and amounts to a general presupposition requiring that in each and every legal order 'the constitution' shall be obeyed.

In the following sentence Professor Stone maintains that I 'now', that is, not earlier than in the second edition of my *Reine Rechtslehre*, insist 'that the basic norm is outside the legal system', but nevertheless 'has legally relevant functions'. That means that – according to Professor Stone – I understand by the 'basic norm' a norm which is not a norm of positive law, and at the same time a norm which is a norm of positive law. This interpretation is without any foundation in my writings. I have always and not only in the second edition of my *Reine Rechtslehre* clearly distinguished between the basic norm presupposed in juristic thinking as the constitution in a legal-logical sense and the constitution in a positive legal sense, and I have always insisted that the basic norm as the constitution in a legal-logical sense – not the constitution in a positive legal sense – is *not* a norm of positive law, that it is not a norm 'posited', i.e., created by a real act of will of a legal organ, but a norm *presupposed in juristic thinking*. It is, unfortunately, not possible to translate adequately into English the German terms by which the difference between the basic norm and a norm of positive law is characterized, namely, that the basic norm is not *gesetzt* by a real act of will, but *vorausgesetzt* in juristic thinking. I refer in this respect to my *Reine Rechtslehre* and my *General Theory of Law and State* which was published in 1945, fifteen years before the second edition of the *Reine Rechtslehre*. It is as a norm presupposed in juristic thinking that the basic norm (if it is presupposed) is 'at the top of the pyramid of norms of each legal order'. It is 'meta-legal' if by this term is understood that the basic norm is not a norm of positive law, that is, not a norm created by a real act of will of a legal organ. It is 'legal' if by this term we understand everything which has legally relevant functions, and the basic norm presupposed in juristic thinking has the function to found the *objective* validity of the subjective meaning of the acts by which the constitution of a community is created. In this respect the theory of the basic norm is – to a certain extent – similar to the natural-law doctrine according to which a positive legal order is valid if it corresponds to the natural law. The natural law is not considered to be 'meta-legal', though it is not *positive* law. But there are also essential differences between the doctrine of the basic norm and the natural-law doctrine, as I have shown in the chapter 'Theorie der Grundnorm und Naturrechtslehre' in my *Reine Rechtslehre*. The main difference is that the *content* of the positive legal order is completely independent of the basic norm from which only *the objective validity* of the norms of the positive legal order, not the content of this order, can be derived; whereas according to the natural-law doctrine a positive legal order is valid only if and insofar as its content corresponds to the natural law. Hence there can be no conflict between a positive legal order and its basic norm, whereas from the point of view of a postivistic theory of law a conflict between positive law and what is supposed to be natural law is quite possible. None of this is mentioned by Professor Stone.

Professor Stone says: '[O]n his [Kelsen's] own argument, the apex norm [thus he calls the basic norm] must be such, not only that the multitude of norms "derive their validity" from it, but also that it guarantees in some way that the system of norms by and large is "effiacious" ...' I do not maintain that the basic norm 'guarantees' the efficacy of the legal order to which it refers. What I say is that the basic norm refers only to a coercive social order which is by and large effective. That means: we presuppose the basic norm only if there exists a coercive social order which is by and large effective. I say in my *Reine Rechtslehre*: '[The] basic norm refers only to a constitution which is the basis of an effective coercive order. Only if the actual behavior of men corresponds, by and large, to the subjective meaning of the acts directed at this behavior, their subjective meaning is considered also as their objective meaning.' And I say further: 'The reason for the objective validity of a legal order is ... the presupposed basic norm according to which one ought to obey a constitution which actually is established and by and large effective; and consequently one ought also to obey the norms created in conformity with the constitution and by and large effective.' Since – according to my theory – the basic norm refers only to a coercive order which is by and large effective, and since the basic norm is adapted – to this coercive order and not the coercive order to the basic norm, it is *in this sense* that in the basic norm the actual establishment of the norms of the coercive order by real acts of will and the efficacy of these norms are made the condition of the objective validity of the coercive order. Hence the basic norm does not 'guarantee' the efficacy of the legal order; it does nothing to make this order effective. Therefore, I do not maintain that the basic norm is a 'self-dependent beginning', as Professor Stone interprets my theory of the basic norm. For the basic norm depends on the normative order to which it refers and does not – as Professor Stone asserts –depend on 'the facts of men's actual behavior and exposure to sanctions'. The *normative* coercive order to which the basic norm refers and on which it depends is not identical with these facts. The efficacy of the normative order is a condition of its validity, not its validity.

In his criticism of my theory of the basic norm Professor Stones asks: '[W]hat can the 'pure' theorist of law, as Professor Kelsen claims to be, tell us about it [the 'nature and origin' of the basic norm]?' And he says – without quoting a statement of my writings: 'Kelsen is frank to say that he can tell us nothing, since the question ... is a meta-legal one.' I have never declared that I can tell nothing about the nature and origin of the basic norm. About no other problem have I said so much as about the basic norm. In the 'Index' of my *General Theory of Law and State* I refer to more than twenty different pages and in the 'Index' of my *Reine Rechtslehre* to twenty-five different pages on which I deal with the basic norm, the *Grundnorm*. The *function* of the basic norm is – as I have frequently said – to make it possible to consider the *subjective* meaning of the law-creating acts – which is an 'ought' – as their *objective meaning*, and thus as objectively valid norms. Professor Stone does not mention this function of the basic norm, which shows that he does not understand the theory which he criticizes.

In view of the specific function of the basic norm presupposed in juristic thinking I call it 'constitution in a legal-logical sense' in contra-distinction to the 'constitution in the sense of positive law'. It is to the constitution in the sense of positive law that the basic norm refers. I distinguish these two concepts as clearly as possible. Hence Professor Stone has no reason to speak as quoted above of an 'ambiguity', 'swinging' between two norms.

An essential point of my theory of the basic norm, which Professor Stone does not present correctly, is that it is not necessary to presuppose the basic norm, that only *if* we presuppose it can we consider a coercive order which is by and large effective as a system of *objectively valid* norms. Consequently, the foundation of the objective validity of the legal norms is conditional, conditioned by the presupposition of the basic norm. Professor Stone's statement on page 200, 'It is precisely because the basic norm is not a legal norm that Kelsen insists that it is only 'hypothetical' ...' does not refer to the decisive point.

The basic norm is presupposed as a *valid* norm. Professor Stone's statement, 'For Kelsen then the apex norm is neither legally valid nor invalid; it is a 'hypothesis'' is without foundation. But it is characteristic of Professor Stone's critique that he *in a footnote* to this statement says: 'Kelsen, however [!] now speaks of the 'validity' of the basic norm in some special sense in which its 'validity' can be presupposed.' There is not the slightest reason to put the term 'validity' between quotation marks, and to say that the basic norm is – according to my theory – 'valid' in a 'special sense'. These manoeuvres cannot hide the fact that Professor Stone withdraws in a footnote the statement he is making in the text. My characterization of the basic norm as 'hypothesis' means exactly the same as its characterization as 'presupposition', which is the literal translation of this Greek term. In *Reine Rechtslehre* I said: 'In this presupposition lies the ultimate but only conditioned and in this sense hypothetical reason for the objective validity of the legal order.'

The problem that leads to the theory of the basic norm – as I explained in my *Reine Rechtslehre* – is how to distinguish a legal command which is considered to be objectively valid, such as the command of a revenue officer to pay a certain sum of money, from a command which has the same subjective meaning but is not considered to be objectively valid, such as the command of a gangster. The difference consists in that we do not consider the subjective meaning of the command of a gangster –as we consider the subjective meaning of the legal command of a revenue officer – as its objective meaning because we do not presuppose in the former case – as we presuppose in the latter case – a basic norm. A Communist may, indeed, not admit that there is an essential difference between an organization of gangsters and a capitalistic legal order which he considers as the means of ruthless exploitation. For he does not presuppose – as do those who interpret the coercive order in question as an objectively valid normative order – the basic norm. He does not deny that the capitalistic coercive order is the law of the State. What he denies is that this coercive order, the law of the State, is objectively valid. The function of the basic norm is not to make it possible to consider a coercive order which is by and large effective as law, for – according to the definition presented by the Pure Theory of Law – a *legal* order is a coercive order by and large effective; the function of the basic norm is to make it possible to consider this coercive order as an *objectively* valid order. In my *Das Problem der Souveranitat und die Theorie des Volkerrechts* I said that it is the 'quest for the reason for the validity of the law' (die Frage nach dem Geltungsgrund des Rechts) which leads to the presupposition of the basic norm. In my *Allgemeine Staatslehre* I said that the *Grundnorm* is the *Geltungsgrund,* that is, the reason for the validity, of the legal system; and further that the function of the *Grundnorm* is 'to achieve the objective validity of the social order, independent of the subject's wishing and willing …' In the Preface of my *General Theory of Law and State* I said: 'The pure theory of law … seeks the basis of law – that is, the reason of its validity … in a juristic hypothesis – that is, a basic norm …' The chapter dealing with this problem is entitled: 'The Reason of Validity: the Basic Norm'; and there I said: '[T]he reason for the validity of a norm is a presupposition, a norm presupposed to be ultimately valid, that is, a basic norm. The quest for the reason of validity of a norm is … terminated by a highest norm which is the last reason of validity within a normative system …' Since it is a peculiarity of law that it regulates its own creation and a legal norm is valid if it is created in a way determined by another legal norm, the basic norm is the ultimate reason for the validity of the legal order because it authorizes the historically first legislator. The basic norm 'being the supreme reason of the validity of the whole legal order constitutes its unity.' I also said with respect to the basic norm: 'The ultimate hypothesis of positivism is the norm authorizing the historically first legislator.' This statement implies that he is a 'legislator', that is, a 'law'-maker, even if we do not presuppose the basic norm. When in the following sentences it is said that the basic norm confers 'law-creating power' on the historically first legislator and makes it possible 'to interpret the empirical material which presents itself as law as such', by 'law' I meant objectively valid norms. This follows from all that is said before about the basic norm as 'the reason of validity'. In my essay: 'On the Basic Norm', I formulated the question which leads to the assumption of the basic norm as follows: 'If we ask for the reason of the validity of a positive legal order Since it is a peculiarity of law that it regulates its own creation and a legal norm is valid if it is created in a way determined by another legal norm, 'the basic norm is the ultimate reason for the validity of the legal order because it authorizes the historically first legislator' – for the 'reason of the validity', not for the criterion of a legal order. Hence Professor Stone's statement: 'Kelsen in fact usually states the criterion for classifying a *legal* norm in terms of the common dependence of the multitude of norms for their validity on that single norm, which *we* propose here to call "the apex norm"', is not correct. The basic norm does not answer the question as to whether the existing order is a *legal* order, but the question as to what is the reason for the validity of this *legal* order. In a following sentence I said with respect to the basic norm:

'This norm is the reason of the validity of the Constitution and hence the basic norm of the legal order established in conformity with the Constitution. It is a norm presupposed in our juristic thinking ...' And finally, in my *Reine Rechtslehre* I said: 'The function of the basic norm is: to found the objective validity of a positive legal order, that is, of norms of a coercive order by and large effective, created by acts of human beings.' In Grand Larousse Encyclopédique, Professor Stone could find the following statement: '*Norme hypothétique* ou *norme fondamentale*, norme supposée par Kelsen comme étant à la base de tout ordre juridique, dont elle constitue la source logique de validité.' Since in my writings the term 'basic norm' has no other meaning, it is without foundation when Professor Stone maintains that without the hypothesis of the basic norm, 'he [Kelsen] cannot decide whether what confronts him is a legal order at all', and that for this reason the Pure Theory of Law is 'empty and inapplicable to any legal problems'.

In his presentation of my distinction between a static and a dynamic principle, characterizing two different types of normative orders, Professor Stone, substituting for my concept of the basic norm his concept of an 'apex norm', confuses the basic norm as a norm presupposed in juristic thinking, which I call 'constitution in a legal-logical sense', with the 'constitution in a positive-legal sense', which I distinguish clearly and expressly from the former. For he says: 'Kelsen asserts that a legal order cannot be 'static' ...' ; and he advances the following against this alleged thesis of the Pure Theory of Law: 'This distinction [between a static and a dynamic principle] cannot be taken so far as to mean that the apex norm of a legal order can never contain static elements. For this is precisely the position with constitutions which include so-called 'bills of rights' ...' I do not assert that a *legal order* cannot he static. I say expressly in my *General Theory of Law and State*: 'The *basic norm* of a positive legal order ... has an entirely dynamic character.' I emphasize in this work: 'The static principle, on the other hand, in turn, gains access to the system of positive law'; and I explain this statement as follows:

> The constitutional legislator does not determine merely organs for legislation, but also a legislative procedure; and, at times, his norms, that is the constitution [in the sense of positive law], determine in the so-called fundamental rights and bills of liberty the content of the laws, when they prescribe a minimum of what they should and should not contain.

And in the Reine Rechtslehre I say:

> The static and the dynamic principle are contained in one and the same system of positive norms, if the presupposed basic norm, according to the dynamic principle, only authorizes a norm-creating authority, and if this authority and the authorities instituted by it establish not only norms which delegate other norm-creating authorities but also norms prescribing a definite behavior of individuals subjected to the norms.

Professor Stone does not mention this essential element of my distinction between the static and dynamic principle. He only says *in a footnote*: 'Kelsen himself in *Theory* 124–25 says the 'material constitution' may determine 'the contents of future laws'.'

Confusing the basic norm as the constitution in a legal-logical sense with the constitution in a positive legal sense, Professor Stone objects to my theory of the basic norm that an apex norm not only delegates norm-making competence but may also designate 'the procedure, or 'manner and form', by which alone 'the designated persons can exercise norm-creating power". I have never denied that the constitution in the positive legal sense may perform such functions. When, in my *General Theory of Law and State*, to which Professor Stone refers, I said that the basic norm merely authorizes a certain authority endowed with norm-creating power, I meant – as is evident from the preceding statements – the basic norm as constitution in the legal-logical sense.

Professor Stone again attacks my theory of the basic norm in a chapter entitled, 'Mystery and Mystique in the Basic Norm'. What he means he explains in seven questions; and my answers to these questions will show that there is nothing 'mysterious' at all in the theory which arouses such an anger in Professor Stone's mind. He asks:

> 1. When Kelsen refers variously to 'basic norm' (*Grundnorm*), 'origin norm' (*Ursprungsnorm*) and 'constitution in the legal-logical sense' (*Verfassung im rechtslogischen Sinne*), is he naming the same entity? If so, are these names semantically appropriate for the same entity?

My answer: That these terms refer to the same entity Professor Stone himself seems to suppose by formulating his question. That they are semantically appropriate for the same thing is indeed my opinion; otherwise I would not use them in this way.

> 2. Does Kelsen offer the 'basic norm' as merely an intellectual construct to aid cognition by jurisprudents of a legal order as a whole? Or does he offer it as *the Ursprungsnorm*, the source to which lawyers too must trace the validity of all the norms of the legal system? In his own language, is it a 'legal-logical' ('transcendental-logical') or is it a 'legal' concept?

The answer is: The basic norm is not an intellectual 'construct' because – as I mentioned before – it is not 'created' by juristic thinking, *but presupposed* in it, if we consider – without referring to a meta-legal authority such as God or nature – the subjective meaning of the acts by which the constitution (in the positive-legal sense of the word) is established and the subjective meaning of the acts established on the basis of this constitution to be their objective meaning, and if we thus consider these meanings (which are norms) as objectively valid. Because this function is of legal importance, and because the question how is it possible to consider the subjective meaning of the acts concerned as their objective meaning is analogous to the question characterized by Kant as transcendental-logical (how is it possible to have a nonmetaphysical interpretation of the facts ascertained in the laws of nature by which the science of nature describes its object) – for these reasons is the basic norm at the same time a transcendental-logical *and* a legal concept.

> 3. In part consequentially on the above, does he say that the 'basic norm' is not a part of the legal order (in our word, 'extra-systemic') but a mere presupposition of the legal order directing obedience to the 'constitution in the legal sense'? Or does he say it is a part of the legal order (in our word, 'intra-systemic'), the apex norm of the system of norms?

This question I have answered in the preceding explanations.

> 4. Again in part consequently, are Kelsen's formulations of the 'basic norm' intended to express a uniform 'basic norm' for all legal orders, of the pattern –

'The constitution in the legal sense ought to be obeyed'? Or are they intended to be a statement matrix with a blank to be separately filled for each legal order, in the pattern 'The constitution in the legal sense of (Legal Order A, or Legal Order B, etc.) ought to be obeyed'? (The latter would yield a different 'basic norm' for each legal order, A, B, etc.) Or does he mean that the blank is in each case to be filled in with the actual norm or norms constituting the particular legal order's 'apex norm'?

Nobody who has read what I have said about the basic norm can have any doubt about my view that for each positive legal order a *specific* basic norm referring to the constitution (in the positive legal sense) of *this* legal order is to be presupposed if the subjective meaning of the acts by which *this* constitution is established, and the subjective meaning of the acts established on the basis of this constitution, creating positive legal norms, are to be interpreted as their objective meaning. Since different legal orders are based on different constitutions, different basic norms are to be presupposed. Each of these different basic norms refers to a different positive constitution. What is common to all these basic norms is that they refer to a positive legal constitution on the basis of which a positive normative coercive order is established which is by and large effective. All this stands to reason and has been questioned only by Professor Stone, though the same Professor Stone, presenting my theory, says: '[T]he difference between different systems of legal norms (English, for example, as opposed to American or Soviet) lies in their respective apex norms ...'

> 5. What does Kelsen mean by calling the 'basic norm' a 'hypothesis' or 'a hypothetical norm'? Are these the same thing? Or are they only related but not identical notions? Or the same notion applied to different entities? Or both of these?

This question is answered in the preceding explanations. In addition, I call the attention of Professor Stone again to the fact that if I call the basic norm a 'hypothesis' or 'hypothetical' I am using the term in its literal meaning: pre-supposition = *Voraus-Setzung*. The term 'hypothetical', it is true, I am using in some connection – *not with respect to the basic norm, but with respect to positive general legal norms* – in the sense in which Kant uses the term when he speaks of 'hypothetical' in contradistinction to 'categorical' *imperatives*. This too is evident to an attentive reader.

> 6. When Kelsen says that the 'validity' of the 'basic norm' is presupposed, does he mean that though its validity is to be established by reference to other norms, these latter are not the concern of the jurisprudent or lawyer? Or does he mean that its validity is to he established by reference to criteria which are factual, and not normative, and also not the concern of the jurisprudent or lawyer? Or does he mean both? Or that it is immaterial which?

There cannot be the slightest doubt about my view that the basic norm – if presupposed to be valid – refers to the norms of a *legal* order and that a condition of their positivity is that they are by and large effective. When Professor Stone imputes to me – without quoting a statement of my writings which could justify it –as possible the stupid opinion that the positive legal norms are 'not the concern of the jurisprudent or lawyer', I am forced to doubt the objectivity of his criticism. This doubt is confirmed also by other passages in Professor Stone's chapter on my theory. For instance, concerning the relationship between the Pure Theory of Law and logic, I have rejected the view expressed by some writers that this theory is merely a juristic logic. I have declared that it is not a juristic logic but a general theory of law which contains certain logical considerations. Professor Stone quite correctly quotes this statement on page 134. My own view concerning the nature of the Pure Theory of Law is for everybody a sufficient reason why this theory is not mentioned in A. G. Conte's 'Bibliografia di Logica Giuridica'. But Professor Stone, in spite of quoting my statement, explains the omission of my work from Conte's *Bibliografia* by the fact that my use of basic terms of formal logic is – as Professor Stone thinks – 'often loose'.

> 7. What is the bearing, if any, of Kelsen's 'purity' thesis on these and other aspects of the 'basic norm'? Is the method of cognition of the 'basic norm' intended to be 'pure'? If so, in what sense? Or does Kelsen's recent reemphasis that the 'basic norm' stands 'outside' the legal system imply that he recognises that the matters affecting the 'basic norm' are also 'outside' his requirement of juristic purity of method?

It stands to reason that the postulate of purity refers to the entire *theory* of law including the theory of the basic norm, and that there is no particular 'bearing' of the 'purity thesis' on any aspect of the basic norm. In which sense the principle of purity is to be understood Professor Stone has quite correctly formulated on page 101 of his book. That I have recently 're-emphasized' that the basic norm stands outside the legal system is simply not true. I have always, and from the very first time I spoke of the basic norm, maintained that this norm is not a positive norm, that is, not a norm created by an act of will of a legal authority but presupposed in juristic thinking. Whether it 'stands outside or inside' the legal system depends – as I said before – on the definition of the concept of 'legal system'. It is difficult to believe that Professor Stone cannot answer all these questions himself, and not to believe that he is unwilling to understand what I say.

At this point it seems fair to introduce the surprising fact that Kelsen's abstract thesis on the relationship between validity and effectiveness has been quoted readily in Appeal Courts in a number of different countries. The cases in question depend on determining not so much what the law is, but whose version of what the law is should prevail: revolutionary situations. The fact is unsurprising in that the section of *Pure Theory of Law* 'Legitimacy and Effectiveness' talks about change of the basic norm at times of revolution (PTL 208–211). 'The change of the basic norm follows the change of the facts that are interpreted as creating and applying valid legal norms. The basic norm refers only to a constitution which is actually established by legislative act or custom, and is effective. A constitution is "effective" if the norms created in conformity with it are by and large applied and obeyed' (PTL 210). But it is nevertheless surprising that this theory is readily used, for two principal reasons, one particular and one general. The particular reason is that Kelsen often describes the basic norm as a **juristic** presupposition, although on occasion it is unclear who this juristic person is, who is to do the presupposing. It is a well known characteristic of the civil law tradition that jurists rather than judges can be relied upon to explore the deeper questions of the meaning of law, or the nature of legal authority. Judges hardly prove themselves, even in the highest appeal courts, to satisfy the demands that might be placed upon them as jurists. And, as is only too obvious in revolutionary situations, judges are in an exceptionally vulnerable position. As Eekelaar demonstrates, their role may exclude them from the necessary intellectual demands, for there is nearly unwavering political pressure on them. Indeed the actions of judges might complete the revolution in law, by their acceptance of the legal authority of the new regime (Eekelaar 1973). The type of reasoning employed by, and the likely political capitulation of judges, in these situations, are unlikely to satisfy the conditions of rigorous, normative reasoning. The general reason, why the use by appeal courts of Kelsen's analysis is surprising, is straightforward. In many respects, the nature of the question that the Courts desire to consider, and which they appear to turn to Kelsen's analysis of the basic norm (or when the basic norm might change) to consider, is not a particularly relevant question to the pure theory. The theory is premised on the view that it is nearly always possible to identify the basic norm in order to apply the theory. The question, which judges are forced to consider in revolutionary situations, goes one step beyond the theory, or perhaps is its weakest part. So, maybe judges refer to Kelsen simply because he has so little of relevance to say on the subject. Others then have picked up these references and used them to judge the theory by, as it were, its Achilles heel. (For criticism of Kelsen's grundnorm in this context see Dias 1968 and Eekelaar 1973, for a defence see Harris 1971.)

3. The nature of legal technique and the nature of freedom

As a final exploration, the implications of the pure theory for the analysis of other political notions, such as freedom, will be briefly considered. The reason for choosing this example is to highlight how the pure theory gives the opportunity to explore political notions (apart from those usually associated with law, such as rights (PTL 125–145), and duties (PTL 114–125)) and at the same time deepens the understanding of law's specific technique. That technique, Kelsen argues, necessarily permits a 'minimum of liberty' (PTL 42). Whereas law can limit freedom by commanding or prohibiting (secondary norms), by authorising sanctions in relation to certain behaviour (primary norms), it is technically impossible 'Even under the most totalitarian legal order' (PTL 43) to positively regulate all human behaviour. And the corollary exists. Whereas freedom exists because of the technically limited possibility of applying legal technique to all behaviour, so what law guarantees as freedom is dependent on what specific guarantees, specific legal rules, the legal order contains. This latter way of considering freedom is more familiar to those who articulate concepts such as 'the rule of law'. However, even this approach to 'freedom under the law' can be considered in terms of its normativisation. In such considerations the long debate between a positive and negative approach to freedom under law is well demonstrated. Consider this short extract.

Kelsen (*Pure Theory of Law*, 42–44)

The minimum of liberty

As a sanction-prescribing social order, the law regulates human behavior in two ways: in a positive sense, commanding such behavior and thereby prohibiting the opposite behavior; and, negatively, by not attaching a coercive act to a certain behavior, therefore not prohibiting this behavior and not commanding the opposite behavior. Behavior that legally is not prohibited is legally permitted in this negative sense. Since human behavior is either prohibited or not prohibited, and since, if not prohibited, is to be regarded as permitted by the legal order, any behavior of an individual subjected to a legal order may be regarded as regulated by it –positively or negatively. Insofar as the behavior of an individual is permitted by the legal order in the negative sense – and that means: not prohibited – the individual is legally free.

The freedom left to the individual by the legal order simply by not prohibiting a certain behavior must be distinguished from the freedom which is positively guaranteed to the individual by that order. The freedom of an individual which consists in permitting him a certain behavior by not prohibiting it, is guaranteed by the legal order only to the extent that the order commands the other individuals to respect this freedom; the order forbids them to interfere in this sphere of freedom, that is, the order forbids a behavior by which an individual is prevented from doing what is not prohibited and what therefore in this sense is permitted to him. Only then can the nonprohibited (in a negative sense permitted) behavior be looked upon as rightful: that is to say, as the content of a right, which is the reflex of a corresponding obligation.

However, not every behavior so permitted – in the negative sense of not being forbidden – is safeguarded by the prohibition of the opposite behavior of others; not every permitted behavior of one individual corresponds to an obligation of another individual. It is possible that a behavior is not prohibited by the legal order (and therefore, in this sense, permitted), without an opposite behavior of others being prohibited by the legal order, so that this opposite behavior is also permitted. A behavior may not be prohibited, for example, because it is not related to other individuals or at least does not hurt anybody. But not even every behavior that *does* hurt others is prohibited. For example, it may not be prohibited that the owner of a house install a ventilator into a wall situated directly at the borderline of his property. But, at the same time, it may not be prohibited that the owner of the neighboring property builds a house whose one wall directly adjoins the ventilator-equipped wall of the first house and thereby nullifies the effect of the ventilator. In this example, one party is permitted to prevent what the other party is permitted to do – namely to pipe air into one of his rooms by a ventilator.

If a behavior opposite to the not prohibited behavior of another individual is not prohibited, then a conflict is possible against which the legal order makes no provision. The legal order does not seek to prevent this conflict, like other conflicts, by prohibiting the opposite behavior. Indeed, the legal order cannot try to prevent all possible conflicts. Only one thing is prohibited practically universally by modern legal orders: to prevent another individual by force from doing what is not prohibited. For the exercise of physical force-coercive action-is prohibited in principle, except where it is positively permitted for certain authorized individuals.

A legal order – like any normative social order – can command only specific acts or omissions of acts; therefore, no legal order can limit the freedom of an individual with respect to the totality of his external and internal behavior, that is, his acting, wishing, thinking, or feeling. The legal order can limit an individual's freedom more or less by commanding or prohibiting more or less. But a minimum of freedom, that is, a sphere of human existence not interfered by command or prohibition, always remains reserved. Even under the most totalitarian legal order there exists something like inalienable freedom; not as a right innate and natural, but as a consequence of the technically limited possibility of positively regulating human behavior. This sphere of freedom, however, can be regarded as legally guaranteed only to the extent that the legal order prohibits interference. In this respect the constitutionally guaranteed so-called civil liberties are politically particularly important. They are established by provisions of the constitution that limit the competence of the legislators to the extent that the latter are not authorized (or so authorized only under exceptional conditions) to issue norms that command or forbid a certain behavior, such as the practice of a certain religion or the expression of certain opinions.

Kelsen's articulation of these issues may not help to resolve political debates about the best way to protect rights or liberties, or freedom under law. But it might be that it clarifies what the debate about the best way to achieve these ends is all about. And, even more than this, it links consistently (to the extent that Kelsen is consistent) to related themes in moral and political philosophy. Consider this final extract from Kelsen. Although it is by no means easy to read, it does at least demonstrate how understanding law as normative might involve conclusions about such large questions as the nature of free will. Indeed this final extract brings us back to the nub of Kelsen's pure theory; that law is normative and thereby a specific technique of social organisation, with necessary preconditions and outcomes.

Kelsen (*Pure Theory of Law*, 91–99)

23. THE PROBLEM OF THE FREEDOM OF WILL

On the fundamental difference between imputation and causality, namely that imputation has an end point whereas causality has not, rests the contrast between the necessity prevailing in nature and the freedom existing in society and so essential for the normative relations between men. That man, as part of nature, is not free means that his behavior, looked upon as a natural fact, is caused by other facts according to the law of nature – that his behavior must be regarded as the effect of these facts and therefore determined by them. But that man, as a moral or legal person, is 'free' and therefore responsible has a different meaning. If a man is held responsible, morally or legally, for his moral or immoral, his legal or illegal behavior, that is, if human behavior is interpreted according to a moral or legal law as merit, sin, or delict; and if to the merit is imputed a reward, to sin a penance, and to the delict a sanction, then this imputation ends in the behavior interpreted as merit, sin, or delict. To be true, it is customary to say that the merit, sin, and delict are imputed to the man responsible for this behavior. But the real meaning of this statement is that the man ought to be rewarded for his merit (more precisely: that the merit of this man ought to be rewarded); that the man ought to do penance for his sin (more precisely: that the sin of this man ought to have its penance); that the criminal ought to be punished (more precisely: that his crime ought to get the punishment it deserves). It is not behavior defined as merit, sin, or crime that is imputed to the man – such an imputation would be superfluous, since human behavior cannot be separated from the behaving human being. If the question of imputation is raised after a man has behaved meritoriously, has sinned, or has committed a crime, then this question is not: who has performed the meritorious deed, who has committed the sin or the crime? – this would be a question of fact; the moral or legal question of imputation is rather: who is responsible for the behavior? And this question means: who ought to be rewarded or who ought to do penance or be punished? It is the reward, the penance, the punishment that are imputed as specific consequences to specific conditions. And the condition is the behavior that represents the merit, sin, or crime. The imputation of the reward to the merit, of the penance to the sin, and of the punishment to the crime includes the imputation to the man, although only this imputation is clearly expressed in the common usage of language.

The problem of moral or legal responsibility is fundamentally connected with that of retribution; retribution is imputation of reward to merit, of penance to sin, of punishment to crime. The principle of retribution connects a behavior which is in conformity to a norm with a reward, a behavior which is in conflict with a norm with penance or punishment. Thus it *presupposes* a norm that commands or prohibits this behavior or *is* a norm that prohibits the behavior just by attaching a punishment to it. But the behavior that constitutes the immediate condition for the reward, the penance, or the punishment may itself be commanded or prohibited as consequence of a definite condition. If by imputation we understand every connection of a human behavior with the condition under which it is commanded or prohibited in a norm, then also the behavior to which, as to its immediate condition, the reward, the penance, or the punishment is imputed, may be imputed to the condition under which it is commanded or prohibited.

For example: Morals command that if someone is in need he ought to be helped; if someone obeys this command, his behavior ought to be approved, if he disobeys, his behavior ought to be disapproved. The sanctions of approval and disapproval are imputed to their immediate condition – the commanded aid and the prohibited nonaid; the commanded aid is imputed to the fact whose immediate condition it is: namely that somebody is in need. This fact is the mediate condition of the approval (functioning as sanction) of rendering aid and of the disapproval of not rendering it. Another example: The law commands that if someone receives a loan and does not repay it, civil execution – as a sanction – ought to be directed into his property. The sanction of civil execution is imputed to the nonrepayment of the loan, defined as a delict – the nonrepayment being the immediate condition for this sanction; the commanded repayment of the loan is imputed to its immediate condition, the receipt of the loan. This fact is the mediate condition of the sanction of the execution. Beyond this mediate condition of the sanction no imputation takes place. But the reward, penance, punishment (including civil execution) are not imputed to their mediate condition, but only to their immediate condition – merit, sin, delict. Reward, penance, punishment are not imputed to the condition under which a certain behavior is commanded as meritorious or prohibited as sinful or unlawful; they are imputed to the man who behaves in conformity or in conflict with the command, or, more precisely: his behavior in conformity with the command is rewarded, his opposite behavior penanced or punished. In this behavior ends the imputation that constitutes his moral or legal responsibility.

If, however, a certain event is the effect of a cause, and if this cause, as always, itself has a cause, then this cause, too, as *causa* remota, is a cause of the event in question. This event is not only referred to its immediate cause, but also to all its mediate causes, and thus is interpreted as the effect of all those causes that form an infinite chain. The decisive point is: the behavior that, under a normative (i.e., a moral or legal) order, is the end point of an imputation, is, under the causal order, no end point (neither as cause nor as effect) but only a link in an infinite chain.

This, then, is the true meaning of the idea that man, as the subject of a moral or legal order, that is, as a member of a society and as a moral or legal person, is 'free'. That man, subjected to a moral or legal order, is 'free' means: he is the end point of an imputation that is possible only on the basis of this normative order. According to the usual view, however, freedom is understood as the opposite of causal determination. To be 'free' means: not to be subjected to the law of causality. It is usually said: Because man is free or has a free will – and this means according to the usual view that his behavior is not subjected to the law of causality that determines it, insofar as his will is the cause of effects, but not the effect of causes –he is responsible, which means, capable of moral or legal imputation. Only because man is free can he be made responsible for his behavior: punishable for crimes, expected to do penance for sins, eligible to be rewarded for merits. The assumption, however, that only man's freedom (that is, the fact that he is not subjected to the law of causality) makes responsibility (and that means: imputation) possible is in open conflict with the facts of social life. The establishment of a normative, behavior-regulating order which is the only basis of imputation, actually presupposes that man's will is causally determinable, therefore not free. For it is the undoubtable function of such an order to induce human beings to observe the behavior commanded by the order – to turn norms that command a certain behavior into possible motives determining man's will to behave according to the norms. But this means that the idea of a norm commanding a certain behavior becomes the cause of a norm conforming behavior. Only because the normative order (as the content of the ideas of men whose conduct the order regulates) inserts itself in the causal process, in the chain of cause and effects, does the order fulfill its social function. And only on the basis of a normative order, that presupposes such causality with respect to the will of the human beings subject to it, is imputation possible.

Earlier, it has been said it would be senseless to issue a norm commanding that something ought to be done of which it is known beforehand that, under a law of nature, it must necessarily, always and everywhere, take place. This seems to admit that normativity and causality are mutually exclusive. However, this is not so. The norm that we ought to speak the truth is not senseless, for we have no reason to assume a law of nature according to which men must speak the truth always and everywhere; we know that men sometimes speak the truth and at other times lie. But when a man speaks the truth or when he lies, then in both cases his behavior is causally determined, that means, determined by a law of nature. Not by a law of nature according to which one must always speak the truth or always lie, but by another law of nature, for example by one according to which man chooses that behavior from which he expects the greatest advantage. The idea of the norm that one ought to speak the truth can be – in conformity with this law of nature – an effective motive for behavior according to the norm. A norm that would prescribe that man ought not to die would be senseless because we know beforehand that all men must die according to the law of nature. The idea of such a norm cannot be an effective motive for a behaviour according to the norm but in contradiction to the law of nature. The idea of such a norm is senseless, precisely because of the lack of the possibility of causal effectiveness.

Sometimes it is admitted that man's will, like all happenings, is actually causally determined, but it is asserted that, in order to make moral-legal imputation possible, man must be regarded *as if* his will were free; that means, one believes it necessary to maintain freedom of will (that is, causal nondetermination) as a necessary fiction.

However, when imputation is recognized as a connection of facts different from causality but by no means in conflict with it, this fiction becomes superfluous.

Since the objective determination of the will according to the laws of causality cannot be denied, some writers believe to be able to base the possibility of imputation upon the subjective fact that man, although not free, erroneously believes himself to be free; they base the assumption that he believes himself to be free on the fact that he feels remorse when he has committed a legal or moral wrong. But this is not correct. By no means do all men feel remorse as a result of a committed wrong. Above all, many do not regard as a wrong that which, according to the legal or moral order under which they are living, is a wrong; besides, what is wrong is different according to different legal or moral orders. Men feel remorse even if they are aware that they have committed a deed they themselves regard as wrong, forced by a motive that was stronger than the one that pressed them to refrain from committing the deed. Even a convinced determinist can feel remorse when he has done something that he considers to be wrong; just as even a convinced determinist does by no means draw from his view the conclusion that a behavior forbidden by morals or law must not be disapproved or not be punished – that no imputation must take place. Imputation presupposes neither the fact or fiction of causal nondetermination, nor the subjective error of man to be free.

Some writers believe they can use the following way to solve the problem of the conflict between freedom of will as an indispensable supposition of imputation and the principle of causality that determines all events: A man is morally or legally responsible for a happening if it was caused either by his act of will or by his failure to perform an act of will that could have prevented the happening. He is not responsible for a happening when it was not caused by his act of will or his failure to perform an act of will that could have prevented the happening. That man is free merely means, according to these writers, his awareness to be able to act as he wishes. These facts, they maintain, are entirely compatible with strict determinism because the act of will or the failure to act are considered as causally determined.

The attempt to maintain the idea of freedom of will by interpreting it as the awareness of the possibility to act as one wishes must fail. For the awareness to be able to act as one wishes, is the knowledge that our acts are caused by our will. But the question is not whether our action is caused by our will – indeterminism does not deny this; but, rather, whether our will is causally determined or not. If the mentioned attempt is not merely a denial of freedom of will, but is to represent a solution of the problem while maintaining the supposition that responsibility is possible only under the condition of freedom of will, then we are merely confronted with a shift of the problem. By presenting the problem in this way, it is merely proved that a moral-legal imputation is possible and actually occurs though the will is causally determined.

The supposition that man has a free will (that is, a causally not determined will), is necessary – so it is frequently argued – to explain why only men, not things, animals, and natural events are made morally-legally responsible; why imputation takes place only with respect to man. However, imputation takes place only with respect to man because and insofar as moral and legal orders command only human behavior; and they do so because it is assumed that the idea of their norms create acts of will only in man – acts that, in turn, cause the commanded behavior. The explanation, therefore, is not the freedom of will, but, to the contrary, the causal determinability of the human will.

Another argument in favor of the dogma of the freedom of will is the reference to the fact that modern legal orders exempt certain cases from responsibility (and that means, from imputation), because, it is said, in these cases it cannot be assumed that a free act of will takes place. Thus, children and the mentally ill are not held responsible for their conduct and its effects, and even mentally sane adults if they are placed under 'irresistible compulsion'. The explanation for the first two cases is the assumption that children and the mentally ill (because of the condition of their consciousness) cannot, or not sufficiently, be caused, by the idea of legal norms, to behave in conformity with these norms; other motives are usually stronger than these ideas especially since these individuals do not even know of legal norms. For mentally sane adults, however, it may be assumed that usually the idea of legal norms and of the evil consequences of their violation is a stronger motive than the motives that lead to an illegal behavior. To be sure, these latter motives may also be stronger in an adult and a mentally sane individual, but this would be the exception. Modern legal orders presuppose an average human being and an average set of external circumstances under which people act causally determined. If such a human being under such circumstances exhibits a conduct that the legal order prohibits, then this human being is responsible for his conduct and its effects according to this legal order. If he, causally determined by circumstances other than those presupposed by the legal order, exhibits a conduct prohibited by the legal order, then he is said to act under irresistible compulsion. Actually man always acts under irresistible compulsion, because his actions are always causally determined; and causality, by its very nature, is irresistible compulsion. That which is called 'irresistible compulsion' in legal terminology actually is only a special case of irresistible compulsion – namely that for which the legal order does not stipulate responsibility. When imputation takes place, irresistible compulsion is always present. But imputation does not take place in every case of irresistible compulsion.

Finally we must mention the view that determinism and moral-legal responsibility can be considered to be compatible only by referring to the fact that our knowledge of the causal determination of human behavior is inadequate – that we do not know, or not know sufficiently, the causes that determine human behavior. If we fully knew these causes we would not be in a position to hold a person responsible for his behavior and their consequences; therefore the proverb: 'To understand everything means to forgive everything'. To understand the behavior of a human being means: to know its causes; to forgive him means: to renounce to hold him responsible for his behavior, to renounce to blame or punish him, to renounce to link his behavior with a sanction – that is, to renounce imputation. But in many cases in which the causes of his behavior are known and hence his behavior is understood, imputation is not renounced, the behavior is not forgiven. The proverb rests on the error that causality excludes imputation.

It follows that it is not freedom, i.e., nondetermination of will, but its very opposite, causal determinability of will, that makes imputation possible. One does not impute a sanction to an individual's behavior because he is free, but the individual is free because one imputed a sanction to his behavior. Imputation and freedom (in this sense) are indeed essentially linked. But this freedom cannot exclude causality, and does in fact not exclude it. If the assertion that man as a moral or legal personality is free, is to have any meaning, then this moral or legal freedom must be compatible with the causal determination of his behavior. Man is free insofar and because reward, penance, or punishment are imputed as consequence to a certain human behavior; not because this conduct is causally indetermined, but although it is causally determined, nay, *because* it is causally determined. Man is free because his behavior is an end point of imputation. And this behavior can be an end point of imputation even if it is causally determined. Therefore the causality of the natural order and freedom under a moral and legal order are not incompatible with each other; even as the natural order and the legal-moral orders are not contradictory – and cannot be contradictory, because the one is an order of something that *is* and the others are orders of something that *ought* to be. Incompatibility as consequence of logical contradiction can exist only between an assertion that something *is* and an assertion that *it is not*, or between an assertion that something *ought* to be and an assertion that it *ought not to be*; but not between an assertion that something is and that it *ought not to be.*

Further Reading

For the shortest statement by Kelsen of the Pure Theory: Kelsen 1966b.

As examples of classic essays by Kelsen: Kelsen 1957a.

For examples of some of the best critical essays on the Pure Theory: Paulson and Paulson 1998; Tur and Twining 1986.

For a critical account of Kelsen's analysis as it might apply to revolutions: Eekelaar 1973.

Questions

1. In writing about the difference between an act of a legal community and that of a gang of robbers, Kelsen says: 'But why do we interpret the subjective meaning of the [first] act also as its objective meaning, but not so of the other act? Why do we suppose that of the two acts, which both have the subjective meaning of an "ought", only one established a valid, that is, binding, norm? In other words: What is the reason for the validity of the norm that we consider to be the objective meaning of this act? This is the decisive question.' Explain what Kelsen has written here, and discuss whether he is right in thinking that this is 'the decisive question'.

2. 'Kelsen seeks to identify what, within the practices of lawyers, constitutes legal

knowledge. As such, Kelsen's goal is a pure science of law, it is not a theory of pure law.' Discuss.

3. Of what use is the grundnorm to a socio-legal researcher, a doctrinal legal scholar, or a judge? In your answer, consider two sets of circumstances: a normally operating legal system, and a situation immediately following a coup d'état.

4. 'If lawyers can identify objectively, on any occasion, what the law requires, it is because the structure of legal knowledge takes the form described in the Pure Theory of Law.' Discuss.

6 Classical Social Theory and Law

Robert Reiner

In this chapter and the one that follows we look at theories which might be said to shift the theoretical 'resource base' upon which the study of law is to be conducted, to give pride of place to the approaches of social science, or 'social theory'. In one respect this can be regarded as continuing the trend set by the positivists in their move away from natural law theories. For the positivist, to understand the law it is essential to regard the law as primarily a social phenomenon. Hart, as you will recall, regarded his own theory as in one respect a descriptive sociology. However, the theories so far, including Hart's, have dealt with concepts, and sought to identify the nature and scope of law as a separate or unique social phenomenon. Whether one accepts positivist or natural law versions of these concepts, one is still arguing over the appropriate way to conceptualise the normative propositions that make up a system of law. And both positivist and natural law theories prioritise the use of reason, identifying appropriate propositions and examining the links between them, with a strong emphasis on philosophical methods and arguments. There is much in this that can lead to a charge of formalism: that law is about identifying the rules of law, and their relationships to each other, or to other types of rules (such as morals). But law is about more than rules and doctrines. What about its relationship to interest groups, human behaviour, politics, or any number of aspects of social life.

In this chapter, we consider the point of view of those who take the claim that legal theory is sociology of law seriously, or literally. Here we will look at the major schools of thought which regard the phenomenon of law as the fit object of study by those using the techniques and ideas of the social sciences, in particular those of sociology. In the next chapter, we will consider two academic movements originating in the United States, American legal realism and critical legal studies. The first departed from classical positivism by expressing strong scepticism about the ability of systems of rules to actually provide coherent guidance to judges, lawyers, and subjects of the law. Rules, they argued, are easily manipulated by lawyers and judges to deliver the result one wants – what really drives particular decisions varies from a judge's political orientation to his temper on the day, 'what he had for breakfast'. For American legal realists, this rule scepticism led to their belief that the law should be reformed; the law would become much more rational if it *adopted* the techniques of the social sciences when it made its decisions. The critical legal studies movement bears a different relationship to the social sciences. Relying strongly on social theoretical understandings about the nature of ideology, and having like the realists a strong scepticism about the efficacy of rules, critical legal scholars characterise the law, roughly, as a site of political confrontation which only appears to be independent and unbiased because of the indoctrination in liberal culture of most of its practitioners.

The relationship between law and society might seem to be of obvious relevance to both lawyers and sociologists. A central concern of sociologists of all theoretical and political persuasions has been with the nature of social order and social change: how can societies composed of differing individuals and groups, with varying, often conflicting, perspectives, values and interests achieve any coherence and develop? Law would seem of obvious relevance to this.

In turn, sociological analysis might seem important to lawyers for both intellectual and practical reasons. Intellectually, lawyers might be expected to have some interest in such issues as the nature and functions of law, and how to account for legal change, questions to which sociological analysis could contribute. Practically, lawyers, judges and legislators might be concerned about the consequences of the laws they administer and develop. What are the social ramifications of one decision rather than another? Do legal reforms achieve their intended outcomes? If not, why not, and how can the objectives of legal changes be achieved?

Despite these points of potential mutual interest, lawyers and sociologists have tended to maintain a distance from each other. Lawyers frequently adopt a view of law, legal argument and decision-making that emphasises formal consistency and predictability as the prime virtues, eschewing concern with the social context or consequences of legal rules. In England in particular judges have tended to adhere to a restricted, declaratory view of their role, avoiding any explicit policy-making or creative role even in 'hard cases'. This contrasts with the United States where the influence of legal realism makes for judgments that are more explicitly informed by political and social considerations, and even social research findings (see Chapter 7).

Many sociologists for their part have tended to play down the role of law in explaining social order and change. They have emphasised the significance of informal processes in the maintenance and reproduction of social order, sometimes even seeing formal law as an epiphenomenal reflection of deeper structures, not an important factor in its own right. Socio-legal researchers have often veered towards rule scepticism, regarding law as a presentational device for legitimating decisions that are actually determined by other social or psychological causes.

To help you with the perspective of those who see theorising about law as something more than what is offered within the traditions that you have so far covered in this book (natural law and legal positivism), one extract is set out here. (In addition, for an important recent debate on the relationship between law and social theory, see Cotterrell 1998 and Nelken 1998.)

Cotterrell (1992, 1–15)

Introduction: Theory and Method in the Study of Law

Suppose that a new piece of legislation comes into existence, created in the proper formal manner by an accepted law-making institution. What happens? Immediately lawyers set to work, digesting and comprehending the changes brought about by the new rules. The new law is probably published in some official form and finds its way into the libraries of law schools, lawyers and administrators. The body of legal doctrine – rules, principles and concepts of law – is slightly, or perhaps fundamentally, altered. The changes are registered in digests of legislation, legal encyclopaedias, lawyers' updates or periodicals. But what then? Does anything else happen? Does the law somehow reach the world beyond this rarefied professional sphere? If so, in what way? With what effect?

Not every such law will even reach the courts of law because no case may arise to raise the issues with which the new law is concerned. Perhaps the matter which is the object of the law is not important in the experience of social life or, if it is, for various reasons the issues are kept away from courts. No one sees fit to raise them. Suppose, however, that the new law is invoked before a judge. Even so the court may refuse to apply it. It may be ruled irrelevant or interpreted in such a way as to remove some or all of its potential effect. But suppose the court does apply the new law to the case under consideration. What effect will the judgment have on the conduct of life outside the courtroom? Very often, surprisingly little may be known by judges and lawyers about the law's potential or actual social effects. Perhaps even more surprisingly, rarely is any systematic attempt made by them to find out.

Practical questions such as these concerning the effects of laws have provided a major impetus for social scientific study of law. Yet they provide only a part of the justification for such study and not necessarily the most important part. A major justification is that law is too important a social phenomenon to be analysed in a way that isolates it from other aspects of society and makes impossible an understanding of the complexity of its relations with other social phenomena, its 'reality' as a part of life and not merely as a technique of professional practice. 'Law permeates all realms of social behaviour. Its pervasiveness and social significance are felt in all walks of life.' One recent writer notes, echoing a theme of such earlier sociologists as Durkheim and Gurvitch, that 'the law in any social system is, in fact, a fundamental framework (a skeleton, if you like) of the nature of all its forms of association and institutions. If we know the law of any society, we have an excellent outline of the nature of the social system as a whole'. For another writer, the effort to understand law's significance 'takes us straight to the heart of ... the major unsolved problems of social theory'. What is common to all such views is that analysis of law is seen as revealing, or having the potential to reveal, more than just law itself. If we understand law as a social phenomenon we understand much about the society in which it exists.

Lawyers' Conceptions of Law

Nevertheless, as every lawyer knows, law can be analysed in its own terms – that is, in terms of the internal logical structure of legal doctrine – at least if logic is tempered with dashes of expediency. What has sometimes been underemphasised by lawyers, however, is that 'pure legal analysis' is a highly problematic concept. The analysis of legal doctrine – the rules, regulations, principles and concepts set out in law books and authoritatively stated in legislation or deduced from judicial decisions – involves numerous decisions as to how far and in what manner logical analysis can be developed. Considerations of policy cannot be excluded from the analysis since legal doctrine is continually being shaped in the practice of courts and other agencies of interpretation by reference to assumed social purposes of law. Further, lawyers' analysis of law is grounded in an array of philosophical assumptions – for example, about the nature of responsibility, obligation, causation and the autonomy of the individual – which often necessarily remain unexamined. These assumptions have, however, increasingly become matters for examination as changes have occurred in the modern political and social context of Western legal systems. With the development of modern forms of legislation, purely 'legal logical' interpretation has seemed ever more problematic as law reflects and embodies policy more explicitly and as the scope and character of regulation changes.

None of this is intended to deny the validity of lawyers' pragmatic rationalisations of legal rules into more or less systematic form. This ordering activity is essential to professional legal practice. But the character of contemporary law – an immense, ever-changing network of legislative rules, judicial precedents, orders, regulations, powers and discretions – is such that these necessary rationalisations are inevitably partial and limited. They serve practical ends. They are part of the technique of orderly application of law; practical instruments in the enterprise of regulating conduct. Systematisation and generalisation of doctrine are tools to be used or put aside depending on the character of the task in hand. Serious problems arise only when it is assumed that the nature of law *in general* can be adequately explained – that comprehensive *theories of law* can be constructed – by logically organising and analysing legal doctrine without relating it to systematic empirical knowledge about the societies in which it exists and in relation to which its concepts acquire their meaning. Theory developed solely through rationalisation of and speculation on the rules, principles, concepts and values considered to be explicitly or implicitly present in legal doctrine can be termed normative legal theory. It constitutes a major focus of past and present legal philosophy. By contrast the empirical legal theory with which this book is concerned proceeds on the basis that an understanding of the nature of law requires not only systematic empirical analysis of legal doctrine and institutions but also of the social environment in which legal institutions exist.

A Variety of Perspectives on Law

To say that law should be analysed empirically as a social phenomenon is one thing. But how should this be done? Is there a single 'social reality of law' to be discovered? A lawyer's professional outlook on law may well differ from that of a social scientist or from the varied conceptions of law that ordinary citizens in different ethnic, occupational or other groups hold. Furthermore, different kinds of social theory will portray law in different ways within the competing pictures of the character of modern Western societies which they present. Law thus has different social realities constructed from different vantage points. Yet some of these perceptions of law have more depth, more explanatory power than others; they take into account more – or more systematically gathered – empirical detail about law. Their theoretical analysis is more fully worked out, more coherent, or more aware of and capable of incorporating or explaining rival hypotheses, competing theories or data relating to the social environment of law. A lawyer may have a far better grasp of the complex patterns of doctrinal development in the law than a sociologist possesses. A social scientist may be able to draw on knowledge of social institutions and social theory seemingly unrelated to law but which, properly interpreted, can illuminate the nature of legal developments in a way that might entirely escape the reflection that lawyers bring to bear on their particular professional experience.

The possibility of ultimately describing and analysing the social reality of law, as the embodiment of knowledge that transcends partial perspectives, is the possibility of *science*. That it remains only a possibility, an aim to work towards, and one that may never be realised is no reason to deny its importance. In the most general sense scientific method involves two elements: first, a clear and explicit recognition that all perspectives on experience are necessarily partial and incomplete and, secondly, the serious (but necessarily never completed) attempt to overcome the limitations of partial perspectives through systematic collection, analysis and interpretation of the empirical data of experience ...

Sociology and Law

It may be asked why a specifically sociological perspective on law is justified and what such a perspective implies. In one sense law and sociology as forms of professional practice are similar in scope yet wholly opposed in method and aims. Law as a scholarly professional practice is concerned with elaboration of the practical art of government through rules. Its concern is prescriptive and technical. Sociology is concerned with the scientific study of social phenomena. Its concern is explanatory and descriptive. The lawyer is essentially a man of affairs entrusted with part of the apparatus of regulation of social relations. The sociologist remains a relatively uncommitted observer. If these stereotypes are often belied in practice they nevertheless broadly point to differences in outlook which appear typical when the respective disciplinary statuses of law and sociology are self-consciously asserted.

Yet both law and sociology are concerned with the whole range of significant forms of social relationships. And in practice the criteria determining which relationships are significant are often similar, deriving from the same cultural assumptions or conceptions of policy relevance. Furthermore, both legal studies and sociological inquiries typically seek to view these phenomena as part of, or potentially part of, an integrated social structure. Thus, despite their radical differences in method and outlook law and sociology share a fundamentally similar basic subject matter. Law is a practical craft of systematic control of social relations and institutions. Sociology is the scientific enterprise that seeks systematic knowledge of them. An American commentator writes, 'Sociology is concerned with values, interaction patterns, and ideologies that underlie the basic structural arrangements in a society, many of which are embodied in law as substantive rules. Both sociology and law are concerned with norms, rules that prescribe the appropriate behaviour for people in a given situation. The study of conflict and conflict resolution are central in both disciplines. Both sociology and law are concerned with the nature of legitimate authority, the mechanisms of social control, issues of civil rights, power arrangements, and the relationship between public and private spheres'.

...

A sociological perspective implies here the kind of broad view expressed by the American historian H. Stuart Hughes. For Hughes, sociology is not 'the highly specialised and fragmented discipline with which we are familiar in the United States' (or in Britain, for that matter) but 'a more universal social theorising in the tradition of Montesquieu or Marx'. Writing of three classic social theorists he notes: 'This was the notion of sociology held by Weber or Durkheim or Pareto. However finite the problems to which they might address themselves, what they were really after was the overall structure of society. And it is significant that they were all men of broad general education who came to sociology only after having received their original training in other fields'. A sociological perspective on law does not require that law should somehow be subsumed as part of academic sociology's territory but that it should be viewed with a 'sociological imagination'. Such an imagination constantly seeks to interpret detailed knowledge of law in a wider social context, consistently looks for the relations between legal development and wider social changes, tries to understand law as interacting in complex ways with the social environment it purports to regulate, and tries always to approach these matters systematically with a constant sensitivity to the need for specific empirical data and rigorous theoretical explanation.

...

The classic social theorists, Max Weber, Karl Marx and Emile Durkheim, whose insights about the character of Western societies inform the pages of this ... [chapter] understood the analysis of social phenomena in this broad sense, although they were far from unworldly or impractical in their concerns. They sought answers to large questions about the nature and direction of social change, the conditions and forms of social order, the relationship between the individual and society. At this level sociological study has contributed much enlightenment, taking up persistent questions of social philosophy but seeking as far as possible to confront theory with empirical data in a serious manner, so as to escape the blind gropings of uncontrolled speculation. It is at this level that sociology can contribute most to an understanding of law. It offers not 'finished' knowledge – a body of technical, scientific prescriptions or diagnoses – but a continually broadening, self-critical effort to explore the conundrums presented by the empirical data of social life.

Compartmentalisation and its Dangers

It should be apparent from what has been said that the sociological study of law hardly forms a neat intellectual compartment – nor should it do so. Its boundaries are set only by the quest for understanding of the character of law as a social phenomenon. The term 'sociology of law', now often used to describe this area of study, is convenient until it is used to justify a rigid disciplinary compartmentalisation which can only hamper development of the field. One writer remarks 'the sociology of law is but a sub-discipline of sociology and, as such, aims at the understanding of that discipline's particular subject-matter'. Yet contemporary sociology as an academic discipline is marked by an immense variety of special concerns and theoretical and methodological approaches. Its character as a resource to be drawn on in the development of knowledge in particular fields – for example, legal study – is perhaps more apparent at the present time than its disciplinary integrity. Although among the classic social theorists Durkheim most strongly promoted sociology as the unifying central discipline of social science, he also clearly and continuously stressed its utility as a resource in the study of particular social fields.

...

Legal Positivism

So far the term 'law' has remained undefined in these considerations ... But it is important to note here a few quite general problems of method which arise as soon as the attempt to study law as an empirical social phenomenon is made. Law is often said to have a double-faceted character which can be expressed in various ways. Thus law consists of prescriptions – 'ought propositions' specifying the way legal subjects ought to behave. Yet at the same time it constitutes a social phenomenon which only 'exists' if the prescriptions of conduct actually have some effect on the way people think or behave. Law is thus both prescriptive norm and descriptive fact. It is to be considered in terms of its validity and also its efficacy. It is *sollen* and *sein* – 'ought' and 'is'. This dualism is much discussed in the literature of jurisprudence. It is seen to pose problems for analysis since, although law appears as both prescriptive norm and empirical fact, 'these two categories logically exclude one other'. In fact the rigid separation of these two aspects of law holds good only if a particular approach to analysis of law is adopted. This approach, which is really a philosophical conception of what constitutes valid knowledge and of how it is to be obtained, has been pervasive in both legal theory and social science and is known as positivism.

It would be impossible in the space available here even to begin to survey all the major ramifications of the positivist outlook in legal study and sociological analysis. Nevertheless, since much of the literature discussed in this book is either informed by positivist assumptions or (particularly in the case of phenomenological and related approaches) is written in more or less explicit criticism or rejection of them, some brief introductory remarks must be offered here. In essence, positivism is a philosophical position which asserts that scientific knowledge derives from observation of the data of experience and not from speculation that seeks to 'look behind' observed facts for ultimate causes, meanings or essences. What we observe is, therefore, what really exists – and, scientifically speaking, all that exists. Hence judgments of value, of what is good or bad, political or policy questions, questions about the ultimate nature of things which cannot be determined by generalisations from observation – all of these are unscientific. Because these matters are subjective, existing only in the minds of individuals, they are unanalysable by scientific means. In the strongest versions of positivism they do not constitute knowledge at all. Fact and value are thus rigidly separated. Science should be 'value free' in two senses. It should not, itself, make value judgments about what it observes. And it should not seek to inquire into the meaning or ultimate significance of the values held by those it observes. This is not to say that values cannot be studied but they can be studied only as the observable preferences and commitments of actual individuals, not as having significance or reality in their own right.

In the Anglo-American legal world, and indeed to a greater or lesser extent in most modern highly-developed legal systems, a positivist outlook on law is the typical outlook of lawyers and informs much legal scholarship and teaching. Law consists of data – primarily rules – which can be recognised as such by relatively simple tests or 'rules of recognition'. A familiar such simple test is that the rules have passed through certain formal stages of a legislative process, or (less simple) that they can be derived from the *ratio decidendi* – the essential grounds of decision – of a case decided by a court having the jurisdiction and authority to lay down new rules in such a case. According to a positivist conception, these rules of law –possibly with some subsidiary legal phenomena – constitute the law, the data which it is the lawyer's task to analyse and order. In this sense, law is a 'given' – part of the data of experience. If it can be recognised as existing according to certain observational tests it can be analysed. The tests by which legal positivism recognises the existence of law or particular laws are thus analogous to those by which a scientist might recognise the presence of a particular chemical.

Some Limitations of Legal Positivism

Although, up to a point, this is an obviously useful way by which the lawyer or legal analyst identifies the subject matter of his or her inquiries it necessarily directs attention away from the idea that law consists of human processes. To treat the data of law merely as legal rules may be a static (and therefore inadequate) representation of a dynamic phenomenon: the reality of regulation as the continually changing outcome of a complex interaction of individuals and groups in society. Legal positivism seeks tests of the 'legal' which make it possible to identify the data of law, as far as possible without looking behind legislative rules to the process by which they were created, and without considering judicial attitudes or values. What is considered to be the justice or injustice, wisdom or efficiency, moral or political significance of a law is not essential to an understanding of it as long as rules of law can be clearly ascertained. Only when the 'data of law' are elusive – when the rules are not clear or their applicability to a new case is in doubt – must these 'non-legal elements' be considered. Since, however, they are by definition external to law they are not necessarily considered systematically but are typically used more or less selectively as rhetorical ammunition in debates on legal interpretation.

Positivism is a primary modem philosophical foundation of legal professional knowledge. Consequently, there are powerful professional reasons for maintenance of a positivist outlook in legal analysis. Yet it is significant that, as a philosophy of law, positivism has come under powerful attack in recent years. It has been charged that it ignores the role of values in law and the way in which law is established in interpretation, that in treating rules as the given data of law it assumes a certainty and clarity in rules that is by no means apparent, that it cannot cope with the complex relationship between rules and discretionary powers of officials in legal regulation in complex contemporary societies, and more generally that it cannot provide an adequate basis for understanding processes of legal change. In this respect, critics of legal positivism refer to theoretical issues about contemporary Western law which are a major focus of sociology of law.

Sociological Positivism Versus 'Interpretive Sociology'

Positivist method, in various manifestations, is also characteristic of certain types of sociology. However, it does not represent, by any means, a universal conception of the nature of sociological knowledge and of the means of acquiring it. Indeed, in much contemporary Western European sociology, positivist approaches are typically either overlaid with many qualifications and modifications or are explicitly rejected. While legal Positivism remains strong in the legal systems of Britain, the United States and other Western states, sociological positivism has been widely challenged by flourishing competing approaches which have stressed the need for interpretive 'understanding' of social phenomena in terms of the motivations of social actors rather than mere observation of behaviour or measurement of attitudes.

Sociological positivism in its most explicit form is typified by Durkheim's famous injunction that we should 'treat social facts as things'. In other words, social phenomena should be measured and analysed in basically the same manner as the natural scientist would measure and analyse substances and processes in laboratory experiments. Durkheim pointed out that, although many social phenomena – for example, the morale or cohesion of a society – are far too intangible to measure directly, it may be possible to discover indicators of these intangible phenomena in more directly observable matters. In his own studies, changes in the law and variations in suicide rates provided two such 'indices' of wider, more nebulous social phenomena. Of course, controlled experiments cannot usually be carried out in the social world in the same manner as in a laboratory although, for example, studies of jury decision-making have made use of 'simulated juries' replicating as far as possible the actual conditions of jury deliberations under experimental conditions. In fact, social science possesses a whole battery of fact-gathering techniques including sophisticated questionnaire survey methods, participant observation, and techniques of conversation analysis, which go some way to meet the claim that observational methods comparable in rigour with those of natural science cannot be used.

The often pointed-out flaw in a strict sociological positivism is that society is not a 'thing' external to the observer. At the same time as social facts appear as things constraining or influencing the actions and attitudes of members of a society they can also be seen as shaped or sustained by the interactions, motivations or beliefs of those same members. As a member of a human society the social scientist is implicated in – a part of – what he or she studies. For this reason, the conception of a totally objective attitude on the part of the observer is very problematic. As a 'social being', such an observer cannot put aside fundamental and perhaps unstated conceptions of social life which are an integral part of his or her personality.

In one sense, however, social science possesses a great methodological advantage over natural science. In social science the observer observes other human beings. Because of the possibility of empathy between observer and observed, between subject and object, the researcher has the chance not only to record behaviour and attitudes but also to understand the motivations of the social actors being studied; to understand social action as *meaningful* to those engaged in it. Because of this commonality of observer and observed the former can legitimately go beyond mere observation to interpretation. This is not to assume that all social action is rational but only that it may be useful to interpret it in terms of models of rationality or of typical expectations about conduct in situations such as those observed. The observer can, and perhaps should, thus attempt to make sense of social phenomena in terms of the outlook of the actors whose conduct constitutes these phenomena.

From this viewpoint sociology's concern is to understand social phenomena in terms of the subjective meaning of actors, rather than merely to measure observable regularities. As Max Weber, the classic exponent of this 'understanding' (*verstehende*) approach to study in sociology expressed the matter, social action – the basic subject matter of sociological analysis – is behaviour that is subjectively meaningful to the individual undertaking it and is directed towards, or takes into account the position of, other actors with whom the individual interrelates. An emphasis on explaining how social phenomena are created in social action or interaction is in no way incompatible with a parallel concern with the mechanisms by which these phenomena control or influence the action of members of a society as long as it is recognised that some individuals or groups in a society may have more power than others to shape social conditions.

That this 'understanding' approach is of the greatest importance as a means of explaining how social phenomena are constructed is illustrated by developments both in legal philosophy and in the sociology of law. The influential legal philosopher H.L.A. Hart introduces in his major work on legal theory the notion that rules are to be understood in terms of their 'internal aspect' which, broadly speaking, is the *subjective* meaning that rules have for those who understand concepts of legal obligation. In the sociology of law much writing now follows directly or indirectly Weber's methodological lead though often mediated through related philosophical conceptions. Law can be seen as consisting of norms – 'ought propositions' – but these norms 'exist' in the experience and reasoning patterns of actual individuals. Hence law as embodied in behaviour and attitudes, as one of the determinants of social action, is a social fact. But at the same time it is a realm of ideas to be understood in terms of the subjective meaning of those ideas for individuals living within a legal order.

...

Objectivity and Values

...

The literature of sociological study of law is a rich tapestry to which many have contributed and which was begun many centuries ago. The ideals of those who have written have been extremely varied. Some have sought a more just legal order; some have hoped for a world that would dispense with law altogether. Many have considered that understanding law meant understanding the great issues of politics and society. Some of the most influential social and political theorists have been legal scholars or trained in law, among them Bodin, Montesquieu, Bentham, Millar, Gumplowicz, Weber, Marx and Lukacs. Today this field is one of the liveliest foci of social research. For some researchers its justification, wholly or partially, is to improve law, to aid the legislator or the judge or, even, to facilitate 'social engineering', a more efficient organisation of society or a more efficient technology of government for realising collective welfare. Whether such aims are appropriate or realistic can be left for the reader to judge in the light of material discussed in subsequent chapters. For this writer, however, its primary objective is to increase understanding of legal phenomena, to contribute to the overcoming of partial perspectives, and so to contribute to wider understanding of the society in which these phenomena exist, and of the conditions and responsibilities of individuals in relation to each other as members of such a society. In this broad sense the objective of the sociology of law is to contribute to an understanding of the meaning and conditions of justice in society.

As the extract by Cotterrell shows, the potential scope of Sociology of Law, in terms of the data that can be analysed and the methods that can be used, is quite vast. As such, it is quite difficult to introduce you to any particular set of materials, and claim that these represent the Sociology of Law. Instead, in this chapter, we have chosen to introduce you to three of the most important figures in the Sociology of Law: Marx, Weber and Durkheim. These three are giants in the intellectual history of Sociology, and they each had things to say that are significant for the study and understanding of law. Each provides us with a means by which to analyse how laws come into being, what interests they serve, and how they contribute to the definition and reproduction of social order. These questions were of great importance to the classical social theorists of the nineteenth and early twentieth centuries, who were concerned to understand the sources and the trajectory of the modern societies developing in the wake of the industrial and democratic political revolutions of the late eighteenth century. In the case of Marx and Durkheim, we see important examples of the 'skeleton' idea referred to by Cotterrell: that the laws of a society reflect, in some reliable and measurable way, its underlying structure. In the case of Marx (or at least some Marxists) we find a theory which seeks to locate the basis of understanding law (as well as politics, education, religion, morality) in a society's economic relations. In the case of Durkheim, we have a theory which analyses the evolution of societies from primitive to modern in terms of changes to the dominant forms of law (from repressive to restitutive) and links this in turn to the underlying basis of cohesion or 'solidarity' in each type of society. With Weber we find something more complex. The evolution of Western capitalist society is analysed by reference to the role played by the forms of law which developed in that same society. Whilst many of the specific views of each of these theorists have been refuted by criticism or the passage of time, their perspectives remain highly relevant to our contemporary problems of dramatic social change and transformation. Our aim in introducing these theorists here, and providing extracts or commentaries on their work, is not to assess the extent to which their analysis is correct. Rather, it should give you a flavour of the wider questions about law which can be asked when one moves from a philosophical to a sociological approach.

Karl Marx (1818–1883)

There are a number of special difficulties in discussing the Marxist perspective on law, despite (or because of?) the existence of a huge amount of literature on it. (Surveys of Marxism and Law can be found in Cain 1974, Cain and Hunt 1979, Phillips 1980, Collins 1982, Vincent 1993.) Because of its history as the inspiration for a political movement and a state that until recently dominated a substantial part of the world, interpretations of Marxism are – and always have been – fraught with political controversy. The writings of Karl Marx have been pored over by generations of political activists and scholars as if they were holy writ, and subjected to similar types of casuistry.

One fundamental issue is the relationship between Marx and Marxism. Marxism is a movement that has assumed various forms over the last century and a half, and bears a complex and vexed relationship to the work of Karl Marx. Marx himself once denied (ironically) that he was a Marxist (see Wheen 1999, 1). Like the Bible, his authority has been called in aid of many conflicting viewpoints. All of Marx's huge corpus of writing can be drawn upon to interpret Marxism, although as with any other writer he changes and develops his perspective over time, and there are inconsistencies as well as continuities in his work.

The general problems of interpreting Marx and Marxism are magnified in relation to the analysis of law. In part this stems from the fact that there is no theory of the state or law explicitly set out in Marx's work. *Capital* is an unfinished project; Marx died with Volume III not yet completed, and what we have is primarily an exposition of Marx's theory of capitalism as an economic system, with his analysis of its political and ideological dimensions – including law – promised but not even begun. There are many passages about aspects of law in the huge corpus of writings by Marx and his patron and collaborator Engels. These are collected and discussed in a substantial library of secondary literature specifically on Marx and law. There are also many analyses of law in the work of subsequent Marxists. However, there is no definitive statement by Marx himself, and different interpretations compete with each other. Many of the more substantial theoretical passages about law are found in Marx's early writings, and thus subject to the debate about whether these works pre-date the development of Marxism as a theoretical system. (The Althusserian reading in fact denies that strictly speaking law is a concept within Marxism at all. On this view Marxism is a specific theory about the conditions of existence, reproduction and development of modes of production, in particular capitalism. Whilst law is clearly an important phenomenon within capitalist systems, it is a concrete historical object to be analysed by the theoretical apparatus of Marxism, but not a conceptual tool in its own right – see Hirst 1975.)

In this chapter we will first look at the implications for law suggested by Marx's theoretical perspective in general. It will then consider the longest discussion of law in Marx's mature work, Chapter 10 of *Capital* Vol 1. This is a concrete historical study of the emergence of one specific set of laws, the Factory Acts of the early nineteenth century, and does not purport to provide a general theory of law. Nonetheless it will be suggested that Marx's historical analysis does imply such a theory. This is arguably as close as we can get to a statement of Marx's own perspective on law. Later in the chapter, using an extract from *Law and Marxism* by Collins, we will explore what is involved in developing a Marxist theory of law.

1. Marxism, Law and Political Economy

Three very broad versions of Marxism as a theoretical perspective can be distinguished: instrumentalism, structuralism, and humanism. Each has different implications for the analysis of law.

Instrumental Marxism is found in its most undiluted form in polemical writing, both Marxist and anti-Marxist. It is the view of law, state, and indeed all of politics and culture as straightforward instruments of a ruling class. Law may purport to represent justice but this is merely an ideological disguise for serving as a tool of the ruling class, advancing their interests and controlling the working class. (This is implied by the novelist Anatole France's frequently cited cynicism about 'the majestic equality of the law, which forbids the rich as well as the poor to sleep under bridges, to beg in the streets, and to steal bread' – *Le Lys Rouge*, 1894.) This view is seldom found in Marxist theoretical work. It is, however, implicit in many empirical studies of the social origins and position of political and legal elites, where this is used to explain the pattern of their decision-making (for example Miliband 1969, Griffith 1997).

Structural Marxism argues that social phenomena cannot be seen straightforwardly as the outcome of human action or the interests of particular groups. Capitalism and other modes of production are systems with characteristic dynamics that structure the actions of actors and institutions (see Poulantzas 1978). The state and the law are themselves structures that cannot be understood separately from their place in the overall reproduction of capitalism. Law is not a tool of the ruling class, but has 'relative autonomy'. It functions to reproduce the conditions of existence of capitalism as a system, not the particular interests of specific people or interests.

Humanist Marxism is most obviously found in Marx's early writings, and structural Marxists such as Althusser claim that it is precisely this position that Marx abandoned in his later writings (particularly in his magnum opus *Capital*). It is also the perspective implicit in Marx's own historical writings, even in his 'mature' years. A well-known aphorism of Marx himself encapsulates this view: 'Men make their own history, but not under conditions of their own choosing'. People have a degree of autonomy as historical agents and not just as bearers of structural forces, but nonetheless are constrained by limits determined by their past and present circumstances. This gives scope not only for human autonomy but also for cultural values to have some independent force. Thus E P Thompson argued that the 'rule of law' was not merely an ideological smokescreen but a human achievement of permanent value resulting from centuries of political struggle, even if it was often deformed in practice (Thompson 1975: for accounts of the debate on Marxism and the rule of law see Collins 1982, Ch 6; Fine 1984; Fine 1994; Cole 2001).

2. The Materialist Conception of History

These three versions of Marxism are all supportable by different aspects of the work of Marx himself. The space for these clashing interpretations is created by ambiguities in Marx's own perspective. This can be illustrated by a frequently discussed passage in which Marx attempted to sum up the methodology of his own researches for his major work *Capital*. In this Marx claimed that 'relations of production' that are 'independent of the will ... constitute the economic structure of society, the real foundations, on which arises a legal and political superstructure, and to which correspond definite forms of social consciousness. The mode of production of material life conditions the general process of social and intellectual life. It is not the consciousness of people that determines their existence, but their social existence that determines their consciousness.' (See extract 1 below.)

This passage is presented as the essence of the historical materialism that Marx thought of as his distinctive contribution to social analysis. It rests on the contrast between economic *base* and political and ideological *superstructure*. The base is the *mode of production*, a distinctive type of economic system, consisting of specific *forces* (technology, materials, know-how etc) and *relations* of production (particular ways of organising the labour process). *Social formations*, specific, concrete societies, correspond more or less to the pure model of a particular mode of production. The mid-nineteenth century United States, for example, was primarily capitalist but also contained elements of the slave and feudal modes of production. History develops through the conflict of forces within particular modes of production, such as the class struggle between capital and labour in capitalism.

The base/superstructure metaphor has led to various interpretations that underlie the conflicting instrumental, structuralist and humanist versions of Marxism (see Collins 1982, Ch 4). How exactly are the crucial terms Marx uses to characterise the base/superstructure relationship, 'conditions' and 'determines', to be interpreted? Do those with economic power (the ruling class) completely control the superstructure in their interests (instrumentalism)? Does the superstructure have relative autonomy to develop according to its own logic, whilst being determined ultimately by the conditions of existence of the base (structuralism)? Do actors have real autonomy to develop various strategies to realise their ideas and values, but constrained by their historical and material circumstances (humanism)? The essence of Marxism is its materialist perspective, the limitation 'in the last instance' of human possibility at any particular time by material exigencies. But there is much scope for varying interpretations of how wide these limits are, and to what extent actions within them are determined by the base.

Marx's own most sustained critique of law is found in Chapter Ten of *Capital* Vol 1 and is an analysis of the Factory Acts in early nineteenth century England (Marx 1976). This critique contains elements of structural, instrumental and humanist analysis.

3. Marx's Analysis of the Factory Acts

The context for Marx's historical study of the Factory Acts in Chapter Ten of *Capital* Vol 1 is his analysis of the dynamics of the capitalist mode of production. The general condition of the working classes at this time is not a consequence of a decline in moral values, such as an increase in greed on the part of the manufacturing classes, but was to be found in more deep seated structural aspects of his own society. Marx argued that a distinctive feature of capitalism is the generalised production of *commodities*, ie of goods intended primarily for exchange rather than immediate use. Marx accepts the labour theory of value that was dominant in the early nineteenth century, seeing labour as the basic source of the creation of value. However, labour has the unique capacity to create new value, in addition to its own cost. In capitalism the worker produces more value than he is paid for, and the capitalist expropriates the surplus.

Surplus labour is not unique to capitalism. It occurs in all historical societies, within a variety of different relations of production, such as slavery or feudalism, in which the extraction of surplus by the ruling class is apparent because it is achieved through direct political and social subordination. One of the unique features of capitalism is that there is an inherent pressure to maximise exploitation built in to capitalist relations of production. In earlier modes of production the extraction of surplus was primarily directed at providing 'use value' (consumption and investment) for the ruling class, and was limited by their customary expectations. In capitalism the primary purpose of production is exchange value, and there is no limit set to this by customary perceptions of need. Capitalists operate under competitive pressures that oblige them to seek to maximise their profits whatever their own aspirations might be. Even the most ascetic or socially conscious owner is subject to this pressure: avarice only makes it easier.

On Marx's analysis class struggle is built in to capitalist relations of production. Competitive pressure drives the owner of the means of production to seek to maximise the extraction of surplus value. This means trying to lengthen the working day, and/or the intensity of effort within it, as much as possible. Workers for their part will seek to resist the continuous extension or intensification of their working day, so there is a perennial potential for conflict.

The legislative history of the nineteenth century presents a clear puzzle for this structural analysis. During this period Parliament passed a series of Factory Acts aimed at protecting the hours and conditions of labour. This was a Parliament elected entirely by the upper and middle classes: workers only began to be enfranchised in gradual stages after 1867. When Marx claimed polemically in the 1848 *Communist Manifesto* that the state was 'but a committee for managing the common affairs of the whole bourgeoisie' (a quintessential statement of instrumental Marxism) this was as much literal description as colourful critique. So how could it come about that the Parliament of the capitalists came to enact a series of measures restricting their exploitation of workers? In essence Marx's account clearly rejected an instrumental interpretation of Marxism (although he evidently indulged in it himself when engaged in polemics against capitalism). Instead he blends elements of structuralist and humanist perspectives to explain the seeming paradox of laws acting against the interest of the classes that dominated the legislature.

Marx's primary explanation of the emergence of the Factory Acts is a (colourfully expressed) structuralist account. The function of law, argues Marx, is to reproduce capitalism as a mode of production. It thus benefits the capitalist class as a whole, but in order to achieve this, law may have to act against the interest of individual capitalists. The remorseless pressures of competitive markets drive individual capitalists to exploit workers ever more intensively but this undermines the viability of the system as a whole as the health of the labour force is undermined. Laws limiting the permitted hours of work relieve the pressures of competition facing capitalists and preserve the fitness and hence productivity of the labour force. Individual capitalists in a competitive environment could not achieve this without legislation, because if any would allow their workers to work less intensively their profitability and hence survival would be threatened. This is not due to the malice of capitalists, nor could it be changed by their benevolence. It requires legal change ensuring that a reduction in working hours (which the more perspicacious capitalists pressed for) did not affect the viability of most firms. The logic of this argument is analogous to many conservative analyses of law, which see its function as being to curb individual freedom for the long-run benefit of all. Marx's account sees law as essentially operating at two levels. Law satisfies the conditions of existence of any viable system of production, thus achieving the common interests of all. However, law particularly benefits the dominant class in the system that is reproduced.

Whilst Marx's primary explanation of the emergence of the Factory Acts is that they mitigate the destructive consequences of undiluted competitive pressure, this could only be achieved through human action. Marx's account examines in detail the political and class struggles that brought about the structurally required legislative changes. His points exemplify some key themes of later sociological analyses of law.

Marx emphasises that the Factory Acts had an important *symbolic* as well as practical role, implying that the law was concerned with the welfare of the working class. The Acts passed in the early part of the nineteenth century (before the 1833 Factory Act) had no impact at all in practice, and were only of significance symbolically. One reason for their ineffectiveness was the minimal change embodied in the legislation. The early Acts only returned hours of work to the level of the late eighteenth century before they had been sharply increased by rapid industrialisation. In addition 'Parliament ... was shrewd enough not to vote a penny for their compulsory implementation' (*Capital*, Vol 1, 1976, 390) – a nice example of what the legal realists were later to call the gap between 'law in the books' and 'law in action'.

The 1833 Act, however, established a Factory Inspectorate to enforce the limits on child and other labour that it ordained. From then on the story largely becomes a running battle between the Inspectorate and the factory owners, who develop a series of techniques of avoidance whereby they could operate within the limits of the law whilst maintaining the level of intensity of labour in their enterprises. Marx argues that the Inspectors were able to succeed only because the balance of forces in the class struggle had tilted towards labour in the 1840s. The capitalist class became increasingly split into two factions, the landowners and the manufacturers, provoked by conflict over the Corn Laws. These were protectionist measures to keep up the price of domestic corn by restricting imports, supported by agricultural interests but opposed by industry (as it raised the cost of living for urban workers). The landowners used the issue of factory conditions as a weapon to discredit the industrialists, and (in Marx's words) 'thundered with philanthropic indignation against the "nefarious practices" of their foes'. For their part, the manufacturers promised the Ten Hour Bill as a way of gaining working class support.

4. Marx's Model of Law

The general conclusion drawn by Marx himself from this narrative was that the law was an arena of struggle in which the principle of equality before the law *could* be built on to achieve reforms that benefited the working class (see Marx 1976, 415–16). Marx evidently seems to reject an instrumental conception of the law as a simple tool of the ruling class. Achieving legal rights that do practically benefit the working class requires effective organisation and tactics, concludes Marx. The success of these is not purely a function of human ingenuity and tactical skill. There are also structural conditions that can make working class struggles for reform more or less successful. Perhaps the most fundamental is the one Marx stresses at the outset of his analysis: whether or not reforms on behalf of the working class are beneficial for the mode of production as a whole (as distinct from the interests of individual members of the ruling class). There also may be specific historical circumstances more conducive to reform, for example the intra-capitalist conflict over the Corn Laws stressed by Marx. The possibility of achieving reforms is more likely when they are seen as a way of dampening down pressures for more radical or revolutionary change.

Marx cautions against excessive optimism about the effects of legal reforms, noting that law has important symbolic as well as practical dimensions, and that the enforcement of law may vary from its formal requirements. Whilst recognising that legal equality is not only compatible with considerable factual inequality but may act as an ideological smokescreen, nonetheless Marx clearly sees the achievement of legal rights for the mass of the population as a desirable advance both in itself and as a platform for other changes.

The first reading below is the short passage from *The Critique of Political Economy* where Marx offers a brief summary of his approach. The second reading is a contemporary discussion by Collins emphasising the complexity of Marx's analysis of law.

Extract I

Karl Marx ('Preface to A Contribution to the Critique of Political Economy' in Marx and Engels *Selected Works* 1970, 181–2)

The first work which I undertook for a solution of the doubts which assailed me was a critical review of the Hegelian philosophy of right, a work the introduction to which appeared in 1844 in the *Deutsch-Franzosische Jahrbucher*, published in Paris. My investigation led to the result that legal relations as well as forms of state are to be grasped neither from themselves nor from the so-called general development of the human mind, but rather have their roots in the material conditions of life, the sum total of which Hegel, following the example of the Englishmen and Frenchmen of the eighteenth century, combines under the name of 'civil society', that, however, the anatomy of civil society is to be sought in political economy. The investigation of the latter, which I began in Paris, I continued in Brussels, whither I had emigrated in consequence of an expulsion order of M. Guizot. The general result at which I arrived and which, once won, served as a guiding thread for my studies, can be briefly formulated as follows: In the social production of their life, men enter into definite relations that are indispensable and independent of their will, relations of production which correspond to a definite stage of development of their material productive forces. The sum total of these relations of production constitutes the economic structure of society, the real foundation, on which rises a legal and political superstructure and to which correspond definite forms of social consciousness. The mode of production of material life conditions the social, political and intellectual life process in general. It is not the consciousness of men that determines their being, but, on the contrary, their social being that determines their consciousness. At a certain stage of their development, the material productive forces of society come in conflict with the existing relations of production, or – what is but a legal expression for the same thing – with the property relations within which they have been at work hitherto. From forms of development of the productive forces these relations turn into their fetters. Then begins an epoch of social revolution. With the change of the economic foundation the entire immense superstructure is more or less rapidly transformed. In considering such transformations a distinction should always be made between the material transformation of the economic conditions of production, which can be determined with the precision of natural science, and the legal, political, religious, aesthetic or philosophic – in short, ideological forms in which men become conscious of this conflict and fight it out. Just as our opinion of an individual is not based on what he thinks of himself, so can we not judge of such a period of transformation by its own consciousness; on the contrary, this consciousness must be explained rather from the contradictions of material life, from the existing conflict between the social productive forces and the relations of production. No social order ever perishes before all the productive forces for which there is room in it have developed; and new, higher relations of production never appear before the material conditions of their existence have matured in the womb of the old society itself. Therefore mankind always sets itself only such tasks as it can solve; since, looking at the matter more closely, it will always be found that the task itself arises only when the material conditions for its solution already exist or are at least in the process of formation. In broad outlines Asiatic, ancient, feudal, and modern bourgeois modes of production can be designated as progressive epochs in the economic formation of society. The bourgeois relations of production are the last antagonistic form of the social process of production – antagonistic not in the sense of individual antagonism, but of one arising from the social conditions of life of the individuals; at the same time the productive forces developing in the womb of bourgeois society create the material conditions for the solution of that antagonism. This social formation brings, therefore, the prehistory of human society to a close.

Extract 2

Collins (1982, 2–14 (edited))

(1) What is Marxism?

...

There seems no alternative, therefore, if we are to proceed further with an investigation of the Marxist approach towards law, but to offer a tentative definition of Marxism. Naturally any proposal will take into account both Marx's writings and the content of works claiming to be Marxist. The definition of Marxism offered here will inevitably be controversial, but I believe that it is possible to identify an underlying unity in the Marxist vision of history. This thread binding the Marxist tradition together can be perceived in two elements of the theory. first, a common methodology for deciphering the meaning of history, and, second, a prediction that the destiny of mankind lies in a Communist society. I shall consider these two themes in turn.

On the matter of methodology, the outstanding characteristic of Marxism is its close affinity to the methods of the natural sciences such as chemistry or biology. In order to establish the meaning of history Marx insisted that we should scrutinize the past to discover the causes of social change and the underlying currents of progress much like a scientist conducting an experiment. Whereas other kinds of historicism had looked for mystical signs, spiritual revelation or relied upon higher faculties of reason to predict the path of civilization Marx rejected all such speculative metaphysics. He insisted that the source of social change lay in the world itself, in the material conditions of life. There were no transcendental forces controlling events on the planet, nor was history dependent upon a process of the resolution of deep structures of ideals and values espoused by men. For Marx the source of social change lay in the material circumstances in which men found themselves and how they responded to their predicament. It followed that his method for constructing an interpretation of the meaning of history lay in a close examination of the material basis of prior civilizations in order to discover how men had reacted to their conditions and to identify the causes of instability which eventually led to successive transformations of that society.

...

The second distinguishing mark of the Marxist tradition is its belief that the destiny of mankind lies in *Communism*. What does this prediction signify? Marx argued in the *Communist Manifesto* that modern society is based upon a capitalist economy. This system is composed of some persons who own the means of production such as factories or land, and these capitalists employ the mass of the population to produce goods to be sold at a profit. Modern society is roughly divided into these two social classes, the owners of the means of production and the proletariat who work for them. Marx predicted that eventually a political struggle would occur as a result of the conflict of interest between the polarized classes of capitalist society. The proletariat would seize power through a revolution and create a new kind of class-less society in which the means of production would be owned in common by the entire community. In addition the social division of labour under which men perform tasks at someone else's beck and call would be abolished. Everyone would then experience true freedom for they would have control over every aspect of their lives. There would be not only an alteration in the organization of political power and the production of wealth but also a transformation in the nature of men themselves for they would attain a higher state of being.

Marx thought that capitalism was the penultimate stage in the process of history. The next and final phase would be Communism, though the timing of the transition was indeterminate, and there would be a period of transition. The course of events would depend not only on economic conditions but also in part upon political action and theoretical work. No wonder Marx regarded his breakthrough as tremendously important! Since theory affects practice, he believed that his solution to the riddle of the meaning of history actually hastened the transition to the utopian destiny of mankind.

...

(2) Is there a Marxist theory of law?

It has often been remarked that there is no Marxist theory of law. At first sight this is a strange assertion for it is in the nature of Marxism as a general theory of the evolution of societies that it will pass comment on significant institutions such as the law. Admittedly the main thrust of Marxist analysis is directed towards the economic infrastructure and the organizations of power in a community. That emphasis stems naturally from Marx's insight that the source of social change and the revelation of the destiny of man can only be discovered from the material circumstances of life and how man has responded to them. It follows that law is not a central focus of concern for Marxists. Neither is law a prominent analytical concept of comparable importance to social class or capitalism for example. Nevertheless legal systems are of considerable interest to Marxists because of the part they play in different social formations such as feudalism or capitalism. Marxists cannot deny the importance of some of the functions performed by legal institutions, but essentially their interest in law is tangential to a predominant focus on the general mode of social organization and the material circumstances in which men are placed. In so far as law has played a part in these decisive factors in the evolution of society then it has been of concern to Marxists.

In fact only a few have troubled themselves to examine law in any detail. For the most part discussions have been restricted to cursory remarks forming a section in work of a broader compass. Thus legal rules are often cited as a means of illustrating the course of political struggles and the evolution of social formations. But the nature of legal institutions themselves remains an unexplored terrain. Apart from extremely recent literature there are only two major works devoted exclusively to the formulation of a Marxist theory of law. Both were composed in the early part of this century. The first was Karl Renner's treatise about the relationship between law and social change, called *The Institutions of Private Law and their Social Functions* (1904). Slightly later, after the 1917 Revolution in the USSR a Soviet jurist named Evgeny Pashukanis outlined a more general theory of law. Recently there has been a flurry of articles and books devoted to Marxist studies of law. They have found their inspiration in historical studies and novel theoretical positions emanating from French and German Marxists. In addition Cain and Hunt have conveniently amassed extracts from the scattered writings of Marx and Engels on law in a book, though it is evident from that collection that neither of the founders of Marxism ever developed a systematic approach to law.

The paucity of Marxist jurisprudence until modern times is probably largely a result of the materialist emphasis of Marxism. Since the primary focus rests on the economy and the corresponding power relations within a society, law is treated as a peripheral concern. Even then it is usually relegated to the position of a relatively unproblematic sector of the State scarcely worthy of detailed consideration. There is, however, a second reason for the absence of a Marxist theory of law in a highly developed form which goes to the roots of our perception of legal institutions.

To demand a general theory of law from a Marxist is to ask him to run the risk of falling prey to what can be termed the fetishism of law ... What is meant by the fetishism of law? In simple terms it is the belief that legal systems are an essential component of social order and civilization. This belief is a pervasive feature of social and political theories outside the Marxist tradition. It serves as the foundation for most liberal political theory. In addition, this notion underlies all the important general theories of law which are in currency today. Because Marxism does not subscribe to the fetishism of law it also resists the directions of speculative thought which seek to provide a general theory of law. We can understand this point more clearly if the attributes of legal fetishism are examined in greater detail.

There are three features of legal fetishism which should be highlighted. In the first place there is the thesis that a legal order is necessary for social order. Unless there is a system of laws designed to ensure compliance with a set of rules which define rights and entitlements then no civilization is possible; if laws and legal institutions were abolished anarchy would immediately break out. H. L. A. Hart expresses this idea with his claim that there must be a minimum content of law. Unless there are rules governing ownership of property and enforcing prohibitions against physical violence, he says, society would be impossible. If a legal system, or at least some kind of coercive system, failed to provide such rules, the community would disintegrate. For those who fetishize law, legal rules are at the centre of social life, forming the basis for peaceful social intercourse. Like other norms such as the conventions on which linguistic communication is based, legal rules provide the foundation for exchanges, reliance, safety, privacy, and satisfy numerous other perennial human wants. It can be added that the greater the sophistication of the legal system, the more effective it will be in the satisfaction of those wants, and the more truly it will be like law. Thus Hart speaks of a transition from purely customary rules of the pre-legal world to the authentic legal order of modern society which has rules to cover all eventualities including mechanisms for altering the existing laws.

A second contention of legal fetishism is that law is a unique phenomenon which constitutes a discrete focus of study. Legal systems are not simply types of a broader species of systems of power, but they possess distinctive characteristics. In particular, modern jurisprudence identifies three exclusive features of legal systems. First, there are regular patterns of institutional arrangements associated with law such as the division between a legislature and a judiciary. Second, lawyers communicate with each other through a distinctive mode of discourse, though the exact nature of legal reasoning remains controversial. Third, legal systems are distinguished from simple exercises of force by one group over another; for legal rules also function as normative guides to behaviour which individuals follow regardless of the presence or absence of officials threatening to impose sanctions for failing to comply with the law. Together these three features of law, its institutional framework, its methodology, and its normativity, are considered to make law a unique phenomenon. They constitute the background for the whole enterprise of modern jurisprudence which seeks to provide a general theory of law. Whereas the first thesis of legal fetishism encouraged us to believe that law contains the answers to the problem of the origin of civilization and thus made a general theory of law of interest, the second feature of legal fetishism, a belief in the uniqueness of law, suggests that it is possible to isolate legal phenomena and to study their nature. A final aspect of legal fetishism makes a general theory of law not only interesting and possible but also crucial to political theory.

This third feature is the doctrine of the Rule of Law ... a crude approximation to its meaning will suffice to demonstrate its link to legal fetishism. The core principle of the doctrine is that political power should be exercised according to rules announced in advance. A political system is analogous to a game: it is only fair to give prior notice of the rules to all the participants and then to insist that everyone abide by them even in adversity. The Rule of Law does not require that the laws should have any particular kind of content, but simply that they should constrain the weak and powerful alike. Such a political principle inhibits arbitrary despots and authoritarian oligarchies from dispossessing citizens of their liberties without cause shown. A substantial portion of the motivation behind the construction of general theories of law lies in a desire to demonstrate that the Rule of Law is a realistic ideal. What has to be proven therefore is that the laws of a society can be identified and then applied impartially. A general theory of law hopes to provide criteria by which laws can be distinguished from other phenomena and then explain how legal rules can be interpreted and applied by judges independently of concern for their own or their friends' material interests. Such a theory is plainly crucial to styles of political legitimation which rest predominately on the ideal of the Rule of Law.

Marxists have rejected these three aspects of legal fetishism. They concede that such ideas represent a persuasive interpretation of reality found in modern society. Few would doubt the important role of law in preventing the disintegration of social order or restricting authoritarian governments. Yet Marxists claim that legal fetishism embodies a distorted image of reality which must be unmasked. To begin with, the notion that society rests on law is too simplistic. It is implausible to think that without law everyone would be at each other's throat, or would use superior physical force to take another's possessions. It is much more likely that informal standards of behaviour based on reciprocity would permit an elementary form of stable community to exist. Clearly there is a subtle relationship between the function of laws and informal customs in constituting the normative basis for a peaceful and prosperous society which will not be revealed if an assumption about the necessity and priority of law is adopted. Growing from that insight, Marxists portray the heavy dependence of organizations of power in modern society upon law as the result of a specific historic conjuncture of circumstances, and argue further that the important role of law today in maintaining social order is not an immutable feature of human civilization in the future.

Equally Marxists deny that there is a special and distinctive phenomenon which we can term law. Because Marxism has approached law tangentially, treating it as one aspect of a variety of political and social arrangements concerned with the manipulation of power and the consolidation of modes of production of wealth, there has been no commitment towards an identification of the unique qualities of legal institutions. Of course the term law is conventionally used to refer to particular kinds of systems of rules which find their paradigm in modern societies, but Marxism has not felt bound by the parameters of linguistic usage when considering law. What is more important for a Marxist is to notice how laws or law-like institutions serve particular functions within a social formation. The focus is switched from proposing a definition and drawing up of lists of functions of law to devising an explanation of the functions which laws together with other social institutions help to perform in particular historical contexts. Guided by the emphasis upon materialism Marxists avoid assumptions about the uniqueness of legal phenomena or their essence, and so they rarely offer a general theory of law, Pashukanis being the obvious exception.

The final aspect of legal fetishism, the doctrine of the Rule of Law, illustrates one of the functions which laws help to perform and as such it has been of great interest to Marxists. Since legal rules can inhibit the arbitrary exercise of power, even if their control is precarious, law can contribute an important dimension to political philosophies seeking to explain or justify the existing structures of political domination on the ground that the powerful are constrained by the demands of due process of law. The ideal of the Rule of Law encapsulates this legitimizing function of legal systems. The bulk of western jurisprudence uses the Rule of Law doctrine as a standard by which to judge the success or desirability of a general theory of law. It is crucial for these legal philosophers to demonstrate the superiority of their approach towards the problem of the identification of the laws of a particular legal system because they can then argue that they have proved the coherence of the predominant legitimating ideology of power in liberal society. Marxists, however, are obviously uninterested in putting forward a theory of their own, for their purpose is to challenge rather than defend the present organization of power. Accordingly you will not find here those elaborate analyses of the structures of legal systems which parade as legal theory in the law schools. Nevertheless the Rule of Law and the function of law in modern theories of the legitimation of power remain of vital interest to Marxists in their search for a critical understanding of the complexities of modern social systems. Therefore, a general theory of law in the conventional mode would be an anathema to Marxism though legal phenomena must constitute a central focus of inquiry.

In summary, general theories of law are predicated on a belief in the nature of law which can be termed legal fetishism Marxists reject such a belief and it follows that they are not inclined to develop a general theory of law as an end in itself. Nevertheless much remains for Marxists to say about law...

Max Weber (1864–1920)

Max Weber's work has usually been characterised as a debate with the ghost of Marx. Certainly their subject matter and key intellectual concerns have many similarities. Weber's central theme, animating his encyclopaedic exploration of social phenomena in many different historical civilisations, was the elucidation and analysis of the historically unique features of Western capitalism. (For a general account of Weber see Turner 1981; Parkin 1982; Albrow 1990. A useful collection of essays is Turner 2000. Specifically on Weber and law, see Albrow 1975; Hunt 1978, Ch 5; Kronman 1983; Turner and Factor 1994.) Weber had originally trained as a lawyer, and law was an important motif in his attempt to characterise the specific features of modern social organisation.

Weber's analysis of capitalism is typically seen as the obverse of Marx. Weber is usually portrayed as rejecting Marx's materialist theory of history in favour of an idealistic approach, emphasising the role of the cultural and political factors that Marxists tend to dismiss as merely an epiphenomenal superstructure shaped by the all important economic base. Weber's best known work *The Protestant Ethic and the Spirit of Capitalism* certainly focussed above all on the role of ideas – the rise of Protestantism – as the key explanation of the rise of modern capitalism. However Weber himself stressed that he emphasised the role of religion (see Weber 1976) because it was the part of the picture left out by the dominant materialistic interpretations advanced by the Marxist movement of his day (the Second International, which was characterised by an extremely deterministic and economistic perspective). Weber distanced himself from *all* one-sided interpretations, idealist as well as materialist.

Weber's account of modern society does highlight key features other than Marx's emphasis on the labour-capital relationship. Weber's characterisation of the unique features of modern capitalism was derived from the fourfold typology that he developed for the analysis of all forms of social action: traditional, affectual, *wertrational* (value-oriented rationality), and *zweckrational* (goal-oriented rationality). On this model, the meaning of action can be interpreted either as a continuation of traditional patterns, or the expression of emotional states, or the direct embodiment of the actor's fundamental values, or as instrumentally directed at achieving the actor's goals. Weber saw the key feature of modern societies as *rationalisation*, the increasing dominance of all action by the fourth of these types, goal-oriented rationality. This involved an instrumentalisation and demystification of social life. 'There are no mysterious, incalculable forces that come into play, but rather one can, in principle, master all things by calculation.' The organisational form that embodied this principle was formal bureaucracy, and the trend towards rationalisation could be traced throughout modern society's diverse features, including law.

Weber emphasised value-freedom as a vital aspect of the methodology of the social sciences, and in accordance with this purported to be describing rather than evaluating the development of modern societies. Nonetheless he explicitly regretted many of the trends he regarded as inescapable, railing against a world dominated by 'specialists without vision, sensualists without heart'. To Weber rationalisation was an 'iron cage', the fate of the world whether welcome or not.

The nature of power and inequality were central issues for Weber. However, Weber's analysis differs significantly from Marx. Weber was as aware of the profound class differences in capitalist societies as Marx was. However, he saw these as stemming from power in the market, not from control of labour in the process of production. To Weber class differences co-existed in capitalism with other inequalities that were of independent significance, status (ie social honour) and political derived power, whereas Marx saw these as ultimately dependent on economic class. Since Weber saw class differences as deriving from the market he regarded them as primarily a feature of capitalist societies, although patterns of domination characterised all societies. In other social orders social and power inequality could be equally or more profound but would not take the form of class differences. Perhaps the most significant implication of this is that for Weber domination is inevitable. Attempts to overthrow one particular pattern of domination invariably produce some other pattern, not the equalisation of power. Whilst Weber's view of the inequalities of capitalism is as dark as Marx's, he did not see a preferable alternative. As Benson puts it, Weber 'goes half-way with Marx – the pessimistic half' (Benson 1978, 53).

Although power differences could not be overcome according to Weber, they could be seen as legitimate, as the exercise of *authority*, not crude domination. Authority was indeed a more stable form of the exercise of power than reliance on the force of sanctions. Power could be legitimised in a variety of ways, reflecting the fundamental types of social action. Weber distinguished three types of authority, varying according to the basis on which legitimacy was conferred on power: traditional, charismatic, and rational-legal (corresponding respectively to traditional, affectual, and goal-directed rational action). A central theme of Weber's analysis of modern capitalism is that power in it is primarily exercised as rational-legal authority (although elements of the other types survive). The emergence of rational-legal authority thus becomes a focal point of Weber's account of modernisation.

Weber devotes much attention to the comparative analysis of law, with a wealth of detailed examples across a wide range of time and space. Underlying the immense detail of different legal systems, however, is a simple typology of law, corresponding to the typologies of action and authority. Law itself is defined in a fundamentally positivist way. To Weber, law is a particular type of order or rule whose 'validity is externally guaranteed by the probability that coercion (physical or psychological), to bring about conformity or to avenge violation, will be applied by a staff of people holding themselves specially ready for that purpose'. Legal systems differ, however, in the way that decisions are reached about what the rules are, and how they are to be applied. Procedures for law-making and adjudication vary in the degree and form of their rationality.

The rationality of modes of legal decision-making can vary along two axes:

a) *Rational/irrational*: To what extent are procedures 'under the control of the intellect'? Are decisions reached in a universalistic way, treating like cases alike according to the consistent application of rules?

b) *Formal/substantive*: How far is the legal system an autonomous realm of formal decision-making according to its own logic and procedures, as opposed to simply reflecting substantive considerations drawn from other institutional spheres (for example politics or religion)? Putting these two dimensions together yields a fourfold typology of legal decision-making:

i)   Substantive irrationality

This refers to decisions reached on a case-by-case basis according to their specific, concrete features, based on the ethical, emotional or political response of the decision-maker. Weber called this Solomonic or Khadi justice: systems in which those perceived as wise adjudicate cases on an ad hoc basis, presumably in accordance with the tacit sense of justice of the community if they are to retain their reputations for wisdom. Aspects of this style may survive in modern systems, and Weber regarded the jury as an example.

ii)   Formal irrationality

By this term Weber meant decisions that were arrived at through processes internal to a distinctively legal institutional realm or logic (and thus 'formal'), but not in consistent and predictable rule-bound ways that were 'under the control of the intellect'. Examples offered by Weber include the consulting of oracles, and trial by ordeal or by battle.

iii) Substantive rationality

This category encompasses decisions that are made consistently with reference to particular principles or norms, but where these are derived from institutions that are not distinctively legal. Examples would include religious courts in a theocracy, or political courts in a totalitarian regime. Elements of this survive in liberal democracies, for example if courts consistently are biased against certain interests or groups, as radical analysts have often suggested.

iv) Formal rationality

Decisions are formally rational when they are based on the internal rules and logic of a specifically legal system. There are two sub-types that can be distinguished, depending on the extent to which decisions depend on extrinsic forms or intrinsic logical principles. In the former, decisions are made primarily according to the significance attached to particular external acts or symbols, for example the validity of a contract may turn on whether the right seal is attached or certain forms of words have been said.

The essence of formal rationality, however, is the reaching of decisions by deduction from a logically closed system of formal rules, and not just the following of external forms. Weber specifies five elements characterising a formally rational legal system:

> First, that every concrete legal decision be the "application" of an abstract legal proposition to a concrete "fact" situation; second, that it must be possible in every concrete case to derive the decision from an abstract legal proposition by means of legal logic; third, that the law must actually or virtually constitute a "gapless" system of legal propositions, or must, at least, be treated as if it were such a gapless system; fourth, that whatever cannot be "construed" legally in rational terms is also logically irrelevant; and fifth, that every social action of human beings must always be visualised as either an "application" or "execution" of legal propositions, or as an "infringement" thereof.

The ideal-type of formal rationality is thus an autonomous and self-reproducing sphere of legal decision-making based on deducing the implications of its rules for particular fact situations.

There is an inescapable tension between formal and substantive rationality, argues Weber. Formal rationality, the strict application of legal rules in specific situations, may often be regarded as unfair or inappropriate according to particular substantive conceptions of justice. On the other hand, reaching decisions on the basis of non-legal substantive considerations can produce outcomes that are 'perverse' from the standpoint of formal legal rationality, say if juries acquit a defendant with whom they sympathise against the weight of the legally valid evidence. Formal rationality necessarily imposes strict boundaries on what factors are deemed legally relevant, in order to achieve logical consistency, and will often exclude considerations that are seen as important from other substantive viewpoints.

Although rejecting any idea of a necessary or inevitable historical evolution, Weber does see formal rationality as particularly associated with modern liberal capitalist societies. This is far from asserting a one-to-one connection. Formal rationality has been approximated to in some earlier legal systems, and is only found in modern societies to a varying and always incomplete extent. Nonetheless Weber does see modern capitalist society as unique in that political domination tends to be legitimated on the rational-legal mode: it is constituted as authority that works according to formal laws that limit and bind it. Law forms an autonomous system developed by professional legal specialists interpreting and applying legal principles according to their internal logic not external substantive criteria.

A distinctive status group of legal professionals on these lines, with a high degree of autonomy from economic, political and religious institutions, has only emerged in modern Western society. It is the form of law most conducive to capitalist development because it maximises the predictability of economic life, whilst freeing it from 'moral' constraints. But although there is an 'elective affinity' between capitalism and formally rational law neither is the historical cause of the other. This emerges from Weber's discussion of the 'England problem' (see Trubek 1972, 720–48; Berman and Reid in Turner 2000). England, the first country to undergo capitalist industrialisation (and, in Weber's day, still the most advanced), had a legal system that was much less close to the model of formal rationality than the German or French. Weber accounts for this by the power of the legal guilds in early modern England, who were able to preserve a training system that they controlled based on apprenticeship, rather than formal academic education in juristic theory. This inhibited the systematisation of law into a formally rational structure logically developed from fundamental principles in favour of a more empirical, practice-based case-law style.

The development of law was neither the straightforward reflection of economic forces (as vulgar Marxism would have it), nor the embodiment of lofty principles of eternal justice (as conservative apologists might claim), on Weber's analysis. It was necessary to examine the particular political and cultural circumstances of different societies, which could differ within a fundamentally similar economic base. Nonetheless economic forces were also important. Thus the congeniality of a formally rational legal system for market societies, because of the predictability it offers for property and other rights, accounted for a process of rationalisation within the structure of common law, bringing its substance closer to the formal rationality of a codified system. Weber argued that the notion of precedent had developed from the drawing of empirical analogies between concrete fact situations to the induction from cases of general rules and principles that are held to be binding.

Many of the criticisms that have been advanced against Weber's analysis seem to attribute to him a more straightforward, less nuanced position than the highly complex, ambivalent account he offered, both of modernity and of the place of law within it. He is typically attacked for seeing formal rationality as the pinnacle of legal development, in both a normative and a descriptive sense. Thus he is criticised for failing to see the negative aspects of formally rational law, as well as its ultimate unattainability. Formal rationality has been caricatured as slot-machine justice: pop in the facts and out comes the verdict as the legal calculator logically applies the relevant rules. Bracketing out many considerations that people might find relevant renders the law out of touch with popular sentiment, delivering asinine verdicts, and worse still miscarriages of justice. 'Irrational' institutions like the jury, that can introduce substantive considerations because they do not have to fit their decisions into the framework of formal legal reasoning, may actually be devices for preserving the legitimacy of the legal process. Weber recognised the increasingly legal nature of governance in modern society, but failed to anticipate the twentieth century trend that as more areas of social life become subject to law the legal institutions applied to them tend to be less formal (for example social security or employment tribunals). Socio-legal researchers point to the substantive factors that underlie the law in action, even if decisions have to be presented as if they fit the rational template of the law in the books. Radicals would argue that the concept of formal legal rationality is an ideological disguise for processes that systematically favour the powerful and the status quo under a cloak of impartial logic.

All these points have some validity but deny the explicit status that Weber claimed for his ideal-types of action, authority, and law, such as formal rationality. These were intended as methodological tools, providing clear, systematic benchmarks for understanding social processes. They were not intended as normative models, nor as descriptions of historical phenomena. They should be assessed for their usefulness in illuminating trends and structures, not their moral appeal or fit with all empirical cases. Formal rationality (and the other types of law) offered a clear vision of how decision-making could operate on different lines, and benchmarks for understanding processes of change. It certainly did not represent what Weber unequivocally thought law should be, nor how modern legal systems operate.

At most Weber was offering the (plausible) hypothesis that modern systems tend to be characterised by formal rationality more than other types. But he was acutely aware of the negative as well as the positive aspects of rationality, in law as in all social action. It flourished because it offered the great appeal of predictability, on the basis of which there could develop far more powerful forms of technology and organisation. Its affinity for efficient systems of production, exchange, and governance made rationality an 'iron cage' (as Weber called it). But there were many negative consequences, ranging from the consolidation of power differences to the disenchantment of demystified and more instrumental social relationships and views of the world. Weber was at least as alarmed and dismayed by the downside of the enormously productive forces unleashed by bourgeois modernity as his supposed arch-opponent Marx was. But whilst Marx thought that an alternative form of social organisation could keep the baby of productive efficiency whilst throwing out the bath water of domination, Weber regarded such hopes as utopian (to use a Marxist phrase). The overthrow of capitalism would result not in the withering away of oppression but simply a modification of its form. The history of the twentieth century certainly gives Weber's analysis much credibility, even if – *pace* many post-1989 suggestions – we are not yet at the end of history.

The first extract which follows is taken from Weber's major work *Economy and Society*. It is Weber's statement of the constituent parts of a legal order which falls within the formal rational type. As a description of a particular kind of law, it has many parallels with what positivists such as Hart and Kelsen describe, without further qualification, as 'Law'. If, as you read this extract, you ask yourself: 'could Hart have written this?', you might come up with some valuable thoughts. You might think that Hart should have written this. Any system of rules operating within an institutional structure needs to take that structure much more seriously than Hart seems to do, and understand more fully the human behaviour that operates within it. (On how Weber's analysis could have advanced Hart's, see Ross 2001.) In the second extract Weber's general analysis of law and the evolution of Capitalism, especially as it relates to England, is discussed critically by Albrow.

Extract I

Max Weber (1978, 217–220)

Legal Authority with a Bureaucratic Administrative Staff

3. Legal Authority: The Pure Type

Legal authority rests on the acceptance of the validity of the following mutually inter-dependent ideas.

1.   That any given legal norm may be established by agreement or by imposition, on grounds of expediency or value-rationality or both, with a claim to obedience at least on the part of the members of the organization. This is, however, usually extended to include all persons within the sphere of power in question – which in the case of territorial bodies is the territorial area – who stand in certain social relationships or carry out forms of social action which in the order governing the organization have been declared to be relevant.

2.   That every body of law consists essentially in a consistent system of abstract rules which have normally been intentionally established. Furthermore, administration of law is held to consist in the application of these rules to particular cases; the administrative process in the rational pursuit of the interests which are specified in the order governing the organization within the limits laid down by legal precepts and following principles which are capable of generalized formulation and are approved in the order governing the group, or at least not disapproved in it.

3.   That thus the typical person in authority, the 'superior', is himself subject to an impersonal order by orienting his actions to it in his own dispositions and commands. (This is true not only for persons exercising legal authority who are in the usual sense 'officials', but, for instance, for the elected president of a state.)

4.   That the person who obeys authority does so, as it is usually stated, only in his capacity as a 'member' of the organization and what he obeys is only 'the law'. (He may in this connection be the member of an association, of a community, of a church, or a citizen of a state.)

5. In conformity with point 3, it is held that the members of the organization, insofar as they obey a person in authority, do not owe this obedience to him as an individual, but to the impersonal order. Hence, it follows that there is an obligation to obedience only within the sphere of the rationally delimited jurisdiction which, in terms of the order, has been given to him.

The following may thus be said to be the fundamental categories of rational legal authority:

(1) A continuous rule-bound conduct of official business.

(2) A specified sphere of competence (jurisdiction). This involves: (a) A sphere of obligations to perform functions which has been marked off as part of a systematic division of labor. (b) The provision of the incumbent with the necessary powers. (c) That the necessary means of compulsion are clearly defined and their use is subject to definite conditions. A unit exercising authority which is organized in this way will be called an 'administrative organ' or 'agency'. There are administrative organs in this sense in large-scale private enterprises, in parties and armies, as well as in the state and the church. An elected president, a cabinet of ministers, or a body of elected 'People's Representatives' also in this sense constitute administrative organs. This is not, however, the place to discuss these concepts. Not every administrative organ is provided with compulsory powers. But this distinction is not important for present purposes.

(3) The organization of offices follows the principle of hierarchy; that is, each lower office is under the control and supervision of a higher one. There is a right of appeal and of statement of grievances from the lower to the higher. Hierarchies differ in respect to whether and in what cases complaints can lead to a 'correct' ruling from a higher authority itself, or whether the responsibility for such changes is left to the lower office, the conduct of which was the subject of the complaint.

(4) The rules which regulate the conduct of an office may be technical rules or norms. In both cases, if their application is to be fully rational, specialized training is necessary. It is thus normally true that only a person who has demonstrated an adequate technical training is qualified to be a member of the administrative staff of such an organized group, and hence only such persons are eligible for appointment to official positions. The administrative staff of a rational organization thus typically consists of 'officials', whether the organization be devoted to political, hierocratic, economic – in particular, capitalistic – or other ends.

(5) In the rational type it is a matter of principle that the members of the administrative staff should be completely separated from ownership of the means of production or administration. Officials, employees, and workers attached to the administrative staff do not themselves own the non-human means of production and administration. These are rather provided for their use, in kind or in money, and the official is obligated to render an accounting of their use. There exists, furthermore, in principle complete separation of the organization's property (respectively, capital), and the personal property (household) of the official. There is a corresponding separation of the place in which official functions are carried out – the 'office' in the sense of premises – from the living quarters.

(6) In the rational type case, there is also a complete absence of appropriation of his

official position by the incumbent. Where 'rights' to an office exist, as in the case of judges, and recently of an increasing proportion of officials and even of workers, they do not normally serve the purpose of appropriation by the official, but of securing the purely objective and independent character of the conduct of the office so that it is oriented only to the relevant norms.

(7) Administrative acts, decisions, and rules are formulated and recorded in writing, even in cases where oral discussion is the rule or is even mandatory. This applies at least to preliminary discussions and proposals, to final decisions, and to all sorts of orders and rules. The combination of written documents and a continuous operation by officials constitutes the 'office' (*Bureau*) which is the central focus of all types of modern organized action.

(8) Legal authority can be exercised in a wide variety of different forms ... The following ideal-typical analysis will be deliberately confined for the time being to the administrative staff that is most unambiguously a structure of domination: 'officialdom' or 'bureaucracy'.

In the above outline no mention has been made of the kind of head appropriate to a system of legal authority. This is a consequence of certain considerations which can only be made entirely understandable at a later stage in the analysis. There are very important types of rational domination which, with respect to the ultimate source of authority, belong to other categories. This is true of the hereditary charismatic type, as illustrated by hereditary monarchy, and of the pure charismatic type of a president chosen by a plebiscite. Other cases involve rational elements at important points, but are made up of a combination of bureaucratic and charismatic components, as is true of the cabinet form of government. Still others are subject to the authority of the chiefs of other organizations, whether their character be charismatic or bureaucratic; thus the formal head of a government department under a parliamentary regime may be a minister who occupies his position because of his authority in a party. The type of rational, legal administrative staff is capable of application in all kinds of situations and contexts. It is the most important mechanism for the administration of everyday affairs. For in that sphere, the exercise of authority consists precisely in administration.

Extract 2

Albrow (1975, 20–25)

Weber's Account of the Development of Modern Law

Weber's historical account of law consists of relatively few themes woven together to give a very rich texture. Bare summary can do scant justice to this richness but bare summary is necessary because too easily is the reader overwhelmed by the erudition and repeated flashes of insight. The themes include the ways in which new law is generated, the relation between law and the economy, in particular the way law facilitates economic development, the weight of economic and political factors in determining the balance of formal and substantive rationality in law, the intellectual outlook and interests of lawyers as a factor in legal development, but above all the tension between formal and substantive rationality as an ever present element.

Right away it must be said that there is clearly an intimate connection between Weber's methodological and definitional approach to law ... and ... the tension between formal and substantive rationality. His sociological positivism in respect of the concept of law excludes the possibility of any kind of consideration of the values which jurists normally discuss. In particular it resolutely and deliberately avoids any discussion of justice or any consideration which might distinguish between enforced codes of rules according to the values which they express. (This is the counterpart in another context of his determination to define the State in terms which exclude any reference to its ends). Weber's formalism in his account of legal thought has the same effect. The lawyer is presented as being ultimately interested in the logical coherence of a system of propositions, and not in the values which those propositions might express. The lawyer then appears as another kind of scientist, dogmatic it is true, but uncommitted to anything except the logic of law.

Now Weber's concept of substantive rationality makes reference to all those aspects which are excluded by his legal positivism. With law defined in the way Weber does and with the lawyer presented as he is, it is no wonder that substantive rationality, namely, all those considerations of public good, welfare, economic advantage, justice and morality about which the legal profession has views as much, if not more than, any other group, and which are incorporated into any legal code appear as in permanent tension with the formal rationality of law.

This can be illustrated from Weber's consideration of the factors involved in the creation of new rules of law. They arise, he says, out of new forms of conduct, which either change the meaning of existing rules, or else result in the creation of new rules. In this creative process new agreements can result in new rules, or these rules can he imposed from above. In both these processes the participation of specialized and trained legal personnel is often decisive in determining the character of the law that is created. In his lengthy discussion of the organization of legal innovation there is only a short reference to what he calls 'purely 'emotional' factors, such as the so-called sense of justice'. He goes on 'Experience shows however, that the 'sense of justice' is very unstable unless it is firmly guided by the 'pragma' of objective or subjective interests. It is, as one can still easily see today, capable of sudden fluctuations and it cannot be expressed except in a few very general and purely formal maxims'. In fact Weber sees this 'sense', being emotional, as a source of irrational adjudication, a 'popular conception' as against the 'lawyer's law' of the professionals. This is interesting because it is one of the few occasions Weber refers to popular conceptions of law and secondly because of the dismissive way he speaks of what is the substance behind formal maxims. The fact that the sense of justice has to be expressed in formal maxims apparently makes it unimportant. The formality of the maxims is what matters.

The dichotomy of form and substance has an equally important part to play in Weber's account of the relations of the economy to law. Questions of economic advantage, welfare, profitability and so on are for him intrinsically heteronomous, non-legal or substantive. By emphasizing the formal nature of law Weber has in fact begun his analysis in such a way that he can stress the independence of the two spheres. He can then treat law and economy as distinct variables and examine their reciprocal interaction.

In his examination of the influence of the economy on law Weber concludes that in general economic interests do not determine the direction of legal rationalization. The invention of the appropriate legal techniques for modern economic life, e.g. agency, negotiable instrument, or assignment depends on the intellectual training and body of legal ideas available to the legal experts of the time. While bourgeois groups demand a calculable law and thus are decisive for a general trend to formal law, they have no influence on the development of the most highly rationalized forms. 'This logical systematization of the law has been the consequence of the intrinsic intellectual needs of the legal theorists and their disciples, the doctors, i.e. of a typical aristocracy of legal literati.' For Weber the test case for the independence of legal structure from economic interests is very much England. The history of the development of the legal structure of organizations is very different in England from that on the continent and yet capitalist development took place in both.

Actually Weber's treatment of the English situation reveals difficulties in his entire discussion of the relations of law and the economy. In any case for him English law was inferior to the continental in its lower degree of rationalization. He sees it as empirical, complicated and expensive and 'it may indeed be said that England achieved capitalistic supremacy among the nations not because of, but rather in spite of, its judicial system'. But at the same time Weber cannot avoid commenting on the class basis of British law. He sees it as a blatant case of one law for the rich and one for the poor. Only the rich can afford litigation and the poor put up with the 'Khadi-justice' of the justices of the peace.

This denial of justice was in close conformity with the interests of the propertied, especially the capitalistic, classes. But such a dual judicial policy of formal adjudication of disputes within the upper class, combined with arbitrariness or *de facto* denotation of justice for the economically weak is not always possible.

Weber's attitude to England is worth a paper in itself, but what must interest us here is that Weber's own judgment on what benefits or does not benefit which class appears indeterminate and uncertain. It is difficult to avoid the conclusion that, even on his account, the structure of legal thought is very epiphenomenal. Economic development takes place regardless. The bourgeoisie always gets the law to suit it. By concentrating on law as technique he makes it appear important for the independence and prosperity of those who live from the law and nothing more.

Nothing could be more indicative of the profound antinomies and paradoxes of his view of the relation of formal and substantive considerations in law than his discussion of contract. For Weber legal rights are the 'reflex' of legal regulation and rights are a source of power. In so far as law creates rights, it gives power to particular individuals which they can then exploit. Certain structures of rights can therefore favour the emergence of certain kinds of economic relation. In the modern world the extent of contractual freedom is so great that one can designate modern society as of the contractual type. Whatever the individual (or corporate group) sees as in his interests, economic or otherwise, he can organize on the basis of a contractual relationship with others which the law will recognize and enforce if need be. The result is that market forces of the economy have a scope for development beyond anything experienced before. This legal 'freedom' becomes the basis of economic servitude for wide strata of society.

On such themes Weber's realism amounts to a critique of contemporary society owing much to and quite as trenchant as Marx's. It would be quite wrong to imagine that because

Weber accepts the bourgeois legal and economic science of his time that this translates itself into a complacent acceptance of the status quo. On the contrary, his whole analysis of rationalization is a despairing indictment of the fate of both bourgeoisie and proletariat.

Now this might appear to be a decisive argument in favour of seeing the development of legal technique as a major factor in economic development, and indeed this appears to be why Weber introduces this theme. But towards the end of *Law in Economy and Society* it appears that the development of modern commercial law in particular has quite another significance, for it gives very full scope to industrial and commercial pressure groups to have transactions defined as commercial even when they are not conducted by merchants, so that out of economic expediency a commercial meaning may be imposed on what was not intended as such. Alternatively, the real intentions of the parties to a contract may be taken into account – and this in Weber's view is equally destructive of the formal character of law. Thus:

In the sphere of private law the concern for a party's mental attitude has quite generally entailed evaluation by the judge. 'Good faith and fair dealing' or the 'good' usage of trade or, in other words, ethical categories have become the test of what the parties are entitled to mean by their 'intention'. Yet, the reference to the 'good' usage of trade implies in substance the recognition of such attitudes which are held by the average party concerned with the case, i.e., a general and purely business criterion of an essentially factual nature, such as the average expectation of the parties in a given transaction. It is this standard which the law has consequently to accept.

So it appears that much of the development of modern law in relation to economic affairs can only derogate from the formality of law and the independence of judicial decision. 'Logically consistent formal legal thinking' is incompatible with the 'fact that the legally relevant agreements and activities of private parties are aimed at economic results and orientated towards economically determined expectations ... Lawyers' law has never been and never will be brought into conformity with lay expectation unless it totally renounces that formal character which is immanent in it.'

As with his discussion of the relation of the economy and law so Weber's analysis of the relations of law and politics is focussed on the tension of formal and substantive rationality. But here Weber sees a more direct influence of political factors on the law, which is hardly surprising since his definition of law contains that element of realism which emphasizes coercion, enforcement agencies and hence political power. In this sense the relations of law and politics are much more conceptual than empirical and this means that the attempt to analyse their relations as two separate variables, contingently related, as Weber does with law and the economy is less possible. Thus Weber shows how the development of much modern law involved the incorporation of separate legal codes into a single jurisdiction through the creation of special rights and that the centralization of the State involves such an extension of legal concepts.

But here too formally rational law finds its independence and clashes with both political expedience and the attempt to regulate State affairs according to moral or economic principles. Indeed Weber develops a theory which sees the lawyers acquiring an independent power position by their ability to become detached from the competing interests in a plural society. The patriarchal monarch would find that in using juristic experts he would have handed over his capacity to organize his affairs autonomously. Formal justice reduces arbitrariness and favours those with economic power at the expense of those with political power. The enlightened despots of the eighteenth century in particular sought to avoid juristic hair-splitting and to avoid the elaboration of law by professional jurists. The Prussian General Code of 1794 was an attempt at systematic rationalism of a substantively rational kind. But for Weber this code, which indeed survived only until 1896, was a failure. Its clarity was obscured by taking 'as its point of departure not formal legal concepts but the practical relations of life'.

This discussion of the Prussian Code leads Weber into an account of the French Civil Code and a concluding general discussion of the conflicts between formal and substantive rationality in modern legal thought. It is at this point that one can see all the more clearly that Weber's analysis must be seen as much as a contribution to juristic debate as to a sociology of law and it becomes quite obvious that Weber is in fact espousing a particular juristic doctrine. The French Code attempts to base its laws on a normative standard of natural law. The sources of natural law doctrine are various, stemming from Stoicism and Christianity, mediaeval English ideas of individual rights, and the eighteenth century enlightenment. In Weber's definition 'Natural law is the sum total of all those norms which are valid independently of, and superior to, any positive law and which owe their dignity not to arbitrary enactment but, on the contrary, provide the very legitimation for the binding force of positive law.'

Natural law was often expressed in very formal axioms but in practice, argues Weber, and indeed necessarily, natural law ideas involve bringing into the discussion of law problems of practicality and usefulness. It involves the English concept of reasonableness rather than rationality of logic of the Roman Law. Such notions, notes Weber, play a vital part in all socialist movements. But nonetheless he considers these metajuristic justifications of law to be everywhere on the retreat. Intellectual scepticism and the relativization of morals has led to seeing such metaphysical claims as the mere expression of compromises between conflicting groups. So legal positivism has advanced irresistibly and the legal profession becomes a conservative force simply concerned to preserve the law of the moment from either proletarian demands for social justice or patriarchal welfare-statism. In this conservatism the command by the legal profession of the technical expertise of formal legal rationality is its great power asset and also its intellectual delight. The formal expertise of the lawyer and the conception of law as a gapless complex of norms, factors which originally facilitated the reception of Roman Civil law, had given to the legal profession that power resource which transcended and indeed made irrelevant the substance of Roman law.

All kinds of countervailing tendencies to the advance of formalistic legal rationalism might exist in the modern world. Weber gives a resume of them. We have already mentioned his view of commercial law. Anglo-American ideas with their low level of rationalism, crude empiricism and relative accessibility to the layman represent an exception. The jury system represents a form of 'popular' and irrational justice. Sometimes jurists themselves, alarmed by the technical perfection they attain, advocate the introduction of substantive considerations into the law and in the short term at least make of law something more than a set of techniques. They react against being 'slot machine' lawyers and advocate judicial creativeness as they believe is characteristic of the Anglo-American system.

Weber allows that these countervailing tendencies have strength but it is quite clear where he feels the future to lie in the legal profession. 'In any case, the juristic precision of judicial opinions will be seriously impaired if sociological, economic, or ethical argument were to take the place of legal concepts', ' … it will be inevitable that, as a result of technical and economic developments, the legal ignorance of the layman will increase. Inevitably the notion must expand that the law is a rational technical apparatus, which is continually transformable in the light of expediential considerations and devoid of all sacredness of content.'

Emile Durkheim (1858–1917)

Law played a central role in Durkheim's analysis of social development, although it was not his primary interest (for general accounts of Durkheim see Lukes 1973; Fenton 1984. The definitive study of his work on law is Cotterrell 1999. Lukes and Scull 1983 is an invaluable collection of extracts from Durkheim's own writings on law, with a critical introduction by the editors). His abiding concern, throughout his work, was with understanding the nature and sources of social solidarity and cohesion, in particular in the problematic context of modern industrial societies. Since Durkheim's work is focused on understanding social order he devotes much attention to the analysis of deviance and law-breaking (he has been a major influence in the development of criminology: Taylor, Walton and Young 1973, Ch 3; Reiner 1984; Garland 1990, Chs 2 and 3; Downes and Rock 1998, Chs 4 and 5). In his early writings in particular Durkheim also examined the relationship between legal and social development in general, and sparked an ongoing debate about his interpretation of legal evolution. Law came to play a vital part in Durkheim's account of modern societies not for its own sake, however, but because he saw law as the crucial empirical indicator of social solidarity, his overriding concern. 'Since law reproduces the principal forms of social solidarity, we have only to classify the different types of law to find therefrom the different types of social solidarity which correspond to it.' By solidarity Durkheim means the 'moral phenomenon' that is a 'social fact' of social coexistence, of 'the general integration of society'.

This argument was most explicit in Durkheim's first book *The Division of Labour in Society*. In this work Durkheim developed a distinction between two types of social solidarity, mechanical and organic. *Mechanical* solidarity is characterised by all individuals uniformly sharing the same values, beliefs and roles, a common *conscience collective*. Solidarity is based on similarity, although individuals are largely self-sufficient and thus solidarity is brittle. This model was attributed by Durkheim to simpler societies with only a rudimentary division of labour. *Organic* solidarity by contrast is based on the mutual interdependence of different units in societies with a highly developed division of labour. Durkheim's key argument was that organic solidarity was the only type possible in complex and differentiated modern societies, although it certainly did not develop automatically and had not yet been realised. Nonetheless the practical interdependence of people in a highly developed division of labour created the potential for solidarity based on a social ethic of respect for individual liberty and difference. Durkheim's concern was to understand the barriers and the possible pathways to the achievement of this form of solidarity, against the background of the processes creating conflict, tension and *anomie* (normlessness) in modern societies.

Law entered Durkheim's argument initially for methodological reasons (although of course a concern for solidarity would lead to an interest in order and deviance in any case). Solidarity was a moral phenomenon which in itself could not be observed or measured. Empirical research on it required an externally observable indicator, and Durkheim claimed that law was the 'visible symbol' of solidarity. This was based on a conception of law as an expression of social consensus, a reflection of shared sentiments and values, so that 'we can thus be certain of finding reflected in law all the essential varieties of social solidarity'. This seems to rule out of account the possibility of law being an arena of conflict or the expression of power (as both Marx and Weber saw it), although indeed Durkheim himself acknowledged that legal rules may reflect class conflict. Nonetheless he adopts a primarily consensus view of law, as a requirement of his methodology, claiming that changing forms of law could be interpreted as indices of changes in the underlying nature of social solidarity. Proceeding on the basis of the positivist claim that the essential character of law is that it is sanctioned conduct, Durkheim argued that we can use the nature of legal sanctions as a measure of the type of law and hence also of social solidarity.

> It is now probable that there is a type [of law] which symbolizes this special solidarity of which the division of labor is the cause. That found, it will suffice, in order to measure the part of the division of labor, to compare the number of juridical rules which express it with the total volume of law ... Every precept of law can be defined as a rule of sanctioned conduct. Moreover, it is evident that sanctions change with the gravity attributed to precepts, the place they hold in the public conscience, the role they play in society. It is right, then, to classify juridical rules according to the different sanctions which are attached to them. (Durkheim 1893/1964, 68–69)

Durkheim distinguished between two types of legal sanctions, arguing that they corresponded in turn to the two forms of solidarity. *Repressive* sanctions involved the infliction of suffering or loss to avenge violations of the law. It was characteristic of mechanical solidarity, expressing the strong, shared sentiments of such societies. Repressive law did not necessarily rest upon any specialised adjudication or enforcement machinery, but could be exercised by the community as a whole. *Restitutive* sanctions involved only the restoration of the status quo that had been disrupted by legal violation, the 're-establishment of troubled relations to their normal state', with no infliction of harm on the violator beyond that. It is concerned with the regulation and co-ordination of the complex relations arising out of the division of labour, not with avenging violations of the shared sentiments and norms of a *conscience collective*. Restitutive law thus corresponds to a highly developed division of labour, and is an anticipation or reflection of the development of organic solidarity. It involves the specialised personnel, organisational machinery and elaborated rules and procedures of a modern legal system.

Durkheim's thesis about legal evolution has attracted much debate, ever since its publication. Durkheim himself responded implicitly to the initial criticism in an 1899 essay, 'Two Laws of Penal Evolution', where he suggested that the growth of state absolutism could produce periods of regression to repressiveness in developed societies, complicating the hypothesis of restitutive law progressively displacing punitive sanctions. This revision of his initial treatment of the subject was intended to counter the criticism that the history of modern societies did not exhibit a straightforward evolution towards restitutive law. The eighteenth century 'age of absolutism', for example, exhibited a trend towards increasingly bloody penal regimes (as of course did the twentieth century experience of totalitarianism, after Durkheim's death).

The main line of criticism of Durkheim's work on legal evolution has been the same for over a century: he got his facts wrong. Anthropological evidence suggests that the simplest societies, with little division of labour, were not characterised by harsh repressive sanctions but on the contrary by order maintenance through a variety of informal processes. This was the conclusion of a seminal 1964 article by Schwartz and Miller that analysed the data recorded by anthropological and historical studies for a sample of 51 non-industrial societies. It showed that there was a close relationship between the social complexity of a society and the evolution of legal systems. Institutions for adjudication and enforcement of norms through formal sanctioning only emerge as societies become more complex. Schwartz and Miller specifically interpret this as a refutation of Durkheim's claim that 'penal law ... occurs in societies with the simplest division of labour'. On the contrary, their 'data show that police are found only in association with a substantial degree of division of labour ... By contrast restitutive sanctions – damages and mediation – which Durkheim believed to be associated with an increasing division of labour, are found in many societies that lack even rudimentary specialisation. Thus Durkheim's hypothesis seems the reverse of the empirical situation.'

Subsequent research has tended to confirm this conclusion, although it has also tended to suggest that the relationship between legal and social development is more complicated than Schwartz and Miller themselves imply. As Durkheim's own auto-critique in 'Two Laws of Penal Evolution' argued, political factors such as the character of the state may cross-cut the influence of social structure, producing for example the move towards greater punitiveness in the eighteenth century that Durkheim himself noted. More fundamentally damaging to Durkheim's perspective is Spitzer's finding that social complexity tends to produce greater social divisions and conflict, and hence more repression, rather than increasing cohesiveness and restitutive law as Durkheim's model of organic solidarity implied. This was shown by a study of the same data base as Schwartz and Miller had analysed. Spitzer concludes that the evolution of punishment is curvilinear: 'Sanctions are lenient in simple egalitarian (reciprocal) societies, severe in non-market (redistributive) complex societies, and lenient in established market societies.' (Spitzer 1975, 633) Another review of anthropological literature, by Robinson and Scaglion, concluded similarly that the emergence of specialised policing institutions was primarily related to the growth of 'economic specialisation and differential control of resources ... in the transition from a kinship – to a class-dominated society'.

Durkheim's work remains significant at the very least in having sparked off an ongoing enquiry and debate into the relationship between law and social evolution, although his picture of this has been apparently refuted. However it also retains its value in a more substantial way, as a thesis about the future of law in modern societies. The notion of organic solidarity was not intended to be an accurate depiction of how industrial societies had actually evolved, but as an 'ideal-type' of the only kind of solidarity that Durkheim thought possible in complex and differentiated modern societies. Although the development of modernity had shattered earlier forms of solidarity based on uniform sharing in a common conscience collective, Durkheim's key point was that the division of labour produced factual interdependence between people at the same time as it generated social differences. This created the potential for a new form of social solidarity based on difference not similarity. (A necessary precondition for this must be in Durkheim's view that differences in economic position should not be so sharp as to preclude their being perceived as just (see Fenton 1983, Ch 2). Socialist calls for redistribution were seen by him not as misguided but as not sufficient for the attainment of solidarity. There was also the need for a suitable social ethic to provide meaning and mutual respect.) The ethic appropriate for this was one of mutual respect and toleration of diversity not the enforcement of a monolithic morality. The form of law appropriate for such a social order could not be one that tried to enforce a common sentiment and consciousness that no longer existed, but one that sought only to repair specific instances of harm by seeking restitutive damages not vengeance. As an account of what has actually happened Durkheim's picture of legal evolution has been refuted many times, but as an agenda for a possible future it retains its power.

The following extract from Reiner provides a summary of the critical debate sparked off by Durkheim's analysis.

Reiner (1984, 176–200)

Durkheim on law, crime and deviance

Law was a fundamental concept in the thesis developed in Durkheim's first book, *The Division of Labour in Society*. Durkheim's main concern here as elsewhere in his work, was with understanding the problems and preconditions of social solidarity in complex, differentiated, industrial societies. Central to his account was the distinction he developed between two contrasting forms of solidarity – 'mechanical' and 'organic'. 'Mechanical' solidarity is said to be characteristic of simple societies with only a rudimentary division of labour. The individual members of society are uniformly enveloped within a common 'conscience collective', sharing the same values, beliefs and roles. Notions of individual difference, rights and responsibilities are only weakly developed, if at all. Solidarity of such societies is mechanical in that it arises from the similarity of the different atoms constituting the whole.

'Organic' by contrast, is that which develops on the basis of an advanced and complex division of labour. Such societies are characterized by the interdependence of units differentiated by economic and social function. Although organically solidarity societies do not have a pervasive collective conscience like that associated with mechanical solidarity. the practical interdependence arising out of the division of labour. if combined with an appropriate social ethic recognizing and based upon respect for the individual differences produced by specialized functions, could bind such societies into tightly knit, albeit differentiated, social organisms.

Durkheim's concern with the solidarity of societies in itself logically indicates an indirect interest in deviation and crime, but he brings law explicitly and centrally into his discussion of solidarity for methodological reasons. He observes that 'social solidarity is a completely moral phenomenon which, taken by itself, does not lend itself to exact observation nor indeed to measurement.' Empirical research requires an externally observable and measurable indicator of solidarity, which cannot be directly apprehended in itself. 'We must substitute for this internal fact which escapes us an external index which synibolises it and study the former in the light of the latter. This visible symbol is law.'

This usage of law as the index of social solidarity is based upon a highly tendentious conception of the law-society relation, which Durkheim explicitly elaborates and defends.

> Social life, especially where it exists durably, tends inevitably to assume a definite form and to organise itself, and law is nothing else than this very organisation in so far as it has greater stability and precision. The general life of society cannot extend its sway without juridical life extending its sway at the same time and in direct relation. We can thus be certain of finding reflected in law all the essential varieties of social solidarity.

Durkheim recognizes that there may be rules and relations, in society which 'fix themselves without assuming a juridical form' and are based on custom. But he sees these as 'assuredly secondary: law produces those which are essential and they are the only ones we need to know'. Custom and law are in conflict only in 'rare and pathological cases which cannot endure without danger'.

Law itself is not explicitly defined by Durkheim. But the implication is that law is the set of rules which are more or less formally promulgated and enforced in a society. It is a kind of legal positivism in that rules need not have any particular substantive content nor any specific formal character to count as law. What is tendentious is the direct linking of law to the moral consensus of a society. This rules out by definitional fiat the exploration of such issues as the conflicting social interests which law might serve, or an adequate account of the process of legislation which may reflect struggles between competing interests and conceptions of morality. The methodological strategy of assuming law to be an index of solidarity seems to presuppose a consensus view of law, even though later in the same book, when discussing the forced division of labour, Durkheim acknowledges that legal rules may reflect and even exacerbate class conflict.

Having established to his satisfaction that 'law reproduces the principal forms of social solidarity', the next task for Durkheim is 'to classify the different types of law to find therefrom the different types of solidarity which correspond to it'. In line with his general conception of sociological method, Durkheim argues that we cannot simply take on board the distinctions already drawn by jurists, such as that between private and public law. 'To proceed scientifically, we must find some characteristic which, while being essential to juridical phenomena, varies as they vary.' He finds this in the essential character of law as 'sanctioned conduct', and develops a distinction between two forms of legal sanction which correspond to the two types of social solidarity.

'Repressive' law is enforced by penal sanctions which 'consist essentially in suffering, or at least a loss, inflicted on the agent'. It is associated with mechanical solidarity in that it expresses strong, shared social sentiments. Violations of these result in sanctions harming the offender and extracting vengeance for the assault on the conscience collective. Repressive law does not necessarily require any specialized judicial machinery for its enforcement – it may be exercised by the collective as a whole, although this must be an organized act.

'Restitutive' law by contrast, 'consists only of *the return of things as they were*, in the reestablishment of troubled relations to their normal state'. It is concerned with the regulation and co-ordination of relations arising from the division of labour. Restitutive sanctions do not result from violations of the conscience collective, and do not reflect the same strong sentiments as those producing a penal reaction. Restitution is 'not expiatory, but consists of a simple *return in state*'. Restitutive law may be negative, involving 'pure abstention', i.e. rules delimiting areas of personal rights such as property, or positive, constituting the co-operative relations of the division of labour, e.g. contract or administrative law. Restitutive law corresponds to a highly developed division of labour. It is more specialized and complex in both substantive content and organizational machinery and personnel for its administration. It is a reflection of a movement towards organic solidarity based upon positive co-operation.

Durkheim's theses about law stimulated a debate about their empirical validity which still flourishes today. Although presented as if it were a readily testable empirical hypothesis, Durkheim's claims about legal evolution are extraordinarily difficult to assess. Durkheim himself states blithely that 'It will suffice, in order to measure the part of the division of labour, to compare the number of juridical rules which express it with the total volume of law'. This, however, is no simple job for a pocket calculator. Given that there is a distinction between 'the law in the books' and 'the law in action', it is not clear that it is satisfactory to take all written codes, statutes and case-law (even if this Herculean task could be accomplished) as corresponding to 'the total volume of law' which is active in a society. This problem applies *a fortiori* to non-literate societies without any 'law in the books'. Nor is there any simple metric for counting the number of rules of different kinds. Is a statute with eight sub-sections detailing special applications one law or nine? Furthermore, the nature of sanctions is postulated as the index of the character of law. But how are these to be assessed precisely? Is a sanction of capital punishment for a particular offence which is seldom applied in practice more or less 'repressive' than a sanction of imprisonment which is regularly applied? As the criminologists and penal reformers of the classical school argued at the turn of the eighteenth century, there is a payoff between the nominal severity of sanctions and the likelihood of their effective application. Which for Durkheim is the most important? As the classicists also argued prevention of crime by professionally organized policing may control society more tightly than the threat of severe sanctions seldom enforced. But is a penal code safeguarded by intensive police patrol and surveillance more or less repressive than one nominally buttressed by severer sanctions which are very uncertainly applied? Does the contention that restitutive law advances in relation to repressive mean that restitutive sanctions displace repressive ones for the same offence, or that new offences with restitutive sanctions are added on in disproportionate volume to the existing penal code? The impression created by Durkheim that the path of legal evolution may be readily charted by a quantification of sanctions is clearly misleading.

Durkheim's interest in social solidarity and the character of legal sanctions as the index of this led him to more specific analyses of crime, deviance and punishment, in *The Division of Labour*, and in some of his later works, particularly *The Rules of Sociological Method*, *Suicide*, and 'Two laws of penal evolution'. The starting point for Durkheim's treatment of crime and deviance is the formulation of a definition of crime which has been highly influential in subsequent criminology, particularly since the development of the 'labelling theory' perspective in the early 1960s. Durkheim rejects the definition of crime which would constitute the commonsense of any society – that crimes are acts which are harmful to society or contrary to natural justice. He points to the enormous variation between societies in the acts which have been regarded as criminal in order to rebut the claim that conceptions of crime are rooted in the social evil represented by particular actions. 'There are many acts which have been and still are regarded as criminal without in themselves being harmful to society.' The only attribute applicable to crimes in general is that they are socially proscribed and punished. 'The only common characteristic of all crimes is that they consist ... in acts universally disapproved of by members of each society ... Crime shocks sentiments which, for a given social system, are found in all healthy consciences.' It is social reaction and labelling, not the intrinsic character of an act, which constitutes it as a crime. 'We must not say that an action shocks the common conscience because it is criminal, but rather that it is criminal because it shocks the common conscience.' To this primary definition Durkheim adds two riders. Crimes are distinguishable from more minor moral peccadilloes by the *strength* of social disapproval. 'The collective sentiments to which crime corresponds must, therefore, singularise themselves from others by some distinctive property, they must have a certain average intensity. Not only are they engraven in all consciences, but they are strongly engraven.' Furthermore, only specific acts can be criminalized, not diffusely defined patterns of conduct, no matter how intense the moral condemnation they attract. 'The wayward son, however, and even the most hardened egotist are not treated as criminals. It is not sufficient, then, that the sentiments be strong, they must be precise.' In sum, 'an act is criminal when it offends strong and defined states of the collective conscience'.

Crime thus defined is a universal feature of all societies argues Durkheim. This is because crime performs a vital social function in any society. Through the punishment of offenders not only are the moral boundaries of the community clearly demarcated, but the strength of attachment to them is reinforced. The purpose of punishment is neither deterrence, rehabilitation of the offender, nor the administration of his just deserts. Punishment strengthens social solidarity through the reaffirmation of moral commitment among the conforming population who witness the suffering and expiation of the offender.

> Its true function is to maintain social cohesion intact, while maintaining all its vitality in the common conscience ... We can thus say without paradox that punishment is above all designed to act upon upright people, for, since it serves to heal the wounds made upon collective sentiments, it can fill this role only where these sentiments exist ... In short, in order to form an exact idea of punishment, we must reconcile the two contradictory theories which deal with it: that which sees it as expiation, and that which makes it a weapon for social defence. It is certain that it functions for the protection of society, but that is because it is expiatory.

To this functionalist argument for the universality of crime and punishment, Durkheim adds another line of reasoning in his later treatment of crime as a 'normal' rather than 'pathological' feature of societies in *The Rules of Sociological Method*. This rests upon the statistical assumption of inevitable variation in individual character. 'It is impossible for all to be alike, if only because each one has his own organism and that these organisms occupy different areas in space.' Although specific offences may become inconceivable due to progressive refinement of the moral sentiments of society, this will make people more sensitive to the marginal failures to conform which inevitably still remain, rather than eliminating crime.

> Imagine a society of saints, a perfect cloister of exemplary individuals. Crimes, properly so called, will there be unknown: but faults which appear venial to the layman will create there the same scandal that the ordinary offense does in ordinary consciousnesses. If, then, this society has the power to judge and punish, it will define these acts as criminal and will treat them as such.

As the final strand of his demonstration of the normality of crime, Durkheim unites the functionalist and statistical arguments in the claim that crime can have a positively beneficial, progressive role in social evolution. Individuals who anticipate necessary adjustments of social morality to changing conditions may be stigmatized as criminal at first. Crime is the precondition and the proof of a society's capacity for flexibility in the face of essential change.

> How many times, indeed, it is only an anticipation of future morality − a step toward what will be! According to Athenian law, Socrates was a criminal, and his condemnation was no more than just. However, his crime, namely, the independence of his thought, rendered a service not only to humanity but to his country.

The conclusion of Durkheim's argument is that contrary to the conventional view that crime is a social pathology that must be eradicated, it is a normal and inescapable phenomenon which can play a useful part in facilitating social progress. So much for the familiar image of Durkheim as the apostle of social control.

> Contrary to current ideas, the criminal no longer seems a totally unsociable being, a sort of parasitic element, a strange and unassimilable body, introduced into the midst of society. On the contrary, he plays a definite role in social life. Crime, for its part, must no longer be conceived as an evil that cannot be too much suppressed. There is no occasion for self-congratulation when the crime rate drops noticeably below the average level, for we may be certain that this apparent progress is associated with some social disorder.

Durkheim stresses that it does not follow from the normality of crime that it is not to be abhorred. His argument is not an apologia for the criminal. Firstly, there is nothing contradictory about abhorring something which is inevitable or even functional, as we do with physical pain in illness. But more fundamentally, it is largely through the process of *punishment* that crime becomes functional, apart from the Socrates-type case of the progressive deviant.

Furthermore, although Durkheim does not bring this out in his general consideration of crime, even if *some* level of crime is necessary in any society, the *actual* rate may well be pathological and a reflection of social disorganization. Durkheim gives us no ready recipe for calculating the 'normal' rate for particular social types, but his treatment elsewhere of specific forms of deviance both illustrates the possibility of pathological levels of crime, and provides a model for its analysis. The best-known and most fully articulated study of a specific kind of deviance is his celebrated *Suicide*, but Durkheim also offers a rather more cursory account of homicide in *Professional Ethics and Civic Morals*, chapter 10.

Durkheim's basic concern is to demonstrate that the rate of suicide (and by extension other kinds of deviation) is a function of the general state of social integration and regulation. His two basic types of suicide, egoistic and anomic, are results of the breakdown of social integration and regulation respectively. The egoistic type of suicide (induced from the greater suicide-propensity of Protestants rather than Catholics, the unmarried and childless rather than the married or those with families, and the drop of suicide rates at times of war or national crisis) is the result of a weakening of bonds integrating individuals into the collectively. The anomic type of suicide (induced mainly from the relationship between suicide and sudden dislocations of economic life) is the product of moral deregulation, a lack of definition of legitimate aspirations through a restraining social ethic which could impose meaning and order on the individual conscience. Both are symptomatic of a failure of economic development and the division of labour to produce that organic solidarity which Durkheim anticipated as the normal condition of industrial societies. The remedy lies in social reconstruction to provide the material and moral preconditions of solidarity. This account of the way that the roots of deviation lay in pathological states of the social order, in particular anomic, has been one of the most influential aspects of Durkheim's work on subsequent criminology.

A decade after his initial treatment of legal evolution in *The Division of Labour*, Durkheim returned to the subject in his essay on 'Two laws of penal evolution', which contains his most developed statement on law, crime and punishment. Paradoxically, he makes no reference to his earlier treatments, even though he clearly takes account of some of the contemporary criticisms of his work.

In this essay Durkheim seeks to establish and explain two laws which he claims have governed the evolution of the apparatus of punishment. The first, which he calls 'the law of quantitative change', he formulates thus: 'The intensity of punishment is the greater the more closely societies approximate to a less developed type – and the more the central power assumes an absolute character.' This is clearly a reformulation of his legal evolution hypothesis from *The Division of Labour*, with the concepts of mechanical and organic solidarity being displaced by a rather looser notion of degrees of development. Most importantly, however, a subsidiary hypothesis relating the penal system to the character of the state has been added, evidently to explain exceptions to the postulated primary 'law'. The second law, 'of qualitative changes', is formulated as: 'Deprivations of liberty, and of liberty alone, varying in time according to the seriousness of the crime, tend to become more and more the normal means of social control.'

To substantiate his first law, Durkheim adduces the augmented forms of the death penalty (discussed in stomach-turning detail) found in some ancient societies. For non-capital offences, physical punishments symbolic of the crime (such as tearing out the tongue of a spy) were used. With the development of 'city states' the augmented forms of capital and corporal punishment decline, a process accelerated in 'Christian societies'. This process of progressive decline in penal harshness is reversed after the fourteenth century as 'the king's power became more and more firmly established', reaching a climacteric in the increasingly severe penal codes of most European countries during the eighteenth century. 'The apogee of the absolute monarchy coincides with the period of the greatest repression.' This interlude is an illustration of the subsidiary hypothesis in Durkheim's first law, relating punishment to state power. The late eighteenth century and nineteenth century witnessed a renewal of the major trajectory towards less severe punishment, as the arguments of the penal reformers such as Beccaria, Bentham and many others began to prevail. The reforms associated with the liberal utilitarians involved not only quantitative declines in harshness of punishment, but the qualitative change to imprisonment as the dominant penal techniques which Durkheim enshrines as his second law.

In explaining the laws Durkheim argues that changing forms of punishment are due to changes in the character of crime, which in turn is related to the form of social solidarity and conscience. 'Since punishment results from crime and expresses the manner in which it affects the public conscience, it is in the evolution of crime that one must seek the cause determining the evolution of punishment.'

Durkheim distinguishes between two kinds of crime. The criminality characteristic of primitive societies offends against sentiments which have *collective* things as their object, as well as being sentiments which are collectively shared. The offended sentiments and objects are imbued with a strong religious element, which gives crime an exceptionally odious character calling down violent repression on the perpetrator. By contrast the crime associated with modern societies offends collective sentiments which have the *individual* as their object, it is a human rather than religious criminality. This lessens the intensity of repression for the 'offence of man against man cannot arouse the same indignation as an offence of man against God'. Moreover, the punishment of the offender evokes sentiments of qualitatively the same kind of horror for individual suffering as that for the victim, thus mitigating the force of the collective sentiment for reprisal. The result is that 'Seeing as, in the course of time, crime is reduced more and more to offences against persons alone, while religious forms of criminality decline, it is inevitable that punishment on the average should become weaker.'

While focussing on the changing character of repressive law (from religious to human) as societies develop, thereby implicitly recognizing the strength of survival of penal law in modern societies, Durkheim does not pursue further *The Division of Labour's* insights into the proliferation of non-penal, restitutive forms of law. The argument that harshness of sanctions is related to absolutist state power allows him to modify his claim that punishment is completely determined by social structure. But the theoretical advance of introducing a political dimension into the explanation of punishment is weakened by his insistence that state forms vary quite independently of the changing social structure … This closes off the possibility of developing a political sociology of punishment which would have to relate state, law, and social structure in a way that explores their interdependence. In effect in the 'Two laws' essay, Durkheim introduces the state as a residual category to explain away apparent deviations from his primary thesis.

The second law postulating the emergence of imprisonment as the dominant penal technique in modern times, is explained largely by the coincidence of the development of a notion of individual rather than collective criminal responsibility, requiring pre-trial detention of offenders, with the practical availability of secure buildings due to social centralization and urbanization. The move towards imprisonment as a pure form of punishment is explained as a corollary of the first law, declining penal harshness, once the means and practice of incarceration had become established. Durkheim's account of the second law is altogether sketchier and subordinate to the first, and he fails to develop in any serious or sustained way the obvious inter-connections between imprisonment and utilitarian penal philosophy which would be consonant with his general conception of modern society, notably its suitability for precisely graded variations of severity. Nor does Durkheim consider the varying penal philosophies which developed in the nineteenth century to justify imprisonment and explain its purpose. He ends rather limply with the vague call for new forms of penal institution to be 'born which correspond better to the new aspirations of the moral conscience'.

...

Durkheim's account of the evolution of law has provoked considerable criticism ever since the initial publication of *The Division of Labour*; indeed 'Two laws of penal evolution' partly represents Durkheim's response to some early critiques. Since the mid-1960s there has been a revival of interest in Durkheim's model of legal evolution, and a steady stream of papers debating it.

The nub of the criticism of Durkheim's thesis has been that he simply got his facts wrong, in particular in characterizing primitive societies as dominated by repressive law which becomes progressively less punitive as societies develop. As Faris forcefully put it in a review of the first English translation of *The Division of Labour*:

> Published when the author was thirty-five years old, the work accepts as accurate the crude misconceptions of the 1880s concerning the life of primitive man as set forth in the books of those who were no more competent to describe them than a botanist would be to write a treatise in his field without ever having seen a plant ... Not to be severe with a writer who, forty-one years ago, accepted what is now known to be untenable, it would at least seem that extended discussion of an argument based on abandoned premises might be considered an unnecessary expenditure of energy.

Despite this warning, many writers have ventured to expend considerable energy in this area. But the conclusion that Durkheim's account was factually wrong has been confirmed by later work. Reviewing *The Division of Labour* and its significance in 1966, Barnes wrote: 'the main weakness ... is that the ethnographic evidence shows that, in general, primitive societies are not characterised by repressive laws'.

What is uncontentious is that Durkheim's work is significant in opening up the issue of the relationship between law and social development, and more broadly emphasizing the social context of law in general. As Sheleff put it: 'Durkhelm was probably right in his theoretical premise that the law is the visible outer symbol of the nature of a society. He was almost certainly wrong in his empirical assessment of the direction of the law from repressive to restitutive.'

As Jones has pointed out, until recently contemporary criminology has been marked by 'a failure to consider the relationships between crime, punishment and social change'. Although in the last few years histories of crime and law have proliferated, recent studies have either been ethnographic rather than theoretical, or subject to 'a discernible trend … to over-compensate for Durkheim's failure by giving too much attention to the role of economic and political interests, at the expense of more sociological concerns'.

The only study actually to provide some empirical support for Durkheim is an analysis of support for capital punishment in different areas of Canada carried out by Chandler. His findings indicate that more mechanically solidary areas (more culturally homogeneous, religious, less developed) will support retribution and induce their MPs to vote for the death penalty'. As Chandler himself recognizes, however, such a cross-sectional analysis cannot in itself be taken as indicating anything about evolution (the same point can be made. of course, about the numerous attempts to refute Durkheim by cross-sectional data). More crucially, support for the death penalty specifically does not tell us anything about the relative preponderance of repressive or restitutive law in general.

The most important deficiency in Durkheim's account of legal evolution is one that he partially acknowledged in the later formulation in 'Two laws' but which remains only sketchy and undeveloped: the relation between the state and law. It is clear that Durkheim himself quickly became aware of the errors in his conception of primitive law as repressive, and the distortions involved in his initial thesis about a unilinear path of evolution towards less punitive law. Some writers have even claimed that Durkheim completely abandoned his views on legal evolution after the first publication of *The Division of Labour* in 1893, as evidenced by the fact that he never again uses the distinctions mechanical versus organic solidarity or repressive versus restitutive law in his later work. But the primary thesis advanced in his first 'law of penal evolution' in the 1900 essay is essentially the same as that proposed in The *Division of Labour*, linking social development to declining punitiveness. The crucial difference is that he introduces the subsidiary clause relating punitiveness to the growth of centralized state power. It seems clear that this is to provide an explanation of an obvious and damaging exception to the first law: the increasing harshness of penalties in seventeenth and eighteenth century Europe that followed in the wake of royal absolutism. Furthermore it is even clearer in the 'Two laws' essay that all Durkheim's evidence about the harshness of primitive law is drawn from fairly advanced and complex ancient societies rather than small, simple tribal societies. Putting together the two aspects of Durkheim's first law the overall pattern of development of punishment predicted is a curvilinear one, with an increase in punitiveness as centralized state powers emerge, followed by declining harshness (or possibly even more complex sequences if the evolutionary starting point is pushed back to tribal societies). Barnes cites a later book review by Durkheim which actually claims the 'role of discipline grows with civilisation', though whether this amounts to a repudiation of the idea of an inverse relationship between social complexity and punitiveness, or merely recognition of the fact that the growth of centralized state power had outweighed the effects of social development to produce a net increase in repressiveness is not clear.

What is evident is that Durkheim did come to see the evolution of law and punishment as related not only to social structure and morality, but also to state power, conceived of by him as an independent variable. Although this is an advance on his earlier formulation, the thesis of the 'Two laws of penal evolution' remains unsatisfactory.

...

Even if Durkheim's account of the evolution of law and punishment is largely discredited at the empirical level, it nonetheless remains of enduring significance in a more substantial sense than merely to have sparked off an important debate. This is because Durkheim's work on legal development has another face than its evolutionary one, as Turkel and Cotterrell in particular have emphasized. Durkheim's overriding theoretical and moral/political concern and project was to identify and understand the problems and prospects of achieving social solidarity in complex and differentiated societies. Giving a substantive account of the path of legal evolution was subordinate to and instrumental for this primary goal. In this perspective Durkheim's contrast between mechanical solidarity with repressive law and organic solidarity with restitutive law can be seen not so much as two concrete poles of an evolutionary progression which had actually occurred in history but rather as ideal-types for elucidating the requirements of solidarity in modern societies. Durkheim's contention is that organic solidarity is possible in complex societies, given both structural change and moral reconstruction ... The form of law appropriate to such a society would be restitutive rather than repressive. It would be concerned with the adjustment and co-ordination of differentiated functions and individuals, and rooted in their diverse conditions of life as expressed by a framework of semi-autonomous corporations, rather than the imposition of a uniform, monolithic morality. The evolutionary flavour of Durkheim's account arises in part because he was anxious to depict organic solidarity not as a remote utopian ideal but as the culmination of virtual tendencies which could already be discerned (although Durkheim undoubtedly exaggerated these and neglected the extent and systematic nature of the conflicts engendered by the forced and anomic forms of division of labour actually prevalent). Durkheim's perspective continues to be of value because he points to problems which conservatives, liberals and Marxists alike tend to ignore. Against conservatives he levels cogent demonstrations that solidarity in modern societies cannot be based on resuscitation of obsolete moral forms. But he also points to the problems of moral cohesion and meaning, and the sociological (as opposed to economic or political) preconditions of this, in terms of the importance of intermediate levels of social organization and grouping between state and citizen, issues which liberals and Marxists are inclined to overlook. However, while his problematic is of continuing relevance, Durkheim's proposals for its achievement are sketchy and unconvincing. In particular, the experience of nearly a century of reform attempts to realize a fairer distribution of rewards and opportunities in industrial societies suggests that both the structural impediments to this and the resistance of the privileged classes pose a more considerable obstacle than he realized to 'the work of justice' which Durkheim saw as 'the task of the most advanced societies'.

At the start of the second millennium we are living through as profound a change in social order throughout the world as the advent of modern industrialisation which formed the crucible for the development of classical social theory. The writings of Marx, Weber and Durkheim remain a useful source of perspectives, models, conceptual tools for trying to understand what is happening, and what the role of law is in reflecting and shaping the changing social order. To what extent does law come to be an instrument of social domination? Can it be a vehicle of reform? Are the virtues of formal logical consistency and predictability achieved at the price of substantive injustice? Is the price of rationality the eclipse of the passions and values that give meaning to human experience? Are social complexity and difference sources of strife and disorientation, or can they be the basis of new forms of solidarity and ethics? The key questions the classical social theorists grappled with remain pertinent, and they provide a range of alternative interpretations that can be drawn upon to illuminate the contemporary predicament. In Part II of this book, in a number of the chapters (especially 18, 19, and 20) you will have an opportunity to explore that predicament and the role of law within it.

Further Reading

If you wish to read more on Marx the potential literature is enormous, but H Collins *Marxism and Law* (1982) is a particularly concise and readable account.

If you wish to read more on Durkheim, R Cotterrell *Emile Durkheim: Law in a Moral Domain* (1999) is a modern tour de force.

With Weber you might like to try something rather different. *Law as a Social Institution* by Ross (2001a) is a short book that demonstrates the interrelation between some of Weber's ideas and those of H L A Hart, and suggests how Hart's *Concept of Law* could have been enhanced by using some of Weber's analysis.

For a more extensive account of many of the issues and ideas developed in this chapter, see Cotterrell 1992.

Questions

1.   'The theories of Marx, Weber and Durkheim are not theories of law but theories about society. However, each of them has profound implications for our understanding of the nature and role of law.' Discuss.

2.   'Law is an expression of the underlying character of society's structure.' Critically assess the theories that take this approach.

3.   Is the best way to approach the question of what law is, to start with the question of what society is?

7 Law as Politics: Progressive American Perspectives

Hugh Collins

Has the United States generated a distinctive contribution to jurisprudence? Perhaps not. There are too many voices, speaking in cultural traditions from all over the globe, either for unifying themes to be discerned, or for some distinctive tenets or theoretical positions to be regarded as uniquely American. Even so, from an English perspective, especially for those grounded in the analytical tradition, there is a distinctive quality in much of American legal theory: its perennial debates about the political quality of law.

The constitutional framework of the United States explains this focus on the political character of law. In America, legislation and the common law developed by the judges depend ultimately for their legal validity on their conformity to the US Constitution. The Bill of Rights appended to the constitution, with its general principles such as liberty, equality, and freedom of speech, provides the opportunity to mount challenges in the courts to the validity of any laws or government actions that might conflict with those general principles. As a result, many of the most controversial political issues are resolved ultimately not through a democratic political process but through the courts' interpretations of the abstract principles of the Bill of Rights. Does the prohibition against denying any person equal protection of the laws render unlawful racially segregated schools: *Brown v Board of Education* 347 US 483 (1954)? Does the prohibition against restrictions on liberty forbid social regulation that restricts freedom of contract and controls the operation of markets: *Lochner v New York* 198 US 45 (1905)? Within the right to liberty, is there an implicit right to privacy, which protects women's right to choose to have an abortion: *Roe v Wade* 410 US 113 (1973)? Inevitably, these cases provoke questions about the political nature of law.

Concern about the legitimacy of judicial decisions also provokes close scrutiny of the methods of legal reasoning employed by the courts. In constitutional 'hard cases', there is plenty of scope to doubt whether the courts are merely applying established rules to the facts of the case. The constitutional rules themselves are often no more than vague general principles, susceptible to a wide range of interpretations. These 'open texture' rules or broad standards undercut any arguments that the courts merely employ a formal process of reasoning in the style of applying a clear rule according to its literal meaning to the facts of a case. But does this indeterminacy lead inexorably to the conclusion that the courts' decisions in these constitutional hard cases are no more than disguised political decisions? Is legal reasoning merely an elaborate camouflage for the exercise by (more or less) unelected and unaccountable judges of their personal political preferences?

These themes about the indeterminacy and political quality of legal reasoning give a distinctive character to much of American legal theory. Bitter controversies have raged among jurists about how these questions should be resolved. The proffered answers have been extremely varied in style, philosophical orientation, constitutional theory, and in their political implications. For brief periods, however, groups of scholars have been lumped together, often by their opponents, as forming a school or movement that is believed to follow a particular set of views on these issues. In this vein, we can discover groups called 'Formalists', the 'Law as Process' school, the 'Law as Social Engineering' group, the 'Law and Society Movement'. Whether or not these groups of jurists were united by a common theory is doubtful. What often bound them together rather more were shared views on the political controversies of the day. This source of unity in shared values is especially true of the two 'progressive' movements to be examined in this chapter: the 'Legal Realists' and the 'Critical Legal Studies Movement'.

In America, the term 'progressive' implies political views that are associated with moderate leftist parties, as opposed to conservative or centrist liberal views. What the Legal Realists, writing mostly in the 1920s and 1930s, and the Critical Legal Studies (CLS) movement in the period 1975–90, have in common is that they used legal theory to criticise and challenge established legal institutions, rules, and practices from a progressive perspective. Inevitably these works provoked fierce reactions from those concerned to reassert the legitimacy of the American legal system and affirm conservative or centrist values. At the cost of distorting the overall picture of American legal theory, we concentrate our attention on these two progressive movements, not only because they represent some of the most distinctive American contributions to legal theory, but also because they have also been a significant influence on English jurisprudence.

Looking at these debates from the other side of the Atlantic, what insights can be obtained? Our constitutional tradition of parliamentary supremacy is rather different. We are not so frequently confronted with judicial decisions about strongly contested political issues. But are judicial decisions in the United Kingdom nevertheless equally political? Does the American progressives' analysis of the indeterminacy and political quality of legal reasoning apply only to the constitutional structure of the United States or does it extend to any modern legal system? If so, what is meant by the claims that judicial decisions are political and that legal reasoning is indeterminate? If judges exercise considerable political power, how should they approach the task of adjudication? Should the judge, for example, explicitly consider the political and economic consequences of the decision, or should the reasoning be confined to legal arguments about established rules and principles? This discussion expands beyond the process of adjudication, because progressive legal theories do not necessarily accept the adequacy of the courts as a mechanism for resolving social and political disputes. Here we examine the answers given to those questions not only by Americans but also by British writers who shared a similar perspective.

The Political Character of Judicial Decisions

The American Legal Realists earned their sobriquet from two starting points in their work. The first was an insistence that there was more to the study of law than learning legal doctrine and rules. It is equally important to study the institutions and practices of the legal system, in order to grasp how they function in practice. In this respect, Realism was a call for what might be termed today 'socio-legal studies'. Secondly, the epithet of Realism also signified an insistence on the instrumental character of law. Realists criticised theories of law that suggested that the content of the law rests ultimately on immutable principles of justice. Such theories they associated with conservative values, because the immutable principles such as the protection of liberty and private property tended to obstruct the use of law for social and welfare goals. Legal Realists insisted rather that law is a means to achieve social goals, that it is mutable, a product of human will, not based on any transcendent principles. Legal Realism thus called for the study of 'law in action', not just the law in the books, and bred a scepticism about the inevitability of any legal outcome, given that law was merely an instrument of government. In these attitudes we can detect both an assertion by professors in the new university law schools that their task was greater than mere instruction of lawyers in legal argument, and a view of the role of law in society that was congenial to progressives who wished to change society through social regulation.

Karl Llewellyn, one of the most prolific and influential writers associated with the Realist movement, stressed the following 'common points of departure' of various Realist scholars (1931, 1222). '(1) The conception of law in flux, of moving law, and of judicial creation of law. (2) The conception of law as a means to social ends and not as an end in itself; so that any part needs constantly to be examined for its purpose, and for its effect, and to be judged in the light of both and of their relation to each other. (3) The conception of society in flux, and in flux typically faster than the law, so that the probability is always given that any portion of law needs re-examination to determine how far it fits the society it purports to serve. (4) The *temporary* divorce of Is and Ought for the purposes of study ... (5) Distrust of traditional legal rules and concepts insofar as they purport to *describe* what either courts or people are actually doing. Hence the constant emphasis on rules as 'generalised predictions of what courts will do' ... (6) Hand in hand with this distrust of traditional rules (on the descriptive side) goes a distrust of the theory that traditional prescriptive rule-formulations are the heavily operative factor in producing court decisions. This involves the tentative adoption of the theory of rationalization for the study of opinions ... (7) The belief in the worthwhileness of grouping cases and legal situations into narrower categories than has been the practice in the past ... (8) An insistence on evaluation of any part of law in terms of its effects, and an insistence on the worthwhileness of trying to find these effects. (9) Insistence on sustained and programmatic attack on the problems of law along any of these lines.'

As well as emphasising the need to study the effects of law in practice and its instrumental character, these propositions also reveal two kinds of scepticism that have been associated ever since with American Legal Realism: rule scepticism and fact scepticism.

1. Rule Scepticism

Rule scepticism holds that judges reach their decisions not in a formalist way by the application of the relevant rules, principles, and concepts to the facts of a particular case: 'General propositions do not decide concrete cases' (Holmes J, *Lochner v New York* 198 US 45 (1905)). One needs to dig behind the legal rhetoric to discover the real motivating factors for a decision. Legal reasoning should be regarded as more a process of rationalisation of a result than as the reason for the outcome. The selection of the result by a judge will normally turn on a broader range of factors than legal rules and principles. The reasons given for the decision in the form of rules and precedents may explain some of the motivation of the judge and help to some extent in a prediction of the result. But their main function may lie rather more in retrospective justification or legitimation, that is to present the judicial decision as legally right and inevitable. To predict accurately the results of cases, which is an important part of the task of lawyers, one needs to understand not only legal doctrine, usually at a lower level of generality than traditional abstract principles, but also the attitude or political opinions of judges.

> 'Rules are important so far as they help you to see or predict what judges will do or so far as they help you to get judges to do something. That is their importance. That is all their importance, except as pretty playthings. But you will discover that you can no more afford to overlook them than you can afford to stop with having learned their words.' (Karl Llewellyn, *The Bramble Bush*)

2. Fact Scepticism

Added to this Realist scepticism about the determining role of legal doctrines and rules in judicial decisions is a hesitant type of fact scepticism. When determining the facts of the case, it is difficult, if not impossible, for a judge to avoid evaluations and interpretations of events. When describing the events, a judge is likely to present the facts in a way that suggests the merits of the outcome that the judge proposes to reach. This process may be completely unconscious, but nevertheless it plays a vital role in determining the outcome of the case and in helping to rationalise the decision. According to the Realists, the facts are not 'out there', but are selected and described with a view both to a rhetorical justification of the judge's decision, and to a construction of events so that a relevant legal rule or principle apparently determines the result.

To illustrate fact scepticism, consider the following descriptions of a well-known contract dispute. A claim was brought by a builder, Ruxley Electronics managed by Mr Hall, for payment of the agreed price of £70,000 for a swimming pool constructed in Mr Forsyth's garden. Mr Forsyth counter-claimed damages of £21,650 for breach of contract on the grounds that the pool had not been finished and did not meet the specifications in the contract because it was too shallow. Here are extracts from the description of the facts by the judges in *Ruxley Electronics and Construction Ltd v Forsyth* in the Court of Appeal [1994] 1 WLR 630 and the House of Lords [1996] AC 344. Which court do you think allowed Mr Forsyth's full counterclaim?

Staughton LJ (in the Court of Appeal): 'The progress of the works was anything but smooth. When the pool was first completed … a crack appeared across the bottom of it … Eventually Mr. Hall agreed that the existing pool would be renewed and replaced … Various defects were asserted by Mr. Forsyth … Some but not all were remedied … Then Mr. Forsyth, who had not previously spent a great deal of time at the house, discovered that the maximum depth of water in the pool was not 7 feet 6 inches … Mr Forsyth had asked for an increase in the maximum depth [from the original specifications] … saying that he was a big man and would feel safer and more comfortable with the greater depth of water.'

Lord Lloyd (in the House of Lords): 'The depth of the pool was to be 6 feet 6 inches at the deep end … Mr. Hall agreed to increase the depth without extra charge … Work started in 1987 … But the subcontractor did not do the job properly … Mr. Hall agreed to remove the existing pool and replace it free of charge. He also agreed to reimburse the professional charges which Mr. Forsyth had incurred … In … 1988 the plaintiffs submitted their invoice. But Mr. Forsyth insisted on a reduction of £10,000 to compensate him for the disturbance which he had suffered during the rebuilding of the pool. Mr. Hall reluctantly agreed. Still Mr. Forsyth did not settle the plaintiff's invoice … The trial [of the builder's claim] commenced … [and after two days] Mr. Forsyth dismissed his solicitors and counsel … [The next day] he amended his counterclaim to raise for the first time the question of the depth of the pool …'

Notice how the Court of Appeal painted a picture of a long-suffering Mr Forsyth dealing with an incompetent builder, whereas the House of Lords told the story of a patient, flexible, and generous contractor dealing with a cantankerous, opportunist, and unreasonable client. Even though the two courts largely agreed about the relevant rules of the law, different outcomes seem inevitable as a result of the rhetorical descriptions of the facts. The Court of Appeal allowed the full counter-claim, whereas the House of Lords rejected it (except for a small claim for loss of amenity).

3. Instrumentalism

These strands of rule and fact scepticism could be combined into a powerful critique of legal reasoning and the scope of the power of the judiciary. If the courts could manipulate the rules and the facts of cases in order to justify the results that they wanted to reach, their position in the constitutional framework appeared indefensible. The judges could not pretend that they were mere oracles of the law, interpreting it rather than making it. And if the judges were making the law, including constitutional law, were they not usurping power from democratic legislatures?

Although such views have often been attributed to American Legal Realists, it is hard to find examples of such extreme positions. On the contrary, the Realists preferred to argue for an approach that might be described as policy science. Many Realists believed that with the knowledge provided by the new disciplines of the social sciences, including careful studies of the operations of the legal system itself, it should be possible to guide courts towards rational and justifiable results. The message was that law was a policy science, which should be applied with the best available information, and careful consideration of the social and political consequences of the possible determinations of a case. The meaning of the legal rules could be determined rationally by reference to their purpose. This argument is now widely accepted and adopted by those judges who use the style of 'purposive interpretation'. This approach to interpretation does suppose that it is possible to reach a determinate conclusion about the purpose of any particular law, which then confines the possible meanings of a legal rule. A purposive approach assumes that behind the legal rules there is a finite list of intelligible and compatible purposes, which can be employed to resolve the problem of linguistic indeterminacy. Examination of purposes opens the door to the deployment of sociological information about the composition of society and economic analysis of the probable effects of alternative interpretations of the law. American Legal Realism thus paved the way for an openness in legal reasoning to interdisciplinary analysis, which has been a distinctive feature of American legal thought.

There was a resonance between this instrumentalist analysis of legal reasoning and early twentieth century philosophical developments in the United States. Under the label of 'Pragmatism', philosophers such as John Dewey and William James had attacked the idea that there were any fundamental or absolute moral truths. They explained the belief in moral absolutes as historically and socially constructed. A moral truth, they argued, was a matter of opinion, legitimated and imposed by powerful groups in society. For this reason, pragmatists were not concerned whether or not some moral precept was true, but asked whether or not the precept was useful and contributed to social and political reform. Drawing on these ideas, Legal Realists could find parallels for their criticisms of formalist legal reasoning, with its frequent (though not necessary) assumption that the law was based upon fundamental principles, and they could also find intellectual support for their instrumental approach to legal reasoning.

This view of law as an instrumental policy science had a lasting effect on the study and approach to most branches of American law. For example, the subject of conflict of laws was transformed by Realists, most notably Walter Wheeler Cook. This branch of the law addresses primarily the question of what rules national legal systems should apply to a dispute with an international element, such as a contract made between parties living in different jurisdictions. The formalist tradition in legal scholarship, most notably Dicey in England, had reduced this branch of the law to a complex set of rules in the formalist style. Throwing out the rule book, Cook argued that decisions about the applicable law should be made instrumentally, with a view to achieving justice between the parties to a particular dispute and in the pursuit of a coherent social policy (Cook, 1924).

The lasting influence of Realism on American legal thought was a pervasive willingness to accept the view that judicial decisions were guided by instrumental considerations. It followed that no clear distinction could be drawn between legal reasoning and broader policy or political reasoning. The legitimacy of judicial decisions was thereafter assessed not only by reference to its conformity to established rules and precedents, but also by reference to its consequences in society.

In their day, however, the Realists were criticised for their legal positivism and moral relativism. By rejecting the idea that law rests on immutable principles of justice, or indeed any fixed set of moral values, but is rather an instrument of government for social ends, the Realists provoked a serious backlash from those theorists sympathetic to natural law ideas. Realists were perceived as undermining the legitimacy of the legal system by sweeping away its foundations in fundamental moral principles. By the late 1930s, Realism was perceived by many theorists as inherently dangerous, because, it was alleged, Realism paved the way for totalitarian systems to use the legal system without any constraints. Conservative critics regarded the Realists' support for Roosevelt's extensive use of the law to reshape society in his New Deal policies as evidence of their support for state power without limits. But even legal theorists such as Fuller, who were sympathetic to social regulation, regarded Realism as a dangerous theory, because it denied the moral foundations of law, an error which Fuller tried to correct in his own work (see Chapter 2).

4. Realist Influences in the United Kingdom

The Realist influence has certainly left its mark on legal thought in the United Kingdom. Although the attachment of the United Kingdom legal community to formal processes of legal reasoning is firmer, today there is a much greater willingness on the part of judges and scholars to discuss openly and carefully the policy implications of alternative legal rules. Although it is not true that 'We are all Realists now', open assessments of the consequences of legal rules for society and the economy have become a characteristic feature of legal reasoning in part due to the influence of American Legal Realism.

What remains different in the United Kingdom is an unwillingness to examine the political values of the senior judges. In the United States, the judges of the Supreme Court of the United States are selected by the President for their general political orientation, and their decisions are closely monitored for their conservative or liberal leanings. In the United Kingdom, however, few people other than lawyers know the names of the Law Lords, and their political dispositions are not generally regarded as either relevant to their appointment or to the decisions which they reach. The prevailing view is rather that the senior judges are appointed according to criteria of intellectual merit and legal expertise. In the future this perspective may change as the courts are invited to exercise their powers under the Human Rights Act 1998 to declare the incompatibility of laws with the European Convention on Human Rights. The senior judges may avoid such exposure to public and political scrutiny by using those new powers sparingly. Nevertheless, there have been elements in British scholarly assessments of the work of the courts that complement fully the most searching Realist criticisms of the political character of the judiciary. Consider this quote from Griffith's book *The Politics of the Judiciary* (1997, 337).

A central thesis of this book is that judges in the United Kingdom cannot be politically neutral because they are placed in positions where they are required to make political choices which are sometimes presented to them, and often presented by them, as determinations of where the public interest lies; that their interpretation of what is in the public interest and therefore politically desirable is determined by the kind of people they are and the position they hold in our society; that this position is a part of established authority and so is necessarily conservative, not liberal. From all this flows that view of the public interest which is shown in judicial attitudes such as tenderness towards private property and dislike of trade unions, strong adherence to the maintenance of order, distaste for minority opinions, demonstrations and protests, support of governmental secrecy, concern for the preservation of the moral and social behaviour to which it is accustomed, and the rest.

But the most important influence of Realism on legal thought in the United Kingdom is to be found, as in the United States, in discussions of the details of every branch of law. Whilst many student texts remain largely faithful to a formalist or 'black-letter tradition' by presenting the law as a set of rules, others emphasise in the Realist fashion the instrumental qualities of legal doctrines and particular precedents. For example, most of the student texts in the 'Law in Context' series share the Realist concerns to examine the purposes and effects of law in its social context, and examine the law critically as an instrument for achieving certain goals.

5. Law as Politics

Once the step is taken of arguing that judicial decisions are reached instrumentally in the pursuit of particular purposes, it becomes possible to argue that in a sense legal reasoning is always political. This argument applies not only to constitutional and public law cases, which raise controversial matters of general public interest that divide politicians, but also to private law cases involving contractual or property disputes. Questions about breach of contract or the determination of proprietary rights are not so obviously political. According to the Realists, however, judges approach such decisions with their own personal set of values and ideals. Although judges may regard these opinions as merely common sense, they comprise a set of values that play a crucial role in all decisions. These values can be linked together into a reasonably coherent set of political ideas, and in that sense all decisions have a political character. For example, in a contractual dispute, a judge may place a high value on respecting freedom of contract, an ideal which can be linked to a broader set of values that prefers free markets rather than state regulation of trade. Alternatively, a judge may decide the same case by seeking to protect the weaker party against the consequences of an improvident bargain, thus leaning against free markets in favour of welfare intervention. In this sense all judicial decisions in both public and private law may be characterised as being motivated by political considerations. What is not suggested by the Realists, of course, is that judges follow slavishly the views of a particular political party.

The Incoherence of Legal Reasoning

As well as linguistic indeterminacy, however, Realists pressed another criticism of formal models of legal reasoning. When judicial precedents were examined carefully, it was possible to discern in many different areas of the common law the use of conflicting rules or the evolution of competing lines of precedent. In the United States, with its 50 state jurisdictions, each developing the common law, it appeared that the same legal doctrines inherited from England could lead to diverse judicial rulings. This obvious disintegration of the consistency of the common law permitted the Realists to argue that the indeterminacy of legal reasoning lay deeper than the vagueness of words. The problem was that there was no agreement about the correct rule or principle to apply to a particular case. Instead, a court often had to choose between competing rules, which had evolved in the different states. In short, the linguistic formulation as well as the meaning of the governing legal norm was indeterminate.

Since the fact of inconsistency among the precedent judicial decisions could not be denied, those scholars and judges who wished nevertheless to claim that the common law retained coherence and consistency were forced to search for these qualities at a higher level of generality. In one form or another the defence against the Realist attack on formalism was always to insist that at the level of principle, precept, purpose, or concept, both coherence and consistency could be discovered in the law (eg Wechsler 1959). The most sophisticated, modern exposition of such a defence is found in Ronald Dworkin's *Law's Empire* (see Chapters 8 and 9 for a full account of Dworkin's exposition). But the general thrust of this defence of the integrity of the law, and the avoidance of the view that judges always have a choice about which rule to apply, is a central theme in American jurisprudence after Realism.

When the CLS movement took up this theme of the indeterminacy of legal reasoning in the late 1970s, therefore, these scholars addressed a different target from the Realists before them. Instead of attacking formalism in rule application, they had to argue that that the appeal to the coherence of underlying principles or purposes could not establish the coherence and determinacy of legal reasoning. The methods they employed for this task of demonstrating the incoherence of the law at the level of principle were extremely varied, without any evident unity of philosophical approach. The CLS arguments are, however, distinguishable from the Realists. Whereas the Realists stressed the extent to which judicial decisions depended upon unarticulated factors outside the legal rules such as policy considerations, the CLS scholars emphasised the contingency of the legal reasoning itself. The legal arguments were indeterminate in themselves, not simply owing to the vagueness of language, but more deeply because of the conflicts of underlying principles or purposes of rules. The contradictions to be discovered in the precedents revealed fundamental disagreements about the policies or principles on which the law should be based.

According to the CLS movement these conflicts or contradictions lie in the foundations of legal reasoning and cannot ever be reconciled. In practice, one principle is treated as dominant, the other exceptional, so that the contradiction is not perceived to present a difficulty for the coherence of law. Nevertheless, the presence and occasional appeal to the disfavoured principle or purpose reveals that the underlying tension in legal thought is never resolved.

> '[A] standard four-part critical method has been used again and again, whether consciously or not. First, the Critics attempted to identify a contradiction in liberal legal thought, a set of paired rhetorical arguments that both resolve cases in opposite, incompatible ways and correspond to distinct visions of human nature and human fulfilment ... Second, the Critics tried to demonstrate that each of the contradictions is utterly pervasive in legal controversy, even in cases where practice is so settled that we nearly invariably forget that the repressed contradictory impulse *could* govern the decision at issue ... Third, Critics have attempted to show that mainstream thought invariably treats one term in each set of contradictory impulses as privileged in three distinct senses. The privileged term is presumptively entitled as a normative matter to govern disputes; it is simply assumed, as a descriptive matter, to govern the bulk of situations; and most subtly, but perhaps most significantly, departures from the purportedly dominant norm, even if they are obviously frequent, are treated as *exceptional*, in need of special justification, a bit chaotic ... Fourth, the Critics note that, closely examined, the "privileged" impulses describe the program of a remarkably right-wing, quasi-libertarian order ...' (Kelman 1987, 3–4)

Notice that the CLS movement does not deny that judges attempt with some success to justify their interpretations of the law by reference to the coherence of underlying principle or purpose. Nor do they deny that it is possible to predict with considerable accuracy the outcome of legal disputes. Their argument is rather that the coherence or integrity of the law is always an illusion, because it involves the marginalisation of other principles or policies that do not fit. Furthermore, they also argue that the vision of coherent principles that is typically favoured by the judges is one that embodies rather right-wing political precepts.

We can use a familiar example from English contract law to illustrate these points. It is generally accepted that a binding contract must be supported by good consideration. A Realist would perhaps point out that the concept of consideration is malleable, and that if a court decides to enforce a promise on grounds of fairness or efficiency, it will, if necessary, invent consideration, either by twisting the meaning of the doctrine or by manipulating the facts of the case. A CLS writer might add, however, that it is also true that judges appear to enforce promises occasionally on the basis of another legal principle, often described as equitable or promissory estoppel. This legal doctrine does not fit easily with the supposed requirement of consideration for a binding contract. It is possible to try to explain away this contradiction by some device such as to claim that there is a difference between common law and equity, or that estoppels only apply to certain types of transactions, or even that judges are not really enforcing promises at all when the doctrine of estoppel is used. But a CLS writer would observe that the formal reconciliation of legal doctrines cannot ultimately solve what is at bottom a fundamental conflict of values or principles: consideration insists that contractual obligations should only arise as part of a consensual exchange, whereas estoppel permits detrimental reliance upon others to provide a source of legal obligation. To this analysis could be added the claim that consideration embodies a view of the obligations owed between citizens that stresses how they should only arise through the pursuit of self-interest, whereas estoppel embodies a precept that citizens owe in addition obligations towards others who reasonably rely upon them. Although this example rather simplifies the arguments, it captures the essential message of the CLS movement that tensions within legal doctrine reveal profound political disagreements, which can never be resolved through legal reasoning, though often the more 'progressive' view is suppressed.

In an early and influential essay in the CLS movement Duncan Kennedy attempted to portray the contradictions in legal doctrine as possessing a common root – a fundamental contradiction in liberal legal thought.

> Here is an initial statement of the fundamental contradiction. Most participants in American legal culture believe that the goal of individual freedom is at the same time dependent on and incompatible with the communal coercive action that is necessary to achieve it. Others (family, friends, bureaucrats, cultural figures, the state) are necessary if we are to become persons at all – they provide us the stuff of our selves and protect us in crucial ways against destruction ... But at the same time that it forms and protects us, the universe of others (family, friendship, bureaucracy, culture, the state) threatens us with annihilation and urges upon us forms of fusion that are quite plainly bad rather than good ... Numberless conformities, large and small abandonments of self to others, are the price of what freedom we experience in society ... The kicker is that the abolition of these illegitimate structures, the fashioning of an unalienated collective existence, appears to imply such a massive increase of collective control over our lives that it would defeat its purpose ... Even this understates the difficulty. It is not just that the world of others is intractable. The very structures against which we rebel are necessarily within us as well as outside us. We are implicated in what we would transform, and it in us ... The fundamental contradiction – that relations with others are both necessary to and incompatible with our freedom – is not only intense. It is also pervasive ... There simply are no legal issues that do not involve directly the problem of the legitimate content of collective coercion, since there is by definition no legal problem until someone has at least imagined that he might invoke the force of the state. And it is not just a matter of definition. The more sophisticated a person's legal thinking, regardless of her political stance, the more likely she is to believe that all issues within a doctrinal field reduce to a single dilemma of the degree of collective as opposed to individual self-determination that is appropriate ... (1979, 209)

Kennedy's purpose was to portray legal reasoning as an unceasing effort to obfuscate, deny, or hide this contradiction. Legal reasoning achieves this purpose partly through its attachment to doctrinal categories, such as contract and tort, which serve to create an illusion of a permanent and coherent resolution of the fundamental contradiction. But all the techniques of legal reasoning, whether they involve formalist rule-application, purposive interpretation, or tests involving the balancing of interests, serve the purpose of mediating and legitimising a particular, contingent, settlement of the fundamental contradiction, one that usually serves the interests of the most powerful groups in society.

One need not accept that there is a single fundamental contradiction in order to pursue the argument that legal reasoning is riddled with deep, unresolved tensions. The following extract concentrates on the competing and contradictory roles of intentionalist and determinist views of human agency for the purpose of criminal responsibility. An intentionalist view regards human actors as always free to make choices, and that criminal responsibility should be confined to instances where an individual has chosen to perform the prohibited act. A determinist analysis emphasises the way in which human action always occurs within social structures, and is causally connected to prior events. Determinism tends not to condemn predetermined events. The author's argument is that both views about when a person should be held to be responsible for an action are always present in legal reasoning, but that determinism with its tendency to absolve people from criminal responsibility is normally suppressed. In addition, this extract deploys a sophisticated version of fact scepticism in order to undermine the superficial coherence legal reasoning. In particular, notice how the discussion of time-frames goes beyond the Realist discussion of the rhetorical use of 'the facts' in order to demonstrate what counts as a relevant fact is a crucial, though often unconscious, part of the construction of a legal argument.

Kelman (1981, 592–672)

By interpretive construction, I refer to a process by which concrete situations are reduced to substantive legal controversies: It refers both to the way we construe a factual situation and to the way we frame the possible rules to handle the situation. What then follows logically, if not chronologically, is rational rhetoricism – the process of presenting the legal conclusions that result when interpretive constructs are applied to the 'facts'. This rhetorical process is the 'stuff' of admirable legal analysis: distinguishing and analysing cases, applying familiar policies to unobvious fact patterns, and emphasizing the degree to which we can rely on the least controversial underlying values. These rhetorical techniques are so intellectually complex that there is a powerful tendency to elevate falsely the importance of intellect in actual legal decision-making, to fail to see the interpretive construction that makes the wise posturing possible. I will look behind (or unpack) this rhetoric to the selection of 'relevant' categories and 'relevant' facts. At the same time, I will try to understand the appeal of the well-argued case, an appeal clearly felt by so many of my colleagues and students.

...

I. A GENERAL SUMMARY OF INTERPRETIVE CONSTRUCTS

Legal argument can be made only *after* a fact pattern is characterized by interpretive constructs. Once these constructs operate, a single legal result seems inevitable, a result seemingly deduced on general principle. These constructs appear both in conscious and unconscious forms in standard legal discourse. Before examining in detail how interpretive constructs reify substantive 'textbook' law, it will be useful to examine them more precisely.

A. FOUR UNCONSCIOUS INTERPRETIVE CONSTRUCTS

Unconscious interpretive constructs shape the way we view disruptive incidents, but they are never identified or discussed by judges or commentators. There are basically four forms of unconscious constructs, two dealing with 'time-framing' and two dealing with problems of categorization. I discuss unconscious constructs before conscious ones because the former are often used to avoid issues inherent in the latter, issues that the legal analysts are most prone to be aware are controversial, perhaps insoluble, and highly politicized.

1. Broad and narrow time frames

We put people on trial. People exist over time; they have long, involved personal histories. We prosecute particular acts – untoward incidents – that these people commit. But even these incidents have a history: Things occur before or after incidents that seem relevant to our judgment of what the perpetrator did. Sometimes we incorporate facts about the defendant's personal history. Other times, we incorporate facts about events preceding or post-dating the criminal incident. But an interpreter can readily focus solely on the isolated criminal incident, as if all we can learn of value in assessing culpability can be seen with that narrower time focus.

Most often, though not invariably, the arational choice between narrow and broad time frames keeps us from having to deal with more explicit political questions arising from one conscious interpretive construct – the conflict between intentionalism and determinism. Often, conduct is deemed involuntary (or determined) rather than freely willed (or intentional) because we do not consider the defendant's earlier decisions that may have put him in the position of apparent choicelessness. Conversely, conduct that could be viewed as freely willed or voluntary if we looked only at the precise moment of the criminal incident is sometimes deemed involuntary because we open up the time frame to look at prior events that seem to compel or determine the defendant's conduct at the time of the incident. The use of 'time-framing' as interpretive *method* blocks the perception that intentionalist or determinist issues could be substantively at stake. If one has somehow convinced oneself that the incident, narrow time-framed focus is the appropriate *technique* for interpreting criminal law material, there is simply no background data one can use, either to provide the grist for a determinist account or to locate a prior sphere of choice in a seemingly constricted world. The interpretive 'choice' between narrow and broad time frames affects not only controversial, doctrinally tricky legal cases, but also 'easy' cases, because narrow time-framing fends off, at the methodological level, the possibility of doing determinist analyses.

2. Disjoined and unified accounts

A second unconscious interpretive construct relating to time involves the tension between disjoined and unified accounts of incidents. Many legally significant situations seem to require a somewhat broad time frame, at least in the sense that we feel we must look beyond a single moment in time and account, in some fashion, for some clearly relevant earlier moment. The earlier 'moment' may be the time at which a defendant made some judgment about the situation she was in, some judgment that at least contributed to the ultimate decision to act criminally. For instance, the defendant negligently believes she must use deadly force to defend herself and then she intentionally kills someone, having formed that belief. Alternatively, the earlier moment may simply be the moment at which the defendant initiated the chain of events that culminated in criminal results. For instance, the defendant may shoot at X, but the bullet will miss X and then kill Y, an unforeseeably present bystander.

Once we agree to look at these earlier moments, we must decide whether to disjoin or unify the earlier moment with the later moment. We can treat all the relevant facts as constituting a single incident, or we can disjoin the events into two separate incidents.

Once this arational interpretive decision is made, the question of criminal culpability is forever biased. Is a negligent decision to kill followed by an intentional killing a negligent or intentional act? Is the person who misses X and shoots Y someone who commits two crimes-attempted murder of X plus, say, reckless homicide of Y – or one crime – an intentional murder of a person? Sometimes, unifying two arguably separate incidents allows us to avoid making a hard-to-justify assertion that the arguably second incident or decision was determined by the first. Often, other interests are at stake in separating or joining a series of incidents.

3. Broad and narrow views of intent

A third unconscious construct involves broad and narrow views of intent. Each time someone acts, we can say with fair confidence that, in the absence of some claim of accident, he intended to do precisely the acts that he has done. But we have difficulty categorizing those acts, because an individual set of acts may, in the observer's eyes, be an instance of a number of different categories of acts. For example, when the defendant intends to undertake certain deeds constituting a particular crime, it feels both misleading in significant ways, and perfectly proper in others, to assert that the defendant intended the particular crime. On one hand, it is odd to think of actors as viewing the world in criminal law categories when they act. On the other hand, it is equally odd to think of actors as focusing in their consciousness only on the most precise physical motions they undertake. Thus, when we talk of the requisite intent to commit assault *with intent* to commit murder, it is peculiar to think *either* that the defendant must have mentally focused his conduct on the broadly interpreted *crime of* murder (with all its complications, eg., that he must intend to act with malice, premeditation, nonprovocation, nonjustification, etc.), or that it is sufficient that he simply focused on the physical *motions* which would predicate the crime (eg., pulling the trigger on the gun, which we may deem murder if, in fact, he acted with what we call malice, nonprovocation, etc.).

Similarly, a defendant may perform suspicious acts not in themselves criminal or abandon a particular criminal attempt. We wonder whether the defendant, in the first case, can accurately be thought of as intending only the precise acts he committed or whether, in some broader sense, he *intended* some apter deeds which we would deem criminal acts. Likewise, in the second case, we wonder whether the defendant abandoned only the one criminal incident or abandoned the criminal category of which that incident is but an instance.

4. Broad and narrow views of the defendant

A fourth unconscious construct is that the interpreter may view defendants in broad or narrow terms. Each defendant is a unique individual, with a unique set of perceptions and capabilities. Every crime is committed in a unique setting. At the same time, every defendant has general human traits, and is thus a representative of the broader category of human beings. Similarly, the setting in which a crime is committed is an instance of those settings in which the crime is generally committed, and the features of the more general situation could be ascribed to the particular situation. By varying our interpretive focus, by particularizing at times and categorizing at others, substantive criminal law reaches all manner of results. Shifts in these perspectives underlie efforts to make doctrinal categories appear more cogent than they actually are.

B. CONSCIOUS INTERPRETIVE CONSTRUCTS

Just as unconscious constructs shape the way we view disruptive incidents, conscious constructs settle doctrinal issues while obscuring the nondeductive nature of legal discourse. I discuss two forms of conscious construction: the choice between intentionalistic and deterministic accounts of human conduct, and the choice between stating legal commands in the form of precise rules or vague ad hoc standards. While judges and commentators seem to be aware of these constructs, they discuss them only as *general* philosophical themes in the criminal law.

But I will argue that any consciously stated 'grand' choices elevating intentionalism or rules, determinism or standards, as *the* solution to legal dilemmas is inevitably partial. The 'victory' of one framework or the other is a temporary one that can never be made with assurance or comfort. Each assertion manifests no more than a momentary expression of feelings that remain contradictory and unresolved. Most significantly, arguments based on these explicitly political issues feel less 'legal' than arguments grounded in traditional doctrinal categories. Perhaps more important for this article, I will also argue that the assertion of the inexorability of applying one or the other poles in these controversies to a particular setting settles many doctrinal issues, though the problematic nature of chosen doctrine would become more apparent if the use of interpretive constructs surfaced. In this sense, these interpretive constructs function just like the four unconscious constructs. Though they are conscious political positions when employed at a general level, they may function as unreasoned presuppositions that solve cases while obscuring the dissonant, fundamentally nondeductive nature of legal discourse.

I. Intentionalism and determinism

Intentionalism is the principle that human conduct results from free choice. An intentionalist interpretation of an incident gives moral weight to autonomous choice and expresses the indeterminacy of future actions. Determinism, on the other hand, implies that subsequent behavior is causally connected to prior events. A determinist interpretation considers behavior by looking backward, and it expresses no moral respect or condemnation of these predetermined acts.

Most basic issues of the criminal law are issues of the applicability of an intentionalist model. Notions of blameworthiness and deterrence are both based on the assumption that criminal actors make intentional choices. Of course, criminal jurisprudence *acknowledges* the plausibility of a determinist discourse, but it *acts* as if the intentionalist discourse is ultimately complete, coherent, and convincing. It is quite apparent, however, that standard criminal law doctrine often interprets facts in deterministic modes. For example, duress, insanity, and provocation are determinist excuses for otherwise criminal conduct.

2. Rules versus standards

An overarching conflict within our legal system pertains to the form that legal pronouncements should take. Our legal system bounces fitfully between 'clearly defined, highly administrable, general rules' and 'equitable standards producing ad hoc decisions with relatively little precedential value'.

Rules seem, on the positive side, capable of uniform and nonprejudicial application. They define spheres of autonomy and privacy and spheres of duty by giving clear notice to citizens of the legal consequences of their conduct. The void-for-vagueness and strict construction doctrines both resonate in the rule-respecting liberal tradition. On the negative side, rules will inevitably be both over- and underinclusive according to the purposes reasonably attributable to the law. This not only leads to random injustice when particular culpable parties are acquitted and nonculpable parties are convicted, but it enables people to calculate privately optimal levels of undesirable behavior that are within the precise confines of the law.

Standards alleviate the problems of nonpurposive applications of legal commands to particular cases. On the other hand, they may be difficult to administer or may be enforced in a biased, unequal, and uncertain fashion. The use of standards in the criminal law is rampant. Whether we are talking about requirements of 'malice' in homicide law, looking at regulatory statutes that are openly vague in proscribing *unreasonable* restraints of trade, or considering the use of discretion in prosecution and sentencing, it is difficult to deny that avoiding vagueness is more important as ideology than in practice. In any argument within our culture, *both* of these modes of framing legal commands are simultaneously appealing and unappealing; neither has killer force. Because neither position can dominate the other, legal arguments about the desirable form of legal commands are not just oscillating, unsettled, and unbalanced, but the choice of one resolution or the other ultimately feels like a product of whim – a reflection of one's most recent overreaction to the follies of the previously adopted form.

...

[Kelman gives many examples of the power of these interpretive constructs in United States criminal law, from which a few examples are taken here.]

The voluntary act requirement. Unconscious shifting between broad and narrow time frames also arises in applying the criminal law's voluntary act requirement. In *Martin v. State* police officers arrested the defendant at his home and took him onto a public highway, where the defendant used loud and profane language. He was convicted under a statute prohibiting public exhibition of a drunken condition. The appellate court reversed, holding that the defendant was involuntarily and forcibly carried to the public place by the arresting officers. The court concluded, uncontroversially, that an involuntary act cannot give rise to liability. But in *People v. Decina*, the court sustained the defendant's conviction for negligent homicide, though at the time his car struck the victims, he was unconscious as a result of an epileptic fit, not voluntarily operating the vehicle. The court held that the defendant was culpable because he had made a conscious decision to drive, knowing that an epileptic attack was possible.

The hidden interpretive time-framing construct becomes visible when one tries to square *Martin* with *Decina*. In *Decina*, the court opened up the time frame, declaring that if the defendant commits a voluntary act at time one which poses a risk of causing an involuntary harm later – drives the car knowing he is a blackout-prone epileptic – then the second act – crashing while unconscious – will be deemed voluntary. But the defendant in *Martin,* as well, may have done *something* voluntarily (before the police came) that posed a risk that he would get arrested and carried into public in his drunken state. While it is plausible that Martin was arrested on an old warrant and could not foresee that he would wind up in public on this occasion, it is quite possible that the defendant was arrested for activity he was engaging in at home: for instance, beating his wife. Why did the court not consider saying that the voluntary act at time one (wife beating) both posed a risk of and caused a harmful involuntary act at time two (public drunkenness) and assessing the voluntariness of the alleged criminal act with reference to the wider time-framed scenario? It cannot be that the involuntary, harmful act at time two was unforeseeable: The probability of an epileptic black-out is almost certainly far lower than the probability of ending up in public after engaging in behavior likely to draw police attention. Arguments that we are less concerned with people 'thinking ahead' to avoid public drunkenness than unconscious driving seem inadequate as well; the penalties for public drunkenness are presumably set lower to reflect the relative lack of gravity of the offense. Ultimately, the *Martin* finding of voluntariness 'works' not because it is 'right,' but because all the hard points disappear in the initial interpretive construction of the potentially relevant facts.

Hostility to strict liability. Commentators who attack the use of strict liability in criminal law invariably use narrow time-framing. They imply that the defendant deemed guilty of an offense which allows no mental state excuses as to some element of the crime is treated unjustly because he could somehow not avoid criminality. Look, for instance, at H.L.A. Hart's comments on criminal responsibility:

> The reason why, according to modern ideas, strict liability is odious, and appears as a sacrifice of a valued principle ... is that those whom we punish should have had, when they acted, the normal capacities ... for doing what the law requires and abstaining from what it forbids ... [The] moral protest is that it is morally wrong to punish because 'he could not have helped it' or 'he could not have done otherwise' or 'he had no real choice'.

But this implication is not valid. Often, the actor could readily avoid liability-so that all metaphors of 'unobeyable laws', or 'helpless victims' are inappropriate – if we simply broaden the time frame. Chief Justice Burger did precisely this in *United States v. Park.* *Park* sustained a conviction of a responsible corporate official for shipping adulterated food, though the official had not been 'aware of wrong-doing'. The Chief Justice argued that corporate officials voluntarily assume a duty to ensure that violations will not occur when they take on managerial responsibility.

The problem is further illuminated by one of the classic – and classically criticized – applications of strict liability in the criminal law: statutory rape cases. Assume that the age of consent is 16. Defendant admits having sexual intercourse with a girl who is 15, but asserts that he reasonably believed she was 16. The narrow time-framed argument against liability is that the defendant, at the time of intercourse, reasonably perceived the girl to be 16; given the defendant's reasonable perception, he did not act in a culpably antisocial fashion; since it is legally acceptable to have sexual relations with 16-year-olds, to punish the defendant is to punish him when he 'did all that could reasonably be expected of him to avoid criminality'.

The narrow time focus obliterates the difficulties of deciding what constitutes a reasonable belief. Should our decision focus on perceptions available at the moment of seduction, or we do require that some checks *prior* to seduction be taken? If one is generally hostile to statutory rape laws, one can readily negate them by *defining* reasonable *perceptions* (negligence vel non) in terms of judgments that can be made, such as judgments about the girl's appearance, at the time of the allegedly criminal incident. But a defendant may deserve little sympathy for being *unable* to avoid crime when he has had prior opportunities to discover the girl's true legal age. If one is interested in using the criminal law to protect the chastity of the young, one should insist that people *take affirmative steps to avoid mistakes of age.* The practical difference between framing this policy in terms of strict liability and instructing a jury that the reasonable person must take affirmative steps to avoid mistakes of age (which would almost certainly eliminate the *practical* effect of the nonnegligent mistake defense) is ultimately insignificant.

...

Consent. Problems of time-framing also appear in deciding whether consent has been given to otherwise criminal acts. Assuming, arguendo, that no action is harmful which the *subject* assents to, we still can *identify* the supposedly consenting subject using either a broad or a narrow time frame. We can look into the subject's past or just at a single moment of assent. Should that moment be immediately before the act is performed? If the victim at one point did not assent to the harmful act but has assented to it right before the act is taken, has he assented to it? When Odysseus demands at one point to be bound up when the Sirens sing, and *later* demands to be released, which choice most fulfills his 'desires'? When someone goes on a diet, do you give him the piece of chocolate cake he begs for if you are trying to do *his* will?

...

In terms of broadening the time frame backward, we must also determine whether the origins of preference formation should he considered. Does it matter if the assent follows threats or bribes (restricted determinism) or a warped childhood (fuller determinism)? Does it matter whether the subject chose these influences or that, ultimately, no one privately chooses the most basic influences? Is the subject we are interested in the developing person or only that person who actually developed?

Just as significant – and perhaps more operationally significant to judicial efforts to define consent – is whether we open the time frame to account for beliefs held subsequent to the action, too. Do we require that the subject not regret or disown the earlier choice before we exculpate the defendant? It is perfectly plausible that a defendant be deemed guilty of a 'harmful' assault if there is ultimately a complainant: that the harm may be revealed only *after* the fact. A philosophical scheme that denies the possibility that one can harm those who have consented to one's acts seems mechanically workable only if we define the consenting subject in the narrowest time frame, accounting only for preferences expressed by the subject at the moment of defendant's conduct. This definition of the consenting subject is hardly compelling, however, since it is unlikely that the victim dissociates himself into a disconnected series of assenters. More likely, the subject views himself as a person with a continuous personal identity, a person concerned about later re-evaluation of current decisions and the impact of past pressures on choice.

...

B. Disjoined and Unified Accounts of "Incidents"

A second unconscious interpretive construct is the choice between 'disjoined' and 'unified' accounts of relevant legal facts. Substantive criminal law unknowingly, or at least without rational argument, shifts between viewing a series of significant events as a single incident or as separate incidents.

1. Imperfect self-defense

Imperfect self-defense doctrine is one example of the arational choice between disjoined and unified accounts of incidents. In these cases, the defendant genuinely believes that the ultimate victim is attacking him with deadly force that cannot be warded off unless he counters with deadly force, but a reasonable person in the defendant's position would not believe this. Holding this negligent but genuine belief, the defendant intentionally kills the victim. Is the homicide intentional or negligent? On the one hand, we might view the killing incident as temporally disjoined; a negligent perception of the need to kill is *followed* by an intentional killing. Under this view, the defendant is more blameworthy than the traditional negligent killer (eg. the bad driver, the person who plays with guns), because he has focused on the issue of whether to take human life and has gone ahead and done it. On the other hand, if the perception of the need to kill and the conduct are unified as a single incident, we will not see the killing as worse than the traditional negligent killing. The Model Penal Code, reflecting a partial judicial and legislative trend, considers such defendants guilty only of negligent homicide. The Code does not recognize, if only to deny its importance, the distinction between deliberately taking human life under unreasonable perceptions and taking life without being subjectively aware of the risk of death.

In contrast, in *United States v Calley*, the defendant deliberately shot Vietnamese villagers after unreasonably believing that he was lawfully ordered to do so. The court held that Calley committed intentional murder, even if he believed he was acting under orders, because: 'The acts of a subordinate done in compliance with an unlawful order given him by his superior are [not] excused ... [if] the superior's order is one which a man of ordinary sense and understanding would, under the circumstances, know to be unlawful ...' The court, without comment or apparent awareness, disjoined a potentially unified incident, classifying negligent perception *followed by* the legally relevant intentional killing as separate incidents, each incident to be judged on its own merits.

One might believe that the intentional killing should be separate from the perception in this particular case because the Calley 'incident' occurred over a longer period than does the typical imperfect self-defense incident. Calley did have a longer time to consider his perceptions *before* he killed intentionally. But that reasoning is hard to fathom: As long as Calley *still* believed at the time he killed that he was acting legally, he is like the imperfect self-defender. Both could say: 'At the moment I pulled the trigger, intentionally killing the victim, I believed that I was legally authorized to kill. Although my belief was unreasonable, it was not based on a misunderstanding of legal duties. I simply misapplied these legal norms to the particulars of this case.'

We must recognize that disjoined time-framing has made a hard case seem easy. The unstated, unjustified, disjoined perspective of *Cally* suppresses the sense that the actor did not kill in the manner the worst intentional killers do – with a subjective sense of wrongfulness. On the other hand, the Model Penal Code's unified perspective similarly suppresses the recognition that negligent self-defenders cause death differently than do ordinary negligent killers in that they at least sense the presence of death.

...

Perhaps we should always ask how culpable the defendant was in *becoming* an intentional criminal. Interpretive construction suppresses this disturbing question: We unify when we want to account for but deny that we are looking at the background of an intentional act; we disjoin and focus on the 'second' incident when we want to obliterate the past altogether.

C. BROAD AND NARROW VIEWS OF INTENT

A third unconscious construct is the unstated choice between broad and narrow views of the actor's intent. A narrow view assumes that the actor intends only the precise physical act he performs. A broad view assumes that the precise act is an instance of some broader category of acts the actor intends.

1. Impossible attempts

The shifting between broad and narrow views that unconsciously occurs in the criminal law is evident in the doctrine of impossible attempts. The typical attempt case has a decidedly temporal dimension; the defendant fails to cause harm because his criminal conduct is incomplete, interrupted, or thwarted. In impossible attempts, the defendant completes the physical acts, yet no criminally cognizable harm occurs.

Courts and commentators must deal with four categories of impossibility: pure legal impossibility, traditional legal impossibility, legal/factual impossibility, and factual impossibility.

...

I believe that the lines drawn among, and the arguments separating, these four categories are generally based on submerged interpretive shifts between broad and narrow views of the defendant's intent. When we view the defendant as intending only precise physical acts, we acquit the defendant because these precise acts do not constitute a crime. On the other hand, when we view the defendant as intending a broader category of acts, an apter version of the acts he did, we inculpate the defendant for attempting a crime. These interpretive shifts can be seen if we analyze the doctrinal positions of the major commentators in two paradigm cases – *Wilson v. State* and *People v. Jaffe*. In *Wilson*, defendant was acquitted of a forgery because he changed numbers rather than letters on a check – a case of traditional legal impossibility, since the change in numbers was not a material alteration of the check and the crime of forgery requires material alterations. In *Jaffe*, the defendant was acquitted of a charge of attempting to receive stolen goods because the stolen goods he thought he was to receive had been recovered by the police, and hence were no longer stolen – a case of legal/factual impossibility.

Lafave and Scott, reflecting both the Model Penal Code and traditional commentators, make nonrational interpretive switches in distinguishing traditional legal impossibility from legal/factual impossibility. They argue:

> In Wilson the defendant may have thought he was committing a crime, but if he did it was not because he intended to do something that the criminal law prohibited but rather because he was ignorant of the material alteration requirement of the crime of forgery. In Jaffe, on the other hand, what the defendant intended to do was a crime and if the facts had been as the defendant believed them to be he would have been guilty of the completed crime.

Lafave and Scott simply interpret, without rationale, Wilson's intent narrowly and Jaffe's intent broadly. They view Wilson as intending the most precise deed imaginable – altering the numbers on the check – rather than as intending a broader category of acts – intending to receive money from a bank by aptly altering an instrument. They view Jaffe as intending a broader category of acts – receiving stolen property – rather than intending a precise act – receiving the particular goods that were actually delivered to him. Viewed narrowly, Jaffe 'thought he was committing a crime' but was not because the criminal law does not prohibit receiving un-stolen goods. Similarly, viewed broadly, Wilson intended to violate the law of forgery; had he *correctly* altered the instrument (so as to make a bank pay him money), he would have been guilty of the completed crime.

...

2. Provocation

The role of broad and narrow views of the defendant is explicit in provocation doctrine. In many jurisdictions, an intentional homicide is punished less severely if the defendant was reasonably provoked; the grade of the crime may be reduced to manslaughter. The problem, as courts and commentators recognize, is that there exists no convincing interpretation of reasonable provocation. The *ordinary* man would *never* be provoked to take another life by jibes, assaults, or even the bad fortune of discovering adultery in progress. So when we say that a defendant was reasonably provoked to kill, we *cannot* mean that the defendant's conduct was typical of people in similar situations. Nor does the narrowest view of reasonableness acceptably define provocation: Someone just like the defendant, with all his fears, foibles, and disabilities, would *obviously* be provoked to kill under the same pressures he faced, because that someone just *did*.

Courts include or exclude certain traits of the defendant in the profile of the typical individual to whom the defendant's conduct is to be compared. For instance, a court may say that it is irrelevant that a particular defendant is generally impotent in assessing whether a prostitute's taunts on the subject are reasonable provoking; commentators respond that the defendant's reaction ought to be compared to the reasonable impotent man's. Presumably, everyone tries to exclude from his vision of the typical man to whom the defendant is to be compared all the narrow-focused traits the defendant has that the criminal law is designed to alter – hotheadedness, hypersensitivity, proclivity toward violence – but this line ultimately collapses. Of course the criminal code is not trying to deter or to blame impotence itself. But if the impotent as a group pose a menace because impotence is associated with hypersensitivity, if they are prone to violence when confronted by situations that routinely confront people, it is not clear why we would want to exculpate them. Ultimately, the real battle here is between our asserted determinist (excusing) notions of impotence and our intentionalist (inculpatory) models of hotheadedness. Unconscious interpretive construction avoids this more openly political battle: As we take a broader, more categorical view of the typical provoked defendant, fewer and fewer defendants appear to have acted reasonably.

...

III. CONSCIOUS INTERPRETIVE CONSTRUCTS

Conscious interpretive constructs, like the unconscious ones, operate to avoid fundamental political problems. This part applies the two conscious constructs to the substantive criminal law.

A. INTENTIONALISM AND DETERMINISM

Anglo-American courts and commentators assert that our criminal justice system is based on the supposition of 'free will' or intentionalistic conduct. Of course, though, in a number of areas we allow determinist excusing conceptions of the defendant to be considered. This residual determinism negates the simplest claims justifying the generally asserted intentionalism, ie., that a determinist discourse is somehow technically infeasible or methodologically inapplicable to legal contexts. The standard methodological objections to a more general determinism are twofold: first, a simple scepticism about the *necessity* of any effect following from any cause, and second, a distrust of our capacity to account for the roots of particular decisions that explain the *precise* conduct that the actor ultimately engaged in. Yet, these objections apply as well to the uses of determinism that we do tolerate.

1. Apparent determinism: duress, subjective entrapment, and provocation.

Ordinarily, we judge criminal liability at the moment the crime occurs. A defendant is guilty if he performs a harmful act in a blameworthy fashion. The origin of a decision to act criminally is ordinarily of no concern.

At times, though, we open the time frame to look at earlier events in the defendant's experience and construct deterministic accounts of the intentional wrongdoing. For instance, a defendant may perjure himself after being threatened. At the moment the defendant is perjuring himself, he is intentionally telling a lie. But the decision to lie under duress may seem normal, expectable, and therefore blameless.

Duress. Some decisions seem explicable, the result of background pressures that rendered the defendant less deterrable or less blameworthy. The duress defense represents a severe threat to ordinary criminal law discourse and is strictly *confined*, in terms of both time and the pressures that may influence the reasonable defendant. For the most part, we accept only discrete incidents as forming the basis of a duress plea, and we demand that these incidents occur close in time to the arguably criminal incident. Furthermore, the pressures must be attributable to a single human agent or group of agents that focuses his or their efforts on inducing the defendant to commit the crime. This second restriction maintains the illusion of an intentionalist discourse, but the relevant will is now that of the *source of* the duress, not that of the defendant. Of course, though, from the vantage point of the defendant on trial, we have shifted to a determinist mode. What is odd is that the 'substitution of wills' metaphor implies that the defendant is acting involuntarily, or at least without exercising normal rational facilities, when he commits the crime. In fact, his conduct may be as voluntary and sensible as any behavior we can imagine, given the background conditions. The defendant is not rendered will-less; it is simply that the *content* of the expressions of his will, in the typically relevant broader time perspective we are suddenly using, is deemed to be determined.

...

V. CONCLUSION

I can interpret my own task of deconstructing rhetoric in three distinct, though not wholly incompatible, fashions. First, I can view the piece as a rather traditional legal realist's plea for the 'politicization' of legal discourse. One might view my arguments as having the following structure: The courts and commentators purport to solve the particular doctrinal dilemma, but their 'solutions' use an unsupportable 'interpretation' or 'characterization' to make the case appear manageable. Had they been doing 'good' legal analysis, they would instead 'balance' the substantive policy concerns at stake to reach a well-reasoned result.

I have very limited sympathy for this account.

...

A second plausible account of my work is that I am attempting to account for the existence of interpretive construction, and that identifying the forms that characterization takes is just one important step towards understanding the process of interpretation at a broader level. At various points I have accounted for the appearance of a particular interpretive construct as manifesting a simple class conflict between those protecting the position that the legal system routinely allows them from sudden, incidental disruption, and those disfavoured by the routine distribution of benefits that the legal system generates.

...

A third account of my enterprise is that the interpretive constructs I note are not politically meaningful at all, but simply inexplicably unpatterned mediators of experience, the inevitably nonrational filters we need to be able to perceive or talk at all. If that were the case, my role would be largely aesthetic: I speak on behalf of those who no longer like to listen to people making arguments that mask a hidden structure of 'nonarguments' with insistent, false rigor. In the preface to their property casebook, Professors Casner and Leach wrote that, 'In order to move the student along the road of becoming a lawyer, he must be subjected to close analytical testing that rejects generalities or approximations. We think this must come at the beginning of his law study to get him to recognize and abhor superficiality.' [Cases and text on Property (2nd edn 1969) vii] I don't know whether to laugh or cry. When the unwarranted conceptualist garbage is cleared away, dominant legal thought is nothing *but* some more or less plausible common-wisdom banalities, superficialities, and generalities, little more on close analysis than a tiresome, repetitive assertion of complacency that 'we do pretty well, all considered, when you think of all the tough concerns we've got to balance'. Legal thought *does* have its rigorous moments, but these are largely grounded in weak and shifting sands. There is some substance, but we tend to run for cover when it appears.

In the criminal law, two substantive concerns recur. Intentional action and rule-like form are purportedly necessary to construct our ordinary jurisprudence. But no one truly believes in absolute intentionalism or in rules, though the departures from the polar positions are vague and weakly defended. We must avoid the issues in order to talk like lawyers, partly because we have so little to say about them that is not deeply contradictory and ambivalent. What is worse for the lawyer rhetoritician is that when we assert a bottom line, we are rarely very convincing. We rarely do more than restate some utterly nonlegal functionalist preference, some pompous version of Pollyanna's principles, or some equally nonlegal anger or contempt for a system in which the comfortable beneficiaries of a rule structure cash in on their strengths and self-righteously condemn those marginalized by the most central social and collective decisions – the decisions about how rights, duties, and privileges are created and enforced. Rather than face our inability to speak, we hide the uses of standards and determinist discourses, or proclaim, loudly if not clearly, that when we are *obviously* using them, we are in an 'exceptional' circumstance.

Most often, we avoid the issues altogether by constructing the legal material in terms of apparently well-established conceptualist dogma, looking to concepts that, at some broad level, are doubtless policy-'justified' (somewhere or other). As best I can tell, we do these interpretive constructions utterly un-self-consciously. I have never seen or heard anyone declare that they are framing time broadly or narrowly, unifying or disjoining an incident, broadly or narrowly categorizing a defendant's actual or required intent or a defendant's being or circumstances, let alone explain why they are doing it. It is illuminating and disquieting to see that we are nonrationally constructing the legal world over and over again; it is a privilege to discern some structure to this madness, a privilege one gets when a system feels unjust and unnatural. The outsider sees patterns that the insider, committed to keeping the enterprise afloat, never sees; structuring the practices of others is a funny and fun form of dismissal.

...

In his closing reflections, Kelman reveals a stance adopted by many members of the CLS movement, which became known as 'trashing' (Kelman 1984). The aim was to reveal the soft foundations of legal reasoning, its lack of grounding in anything but unconscious, unreasoned, superficial choices. The claim is not that the outcomes of legal disputes are unpredictable, because persistent patterns of dominant and submerged principles are revealed by the analysis of cases. The claim is rather that legal reasoning does not provide a coherent explanation and justification for this pattern. Trashing was, of course, a red rag to the bull for the bulk of law professors, for it denied that they had anything useful or intellectually rigorous to teach aspiring lawyers.

This concentration on the incoherence of legal reasoning was linked to the concern of leftist intellectual thought, particularly the traditions of Western Marxism, to reveal systems of thought as ideological in the sense that systems of belief conceal the vested interests that they serve. The CLS movement concentrated its attention on legal reasoning rather than broader ideologies, with a view to exposing its contradictions and undermining is legitimating power. In pursuing this task, CLS writers borrowed many of the standard methods for criticising ideological constructs, including techniques called 'deconstruction'. This method pays close attention to the use of language or rhetoric in order to expose shifts in meaning that betray an underlying incoherence of thought. Here is an illustration of this method of deconstruction using familiar English examples.

Collins (1987, 92–96)

TWO CONCEPTIONS OF PRIVACY

The first conception of privacy insists that an individual owes no legal obligations to a stranger. This 'estrangement' conception of privacy confines legal obligation to those persons who have deliberately chosen to bind themselves towards one another. Thus contractual obligations created by agreement between the parties must constitute the paradigm form of legal obligation.

...

[An] example of the implications of the estrangement conception of privacy arose in the law of tort in the nineteenth century on account of its resistance to the imposition of liability on manufacturers for defective products towards the ultimate consumer because of the absence of a contractual relation between them ... Similarly, in the law of contract, by virtue of the doctrine of privity, an agreement cannot give rise to legal obligations owed to third persons, even though these person may have been intended to benefit from the performance of the contractual undertaking ... The first conception of privacy thus regards both the ultimate consumer and the third party beneficiary as a stranger to whom no private legal obligations can be owed. But this estrangement conception of privacy jostles with another in private law.

The second conception of privacy insists that an individual owes no legal obligations to intimates. Again, respect for the value of privacy prevents any legal obligations from arising, but this 'intimacy' conception of privacy gives as its reason the principle that legal rights and duties are inappropriate for social and domestic relations. Few commentators doubt that the courts will refuse to enforce such agreement as invitations to dinner and agreements to pay a fixed sum of housekeeping money to a spouse. Often the courts achieve this result by declaring the absence of consideration to support such agreements ... Similarly, in the law of tort, although the modern law imposes a broad liability for negligent misrepresentations, the courts decline to find such an obligation when the misleading advice or information was given on a social occasion, such as a doctor or a lawyer giving her opinion about a case at a party.

...

These two conceptions of privacy focus on the same legal question: is a particular relationship a suitable target for private legal obligation? Yet they suggest two very different reasons for declining to grant a legal remedy. The estrangement conception of privacy insists that legal obligations should be denied unless the parties have formed close relationships by agreement or some other voluntary assumption of responsibility. The intimacy conception of privacy, in contrast, excludes legal obligations unless the parties are dealing at arm's length, in the stance of self-interested strangers.

A DANGEROUS SUPPLEMENT

When courts decline to find legal obligations on the ground of privacy, they frequently employ a group of rhetorical words and phrases which express this perspective on the situation.

...

In the context of the estrangement conception of privacy, the courts often use the word 'stranger' itself to describe the person to whom no legal obligations are owed. Consider, for example, this formulation of the doctrine of privity:

> Although I may regret it, I find it impossible to deny the existence of the general rule that a stranger to a contract cannot in a question with either of the contracting parties take advantage of provisions of the contract, even where it is clear from the contract that some provision in it was intended to benefit him. (Lord Reid, *Scruttons Ltd v Midland Silicones Ltd* [1962] AC 446, 473)

Alternatively, the estrangement conception of privacy can be expressed by stressing the intimacy of the parties, thereby asserting a justification for cloaking them in legal obligations towards each other. The growth of a duty of care owed to persons other than parties to a contract was expressed in the rhetoric of neighbours in order to over come the objection grounded in the estrangement conception of privacy that these strangers were insufficiently close for private law obligations to arise. In Lord Atkin's famous formulation the word 'neighbour' translates the stranger into an intimate:

> The rule that you are to love your neighbour becomes, in law, you must not injure your neighbour ... Who, then, in law is my neighbour? The answer seems to be – persons who are so closely and directly affected by my act that I ought reasonably to have them in contemplation as being so affected when I am directing my mind to the acts or omissions which are called in question. (*Donoghue v Stevenson* [1932] AC 562, 580)

In contrast, in order to express the intimacy conception of privacy, the courts frequently stress the informal and social nature of the relations. The sentiments of love and affection exclude the law of contract in another of Lord Atkin's famous judgments:

> Agreements such as these are outside the realm of contracts altogether. The common law does not regulate the form of agreements between spouses. There promises are not sealed with seals and sealing wax. The consideration that really obtains for them is that natural love and affection which counts for so little in these cold Courts ... In respect of these promises each home is a domain into which the King's write does not seek to run, and to which his officers do not seek to be admitted. (*Balfour v Balfour* [1919] 2 KB 571)

Another way of expressing the intimacy conception of privacy is to label a relationship as a private one in contrast to the public relations between citizens.

...

These few examples convey some of the themes of judicial rhetoric. Yet they exhibit a disturbing characteristic. Our initial distinction between the two conceptions of privacy appears to melt away before our eyes. We said that the estrangement conception of privacy insists that strangers and remote actors cannot have legal obligations thrust upon them, for that would violate their private autonomy. Yet we have also noted that friends and intimates cannot have legal obligations imposed upon them, for that would subvert the bonds of trust and affection which sustain their private relations. The estrangement conception of privacy restricts legal obligations to intimates, whereas the intimacy conception only permits obligations between strangers. At one moment in judicial rhetoric, words and phrases denoting intimacy, proximity, and neighbourliness provide a reason for the imposition of legal obligations, but at the next the same words justify the denial of a legal remedy. Similarly, the emphasis upon the distance between the litigants, their self-interested independence, and the absence of ties of sentiment, authority or dependence provides a reason both for granting legal rights, as in domestic contracts, and for refusing rights, as in the privity of contract doctrine. Is this a contradiction lurking the rhetoric or privacy?

I think that to speak of contradictions in legal rhetoric is a mistake. This kind of legal discourse expresses values and political principles which provide generalised justifications for decisions rather than precise legal rules which may conflict in a contradictory way. Tensions in legal rhetoric are often better described as 'dangerous supplements'. Like the green and black colours on the monitor before me, the terms strangers and intimates define themselves in opposition to each other. Their meaning depends upon the sense of contrast or *différance* [Derrida 1973; Culler 1981]. One term cannot be understood without reference to the other: to be a stranger one must not be an intimate; to be an intimate, one must not be a stranger. Where the meaning of terms depends upon such fragile contrasts, rhetorical justifications necessarily employ both terms, if only by implication. Hence the assertion that a third party is a stranger implies a meaning for intimacy at the same time as it identifies the stranger.

But each term also presents a danger to the other on account of the two conceptions of privacy. An assertion that persons are intimates rather than strangers in order to justify the imposition of legal obligation always runs the risk of running foul of the second conception of privacy in which intimacy abhors legal obligations. To take such concepts as intimacy or estrangement to their logical conclusion would have the effect of depriving the other of any content. For example, it was suggested above that the estrangement conception of privacy generates a justification for the doctrine of privity of contract. The principle that obligations can only be created between close associates requires that third parties cannot gain rights under a contract because they are strangers. By virtue of the intimacy conception of privacy, however, it is precisely the fact that third parties are strangers and not intimates which provides a reason for legal protection of their interests. The interplay of the two conceptions of privacy thus produces apparent incoherence in the law of privity of contract, for whilst the estrangement conception restricts legal obligations to parties to the agreement, the intimacy conception perceives the importance of attaching legal obligations to dealings between strangers. In this realm of legal rhetoric, the concepts of intimacy and estrangement threaten to subvert each other's values, yet they depend upon each other implicitly for their meaning. In this sense, they function as dangerous supplements for each other.

While the preceding discussion examines legal reasoning at the level of judicial rhetoric, a more ambitious use of deconstruction seeks to demonstrate how whole branches of law rest upon the unstable foundations of dangerous supplements. In an especially powerful example of such an argument, Frug exposes the shifting sands on which both administrative law and company law are based. He argues that we share an ambiguous attitude towards bureaucracies or organisations. On the one hand, we appreciate that bureaucracies are necessary for governments and businesses to achieve worthwhile goals effectively, on the other hand we appreciate that bureaucratic power may be misused. Frug describes the history of administrative law and company law as a series of attempts to legitimise the role of bureaucracies. But he argues that all these efforts ultimately fail because they dissolve into incoherence. The legitimating stories always attempt both to demonstrate that bureaucracies serve our subjective desires such as the government's pursuit of the democratic wishes of the people, and that bureaucracies are subject to some kind of objective constraint that prevents the bureaucracy from misusing it power. The underlying problem is the difficulty of separating in any way the 'subjective' ground for legitimacy, that is the idea the bureaucracies pursue our chosen aims, for the 'objective' ground for legitimacy, that is the idea that bureaucracies are subject to constraints that prevent the misuse of power. The notion that the law controls bureaucracy by reference to objective standards is constantly undermined by the need to recognise and permit subjective standards to predominate in order that bureaucracy may implement people's wishes. But once bureaucracy is granted discretion to pursue subjectively chosen goals, this immediately threatens the protection against the misuse of power allegedly supplied by the objective legal standards. For example, if we argue that governments pursue subjectively chosen goals within objective constraints provided by law, we encounter disputes about whether or not administrative decisions are permitted interpretations of the goal. At that point, a court typically accepts that a government must be granted some discretion in view of its superior expertise in its decisions with respect to how to interpret and achieve the goal. The expertise of government provides an objective basis for legitimacy. Yet plainly the courts cannot defer entirely to that claim of expertise, for otherwise the law would impose no controls against the misuse of power. Judicial review of administrative action has to rely simultaneously on the claim that judges can understand the subjective aim of the legislation under which government acts and use that understanding to impose objective constraints, and at the same time acknowledge that the government has more objective expertise in interpreting the subjective aim of the legislation, and that therefore judges should refrain from reviewing administrative decisions lest they impose their own subjective preferences. However, judges also claim an objective expertise, namely an understanding of the principles of legality, so that they should be permitted to intervene when in their expert judgement the principles of legality have been violated. The problem is, of course, that such judicial expertise may be misused to subvert the democratic choice represented by the administrative decision. This argument may sound confusing, even incoherent, but that is of course precisely Frug's point: administrative law is ultimately incoherent. The following passage illustrates his argument in relation to a standard problem that arises in administrative law.

Frug (1984, 1334–1340)

The judicial review model assigns the role of police officer to the courts, and the model's ability to legitimate bureaucracy rests on this judicial role. Bureaucratic legitimacy is derived from the courts' own legitimacy: it is because we can trust the courts that we can trust the bureaucracy.

...

Whichever description of the judicial function one adopts, the critical task for the judicial review model is drawing the proper line between the role of the bureaucracy and the role of the courts. Too little judicial intervention would render the bureaucracy uncontrolled and allow it to exercise arbitrary power. But too much intervention would prevent the bureaucracy from adequately performing its functions and would jeopardize its important role in society. The boundary between courts and bureaucracy must therefore enable the judiciary to deter bureaucratic abuse while permitting the bureaucracy to exercise necessary freedom of action.

...

As this description of the judicial role indicates, judicial review theorists have sought to distinguish and render compatible the subjective and objective aspects of life on both sides of the court/bureaucracy boundary. First and foremost, they have tried to describe the judicial role as both subjective and objective. They have generally rejected rigid attempts to circumscribe the court's role; judicial discretion about when and how to intervene is essential. But if judicial intervention were too subjective, it would belie the assertion that the courts are applying legal – not personal – judgment in restraining the bureaucracy. Thus, the courts must act professionally and rationally while exercising their flexibility and discretion. To be effective, these objective restraints must not be invaded by the exercise of judicial subjectivity.

The need to separate yet combine the subjective and objective elements exists on the bureaucracy side of the boundary as well. Judicial review theorists recognize that no model of bureaucracy can eliminate the exercise of bureaucratic discretion, and they also understand that each model imposes some objective limits on that discretion. Accordingly, courts must respect 'appropriate' bureaucratic subjectivity and eliminate only 'improper' subjectivity. Similarly, they need to be able to tell when objective constraints on the bureaucracy are working properly and when they are not. In short, courts need to ensure that the bureaucracy properly melds its subjective and objective elements.

...

The coincidence of subjectivity and objectivity – and the consequent need to divide them – is increased geometrically. Everywhere one turns, there is a problem that requires an objective/subjective distinction. As a result, the judicial review model enunciates thousands of 'tests' and judicial techniques that restate over and over again the attempt to combine – yet separate – subjectivity and objectivity.

...

Consider how the courts are supposed to decide what the key terms in the substantive tests mean. In *Universal Camera Corp. v. NLRB*, a paradigmatic instance of the judicial review model in administrative law, Justice Frankfurter addressed an important test setting the court/bureaucracy boundary: an administrative factfinding shall be conclusive if supported by substantial evidence on the record considered as a whole. Describing how the courts should apply this standard, Justice Frankfurter recognized that the substantial evidence test did not furnish a 'calculus of value by which a reviewing court can assess the evidence' underlying a bureaucratic factfinding. 'We cannot escape', he said, 'the use of undefined defining terms.' But if the words of the test do not help, what will? Justice Frankfurter answered first with the language of expertise:

> Enforcement of such broad standards implies subtlety of mind and solidity of judgment ... It cannot be too often repeated that judges are not automata. The ultimate reliance for the fair operation of any standard is a judiciary of high competence and character and the constant play of an informed professional critique upon its work.

But this reference to the character of the judiciary relied too heavily on judicial discretion; he therefore immediately supplemented it with an appeal to the will of the legislature, the language of formalism:

> But a standard leaving an unavoidable margin for individual judgment does not leave the judicial judgment at large even though the phrasing of the standard does not wholly fence it in. The legislative history of these Acts demonstrates a purpose to impose on courts a responsibility which has not always been recognized ... We should fail in our duty to effectuate the will of Congress if we denied recognition to expressed Congressional disapproval of the finality accorded to [agency] findings by some decisions of this and lower courts, or even of the atmosphere which may have favored those decisions.

Justice Frankfurter thus defined and circumscribed the court's role by understanding it in joint formalist-expertise terms. He envisioned the courts as organizations that could successfully combine the features of apparently antithetical models of bureaucratic legitimacy.

In doing so, Justice Frankfurter had to avoid transparently contradictory combinations of the two models. Contradictory pairings are certainly possible: a formalist-objective message (restrain yourself – obey the legislative will) can be combined with an expertise – subjective message (intervene – use your expertise), or a formalist-subjective message (intervene – obey the legislative will) can be combined with an expertise-objective message (restrain yourself – be limited by your expertise). Justice Frankfurter could avoid these undesirable expertise-formalism combinations because of the manipulability of the formalist and expertise structures. Formalist and expertise rhetoric can be combined to appear consistent with each other because any specific bureaucratic or judicial action can be justified separately by using either rhetoric. A legislative attempt to deny jurisdiction to the courts can routinely be 'narrowly construed' to allow the intervention demanded by expertise, just as a broad legislative authorization of intervention can be construed to require no more than the courts are competent to handle. It is this malleability that enables the courts to make the combination of formalism and expertise appear convincing.

Even so, the formalism-expertise combination can be interpreted in two antithetical ways: legislation and judicial expertise can either impose a double constraint on judicial intervention or provide a double authorization for judges to employ their discretion in reviewing the bureaucracy's actions. The possibility of both readings means that the judicial review model gives the courts a divided message: be limited by your expertise and by the will of the legislature (objectivity) and be empowered by your expertise and the will of the legislature, as you interpret it, to prevent bureaucratic abuse (subjectivity). Early interpretations of the model emphasized the objective side of this message and the importance of judicial modesty, while later interpretations focused on the subjective side and the importance of the judicial check on bureaucratic abuse. Yet neither reading could conceivably be the 'right' one. The judicial review model adopts both interpretations of the judicial role simultaneously. The 'objective' reading can only be understood by incorporating within its definition of objectivity a subjective supplement, and the subjective reading has no meaning without an objective supplement.

...

Similar arguments may be used to undermine the coherence of company law. Here the problem is the potential misuse of power by the managers or directors of a company in ways that thwart the wishes of the shareholders. One legal solution to the problem of the misuse of corporate power is to impose fiduciary duties upon the directors of company to act in the best interests of the shareholders. Yet this legal constraint must not obstruct the ability of the directors to manage the company in an entrepreneurial way, which is the wish of the shareholders.

> The second mechanism for controlling managerial power which was singled out in the legal model was the fiduciary duties imposed upon the directors and officers of the company. The duties can be formulated as three distinct rules. Directors owe a duty of care and skill; a duty of loyalty; and a duty to act *bona fide* in the best interests of the company and not for any improper purpose. One analysis of the function of these duties is that they ensure that the directors of the company have sufficient discretion and flexibility to be able to manage the company efficiently, whilst precluding them from exercising this discretion contrary to the interests of the shareholders ... In administrative law the theory is that the courts are simply implementing the will of the legislature by subjecting the exercise of discretionary power to these standards of review. In company law it can equally be argued that by casting trustee-like duties on directors so that they are required to act only in the interests of the shareholders the law aims to ensure that the will of the shareholders is implemented. If this is the object of imposing fiduciary duties on directors it fails. This is because in considering what are the interests of the shareholders the directors are not obliged actually to consider what the subjective desires of the shareholders might be. The interests of the shareholders become an objective standard to govern the actions of the directors. Yet it is an objective standard which the directors themselves define, and not one that is imposed upon them by the courts, who regard it as illegitimate to substitute their own view of what constitutes the best interests of the company or the shareholders for that of the directors of the company. So the injunction to directors is that they must act *bona fide* in what they, and not the court, thinks are the best interests of the company. (Stokes 1986, 169–70)

These demonstrations of the incoherence of law through the presence of deeply opposed principles or concepts, without any apparent mechanism for reconciling them other than an unexplained privileging of one principle over another, could not in the end achieve the objective of the CLS movement. What was required, in addition, was a demonstration that it was impossible to find a coherent reconciliation of principles. Opponents of the CLS movement such as Dworkin (see the remaining chapters of Part I) could concede that the law was full of rival principles, which had to be reconciled in hard cases by a process of sophisticated moral and political reasoning. What these opponents were unable to accept was that, armed with a suitably sophisticated theory, it would be impossible to achieve an intellectually coherent explanation of how the principles fitted together in relation to particular legal problems.

In response to this challenge, members of the CLS movement attempted what was variously called the 'critique of liberal legalism' and the 'critique of objectivism'. The general aim of this work was to show that the belief that conflicting principles can be reconciled rests ultimately on a view that certain institutional patterns at the foundations of society are necessarily linked together. If these institutional arrangements are bound together by some type of logical necessity, it makes sense to think that the fundamental institutional arrangements can provide the key to showing how the competing principles should be reconciled. The kinds of fundamental institutional arrangements that the CLS movement had in mind were private property rights, free markets, the traditional nuclear family, the rule of law, and democratic government. The target of CLS attacks was therefore any view that suggested the existence of necessary connections between institutions such as private property rights and efficient markets, or between free markets and democratic government, or between the rule of law and democracy. The targets of such attacks occupy the whole political spectrum, not only conservatives such as Hayek who asserts an essential connection between free markets and the Rule of Law, Marxists who build models of highly determined links between economic systems and political institutions, and centrist liberals like Dworkin, who relies upon institutional structures to account for the coherence of law. One important stand in the work of the CLS movement was a sustained attempt to write legal history that explained the contingency of the formation of legal rules and institutions on political struggles conducted through the courts (Gordon 1984; Klare 1978; Horwitz 1977). Demonstrations that rules of private property, contract, and tort have never been fixed, have always been the site of struggle, and are merely temporary and contingent outcomes, serves the purpose of undermining any view that certain institutional arrangements fit together into a coherent pattern. In the next extract, this critique of the 'logic of social types' is used in an attempt to remove the foundations of any claim that competing principles in legal doctrine might be coherently reconciled.

Unger (1983, 564–76)

THE critical legal studies movement has undermined the central ideas of modern legal thought and put another conception of law in their place. This conception implies a view of society and informs a practice of politics.

...

The ideas and activities of the movement respond to a familiar situation of constraint upon theoretical insight and transformative effort. This situation is exemplary: its dangers and opportunities reappear in many areas of contemporary politics and thought. Our response may, therefore, also have an exemplary character.

One of the most important obligations anybody has toward a movement in which he participates is to hold up before it what, to his mind, should represent its highest collective self-image. My version of this image of critical legal studies is more proposal than description. It may meet with little agreement among the critical legal scholars. But I have unequivocally preferred the risks of repudiation to those of indefinition. In this, if in nothing else, my statement will exemplify the spirit of our movement.

It may help to begin by placing critical legal studies within the tradition of leftist tendencies in modern legal thought and practice. Two overriding concerns have marked this tradition.

The first concern has been the critique of formalism and objectivism. Let me pause to define formalism and objectivism carefully, for these ideas will play an important role in later stages of my argument. By formalism I do not mean what the term is usually taken to describe: belief in the availability of a deductive or quasi-deductive method capable of giving determinate solutions to particular problems of legal choice. What I mean by formalism in this context is a commitment to, and therefore also a belief in the possibility of, a method of legal justification that can be clearly contrasted to opened disputes about the basic terms of social life, disputes that people call ideological, philosophical, or visionary. Though such conflicts may not be entirely bereft of criteria, they fall far short of the rationality that the formalist claims for legal analysis. The formalism I have in mind characteristically invokes impersonal purposes, policies, and principles as an indispensable component of legal reasoning. Formalism in the conventional sense – the search for a method of deduction from a gapless system of rules – is merely the anomalous, limiting case of this jurisprudence.

You might add a second distinctive formalist thesis: that only through such a restrained, relatively apolitical method of analysis is legal doctrine possible. By legal doctrine or legal analysis, in turn, I mean a form of conceptual practice that combines two characteristics: the willingness to work from the institutionally defined materials of a given collective tradition and the claim to speak authoritatively within this tradition, to elaborate it from within in a way that is meant, at least ultimately, to affect the application of state power. Doctrine can exist – the formalist says or assumes – because of a contrast between the more determinate rationality of legal analysis and the less determinate rationality of ideological contests.

This thesis can be restated as the belief that lawmaking and law application differ fundamentally, as long as legislation is seen to be guided only by the looser rationality of ideological conflict. Lawmaking and law application diverge in both how they work and how their results may properly be justified. To be sure, law application may have an important creative element. But in the politics of lawmaking the appeal to principle and policy – when it exists at all – is supposed to be both more controversial in its foundations and more indeterminate in its implications than the corresponding features of legal analysis. Other modes of justification allegedly compensate for the diminished force and precision of the ideal element in lawmaking. Thus, legislative decisions may be validated as results of procedures that are themselves legitimate because they allow all interest groups to be represented and to compete for influence or, more ambitiously, because they enable the wills of citizens to count equally in choosing the laws that will govern them.

By objectivism I mean the belief that the authoritative legal materials – the system of statutes, cases, and accepted legal ideas – embody and sustain a defensible scheme of human association. They display, though always imperfectly, an intelligible moral order. Alternatively they show the results of practical constraints upon social life – constraints such as those of economic efficiency – that, taken together with constant human desires, have a normative force. The laws are not merely the outcome of contingent power struggles or of practical pressures lacking in rightful authority.

The modern lawyer may wish to keep his formalism while avoiding objectivist assumptions. He may feel happy to switch from talk about interest group politics in a legislative setting to invocations of impersonal purpose, policy, and principle in an adjudicative or professional one. He is plainly mistaken; formalism presupposes at least a qualified objectivism. For if the impersonal purposes, policies, and principles on which all but the most mechanical versions of the formalist thesis must rely do not come, as objectivism suggests, from a moral or practical order exhibited, however partially and ambiguously, by the legal materials themselves, where could they come from? They would have to be supplied by some normative theory extrinsic to the law. Even if such a theory could be convincingly established on its own ground, it would be a sheer miracle for its implications to coincide with a large portion of the received doctrinal understandings. At least it would be a miracle unless you had already assumed the truth of objectivism. But if the results of this alien theory failed to overlap with the greater part of received understandings of the law, you would need to reject broad areas of established law and legal doctrine as 'mistaken'. You would then have trouble maintaining the contrast of doctrine to ideology and political prophecy that represents an essential part of the formalist creed: you would have become a practitioner of the free-wheeling criticism of established arrangements and received ideas. No wonder theorists committed to formalism and the conventional view of doctrine have always fought to retain some remnant of the objectivist thesis. They have done so even at a heavy cost to their reputation among the orthodox, narrow-minded lawyers who otherwise provide their main constituency.

Another, more heroic way to dispense with objectivism would be to abrogate the exception to disillusioned, interest group views of politics that objectivist ideas at least implicitly make. This could be accomplished by carrying over to the interpretation of rights the same shameless talk about interest groups that is thought permissible in a legislative setting. Thus, if a particular statute represented a victory of the sheep-herders over the cattlemen, it would be applied, strategically, to advance the former's aims and to confirm the latter's defeat. To the objection that the correlation of forces underlying a statute is too hard to measure, the answer may be that this measurement is no harder to come by than the identification and weighting of purposes, policies, and principles that lack secure footholds in legislative politics. This 'solution', however, would escape objectivism only by discrediting the case for doctrine and formalism. Legal reasoning would turn into a mere extension of the strategic element in the discourse of legislative jostling. The security of rights, so important to the ideal of legality, would fall hostage to context-specific calculations of effect.

If the criticism of formalism and objectivism is the first characteristic theme of leftist movements in modern legal thought, the purely instrumental use of legal practice and legal doctrine to advance leftist aims is the second. The connection between these two activities – the skeptical critique and the strategic militancy – seems both negative and sporadic. It is negative because it remains almost entirely limited to the claim that nothing in the nature of law or in the conceptual structure of legal thought – neither objectivist nor formalist assumptions – constitutes a true obstacle to the advancement of leftist aims. It is sporadic because short-run leftist goals might occasionally be served by the transmutation of political commitments into delusive conceptual necessities.

These themes of leftist legal thought and practice have now been reformulated in the course of being drawn into a larger body of ideas. The results offer new insight into the struggle over power and right, within and beyond the law, and they redefine the meaning of radicalism.

II. THE CRITICISM OF LEGAL THOUGHT

We have transformed the received critique of formalism and objectivism into two sets of more specific claims that turn out to have a surprising relation. The two groups of critical ideas state the true lesson of the law curriculum – what it has actually come to teach, rather than what the law professors say it teaches, about the nature of law and legal doctrine. The recitation of this lesson carries the critique of formalist and objectivist ideas to an unprecedented extreme. This very extremism, however, makes it possible to draw from criticism elements of a constructive program.

A. The Critique of Objectivism

Take first the way we have redefined the attack upon objectivism. Our key idea here is to reinterpret the situation of contemporary law and legal doctrine as the ever more advanced dissolution of the project of the classical, nineteenth century jurists conceived in a certain way. Because both the original project and the signs of its progressive breakdown remain misunderstood, the dissolution has not yet been complete and decisive. The nineteenth century jurists were engaged in a search for the built-in legal structure of the democracy and the market. The nation, at the Lycurgan moment of its history, had opted for a particular type of society: a commitment to a democratic republic and to a market system as a necessary part of that republic. The people might have chosen some other type of social organization. But in choosing this one, in choosing it for example over an aristocratic and corporatist polity on the old-European model, they also chose the legally defined institutional structure that went along with it. This structure provided legal science with its topic and generated the purposes, policies, and principles to which legal argument might legitimately appeal. Thus, two ideas played the central role in this enterprise. One was the distinction between the foundational politics, responsible for choosing the social type, and the ordinary politics, including the ordinary legislation, operating within the framework established at the foundational moment. The other idea was the existence of an inherent and distinct legal structure of each type of social organization.

Many may be tempted to dismiss out of hand as wholly implausible and undeserving of criticism this conception of a logic of social types, each type with its intrinsic institutional structure. It should be remembered, however, that in less explicit and coherent form the same idea continues to dominate the terms of modern ideological debate and to inform all but the most rigorous styles of microeconomics and social science. It appears, for example, in the conceit that we must choose between market and command economies or at most combine into a 'mixed economy' these two exhaustive and well-defined institutional options. The abstract idea of the market as a system in which a plurality of economic agents bargain on their own initiative and for their own account becomes more or less tacitly identified with the particular set of market institutions that triumphed in modern Western history. Moreover, the abandonment of the objectivist thesis would leave formalism, and the kinds of doctrine that formalism wants to defend, without a basis, a point to which my argument will soon return. The critique of objectivism that we have undertaken is essentially the critique of the idea of types of social organization with a built-in legal structure and of the more subtle but still powerful successors of this idea in current conceptions of substantive law and doctrine. We have conducted this assault on more than one front.

Historical study has repeatedly shown that every attempt to find the universal legal language of the democracy and the market revealed the falsehood of the original idea. An increasing part of doctrinal analysis and legal theory has been devoted to containing the subversive implications of this discovery.

The general theory of contract and property provided the core domain for the objectivist attempt to disclose the built-in legal content of the market just as the theory of protected constitutional interests and of the legitimate ends of state action was designed to reveal the intrinsic legal structure of a democratic republic. But the execution kept belying the intention. As the property concept was generalized and decorporealized, it faded into the generic conception of right, which in turn proved to be systematically ambiguous (e.g., Hohfeld) if not entirely indeterminate. Contract, the dynamic counterpart to property, could do no better. The generalization of contract theory revealed, alongside the dominant principles of freedom to choose the partner and the terms, the counterprinciples: that freedom to contract would not be allowed to undermine the communal aspects of social life and that grossly unfair bargains would not be enforced. Though the counterprinciples might be pressed to the corner, they could be neither driven out completely nor subjected to some system of metaprinciples that would settle, once and for all, their relation to the dominant principles. In the most contested areas of contract law, two different views of the sources of obligation still contend. One, which sees the counterprinciples as mere ad hoc qualifications to the dominant principles, identifies the fully articulated act of will and the unilateral imposition of a duty by the state as the two exhaustive sources of obligation. The other view, which treats the counterprinciples as possible generative norms of the entire body of law and doctrine, finds the standard source of obligations in the only partially deliberate ties of mutual dependence and redefines the two conventional sources as extreme, limiting cases. Which of these clashing conceptions provides the real theory of contract? Which describes the institutional structure inherent in the very nature of a market?

The development of constitutional law and constitutional theory throughout the late nineteenth and the twentieth centuries tells a similar story of the discovery of indeterminacy through generalization. This discovery was directly connected with its private law analogue. The doctrines of protected constitutional interests and of legitimate ends of state action were the chief devices for defining the intrinsic legal-institutional structure of the scheme of ordered liberty. They could not be made coherent in form and precise in implication without freezing into place, in a way that the real politics of the republic would never tolerate, some particular set of deals between the national government and organized groups. Legitimate ends and protected interests exploded into too many contradictory implications; like contract and property theory, they provided in the end no more than retrospective glosses on decisions that had to be reached on quite different grounds.

The critique of this more specific brand of objectivism can also be pressed through the interpretation of contemporary law and doctrine. The current content of public and private law fails to present a single, unequivocal version of the democracy and the market. On the contrary, it contains in confused and undeveloped form the elements of different versions. These small-scale variations, manifest in the nuances of contemporary doctrine, may suggest larger possible variations.

The convergent result of these two modes of attack upon objectivism – the legal-historical and the legal-doctrinal – is to discredit, once and for all, the conception of a system of social types with a built-in institutional structure. The very attempt to work this conception into technical legal detail ends up showing its falsehood. Thus, the insight required to launch the attack against objectivism – the discovery of the indeterminate content of abstract institutional categories like democracy or the market – with its far-reaching subversive implications, was partly authored by a cadre of seemingly harmless and even toadying jurists. Those who live in the temple may delight in the thought that the priests occasionally outdo the prophets.

B. The Critique of Formalism

We have approached the critique of formalism from an angle equally specific. The starting point of our argument is the idea that every branch of doctrine must rely tacitly if not explicitly upon some picture of the forms of human association that are right and realistic in the areas of social life with which it deals. If, for example, you are a constitutional lawyer, you need a theory of the democratic republic that would describe the proper relation between state and society or the essential features of social organization and individual entitlement that government must protect come what may.

Without such a guiding vision, legal reasoning seems condemned to a game of easy analogies. It will always be possible to find, retrospectively, more or less convincing ways to make a set of distinctions, or failures to distinguish, look credible. A common experience testifies to this possibility; every thoughtful law student or lawyer has had the disquieting sense of being able to argue too well or too easily for too many conflicting solutions. Because everything can be defended, nothing can; the analogy-mongering must be brought to a halt. It must be possible to reject some of the received understandings and decisions as mistaken and to do so by appealing to some background normative theory of the branch of law in question or of the realm of social practice governed by that part of the law.

Suppose that you could determine on limited grounds of institutional propriety how much a style of doctrinal practice may regularly reject as mistaken. With too little rejection, the lawyer fails to avoid the suspect quality of endless analogizing. With too much, he forfeits his claim to be doing doctrine as opposed to ideology, philosophy, or prophecy. For any given level of revisionary power, however, different portions of the received understandings in any extended field of law may be repudiated.

To determine which part of established opinion about the meaning and applicability of legal rules you should reject, you need a background prescriptive theory of the relevant area of social practice, a theory that does for the branch of law in question what a doctrine of the republic or of the political process does for constitutional argument. This is where the trouble arises. No matter what the content of this background theory, it is, if taken seriously and pursued to its ultimate conclusions, unlikely to prove compatible with a broad range of the received understandings. Yet just such a compatibility seems to be required by a doctrinal practice that defines itself by contrast to open-ended ideology. For it would be strange if the results of a coherent, richly developed normative theory were to coincide with a major portion of any extended branch of law. The many conflicts of interest and vision that lawmaking involves, fought out by countless minds and wills working at cross-purposes, would have to be the vehicle of an immanent moral rationality whose message could be articulated by a single cohesive theory. This daring and implausible sanctification of the actual is in fact undertaken by the dominant legal theories and tacitly presupposed by the unreflective common sense of orthodox lawyers. Most often, the sanctification takes the form of treating the legal order as a repository of intelligible purposes, policies, and principles, in abrupt contrast to the standard disenchanted view of legislative politics.

This argument against formalism may be criticized on the ground that the claimed contrast between the game of analogy and the appeal to a background conception of right is untenable; from the outset analogy is guided by such a conception, so the criticism would suggest. But for the analogy to be guided by such a conception would require precisely the miracle to which I just referred: the preestablished harmony between the content of the laws and the teachings of a coherent theory of right. Or, again, it may be objected that in law such background views benefit from a self-limiting principle: the principle introduced by the constraints of institutional context. Such a principle, however, must rely either upon a more or less tacit professional consensus about the rightful limits of institutional roles or upon an explicit and justifiable theory of institutional roles. Even if a consensus of this sort could claim authority, it simply does not exist. The proper extent of the revisionary power – the power to declare some portion of received legal opinion mistaken – remains among the most contested subjects of legal controversy, as the American debates about judicial 'activism' and 'self-restraint' show. An explicit theory of institutional roles can make sense and find support only within a substantive theory of politics and rights. We thus return to the initial implausibility of a widespread convergence of any such theory with the actual content of a major branch of law.

Having recognized this problem with doctrine, modern legal analysis tries to circumvent it in a number of ways. It may, for example, present an entire field of law as the expression of certain underlying theoretical approaches to the subject. These implicit models, it is suggested, fit into some coherent scheme or, at least, point toward a synthesis. In this way it seems possible to reconcile the recognition that legal analysis requires an appeal to an underlying theory of right and social practice with the inability to show that the actual content of law and doctrine in any given area coincides, over an appreciable area of law, with a particular theory. But this recourse merely pushes the problem to another level. No extended body of law in fact coincides with such a metascheme, just as no broad range of historical experience coincides with the implications of one of the evolutionary views that claim to provide a science of history. (That this counts as more than a faint resemblance is a point to which I shall return.) It is always possible to find in actual legal materials radically inconsistent clues about the range of application of each of the models and indeed about the identity of the models themselves.

Once the lawyer abandons these methods of compensation and containment, he returns to a cruder and more cynical device. He merely imposes upon his background conceptions – his theories of right and social practice – an endless series of ad hoc adjustments. The looseness of the theories and the resulting difficulty of distinguishing the ad hoc from the theoretically required make this escape all the easier. Thus, there emerges the characteristic figure of the modern jurist who wants – and needs – to combine the cachet of theoretical refinement, the modernist posture of seeing through everything, with the reliability of the technician whose results remain close to the mainstream of professional and social consensus. Determined not to miss out on anything, he has chosen to be an outsider and an insider at the same time. To the achievement of this objective he has determined to sacrifice the momentum of his ideas. We have denounced him wherever we have found him, and we have found him everywhere.

One more objection might be made to this attack upon formalism and upon the type of doctrinal practice that formalism justifies. According to this objection, the attack succeeds only against the systematic constructions of the most ambitious academic jurists, not against the specific, problem-oriented arguments of practical lawyers and judges. It is hard, though, to see how such arguments could be valid, how indeed they might differ from rhetorical posturing, unless they could count as tentative fragments of a possible cohesive view of an extended body of law.

The implication of our attack upon formalism is to undermine the attempt to rescue doctrine through these several stratagems. It is to demonstrate that a doctrinal practice that puts its hope in the contrast of legal reasoning to ideology, philosophy, and political prophecy ends up as a collection of makeshift apologies.

C. The Critiques of Objectivism and Formalism Related: Their Significance for Current Legal Theories

Once the arguments against objectivism and formalism have been rendered in these specific ways, their relation to each other gains a new and surprising clarity. As long as the project of the nineteenth century jurists retained its credibility, the problem of doctrine did not emerge. The miracle required and promised by objectivism could take place: the coincidence of the greater part of substantive law and doctrine with a coherent theory, capable of systematic articulation and relentless application. The only theory capable of performing the miracle would have been one that described the inner conceptual and institutional structure of the type of social and governmental organization to which the nation had committed itself at its foundational moment. Such a theory would not have needed to be imported from outside. It would not have been just somebody's favorite system. It would have translated into legal categories the abiding structure of ordinary political and economic activity. Once the objectivist project underlying the claim to reveal the inherent content of a type of social organization ceased to be believable, doctrine in its received form was condemned to the self-subversion that our critique of formalism has elucidated. But because the nature and defects of the project appeared only gradually, the permanent disequilibrium of doctrine became manifest little by little.

This view of the flaws in objectivism and formalism and of the close link between the two sets of ideas and the two critiques explains our approach to the most influential and symptomatic legal theories in America today: the law and economics and the rights and principles schools. Each of these theories is advanced by a group that stands at the margin of high power, that despairs of seeing its aims triumph through the normal means of governmental politics, and that appeals to some conceptual mechanism designed to show that the advancement of its program is a practical or moral necessity. The law and economics school has mainly addressed private law; the rights and principles school, public law. The law and economics school has invoked practical requirements (with normative implications) that supposedly underlie the legal system and its history; the rights and principles school, moral imperatives allegedly located within the legal order itself. The law and economics school has chiefly served the political right; the rights and principles school, the liberal center. But both theoretical tendencies can best be understood as efforts to recover the objectivist and formalist position. It is as restatements of objectivism and formalism that we have rejected them.

The chief instrument of the law and economics school is the equivocal use of the market concept. These analysts give free rein to the very mistake that the increasing formalization of microeconomics was largely meant to avoid: the identification of the abstract market idea or the abstract circumstance of maximizing choice with a particular social and institutional complex. As a result, an analytic apparatus intended, when rigorous, to be entirely free of restrictive assumptions about the workings of society and entirely subsidiary to an empirical or normative theory that needs independent justification gets mistaken for a particular empirical and normative vision. More particularly, the abstract market idea is identified with a specific version of the market – the one that has prevailed in most of the modern history of most Western countries – with all its surrounding social assumptions, real or imagined. The formal analytic notion of allocational efficiency is identified with a specific theory of economic growth or, quite simply, with the introduction, the development, or the defense of this particular institutional and social order. Such are the sophistries by which the law and economics school pretends to discover both the real basis for the overall evolution of the legal order and the relevant standard by which to criticize occasional departures of that order from its alleged vocation. From this source supposedly come the purposes and policies that do and should play the paramount role in legal reasoning.

The rights and principles school achieves similar results through very different means. It claims to discern in the leading ideas of the different branches of law, especially when illuminated by a scrupulous, benevolent, and well-prepared professional elite, the signs of an underlying moral order that can then serve as the basis for a system of more or less natural rights. This time, the objective order that guides the main line of legal evolution and serves to criticize the numerous though marginal aberrations is a harshly simplified version of moral ideas supposedly expressed in authoritative legal materials.

No longer able to appeal to the idea of the built-in institutional structure of a type of social organization, this school alternates confusedly between two options, both of which it finds unacceptable as a basis for legal theory. One option is that moral consensus (if only it could actually be identified) carries weight just because it exists. The alternative view is that the dominant legal principles count as the manifestations of a transcendent moral order whose content can be identified quite apart from the history and substance of a particular body of law. The third, mediating position for which the school grasps – that consensus on the received principles somehow signals a moral order resting mysteriously upon more than consensus – requires several connected intellectual maneuvers. One is a drastic minimization of the extent to which the law already incorporates conflict over the desirable forms of human association. Another is the presentation of the dominant legal ideas as expressions of higher moral insight, an insight duly contained and corrected by a fidelity to the proprieties of established institutional roles, a fidelity that must itself be mandated by the moral order. Yet another is the deployment of a specific method to reveal the content and implications of this order: generalize from particular doctrines and intuitions, then hypostasize the generalizations into moral truth, and finally use the hypostasis to justify and correct the original material. The intended result of all this hocus-pocus is far clearer than the means used to achieve it. The result is to generate a system of principles and rights that overlaps to just the appropriate extent with the positive content of the laws. Such a system has the suitable degree of revisionary power, the degree necessary to prove that you are neither an all-out and therefore ineffective apologist nor an irresponsible revolutionary.

The law and economics and the rights and principles schools supply a watered-down version of the enterprise of nineteenth century legal science. The endeavor of the classical nineteenth century jurists in turn represented a diluted version of the more common, conservative social doctrines that preceded the emergence of modern social theory. These doctrines pretended to discover a canonical form of social life and personality that could never be fundamentally remade and reimagined even though it might undergo corruption or regeneration. At each succeeding stage of the history of these ideas, the initial conception of a natural form of society becomes weaker: the categories more abstract and indeterminate, the champions more acutely aware of the contentious character of their own claims. Self-consciousness poisons their protestations. Witnessing this latest turn in the history of modern legal thought, no one could be blamed for recalling hopefully Novalis' remark that 'when we dream that we dream we are about to awake'.

A large part of this history consists in the attempt to deflect the critique of formalism and objectivism by accepting some of its points while saving increasingly less of the original view. The single most striking example in twentieth century American legal thought has been the development of a theory of legal process, institutional roles, and purposive legal reasoning as a response to legal realism. Perhaps the most creditable pretext for these endless moves of confession and avoidance has been the fear that, carried to the extreme, the critique of objectivism and formalism would leave nothing standing. The very possibility of legal doctrine, and perhaps even of normative argument generally, might be destroyed. Thus, ramshackle and plausible compromises have been easily mistaken for theoretical insight. For many of us, the turning point came when we decided, at the risk of confusion, paralysis, and marginality, to pursue the critical attack a outrance. When we took the negative ideas relentlessly to their final conclusions, we were rewarded by seeing these ideas turn into the starting points of a constructive program.

The ambition of the CLS movement was to demonstrate that even the most sophisticated defences of the coherence or integrity of legal reasoning, which deployed arguments of purpose or principle in an effort to resolve tensions within the doctrine, could never achieve their goal. These defences of the legitimacy of the legal system had to fail, it was argued, because the principles merely restated at a higher level of generality the underlying contradictory values on which the legal order was based. No resolution could be found in appeals to the basic institutional arrangements of society, because all such arrangements are contingent and malleable (Unger 1987). Having dismissed most of the legal theory in this book as either 'specious' or 'hocus-pocus', what could the CLS movement offer in its place?

A Radical Agenda?

Plainly what the CLS movement hoped to achieve was a recognition of the possibility of more radical social change through law. This desire to use law for social change arose from a perception that despite some important progressive measures since 1945, such as the Civil Rights Act 1964 and some improvements to equality through constitutional adjudication, the American legal system represented a major obstacle to social change. To liberate the law, so that it could supply a powerful tool for progressive political measures, what was required was to realise the potential that lay within its indeterminacy and incoherence. The CLS movement was sustained in both the United States and in Britain by regular conferences, where all the exotic varieties of progressive and leftist political thought explored these possibilities for critical legal practice.

The question was asked, of course, about the direction to which this potential for the progressive use of law might lead. Most authors in the CLS movement avoided this question (see Fischl 1992), focussing instead upon demonstrating the possibility for the law to take a different view of the rights and obligations which it recognised. What seems to be proposed is a critical practice rather than any kind of blueprint for society (see Gabel and Harris 1983). This practice might occur in any context, not only in the traditional locations of workers' organisations and community action groups, but also within universities and firms of lawyers. The CLS movement provoked its most venomous attacks when it challenged the structures and practices of lawyers themselves (see Menand 1986). For example, Kennedy (1983) analyses the way in which law schools use systems of domination such as that of professors over students, in order to train lawyers to accept and reinforce later the hierarchies of the legal system. Suggested solutions included doing away with grading and degree classifications, admissions by lottery, and ensuring that everyone employed by the institution is regarded and rewarded equally. Similarly he encouraged lawyers working for large corporate clients to question whether they should always act in ways that placed their own client's interests first over other community and environmental interests (see Kennedy 1981). This critical practice, which clearly resonates with the student radicalism of the 1960s, involves the politicisation of all aspects of law, legal practice, and legal education, not just highly contested constitutional issues.

But what, it may be insisted, was the political objective of this critical practice (see Johnson 1984)? Unger once described the CLS values as 'super-liberalism', because the core principles seem to be liberty and equality. Of course, the CLS movement believed that the traditional liberal accounts of those ideals were fundamentally inadequate. In relation to liberty, it is possible to detect the influence of Marcuse (1986/ 1964) whose argument that the tolerance of American society was ultimately deceptive and repressive had appealed to student radicals in the 1960s. Those students later became of course many of the leading figures of the CLS movement. With respect to equality, what was sought from the legal system was not just formal equality before the law, but a more pervasive attack on the sources of substantive inequality in wealth and power. For this purpose what was required was more than criticism of particular rules of law. The task demanded a critical examination of how the law constituted institutional arrangements in society: its scheme of property rights, market transactions, and governmental and corporate organisations. It was these basic institutional arrangements, constituted and protected by the law, which presented the fundamental obstacle to the better realisation of liberty and equality.

Yet, if law is an obstacle to radical change, how could the law become an instrument of social transformation? Although some strands in the CLS movement followed the pessimism of Marxists in this respect, there was a vibrant strand of theory, which argued for the possibility of radical action through the manipulation of legal doctrine. Unger called this practice 'deviationist doctrine' or 'expanded doctrine'. This practice involves bringing to the surface of legal argument the deeper controversies over what is the right and feasible structure for society. Three forms of deviationist doctrine may be distinguished.

A vertical analysis traces legal principles back to their empirical and normative foundations. Having demonstrated those beliefs to be no longer plausible in a modern context, adjustments to legal doctrine can be proposed that better fulfil the normative foundations in the contemporary empirical context. For example, if the original structure of company law was designed to protect shareholders as the investors in a company, it might be demonstrated that in a contemporary context of large corporations the legal mechanisms such as fiduciary duties no longer achieve the goal of providing adequate protection to shareholders. Adjustments to the fiduciary duties might be proposed that better protect the shareholders. Furthermore, it might be argued that other groups such as workers also invest in the success of the company by devoting their energy and skills, so that in a knowledge-based economy they also deserve protection from misuse of management power under the original rationale for corporate structures.

A horizontal analysis challenges the sharp boundaries that the law draws between different spheres of social life. For example, the law often draws a sharp distinction between the public and the private. As a citizen, for instance, the law provides guarantees of civil liberties and fair procedures against the power of government. But those same rights are usually denied in the context of the workplace, which is regarded as a private sphere governed by contract. Horizontal analysis chips away at such sharp divides, suggesting for instance that employers should also be bound in their dealings with workers by respect for human rights and a requirement to follow fair procedures. This analysis requires both a challenge to settled assumptions of the law about where the pubic/private line should be drawn, and also to its empirical foundations that there is a difference in kind between state power and the employers' power.

A third type of deviationist doctrine attempts to restate some branch of the law in a way that systematically emphasises the significance of the suppressed principle and undermines the apparent strength of the dominant principle. In our earlier example of the relation in the law of contract between consideration and promissory estoppel, we noted that the former tended to dominate accounts of the law. A deviationist approach would first doubt the coherence of the doctrine of consideration itself, perhaps pointing to ambiguities in the idea or the way in which courts construct facts in order to satisfy the doctrine. The next step would emphasise the persistent significance of the alternative test for legal enforceability presented by a doctrine of promissory estoppel. The underlying objective of this deviationist doctrine would be to reorient the law towards the values or principles expressed by the submerged principle. It might even be suggested that the protection of reliance is the dominant principle, and that the test of consideration is a marginal, historically anachronistic, and incoherent special case of contractual liability.

One might argue plausibly that deviationist doctrine has been the work of legal scholars for centuries, for the greatest have constructed imaginative and fresh interpretations of established doctrines with which to tackle new problems and to revise the law. For instance, the article by Fuller and Perdue, 'The Reliance Interest in Contract Damages', and the later work in England by Atiyah, came very close to articulating the type of argument about the role of consideration that was suggested in the previous paragraph. Where CLS writers differed was in the degree to which they were prepared to question and revise the established legal orthodoxy. For example, in a typical CLS work, Singer argues that promissory estoppel and analogous doctrines provide the legal foundation for workers and the local community to intervene to prevent the owners of a large steel mill from closing it down (Singer 1988). Such a claim challenges the institutional foundations of a market economy by suggesting that legal doctrine provides the basis for controls over when capitalists can alter their investments.

Even though it may be conceded that deviationist doctrine might in the hands of members of the CLS movement suggest more radical revisions of our institutional arrangements, a sceptic might justly question whether law review articles could ever have any significant contribution to make to progressive political achievements. Furthermore, the fact that the CLS movement faded away or disintegrated into many different strands, such as radical feminism and critical race theory, casts doubt on its ability to use the tools of critique and deviationist doctrine to any great effect. No doubt the CLS movement was in part suppressed in America by Deans of law schools who tried to prevent 'Crits' from obtaining faculty appointments. But even in Britain, where there was usually less heat in the debates, the Crits were marginalised and do not seem to have had a lasting influence. The problem confronting the CLS movement was not just resistance to progressive political positions, but rejection of the analysis of the incoherence of legal doctrine and the (alleged) liberating potential that followed from that insight (see Finnis 1987b). Steeped in the doctrinal learning of the common law, few law professors, judges, or lawyers could bring themselves to think that they had always been just 'making sense out of nonsense' (see Howarth 1992). This view was unthinkable because not only did it call into question all legal institutions and any belief in justice through law, but also at a personal level it questioned whether a life in the law was a meaningful life at all. Few lawyers were prepared to confront such a question, and many of those Crits who peered into the abyss withdrew to more conventional types of legal scholarship.

The final extract in this chapter tries to address this problem that confronts radical progressive movements in law. Roberto Unger investigates how and why the idea that lawyers are making sense of nonsense is repressed and denied, because lawyers work under 'the spell of rationalising legal analysis'. He bemoans the 'arrested development of legal thought', because lawyers have ceased to work imaginatively towards the creation of revised institutions. Unger suggests a way out of this impasse through mapping and criticism. But we can easily see the flaw in this programme for progressive movements that it may never get beyond critical analysis of existing law and institutions to the development of radically new structures for society (for a reply to Unger, see Chrisodoulidis 1996).

Unger (1996, 1–6, 19–23)

The arrested development of legal thought

THE GENIUS OF CONTEMPORARY LAW

To grasp the potential of legal analysis to become a master tool of institutional imagination in a democratic society we must begin by understanding what is most distinctive about law and legal thought in the contemporary industrial democracies. In this effort no contrast is more revealing than the comparison of the substantive law and legal methods of today with the project of nineteenth-century legal science and the law of nineteenth-century commercial economies.

Consider how the law and legal thought of today may look to a future student who tries to identify its deepest and most original character within the larger sequence of legal history. Suppose that we use in this endeavour less the search for recurrent doctrinal categories and distinctions Holmes pursued in *The Common Law* than the reciprocal reading of vision and detail von Jhering offered in *The Spirit of the Roman Law*. The latter method rather than the former respects the place of law between imagination and power, and connects the self-understanding of legal thought to the central tradition of modern social theory founded by Montesquieu. Viewed in this light, the overriding theme of contemporary law and legal thought, and the one defining its genius, is the commitment to shape a free political and economic order by combining rights of choice with rules designed to ensure the effective enjoyment of these rights. Little by little, and in country after country of the rich Western world and of its poorer emulators, a legal consciousness has penetrated and transformed substantive law, affirming the empirical and defensible character of individual and collective self-determination: its dependence upon practical conditions of enjoyment, which may fail.

This conception stands out by contrast to the single most influential idea in the law and legal thought of the nineteenth century, an idea developed as much in the case-oriented discourse of American and English jurists, or the aphoristic and conclusory utterances of French lawyers, as in the relentless category-grinding of the German pandectists. According to this earlier idea a certain system of rules and rights defines a free political and economic order. We uphold the order by clinging to the predetermined system of rules and rights by preventing its perversion through politics, especially the politics of privilege and redistribution.

A consequence of this animating idea of contemporary law has been the reorganisation of one branch of law and legal doctrine after another as a binary system of rights of choice and of arrangements withdrawn from the scope of choice the better to make the exercise of choice real and effective. The governing aim of this dialectical organisation is to prevent the system of rules and rights from becoming or remaining a sham, concealing subjugation under the appearance of coordination.

Sometimes this binary reshaping takes place by marshalling countervailing rules and doctrines within a single branch of law, as when the doctrine of economic duress and of unequal bargaining power complements and qualifies the core rules of contract formation and enforceability, or when freedom to choose the terms in a labour contract is restricted by selective direct legal regulation of the employment relation. At other times the dual structure works by assigning the choice-restricting and freedom-sustaining arrangements to a distinct branch of law, as when collective bargaining law attempts to correct the inability of individual contract to compensate for the power disparities of the employment relation. At yet other times the dual structure has taken the form of a coexistence of two legal regimes for the governance of overlapping social problems. Thus, fault-based liability may be strengthened rather than undermined by the refusal to extend it to the compensation for the actualisation of the risks inherent in a line of business, and by the development of insurance systems disregarding fault-oriented standards of compensation.

The binary structure that has reorganised private law in every industrial democracy recurs, on a larger scale, in the relation of governmental regulation to private law as a whole. The entitlements afforded by the welfare state, and the enjoyment by workers of prerogatives relatively secure against labour-market instability and the business cycle, have been understood and developed by twentieth-century lawyers as devices for guaranteeing the effective enjoyment of the public-law and private-law rights of self-determination. If the market economy, representative democracy, and free civil society have certain inherited and necessary forms, these forms must nevertheless be refined and completed so that they may provide the reality as well as the appearance of free choice and coordination to every rights-bearing individual.

The supreme achievement of this sustained exercise in correction is to make the individual effectively able to develop and deploy a broad range of capacities. He can then form and execute his life projects, including those most important ones that he may need to imagine and advance through free association with other people. Class hierarchies may nevertheless have persisted with barely diminished force. The majority of the people may be an angry and marginalised although fragmented mass of individuals, who feel powerless at their jobs and hopeless about their national politics, while seeking solace and escape in private pleasure, domestic joys, and nostalgic traditionalism. According to this mode of thought, however, these burdens of history and imperfection merely show that we must patiently continue the work of securing the effective enjoyment of rights.

The theme of the dialectic between the realm of free economic and political choice and the realm of that which is withdrawn from choice for the sake of choice is all the more remarkable because it fails to track any specific ideological position within the debates of modem politics and modem political thought. It merely excludes positions that from the vantage point of those who inhabit this imaginative world may seem extremist. It excludes the old nineteenth-century idea that a particular scheme of private and public rights will automatically secure economic and political freedom if only it can be protected against redistributive interventionism. It also repels the radically reconstructive idea that no real and widely shared experience of individual and collective self-determination will be possible unless we revolutionise the present institutional system by substituting, for example, 'socialism' for 'capitalism'. Yet while the spirit of contemporary law may seem to antagonise only unbelievable or insupportable alternatives, it generates, in detail, endless practical and argumentative work for the analyst and the reformer. Thus, it resembles, in the generality of its scope and the fecundity of its effects, the general conception that preceded it in the history of law and legal thought: the project of a legal science that would reveal the in-built legal and institutional content of a free society and police its boundaries against invasion by politics.

THE LIMIT OF CONTEMPORARY LEGAL THOUGHT

There is nevertheless a riddle in the career of this idea. Until we solve this riddle, we cannot correctly understand the genius – and the self-imposed poverty – of contemporary legal thought, nor can we fully appreciate the extent to which the development of law remains bound up with the fate of democratic experimentalism. When we begin to explore ways of ensuring the practical conditions for the effective enjoyment of rights, we discover at every turn that there are alternative plausible ways of defining these conditions, and then of satisfying them once they have been defined. For every right of individual or collective choice, there are different plausible conceptions of its conditions of effective realisation in society as now organised. For every such conception, there are different plausible strategies to fulfil the specified conditions.

Some of these conceptions and strategies imply keeping present institution arrangements while controlling their consequences: by counteracting, for example through tax-and-transfer or through preferment for disadvantaged groups, their distributive consequences. Other conceptions and strategies, however, imply a piecemeal but cumulative change of these institutional arrangements. These structure-defying and structure-transforming solutions may in turn go in alternative directions. They may mark the initial moves in different trajectories of structural change.

Thus, the reach toward a recognition of the empirical and defensible character of the rights of choice should be simply the first step in a two-step movement. The second step, following closely upon the first, would be the legal imagination and construction of alternative pluralisms: the exploration, in programmatic argument or in experimental reform, of one or another sequence of institutional change. Each sequence would redefine the rights, and the interests and ideals they serve, in the course of realising them more effectively. Contemporary legal theory and doctrine and substantive law itself, almost never take this second step. Theirs is a striking instance of arrested development.

The failure to turn legal analysis into institutional imagination – the major consequence of the arrested development of legal thought – has special meaning and poignancy in the United States. For surely one of the flaws in American civilisation has been the effort to bar the institutional structure of the country against effective challenge; to see America's 'scheme of ordered liberty' as a definitive escape from the old history of classes and ideologies; to refuse to recognise that the spiritual and political ideals of a civilisation remain fastened to the special practices and institutions representing them in fact. Experimentalism has been the most defensible part of American exceptionalism; yet only under the pressure of extreme crisis have Americans brought the experimentalist impulse to bear upon their institutions. Those American thinkers have been the greatest who, like Jefferson and Dewey, tried to convince their contemporaries to trade in some bad American exceptionalism for some good American experimentalism. Those periods of American history have been the most significant when interests became entangled in ideals because both ideals and interests collided with institutional arrangements.

STRUCTURAL BUT EPISODIC INTERVENTION

What force arrests the development of legal thought in the move from the discovery of the institutional indeterminacy of free economies, societies, and polities to the exploration of their diversity of possible institutional forms? We can shed an oblique but revealing light on this riddle by reconsidering it from the perspective of what has come to be known in American law as the problem of complex enforcement and structural injunctions. Although the procedural device has developed more fully in the United States than anywhere else, the opportunity it exploits in the relation of law to society is fast becoming universal. The new mode of procedural intervention seems like a natural extension and instrument of the central idea of contemporary law. Nevertheless, the incongruities of its theory and practice makes the arrested development of this idea all the more startling.

Alongside the traditional style of adjudication, with its emphasis upon the structure-preserving assignment of rights among individual litigants, there has emerged a different adjudicative practice, with agents, methods, and goals different from those of the traditional style. The agents of this alternative practice are collective rather than individual although they may be represented by individual litigants. The class-action lawsuit is the most straightforward tool of this redefinition of agents.

The aim of the intervention is to reshape an organisation or a localised area of social practice frustrating the effective enjoyment of rights. The characteristic circumstance of frustration is one in which the organisation or the practice under scrutiny has seen the rise of disadvantage and marginalisation that their victims are powerless to escape. Subjugation, localised and therefore remediable, is the paradigmatic evil addressed by the reconstructive intervention.

The method is the effort to advance more deeply into the causal background of social life than traditional adjudication would countenance, reshaping the arrangements found to be most immediately and powerfully responsible for the questioned evil. Thus, the remedy may require a court to intervene in a school, a prison, a school system, or a voting district, and to reform and administer the organisation over a period of time. Complex enforcement will demand a more intimate and sustained combination of prescriptive argument and causal inquiry than has been characteristic of lawyers' reasoning.

The basic problem in the theory and practice of structural injunctions is the difficulty of making sense of their limits. Once we begin to penetrate the causal background of contested practices and powers why should we stop so close to the surface? The evils of unequal education for different races, for example, may soon lead an American structural reform in one direction to question the legitimacy of local financial responsibility for public schools and in another direction to challenge the institutional arrangements, such as subcontracting and temporary hiring, that help reproduce an underclass by segmenting the labour force. The more circumscribed corrective intervention is likely to prove ineffective. If causal efficacy is the standard of remedial success, one foray into the structural background of rights-frustration should lead to another. Once we start to tinker with relatively peripheral organisations such as prisons and asylums and to reshape them in the image of ideals imputed to substantive law, why should we not keep going until we reach firms and bureaucracies, families and local governments? As we deepened the reach and extended the scope of intervention, the reconstructive activities of complex enforcement would become evermore ambitious, exercising greater powers, employing bigger staffs, and consuming richer resources.

THE MISSING AGENT

None of this, of course, will happen. It will not happen because no society, not even the United States, will allow a vanguard of lawyers and judges to reconstruct its institutions little by little under the transparent disguise of interpreting the law. The mass of working people may be asleep. The educated and propertied classes are not. They will not allow their fate to be determined by a closed cadre of priestly reformers lacking in self-restraint. They will put these reformers in their place, substituting for them successors who no longer need to be put in their place.

The deepening of the reach and the broadening of the scope of complex enforcement would soon outrun the political legitimacy of the judiciary and exhaust its practical and cognitive resources. Moreover, in the name of the mandate to intervene the better to secure the effective enjoyment of rights, judges would usurp an increasing portion of the real power of popular self-government.

So what should the judges do, and what do they do in fact? Judges in the United States have sometimes seemed to want to do as much as they could get way with: better some penetration of the structural background to subjugation than none; better marginal social organisations than no organisations at all. The difficulty arises from the disproportion between the reconstructive mission and its institutional agent. Complex enforcement is both structural and episodic. The work of structural and episodic intervention seems required if we are to ensure the effective enjoyment of rights and execute the mandate of substantive law. It is a necessary procedural complement, not a casual afterthought to the genius of contemporary law. But who should execute such structural and episodic work in contemporary democratic government?

No branch of present-day presidential or parliamentary regimes seems well equipped, by reason of political legitimacy or practical capability, to do it. The majority-based government of the parliamentary system, or the executive branch of the presidential regime, cannot reinterpret rights and reshape rights-based arrangements in particular corners of social life without danger to the freedom of citizens. Moreover, they would soon find themselves distracted and demoralised by countless forms of petty anxiety and resistance. The administrative agencies or civil service might have more detachment and expertise but correspondingly less authority in the choice of a reconstructive direction or in the exercise of a power free to forge singular solutions to localised problems. Legislatures and parliaments would become both despotic and ineffective if they were to deal, in an individualised and episodic manner, with structural problems and institutional rearrangements. The judiciary lacks both the practical capability and the political legitimacy to restructure, and to manage during restructuring, the deserving objects of complex enforcement. Its unsuitability to the task will be all the more manifest if the frustration of enjoyment of rights by intractable disadvantage turns out to be a common incident of social life, and if the cure demands an increasingly invasive reach into the background of practices and institutions.

The truth is that no part of present-day government is well suited, by virtue of practical capacity or political intervention, to undertake the job of structural and episodic reconstruction. The mission lacks – as every novel and serious mission in the world does – its proper agent. The best response is then to forge the new agent: another branch of government, another power in the state, designed, elected, and funded with the express charge of carrying out this distinctive, rights-ensuring work. Such a move, however, would demand the very openness to institutional experimentalism in which contemporary law and contemporary democracies have proved so markedly deficient. It would require us, as lawyers and as citizens, to complete the move from the accomplished first step of insistence upon the effectiveness of the enjoyment of rights to the missing second step of institutional reimagination and reconstruction.

In the absence of such an extension of the cast of available agents, any of the existing, somewhat unsuitable agents might accept or refuse the work, and then, having accepted it, push it as far as it wanted or could. In the United States, the judiciary, especially the federal judiciary, has been this incongruous, sometime, and half-hearted agent. In other countries it could be any other power in the state. From this marriage of the indispensable work to the unsuitable agent there arises the implicit theory of the structural injunctions in American law. This theory requires us to split the difference between two persuasive and incompatible propositions: the maxim that we must carry out the mandate of substantive law whether or not we have available the right agents and instruments, and the contrasting maxim that the implementation of law must take place under the discipline of institutional propriety and capability.

Thus the problem of complex enforcement sheds a double light upon the arrested development of contemporary legal thought. It shows how fidelity to law and to its imputed ideals may drive, unwittingly and on a small scale, into the institutional experiments that we have refused straightforwardly to imagine and to achieve. It also demonstrates how our failure to take the second step disorients and inhibits our small-time reconstructive work. This chapter in the history of contemporary law wonderfully illustrates the combination of self-concealment and self-disclosure in a ruling vision.

...

AIMS OF A REVISED PRACTICE OF LEGAL ANALYSIS

Implicit in my discussion of rationalising legal analysis are a series of connected standards by which to guide and to assess the redirection of legal thought outside adjudication. These standards converge to yield the idea of legal analysis as institutional imagination.

Thus, the method we need should be free of the taint of institutional fetishism and structure fetishism. Institutional fetishism is the identification of abstract institutional conceptions like the market economy or representative democracy with a particular repertory of contingent arrangements. Structure fetishism is its higher-order counterpart: the failure to recognise that the institutional and imaginative orders of social life differ in their entrenchment as well as in their Content: that is to say, in the relation to the structure-defying and structure- transforming freedom of action and insight they constrain. The method should help us identify and resolve the internal instability characteristic of programmatic positions in contemporary law and politics: the conflict between the commitment to defining ideals, and the acquiescence in arrangements that frustrate the realisation of those ideals, or impoverish their meaning. Consequently, it should seize upon the internal relation between thinking about ideals or interests and thinking about institutions or practices. When so doing, it can gain energy and direction from a larger conception of the democratic project as well as from more particular professed ideas and recognised interests, for the democratic project, properly interpreted, is both our most powerful family of ideals and our most promising way to reconcile our devotion to these ideals with the pursuit of our material interests.

To these ends, the method should make good on the capacity of law and legal thought to move at the level of full detail in representing the relation of practices and institutions to interests and ideals, and in connecting the realities of power to the discourse of aspiration. To mobilise these resources, it must rid itself of the anti-analogical prejudice; of the illusory belief in rational reconstruction as the necessary and sufficient antidote to arbitrariness in law; of the confusions and equivocations of conservative reformism, particularly in the variant of pessimistic progressive reformism; and of the obsession with judges and the ways they decide cases. It must elect the citizenry as its primary and ultimate interlocutor. It must imagine its work to be that of informing the conversation in a democracy about its present and alternative futures.

MAPPING AND CRITICISM

These aims come together in the practice of legal analysis as institutional imagination. This practice has two, dialectically linked moments: mapping and criticism. Give the name *mapping* to the suitably revised version of the low-level, spiritless analogical activity, the form of legal analysis that leaves the law an untransformed heap. Mapping is the attempt to describe in detail the legally defined institutional microstructure of society in relation to its legally articulated ideals. Call the second moment of this analytic practice *criticism:* the revised version of what the rationalistic jurists deride as the turning of legal analysis into ideological conflict. Its task is to explore the interplay between the detailed institutional arrangements of society as represented in law, and the professed ideals or programmes these arrangements frustrate and make real.

Mapping is the exploration of the detailed institutional structure of society, as it is legally defined. It would he naive positivism to suppose that this structure is uncontroversially manifest, and can be portrayed apart from theoretical preconceptions. The crucial point of mapping is to produce a detailed, although fragmentary, legal-institutional analysis replacing one such set of preconceptions by another.

The perspective to be adopted is the standpoint of the second moment of the revised practice of legal analysis I am sketching: the moment of criticism. Thus, the two moments connect closely; they are related – to use one vocabulary – dialectically – and to use another – internally. Mapping serving the purpose of criticism is an analysis exhibiting the formative institutions of society and its enacted dogmas about human association as a distinct and surprising structure and, above all, as a structure that can be revised part by part. The established system of such arrangements and beliefs both constrains the realisation of our professed social ideals and recognised group interests and gives them much of their tacit meaning.

The preconceptions to be replaced negate the possibility or the significance criticism. Such preconceptions present the greater part of any extended a received body of law and legal understandings as an expression of a cohesive moral and political vision, or of a set of practical necessities, or of a lawlike evolutionary sequence.

One set of such anti-critical abstractions exercising especially great influence in contemporary law and legal thought is the second-order Lochnerism explored earlier. Remember that the earlier, cruder, repudiated Lochnerism is the contrast between a law that is just there, prepolitically, as the built-in legal structure of an accepted and established type of economic and governmental organisation – call it liberal capitalist democracy or whatever – and a law that represents the unprincipled, faction-driven, redistributive intervention of government in this core legal structure. That is the Lochnerism American notables – and their Europe counterparts – rejected, although they still have not rejected it completely and unequivocally. The Lochnerism that survives, generating a steady stream of abstractions that prevent the work of mapping-criticism, is the Lochnerism meant to distinguish concessions to factional interest or outlook from expressions of impersonal moral and political vision or practical necessity. The expressions must be rescued from the concessions, and it is on the basis of invocations of the former and denunciations of the latter that rationalising legal analysis does its work.

The language of contemporary politics commonly superimposes such reassuring ideological abstractions, more or less directly, upon low-level promises to particular organised interests. At every turn it becomes impossible to tell whether the abstractions serve as an ideological disguise for the pursuit of the interests, or whether, on the contrary, the pursuit of the interests is being disoriented by the abstractions. What we chiefly lack is what should be the very heart of political discourse: the middle ground of alternative trajectories of institutional and policy change. To help develop this middle ground is one of the tasks of the combined practice of mapping and criticism. A requirement for the accomplishment of this task is that we resist the impulse to rationalise or to idealise the institutions and laws we actually have.

What type of insight may one hope to develop through the practice of mapping? Consider the example of the relation of the traditional property right to the many exceptions that begin to surround it. The property right, bringing together many faculties assigned to the same right-holder, is the very model of the modern idea of right, and the central mechanism for the allocation of decentralised claims to capital. Yet we find in contemporary legal systems many areas of law and practice that settle matters in ways departing from the logic of this property entitlement. In agriculture, for example, there may be a partnership between the government and the family farmer decomposing the property right and limiting the absoluteness of the property owner's right in exchange for varieties of governmental support. In the defence-procurement industry, and even more under the conditions of war capitalism, a similar decomposition in the form of collaboration between public power and the private producer may occur. In the development of contemporary capital markets we see a continuous creation of new markets in particular faculties abstracted out of the comprehensive property entitlement. The situation then begins to look like this: the main mechanism is surrounded by a growing number of exceptions. However, even if traditional property had been eviscerated more than it in fact has been, it would continue to occupy the vital role of holding the space that any other generalised form of decentralised allocation of capital would hold. It holds the place that would be occupied by the alternative method of decentralised capital allocation already prefigured in the current exceptions to the unified property right. This is a typical example of the type of combination of sameness and variety one might hope to discover through mapping.

The second moment of this revised practice of legal analysis is criticism. Criticism explores the disharmonies between the professed social ideals and programmatic commitments of society, as well as the recognised group interests, and the detailed institutional arrangements that not only constrain the realisation of those ideals, programmes, and interests, but also give them their developed meaning.

The relation between criticism and mapping can now come more clearly into focus. Mapping provides materials for criticism, and criticism sets the perspective and the agenda for mapping. Nothing in my account of the revised practice of legal analysis defines the extent to which criticism can itself be informed or guided by a more context-independent type of moral and political argument. Rather than addressing that issue now, however, it is enough to recognise how little we need a prior and confident view of it, to begin revising the practice of legal analysis in this way and to begin practising the revision. The reoriented approach may prove compatible with a broad range of positions about our ability to connect with a less history-bound mode of judgement. Moreover, the new practice may itself have something to teach us about the relative merits of different views of authority beyond context in moral and political disputes.

Consider now some lines along which we might work out the anti-rationalising response to the circumstance of contemporary law and legal thought. The first task – the task of the mapping moment – is to understand the existing institutional situation as the complex and contradictory structure that it really is, as the strange and surprising settlement that you could never guess from abstractions like 'the mixed economy', 'representative democracy', or 'industrial society.' In this view, the jurist should work as an enlarger of the collective sense of reality and possibility. He must imitate the artist who makes the familiar strange, restoring to our understanding of our situation some of the lost and repressed sense of transformative opportunity.

The focus of mapping is the attempt to construct a picture of our institutions – of the government, of the economy, the family – out of the stuff of law and legal doctrine. It is a hard task; the material wears no particular picture on its face. What kind of picture do we want? First, we want a view that defines itself by contrast to the rationalising account. This account – remember – wants to present the stuff of law as tied together in a way that justifies most of it while rejecting a minor part of it. Rational reconstruction in law justifies and interprets the greater part of the law and of the received legal understandings either as the expression of an evolving system of moral and political conceptions or as the outcome of inexorable functional requirements. Affirmatively, the view we want is the view serving the purposes of the second moment of this analytic practice: the moment of criticism, when we focus on the disharmonies of the law and on the way in which the ideal conceptions, expressed in policies and principles, or the group interests represented by programmes and strategies, get truncated in their fulfilment and impoverished in their meaning by their received institutional forms.

I have already offered a number of examples of the mapping exercise: the partial alternatives to the unified property idea that we can already witness in current law and practice; the relation of traditional rights adjudication to the structural but episodic intervention of complex enforcement; and, more generally, the dialectical organisation of contemporary law in each of its branches as a duality of rights of personal choice and popular self-government and rights designed to ensure the reality of individual and collective self-determination.

Do we need a full-blown theory, a practice of social explanation, a set of programmatic ideas, and a conception of the relation between programmatic thinking and social explanation to inform mapping? The answer is yes and no. We need such ideas fully to develop and elucidate the revised practice of legal analysis. But we need not have such a theory to begin the mapping.

We already have two points of departure at hand. One starting point is the effort to radicalise the professed social ideals or party programmes, to take them beyond their existing institutional constraints, and to change their meaning in the course of doing so. Another point of departure is the negativistic work of demolishing the rationalising conceptions and interpretations of contemporary law.

Thus, this mapping involves no naive acceptance of the low-level, analogical, glossatorial picture of law as an unshapen, undigested heap. It demands a radical redrawing of that picture from the standpoint of the precommitments of criticism. The moments of mapping and criticism form a dialectical unity. We can nevertheless claim for the low-level, analogical conception of law certain advantages. It presents extant law and received legal understanding free – or freer – from the rationalising spell and from the special outlook of the Madisonian notables, ever anxious for a view of law on which, as judges or publicists, they can act with the least embarrassment.

Is criticism more likely to occur under conditions in which mapping dominates the legal culture, or in situations in which rationalisation does? To answer this question, we must begin by remembering that mapping and criticism are indissoluble; they are aspects or moments of the same practice. Just as mapping provides materials for criticism, it is already done with the interests of criticism in mind. Moreover, as a practical matter, the formation of such a transformative analytic practice is possible only in the historical circumstance in which we can rebel against runaway rationalisation. For, even as rationalising analysis in law and in the corresponding areas of political and social thought, mythologises our institutions, it also generalises our ideals. It thus sets the stage on which the mapper-critic can go to work.

Further Reading

On American Legal Realism and American Jurisprudence in general: Summers 1982, Twining 1985, Duxbury 1995.

On the critical legal studies movement: Hutchinson 1989.

For selected American critical legal studies essays: Kairys 1990.

For selected British critical legal studies essays: Grigg-Spall and Ireland 1992.

For criticism of the CLS movement: Finnis 1987b.

Questions

1. Are you a sceptic about rules, or principles, or facts, or all, or none? Why, or why not?

2. 'The apparent objectivity of law is a product of disguised contradictions.' Discuss.

3. 'So called Realist and Critical Legal Theories might be more real and critical than other theories but never do or could amount to legal theories in themselves.' Discuss.

8 Law and Adjudication: Dworkin's Critique of Positivism

James Penner

While we have seen in previous chapters that there are different versions of positivism, the success of Hart's criticism of his predecessors, in particular Austin, and the compelling way in which he presented his own theory, made Hart's characterisation of positivism the one which has since attracted the most attention in the English speaking world; in a sense, for those pursuing an anti-positivist line, Hart's theory has become the 'one to beat'. Of all Hart's critics, his successor in the Chair of Jurisprudence at Oxford, Ronald Dworkin, has engaged in the most sustained, indeed decades long, project of showing how the central elements of Hart's positivism, and moreover, any 'Hartian' version of positivism, are flawed. Dworkin's claims have ranged from straightforward arguments that Hart has mistaken the facts of legal practice, to arguments that basic concepts of his theory, like the rule of recognition, are unsound, to the claim that the project of positivism itself, and in particular Hart's rendering of it, is actually incoherent.

Before beginning to assess Dworkin's philosophy of law, a couple of things should be borne in mind. First, most people find Dworkin a very engaging and persuasive writer. However, it is not always easy to say with precision exactly what Dworkin believes or intends about certain issues given his propensity to revisit these issues many times in his large body of work. He has framed his views in many different ways, and it is not always easy to say with assurance that Dworkin's actual view is this rather than that. Moreover, Dworkin has proven to be an astoundingly good respondent to the various criticisms that have been made of his own work, and much of his writing amounts to the careful and compelling re-casting of his views to blunt or deflect what can appear, at first glance at least, to be devastating blows; this, of course, only compounds the problem of determining with assurance what, at a detailed level, Dworkin actually holds. By and large, this creative engagement of Dworkin with his critics has been a hugely productive engine of legal philosophy. However, in some respects, it has removed the legal philosophical debate to some of the most arcane, even baroque, exercises in inward-looking interpretation to determine 'what Hart *really* meant' in *The Concept of Law* and 'what Dworkin *really* means' by 'legal principle' or 'law as integrity' and so on. Here we try to avoid entering into those realms, on the following principle: every philosopher makes mistakes. Plato and Aristotle made mistakes; Kant and Hegel made mistakes. Hart made mistakes too, and so has Dworkin. (One of the testaments to Hart's greatness as a philosopher was his willingness to admit where he had gone wrong.) Therefore, there is no need to go searching in anyone's body of work for mistakes that are somehow *difficult* to detect, in the sense that they can only be revealed by interpreting the work in some terribly demanding way, for example by showing that there is some deep tension in Hart's or Dworkin's methodological presuppositions. We will find lots to chew on simply by looking at what these authors more or less literally say and assessing the arguments they more or less literally present. To go on in this way is not to deny that deeper problems or contradictions may lie in a philosopher's work, nor that these deeper things may not be of great importance. But it is to take these authors' work seriously according to their own self-presentation. Hart worked and Dworkin works within a tradition of philosophy sometimes called the Anglo-American analytic or analytical tradition in which a great premium is placed upon clarity and the straightforward elaboration of one's views. So it seems reasonable to read, in the first instance at least, their works in the way they were intended, as attempts to more or less literally say what they mean.

In this chapter and the next we will be looking at Dworkin's theory of the nature of law. Because Dworkin developed it in response to Hart's positivism, it begins with a rather negative 'moment' and then increasingly turns to the more positive moment in which he steps forward to reveal his own understanding of law (though his criticisms of positivism continue to inform the account throughout). Dworkin's work can be presented in three stages (which I've largely drawn from Raz 1986), though take this division as provisional and after exploring the body of Dworkin's work decide for yourself whether it really works.

The first stage, roughly what Dworkin produced in the 1960s, was his 'rules and principles' critique of Hart's positivism. Here, in his paper 'Is Law a System of Rules?' (also published under the title 'The Model of Rules I'), Dworkin argued that Hart's positivism failed because his rule of recognition failed to account for the role of principles, as opposed to rules, in the law. Here he foreshadowed his project of producing a better general theory, but it was not outlined in assessable detail. In the next stage, which seems to fit nicely into the decade of the 70s, Dworkin took on the sustained project of developing his alternative theory, the most systematic statement of which is found in his paper 'Hard Cases'. Here Dworkin elaborated the most controversial and interesting theses of his theory of law: that judges do not have any significant discretion in deciding cases where the law is uncertain, that there is always a right answer to a legal question, and that judges are engaged in a project which requires them to approach their decision-making task in the spirit of philosophers engaged in elaborating and defending theories about what is morally and politically just. In this paper he also introduced the figure of Hercules, a judge with unlimited intelligence, knowledge, and time to think out problems, whose method of deciding cases is intended to serve as an idealised model of what judges (or at least common law judges) really do. In the 80s, Dworkin entered the 'third stage' of developing his views; he altered or enhanced his theory (depending upon your viewpoint), but definitely took it in a different direction; he took what is now sometimes called the 'interpretive turn'. It is a commonplace that much of what lawyers and judges do is 'interpretation': they interpret statutes and judicial decisions, and largely on the basis of what they make of them, how they interpret them, they decide how to act in the case before them. In short, finding the law to apply in the case before one is a matter of interpreting what one finds in the books, statute books and books of cases. Dworkin seized upon this aspect of lawyerly practice to argue that, properly understood, legal interpretation was akin to literary interpretation, in particular that the goal of legal interpretation was to make of the law the best law that it could be (on certain criteria of what 'best' amounts to) in the same way that (according to Dworkin) the goal of literary interpretation, or the interpretation of art generally, was to reveal the work of art as the best work of art it could be within the genre to which it was taken to belong. In this way, Dworkin characterised the theory-making judge of 'Hard Cases' as a kind of literary critic, and making a judicial decision as a bit like adding another chapter to a novel in progress.

In this chapter, we will discuss the first two stages of Dworkin's work, the 60s and 70s stages, in which he laid out his basic disquiet with positivism, and tried to show how it was possible to do better.

At this stage it is worthwhile reviewing Chapter 4 to refresh your memory about Hart's theory of law.

Although some of the criticisms Dworkin makes of Hart in 'Is Law a System of Rules?' were foreshadowed or made in part by others, this essay was immediately noticed because carefully working his way through the *implications* of these criticisms as he did, Dworkin appeared to show that the whole positivist position was fundamentally unsound, truly rotten at its core, because he appeared to show that the Rule of Recognition didn't *work*.

Now, how did Dworkin show that? The argument proceeds in several steps.

Step 1 – The characterisation of positivism: According to Dworkin, positivism relies upon a sharp distinction between what is law and what is not. If there is a law that you can't park on double-yellow lines, then you have legal reason for not doing so. If there is no such law, you don't. In particular, positivists draw a distinction between legal reasons and moral reasons. If there is a law prohibiting murder, then you have a legal duty not to commit murder. You also have a moral duty not to do so, but that is not because there is any law not to commit murder, but because murder is wicked. Morality and law are in this way distinct. You may have a moral duty to rescue a small child drowning in a stream, but no legal duty to do so, because there is no law that you must. Conversely, you may have a legal duty not to smoke cannabis, even though you have no moral duty not to do so. While positivists generally regard it as a deficiency of the law when it is seriously out of step with morality, they insist that the two are distinct. But in order to maintain this distinction, there must be a way of identifying what the law is which doesn't involve recourse to moral evaluation. Obviously, if a positivist were asked – 'what is the law on x (murder, smoking cannabis, what have you)?', and the answer was: 'The law is whatever morality dictates' then no such distinction between what the law says and what morality says would exist. So the first step of Dworkin's argument, in part (a) of the passage below, is to insist that positivists need some method to identify law; he then draws the implications of (a) in parts (b) and (c) of the passage.

Dworkin (1977, 17)

Positivism has a few central and organizing propositions ... These key tenets may be stated as follows:

(a) The law of a community is a set of special rules used by the community directly or indirectly for the purpose of determining which behavior will be punished or coerced by the public power. These special rules can be identified or distinguished by specific criteria, by tests having to do not with their content but with their *pedigree* or the manner in which they were adopted or developed. These tests of pedigree can be used to distinguish valid legal rules from spurious legal rules (rules which lawyers and litigants wrongly argue are rules of law) and also from other sorts of social rules (generally lumped together as 'moral rules') that the community follows but does not enforce through public power.

(b) The set of these valid legal rules is exhaustive of 'the law', so that if someone's case is not clearly covered by such a rule (because there is none that seems appropriate, or those that seem appropriate are vague, or for some other reason) then that case cannot be decided by 'applying the law'. It must be decided by some official, like a judge, 'exercising his discretion', which means reaching beyond the law for some other sort of standard to guide him in manufacturing a fresh legal rule or supplementing an old one.

(c) To say that someone has a 'legal obligation' is to say that his case falls under a valid legal rule that requires him to do or to forbear from doing something. (To say he has a legal right, or has a legal power of some sort, or a legal privilege or immunity, is to assert, in a shorthand way, that others have actual or hypothetical legal obligations to act or not to act in certain ways touching him.) In the absence of such a valid rule there is no legal obligation; it follows that when a judge decides an issue by exercising his discretion, he is not enforcing a legal right as to that issue.

Step 2 – Having thus laid out the core tenets of positivism, Dworkin then begins his attack by arguing that the positivist's idea of law as a system of rules is flawed, because the law contains more than rules: it also contains 'non-rule' standards, in particular, principles.

Dworkin (1977, 22–28)

[W]hen lawyers reason or dispute about legal rights and obligations, particularly in those hard cases when our problems with these concepts seem most acute, they make use of standards that do not function as rules, but operate differently as principles, policies, and other sorts of standards. Positivism, I shall argue, is a model of and for a system of rules, and its central notion of a single fundamental test for law forces us to miss the important roles of these standards which are not rules ... Most often I shall use the term 'principle' generically ... occasionally, however, I shall be more precise, and distinguish between principles and policies ... I call a 'policy' that kind of standard that sets out a goal to be reached, generally an improvement in some economic, political, or social feature of the community, (though some goals are negative, in that they stipulate some present feature is to be protected from adverse change). I call a 'principle' a standard that is to be observed, not because it will advance or secure an economic, political, or social situation deemed desirable, but because it is a requirement of justice or fairness or some other dimension of morality.

...

My immediate purpose, however, is to distinguish principles in the generic sense from rules, and I shall start by collecting some examples of the former. The examples I offer are chosen haphazardly; almost any case in a law school casebook would provide examples that would serve as well. In 1889 a New York court, in the famous case of *Riggs v. Palmer*, had to decide whether an heir named in the will of his grandfather could inherit under that will, even though he had murdered his grandfather to do so. The court began its reasoning with this admission: 'It is quite true that statutes regulating the making, proof and effect of wills, and the devolution of property, if literally construed, and if their force and effect can in no way and under no circumstances be controlled or modified, give this property to the murderer.' But the court continued to note that 'all laws as well as all contracts may be controlled in their operation and effect by general, fundamental maxims of the common law. No one shall be permitted to profit by his own fraud, or to take advantage of his own wrong, or to found any claim upon his own iniquity, or to acquire property by his own crime.' The murderer did not receive his inheritance.

In 1960, a New Jersey court was faced, in *Henningsen v. Bloomfield Motors, Inc.* with the important question of whether (or how much) an automobile manufacturer may limit his liability in case the automobile is defective. Henningsen had bought a car, and signed a contract which said that the manufacturer's liability for defects was limited to 'making good' defective parts – 'this warranty being expressly in lieu of all other warranties, obligations or liabilities.' Henningsen argued that, at least in the circumstances of his case, the manufacturer ought not to be protected by this limitation, and ought to be liable for the medical and other expenses of persons injured in a crash. He was not able to point to any statute, or to any established rule of law, that prevented the manufacturer from standing on the contract. The court nevertheless agreed with Henningsen. At various points in the court's argument the following appeals to standards are made: (a) '[W]e must keep in mind the general principle that, in the absence of fraud, one who does not choose to read a contract before signing it cannot later relieve himself of its burdens.' (b) 'In applying that principle, the basic tenet of freedom of competent parties to contract is a factor of importance.' (c) 'Freedom of contract is not such an immutable doctrine as to admit of no qualification in the area in which we are concerned.' (d) 'In a society such as ours, where the automobile is a common and necessary adjunct of daily life, and where its use is so fraught with danger to the driver, the passengers and the public, the manufacturer is under a special obligation in connection with the construction, promotion and sale of his cars. Consequently, the courts must examine purchase agreements closely to see if consumer and public interests are treated fairly.' (e) '[I]s there any principle which is more familiar or more firmly embedded in the history of Anglo-American law than the basic doctrine that the courts will not permit themselves to be used as instruments of inequity and injustice?' (f) 'More specifically the courts generally refuse to lend themselves to the enforcement of a 'bargain' in which one party has unjustly taken advantage of the economic necessities of other ...'

The standards set out in these quotations are not the sort we think of as legal rules. They seem very different from propositions like 'The maximum legal speed on the turnpike is sixty miles an hour' or 'A will is invalid unless signed by three witnesses'. They are different because they are legal principles rather than legal rules.

The difference between legal principles and legal rules is a logical distinction. Both sets of standards point to particular decisions about legal obligation in particular circumstances, but they differ in the character of the direction they give. Rules are applicable in an all-or-nothing fashion. If the facts a rule stipulates are given, then either the rule is valid, in which case the answer it supplies must be accepted, or it is not, in which case it contributes nothing to the decision.

This all-or-nothing is seen most plainly if we look at the way rules operate, not in law, but in some enterprise they dominate – a game, for example. In baseball a rule provides that if the batter has had three strikes, he is out. An official cannot consistently acknowledge that this is an accurate statement of a baseball rule, and decide that a batter who has had three strikes is not out. Of course, a rule may have exceptions (the batter who has taken three strikes is not out if the catcher drops the third strike). However, an accurate statement of the rule would take this exception into account, and any that did not would be incomplete. If the list of exceptions is very large, it would be too clumsy to repeat them each time the rule is cited; there is, however, no reason in theory why they could not all be added on, and the more that are, the more accurate is the statement of the rule.

If we take baseball rules as a model, we find that rules of law, like the rule that a will is invalid unless signed by three witnesses, fit the model well. If the requirement of three witnesses is a valid legal rule, then it cannot be that a will has been signed by only two witnesses and is valid. The rule might have exceptions, but if it does then it is inaccurate and incomplete to state the rule so simply, without enumerating the exceptions. In theory, at least, the exceptions could all be listed, and the more of them that are, the more complete is the statement of the rule.

But this is not the way the sample principles in the quotations operate. Even those which look most like rules do not set out legal consequences that follow automatically when the conditions provided are met. We say that our law respects the principle that no man may profit from his own wrong, but we do not mean that the law never permits a man to profit from wrongs he commits. In fact, people often profit, perfectly legally, from their legal wrongs. The most notorious case is adverse possession – if I trespass on your land long enough, some day I will gain a right to cross your land whenever I please. There are many less dramatic examples. If a man leaves one job, breaking a contract, to take a much higher paying job, he may have to pay damages to his first employer, but he is usually entitled to keep his new salary. If a man jumps bail and crosses state lines to make a brilliant investment in another state, he may be sent back to jail, but he will keep his profits. We do not treat these – and countless other counter-instances that can easily be imagined – as showing that the principle about profiting from one's wrongs is not a principle of our legal system, or that it is incomplete and needs qualifying exceptions. We do not treat counter-instances as exceptions (at least not exceptions in the way in which a catcher's dropping the third strike is an exception) because we could not hope to capture these counter-instances simply by a more extended statement of the principle. They are not, even in theory, subject to enumeration, because we would have to include not only these cases (like adverse possession) in which some institution has already provided that profit can be gained through a wrong, but also those numberless imaginary cases in which we know in advance that the principle would not hold. Listing some of these might sharpen our sense of the principle's weight (I shall mention that dimension in a moment), but it would not make for a more accurate or complete statement of the principle.

A principle like 'No man may profit from his own wrong' does not even purport to set out conditions that make its application necessary. Rather, it states a reason that argues in one direction, but does not necessitate a particular decision. If a man has or is about to receive something, as a direct result of something illegal he did to get it, then that is a reason which the law will take into account in deciding whether he should keep it. There may be other principles or policies arguing in the other direction – a policy of securing title, for example, or a principle limiting punishment to what the legislature has stipulated. If so our principle may not prevail, but that does not mean that it is not a principle of our legal system, because in the next case, when these contravening considerations are absent or less weighty, the principle may be decisive. All that is meant, when we say that a particular principle is a principle of our law, is that the principle is one which officials must take into account, if it is relevant, as a consideration inclining in one direction or another.

...

This first difference between rules and principles entails another. Principles have a dimension that rules do not – the dimension of weight or importance. When principles intersect (the policy of protecting automobile consumers intersecting with principles of freedom of contract, for example), one who must resolve the conflict has to take into account the relative weight of each. This cannot be, of course, an exact measurement, and the judgment that a particular principle or policy is more important than another will often be a controversial one. Nevertheless, it is an integral part of the concept of a principle that it has this dimension, that it makes sense to ask how important or how weighty it is.

Rules do not have this dimension. We can speak of rules as being functionally important or unimportant (the baseball rule that three strikes are out is more important than the rule that runners may advance on a balk, because the game would be much more changed with the first rule altered than the second). In this sense, one legal rule may be more important than another because it has a greater or more important role in regulating behavior. But we cannot say that one rule is more important than another within the system of rules, so that when two rules conflict one supersedes the other by virtue of its greater weight. If two rules conflict, one of them cannot be a valid rule. The decision as to which is valid, and which must be abandoned or recast, must be made by appealing to considerations beyond the rules themselves. A legal system might regulate such conflicts by other rules, which prefer the rule enacted by the higher authority, or the rule enacted later, or the more specific rule, or something of that sort. A legal system may also prefer the rule supported by the more important principles. (Our own legal system uses both of these techniques.)

It is not always clear from the form of a standard whether it is a rule or a principle. 'A will is invalid unless signed by three witnesses' is not very different in form from 'A man may not profit from his own wrong', but one who knows something of American law knows that he must take the first as stating a rule and the second as stating a principle. In many cases the distinction is difficult to make – it may not have been settled how the standard should operate, and this issue may itself be a focus of controversy. The first amendment to the United States Constitution contains the provision that Congress shall not abridge freedom of speech. Is this a rule, so that if a particular law does abridge freedom of speech, it follows that it is unconstitutional? Those who claim that the first amendment is 'an absolute' say that it must be taken in this way, that is, as a rule. Or does it merely state a principle, so that when an abridgement of speech is discovered, it is unconstitutional unless the context presents some other policy or principle which in the circumstances is weighty enough to permit the abridgement? That is the position of those who argue for what is called the 'clear and present danger' test or some other form of 'balancing'.

Sometimes a rule and a principle can play much the same role, and the difference between them is almost a matter of form alone. The first section of the Sherman Act states that every contract in restraint of trade shall be void. The Supreme Court had to make the decision whether this provision should be treated as a rule in its own terms (striking down every contract 'which restrains trade', which almost any contract does) or as a principle, providing a reason for striking down a contract in absence of effective contrary policies. The Court construed the provision as a rule, but treated that rule as containing the word 'unreasonable' and as prohibiting only 'unreasonable' restraints of trade. This allowed the provision to function logically as a rule (whenever a court finds that the restraint is 'unreasonable' it is bound to hold the contract invalid) and substantially as a principle (a court must take into account a variety of other principles and policies in determining whether a particular restraint in particular economic circumstances is 'unreasonable').

Words like 'reasonable', 'negligent', 'unjust', and 'significant' often perform just this function. Each of these terms makes the application of the rule which contains it depend to some extent upon principles or policies lying beyond the rule, and in this way makes that rule itself more like a principle. But they do not quite turn the rule into a principle, because even the least confining of these terms restricts the *kind* of other principles and policies on which the rule depends. If we are bound by a rule that says that 'unreasonable' contracts are void, or that grossly 'unfair' contracts will not be enforced, much more judgment is required than if the quoted terms were omitted. But suppose a case in which some consideration of policy or principle suggests that a contract should be enforced even though its restraint is not reasonable, or even though it is grossly unfair. Enforcing these contracts would be forbidden by our rules, and thus permitted only if these rules were abandoned or modified. If we were dealing, however, not with a rule but with a policy against enforcing unreasonable contracts, or a principle that unfair contracts ought not to be enforced, the contracts could be enforced without alteration of the law.

Step 3 – With the rules/principles distinction in hand, Dworkin denies that judges in a common law system have any discretion to make new law.

Dworkin (1977, 29–36)

An analysis of the concept of legal obligation must … account for the important role of principles in reaching particular decisions of law. There are two very different tacks we might take:

(a)　We might treat legal principles the way we treat legal rules and say that some principles are binding as law and must be taken into account by judges and lawyers who make decisions of legal obligation. If we took this tack, we should say that in the United States, at least, the 'law' includes principles as well as rules.

(b)　We might, on the other hand, deny that principles can be binding the way some rules are. We would say, instead, that in cases like Riggs or Henningsen the judge reaches beyond the rules that he is bound to apply (reaches, that is, beyond the 'law') for extra-legal principles he is free to follow if he wishes.

One might think that there is not much difference between these two lines of attack, that it is only a verbal question of how one wants to use the word 'law'. But that is a mistake, because the choice between these two accounts has the greatest consequences for an analysis of legal obligation. It is a choice between two *concepts* of a legal principle, a choice we can clarify by comparing it to a choice we might make between two concepts of a legal rule. We sometimes say of someone that he 'makes it a rule' to do something, when we mean that he has chosen to follow a certain practice. We might say that someone has made it a rule, for example, to run a mile before breakfast because he wants to be healthy and believes in a regimen. We do not mean, when we say this, that he is bound by the rule that he must run a mile before breakfast, or even that he regards it as binding upon him. Accepting a rule as binding is something different from making it a rule to do something. If we use Hart's example again, there is a difference between saying that Englishmen make it a rule to see a movie once a week, and saying that the English have a rule that one must see a movie once a week. The second implies that if an Englishman does not follow the rule, he is subject to criticism or censure, but the first does not. The first does not exclude the possibility of a sort of criticism – we can say that one who does not see movies is neglecting his education – but we do not suggest that he is doing something wrong just in not following the rule. If we think of the judges of a community as a group, we could describe the rules of law they follow in these two different ways. We could say, for instance, that in a certain state the judges make it a rule not to enforce wills unless there are three witnesses. This would not imply that the rare judge who enforces such a will is doing anything wrong just for that reason. On the other hand we can say that in that state a rule of law requires judges not to enforce such wills; this does imply that a judge who enforces them is doing something wrong. Hart, Austin and other positivists, of course, would insist on this latter account of legal rules; they would not at all be satisfied with the 'make it a rule' account. It is not a verbal question of which account is right. It is a question of which describes the social situation more accurately. Other important issues turn on which description we accept.

If judges simply 'make it a rule' not to enforce certain contracts, for example, then we cannot say, before the decision, that anyone is 'entitled' to that result, and that proposition cannot enter into any justification we might offer for the decision.

The two lines of attack on principles parallel these two accounts of rules. The first tack treats principles as binding upon judges, so that they are wrong not to apply the principles when they are pertinent. The second tack treats principles as summaries of what most judges 'make it a principle' to do when forced to go beyond the standards that bind them. The choice between these approaches will affect, perhaps even determine, the answer we can give to the question whether the judge in a hard case like Riggs or Henningsen is attempting to enforce pre-existing legal rights and obligations. If we take the first tack, we are still free to argue that because such judges are applying binding legal standards they are enforcing legal rights and obligations. But if we take the second, we are out of court on that issue, and we must acknowledge that when a case is not covered by a clear rule, a judge must exercise his discretion to decide that case, by what amounts to a fresh piece of legislation.

...

Sometimes we use 'discretion' in a weak sense, simply to say that for some reason the standards an official must apply cannot be applied mechanically but demand the use of judgment. We use this weak sense when the context does not already make that clear, when the background our audience assumes does not contain that piece of information. Thus we might say, 'The sergeant's orders left him a great deal of discretion', to those who do not know what the sergeant's orders were or who do not know something that made those orders vague or hard to carry out. It would make perfect sense to add, by way of amplification, that the lieutenant had ordered the sergeant to take his five most experienced men on patrol but that it was hard to determine which were the most experienced.

Sometimes we use the term in a different weak sense, to say only that some official has final authority to make a decision and cannot be reviewed and reversed by any other official. We speak this way when the official is part of a hierarchy of officials structured so that some have higher authority but in which the patterns of authority are different for different classes of decision. Thus we might say that in baseball certain decisions, like the decision whether the ball or the runner reached second base first, are left to the discretion of the second base umpire, if we mean that on this issue the head umpire has no power to substitute his own judgment if he disagrees.

I call both of these senses weak to distinguish them from a stronger sense. We use 'discretion' sometimes not merely to say that an official must use judgment in applying the standards set him by authority, or that no one will review that exercise of judgment, but to say that on some issue he is simply not bound by standards set by the authority in question. In this sense we say that a sergeant has discretion who has been told to pick any five men for patrol he chooses or that a judge in a dog show has discretion to judge airedales before boxers if the rules do not stipulate an order of events. We use this sense not to comment on the vagueness or difficulty of the standards, or on who has the final word in applying them, but on their range and the decisions they purport to control. If the sergeant is told to take the five most experienced men, he does not have discretion in this strong sense because that order purports to govern his decision.

The boxing referee who must decide which fighter has been the more aggressive does not have discretion, in the strong sense, for the same reason ... We must avoid one tempting confusion. The strong sense of discretion is not tantamount to license, and does not exclude criticism. Almost any situation in which a person acts (including those in which there is no question of decision under special authority, and so no question of discretion) makes relevant certain standards of rationality, fairness, and effectiveness ... So we can say that the sergeant who was given discretion (in the strong sense) to pick a patrol did so stupidly or maliciously or carelessly, or that the judge who had discretion in the order of viewing dogs made a mistake because he took boxers first although there were only three airedales and many more boxers. An official's discretion means not that he is free to decide without recourse to standards of sense and fairness, but only that his decision is not controlled by a standard furnished by the particular authority we have in mind when we raise the question of discretion. ... We may now return, with these observations in hand, to the positivists' doctrine of judicial discretion. That doctrine argues that if a case is not controlled by an established rule, the judge must decide it by exercising discretion. We want to examine this doctrine and to test its bearing on our treatment of principles.

...

Hart ... says that when the judge's discretion is in play, we can no longer speak of his being bound by standards, but must speak rather of what standards he 'characteristically uses'. Hart thinks that when judges have discretion, the principles they cite must be treated on our second approach, as what courts 'make it a principle' to do. It therefore seems that positivists, at least sometimes, take their doctrine in the third, strong sense of discretion. In that sense it does bear on the treatment of principles; indeed, in that sense it is nothing less than a restatement of our second approach. It is the same thing to say that when a judge runs out of rules he has discretion, in the sense that he is not bound by any standards from the authority of law, as to say that the legal standards judges cite other than rules are not binding on them.

So we must examine the doctrine of judicial discretion in the strong sense. (I shall henceforth use the term 'discretion' in that sense.) Do the principles judges cited in cases like *Riggs* or *Henningsen* control their decisions, as the sergeant's orders to take the most experienced men or the referee's duty to choose the more aggressive fighter control the decisions of these officials? What arguments could a positivist supply to show that they do not?

(1) A positivist might argue that principles cannot be binding or obligatory. That would be a mistake. It is always a question, of course, whether any particular principle is *in fact* binding upon some legal official. But there is nothing in the logical character of a principle that renders it incapable of binding him. Suppose that the judge in *Henningsen* had failed to take any account of the principle that automobile manufacturers have a special obligation to their consumers, or the principle that the courts seek to protect those whose bargaining position is weak, but had simply decided for the defendant by citing the principle of freedom of contract without more. His critics would not have been content to point out that he had not taken account of considerations that other judges have been attending to for some time. Most would have said that it was his duty to take the measure of these principles and that the plaintiff was entitled to have him do so.

We mean no more, when we say that a *rule* is binding upon a judge, than that he must follow it if it applies, and that if he does not he will on that account have made a mistake.

It will not do to say that in a case like *Henningsen* the court is only 'morally' obligated to take particular principles into account, or that it is 'institutionally' obligated, or obligated as a matter of judicial 'craft', or something of that sort. The question will still remain why this type of obligation (whatever we call it) is different from the obligation that rules impose upon judges, and why it entitles us to say that principles and policies are not part of the law but are merely extra-legal standards 'courts characteristically use'.

(2) A positivist might argue that even though some principles are binding, in the sense that the judge must take them into account, they cannot determine a particular result. This is a harder argument to assess because it is not clear what it means for a standard to 'determine' a result. Perhaps it means that the standard *dictates* the result whenever it applies so that nothing else counts. If so, then it is certainly true that the individual principles do not determine results, but that is only another way of saying that principles are not rules. Only rules dictate results, come what may. When a contrary result has been reached, the rule has been abandoned or changed. Principles do not work that way; they incline a decision one way, though not conclusively, and they survive intact when they do not prevail. This seems no reason for concluding that judges who must reckon with principles have discretion because a set of principles can dictate a result. If a judge believes that principles he is bound to recognize point in one direction and that principles pointing in the other direction, if any, are not of equal weight, then he must decide accordingly, just as he must follow what he believes to be a binding rule. He may, of course, be wrong in his assessment of the principles, but he may also be wrong in his judgment that the rule is binding.

...

(3) A positivist might argue that principles cannot count as law because their authority, and even more so their weight, are congenitally *controversial*. It is true that generally we cannot *demonstrate* the authority or weight of a particular principle as we can sometimes demonstrate the validity of a rule by locating it in an act of Congress or in the opinion of an authoritative court. Instead, we make a case for a principle, and for its weight, by appealing to an amalgam of practice and other principles in which the implications of legislative and judicial history figure along with appeals to community practices and understandings. There is no litmus paper for testing the soundness of such a case – it is a matter of judgment, and reasonable men may disagree. But again this does not distinguish the judge from other officials who do not have discretion. The sergeant has no litmus paper for experience, the referee none for aggressiveness. Neither of these has discretion, because he is bound to reach an understanding, controversial or not, of what his orders or the rules require, and to act on that understanding. That is the judge's duty as well.

Step 4 – Finally, Dworkin makes the last move in his argument, to show that Hart's rule of recognition cannot function as it is supposed to do. He begins by turning the tables on the positivists, arguing that principles, rather than being extraneous extras to the body of rules, are essential for the functioning of the law in common law systems.

Dworkin (1977, 37–44)

Unless at least some principles are acknowledged to be binding upon judges, requiring them as a set to reach particular decisions, then no rules, or very few rules, can be said to be binding upon them either.

In most American jurisdictions, and now in England also, the higher courts not infrequently reject established rules. Common law rules – those developed by earlier court decisions – are sometimes overruled directly, and sometimes radically altered by further development. Statutory rules are subjected to interpretation and reinterpretation, sometimes even when the result is not to carry out what is called the 'legislative intent'. If courts had discretion to change established rules, then these rules would of course not be binding upon them, and so would not be law on the positivists' model. The positivist must therefore argue that there are standards, themselves binding upon judges, that determine when a judge may overrule or alter an established rule, and when he may not.

When, then, is a judge permitted to change an existing rule of law? Principles figure in the answer in two ways. First, it is necessary, though not sufficient, that the judge find that the change would advance some principle, which principle thus justifies the change. In *Riggs* the change (a new interpretation of the statute of wills) was justified by the principle that no man should profit from his own wrong; in *Henningsen* the previously recognized rules about automobile manufacturers' liability were altered on the basis of the principles I quoted from the opinion of the court.

But not any principle will do to justify a change, or no rule would ever be safe. There must be some principles that count and others that do not, and there must be some principles that count for more than others. It could not depend on the judge's own preferences amongst a sea of respectable extra-legal standards, any one in principle eligible, because if that were the case we could not say that any rules were binding. We could always imagine a judge whose preferences amongst extra-legal standards were such as would justify a shift or radical reinterpretation of even the most entrenched rule.

Second, any judge who proposes to change existing doctrine must take account of some important standards that argue against departures from established doctrine, and these standards are also for the most part principles. They include the doctrine of 'legislative supremacy', a set of principles that require the courts to pay a qualified deference to the acts of the legislature. They also include the doctrine of precedent, another set of principles reflecting the equities and efficiencies of consistency. The doctrines of legislative supremacy and precedent incline toward the status quo, each within its sphere, but they do not command it. Judges are not free, however, to pick and choose amongst the principles and policies that make up these doctrines – if they were, again, no rule could be said to be binding.

Consider, therefore, what someone implies who says that a particular rule is binding. He may imply that the rule is affirmatively supported by principles the court is not free to disregard, and which are collectively more weighty than other principles that argue for a change. If not, he implies that any change would be condemned by a combination of conservative principles of legislative supremacy and precedent that the court is not free to ignore. Very often, he will imply both, for the conservative principles, being principles and not rules, are usually not powerful enough to save a common law rule or an aging statute that is entirely unsupported by substantive principles the court is bound to respect. Either of these implications, of course, treats a body of principles and policies as law in the sense that rules are; it treats them as standards binding upon the officials of a community, controlling their decisions of legal right and obligation.

...

Most rules of law, according to Hart, are valid because some competent institution enacted them. Some were created by a legislature, in the form of statutory enactments. Others were created by judges who formulated them to decide particular cases, and thus established them as precedents for the future. But this test of pedigree will not work for the *Riggs* and *Henningsen* principles. The origin of these as legal principles lies not in a particular decision of some legislature or court, but in a sense of appropriateness developed in the profession and the public over time. Their continued power depends upon this sense of appropriateness being sustained. If it no longer seemed unfair to allow people to profit by their wrongs, or fair to place special burdens upon oligopolies that manufacture potentially dangerous machines, these principles would no longer play much of a role in new cases, even if they had never been overruled or repealed. (Indeed, it hardly makes sense to speak of principles like these as being 'overruled' or 'repealed'. When they decline they are eroded, not torpedoed.)

True, if we were challenged to back up our claim that some principle is a principle of law, we would mention any prior cases in which that principle was cited, or figured in the argument. We would also mention any statute that seemed to exemplify that principle (even better if the principle was cited in the preamble of a statute, or in the committee reports or other legislative documents that accompanied it). Unless we could find some institutional support, we would probably fail to make out our case, and the more support we found, the more weight we could claim for our principle.

Yet we could not devise any formula for testing how much and what kind of institutional support is necessary to make a principle a legal principle, still less to fix its weight at a particular order of magnitude. We argue for a principle by grasping a whole set of shifting, developing and interacting standards (themselves principles rather than rules) about institutional responsibility, statutory interpretation, the persuasive force of various sorts of precedent, the relation of all of these to contemporary moral practices, and hosts of other such standards. We could not bolt all of these together into a single 'rule', even a complex one, and if we could the result would bear little relation to Hart's picture of a rule of recognition, which is the picture of a fairly stable master rule specifying 'some feature or features possession of which by a suggested rule is taken as a conclusive affirmative indication that it is a rule ...'

Moreover, the techniques we apply in arguing for another principle do not stand (as Hart's rule of recognition is designed to) on an entirely different level from the principles they support. Hart's sharp distinction between acceptance and validity does not hold. If we are arguing for the principle that a man should not profit from his own wrong, we could cite the acts of courts and legislatures that exemplify it, but this speaks as much to the principle's acceptance as its validity. (It seems odd to speak of a principle as being valid at all, perhaps because validity is an all-or-nothing concept, appropriate for rules, but inconsistent with a principle's dimension of weight.) If we are asked (as we might well be) to defend the particular doctrine of precedent, or the particular technique of statutory interpretation, that we used in this argument, we should certainly cite the practice of others in using that doctrine or technique. But we should also cite other general principles that we believe support that practice, and this introduces a note of validity into the chord of acceptance. We might argue, for example, that the use we make of earlier cases and statutes is supported by a particular analysis of the point of the practice of legislation or the doctrine of precedent, or by the principles of democratic theory, or by a particular position on the proper division of authority between national and local institutions, or something else of that sort. Nor is this path of support a one-way street leading to some ultimate principle resting on acceptance alone. Our principles of legislation, precedent, democracy, or federalism might be challenged too; and if they were we should argue for them, not only in terms of practice, but in terms of each other and in terms of the implications of trends of judicial and legislative decisions, even though this last would involve appealing to those same doctrines of interpretation we justified through the principles we are now trying to support. At this level of abstraction, in other words, principles rather hang together than link together.

So even though principles draw support from the official acts of legal institutions, they do not have a simple or direct enough connection with these acts to frame that connection in terms of criteria specified by some ultimate master rule of recognition. Is there any other route by which principles might be brought under such a rule?

Hart does say that a master rule might designate as law not only rules enacted by particular legal institutions, but rules established by custom as well. He has in mind a problem that bothered other positivists, including Austin. Many of our most ancient legal rules were never explicitly created by a legislature or a court. When they made their first appearance in legal opinions and texts, they were treated as already being part of the law because they represented the customary practice of the community, or some specialized part of it, like the business community ... The master rule, he says, might stipulate that some custom counts as law even before the courts recognize it. But he does not face the difficulty this raises for his general theory because he does not attempt to set out the criteria a master rule might use for this purpose. It cannot use, as its only criterion, the provision that the community regard the practice as morally binding, for this would not distinguish legal customary rules from moral customary rules, and of course not all of the community's long-standing customary moral obligations are enforced at law. If, on the other hand, the test is whether the community regards the customary practice as legally binding, the whole point of the master rule is undercut, at least for this class of legal rules. The master rule, says Hart, marks the transformation from a primitive society to one with law, because it provides a test for determining social rules of law other than by measuring their acceptance. But if the master rule says merely that whatever other rules the community accepts as legally binding are legally binding, then it provides no such test at all, beyond the test we should use were there no master rule. The master rule becomes (for these cases) a non-rule of recognition; we might as well say that every primitive society has a secondary rule of recognition, namely the rule that whatever is accepted as binding is binding. Hart himself, in discussing international law, ridicules the idea that such a rule could be a rule of recognition, by describing the proposed rule as 'an empty repetition of the mere fact that the society concerned ... observes certain standards of conduct as obligatory rules'.

Hart's treatment of custom amounts, indeed, to a confession that there are at least some rules of law that are not binding because they are valid under standards laid down by a master rule but are binding – like the master rule – because they are accepted as binding by the community. This chips at the neat pyramidal architecture we admired in Hart's theory: we can no longer say that only the master rule is binding because of its acceptance, all other rules being valid under its terms.

This is perhaps only a chip, because the customary rules Hart has in mind are no longer a very significant part of the law. But it does suggest that Hart would be reluctant to widen the damage by bringing under the head of 'custom' all those crucial principles and policies we have been discussing. If he were to call these part of the law and yet admit that the only test of their force lies in the degree to which they are accepted as law by the community or some part thereof, he would very sharply reduce that area of the law over which his master rule held any dominion. It is not just that all the principles and policies would escape its sway, though that would be bad enough. Once these principles and policies are accepted as law, and thus as standards judges must follow in determining legal obligations, it would follow that rules like those announced for the first time in *Riggs* and *Henningsen* owe their force at least in part to the authority of principles and policies, and so not entirely to the master rule of recognition.

So we cannot adapt Hart's version of positivism by modifying his rule of recognition to embrace principles. No tests of pedigree, relating principles to acts of legislation, can be formulated, nor can his concept of customary law, itself an exception to the first tenet of positivism, be made to serve without abandoning that tenet altogether. One more possibility must be considered, however. If no rule of recognition can provide a test for identifying principles, why not say that principles are ultimate, and form the rule of recognition of our law? The answer to the general question 'What is valid law in an American jurisdiction?' would then require us to state all the principles (as well as ultimate constitutional rules) in force in that jurisdiction at the time, together with appropriate assignments of weight. A positivist might then regard the complete set of these standards as the rule of recognition of the jurisdiction. This solution has the attraction of paradox, but of course it is an unconditional surrender. If we simply designate our rule of recognition by the phrase 'the complete set of principles in force', we achieve only the tautology that law is law. If, instead, we tried actually to list all the principles in force we would fail. They are controversial, their weight is all important, they are numberless, and they shift and change so fast that the start of our list would be obsolete before we reached the middle. Even if we succeeded, we would not have a key for law because there would be nothing left for our key to unlock.

I conclude that if we treat principles as law we must reject the positivists' first tenet, that the law of a community is distinguished from other social standards by some test in the form of a master rule. We have already decided that we must then abandon the second tenet the doctrine of judicial discretion – or clarify it into triviality. What of the third tenet, the positivists' theory of legal obligation?

This theory holds that a legal obligation exists when (and only when) an established rule of law imposes such an obligation. It follows from this that in a hard case – when no such established rule can be found – there is no legal obligation until the judge creates a new rule for the future. The judge may apply that new rule to the parties in the case, but this is ex post facto legislation, not the enforcement of an existing obligation.

> The positivists' doctrine of discretion (in the strong sense) required this view of legal obligation, because if a judge has discretion there can be no legal right or obligation – no entitlement – that he must enforce. Once we abandon that doctrine, however, and treat principles as law, we raise the possibility that a legal obligation might be imposed by a constellation of principles as well as by an established rule. We might want to say that a legal obligation exists whenever the case supporting such an obligation, in terms of binding legal principles of different sorts, is stronger than the case against it.

Dworkin's ingenious argument can be summarised as follows: According to positivism, the law is composed of a system of rules which are identified as valid parts of the system by means of a master pedigree rule, the rule of recognition. But if we look at judicial practice, we see that judges do not only apply rules and then exercise their discretion in cases where the rules are not clearly determinative, but in hard cases of this kind, apply more general considerations, principles, to decide hard cases; but principles are not identifiable as 'valid' principles of the system by some master pedigree rule; rather, lawyers and judges make a case for the applicability of principles, based upon considerations of the history of the law, the practice of judges and lawyers in deciding cases, and general considerations of justice and morality; if this is right, then positivism is faced with a further problem: *because* it is clear that established rules can be overturned by judges' taking principles into consideration, and so rules cannot be established as necessarily valid rules of the system by a pedigree test alone for their status as rules can be upset by principles which are not identified by the pedigree test, *it follows that the whole body of rules is subject to revision by principles, which cannot be accounted for by the pedigree test, and so not the slightest part of the whole body of law can be ascertained, ie determined with certainty to be valid, by a pedigree test alone.* Finally, Hart cannot avoid this conclusion by treating the rule of recognition not so much as a rule, but a customary judicial practice, on the view that principles are like customs recognised by the law. The reason is that customs, like principles, are customs only in so far as they are *accepted* – one makes a case for a custom just as one does for a principle – but the fact that a custom has become socially accepted, ie is practised, does not distinguish *legal* customs, ie the customs the law will recognise and enforce, from all other social customs, which it does not; just as with principles, there is no particular *test* which identifies legal customs from all others, so Hart cannot simply cite the case of customary law to refute Dworkin's argument, for as far as Dworkin is concerned, the existence of customary law, like the existence of legal principles, undermines the possibility of a feasible rule of recognition.

Dworkin's argument was subjected to a number of criticisms, and here we hope to identify the ones which are the most important, and in respect of which we can ask whether Dworkin's later work provided a convincing response. First, a few points to notice. There is a large difference in the starting points of Hart and Dworkin in their attempts to describe what the law is. Choosing the neutral term 'standards', it is obvious that Hart's chief concern was to describe the social institutional basis for there being in society a set of standards to guide the behaviour of individuals, standards which were not merely the generally accepted standards of social morality. Dworkin, by contrast, regards the law as that body of standards to which judges may make recourse in rendering decisions in cases that come before them. Now, one would hope that these sets of standards are identical, so that the standards which legal institutions set to guide the behaviour of subjects of law outside the court are also the ones that judges apply in court. But taking these two different starting positions will cause one to emphasise different things. Hart's concern to provide a rule of recognition is obvious from his perspective, for there must be some functioning way to distinguish legal from other obligations (even if that might require that a subject in a sophisticated and complex system seek legal advice to do so). From Dworkin's perspective, the matter is not so much one of guiding people's behaviour outside of court, but in resolving disputes between litigants in a way that can be justified – to decide cases *according* to law requires that a sound characterisation of the considerations judges bring to bear must reflect the wealth of considerations we see judges actually employing. We might also notice here a distinction between the adjectives 'valid' and 'binding' as applied to rules or principles of law. (It is worthwhile noting when Dworkin uses one rather than the other.) When Hart wrote about the rule of recognition he was clearly concerned to describe how legal systems create *valid* standards of the system; the rule of recognition is that rule which dictates those processes which create valid standards. It does not necessarily follow that in any particular case before the court all the validly created relevant standards are *binding* on the judge (though of course one would expect that in most cases this would be so). An old statutory provision prohibiting 'witchcraft' may be a valid legal standard, just because it was validly created by a source (parliamentary legislation) recognised by the rule of recognition, but other valid standards of the system, such as a rule about applying laws which have fallen out of use, may mean that a court will not treat it as binding. The same point can be made even more obviously in the case of rules and principles established by judicial precedent. In contrast, Dworkin is clearly concerned with standards that are *binding* upon judges – what standards bind, and how they do so.

Once we take into account these different perspectives, we can understand why one response to the Hart/Dworkin argument was 'What's all the fuss about?' Didn't Dworkin only fill out or complete Hart's account of the nature of law by showing that Hart neglected to produce a properly refined characterisation of the different kinds of standards operating in the law, and so required an amendment to the positivist theory to incorporate standards like principles, and furthermore, that his theory lacked a theory of adjudication? Perhaps. But what continues to distinguish Hartian positivists from Dworkinians is the way they characterise this 'amendment' or 'completion'. A positivist would say that, true, judges apply principles in hard cases to develop the law, but in doing so they genuinely *develop* or *modify* the law. Where the law is unsettled, a subject of the law is faced with a genuine problem because the law itself is uncertain; when his case goes to court the judge, in deciding, will establish new law to cover his case which was just not there before. Positivists, in general, simply do not share Dworkin's democratic concerns about the legitimacy of judges legislating in this way. For a positivist, under the typical political settlement in most modern countries judges simply have the power to make law in this gap-filling, interstitial way, and everyone recognises that, and accepts it as an ineradicable feature of the fact that it would be inconvenient to have to send all cases of unsettled law back to the legislature for 'democratic' determination. (The French tried this for a time following the revolution, but soon gave it up as hopeless.) For Dworkin, on the other hand, there must be a better way of describing what judges do in hard cases; he regards the positivist response as complacent and simplistic. The law has intellectual resources which allows it to provide answers which are not simply 'new law', but answers which in a fairly robust way *follow* from the law that has gone before. Of course positivists don't believe that a judge, in a hard case, can decide the case any way he wants, for any reason. But positivists insist that constraints though there are, where the law is unsettled the judge really is faced with a choice, and the fact that there are lots of intellectual resources available to guide him does not let him off the hook – he is exercising genuine political power to make law, and so should acquit himself appropriately when he exercises that power. At the end of the day, (at least at this stage of the debate), it is fair to say that one's preference for Hart or Dworkin over this is largely a matter of judgment about which reasonable people can disagree. It largely depends upon your own sense of how lawyers and judges and subjects of the law regard the judicial development of the law.

Joseph Raz is probably H L A Hart's most important intellectual heir, and is one of Dworkin's longest-standing critics. We will visit his work again, but here we examine Raz's (1972) response to Dworkin's principles-based critique of Hart's positivism. Roughly, Raz argues that Dworkin mischaracterises legal principles; once we have a better grasp of principles, we see that Dworkin's conclusions are unsupported. His first criticism concerns the distinction between statements *of law* and statements *about the law.*

Consider the following series of statements:

(1) Act justly.

(2) Keep your agreements.

(3) Meet all your contractual obligations.

(4) Meet your obligations under your contract of employment with the LSE.

(5) Mark your students' exam scripts on time.

In one way or another, all of these can be regarded as propositions of or about the law. Perhaps (1) and (2) might be regarded as general principles guiding the law. (3) is certainly a true statement of the force of the law, although obviously subject to various exceptions. Assuming the existence of such a contract, (4) can count as a true statement of the law in the sense that a lawyer who advised a client to meet his obligations under a specific contract would be expressing the force of the law, and (5) is a similar kind of statement, though an even more specific one. Only (3), however, is plausibly a statement, albeit a general one, *of the law*, ie a plausible candidate for a law of the system. (1) and (2) are just far too abstract and imprecise to do any practical work in guiding the behaviour of subjects of the law; (4) and (5) are not statements of laws, but are rather statements of the effect of the law in concrete cases. (Hypothetically, though not practically, we *might* have just one 'law' of the system, something like (1), and regard any more specific statements about what (1) entailed as mere applications of (1) to concrete circumstances. Or, from the opposite extreme, we could hypothetically, though again not practically, treat statements like (5) as individual laws; on this view, the making of a contract would be a law-creating act. Of course we do neither; our understanding of laws, or rules of law, is that they are there to give more or less specific guidance to more or less all the subjects of the law. Thus a functioning system of laws requires laws, or rules of law, to be framed at the right level of generality to provide practical guidance for the subjects of the law – general enough to cover all the fact situations in which the concern behind the law arises, but specific enough so that they can be applied more or less straightforwardly in those fact situations.) Thus we see that (1) and (2) are, if anything, general statements *about the law*, ie descriptions of what the law requires, even though they are *framed as directives* which at first glance might look as standards of the law, that is, abstract legal principles; (4) and (5) are similarly statements *about the law*, ie about what the law requires in specific instances.

Raz criticises Dworkin for neglecting to consider this distinction:

> We often have need to refer summarily to a body of legal rules without specifying their content in detail. Such references are frequently made by courts in the course of justifying their decisions. These references usually take the form of a statement of a principle, but they are not statements of the contents of laws of a special type, namely principles. They are merely a brief allusion to a number of rules. Someone may say that in his country the principle of freedom of speech is recognised by law. When asked what he means he may say that the only laws setting limits to the liberty to express opinions are concerned with libel and military security; that censorship of films, books, and the theatre must be justified by the protection of infants; that there are detailed regulations guaranteeing access to the mass media to people representing all shades of opinion on public matters; and so on. His statement that in his country freedom of speech is recognised by law can thus be seen to be a summary reference to a great number of laws, not a statement of the content of a single law. Another person, by contrast, may say that a certain legal system incorporates the principle of freedom of speech because it contains a law instructing the courts and all public officials to protect freedom of speech in all cases, even those not governed by specific rules. This person's statement *is* a statement of the content of one particular law, and it is a principle in the sense in which Professor Dworkin employs the term. It imposes an obligation and guides the action of courts and officials. (Raz 1972, 828)

What flows from this? The first point is that there may be fewer true principles in the law than appear at first glance, for summary statements of the law in an area are statements *about* the law, descriptions of it, not statements *of* law which would count as legally-binding standards courts must enforce. This leads to a tricky point for Dworkin – to the extent that judges decide hard cases with reference to their descriptions of a general area of law, say their depiction of the law as by and large favouring freedom of contract, such statements not being binding principles *of* law, but merely summary statements of the law in an area, *to that extent judges are not deciding the case according to binding legal standards*; rather they are exercising their discretion to develop the law in the way they think is most in keeping with the general trend of the law as it stood prior to their decision. Thus, to the extent that Dworkin sees 'principles' everywhere in hard cases, 'principles' which are the deciding factors in those cases, but at the same time he fails to distinguish 'principles' which are merely descriptions of the law, ie statements *about* the law, from true principles *of law*, he is playing into the positivists' hands by inadvertently adopting the view that judges decide cases for non-legally binding reasons (however sensible those reasons might be).

Secondly, Raz outlines a completely different distinction between rules and principles, and on the basis of it argues that the existence of legal principles, rather than showing that judges have no true discretion, *are the best evidence that judges do have discretion* to make new law.

Raz (1972, 838–47)

The distinction between rules and principles of obligation both in law and outside it turns on the character of the norm-act prescribed. Rules prescribe relatively specific acts; principles prescribe highly unspecific actions. Generic acts, types of acts, are of various degrees of specificity. An act is highly unspecific if it can be performed on different occasions by the performance of a great many heterogeneous generic acts on each occasion. It is more specific to the extent to which there is only a small number of generic acts by the performance of which it is performed. Smoking is a highly specific act which is performed by smoking a pipe, a cigarette or a cigar, but not by many other generic acts. Assault, murder, rape, and speeding are likewise relatively specific acts. Promoting human happiness, respecting human dignity, increasing productivity, and behaving negligently or unjustly or unreasonably are highly unspecific acts. It is because of this that we say rules prescribe or proscribe the first class of acts, whereas principles prescribe the second (to the extent that these types of behavior are governed by norms at all). The distinction between rules and principles is, on this analysis, one of degree, since there is no hard and fast line between acts which are specific and those which are unspecific. Consequently, there will be many borderline cases where it will be impossible to say that we definitely have a rule or definitely a principle.

The suggestion that it is this logical distinction between the type of norm-acts prescribed which underlies much of our ordinary usage of the terms 'rules' and 'principles' may be greeted with some suspicion. We feel that rules and principles play different roles in practical reasoning whether in the law or outside it and that the suggested distinction does not seem to explain this. In fact, however, the logical distinction does explain some of these differences and it indicates how to explain the rest. Since highly unspecific acts can be performed by performing on different occasions a variety of more specific acts, the opportunities for performing them encompass the opportunities for performing the more specific acts and are more general than the latter. Norms prescribing highly unspecific acts, consequently, must be justified by more general considerations bearing on a wider area of human activity. Since we justify considerations which apply to a limited range of situations and actions by more general considerations, principles can be used to justify rules but not vice versa. This is, perhaps, the most important difference in the role of rules and principles in practical reasoning in general, and it can be explained by means of the distinction I have suggested. This does not explain all the differences between rules and principles in the law. These, though dependent on the logical distinction, do not derive from it alone. They depend also on various constraints imposed by general legal policies and goals.

D. THE ROLE OF PRINCIPLES IN THE LAW

Let me start with a brief survey of five different purposes for which principles are used in the law. I will then make a general comment on their relation to other laws. The extent to which principles are used for these different purposes varies greatly among different legal systems. Even within one legal system some principles are used for all of them, while others are restricted to a few; and in some branches of the law principles are relied on more extensively than in others. I will not try to analyze in detail the role of principles in any particular legal system. My aim is only to isolate some of the different tasks principles may be assigned.

...

1. *Principles as grounds for interpreting laws.* This is perhaps the most extensive and least inhibited use to which virtually all principles are put. Principles are used for the interpretation of all laws, including other principles of a more restricted application. There is a very strong presumption in most legal systems that other things being equal an interpretation which makes a law conform to a principle is to be preferred to one which does not. Obviously, some interpretations often conform better to some principles than others, and the courts have to decide which interpretation to prefer. This role of principles is of the utmost importance since it is a crucial device for ensuring coherence of purpose among various laws bearing on the same subject. The importance of this function of principles can he gathered by comparing various legal systems which, despite great similarity in their rules, reach different conclusions in many cases because they apply different principles for their interpretation.

2. *Principles as grounds for changing laws.* The first function of principles merges into the second, since the borderline between an interpretation of a law and its amendment is notoriously a blurred one. Nevertheless the two functions are distinct, and it is not difficult to distinguish between them in the majority of cases. The doctrine of precedent, where accepted, commonly includes the understanding that laws developed through precedent are subject to amendment by the use of principles. This does not mean that judge-made rules are often upset; for, as Professor Dworkin reminds us, principles are often conservative in nature.

...

3. *Principles as grounds for particular exceptions to laws.* Sometimes a law is not applied to a case on which it bears on the ground that to do so in those particular circumstances would sacrifice important principles; but the law is not thereby modified. This may often occur in countries where the doctrine of precedent is not recognized but where principles are allowed to override rules in particular circumstances. In common law countries this use of principles is more restricted, but nonetheless of considerable importance. The principle of laches [the principle by which a plaintiff cannot succeed if he has unreasonably delayed enforcing his rights] for example, is one of a group of principles of equity which is characteristically used in this way. In contrast we may remember that the principle 'no one may profit from his own wrong' is characteristically

used in the second manner described earlier, i.e., as ground far changing and qualifying rules.

4. *Principles as grounds for making new rules.* When principles but no other laws apply to a certain range of problems, courts act to regulate the area by making new rules. This is a very important way in which the common law develops: new rules are made on the basis of established principles.

5. *Principles as the sole ground for action in particular cases.* There are situations in which what ought legally to be done is determined directly by the application of various principles to the case. This function of principles is radically different from those previously mentioned, for here principles do not operate through the mediation of rules. They are not grounds for the interpretation or modification of rules, nor do they compete with them or serve as grounds for creating them. It is easy to underestimate the extent to which principles are used in this way in most countries. The whole area of sentencing is governed almost exclusively by principles. The activities of public officials and administrative agencies are largely governed by principles in this fashion. The law confers certain powers on the agency and directs it to use them to promote certain policy goals in accordance with general principles. The exercise of discretionary powers is typically guided by principles rather than rules.

It is true, nevertheless, that on the whole there is a marked tendency in the law of many countries not to rely on the direct application of principles but to use them to govern the operation of rules in the ways indicated above. This is particularly true when individuals rather than courts and officials are the norm-subjects of the principles.

Some of the reasons for preferring rules to principles in the direct regulation of behavior have to do with the particular conditions of various countries or of different branches of the law. But at least one general reason for this preference is fairly obvious. Principles, because they prescribe highly unspecific acts, tend to be more vague and less certain than rules. On the other hand, and for the same reason, they are particularly suitable for incorporating into the law very general goals and values, whereas rules are more apt to reflect more concrete considerations which apply to particular situations.

Since the law should strive to balance certainty and reliability against flexibility, it is on the whole wise legal policy to use rules as much as possible for regulating human behavior because they are more certain than principles and lend themselves more easily to uniform and predictable application. It is on the whole advisable to limit the use of principles to govern the creation and application of rules in order to ensure adequate flexibility in changing them and to prevent some of their unforeseen and undesirable effects. Some areas, such as governmental activities, cannot be adequately regulated by rules, and they must be directly governed by principles. But these cases are exceptional. Since in the use of rules the premium should be on certainty, whereas in the use of principles the premium is on flexibility, it is wise to accept relatively simple methods of resolving conflicts between rules which will not detract from the predictability of their application. No similar reasons apply to the methods of resolving conflicts between principles ... The difference stems from reasons of legal policy. It is not a logical difference between the concepts of a rule and a principle.

In fact, all the comments made in this section concerning the relative roles of rules and principles apply only to their use in the law and similar institutions and are not entailed by the concepts of a rule and a principle. In morality, where certainty and uniformity are generally less valued than correctness of judgment, rules have a much more limited role to play than in the law.

...

PRINCIPLES AND THE LIMITS OF LAW

By the thesis of the 'limits of law' I mean the position that there is a test which distinguishes what is law from what is not.

...

Professor Dworkin argues that (1) the law includes some principles as well as rules. From this he concludes that (2) the courts never have discretion in the strong sense. It follows, though he does not draw the conclusion at this point, that (3) the thesis of the limits of law is wrong. I shall argue that (3) does indeed follow from (2), but that (2) does not follow from (1) and is in any case wrong.

...

Professor Dworkin is primarily concerned to argue that there are legally binding principles. But this has never been denied by anyone, least of all by the positivists. Indeed, Austin could not have denied that some principles are legally binding while remaining true to his theory of law. The most fundamental tenet of his theory is that the commands of a sovereign are law, and there is nothing to prevent a sovereign from commanding that a principle shall be binding. Professor Dworkin's mistake lies in assuming that when Austin was talking about commands he was referring to what Professor Dworkin calls rules. But this is not the case. Neither does Hart use 'rules' in the same sense as Professor Dworkin. By 'rules' he means what Professor Dworkin seems to mean by 'standards', namely rules, principles or any other type of norm (whether legal or social).

The crux of the argument lies in the inference that since some principles are law judicial discretion does not exist. Professor Dworkin says very little on this. The reason, I suspect, is that he rightly sees that other theorists, not only the positivists, exaggerated the scope of judicial discretion because they failed to attend to the role principles play in the law. They tended to assume that whenever a rule is vague the court has discretion and did not see that sometimes the rule when read in light of some principles is not vague and does not leave room for discretion. 'A set of principles', as Professor Dworkin reminds us, 'can dictate a result'. But that it sometimes can does not mean that it always does. And it is this that Professor Dworkin has to establish to make his case against judicial discretion. Unfortunately, he does not even try to establish this point. I suppose that there might be a legal system which contains a rule that whenever the courts are faced with a case for which the law does not provide a uniquely correct solution they ought to refuse to render judgment. In such a system there would be no judicial discretion. But, whether or not such a system can exist, few if any legal systems in fact contain such a rule. In most legal systems there are at least three different sources of judicial discretion. Let me survey them briefly.

1. *Vagueness.* Vagueness is inherent in language. It is a problem courts have to face very frequently. As noted above, principles as well as rules of interpretation can sometimes solve problems of vagueness without leaving room for discretion. But principles

themselves are vague, and discretion in cases of vagueness cannot be dispensed with so long as courts are entitled to render judgment in such cases.

2. *Weight.* Though principles sometimes limit the scope of the courts' discretion, they tend on the whole to expand it ... the law usually determines with precision the relative weight of rules. Not so with principles. The law characteristically includes only incomplete indications as to their relative weight and leaves much to judicial discretion to be exercised in particular cases. The scope of discretion is in fact doubly extended, since not only must the relative importance of principles be determined, but also the importance relative to each principle of deviating from it or of following it on particular occasions. This matter is usually entrusted to judicial discretion. That courts have discretion as to weight does not, of course, mean that the law has nothing to contribute to the solution of the case. It contributes some of the elements for a solution, but not all the elements necessary to dictate a uniquely correct solution. In such cases the law dictates what considerations have to be taken into account, but not what weight to assign to each of them or to actions in accordance with or contrary to each of them in particular cases.

3. *Laws of discretion.* Most legal systems contain laws granting courts discretion, not only as to the weight of legally binding considerations, but also to act on considerations which are not legally binding. Such discretion may be, and usually is, guided by principles. These principles, however, do not dictate the considerations to be taken into account, but merely limit the range of the considerations.

One may distinguish between substantive principles, which dictate a goal to be pursued or a value to be protected, and principles of discretion, which guide discretion by stipulating what type of goals and values the judge may take into account in exercising his discretion. Compare the following two sets of hypothetical principles. (a) 'Car manufacturers have a duty to protect the public from accidents.' 'Increased productivity and efficiency should be the prime objective of public corporations.' 'The validity of standard contracts is contingent on their not taking advantage of the economic necessities of the weaker party.' 'The law favors security of title.' (b) 'The courts will not enforce unjust contracts.' 'Public corporations should act for the general good.' 'Whatever is contra *bonos mores et decorum* the principles of our law prohibit.' The first group of principles set particular considerations to be acted on. They may be vague and they do not specify the weight to be given to each consideration, but the consideration prescribed is clear enough and is not a matter left to the courts' discretion. Principles of the second group, on the other hand, do not stipulate what considerations should be acted on. They merely specify the type of considerations which may be taken into account and leave the rest to the officials or the courts addressed by the principles. Rather than negating discretion, they presuppose its existence and guide it.

...

We must conclude that legal principles do not exclude judicial discretion; they presuppose its existence and direct and guide it. The argument from the absence of judicial discretion against the thesis of the limits of law must therefore be rejected. It should be noted, however, that judicial discretion is not arbitrary judgment. Courts are never allowed to act arbitrarily. Even when discretion is not limited or guided in any specific direction the courts are still legally bound to act as they think is best according to their beliefs and values. If they do not, if they give arbitrary judgment by tossing a coin, for example, they violate a legal duty.

Having outlined his understanding of principles, Raz then sets out to show that there can be a workable criterion of identity for principles of a legal system. First of all he points out that, as Dworkin acknowledges, principles can enter the legal system by way of legislation or judicial precedent:

> Legal principles, like other laws, can be enacted or repealed by legislatures and administrative authorities. They can also become legally binding through establishment by the courts. Many legal systems recognize that both rules and principles can he made into law or lose their status as law through precedent. Rules and principles differ in this respect. A court can establish a new rule in a single judgment which becomes a precedent. Principles are not made into law by a single judgment; they evolve rather like a custom and are binding only if they have considerable authoritative support in a line of judgments. Like customary law, judicially adopted principles need not be formulated very precisely in the judgments which count as authority for their existence. All that has to be shown is that they underlie a series of courts' decisions, that they were in fact a reason operating in a series of cases. (Raz 1972, 848)

But Raz disputes Dworkin's further claim that (on some occasions) moral standards accepted by the community count as legal principles by that fact alone, erasing the distinction between legal and moral standards. Raz agrees that in most countries the exercise of judicial discretion is constrained by a very general principle that judges should only act on those values and opinions that have the support of some important segment of the population; or perhaps it should be said that judges should not exercise their discretion in a way which is significantly in conflict with the moral views of a broad segment of the community. But, Raz argues, it is entirely wrong to conclude that such principles *convert* any specific social norms into legally binding principles. First, it is a myth that within most modern states there exists any 'common morality' to which all adhere. Secondly, even to the extent that there is a widely accepted 'common morality', this common morality is far too vague and abstract to provide any *specific* moral norms that are equally widely accepted, norms specific enough to be helpful when judges must exercise their discretion and decide difficult cases. Raz acknowledges that too often, judges do like to claim that their decisions reflect not just the values of some, but attract national support, or the spirit of the nation ('American values', 'British fair play' etc), but this rhetoric should be firmly resisted.

> The courts tend all too often to claim that a specific policy is entailed by belief in some general value, thus avoiding a concrete justification of their decision, maintaining the rhetoric of common goals and community values and endorsing partisan positions without admitting it. Some judges may themselves be captives of the myths they help to perpetuate. But the fact that they are misled should not mislead us. Occasional deviations from the canons of good reasoning can be dismissed as mistakes, but when constant use is made of a pattern of argumentation completely devoid of logical validity it is time to distinguish between myth and rhetoric on the one hand and reality on the other. And the law should be understood to encompass reality, not rhetoric. (Raz 1972, 850–51)

Raz then addresses the central difficulty, how a rule of recognition can account for the way in which principles of the common law arise over the historical course of a series of decisions. He argues that there is such a workable rule of recognition, although explaining it this will entail a modification of Hart's own description of rule of recognition as originally stated.

Raz (1972, 851–854)

THE POSSIBILITY OF A CRITERION OF IDENTITY

If the thesis of the limits of law is right, there must be a criterion of identity which sets necessary and sufficient conditions, satisfaction of which is a mark that a standard is part of a legal system ... Professor Dworkin claims that no adequate criterion of identity can be formulated and that therefore the thesis of the limits of law must be rejected ... Legal principles may be valid in precisely the same way that rules are. They may, for example, be enacted in the constitution or in a statute, as some of Professor Dworkin's own examples show. It is true, though, that some legal principles are law because they are accepted by the judiciary. But this is true of rules as well as principles. It is, however, an important point which does necessitate a modification of Hart's criterion of identity. But here again Professor Dworkin claims too much. He claims that if the master rule says merely that whatever other rules the community accepts are legally binding then it fails to act as an identifying criterion distinguishing between law and social norms. Had all social customs in all countries been legally binding this would have been a valid criticism. Some countries, however, do not recognize custom as a source of law at all. Those legal systems which do regard customs as legally binding do so only if they pass certain tests. These tests, if they are not set out in a statute or some other law, are laid down by the rule of recognition, which determines under what conditions social customs are binding in law.

The rule of recognition, therefore, does serve to explain the legal status of general community customs. It cannot, however, explain in the same way the legal status of judicial customs. Since it is itself a judicial custom it cannot confer any special status on other judicial customs. Judicial rule-making ... differs in this respect from the evolution of principles by the courts. A rule becomes binding by being laid down in one case as a precedent. It does not have to wait until it is accepted in a series of cases to be binding. It is binding because of the doctrine of precedent which is part of our rule of recognition. Principles evolved by the courts become binding by becoming a judicial custom. They are part of the law because they are accepted by the courts, not because they are valid according to the rule of recognition.

Hart's criterion of identity must be modified. A legal system consists not only of one customary rule of the law enforcing agencies and all the laws recognized by it, but of all the customary rules and principles of the law enforcing agencies and all the laws recognized by them. This is an important modification, but it preserves the fundamental point underlying Hart's criterion and shared by many: namely, that law is an institutionalized normative system and that the fact that the enforcement of its standards is a duty of special law-enforcing agencies is one important feature which distinguishes it from many other normative systems. The importance of this feature of law is made manifest by distinguishing between legal and non-legal standards according to whether or not the courts have an obligation to apply them, either because they are themselves judicial custom or because judicial customs make their application obligatory.

Professor Dworkin has a second argument disputing the possibility of formulating an adequate criterion of identity. 'True,' he says, 'if we were challenged to back up our claim that some principle is a principle of law, we would mention any prior cases in which that principle was cited, or figured in the argument ... Unless we could find some such institutional support, we would probably fail to make out our case ... Yet we could not devise any formula for testing how much and what kind of institutional support is necessary to make a principle a legal principle.' In this passage Professor Dworkin is rejecting not merely Hart's version of the thesis of the limits of law but all versions of this thesis. He agrees that if legal and non-legal standards can be distinguished this could only he done by relying on the fact that only legal standards have adequate institutional support in the practice of the courts. He denies, however, the possibility of a general explanation of what counts as adequate institutional support. It follows that it is impossible to provide a general account of the difference between legal and non-legal standards and the thesis of the limits of law must be abandoned. What is the force of this argument? If a legal system consists, as I have suggested, of those standards which the courts are bound to recognize, we must agree with Professor Dworkin that we need a general explanation of what counts as adequate institutional support. For laws are binding on the courts either because judicial customs make their recognition obligatory or because they are themselves judicial customs. Thus the acceptability of the thesis of the limits of law depends on our ability to explain the concept of a judicial custom. But judicial customs are but a special case of social customs.

What we need is an adequate explanation of the concept of a customary norm. Once we have it we will know what judicial custom is and will have a complete criterion of identity. Hart has provided such an explanation. No doubt it is possible to improve on it, but there is no reason to suppose that the concept of a customary norm defies analysis. It is true that an analysis of the concept does not give us a decision procedure determining for every principle or rule whether or not it has sufficient support to be regarded as a judicial custom. Borderline cases will remain; they must remain, for customary norms evolve gradually. But Dworkin's is a very weak argument, which rejects a distinction because it admits the existence of borderline cases.

Raz's claim for the theoretical soundness of the rule of recognition has never abated. In response to a more recent formulation by Dworkin of his view, he said the following:

Recently Dworkin attempted to explain that his argument was that one cannot find 'any single master rule, accepted by the great majority of legal officials, which identifies all and only those principles to which judges have appealed in argument.' (A Reply by Ronald Dworkin in RONALD DWORKIN AND CONTEMPORARY JURISPRUDENCE 247, 261, M. Cohen, ed. 1984). But this point simply supports Hart's argument for the existence of judicial discretion ... an argument which Dworkin claimed to have been challenging. For if Hart is right to claim that there is judicial discretion, then it must be the case that there is no Rule of Recognition that captures all the standards appealed to by the courts. The fact that there are standards that are quite properly appealed to by courts, but are

not binding under the Rule of Recognition proves, to Hart, the existence of judicial
discretion. (Raz 1986, 1105 fn 10)

From one perspective, almost all of Dworkin's subsequent work can be regarded as a
response to Raz's claim that his argument against a 'positivist' notion of a judicial
custom underpinning the rule of recognition was a weak one. He continued to press,
and elaborate upon, his point that the way in which judges and lawyers determine what
count as legal considerations does not, in hard cases at least, depend solely upon some
exercise in determining whether a particular consideration is legal in virtue of past
historical practice, but depends rather on whether one can establish by moral and political
theoretical argument whether a standard is in some sense an appropriate consideration.
In this way, the determination of what is law cannot be purely a matter of historical
social fact, ie upon what the legislatures and courts *have done*, but depends upon
what is actually morally or politically 'correct' or 'right' in the circumstances.

The 1975 paper 'Hard Cases' comes closest to capturing the essence of Dworkin's
own theory of law, so what follows is a large part of the original paper. It is best to read
it carefully all at one go, for it flows almost seamlessly from one issue to the next.
However, here is a basic roadmap: This piece reformulates and elaborates many of the
themes of his original 'rules and principles' attack on positivism. Dworkin begins by
re-visiting the principle/policy distinction that he made in the first reading we looked
at, though here much greater weight is placed upon it. Judges are to decide cases on
the basis of principle, not policy. Dworkin argues that, while the judicial function is
thoroughly political, it is not political in the way that legislative politics is, for judges
are not to decide cases on the basis of policies, but on the basis of legal principle. The
particulars of Dworkin's principle/policy distinction have been criticised, but Dworkin
draws a genuine distinction here that responds to our intuitions. There is a difference
between deciding a case on the basis of what, all things considered, appears to be the
best way forward to achieve our goals (a decision on the basis of policy), and deciding
a case in terms of what *follows from* our past decisions of similar kinds (a decision of
principle). The latter kind of decision is one in which we decide one way rather than
another because we are, somewhat implicitly to be sure, *already committed* to that
decision. Of course a positivist can accept the distinction but still argue (1) that the
cases show that judges do decide on the basis of policy, and (2) that even where judges
would prefer to decide on the basis of principle, ie would like to act in accordance with
past normative commitments, the past normative commitments do not identify a
particular decision, and so judges must simply choose to decide in the way they think
best. But Dworkin disagrees: what the law is, in particular in hard cases where the law
at first glance looks uncertain, is what flows from the moral/political theory which makes
best sense of the past constitutional and legislative enactments and judicial decisions
in the jurisdiction. Thus, if the most coherent, theoretically sound rendering of New
York State law, taking into account all the relevant constitutional provisions, statutes
and judicial decisions, inclines one to the view that a murderer cannot inherit from his
victim, then *it is the law* that a murderer cannot inherit from his victim. The paper thus
frames two of Dworkin's most famous 'theses'. The 'rights thesis' holds that individual
litigants have a right to a judicial decision which is decided in the way just set out; their
cases are not to be disposed of by a judge pursuing a policy goal, but by determining

what their rights are, rights which flow from the best rendering of the principled reasons underlying all the relevant constitutional provisions, statutes and cases. Secondly, Dworkin subscribes to a 'right answer' thesis, which holds that, in principle at least, the body of law of a jurisdiction, once properly examined and accounted for, will always yield a single, correct, legal answer in a disputed case. Of course, determining what the right answer is in any particular case may be no mean feat, and in this paper Dworkin introduces Hercules, a judge of unlimited intelligence and knowledge of the law, and all the time in the world to decide any case. He is, it goes without saying, an ideal rather than realistic rendering of what a workaday judge is up to. But Dworkin intends him seriously as a model, carried to the logical extreme, of what lawyers and judges actually do when they consider issues of law.

Dworkin (1975, 1058–65, 1078–1101, 1109)

A. THE RIGHTS THESIS

...

Arguments of policy justify a political decision by showing that the decision advances or protects some collective goal of the community as a whole. The argument in favor of a subsidy for aircraft manufacturers, that the subsidy will protect national defense, is an argument of policy. Arguments of principle justify a political decision by showing that the decision respects or secures some individual or group right. The argument in favor of anti-discrimination statutes, that a minority has a right to equal respect and concern, is an argument of principle. These two sorts of argument do not exhaust political argument. Sometimes, for example, a political decision, like the decision to allow extra income tax exemptions for the blind, may be defended as an act of public generosity or virtue rather than on grounds of either policy or principle. But principle and policy are the major grounds of political justification.

The justification of a legislative program of any complexity will ordinarily require both sorts of argument. Even a program that is chiefly a matter of policy, like a subsidy program for important industries, may require strands of principle to justify its particular design. It may be, for example, that the program provides equal subsidies for manufacturers of different capabilities, on the assumption that weaker aircraft manufacturers have some right not to be driven out of business by government intervention, even though the industry would be more efficient without them. On the other hand, a program that depends chiefly on principle, like an antidiscrimination program, may reflect a sense that rights are not absolute and do not hold when the consequences for policy are very serious. The program may provide, for example, that fair employment practice rules do not apply when they might prove especially disruptive or dangerous. In the subsidy case we might say that the rights conferred are generated by policy and qualified by principle; in the antidiscrimination case they are generated by principle and qualified by policy.

It is plainly competent for the legislature to pursue arguments of policy and to adopt programs that are generated by such arguments. If courts are deputy legislatures, then it must be competent for them to do the same. Of course, unoriginal judicial decisions that merely enforce the clear terms of some plainly valid statute are always justified on arguments of principle, even if the statute itself was generated by policy. Suppose an aircraft manufacturer sues to recover the subsidy that the statute provides. He argues his right to the subsidy; his argument is an argument of principle. He does not argue that the national defense would be improved by subsidizing him; he might even concede that the statute was wrong on policy grounds when it was adopted, or that it should have been repealed, on policy grounds, long ago. His right to a subsidy no longer depends on any argument of policy because the statute made it a matter of principle.

But if the case at hand is a hard case, when no settled rule dictates a decision either way, then it might seem that a proper decision could be generated by either policy or principle. Consider, for example, the problem of the recent Spartan Steel case. The defendant's employees had broken an electrical cable belonging to a power company that supplied power to the plaintiff, and the plaintiff's factory was shut down while the cable was repaired. The court had to decide whether to allow the plaintiff recovery for economic loss following negligent damage to someone else's property. It might have proceeded to its decision by asking either whether a firm in the position of the plaintiff had a right to a recovery, which is a matter of principle, or whether it would be economically wise to distribute liability for accidents in the way the plaintiff suggested, which is a matter of policy.

If judges are deputy legislators, then the court should be prepared to follow the latter argument as well as the former, and decide in favor of the plaintiff if that argument recommends. That is, I suppose, what is meant by the popular idea that a court must be free to decide a novel case like *Spartan Steel* on policy grounds; and indeed Lord Denning described his own opinion in that case in just that way. I do not suppose he meant to distinguish an argument of principle from an argument of policy in the technical way I have, but he in any event did not mean to rule out an argument of policy in that technical sense.

I propose, nevertheless, the thesis that judicial decisions in civil cases, even in hard cases like *Spartan Steel*, characteristically are and should be generated by principle not policy. That thesis plainly needs much elaboration, but we may notice that certain arguments of political theory and jurisprudence support the thesis even in its abstract form. These arguments are not decisive, but they are sufficiently powerful to suggest the importance of the thesis, and to justify the attention that will be needed for a more careful formulation.

B. PRINCIPLES AND DEMOCRACY

The familiar story, that adjudication must be subordinated to legislation, is supported by two objections to judicial originality. The first argues that a community should be governed by men and women who are elected by and responsible to the majority. Since judges are, for the most part, not elected, and since they are not, in practice, responsible to the electorate in the way legislators are, it seems to compromise that proposition when judges make law. The second argues that if a judge makes new law and applies it retroactively in the case before him, then the losing party will be punished, not because he violated some duty he had, but rather a new duty created after the event.

These two arguments combine to support the traditional ideal that adjudication should be as unoriginal as possible. But they offer much more powerful objections to judicial decisions generated by policy than to those generated by principle. The first objection, that law should be made by elected and responsible officials, seems unexceptionable when we think of law as policy; that is, as a compromise among individual goals and purposes in search of the welfare of the community as a whole. It is far from clear that interpersonal comparisons of utility or preference, through which such compromises might be made objectively, make sense even in theory; but in any case no proper calculus is available in practice. Policy decisions must therefore be made through the operation of some political process designed to produce an accurate expression of the different interests that should be taken into account. The political system of representative democracy may work only indifferently in this respect, but it works better than a system that allows nonelected judges, who have no mail bag or lobbyists or pressure groups, to compromise competing interests in their chambers.

The second objection is also persuasive against a decision generated by policy. We all agree that it would be wrong to sacrifice the rights of an innocent man in the name of some new duty created after the event; it does, therefore, seem wrong to take property from one individual and hand it to another in order just to improve overall economic efficiency. But that is the form of the policy argument that would be necessary to justify a decision in *Spartan Steel*. If the plaintiff had no right to the recovery and the defendant no duty to offer it, the court could be justified in taking the defendant's property for the plaintiff only in the interest of wise economic policy.

But suppose, on the other hand, that a judge successfully justifies a decision in a hard case, like *Spartan Steel*, on grounds not of policy but of principle. Suppose, that is, that he is able to show that the plaintiff has a right to recover its damages. The two arguments just described would offer much less of an objection to the decision. The first is less relevant when a court judges principle, because an argument of principle does not often rest on assumptions about the nature and intensity of the different demands and concerns distributed throughout the community. On the contrary, an argument of principle fixes on some interest presented by the proponent of the right it describes, an interest alleged to be of such a character as to make irrelevant the fine discriminations of any argument of policy that might oppose it. A judge who is insulated from the demands of the political majority whose interests the right would trump is, therefore, in a better position to evaluate the argument.

The second objection to judicial originality has no force against an argument of principle. If the plaintiff has a right against the defendant, then the defendant has a corresponding duty, and it is that duty, not some new duty created in court, that justifies the award against him. Even if the duty has not been imposed upon him by explicit prior legislation, there is, but for one difference, no more injustice in enforcing the duty than if it had been.

The difference is, of course, that if the duty had been created by statute the defendant would have been put on much more explicit notice of that duty, and might more reasonably have been expected to arrange his affairs so as to provide for its consequences. But an argument of principle makes us look upon the defendant's claim, that it is unjust to take him by surprise, in a new light. If the plaintiff does indeed have a right to a judicial decision in his favor, then he is entitled to rely upon that right. If it is obvious and uncontroversial that he has the right, the defendant is in no position to claim unfair surprise just because the right arose in some way other than by publication in a statute. If, on the other hand, the plaintiff's claim is doubtful, then the court must, to some extent, surprise one or another of the parties; and if the court decides that on balance the plaintiff's argument is stronger, then it will also decide that the plaintiff was, on balance, more justified in his expectations. The court may, of course, be mistaken in this conclusion; but that possibility is not a consequence of the originality of its argument, for there is no reason to suppose that a court hampered by the requirement that its decisions be unoriginal will make fewer mistakes of principle than a court that is not.

C. JURISPRUDENCE

We have, therefore, in these political considerations, a strong reason to consider more carefully whether judicial arguments cannot be understood, even in hard cases, as arguments generated by principle. We have an additional reason in a familiar problem of jurisprudence. Lawyers believe that when judges make new law their decisions are constrained by legal traditions but are nevertheless personal and original. Novel decisions, it is said, reflect a judge's own political morality, but also reflect the morality that is embedded in the traditions of the common law, which might well be different. This is, of course, only law school rhetoric, but it nevertheless poses the problem of explaining how these different contributions to the decision of a hard case are to be identified and reconciled.

One popular solution relies on a spatial image; it says that the traditions of the common law contract the area of a judge's discretion to rely upon his personal morality, but do not entirely eliminate that area. But this answer is unsatisfactory on two grounds. First, it does not elucidate what is at best a provocative metaphor, which is that some morality is embedded in a mass of particular decisions other judges have reached in the past. Second, it suggests a plainly inadequate phenomenological account of the judicial decision. Judges do not decide hard cases in two stages, first checking to see where the institutional constraints end, and then setting the books aside to stride off on their own. The institutional constraints they sense are pervasive and endure to the decision itself. We therefore need an account of the interaction of personal and institutional morality that is less metaphorical and explains more successfully that pervasive interaction.

The rights thesis, that judicial decisions enforce existing political rights, suggests an explanation that is more successful on both counts. If the thesis holds, then institutional history acts not as a constraint on the political judgment of judges but as an ingredient of that judgment, because institutional history is part of the background that any plausible judgment about the rights of an individual must accommodate. Political rights are creatures of both history and morality: what an individual is entitled to have, in civil society, depends upon both the practice and the justice of its political institutions. So the supposed tension between judicial originality and institutional history is dissolved: judges must make fresh judgments about the rights of the parties who come before them, but these political rights reflect, rather than oppose, political decisions of the past. When a judge chooses between the rule established in precedent and some new rule thought to be fairer, he does not choose between history and justice. He rather makes a judgment that requires some compromise between considerations that ordinarily combine in any calculation of political right, but here compete.

The rights thesis therefore provides a more satisfactory explanation of how judges use precedent in hard cases than the explanation provided by any theory that gives a more prominent place to policy. Judges, like all political officials, are subject to the doctrine of political responsibility. This doctrine states, in its most general form, that political officials must make only such political decisions as they can justify within a political theory that also justifies the other decisions they propose to make. The doctrine seems innocuous in this general form; but it does, even in this form, condemn a style of political administration that might be called, following Rawls, intuitionistic. It condemns the practice of making decisions that seem right in isolation, but cannot be brought within some comprehensive theory of general principles and policies that is consistent with other decisions also thought right. Suppose a Congressman votes to prohibit abortion, on the ground that human life in any form is sacred, but then votes to permit the parents of babies born deformed to withhold medical treatment that will keep such babies alive. He might say that he feels that there is some difference, but the principle of responsibility, strictly applied, will not allow him these two votes unless he can incorporate the difference within some general political theory he sincerely holds.

The doctrine demands, we might say, articulate consistency. But this demand is relatively weak when policies are in play. Policies are aggregative in their influence on political decisions and it need not be part of a responsible strategy for reaching a collective goal that individuals be treated alike. It does not follow from the doctrine of responsibility, therefore, that if the legislature awards a subsidy to one aircraft manufacturer one month it must award a subsidy to another manufacturer the next. In the case of principles, however, the doctrine insists on distributional consistency from one case to the next, because it does not allow for the idea of a strategy that may be better served by unequal distribution of the benefit in question. If an official believes, for example, that sexual liberty of some sort is a right of individuals, then he must protect that liberty in a way that distributes the benefit reasonably equally over the class of those whom he supposes to have the right. If he allows one couple to use contraceptives on the ground that this right would otherwise be invaded, then he must, so long as he does not recant that earlier decision, allow the next couple the same liberty. He cannot say that the first decision gave the community just the amount of sexual liberty it needed, so that no more is required at the time of the second.

Judicial decisions are political decisions, at least in the broad sense that attracts the doctrine of political responsibility. If the rights thesis holds, then the distinction just made would account, at least in a very general way, for the special concern that judges show for both precedents and hypothetical examples. An argument of principle can supply a justification for a particular decision, under the doctrine of responsibility, only if the principle cited can be shown to be consistent with earlier decisions not recanted, and with decisions that the institution is prepared to make in the hypothetical circumstances. That is hardly surprising, but the argument would not hold if judges based their decisions on arguments of policy. They would be free to say that some policy might be adequately served by serving it in the case at bar, providing, for example, just the right subsidy to some troubled industry, so that neither earlier decisions nor hypothetical future decisions need be understood as serving the same policy.

...

III. INSTITUTIONAL RIGHTS

...

Institutional rights may be found in institutions of very different character. A chess player has a 'chess' right to be awarded a point in a tournament if he checkmates an opponent. A citizen in a democracy has a legislative right to the enactment of statutes necessary to protect his free speech. In the case of chess, institutional rights are fixed by constitutive and regulative rules that belong distinctly to the game, or to a particular tournament. Chess is, in this sense, an autonomous institution; I mean that it is understood, among its participants, that no one may claim an institutional right by direct appeal to general morality. No one may argue, for example, that he has earned the right to be declared the winner by his general virtue. But legislation is only partly autonomous in that sense. There are special constitutive and regulative rules that define what a legislature is, and who belongs to it, and how it votes, and that it may not establish a religion. But these rules belonging distinctly to legislation are rarely sufficient to determine whether a citizen has an institutional right to have a certain statute enacted; they do not decide, for example, whether he has a right to minimum wage legislation. Citizens are expected to repair to general considerations of political morality when they argue for such rights.

The fact that some institutions are fully and others partly autonomous has the consequence mentioned earlier, that the institutional rights a political theory acknowledges may diverge from the background rights it provides. Institutional rights are nevertheless genuine rights. Even if we suppose that the poor have an abstract background right to money taken from the rich, it would be wrong, not merely unexpected, for the referees of a chess tournament to award the prize money to the poorest contestant rather than the contestant with the most points. It would provide no excuse to say that since tournament rights merely describe the conditions necessary for calling the tournament a chess tournament, the referee's act is justified so long as he does not use the word 'chess' when he hands out the award. The participants entered the tournament with the understanding that chess rules would apply; they have genuine rights to the enforcement of these rules and no others.

Institutional autonomy insulates an official's institutional duty from the greater part of background political morality. But how far does the force of this insulation extend? Even in the case of a fully insulated institution like chess some rules will require interpretation or elaboration before an official may enforce them in certain circumstances. Suppose some rule of a chess tournament provides that the referee shall declare a game forfeit if one player 'unreasonably' annoys the other in the course of play. The language of the rule does not define what counts as 'unreasonable' annoyance; it does not decide whether, for example, a player who continually smiles at his opponent in such a way as to unnerve him, as the Russian grandmaster Tal once smiled at Fischer, annoys him unreasonably.

The referee is not free to give effect to his background convictions in deciding this hard case. He might hold, as a matter of political theory, that individuals have a right to equal welfare without regard to intellectual abilities. It would nevertheless be wrong for him to rely upon that conviction in deciding difficult cases under the forfeiture rule. He could not say, for example, that annoying behavior is reasonable so long as it has the effect of reducing the importance of intellectual ability in deciding who will win the game. The participants, and the general community that is interested, will say that his duty is just the contrary. Since chess is an intellectual game, he must apply the forfeiture rule in such a way as to protect, rather than jeopardize, the role of intellect in the contest.

We have, then, in the case of the chess referee, an example of an official whose decisions about institutional rights are understood to be governed by institutional constraints even when the force of these constraints is not clear. We do not think that he is free to legislate interstitially within the 'open texture' of imprecise rules. If one interpretation of the forfeiture rule will protect the character of the game, and another will not, then the participants have a right to the first interpretation. We may hope to find, in this relatively simple case, some general feature of institutional rights in hard cases that will bear on the decision of a judge in a hard case at law.

I said that the game of chess has a character that the referee's decisions must respect. What does that mean? How does a referee know that chess is an intellectual game rather than a game of chance or an exhibition of digital ballet? He may well start with what everyone knows. Every institution is placed by its participants in some very rough category of institution; it is taken to be a game rather than a religious ceremony or a form of exercise or a political process. It is, for that reason, definitional of chess that it is a game rather than an exercise in digital skill. These conventions, exhibited in attitudes and manners and in history, are decisive. If everyone takes chess to be a game of chance, so that they curse their luck and nothing else when a piece en prise happens to be taken, then chess is a game of chance, though a very bad one.

But these conventions will run out, and they may run out before the referee finds enough to decide the case of Tal's smile. It is important to see, however, that the conventions run out in a particular way. They are not incomplete, like a book whose last page is missing, but abstract, so that their full force can be captured in a concept that admits of different conceptions; that is, in a contested concept. The referee must select one or another of these conceptions, not to supplement the convention, but to enforce it. He must construct the game's character by putting to himself different sets of questions. Given that chess is an intellectual game, is it, like poker, intellectual in some sense that includes ability at psychological intimidation? Or is it, like mathematics, intellectual in some sense that does not include that ability? This first set of questions asks him to look more closely at the game, to determine whether its features support one rather than the other of these conceptions of intellect. But he must also ask a different set of questions. Given that chess is an intellectual game of some sort, what follows about reasonable behavior in a chess game? Is ability at psychological intimidation, or ability to resist such intimidation, really an intellectual quality? These questions ask him to look more closely at the concept of intellect itself.

The referee's calculations, if they are self-conscious, will oscillate between these two sets of questions, progressively narrowing the questions to be asked at the next stage. He might first identify, by reflecting on the concept, different conceptions of intellect. He might suppose at this first stage, for example, that physical grace of the sort achieved in ballet is one form of intelligence. But he must then test these different conceptions against the rules and practices of the game. That test will rule out any physical conception of intelligence. But it may not discriminate between a conception that includes or a conception that rejects psychological intimidation, because either of these conceptions would provide an account of the rules and practices that is not plainly superior, according to any general canons of explanation, to the account provided by the other. He must then ask himself which of these two accounts offers a deeper or more successful account of what intellect really is. His calculations, so conceived, oscillate between philosophy of mind and the facts of the institution whose character he must elucidate.

This is, of course, only a fanciful reconstruction of a calculation that will never take place; any official's sense of the game will have developed over a career, and he will employ rather than expose that sense in his judgments. But the reconstruction enables us to see how the concept of the game's character is tailored to a special institutional problem. Once an autonomous institution is established, such that participants have institutional rights under distinct rules belonging to that institution, then hard cases may arise that must, in the nature of the case, be supposed to have an answer. If Tal does not have a right that the game be continued, it must be because the forfeiture rule, properly understood, justifies the referee's intervention; if it does, then Fischer has a right to win at once. It is not useful to speak of the referee's 'discretion' in such a case. If some weak sense of discretion is meant, then the remark is unhelpful; if some strong sense is meant, such that Tal no longer has a right to win, then this must be, again, because the rule properly understood destroys the right he would otherwise have. Suppose we say that in such a case all the parties have a right to expect is that the referee will use his best judgment. That is, in a sense, perfectly true, because they can have no more, by way of the referee's judgment, than his best judgment. But they are nevertheless entitled to his best judgment about which behavior is, in the circumstances of the game, unreasonable; they are entitled, that is, to his best judgment about what their rights are. The proposition that there is some 'right' answer to that question does not mean that the rules of chess are exhaustive and unambiguous; rather it is a complex statement about the responsibilities of its officials and participants.

But if the decision in a hard case must be a decision about the rights of the parties, then an official's reason for that judgment must be the sort of reason that justifies recognizing or denying a right. He must bring to his decision a general theory of why, in the case of his institution, the rules create or destroy any rights at all, and he must show what decision that general theory requires in the hard case. In chess the general ground of institutional rights must be the tacit consent or understanding of the parties. They consent, in entering a chess tournament, to the enforcement of certain and only those rules, and it is hard to imagine any other general ground for supposing that they have any institutional rights. But if that is so, and if the decision in a hard case is a decision about which rights they actually have, then the argument for the decision must apply that general ground to the hard case.

The hard case puts, we might say, a question of political theory. It asks what it is fair to suppose that the players have done in consenting to the forfeiture rule. The concept of a game's character is a conceptual device for framing that question. It is a contested concept that internalizes the general justification of the institution so as to make it available for discriminations within the institution itself. It supposes that a player consents not simply to a set of rules, but to an enterprise that may be said to have a character of its own; so that when the question is put – To what did he consent in consenting to that? – the answer may study the enterprise as a whole and not just the rules.

IV. LEGAL RIGHTS

A. LEGISLATION

Legal argument, in hard cases, turns on contested concepts whose nature and function are very much like the concept of the character of a game. These include several of the substantive concepts through which the law is stated, like the concepts of a contract and of property. But they also include two concepts of much greater relevance to the present argument. The first is the idea of the 'intention' or 'purpose' of a particular statute or statutory clause. This concept provides a bridge between the political justification of the general idea that statutes create rights and those hard cases that ask what rights a particular statute has created. The second is the concept of principles that 'underlie' or are 'embedded in' the positive rules of law. This concept provides a bridge between the political justification of the doctrine that like cases should be decided alike and those hard cases in which it is unclear what that general doctrine requires. These concepts together define legal rights as a function, though a very special function, of political rights. If a judge accepts the settled practices of his legal system – if he accepts, that is, the autonomy provided by its distinct constitutive and regulative rules – then he must, according to the doctrine of political responsibility, accept some general political theory that justifies these practices. The concepts of legislative purpose and common law principles are devices for applying that general political theory to controversial issues about legal rights.

We might therefore do well to consider how a philosophical judge might develop, in appropriate cases, theories of what legislative purpose and legal principles require. We shall find that he would construct these theories in the same manner as a philosophical referee would construct the character of a game. I have invented, for this purpose, a lawyer of superhuman skill, learning, patience and acumen, whom I shall call Hercules. I suppose that Hercules is a judge in some representative American jurisdiction. I assume that he accepts the main uncontroversial constitutive and regulative rules of the law in his jurisdiction. He accepts, that is, that statutes have the general power to create and extinguish legal rights, and that judges have the general duty to follow earlier decisions of their court or higher courts whose rationale, as lawyers say, extends to the case at bar.

1. The Constitution. – Suppose there is a written constitution in Hercules' jurisdiction which provides that no law shall be valid if it establishes a religion. The legislature passes a law purporting to grant free busing to children in parochial schools. Does the grant establish a religion? The words of the constitutional provision might support either view. Hercules must nevertheless decide whether the child who appears before him has a right to her bus ride.

He might begin by asking why the constitution has any power at all to create or destroy rights. If citizens have a background right to salvation through an established church, as many believe they do, then this must be an important right. Why does the fact that a group of men voted otherwise several centuries ago prevent this background right from being made a legal right as well? His answer must take some form such as this. The constitution sets out a general political scheme that is sufficiently just to be taken as settled for reasons of fairness. Citizens take the benefit of living in a society whose institutions are arranged and governed in accordance with that scheme, and they must take the burdens as well, at least until a new scheme is put into force either by discrete amendment or general revolution. But Hercules must then ask just what scheme of principles has been settled. He must construct, that is, a constitutional theory; since he is Hercules we may suppose that he can develop a full political theory that justifies the constitution as a whole. It must be a scheme that fits the particular rules of this constitution, of course. It cannot include a powerful background right to an established church. But more than one fully specified theory may fit the specific provision about religion sufficiently well. One theory might provide, for example, that it is wrong for the government to enact any legislation that will cause great social tension or disorder; so that, since the establishment of a church will have that effect, it is wrong to empower the legislature to establish one. Another theory will provide a background right to religious liberty, and therefore argue that an established church is wrong, not because it will be socially disruptive, but because it violates that background right. In that case Hercules must turn to the remaining constitutional rules and settled practices under these rules to see which of these two theories provides a smoother fit with the constitutional scheme as a whole.

But the theory that is superior under this test will nevertheless be insufficiently concrete to decide some cases. Suppose Hercules decides that the establishment provision is justified by a right to religious liberty rather than any goal of social order. It remains to ask what, more precisely, religious liberty is. Does a right to religious liberty include the right not to have one's taxes used for any purpose that helps a religion to survive? Or simply not to have one's taxes used to benefit one religion at the expense of another? If the former, then the free transportation legislation violates that right, but if the latter it does not. The institutional structure of rules and practice may not be sufficiently detailed to rule out either of these two conceptions of religious liberty, or to make one a plainly superior justification of that structure. At some point in his career Hercules must therefore consider the question not just as an issue of fit between a theory and the rules of the institution, but as an issue of political philosophy as well. He must decide which conception is a more satisfactory elaboration of the general idea of religious liberty. He must decide that question because he cannot otherwise carry far enough the project he began. He cannot answer in sufficient detail the question of what political scheme the constitution establishes.

So Hercules is driven, by this project, to a process of reasoning that is much like the process of the self-conscious chess referee. He must develop a theory of the constitution, in the shape of a complex set of principles and policies that justify that scheme of government, just as the chess referee is driven to develop a theory about the character of his game. He must develop that theory by referring alternately to political philosophy and institutional detail. He must generate possible theories justifying different aspects of the scheme and test the theories against the broader institution. When the discriminating power of that test is exhausted, he must elaborate the contested concepts that the successful theory employs.

2. Statutes. – A statute in Hercules' jurisdiction provides that it is a federal crime for someone knowingly to transport in interstate commerce 'any person who shall have been unlawfully seized, confined, inveigled, decoyed, kidnapped, abducted, or carried away by any means whatsoever …' Hercules is asked to decide whether this statute makes a federal criminal of a man who persuaded a young girl that it was her religious duty to run away with him, in violation of a court order, to consummate what he called

a celestial marriage. The statute had been passed after a famous kidnapping case, in order to enable federal authorities to join in the pursuit of kidnappers. But its words are sufficiently broad to apply to this case, and there is nothing in the legislative record or accompanying committee reports that says they do not.

Do they apply? Hercules might himself despise celestial marriage, or abhor the corruption of minors, or celebrate the obedience of children to their parents. The groom nevertheless has a right to his liberty, unless the statute properly understood deprives him of that right; it is inconsistent with any plausible theory of the constitution that judges have the power retroactively to make conduct criminal. Does the statute deprive him of that right? Hercules must begin by asking why any statute has the power to alter legal rights. He will find the answer in his constitutional theory: this might provide, for example, that a democratically elected legislature is the appropriate body to make collective decisions about the conduct that shall be criminal. But that same constitutional theory will impose on the legislature certain responsibilities: it will impose not only constraints reflecting individual rights, but also some general duty to pursue collective goals defining the public welfare. That fact provides a useful test for Hercules in this hard case. He might ask which interpretation more satisfactorily ties the language the legislature used to its constitutional responsibilities. That is like the referee's question about the character of a game. It calls for the construction, not of some hypotheses about the mental state of particular legislators, but of a special political theory that justifies this statute, in the light of the legislature's more general responsibilities, better than any alternative theory.

Which arguments of principle and policy might properly have persuaded the legislature to enact just that statute? It should not have pursued a policy designed to replace state criminal enforcement by federal enforcement whenever constitutionally possible. That would represent an unnecessary interference with the principle of federalism that must be part of Hercules' constitutional theory. It might, however, responsibly have followed a policy of selecting for federal enforcement all crimes with such an interstate character that state enforcement was hampered. Or it could responsibly have selected just specially dangerous or widespread crimes of that character. Which of these two responsible policies offers a better justification of the statute actually drafted? If the penalties provided by the statute are large, and therefore appropriate to the latter but not the former policy, the latter policy must be preferred. Which of the different interpretations of the statute permitted by the language serves that policy better? Plainly a decision that inveiglement of the sort presented by the case is not made a federal crime by the statute.

I have described a simple and perhaps unrepresentative problem of statutory interpretation, because I cannot now develop a theory of statutory interpretation in any detail. I want only to suggest how the general claim, that calculations judges make about the purposes of statutes are calculations about political rights, might be defended. There are, however, two points that must be noticed about even this simple example. It would be inaccurate, first, to say that Hercules supplemented what the legislature did in enacting the statute, or that he tried to determine what it would have done if it had been aware of the problem presented by the case. The act of a legislature is not, as these descriptions suggest, an event whose force we can in some way measure so as to say it has run out at a particular point; it is rather an event whose content is contested in the way in which the content of an agreement to play a game is contested. Hercules constructs his political theory as an argument about what the legislature has, on this occasion, done. The contrary argument, that it did not actually do what he said, is not a realistic piece of common sense, but a competitive claim about the true content of that contested event.

Second, it is important to notice how great a role the canonical terms of the actual statute play in the process described. They provide a limit to what must otherwise be, in the nature of the case, unlimited. The political theory Hercules developed to interpret the statute, which featured a policy of providing federal enforcement for dangerous crimes, would justify a great many decisions that the legislature did not, on any interpretation of the language, actually make. It would justify, for example, a statute making it a federal crime for a murderer to leave the state of his crime. The legislature has no general duty to follow out the lines of any particular policy, and it would plainly be wrong for Hercules to suppose that the legislature had in some sense enacted that further statute. The statutory language they did enact enables this process of interpretation to operate without absurdity; it permits Hercules to say that the legislature pushed some policy to the limits of the language it used, without also supposing that it pushed that policy to some indeterminate further point.

B. THE COMMON LAW

I. Precedent. – One day lawyers will present a hard case to Hercules that does not turn upon any statute; they will argue whether earlier common law decisions of Hercules' court, properly understood, provide some party with a right to a decision in his favor. *Spartan Steel* was such a case. The plaintiff did not argue that any statute provided it a right to recover its economic damages; it pointed instead to certain earlier judicial decisions that awarded recovery for other sorts of damage, and argued that the principle behind these cases required a decision for it as well.

Hercules must begin by asking why arguments of that form are ever, even in principle, sound. He will find that he has available no quick or obvious answer. When he asked himself the parallel question about legislation he found, in general democratic theory, a ready reply. But the details of the practices of precedent he must now justify resist any comparably simple theory.

He might, however, be tempted by this answer. Judges, when they decide particular cases at common law, lay down general rules that are intended to benefit the community in some way. Other judges, deciding later cases, must therefore enforce these rules so that the benefit may be achieved. If this account of the matter were a sufficient justification of the practices of precedent, then Hercules could decide these hard common law cases as if earlier decisions were statutes, using the techniques he worked out for statutory interpretation. But he will encounter fatal difficulties if he pursues that theory very far. It will repay us to consider why, in some detail, because the errors in the theory will be guides to a more successful theory.

Statutory interpretation, as we just noticed, depends upon the availability of a canonical form of words, however vague or unspecific, that set limits to the political decisions that the statute may be taken to have made. Hercules will discover that many of the opinions that litigants cite as precedents do not contain any special propositions taken to be a canonical form of the rule that the case lays down. It is true that it was part of Anglo-American judicial style, during the last part of the nineteenth century and the first part of this century, to attempt to compose such canonical statements, so that one could thereafter refer, for example, to the rule in *Rylands v. Fletcher*. But even in this period, lawyers and textbook writers disagreed about which parts of famous opinions should be taken to have that character. Today, in any case, even important opinions rarely attempt that legislative sort of draftsmanship. They cite reasons, in the form of precedents and principles, to justify a decision, but it is the decision, not some new and stated rule of law, that these precedents and principles are taken to justify. Sometimes a judge will acknowledge openly that it lies to later cases to determine the full effect of the case he has decided.

Of course, Hercules might well decide that when he does find, in an earlier case, a canonical form of words, he will use his techniques of statutory interpretation to decide whether the rule composed of these words embraces a novel case. He might well acknowledge what could be called an enactment force of precedent. He will nevertheless find that when a precedent does have enactment force, its influence on later cases is not taken to be limited to that force. Judges and lawyers do not think that the force of precedents is exhausted, as a statute would be, by the linguistic limits of some particular phrase. If *Spartan Steel* were a New York case, counsel for the plaintiff would suppose that Cardozo's earlier decision in *MacPherson v. Buick*, in which a woman recovered damages for injuries from a negligently manufactured automobile, counted in favor of his client's right to recover, in spite of the fact that the earlier decision contained no language that could plausibly be interpreted to enact that right. He would urge that the earlier decision exerts a gravitational force on later decisions even when these later decisions lie outside its particular orbit.

This gravitational force is part of the practice Hercules' general theory of precedent must capture. In this important respect, judicial practice differs from the practice of officials in other institutions. In chess, officials conform to established rules in a way that assumes full institutional autonomy. They exercise originality only to the extent required by the fact that an occasional rule, like the rule about forfeiture, demands that originality. Each decision of a chess referee, therefore, can be said to be directly required and justified by an established rule of chess, even though some of these decisions must be based on an interpretation, rather than on simply the plain and unavoidable meaning, of that rule.

Some legal philosophers write about common law adjudication as if it were in this way like chess, except that legal rules are much more likely than chess rules to require interpretation. That is the spirit, for example, of Professor Hart's argument that hard cases arise only because legal rules have what he calls 'open texture'. In fact, judges often disagree not simply about how some rule or principle should be interpreted, but whether the rule or principle one judge cites should be acknowledged to be a rule or principle at all. In some cases both the majority and the dissenting opinions recognize the same earlier cases as relevant, but disagree about what rule or principle these precedents should be understood to have established. In adjudication, unlike chess, the argument for a particular rule may be more important than the argument from that rule to the particular case; and while the chess referee who decides a case by appeal to a rule no one has ever heard of before is likely to be dismissed or certified, the judge who does so is likely to be celebrated in law school lectures.

Nevertheless, judges seem agreed that earlier decisions do contribute to the formulation of new and controversial rules in some way other than by interpretation;

they are agreed that earlier decisions have gravitational force even when they disagree about what that force is. The legislator may very often concern himself only with issues of background morality or policy in deciding how to cast his vote on some issue. He need not show that his vote is consistent with the votes of his colleagues in the legislature, or with those of past legislatures. But the judge very rarely assumes that character of independence. He will always try to connect the justification he provides for an original decision with decisions that other judges or officials have taken in the past.

In fact, when good judges try to explain in some general way how they work, they search for figures of speech to describe the constraints they feel even when they suppose that they are making new law, constraints that would not be appropriate if they were legislators. They say, for example, that they find new rules imminent in the law as a whole, or that they are enforcing an internal logic of the law through some method that belongs more to philosophy than to politics, or that they are the agents through which the law works itself pure, or that the law has some life of its own even though this belongs to experience rather than to logic. Hercules must not rest content with these famous metaphors and personifications, but he must also not be content with any description of the judicial process that ignores their appeal to the best lawyers.

The gravitational force of precedent cannot be captured by any theory that takes the full force of precedent to be its enactment force as a piece of legislation. But the inadequacy of that approach suggests a superior theory. The gravitational force of a precedent may be explained by appeal, not to the wisdom of enforcing enactments, but to the fairness of treating like cases alike. A precedent is the report of an earlier political decision; the very fact of that decision, as a piece of political history, provides some reason for deciding other cases in a similar way in the future. This general explanation of the gravitational force of precedent accounts for the feature that defeated the enactment theory, which is that the force of a precedent escapes the language of its opinion. If the government of a community has forced the manufacturer of defective motor cars to pay damages to a woman who was injured because of the defect, then that historical fact must offer some reason, at least, why the same government should require a contractor who has caused economic damage through the defective work of his employees to make good that loss. We may test the weight of that reason, not by asking whether the language of the earlier decision, suitably interpreted, requires the contractor to pay damages, but by asking the different question whether it is fair for the government, having intervened in the way it did in the first case, to refuse its aid in the second.

Hercules will conclude that this doctrine of fairness offers the only adequate account of the full practice of precedent. He will draw certain further conclusions about his own responsibilities when deciding hard cases. The most important of these is that he must limit the gravitational force of earlier decisions to the extension of the arguments of principle necessary to justify those decisions. If an earlier decision were taken to be entirely justified by some argument of policy, it would have no gravitational force. Its value as a precedent would be limited to its enactment force, that is, to further cases captured by some particular words of the opinion. The distributional force of a collective goal, as we noticed earlier, is a matter of contingent fact and general legislative strategy. If the government intervened on behalf of Mrs. MacPherson, not because she had any right to its intervention, but only because wise strategy suggested that means of pursuing some collective goal like economic efficiency, there can be no effective argument of fairness that it therefore ought to intervene for the plaintiff in Spartan Steel.

...

So Hercules, when he defines the gravitational force of a particular precedent, must take into account only the arguments of principle that justify that precedent. If the decision in favor of Mrs. MacPherson supposes that she has a right to damages, and not simply that a rule in her favor supports some collective goal, then the argument of fairness, on which the practice of precedent relies, takes hold. It does not follow, of course, that anyone injured in any way by the negligence of another must have the same concrete right to recover that she has. It may be that competing rights require a compromise in the later case that they did not require in hers. But it might well follow that the plaintiff in the later case has the same abstract right, and if that is so then some special argument citing the competing rights will be required to show that a contrary decision in the later case would be fair.

2. The Seamless Web. – Hercules' first conclusion, that the gravitational force of a precedent is defined by the arguments of principle that support the precedent, suggests a second. Since judicial practice in his community assumes that earlier cases have a general gravitational force, then he can justify that judicial practice only by supposing that the rights thesis holds in his community. It is never taken to be a satisfactory argument against the gravitational force of some precedent that the goal that precedent served has now been served sufficiently, or that the courts would now be better occupied in serving some other goal that has been relatively neglected, possibly returning to the goal the precedent served on some other occasion. The practices of precedent do not suppose that the rationales that recommend judicial decisions can be served piecemeal in that way. If it is acknowledged that a particular precedent is justified for a particular reason; if that reason would also recommend a particular result in the case at bar; if the earlier decision has not been recanted or in some other way taken as a matter of institutional regret; then that decision must be reached in the later case.

Hercules must suppose that it is understood in his community, though perhaps not explicitly recognized, that judicial decisions must be taken to be justified by arguments of principle rather than arguments of policy. He now sees that the familiar concept used by judges to explain their reasoning from precedent, the concept of certain principles that underlie or are embedded in the common law, is itself only a metaphorical statement of the rights thesis. He may henceforth use that concept in his decisions of hard common law cases. It provides a general test for deciding such cases that is like the chess referee's concept of the character of a game, and like his own concept of a legislative purpose. It provides a question – What set of principles best justifies the precedents? – that builds a bridge between the general justification of the practice of precedent, which is fairness, and his own decision about what that general justification requires in some particular hard case.

Hercules must now develop his concept of principles that underlie the common law by assigning to each of the relevant precedents some scheme of principle that justifies the decision of that precedent. He will now discover a further important difference between this concept and the concept of statutory purpose that he used in statutory interpretation. In the case of statutes, he found it necessary to choose some theory about the purpose of the particular statute in question, looking to other acts of the legislature only insofar as these might help to select between theories that fit the statute about equally well. But if the gravitational force of precedent rests on the idea that fairness requires the consistent enforcement of rights, then Hercules must discover principles that fit, not only the particular precedent to which some litigant directs his attention, but all other judicial decisions within his general jurisdiction and, indeed, statutes as well, so far as these must be seen to be generated by principle rather than policy. He does not satisfy his duty to show that his decision is consistent with established principles, and therefore fair, if the principles he cites as established are themselves inconsistent with other decisions that his court also proposes to uphold.

Suppose, for example, that he can justify Cardozo's decision in favor of Mrs. MacPherson by citing some abstract principle of equality, which argues that whenever an accident occurs then the richest of the various persons whose acts might have contributed to the accident must bear the loss. He nevertheless cannot show that that principle has been respected in other accident cases, or, even if he could, that it has been respected in other branches of the law, like contract, in which it would also have great impact if it were recognized at all. If he decides against a future accident plaintiff who is richer than the defendant, by appealing to this alleged right of equality, that plaintiff may properly complain that the decision is just as inconsistent with the government's behavior in other cases as if MacPherson itself had been ignored. The law may not be a seamless web; but the plaintiff is entitled to ask Hercules to treat it as if it were.

You will now see why I called our judge Hercules. He must construct a scheme of abstract and concrete principles that provides a coherent justification for all common law precedents and, so far as these are to be justified on principle, constitutional and statutory provisions as well. We may grasp the magnitude of this enterprise by distinguishing, within the vast material of legal decisions that Hercules must justify, a vertical and a horizontal ordering. The vertical ordering is provided by distinguishing layers of authority; that is, layers at which official decisions might be taken to be controlling over decisions made at lower levels. In the United States the rough character of the vertical ordering is apparent. The constitutional structure occupies the highest level, the decisions of the Supreme Court and perhaps other courts interpreting that structure the next, enactments of the various legislatures the next and decisions of the various courts developing the common law different levels below that. Hercules must arrange justification of principle at each of these levels so that the justification is consistent with principles taken to provide the justification of higher levels. The horizontal ordering simply requires that the principles taken to justify a decision at one level must also be consistent with the justification offered for other decisions at that level.

Suppose Hercules, taking advantage of his unusual skills, proposed to work out this entire scheme in advance, so that he would be ready to confront litigants with an entire theory of law should this be necessary to justify any particular decision. He would begin, deferring to vertical ordering, by setting out and refining the constitutional theory he has already used. That constitutional theory would be more or less different from the theory that a different judge would develop, because a constitutional theory requires judgments about complex issues of institutional fit, as well as judgments about political and moral philosophy, and Hercules' judgments will inevitably differ from those other judges would make. These differences at a high level of vertical ordering will exercise considerable force on the scheme each judge would propose at lower levels. Hercules might think, for example, that certain substantive constitutional constraints on legislative power are best justified by postulating an abstract right to privacy against the state, because he believes that such a right is a consequence of the even more abstract right to liberty that the constitution guarantees. If so, he would regard the failure of the law of tort to recognize a parallel abstract right to privacy against fellow citizens, in some concrete form, as an inconsistency. If another judge did not share his beliefs about the connection between privacy and liberty, and so did not accept his constitutional interpretation as persuasive, that judge would also disagree about the proper development of tort.

So the impact of Hercules' own judgments will be pervasive, even though some of these will be controversial. But they will not enter his calculations in such a way that different parts of the theory he constructs can be attributed to his independent convictions rather than to the body of law that he must justify. He will not follow those classical theories of adjudication I mentioned earlier, which suppose that a judge follows statutes or precedent until the clear direction of these runs out, after which he is free to strike out on his own. His theory is rather a theory about what the statute or the precedent itself requires, and though he will, of course, reflect his own intellectual and philosophical convictions in making that judgment, that is a very different matter from supposing that those convictions have some independent force in his argument just because they are his.

3. Mistakes. – I shall not now try to develop, in further detail, Hercules' theory of law. I shall mention, however, two problems he will face. He must decide, first, how much weight he must give, in constructing a scheme of justification for a set of precedents, to the arguments that the judges who decided these cases attached to their decisions. He will not always find in these opinions any proposition precise enough to serve as a statute he might then interpret. But the opinions will almost always contain argument, in the form of propositions that the judge takes to recommend his decision. Hercules will decide to assign these only an initial or prima facie place in his scheme of justification. The purpose of that scheme is to satisfy the requirement that the government must extend to all the rights it supposes some to have. The fact that one officer of the government offers a certain principle as the ground of his decision may be taken to establish prima facie that the government does rely that far upon that principle.

But the main force of the underlying argument of fairness is forward-looking, not backward-looking. The gravitational force of Mrs. MacPherson's case depends not simply on the fact that she recovered for her Buick, but also on the fact that the government proposes to allow others in just her position to recover in the future. If the courts proposed to overrule the decision, no substantial argument of fairness, fixing on the actual decision in the case, survives in favor of the plaintiff in *Spartan Steel*. If, therefore, a principle other than the principle Cardozo cited can be found to justify MacPherson, and if this other principle also justifies a great deal of precedent that Cardozo's does not, or if it provides a smoother fit with arguments taken to justify decisions of a higher rank in vertical order, then this new principle is a more satisfactory basis for further decisions. Of course, this argument for not copying Cardozo's principle is unnecessary if the new principle is more abstract, and if Cardozo's principle can be seen as only a concrete form of that more abstract principle. In that case Hercules incorporates, rather than rejects, Cardozo's account of his decision. Cardozo, in fact, used the opinion in the earlier case of *Thomas v. Winchester*, on which case he relied, in just that fashion. It may be, however, that the new principle strikes out on a different line, so that it justifies a precedent or a series of precedents on grounds very different from what their opinions propose. Brandeis' and Warren's famous argument about the right to privacy is a dramatic illustration: they argued that this right was not unknown to the law but was, on the contrary, demonstrated by a wide variety of decisions, in spite of the fact that the judges who decided these cases mentioned no such right. It may be that their argument, so conceived, was unsuccessful, and that Hercules in their place, would have reached a different result. Hercules' theory nevertheless shows why their argument, sometimes taken to be a kind of brilliant fraud, was at least sound in its ambition.

Hercules must also face a different and greater problem. If the history of his court is at all complex, he will find, in practice, that the requirement of total consistency he has accepted will prove too strong, unless he develops it further to include the idea that he may, in applying this requirement, disregard some part of institutional history as a mistake. For he will be unable, even with his superb imagination, to find any set of principles that reconciles all standing statutes and precedents. This is hardly surprising: the legislators and judges of the past did not all have Hercules' ability or insight, nor were they men and women who were all of the same mind and opinion. Of course, any set of statutes and decisions can be explained historically, or psychologically, or sociologically, but consistency requires justification, not explanation, and the justification must be plausible and not sham. If the justification he constructs makes distinctions that are arbitrary and deploys principles that are unappealing, then it cannot count as a justification at all.

...

Hercules must expand his theory to include the idea that a justification of institutional history may display some part of that history as mistaken. But he cannot make impudent use of this device, because if he were free to take any incompatible piece of institutional history as a mistake, with no further consequences for his general theory, then the requirement of consistency would be no genuine requirement at all. He must develop some theory of institutional mistakes, and this theory of mistakes must have two parts. It must show the consequences for further arguments of taking some institutional event to be mistaken; and it must limit the number and character of the events than can be disposed of in that way.

He will construct the first part of this theory of mistakes by means of two sets of distinctions. He will first distinguish between the specific authority of any institutional event, which is its power as an institutional act to effect just the specific institutional consequences it describes, and its gravitational force. If he classifies some event as a mistake, then he does not deny its specific authority, but he does deny its gravitational force, and he cannot consistently appeal to that force in other arguments. He will also distinguish between embedded and corrigible mistakes; embedded mistakes are those whose specific authority is fixed so that it survives their loss of gravitational force; corrigible mistakes are those whose specific authority depends on gravitational force in such a way that it cannot survive this loss.

The constitutional level of his theory will determine which mistakes are embedded. His theory of legislative supremacy, for example, will insure that any statutes he treats as mistakes will lose their gravitational force but not their specific authority. If he denies the gravitational force of the aircraft liability limitation statute, the statute is not thereby repealed; the mistake is embedded so that the specific authority survives. He must continue to respect the limitations the statute imposes upon liability, but he will not use it to argue in some other case for a weaker right. If he accepts some strict doctrine of precedent, and designates some judicial decision, like the decision denying a right in negligence against an accountant, a mistake, then the strict doctrine may preserve the specific authority of that decision, which might be limited to its enactment force, but the decision will lose its gravitational force; it will become, in Justice Frankfurter's phrase, a piece of legal flotsam or jetsam. It will not be necessary to decide which.

That is fairly straightforward, but Hercules must take more pains with the second part of his theory of mistakes. He is required, by the justification he has fixed to the general practice of precedent, to compose a more detailed justification, in the form of a scheme of principle, for the entire body of statutes and common law decisions. But a justification that designates part of what is to be justified as mistaken is prima facie weaker than one that does not. The second part of his theory of mistakes must show that it is nevertheless a stronger justification than any alternative that does not recognize any mistakes, or that recognizes a different set of mistakes. That demonstration cannot be a deduction from simple rules of theory construction, but if Hercules bears in mind the connection he earlier established between precedent and fairness, this connection will suggest two guidelines for his theory of mistakes. In the first place, fairness fixes on institutional history, not just as history but as a political program that the government proposed to continue into the future; it seizes, that is, on forward-looking, not the backward-looking implications of precedent. If Hercules discovers that some previous decision, whether a statute or a judicial decision, is now widely regretted within the pertinent branch of the profession, that fact in itself distinguishes that decision as vulnerable. He must remember, second, that the argument from fairness that demands consistency is not the only argument from fairness to which government in general, or judges in particular, must respond. If he believes, quite apart from any argument of consistency, that a particular statute or decision was wrong because unfair, within the community's own concept of fairness, then that belief is sufficient to distinguish the decision, and make it vulnerable. Of course, he must apply the guidelines with a sense of the vertical structure of his overall justification, so that decisions at a lower level are more vulnerable than decisions at a higher.

Hercules will therefore apply at least two maxims in the second part of his theory of mistakes. If he can show, by arguments of history or by appeal to some sense of the legal community, that a particular principle, though it once had sufficient appeal to persuade a legislature or court to a legal decision, has now so little force that it is unlikely to generate any further such decisions, then the argument from fairness that supports that principle is undercut. If he can show by arguments of political morality that such a principle, apart from its popularity, is unjust, then the argument from fairness that supports that principle is overridden. Hercules will be delighted to find that these discriminations are familiar in the practice of other judges. The jurisprudential importance of his career does not lie in the novelty, but just in the familiarity, of the theory of hard cases that he has now created.

...

Hercules' technique encourages a judge to make his own judgments about institutional rights. The argument from judicial fallibility might be thought to suggest two alternatives. The first argues that since judges are fallible they should make no effort at all to determine the institutional rights of the parties before them, but should decide hard cases only on grounds of policy, or not at all. But that is perverse; it argues that because judges will often, by misadventure, produce unjust decisions they should make no effort to produce just ones. The second alternative argues that since judges are fallible they should submit questions of institutional right raised by hard cases to someone else. But to whom? There is no reason to credit any other particular group with better facilities of moral argument; or, if there is, then it is the process of selecting judges, not the techniques of judging that they are asked to use, that must be changed. So this form of skepticism does not in itself argue against Hercules' technique of adjudication, though of course it serves as a useful reminder to any judge that he might well be wrong in his political judgments, and that he should therefore decide hard cases with humility.

Perhaps the single most striking aspect of Dworkin's theory as described in 'Hard Cases' is his insistence that the law is a philosophical or theoretical enterprise, that it is the essence of the law that judges only provide reasons properly for their decisions when they do so in a way which, appearance notwithstanding, can be regarded as a real contribution to moral and political theory. Though this appears very flattering to judges, do you agree that judges are theorists of this kind? If not, should they be?

Recall also this claim:

Judges, like all political officials, are subject to the doctrine of political responsibility. This doctrine states, in its most general form, that political officials must make only such political decisions as they can justify within a political theory that also justifies the other decisions they propose to make.

It is worth thinking about this statement for a moment. The duty one would naturally ascribe to political officials is to serve only the interests of their subjects to the best of their ability (in particular not abuse their office by serving their own interests), for acting in this way justifies their holding office. While acting in contradictory ways which defeat their honest objectives would be a bad thing, it would seem novel to impose a duty on officials not only to make 'honest best efforts' but to achieve as well a rather high 'cognitive' standard in justifying their actions, ie to act only in ways which they can explicitly justify as part of a theoretically coherent political programme. As far as I know only certain totalitarian Marxist regimes states have ever officially set themselves this sort of goal. Consider also the common, and perhaps 'common sense', view that the law is not a 'seamless web', however much a theory might present it so. The law is a jumble, an agglomeration, of norms created at particular times for particular reasons. It would seem purely fanciful to think that most judges and lawyers *have acted* on the doctrine of political responsibility Dworkin proposes. So the question we must ask is whether, given this is so, it is reasonable to believe that judges do have the political responsibility of theorising the law so that it reads like this doctrine of political responsibility has been, for the most part, adhered to.

In any case, the effect of treating *the results of theorising* to justify the coherence of the law *as law* is massively to expand what counts as a legal reason, ie a reason a judge may properly draw upon to decide a case. Any thought that contributes to rendering a proper philosophical account of the law of a jurisdiction, a philosophical account which shows the law to be as coherent a programme to do justice amongst the subjects of a jurisdiction as it can be, is a thought that can be drawn upon by a judge as a legal reason for deciding the case one way rather than another. For obvious reasons, this bolsters Dworkin's 'right answer thesis' ie the idea that there will always be law to determine a hard case. It seems pretty clear that, given that there will always be some reasons to decide a case one way rather than another, (Dworkin admits that in a very simple legal system there might simply not be enough norms or principles to favour one theory over another, in which case there might be an actual 'tie' between competing views, but that is not a problem for any modern legal system (Dworkin 1977, 286)), the more of those reasons which count as legal reasons, the more law there is to determine an answer to a case. And it is difficult not to think that any sensible reason for deciding a case could not be scooped into the net once all considerations that contribute to a sensible theoretical accounting of the law are themselves regarded as legal considerations.

A final point to consider is the 'coherentist' nature of the task Dworkin sets judges. On this view the law can be regarded as not only the explicit law (the sort of rules and principles which a rule of recognition might easily pick out, like statutes or common law rules established in precedents), but all those implicit norms which would coherently flow from this explicit law, their coherence with the explicit law being established by recourse to an abstract moral/political theory of the law of the jurisdiction. Thus the boundaries of the law are moved outward from the positivist model via the imposition upon judges of the task of thinking theoretically beyond the explicit law. Is there not an inherent conservatism in this coherentist model of the scope of the law? As critics pointed out, 'Hard Cases' appears to suggest that judges decide hard cases in a way which fits with the general trend of the law of the jurisdiction, for only then will that decision 'cohere' with the explicit law. But do judges decide hard cases this way, and should they? Consider the case of South African judges operating under the apartheid regime. When hard cases came before them, did they decide those cases in a way that was most in keeping, that most cohered, with the racist assumptions underlying apartheid? If they didn't, would they, according to Dworkin, have been acting 'unjudicially', breaching the doctrine of political responsibility?

Further Reading

The most important goal of your further reading at this stage should be better to acquaint yourself with Dworkin's thought during this period of his career. The best source is Dworkin 1977, a collection of his essays; in Ch 3 he responds to critics of his first 'rules and principles' critique of Hart; Chs 1, 8 and 13 are also very informative. For comparison, Simpson 1987 provides a very interesting alternative critique of Hart's theory, with particular reference to the rule of recognition, in so far as it applies to the common law, though Simpson draws a significantly different conclusion from Dworkin.

Questions

1. Explain Dworkin's claim that, once the distinction between rules and principles is observed, we see that the rule of recognition cannot work as positivists claim. How would you have expected Hart to respond?

2. Critically assess Dworkin's claim that judges do not have any discretion to make law.

3. What are the various ways of distinguishing between different kinds of standards, in particular, how do Dworkin and Raz distinguish between rules and principles? Can their accounts be combined, or are they fundamentally at odds?

4. Does Dworkin's thesis in 'Hard Cases' in any way really depend upon his earlier 'rules and principles' critique of positivism?

5. What is the 'rights thesis'?

6. To what extent does Hercules serve as a reasonable ideal for the common law judge?

7. According to Dworkin in 'Hard Cases', what is the law of any jurisdiction?

8. It has been often argued that Dworkin provides not a theory of law, but a theory of adjudication. Discuss.

9 Law as Integrity: Dworkin's Interpretive Turn

James Penner

In this chapter we investigate Dworkin's 'interpretive turn'. In the 1980s Dworkin essentially completed the development of his general theory of law. The basic character of the theory remained. Judges are theorists of the law, and the conclusions they reach in their theoretical reflections concerning the general justifying principles of the law are to be regarded as much a part of the law as the explicit law 'on the books', thus providing legal grounds for deciding cases. What changed was the description of the theoretical enterprise in which they were engaged. In 'Hard Cases', Hercules appears very much as a straightforward moral/political philosopher, whose moral/political theoretical musings are constrained by his duty to articulate the moral point, purpose, or sense of the law. The judge's theoretical project is thus to find the most morally compelling theory that can be found within the history of the legal regulation of human affairs in his jurisdiction. In the 1980s, Dworkin recharacterised, or elaborated, (depending on your assessment), this theoretical project, by comparing the judge's efforts to articulate the sense of the law with the literary critic's effort to provide the best interpretation of a work of literature. Many metaphors were loosed by Dworkin in this process, the most telling perhaps is his claim that, in the same way that a critic (supposedly) interprets a work of art to show it 'in its best light', to reveal it as the best example it can be of a work of the genre to which it is taken to belong, the judge interprets the law of his jurisdiction to reveal it as the most morally sound body of law it can be, given the actual legal history the judge finds.

Dworkin (1986, 146–47, 149–53, 158–62, 164–66)

What are propositions of law really about? What in the world could make them true or false? The puzzle arises because propositions of law seem to be descriptive – they are about how things are in the law, not about how they should be – and yet it has proved extremely difficult to say exactly what it is that they describe. Legal positivists believe that propositions of law are indeed wholly descriptive: they are pieces of history.

A proposition of law, in their view, is true just in case some event of a designated lawmaking kind has taken place, and otherwise not. This seems to work reasonably well in very simple cases. If the Illinois legislature enacts the words 'No will shall be valid without three witnesses', then the proposition of law, that an Illinois will needs three witnesses, seems to be true only in virtue of that historical event.

But in more difficult cases the analysis fails. Consider the proposition that a particular affirmative action scheme (not yet tested in the courts) is constitutionally valid. If that is true, it cannot be so just in virtue of the text of the Constitution and the fact of prior court decisions, because reasonable lawyers who know exactly what the Constitution says and what the courts have done may yet disagree whether it is true. (I am doubtful that the positivists' analysis holds even in the simple case of the will; but that is a different matter I shall not argue here.)

What are the other possibilities? One is to suppose that controversial propositions of law, like the affirmative action statement, are not descriptive at all but are rather expressions of what the speaker wants the law to be. Another is more ambitious: controversial statements are attempts to describe some pure objective or natural law, which exists in virtue of objective moral truth rather than historical decision. Both these projects take some legal statements, at least, to be purely evaluative as distinct from descriptive: they express either what the speaker prefers – his personal politics – or what he believes is objectively required by the principles of an ideal political morality. Neither of these projects is plausible, because someone who says that a particular untested affirmative action plan is constitutional does mean to describe the law as it is rather than as he wants it to be or thinks that, by the best moral theory, it should be. He might say that he regrets that the plan is constitutional and thinks that, according to the best moral theory, it ought not to be.

There is a better alternative: propositions of law are not merely descriptive of legal history, in a straightforward way, nor are they simply evaluative in some way divorced from legal history. They are interpretive of legal history, which combines elements of both description and evaluation but is different from both.

LITERATURE

THE AESTHETIC HYPOTHESIS

If lawyers are to benefit from a comparison between legal and literary interpretation, however, they must see the latter in a certain light, and in this section I shall try to say what that is. (I would prefer the following remarks about literature to be uncontroversial among literary scholars, but I am afraid they will not be.) Students of literature do many things under the titles of 'interpretation' and 'hermeneutics', and most of them are also called 'discovering the meaning of a text'. I shall not be interested, except incidentally, in one thing these students do, which is trying to discover the sense in which some author used a particular word or phrase. I am interested instead in arguments which offer some sort of interpretation of the meaning of a work as a whole. These sometimes take the form of assertions about characters: that Hamlet really loved his mother, for example, or that he really hated her, or that there really was no ghost but only Hamlet himself in a schizophrenic manifestation. Or about events in the story behind the story: that Hamlet and Ophelia were lovers before the play begins (or were not). More usually they offer hypotheses directly about the 'point' or 'theme' or 'meaning' or 'sense' or 'tone' of the play as a whole: that Hamlet is a play about death, for example, or about generations, or about politics. These interpretive claims may have a practical point. They may guide a director staging a new performance of the play, for example. But they may also be of more general importance, helping us to an improved understanding of important parts of our cultural environment. Of course, difficulties about the speaker's meaning of a particular word in the text (a 'crux' of interpretation) may bear upon these larger matters. But the latter are about the point or meaning of the work as a whole, rather than the sense of a particular phrase.

Critics much disagree about how to answer such questions. I want, so far as is possible, not to take sides but to try to capture the disagreements in some sufficiently general description of what they are disagreeing about. My apparently banal suggestion (which I shall call the 'aesthetic hypothesis') is this: an interpretation of a piece of literature attempts to show which way of reading (or speaking or directing or acting) the text reveals it as the best work of art. Different theories or schools or traditions of interpretation disagree on this hypothesis, because they assume significantly different normative theories about what literature is and what it is for and about what makes one work of literature better than another.

I expect that this suggestion, in spite of its apparent weakness, will be rejected by many scholars as confusing interpretation with criticism or, in any case, as hopelessly relativistic, and therefore as a piece of skepticism that really denies the possibility of interpretation altogether. Indeed the aesthetic hypothesis might seem only another formulation of a theory now popular, which is that since interpretation creates a work of art and represents only the fiat of a particular critical community, there are only interpretations and no best interpretation of any particular poem or novel or play. But the aesthetic hypothesis is neither so wild nor so weak nor so inevitably relativistic as might first appear.

Interpretation of a text attempts to show it as the best work of art it can be, and the pronoun insists on the difference between explaining a work of art and changing it into a different one. Perhaps Shakespeare could have written a better play based on the sources he used for Hamlet than he did, and in that better play the hero would have been a more forceful man of action. It does not follow that Hamlet, the play he wrote, really is like that after all. Of course, a theory of interpretation must contain a subtheory about identity of a work of art in order to be able to tell the difference between interpreting and changing a work. (Any useful theory of identity will be controversial, so that this is one obvious way in which disagreements in interpretation will depend on more general disagreements in aesthetic theory.)

Contemporary theories of interpretation all seem to use, as part of their response to that requirement, the idea of a canonical text (or score, in the case of music, or unique physical object, in the case of most art). The text provides one severe constraint in the name of identity: all the words must be taken account of and none may be changed to make 'it' a putatively better work of art. (This constraint, however familiar, is not inevitable. A joke, for example, may be the same joke though told in a variety of forms, none of them canonical; an interpretation of a joke will choose a particular way in which to put it, and this may be wholly original, in order to bring out its 'real' point or why it is 'really' funny.) So any literary critic's style of interpretation will be sensitive to his theoretical beliefs about the nature of and evidence for a canonical text.

An interpretive style will also be sensitive to the interpreter's opinions about coherence or integrity in art. An interpretation cannot make a work of art more distinguished if it makes a large part of the text irrelevant, or much of the incident accidental, or a great part of the trope or style unintegrated and answering only to independent standards of fine writing. So it does not follow, from the aesthetic hypothesis, that because a philosophical novel is aesthetically more valuable than a mystery story, an Agatha Christie novel is really a treatise on the meaning of death. This interpretation fails not only because an Agatha Christie, taken to be a tract on death, is a poor tract less valuable than a good mystery, but because the interpretation makes the novel a shambles. All but one or two sentences would be irrelevant to the supposed theme; and the organisation, style, and figures would be appropriate not to a philosophical novel but to an entirely different genre. Some books originally offered to the public as mysteries or thrillers (and perhaps thought of by their authors that way) have indeed been 'reinterpreted' as something more ambitious. The present critical interest in Raymond Chandler is an example. But the fact that this reinterpretation can be successful in the case of Chandler, but not Christie, illustrates the constraint of integrity.

There is nevertheless room for much disagreement among critics about what counts as integration, about which sort of unity is desirable and which irrelevant or undesirable. Is it really an advantage that the tongue of the reader, in reading a poem aloud, must 'mime' motions or directions that figure in the tropes or narrative of the poem? Does this improve integrity by adding yet another dimension of coordination? Is it an advantage when conjunctions and line endings are arranged so that the reader 'negotiating' a poem develops contradictory assumptions and readings as he goes on, so that his understanding at the end is very different from what it was at discrete points along the way? Does this add another dimension of complexity to unity, or does it rather compromise unity because a work of literature should be capable of having the same meaning or import when read a second time? Schools of interpretation will rise or fall in response to these questions of aesthetic theory, which is what the aesthetic hypothesis suggests.

The major differences among schools of interpretation are less subtle, however, because they touch not these quasi-formal aspects of art but the function or point of art more broadly conceived. Does literature have (primarily or substantially) a cognitive point? Is art better when it is in some way instructive, when we learn something from it about how people are or what the world is like? If so and if psychoanalysis is true (please forgive that crude way of putting it), then a psychoanalytic interpretation of a piece of literature will show why it is successful art. Is art good insofar as it is successful communication in the ordinary sense? If so, then a good interpretation will focus on what the author intended, because communication is not successful unless it expresses what a speaker wants it to express. Or is art good when it is expressive in a different sense, insofar as it has the capacity to stimulate or inform the lives of those who experience it? If so, then interpretation will place the reader (or listener or viewer) in the foreground. It will point out the reading of the work that makes it most valuable – best as a work of art – in that way.

Theories of art do not exist in isolation from philosophy, psychology, sociology, and cosmology. Someone who accepts a religious point of view will probably have a different theory of art from someone who does not, and recent critical theories have made us see how far interpretive style is sensitive to beliefs about meaning, reference, and other technical issues in the philosophy of language. But the aesthetic hypothesis does not assume that anyone who interprets literature will have a fully developed and self-conscious aesthetic theory. Nor that everyone who interprets must subscribe entirely to one or another of the schools I crudely described. The best critics, I think, deny that there is one unique function or point of literature. A novel or a play may be valuable in any number of ways, some of which we learn by reading or looking or listening, rather than by abstract reflection about what good art must be like or for.

Nevertheless, anyone who interprets a work of art relies on beliefs of a theoretical character about identity and other formal properties of art, as well as on more explicitly normative beliefs about what is good in art. Both sorts of beliefs figure in the judgment that one way of reading a text makes it a better text than another way. These beliefs may be inarticulate (or 'tacit'). They are still genuine beliefs (and not merely 'reactions') because their force for any critic or reader can be seen at work not just on one isolated occasion of interpretation but in any number of other occasions, and because they figure in and are amenable to argument. (These weak claims do not take sides in the running debate whether there are any necessary or sufficient 'principles of value' in art or whether a theory of art could ever justify an interpretation in the absence of direct experience of the work being interpreted.)

None of this touches the major complaint I anticipated against the aesthetic hypothesis: that it is trivial. Obviously (you might say) different interpretive styles are grounded in different theories of what art is and what it is for and what makes art good art. The point is so banal that it might as well be put the other way around: different theories of art are generated by different theories of interpretation. If someone thinks stylistics are important to interpretation, he will think a work of art better because it integrates pronunciation and trope; if someone is attracted by deconstruction, he will dismiss reference in its familiar sense from any prominent place in an account of language. Nor does my elaboration of the hypothesis in any way help to adjudicate among theories of interpretation or to rebut the charge of nihilism or relativism. On the contrary, since people's views about what makes art good art are inherently subjective, the aesthetic hypothesis abandons hope of rescuing objectivity in interpretation except, perhaps, among those who hold very much the same theory of art, which is hardly very helpful.

No doubt the aesthetic hypothesis is in important ways banal – it must be abstract if it is to provide an account of what a wide variety of theories disagree about – but it is perhaps not so weak as all that. The hypothesis has the consequence that academic theories of interpretation are no longer seen as what they often claim to be – analyses of the very idea of interpretation – but rather as candidates for the best answer to the substantive question posed by interpretation. Interpretation becomes a concept of which different theories are competing conceptions. (It follows that there is no radical difference but only a difference in the level of abstraction between offering a theory of interpretation and offering an interpretation of a particular work of art.) The hypothesis denies, moreover, the sharp distinctions some scholars have cultivated. There is no longer a flat distinction between interpretation, conceived as discovering the real meaning of a work of art, and criticism, conceived as evaluating its success or importance. Some distinction remains, because there is always a difference between saying how good a particular work can be made to be and saying how good that is. But evaluative beliefs about art figure in both these judgments.

Objectivity is another matter. It is an open question, I think, whether the main judgments we make about art can properly be said to be true or false, valid or invalid. This question is part of the more general philosophical issue of objectivity, presently much discussed in both ethics and the philosophy of language, and no one is entitled to a position who studies the case of aesthetic judgment alone. Of course no important aesthetic claim can be 'demonstrated' to be true or false; no argument can be produced for any interpretation which we can be sure will commend itself to everyone, or even everyone with experience and training in the appropriate form of art. If this is what it means to say that aesthetic judgments are subjective – that they are not demonstrable – then they are subjective. But it does not follow that no normative theory about art is better than any other, nor that one theory cannot be the best that has so far been produced.

...

LAW AND LITERATURE

THE CHAIN OF LAW

These sketchy remarks about literary interpretation may have suggested too sharp a distinction between the role of the artist in creating a work of art and that of the critic in interpreting it later. The artist can create nothing without interpreting as he creates; since he intends to produce art, he must have at least a tacit theory of why what he produces is art and why it is a better work of art through this stroke of the pen or the brush or the chisel rather than that. The critic, for his part, creates as he interprets; for though he is bound by the fact of the work, defined in the more formal and academic parts of his theory of art, his more practical artistic sense is engaged by his responsibility to decide which way of seeing or reading or understanding that work shows it as better art. Nevertheless, there is a difference between interpreting while creating and creating while interpreting, and therefore a recognisable difference between the artist and the critic.

I want to use literary interpretation as a model for the central method of legal analysis, and I therefore need to show how even this distinction between artist and critic might be eroded in certain circumstances. Suppose that a group of novelists is engaged for a particular project and that they draw lots to determine the order of play. The lowest number writes the opening chapter of a novel, which he or she then sends to the next number, who adds a chapter, with the understanding that he is adding a chapter to that novel rather than beginning a new one, and then sends the two chapters to the next number, and so on. Now every novelist but the first has the dual responsibilities of interpreting and creating because each must read all that has gone before in order to establish, in the interpretivist sense, what the novel so far created is. He or she must decide what the characters are 'really' like; what motives guide them; what the point or theme of the developing novel is; how far some literary device or figure, consciously or unconsciously used, contributes to these, and whether it should be extended or refined or trimmed or dropped in order to send the novel further in one direction rather than another. This must be interpretation in a non-intention-bound style because, at least for all novelists after the second, there is no single author whose intentions any interpreter can, by the rules of the project, regard as decisive.

Some novels have in fact been written in this way (including the softcore pornographic novel Naked Came the Stranger), though for a debunking purpose; and certain parlor games, for rainy weekends in English country houses, have something of the same structure. But in my imaginary exercise the novelists are expected to take their responsibilities seriously and to recognize the duty to create, so far as they can, a single, unified novel rather than, for example, a series of independent short stories with characters bearing the same names. Perhaps this is an impossible assignment; perhaps the project is doomed to produce not just a bad novel but no novel at all, because the best theory of art requires a single creator or, if more than one, that each have some control over the whole. But what about legends and jokes? I need not push that question further because I am interested only in the fact that the assignment makes sense, that each of the novelists in the chain can have some idea of what he or she is asked to do, whatever misgivings each might have about the value or character of what will then be produced.

Deciding hard cases at law is rather like this strange literary exercise. The similarity is most evident when judges consider and decide common law cases; that is, when no statute figures centrally in the legal issue, and the argument turns on which rules or principles of law 'underlie' the related decisions of other judges in the past. Each judge is then like a novelist in the chain. He or she must read through what other judges in the past have written not only to discover what these judges have said, or their state of mind when they said it, but to reach an opinion about what these judges have collectively done, in the way that each of our novelists formed an opinion about the collective novel so far written. Any judge forced to decide a lawsuit will find, if he looks in the appropriate books, records of many arguably similar cases decided over decades or even centuries past by many other judges of different styles and judicial and political philosophies, in periods of different orthodoxies of procedure and judicial convention. Each judge must regard himself, in deciding the new case before him, as a partner in a complex chain enterprise of which these innumerable decisions, structures, conventions, and practices are the history; it is his job to continue that history into the future through what he does on the day. He must interpret what has gone before because he has a responsibility to advance the enterprise in hand rather than strike out in some new direction of his own. So he must determine, according to his own judgment, what the earlier decisions come to, what the point or theme of the practice so far, taken as a whole, really is.

The judge in the hypothetical case ... about an aunt's emotional shock, must decide what the theme is not only of the particular precedent of the mother in the road but of accident cases, including that precedent, as a whole. He might be forced to choose, for example, between these two theories about the 'meaning' of that chain of decisions. According to the first, negligent drivers are responsible to those whom their behavior is likely to cause physical harm, but they are responsible to these people for whatever injury – physical or emotional – they in fact cause. If this is the correct principle, then the decisive difference between that case and the aunt's case is just that the aunt was not within the physical risk, and therefore she cannot recover. On the second theory, however, negligent drivers are responsible for any damage they can reasonably be expected to foresee if they think about their behavior in advance. If that is the right principle, then the aunt may yet recover. Everything turns on whether it is sufficiently foreseeable that a child will have relatives, beyond his or her immediate parents, who may suffer emotional shock when they learn of the child's injury. The judge trying the aunt's case must decide which of these two principles represents the better 'reading' of the chain of decisions he must continue.

Can we say, in some general way, what those who disagree about the best interpretation of legal precedent are disagreeing about? I said that a literary interpretation aims to show how the work in question can be seen as the most valuable work of art, and so must attend to formal features of identity, coherence, and integrity as well as more substantive considerations of artistic value. A plausible interpretation of legal practice must also, in a parallel way, satisfy a test of two dimensions: it must both fit that practice and show its point or value. But point or value here cannot mean artistic value because law, unlike literature, is not an artistic enterprise. Law is a political enterprise, whose general point, if it has one, lies in coordinating social and individual effort, or resolving social and individual disputes, or securing justice between citizens and between them and their government, or some combination of these. (This characterization is itself an interpretation, of course, but allowable now because relatively neutral.) So an interpretation of any body or division of law, like the law of accidents, must show the value of that body of law in political terms by demonstrating the best principle or policy it can be taken to serve.

We know from the parallel argument in literature that this general description of interpretation in law is not license for each judge to find in doctrinal history whatever he thinks should have been there. The same distinction holds between interpretation and ideal. A judge's duty is to interpret the legal history he finds, not to invent a better history. The dimensions of fit will provide some boundaries. There is, of course, no algorithm for deciding whether a particular interpretation sufficiently fits that history not to be ruled out. When a statute or constitution or other legal document is part of the doctrinal history, speaker's meaning will play a role. But the choice of which of several crucially different senses of speaker's or legislator's intention is the appropriate one cannot itself be referred to anyone's intention but must be decided, by whoever must make the decision, as a question of political theory. In the common law cases the question of fit is more complex. Any particular hypothesis about the point of a string of decisions ('these decisions establish the principle that no one can recover for emotional damage who did not lie within the area of physical danger himself') is likely to encounter if not flat counter-examples in some earlier case at least language or argument that seems to suggest the contrary. So any useful conception of interpretation must contain a doctrine of mistake – as must any novelist's theory of interpretation for the chain novel. Sometimes a legal argument will explicitly recognize such mistakes: 'Insofar as the cases of A v. B and C v. D may have held to the contrary, they were, we believe, wrongly decided and need not be followed here.' Sometimes the doctrine of precedent forbids this crude approach and requires something like: 'We held, in E v. F, that such-and-such, but that case raised special issues and must, we think, be confined to its own facts' (which is not quite so disingenuous as it might seem).

This flexibility may seem to erode the difference on which I insist, between interpretation and a fresh, clean-slate decision about what the law ought to be. But there is nevertheless this overriding constraint. Any judge's sense of the point or function of law, on which every aspect of his approach to interpretation will depend, will include or imply some conception of the integrity and coherence of law as an institution, and this conception will both tutor and constrain his working theory of fit – that is, his convictions about how much of the prior law an interpretation must fit, and which of it, and how. (The parallel with literary interpretation holds here as well.)

It should be apparent, however, that any particular judge's theory of fit will often fail to produce a unique interpretation. (The distinction between hard and easy cases at law is perhaps just the distinction between cases in which they do and do not.) Just as two readings of a poem may each find sufficient support in the text to show its unity and coherence, two principles may each find enough support in the various decisions of the past to satisfy any plausible theory of fit. In that case substantive political theory (like substantive considerations of artistic merit) will play a decisive role. Put bluntly, the interpretation of accident law, that a careless driver is liable to those whose damage is both substantial and foreseeable, is probably a better interpretation, if it is, only because it states a sounder principle of justice than any principle that distinguishes between physical and emotional damage or that makes recovery for emotional damage depend on whether the plaintiff was in danger of physical damage. (I should add that this issue, as an issue of political morality, is very complex, and many distinguished judges and lawyers have taken each side.)

We might summarize these points this way. Judges develop a particular approach to legal interpretation by forming and refining a political theory sensitive to those issues on which interpretation in particular cases will depend; and they call this their legal philosophy. It will include both structural features, elaborating the general requirement that an interpretation must fit doctrinal history, and substantive claims about social goals and principles of justice. Any judge's opinion about the best interpretation will therefore be the consequence of beliefs other judges need not share. If a judge believes that the dominant purpose of a legal system, the main goal it ought to serve, is economic, then he will see in past accident decisions some strategy for reducing the economic costs of accidents overall. Other judges, who find any such picture of the law's function distasteful, will discover no such strategy in history but only, perhaps, an attempt to reinforce conventional morality of fault and responsibility. If we insist on a high order of neutrality in our description of legal interpretation, therefore, we cannot make our description of the nature of legal interpretation much more concrete than I have.

...

POLITICS IN INTERPRETATION

If my claims about the role of politics in legal interpretation are sound, then we should expect to find distinctly liberal or radical or conservative opinions not only about what the Constitution and laws of our nation should be but also about what they are. And this is exactly what we do find. Interpretation of the equal protection clause of the United States Constitution provides especially vivid examples. There can be no useful interpretation of what that clause means which is independent of some theory about what political equality is and how far equality is required by justice, and the history of the last half-century of constitutional law is largely an exploration of exactly these issues of political morality. Conservative lawyers argued steadily (though not consistently) in favor of an author's intentions style of interpreting this clause, and they accused others, who used a different style with more egalitarian results, of inventing rather than interpreting law. But this was bluster meant to hide the role their own political convictions played in their choice of interpretive style, and the great legal debates over the equal protection clause would have been more illuminating if it had been more widely recognized that reliance on political theory is not a corruption of interpretation but part of what interpretation means.

Dworkin's metaphor of the 'chain novel' (though the metaphor of a never-ending soap opera might work better) describes how judges develop the law in such a way as to show fidelity to the past, but also in a way that requires them to make creative judgments which reflect their own evaluations as to the best way to proceed. The past 'law' constrains what they can do, but they are nevertheless required to show genuine evaluative judgment in going on. They are therefore not slaves to the past law, but neither are they free to 'strike off on their own' so as to depart radically from what has gone before.

Dworkin wrote this article at the height of the critical legal studies movement's influence, one of whose central claims (recall Chapter 7) was that the law does not provide any apolitical constraints upon what judges could decide; rather, judges give decisions which reflect their (largely centrist) political orientations. The extant past law does not provide any determinate guidance as to how cases should be decided – by cleverly manipulating precedents and statutes, a clever judge can 'find' textual support for almost any decision. The only thing that keeps the law in some sort of consistent shape is the fact that judges and lawyers are by and large successfully indoctrinated in the more or less liberal, centrist, political tradition; thus the constraints upon their decision-making power are ideological, not a matter of the substance of the law. Dworkin appears to provide an answer: we first identify a work of art, then seek to interpret it to make of it the best work of art it can be; by analogy, one presumes there is a pre-interpretive body of law which we can identify, and then set out to interpret so as to make of this law the most morally compelling it can be. Because there is this pre-interpretive body of law, a judge *cannot* just decide a case any way he likes; he cannot manipulate statutes and precedents to reach any result he desires, for that would not be interpreting the law as he finds it. Thus the pre-interpretive body of law constrains the range of interpretations a judge can make of it; the 'infinite manipulability' of the law is a sceptical myth. However, in the next reading, Fish argues that the constraint Dworkin wishes to find in the pre-interpretive identification of works of art and in pre-interpretive bodies of law is itself mythical.

Fish (1982, 552–60, 562, 565–67)

We can begin by focusing on the most extended example in his essay of a 'chain enterprise', the imagined literary example of a novel written not by a single author but by a group of co-authors, each of whom is responsible for a separate chapter … Now every novelist but the first has the dual responsibilities of interpreting and creating, because each must read all that has gone before in order to establish, in the interpretivist sense, what the novel so far created is. He or she must decide what the characters are 'really' like; what motives in fact guide them; what the point or theme of the developing novel is; how far some literary device or figure, consciously or unconsciously used, contributes to these, and whether it should be extended or refined or trimmed or dropped in order to send the novel further in one direction rather than another.

In its deliberate exaggeration, this formulation of a chain enterprise is helpful and illuminating, but it is also mistaken in several important respects. First of all, it assumes that the first person in the chain is in a position different in kind from those who follow him because he is only creating while his fellow authors must both create and interpret. In an earlier draft of the essay Dworkin had suggested that as the chain extends itself the freedom enjoyed by the initiator of the sequence is more and more constrained, until at some point the history against which 'late novelists' must work may become so dense 'as to admit only one good-faith interpretation'; and indeed that interpretation will not be an interpretation in the usual sense because it will have been demanded by what has already been written. Dworkin has now withdrawn this suggestion (which he had qualified with words like 'probably'), but the claim underlying it – the claim that constraints thicken as the chain lengthens – remains as long as the distinction between the first author and all the others is maintained. The idea is that the first author is free because he is not obliged 'to read all that has gone before' and therefore doesn't have to decide what the characters are 'really' like and what motives guide them, and so on. But in fact the first author has surrendered his freedom (although, as we shall see, surrender is exactly the wrong word) as soon as he commits himself to writing a novel, for he makes his decision under the same constraints that rule the decisions of his collaborators. He must decide, for example, how to begin the novel, but the decision is not 'free' because the very notion 'beginning a novel' exists only in the context of a set of practices that at once enable and limit the act of beginning. One cannot think of beginning a novel without thinking within, as opposed to thinking 'of', these established practices, and even if one 'decides' to 'ignore' them or 'violate' them or 'set them aside', the actions of ignoring and violating and setting aside will themselves have a shape that is constrained by the preexisting shape of those practices. This does not mean that the decisions of the first author are wholly determined, but that the choices available to him are 'novel writing choices', choices that depend on a prior understanding of what it means to write a novel, even when he 'chooses' to alter that understanding. In short he is neither free nor constrained (if those words are understood as referring to absolute states), but free and constrained. He is free to begin whatever kind of novel he decides to write, he is constrained by the finite (although not unchanging) possibilities that are subsumed in the notions 'kind of novel' and 'beginning a novel'.

Moreover, those who follow him are free and constrained in exactly the same way. When a later novelist decides to 'send the novel further in one direction rather than in another', that decision must follow upon a decision as to what direction has already been taken; and that decision will be an interpretive one in the sense that it will not be determined by the independent and perspicuous shape of the words, but will be the means by which the words are given a shape. Later novelists do not read directly from the words to a decision about the point or theme of the novel, but from a prior understanding (which may take a number of forms) of the points or themes novels can possibly have to a novelistic construction of the words. Just as the first novelist 'creates' within the constraints of 'novel-practice' in general, so do his successors on the chain interpret him (and each other) within those same constraints. Not only are those constraints controlling, but they are uniformly so; they do not relax or tighten in relation to the position an author happens to occupy on the chain. The last author is as free, within those constraints, to determine what 'the characters are really like' as is the first. It is of course tempting to think that the more information one has (the more history) the more directed will be one's interpretation; but information only comes in an interpreted form (it does not announce itself). No matter how much or how little you have, it cannot be a check against interpretation because even when you first 'see' it, interpretation has already done its work. So that rather than altering the conditions of interpretation, the accumulation of chapters merely extends the scope of its operation.

If this seems counterintuitive, imagine the very real possibility of two (or more) 'later' novelists who have different views of the direction the novel has taken and are therefore in disagreement as to what would constitute a continuation of 'that' novel as opposed to 'beginning a new one'. To make the example more specific, let us further imagine that one says to another, 'Don't you see that it's ironic, a social satire?', and the second replies, 'Not at all, at most it's a comedy of manners', while a third chimes in, 'You're both wrong; it's obviously a perfectly straightforward piece of realism'. If Dworkin's argument is to hold, that is, if the decisions he talks about are to be constrained in a strong sense by an already-in-place text, it must be possible to settle this disagreement by appealing to that text. But it is precisely because the text appears differently in the light of different assumptions as to what is its mode that there is a disagreement in the first place. Or, to put it another way, 'social satire', 'comedy of manners', and 'piece of realism' are not labels applied mechanically to perspicuous instances; rather, they are names for ways of reading, ways which when put into operation render from the text the 'facts' which those who are proceeding within them then cite. It is entirely possible that the parties to our imagined dispute might find themselves pointing to the same 'stretch of language' (no longer the same, since each would be characterizing it differently) and claiming it as a 'fact' in support of opposing interpretations. (The history of literary criticism abounds in such scenarios.) Each would then believe, and be able to provide reasons for his belief, that only he is continuing the novel in the direction it has taken so far and that the others are striking out in a new and unauthorized direction.

Again, this does not mean that a late novelist is free to decide anything he likes (or that there is no possibility of adjudicating a disagreement), but that within the general parameters of novel reading practice, he is as free as anyone else, which means that he is as constrained as anyone else. He is constrained in that he can only continue in ways that are recognizable novel ways (and the same must be said of the first novelist's act of 'beginning'), and he is free in that no amount of textual accumulation can make his choice of one of those ways inescapable. Although the parameters of novel practice mark the limits of what anyone who is thinking within them can think to do, within those limits they do not direct anyone to do this rather than that. (They are not a 'higher' text.) Every decision a late novelist makes will rest on his assessment of the situation as it has developed; but that assessment will itself be an act of interpretation which will in turn rest on an interpreted understanding of the enterprise in general.

This, then, is my first criticism of Dworkin's example: the distinction it is supposed to illustrate – the distinction between the first and later novelists – will not hold up because everyone in the enterprise is equally constrained. (By 'equally' I mean equally with respect to the condition of freedom; I am making no claims about the number or identity of the constraints.) My second criticism is that in his effort to elaborate the distinction Dworkin embraces both of the positions he criticizes. He posits for the first novelist a freedom that is equivalent to the freedom assumed by those who believe that judges (and other interpreters) are bound only by their personal preferences and desires; and he thinks of later novelists as bound by a previous history in a way that would be possible only if the shape and significance of that history were self-evident. Rather than avoiding the Scylla of legal realism ('making it up wholesale') and the Charybdis of strict constructionism ('finding the law just "there"'), he commits himself to both. His reason for doing so becomes clear when he extends the example to an analysis of the law:

> Deciding hard cases at law is rather like this strange literary exercise. The similarity is most evident when judges consider and decide 'common-law' cases; that is, when no statute figures centrally in the legal issue, and the argument turns on which rules or principles of law 'underlie' the related decisions of other judges in the past. Each judge is then like a novelist in the chain. He or she must read through what other judges in the past have written not simply to discover what these judges have said, or their state of mind when they said it, but to reach an opinion about what these other judges have collectively done, in the way that each of our novelists formed an opinion about the collective novel so far written. Any judge forced to decide any law suit will find, if he looks in the appropriate books, records of many arguably similar cases decided over decades or even centuries past by many other judges of different styles and judicial and political philosophies, in periods of different orthodoxies of procedure and judicial convention. Each judge must regard himself, in deciding the case before him, as a partner in a complex chain enterprise of which these innumerable decisions, structures, conventions and practices are the history; it is his job to continue that history into the future through what he does. He must interpret what has gone before because he has a responsibility to advance the enterprise in hand rather than strike out in some new direction of his own.

The emphasis on the word 'must' alerts us to what is at stake for Dworkin in the notion of a chain enterprise. It is a way of explaining how judges are kept from striking out in a new direction, much as later novelists are kept by the terms of their original agreement from beginning a new novel. Just as it is the duty of a later novelist to continue the work of his predecessors, so it is the duty of a judge to 'advance the enterprise in hand'. Presumably, the judge who is tempted to strike out in 'some direction of his own' will be checked by his awareness of his responsibility to the corporate enterprise; he will then comport himself as a partner in the chain rather than as a free and independent agent.

The force of the account, in other words, depends on the possibility of judges comporting themselves in ways other than the 'chain-enterprise' way. But is there in fact any such possibility? What would it mean for a judge to strike out in a new direction?

Dworkin doesn't tell us, but presumably it would mean deciding a case in such a way as to have no relationship to the history of previous decisions. It is hard to imagine what such a decision would be like since any decision, to be recognized as a decision by a judge, would have to be made in recognizably judicial terms. A judge who decided a case on the basis of whether or not the defendant had red hair would not be striking out in a new direction; he would simply not be acting as a judge, because he could give no reasons for his decision that would be seen as reasons by competent members of the legal community. (Even in so extreme a case it would not be accurate to describe the judge as striking out in a new direction; rather he would be continuing the direction of an enterprise – perhaps a bizarre one – other than the judicial.) And conversely, if in deciding a case a judge is able to give such reasons, then the direction he strikes out in will not be new because it will have been implicit in the enterprise as a direction one could conceive of and argue for. This does not mean that his decision will be above criticism, but that it will be criticized, if it is criticized, for having gone in one judicial direction rather than another, neither direction being 'new' in a sense that would give substance to Dworkin's fears.

Those fears are equally groundless with respect to the other alternative Dworkin imagines, the judge who looks at the chain of previous decisions and decides to see in it 'whatever he thinks should have been there'. Here the danger is not so much arbitrary action (striking out in a new direction) as it is the wilful imposition of a personal perspective on materials that have their own proper shape. 'A judge's duty', Dworkin asserts, 'is to interpret the legal history he finds and not to invent a better history'. Interpretation that is constrained by the history one finds will be responsible, whereas interpretation informed by the private preferences of the judge will be wayward and subjective. The opposition is one to which Dworkin repeatedly returns in a variety of forms, but in whatever form it is always vulnerable to the same objection: neither the self-declaring or 'found' entity nor the dangerously free or 'inventing' agent is a possible feature of the enterprise.

First of all, one doesn't just find a history; rather one views a body of materials with the assumption that it is organized by judicial concerns. It is that assumption which gives a shape to the materials, a shape that can then be described as having been 'found'. Moreover, not everyone will find the same shape because not everyone will be proceeding within the same notion of what constitutes a proper judicial concern, either in general or in particular cases. One sees this clearly in Dworkin's own account of what is involved in legal decision making. A judge, he explains, will look in the 'appropriate books' for cases 'arguably similar' to the one before him. Notice that the similarity is 'arguable', which means that it must be argued for; similarity is not something one finds, but something one must establish, and when one establishes it one establishes the configurations of the cited cases as well as of the case that is to be decided. Similarity, in short, is not a property of texts (similarities do not announce themselves), but a property conferred by a relational argument in which the statement A is like B is a characterization (one open to challenge) of both A and B. To see a present day case as similar to a chain of earlier ones is to reconceive that chain by finding in it an applicability that has not always been apparent. Paradoxically, one can be faithful to legal history only by revising it, by redescribing it in such a way as to accommodate and render manageable the issues raised by the present. This is a function of the law's conservatism, which will not allow a case to remain unrelated to the past, and so assures that the past, in the form of the history of decisions, will be continually rewritten. In fact, it is the duty of a judge to rewrite it (which is to say no more than that it is the duty of a judge to decide), and therefore there can be no simply 'found' history in relation to which some other history could be said to be 'invented'. All histories are invented in the weak sense that they are not simply 'discovered', but assembled under the pressure of some present urgency; no history is invented in the strong sense that the urgency that led to its assembly was unrelated to any generally acknowledged legal concern.

...

As one reads Dworkin's essay the basic pattern of his mistakes becomes more and more obvious. He repeatedly makes two related and mutually reinforcing assumptions: he assumes that history in the form of a chain of decisions has, at some level, the status of a brute fact; and he assumes that wayward or arbitrary behavior in relation to that fact is an institutional possibility. Together these two assumptions give him his project, the project of explaining how a free and potentially irresponsible agent is held in check by the self-executing constraints of an independent text. Of course by conceiving his project in this way – that is, by reifying the mind in its freedom and the text in its independence – he commits himself to the very alternatives he sets out to avoid, the alternatives of legal realism on the one hand and positivism on the other. As a result, these alternatives rule his argument, at once determining its form and emerging, again and again, as its content.

An example, early in the essay, involves the possibility of reading an Agatha Christie mystery as a philosophical novel. Such a reading, Dworkin asserts, would be an instance of 'changing' the text rather than 'explaining' it because the text as it is will not yield to it without obvious strain or distortion. 'All but one or two sentences would be irrelevant to the supposed theme, and the organization, style and figures would be appropriate not to a philosophical novel but to an entirely different genre ...' The assumption is that sentences, figures, and styles announce their own generic affiliation, and that a reader who would claim them for an inappropriate genre would be imposing his will on nature. It is exactly the same argument by which judges are supposedly constrained by the obvious properties of the history they are to continue, and it falls by the same analysis. First of all, generic identification, like continuity between cases, is not something one finds, but something one establishes, and one establishes it for a reason. Readers don't just 'decide' to recharacterize a text; there has to be some reason why it would occur to someone to treat a work identified as a member of one genre as a possible member of another. There must already be in place ways of thinking that will enable the recharacterization to become a project, and there must be conditions in the institution such that the prosecution of that project seems attractive and potentially rewarding. With respect to the project Dworkin deems impossible, those ways and conditions already exist. It has long been recognized that authors of the first rank – Poe, Dickens, Dostoyevski – have written novels of detection, and the fact that these novels have been treated seriously means that the work of less obviously canonical authors – Wilkie Collins, Conan Doyle, among others – are possible candidates for the same kind of attention. Once this happens, and it has already happened, any novel of detection can, at least provisionally, be considered as a 'serious' work without a critic or his audience thinking that he is doing something bizarre or irresponsible; and in recent years just such consideration has been given to the work of Hammet, Chandler (whom Dworkin mentions), Highsmith, Sayers, Simenon, Freeling, and MacDonald (both Ross and John D.) ... Given these circumstances (and others that could be enumerated), it would be strange if a sociological or anthropological or philosophical interpretation of Agatha Christie had not been put forward (in fact, here we have an embarrassment of riches).

...

To explain a work is to point out something about it that had not been attributed to it before and therefore to change it by challenging other explanations that were once changes in their turn. Explaining and changing cannot be opposed activities (although they can be the names of claims and counterclaims) because they are the same activities. Dworkin opposes them because he thinks that interpretation is itself an activity in need of constraints, but what I have been trying to show is that interpretation is a structure of constraints, a structure which, because it is always and already in place, renders unavailable the independent or uninterpreted text and renders unimaginable the independent and freely interpreting reader. In searching for a way to protect against arbitrary readings (judicial and literary), Dworkin is searching for something he already has and could not possibly be without. He conducts his search by projecting as dangers and fears possibilities that could never be realized and by imagining as discrete concepts entities that are already filled with the concerns of the enterprise they supposedly threaten.

...

I cannot conclude without calling attention to what is perhaps the most curious feature of Dworkin's essay, the extent to which it contains its own critique. Indeed, a reader sympathetic to Dworkin might well argue that he anticipates everything I have said in the preceding pages. He himself says that 'the artist can create nothing without interpreting as he creates, since ... he must have at least a tacit theory of why what he produces is art'; and he also points out that the facts of legal history do not announce themselves but will vary with the beliefs of particular judges concerning the general function of the law. In another place he admits that the constraint imposed by the words of a text 'is not inevitable', in part because any theory of identity (i.e., any theory of what is the same and what is different, of what constitutes a departure from the same) 'will be controversial'. And after arguing that the 'constraint of integrity' (the constraint imposed by a work's coherence with itself) sets limits to interpretation, he acknowledges that there is much disagreement 'about what counts as integration'; he acknowledges in other words that the constraint is itself interpretive.

Even more curious than the fact of these reservations and qualifications is Dworkin's failure to see how much they undercut his argument. Early in the essay he distinguishes between simple cases in which the words of a statute bear a transparent relationship to the actions they authorize or exclude (his sample statute is 'No will shall be valid without three witnesses'), and more difficult cases in which reasonable and knowledgeable men disagree as to whether some action or proposed action is lawful. But immediately after making the distinction he undermines it by saying (in a parenthesis), 'I am doubtful that the positivists' analysis holds even in the simple case of the will; but that is a different matter I shall not argue here'. It is hard to see how this is a different matter, especially since so much in the essay hangs on the distinction. One doesn't know what form the argument Dworkin decides not to make would take, but it might take the form of pointing out that even a simple case the ease and immediacy with which one can apply the statute to the facts is the result of the same kind of interpretive work that is more obviously required in the difficult cases. In order for a case to appear readable independently of some interpretive strategy consciously employed, one must already be reading within the assumption of that strategy and employing, without being aware of them, its stipulated (and potentially controversial) definitions, terms, modes of inference, etc. This, at any rate, would be the argument I would make, and in making it I would be denying the distinction between hard and easy cases, not as an empirical fact (as something one might experience), but as a fact that reflected a basic difference between cases that are self-settling and cases that can be settled only by referring them to the history of procedures, practices, and conventions. All cases are so referred (not after reading but in the act of reading) and they could not be anything but so referred and still be seen as cases. The point is an important one because Dworkin later says that his account of chain enterprises is offered as an explanation of how we decide 'hard cases at law'; that is, his entire paper depends on a distinction that he himself suggests may not hold, and therefore, as we have seen, his entire paper depends on the 'positivist analysis' he rejects in the parenthesis.

One can only speculate as to what Dworkin intends by these qualifications, but whether they appear in a parenthesis or in an aside or in the form of quotation marks around a key word, their effect is the same: to place him on both sides of the question at issue and to blur the supposedly hard lines of his argument. As a result we are left with two ways of reading the essay, neither of which is comforting. If we take the subtext of reservation and disclaimer seriously it so much weakens what he has to say that he seems finally not to have a position at all; and if we disregard the subtext and grant his thesis its strongest form, he will certainly have a position, but it will be, in every possible way, wrong.

Fish and Dworkin have joined issue over the nature of interpretive constraints in subsequent writings (Fish 1983, 1987; Dworkin 1983), and to some extent the debate looks as if they've been speaking at cross purposes. Fish's basic position is not that the distinction between interpreting a text and 'striking off on one's own' or 'inventing' something different is a distinction that is felt within an interpretive community as an element of the currently reigning understanding of what is reasonable and what is unreasonable to say about a particular work of art or a particular area of law. But these elements are not guaranteed by the words on the page of a novel or the history of the law, but are guaranteed by the socially (including politically and philosophically) constructed sense of what makes sense. Dworkin, in reply, has basically stated that he accepts the social constructedness of all interpretations, and that determining what a text is, as well as interpreting it to make of it the best it can be, is an interpretive judgment; but he does want to maintain that there are convictions generated by the activity of 'interpreting for fit', 'convictions about form', that constrain one's 'convictions' about substance. In short, he wants to defend a view of interpretation in which there are two kinds of interpretive judgments which together provide limits on the sort of aesthetic interpretation one can make of a work of art, or limits on the characterisation one will make of the law.

Dworkin (1986, 169–171)

Is the … objection [that interpretation, on my account, really is no different from invention] right? It declares that if all parts of an interpretation are theory-dependent in the way I say they are, then there can be no difference between interpreting and inventing because the text can exercise only an illusory constraint over the result. I anticipated this objection in my argument that interpretive convictions can act as checks on one another in the way necessary to avoid this circularity and give bite to interpretive claims. I divided interpretive convictions into two groups – convictions about form and about substance – and suggested that in spite of the obvious interactions these two groups were nevertheless sufficiently disjoint to allow the former to constrain the latter in the way I used the chain novel example to suggest. [This] objection might challenge my argument at wholesale or retail. It might deny the very possibility that different parts of a general theoretical structure could ever act as constraints of checks on one another. Or it might accept this possibility but deny its application to the case of literary or legal interpretation. If the challenge is wholesale, denying the possibility of internal theoretical constraint, it contradicts an important theme in contemporary philosophy of science. For it is a familiar thesis in that discipline that none of the beliefs we have, about the world and what is in it, is forced upon us by a theory-independent recalcitrant reality; that we have the beliefs we do only in consequence of having accepted some particular theoretical structure. According to one prominent version of this view, the entire body of our convictions about logic, mathematics, physics, and the rest confronts experience together, as one interdependent system, and there is no part of this system which could not, in principle, be revised and abandoned if we were willing and able to revise and adjust the rest. If we held very different beliefs about the theoretical parts of physics and the other sciences, we would, in consequence, divide the world into very different entities, and the facts we 'encountered' about these different entities would be very different from the facts we now take to be unassailable.

Now suppose we accepted this general view of knowledge and drew from it the startling conclusion that discrete scientific hypotheses cannot be tested against facts at all, because once a theory has been adopted there are no wholly independent facts against which to test that theory. We would have misunderstood the philosophical thesis we meant to apply. For the point of that thesis is not to deny that facts constrain theories but to explain how they do. There is no paradox in the proposition that facts both depend on and constrain the theories that explain them. On the contrary, that proposition is an essential part of the picture of knowledge just described, as a complex and interrelated set of beliefs confronting experience as a coherent whole … Facts check theories in science because the overall theoretical structure of science is complex enough to allow internal tensions, checks, and balances. This would be impossible if there were no functional distinctions with the system of scientific knowledge among various kinds and levels of belief. If we did not have special and discrete opinions about what counts as an observation, for example, we could not disprove established theories by fresh observations. The … objection should be read as complaining that our interpretive systems are in this way much less complex than our scientific systems, that the former lack the requisite internal structure to allow the internal constraint that is a feature of the latter.

It is, I think, an insight that the distinction between judgment and taste often turns on the complexity or simplicity of theoretical apparatus. It would be silly to claim that our preferences for chocolate over vanilla, for example, were judgments constrained by the facts about the ice cream itself. The obvious 'subjectivity' of this kind of taste is often taken as an opening wedge for general aesthetic and even moral skepticism. But it is easy enough to explain the ice cream case in a way that distinguishes rather than implicates more complex judgments. Ice cream opinions are not sufficiently interconnected with and dependent upon other beliefs and attitudes to allow a taste for chocolate, once formed, to conflict with anything else. So the question raised by the ... objection, taken in the more interesting way, can be stated bluntly: are interpretive claims of the sort critics and lawyers make more like scientific claims, in this respect, or more like tastes in ice cream? Do they have or lack the necessary structure to permit a useful degree of internal constraint?

[I have] tried to show that they do have the necessary structure, and there is no point repeating my arguments. I emphasised the difference between what I called convictions about integrity, pertinent to the dimensions of fit, and convictions about artistic merit, pertinent to the dimensions of value. I tried to show how each interpreter finds, in the interaction between these two sets of attributes and beliefs, not only constraints and standards for interpretation but the essential circumstance of that activity, the grounds of his capacity to give discrete sense to interpretive judgments. It is true that these two departments of interpretive convictions are not wholly insulated from each other; my claim is rather that they are, for each person, sufficiently insulated to give friction and therefore sense to anyone's interpretive analysis. It is a further question how far interpretive convictions of either sort are – or must be – shared within a community of people who talk and argue about interpretation among themselves.

This 'complexity' analysis has not convinced everyone, in particular in the case of law. On Dworkin's interpretive theory, deciding what forms part of the legal history that an interpretation must 'fit' if it is to be an interpretation, rather than an 'invention', is ultimately, as Dworkin puts it, 'a question of political theory'. But the considerations of moral and political values which make 'best account' of the legal history are also, obviously, a matter of political theory. So the problem, as critics such as Simmonds (1987) and Marmor (1992) see it, is that both 'fit' and moral/political value are criteria which ultimately turn on the same sort of evaluation: the two elemental criteria which a judge has to weigh against each other in coming to his interpretive conclusions are not, therefore, sufficiently independent of each other, are not 'disjoint' in the way Dworkin requires them to be, to provide the 'friction' that makes them constrain each other. For what you believe to be important in terms of political and moral justification of law will colour (perhaps establish) your ideas about what counts *as a law*. Remember, for example, how Austin's command theory of the law (his view about how the point of law was to express and enforce the wishes of the sovereign) required him to withhold the status of 'law properly so called' from constitutional law. The point is not, of course, that we don't generally share more or less equivalent beliefs about what counts as law – statutes are law, cases establish rules of law, and so on – we do. The point about this objection is that it is not clear how Dworkin can explain this. Given that fit is apparently significantly shaped by the dimension of moral value, his theory would seem to indicate that peoples' notion of fit can, and perhaps might be expected to, differ radically, in which case he has provided no workable 'constraint' of 'fit'. (You can modify this to make the same argument against Hercules's philosophical theorising about the law in Hard Cases; recall that Hercules has a theory of mistakes, ie a theory about determining that a past statute or case counts as mistakenly included in the law, and so can be jettisoned, in order to allow the body of law to be characterised overall by a more appealing moral/political justification. One might ask whether the theory of mistakes does not really just collapse into the project of providing a morally and politically attractive account of the law, for, depending upon what moral/political theory appeals to a theorist, different historical legal standards, and different quantities of this historical material, will appear right to discard.) Marmor denies that the 'complexity' solution Dworkin offers to explain the 'friction' necessary for scientific explanation works by analogy with his interpretive theory of law.

Marmor (1992, 84)

A theory is warranted in relying on the complexity thesis if it accounts for beliefs which (at least prima facie) are different in kind or source. This is a crucial point; consider what the concept of fit involves in a physical theory. It embraces notions such as sense datum, prediction, logic, mathematics, laws or regularities, probabilities, and so forth. At least some of the beliefs embodied in these concepts differ in kind or origin, and even belong to very different realms of knowledge. This is why the idea of complexity can play a significant role in such a theory.

Does Dworkin's interpretative theory of law meet these criteria? Hardly, since our convictions with regard to both identity and fit so clearly depend on the substantive justification. The whole idea of 'checks and balances' becomes suspect when it turns out that everything emerges from the same evaluative judgement, that is, coherence. In other words, it is not value dependence, per se, which undermines the idea of complexity in Dworkin's legal theory, but the fact that all the elements of interpretation seem to depend on the proposed value.

A further criticism is more specifically directed to the idea that the criteria of fit and moral/political value that Dworkin identifies will serve to guide judges in finding a uniquely correct decision in a hard case; they will not, argues Finnis, because these criteria represent incommensurable values. The phenomenon of incommensurability can be best explained by an example. Say, for example, that this evening you have a choice of going to a film you're interested in seeing, or going to the pub with friends. You can't decide what to do. Now assume that you find out that a friend you haven't seen in a while will be at the pub. This definitely makes the pub option more attractive than before; but you *still* can't decide. The analysis that values are incommensurable is meant to explain this sort of phenomenon (amongst others). The idea is that the aesthetic value of seeing the film, and the value of friendship that characterises spending time with your friends in a pub, can not be *commensurated* in the sense that there is no common scale, or metric, which allows a certain amount of one to be treated as an equivalent amount of the other. A well-lived life will involve the experience of both, and no amount of one will make up for the lack of the other. The commensurability analysis is also used to explain why success in one's career is no substitute for love, or to explain why we are troubled by the idea that any amount of money would be sufficient to compensate one, for example, for the loss of one's eyesight. The point is not that people cannot choose between values. It is a fact of life that we must, and we weigh the considerations and do our best. The point is that we cannot justify our choices by claiming that, for example, seeing a good film provides us with the equivalent in value of seeing our friends, so that if we could see more films we could drop five of our friends and suffer no loss. Finnis makes the same point about the criteria of fit and moral/political value. These two dimensions do not weigh up on the same scale, and so there is no way of determining a single right answer on the basis of them, eg by showing that decision A with five units of fit and seven units of value comes out better than decision B with six units of fit but only four units of value.

Finnis (1987a, 372–75)

Hercules himself, no matter how superhuman, could not justifiably claim unique correctness for his answer to a hard case (as lawyers in sophisticated legal systems use that term). For in such a case, a claim to have found the right answer is senseless, in much the same way as it is senseless to claim to have identified the English novel which meets the two criteria 'shortest and most romantic' (or 'funniest and best', or 'most English and most profound'). Two incommensurable criteria of judgment are proposed – in Dworkin's theory, 'fit' (with past political decisions) and 'justifiability' (inherent substantive moral soundness). A hard case is hard (not merely novel) when not only is there more than one answer which violates no applicable rule, but the answers thus available are ranked in different orders along each of the available criteria of evaluation: brevity, humour, Englishness, fit (integrity), romance, inherent 'quality', profundity, inherent 'justifiability' and so forth.

In earlier works, Dworkin tried to head off the problem of incommensurability of criteria by proposing a kind of lexical ordering; candidates (theories of law) must fit *adequately*, and of those which satisfy this 'threshold' criterion, that which ranks highest in soundness is 'the best' even though it fits less well than (an)other(s). This solution was empty, for he identified no criteria, however sketchy or 'in principle', for specifying when fit is 'adequate', i.e, for locating the threshold of fit beyond which the criterion of soundness would prevail. Presumably, candidates for 'the right answer' to the question 'When is fit adequate?' would themselves be ranked in terms both of fit and of soundness. An infinite regress, of the vicious sort which nullify purported explanations, was well under way.

In Law's Empire, Dworkin abandons the simple picture of a lexical ordering between the dimensions of fit and soundness. He stresses that within the second dimension 'questions of fit surface again, because an interpretation is *pro tanto* more satisfactory if it shows less damage to integrity than its rival'; 'even when an interpretation survives the threshold requirement, any infelicities of fit will count against it ... in the general balance of political virtues'. This is a gain in moral realism. But it strips away the last veil hiding the problem of the incommensurability of the criteria proposed for identifying a best or uniquely right interpretation, theory or answer. We are left with the metaphor 'balance' – as in 'the general balance of political virtues' embodied in competing interpretations. But in the absence of any metric which could commensurate the different criteria (the dimensions of fit and inherent moral merit), the instruction to 'balance' (or, earlier, to 'weigh') can legitimately mean no more than bear in mind, conscientiously, all the relevant factors, and *choose*.

It is a feature of the phenomenology of choice that after one has chosen, the factors favouring the chosen alternative will usually seem to outweigh or overbalance those favouring the rejected alternatives. The chosen alternative will seem to have a supremacy, a unique rightness. But the truth is that the choice was not guided by 'the right answer', but rather *established* it in the sentiments, the dispositions, of the chooser. When the choice is that of the majority in the highest relevant appeal court (a mere brute fact), the unique rightness of the answer is established not only for the attitude of those who have chosen it, but also for the legal system or community for which it has thus been authoritatively chosen and laid down as or in a *rule*.

In the real world, of course, the problem of commensurability is much more intense than I have portrayed it; for there is not just one dimension of soundness or substantive political justifiability, but many incommensurable dimensions. Their incommensurability is profoundly important for ethics and political, not merely for legal, adjudication. It has not been sufficiently noted, in debate on Dworkin's work, how thoroughly he shares utilitarianism's deepest and most flawed assumption: the assumption of the commensurability of basic goods and thus of the states of affairs which instantiate them. And this assumption is not marginal to his theory of law, as his denial of absolute rights, though important, can perhaps be said to be marginal; it is of its essence.

In sum: there are countless ways of going wrong in a hard case; the judgment that Mrs. McLoughlin and her legal advisers should be summarily executed and their property distributed to the defendant can head a list of possible but erroneous judgments which has no end. A case is hard, in the sense which interests lawyers, when there is more than one right, i.e. not wrong, answer. Dworkin's discussion of the two dimensions has made this clearer than ever.

Dworkin's basic response to this sort of challenge is to shift the burden of proof: since we all think there are right answers in the law, or at least that we can clearly form reasonable opinions to prefer one answer to all the others taking into account a multiplicity of criteria, why do we give any credence to the incommensurability argument? It appears to be a concocted theoretical objection with no foundation in reality, that is, in our actual practice of making judgments. There must be an argument, *in specific cases*, that different values cannot be weighed. (See Dworkin 1996.) Having provided in *Law's Empire* a detailed account of Hercules's weighing considerations of fit and moral/political value, Dworkin sees no reason to believe that these two interpretive criteria are incommensurable. Dworkin does not deny that the possibility of incommensurability. Probably the most famous example of this is Kierkegaard's retelling of the Abraham and Isaac story. God told Abraham to sacrifice Isaac, and thus presented Abraham with a pure choice of incommensurable values: the value of following God's will in killing Isaac was at complete odds with every other human value Abraham cherished, in particular the value of his son. Choosing to kill Isaac or not, and thus choosing to pursue one of these values, would be to choose one to the complete renunciation of the other. As Dworkin has put it in conversation, one can 'see clear to the bottom' of these values and see that they have no interaction with each other. This is a truly *radical* choice between incommensurable values. But Dworkin denies that most of our decisions are radical choice like this. Our various values interact and colour each other; this is not to say that they are all of a piece, but that we do, in various complex and sophisticated ways, value them against each other. Thus, according to Dworkin, the incommensurability analysis doesn't apply.

In *Law's Empire* (Dworkin 1986) Dworkin explained at length his interpretive theory of law, 'law as integrity'. Why 'integrity'? 'Integrity' is a value in aesthetic and legal interpretation; a good interpretation of a work shows how a work is coherent, how all of the parts hang together (to the extent that they do) to produce a valuable aesthetic experience for the observer. Similarly with interpretations of law; a good interpretation of the law shows how the law is coherent, how there can be discerned within it a principled body of decisions to respect the rights of its subjects, rights which reflect a sound moral and political viewpoint. What integrity amounts to will be controversial; different interpreters will have different beliefs about what the constraint of integrity requires; interpretation is a theoretical or philosophical enterprise. Thus we see that Dworkin's adoption of an 'interpretive' theory of legal discourse is a *specification* or *refinement* of his earlier claim that legal discourse reveals the law to be a theoretical or philosophical enterprise; the Hercules of *Law's Empire,* as we are about to see, is not very different from the Hercules of 'Hard Cases'.

Dworkin (1986, 65–66, 93–96, 225–28, 238–39, 243–49)

STAGES OF INTERPRETATION

We must begin to refine constructive interpretation into an instrument fit for the study of law as a social practice. We shall need an analytical distinction among the following three stages of an interpretation, noticing how different degrees of consensus within a community are needed for each stage if the interpretive attitude is to flourish there. First, there must be a 'preinterpretive' stage in which the rules and standards taken to provide the tentative content of the practice are identified. (The equivalent stage in literary interpretation is the stage at which discrete novels, plays, and so forth are identified textually, that is, the stage at which the text of *Moby-Dick* is identified and distinguished from the text of other novels.) I enclose 'preinterpretive' in quotes because some kind of interpretation is necessary even at this stage. Social rules do not carry identifying labels. But a very great degree of consensus is needed – perhaps an interpretive community is usefully defined as requiring consensus at this stage – if the interpretive attitude is to be fruitful, and we may therefore abstract from this stage in our analysis by presupposing that the classifications it yields are treated as given in day-to-day reflection and argument.

Second, there must be an interpretive stage at which the interpreter settles on some general justification for the main elements of the practice identified at the preinterpretive stage. This will consist of an argument why a practice of that general shape is worth pursuing, if it is. The justification need not fit every aspect or feature of the standing practice, but it must fit enough for the interpreter to be able to see himself as interpreting that practice, not inventing a new one. Finally, there must be a postinterpretive or reforming stage, at which he adjusts his sense of what the practice 'really' requires so as better to serve the justification he accepts at the interpretive stage.

...

Political philosophy thrives ... in spite of our difficulties in finding any adequate statement of the concept of justice. Nevertheless I suggest the following as an abstract account that organizes further argument about law's character. Governments have goals: they aim to make the nations they govern prosperous or powerful or religious or eminent; they also aim to remain in power. They use the collective force they monopolize to these and other ends. Our discussions about law by and large assume, I suggest, that the most abstract and fundamental point of legal practice is to guide and constrain the power of government in the following way. Law insists that force not be used or withheld, no matter how useful that would be to ends in view, no matter how beneficial or noble these ends, except as licensed or required by individual rights and responsibilities flowing from past political decisions about when collective force is justified.

The law of a community on this account is the scheme of rights and responsibilities that meet that complex standard: they license coercion because they flow from past decisions of the right sort. They are therefore 'legal' rights and responsibilities. This characterization of the concept of law sets out, in suitably airy form, what is sometimes called the 'rule' of law. It is compatible with a great many competing claims about exactly which rights and responsibilities, beyond the paradigms of the day, do follow from past political decisions of the right sort and for that reason do license or require coercive enforcement. It therefore seems sufficiently abstract and uncontroversial to provide, at least provisionally, the structure we seek. No doubt there are exceptions to this claim, theories that challenge rather than elaborate the connection it assumes between law and the justification of coercion. But not as many as there might seem to be at first glance.

Conceptions of law refine the initial, uncontroversial interpretation I just suggested provides our concept of law. Each conception furnishes connected answers to three questions posed by the concept. First, is the supposed link between law and coercion justified at all? Is there any point to requiring public force to be used only in ways conforming to rights and responsibilities that 'flow from' past political decisions? Second, if there is such a point, what is it? Third, what reading of 'flow from' – what notion of consistency with past decisions – best serves it? The answer a conception gives to this third question determines the concrete legal rights and responsibilities it recognizes.

...

[W]e shall study three rival conceptions of law, three abstract interpretations of our legal practice that I have deliberately constructed on this model as answers to this set of questions. These conceptions are novel in one way: they are not meant precisely to match [particular] 'schools' of jurisprudence ... and perhaps no legal philosopher would defend either of the first two exactly as I describe it. But each captures themes and ideas prominent in that literature, now organized as interpretive ... claims ... I shall call these three conceptions 'conventionalism', 'legal pragmatism', and 'law as integrity'. I shall argue that the first of these, though it seems initially to reflect the ordinary citizen's understanding of law, is the weakest; that the second is more powerful and can be defeated only when our theater of argument expands to include political philosophy; and that the third is, all things considered, the best interpretation of what lawyers, law teachers, and judges actually do and much of what they say.

Conventionalism gives an affirmative answer to the first question posed by our 'conceptual' description of law. It accepts the idea of law and legal rights. It argues, in answer to the second question, that the point of law's constraint, our reason for requiring that force be used only in ways consistent with past political decisions, is exhausted by the predictability and procedural fairness this constraint supplies, though … conventionalists divide about the exact connection between law and these virtues. It proposes, in answer to the third question, a sharply restricted account of the form of consistency we should require with past decisions: a right or responsibility flows from past decisions only if it is explicit within them or can be made explicit through methods or techniques conventionally accepted by the legal profession as a whole. Political morality, according to conventionalism, requires no further respect for the past, so when the force of convention is spent judges must find some wholly forward-looking ground of decision.

Legal pragmatism is, from the point of view of my conceptual suggestion, a skeptical conception of law. It answers the first question I listed in the negative: it denies that a community secures any genuine benefit by requiring that judges' adjudicative decisions be checked by any supposed right of litigants to consistency with other political decisions made in the past. It offers a very different interpretation of our legal practice: that judges do and should make whatever decisions seem to them best for the community's future, not counting any form of consistency with the past as valuable for its own sake. So pragmatists, strictly speaking, reject the idea of law and legal right deployed in my account of the concept of law, though as we shall see, they insist that reasons of strategy require judges sometimes to act 'as if' people have some legal rights.

Like conventionalism, law as integrity accepts law and legal rights wholeheartedly. It answers the second question, however, in a very different way. It supposes that law's constraints benefit society not just by providing predictability or procedural fairness, or in some other instrumental way, but by securing a kind of equality among citizens that makes their community more genuine and improves its moral justification for exercising the political power it does. Integrity's response to the third question – its account of the character of consistency with past political decisions that law requires – is correspondingly different from the answer given by conventionalism. It argues that rights and responsibilities flow from past decisions and so count as legal, not just when they are explicit in these decisions but also when they follow from the principles of personal and political morality the explicit decisions presuppose by way of justification.

…

INTEGRITY AND INTERPRETATION

The adjudicative principle of integrity instructs judges to identify legal rights and duties, so far as possible, on the assumption that they were all created by a single author – the community personified – expressing a coherent conception of justice and fairness. We form our third conception of law, our third view of what rights and duties flow from past political decisions, by restating this instruction as a thesis about the grounds of law. According to law as integrity, propositions of law are true if they figure in or follow from the principles of justice, fairness, and procedural due process that provide the best constructive interpretation of the community's legal practice. Deciding whether the law grants Mrs. McLoughlin compensation for her injury, for example, means deciding whether legal practice is seen in a better light if we assume the community has accepted the principle that people in her position are entitled to compensation.

Law as integrity is therefore more relentlessly interpretive than either conventionalism or pragmatism. These latter theories offer themselves as interpretations. They are conceptions of law that claim to show our legal practices in the best light these can bear, and they recommend, in their postinterpretive conclusions, distinct styles or programs for adjudication. But the programs they recommend are not themselves programs of interpretation: they do not ask judges deciding hard cases to carry out any further, essentially interpretive study of legal doctrine. Conventionalism requires judges to study law reports and parliamentary records to discover what decisions have been made by institutions conventionally recognized to have legislative power. No doubt interpretive issues will arise in that process: for example, it may be necessary to interpret a text to decide what statutes our legal conventions construct from it. But once a judge has accepted conventionalism as his guide, he has no further occasion for interpreting the legal record as a whole in deciding particular cases. Pragmatism requires judges to think instrumentally about the best rules for the future. That exercise may require interpretation of something beyond legal material: a utilitarian pragmatist may need to worry about the best way to understand the idea of community welfare, for example. But once again, a judge who accepts pragmatism is then done with interpreting legal practice as a whole.

Law as integrity is different: it is both the product of and the inspiration for comprehensive interpretation of legal practice. The program it holds out to judges deciding hard cases is essentially, not just contingently, interpretive; law as integrity asks them to continue interpreting the same material that it claims to have successfully interpreted itself. It offers itself as continuous with – the initial part of – the more detailed interpretations it recommends.

...

History matters in law as integrity: very much but only in a certain way. Integrity does not require consistency in principle over all historical stages of a community's law; it does not require that judges try to understand the law they enforce as continuous in principle with the abandoned law of a previous century or even a previous generation. It commands a horizontal rather than vertical consistency of principle across the range of the legal standards the community now enforces. It insists that the law – the rights and duties that flow from past collective decisions and for that reason license or require coercion – contains not only the narrow explicit content of these decisions but also, more broadly, the scheme of principles necessary to justify them. History matters because that scheme of principle must justify the standing as well as the content of these past decisions. Our justification for treating the Endangered Species Act as law, unless and until it is repealed, crucially includes the fact that Congress enacted it, and any justification we supply for treating that fact as crucial must itself accommodate the way we treat other events in our political past.

Law as integrity, then, begins in the present and pursues the past only so far as and in the way its contemporary focus dictates. It does not aim to recapture, even for present law, the ideals or practical purposes of the politicians who first created it. It aims rather to justify what they did (sometimes including, as we shall see, what they said) in an overall story worth telling now, a story with a complex claim: that present practice can be organized by and justified in principles sufficiently attractive to provide an honorable future. Law as integrity deplores the mechanism of the older 'law is law' view as well as the cynicism of the newer 'realism'. It sees both views as rooted in the same false dichotomy of finding and inventing law. When a judge declares that a particular principle is instinct in law, he reports not just a simple-minded claim about the motives of past statesmen, a claim a wise cynic can easily refute, but an interpretive proposal: that the principle both fits and justifies some complex part of legal practice, that it provides an attractive way to see, in the structure of that practice, the consistency of principle that integrity requires.

...

Law as integrity asks a judge deciding a common-law case like McLoughlin to think of himself as an author in the chain of common law. He knows that other judges have decided cases that, although not exactly like his case, deal with related problems; he must think of their decisions as part of a long story he must interpret and then continue, according to his own judgment of how to make the developing story as good as it can be. (Of course the best story for him means best from the standpoint of political morality, not aesthetics.) We can make a rough distinction once again between two main dimensions of this interpretive judgment. The judge's decision – his postinterpretive conclusions – must be drawn from an interpretation that both fits and justifies what has gone before, so far as that is possible. But in law as in literature the interplay between fit and justification is complex. Just as interpretation within a chain novel is for each interpreter a delicate balance among different types of literary and artistic attitudes, so in law it is a delicate balance among political convictions of different sorts; in law as in literature these must be sufficiently related yet disjoint to allow an overall judgment that trades off an interpretation's success on one type of standard against its failure on another. I must try to exhibit that complex structure of legal interpretation, and I shall use for that purpose an imaginary judge of superhuman intellectual power and patience who accepts law as integrity.

Call him Hercules.

...

Law as integrity asks judges to assume, so far as this is possible, that the law is structured by a coherent set of principles about justice and fairness and procedural due process, and it asks them to enforce these in the fresh cases that come before them, so that each person's situation is fair and just according to the same standards. That style of adjudication respects the ambition integrity assumes, the ambition to be a community of principle ... [I]ntegrity does not recommend what would be perverse, that we should all be governed by the same goals and strategies of policy on every occasion. It does not insist that a legislature that enacts one set of rules about compensation today, in order to make the community richer on the whole, is in any way committed to serve that same goal of policy tomorrow. For it might then have other goals to seek, not necessarily in place of wealth but beside it, and integrity does not frown on this diversity. Our account of interpretation, and our consequent elimination of [a possible] interpretation read as a naked appeal to policy, reflects a discrimination already latent in the ideal of integrity itself.

We reach the same conclusion ... through a different route, by further reflection on what we have learned about interpretation. An interpretation aims to show what is interpreted in the best light possible, and an interpretation of any part of our law must therefore attend not only to the substance of the decisions made by earlier officials but also to how – by which officials in which circumstances – these decisions were made. A legislature does not need reasons of principle to justify the rules it enacts about driving, including rules about compensation for accidents, even though these rules will create rights and duties for the future that will then be enforced by coercive threat. A legislature may justify its decision to create new rights for the future by showing how these will contribute, as a matter of sound policy, to the overall good of the community as a whole. There are limits to this kind of justification ... The general good may not be used to justify the death penalty for careless driving. But the legislature need not show that citizens already have a moral right to compensation for injury under particular circumstances in order to justify a statute awarding damages in those circumstances.

Law as integrity assumes, however, that judges are in a very different position from legislators. It does not fit the character of a community of principle that a judge should have authority to hold people liable in damages for acting in a way he concedes they had no legal duty not to act. So when judges construct rules of liability not recognized before, they are not free in the way I just said legislators are. Judges must make their common law decisions on grounds of principle, not policy: they must deploy arguments why the parties actually had the 'novel' legal rights and duties they enforce at the time the parties acted or at some other pertinent time in the past. A legal pragmatist would reject that claim. But Hercules rejects pragmatism. He follows law as integrity and therefore wants an interpretation of what judges did in the earlier emotional damage cases that shows them acting in the way he approves, not in the way he thinks judges must decline to act.

...

Law as integrity, then, requires a judge to test his interpretation of any part of the great network of political structures and decisions of his community by asking whether it could form part of a coherent theory justifying the network as a whole. No actual judge could compose anything approaching a full interpretation of all of his community's law at once. That is why we are imagining a Herculean judge of superhuman talents and endless time. But an actual judge can imitate Hercules in a limited way. He can allow the scope of his interpretation to fan out from the cases immediately in point to cases in the same general area or department of law, and then still farther, so far as this seems promising. In practice even this limited process will be largely unconscious: an experienced judge will have a sufficient sense of the terrain surrounding his immediate problem to know instinctively which interpretation of a small set of cases would survive if the range it must fit were expanded. But sometimes the expansion will be deliberate and controversial. Lawyers celebrate dozens of decisions of that character, including several on which the modern law of negligence was built. Scholarship offers other important examples.

Suppose a modest expansion of Hercules' range of inquiry does show that plaintiffs are denied compensation if their physical injury was not reasonably foreseeable at the time the careless defendant acted, thus ruling out [one possible] interpretation [but not others]. He must expand his survey further. He must look also to cases involving economic rather than physical or emotional injury, where damages are potentially very great: for example, he must look to cases in which professional advisers like surveyors or accountants are sued for losses others suffer through their negligence. [On one interpretation] such liability might be unlimited in amount, no matter how ruinous in total, provided that the damage is foreseeable, but [another interpretation] suggests, on the contrary, that liability is limited just because of the frightening sums it might otherwise reach. If one interpretation is uniformly contradicted by cases of that sort and finds no support in any other area of doctrine Hercules might later inspect, and the other is confirmed by the expansion, he will regard the former as ineligible, and the latter alone will have survived. But suppose he finds, when he expands his study in this way, a mixed pattern. Past decisions permit extended liability for members of some professions but not for those of others, and this mixed pattern holds for other areas of doctrine that Hercules, in the exercise of his imaginative skill, finds pertinent.

The contradiction he has discovered, though genuine, is not in itself so deep or pervasive as to justify a skeptical interpretation of legal practice as a whole, for the problem of unlimited damages, while important, is not so fundamental that contradiction within it destroys the integrity of the larger system. So Hercules turns to the second main dimension, but here, as in the chain-novel example, questions of fit surface again, because an interpretation is *pro tanto* more satisfactory if it shows less damage to integrity than its rival. He will therefore consider whether [one] interpretation fits the expanded legal record better than [the other]. But this cannot be a merely mechanical decision; he cannot simply count the number of past decisions that must be conceded to be 'mistakes' on each interpretation. For these numbers may reflect only accidents like the number of cases that happen to have come to court and not been settled before verdict. He must take into account not only the numbers of decisions counting for each interpretation, but whether the decisions expressing one principle seem more important or fundamental or wide-ranging than the decisions expressing the other. Suppose [one] interpretation fits only those past judicial decisions involving charges of negligence against one particular profession – say, lawyers – and [the other] interpretation justifies all other cases, involving all other professions, and also fits other kinds of economic damage cases as well. [The latter] [i]nterpretation then fits the legal record better on the whole, even if the number of cases involving lawyers is for some reason numerically greater, unless the argument shifts again, as it well might, when the field of study expands even more.

Now suppose a different possibility: that though liability has in many and varied cases actually been limited to an amount less than [one] interpretation would allow, the opinions attached to these cases made no mention of the principle [underlying the contrary] interpretation, which has in fact never before been recognized in official judicial rhetoric ... Judges in fact divide about this issue of fit. Some would not seriously consider [an] interpretation [based upon a principle] if no past judicial opinion or legislative statement had ever explicitly mentioned its principle. Others reject this constraint and accept that the best interpretation of some line of cases may lie in a principle that has never been recognized explicitly but that nevertheless offers a brilliant account of the actual decisions, showing them in a better light than ever before. Hercules will confront this issue as a special question of political morality. The political history of the community is *pro tanto* a better history, he thinks, if it shows judges making plain to their public, through their opinions, the path that later judges guided by integrity will follow and if it shows judges making decisions that give voice as well as effect to convictions about morality that are widespread through the community. Judicial opinions formally announced in law reports, moreover, are themselves acts of the community personified that, particularly if recent, must be taken into the embrace of integrity. These are among his reasons for somewhat preferring an interpretation that is not too novel, not too far divorced from what past judges and other officials said as well as did. But he must set these reasons against his more substantive political convictions about the relative moral value of the two interpretations, and if he believes that [one] interpretation is much superior from that perspective, he will think he makes the legal record better overall by selecting it even at the cost of the more procedural values. Fitting what judges did is more important than fitting what they said.

Now suppose an even more unpatterned record. Hercules finds that unlimited liability has been enforced against a number of professions but has not been enforced against a roughly equal number of others, that no principle can explain the distinction, that judicial rhetoric is as split as the actual decisions, and that this split extends into other kinds of actions for economic damage. He might expand his field of survey still further, and the picture might change if he does. But let us suppose he is satisfied that it will not. He will then decide that the question of fit can play no more useful role in his deliberations even on the second dimension. He must now emphasize the more plainly substantive aspects of that dimension: he must decide which interpretation shows the legal record to be the best it can be from the standpoint of substantive political morality. He will compose and compare two stories. The first supposes that the community personified has adopted and is enforcing the principle of foreseeability as its test of moral responsibility for damage caused by negligence, that the various decisions it has reached are intended to give effect to that principle, though it has often lapsed and reached decisions that foreseeability would condemn. The second supposes, instead, that the community has adopted and is enforcing the principle of foreseeability limited by some overall ceiling on liability, though it has often lapsed from that principle. Which story shows the community in a better light, all things considered, from the standpoint of political morality?

Hercules' answer will depend on his convictions about the two constituent virtues of political morality we have considered: justice and fairness. It will depend, that is, not only on his beliefs about which of these principles is superior as a matter of abstract justice but also about which should he followed, as a matter of political fairness, in a community whose members have the moral convictions his fellow citizens have.

These passages from *Law's Empire* mainly concern Dworkin's own favoured interpretive theory, 'law as integrity', but a bit of time should be spent on 'conventionalism' and 'pragmatism', the two alternative 'interpretive' theories he discusses and rejects. Broadly speaking, conventionalism and pragmatism are Dworkin's 'interpretive' versions of positivism (Chapters 3, 4, 5) and American legal realism (Chapter 7) respectively. For a conventionalist, like the positivist, the law can 'run out' in a hard case; there may be no settled legal rules or conventions determining the case one way or another, and thus to reach a decision the court will have to make new law. Conventionalism can be characterised as the 'fair warning' or 'protected expectations' theory of law; if there is an established legal standard governing a case, then the parties' have fair warning about how the law will deal with them, and they have legally protected expectations that the law will be applied by judges accordingly; where there is no such established legal standard, there can be no protected expectations and they will have to live with the fact that judges have the power to make new law to settle the dispute. For his part, the pragmatist interprets judicial practice to reach a sceptical conclusion about the character of the law. The pragmatist believes that judges are not truly constrained by past political decisions made by legislatures or the courts; rather, decisions are to be justified on the basis of any and all factors that are relevant to determining whether the decision is a good one; thus the pragmatist does not, *as a matter of principle*, give any weight to the fact that the case before him might be covered by prior judicial or statutory rules or principles. However, pragmatism will appear less radical in practice than in theory because pragmatists do see that judges *appear* to decide cases on the basis of past rules and principles that have been 'established in the law'. They argue, however, that judges do so as a matter of political tactics or strategy. Consistency and certainty are values in themselves, which 'go into the pot' of considerations for decisions, and so, unsurprisingly, many judges' decisions will appear to adhere to the prior law. What the pragmatist denies is that this kind of conventionalism reflects any true legal duty or obligation to treat these established rules as genuinely binding. The power of judges to use the coercive power of the state is in principle unlimited, but is in practice constrained by the duty to use that power in ways which will, all things considered, achieve the best result.

One of the difficulties of assessing these 'interpretive versions' of positivism and American legal realism is the fact that they must be conceived as interpretive theories of law which meet Dworkin's abstract concept of such interpretive theories; recall what he says about this:

> ... I suggest, that the most abstract and fundamental point of legal practice is to guide and constrain the power of government in the following way. Law insists that force not be used or withheld, no matter how useful that would be to ends in view, no matter how beneficial or noble these ends, except as licensed or required by individual rights and responsibilities flowing from past political decisions about when collective force is justified.

Simmonds, in particular, has objected to Dworkin's characterisation of conventionalism precisely on the ground that Dworkin cannot do justice to it given that it must fit this abstract characterisation of law, which is quite clearly fairly controversial – is it plausible that the *chief* function of the law is to *restrain* government coercion? To many minds, this is getting it precisely backward: the fundamental point of the law is to *exercise* state coercion, albeit in a different way than when the state exercises executive power. Consider the following counterclaims by Simmonds on behalf of conventionalism.

Simmonds (1990, 68, 70–72)

Notice first of all that [Dworkin's] abstract description treats legal sanctions as a matter of organised force deployed by the government to advance governmental objectives.

That seems to entail a coercive and instrumentalist view of sanctions. It rules out any thoroughgoing retributivist stance which regards legal sanctions as a just punishment for the violation of legal rules. Retributivism may be false, but it cannot be dismissed as uncontroversially false. It is therefore very odd to propose, as an agreed plateau from which theoretical debate can proceed, an account that is inconsistent with retributivism.

The abstract description of law treats law as guiding and constraining the use of force in the pursuit of governmental objectives. This naturally inclines us towards the view that law is a matter of the form in which governmental objectives are to be pursued. Yet is not the provision of a system of law itself a central (perhaps the central) governmental objective? By making the distinction between governmental objectives on the one hand, and law as a constraint on the pursuit of those objectives on the other hand, Dworkin furthers that suppression of the mundane ordering aspects of law which is a major feature of his work.

...

Dworkin argues [that] conventionalism proposes a trade-off between flexibility and predictability, but only in one particular way: where a case falls within a clear rule, one must respect the value of predictability, allowing considerations of flexibility to have force only in cases not covered by a clear rule. This strategy imposes an arbitrary constraint on the process of trading off two values against each other. If the basic object is to trade off predictability against flexibility, the trade-off should be carried out in a case by case manner. In each individual case, the argument in favour of enforcing the rules should be weighed against the arguments favouring non-enforcement. This means that in each case the appropriateness of rule-enforcement would be an open question: the judge would never really be bound by the rules. Conclusion: conventionalism is either i. descriptively inaccurate, or ii. irrational, or iii. collapses into pragmatism.

It seems to me that this argument is valid. But it is valid only against the 'fair warning' version of conventionalism. If the point of rules is to give fair warning of the use of organised force, the strength of the argument (in any individual case) for enforcing the rules is a function of the weight we attach to the expectations created by the rules. If we give fair warning and no one takes any notice, there is no reason to enforce the rule (setting to one side all reasons that flow from the rule's content). If rule enforcement is indeed a matter of 'fair warning' and protecting the expectations created by the rule, it would be irrational to adopt a policy of rigid rule enforcement (at least if we set on one side all questions of administrative costs). Far better to adopt a situation sensitive, pragmatist approach that can examine the strength of the expectations created in reliance on the rule. Dworkin's argument against conventionalism thus relies squarely on the 'fair warning' account of conventionalism. The 'fair warning' account relies in turn upon our acceptance of Dworkin's 'abstract description of the point of law'.

Earlier I pointed out that the 'abstract description' treats law as a constraint on the pursuit of governmental objectives. The 'fair warning' version of conventionalism builds on the abstract description by spelling out (in one particular way) the nature of, and for, that constraint. But, as I objected earlier, is not the provision of a system of law itself a central, or the central, governmental objective? This may initially have struck the reader as a footling objection, but I hope now to convince him or her that it is not.

...

I suspect that no one coming to the question cold would think of the 'fair warning' account as a natural and obvious account of conventionalism. We are led to adopt the 'fair warning' version because it fits the structure of the 'abstract description'. The abstract description separates law, on the one hand, from governmental objectives on the other: law becomes a matter of form or constraint. To achieve a better account of conventionalism, we need to break with the 'abstract description' and to re-locate law within the realm of governmental objectives.

A more natural account of conventionalism would be something like this. Social order requires the regulation of conduct by rules. It might be possible to maintain order in other ways: societies with complex interlocking kinship structures can be very successful at minimizing violence and resolving disputes by putting pressure on the parties to compromise. It is probably unhelpful to think of such societies in terms of 'law'. However, where every dispute must be resolved by compromise, no individual can have clearly demarcated and reliable entitlements. That in turn means that such a society cannot adequately protect liberty, since liberty means nothing if it is not the liberty to do things that others will bitterly oppose and object to. The maintenance of order consistently with liberty therefore requires the enforcement of rules. Such rules might in principle be informal social rules, not formal legal rules. But informal rules are likely, in a complex society, to suffer from an unacceptably high degree of vagueness and uncertainty. Even when reasonably settled informal rules exist, disputes can only be contained and limited (otherwise than by forced compromise) if there is some authoritative organ for decision on the content and applicability of the rules. It is conceivable that such decisions might be authoritative and binding only for the parties in the individual dispute, so that the rules might be construed differently in different cases. The overall number of disputes would be reduced, however, if decisions were treated as generally authoritative, as settling particular points for future cases.

At this stage in the argument a somewhat different range of considerations can be introduced. One's ability to formulate and execute medium to long term projects depends on the degree of predictability exhibited by the social world. My projects are likely to presuppose the continuance of certain states of affairs, and the likely responses of others to my actions. For social life to exhibit the degree of predictability required by the exercise of projective autonomy, human conduct must be governed by rules. Rules are therefore required for (at least) two related reasons: i. they define entitlements, thereby making possible the authoritative resolution of disputes consistently with some degree of liberty; ii. they give rise to a stable set of expectations about the conduct of other actors, thereby making the formulation and execution of medium to long term projects possible.

This seems to me a fairly plausible position which echoes themes to be found in writers such as Hart, Fuller, and Hayek. Surely this is a more natural account of 'conventionalism' than Dworkin's 'fair warning' version. We are now in a position to see why conventionalism, on our revised account, does not collapse into pragmatism.

According to the revised account of conventionalism, a major object of government is the provision of a system of enforceable rules. Such a system of rules is necessary if we are to have a complex society which is nevertheless characterised by stable expectations. The point of the rules is, at least in part, the *creation* of stable expectations. Once we have grasped this feature of conventionalism, we can understand why the pragmatist strategy is rationally inferior to the conventionalist one. For the pragmatist judge, the arguments for enforcing a rule are a function of the expectations actually created by the rule. This makes it very hard for the rules to create stable expectations. If I know that a rule will be enforced only if it has created sufficiently numerous and weighty expectations, I do not know whether to expect its enforcement until I have examined the expectations of my fellow citizens. They, however, are in exactly same position as I am myself, and consequently do not know whether to expect the enforcement of the rule. Under a pragmatist judiciary, the fact that a particular rule had been enacted (as opposed to the content of the rule) could create expectations of enforcement only by accident, as a result of people making a mistake about the nature of judicial activity. The best strategy for the creation of stable expectations is an advance commitment to rule-enforcement, irrespective of whether or not the rule has actually succeeded in creating expectations of enforcement.

Finnis makes a similar point, doubting whether Dworkin's interpretive theory can amount to a comprehensive theory of law. For while aspects of legal practice are interpretive, not all aspects of legal practice are. In particular, it is hard to regard the exercise of practical reason involved in legislating (and legislation is a significant part of legal practice) as merely an act of interpretation.

Finnis (1987a, 362–63)

[I]nterpretation according to Dworkin is to be understood on the model of purpose, practical reasoning, and intention. This understanding lends power and illumination to his account of the interpretative attitude and its role in and in relation to law. But there is an irreducible passivity or derivativeness about the concept of interpretation, even after it has been transmuted by Dworkin from 'of created reality' to 'a creating and imposing of the interpreter's purpose' (and after 'construction' has likewise slid from 'construing' to 'creation'). Interpretation resists being taken for the whole of practical reasoning; or perhaps, more clearly, practical reasoning – e.g., political *praxis* – resists being rendered as 'interpretation of a practice'. Adjudication and juristic interpretation resist being taken for the constitutive and legislative moments in the life of the law; those moments resist being understood, through and through, as interpretive. These resistances show up as missing or underdeveloped elements in the book's depiction of law's empire – an empire which is thus treated as if it were *acquired* in the way the British (some say) acquired theirs: in a fit of absence of mind.

In short: even if Dworkin succeeded in showing that his account of interpretation and the interpretative attitude in legal practice is the best account, he would not thereby have shown (nor does he otherwise show) that law and legal practice and its point are adequately described and explained by that account.

How do you think Dworkin would respond to this criticism? Recall his description of the various stages of interpretation. Can Dworkin argue that the concept of law that he is defending is one which is post-interpretive, and thus one that clearly relies upon a prior, pre-interpretive practice of some kind? Thus that the empire of law that he describes is a modern one which accepts the existence of a 'non-interpretive' past?

Might he claim that our understanding of law *now* is such that we no longer believe that there are non-interpretive, purely 'creative' moments? Thus can Dworkin reframe Finnis's claim, to say that law's empire was (in part) *acquired,* but not in a fit of absence of mind, but in a pre-interpretive stage in which the participants of the social practice had not developed the full interpretive attitude which we now have, and now appreciate to be the only way to think about law now?

To conclude this chapter, we return to the common sense distinction that does seem to exist between (1) the generally accepted, uncontroversial body of law – on Dworkin's view the 'pre-interpretive' law, and (2) what might lay implicitly within it which can be teased out by creatively interpreting the law, or, to put this in a more 'Hard Cases' sort of way, what might appear to flow from the explicit law as a matter of moral and political principle. The issue which must now be faced is whether Dworkin's reliance on a distinction of this kind does not play right into the hands of positivists, as Fish apparently seems to think it does, leaving Dworkin pretty much where he began. This seems to be the view of Raz, who in the following reading argues that Dworkin has never really overcome the need for something like a rule of recognition which serves to identify (in a common sense way) what the law to be theorised about or interpreted is. As for Dworkin's interpretive theory of adjudication Raz, to put it bluntly, essentially says that it reduces to the truism that judges must both apply the law on the books as well as develop it on the basis of moral considerations. The following reading also provides Raz's critical overview of Dworkin's development of his theory from the 60s to the 80s.

Raz (1986, 1104–09, 1111–12, 1115–19)

Dworkin's views roughly divide into three phases. In the first, mostly in the 1960's, Dworkin is not yet propounding a comprehensive theory of law, but is rather concerned to criticize Hart's. On the surface the critique centers on the alleged inability of a theory like Hart's to allow for the existence of legal standards which have merely a prima facie rather than a conclusive force. Dworkin explains, coining his own terminology, that positivism only allows for the existence of legal 'rules' which apply in an all-or-nothing fashion, so that 'if the facts a rule stipulates are given, then either the rule is valid, in which case the answer it supplies must be accepted, or it is not, in which case it contributes nothing to the decision.' In contrast, a legal 'principle' simply 'states a reason which argues in one direction, but does not necessitate a particular decision.' However, according to Dworkin's own argument during that period, some of the most important principles of American law have been laid down in the Constitution. Dworkin would require different arguments, some of which he has indeed deployed in later years, to show that Hart's theory cannot allow for the Constitution being part of American law. His stated criticism is so obviously unsustainable that one is compelled to conclude that his real target lay elsewhere. What it might have been is open to speculation.

One suggestion is that Dworkin was implicitly arguing that Hart's theory recognizes as law only, to use Lyons's term, 'explicit' law and denies the existence of 'implicit' law. Two points have to be distinguished in evaluating this possible criticism. First, to understand what the law states, to understand the plain meaning of statutes and judicial decisions, requires a good deal of background information. To start with, it requires knowledge of English, or any other languages in which the law is stated. It also requires familiarity with the beliefs about the natural and social world common in the society concerned. Without such background knowledge, much of the legal source material would literally make no sense at all. The law itself, and not simply its social and economic consequences, would defy comprehension. But it does not follow that all that background information is part of the law. Neither English nor the rules of its grammar are part of English or American law. They are merely background information necessary for its comprehension. When referring to implied law one has in mind not these prerequisites of intelligibility but the familiar fact that the law says more than it explicitly states, that there is more to its content than is explicitly stated in its sources, such as statutes and judicial decisions.

This thought must be self-evident to anyone who conceives of the law as the creation of human actions, and particularly as emerging from communicative acts such as the promulgation of statutes or the rendering of judgments in court. It is a universal feature of human communication that what is said or communicated is more than what is explicitly stated and includes what is implied. Notice that this very statement assumes that the distinction between what is stated and what is implied is valid. It employs the distinction to say that in using language we say by implication more than we explicitly state.

...

Even if Hart cannot be charged with deliberate denial of the existence of implicit law it is possible that his theory fails to allow room for it. It is this claim that I am speculatively attributing to the Dworkin of the first phase. More specifically Dworkin's criticism might run as follows: According to Hart law is identified by criteria of validity incorporated in a Rule of Recognition. But no general criteria of validity can be formulated which identify all the implicit law and nothing else. Hence Hart's theory fails to allow for the existence of implicit law. This criticism is right about one point. There is no test by which all that is implied by what is stated by a person or an institution can be identified, other than the simple test that it is so implied. To that extent, it is true that the Rule of Recognition does not and cannot include criteria which identify the implied law. But do we need such criteria? Isn't it enough to say that what is implied by legislation and precedent is law as well?

To expect the Rule of Recognition to include criteria for the identification of implied law is to misconceive its function. In a sense it does not even contain criteria for the identification of explicit law. All it does, and all it is meant to do, is to identify which acts are acts of legislation and which are the rendering of binding judicial decisions, or more generally, which acts create law. The Rule of Recognition does not help one to understand what is the law thus created, whether it is stated or implied. To understand that, one requires the general ability to interpret linguistic utterances, as well as the specific background information necessary to interpret the law-creating acts in whatever society is under consideration. Thus this particular criticism of Hart's theory is unwarranted.

Whether or not Dworkin had something like that in mind in the sixties ceased to matter in the seventies. For once the first version of his own theory of law emerged it was clear that he was now treading a different path. It is true that something like the distinction between implicit and explicit law was crucial to his theory as it then was. But implicit law is understood in a very different way from that suggested by the communication model discussed above. Given the change it may be best not to refer any more to the distinction between explicit and implicit law, as the very terms imply the communication model of interpretation. Instead I shall refer to source-based and non-source-based law. Elsewhere I have explained that according to the first version of Dworkin's theory, to establish the content of the law of a certain country one first finds out what are the legal sources valid in that country and then one considers one master question: Assuming that all the laws ever made by these sources which are still in force, were made by one person, on one occasion, in conformity with a complete and consistent political morality ... what is the morality? The answer to the master question and all that it entails, in combination with other true premises is ... the law.

Notice first that the theory accords pride of place to legal sources, and Dworkin provides no alternative method to Hart's Rule of Recognition regarding the task of identifying them. Secondly, the law includes all the law generated by these sources. Beyond this source-based law, there is the non-source-based law. According to Dworkin, non-source-based law includes not what is implied by the legal sources, but what coheres with it, i.e., all the other implications of the political morality which justify the source-based law in accordance with the test of the master question. While what people and institutions imply is part of what they actually communicate, Dworkin's coherence test ignores the 'implications' of acts of communication, and focuses on a certain mode of hypothetical, rational reconstruction of the 'meaning' of the legal sources. Where non-source-based law is concerned these sources are understood in an ahistorical way, independent of whatever intentions and beliefs the law-makers actually have or happened to have. Thus Dworkinian 'implicit law' includes much that was not communicated by anyone, explicitly or by implication, may have never been in anyone's mind, and which may bear no relation to the political ideas or programs of anyone who ever wielded legal or political power.

'Hard Cases' changed our understanding of the direction of Dworkin's attack on Hart and on legal positivism generally. It is not, or is no longer, a criticism of the notion of the Rule of Recognition as the means of identifying legal sources. I venture to suggest that Dworkin's theory implies the acceptance of something that is at least like the Rule of Recognition as a necessary means for the identification of legal sources. Instead Dworkin challenges the way these legal sources are relevant to the understanding of law. He offers in effect a two-tier theory. The law consists of what the legal sources directly make into law, and of everything which coheres with this part of the law in the way explained above. The communication model for the understanding of implied law is replaced by a coherence model for non-source-based law.

Most commentators, and I suspect most readers, myself included, took Dworkin to be advocating what is essentially a hybrid theory: a communication model of source-based law and a coherence model of the rest. Legal sources are to be interpreted in accordance with the communication model to yield the source-based law. That law is then used as the basis of the coherence test to yield the rest of the law.

...

I described the theory commonly attributed to Dworkin in the seventies as a hybrid theory combining the communication and the coherence models. This combination has a political logic of its own: it represents a conservative political view of the role of the judiciary. The fact that almost all Dworkin's political polemics are directed at the Right should not be allowed to disguise this fact. The two-stage procedure that his theory involves puts coherence at the moral service of the powers that be. Their ideology naturally dominates the law directly derived from the legal sources in accordance with the communication model. The coherence thesis then requires the courts to apply that same dominant ideology to hard cases that cannot be resolved by the application of the communication model. Here Dworkin clearly parts company with the legal positivists whose theory of law makes room for a theory of adjudication calling on the courts to counter rather than to propagate the ideology which underlies unsatisfactory source-based law.

Several commentators criticised this conservative tendency of Dworkin's apparent theory, in particular in its implications for countries such as South Africa where the pervasiveness of the injustice in their source-based law (i.e., their law inasmuch as it is determined by the communication model) means that the coherence test requires further injustices to be perpetuated in 'hard cases' in the name of coherence. Those theorists wondered why the courts should not be morally required, when handling cases not completely regulated by source-based law, to mitigate the injustices of such legal regimes. Dworkin responded to this criticism in the late seventies in part by indicating his willingness to give less importance to source-based law in his general theory of the law.

...

Hart's position is that courts should follow the law and have discretion when the law does not determine a uniquely correct outcome in the case before them. When the law does not directly incorporate moral precepts (e.g., by abolishing the death penalty) but endorses their application by reference to them through the enactment of very general standards ('cruel and unusual punishment'), then it grants courts discretion to apply moral considerations to the case. This grant of discretion does not mean, according to Hart and others whose theories followed and developed his views, that the courts can act arbitrarily, or do whatever they like. It means that they ought to apply their judgment to the moral issue that the general standard directs them to consider. They are not free to act on any moral considerations in which they happen to believe. Even when courts have discretion, their discretion is almost invariably guided by law which requires it to be exercised in a certain manner and on the basis of a certain range of considerations and on no others.

In this respect courts are in a position similar to delegated legislators and administrative authorities. When these officials have discretion to make rules and regulations, or to issue decisions in individual cases, they are typically guided by law to exercise their discretion to promote goals set by statute (e.g., workplace safety) or to have regard for certain considerations stipulated by it (e.g., respecting landlords' rights, or having regard to the housing needs of the sitting tenants). Anyone who is tempted to deny that courts have discretion when they are directed to apply a preexisting law with very general standards of application, on the ground that morality has been made into law by the directive to the courts to apply moral standards, will have a hard time to avoid denying that delegated legislators and administrative agencies ever have rulemaking powers. What appears to be the making of a new law will, on this view, be no more than a declaration of the discovery of a preexisting law.

Dworkin used to be associated with such a view. In fact he first attracted widespread attention with an article saying that courts never make law, never have discretion, that their only role is to discover and enforce preexisting law. His main article on legal theory to date is dedicated to the support of this thesis. But all this is abandoned in the present volume. We are still told that the law always provides right answers to all legal cases, and this presumably includes the denial that courts have discretion. But the suggestion that the right answers are there to be discovered by judges, the claim that courts never make law but merely apply it, and related claims which many have come to regard as the hallmark of Dworkin's theory of law, have apparently been jettisoned. Instead we are told that 'the ways in which interpretive arguments may be said to admit of right answers are sufficiently special, and complex, … [that] there is little point in either asserting or denying an "objective" truth for legal claims'. Judicial decisions as interpretations of the law both apply the law and create law at the same time. Courts are like authors of chapters of chain novels, who add new chapters in a way which reflects their understanding of the story so far.

All this makes it sound as if the claim that there are right answers to all legal questions, in the special and complex meaning given it by Dworkin, is the claim that judges may not decide any way they wish, and that their decisions can be evaluated as better or worse in terms of criteria which should have guided their judgment in the first place. To my knowledge, only some Realist writers and skeptics have denied that. Hart has never done so, and has done a good deal to refute the skeptics' arguments. I am not claiming that every nonskeptic shares Dworkin's view of how judges should decide cases. Dworkin's main doctrine of adjudication is that judges should settle cases by a coherence test that he has proposed. Many would dispute it. My point is that the affirmation of the universal existence of right answers, and the denial of judicial creativity and of judicial discretion, appear to have been whittled down to the point where few would disagree. In particular, Dworkin has made these arguments compatible with the claim that judges have discretion as it is understood by Hart and by many other writers.

Much of legal theory can be seen as an attempt better to understand what a court takes from the law and what it gives to it, where the application of the law stops and judicial discretion begins, what the boundary is between the law the court finds and the law it creates. The attempt does not suppose that one can distinguish among the different acts and pronouncements of courts those which belong to the one class from those which belong to the other. It supposes, however, that since we say that courts both apply and create law, it is possible to identify which aspects of their activities make them law-applying acts, and which make them law-creating acts. While Dworkin appeared to be claiming that courts are only engaged in discovering preexisting law and nothing else, he was exempt from facing the question. Now that he has joined other legal scholars in recognizing their creative role, readers will be curious to know what analysis of the distinction he offers to rival the account of Hart or other contemporary writers.

The answer lies in his claim that judges interpret law. The conception of judicial activity as an interpretation dominates the picture of law given in the book. Law is explained through an analogy between legal and literary interpretation, an analogy meant to serve two aims. On the one hand, it is used to argue for the dependence of judicial decisions on the court's view of substantive moral and political issues. On the other hand, it is used to illustrate the complex relations between discovery and creation, and between subjective judgment and objective truth in the law.

Legal interpretation resembles literary interpretation in that both activities are governed by the aesthetic thesis. Regarding works of art, the thesis says that the role of interpretation is to show which way of understanding the text shows it as the best work of art. Regarding law, the thesis is that interpretation shows which way of understanding the law shows it as the best law. Inasmuch as the literary analogy supports the application to the law of the aesthetic thesis, it is used to illustrate the alleged dependence of the question, 'What is the law?' on moral and political issues. I shall return to this question below. It is also used as a reminder of the involved relations between creation and discovery, objectivity, and subjectivity. But here law is somewhat unlike literature, for the courts combine the role of creative artist and critic. They generate new chapters of law on the basis of an interpretation of the previous chapters.

In this respect Dworkin can be seen as joining forces with Hart in fighting the Realists and skeptics, who deny the rational dependence of the new chapters on the past, and the formalists and neutralists, who deny that courts have any business engaging in moral argument. It is true that Hart and others make this point by saying that courts have both to apply the law and to use discretion, within the bounds it allows, to develop it. Dworkin points out that both functions are encompassed within the notion of interpretation, so that in saying that judges interpret the law one is pointing both to their faithfulness to the past, and to their reliance on moral considerations which may never have entered the minds of judges and legislators in the past. In this he highlights the close interrelationship between the two aspects of the judicial activity. But he offers no analysis of their contrasting nature which could match alternative analyses offered by other writers. Saying that the answer to legal questions depends both on considerations of fit and on moral considerations is allowing that the problem exists rather than solving it.

...

This lacuna in Dworkin's theory is compounded in its current version because of the as yet incomplete attempt to rid the theory of its hybrid character the issue with which I started and to which we must now return. The law, we are told, consists in the best interpretation of the country's legal history. The best interpretation is the one which shows it in the best possible moral light. That interpretation may require us to interpret the Constitution, statutes, and other relevant legal sources in accordance with the intention of the legislator or it may not. It will also specify which intentions count and what weight to give to them. The communication model is not so much discarded as subdued and humbled. It is relegated to a secondary role within the general coherence-based theory of law.

I doubt however whether the book succeeds in subduing the force of the communication model. The reason is that Dworkin wishes, as of course he should, to maintain the distinction 'between interpretation and ideal. A judge's duty is to interpret the legal history as he finds it, not to invent a better history'. That seems to mean that the coherence method applies to a given set of legal material, statutes and decisions, which constitute the legal history. It may disregard some legal material but it must make sense of much of it or it would be an invention of an ideal rather than an interpretation of an existing history. But what is this legal material? It is not a set of meaningless inscriptions on paper, etc. It is a body of interpreted history, of meaningful documents. Otherwise why fix on this legal history? If you regard the Constitution as an uninterpreted jumble of ink scratchings and regard legal theory as designed to give it meaning in accordance with the best moral theory there is, then there is no gap between ideal law and an interpretation of existing law. Under these conditions one can interpret the Constitution to mean anything at all. It can be read to mean the same as Shakespeare's Hamlet. (If, for example, it has double the number of words as the number of sentences in Hamlet, all you have to do is to read every two words as if they meant one sentence in Hamlet.) Dworkin is of course aware of this. His method of coherence can only apply to the legal documents which are given their plain meaning. 'When a statute or constitution or other legal document is part of the doctrinal history,' he observes, 'speaker's meaning will play a role'.

Speaker's meaning is presupposed by the coherence doctrine. Once more we have the same hybrid theory we had all along. To determine the content of the law we need first something like a Rule of Recognition to identify what belongs to the doctrinal history, and that doctrinal history will be understood in accordance with the communication model to generate the material which sets the limits to what the coherence model can do. It can discard some of that legal material as mistaken, but it must cohere with much of it. Dworkin seems to claim more than his theory can deliver when he claims that legislator's intent has only the modest role assigned it by the coherence model. It is more nearly the other way round. The coherence model applies only within the limits allowed by the communication model.

Further reading

As in the last chapter, the first goal of your further reading should be to deepen your understanding of Dworkin's theory. Both Dworkin 1985 and Dworkin 1986 are invaluable. Guest 1991 provides an overview and analysis of Dworkin's project. As to criticism, a reading in full of any of the works from which readings were taken for this chapter is a good place to start. Hunt 1991 is a collection of essays on Dworkin from a critical legal perspective. For those interested in the general issue of interpretation and law, Marmor 1995 is an excellent collection of essays on the topic. Fish 1989 collects many of his essays on law, literature, and interpretation. For a very accessible consideration of the debate about the nature of legal interpretation in the course of assessing the consequences for democracy of the United Kingdom's incorporation into domestic law of the European Convention on Human Rights, see Campbell 2001. Finally, Marmor 1998 is an important essay exploring the way in which legal rules, in particular the rule of recognition, can be explained on conventionalist grounds.

Questions

1. How much does Dworkin's 'interpretive turn' alter his theory of law from his statement of it in 'Hard Cases'?

2. What value is there in Dworkin's chain novel model of law? Are Fish's criticism's fatal to its usefulness?

3. What, according to Dworkin, is conventionalism? What is it according to Simmonds? Who, if either, has the better characterisation?

4. In what way can it be said that Dworkin's claim that there are two different interpretive tasks, one to determine fit, the other to determine moral value, plays into the hands of his positivist opponents? Can Dworkin avoid this result?

5. Is Dworkin's explanation of the way that 'fit' serves to constrain interpretations of law successful?

6. Explain the significance of this statement by Raz: 'To expect the Rule of Recognition to include criteria for the identification of implied law is to misconceive its function. In a sense it does not even contain criteria for the identification of explicit law. All it does, and all it is meant to do, is to identify which acts are acts of legislation and which are the rendering of binding judicial decisions, or more generally, which acts create law. The Rule of Recognition does not help one to understand what is the law thus created, whether it is stated or implied. To understand that, one requires the general ability to interpret linguistic utterances, as well as the specific background information necessary to interpret the law-creating acts in whatever society is under consideration.'

7. Explain what Finnis means when he says that Dworkin's description of law's empire is as of an empire which is treated 'as if it were *acquired* in the way the British (some say) acquired theirs: in a fit of absence of mind'. Is the criticism just?

8. Critically assess Finnis's incommensurability argument against Dworkin.

10 The Current Debate: The Semantic Sting, 'Soft Positivism', and the Authority of Law according to Raz

James Penner

In the last two chapters we examined Dworkin's criticism of positivism and his own theory of the nature of law. In this final chapter of Part I we look at three issues which have shaped much of the recent debate amongst Anglo-American philosophers of law. The first concerns the nature of jurisprudence, and revolves around Dworkin's claim that jurisprudence is just legal reasoning at an abstract level. Thus the workaday activity of lawyers and judges is essentially the same work as is done by philosophers of the law, although their work is done at a less abstract level; by the same token, despite appearances, the work of legal philosophers really amounts to their making claims about what the law of a particular jurisdiction (or several jurisdictions) is. 'Soft positivism' is our second topic. Soft positivism forms a sort of 'half-way' house between Dworkin's theory of law, in which the law is seen as co-extensive with political morality (in the particular way his interpretive theory of law says it is) and traditional modern positivism, in which the law is seen as clearly separate from morality. The soft positivist argues that though the law is not necessarily connected to morality, the law *can* incorporate moral criteria in the rule of recognition. So, for example, if a bill of rights introduces a requirement of fair procedure, the soft positivist would accept that what the law is depends on what the morality of fairness requires. So in particular areas of law where the rule of recognition incorporates moral criteria, the law is just as Dworkin would depict it – what the law is is what morality requires, and judges do not exercise discretion when they decide a hard case and state in a case what the law requires; rather, they declare what the law, as determined by the best moral argument, already is. Finally, we look at Raz's positivist theory of law, which turns heavily on the notion of authority. According to Raz, the key insight for understanding the nature of law, an insight which also shows the truth of traditional positivism, is the fact that the law is authoritative. By probing the nature of authority, we are invited to see how both Dworkin's theory and soft positivism are mistaken. In the final part of this chapter, we step back and take a look at the 'big picture', and try to describe as well as we can the fundamental differences in outlook which distinguish the different viewpoints that have occupied our attention in Chapters 8, 9, and 10.

The semantic sting and the nature of jurisprudence

The 'semantic sting' argument forms part of a larger claim that Dworkin makes about the nature of jurisprudence. According to him, jurisprudence or legal theory is not merely descriptive of the law, but is *evaluative* as well; that is to say, you cannot produce a theory of the law without at the same time taking a stand on large moral and political issues about what amounts to a *good* legal system, what rights people actually have, what the value of equality is, and so forth. Secondly, positivism, because it fails to deal adequately with the evaluative element of theorising, cannot therefore produce a meaningful theory of law. Dworkin gives a particular name to this failing of positivism; he says that positivism administers 'the semantic sting' to those who follow it. Because positivists do not properly address the evaluative dimension of legal theory, Dworkin claims that they, Hart in particular, try to explain the arguments of law that lawyers and judges make in terms of ideas drawn from the philosophy of language, in particular ideas about the meaning of words. 'Semantics' is the study of the meaning of words, and therefore Dworkin claims that positivists have lost their way by thinking that legal philosophy is really about the meaning of words like 'law', hence they have been 'stung' by semantics. In the following passages from *Law's Empire*, Dworkin sets this out. Pay particular attention to the way the argument builds. He begins by trying to explain the characteristic way in which lawyers and judges argue and disagree with each other in hard cases, and by describing how positivists have tried to account for this disagreement, and why they fail to explain it adequately. He then diagnoses what he sees as the positivist's problem. Trapped by a 'semantic' philosophical orientation, positivists are trapped into saying that legal argument is either bickering about the meaning of words, or is a disguised argument about what the law *ought to be*, not what the law *is*. Positivists therefore arrive at their major theoretical conclusion – that there is a sharp distinction between legal and moral argument (and between law and morality) and that judges use their discretion to decide cases on moral grounds when the law runs out – not as a result of their trying to describe what actually goes on in legal argument, but because their philosophical prejudices drive them to this result – it is the only explanation their theory will admit. Their philosophical prejudices leave them with nothing else to say about legal argument, however poorly it describes what actually goes on.

Dworkin (1986, 4–7, 8–9, 10–11, 31–33, 34, 37–38, 39–42, 43–46)

Let us call 'propositions of law' all the various statements and claims people make about what the law allows or prohibits or entitles them to have. Propositions of law can be very general – 'the law forbids states to deny anyone equal protection within the meaning of the Fourteenth Amendment' – or much less general – 'the law does not provide compensation for fellow-servant injuries' – or very concrete – 'the law requires Acme Corporation to compensate John Smith for the injury he suffered in its employ last February'. Lawyers and judges and ordinary people generally assume that some propositions of law, at least, can be true or false. But no one thinks they report the declarations of some ghostly figure: they are not about what Law whispered to the planets. Lawyers, it is true, talk about what the law 'says' or whether the law is 'silent' about some issue or other. But these are just figures of speech.

Everyone thinks that propositions of law are true or false (or neither) in virtue of other, more familiar kinds of propositions on which these propositions of law are (as we might put it) parasitic. These more familiar propositions furnish what I shall call the 'grounds' of law. The proposition that no one may drive over 55 miles an hour in California is true, most people think, because a majority of that state's legislators said 'aye' or raised their hands when a text to that effect lay on their desks. It could not be true if nothing of that sort had ever happened; it could not then be true just in virtue of what some ghostly figure had said or what was found on transcendental tablets in the sky.

Now we can distinguish two ways in which lawyers and judges might disagree about the truth of a proposition of law. They might agree about the grounds of law – about when the truth or falsity of other, more familiar propositions makes a particular proposition of law true or false – but disagree about whether those grounds are in fact satisfied in a particular case. Lawyers and judges might agree, for example, that the speed limit is 55 in California if the official California statute book contains a law to that effect, but disagree about whether that is the speed limit because they disagree about whether, in fact, the book does contain such a law. We might call this an empirical disagreement about law. Or they might disagree about the grounds of law, about which other kinds of propositions, when true, make a particular proposition of law true. They might agree, in the empirical way, about what the statute books and past judicial decisions have to say about compensation for fellow-servant injuries, but disagree about what the law of compensation actually is because they disagree about whether statute books and judicial decisions exhaust the pertinent grounds of law. We might call that a 'theoretical' disagreement about the law.

...

[L]awyers and judges do disagree theoretically. They disagree about what the law really is, on the question of racial segregation or industrial accidents, for example, even when they agree about what statutes have been enacted and what legal officials have said and thought in the past. What kind of disagreement is this? How would we ourselves judge who has the better of the argument?

The general public seems mainly unaware of that problem; indeed it seems mainly unaware of theoretical disagreement about law. The public is much more occupied with the issue of fidelity. Politicians and editorial writers and ordinary citizens argue, sometimes with great passion, about whether judges in the great cases that draw public attention 'discover' the law they announce or 'invent' it and whether 'inventing' law is statecraft or tyranny. But the issue of issue of fidelity is almost never a live one in Anglo-American courts; our judges rarely consider whether they should follow the law once they have settled what it really is, and the public debate is actually an example, though a heavily disguised one, of theoretical disagreement about law.

In a trivial sense judges unquestionably 'make new law' every time they decide an important case. They announce a rule or principle or qualification or elaboration – that segregation is unconstitutional or that workmen cannot recover for fellow-servant injuries, for example – that has never been officially declared before. But they generally offer these 'new' statements of law as improved reports of what the law, properly understood, already is. They claim, in other words, that the new statement is required by a correct perception of the true grounds of law even though this has not been recognized previously, or has even been denied. So the public debate about whether judges 'discover' or 'invent' law is really about whether and when that ambitious claim is true. If someone says the judges discovered the illegality of school segregation, he believes segregation was in fact illegal before the decision that said it was, even though no court had said so before. If he says they invented that piece of law, he means segregation was not illegal before, that the judges changed the law in their decision. This debate would be clear enough – and could easily be settled, at least case by case – if everyone agreed about what law is, if there were no theoretical disagreement about the grounds of law. Then it would be easy to check whether the law before the Supreme Court's decision was indeed what that decision said it was. But since lawyers and judges do disagree in the theoretical way, the debate about whether judges make or find law is part of that disagreement, though it contributes nothing to resolving it because the real issue never rises to the surface.

THE PLAIN-FACT VIEW

Incredibly, our jurisprudence has no plausible theory of theoretical disagreement in law. Legal philosophers are of course aware that theoretical disagreement is problematic, that it is not immediately clear what kind of disagreement it is. But most of them have settled on what we shall soon see is an evasion rather than an answer. They say that theoretical disagreement is an illusion, that lawyers and judges all actually agree about the grounds of law. I shall call this the 'plain fact' view of the grounds of law; here is a preliminary statement of its main claims. The law is only a matter of what legal institutions, like legislatures and city councils and courts, have decided in the past. If some body of that sort has decided that workmen can recover compensation for injuries by fellow workmen, then that is the law. If it has decided the other way, then that is the law. So questions of law can always be answered by looking in the books where the records of institutional decisions are kept. Of course it takes special training to know where to look and how to understand the arcane vocabulary in which the decisions are written. The layman does not have this training or vocabulary, but lawyers do, and it therefore cannot be controversial among them whether the law allows compensation for fellow-servant injuries, for example, unless some of them have made an empirical mistake about what actually was decided in the past. 'Law exists as a plain fact, in other words, and what the law is in no way depends on what it should be. Why then do lawyers and judges sometimes appear to be having a theoretical disagreement about the law? Because when they appear to be disagreeing in the theoretical way about what the law is, they are really disagreeing about what it should be. Their disagreement is really over issues of morality and fidelity, not law.'

...

Most laymen assume that there is law in the books decisive of every issue that might come before a judge. The academic version of the plain-fact view denies this. The law may be silent on the issue in play, it insists, because no past institutional decision speaks to it either way. Perhaps no competent institution has ever decided either that workmen can recover for fellow-servant injuries or that they cannot. Or the law may be silent because the pertinent institutional decision stipulated only vague guidelines by declaring, for example, that a landlord must give a widow a 'reasonable' time to pay her rent. In these circumstances, according to the academic version, no way of deciding can count as enforcing rather than changing the law. Then the judge has no option but to exercise a discretion to make new law by filling gaps where the law is silent and making it more precise where it is vague.

None of this qualifies the plain-fact view that law is always a matter of historical fact and never depends on morality. It only adds that on some occasions trained lawyers may discover that there is no law at all. Every question about what the law is still has a flat historical answer, though some have negative answers. Then the question of fidelity is replaced with a different question, equally distinct from the question of law, which we may call the question of repair. What should judges do in the absence of law? This new political question leaves room for a division of opinion very like the original division over the question of fidelity. For judges who have no choice but to make new law may bring different ambitions to that enterprise. Should they fill gaps cautiously, preserving as much of the spirit of the surrounding law as possible? Or should they do so democratically, trying to reach the result they believe represents the will of the people? Or adventurously, trying to make the resulting law as fair and wise as possible, in their opinion? Each of these very different attitudes has its partisans in law school classrooms and after-dinner speeches at professional organizations.

...

The plain-fact view is not, I must add, accepted by every one. It is very popular among laymen and academic writers whose specialty is the philosophy of law. But it is rejected in the accounts thoughtful working lawyers and judges give of their work. They may endorse the plain-fact picture as a piece of formal jurisprudence when asked in properly grave tones what law is. But in less guarded moments they tell a different and more romantic story. They say that law is instinct rather than explicit in doctrine, that it can be identified only by special techniques best described impressionistically, even mysteriously. They say that judging is an art not a science, that the good judge blends analogy, craft, political wisdom, and a sense of his role into an intuitive decision, that he 'sees' law better than he can explain it, so his written opinion, however carefully reasoned, never captures his full insight.

Very often they add what they believe is a modest disclaimer. They say there are no right answers but only different answers to hard questions of law, that insight is finally subjective, that it is only what seems right, for better or worse, to the particular judge on the day. But this modesty in fact contradicts what they say first, for when judges finally decide one way or another they think their arguments better than, not merely different from, arguments the other way; though they may think this with humility, wishing their confidence were greater or their time for decision longer, this is nevertheless their belief. In that and other ways the romantic 'craft' view is unsatisfactory; it is too unstructured, too content with the mysteries it savors, to count as any developed theory of what legal argument is about. We need to throw discipline over the idea of law as craft, to see how the structure of judicial instinct is different from other convictions people have about government and justice.

SEMANTIC THEORIES OF LAW

Earlier ... I described what I called the plain-fact view of law. This holds that law depends only on matters of plain historical fact, that the only sensible disagreement about law is empirical disagreement about what legal institutions have actually decided in the past, that what I called theoretical disagreement is illusory and better understood as argument not about what law is but about what it should be. [Hard cases] seem counterexamples to the plain-fact view: the arguments in these cases seem to be about law, not morality or fidelity or repair. We must therefore put this challenge to the plain-fact view: why does it insist that appearance is here an illusion? Some legal philosophers offer a surprising answer. They say that theoretical disagreement about the grounds of law must be a pretense because the very meaning of the word 'law' makes law depend on certain specific criteria, and that any lawyer who rejected or challenged those criteria would be speaking self-contradictory nonsense.

We follow shared rules, they say, in using any word: these rules set out criteria that supply the word's meaning. Our rules for using 'law' tie law to plain historical fact. It does not follow that all lawyers are aware of these rules in the sense of being able to state them in some crisp and comprehensive form. For we all follow rules given by our common language of which we are not fully aware. We all use the word 'cause', for example, in what seems to be roughly the same way – we agree about which physical events have caused others once we all know the pertinent facts – yet most of us have no idea of the criteria we use in making these judgments, or even of the sense in which we are using criteria at all. It falls to philosophy to explicate these for us. This may be a matter of some difficulty, and philosophers may well disagree. Perhaps no set of criteria for using the word 'cause' fits ordinary practice exactly, and the question will then be which set provides the overall best fit or best fits the central cases of causation. A philosopher's account of the concept of causation must not only fit, moreover, but must also be philosophically respectable and attractive in other respects. It must not explain our use of causation in a question-begging way, by using that very concept in its description of how we use it, and it must employ a sensible ontology. We would not accept an account of the concept of causation that appealed to causal gods resident in objects. So, according to the view I am now describing, with the concept of law. We all use the same factual criteria in framing, accepting, and rejecting statements about what the law is, but we are ignorant of what these criteria are. Philosophers of law must elucidate them for us by a sensitive study of how we speak. They may disagree among themselves, but that alone casts no doubt on their common assumption, which is that we do share some set of standards about how 'law' is to be used.

Philosophers who insist that lawyers all follow certain linguistic criteria for judging propositions of law have produced theories identifying these criteria. I shall call these theories collectively semantic theories of law, but that name itself requires some elaboration. For a long time philosophers of law packaged their products as definitions of law. John Austin, for example, ... said he was explicating the 'meaning' of law. When philosophers of language developed more sophisticated theories of meaning, legal philosophers became more wary of definitions and said, instead, that they were describing the 'use' of legal concepts, by which they meant, in our vocabulary, the circumstances in which propositions of law are regarded by all competent lawyers as true or as false. This was little more than a change in packaging, I think; in any case I mean to include 'use' theories in the group of semantic theories of law, as well as the earlier theories that were more candidly definitional.

LEGAL POSITIVISM

Semantic theories suppose that lawyers and judges use mainly the same criteria (though these are hidden and unrecognized) in deciding when propositions of law are true or false; they suppose that lawyers actually agree about the grounds of law. These theories disagree about which criteria lawyers do share and which grounds these criteria do stipulate. Law students are taught to classify semantic theories according to the following rough scheme. The semantic theories that have been most influential hold that the shared criteria make the truth of propositions of law turn on certain specified historical events. These positivist theories, as they are called, support the plain-fact view of law, that genuine disagreement about what the law is must be empirical disagreement about the history of legal institutions. Positivist theories differ from one another about which historical facts are crucial, however, and two versions have been particularly important in British jurisprudence. John Austin, a nineteenth-century English lawyer and lecturer, said that a proposition of law is true within a particular political society if it correctly reports the past command of some person or group occupying the position of sovereign in that society ... Hart rejected Austin's account of legal authority as a brute fact of habitual command and obedience. He said that the true grounds of law lie in the acceptance by the community as a whole of a fundamental master rule (he called this a 'rule of recognition') that assigns to particular people or groups the authority to make law. So propositions of law are true not just in virtue of the commands of people who are habitually obeyed, but more fundamentally in virtue of social conventions that represent the community's acceptance of a scheme of rules empowering such people or groups to create valid law. For Austin the proposition that the speed limit in California is 55 is true just because the legislators who enacted that rule happen to be in control there; for Hart it is true because the people of California have accepted, and continue to accept, the scheme of authority deployed in the state and national constitutions. For Austin the proposition that careless drivers are required to compensate mothers who suffer emotional injury at the scene of an accident is true in Britain because people with political power have made the judges their lieutenants and tacitly adopt their commands as their own. For Hart that proposition is true because the rule of recognition accepted by the British people makes judges' declarations law subject to the powers of other officials – legislators – to repeal that law if they wish.

...

Defending Positivism I shall concentrate on legal positivism because ... this is the semantic theory that supports the plain-fact view and the claim that genuine argument about law must be empirical rather than theoretical. If positivism is right, then the appearance of theoretical disagreement about the grounds of law, in [hard cases] is in some way misleading. In these cases past legal institutions had not expressly decided the issue either way, so lawyers using the word 'law' properly according to positivism would have agreed there was no law to discover. Their disagreement must therefore have been disguised argument about what the law should be. But we can restate that inference as an argument against positivism. For why should lawyers and judges pretend to theoretical disagreement in cases like these? Some positivists have a quick answer: judges pretend to be disagreeing about what the law is because the public believes there is always law and that judges should always follow it. On this view lawyers and judges systematically connive to keep the truth from the people so as not to disillusion them or arouse their ignorant anger.

This quick answer is unpersuasive. It is mysterious why the pretense should be necessary or how it could be successful. If lawyers all agree there is no decisive law in cases like our sample cases, then why has this view not become part of our popular political culture long ago? And if it has not — if most people still think there is always law for judges to follow — why should the profession fear to correct their error in the interests of a more honest judicial practice? In any case, how can the pretense work? Would it not be easy for the disappointed party to demonstrate that there really was no law according to the grounds everyone knows are the right grounds? And if the pretense is so easily exposed, why bother with the charade? Nor is there any evidence in [hard] cases that any of the lawyers or judges actually believed what this defense attributes to them. Many of their arguments would be entirely inappropriate as arguments for either the repair or the improvement of law; they make sense only as arguments about what judges must do in virtue of their responsibility to enforce the law as it is.

...

In fact there is no positive evidence of any kind that when lawyers and judges seem to be disagreeing about the law they are really keeping their fingers crossed. There is no argument for that view of the matter except the question-begging argument that if the plain-fact thesis is sound they just must be pretending. There is, however, a more sophisticated defense of positivism, which concedes that lawyers and judges in our sample cases thought they were disagreeing about the law but argues that for a somewhat different reason this self-description should not be taken at face value. This new argument stresses the importance of distinguishing between standard or core uses of the word 'law' and borderline or penumbral uses of that word. It claims that lawyers and judges all follow what is mainly the same rule for using 'law' and therefore all agree about, for example, the legal speed limit in California and the basic rate of tax in Britain. But because rules for using words are not precise and exact, they permit penumbras or borderline cases in which people speak somewhat differently from one another. So lawyers may use the word 'law' differently in marginal cases when some but not all of the grounds specified in the main rule are satisfied. This explains, according to the present argument, why they disagree in hard cases ... Each uses a slightly different version of the main rule, and the differences become manifest in these special cases. In this respect, the argument continues, our use of 'law' is no different from our use of many other words we find unproblematical. We all agree about the standard meaning of 'house', for example. Someone who denies that the detached one-family residences on ordinary suburban streets are houses just does not understand the English language. Nevertheless there are borderline cases. People do not all follow exactly the same rule; some would say that Buckingham Palace is a house while others would not.

...

The new story is in one way like the fingers-crossed story, however: it leaves wholly unexplained why the legal profession should have acted for so long in the way the story claims it has. For sensible people do not quarrel over whether Buckingham Palace is really a house; they understand at once that this is not a genuine issue but only a matter of how one chooses to use a word whose meaning is not fixed at its boundaries. If 'law' is really like 'house', why should lawyers argue for so long about whether the law really gives the secretary of the interior power to stop an almost finished dam to save a small fish, or whether the law forbids racially segregated schools? How could they think they had arguments for the essentially arbitrary decision to use the word one way rather than another? How could they think that important decisions about the use of state power should turn on a quibble? It does not help to say that lawyers and judges are able to deceive themselves because they are actually arguing about a different issue, the political issue whether the secretary should have that power or whether states should be forbidden to segregate their schools. We have already noticed that many of the arguments judges make to support their controversial claims of law are not appropriate to those directly political issues. So the new defense of positivism is a more radical critique of professional practice than it might at first seem. The crossed-fingers defense shows judges as well-meaning liars; the borderline-case defense shows them as simpletons instead.

The borderline defense is worse than insulting, moreover, because it ignores an important distinction between two kinds of disagreements, the distinction between borderline cases and testing or pivotal cases. People sometimes do speak at cross-purposes in the way the borderline defense describes. They agree about the correct tests for applying some word in what they consider normal cases but use the word somewhat differently in what they all recognize to be marginal cases, like the case of a palace. Sometimes, however, they argue about the appropriateness of some word or description because they disagree about the correct tests for using the word or phrase on any occasion. We can see the difference by imagining two arguments among art critics about whether photography should be considered a form or branch of art. They might agree about exactly the ways in which photography is like and unlike activities they all recognize as 'standard' uncontroversial examples of art like painting and sculpture. They might agree that photography is not fully or centrally an art form in the way these other activities are; they might agree, that is, that photography is at most a borderline case of an art. Then they would probably also agree that the decision whether to place photography within or outside that category is finally arbitrary, that it should be taken one way or another for convenience or case of exposition, but that there is otherwise no genuine issue to debate whether photography is 'really' an art. Now consider an entirely different kind of debate. One group argues that (whatever others think) photography is a central example of an art form, that any other view would show a deep misunderstanding of the essential nature of art. The other takes the contrary position that any sound understanding of the character of art shows photography to fall wholly outside it, that photographic techniques are deeply alien to the aims of art. It would be quite wrong in these circumstances to describe the argument as one over where some borderline should be drawn. The argument would be about what art, properly understood, really is; it would reveal that the two groups had very different ideas about why even standard art forms they both recognize – painting and sculpture – can claim that title.

You might think that the second argument I just described is silly, a corruption of scholarship. But whatever you think, arguments of that character do occur, and they are different from arguments of the first kind. It would be a serious misunderstanding to conflate the two or to say that one is only a special case of the other. The 'sophisticated' defense of positivism misunderstands judicial practice in just that way.

The various judges and lawyers who argued [hard cases] did not think they were defending marginal or borderline claims. Their disagreements about legislation and precedent were fundamental ... They disagreed about what makes a proposition of law true not just at the margin but in the core as well. [Hard] cases were understood by those who argued about them in courtrooms and classrooms and law reviews as pivotal cases testing fundamental principles, not as borderline cases calling for some more or less arbitrary line to be drawn.

THE REAL ARGUMENT FOR SEMANTIC THEORIES

If legal argument is mainly or even partly about pivotal cases, then lawyers cannot all be using the same factual criteria for deciding when propositions of law are true and false. Their arguments would be mainly or partly about which criteria they should use. So the project of the semantic theories, the project of digging out shared rules from a careful study of what lawyers say and do, would be doomed to fail. The waiting challenge has now matured. Why are positivists so sure that legal argument is not what it seems to be? Why are they so sure, appearances to the contrary, that lawyers follow common rules for using 'law'? It cannot be experience that convinces them of this, for experience teaches the contrary. They say judicial and legal practice is not what it seems. But then why not? The symptoms are classic and my diagnosis familiar. The philosophers of semantic theory suffer from some block. But what block is it? Notice the following argument. If two lawyers are actually following different rules in using the word 'law', using different factual criteria to decide when a proposition of law is true or false, then each must mean something different from the other when he says what the law is ... They are only talking past one another. Their arguments are pointless in the most trivial and irritating way, like an argument about banks when one person has in mind savings banks and the other riverbanks. Worse still, even when lawyers appear to agree about what the law is, their agreement turns out to be fake as well, as if the two people I just imagined thought they agreed that there are many banks in North America.

These bizarre conclusions must be wrong. Law is a flourishing practice, and though it may well be flawed, even fundamentally, it is not a grotesque joke. It means something to say that judges should enforce rather than ignore the law, that citizens should obey it except in rare cases, that officials are bound by its rule. It seems obtuse to deny all this just because we sometimes disagree about what the law actually is. So our legal philosophers try to save what they can. They grasp at straws: they say that judges in hard cases are only pretending to disagree about what the law is, or that hard cases are only borderline disputes at the margin of what is clear and shared. They think they must otherwise settle into some form of nihilism about law. The logic that wreaks this havoc is the logic just described, the argument that unless lawyers and judges share factual criteria about the grounds of law there can be no significant thought or debate about what the law is. We have no choice but to confront that argument.

...

I shall call the argument I have just described, which has caused such great mischief in legal philosophy, the semantic sting. People are its prey who hold a certain picture of what disagreement is like and when it is possible. They think we can argue sensibly with one another if, but only if, we all accept and follow the same criteria for deciding when our claims are sound, even if we cannot state exactly, as a philosopher might hope to do, what these criteria are. You and I can sensibly discuss how many books I have on my shelf, for example, only if we both agree, at least roughly, about what a book is. We can disagree over borderline cases: I may call something a slim book that you would call a pamphlet. But we cannot disagree over what I called pivotal cases. If you do not count my copy of Moby-Dick as a book because in your view novels are not books, any disagreement is bound to be senseless. If this simple picture of when genuine disagreement is possible exhausts all possibilities, it must apply to legal concepts, including the concept of law. Then the following dilemma takes hold. Either, in spite of first appearances, lawyers actually all do accept roughly the same criteria for deciding when a claim about the law is true or there can be no genuine agreement or disagreement about law at all, but only the idiocy of people thinking they disagree because they attach different meanings to the same sound. The second leg of this dilemma seems absurd. So legal philosophers embrace the first and try to identify the hidden ground rules that must be there, embedded, though unrecognised, in legal practice. They produce and debate semantic theories of law.

Unfortunately for these theories, this picture of what makes disagreement possible fits badly with the kinds of disagreements lawyers actually have. It is consistent with lawyers and judges disagreeing about historical or social facts, about what words are to be found in the text of some statute or what the facts were in some precedent judicial decision. But much disagreement in law is theoretical rather than empirical. Legal philosophers who think there must be common rules try to explain away the theoretical disagreement. They say that lawyers and judges are only pretending or that they disagree only because the case before them falls in some gray or borderline area of the common rules. In either case (they say) we do better to ignore the words judges use and to treat them as disagreeing about fidelity or repair, not about law. There is the sting; we are marked as its target by too crude a picture of what disagreement is or must be like.

Dworkin's argument contains a number of particular elements, and it is best to look at each of them in turn.

1. Disagreement in law

The 'keystone' of the argumentative arch is the way Dworkin describes disagreement in hard cases. It is 'theoretical', rather than 'empirical'. I think we can all agree that there is very little so-called 'empirical' disagreement in law, as Dworkin defines the term. There is very little argument in an appeal case, for example, about what the words of a statute are, or whether it was properly passed by Parliament; likewise, rarely is there disagreement about what the actual words of a judge's opinion are (occasionally in the past there were two or more inconsistent published reports), or whether the opinion was properly given to resolve a case. Legal disagreement is typically about other things. So if 'theoretical' disagreement is a category which is defined by the exclusion of 'empirical' disagreement, most legal argument is 'theoretical'. But one cannot conclude from this that the disagreement is theoretical in the sense that it is 'interpretive' in the way that Dworkin characterises it, as argument about what the law 'really' is according to the way Hercules would see it. Dworkin may be right that legal disagreement is 'interpretive', but he hasn't shown this simply by pointing out that it is not 'empirical'.

A positivist like Hart or Raz would characterise non-empirical disagreement in law differently, roughly along the same lines as they would characterise those situations where the law is uncertain, requiring judicial discretion to settle the issue. But perhaps the most common source of disagreement in law is the problem which arises naturally from what Raz dubs the 'communicative' model of legislation (whether statutory or judicial) (outlined in the Raz 1986 reading in the last chapter); we say more than we literally state by the form of words we use. What we communicate depends upon what we state in the context of stating it, and therefore to ascertain what a judge communicated when he delivered his opinion in a case will require us to interpret his words in context, in terms of the way he characterised the facts, in terms of other decisions and statutes he cited, in terms of the way he framed the issues, and so on. There is no simple formula for doing this. Different readers will disagree about what the best interpretation of a judge's opinion is, in the same way that people might disagree about what Jesus really intended by particular passages in the Sermon on the Mount while fully agreeing upon the particular words and sentences he used. This is an interpretive disagreement to be sure, but it is not an 'interpretive' disagreement in the way that Dworkin means interpretive disagreement in law, in the Herculean sense. A positivist can even agree with Dworkin that this particular interpretive disagreement can be about what the law really is, because the positivist can accept that the law is not just what is explicitly stated, but what is also implicitly intended by any communication which counts as a source of law, and obviously there are better and worse interpretations (though it is typical of barristers to have a go even at a weak interpretation if it would advance their case). Of course a positivist will also say that there is no sharp dividing line between finding the implicit law in these circumstances and dealing with any uncertainty by just choosing one 'interpretation' which is a possible one but also appeals for other reasons. Various canons of statutory interpretation operate in both of these ways. Because we can assume that legislative draftsmen are aware of these canons, we can sometimes impute a particular interpretation to a statute in the belief that given the conventions of statute writing, this is what the statute intends; in other circumstances, such canons provide grounds for a judge to make the law by determining a particular meaning for the statute even though it does not seem very likely that such a result was contemplated when the statute was passed.

Secondly, however, the positivist would simply disagree with the essence of Dworkin's claim, that judges and lawyers consistently present themselves in their legal arguments as arguing for what the law *is*, rather than what the law *ought to be*. They would interpret the more 'romantic' vision that Dworkin cites – according to which lawyers and judges regard legal argument and deciding cases as an art rather than a science, as more instinct than explicit application of doctrine, as blending analogy, craft, political wisdom and a sense of their role in the legal institution – as the practitioner's recognition that they both apply and make the law in their practice, which dual task charges them with a political responsibility which is greater than if they were mere functionaries straightforwardly 'applying' the law to cases. Rather than finding the following statement that practitioners 'often make' contradictory, as Dworkin does, a positivist would accept it at face value:

They say there are no right answers but only different answers to hard questions of law, that insight is finally subjective, that it is only what seems right, for better or worse, to the particular judge on the day.

2. Linguistic philosophy and the source of positivism's error

What the semantic sting purports to show is that positivists have been going about their philosophical task *in the wrong way* when they've tried to explain law. A belief in the power of the philosophy of language leads them to believe that the best way to understand the phenomenon of law is to analyse the meaning of the word 'law', on the following supposition: all competent speakers who use the word 'law', in particular lawyers, know the grammatical rules for applying the word law to particular cases, even if they are not able explicitly to state these rules; therefore a philosopher can, by looking carefully at the use of 'law' unearth or make explicit the rules which determine when 'law' is used correctly. So, once these rules are made explicit, we will have an explicit characterisation of when a person properly uses the word law, and thus the rules when it is appropriate to say, for example, that 'it is a law that the speed limit is 70 mph on the motorway', ie we will have before us the rules which tell us what is, and what is not, a proposition of law.

Of all the claims that Dworkin has made against Hart and other positivists, this is probably the one that has been regarded as the most wrong, perhaps even outrageous. In the case of Hart, it appears to take Hart's partial reliance on J L Austin's method of using 'a sharpened awareness of words to sharpen our perception of the phenomenon' to generate certain insights, such as the distinction between 'being obliged' and 'having an obligation' (Hart 1994, vi), and treat that reliance as the basis of the claim that Hart proposed a 'linguistic' or 'semantic' theory of law, ie that he was providing some kind of philosophical analysis of the word 'law' and when it may properly be used, rather than trying to describe the essential elements of law or legal systems. This Hart flatly denied:

> Though … I am classed with Austin as a semantic theorist and so as deriving a plain-fact positivist theory of law from the meaning of the word 'law', and suffering from the semantic sting, in fact nothing in my book or in anything else I have written supports such an account of my theory. Thus, my doctrine that developed municipal legal systems contain a rule of recognition specifying the criteria for the identification of the laws the courts have to apply may be mistaken, but I nowhere base this doctrine on the mistaken idea that it is part of the meaning of the word 'law' that there should be such a rule of recognition in all legal systems, or on the even more mistaken idea that if the criteria for the identification of the grounds of law were not uncontroversially fixed, 'law' would mean different things to different people. (Hart 1994, 246; see also Raz 1998, for the view that Hart's reliance on the philosophy of language was ultimately of very little value, but not because his philosophy of language was flawed, but because of other philosophical problems Hart faced which the philosophy of language was not apt to sort out.)

In any case, Hart thinks that Dworkin is simply confused here. Dworkin elides knowing what law is with knowing what *the law* of any particular jurisdiction is, and these two are simply not the same thing. Hart said:

> A semantic theory of law is said by Dworkin to be a theory that the very meaning of the word 'law' makes law depend on certain specific criteria. But propositions of law are typically statements not of what 'law' is but of what *the law* is, i.e. what the law of some system permits or requires or empowers people to do ... This would only be the case if the criteria provided by a system's rule of recognition and the need for such a rule were derived from the meaning of the word 'law'. But there is no trace of such a doctrine in my work. (Hart 1994, 247)

Many have found this claim an almost incomprehensible feature of *Law's Empire*; Finnis seems flabbergasted by:

> Dworkin's failure, both when defining vicious semanticism [ie the semantic sting], and when speaking in his own voice, to distinguish between 'the law' (of a particular community, the topic of thought by that community's lawyers and judges) and 'law' (a topic of thought of anthropologists, sociologists, other historians, moralists and jurisprudents such as Hart, Kelsen, and Dworkin). Dworkin treats 'the law' and 'law' as synonymous, and I fail to see how he can be so indifferent to the manifest difference between the two terms, corresponding to the difference between the two sorts of intellectual enterprise which I have just indicated. (Finnis 1987a, 368)

One of the strange features of this particular conflict is that Dworkin *embraces* the very idea that others find nonsensical, ie that there *is no genuine distinction* between talking about or theorising about law, ie the general phenomenon of law as found throughout history in different cultures and different institutional forms, and talking about or theorising about *the* law of any particular jurisdiction. (Which is not to say that therefore Dworkin is obviously wrong, and the others right – revolutions in philosophy do occur.) As we will look at in more detail below, for Dworkin any legal argument about the law of a particular jurisdiction is merely a more specific part of the project of theorising about law *per se*. And his argument, in part, is that positivists have obscured this truth from themselves, with the result that they have not seen what their theories actually amount to. So we must ask whether there is a subtlety in Dworkin's claim his critics may have missed. Consider again this passage:

> When philosophers of language developed more sophisticated theories of meaning, legal philosophers became more wary of definitions and said, instead, that they were describing the 'use' of legal concepts, *by which they meant, in our vocabulary, the circumstances in which propositions of law are regarded by all competent lawyers as true or as false.* (my italics)

At first glance, this seems obviously false. When legal philosophers described the use of legal concepts, they were trying to explain what these concepts, like 'law', 'rule', 'obligation' and so forth, mean. Now of course, understanding what these concepts mean would be important knowledge in assessing what competent lawyers do when they determine whether propositions of law, such as 'It is the law that enforceable agreements require consideration', are true or false. But determining the use or meaning of legal concepts does not at all suggest that, having these meanings in hand, one can then determine the circumstances in which propositions of law are true or false in any particular legal jurisdiction. Knowing what the word 'law' means is essential to understanding what a French lawyer or a German lawyer means when they say 'In France the law is such and such' or in 'Germany the law is so and so', but having the meaning of the word law under your belt *tells you nothing* about what particular rules determine whether something is a valid law or not in these jurisdictions, and no positivist has ever said anything so foolish.

Now, Dworkin might mean instead something like the following: according to positivists, if we have a knowledge of what the word 'law' means, we understand how to apply the word, and so we will have the ability to classify certain things as laws and also be able to say that certain other things are not laws; therefore, the meaning of the word 'law' sets boundaries on what we count as a law; thus certain kinds of things are ruled out as laws; thus certain *propositions* can not be called 'propositions of law' because they fall outside the boundaries set by the meaning of the word 'law'. This is, however, also false. Certainly, all kinds of things are ruled out as 'laws' or 'propositions of law' because they fall outside the meaning of the word 'law', although the better way of putting this is to say that certain things cannot be called 'laws' because they are not laws, that is they do not fall into the class of things to which the word 'law' refers, and knowing the meaning of 'law' is to understand what things fall into the class and which do not (though there may be problematic borderline cases). Bicycles, for example, are not laws, and neither is the taste of champagne. If you can't see straightforwardly, automatically really, that bicycles or the taste of champagne do not count as laws, then you don't have the concept *law* under your belt. But different kinds of proposition are just the sorts of thing that *are* candidates for being a law. 'The speed limit on the motorway is 15 mph' *could* be a true proposition of law in some jurisdiction that found setting the speed limit this low a sensible thing to do. That the meaning of 'law' rules out certain things as 'propositions of law' (bicycles, the taste of champagne) doesn't mean that it also rules out all propositions which happen not to be propositions of law, so that, by knowing the word 'law' one can by knowing just that tell whether a particular proposition is a true proposition of law in some jurisdiction. This is not a special feature of the word 'law', by the way, but is true of all kinds of words. Consider 'animal'. Knowing the meaning of the word animal will tell you that apple crumble is not an 'animal', nor is 'the peace that passeth all understanding'. By the same token however, you'd better believe that unicorns and dragons are animals, *if* there are unicorns or dragons. But knowing the meaning of 'animal', and that unicorns and dragons are candidate animals, doesn't tell you whether there are any unicorns or dragons. You have to look around the world and check. Likewise, there's nothing in the concept *law* to rule out or rule in any possible proposition of law – to determine that, *you have to go and look at the world and check*; you have to go and see whether that proposition has been made part of a legal system, by legislation for instance. Again, so far as I know, no philosopher of law has ever claimed that having acquired the concept *law* provides one *ipso facto* with a capacity to know whether any candidate proposition is the law of some jurisdiction.

Let's try once more. Perhaps what Dworkin is getting at is the idea that if one undertakes a philosophical analysis of a concept like *law*, typically by attending to the various cases in which people who have the concept use it, one *can learn* something about the law itself, in particular, one can learn something about the circumstances in which we judge propositions to be propositions of law. And philosophers *have* made this claim. Hart, to the extent to which he relied upon Austin's method of attending to the use of words, certainly thought something like this. He claimed, roughly, that one chief function of the concept *law* was to represent a *subset* of all the normative standards which exist in society: Not all norms are laws; principles of morality are not *ipso facto* principles of the legal system of any jurisdiction; thus implicit in the concept *law* itself is the idea that there is a means of identifying this subset. Now, although this is controversial, I think this is basically all Hart managed to glean from his analysis of the concept *law*. I think his claim that laws were certain kinds of *institutionalised social standards* drew more upon his 'armchair' sociology than any linguistic analysis (for a different view, see Stavropoulous 2001). But one can probably say that his claim about the necessity of a 'rule of recognition' in each legal system owed something to his linguistic analysis (consider again the differences he revealed between 'being obliged' and 'having an obligation', and doing something 'as a rule' and being bound by a rule), because given that he felt the concept *law* picked out only a subset of all social standards it seems implicit then that anyone having the concept *law* would understand (if only implicitly) that laws were only some subset of all social standards, *and* that there must be some means of identifying which of these standards were laws. Alright, so far, so good. Dworkin can probably rightly claim that linguistic analysis led some philosophers to claim that any legal system needed some kind of 'rule of recognition', some means to identify laws as distinct from all other social standards. But again, it would be an error to conclude from this that Hart or any other positivist believed (what is clearly false) that having the concept *law* and therefore understanding that there must be some means of identifying laws out of all social standards, would also entail knowing what *particular* means any society or jurisdiction used to determine whether a particular social standard was a law or not. And one would have to make this kind of charge stick against Hart in order for Dworkin's statement to be an accurate characterisation. With respect, I can see no textual evidence in anything Hart wrote to support such a charge, though you are more than welcome to look for yourself.

3. 'Paradigm cases' and 'cases pivotal for a theory'

There is another element of Dworkin's semantic sting argument which we must consider. Recall that Dworkin lambastes legal positivists for treating theoretical disagreement as borderline disagreements over the meaning of words. To quote again a passage from *Law's Empire* provided above:

> The borderline defense is worse than insulting, moreover, because it ignores an important distinction between two kinds of disagreements, the distinction between borderline cases and testing or pivotal cases. People sometimes do speak at cross-purposes in the way the borderline defense describes. They agree about the correct tests for applying some word in what they consider normal cases but use the word somewhat differently in what they all recognize to be marginal cases, like the case of a palace. Sometimes, however, they argue about the appropriateness of some word or description because they disagree about the correct tests for using the word or phrase on any occasion. We can see the difference by imagining two arguments among art

critics about whether photography should be considered a form or branch of art. They might agree about exactly the ways in which photography is like and unlike activities they all recognize as 'standard' uncontroversial examples of art like painting and sculpture. They might agree that photography is not fully or centrally an art form in the way these other activities are; they might agree, that is, that photography is at most a borderline case of an art. Then they would probably also agree that the decision whether to place photography within or outside that category is finally arbitrary, that it should be taken one way or another for convenience or case of exposition, but that there is otherwise no genuine issue to debate whether photography is 'really' an art. Now consider an entirely different kind of debate. One group argues that (whatever others think) photography is a central example of an art form, that any other view would show a deep misunderstanding of the essential nature of art. The other takes the contrary position that any sound understanding of the character of art shows photography to fall wholly outside it, that photographic techniques are deeply alien to the aims of art. It would he quite wrong in these circumstances to describe the argument as one over where some borderline should be drawn. The argument would be about what art, properly understood, really is; it would reveal that the two groups had very different ideas about why even standard art forms they both recognize – painting and sculpture – can claim that title.

You might think that the second argument I just described is silly, a corruption of scholarship. But whatever you think, arguments of that character do occur, and they are different from arguments of the first kind. It would be a serious misunderstanding to conflate the two or to say that one is only a special case of the other. The 'sophisticated' defense of positivism misunderstands judicial practice in just that way.

This passage forms one aspect of Dworkin's argument that positivists cannot properly describe theoretical disagreement in law, whereas he can. However, it is certainly arguable that his claim is mistaken, because he fails properly to distinguish the issues involved in something being a paradigm case of an x, and something being a pivotal case for someone's theory of the nature of an x.

A paradigm case is the sort of case one draws someone's attention to when teaching certain kinds of word, or assuring oneself that someone has a concept. Consider a concept like 'dog'. A Labrador retriever is a dog if anything is, and if someone started arguing with you that a Labrador retriever was not a dog, you would conclude he did not know what a the word 'dog' meant. That's why a Labrador retriever is a paradigm case. On the other hand, you might not draw the same conclusion, especially in judging a child, if they were uncertain whether or reluctant to call a Chihuahua a 'dog', or a hyena or a fox. For whatever else they are, these are not paradigm cases of dogs: they have some similarities to paradigm cases, but also dissimilarities. The idea of a paradigm case is important, because for words which are taught, explained, and applied on the basis of paradigms, the disposition of all competent speakers to *treat certain cases – like the Labrador retriever in the case of 'dog' – as paradigm cases*, is what secures the meaning of the word, secures that you and I and everyone else means the same thing by the use of 'dog'. Not all words are taught and depend upon paradigm cases like this. The meaning of some words depends upon definitions, for example 'prime' as in prime number. We are not taught prime on the basis of having 2, 3, 7 and 13 just pointed out to us, and told to apply the word in the same way. We are given a definition, something like 'prime numbers are those divisible by no natural numbers other than themselves and 1' (I expect a mathematician might put this better). Other words might be called 'theoretical' words, words whose meaning depends upon the way in which they figure in a theory, in particular, scientific theories. 'Proton' may serve as an example. We learn the meaning of proton by seeing how protons play a part in a theory in physics which describes the nature of matter. (Which doesn't mean that protons are not 'real', or are just some kind of 'theoretical construct'; whether protons are real, whether there are protons, depends upon whether physics has understood the nature of matter aright. It just means that to understand what protons are and thus what 'proton' means you must understand (some of) the theory in physics too.)

A *case pivotal for a theory* is different. Here's a real life example from science. Consider two different theories about the nature of animal classes. According to one theorist, the essence of animal classes lies in their evolutionary history, particularly in the process of speciation (the way in which different species arise from common ancestors), and his test for membership of a species is whether a candidate member can interbreed with others of that class. It turns out that wolves and dogs interbreed, much more than was previously thought, and so according to this theorist, wolves *are dogs*, however surprising that sounds. Another theorist, an animal behaviourist, would draw the boundary of 'animal classes' by classing together those animals that have a behavioural repertoire sufficiently alike. For him, the behaviour of wolves is distinct enough from that of dogs (understandable given the millennial co-evolution of dogs with humans) to show that wolves are not dogs. Now assume that these two theorists have an argument as to which of them has the better theory of animal classes. The status of wolves is a pivotal case in this dispute. For whether we are willing or not to class wolves with dogs will be a crucial element of whether we adopt one theory or another. We might say, with the animal behaviourist, that however informative the genetic interbreeding story is, it is an unsound way to classify animals, because it leads to the bizarre result that wolves are dogs. Or we might conclude with the interbreeding test theorist, that focussing on behaviour provides an insufficiently rigorous classification scheme, and that whether or not animals interbreed (or can do) is a more essential criterion of their nature; on this score wolves really are dogs. Now the point to notice about this case, where the status of wolves provides a pivotal case for the truth of these opposing theories, is that on neither theory do wolves count as paradigm cases of dogs. Neither theorist would say that a wolf was a typical dog, or start teaching his child the world 'dog' by pointing out a wolf. They would teach their children the word dog as we all do, pointing out Labrador retrievers, for example. Paradigm cases of a word or concept are just not the same thing as pivotal cases in a clash of theories about what the concept is a concept of, or what a word refers to.

Now, in the passage above, Dworkin says that people who believe that certain words are paradigm case words, like 'dog', will disagree about the use of such words only in borderline cases. People who know the meaning of 'dog' may have difficulty with borderline cases like Chihuahuas. This seems true enough. But even though they will only disagree about the correct use of the word 'dog' in borderline cases, that does not mean that they won't have disagreements about dogs, or the nature of dogs, theoretical disagreements if you will. We have just seen an example of this in the case of the scientific dog theorists.

Here's how. People mean the same thing by a word when they treat the same sorts of things as paradigm cases to which the word applies. But sharing the meaning of a word with someone in no way guarantees that they each have the same *beliefs* about the thing the word refers to. It is crucial to understand that knowing the meaning of a word does not make one an immediate know-it-all about whatever the word refers to. Knowing 'dog' does not tell one everything important or significant about dogs. In relative terms, the meanings of words come cheap, in the sense that one learns words fairly easily either by direct exposure to the paradigm cases or by being informed about those instances in various ways by others (think about teaching a child in the United Kingdom what 'kangeroo' or 'giraffe' mean), but that knowledge of the things the words refer to is hard won – knowledge requires investigation and thought. Think of it this way: learning a word is like opening a file on a research project. Learning 'dog', so that one can call the right things dogs may not require much more than having dogs pointed out to one a couple of times; children seem to learn to pick out dogs very easily. But getting that under one's belt does not guarantee one much, if anything, in the way of knowledge. There is a lot to learn about dogs. As a result, we can share the meaning of words but have many different beliefs about what the words refer to. We can have all kinds of beliefs about dogs, including scientific or other 'theoretical' beliefs, and we can disagree about our theoretical or scientific or religious beliefs about dogs (dogs are man's best friend, dogs are genetically closely related to wolves, dogs are especially prized by the gods) safe in the knowledge that we are disagreeing *about* dogs, and not arguing at cross purposes. And so, to return to Dworkin's example, if we assume that 'art' is a paradigm case word, ie we learn the word 'art' by being shown paradigm cases of art, paintings, sculptures, and so on, we can still have all kinds of disagreement about art, including theoretical disagreements about art, For example I may say that the value of all art lies in how beautiful it is, whereas you may say the true value in art lies in its ability to depict the anxiety underlying the human condition. So, it is simply not true that those who believe that certain words are secured in their meaning by general agreement on paradigm cases, cannot account for theoretical disagreement about the things those words refer to. Indeed, one theorist who takes a broadly Dworkinian line on legal philosophy, Nicos Stavropoulos, has tried to explain the nature of theoretical disagreement in Dworkin's theory roughly along these lines, by distinguishing our understanding of the meaning of words from our beliefs, including our theoretical beliefs, about what our words refer to (Stavropoulos 1996; although Stavropoulos finds fault with the paradigm case characterisation of word meaning, opposing it to a 'causal' theory of meaning, this disagreement does not alter the distinction between knowing the meaning of a word and having beliefs about what a word refers to which is the matter in question here; for details see Penner 1997a).

The paradigm case proponent, ie the one who believes that a word's meaning is secured by agreement amongst speakers about what counts as paradigm cases for the use of a word, can also account for the 'central' or 'pivotal' case disagreement, as the theoretical fight about wolves just described demonstrates. To consider Dworkin's own example: two theorists of art argue over the case of photography. These theorists agree that painting and sculpture are standard art forms, paradigm cases of art. However they have very different theories about why these are standard art forms. So, they have very different theories about the nature of art. This doesn't impugn in the least the paradigm case proponent, for as just explained, sharing the meaning of a word on the basis that one shares paradigm cases to which it applies is fully compatible with all manner of differences in beliefs, including theoretical differences, about the nature of what the word refers to. Now, to carry on with the example, one theorist's theory tells him that photography is a central case of art, and the other thinks it is not art at all. What should we say about this? Well, it depends upon what these two theorists will *do* in response to their theories.

Dworkin seems to suggest that one's theoretical beliefs about art will determine what counts as a paradigm instances of art. Thus if your theory of art and my theory of art pick out different pivotal or central cases, pivotal or central *for the truth* of our theories, we will have different paradigm cases for what art is. But this is not necessarily so. We might argue strenuously with each other over whether photography is art, and you might regard photography as an unhitherto realised marvellous example of all the artistic values. Nevertheless, we may go on teaching our children the word 'art' by pointing out painting and sculpture as the paradigm cases of art. We will teach our children what art is by pointing to the same examples, and we will test whether they know what art is by seeing how they respond or deal with those examples. Our deep theoretical disagreements may remain, but so long as we do not diverge in treating the standard cases as standard cases, we rest safe in the knowledge that our theoretical disagreements concern the same thing. However, we may not carry on as before. On the strength of our views, we may begin to teach our children differently, you pointing out photography as a paradigm case of art, my not doing so. But if this latter course of action occurs, on what basis can we now say that I and my child and you and yours share the same meaning for the word 'art'? We look to different things in the world and treat those as examples of art, and we have clearly conflicting beliefs about what art is. The only thing we seem to share is the word 'art'. If you and I start arguing about 'art', how can we not be arguing at cross purposes, as in the case where I'm claiming things about river banks and you're claiming things about merchant banks? The paradigm case proponent thus explains that there may be different meanings for the word 'art', and that conceptual confusions may arise because words have similar meanings (they share some paradigm cases) but are actually different. It is clear that this does sometime happen. Sometimes divergence in paradigms will occur, and sometimes we really do have arguments at cross purposes, though the meaning of the different words will often be fairly similar. It is arguable, for example, that a word like 'democratic' does mean different (though related) things to different people – for example, some people would look simply to structural forms of political practice (elections, universal suffrage, etc) as examples of what is 'democratic', whereas for others, 'democratic' refers to a kind of political value akin to solidarity or equality, that different forms of government may manifest irrespective of those structural political forms. So someone might say that, despite universal suffrage and its electoral system, the United States is not *really* democratic so long as the mass media is in the hands of a few corporate giants. And if people who don't share the same meaning for the word democracy start arguing about what 'democracy' is really about, then their argument will be at cross-purposes. Anyone who has ever engaged in a political argument will know how often this does occur.

If the outline of the way paradigm case words work, as just presented, is correct, then Dworkin has not shown that the paradigm case proponent cannot account for theoretical disagreement. Indeed, rather than explaining theoretical disagreement over art, Dworkin's own example and the way he discusses it puts him in danger of being unable to explain theoretical disagreement, characterising the theoretical disagreement between the art theorists as one where they are merely 'talking past one another', having an argument which is 'pointless in the most trivial and irritating way'. For if one of these theorists would treat photography as a genuine paradigm case, and the other wouldn't, and would therefore apply the word differently and teach their children differently in consequence, then it would seem quite clear that they have different (though related) concepts of art.

Nevertheless, all of the above doesn't mean (1) that the paradigm case proponent has explained theoretical disagreement in law, nor (2) that Dworkin cannot. As to (1), it may be the case that the meaning of (at least some) legal words is not determined by our sharing of paradigm cases. As to (2) it may be the case that many legal words express 'interpretive concepts', as Dworkin would say, and so 'theoretical' disagreement in law is what he would call 'interpretive' disagreement. Our concepts are interpretive once we take the 'interpretive' attitude to them. Taking the interpretive attitude is what Dworkin explains in his characterisation of the three stages of interpretation, the pre-interpretive, the interpretive, and the post-interpretive stages as we saw in the last chapter (Dworkin 1986). In a sense, our concepts are interpretive when we take our theories about what the concept represents in a certain way. With a word that expresses an interpretive concept, there is no sharp distinction between what the word means and what we believe about the thing to which it refers. So for example, if 'contract' expresses an interpretive concept, then our theories of contract are part of the meaning of the word 'contract'. We do not know, and share with others, the meaning of 'contract' because we have learned to apply 'contract' to paradigm cases of contracts, the same cases as everyone else, but because we share some central theoretical beliefs about what contracts *really* are. So, you might ask, if we share the meaning of the word contract because we share the same theoretical beliefs about it, how can we have any theoretical disagreement about the nature of contracts? Easy – while we share a broad theoretical belief that secures us in meaning the same thing by contract, we can diverge in our more specific theoretical beliefs. Dworkin regards *law* as an interpretive concept, and recall (Chapter 9, Dworkin 1996) that he suggests that we all share the belief that:

> the most abstract and fundamental point of legal practice is to guide and constrain the power of government in the following way. Law insists that force not be used or withheld, no matter how useful that would be to ends in view, no matter how beneficial or noble these ends, except as licensed or required by individual rights and responsibilities flowing from past political decisions about when collective force is justified.

Now it is not to the point here whether or not Dworkin has pinpointed the right theoretical belief about law that we all share (presumably he has not, since many (eg Simmonds 1990, Chapter 9) who count as having the concept law would disagree strenuously that they share this fundamental theoretical belief), for one might do better in isolating the theoretical belief that we all share. The point is that though we share such a belief, we can still disagree on further theoretical beliefs about the law.

Where we end up, then, is faced with the question whether legal concepts, and the words that express them, are sometimes? always? typically? paradigm case concepts or interpretive concepts (or perhaps other kinds of concepts altogether, defined concepts (akin to prime) or theoretical concepts (akin to proton), for example). It does not seem necessary to choose between paradigm case concepts and interpretive concepts to explain 'theoretical' disagreement in law, so it does not seem that Dworkin can establish that all legal concepts are interpretive on that basis. By way of his explanation of the pre-interpretive, interpretive, and post-interpretive stages, Dworkin invites us to share with him the view that we take an interpretive attitude to *law* and legal concepts like *contract, murder, property*, and so on. It is suggested, however, that the only plausible way to determine this question is to look at individual concepts one by one, *law, contract, murder, property*, and so on, and try to see how people acquire their meanings and use them. (There may also be other reasons, owing to different philosophical considerations, for preferring one characterisation of concepts over another, which cannot be explored here; for the nonce we are assuming that both paradigm case explanations and interpretive explanations are plausible enough to deserve consideration.) Only then should we feel secure in preferring Dworkin's claim that 'theoretical' disagreement in law is 'interpretive' in the way he means that.

4. The evaluative element of legal theory, and the question whether the philosophy of law is continuous with workaday legal reasoning

There is, finally, one more aspect to the semantic sting argument. Dworkin claims that by focussing on the meaning of the word 'law', positivists have adopted the position of an external observer of the law, to describe law objectively without taking part in the ongoing debates that lawyers and judges conduct in trying to determine the grounds of law. The positivist reliance upon linguistic philosophy, to provide a semantics for the word 'law', is, in this version of the semantic sting argument, really more a symptom of the problem than its cause, for the linguistic approach is just one of different possible 'external observer' approaches to understanding law. Thus to describe law by describing how the word 'law' is used is to try to describe the law as an external observer would, by noting the regularities in the participants' use of language. This approach can be contrasted with an 'internal' one, by which the theorist wishes to understand how the participants themselves understand what they are up to. Dworkin claims that any external approach is doomed to fail, because any proper theory of a social practice in which the participants are themselves interpreters of their practice will require the theorist to become a full, interpreting participant in order that he or she may fully capture the nature of that practice. The theorist as participant will not only describe the practice, but *evaluate* it, that is, judge its moral merit, and will seek to interpret the practice to show it in its best light as do all the other participants. In this way, doing jurisprudence is only doing at a more abstract level what lawyers and judges do everyday. In the same way that judges and lawyers bring to bear their substantial commitments about justice, equality, and so forth to bear when they make arguments and render decisions, so must a legal theorist bring to bear his own substantial moral and political views when he tries to produce a good theory of the nature of law. Again, we look at passages from *Law's Empire*.

Dworkin (1986, 62–64, 90)

Someone might say that interpretation of a social practice means discovering the purposes or intentions of the other participants in the practice ... Or that it means discovering the purposes of the community that houses the practice, conceived as itself having some form of mental life or group consciousness. The first of these suggestions seems more attractive because less mysterious. But it is ruled out by the internal structure of an argumentative social practice, because it is a feature of such practices that an interpretive claim is *not* just a claim about what other interpreters think. Social practices are composed, of course, of individual acts. Many of these acts aim at communication and so invite the question, 'What did he mean by that?', or 'Why did he say it just then?' ... But a social practice creates and assumes a crucial distinction between interpreting the acts and thoughts of participants one by one, in that way, and interpreting the practice itself, that is, interpreting what they do collectively. It assumes that distinction because the claims and arguments participants make, licensed and encouraged by the practice, are about what *it* means, not what *they* mean.

That distinction would be unimportant for practical purposes if the participants in a practice always agreed about the best interpretation of it. But they do not agree ... So each of the participants in a social practice must distinguish between trying to decide what other members of his community think the practice requires and trying to decide, for himself, what it really requires ... A social scientist who offers to interpret the practice must make the same distinction. He can, if he wishes, undertake only to report the various opinions different individuals in the community have about what the practice demands. But that would not constitute an interpretation of the practice itself; if he undertakes that different project he must ... use the methods his subjects use in forming their own opinions about what [the social practice] really requires. He must, that is, join the practice he proposes to understand; his conclusions are then not neutral reports about what the citizens [who participate in the practice] think but claims about [the practice] *competitive* with theirs.

...

Legal philosophers are in the same situation as the philosopher of [a social practice]. They cannot produce useful semantic theories of law. They cannot expose the common criteria or ground rules lawyers follow for pinning legal labels onto facts, for there are no such rules. General theories of law ... must be abstract because they aim to interpret the main point and structure of legal practice, not some particular part or department of it. But for all their abstraction, they are constructive interpretations: they try to show legal practice as a whole in its best light, to achieve equilibrium between legal practice as they find it and the best justification of that practice. So no firm line divides jurisprudence from adjudication or any other aspect of legal practice. Legal philosophers debate about the general part, the interpretive foundation any legal argument must have. We may turn that coin over. Any practical legal argument, no matter how detailed and limited, assumes the kind of abstract foundation jurisprudence offers, and when rival foundations compete, a legal argument assumes one and rejects others. So any judge's opinion is itself a piece of legal philosophy, even when the philosophy is hidden and the visible argument is dominated by citation and lists of facts. Jurisprudence is the general part of adjudication, silent prologue to any decision at law.

Hart rejected this characterisation of jurisprudence root and branch. Hart, of course, famously drew attention to the character of the law as a social practice to show that participants took the 'internal' point of view of the practice, argued that legal theorists must take this into account in their theories, and in so doing himself tried to show how law was a normative practice, an 'affair' of rules. Nevertheless Hart never wavered from his view that legal theory's main goal was to provide an appropriately sophisticated account or description of the social phenomenon of law. He believed that a good description of the law required taking into account facts of this kind, but that didn't turn the enterprise into one whereby the theorist had to join the practice and become one of the participants. 'It is true that … the descriptive legal theorist must *understand* what it is to adopt the internal point of view and in that limited sense must be able to put himself in the place of an insider; but this is not to accept the law or share or endorse the insider's internal point of view or in any other way to surrender his descriptive stance.' (Hart 1994, 242)

Intuitively there seems no reason to doubt that a descriptive stance, as Hart characterises it, towards law or any other social practice is possible. This is true even of 'interpretive' or 'argumentative' social practices, if that is thought to make a difference. There seems to be no reason in principle why one cannot be an historian or sociologist or philosopher of religion or science, describing the internal debates and arguments of religion or science, without oneself having to adopt religious beliefs or adhere to particular controversial scientific theories.

This is not to say, of course, that a theory of law, or a theory of anything for that matter, is not evaluative *in any way*. It is to say that in order to describe a practice, one need not make the same *kind* of evaluations about the practice as its participants do. The participants value and evaluate the practice in so far as the practice contributes to their lives. Someone describing the practice, on the other hand, evaluates the practice in terms of picking and choosing what aspects of the practice seem to contribute to *acquiring knowledge of* or *understanding of* the practice, given his theoretical (eg historical, philosophical, sociological) or other (eg moral) interests in it. As Raz puts it (Raz 1994, 193), the justification of a particular theory about the nature of the law 'is tied to an evaluative judgment about the relative importance of various features of social organisations, and these reflect our moral and intellectual concerns'. These concerns, however, and thus these evaluative choices, will be those of the describer, not those of the participants. And as is well known, even a participant can 'stand back' from his own beliefs about the value of a practice, whether religious, or scientific, or aesthetic, to inquire into the practice to obtain knowledge of it for intellectual, historical, or other purposes. Moreover, within the constellation of various interests or concerns which might attend one's inquiry into the law, it is certainly arguable that one interest or concern stands out: what is essential or necessary or particular or peculiar about this thing in the world (this social practice) we call 'law', that *makes* it what it *is*. As Coleman puts it:

> [Jurisprudence] begins by asking whether there are features of law that are essential, or, in an appropriate sense, necessary to law or to our concept of it: essential in the sense that a social practice that fails to have them could not qualify as law. If they exist, these features do not depend upon a controversial theory of law's proper function, but on an understanding of what the law is. (Coleman 1998, 389–90)

Nothing said here, of course, is meant to deny the point that people often approach their inquiries with mixed motives, unconscious biases, ideological commitments, and so on, which often colour and prejudice those inquiries. But the very fact that we find it so important to look for these kind of 'cognitive' impediments shows that we are capable of making the distinction between different ways in which a practice, or anything else for that matter, can be valued and evaluated.

Nevertheless, this sort of reaction to Dworkin's claim may misunderstand it. Consider again this passage:

> ... A social scientist who offers to interpret the practice must make the same distinction. He can, if he wishes, undertake only to report the various opinions different individuals in the community have about what the practice demands. But that would not constitute an interpretation of the practice itself; if he undertakes that different project he must ... use the methods his subjects use in forming their own opinions about what [the social practice] really requires. He must, that is, join the practice he proposes to understand; his conclusions are then not neutral reports about what the citizens [who participate in the practice] think but claims about [the practice] *competitive* with theirs
> ...

Dworkin clearly believes that in respect of interpretive practices as he defines them, and of course law is one, the true 'meaning' or nature of a practice, in the same way as what the law of a jurisdiction *really* is, is a controversial matter, and the only way for participants of the practice, lawyers and judges and interested laypeople, to approach understanding what the law 'really' requires, is to engage in a philosophical/theoretical/ interpretive exercise a la Hercules. In this way, participating in law *is* participating in a kind of theory or a kind of philosophy; that, of course, is one of Dworkin's most provocative claims, one with which we are already familiar. If Dworkin is right about this, then it is true that legal argument is continuous with a kind of philosophy, for legal argument just amounts to a kind of philosophy. And Dworkin might be claiming that legal theorists ought themselves to be engaged in this kind of philosophy, and that we should call this activity legal philosophy. But that exhortation or definitional manoeuvre doesn't rule out of order the sort of legal philosophical stance that everyone else, from natural lawyers to Kelsen to Raz have taken. Alternatively, Dworkin might take the philosophy of law to be the 'philosophy of practice' in the following sense: in a way, one supposes, only practicing lawyers will be able to convincingly say, or argue about, what it's really like to practice law, what the practice really demands of one, or that only practising Roman Catholics can say, or argue about, what it's really like to be a practising Roman Catholic, what being a practising Roman Catholic really demands of one. Different lawyers and different Roman Catholics might form controversial views about what it's really like, and argue about it, so we could have theory or philosophy about what it's really like to be a lawyer or a Roman Catholic. But again, it would seem another definitional manoeuvre to claim that 'jurisprudence' just is this 'philosophy of what it's like' to be a lawyer or a Roman Catholic.

Two final points that can be made. First, to the extent that the law is regarded as having other functions than resolving disputes in court, for example, guiding the behaviour of subjects outside of the court, the practice of law by lawyers and judges will not look like the central phenomenon which jurisprudence must address. The point here is that while law is a 'social practice', in the sense that it is a purposive social activity, it may be a mistake to identify this activity only with the 'practice of law' in the narrow sense of what lawyers and judges do. If that is right, then it would be a simple mistake to think that explaining law would be explaining what being a lawyer is like, or explaining what legal practice *really* demands of lawyers and judges.

Secondly, it clear that engaging in any old practice does not amount to theorising about the nature of the practice willy nilly. I may play cricket or chess, without having any view at all about what the essence of cricket or chess is; I am perfectly capable of engaging in the social practice of speaking English, but might have no thoughts whatever about what the essence of English grammar or vocabulary is, or how it all works. It would be nonsense to say that having played cricket I have unknowingly been formulating or criticising theories of cricket all along, or that by speaking English I have been critically assessing Chomsky's linguistic theory. Dworkin's claim is that true though this may be of these sorts of practices, it is different with 'interpretive' or 'theoretical' practices. By practicing law, I have indeed unknowingly engaged Hart and Dworkin, adopted Razian views or decided that natural law is sound. Those many capable and exceptional lawyers who are rather smugly content to deny that they hold any theory of law at all, and who dismiss doing jurisprudence as a waste of time which would prevent them from improving their legal knowledge and ability (as a law student having just worked through ten chapters on the subject, you may be of the same mind), are, according to Dworkin, mistaken; they do not realise that they have been legal theorists all along. How do we decide who's right here? It is, perhaps, worthwhile considering whether constructing theories is inherently a *conscious* activity, an activity in its own right. Theorising *about* an activity, about, eg the practice of law, would seem to be an activity in itself, distinct from practicing law. One is always theorising about some particular thing, which is not the same as doing that particular thing, even if that thing is itself theoretical or interpretive. Philosophy is a philosophical practice if anything is, but philosophers are not for that reason always philosophising about philosophy. Literary criticism is an interpretive activity if anything is, but literary critics are not therefore always interpreting the practice of literary criticism. And so with law: thinking about the practice of law, philosophically reflecting on it, cannot be the same thing as engaging in law, ie in practising law. Or so, at least, it would seem.

Soft Positivism

As we have seen, one of Dworkin's most insistent claims about adjudication is that lawyers and judges bring to bear moral considerations in determining what the law *is*, not merely in the course of exercising a discretion to make new law, but because these moral considerations, to the extent they figure in a sound justification of the law, are grounds of law. In response to this claim, a version of positivism called 'soft positivism' or 'inclusive positivism' or 'incorporationism' has arisen. A soft positivist believes that while there is no requirement that any legal system's rule of recognition require judges to treat moral considerations as grounds of law, a rule of recognition *can* incorporate moral criteria, so that what the law is will depend, with respect to certain parts of the law, on moral considerations. In short, to borrow from Coleman (1998, 382), soft positivism 'allows that morality can be a condition of legality: that the legality of norms can sometimes depend on their substantive moral merits, not just their pedigree or social source'. In his postscript, Hart identified himself as a kind of soft positivist (Hart 1994, 250–54). In particular, he said that, 'the rule of recognition may incorporate as criteria of legal validity conformity with moral principles or substantive values'. (Hart 1994, 250)

Note that soft positivists do not claim, as Dworkin does, that judges never have the discretion to make law; rather, they agree with Dworkin that in some cases the law *may* incorporate moral criteria for identifying what the law is.

Now it is very important to identify precisely what soft positivism amounts to. The claim is not simply that judges may be required to decide cases on the basis of moral criteria. Any positivist would allow that. If there is a constitutional or statutory or precedential rule that requires judges to decide a case on, say, considerations of justice and fairness, judges will be required to decide the case on basis of their assessment of what those moral values require. The fact, which all accept, that judges may decide cases in this way does not resolve any issues between positivists and their opponents. It is how positivists *describe* what is going on in such cases which is controversial. For a positivist, when a judge decides a case on the basis of moral criteria, he is *making* new law. Recall Raz's characterisation of legal principles. For Raz, these principles are the best evidence of the discretion of judges to make law, for by directing judges to decide on the basis of principles, judges are directed to make *specific* rules covering those cases which come before them, specific rules which give effect to the general guidance of the principle in question. So the fact that the law incorporates moral criteria in its directions to judges about how they decide cases is something all positivists can happily accept. The novelty of soft positivism is its acceptance that the *rule of recognition*, the rule that *identifies what the law is*, contains moral criteria. If the rule of recognition identifies what the law is (in certain cases) by whether the law meets a moral requirement, eg that the law is just, or is reasonable, or promotes equality, and so on, then the very act of identifying the law will engage lawyers and judges in moral argument, for morality is controversial. So in those cases where the moral criteria component of the rule of recognition operates, this moral controversy ensures that the law is radically uncertain – no one can be sure in advance how it will apply in a case, and, as Dworkin would rightly characterise the results of adjudication in cases where such moral criteria operate, though a judge in such a case provides his best opinion as to what the law is, his opinion is not to be regarded as settling the law; rather, his opinion deserves great respect from, and must be taken account of in the reasoning of, subsequent judges and lawyers who are faced with cases in areas of law where such criteria would operate.

Hart considered whether the uncertainty generated by the admittance of such criteria into the rule of recognition was fatal to the overall positivist orientation of his theory.

For uncertainty is the very problem which, according to regular or 'hard' positivists, the rule of recognition is there to address. After all, did Hart not introduce the rule of recognition as that secondary rule whose purpose was to deal with the problem of uncertainty in a 'primitive' legal system? Hart said:

> This criticism ... seems to me to exaggerate both the degree of certainty which a consistent positivist must attribute to a body of legal standards and the uncertainty which will result if the criteria of legal validity include conformity with specific moral principles or values. It is of course true that an important function of the rule of recognition is to promote the certainty with which the law may be ascertained. This is would fail to do if the tests which it introduced for law not only raise controversial issues in some cases but raise them in all or most cases. But the exclusion of all uncertainty at whatever costs in other values is not a goal which I have ever envisaged for the rule of recognition. (Hart 1994, 251)

However, is this a workable response? Consider the obvious sort of candidate for a moral criterion embedded in the rule of recognition, for example the constitutional principle that all laws must treat citizens 'equally', or that each must receive the 'equal protection' of the law. Such a moral criterion would render all of the law uncertain; or rather, the law would only be as certain as whatever moral consensus or convergence happened to exist amongst legal practitioners. And it is this sort of certainty or stability, the stability of moral consensus or convergence to which Dworkin attributes the stability of law at any given time. Once a soft positivist grants the anti-positivist this sort of inroad into the rule of recognition, how can he find any principled stopping point which prevents the incorporation of a general moral criterion which leads to this result? Can a soft positivist say, *that as a matter of the nature of law*, the rule of recognition allows only those moral criteria for the identification of law which operate in restricted areas of the law?

It may be the case that Hart had some misgivings about the way his claim to be a 'soft positivist' ought to be treated, which is perhaps revealed by his response to an argument of Dworkin's. Dworkin (1983, 250) argued that in order for soft positivism to retain its orientation towards the objective determination of the law, then the moral criterion in the rule of recognition would have to concern objective moral values, ie moral values in respect of which we could make objective judgments; only then would such a criterion in the rule of recognition identify laws in a way in which all would agree. But this would require soft positivism to endorse a controversial philosophical theory about moral values and moral judgments, for it is controversial whether moral values and judgments are objective. Hart responded in this way:

> [W]hatever is the answer is to [the question whether moral judgments are objective] the judge's duty will be the same: namely, to make the best moral judgment he can on any moral issues he may have to decide. It will not matter for any practical purpose whether in so deciding cases the judge is *making* law in accordance with morality (subject to whatever constraints are imposed by law) or alternatively is guided by his moral judgment as to what already *existing* law is revealed by a moral test for law. Of course, if the question of the objective standing of moral judgments is left open by legal theory,

> as I claim it should be, then soft positivism cannot be simply characterised as the theory that moral principles or values may be among the criteria of legal validity, since if it is an open question whether moral principles and values have objective standing, it must also be an open question whether 'soft positivist' provisions purporting to include conformity with them among the tests for existing law can have that effect or instead, can only constitute directions to courts to *make* law in accordance with morality.
>
> It is to be observed that some theorists, notably Raz, hold that whatever the status of moral judgments may be, whenever the law requires courts to apply moral standards to determining the law it thereby grants the courts discretion and directs them to use it according to their best moral judgment in making what is a new law; it does not thereby convert morality into pre-existing law. (Hart 1994, 254, italics original)

Here Hart seems to take away with one hand what he gave with the other, for the only significant claim that soft positivism makes is that it is possible in some cases for the *existing* law to be determined only by moral criteria. To equivocate at this stage, and suggest, in particular by concluding with a nod to Raz, that soft positivism may really only be claiming that *new law is made* according to moral criteria, strongly weakens Hart's endorsement of soft positivism. It seems to suggest that according to Hart, soft positivists only claim that the law can include directions to judges to make new law, ie exercise their discretion, but do so by reference to moral criteria. No hard positivist has ever denied that, nor would they have any reason to.

Raz remains an 'exclusive' or 'hard' positivist, but his argument against soft positivism differs from the ones we have examined above. His rejection of soft positivism is based upon his concern for the authoritative nature of law. It is best to look at that theory first, and then revisit briefly the question of soft positivism and see Raz's criticism (which indeed is obvious once you understand his theory of authority). So to that we now turn.

The Authority of Law According to Raz

If the law is to work as the law must, it must be able to guide the behaviour of the subjects of the law. We all know how the law typically does this: it issues rules telling us what to do. In this sense, Raz describes the law as an authority, or as 'having' authority – it claims the right to tell us what to do. Secondly, Raz explains that if the law is a *legitimate* authority, it tells us to do what we ought to do.

The comparison with another kind of authority is helpful here. Consider a medical doctor. A medical doctor is a medical authority in respect of his patients because he is able to tell them what to do when they are unwell (in some cases at least). Now the medical doctor doesn't make up the relevant facts about your case and the science of medicine when you walk into their office seeking treatment. Those facts exist independently of the doctor, and if you had the time and the wit you could go to medical school or in some other way learn the facts and diagnose yourself. The medical doctor is a legitimate authority not because he has the right to tell you to do whatever he wants, but because *he has the knowledge, ie of medicine* that enables him to tell you what sort of treatment is indicated in your case. So the idea is that in the case of a legitimate authority, the authority has authority not just because it claims the right to tell you what to do, but because it can and will tell you how to do what's right. In other words, a legitimate authority is one which assists us in doing what we ought to do by doing the hard work of figuring out what we ought to do (whether we ought to wear seat-belts to avoid injuries, etc, whether there ought to be such and such regulations concerning food purity, etc) and then telling us to do it.

Now, you'll notice that if you already have all the knowledge necessary to properly guide your own behaviour in some area of activity, medicine, for example, then you don't have need of an authority. But likewise, if you don't have all the knowledge necessary to guide your behaviour, it does you no good whatsoever for the authority to tell you: 'do the right thing!' Of course you want to do that; that's why you've come to the authority; what you want the authority to do is *tell* you what the right thing is, whether it's how to create a will or how to be relieved of 'flu. In technical Razian terms, to be effective authorities must 'mediate' between the reasons which apply to a subject's case and the subject himself. The medical authority stands between the facts of medicine and his patient and serves the patient by telling him what to do without making him do a degree in medicine, which would of course bring the facts of medicine to his patient's understanding directly. Similarly, the law isn't an effective authority if doesn't tell you what to do in more or less straightforward terms, but rather gives you all the facts relevant to the circumstances and tells you to figure it out for yourself. The law doesn't tell you to weigh up all the fiscal, economic, social, and moral factors, and then tell you to decide what the basic rate of tax is that you ought to pay. The law does all that for you and then just tells you to fork out 20% or whatever.

And this explains Raz's trouble with soft positivism, and Dworkin's theory of law as well. The law cannot guide the behaviour of its subjects if it gives them directions which require them themselves to engage in moral investigation before they know what they have to do. For doing that is like giving them no guidance at all. And whatever you might call a 'legal system' which gave no guidance or only useless guidance of this kind, you could not call it an authority, and for Raz the one thing that is true about law is that it does claim the authority to tell you what to do. Therefore, Raz holds that whenever judges are entitled to decide a case or formulate a rule on the basis of moral considerations, they are *creating* new law, not applying law that already exists, because the only thing that already exists in such a case are the various moral considerations that anyone would look at to decide how to act. To tell your subjects to make reference to those and act is abdicating the responsibility of serving as an authority, for in that case you are not mediating between all the considerations that apply to a subject's case and the subject himself. You're leaving them to plot their own course of action on their own.

Our understanding of this is sharpened by a distinction Raz makes between the *deliberative* and *executive* stages of practical reason. In the first stage we weigh up all the various considerations that apply to our situation, and decide what the best course of action is. In the executive phase, we follow that particular course of action. The function of authorities is to carry out the deliberation for the authorities' subjects and produce rules or other standards which the subjects then execute. In this respect legal rules are *decisions*. They are the decisions of legal authorities which result from their deliberations. For a legal standard to exist, the law must have decided to guide its subjects to act in one way rather than another. Telling the subjects to do the deliberation themselves is to make no decision at all, or rather, it is to abdicate authority in that area of human activity, which the law, of course, does. The law, for example, refuses to regulate how many Christmas presents you should give. Decide for yourself, for heaven's sake. And in cases where the law hasn't made up its mind, in cases where what the law 'is' still depends on weighing up various moral considerations, there is no law at all – there is a gap in the law, a gap which will be filled when the legislature passes some more or less specific guidance or a court itself weighs up all the factors and provides some more or less determinative standard for subjects of the law to follow. On this account, the legislature or the courts often *defers* making up their minds and giving determinative guidance; instead they produce broad or vague directions and leave it to the courts, or to later courts, to give workable guidance on a case by case basis.

In the reading below, we have a fairly concise statement by Raz of his authority-centred theory of the nature of law. He begins, however, by taking issue with Dworkin over the proper perspective to take on the law, denying that the lawyer's perspective on the law is the appropriate one. Read carefully why he denies this, and think about how Raz would respond to the claim Dworkin makes, which we examined in Part I, that legal theorists are engaged in legal reasoning, and lawyers in jurisprudence.

Raz (1994, 186–192, 194, 199–200, 202–203, 207–210)

Legal theory in America has always been dominated by the thought that law is just what the courts do. American theorists not only embraced the lawyer's perspective but jumped to the conclusion that all the considerations which courts may use are legal. The most sophisticated and accomplished representative of this tradition is R. M. Dworkin who, in a series of articles during the last fifteen years, developed a theory of law out of a theory of adjudication. In fact he developed a theory of adjudication and regards it willy-nilly and without further argument as a theory of law. Dworkin points out that judges must use moral considerations in addition to enacted and case law. He argues that the moral considerations which they should use are those which belong to a moral theory justifying the enacted and case law binding on them, i.e., that moral theory which constitutes the ideology of the law. One may agree or disagree with this theory of adjudication. Either way one has to ask a separate question: which of all these considerations constitute the law? Dworkin, however, does not pause to ask this question. He unquestioningly assumes, without ever stating the assumption or providing any reason for it, that all the considerations which courts legitimately use are legal considerations. Dworkin's identification of a theory of adjudication with a theory of law looks, however, very natural from the lawyer's perspective. Lawyers' activities ... revolve, directly or indirectly, round litigation in the courts. From the lawyer's perspective all the considerations pertaining to judicial reasoning are equally relevant. A lawyer has to concern himself not only with legislation and precedent but also with other considerations relevant to judicial reasoning. A lawyer, therefore, fortified ... with the knowledge that the law has to do with judicial reasoning, finds no reason from the perspective of his own professional preoccupations to stop short of identifying the theory of law with a theory of adjudication.

...

Yet there is something inherently implausible in adopting the lawyer's perspective as one's fundamental methodological stance. There is no doubting the importance of the legal profession and of the judicial system in society. It is entirely appropriate to make them the object of a separate study and to regard legal theory as that study. It is, however, unreasonable to study such institutions exclusively from the lawyer's perspective. Their importance in society results from their interaction with other social institutions and their centrality in the wider context of society. The law is of interest to students of society generally, and legal philosophy, especially when it inquires into the nature of law, must stand back from the lawyer's perspective, not in order to disregard it, but in order to examine lawyers and courts in their location in the wider perspective of social organization and political institutions generally.

...

It is entirely plausible to regard the notion of law as bound up with that of a judicial system, but what are the essential characteristics of a court and why are they important to the political organization of society? Three features characterize courts of law:

1.   They deal with disputes with the aim of resolving them.

2.   They issue authoritative rulings which decide these disputes.

3.   In their activities they are bound to be guided, at least partly, by positivist authoritative considerations.

The first point does not imply that courts of law do not engage in other activities than settling disputes. They often administer estates and bankruptcies, conduct the affairs of certain categories of people, etc. The first point simply asserts that, however many other activities lawcourts engage in, they are courts because, among other things, they strive to settle disputes.

...

The second limb of the above definition of a court of law, i.e. that it issues authoritative rulings, may seem self-evident. A few words of explanation concerning the sense of 'authoritative' rulings may nevertheless be called for. First, let me make clear that both here and below I am using 'authoritative' as short for 'claimed to be authoritative', i.e. by the court or person concerned or the organization to which they belong or which they represent. There is no suggestion that the claim is morally warranted. A court's opinion on the merits of a dispute is authoritative and binding in a way in which my opinion is not, not because I have no opinion on such disputes (which I sometimes have), not because my opinion is not an expert's opinion (which it may be), nor again because courts never err (they sometimes do). The reason is that the court's very utterance of its opinion is claimed by it to be a reason for following it, whereas my utterance of my opinion is not claimed to be a reason for following it. At best it amounts to informing the persons concerned of the existence of reasons which are themselves quite independent of my utterance.

The need for the third limb of the definition, that courts of law be, at least partly, guided by authoritative positivist considerations, is clearly seen by contemplating its negation. There are forms of arbitration in which the arbitrator is instructed merely to judge the merits of the case and to issue a just judgment, without being bound to follow any authoritative positivist standard. We can imagine a purely moral adjudication taking the same form. Positivist considerations are those the existence and content of which can be ascertained without resort to moral argument. Statutes and precedents are positivist considerations whereas the moral principles of justice are not. A moral adjudicator will rely in his deliberation on the existence of positivistic standards, but he is not bound to regard them as authoritative. But one does not have a court of law unless it is bound to take as authoritative some positivist standards such as custom, legislation, or precedent.

So much we can learn from our intuitive understanding of the nature of courts of law as a political institution. How can we use this understanding as a base on which to anchor a complete doctrine on the nature of law? The clue is in the emergence of authoritative positivist considerations as crucial to our conception of courts of law which ... provide the institutional key to the nature of law. We can formulate an additional constraint on an adequate doctrine of the nature of law:

Law consists only of authoritative positivist considerations.

An analogy with personal action will help to explain the point. It is possible to distinguish between a deliberative and an executive stage in a person's attitude to the prospect of a certain action. The deliberative stage, in which the person considers the merits of alternative courses of action, terminates when he reaches a conclusion as to what he should do. It is followed by an executive stage if and when he forms an intention to perform a certain act. In the executive stage he is set to act if and when the occasion arrives. When an intention is formed deliberation will terminate, though it may be restarted and the intention suspended or even revoked. Sometimes the intention will harden into a decision, indicating reluctance to reopen deliberation. In any case, the existence of an intention indicates that the question what to do has been settled and that the person is ready to act. Not every action is preceded by both stages or by one of them. Sometimes one just acts without prior deliberation or intention. Sometimes one or the other stage exists without the other, and very often when both exist the boundaries between them are extremely fuzzy. Yet the general distinction is of great importance: just as the deliberative stage is necessary for people to be able to form considered views on the merits of alternative courses of action, so the executive stage is necessary to enable people to plan ahead, to determine themselves to act in advance of the occasion for the action. For large organizations a distinction between deliberative and executive stages is essential to secure planned and efficient institutional action. In institutions such division often includes a division of responsibility between different persons. Some will be responsible for deliberating and deciding, others for executing those decisions. In general, social co-operation, either negative (people refraining from hurting each other) or positive, can be viewed as a form of social action decided upon by some social institutions and carried out by individuals. Some societies allow individuals a share in deciding on their schemes of co-operative action and other plans. But even they have to distinguish between the deliberative stage, where individuals contribute to the decision-making process, and the executive stage, where perhaps those very same individuals are bound to observe those decisions.

In the deliberative stage the question what is to be done is open to argument based on all sorts of considerations. Reasons of a moral character will often dominate. Once the matter has been decided to the satisfaction of the social institution involved, its appropriate organ will formulate 'the social intention', i.e. it issues an authoritative instruction. Since this instruction represents the conclusion of the deliberative stage and belongs itself to the executive stage, it will be identifiable without resort to further moral argument. Those belong by definition to the deliberative stage. Only positivist considerations can belong to the executive stage. Furthermore, executive considerations are authoritatively binding. Those subject to them are not normally allowed, by the social institution concerned, to challenge or query their validity or conclusiveness. To do so is to reopen the deliberative process, and unless there are limitations on the freedom with which this can be done the considerations cannot be regarded as executive. So long as argument is free the executive stage has not been reached.

Executive considerations are, therefore, authoritative positivist considerations. This brings us back to the definition of courts of law. It included the fact that they are guided in part by authoritative positivist considerations, and that they issue authoritative rulings (which, being issued by the action of members of the court, are themselves authoritative positivist rulings). This suggests that the law consists of the authoritative positivist considerations binding on the courts and belongs essentially to the executive stage of the political institution (the state, the church, etc.) of which it is a part. The resulting picture has the courts applying both legal (i.e. authoritative positivist) and non-legal considerations. They rely both on executive and deliberative reasons, yet the law belongs to the first kind only.

The two-stage picture presented above may make one surprised with a doctrine by which the courts are guided by considerations belonging to both stages. But the surprise is due merely to the oversimplification in the representation of the two stages above. Consider again the case of the individual. A person may stagger the process of decision-making, moving towards the 'pure' executive stage in several separate steps. First, for example, he decides to act on the balance of economic considerations and to discount considerations of prestige. Then he decides that one of the half-dozen alternatives open to him is to be rejected, since at least one of the others is better supported by economic considerations, etc. The law often proceeds in a similar way. On many issues statutes represent but the first step towards a 'pure' executive stage. They may have to be supplemented by delegated legislation and perhaps even by further administrative action. Sometimes litigation reaches the courts in matters which have not reached a 'pure' executive stage in the matter at issue and the courts have to resort to non-legal, i.e. non-executive, considerations to resolve the dispute. Even this picture is oversimplified. It suggests, for example, that the survival of a deliberative stage down to the adjudicative level is always to he regretted. This is far from the truth. It is often advantageous for a person while forming a general intention in advance (I'll stay the night in Nottingham) to leave the precise details to the last moment (I'll choose a hotel when there). The same kind of reason suggests that often, especially when dealing with very broad categories, it is better not to fix too inflexibly the precise details in advance. It is better to settle for executive reasons, i.e. laws, which fix the framework only and leave the courts room to apply deliberative reasons within that framework.

Be that as it may, our concern here is not to comment on various law-making policies but on the nature of law. Our analysis has yielded only one element: the law consists of authoritative positivist considerations enforceable by courts. Clearly, not all the considerations which meet this condition are part of the law. Other conditions have to be added. However, the fact that law consists of considerations enforceable by courts ... which are authoritative and positivist is suggested by the definition of a legal court, and is supported by the common distinction between the two functions of the courts as law-makers and law-appliers which roughly coincides with the distinction between cases where the law is unsettled and those where it is not. It is further supported by the fact that any analysis of law based in part on this feature focuses on a distinction of paramount importance to social organization: the distinction between the deliberative and the executive stages.

...

H. L. A. Hart is heir and torch-bearer of a great tradition in the philosophy of law which is realist and unromantic in outlook. It regards the existence and content of the law as a matter of social fact whose connection with moral or any other values is contingent and precarious. His analysis of the concept of law is part of the enterprise of demythologizing the law, of instilling rational critical attitudes to it. Right from his inaugural lecture in Oxford he was anxious to dispel the philosophical mist which he found in both legal culture and legal theory. In recent years he has shown time and again how much the rejection of the moralizing myths which accumulated around the law is central to his whole outlook. His essays on 'Bentham and the Demystification of the Law' and on 'The Nightmare and the Noble Dream' showed him to be consciously sharing the Benthamite sense of the excessive veneration in which the law is held in common-law countries, and its deleterious moral consequences. His fear that in recent years legal theory has lurched back in that direction, and his view that a major part of its role is to lay the conceptual foundation for a cool and potentially critical assessment of the law are evident.

This attitude strikes at the age-old question of the relation between morality and law. In particular it concerns the question whether it is ever the case that a rule is a rule of law because it is morally binding, and whether a rule can ever fail to be legally binding on the ground that it is morally unacceptable. As so often in philosophy, a large part of the answer to this question consists in rejecting it as simplistic and misleading, and substituting more complex questions concerning the relation between moral worth and legal validity.

...

AUTHORITY AND THE LAW

I will assume that necessarily law, every legal system which is in force anywhere, has *de facto* authority. That entails that the law either claims that it possesses legitimate authority or is held to possess it, or both. I shall argue that, though a legal system may not have legitimate authority, or though its legitimate authority may not be as extensive as it claims, every legal system claims that it possesses legitimate authority. If the claim to authority is part of the nature of law, then whatever else the law is it must be capable of possessing authority. A legal system may lack legitimate authority. If it lacks the moral attributes required to endow it with legitimate authority then it has none. But it must possess all the other features of authority, or else it would be odd to say that it claims authority. To claim authority it must be capable of having it, it must be a system of a kind which is capable in principle of possessing the requisite moral properties of authority.

...

The claims the law makes for itself are evident from the language it adopts and from the opinions expressed by its spokesmen, i.e. by the institutions of the law. The law's claim to authority is manifested by the fact that legal institutions are officially designated as 'authorities', by the fact that they regard themselves as having the right to impose obligations on their subjects, by their claims that their subjects owe them allegiance, and that their subjects ought to obey the law as it requires to be obeyed (i.e. in all cases except those in which some legal doctrine justifies breach of duty). Even a bad law, is the inevitable official doctrine, should be obeyed for as long as it is in force, while lawful action is taken to try and bring about its amendment or repeal. One caveat needs be entered here. In various legal systems certain modes of conduct are technically unlawful without being so in substance. It is left to the prosecutorial authorities to refrain from prosecuting for such conduct, or to the courts to give absolute discharge. Where legally recognized policies direct such authorities to avoid prosecution or conviction, the conduct should not be regarded as unlawful except in a technical sense, which is immaterial to our considerations.

...

We will concentrate on two features which must be possessed by anything capable of being authoritatively binding ... It is convenient to concentrate attention on instructions or directives. The terms are used in a wide sense which can cover propositions, norms, rules, standards, principles, doctrines, and the like. In that sense the law is a system of directives, and it is authoritative if and only if its directives are authoritatively binding. Likewise, whoever issues the directives has authority if and only if his directives are authoritatively binding because he makes them, that is (1) they are authoritative, and (2) part of the reason is that he made them.

The two features are as follows. First, a directive can be authoritatively binding only if it is, or is at least presented as, someone's view of how its subjects ought to behave. Second, it must be possible to identify the directive as being issued by the alleged authority without relying on reasons or considerations on which [the] directive purports to adjudicate. The first feature reflects the mediating role of authority. It is there to act on reasons which apply to us anyway, because we will more closely conform to those reasons if we do our best to follow the directives of the authority than if we try to act on those reasons directly. Hence, though the alleged authoritative instruction may be wrongly conceived and misguided, it must represent the judgment of the alleged authority on the reasons which apply to its subjects, or at least it must be presented as the authority's judgment. Otherwise it cannot be an authoritative instruction. It fails not because it is a bad instruction, but because it is not an instruction of the right kind. It may be an instruction given for some other occasion, or in jest, or an order or threat of a gangster who cares for and considers only his own good. Strictly speaking, to be capable of being authoritative a directive or a rule has actually to express its author's view on what its subjects should do. But given that this element is one where pretence and deceit are so easy, there is little surprise that appearances are all one can go by here, and the concept of *de facto* authority, as well as all others which presuppose capacity to have authority, are based on them. If the rule is presented as expressing a judgment on what its subjects should do, it is capable of being authoritative.

The second feature too is closely tied to the mediating role of authority. Suppose that an arbitrator, asked to decide what is fair in a situation, has given a correct decision. That is, suppose there is only one fair outcome, and it was picked out by the arbitrator. Suppose that the parties to the dispute are told only that about his decision, i.e. that he gave the only correct decision. They will feel that they know little more of what the decision is than they did before. They were given a uniquely identifying description of the decision and yet it is an entirely unhelpful description. If they could agree on what was fair they would not have needed the arbitrator in the first place. A decision is serviceable only if it can be identified by means other than the considerations the weight and outcome of which it was meant to settle.

This applies to all decisions, as much to those that a person takes for himself as to those taken for him by others. If I decide what would be the best life insurance to buy, it is no good trying to remind me of my decision by saying that I decided to buy the policy which it is best to buy. It means that I have to decide again in order to know what I decided before, so the earlier decision might just as well never have happened. The same applies to the subjects of any authority. They can benefit by its decisions only if they can establish their existence and content in ways which do not depend on raising the very same issues which the authority is there to settle.

…

Enough of Dworkin's thought is clear to show that its moving ideas are two. First, that judges' decisions, all their decisions, are based on considerations of political morality. This is readily admitted regarding cases in which source-based laws are indeterminate or where they conflict. Dworkin insists that the same is true of ordinary cases involving, say, simple statutory interpretation or indeed the decision to apply a statute at all. This does not mean that every time judges apply statutes they consider and re-endorse their faith in representative democracy, or in some other doctrine of political morality from which it follows that they ought to apply these statutes. It merely means that they present themselves as believing there is such a doctrine. Their decisions are moral decisions in expressing a moral position. A conscientious judge actually believes in the existence of a valid doctrine, a political morality, which supports his action.

If I interpret Dworkin's first leading idea correctly and it is as stated above, then I fully share it. I am not so confident about his second leading idea. It is that judges owe a duty, which he sometimes calls a duty of professional responsibility, which requires them to respect and extend the political morality of their country. Roughly speaking, Dworkin thinks that morality (i.e. correct or ideal morality) requires judges to apply the source-based legal rules of their country, and, where these conflict or are indeterminate, to decide cases by those standards of political morality which inform the source-based law, those which make sense if it is an expression of a coherent moral outlook.

Notice how far-reaching this second idea is. Many believe that the law of their country, though not perfect, ought to be respected. It provides reasonable constitutional means for its own development. Where reform is called for, it should be accomplished by legal means. While the law is in force it should be respected. For most, this belief depends to a large degree on the content of the law. They will deny that the laws of Nazi Germany deserved to be respected. Dworkin's obligation of professional responsibility is different. It applies to every legal system simply because it is a legal system, regardless of its content. Furthermore, it is an obligation to obey not merely the letter of the law but its spirit as well. Judges are called upon to decide cases where source-based law is indeterminate, or includes unresolved conflicts, in accordance with the prevailing spirit behind the bulk of the law. That would require a South African judge to use his power to extend apartheid.

...

It is easy to see that Dworkin's conception of law contradicts the two necessary features of law argued for above. First, according to him there can be laws which do not express anyone's judgment on what their subjects ought to do, nor are they presented as expressing such a judgment. The law includes the best justification of source-based law ... The best justification, or some aspects of it, may never have been thought of, let alone endorsed by anyone. Dworkin draws our attention to this fact by saying that it requires a Hercules to work out what the law is. Nor does Dworkin's best justification of the law consist of the implied consequences of the political morality which actually motivated the activities of legal institutions. He is aware of the fact that many different and incompatible moral conceptions influenced different governments and their officials over the centuries. His best justification may well be one which was never endorsed, not even in its fundamental precepts, by anyone in government. Much of the law of any country may, according to Dworkin, be unknown. Yet it is already legally binding, waiting there to be discovered. Hence it neither is nor is presented as being anyone's judgment on what the law's subjects ought to do.

Second, the identification of much of the law depends, according to Dworkin's analysis, on considerations which are the very same considerations which the law is there to settle ... Establishing what the law is involves judgment on what it ought to be. Imagine a tax problem on which source-based law is indeterminate. Some people say that in such a case there is no law on the issue. The court ought to ask what the law ought to be and to decide accordingly. If it is a higher court whose decision is a binding precedent, it will have thereby made a new law. Dworkin, on the other hand, says that there is already law on the matter. It consists in the best justification of the source-based law. So in order to decide what the tax liability is in law, the court has to go into the issue of what a fair tax law would be and what is the least change in it which will make source-based law conform to it. This violates the second feature of the law argued for above.

It is important to realize that the disagreement I am pursuing is not about how judges should decide cases. In commenting on Dworkin's second leading idea I expressed doubts regarding his view on that. But they are entirely irrelevant here. So let me assume that Dworkin's duty of professional responsibility is valid and his advice to judges on how to decide cases is sound. We still have a disagreement regarding what judges do when they follow his advice. We assume that they follow right morality, but do they also follow the law or do they make law? My disagreement with Dworkin here is that, in saying that they follow pre-existing law, he makes the identification of a tax law, for example, depend on settling what a morally just tax law would be, i.e. on the very considerations which a tax law is supposed to have authoritatively settled.

...

Dworkin's theory, one must conclude, is inconsistent with the authoritative nature of law. That is, it does not allow for the fact that the law necessarily claims authority and that it therefore must be capable of possessing legitimate authority. To do so it must occupy, as all authority does, a mediating role between the precepts of morality and their application by people in their behaviour. It is this mediating role of authority which is denied to the law by Dworkin's conception of it.

Dworkin (2002) has recently assessed Raz's claims about the authority of law. While he points out various features of Raz's account which he finds wanting, he frames his central criticism in the following passage, where he considers Raz's central claim that for a directive to be authoritative, it cannot require the person who must follow the directive to engage in moral reasoning to discover how he or she must act:

Suppose a nation's legislature adopts a law declaring that henceforth, on pain of severe criminal punishment, subjects must never act immorally in any aspect of their lives. That is an exceptionally silly statute, and life in that nation will thereafter be repulsive as well as dangerous. According to Raz, however, it would be a conceptual mistake to describe the statute as law at all. Even in this extreme example, his claim seems too strong. The statute, after all, has normative consequences for those disposed to accept its authority. They now have an additional reason to reflect carefully on the moral quality of everything they do and to act punctiliously, not only because they are now subject to official sanction, but also because their community has declared, through its criminal law, the cardinal importance of moral diligence. They would not be making a conceptual mistake if they said they were behaving differently out of deference to the authority of the new law. They would not say, however, that the statute had merely empowered officials to judge their conduct according to the officials' own moral standards. If they were jailed for an act they thought scrupulously moral, they would insist they had been jailed contrary to law.

... [N]othing in the ordinary concept of authority prevents us from treating as authoritative a rule or principle that incorporates a moral standard. Suppose that a businessman in a trade where 'caveat emptor' prevails converts to a religion whose sacred text enjoins its adherents to deal 'honestly and fairly' in commerce. He will behave differently, and he will sensibly say that in doing so, he is deferring to the authority of his new religion – even though he must ponder the same reasons he always had to decide what that authority commands. Suppose he wonders one day whether it would be unfair not to disclose an evident defect to a buyer who has not noticed it. If he decides that it would be unfair and discloses the defect, he can sensibly say that he has deferred to religious authority. Sacred text forbids what is unfair; non-disclosure is unfair; therefore sacred text requires disclosure. It would be inaccurate to say that the sacred text has not directed him to disclose, but only to consider whether non-disclosure is unfair. His religion tells him to avoid what is unfair, not to avoid what he judges to be unfair. If he decides after careful reflection that non-disclosure is perfectly fair but years later changes his mind, he will then think that he once disobeyed a religious command. (Dworkin 2002, 1673–74)

This passage deserves, and rewards, careful scrutiny. It directly challenges Raz's view of authority, persuasively urging that our intuitions about the nature of authority will pull us away from Raz's explanation of it. Are you convinced by the examples Dworkin gives, and his characterisation of them. How do you think Raz would respond?

As our final reading, in the following passages Coleman provides a characterisation of what divides Dworkin and positivists: as he sees it, the divide turns on what each side regards as the most essential or central element of the law, that is, either (1) as an institution which creates a system of rules to guide the citizens of a jurisdiction, ie to guide them in their daily affairs *outside* of courts or in the absence of any legal officials like police officers or lawyers, or (2) as an institution which resolves disputes between citizens *in a rational way*, and so is essentially committed to providing a sound basis upon which judicial decisions can aim to be reasonable and just.

Coleman (2001, 162, 165–68, 171–72)

To his credit, Dworkin has done more than anyone else to develop a general theory of legal content. On his account, legal content is a function of *constructive interpretation*, an activity that Dworkin understands as having two elements: fit and value. An interpretation operates on the set of authoritative legal pronouncements as the 'data points' of the interpretation of the law of a community. The interpretation must fit its authoritative pronouncements (and history) in roughly the same way that an interpretation of a novel must fit the themes, plot lines, and characters of the novel. By contrast, the value dimension of the interpretation invokes the norms appropriate to the kind of object being interpreted. Because law involves the coercive authority of the state, the norms to which an interpretation of law must turn are those governing the political morality of coercive authority. The object of the interpretation is to show the law of a particular community 'in its best light' – to understand it as adhering to and embodying the norms of the relevant institutional political morality to the greatest extent it can, consistent with the official pronouncements the interpretation must fit.

...

While I have no developed theory of legal content to oppose to Dworkin's, I do have certain reservations about his account, as well as some thoughts about the way in which any positivist theory of content is likely to differ from his.

...

On Dworkin's view, authoritative pronouncements are the data points that constrain the interpretive theory. The theory is no good unless it fits them in such a way that they can be seen as contributing to the 'legal themes' by which the theory fleshes out the content of the community law. Official legal pronouncements thus enter primarily as constraints on the interpretive theory. For positivists, by contrast, the rules or standards that satisfy the criteria of legality are not merely data points or parameters on which, or within which, an interpretive theory is to operate. These pronouncements are, in the first instance, potential guides to human conduct. This is one important reason why positivists might object to thinking of legal content as analogous to literary or artistic content. It is plausible to assert that in order to grasp the content of a work of fiction, for example, we must view the themes, plot line, events, and characters holistically; none of these discrete elements can plausibly be said to have an artistic meaning independently of the work of which it is a part. Particular authoritative pronouncements in law, however, often do seem to play a discretely analyzable role in guiding conduct. Positivists focus on this role in conceiving of legal rules as creating reasons for action.

There appears to be no evidence that Dworkin sees legal rules as having the function of offering those governed by them reasons for action. Indeed, we might even read him as denying that rules constitute any part of the law's content; rather, legal content resides in the principles, to which the rules are transparent. Thus, the authoritative pronouncements are insignificant in the Dworkinian picture beyond the role they play as constraints on the interpretive theory, whereas these pronouncements are essential to the positivist picture.

This difference is extremely important in several ways. The first concerns the role that the set of authoritative pronouncements plays within the theory. In both Dworkin's account and the positivist's the binding legal standards are linguistic entities that have prepositional content. So we need a way of determining their content, regardless of the role they ultimately must play in the theory. For Dworkin, however, these pronouncements have no guidance function. Thus their status as binding, and their content, are altogether provisional and revisable in the light of the theory of content. That theory, in turn, is oriented toward determining right answers to particular disputes and not toward guiding the conduct of ordinary folk. Thus, for Dworkin, the only point of identifying the authoritative pronouncements and ascribing content to them is to construct legal content. The authoritative standards at this juncture in the argument are no more than raw material for a theory of content. That theory itself then provides all the warrant one needs to revise the set of authoritative pronouncements. In Dworkin's theory the actual set of binding legal standards − or authoritative pronouncements − falls out of the theory of content.

When Dworkin's view is understood in this way, several familiar objections to his account are seen to be misplaced. For example, the claim that Dworkin is himself committed to a rule of recognition for identifying the set of binding legal standards on which the theory of interpretation operates is misleading in several ways. First, of course, the rule of recognition is always conventional, and Dworkin rejects conventionalism of all kinds and at every turn. Second, and much more important in this context, the provisional set of authoritative pronouncements are not, in the end, the binding set of legal standards. They are the raw materials for the theory of content. Once a theory of content is constructed, the set of binding and authoritative pronouncements falls out of that theory. This is the sense in which it is both accurate and illuminating to see Dworkin as, in effect, developing a theory of law from a theory of adjudication.

While the above objection to Dworkin is misplaced, Dworkin's approach does leave him open to the charge that, in his account, there never really are binding authoritative pronouncements, only provisional ones. Those standards that are provisional at time T1, allow us to construct a theory of content, from which fall out the 'binding' legal standards at T2. But there is no meaningful or interesting sense in which those standards are binding. Because of the way the theory is constructed, they are no more than the set of provisional standards at T2, on which the theory of content operates. This is a feature of Dworkin's emphasis on what I am calling 'adjudicatory legal content': the set of authoritative standards are relevant in his view only for the purpose of determining legal content, but not for the guidance of conduct. The rules are seen not from the perspective of governing the conduct of ordinary folk, but rather as the raw materials for the theory of legal content that guides judges in resolving disputes. One effect of this picture of legal practice is that the notion of a binding legal standard has to be rethought or eliminated. The difference between binding and provisional is lost.

The problem is deeper, however. It is not just that such a view cannot make sense of the ordinary distinction between binding and provisional standards – the theory cannot even get off the ground. For we cannot infer that a determinate answer to a legal dispute is, for that reason alone, a statement of the law. Here is the problem. Suppose one holds that it is a conceptual truth about law that something is law only if it is capable of guiding conduct, and a norm, decision, or rule is capable of guiding conduct only if those to whom the law is addressed can know in advance what it requires of them. On this view, determinate answers to disputes state the law only if they are knowable in advance. Thus even a decision reached by applying authoritative sources and those to which one is authoritatively directed and doing so in an appropriate or authorized way, need not state the *law*. That depends on what one's theory of *law* is.

In entertaining this view I am not defending it, nor am I asserting that the determinate answers derivable from the Dworkinian account will fail to meet this conceptual constraint on legality or legal content. The point I am making is more general. Dworkin attempts to derive a theory of what law is from a theory of determinate *adjudicatory* content. The point of the example is to express doubt about this strategy. Adjudicatory content is not, by that fact alone, legal content. Because it is not a theory of *legal content* without a theory of law, we cannot derive a theory of *law* from a theory of adjudicatory content. And if we cannot derive a theory of legal content from a theory of adjudicatory content, we cannot derive an account of what is to count as legal binding standards or authoritative pronouncements from the Dworkinian theory of content.

...

I think these points can be illuminated further by drawing out a useful distinction between Dworkin and positivists that flatters both equally and subjects both to criticism. Take Hart as a typical, thoughtful positivist. One way of looking at Hart's position is that when cases fall within the core of rules, the law guides conduct well and there are right answers as a matter of law that are unique, determinate, and by and large determinable. When there are no right answers, when there is substantial disagreement about what the law requires, when we are in the penumbra ... the judge must revise the law. There is no answer as a matter of law to what conduct is required, permitted, or prohibited; the law must be revised if it is to provide an answer. The problem is that positivists have no theory of revision. Hart certainly did not. He tells us only that to resolve the dispute and in effect therefore to revise the law, the judge must exercise discretion.

On the other hand, discretion is a rational and not a random procedure. It is governed by norms and reason; a discretionary decision is still one that should, in this sense, be rationalized. Of course, the question is how – to which the typical positivist has no answer at all. If Hart is the paradigm, a critic could with warrant claim that positivism thus has a nice explanation of what is going on in the standard case, why things work and how they work; but no theory of any use about how to revise the law, when the law is indeterminate and need fixing.

In contrast, if we look at Dworkin's theory of legal content as instead an account how judges should (and do) revise the law rationally when the law needs to be revised, then it is … a perfectly attractive and sensible theory. It probably comes reasonably close to describing what judges in fact do when they revise the law. That is, they ask themselves what the binding sources are, how best to put them together in a way that flatters the enterprise of governance by law, and then ask what decision would fit best with that larger conception. The problem with Dworkin's view is that he has no way of telling which cases call for revision. His theory of revision is his theory of law. His theory of law answers a political question: when is the coercive authority of the state legitimately imposed? It does not answer a practical question: is the law adequate to its practical purposes? If positivists can be charged with offering the label 'discretion' instead of a theory of revision, then what Dworkin offers is a theory of revision masquerading as a theory of law.

The last point Coleman puts should probably be made more charitably: For Dworkin, a theory of revision is not masquerading as a theory of law; it *is* a theory of law, as Coleman should recognise, given Dworkin's starting premise – that the central function of the institution of the law is not to provide guidance to citizens in their affairs, but to *rationally* resolve actual disputes between citizens that come before it. On this view a theory of law *is* a theory of content, or a theory of the revision of legal content, for *the law* is that intellectual activity of resolving disputes on a rational basis. That the dispute resolution be *rational* is an essential feature of this rendering of law. For only on the premise that law resolves disputes in a rational way does Dworkin claim that law is an interpretive and theoretical enterprise, that is, an enterprise which seeks to provide good reasons for its action.

Concluding thoughts

As the final reading of Coleman helps to point out, the debates between Dworkin, Hart, Raz, Fish, Coleman, Simmonds, Marmor and others capture more in the way of disagreement than minor points of philosophical technicality. They embrace large issues about the right perspective to take on law, the nature of legal reasoning, and the place where law fits into the political and social structure of society. We cannot neglect the minor points of detail, for in jurisprudence as elsewhere, the devil is in the detail. But at the same time, it is essential to keep one's head up and keep track of where any individual step in an argument may be leading. In this last part, we raise once again a point mentioned first in Chapter 8, ie the different starting points or general perspectives which seem to motivate these theorists' efforts, and consider an analogy with the institution of a university to help us do so.

What is a university? What is its point, function, or purpose? This is an institution with which you are familiar, and undoubtedly have views. But there may be perspectives on the university which, despite this familiarity, you mightn't have considered. Here are four candidates for the point, function, or purpose of a university:

1. The purpose of the university is to provide post-secondary training, to enhance the skills of students so that upon graduation they will be able to undertake the sophisticated work demanded of participants in a 'knowledge' economy. Besides increasing the individual earning potential of graduates, there will be a general economic benefit in the enlarged GDP which accompanies the application of such a skilled labour force in 'knowledge'-based industries. This view of the university is particularly popular with certain sorts of politician, and has various consequences. Students, on this model, are consumers of a product, skills-enhancement, which increases their earning potential, and therefore, in principal, they should pay for this personal benefit as they would for any other investment product they choose. Universities, and their employees, the teachers, are to be judged on how efficiently they turn out skilled graduates. If they can increase the throughput, say by doubling class sizes, without any measurable 'decline in quality', they should of course do so.

2. The purpose of the university is to perpetuate a social and political elite. A university degree is a badge of status. While in the past this status was associated in part with becoming a gentleman – someone who didn't work with their hands – and so study tended to focus upon the practically useless, classical studies, Greek and Latin and so on, our 'meritocratic' conceits now compel us to regard the true mark of this status as lying in the 'intellectuality' of the atmosphere of the university and the achievement of an erudition which marks the university graduate apart, and makes him or her 'the right stuff' for various kinds of social and economic positions. To put it perhaps crudely, in the same way in which attendance at a famous public school makes one an Etonian or a Wykehamist for life, so one may become an 'Oxford' or a 'Harvard' man or woman, and which opens various doors to power and privilege as a result. Where one goes, of course, matters a lot. Those familiar with 'Yes, Minister' may recall the number of occasions when Sir Humphrey (an Oxford man) would put his frustration with Jim Hacker down to the fact that the latter went to the LSE (of all places).

3. The university forms part of the broader cultural, scientific, and social policy industries. Universities in their 'research activities' contribute to culture and science and informed opinion, producing critical works in the form of books, journals, policy papers, and so on, which shape society's cultural activity, in particular as it is continuous with other cultural, scientific and social policy activities, like the BBC, newspapers, various institutions like museums and opera and theatre companies, symphony orchestras, the chemical and pharmaceutical and engineering industries, think tanks, and the civil service. And in their teaching function, they provide training for future workers in these activities.

4. Finally, and perhaps most strange-sounding to modern ears, the university has an intrinsic function largely unrelated to, and perhaps actually hostile to, the wider

world of economic, social and political activity. Caricatured as the ivory tower, on this understanding the university keeps a certain kind of enlightenment alive, whether religious, in seeking a better understanding of creation, or humanist, to ask why? and how? of both us and the world we find ourselves in. Moreover, this is done for its own sake, whether the broader world benefits or not. On this view, the university cannot *earn* its keep in any way, and depends upon enough people outside the university caring for its project enough to give it the resources it needs, in much the way that the Church so depends. And students, on this view, much as their clerical counterparts, are novices, not consumers. The university needs students because it must find people to carry on its project for the next generation.

Now dissecting these various purposes or functions of the university is artificial; they clearly overlap, and the institution in various ways embodies all four. And you can no doubt think of others. What this elaboration of functions shows, however, is that it would be perfectly sensible to choose one or two of these functions as the central ones. Certainly it is arguable that many latter day politicians focus almost exclusively on (1) and perhaps (3), for obvious reasons.

As a 'take-home' problem, try to do the same thing for the institution of law. One might start by roughly setting a Dworkinian view against a Hartian one; for Dworkin, the central function of law would appear to lie in the court-centred activity of resolving disputes; for Hart, the central function of law would appear to lie in the promulgation of standards to guide the law's subjects so they don't get into disputes and stay out of court. But of course these two functions are related. And you can no doubt think of others. What would a critical legal theorist identify as the most significant function of the legal system? And here is a final question: How would different theorists express the way that law fits into the general political settlement of a society, into its economic system, into its pattern of social divisions or distinctions? And ask yourself – could you give reasons for saying that one sort of function or perspective on law was the *true* one, or the *fundamental* one. What sorts of reason would they be?

The point of doing this is to help you identify what you think is most important or essential about the law, what jurisprudence or the philosophy of law or legal theory must first explain if it is to be a good theory. In the same way that your 'theory of the university' would differ markedly if you chose function (2) rather than function (1) as its most important or essential function, then so would your legal theory reflect your best understanding of what the law most characteristically is, and does.

Further Reading

For a more recent statement by Dworkin of his theory see Dworkin 1997. For a difficult but rewarding critique of both Hart's 'linguistic' jurisprudence and the semantic sting argument, see Raz 1998; see also Endicott 1998 and Stavropoulos 2001. For a recent overview of the philosophical issues raised by soft positivism, including attempts to make it compatible with the authoritative nature of law, see Marmor 2002 and Himma 2002. The best challenge to Raz's authority-centred theory of law as well as to Coleman's views is Dworkin 2002, which was quoted from above, and which you might read in full. For an interesting thesis that the positivism and anti-positivism debate is irresolvable, reflecting a tension at the heart of law, see Shiner 1992.

Questions

1. Explain in your own words what Dworkin means by 'the semantic sting', and evaluate it.

2. In what respect is a theory of law *evaluative*?

3. Are Hart's responses to Dworkin's claims about the linguistic, descriptive, and non-interpretive character of Hart's theory successful?

4. What is 'soft positivism'? Is it plausible?

5. What makes authority so central to Raz's understanding of law? Should it be so central?

6. Is Dworkin's critique of Raz's claim about the authority of law effective? Can Raz offer a response to Dworkin's response? Is Raz's account vulnerable to other arguments?

7. What is Coleman's analysis of the real division between positivists and Dworkin? Is his analysis fair to both sides, and more importantly, is it right?

8. In 1966, the House of Lords issued a 'practice direction' (*Practice Direction* [1966] 1 WLR 1234), stating that it would depart from its previous decisions in cases where it seemed right to do so, 'overruling' its 1898 holding (*London Street Tramways v LCC* [1898] AC 735) that it was bound by its previous decisions (such that only Parliament could alter the law once the House had pronounced upon it). How would (a) a positivist, and (b) Dworkin, describe what happened when the House did this?

Part II Extensions and Negations

Introducing Part II – Extensions and Negations

You are now through Part I of this book. You are entitled to take a deep breath. The number of ideas that have faced you, and the way in which they seem to struggle against each other, should rightly strike you as dumping a difficult project in your lap, the difficult project of sorting them all out. Of course to do that, you must first have substantially assimilated the different views we have presented, to distinguish them reasonably clearly, to see the pressure points where they come into conflict with each other. That is the first step, and helping you to that first step has been our purpose in Part I. We hope you have begun 'step two', trying to sort them all out. But unless you are a very, very clever person, it is unlikely that you will have sorted them out already to the satisfaction of yourself, and perhaps more pertinently, to the satisfaction of your tutors; indeed, the chance of your having done so is vanishingly small, because your tutors are themselves students of this subject, and no legal theorist however eminent believes that he or she has sorted it all out either (perhaps there is an exception or two). What you must try to do is put yourself in the position of a decently critical assessor of the various ideas you have looked at, and begin the process of forming an overview that allows you to frame for yourself which ideas and arguments are hopeless, which plausible but flawed, which hopeful but insufficiently developed, and which strike you as really compelling, an overview you would feel capable of defending, by defending the way in which you would weigh these ideas against each other with some rigour. Keeping this 'sorting it all out' project in mind is the best way to attack your revision of the Part I material for essays and exams. At this stage we hope to have got you to step one, and prepared to embark on step two. We hope to have left you undecided, perhaps troubled, but not confused.

Much of Part I has dealt with the natural law/positivism opposition. In Part II, you will have the opportunity to engage with theories which reject the centrality of positivism and its interminable debate with natural law, in favour of much broader questions and quite different approaches to the study of law. These include feminist theories, economic analysis of law, legal autopoiesis, Foucault's analysis of power, and other developments in legal theory. Part I may also have given the impression that the function of natural law and positivist theories is solely to conduct a debate with each other. Not so. These theories have important things to say in their own right. In Part II we also look at some of these insights. Natural law has generated modern theories of disobedience, punishment, and justice; Positivism has generated theories for the analysis of legal concepts and legal reasoning.

Part II of this book is entitled 'Extensions and Negations'. The important point to remember about this title is not that some theorists or theories seem to build on those encountered in Part I while others reject them, but that they are intelligible (or more intelligible) in their relation to the materials that you have already encountered than as discrete pieces of knowledge in their own right. Some of this will appear quite obvious. For example, in economic analysis of law you will find a theory that hopes to improve on indeterminate arguments about what the law ought to be through the use of economic analysis. And you will also find our old friend Dworkin arguing that judges, as moral persons, would be unlikely to use economic analysis in this way. Other connections are less direct than this. Understanding Foucault, and the implications of his writings for our understanding of law, would be more difficult if you were not already familiar with the fact that social theories about the nature of order, and the basis of historical change (most particularly the change from feudal to modern society) have implications for our understanding of the nature and functions of law (don't forget what you tackled in chapter 6).

The links between Parts I and II should not lead you to believe that the subjects in Part II are like the blades of a fan, linked to a common core but not to each other. Just as those who write about jurisprudence and legal theory are conscious of, and orientate themselves around, what has gone before, they are similarly aware of the different theories developing contemporaneously alongside their own. And even if they were not, there is nothing quite like a rival theory or approach to help you to think about the implications and limitations of the one you are presently studying. Asking the question 'What does accepting the approach of theory X mean for theory Y?' (perhaps legal autopoiesis and economic analysis of law) is a very good way of starting to comprehend each of the theories you encounter. The links you make, whether by way of observing contrasts or supplements, and whether you look backwards or sideways, will all contribute to your understanding.

Your teachers will decide which of the topics in Part II they want you to tackle. There is no maximum or minimum number of chapters necessary for the study of jurisprudence and legal theory. More is not always better, especially when breadth is exchanged for depth.

11 Disobedience

David Schiff

There are times when people claim that it is right for them to break the law. Such claims offer a significant challenge in at least two ways. They challenge the legal system and in particular its attempts to enforce its laws, and justify that enforcement. The claim that it is right to break the law takes some of the ground away from those justifications. The challenge is: 'although you may normally claim that enforcement of the law is justified, in this case I am right to break the law, so those normal justifications cannot simply apply'. Such claims also challenge the coherence of theories of law, and whether they have any practical relevance. Do theories of law offer a coherent account of both the nature of our obligation to law, and the circumstances under which disobedience to the law can be justified? Do theories of law offer any practical guidance to those who disobey law and wish to claim that they are right to do so; guidance that allows them to see more clearly what the implications of their actions are. And, what are the implications of such claims for those, operating as legal officials, in deciding how to respond to particular kinds of disobedience? It is possible to address the advantages and disadvantages of different theories of law by testing them against the yardstick of how well or badly they cope with, or how useful or useless they are when faced with, the claim of justified disobedience.

Of course justified disobedience to law offers a number of practical challenges. But additionally, at the theoretical level, it goes to the roots or foundation of many theories of law. Wherever we have law, there is at least an implicit demand that human actions are in some sense no longer a matter of free choice. This demand, which is often explicit, is directed towards all of us, that we should/must obey. It is, especially if one were to accept Kelsen's reasoning, directed acutely at those operating the machinery of the legal system, that they should/must obey. Such demands are intrinsic to the rules themselves. The language of criminal legal rules is the language of what one should or should not do. The language of much civil law might not appear to be directly about obligation in the sense of what one should or should not do, but that it is right for one to obey remains implicit in it. Take the example of rules about contracts, which are premised on the obligatoriness of keeping to one's promises. Or the rules relating to property premised on the duty not to interfere with another's possessions. Or rules dealing with the powers of officials, such as judicial powers, which are premised on the need for such persons to live up to the demands placed upon them, in the name of the law. It is not surprising that some theorists have stated that the nature of obligation to obey law (and its corollary, the circumstances in which it is justifiable to disobey) are at the heart of any theory of law, what each and every theory needs to have an explanation of.

At a more practical level, facing the issues raised by justified disobedience is a rare but ever present challenge. Not only citizens, but also lawyers in particular will be in situations, at some time or other, where such a challenge arises. At every point in modern life one is faced with law and its obligations. At some points one will think about disobeying. On some occasions one will think about whether it is right to disobey. At other times one will be convinced that it is right, and even believe that one's obligation to do so is paramount. Many historical examples demonstrate that among those most likely to get involved in the latter situation are lawyers, who face the law's demands more directly than other citizens every day of their working lives.

What do theories of law tell us about the nature of obligation to law

If you think about the word obligation and the word duty you will soon realise that they can be and are used in many different situations. Finnis (1980, 297), for example, describes the semantic and cultural difficulties involved in discussions of obligation. 'Discussion of obligation is burdened by the cultural particularity of the word "obligation". Philosophers and moralists find the grammatical substantive form "obligation" convenient for signifying a wide range of notions: that there are things within our power either to do or not to do, which (whatever we desire) we *have* to do (but not because we are forced to), or *must* do, which it is our *duty to* do, which it is *wrong not to* do, or *shameful not to*, which one *morally* (or *legally*) *ought to* do, which (in Latin) *oportet facere* or (in French) *il faut faire*, one's *devoir* in French, *to deon* in the Greek of Aristotle and Euripedes, *swanelo* among the Barotse of southern Africa.' At one level, obligation and duty seem to involve moral or ethical reasoning. At another level, it is clear that our talk of legal duties and obligations may or may not refer back to their moral counterparts. And we also talk of political obligations and social obligations, the obligations of the citizen, or of the parent. Since our focus is 'law' there is some advantage in starting with the phrase 'legal obligation' and exploring what different meanings it might have.

So let's start with the meaning of legal obligation that can be gleaned from the positivism of John Austin. Citizens are, apparently, under an obligation or duty to the sovereign source of law's commands. 'Being liable to evil from you if I comply not with a wish which you signify, I am *bound* or *obliged* by your command, or I lie under a *duty* to obey it. If, in spite of that evil in prospect, I comply not with the wish which you signify, I am said to disobey your command, or to violate the duty which it imposes.' (Austin

1955/1863, 14) He uses the word duty, but the only reason that is implied for that use is the sanction. Thus legal obligation appears to flow from being subjected to sanctions for disobedience. If that is the case then we have at best a pragmatic notion of obligation. One ought not to do what will result in one suffering a sanction. Or we might call this empirical, because you **will** suffer a sanction. The Scandinavian Realist writer Karl Olivecrona (1939, 12–13) has a standard criticism of such a notion of obligation '… we might as well say that there is a binding rule forbidding people to put their hands into the fire. The consequences of such an act are most unpleasant. But we are not on that account deemed to be *bound* to avoid the act. It is not said to be a duty to keep away from the fire. It is in our interest, only, to do so. But the law is thought to be "binding" regardless of our own interests.' That criticism amounts to saying that the use of the word obligation in those terms is meaningless, it adds nothing to the 'real' situation that can be described without reference to it. However, if you do not accept that criticism, then you are left with the idea that one ought to obey the party who has the ability to sanction: centralised authority. It is typical to make such a transition from this intuition to a moral claim. The claim that obligation exists whenever one has the power to command obedience is a version of natural law commonly associated with Hobbes, who argues that order is superior to anarchy, and the former is only possible where one has rulers. The necessity for rulers (and order) as a pre-condition to any moral life (or moral order) leads to a claim that obedience to authority has value in and of itself.

To move beyond such a limited concept of legal obligation, a next step is try to understand legal obligation in terms of the needs of institutions rather than their sanctioning practices. For this understanding Hart's positivism is more informative than Austin's is. Legal officials have an obligation to follow legal rules; they are not merely obliged to them because of the consequences that might flow from disobedience. That obligation is an institutional prerequisite. Gewirth (1970, 55–56) describes this idea of obligation well. 'An institution is a standardized arrangement whereby persons jointly pursue or participate in some purposive activity which is socially approved on the ground of its value for society … institutions are constituted by rules which define what men are required to do if they are to participate in the respective functions or activities; and these requirements are the obligations which men have qua such participants.' The type of obligation described here is principally conceptual or, as Gewirth calls it, 'logical'. Once the institution has defined its rules, those rules constitute it, and the idea of obligation is the conceptual link between those rules and the institution's participants. So, for Hart, there is no doubt that legal officials can be described as being under an obligation to legal rules. But this idea of obligation is not, for him, a moral obligation, neither is it definitive in the sense that judges cannot use their discretion to determine its limits. Obligation within law has no different status from that within games. Law is the game that officials, particularly judges, play. They are conceptually or logically required, and can therefore only act consistently in relation to their legal obligations (play the game of law) by obeying the law, although they might be able to show that apparent disobedience does not amount to actual disobedience under the rules. Where the rules are unclear they are entitled, consistently with their responsibilities, to determine what the limits of the rules and therefore of their legal obligations are. From this it appears that Hart's idea of legal obligation, as an institutional obligation, might tell us something about the activities of officials, but much less about the activities of ordinary citizens. Because the degree of participation of the ordinary citizen is so much less than that of the official, it is difficult for this notion of legal obligation to clarify the nature of the citizen's obligation to law.

While Hart's approach to legal obligation is positivistic, in the sense that he claims that no legal system need have any particular connection with morality, nevertheless, he accepts that legal systems can be established which seek to incorporate moral values. (But remember the objections to such 'soft positivism' discussed in Chapter 10.) For such legal systems, the concepts, ideas and understandings which enable officials to make sense of the institution of which they are a part, will also include moral values. For example, if one placed a particular legal system into its political background, such as that of liberal democracy, then it might be possible to construct a notion of obligation that was implicit in the legal system pertaining to liberal democracy. This is exactly what, in the opinion of this writer, Dworkin undertakes when he writes of obligation to and disobedience of law. We will consider his enterprise later in this chapter. A clear example of this type of argument for 'the right to disobey' is presented by Zweibach. He argues that one has a right to disobey, but not because a law may be judged morally wrong or wicked, but because the act of disobedience in question is an assertion of a right, which assertion is consistent with the rights constituted within the system of law. Thus 'A right to disobey exists because the protection of certain rights is the condition of the authority of the regime and the legitimacy of the common life it represents.' (1975, 148) The slang phrase for this is 'being hoisted on one's own petard' – seeking to hold legal regimes up to the values which are claimed for the system, by using these values to ground rights to disobey. Such reasoning may extend to citizens. While Zweibach focuses on liberal democracies, he sees all legal systems as being constituted by standards that are, in some form or other, non-arbitrary (a similar structure of argument is used in the extract from Rawls later in this chapter).

If one can accept that legal systems must (or can) incorporate moral values, and give rise to moral obligations, the next step is to consider how this may occur. Lon Fuller (1969) relies on the need for law to communicate its demands for obedience, which he uses to develop a procedural form of natural law. If law is non-arbitrary communication, then what is constituted within its standards are at least procedural rights. These rights cannot be withdrawn, or at least any attempt to do so is self-contradictory. One cannot be said to have disobeyed laws which, for procedural reasons, were never capable of being obeyed in the first place. Intentional disobedience to law requires the law to meet Fuller's procedural conditions. Fuller's theory will not ground a right of disobedience to particular laws short of a failure of the whole system to be 'legal'.

A more substantive concept of legal obligation will seek to link law to notions, such as promises. Obligations that arise from promises are limited by the nature of the promise and by the circumstances of its operation. With the promissory version of legal obligation, ie that legal obligation flows from being a party to a 'social contract', disobedience can be justified where there is no conflict between what one must be assumed to have promised and what actions one now wishes to take. Here, as everywhere within discussion of obligation, there are large semantic difficulties. In this instance those difficulties arise both in relation to deciding what amounts to an obligation, and also what amounts to a promise. In what sense is the citizen promising

– by voting, by accepting the benefits that flow from the obedience of others, by accepting the ordered society that she/he lives in? Legal obligation does not flow directly from any particular promise, there can only be a fictitious promise, except possibly in some very small scale societies. Ordinarily then promising can only be constructed through a political notion such as that of a 'social contract'. Whatever problems one may have in identifying the scope of a full/real/typical promise, one has greater difficulties with fictitious situations such as this, where only some of the characteristics of a full/real/typical promise are present. What this form of understanding legal obligation usually implies is some kind of intentionality. A citizen is bound because of what they did or how they acted, they committed themselves to the system of law, and therefore 'intended' that they should be bound by its obligations. An alternative form of social contract argued for by John Rawls (explored in greater depth in Chapter 15) is a promise which one would have undertaken, if asked, if one was being 'fair' to one's fellow citizens. If citizens are bound in modern societies by legal obligations that they have promised to undertake, then the conditions of such promising can only be complex. They depend on practices that are partially legal, but are also political and social. If you were inclined to think about legal obligation in these terms then it is less likely that you would apply the idea to citizens who were unable to participate in the benefits that flow from the particular society's rules or political practices. For John Rawls obligation to law only arises in a 'nearly just' society. A 'nearly just' society is one in which the legal and political institutions produce the conditions of individual liberty, equal opportunity, and only limited inequality (Rawls 1973, see Chapter 15). In this version of what legal obligation means, relying on promises and a form of social contract, some notion of 'the common good' is implicated. Most significantly it is possible to argue that where the application of the law produces substantial injustice contrary to the common good, no promise to obey can be implied.

From a starting point that legal obligation is a necessary consequence of law's existence as an institution, we have progressed to those, like Rawls, who seek to link legal obligation to concepts of the common good. From here, it is only a short step to a full natural law position: if law 'obliges in conscience' then legal obligation is a type of moral obligation. Whether all law must 'oblige in conscience' or only some, and whether such an obligation is absolute, prima facie (and thus can be overridden), or conditional are different questions. But, in whatever form this version of legal obligation arises, it assumes that one ought to obey some laws on some occasions simply because they are laws; and that such a conclusion is the result of the fact that legal obligation has a necessary (although not necessarily absolute) moral quality. In the writings of different natural lawyers this type of understanding of legal obligation arises. With it comes an approach to the question of justified disobedience. To some extent or other, such disobedience needs to be justified by reference to moral reasoning, since one 'ought' to obey the law. When attempted justifications are given what can be expected is that they are formulated consistently, namely that they fully recognise the particular meaning that has been given to legal obligation as a species of moral obligation. Thus, without a moral justification for disobedience, such action would be wrong.

What has been shown is that theories of law say quite a lot about the nature of obligation to law, and in doing so none of them simply ignore that question but approach it from different starting points. You might want to go further and say that some legal theories give the question more weight or substance than others. Just because the meaning of the word obligation is so difficult to substantiate, you should not conclude that discussing it is a waste of time. Although it must be admitted that one branch of legal theory gets close to that position. (Namely the branch of legal theory known as Scandinavian Realism, whose originator was Axel Hagerstrom (1868–1939). 'With regard to the concepts of right and duty, which form the basis of the whole system of legal concepts, Hagerstrom begins by asking, what is in our mind when we speak of rights and duties in the usual way. His analysis leads to the result that these concepts are metaphysical sham-concepts: it is impossible to identify that which we call a right or a duty with any fact ... If rights and duties in such a sense are assumed to be objectively existing, this necessarily leads to a metaphysical conception of law; for those powers and bonds can never be derived from actual facts.' Olivecrona 1953, XXII.)

Having explored the nature of legal obligation in different legal theories it is now possible to turn to the issue of what the extent of that obligation is. You should now be aware that what legal obligation is, remains in dispute, and therefore from the different starting points different answers will be given to the extent of that obligation. And I will leave you to try to apply the following analysis to those different starting points. But the next task for this chapter is to assume the strongest claim for 'legal obligation' namely that it is a type of moral obligation. If legal obligation is best understood as a type of moral obligation then what are the implications of this for various ideas of the extent or limits of that obligation?

Levels of Obligation to obey law: Absolute, Prima Facie, General, Individual, None

The extracts which follow deal with the extent of a citizen's obligation to obey law. There will be a sense in which you will find yourself being asked to decide on the level of that obligation. Is it absolute, or something weaker? But be careful. Not all of the authors of these extracts are as informed as you are about the difficulties of identifying 'the law' whose moral obligation is being explored. For example, if you were to find that the type of thing which Smith (see extract below) would call law comes closest to a positivist model of law, then you will not be surprised to discover that he concludes that law carries no necessary moral obligation at all. You could have told him that without reading his article.

The idea that there is an absolute obligation to obey the law implies that illegality and immorality are corollaries. Every time someone disobeys the law they are acting immorally. Various religious texts can be used to illustrate this claim, such as St Paul's letter to the Romans in which he writes: 'Let every soul be subject unto the higher powers. For there is no power but of God: the powers that be are ordained of God. Whosoever therefore resisteth the power, resisteth the ordinance of God: and they that resist shall receive to themselves damnation. For rulers are not a terror to good works, but to the evil.' However, as you would expect, such an argument will only arise from a clear view that law is, and can only be, morally legitimate. If it is not morally legitimate then it is better described as violence or terror, and 'may under no circumstances be obeyed'. (Aquinas 1959, 137)

With that background understanding take a look at the classic(al) reasoned account of why a bad law, wrongly applied, nevertheless ought to be obeyed. This extract is taken from Plato's account of 'The Last Days of Socrates'. The extract is a combination of Socrates' defence to the charge of corrupting the youth of Athens (The Apology) and his reasons for not escaping but accepting the punishment decreed, namely execution (Crito). These extracts have been explored and commented on ad infinitum. Socrates' arguments go a long way towards the absolute obligation position but leave open the possibility that such a position will not apply in all circumstances. It may not necessarily apply as much to the young as to the old, to those who have participated less or benefited less from their particular society than Socrates did of his, etc (see Woozley 1979).

Plato (1969, 45, 52–3, 65–6, 73–3, 76 and 79–96 (edited))

THE APOLOGY

[The principal charge faced by Socrates was that he 'corrupted the minds of the young'. The prosecution relied mainly on religious and political hostility and his unpopularity with those that he had offended. The Apology consists of three separate speeches: (1) Socrates' defence, (2) his counter-proposal for the penalty, and (3) a final address to the Court. The net result of these speeches (of which only a few short extracts are given below) is that Socrates denied the validity of the charge and denounced those who made it. He demonstrated that he acted only as his conscience demands. And he showed respect for the responsibilities of those, such as the jury, who had to decide his fate.]

I do not know what effect my accusers have had upon you, gentlemen, but for my own part I was almost carried away by them; their arguments were so convincing. On the other hand, scarcely a word of what they said was true.

…

There is another reason for my being unpopular. A number of young men with wealthy fathers and plenty of leisure have deliberately attached themselves to me because they enjoy hearing other people cross-questioned. These often take me as their model, and go on to try to question other persons; whereupon, I suppose, they find an unlimited number of people who think that they know something, but really know little or nothing. Consequently their victims become annoyed, not with themselves but with me; and they complain that there is a pestilential busybody called Socrates who fills young people's heads with wrong ideas.

…

You will find that throughout my life I have been consistent in any public duties that I have performed, and the same also in my personal dealings: I have never countenanced any action that was incompatible with justice, on the part of any person, including those whom some people maliciously call my pupils. I have never set up as any man's teacher; but if anyone, young or old, is eager to hear me conversing and carrying out my private mission, I never grudge him the opportunity; nor do I charge a fee for talking to him, and refuse to talk without one; I am ready to answer questions for rich and poor alike, and I am equally ready if anyone prefers to listen to me and answer my questions. If any given one of these people becomes a good citizen or a bad one, I cannot fairly be held responsible, since I have never promised or imparted teaching to anybody; and if anyone asserts that he has ever learned or heard from me privately anything which was not open to everyone else, you may be quite sure that he is not telling the truth.

…

Well, gentlemen, for the sake of a very small gain in time you are going to earn the reputation – and the blame from those who disparage our city – of having put Socrates to death, 'that wise man' … If you had waited just a little while, you would have had your way in the course of nature. You can see that I am well on in life and near to death. I am saying this not to all of you but to those that voted for my execution, and I have something else to say to them as well.

…

In a court of law, just as in warfare, neither I nor any other ought to use his wits to escape death by any means. In battle it is often obvious that you could escape being killed by giving up your arms and throwing yourself upon the mercy of your pursuers; and in every kind of danger there are plenty of devices for avoiding death if you are unscrupulous enough to stick at nothing. But I suggest, gentlemen, that the difficulty is not so much to escape death; the real difficulty is to escape from doing wrong, which is far more fleet of foot.

…

You too, gentlemen of the jury, must look forward to death with confidence, and fix your minds on this one belief, which is certain: that nothing can harm a good man either in life or after death, and his fortunes are not a matter of indifference to the gods. This present experience of mine has not come about mechanically; I am quite clear that the time had come when it was better for me to die and be released from my distractions. That is why my sign never turned me back. For my part I bear no grudge at all against those who condemned me and accused me, although it was not with this kind intention that they did so, but because they thought that they were hurting me; and that is culpable of them.

CRITO

A room in the State prison at Athens in the year 399 B.C. Socrates is awaiting execution. CRITO, a friend of Socrates, tries to persuade him to escape.

…

CRITO: … Socrates, it is still not too late to take my advice and escape. Your death means a double calamity for me: quite apart from losing a friend whom I can never possibly replace, I'll have this additional problem, that a great many people who don't know you and me very well will think that I let you down, saying that I could have saved you if I had been willing to spend the money; and what could be more shameful than to get a name for thinking more of money than of your friends? Most people will never believe that it was you who refused to leave this place when we tried our hardest to persuade you.

SOCRATES: But my dear Crito, why should we pay so much attention to what 'most people' think? The most sensible people, who have more claim to be considered, will believe that things have been done exactly as they have.

CRITO: As you can see for yourself, Socrates, one is obliged to bear in mind popular opinion as well. Present circumstances are quite enough to show that the capacity of ordinary people for doing one harm is not confined to petty annoyances, but has hardly any limits if you once get a bad name with them.

SOCRATES: I only wish that ordinary people had an unlimited capacity for doing harm; that would mean they had an unlimited power for doing good, which would be a splendid thing. In actual fact they have neither. They cannot make a man wise or foolish; they achieve whatever luck would have it.

CRITO: Have it that way if you like; but tell me this, Socrates. I hope that you aren't worrying about the possible effects on me and the rest of your friends, and thinking that if you escape we shall have trouble with informers for having helped you to get away, and have to forfeit all our property or pay an enormous fine, or even incur some further punishment? If any idea like that is troubling you, dismiss it altogether. It's surely right for us to run that risk in saving you, and even worse, if necessary. Take my advice, and do as I bid.

SOCRATES: All that you say is very much in my mind, Crito, and a great deal more besides.

CRITO: Please don't be afraid of these things. Actually it's quite a moderate sum that certain people want for rescuing you from here and getting you out of the country. And then surely you realize how cheap these informers are to buy off; we wouldn't need much money to settle them. You've got my money at your disposal – that'll be enough, I think; but supposing that in your anxiety for my safety you feel that you oughtn't to spend my money, there are these foreign gentlemen staying in Athens who are quite willing to spend theirs. One of them, Simmias of Thebes, has actually brought enough money with him for this very purpose; and Cebes and a number of others are quite ready to do the same. So as I say, you mustn't let any fears like this make you dispirited about escaping; and you mustn't feel any misgivings like those you mentioned at your trial, that you wouldn't know what to do with yourself if you left this country. Wherever you go, there are plenty of places where you will find a welcome, particularly if you choose to go to Thessaly – I have friends there who will make much of you and give you complete protection, so that no one in Thessaly can interfere with you. Besides, Socrates, I don't even feel that it is just for you to do what you are doing, throwing away your life when you might save it. You are doing your best to treat yourself in exactly the same way as your enemies would, or rather did, when they wanted to ruin you. What is more, it seems to me that you are betraying your sons too. You have it in your power to finish bringing them up and educating them, and instead of that you're proposing to go off and desert them, and so far as you are concerned they'll be left to get along as the whim of fortune determines. They will probably have the kind of luck that usually comes to orphans when they lose their parents. Either one ought not to have children at all, or one ought to see their upbringing and education through to the end, but it strikes me that you are taking the most irresponsible course. You ought to make the choice of a good man and a brave one, considering that you profess to have made goodness your principal concern all through life. Really, I am ashamed, both on your account and on ours your friends; it will look as though we had played something like a coward's part all through this affair of yours. First there was the way you came into court when it was quite unnecessary – that was the first act; then there was the conduct of the defence – that was the second; and finally, to complete the farce, we get this situation, which makes it appear that we have let you slip out of our hands through some lack of courage and enterprise on our part, because we didn't save you, and you didn't save yourself, when it would have been quite possible and practicable, if we had been any use at all. There, Socrates; if you aren't careful, besides the harm there will be all this disgrace for you and us to bear. Come, make your plans. Really it's past the time for that now; the decision should have been made already. There is only one plan – the whole thing must be carried through during this coming night. If we lose any more time, it can't be done, it will be too late. I appeal to you, Socrates, on every ground; take my advice and please do as I say!

SOCRATES: My dear Crito, I would greatly appreciate your enthusiasm if it is right and proper; if not, the stronger it is, the more of a problem it is. Therefore we should consider whether we ought to follow your advice or not; my attitude is not unprecedented, for it's always been my nature never to accept advice from any of my 'friends' except the argument that seems best on reflection. I cannot abandon the arguments which I used to expound in the past simply because this accident has happened to me ... Suppose that we begin by reverting to your point about people's opinions. Was it always right to argue that some opinions should be taken seriously but not others? Or was it always wrong? Perhaps it was right before the question of my death arose, but now we can see clearly that we were pointlessly persisting in a theory which was really childish nonsense. I should like very much to inquire into this problem, Crito, with your help, and to see whether the argument will appear in any different light to me now that I am in this position, or whether it will remain the same; and whether we shall dismiss it or accept it.

People with something to say, I believe, have always stated some such view as the one which I mentioned just now: that some of the opinions which people entertain should be taken seriously, and others not. Now I ask you, Crito, don't you think this is a fair proposition? – You are safe from the prospect of dying tomorrow, in all human probability; and you are not likely to have your judgement upset by this impending calamity. Consider, then; don't you think that it is good enough to say that one should not value all the opinions that people hold, but only some and not others? What do you say? Isn't that a fair statement?

CRITO: Fair enough.

SOCRATES: In other words, one should regard the sound ones and not the flawed?

CRITO: Yes.

SOCRATES: The opinions of the wise being sound, and the opinions of the foolish flawed?

CRITO: Naturally.

SOCRATES: To pass on, then: what do you think of the sort of illustration that I used to employ? When a man is in training, and taking it seriously, does he pay attention to all praise and criticism and opinion indiscriminately, or only when it comes from the one qualified person, the actual doctor or trainer?

CRITO: Only when it comes from the one qualified person.

...

SOCRATES: Very good. Well now, tell me, Crito – we don't want to go through all the examples one by one – does this apply as a general rule, and above all to the issues which we are trying now to resolve: just and unjust, honourable and dishonourable, good and bad? Ought we to be guided and intimidated by the opinion of the many or by that of the one – assuming that there is someone with expert knowledge? Is it true that we ought to respect and fear this person more than all the rest put together; and that if we do not follow his guidance we shall spoil and impair that part of us which, as we used to say, is improved by just conduct and ruined by unjust? Or is this all nonsense?

CRITO: No, I think it is true, Socrates.

SOCRATES: Then consider the next step. There is a part of us which is improved by healthy actions and ruined by unhealthy ones. If we completely wreck it by taking advice contrary to that of the experts, will life be worth living when this part is once ruined? The part I mean is the body; do you accept this?

CRITO: Yes.

SOCRATES: Well, is life worth living with a body which is worn out and ruined?

CRITO: Certainly not.

...

SOCRATES: In that case, my dear fellow, what we ought to worry about is not so much what people in general will say about us but what the expert in justice and injustice says, the single authority and with him the truth itself. So in the first place your proposal is not well-founded when you claim that we must consider popular opinion about what is just and honourable and good, or the opposite. 'But all the same', one might object, 'the people have the power to put us to death.'

CRITO: That's clear enough! It would be said, Socrates; you're quite right.

...

SOCRATES: Then in the light of this admission we must consider whether or not it is just for me to try to get away without being released by the Athenians. If it turns out to be just, we must make the attempt; if not, we must drop it. As for the considerations you raise about expense and reputation and bringing up children, I am afraid, Crito, that these are the concerns of the ordinary public, who think nothing of putting people to death, and would bring them back to life if they could, with equal indifference to reason. Our real task, I fancy, since the argument leads that way, is to consider one question only, the one which we raised just now: shall we be acting justly in paying money and showing gratitude to these people who are going to rescue me, and in escaping or arranging the escape ourselves, or shall we really be acting unjustly in doing all this? If it becomes clear that such conduct is unjust, I cannot help thinking that the question whether we are sure to die, or to suffer any other ill-effect for that matter, if we stand our ground and take no action, ought not to weigh with us at all in comparison with the risk of acting unjustly.

CRITO: I agree with what you say, Socrates; now consider what we are to do.

SOCRATES: Let us look at it together, Crito; and if you can challenge any of my arguments, do so and I will listen to you; but if you can't, be a good fellow and stop telling me over and over again that I ought to leave this place without official permission. I am very anxious to obtain your approval before I adopt the course which I have in mind; I don't want to act against your convictions. Now give your attention to the starting point of this inquiry if you are happy with the way I've put it, and try to answer my questions to the best of your judgement.

CRITO: Well, I will try.

SOCRATES: Do we say that there is no way that one must ever willingly commit injustice, or does it depend upon circumstance? Is it true, as we have often agreed before, that there is no sense in which an act of injustice is good or honourable? Or have we jettisoned all our former convictions in these last few days? Can you and I at our age, Crito, have spent all these years in serious discussions without realizing that we were no better than a pair of children? Surely the truth is just what we have always said. Whatever the popular view is, and whether the consequence is pleasanter than this or even tougher, the fact remains that to commit injustice is in every case bad and dishonourable for the person who does it. Is that our view, or not?

CRITO: Yes, it is.

SOCRATES: Then in no circumstances must one do wrong.

CRITO: No.

SOCRATES: In that case one must not even return injustice when one is wronged, which most people regard as the natural course.

CRITO: Apparently not.

...

SOCRATES: So one ought not to return an injustice or an injury to any person, whatever the provocation. Now be careful, Crito, that in making these single admissions you do not end by admitting something contrary to your real beliefs. I know that there are and always will be few people who think like this; and consequently between those who do think so and those who do not there can be no shared deliberation; they must always feel contempt when they observe one another's decision. I want even you to consider very carefully whether you share my views and agree with me, and whether we can proceed with our discussion from the established hypothesis that it is never right to commit injustice or return injustice or defend one's self against injury by retaliation; or whether you dissociate yourself from any share in this view as a basis for discussion. I have held it for a long time, and still hold it; but if you have formed any other opinion, say so and tell me what it is. If, on the other hand, you stand by what we have said, listen to my next point.

CRITO: Yes, I stand by it and agree with you. Go on.

SOCRATES: Well, here is my next point, or rather question. Ought one to fulfil all one's agreements, provided that they are just, – or break them?

CRITO: One ought to fulfil them.

SOCRATES: Then consider the logical consequence. If we leave this place without first persuading the state to let us go, are we or so are we not doing an injury, and doing it to those we've least excuse for injuring? Are we or are we not abiding by our just agreements?

CRITO: I can't answer your question, Socrates; I am not clear in my mind.

...

SOCRATES: Look at it in this way. Suppose that while we were preparing to run away from here (or however one should describe it) the Laws and communal interest of Athens were to come and confront us with this question: 'Now, Socrates, what are you proposing to do? Can you deny that by this act which you are contemplating you intend, so far as you have the power, to destroy us, the Laws, and the whole State as well? Do you imagine that a city can continue to exist and not be turned upside down, if the legal judgements which are pronounced in it have no force but are nullified and destroyed by private persons?' – how shall we answer this question, Crito, and others of the same kind? There is much that could be said, especially by an orator, to protest at the abolition of this law which requires that judgements once pronounced shall be binding. Shall we say, 'Yes: the State is guilty of an injustice against me, you see, by passing a faulty judgement at my trial'? Is this to be our answer, or what?

CRITO: What you have said, certainly, Socrates.

SOCRATES: Then what if the Laws say, 'Was there provision for this in the agreement between you and us, Socrates? Or did you undertake to abide by whatever judgements the State pronounced?' If we expressed surprise at such language, they would probably say: 'Don't be surprised at what we say, Socrates, but answer our questions; after all, you are accustomed to the method of question and answer. Come now, what charge do you bring against us and the State, that you are trying to destroy us? Did we not give you life in the first place? Was it not through us that your father married your mother and brought you into this world? Tell us, have you any complaint against those of our Laws that deal with marriage?' 'No, none,' I should say. 'Well, have you any against the Laws which deal with children's upbringing and education, such as you had yourself? Are you not grateful to those of our Laws which were put in control of this, for requiring your father to give you an education in music and gymnastics?' 'Yes', I should say. 'Very good. Then since you have been born and brought up and educated, can you deny, in the first place, that you were our child and slave, both you and your ancestors? And if this is so, do you imagine that your rights and ours are on a par, and that whatever we try to do to you, you are justified in retaliating? Though you did not have equality of rights with your father, or master if you had one, to enable you to retaliate, and you were not allowed to answer back when you were scolded nor to hit back when you were beaten, nor to do a great many other things of the same kind, will you be permitted to do it to your country and its Laws, so that if we try to put you to death in the belief that it is just to do so, you on your part will try your hardest to destroy your country and us its Laws in return? And will you, the true devotee of goodness, claim that you are justified in doing so? Are you so wise as to have forgotten that compared with your mother and father and all the rest of your ancestors your country is something far more precious, more venerable, more sacred, and held in greater honour both among gods and among all reasonable men? Do you not realize that you are even more bound to respect and placate the anger of your country than your father's anger? That you must either persuade your country or do whatever it orders, and patiently submit to any punishment that it imposes, whether it be flogging or imprisonment? And if it leads you out to war, to be wounded or killed, you must comply, and it is just that this should be so – you must not give way or retreat or abandon your position. Both in war and in the law courts and everywhere else you must do whatever your city and your country commands, or else persuade it that justice is on your side; but violence against mother or father is an unholy act, and it is a far greater sin against your country.' – What shall we say to this, Crito? That what the Laws say is true, or not?

CRITO: Yes, I think so.

SOCRATES: 'Consider, then, Socrates,' the Laws would probably continue, 'whether it is also true for us to claim that what you are now trying to do to us is not just. Although we have brought you into the world and reared you and educated you, and given you and all your fellow-citizens a share in all the good things at our disposal, nevertheless by the very fact of granting our permission we openly proclaim this principle: that any Athenian, on attaining to manhood and seeing for himself the political organization of the State and us its Laws, is permitted, if he is not satisfied with us, to take his property and go away wherever he likes. If anyone of you chooses to go to one of our colonies, supposing that he should not be satisfied with us and the State, or to emigrate to any other country, not one of us Laws hinders or prevents him from going away wherever he likes, without any loss of property. On the other hand, if any one of you stands his ground when he can see how we administer justice and the rest of our public organization, we hold that by so doing he has in fact undertaken to do anything that we tell him; and we maintain that anyone who disobeys is guilty of doing wrong on three separate counts: first because we brought him into this world, and secondly because we reared him; and thirdly because, after promising obedience, he is neither obeying us nor persuading us to change our decision if we are at fault in any way; and although we set a choice before him and do not issue savage commands, giving him the choice of either persuading us or doing what we say, he is actually doing neither. These are the charges, Socrates, to which we say that you too will be liable if you do what you are contemplating; and you'll not be the least culpable of the Athenians, but one of the most guilty.' If I said, 'Why do you say that?' they would no doubt pounce upon me with perfect justice and point out that there are very few people in Athens who have entered into this agreement with them as explicitly as I have. They would say, 'Socrates, we have substantial evidence that you are satisfied with us and with the State. Compared with all other Athenians, you would not have been so exceptionally much in residence if it had not been exceptionally pleasing to you. You have never left the city to attend a festival – except once to the Isthmus – nor for any other purpose except on some military expedition; you have never travelled abroad as other people do, and you have never felt the impulse to acquaint yourself with another country or other laws; you have been content with us and with our city. So deliberately have you chosen us, and undertaken to observe us in all your activities as a citizen, that you have actually fathered children in it because the city suits you. Furthermore, even at the time of your trial you could have proposed the penalty of banishment, if you had chosen to do so; that is, you could have done then with the sanction of the State what you are now trying to do without it. But whereas at that time you made a fine show of your indifference if you had to die, and in fact preferred death, as you said, to banishment, now you show no respect for your earlier professions, and no regard for us, the Laws, whom you are trying to destroy; you are behaving like the lowest slave, trying to run away in spite of the contracts and undertakings by which you agreed to act as a member of our State. Now first answer this question: Are we or are we not speaking the truth when we say that you have undertaken, in deed and not in word, to play the role of citizen in obedience to us?' What are we to say to that, Crito? Are we not bound to admit it?

CRITO: We must. Socrates.

SOCRATES: 'It is a fact, then,' they would say, 'that you are breaking covenants and undertakings made with us, although you made them under no compulsion or misunderstanding, and were not compelled to decide in a limited time; you had seventy years in which you could have left the country, if you were not satisfied with us or felt that the agreements were unjust. You did not choose Sparta or Crete – your favourite models of good government – or any other Greek or foreign state; you could not have absented yourself from the city less if you had been lame or blind or decrepit in some other way. It is quite obvious that you outstrip all other Athenians in your satisfaction with this city – and for us its Laws, for who could be pleased with a city without its laws? And now, after all this, are you not going to stand by your agreement? Yes, you are, Socrates, if you will take our advice; and then you will at least escape being laughed at for leaving the city.

'Just consider, what good will you do yourself or your friends if you breach this agreement and fall short in one of these requirements. It is fairly obvious that the risk of being banished and either losing their citizenship or having their property confiscated will extend to your friends as well. As for yourself, if you go to one of the neighbouring states, such as Thebes or Megara which are both well governed, you will enter them as an enemy to their constitution, and all good patriots will eye you with suspicion as a destroyer of laws. You will confirm the opinion of the jurors, so that they'll seem to have given a correct verdict – for any destroyer of laws might very well be supposed to have a destructive influence upon young and foolish human beings. Do you intend, then, to avoid well-governed states and the most disciplined people? And if you do, will life be worth living? Or will you approach these people and have the impudence to converse with them? What subjects will you discuss, Socrates? The same as here, when you said that goodness and justice, institutions and laws, are the most precious possessions of mankind? Do you not think that Socrates and everything about him will appear in a disreputable light? You certainly ought to think so. But perhaps you will retire from this part of the world and go to Crito's friends in Thessaly? There you'll find disorder and indiscipline and no doubt they would enjoy hearing the amusing story of how you managed to run away from prison by arraying yourself in some costume – putting on a shepherd's smock or some other conventional runaway's disguise, and altering your personal appearance. And will no one comment on the fact that an old man of your age, probably with only a short time left to live, should dare to cling so greedily to life, at the price of violating the most stringent laws? Perhaps not, if you avoid irritating anyone.

Otherwise, Socrates, you'll be the object of a good many humiliating comments. So you will live as the toady and slave of all the populace, literally "roistering in Thessaly", as though you had left this country for Thessaly to attend a banquet there; and where will your discussions about justice and other good qualities be then, we should like to know? But of course you want to live for your children's sake, so that you may be able to bring them up and educate them. Indeed! by first taking them off to Thessaly and making foreigners of them, so that they'll have that to enjoy too? Or if that is not your intention, supposing that they are brought up here, will they be better cared for and educated because of your being alive, even without you there? Yes, your friends will take care of them. But will they look after your children if you go away to Thessaly, and not if you go off to the next world? Surely if those who profess to be your friends are worth anything, you must believe that they would care for them.

'No, Socrates; be advised by us who raised you – do not think more of your children or of your life or of anything else than you think of what is just; so that when you enter the next world you may have all this to plead in your defence before the authorities there. Neither in this world does doing this appear to be any better, or more just, or more holy – not to you nor to any of your family – nor will it be better for you when you reach the next world. As it is, you will leave this place, when you do, as the victim of a wrong done not by us, the Laws, but by your fellow men. But if you leave in that dishonourable way, returning injustice for injustice and injury for injury, breaking your agreements and covenants with us, and injuring those whom you least ought to injure – yourself, your friends, your country, and us – then you will have to face *our* anger while you live, and in that place beyond when our brothers, the Laws of Hades, know that you have done your best to destroy even us, they will not receive you with a kindly welcome. Do not take Crito's advice in preference to ours.'

That, my dear friend Crito, I do assure you, is what I seem to hear them saying, just as a mystic seems to hear the strains of pipes; and the sound of their arguments rings so loudly in my head that I cannot hear the other side. I warn you that, as my opinion stands at present, it will be useless to urge a different view. However, if you think that you will do any good by it, speak up.

CRITO: No, Socrates, I have nothing to say.

SOCRATES: Then give it up, Crito, and let us follow this course, since God leads the way.

Wasserstrom's extract that follows next is built out of criticism of the absolute obligation position. He criticises the way in which that position might be justified – that all laws are necessarily moral, that **any** disobedience is likely to lead to chaos, that one's promise to obey law is absolute, that receiving the benefits of society implies an absolute commitment to the burdens that it's laws impose on you. He presents arguments for a prima facie obligation position, one that is close to but can be distinguished from a general obligation position. He clearly favours the former. To support his argument he uses a particular example, that of a doctor, in a society that makes performing an abortion a crime, faced with a young woman who has become pregnant after being raped by an escapee from a mental institution. Of course you need to think carefully about the substance of his arguments, but also about his use of this particular example. Does it have elements that strengthen his argument but are not necessarily implicit in other examples? Remember that professions tend to establish their own ethical standards. The medical profession construct their ethical standards around the Hypocratic Oath. Is the ordinary citizen faced with the question of disobedience in a similar position?

Wasserstrom (1963, 780)

I

...

... I am concerned here with *arguments* – with those arguments which have been or which might be given in support of the claim that because one does have an obligation to obey the law, one ought not ever disobey the law.

To describe the focus of the article in this manner is, however, to leave several crucial matters highly ambiguous. And thus, before the arguments can be considered properly, the following matters must be clarified.

A. There are several different views which could be held concerning the nature of the stringency of one's obligation to obey the law. One such view, and the one which I shall be most concerned to show to be false, can be characterized as holding that one has an *absolute* obligation to obey the law. I take this to mean that a person is never justified in disobeying the law; to know that a proposed action is illegal is to know all one needs to know in order to conclude that the action ought not to be done; to cite the illegality of an action is to give a sufficient reason for not having done it. A view such as this is far from uncommon. President Kennedy expressed the thoughts of many quite reflective people when he said:

> ... [O]ur nation is founded on the principle that observance of the law is the eternal safeguard of liberty and defiance of the law is the surest road to tyranny.

> The law which we obey includes the final rulings of the courts as well as the enactments of our legislative bodies. Even among law-abiding men few laws are universally loved.

> But they are universally respected and not resisted.

> Americans are free, in short, to disagree with the law, but not to disobey it. For in a government of laws and not of men, no man, however prominent or powerful, and no mob, however unruly or boisterous, is entitled to defy a court of law.

> If this country should ever reach the point where any man or group of men, by force or threat of force, could long deny the commands of our court and our Constitution, then no law would stand free from doubt, no judge would be sure of his writ and no citizen would be safe from his neighbors.

A more moderate or weaker view would be that which holds that, while one does have an obligation to obey the law, the obligation is a prima facie rather than absolute one. If one knows that a proposed course of conduct is illegal then one has a good – but not necessarily a sufficient – reason for refraining from engaging in that course of conduct.

Under this view, a person may be justified in disobeying the law, but an act which is in disobedience of the law does have to be justified, whereas an act in obedience of the law does not have to be justified.

It is important to observe that there is an ambiguity in this notion of a prima facie obligation. For the claim that one has a prima facie obligation to obey the law can come to one of two different things. On the one hand, the claim can be this: the fact that an action is an act of disobedience is something which always does count against the performance of the action. If one has a prima facie obligation to obey the law, one always has that obligation – although, of course, it may be overridden by other obligations in any particular case. Thus the fact that an action is illegal is a relevant consideration in every case and it is a consideration which must be outweighed by other considerations before the performance of an illegal action can be justified.

On the other hand, the claim can be weaker still. The assertion of a prima facie obligation to obey the law can be nothing more than the claim that as a matter of fact it is *generally* right or obligatory to obey the law. As a rule the fact that an action is illegal is a relevant circumstance. But in any particular case, after deliberation, it might very well turn out that the illegality of the action was not truly relevant. For in any particular case the circumstances might be such that there simply was nothing in the fact of illegality which required overriding – e.g., there were no bad consequences at all which would flow from disobeying the law in this case.

The distinction can be made more vivid in the following fashion. One person, A, might hold the view that any action in disobedience of the law is intrinsically bad. Some other person, B, might hold the view that no action is intrinsically bad unless it has the property, P, and that not all actions in disobedience of the law have that property. Now for A, the fact of disobedience is *always* a relevant consideration, for B, the fact of disobedience may always be initially relevant because of the existence of some well-established hypothesis which asserts that the occurrence of any action of disobedience is correlated highly with the occurrence of P. But if in any particular case disobedience does not turn out to have the property, P, then, upon reflection, it can be concluded by B that the fact that disobedience is involved is not a reason which weighs against the performance of the act in question. To understand B's position it is necessary to distinguish the relevance of *considering* the fact of disobedience from the relevance of the fact of disobedience. The former must always be relevant, the latter is not.

Thus there are at least three different positions which might be taken concerning the character of the obligation to obey the law or the rightness of disobedience to the law. They are: (1) One has an absolute obligation to obey the law; disobedience is never justified. (2) One has an obligation to obey the law but this obligation can be overridden by conflicting obligations; disobedience can be justified, but only by the presence of outweighing circumstances. (3) One does not have a special obligation to obey the law, but it is in fact usually obligatory, on other grounds, to do so; disobedience to law often does turn out to be unjustified.

B. It must also be made clear that when I talk about the obligation to obey the law or the possibility of actions which are both illegal and justified. I am concerned solely with *moral obligations* and *morally justified* actions. I shall be concerned solely with arguments which seek to demonstrate that there is some sort of a connection between the legality or illegality of an action and its morality or immorality. Concentration on this general topic necessarily renders a number of interesting problems irrelevant. Thus, I am not at all concerned with the question of why, in fact, so many people do obey the law. Nor, concomitantly, am I concerned with the nonmoral reasons which might and do justify obedience to law – of these, the most pertinent, is the fact that highly unpleasant consequences of one form or another are typically inflicted upon those who disobey the law. Finally there are many actions which are immoral irrespective of whether they also happen to be illegal. And I am not, except in one very special sense, concerned with this fact either. I am not concerned with the fact that the immorality of the action itself may be a sufficient reason for condemning it regardless of its possible illegality.

...

II

One kind of argument in support of the proposition that one cannot be justified in disobeying the law is that which asserts the existence of some sort of *logical* or conceptual relationship between disobeying the law and acting immorally. If the notion of illegality entails that of immorality then one is never justified in acting illegally just because part of the meaning of *illegal* is *immoral;* just because describing an action as illegal is – among other things – to describe it as unjustified.

A claim such as this is extremely difficult to evaluate.

...

Consider the case of a law that makes it a felony to perform an abortion upon a woman unless the abortion is necessary to preserve her life. Suppose a teenager, the daughter of a local minister, has been raped on her way home from school by an escapee from a state institution for mental defectives. Suppose further that the girl has become pregnant and has been brought to a reputable doctor who is asked to perform an abortion. And suppose, finally, that the doctor concludes after examining the girl that her life will not be endangered by giving birth to the child. An abortion under these circumstances is, it seems fair to say, illegal. Yet, we would surely find both intelligible and appealing the doctor's claim that he was nonetheless justified in disobeying the law by performing an abortion on the girl. I at least can see nothing logically odd or inconsistent about recognizing both that there is a law prohibiting this conduct and that further questions concerning the rightness of obedience would be relevant and, perhaps, decisive. Thus I can see nothing logically odd about describing this as a case in which the performance of the abortion could be both illegal and morally justified.

There is, no doubt, a heroic defense which can be made to the above. it would consist of the insistence that the activity just described simply cannot be both illegal and justified. Two alternatives are possible. First, one might argue that the commission of the abortion would indeed have been justified if it were not proscribed by the law. But since it is so prohibited, the abortion is wrong. Now if this is a point about the appropriateness of kinds of reasons, I can only note that referring the action to a valid law does not seem to preclude asking meaningful questions about the obligatoriness of the action. If this is a point about language or concepts it does seem to be perfectly intelligible to say that the conduct is both illegal and morally justified. And if this is, instead, an *argument* for the immorality of ever disobeying a valid law, then it surely requires appreciable substantiation and not mere assertion.

Second, one might take a different line and agree that other questions can be asked about the conduct, but that is because the commission of the abortion under these circumstances simply cannot be illegal. The difficulty here, however, is that it is hard to understand what is now meant by *illegal*. Of course, I am not claiming that in the case as I have described it, it is clear that the performance of the abortion must be illegal. It might not be. But it might be. Were we to satisfy all the usual tests that we do invoke when we determine that a given course of conduct is illegal, and were someone still to maintain that because the performance of the abortion is here morally justified it cannot be illegal, then the burden is on the proponent of this view to make clear how we are to decide when conduct is illegal. And it would further be incumbent upon him to demonstrate what seems to be highly dubious, namely, that greater clarity and insight could somehow be attained through a radical change in our present terminology. It appears to be a virtually conclusive refutation to observe that there has never been a legal system whose criteria of validity – no matter how sophisticated, how rational and how well defined-themselves guaranteed that morally justified action would never be illegal.

… Perhaps it is correct that *illegal* does not entail *immoral*; *illegal* might nevertheless entail *prima facie immoral*. The evidence adduced tends to show that among one's moral obligations is the prima facie duty to obey the law.

Once again, it is somewhat difficult to know precisely what to make of such a claim. It is hard to see how one would decide what was to count as evidence or whether the evidence was persuasive. At a minimum, it is not difficult to imagine several equally plausible alternative explanations of the disturbing character of accusations of illegal activity. In addition, to know only that one has a prima facie duty to obey the law is not to know a great deal. In particular, one does not know how or when that obligation can be overridden. And, of course, even if it is correct that acting illegally logically implies acting prima facie immorally, this in no way shows that people may not often be morally justified in acting illegally. At most, it demands that they have some good reason for acting illegally; at best, it requires what has already been hypothesized, namely, that the action in question, while illegal, be morally justified.

Thus, it is clear that if the case against ever acting illegally is to be made out, conceptual analysis alone cannot do it. Indeed, arguments of quite another sort must be forthcoming. And it is to these that I now turn.

III

One such argument, and the most common argument advanced, goes something like this: The reason why one ought never to disobey the law is simply that the consequences would be disastrous if everybody disobeyed the law. The reason why disobedience is never right becomes apparent once we ask the question 'But what if everyone did that?'

Consider again the case of the doctor who has to decide whether he is justified in performing an illegal abortion. If he only has a prima facie duty to obey the law it looks as though he might justifiably decide that in this case his prima facie obligation is overridden by more stringent conflicting obligations. Or, if he is simply a utilitarian, it appears that he might rightly conclude that the consequences of disobeying the abortion law would be on the whole and in the long run less deleterious than those of obeying. But this is simply a mistake. The doctor would inevitably be neglecting the most crucial factor of all, namely, that in performing the abortion he was disobeying the law. And imagine what would happen if everyone went around disobeying the law. The alternatives are obeying the law and general disobedience. The choice is between any social order and chaos. As President Kennedy correctly observed, if any law is disobeyed, then no law can be free from doubt, no citizen safe from his neighbor.

Such an argument, while perhaps overdrawn, is by no means uncommon. Yet, as it stands, it is an essentially confused one. Its respective claims, if they are to be fairly evaluated, must be delineated with some care.

At a minimum, the foregoing attack upon the possibility of justified disobedience might be either one or both of two radically different kinds of objection. The first, which relates to the consequences of an act of disobedience, is essentially a *causal* argument. The second questions the *principle* that any proponent of justified disobedience invokes. As to the causal argument, it is always relevant to point out that any act of disobedience may have certain consequences simply because it is an act of disobedience. Once the occurrence of the act is known, for example, expenditure of the state's resources may become necessary. The time and energy of the police will probably be turned to the task of discovering who it was who did the illegal act and of gathering evidence relevant to the offense. And other resources might be expended in the prosecution and adjudication of the case against the perpetrator of the illegal act. Illustrations of this sort could be multiplied, no doubt, but I do not think either that considerations of this sort are very persuasive or that they have been uppermost in the minds of those who make the argument now under examination. Indeed, if the argument is a causal one at all, it consists largely of the claim that any act of disobedience will itself cause, to some degree or other, general disobedience of all laws; it will cause or help to cause the overthrow or dissolution of the state. And while it is possible to assert that any act of disobedience will tend to further social disintegration or revolution, it is much more difficult to see why this must be so.

The most plausible argument would locate this causal efficacy in the kind of example set by any act of disobedience. But how plausible is this argument? It is undeniable, of course, that the kind of example that will be set is surely a relevant factor. Yet, there is nothing that precludes any proponent of justified disobedience from taking this into account. If, for example, others will somehow infer from the doctor's disobedience of the abortion law that they are justified in disobeying any law under *any* circumstances, then the doctor ought to consider this fact. This is a consequence – albeit a lamentable one of his act of disobedience. Similarly, if others will extract the proper criterion from the act of disobedience, but will be apt to misapply it in practice, then this too ought to give the doctor pause. It, too, is a consequence of acting. But if the argument is that disobedience would be wrong even if no bad example were set and no other deleterious consequences likely, then the argument must be directed against the principle the doctor appeals to in disobeying the law, and not against the consequences of his disobedience at all.

As to the attack upon a principle of justified disobedience, as a principle, the response 'But what if everyone disobeyed the law?' does appear to be a good way to point up both the inherent inconsistency of almost any principle of justified disobedience and the manifest undesirability of adopting such a principle. Even if one need not worry about what others will be led to do by one's disobedience, there is surely something amiss if one cannot consistently defend his right to do what one is claiming he is right in doing.

In large measure, such an objection is unreal. The appeal to 'But what if everyone did that?' loses much, if not all, of its persuasiveness once we become clearer about what precisely the 'did that' refers to. If the question 'But what if everyone did that?' is simply another way of asking 'But what if everybody disobeyed the law?' or 'But what if people generally disobeyed the laws?' then the question is surely quasi-rhetorical. To urge general or indiscriminate disobedience to laws is to invoke a principle that, if coherent, is manifestly indefensible. It is equally plain, however, that with few exceptions such a principle has never been seriously espoused. Anyone who claims that there are actions that are both illegal and justified surely need not be thereby asserting that it is right generally to disobey all laws or even any particular law. It is surely not inconsistent to assert both that indiscriminate disobedience is indefensible and that discriminate disobedience is morally right and proper conduct. Nor, analogously, is it at all evident that a person who claims to be justified in performing an illegal action is thereby committed to or giving endorsement to the principle that the entire legal system ought to be overthrown or renounced. At a minimum, therefore, the appeal to 'But what if everyone did that?' cannot by itself support the claim that one has an absolute obligation to obey the law – that disobeying the law can never be truly justified.

There is, however, a distinguishable but related claim which merits very careful attention – if for no other reason than the fact that it is so widely invoked today by moral philosophers. The claim is simply this: While it may very well be true that there are situations in which a person will be justified in disobeying the law, it is surely not true that disobedience can ever be justified solely on the grounds that the consequences of disobeying the particular law were in that case on the whole less deleterious than those of obedience.

This claim is particularly relevant at this juncture because one of the arguments most often given to substantiate it consists of the purported demonstration of the fact that any principle which contained a proviso permitting a general appeal to consequences must itself be incoherent. One of the most complete statements of the argument is found in Marcus Singer's provocative book, *Generalization in Ethics:*

> Suppose ... that I am contemplating evading the payment of income taxes. I might reason that I need the money more than the government does, that the amount I have to pay is so small in comparison with the total amount to be collected that the government will never miss it. Now I surely know perfectly well that if I evade the payment of taxes this will not cause others to do so as well. For one thing, I am certainly not so foolish as to publicize my action. But even if I were, and the fact became known, this would still not cause others to do the same, unless it also became known that I was being allowed to get away with it. In the latter case the practice might tend to become widespread, but this would be a consequence, not of my action, but of the failure of the government to take action against me. Thus there is no question of my act being wrong because it would set a bad example. It would set no such example, and to suppose that it must, because

it would be wrong, is simply a confusion ... Given all this, then if the reasons mentioned would justify me in evading the payment of taxes, they would justify everyone whatsoever in doing the same thing. For everyone can argue in the same way – everyone can argue that if he breaks the law this will not cause others to do the same. The supposition that this is a justification, therefore, leads to a contradiction.

I conclude from this that, just as the reply 'Not everyone will do it' is irrelevant to the generalization argument, so is the fact that one knows or believes that not everyone will do the same; and that, in particular, the characteristic of knowing or believing that one's act will remain exceptional cannot be used to define a class of exceptions to the rule. One's knowledge or belief that not everyone will act in the same way in similar circumstances cannot therefore be regarded as part of the circumstances of one's action. One's belief that not everyone will do the same does not make one's circumstances relevantly different from the circumstances of others, or relevantly different from those in which the act is wrong. Indeed, on the supposition that it does, one's circumstances could never be specified, for the specification would involve an infinite regress.

Singer's argument is open to at least two different interpretations. One quite weak interpretation is this: A person cannot be morally justified in acting as he does unless he is prepared to acknowledge that everyone else in the identical circumstances would also be right in acting the same way. If the person insists that he is justified in performing a certain action because the consequences of acting in that way are more desirable than those of acting in any alternative fashion, then he must be prepared to acknowledge that anyone else would also be justified in doing that action whenever the consequences of doing that action were more desirable than those of acting in any alternative fashion. To take Singer's own example: A person, A, could not be morally justified in evading the payment of his taxes on the grounds that the consequences of nonpayment were *in his case* more beneficial, all things considered, than those of payment, unless A were prepared to acknowledge that any other person, X, would also be justified in evading his, *i.e.*, X's taxes, if it is the case that the consequences of X's nonpayment would in X's case be more beneficial, all things considered, than those of payment. If this is Singer's point, it is, for reasons already elaborated, unobjectionable.

But Singer seems to want to make a stronger point as well. He seems to believe that even a willingness to generalize in this fashion could not justify acting in this way. In part his argument appears to be that this somehow will permit everyone to justify nonpayment of taxes; and in part his argument appears to be that there is a logical absurdity involved in attempting to make the likelihood of other people's behavior part of the specification of the relevant consequences of a particular act. Both of these points are wrong. To begin with, on a common sense level it is surely true that the effect which one's action will have on other people's behavior is a relevant consideration. For as was pointed out earlier, if A determines that other people will be, or may be, led to evade *their* taxes even when the consequences of nonpayment will in their cases be less beneficial than those of payment, then this is a consequence of A's action which he must take into account and attempt to balance against the benefits which would accrue to society from his nonpayment. Conversely, if for one reason or another A can determine that his act of nonpayment will not have this consequence, this, too, must be relevant. In this sense, at least, other people's prospective behavior is a relevant consideration.

More importantly, perhaps, it is surely a mistake – although a very prevalent one in recent moral philosophy – to suppose that permitting a general appeal to consequences would enable everyone to argue convincingly that he is justified in evading his taxes. Even if I adopt the principle that everyone is justified in evading his taxes whenever the consequences of evasion are on the whole less deleterious than those of payment, this in no way entails that I or anyone else will always, or ever, be justified in evading my taxes. It surely need not turn out to be the case even if no one else will evade his taxes – that the consequences will on the whole be beneficial if I succeed in evading mine. It might surely be the case that I will spend the money saved improvidently or foolishly; it might very well be true that the government will make much better use of the money. Indeed, the crucial condition which must not be ignored and which Singer does ignore is the condition which stipulates that the avoidance of one's taxes in fact be optimific, that is, more desirable than any other course of conduct.

The general point is simply that it is an empirical question – at least in theory – what the consequences of any action will be. And it would surely be a mistake for me or anyone else to suppose that that action whose consequences are most pleasing to me – in either the short or long run – will in fact be identical with that action whose consequences are on the whole most beneficial to society. Where the demands of self-interest are strong, as in the case of the performance of an unpleasant task like paying taxes, there are particular reasons for being skeptical of one's conclusion that the consequences of nonpayment would in one's own case truly be beneficial. But once again there is no reason why there might not be cases in which evasion of taxes would be truly justified, nor is there any reason why someone could not consistently and defensibly endorse nonpayment whenever these circumstances were in fact present.

There is one final point which Singer's discussion suggests and which does appear to create something of a puzzle. Suppose that I believe that I am justified in deliberately trespassing on an atomic test site, and thereby disobeying the law, because I conclude that this is the best way to call attention to the possible consequences of continued atmospheric testing or nuclear war. I conclude that the consequences of trespassing will on the whole be more beneficial than any alternative action I can take. But suppose I also concede – what very well may be the case that if everyone were to trespass, even for this same reason and in the same way, the consequences would be extremely deleterious. Does it follow that there is something logically incoherent about my principle of action? It looks as though there is, for it appears that I am here denying others the right to do precisely what I claim I am right in doing. I seem to be claiming, in effect, that it is right for me to trespass on government property in order to protest atomic testing only if it is the case that others, even under identical circumstances, will not trespass. Thus, it might be argued, I appear to be unwilling or unable to generalize my principle of conduct.

This argument is unsound, for there is a perfectly good sense in which I am acting on a principle which is coherent and which is open to anyone to adopt. It is simply the principle that one is justified in trespassing on government property whenever – among other things – it happens to be the case that one can say accurately that others will not in fact act on that same principle. Whether anyone else will at any given time act on any particular principle is an empirical question. It is, to repeat what has already been said, one of the possible circumstances which can be part of the description of a class of situations. There is, in short, nothing logically self-contradictory or absurd about making the likelihood of even identical action one of the relevant justifying considerations. And there is, therefore, no reason why the justifiability of any particular act of disobedience cannot depend, among other things, upon the probable conduct of others.

IV

It would not be at all surprising if at this stage one were to feel considerable dissatisfaction with the entire cast of the discussion so far. In particular, one might well believe that the proverbial dead horse has received still another flaying for the simple reason that no one has ever seriously argued that people are never justified in disobeying the law. One might insist, for instance, that neither Socrates nor President Kennedy was talking about all law in all legal systems everywhere. And one might urge, instead, that their claims concerning the unjustifiability of any act of disobedience rest covertly, if not overtly, on the assumption that the disobedience in question was to take place in a society in which the lawmaking procedures and other political institutions were those which are characteristic of an essentially democratic, or free, society. This is, of course, an important and plausible restriction upon the original claim, and the arguments which might support it must now be considered.

While there are several things about a liberal, democratic or free society which might be thought to preclude the possibility of justified disobedience, it is evident that the presence of all the important constitutive institutions cannot guarantee that unjust or immoral laws will not be enacted. For the strictest adherence to principles of representative government, majority rule, frequent and open elections and, indeed, the realization of all of the other characteristics of such a society, in no way can insure that laws of manifest immorality will not be passed and enforced. And if even the ideal democratic society might enact unjust laws, no existing society can plausibly claim as much. Thus, if the case against the possibility of justified disobedience is to depend upon the democratic nature of the society in question, the case cannot rest simply on the claim that the only actions which will be made illegal are those which are already immoral.

What then are the arguments which might plausibly be advanced? One very common argument goes like this: It is, of course, true that even democratically selected and democratically constituted legislatures can and do make mistakes. Nevertheless, a person is never justified in disobeying the law as long as there exist alternative, 'peaceful' procedures by which to bring about the amendment or repeal of undesirable or oppressive laws. The genuine possibility that rational persuasion and argument can bring a majority to favor any one of a variety of competing views, both requires that disapproval always be permitted and forbids that disobedience ever be allowed. This is so for several reasons.

First, it is clearly unfair and obviously inequitable to accept the results of any social decision-procedure only in those cases in which the decision reached was one of which one approves, and to refuse to accept those decisions which are not personally satisfying. If there is one thing which participation, and especially voluntary participation, in a decision-procedure entails, it is that all of the participants must abide by the decision regardless of what it happens to be. If the decision-procedure is that of majority rule, then this means that any person must abide by those decisions in which he was in a minority just as much as it means that he can insist that members of the minority abide when he is a member of the majority.

As familiar as the argument is, its plausibility is far from assured. On one reading, at least, it appears to be one version of the universalization argument. As such, it goes like this. Imagine any person, A, who has voted with the majority to pass a law making a particular kind of conduct illegal. A surely would not and could not acknowledge the right of any person voting with the minority justifiably to disobey that law. But, if A will not and cannot recognize a right of justified disobedience here, then A certainly cannot consistently or fairly claim any right of justified disobedience on his part in those cases in which he, A, happened to end up being in a minority. Thus, justified disobedience can never be defensible.

This argument is fallacious. For a person who would insist that justified disobedience was possible even after majoritarian decision-making could very plausibly and consistently acknowledge the right of any person to disobey the law under appropriate circumstances regardless of how that person had voted on any particular law. Consider, once again, the case already put of the doctor and the pregnant girl. The doctor can surely be consistent in claiming both that circumstances make the performance of the illegal abortion justified and that any comparable action would also be right irrespective of how the actor, or the doctor, or anyone else, happened to have voted on the abortion law, or any other law. The point is simply that there is no reason why any person cannot consistently: (1) hold the view that majority decision-making is the best of all forms of decision-making; (2) participate voluntarily in the decision-making process; and (3) believe that it is right for *anyone to* disobey majority decisions whenever the relevant moral circumstances obtain, e.g., whenever the consequences of disobedience to that law at that time would on the whole be more deleterious than those of obedience.

But this may be deemed too facile an answer; it also may be thought to miss the point. For it might be argued that there is a serious logical inconsistency of a different sort which must arise whenever a voluntary participant in a social decision-procedure claims that not all the decisions reached in accordance with that procedure need be obeyed. Take the case of majority rule. It is inconsistent for anyone voluntarily to participate in the decision-process and yet at the same time to reserve the right to refuse to abide by the decision reached in any particular case. The problem is not an inability to universalize a principle of action. The problem is rather that of making any sense at all out of the notion of having a majority decide anything – of having a procedure by which to make group decisions. The problem is, in addition, that of making any sense at all out of the fact of voluntary participation in the decision-procedure – in knowing what this participation can come to if it does not mean that every participant is bound by all of the decisions which are reached. What can their participation mean if it is not an implicit promise to abide by all decisions reached? And even if the point is not a logical one, it is surely a practical one. What good could there possibly be to a scheme, an institutional means for making social decisions, which did not bind even the participants to anything?

The answer to this argument – or set of arguments – is wholly analogous to that which has been given earlier. But because of the importance and prevalence of the argument some repetition is in order.

One can simply assert that the notion of any social decision-making procedure is intelligible only if it entails that all participants always abide by all of the decisions which are made, no matter what those decisions are. Concomitantly, one can simply insist that any voluntary participant in the decision-process must be consenting or promising to abide by all decisions which are reached. But one cannot give as a plausible reason for this assertion the fact that the notion of group decision-making becomes incoherent if anything less in the way of adherence is required of all participants. And one cannot cite as a plausible reason for this assertion the fact that the notion of voluntary participation loses all meaning if anything less than a promise of absolute obedience is inferred.

It is true that the notion of a group decision-making procedure would be a meaningless notion if there were no respects in which a group decision was in any way binding upon each of the participants. Decisions which in no way bind anyone to do anything are simply not decisions. And it is also true that voluntary participation is an idle, if not a vicious, act if it does not commit each participant to something. If any voluntary participant properly can wholly ignore the decisions which are reached, then something is surely amiss.

But to say all this is not to say very much. Group decision-making can have a point just because it does preclude any participant from taking some actions which, in the absence of the decision, he might have been justified in performing. And voluntary participation can still constitute a promise of sorts that one will not perform actions which, in the absence of voluntary participation, might have been justifiable. If the fact of participation in a set of liberal political institutions does constitute a promise of sorts, it can surely be a promise that the participant will not disobey a law just because obedience would be inconvenient or deleterious to him. And if this is the scope of the promise, then the fact of voluntary participation does make a difference. For in the absence of the participation in the decision to make this conduct illegal, inconvenience to the actor might well have been a good reason for acting in a certain way. Thus, participation can create new obligations to behave in certain ways without constituting a promise not to disobey the law under any circumstances. And if this is the case, adherence to a principle of justified disobedience is not inconsistent with voluntary participation in the decision-making process.

Indeed, a strong point can be made. The notion of making laws through voluntary participation in democratic institutions is not even inconsistent with the insistence that disobedience is justified whenever the consequences of disobedience are on the whole more beneficial than those of obedience. This is so because a promise can be a meaningful promise even if an appeal to the consequences of performing the promise can count as a sufficient reason for not performing the promise. And if this is the case for promises generally, it can be no less the case for the supposed promise to obey the law.

Finally, even if it were correct that voluntary participation implied a promise to obey, and even if it were the case that the promise must be a promise not to disobey on consequential grounds, all of this would still not justify the conclusion that one ought never to disobey the law. It would, instead, only demonstrate that disobeying the law must be prima facie wrong, that everyone has a prima facie obligation to obey the law. This is so just because it is sometimes right even to break one's own promises. And if this, too, is a characteristic of promises generally, it is, again, no less a characteristic of the promise to obey the law.

The notions of promise, consent, or voluntary participation do not, however, exhaust the possible sources of the obligation to obey the laws of a democracy. In particular, there is another set of arguments which remains to be considered. It is that which locates the rightness of obedience in the way in which any act of disobedience improperly distributes certain burdens and benefits among the citizenry. Professor Wechsler, for example, sees any act of disobedience to the laws of the United States as 'the ultimate negation of all neutral principles, to take the benefits accorded by the constitutional system, including the national market and common defense, while denying it allegiance when a special burden is imposed. That certainly is the antithesis of law'.

On the surface, at least, Professor Wechsler's claim seems overly simple: it appears to be the blanket assertion that the receipt by any citizen, through continued, voluntary presence of benefits of this character necessarily implies that no act of disobedience could be justified. To disobey any law after having voluntarily received these benefits would be, he seems to suggest, so unjust that there could never be overriding considerations. This surely is both to claim too much for the benefits of personal and commercial security and to say too little for the character of all types of disobedience. For even if the receipt of benefits such as these did simply impose an obligation to obey the law, it is implausible to suppose that the obligation thereby imposed would be one that stringent.

But there is a more involved aspect of Professor Wechsler's thesis – particularly in his insistence that disobedience of the law, where benefits of this kind have been received, is the negation of all neutral principles. I am not at all certain that I understand precisely what this means, but there are at least two possible interpretations: (1) Unless everyone always obeyed the law no one would receive these obviously valuable benefits. (2) Since the benefits one receives depend upon the prevalence of conditions of uniform obedience, it follows that no one who willingly receives these benefits can justly claim them without himself obeying. The first has already been sufficiently considered. The second, while not unfamiliar, merits some further attention.

In somewhat expanded form, the argument is simply this. What makes it possible for any particular person to receive and enjoy the benefits of general, personal and economic security is the fact that everyone else obeys the law. Now, if injustice is to be avoided, it is surely the case that any other person is equally entitled to these same benefits. But he will have this security only if everyone else obeys the law. Hence the receipt of benefits at others' expense requires repayment in kind. And this means universal obedience to the law.

There are two features of this argument which are puzzling. First, it is far from clear that the benefits of security received by anyone necessarily depend upon absolute obedience on the part of everyone else. It just might be the case that an even greater quantum of security would have accrued from something less than total obedience. But even if I am wrong here, there is a more important point at issue. For reasons already discussed, it is undeniable that even in a democracy a price would be paid for universal obedience – the price that might have to be paid, for instance, were the doctor to refuse to perform the abortion because it was illegal. If this is so, then the fact that a person received benefits from everyone else's obedience does not necessarily entail that it is unjust for him to fail to reciprocate in kind. The benefit of general security might not have been worth the cost. A greater degree of flexibility on the part of others, a general course of obedience except where disobedience was justified, might have yielded a greater benefit. People may, in short, have done more or less than they should have. And if they did, the fact that anyone or everyone benefitted to some degree in no way requires that injustice can only be avoided through like and reciprocal conduct. If it is better, in at least some circumstances, to disobey a law than to obey it, there is surely nothing unjust about increasing the beneficial consequences to all through acts of *discriminate* disobedience.

If the argument based upon the effect of receipt of certain benefits is therefore not very persuasive, neither in most cases is the argument which is derived from the way in which any act of disobedience is thought to distribute burdens unfairly among the citizenry. The argument can be put very briefly: If there is one thing which any act of disobedience inevitably does, it is to increase the burdens which fall on all the law-abiding citizens. If someone disobeys the law even for what seems to be the best of reasons, he inevitably makes it harder – in some quite concrete sense – on everyone else. Hence, at a minimum this is a good reason not to disobey the law, and perhaps a sufficient reason as well.

This argument is appealing because there is at least one kind of case it fits very well. It is the case of taxation. For suppose the following, only somewhat unreal, conditions: that the government is determined to raise a specified sum of money through taxation, and that, in the long, if not the short, run it will do so by adjusting the tax rate to whatever percentage is necessary to produce the desired governmental income. Under such circumstances it could plausibly be argued that one of the truly inevitable results of a successfully executed decision to evade the payment of one's taxes – a decision made, moreover, on ostensibly justifiable grounds – is that every other member of society will thereby be required to pay a greater tax than would otherwise have been the case. Thus in some reasonably direct and obvious fashion any act of disobedience – particularly if undetected – does add to the burdens of everyone else. And surely this is to make out at least a strong case of prima facie injustice.

Now, for reasons already elaborated, it would be improper to conclude that evasion of one's taxes could never be justified. But the argument is persuasive in its insistence that it does provide a very good reason why evasion always must be justified and why it will seldom be justifiable. But even this feature of disobedience is not present in many cases. Tax evasion, as opposed to other kinds of potentially justified disobedience, is a special, far from typical case. And what is peculiar to it is precisely the fact that any act of disobedience to the tax laws arguably shifts or increases the burden upon others. Such is simply not true of most types of acts of disobedience because most laws do not prohibit or require actions which affect the distribution of resources in any very direct fashion.

Thus, if we take once again the case of the doctor who has decided that he is justified in performing an illegal abortion on the pregnant girl, it is extremely difficult, if not impossible, to locate the analogue of the shifting of burdens involved in tax evasion. How does the performance of the abortion thereby increase the 'costs' to anyone else? The only suggestion which seems at all plausible is that which was noted earlier in a somewhat different context. Someone might argue that it is the occurrence of illegal actions which increases the cost of maintaining a police force, a judiciary and suitable correctional institutions. This cost is a burden which is borne by the citizenry as a whole. And hence, the doctor's illegal acts increase their burdens – albeit very slightly. The difficulty here is threefold. First, if the doctor's act is performed in secret and if it remains undetected, then it is hard to see how there is any shift of economic burden at all. Second, given the fact that police forces, courts and prisons will always be necessary as long as unjustified acts of disobedience are a feature of social existence, it is by no means apparent that the additional cost is anything but truly de minimis. And third, the added costs, if any, are in the doctor's case assumed by the doctor *qua* member of the citizenry. He is not avoiding a burden; at most he adds something to everyone's – including his own – existing financial obligations. Thus, in cases such as these, it is not at all evident that disobedience need even be prima facie unjust and hence unjustified.

V

There is one final argument which requires brief elucidation and analysis. It is in certain respects a peculiarly instructive one both in its own right and in respect to the thesis of this article.

It may be true that on some particular occasions the consequences of disobeying a law will in fact be less deleterious on the whole than those of obeying it – even in a democracy. It may even be true that on some particular occasions disobeying a law will be just whereas obeying it would be unjust. Nevertheless, the reason why a person is never justified in disobeying a law – in a democracy – is simply this: The chances are so slight that he will disobey only those laws in only those cases in which he is in fact justified in doing so, that the consequences will on the whole be less deleterious than if he never disobeys any law. Furthermore, since anyone must concede the right to everyone to disobey the law when the circumstances so demand it, the situation is made still worse. For once we entrust this right to everyone we can be sure that many laws will be disobeyed in a multitude of cases in which there was no real justification for disobedience. Thus, given what we know of the possibilities of human error and the actualities of human frailty, and given the tendency of democratic societies to make illegal only those actions which would, even in the absence of a law, be unjustified, we can confidently conclude that the consequences will on the whole and in the long run be best if no one ever takes it upon himself to 'second-guess' the laws and to conclude that in his case his disobedience is justified.

The argument is, in part, not very different from those previously considered. And thus, what is to be said about it is not very different either. Nonetheless, upon pain of being overly repetitive, I would insist that there is a weak sense in which the argument is quite persuasive and a strong sense in which it is not. For the argument makes, on one reading, too strong an empirical claim – the claim that the consequences will in the long run always in fact be better if no one in a democracy ever tries to decide when he is justified in disobeying the law. As it stands, there is no reason to believe that the claim is or must be true, that the consequences will always be better. Indeed, it is very hard to see why, despite the hypothesis, someone might still not be justified in some particular case in disobeying a law. Yet, viewed as a weaker claim, as a summary rule, it does embody a good deal that is worth remembering. It can, on this level, be understood to be a persuasive reminder of much that is relevant to disobedience: that in a democracy the chances of having to live under bad laws are reduced; that in a democracy there are typically less costly means available, by which to bring about changes in the law; that in a democracy – as in life in general – a justified action may always be both inaptly and ineptly emulated; and that in a democracy – as in life in general – people often do make mistakes as to which of their own actions are truly justified. These are some of the lessons of human experience which are easy to forget and painful to relearn.

But there are other lessons, and they are worth remembering too. What is especially troubling about the claim that disobedience of the law is never justified, what is even disturbing about the claim that disobedience of the law is never justified in a democratic or liberal society, is the facility with which its acceptance can lead to the neglect of important moral issues. If no one is justified in disobeying the Supreme Court's decision in *Brown v. Board of Education* this is so because, among other things, there is much that is wrong with segregation. If there was much that was peculiarly wrong in Mississippi in 1963, this was due to the fact, among other facts, that a mob howled and a governor raged when a court held that a person whose skin was black could go to a white university. Disobeying the law is often – even usually – wrong; but this is so largely because the illegal is usually restricted to the immoral and because morally right conduct is still less often illegal. But we must always be sensitive to the fact that this has not always been the case, is not now always the case and need not always be the case in the future. And under concentration upon what is wrong with disobeying the law rather than upon the wrong which the law seeks to prevent can seriously weaken and misdirect that awareness.

As mentioned earlier, the extract that follows from Smith may be dependent on his view of 'the law'. His conclusion that there is, at best, an individual obligation to obey laws also relies on a particular example. Again, you need to think both about the substance of his arguments, and the example that he uses. On the latter question, you have to see whether his example can be generalised to apply to other examples, or whether it is too specialised. The reason why you have to think about that question goes to the roots of the type of discussion that is involved. When discussing issues of moral obligation and other aspects of ethical theory or moral philosophy, one has at least to attempt to maintain some consistency between one's arguments and to see whether it is possible and how far it is possible for them to be generalised.

Smith (1973, 950–76)

Many political philosophers have thought it obvious that there is a prima facie obligation to obey the law; and so, in discussing this obligation, they have thought their task to be more that of explaining its basis than of arguing for its existence. John Rawls has, for example, written:

> I shall assume, as requiring no argument, that there is, at least in a society, such as ours, a moral obligation to obey the law, although it may, of course, be overriden in certain cases by other more stringent obligations.

As against this, I suggest that it is not at all obvious that there is such an obligation, that this is something that must be shown, rather than so blithely assumed. Indeed, were he uninfluenced by conventional wisdom, a reflective man might on first considering the question be inclined to deny any such obligation: As H. A. Prichard once remarked, 'the mere receipt of an order backed by force seems, if anything, to give rise to the duty of resisting, rather than obeying'.

I shall argue that, although those subject to a government often have a prima facie obligation to obey particular laws (e.g., when disobedience has seriously untoward consequences or involves an act that is *mala in se*), they have no prima facie obligation to obey all its laws. I do not hope to prove this contention beyond a reasonable doubt: My goal is rather the more modest one of showing that it is a reasonable position to maintain by first criticizing arguments that purport to establish the obligation and then presenting some positive argument against it.

...

Now, the question of whether there is a prima facie obligation to obey the law is clearly about a generic obligation [one that asserts that everyone who meets a certain description has a prima facie obligation to perform a certain kind of act whenever he has an opportunity to do so]. Everyone, even the anarchist, would agree that in many circumstances individuals have specific prima facie obligations to obey specific laws. Since it is clear that there is in most circumstances a specific prima facie obligation to refrain from murder, rape, or breach of contract, it is plain that in these circumstances each of us has a specific prima facie obligation not to violate laws which prohibit these acts. Again, disobeying the law often has seriously untoward consequences; and, when this is so, virtually everyone would agree that there is a specific prima facie obligation to obey. Therefore, the interesting question about our obligation vis-a-vis the law is not 'Do individual citizens ever have specific prima facie obligations to obey particular laws?', but rather 'Is the moral relation of any government to its citizens such that they have a prima facie obligation to do certain things merely because they are legally required to do so?' This is, of course, equivalent to asking 'Is there a generic prima facie obligation to obey the law?' Hereafter, when I use the phrase 'the prima facie obligation to obey the law' I shall be referring to a generic obligation.

...

I

The arguments I shall examine fall into three groups: First, those which rest on the benefits each individual receives from government: second, those relying on implicit consent or promise; third, those which appeal to utility or the general good. I shall consider each group in turn.

Of those in the first group, I shall begin with the argument from gratitude. Although they differ greatly in the amount of benefits they provide, virtually all governments do confer substantial benefits on their subjects. Now, it is often claimed that, when a person accepts benefits from another, he thereby incurs a debt of gratitude towards his benefactor. Thus, if it be maintained that obedience to the law is the best way of showing gratitude towards one's government, it may with some plausibility be concluded that each person who has received benefits from his government has a prima facie obligation to obey the law.

On reflection, however, this argument is unconvincing. First, it may reasonably be doubted whether most citizens have an obligation to act gratefully towards their government. Ordinarily, if someone confers benefits on me without any consideration of whether I want them, and if he does this in order to advance some purpose other than promotion of my particular welfare, I have no obligation to be grateful towards him. Yet the most important benefits of government are not accepted by its citizens, but are rather enjoyed regardless of whether they are wanted. Moreover, a government typically confers these benefits, not to advance the interests of particular citizens, but rather as a consequence of advancing some purpose of its own. At times, its motives are wholly admirable, as when it seeks to promote the general welfare; at others, they are less so, as when it seeks to stay in power by catering to the demands of some powerful faction. But, such motives are irrelevant: Whenever government forces benefits on me for reasons other than my particular welfare, I clearly am under no obligation to be grateful to it.

Second, even assuming *arguendo* that each citizen has an obligation to be grateful to his government, the argument still falters. It is perhaps true that cheerful and willing obedience is the best way to show one's gratitude towards government, in that it makes his gratitude unmistakable. But, when a person owes a debt of gratitude towards another, he does not necessarily acquire a prima facie obligation to display his gratitude in the most convincing manner: A person with demanding, domineering parents might best display his gratitude towards them by catering to their every whim, but he surely has no prima facie obligation to do so. Without undertaking a lengthy case-by-case examination, one cannot delimit the prima facie obligation of acting gratefully, for its existence and extent depends on such factors as the nature of the benefits received, the manner in which they are conferred, the motives of the benefactor, and so forth. But, even without such an examination, it is clear that the mere fact that a person has conferred on me even the most momentous benefits does not establish his right to dictate all of my behavior; nor does it establish that I always have an obligation to consider his wishes when I am deciding what I shall do. If, then, we have a prima facie obligation to act gratefully towards government, we undoubtedly have an obligation to promote its interests when this does not involve great sacrifice on our part and to respect some of its wishes concerning that part of our behavior which does not directly affect its interests. But, our having this obligation to be grateful surely does not establish that we have a prima facie obligation to obey the law.

A more interesting argument from the benefits individuals receive from government is the argument from fair play. It differs from the argument from gratitude in contending that the prima facia obligation to obey the law is owed, not to one's government but rather to one's fellow citizens. Versions of this argument have been offered by H.L.A. Hart and John Rawls.

According to Hart, the mere existence of cooperative enterprise gives rise to a certain prima facie obligation. He argues that:

> when a number of persons conduct any joint enterprise according to rules and thus restrict their liberty, those who have submitted to these restrictions when required have a right to a similar submission from those who have benefitted by their submission. The rules may provide that officials should have authority to

enforce obedience and make further rules, and this will create a structure of legal rights and duties, but the moral obligation to obey the rules in such circumstances is *due to* the cooperating members of the society, and they have the correlative moral right to obedience.

Rawls' account of this obligation in his essay, *Legal Obligation and the Duty of Fair Play*, is rather more complex. Unlike Hart, he sets certain requirements on the kinds of cooperative enterprises that give rise to the obligation: First, that success of the enterprise depends on near-universal obedience to its rules, but not on universal cooperation; second, that obedience to its rules involves some sacrifice, in that obeying the rules restricts one's liberty; and finally, that the enterprise conform to the principles of justice. Rawls also offers an explanation of the obligation: He argues that, if a person benefits from participating in such an enterprise and if he intends to continue receiving its benefits, he acts unfairly when he refuses to obey its rules. With Hart, however, Rawls claims that this obligation is owed not to the enterprise itself, nor to its officials, but rather to those members whose obedience has made the benefits possible. Hart and Rawls also agree that this obligation of fair play – 'fair play' is Rawls' term – is a fundamental obligation, not derived from utility or from mutual promise or consent. Finally, both Hart and Rawls conceive of legal systems, at least those in democratic societies, as complex practices of the kind which give rise to the obligation of fair play; and they conclude that those who benefit from such legal systems have a prima facie obligation to obey their laws.

These arguments deserve great respect. Hart and Rawls appear to have isolated a kind of prima facie obligation overlooked by other philosophers and have thereby made a significant contribution to moral theory. However, the significance of their discovery to jurisprudence is less clear. Although Hart and Rawls have discovered the obligation of fair play, they do not properly appreciate its limits. Once these limits are understood, it is clear that the prima facie obligation to obey the law cannot be derived from the duty of fair play.

The obligation of fair play seems to arise most clearly within small, voluntary cooperative enterprises. Let us suppose that a number of persons have gone off into the wilderness to carve out a new society, and that they have adopted certain rules to govern their communal life. Their enterprise meets Rawls' requirements on success, sacrifice, and justice. We can now examine the moral situation of the members of that community in a number of circumstances, taking seriously Hart's insistence that cooperating members have a right to the obedience of others and Rawls' explanation of this right and its correlative obligation on grounds of fairness.

Let us take two members of the community, A and B. B, we may suppose, has never disobeyed the rules and A has benefitted from B's previous submission. Has B a right to A's obedience? It would seem necessary to know the consequences of A's obedience. If, in obeying the rules, A will confer on B a benefit roughly equal to those he has received from B, it would be plainly unfair for A to withhold it from B; and so, in this instance, B's right to A's obedience is clear. Similarly, if, in disobeying the rule, A will harm the community, B's right to A's obedience is again clear. This is because in harming the community A will harm B indirectly, by threatening the existence or efficient functioning of an institution on which B's vital interests depend. Since A has benefitted from B's previous submission to the rules, it is unfair for A to do something which will lessen B's chances of receiving like benefits in the future. However, if A's compliance with some particular rule does not benefit B and if his disobedience will not harm the community, it is difficult to see how fairness to B could dictate that A must comply. Surely, the fact that A has benefitted from B's submission does not give B the right to insist that A obey when B's interests are unaffected. A may in this situation have an obligation to obey, perhaps because he has promised or because his disobedience would be unfair to some other member; but, if he does disobey, he has surely not been unfair to B.

We may generalize from these examples. Considerations of fairness apparently do show that, when cooperation is perfect and when each member has benefitted from the submission of every other, each member of an enterprise has a prima facie obligation to obey its rules when obedience benefits some other member or when disobedience harms the enterprise. For, if in either circumstance a member disobeys, he is unfair to at least one other member and is perhaps unfair to them all. However, if a member disobeys when his obedience would have benefitted no other member and when his disobedience does no harm, his moral situation is surely different. If his disobedience is then unfair, it must be unfair to the group but not to any particular member. But this, I take it, is impossible: Although the moral properties of a group are not always a simple function of the moral properties of its members, it is evident that one cannot be unfair to a group without being unfair to any of its members. It would seem, then, that even when cooperation is perfect, considerations of fairness do not establish that members of a cooperative enterprise have a simple obligation to obey all of its rules, but have rather the more complex obligation to obey when obedience benefits some other member or when disobedience harms the enterprise. This does not, it is worth noting, reduce the obligation of fair play to a kind of utilitarian obligation, for it may well be that fair play will dictate in certain circumstances that a man obey when disobedience would have better consequences. My point is merely that the obligation of fair play governs a man's actions only when some benefit or harm turns on whether he obeys. Surely, this is as should be, for questions of fairness typically arise from situations in which burdens or benefits are distributed or in which some harm is done.

The obligation of fair play is therefore much more complex than Hart or Rawls seem to have imagined. Indeed, the obligation is even more complex than the above discussion suggests, for the assumption of perfect cooperation is obviously unrealistic. When that assumption is abandoned, the effect of previous disobedience considered, and the inevitable disparity among the various members' sacrifice in obeying the rules taken into account, the scope of the obligation is still further limited; we shall then find that it requires different things of different members, depending on their previous pattern of compliance and the amount of sacrifice they have made. These complications need not detain us, however, for they do not affect the fact that fairness requires obedience only in situations where noncompliance would withhold benefits from someone or harm the enterprise. Now it must be conceded that all of this makes little difference when we confine our attention to small, voluntary, cooperative enterprises. Virtually any disobedience may be expected to harm such enterprises to some extent, by diminishing the confidence of other members in its probable success and therefore reducing their incentive to work diligently towards it. Moreover, since they are typically governed by a relatively small number of rules, none of which ordinarily require behavior that is useless to other members, we may expect that when a member disobeys he will probably withhold a benefit from some other member and that he has in the past benefitted significantly from that member's obedience. We may therefore expect that virtually every time the rules of a small, voluntary enterprise call on a member to obey he will have a specific prima facie obligation to do so because of his obligation of fair play.

In the case of legal systems, however, the complexity of the obligation makes a great deal of difference. Although their success may depend on the 'habit of obedience' of a majority of their subjects, all legal systems are designed to cope with a substantial amount of disobedience. Hence, individual acts of disobedience to the law only rarely have an untoward effect on legal systems. What is more, because laws must necessarily be designed to cover large numbers of cases, obedience to the law often benefits no one. Perhaps the best illustration is obedience of the traffic code: Very often I benefit no one when I stop at a red light or observe the speed limit. Finally, virtually every legal system contains a number of pointless or even positively harmful laws, obedience to which either benefits no one or, worse still, causes harm. Laws prohibiting homosexual activity or the dissemination of birth control information are surely in this category. Hence, even if legal systems are the kind of cooperative enterprise that gives rise to the obligation of fair play, in a great many instances that obligation will not require that we obey specific laws. If, then, there is a generic prima facie obligation to obey the laws of any legal system, it cannot rest on the obligation of fair play. The plausibility of supposing that it does depends on an unwarranted extrapolation from what is largely true of our obligations within small, cooperative enterprises to what must always be true of our obligations within legal systems.

...

II

The second group of arguments are those from implicit consent or promise. Recognizing that among the clearest cases of prima facie obligation are those in which a person voluntarily assumes the obligation, some philosophers have attempted to found the citizen's obligation to obey the law upon his consent or promise to do so. There is, of course, a substantial difficulty in any such attempt, viz the brute fact that many persons have never so agreed. To accommodate this fact, some philosophers have invoked the concept of implicit promise or consent. In the *Second Treatise*, Locke argued that mere residence in a country, whether for an hour or a lifetime, constitutes implicit consent to its law. Plato and W. D. Ross made the similar argument that residence in a country and appeal to the protection of its laws constitutes an implicit promise to obey.

Nevertheless, it is clear that residence and use of the protection of the law do not constitute any usual kind of consent to a government nor any usual kind of promise to obey its laws. The phrases 'implicit consent' and 'implicit promise' are somewhat difficult to understand, for they are not commonly used; nor does Locke, Plato, or Ross define them. Still, a natural way of understanding them is to assume that they refer to acts which differ from explicit consent or promise only in that, in the latter cases, the person has said 'I consent ...' or 'I promise ...' whereas in the former, he has not uttered such words but has rather performed some act which counts as giving consent or making a promise. Now, as recent investigation in the philosophy of language has shown, certain speech acts are performed only when someone utters certain words (or performs some other conventional act) with the intention that others will take what he did as being an instance of the particular act in question. And it is certain that, in their ordinary usage, 'consenting' and 'promising' refer to speech acts of this kind. If I say to someone, 'I promise to give you fifty dollars', but it is clear from the context that I do not intend that others will take my utterance as a promise, no one would consider me as having promised. Bringing this observation to bear on the present argument, it is perhaps possible that some people reside in a country and appeal to the protection of its laws with the intention that others will take their residence and appeal as consent to the laws or as a promise to obey; but this is surely true only of a very small number, consisting entirely of those enamoured with social contract theory.

It may be argued, however, that my criticism rests on an unduly narrow reading of the words 'consent' and 'promise'. Hence, it may be supposed that, if I am to refute the implicit consent or promise arguments, I must show that there is no other sense of the words 'consent' or 'promise' in which it is true that citizens, merely by living in a state and going about their usual business, thereby consent or promise to obey the law. This objection is difficult to meet, for I know of no way to show that there is no sense of either word that is suitable for contractarian purposes. However, I can show that two recent attempts, by John Plamenatz and Alan Gewirth, to refurbish the implicit consent argument along this line have been unsuccessful. I shall not quarrel with their analyses of 'consent', though I am suspicious of them; rather, I shall argue that given their definitions of 'consent' the fact that a man consents to government does not establish that he has a prima facie obligation to obey the law.

Plamenatz claims that there are two kinds of consent. The first, which is common garden-variety consent, he terms 'direct'. He concedes that few citizens directly consent to their government. He suggests, however, that there is another kind of consent, which he calls 'indirect', and that, in democratic societies, consent in this sense is widespread and establishes a prima facie obligation to obey the law. Indirect consent occurs whenever a person freely votes or abstains from voting. Voting establishes a prima facie obligation of obedience because:

> Even if you dislike the system and wish to change it, you put yourself by your vote under a [prima facie] obligation to obey whatever government comes legally to power ... For the purpose of an election is to give authority to the people who win it and, if you vote knowing what you are doing and without being compelled to do it, you voluntarily take part in a process which gives authority to these people.

Plamenatz does not explain why abstention results in a prima facie obligation, but perhaps his idea is that, if a person abstains, he in effect acknowledges the authority of whoever happens to win.

The key premise then in the argument is that 'the purpose of an election is to give authority to the people who win it', and it is clear that Plamenatz believes that this implies that elections do give authority to their winners. In assessing the truth of these contentions, it is, of course, vital to know what Plamenatz means by 'authority'. Unfortunately, he does not enlighten us, and we must therefore speculate as to his meaning. To begin, the word 'authority', when used without qualification, is often held to mean the same as 'legitimate authority'. Since prima facie obligation is the weakest kind of obligation, part of what we mean when we ascribe authority to some government is that those subject to it have at least a prima facie obligation to obey. However, if this is what Plamenatz means by 'authority', his argument simply begs the question: For, in order to be justified in asserting that the purpose of an election is to confer authority and that elections succeed in doing this, he must first show that everyone subject to an elected government has a prima facie obligation to obey its law, both those eligible to vote and those ineligible.

It is possible, however, that Plamenatz is using 'authority' in some weaker sense, one that does not entail that everyone subject to it has a prima facie obligation to obey. If this is so, his premises will perhaps pass, but he must then show that those who are eligible to take part in conferring authority have a prima facie obligation to obey it. However, it is difficult to see how this can be done. First, as Plamenatz recognizes, voting is not necessarily consenting in the 'direct' or usual sense, and merely being eligible to vote is even more clearly not consenting. Hence, the alleged prima facie obligation of obedience incurred by those eligible to vote is not in consequence of their direct consent. Second, Plamenatz cannot appeal to 'common moral sentiment' to bolster his argument: This is because if we really believed that those eligible to vote have a prima facie obligation to obey, an obligation not incurred by the ineligible, we should then believe that the eligible have a stronger obligation than those who are ineligible. But, as far as I can tell, we do not ordinarily think that this is true. Finally, Plamenatz cannot rely on a purely conceptual argument to make his point. It is by no means an analytic truth that those subject to elected governments have a prima facie obligation to obey the law. The radical who says, 'The present government of the United States was freely elected, but because it exploits people its citizens have no obligation to obey it', has perhaps said something false, but he has not contradicted himself. Plamenatz's argument is therefore either question-begging or inconclusive, depending on what he means by 'authority'.

Gewirth's argument is similar to Plamenatz's in that he also holds that a person's vote establishes his prima facie obligation of obedience. He argues that men consent to government when 'certain institutional arrangements exist in the community as a whole', including 'the maintenance of a method which leaves open to every sane, noncriminal adult the opportunity to discuss, criticize, and vote for or against the government'. He holds that the existence of such consent 'justifies' government and establishes the subject's prima facie obligation to obey because:

> The method of consent combines and safeguards the joint values of freedom and order as no other method does. It provides a choice in the power of government which protects the rights of the electorate more effectively than does any other method. It does more justice to man's potential rationality than does any other method, for it gives all men the opportunity to participate in a reasoned discussion of the problem of society and to make their discussion effective in terms of political control.

As it stands, Gewirth's argument is incomplete. He makes certain claims about the benefits of government by consent which are open to reasonable doubt. Some communists, for example, would hold that Gewirth's method of consent has led to exploitation, and that human rights and freedom are better protected by the rule of the party. This aside, Gewirth's argument still needs strengthening. The fact that certain benefits are given only by government with a method of consent establishes only that such a government is better than one which lacks such a method. But, to show that one government is better than another, or even to show that it is the best possible government, does not prove that its subjects have a prima facie obligation to obey its laws: There is a prior question, which remains to be settled, as to whether there can be a prima facie obligation to obey any government. Gewirth does not carry the argument farther in his discussion of 'consent', but earlier in his paper he hints as to how he would meet this objection. He argues that 'government as such' is justified, or made legitimate, by its being necessary to avoid certain evils. Indeed, although he does not explicitly so state, he seems to think that utilitarian considerations demonstrate that there is a prima facie obligation to obey any government that protects its subjects from these evils, but that there is an additional prima facie obligation to obey a government with a method of consent because of the more extensive benefits it offers. In the next section, I shall discuss whether a direct appeal to utility can establish a prima facie obligation to obey the law.

III

I shall consider three utilitarian arguments: the first appealing to a weak form of act-utilitarianism, the second and third to rule-utilitarian theories. To my knowledge, the first argument has never been explicitly advanced. It is nevertheless worth considering, both because it possesses a certain plausibility and because it has often been hinted at when philosophers, lawyers, and political theorists have attempted to derive an obligation to obey the law from the premise that government is necessary to protect society from great evil. The argument runs as follows:

> There is obviously a prima facie obligation to perform acts which have good consequences. Now, government is absolutely necessary for securing the general good: The alternative is the state of nature in which everyone is miserable, in which life is 'solitary, poor, nasty, brutish and short'. But, no government can long stand in the face of widespread disobedience, and government can therefore promote the general good only so long as its laws are obeyed. Therefore, obedience to the law supports the continued existence of government and, hence, always has good consequences. From this it follows that there is a prima facie obligation to obey the law.

On even brief scrutiny, however, this argument, quickly disintegrates. The first thing to be noticed is that its principle of prima facie obligation is ambiguous. It may be interpreted as postulating either (a) an obligation to perform those acts which have any good consequences, or (b) an obligation to perform optimific acts (i.e., those whose consequences are better than their alternatives). Now, (a) and (b) are in fact very different principles. The former is obviously absurd. It implies, for example, that I have a prima facie obligation to kill whomever I meet, since this would have the good consequence of helping to reduce over-population. Thus, the only weak act-utilitarian principle with any plausibility is (b). But, regardless of whether (b) is acceptable – and some philosophers would not accept it – the conclusion that there is a prima facie obligation to obey the law cannot be derived from it, inasmuch as there are obvious and familiar cases in which breach of a particular law has better consequences than obedience. The only conclusion to be derived from (b) is that there is a specific prima facie obligation to obey the law whenever obedience is optimific. But no generic prima facie obligation to obey can be derived from weak act-utilitarianism.

The second utilitarian argument appeals not to the untoward consequences of individual disobedience, but rather to those of general disobedience. Perhaps the most common challenge to those who defend certain instances of civil disobedience is 'What would happen if everyone disobeyed the law?' One of the arguments implicit in this question is the generalization argument, which may be expanded as follows:

> No one can have a right to do something unless everyone has a right to do it. Similarly, an act cannot be morally indifferent unless it would be morally indifferent if everyone did it. But, everyone's breaking the law is not a matter of moral indifference; for no government can survive in such a circumstance and, as we have already agreed, government is necessary for securing and maintaining the general good. Hence, since the consequences of general disobedience would be disastrous, each person subject to law has a prima facie obligation to obey it.

In assessing this argument, we must first recognize that the generalization argument is a moral criterion to be applied with care, as virtually everyone who has discussed it has recognized. If we simply note that if everyone committed a certain act there would be disastrous consequences and thereupon conclude that there is a prima facie obligation not to commit acts of that kind, we will be saddled with absurdities. We will have to maintain, for example, that there is a prima facie obligation not to eat dinner at five o'clock, for if everyone did so, certain essential services could not be maintained. And, for similar reasons, we will have to maintain that there is a prima facie obligation not to produce food. Now, those who believe that the generalization argument is valid argue that such absurdities arise when the criterion is applied to acts which are either too generally described or described in terms of morally irrelevant features. They would argue that the generalization argument appears to go awry when applied to these examples because the description 'producing food' is too general to give the argument purchase and because the temporal specification in 'eating dinner at five o'clock' is morally irrelevant.

However, such a restriction on the generalization argument is fatal to its use in proving a prima facie obligation to obey the law. This is because a person who denies any such obligation is surely entitled to protest that the description 'breaking the law' is overly general, on the ground that it refers to acts of radically different moral import. Breaking the law perhaps always has some bad consequences; but sometimes the good done by it balances the bad or even outweighs it. And, once we take these differences in consequences into account, we find that utilitarian generalization, like weak act-utilitarianism, can only establish a specific prima facie obligation to obey the law when obedience is optimific. Were everyone to break the law when obedience is optimific, the consequences would undoubtedly be disastrous; but it is by no means clear that it would be disastrous if everyone broke the law when obedience is not optimific. Since no one knows, with respect to any society, how often obedience is not optimific, no one can be certain as to the consequences of everyone acting in this way. Indeed, for all we know, if everyone broke the law when obedience was not optimific the good done by separate acts of law-breaking might more than compensate for any public disorder which might result. In sum, even if the generalization argument is regarded as an acceptable principle of prima facie obligation, the most it demonstrates is that there is a specific prima facie obligation to obey the law whenever the consequences of obedience are optimific.

...

... Now, to many it may seem obvious that the ideal set of rules for any society will contain the rule 'Obey the law', on the ground that, were its members not generally convinced of at least a prima facie obligation to obey, disobedience would be widespread, resulting in a great many crimes against person and property. But, there are two reasons to doubt such a gloomy forecast. First, we must surely suppose that in this hypothetical society the laws are still backed by sanctions, thereby giving its members a strong incentive to obey its laws. Second, we must also assume that the members of that society accept other moral rules (e.g., 'Do not harm others', 'Keep promises', 'Tell the truth') which will give them a moral incentive to obey the law in most circumstances. It is, in short, a mistake to believe that unless people are convinced that they have a generic prima facie obligation to obey the law, they cannot be convinced that in most circumstances they have a specific prima facie obligation to obey particular laws. We may therefore expect that, even though members of our hypothetical society do not accept a moral rule about obedience to the law per se, they will still feel a prima facie obligation to act in accordance with the law, save when disobedience does no harm. There is, then, no reason to think that an orgy of lawbreaking would ensue were no rule about obedience to the law generally recognized; nor, I think, is there any good reason to believe that acceptance of the rule 'Obey the law' would in any society have better consequences than were no such rule recognized. And, if this is so, there is surely no reason to think that recognition of this rule would have better consequences than recognition of some alternative rule.

...

IV

In the foregoing discussion, I have played the skeptic, contending that no argument has as yet succeeded in establishing a prima facie obligation to obey the law. I want now to examine this supposed obligation directly. I shall assume *arguendo* that such an obligation exists in order to inquire as to how it compares in moral weight with other prima facie obligations. As we shall see, this question is relevant to whether we should hold that such an obligation exists.

To discuss this question, I must, of course, first specify some test for determining the weight of a prima facie obligation. It will be recalled that I defined 'prima facie obligation' in terms of wrongdoing: To say that a person S has a prima facie obligation to do an act X is to say that S has a moral reason to do X which is such that, unless he has a reason not to do X that is at least as strong, S's failure to do X is wrong. Now, we are accustomed, in our reflective moral practice, to distinguish degrees of wrongdoing. And so, by appealing to this notion, we can formulate two principles that may reasonably be held to govern the weight of prima facie obligations: First, that a prima facie obligation is a serious one if, and only if, an act which violates that obligation and fulfills no other is seriously wrong; and, second, that a prima facie obligation is a serious one if, and only if, violation of it will make considerably worse an act which on other grounds is already wrong. These principles, which constitute tests for determining an obligation's weight, are closely related, and application of either to a given prima facie obligation is a sufficient measure; but I shall apply both to the presumed prima facie obligation to obey the law in order to make my argument more persuasive.

First, however, we should convince ourselves of the reliability of these tests by applying them to some clear cases. I suppose it will be granted that we all have a prima facie obligation not to kill (except perhaps in self-defense), and that this obligation is most weighty. Our first test corroborates this, for, if a person kills another when he is not defending himself and if he has no specific prima facie obligation to kill that person, his act is seriously wrong. By contrast, our prima facie obligation to observe rules of etiquette – if indeed there is any such obligation – is clearly trifling. This is borne out by our test, for if I belch audibly in the company of those who think such behavior rude, my wrongdoing is at most trivial. The same results are obtained under our second test. If I attempt to extort money from someone my act is much worse if I kill one of his children and threaten the rest than if I merely threatened them all; and so the obligation not to kill again counts as substantial. Similarly, the prima facie obligation to observe the rules of etiquette is again trivial, for if I am rude during the extortion my act is hardly worse than it would have been had I been polite.

By neither of these tests, however, does the prima facie obligation to obey the law count as substantial. As for the first test, let us assume that while driving home at two o'clock in the morning I run a stop sign. There is no danger, for I can see clearly that there was no one approaching the intersection, nor is there any impressionable youth nearby to be inspired to a life of crime by my flouting of the traffic code. Finally, we may assume that I nevertheless had no specific prima facie obligation to run the stop sign. If, then, my prima facie obligation to obey the law is of substantial moral weight, my action must have been a fairly serious instance of wrongdoing. But clearly it was not. If it was wrong at all – and to me this seems dubious – it was at most a mere peccadillo. As for the second test, we may observe that acts which are otherwise wrong are not made more so – if they are made worse at all – by being illegal. If I defraud someone my act is hardly worse morally by being illegal than it would have been were it protected by some legal loophole. Thus, if there is a prima facie obligation to obey the law, it is at most of trifling weight.

This being so, I suggest that considerations of simplicity indicate that we should ignore the supposed prima facie obligation to obey the law and refuse to count an act wrong merely because it violates some law. There is certainly nothing to be lost by doing this, for we shall not thereby recommend or tolerate any conduct that is seriously wrong, nor shall we fail to recommend any course of action that is seriously obligatory. Yet, there is much to be gained, for in refusing to let trivialities occupy our attention, we shall not be diverted from the important questions to be asked about illegal conduct, viz., 'What kind of act was it?', 'What were its consequences?', 'Did the agent intend its consequences?', and so forth. Morality is, after all, a serious business; and we are surely right not to squander our moral attention and concern on matters of little moral significance.

To illustrate what can be gained, let us consider briefly the issue of civil disobedience. Most philosophers who have written on the subject have argued that, at least in democratic societies, there is always a strong moral reason to obey the law. They have therefore held that civil disobedience is a tactic to be employed only when all legal means of changing an unjust law have failed, and that the person who engages in it must willingly accept punishment as a mark of respect for the law and recognition of the seriousness of lawbreaking. However, once we abandon the notion that civil disobedience is morally significant per se, we shall judge it in the same way we judge most other kinds of acts, that is, on the basis of their character and consequences. Indeed, we can then treat civil disobedience just as we regard many other species of illegal conduct. If breaking the law involves an act which is *mala in se* or if it has untoward consequences, we are ordinarily prepared to condemn it and to think that the malefactor ought to accept punishment. But if law-breaking does not involve an act that is *mala in se and* if it has no harmful consequences, we do not ordinarily condemn it, nor do we think that its perpetrator must accept punishment, unless evading punishment itself has untoward consequences. If we adopt this view of civil disobedience, we shall have done much to escape the air of mystery that hovers about most discussions of it.

Of course, this is not to say it will be easy to determine when civil disobedience is justified. Some have maintained that the civil disobedience of the last decade has led to increasing violation of laws which safeguard people and property? If this is true, each instance of disobedience which has contributed to this condition has a share in the evil of the result. Others maintain that such disobedience has had wholly good consequences, that it has helped to remedy existing injustice and to restrain government from fresh injustice. Still others think its consequences are mixed. Which position is correct is difficult to determine. I myself am inclined to believe that, although the consequences have been mixed, the good far outweigh the bad; but I would be hard pressed to prove it. What is clear, however, is that either abandoning or retaining the supposed prima facie obligation to obey the law will not help settle these questions about consequences. But, if we do abandon it, we shall then at least be able to focus on these questions without having to worry about a prima facie obligation of trivial weight that must nevertheless somehow be taken into account. Finally, if we abandon the prima facie obligation to obey the law, we shall perhaps look more closely at the character of acts performed in the course of civil disobedience, and this may, in turn, lead to fruitful moral speculation. For example, we shall be able to distinguish between acts which cannot conceivably violate the obligation of fair play (e.g., burning one's draft card) and acts which may do so (e.g., tax refusal or evasion of military service). This in turn may provide an incentive to reflect further on the obligation of fair play, to ask, for example, whether Rawls is right in his present contention that a person can incur the obligation of fair play only so long as his acceptance of the benefits of a cooperative enterprise is wholly voluntary.

V

... I suggest that all of this makes it reasonable to maintain that there is in no society a prima facie obligation to obey the law.

Before I conclude my discussion, however, I want to tie up one loose thread. Near the beginning of my argument I distinguished the question to be discussed from that which

I called the lawyer's question, 'May a reasonable man take mere illegality to be sufficient evidence that an act is morally wrong, so long as he lacks specific evidence that tends to show that it is right?' Since I have raised the question, I believe that, for the sake of completeness, I should consider it, if only briefly. To begin, it seems very doubtful that there is, in the lawyer's sense, a prima facie obligation to obey the law. It is undoubtedly true that most instances of lawbreaking are wrong, but it is also true that many are not: This is because there are, as Lord Devlin once remarked, 'many fussy regulations whose breach it would be pedantic to call immoral', and because some breaches of even non-fussy regulations are justified. Now, unless – as in a court of law – there is some pressing need to reach a finding, the mere fact that most As are also B does not, in the absence of evidence that a particular A is not B, warrant an inference that the A in question is also a B: In order for this inference to be reasonable, one must know that virtually all As are Bs. Since, then, it rarely happens that there is a pressing need to reach a moral finding, and since to know merely that an act is illegal is not to know very much of moral significance about it, it seems clear that, if his only information about an act was that it was illegal, a reasonable man would withhold judgment until he learned more about it. Indeed, this is not only what the fictitious reasonable man would do, it is what we should expect the ordinary person to do. Suppose we were to ask a large number of people: 'Jones has broken a law; but I won't tell you whether what he did is a serious crime or merely violation of a parking regulation, nor whether he had good reason for his actions. Would you, merely on the strength of what I have just told you, be willing to say that what he did was morally wrong?' I have conducted only an informal poll; but, on its basis, I would wager that the great majority would answer 'I can't yet say – you must tell me more about what Jones did.'

More importantly, it appears to make little difference what answer we give to the lawyer's question. While an affirmative answer establishes a rule of inference that an illegal act is wrong in the absence of specific information tending to show it to be right, it is a rule that would in fact virtually never be applied in any reasonable determination of whether an illegal act is wrong. If, on the one hand, we have specific information about an illegal act which tends to show it to be right, then the rule is irrelevant to our determination of the act's moral character. Should we be inclined, in this instance, to hold the act wrong we must have specific information which tends to show this: and it is clear that our conclusions about its moral character must be based on this specific information, and not on the supposed reasonableness of holding illegal conduct wrong in the absence of specific information tending to show it is right. On the other hand, if we have specific information tending to show that an illegal act is wrong and no information tending to show it is right, the rule is applicable but otiose: Since we have ample specific reason to condemn the act, the rule is superfluous to our judgment. It would seem, then, that the rule is relevant only when we have no specific information about the illegal conduct's rightness or wrongness: and this, I suggest, is something that virtually never occurs. When we are prompted to make a moral judgment about an illegal act, we virtually always know something of its character or at least its consequences; and it is these that we consider important in determining the rightness or wrongness of lawbreaking. In short, it seems to make little difference what answer we give to the lawyer's question; I raise it here only that it may hereafter be ignored.

In conclusion, it is, I think, important to recognize that there is nothing startling in what I am recommending, nothing that in any way outrages common sense. Even the most conscientious men at times violate trivial and pointless laws for some slight gain in convenience and, when they do so, they do not feel shame or remorse. Similarly, when they observe other men behaving in a like fashion, they do not think of passing moral censure. For most people, violation of the law becomes a matter for moral concern only when it involves an act which is believed to be wrong on grounds apart from its illegality. Hence, anyone who believes that the purpose of normative ethics is to organize and clarify our reflective moral practice should be skeptical of any argument purporting to show that there is a prima facie obligation to obey the law. It is necessary to state this point with care: I am not contending that reflective and conscientious citizens would, if asked, deny that there is a prima facie obligation to obey the law. Indeed, I am willing to concede that many more would affirm its existence than deny it. But, this is in no way inconsistent with my present point. We often find that reflective people will accept general statements which are belied by their actual linguistic practice. That they also accept moral generalizations that are belied by their actual reflective moral practice should occasion no surprise.

This last point may, however, be challenged on the ground that it implies that there is in our reflective moral practice no distinction between raw power and legitimate authority. As I noted above, the concept of legitimate authority is often analyzed in terms of the right to command, where 'right' is used in the strict sense as implying some correlative obligation of obedience. Given this definition, if it is true that the principle 'There is a prima facie obligation to obey the law' is not observed in our reflective moral practice, it follows that we do not really distinguish between governments which possess legitimate authority (e.g., that of the United States) and those which do not (e.g., the Nazi occupation government of France). And this, it may justly be held, is absurd. What I take this argument to show, however, is not that the principle is enshrined in our reflective morality, but rather that what we ordinarily mean when we ascribe legitimate authority to some government is not captured by the usual analysis of 'legitimate authority'. It is a mistake to believe that, unless we employ the concept of authority as it is usually analyzed, we cannot satisfactorily distinguish between the moral relation of the government of the United States vis-a-vis Americans and the moral relation of the Nazi occupation government vis-a-vis Frenchmen. One way of doing this, for example, is to define 'legitimate authority' in terms of 'the right to command and to enforce obedience', where 'right' is used in the sense of 'what is morally permissible'. Thus, according to this analysis of the notion, the government of the United States counts as having legitimate authority over its subjects because within certain limits there is nothing wrong in its issuing commands to them and enforcing their obedience, whereas the Nazi occupation government lacked such authority because its issuing commands to Frenchmen was morally impermissible. It is not my intention to proffer this as an adequate analysis of the notion of legitimate authority or to suggest that it captures what we ordinarily mean when we ascribe such authority to some government. These are difficult matters, and I do not wish to address myself to them here. My point is rather that the questions 'What governments enjoy legitimate authority?' and 'Have the citizens of any government a prima facie obligation to obey the law?' both can be, and should be, kept separate.

The arguments raised in the three extracts that you have just read are examples of a large literature. Many writers have explored these questions and have, through their reasoning, changed the emphasis of, or nature of, the moral obligation that they see as implicit in or characteristic of law. That this literature is itself large is interesting. It represents the fact that conscientious disobedience to law is often challenging both in practice and theoretically, and that when it arises theorists will adapt to the particular circumstances that generated it and attempt to reformulate ideas about obligation to law and justified disobedience of it. Out of such re-formulations the large literature has arisen. It can appear that what is represented is like adding 'angels to a pin-head', the differences become very small. On the other hand some highly influential literature has developed from these exercises, such as that written by Mohatma Ghandi and Martin Luther King (see Bedau 1991, Pennock and Chapman 1970, Christenson 1986).

To complete this section of this chapter, what follows is a short extract from the nineteenth century writer Henry Thoreau who is thought of as the first explicitly to develop and use the idea of civil disobedience as a form of political protest, short of revolution. In his case the protest was against slavery and the government's use of revenues in support of it. Civil disobedience is often, in the literature, used to signify the difference between the revolutionary and the protester whose aim is not revolution. It can be understood as representing that person who generally accepts the legitimacy of the government and society within which she/he lives, but not one particular branch of executive policy and the laws associated with it. Thoreau makes out a case for civil disobedience as a right. His case is different from that of Zweibach, set out earlier. It is a case that seems to imply a position as far away from Socrates as is possible within the arguments of those not set on revolution. It is a position that argues positively for the right to disobey as a moral right (rather than Smith's whose argument is constructed as a negative, having disputed other positions). Thus, for Thoreau, there is no moral obligation to obey the law, only one to obey one's own conscience.

Thoreau (1849)

[The original title of this essay was 'Resistance to Civil Government'. It has been reprinted in many places, such as, in the form of a Peace News Pamphlet in 1963. The pamphlet's significance seems to stem from its relevance to Mohatma Ghandi who apparently came across it while in prison (borrowing it from the prison library) following his imprisonment after taking part in a civil disobedience protest.]

… Must the citizen ever for a moment, or in the least degree, resign his conscience to the legislator? Why has every man a conscience, then? I think that we should be men first, and subjects afterward. It is not desirable to cultivate a respect for the law, so much as for the right. The only obligation which I have a right to assume, is to do at any time what I think right. It is truly enough said, that a corporation has no conscience; but a corporation of conscientious men is a corporation *with* a conscience. Law never made men a whit more just; and, by means of their respect for it, even the well-disposed are daily made the agents of injustice. A common and natural result of an undue respect for law is, that you see a file of soldiers, colonel, captain, corporal, privates, powder-monkeys, and all, marching in admirable order over hill and dale to the wars, against their wills, ay, against their common sense and consciences, which makes it very steep marching indeed, and produces a palpitation of the heart.

…

The mass of men serve the state thus, not as men mainly, but as machines, with their bodies. They are the standing army, and the militia, jailers, constables, *posse comitatus*, etc. In most cases there is no free exercise whatever of the judgment or of the moral sense; but they put themselves on a level with wood and earth and stones; and wooden men can perhaps be manufactured that will serve the purpose as well.

...

Unjust laws exist; shall we be content to obey them, or shall we endeavour to amend them, and obey them until we have succeeded, or shall we transgress them at once? Men generally, under such a government as this, think that they ought to wait until they have persuaded the majority to alter them. They think that, if they should resist, the remedy would be worse than the evil. But it is the fault of the government itself that the remedy is worse than the evil. *It* makes it worse. Why is it not more apt to anticipate and provide for reform? Why does it not cherish its wise minority? Why does it cry and resist before it is hurt? Why does it not encourage its citizens to be on the alert to point out its faults, and *do* better than it would have them? Why does it always crucify Christ, and excommunicate Copernicus and Luther, and pronounce Washington and Franklin rebels?

...

If the injustice is part of the necessary friction of the machine of government, let it go, let it go: perchance it will wear smooth – certainly the machine will wear out. If the injustice has a spring, or a pulley, or a rope, or a crank, exclusively for itself then perhaps you may consider whether the remedy will not be worse than the evil; but if it is of such a nature that it requires you to be the agent of injustice to another, then, I say, break the law. Let your life be a counter friction to stop the machine. What I have to do is to see, at any rate, that I do not lend myself to the wrong which I condemn.

As for adopting the way which the State has provided for remedying the evil, I know not of such ways. They take too much time, and a man's life will be gone. I have other affairs to attend to.

...

I do not hesitate to say, that those who call themselves Abolitionists should at once effectively withdraw their support, both in person and in property, from the government of Massachusetts, and not wait until they constitute a majority of one, before they suffer the right to prevail through them. I think that it is enough that they have God on their side, without waiting for that other one. Moreover, any man more right than his neighbours constitutes a majority of one already.

...

I have paid no poll-tax for six years. I was put into a jail once on this account, for one night; and, as I stood considering the walls of solid stone, two or three feet thick, the door of wood and iron, a foot thick, and the iron grating which strained the light, I could not help being struck with the foolishness of that institution which treated me as if I were mere flesh and blood and bones, to be locked up. I wondered that it should have concluded at length that this was the best use that it could put me to, and had never thought to avail itself of my services in some way. I saw that, if there was a wall of stone between me and my townsmen, there was a still more difficult one to climb or break through, before they could get to be as free as I was. I did not for a moment feel confined, and the walls seemed a great waste of stone and mortar. I felt as I alone of all my townsmen had paid my tax.

...

I have never declined paying the highway tax, because I am as desirous of being a good neighbour as I am of being a bad subject; and, as for supporting schools, I am doing my part to educate my fellow-countrymen now. It is for no particular item in the tax-bill that I refuse to pay it.

...

I do not wish to quarrel with any man or nation. I do not wish to split hairs to make fine distinctions, or set myself up as better than my neighbours. I seek rather, I may say, even an excuse for conforming to the laws of the land. I am but too ready to conform to them ... the Constitution with all its faults, is very good; the law and the courts are very respectable; even this Sate and this American government are, in many respects, very admirable and rare things, to be thankful for.

...

The authority of government, even such as I am willing to submit to – for I will cheerfully obey those who know and can do better than I, and in many things even those who neither know nor can do so well – is still an impure one: to be strictly just, it must have the sanction and consent of the governed. It can have no pure right over my person and property but what I concede to it. The progress from an absolute to a limited monarchy, from a limited monarchy to a democracy, is a progress toward a true respect for the individual. Even the Chinese philosopher was wise enough to regard the individual as the basis of the empire. Is a democracy, such as we know it, the last improvement possible in government? Is it not possible to take a step further towards recognising and organising the rights of man? There will never be a really free and enlightened State, until the State comes to recognise the individual as a higher and independent power, from which all its own power and authority are derived, and treats him accordingly.

...

Dworkin: integrating legal theory and the justification for disobedience to law

In an earlier piece of writing on 'Civil Disobedinece', Dworkin explored the possibilities for justified disobedience through applying his theory of law that sees law as containing right answers to legal decisions, but allowing for considerable dispute about what those right answers might be (Dworkin 1977, Chapter 8). Such dispute facilitates justified disobedience. Dworkin rejects the idea that a citizen is committed to strict interpretation of the law that allows no scope for his/her own evaluation of its validity. The development of the law, he argues, should be permitted through testing questions of validity in the courts. Thus, disobedience of the law might be justified as long as the individual citizen submits themselves to the courts to test out their view of what the law is and their obligation to it. But, he goes further than this. He rejects the idea that once the court, even the highest court, has decided the matter the citizen's obligation to obey becomes absolute. He illustrates how highest appeal courts (in his examples, the Supreme Court of the United States) overrule earlier judgments, and how this leaves further opportunity for justified disobedience to test the validity of the law in question. He believes that 'In the United States, at least, almost any law which a significant number of people would be tempted to disobey on moral grounds would be doubtful – if not clearly invalid – on constitutional grounds as well. The constitution makes our conventional political morality relevant to the question of validity ...' (Dworkin 1977, 208) And, what the court has determined to be one's obligation is not decisive. 'A person's allegiance is to the law, not to any particular person's view of what the law is.' (Dworkin 1977, 214) (The relevance of this argument to those who participate in civil disobedience campaigns should not be ignored. Consider this example. Many anti-nuclear weapons protestors have over the years been charged with a variety of offences: public order offences associated with breach of the peace, criminal damage and criminal trespass offences at military bases. Some protestors refuse to raise 'technical' defences. Others are happy to do so. Such defences, which amount to questioning what the valid law relevant to the situation is, take a number of forms. On trespass and damage to military land, defences are raised about bye-laws demarcating such land as military land. On public order offences connected to breach of the peace, defences are raised that the aims of the protest are to 'keep the peace', and in support of this the argument is presented that, since any use of nuclear weapons would be illegal under international law, there is legal justification in preventing preparation for such use. The Criminal Law Act 1967, s 3, that permits reasonable action to prevent a crime, is raised in justification.)

For Dworkin, an earlier court's decision on the issue becomes only one factor that needs to be considered in determining 'allegiance' to law. Dworkin regards the identification of what is law as something that ordinary people can participate in. And because he believes that the identification of law is, to some significant degree, synonymous with identifying what is just and moral (see Chapters 8 and 9) the opinions of citizens as to what is so wrong as to require disobedience are an important source of data in such an exercise. Officials who encounter citizens challenging laws that they regard as unjust, have an opportunity to consider whether, in fact, the unjust law is truly law. For Dworkin, this is such a useful exercise that one cannot have too many opportunities (making the fact of a recent legal ruling less than definitive of the issue). Earlier in this chapter this was described as constructing a notion of obligation that is implicit in the legal system pertaining to liberal democracy. One that allows for a right to disobey in circumstances in which the act of disobedience in question is an assertion of a right, which assertion is consistent with the rights constituted within the system of law. For Dworkin, the right in question is the right of every citizen to form their own view on what the law is, and if necessary, through their 'disobedience', to uphold it.

Dworkin thinks that not only the citizen but also legal officials should try to respect that right by, for example, deciding not to prosecute certain potential civil disobedience defendants, acquitting those defendants, or accepting mitigation of sentence if prosecuted and found guilty. And those in positions of legislative competence should review laws that provoke such disobedience with a view to their amendment. His conclusions to these arguments are set out below.

Dworkin (1977, 220–221)

… It does not follow from the fact that our practice facilitates adjudication, and renders it more useful in developing the law, that a trial should follow whenever citizens do act by their own lights. The question arises in each case whether the issues are ripe for adjudication, and whether adjudication would settle these issues in a manner that would decrease the chance of, or remove the grounds for, further dissent.

In the draft cases, the answer to both these questions was negative: there was much ambivalence about the war, and uncertainty and ignorance about the scope of the moral issues involved in the draft. It was far from the best time for the court to pass on these issues, and tolerating dissent for a time was one way of allowing the debate to continue until it produced something clearer. Moreover, it was plain that an adjudication of the constitutional issues would not settle the law. Those who had doubts whether the draft was constitutional had the same doubts even after the Supreme Court said that it was. This is one of those cases, touching fundamental rights, in which our practices of precedent encourage such doubts.

Even if the prosecutor does not act, however, the underlying problem will be only temporarily relieved. So long as the law appears to make acts of dissent criminal, a man of conscience will face danger. What can Congress, which shares the responsibility of leniency, do to lessen this danger?

Congress can review the laws in question to see how much accommodation can be given the dissenters. Every program a legislature adopts is a mixture of policies and restraining principles. We accept loss of efficiency in crime detection and urban renewal, for example, so that we can respect the rights of accused criminals and compensate property owners for their damages. Congress can properly defer to its responsibility towards the dissenters by adjusting or compromising other policies. The relevant questions are these: What means can be found for allowing the greatest possible tolerance of conscientious dissent while minimizing its impact on policy? How strong is the government's responsibility for leniency in this case – how deeply is conscience involved, and how strong is the case that the law is invalid after all? How important is the policy in question – is interference with that policy too great a price to pay? These questions are no doubt too simple, nut they suggest the heart of the choices that must be made.

For the same reasons that those who counseled resistance should not have been prosecuted, I think that the law that makes this a crime should be repealed. The case is strong that this law abridges free speech. It certainly coerces conscience, and it probably serves no beneficial effect. If counseling would persuade only a few to resist who otherwise would not, the value of the restraint is small; if counseling would persuade many, that is an important political fact that should be known.

The issues are more complex, again, in the case of draft resistance itself. Those who believed that the war in Vietnam was itself a grotesque blunder would have favored any change in the law that made peace more likely. But if we take the position of those who think the war was necessary, then we must admit that a policy that continued the draft but wholly exempted dissenters would have been unwise. Two less drastic alternatives should have been considered, however: a volunteer army, and an expanded conscientious objector category that included those that found the war immoral. There is much to be said against both proposals, but once the requirement of respect for dissent is recognised, the balance of principle may be tipped in their favour.

So the case for not prosecuting conscientious draft offenders, and for changing the laws in their favour, was a strong one. It would have been unrealistic to expect this policy to prevail, however, for political pressures opposed it.

We must consider, therefore, what the courts could and should have done. A court might, of course, have upheld the arguments that the draft laws were in some way unconstitutional, in general or as applied to the defendants in the case at hand. Or it might acquit the defendants because the facts necessary for conviction are not proved. I shall not argue the constitutional issues, or the facts of any particular case. I want instead to suggest that a court ought not to convict, at least in some circumstances, even if it sustains the statutes and finds the facts as charged. The Supreme Court had not ruled on the chief arguments that the draft was unconstitutional, nor had it held that these arguments raised political questions that are not within its jurisdiction, when several of the draft cases arose. There are strong reasons why a Court should acquit in these circumstances even if it does then sustain the draft. It ought to acquit on the ground that before its decision the validity of the draft was doubtful, and it is unfair to punish men for disobeying a doubtful law.

There would be precedent for a decision along these lines. The Court has several times reversed criminal convictions, on due process grounds, because the law in question was too vague.

How far does this approach take us? It can be argued that it tells us very little about the justification for disobedience, or about the quality of acts of civil disobedience. Since the disobedience relates to a law whose constitutional validity is in question, the premise of the act of disobedience is that it is itself legal, rather than illegal action. Namely, if the authorities operated correctly they would determine either that it was premature to reach a final adjudication on these matters, or that no valid law has in fact been broken and therefore no punishment can be justified. It challenges those in authority to operate on the basis of a broad understanding of what the law is, one that at least permits questions of justice and rights to be explored as part of that understanding. And it treats cases of civil disobedience as opportunities for the law to test those criteria and allow the law to flourish. However, the tendency of such an argument is to accept that there is an absolute obligation to obey 'law', but that there are practically useful ways to allow citizens to challenge what the law is in particular circumstances. As a political practice this approach has limited scope. Most examples of civil disobedience revolve around disobeying a clear law rather than an unclear law. Just because there are always opportunities for those who disobey to follow a route of finding technical 'legal' arguments to justify their actions 'legally', in practice that is hardly the point of their actions. Simply put, in most cases they will be arguing that the law is clear, and clearly wrong, and that they are clearly right to disobey it. They raise the issue of the 'rightness' of their act, not simply its legality. To this argument Dworkin's defence might be that, in a liberal democratic society such as the United States with its particular constitutional arrangements, it is nearly always possible to subsume the first issue (the 'rightness' of the law) within the second (its legality).

Dworkin's second attempt to deal with these issues is more substantial, or at least addresses the claim of justified disobedience more squarely (Dworkin 1985, Chapter 4). However, it retains the link to his overall theory about the meaning of law, and needs to be evaluated in the context of that theory (see Chapters 8 and 9 above). Although he does not attempt to define civil disobedience, his arguments are based on the premise that those who undertake such action 'accept the fundamental legitimacy of both government and community: they act to acquit rather than to challenge their duty as citizens'. (Dworkin 1985, 105) His overall aim is a '*working* theory' (Dworkin 1985, 106). Dworkin assumes, and there is good reason to accept such an assumption, that acts of disobedience to law can be acts responding to all sorts of different laws about which people have strongly differing views, whether those views can be described as moral or political. If disobedience can only be justified by adjudicating on which of those views are sound and which not, then in a heterogeneous society no progress toward consistent standards of reasoning is likely. Indeed, as he shows in the course of his theory of law, questions attaching to law can be understood to reflect policy debates (the subject of politics) but are better interpreted as reflecting those of principle (the subject of law). Then how should we approach questions of principle? The key is to accept whatever strong convictions motivate the person who disobeys law out of conscience, rather than test the soundness of those convictions. Of course there might be some dispute as to what convictions merit any respect at all. But beyond such disputes 'we can at least hope to find rough agreement about the best answers to these questions [those relating to justified disobedience], even though we lack consensus about the substantive moral and strategic convictions in play.' (Dworkin 1985, 106) The soundness of the motivating conviction is thus not relevant to the working theory, only the fact that the act of disobedience in question is motivated by it. On this basis Dworkin distinguishes different motivations as representing different types of civil disobedience. These he classifies as 'integrity-based', 'justice-based' and 'policy-based'. Let us see how Dworkin describes these, while recognising that there may be a mix of motivations operating in respect of either individual acts of disobedience, or those reflected in group protest.

Dworkin (1985, 106–108)

When we take up the first question – about the right thing for people to do who believe laws are wrong – everything depends on which general *type* of civil disobedience we have in mind. I have so far been speaking as if the famous acts of civil disobedience all had the same motives and circumstances. But they did not, and we must now notice the differences. Someone who believes it would be deeply wrong to deny help to an escaped slave who knocks at the door, and even worse to turn him over to the authorities, thinks that the Fugitive Slave Act requires him to behave in an immoral way. His personal integrity, his conscience, forbids him to obey. Soldiers drafted to fight in a war they deem wicked are in the same position. I shall call civil disobedience by people in that circumstance 'integrity based'.

Contrast the moral position of the blacks who broke the law in the civil rights movement, who sat at forbidden lunch counters seeking the privilege of eating greasy hamburgers next to people who hated them. It would miss the point to say that they were there in deference to conscience, that they broke the law because they could not, with integrity, do what the law required. No one has a general moral duty to seek out and claim rights that he believes he has. They acted for a different reason: to oppose and reverse a program they believed unjust, a program of oppression by a majority of a minority. Those in the civil rights movement who broke the law and many civilians who broke it protesting the war in Vietnam thought the majority was pursuing its own interests and goals unjustly because it disregard of the rights of others, the rights of a domestic minority in the case of the civil rights movement and of another nation in the case of the war. This is 'justice-based' civil disobedience.

These first two kinds of civil disobedience involve, though in different ways, convictions of principle. There is a third kind which involves judgments of policy instead. People sometimes break the law not because they believe the program they oppose is immoral or unjust, in the ways described, but because they believe it very unwise, stupid, and dangerous for the majority as well as any minority. The recent protests against the deployment of American missiles in Europe, so far as they violated local law, were for the most part occasions of this third kind of civil disobedience, which I shall call 'policy-based'. If we tried to reconstruct the beliefs and attitudes of the women of Greenham Common in England, or of the people who occupied military bases in Germany, we would find that most – not all but most – did not believe that their government's decision to accept the missiles was the act of a majority seeking its own interest in violation of the rights of a minority or of another nation. They thought, rather, that the majority had made a tragically wrong choice from the common standpoint, from the standpoint of its own interests as much as those of anyone else. They aim, not to force the majority to keep faith with principles of justice, but simply to come to its senses.

There is an obvious danger in any analytic distinction that rests, as this one does, on differences between states of mind. Any political movement or group will include people of very different beliefs and convictions. Nor will any one person's convictions necessarily fall neatly into a prearranged category. Most of those who protested against the American war in Vietnam, for example, believed their government's policy was *both* unjust and stupid. Nevertheless, the distinction among types of civil disobedience (and the further distinctions I shall draw) are useful and important, because they allow us to ask hypothetical questions in something like the following way. We can try to identify the conditions under which acts of civil disobedience would be justified if the beliefs and motives of the actors were those associated with each type of disobedience, leaving us a further question whether the beliefs in play on a particular occasion might plausibly be thought to be or include beliefs of that sort.

In addition to considering the motive for disobeying, Dworkin considers the type of laws disobeyed and what he calls 'persuasive' and 'nonpersuasive' strategies of disobedience. Take the example of the integrity-based motive to disobey, 'when the law requires people to do what their conscience absolutely forbids'. (Dworkin 1985, 108) Does such a motive justify breaking any and every law? Dworkin's answer is no. 'Of course, violence and terrorism cannot be justified in this way. If someone's conscience will not let him obey some law, neither should it let him kill or harm innocent people.' (Dworkin 1985, 108) Some of the militant activities of anti-abortion campaigners in the United States, and some of those of militant anti-animal experiment campaigners in this country would run foul of Dworkin's prohibition here. However, their case is that Dworkin misleads by implying that the activities of these people are 'innocent'. In other words, as a working theory, it is of little value to those who have such strong moral objection to the activities of others, although it may be of importance to those in authority in justifying their actions (coercion) in response. Outside such 'extreme' cases, Dworkin sees no other necessary limitations to disobedience that is motivated in this way. In particular, because he recognises that it is principally 'defensive' rather than 'strategic', it often entails urgent action and therefore cannot wait for the deliberations of courts or legislatures. In this sense it can be nonpersuasive. Whereas a persuasive strategy 'hopes to force the majority to listen to arguments against its program', a nonpersuasive one aims 'to increase the cost of pursuing the program ... in the hope that the majority will find the new cost unacceptably high'. (Dworkin 1985, 109) With these elements Dworkin is able to prioritise those acts of disobedience that, he believes, a liberal democratic society ought to respect and try to accommodate, rather than those that are motivated by strong moral conviction, but nevertheless should not be tolerated. Here is Dworkin's analysis.

Dworkin (1985, 109–113)

... Integrity-based disobedience is defensive: it aims only that the actor not do something his conscience forbids. Justice-based disobedience is, in contrast, instrumental and strategic: it aims at an overall goal – the dismantling of an immoral political program. So consequentialist qualifications appear in our theory of the latter that are out of place in any theory of the former. And a new distinction becomes imperative. Justice-based disobedience might use two main strategies to achieve its political goals. We might call the first a persuasive strategy. It hopes to force the majority to listen to arguments against its program, in the expectation that the majority will then change its mind and disapprove that program. The second strategy, then, is nonpersuasive. It aims not to change the majority's mind, but to increase the cost of pursuing the program the majority still favors, in the hope that the majority will find the new cost unacceptably high. There are many different forms of nonpersuasive strategy – many different ways of putting up the price – and some of them are more attractive, when available, than others. A minority may put up the price, for example, by making the majority choose between abandoning the program and sending them to jail. If the majority has the normal sympathies of decent people, this nonpersuasive strategy may be effective. At the other extreme lie nonpersuasive strategies of intimidation, fear, and anxiety, and in between strategies of inconvenience and financial expense: tying up traffic or blocking imports or preventing official agencies or departments from functioning effectively or functioning at all.

Obviously, persuasive strategies improve the justification for justice-based disobedience. But they do so only when conditions are favorable for their success. Conditions were indeed favorable for the civil rights movement in the United States in the 1960s. The rhetoric of American politics had for some decades been freighted with the vocabulary of equality, and the Second World War had heightened the community's sense of the injustice of racial persecution. I do not deny that there was and remains much hypocrisy in that rhetoric and alleged commitment. But the hypocrisy itself provides a lever for persuasive strategies. The majority, even in the South, blushed when it was forced to look at its own laws. There was no possibility of a political majority saying, 'Yes, that is what we're doing. We're treating one section of the community as inferior to ourselves'. And then turning aside from that with equanimity. Civil disobedience forced everyone to look at what the majority could no longer, for a variety of reasons, ignore. So minds were changed, and the sharpest evidence of the change is the fact that halfway through the battle the law became an ally of the movement rather than its enemy.

Sometimes, however, persuasive strategies offer no great prospect of success because conditions are far from favorable, as in, perhaps, South Africa. When, if ever, are nonpersuasive strategies justified in justice-based disobedience? It goes too far, I think, to say they never are. The following carefully guarded statement seems better. If someone believes that a particular official program is deeply unjust, if the political process offers no realistic hope of reversing that program soon, if there is no possibility of effective persuasive civil disobedience, if nonviolent nonpersuasive techniques are available that hold out a reasonable prospect of success, if these techniques do not threaten to be counterproductive, then that person does the right thing, given his convictions, to use those nonpersuasive means. This may strike some readers as excessively weak; but each of the qualifications I listed seems necessary.

I come finally to policy-based civil disobedience: when the actors seek to reverse a policy because they think it dangerously unwise. They believe the policy they oppose is a bad policy for everyone, not just for some minority; they think they know what is in the majority's own interest, as well as their own, better than the majority knows. Once again we can distinguish persuasive from nonpersuasive strategies in this new context. Persuasive strategies aim to convince the majority that its decision, about its own best interests, is wrong, and so to disfavor the program it formerly favored. Nonpersuasive strategies aim rather to increase the price the majority must pay for a program it continues to favor.

The distinction between persuasive and nonpersuasive strategies is even more important in the case of policy-based than justice-based disobedience, because it seems problematic that nonpersuasive strategies could ever be justified in a working theory of the former. In order to see why, we must notice a standing problem for any form of civil disobedience. Most people accept that the principle of majority rule is essential to democracy; I mean the principle that once the law is settled, by the verdict of the majority's representatives, it must be obeyed by the minority as well. Civil disobedience, in all its various forms and strategies, has a stormy and complex relationship with majority rule. It does not reject the principle entirely, as a radical revolutionary might; civil disobedients remain democrats at heart. But it claims a qualification or exception of some kind, and we might contrast and judge the different types and strategies of disobedience in combination, by asking what kind of exception each claims, and whether it is consistent to demand that exception and still claim general allegiance to the principle as a whole.

Persuasive strategies, whether they figure in justice-based or policy-based disobedience, have a considerable advantage here. For someone whose goal is to persuade the majority to change its mind, by accepting arguments he believes are sound arguments, plainly does not challenge the principle of majority rule in any fundamental way. He accepts that in the end the majority's will must be done and asks only, by way of qualification or annex to this principle, that the majority be forced to consider arguments that might change its mind even when it seems initially unwilling to do so. Nonpersuasive strategies lack this explanation, and that is why, particularly in a democracy, they are always inferior from a moral point of view. But when nonpersuasive strategies are used, subject to the conditions I listed, in justice-based disobedience, they can at least appeal to a standing and well-understood exception to the majority-rule principle, not only in the United States but in Germany and many other countries as well. I mean the exception assumed by the constitutional power of judges to hold acts of the majority's representatives void when, in the judge's view, these decisions outrage the principles of justice embedded in the Constitution. That power assumes that the majority has no right to act unjustly, to abuse the power it holds by serving its own interests at the expense of a minority's rights. I do not claim that judicial review by a constitutional court is a kind of nonpersuasive civil disobedience. But only that judicial review rests on a qualification to the principle of majority rule-the qualification that the majority can be forced to be just, against its will-to which nonpersuasive strategies might also appeal in order to explain why their challenge to majority rule is different from outright rejection of it.

Policy-based disobedience cannot make that appeal, because the standing qualification I just named does not extend to matters of policy. Once it is conceded that the question is only one of the common interest – that no question of distinct majority and minority interests arises – the conventional reason for constraining a majority gives way, and only very dubious candidates apply for its place. Someone who hopes not to persuade the majority to his point of view by forcing it to attend to his arguments, but rather to make it pay so heavily for its policy that it will give way without having been convinced, must appeal to some form of elitism or paternalism to justify what he does. And any appeal of *that* form does seem to strike at the roots of the principle of majority rule, to attack its foundations rather than simply to call for an elaboration or qualification of it. If that principle means anything, it means that the majority rather than some minority must in the end have the power to decide what is in their common interest.

So nonpersuasive means used in policy-based disobedience seems the least likely to be justified in any general working theory. I said earlier that most of those who sit in and trespass to protest the deployment of nuclear missiles in Europe have motives that make their disobedience policy-based. It is therefore important to consider whether they can plausibly consider the means they use to be persuasive means, and this in turn depends on whether conditions are sufficiently favorable for success of a persuasive strategy. The contrast between the civil rights movement and the antinuclear movement is in this respect reasonably sharp. It was obvious early in the civil rights movement that the sit-ins and other techniques of disobedience had persuasive force, because it was obvious that the issue was an issue of justice and that the movement had rhetorical tradition as well as justice on its side. It was only necessary to force enough people to look who would be ashamed to turn away. The questions of policy at the bottom of the nuclear controversy are, by contrast, signally complex. It is plainly not obvious, one way or the other, whether deployment of missiles in Europe is more likely to deter or provoke aggression, for example, or even what kind of an argument would be a good argument for either view. It is hard to see in these circumstances how discussion could be illuminated or debate strengthened by illegal acts. On the contrary, such acts seem likely to make the public at large pay less attention to the complex issues on which any intelligent view must be based, because it will think it has at least one simple and easy-to-understand reason for sticking with the policy its leaders have adopted: that any change in that policy would mean giving way to civil blackmail.

If this is right, those who now support trespass and other illegal acts as protest against nuclear policy must, if they are honest with themselves, concede that they have in mind a nonpersuasive strategy. They aim to raise the price of a policy they believe a tragic mistake, to make that price so high that the majority will yield, though this means surrendering to minority coercion. So they must face the question I said is highly problematic, whether a robust working theory could justify that kind of disobedience. It might be helpful to consider whether we would think nonpersuasive means proper as acts of disobedience protesting other, non-nuclear policies many people think gravely mistaken. Would nonpersuasive disobedience be justified against bad economic policy? The governments of the United States and Britain are now following economic policies that I think unwise because they will work against the general interest in the long as well as the short run. I also think, as it happens, that these economic policies are unjust; even if they were in the best interests of the majority, they would still be unfair to a minority that has rights against that majority. But I mean to set that further claim of injustice aside for this argument and assume only that many people like me think monetarist policy bad from everyone's point of view. Would the fact that we believed this justify illegal acts whose point was to impose so high a price, in inconvenience and insecurity, that the majority would abandon its economic policy, though it remained convinced that it was the best policy?

I think the answer is no. But of course the risks of bad nuclear strategy are vastly greater than the risks of mistaken economic policy. Does the fact that so much more is at stake destroy the analogy? Jurgen Habermas has argued that political legitimacy is threatened when decisions of enormous consequence are taken though only something like a bare or thin majority supports the decision. Can we justify nonpersuasive civil disobedience against the decision to accept the missiles by appealing to that principle? The difficulty is evident. For exactly the same principle would argue against government's deciding not to deploy the missiles. That is as much a decision as the decision to adopt them, and it appears from recent polls that it would not command even a bare majority much less the extraordinary majority Habermas' principle would require. The present controversy, in short, is symmetrical in a way that undermines the value of his principle. Those who oppose the missiles believe that deployment will cause irreparable harm because it threatens the very existence of the community. But that is exactly what people on the other side – and we are assuming that there are slightly more of these – would think about a decision not to deploy the missiles. They think that this decision would make nuclear war more likely, and threaten the existence of the community. So no government violates any principle of legitimacy in accepting missiles that it would not have violated by rejecting them.

We cannot be dogmatic that no argument, better than I have been able to construct, will be found for civil disobedience in these circumstances. We are justified only in the weaker conclusion that those who advocate this form of disobedience now have the burden of showing how a working theory could accept it. They may say that this challenge is irrelevant; that nice questions about which justifications could be accepted by all sides to a dispute become trivial when the world is about to end. There is wisdom in this impatience, no doubt, which I do not mean to deny. But once we abandon the project of this essay, once we make the rightness of what we do turn entirely on the soundness of what we think, we cannot expect honor or opportunity from those who think it is we who are naive and stupid.

There is, in Dworkin's reasoning, as coherent or incoherent, useful or useless as you might judge it, a particular strand. It is that law, especially when dealing with hard cases, is involved in a search for the 'right' answer. When citizens engage in acts of disobeying the law they are to be respected for acquitting, rather than denying, their duties as citizens. To encapsulate the underlying political morality of liberal democracy into legal reasoning involves citizens as well as lawyers and judges. Whereas legal positivists seem to have a highly restricted role for, and idea of, the legal obligations of citizens vis-à-vis the law, Dworkin tries to bring the activities of ordinary citizens within the parameters of legal theory. Thus, he has to try to accommodate the activities of citizens when they disobey, and show how legal officials can consistently respond without necessarily assuming that all disobedience is either simply illegal or deserving of punishment.

A comparison and contrast with another theorist may be useful. You have the opportunity to study this theorist, another liberal political theorist, John Rawls and his *A Theory of Justice*, in Chapter 15.

John Rawls on civil disobedience and conscientious objection

Rawls defines civil disobedience as 'a public, nonviolent, conscientious yet political act contrary to law usually done with the aim of bringing about a change in the law or policies of the government'. Like Dworkin he attempts to account for the 'appropriateness of this form of protest within a free society'. However the sole criterion that this political act relies on is the 'sense of justice of the majority of the community' (Rawls 1973, 364). Thus he argues:

> It should also be noted that civil disobedience is a political act not only in the sense that it is addressed to the majority that holds political power, but also because it is an act guided and justified by political principles, that is, by the principles of justice which regulate the constitution and social institutions generally. In justifying civil disobedience one does not appeal to principles of personal morality or to religious doctrines, though these may coincide with and support one's claims; and it goes without saying that civil disobedience cannot be grounded solely on group or self-interest. Instead one invokes the commonly shared conception of justice that underlies the political order. It is assumed that in a reasonably just democratic regime there is a public conception of justice by reference to which citizens regulate their political affairs and interpret the constitution. The persistent and deliberate violation of the basic principles of this conception over any extended period of time, especially the infringement of the fundamental equal liberties, invites either submission or resistance. By engaging in civil disobedience a minority forces the majority to consider whether it wishes to have its actions construed in this way, or whether, in view of the common sense of justice, it wishes to acknowledge the legitimate claims of the minority. (Rawls 1973, 365–66)

As far as the means available to the person engaged in civil disobedience, Rawls believes that the act must be public, 'engaged in openly with fair notice', nonviolent and accepting of the legal consequences (the punishment). 'It expresses disobedience to law within the limits of fidelity to law, although it is at the outer edge thereof.' (Rawls 1973, 366) And, if civil disobedience fails, then Rawls sees a possible justification for 'militant action or other kinds of resistance', although he does not explore these matters in depth, which might operate outside a 'nearly just constitutional regime' (Rawls 1973, 368).

With his analysis of civil disobedience Rawls can be seen to offer a similar variant to Dworkin's justice-based disobedience, but does not, in contrast, appear to accept the reasoning that Dworkin offers for integrity-based disobedience. Indeed, that category Rawls mainly refers to as conscientious refusal. Unlike civil disobedience, which Rawls accepts as potentially legitimate within certain bounds: 'I assume that there is a limit on the extent to which civil disobedience can be engaged in without leading to a breakdown in the respect for law and the constitution thereby setting in motion consequences unfortunate for all. There is also an upper bound on the ability of the public forum to handle such forms of dissent ... the effectiveness of civil disobedience as a form of protest declines beyond a certain point; and those contemplating it must consider these constraints.' (Rawls 1973, 374), Rawls also has serious reservations about the legitimacy of conscientious refusal in a nearly just society.

His explanation, which you can consider either for its potential criticism of, or further elaboration on Dworkin's reasoning, is set out below.

Rawls (1973, 368–371)

56. THE DEFINITION OF CONSCIENTIOUS REFUSAL

...

Conscientious refusal is noncompliance with a more or less direct legal injunction or administrative order. It is refusal since an order is addressed to us and, given the nature of the situation, whether we accede to it is known to the authorities. Typical examples are the refusal of the early Christians to perform certain acts of piety prescribed by the pagan state, and the refusal of the Jehovah's Witnesses to salute the flag. Other examples are the unwillingness of a pacifist to serve in the armed forces, or of a soldier to obey an order that he thinks is manifestly contrary to the moral law as it applies to war. Or again, in Thoreau's case, the refusal to pay a tax on the grounds that to do so would make him an agent of grave injustice to another. One's action is assumed to be known to the authorities, however much one might wish, in some cases, to conceal it. Where it can be covert, one might speak of conscientious evasion rather than conscientious refusal. Covert infractions of a fugitive slave law are instances of conscientious evasion.

There are several contrasts between conscientious refusal (or evasion) and civil disobedience. First of all, conscientious refusal is not a form of address appealing to the sense of justice of the majority. To be sure, such acts are not generally secretive or covert, as concealment is often impossible anyway. One simply refuses on conscientious grounds to obey a command or to comply with a legal injunction. One does not invoke the convictions of the community, and in this sense conscientious refusal is not an act in the public forum. Those ready to withold obedience recognize that there may be no basis for mutual understanding; they do not seek out occasions for disobedience as a way to state their cause. Rather, they bide their time hoping that the necessity to disobey will not arise. They are less optimistic than those undertaking civil disobedience and they may entertain no expectation of changing laws or policies. The situation may allow no time for them to make their case, or again there may not be any chance that the majority will be receptive to their claims.

Conscientious refusal is not necessarily based on political principles; it may be founded on religious or other principles at variance with the constitutional order. Civil disobedience is an appeal to a commonly shared conception of justice, whereas conscientious refusal may have other grounds. For example, assuming that the early Christians would not justify their refusal to comply with the religious customs of the Empire by reasons of justice but simply as being contrary to their religious convictions, their argument would not be political; nor, with similar qualifications, are the views of a pacifist, assuming that wars of self-defense at least are recognized by the conception of justice that underlies a constitutional regime. Conscientious refusal may, however, be grounded on political principles. One many decline to go along with a law thinking that it is so unjust that complying with it is simply out of the question. This would be the case if, say, the law were to enjoin our being the agent of enslaving another, or to require us to submit to a similar fate. These are patent violations of recognized political principles.

It is a difficult matter to find the right course when some men appeal to religious principles in refusing to do actions which, it seems, are required by principles of political justice. Does the pacifist possess an immunity from military service in a just war, assuming that there are such wars? Or is the state permitted to impose certain hardships for noncompliance? There is a temptation to say that the law must always respect the dictates of conscience, but this cannot be right. As we have seen in the case of the intolerant, the legal order must regulate men's pursuit of their religious interests so as to realize the principle of equal liberty; and it may certainly forbid religious practices such as human sacrifice, to take an extreme case. Neither religiosity nor conscientiousness suffice to protect this practice. A theory of justice must work out from its own point of view how to treat those who dissent from it. The aim of a well-ordered society, or one in a state of near justice, is to preserve and strengthen the institutions of justice. If a religion is denied its full expression, it is presumably because it is in violation of the equal liberties of others. In general, the degree of tolerance accorded opposing moral conceptions depends upon the extent to which they can be allowed an equal place within a just system of liberty.

If pacificism is to be treated with respect and not merely tolerated, the explanation must be that it accords reasonably well with the principles of justice, the main exception arising from its attitude toward engaging in a just war (assuming here that in some situations wars of self-defense are justified). The political principles recognized by the community have a certain affinity with the doctrine the pacifist professes. There is a common abhorrence of war and the use of force, and a belief in the equal status of men as moral persons. And given the tendency of nations, particularly great powers, to engage in war unjustifiably and to set in motion the apparatus of the state to suppress dissent, the respect accorded to pacifism serves the purpose of alerting citizens to the wrongs that governments are prone to commit in their name. Even though his views are not altogether sound, the warnings and protests that a pacifist is disposed to express may have the result that on balance the principles of justice are more rather than less secure. Pacifism as a natural departure from the correct doctrine conceivably compensates for the weakness of men in living up to their professions.

It should be noted that there is, of course, in actual situations no sharp distinction between civil disobedience and conscientious refusal. Moreover the same action (or sequence of actions) may have strong elements of both. While there are clear cases of each, the contrast between them is intended as a way of elucidating the interpretation of civil disobedience and its role in a democratic society. Given the nature of this way of acting as a special kind of political appeal, it is not usually justified until other steps have been taken within the legal framework. By contrast this requirement often fails in the obvious cases of legitimate conscientious refusal. In a free society no one may be compelled, as the early Christians were, to perform religious acts in violation of equal liberty, nor must a soldier comply with inherently evil commands while waiting an appeal to higher authority. These remarks lead up to the question of justification.

Addendum

The materials and commentary found in this chapter do not cover all of the philosophical argument that can be made. In addition, disobedience to law is not simply a philosophical question. Abstract discussion of the individual's right to disobey law ignores the actual circumstances that lead to politically significant claims of legitimate disobedience. If acknowledged at all in the theories discussed in this chapter, those claims become examples that illustrate, or inspire, abstract categories of justified disobedience (as we have seen with Dworkin's analysis). This approach fails to recognise the fact that politically significant disobedience to law is not simply an individual matter, but a clash between law and other institutions, belief systems, knowledges or systems of communication. And this approach also engenders a debate that assumes the centrality of law. Some of the other theories explored in this book invite one to view this topic in a completely different manner. For example, what Dworkin calls 'integrity-based' disobedience can be re-stated within autopoietic theory (see Chapter 18) as 'deafness' to law, a consequence of a rival system of communication that gives meaning to its own operations in a manner which gives legal communications no purchase on events. Foucaultian analysis (see Chapter 19) invites one to engage with the conditions that make obedience to law possible. The sovereign's edict, accompanied by a threat of violence, penetrates only marginally into social life, unless it can ride on the back of technologies and knowledges that create subjects who can transmit power. The technologies and knowledges that transmit power also create the conditions for its resistance. Such resistance or disobedience does not assume the centrality of law, it creates the conditions for governmentality as a condition for law. Both of these theories challenge the assumptions that underlie the philosophical discussion in this chapter of the basis and limits of law's power, or its relevance to understanding real events.

It seems appropriate to conclude this chapter by expressing a particular point of view. Civil disobedience as a political praxis is an attempt to demonstrate that acts of disobedience have greater moral value, in the particular circumstances, than the actions of those with legal authority. It operates from the premise that those with legal authority 'ought' to be acting with moral authority as well. This is reminiscent of the famous statement by Eldridge Cleaver, the writer who you might recall reading in the introductory chapter to this book: 'What we're saying today is that you're either part of the solution or you're part of the problem.' (Speech in San Francisco, 1968, in Scheer 1969, 32) One is appealing to some model of what legal authority ought to be, or how it ought to react. As such, legal positivism, which concentrates on the ability of law to exist without morality, and neglects the bases through which law might be moral, says nothing about the model, or premise, through which this praxis is legitimated. Thus civil disobedience as a form of praxis, or a philosophy about that praxis, remains locked inside the natural law tradition.

Further Reading

Many of the references given in this chapter could usefully be followed up if you wish to undertake further reading. But, in addition, some of the classic essays on civil disobedience can be found in Bedau 1990. Some further essays that develop the kinds of analysis presented in this chapter can be found in Edmundson 1999, Pennock and Chapman 1970. For a historical account of 'political trials' arising from disobedience to law, Christenson 1986. For a critical attack on any limits to disobeying the law (and thus on much of the reasoning in this chapter), Zinn 1968. As alternative introductions to the issues developed here, McCoubrey 1997 (with a focus on legal theory), Greenwalt 1987 (with a focus on ethics).

Questions

1. Breaking the law can have many and varied consequences. To what extent (if at all) are these relevant for determining whether there is an obligation to obey the law? Are these concerns of especial relevance to cases of civil disobedience?

2. 'It is logically inconsistent to argue for the morality of civil disobedience and claim to accept that there is a moral obligation to obey law.' Discuss.

3. Dworkin writes: 'Our legal system ... invites citizens to decide the strengths and weaknesses of legal arguments for themselves ... and to act on those judgements, although that permission is qualified by the limited threat that they may suffer if the courts do not agree.' Explain how this statement expresses elements of Dworkin's theory of civil disobedience. Does the statement accurately describe the citizen's obligation to the law?

4. 'Civil disobedience threatens to undermine what law promises: obligation without morality.' Discuss.

12 Punishment

James Penner

The justification of punishment poses one of the most difficult jurisprudential issues. There are several reasons for this. First, it is clearly one topic in philosophy upon which everyone has a view, regardless of how much they've thought about it. So there tends to be, at the outset, a lot of what might be called attitudinal or emotional noise surrounding the subject which can make it hard to focus on the merits or demerits of a particular argument. Our gut reactions can get in the way of our ability to appreciate the various positions. On the other hand of course, these initial dispositions, however untutored, are not inherently irrational; they've been formed from experience, and they provide an interest in the subject which may be wanting in others, and no philosopher will look down his nose at a vigorous discussion, however prompted. Light can arise from heat. Secondly, for any person with any moral sensitivity whatsoever, our intuitions seem to cut both ways: punishment seems to be, like war, something which regardless of the good it may do, or the rightfulness of doing it, has a kind of intrinsic nastiness, or callousness, or wastefulness, which is offensive. Nevertheless, given human nature, or the human condition, or the human predicament, punishing people seems to be something that, sometimes, it is right to do, or that we must do. It therefore seems plausible, despite the prima facie wrong that punishment presents, that we can justify the practice in one way or another (though not all would agree; the outright abolition of punishment has been pressed).

In this chapter we will look at (1) the debate between retributivists (desert theorists) and deterrence theorists over the justification of punishment; (2) Expressive or communicative theories of punishment; and (3) the anti-punishment perspective surrounding the 'restorative justice' movement.

I Deterrence Theory versus Retributivism (or Desert Theory)

The debate between (1) those who justify punishment on the basis that the evil of treating criminals harshly is outweighed by the good is does by *deterring* people from committing crimes, and (2) those who claim that punishment is the appropriate moral response to criminal acts because the perpetrators *deserve* to be punished, is the traditional clash of viewpoints that colours all other discussions of the subject. What is sometimes missed in observing the contest between them is what these theories actually share. Both deterrence theorists and retributivists wish to explain why it is legitimate to inflict harm on certain kinds of offenders of morality, those who act wickedly or evilly or criminally; at heart, both of these theories defend punishment as morally just. Secondly, both roughly share the commitment to the view that the severity of punishment should be in proportion to the seriousness of the crime (for the deterrence theorist, so as to cause the least disutility to the offender that will at the same time effectively deter others from offending and thereby causing a similar disutility, the (ultimately contingent but widely shared) presumption being that more serious crimes will warrant more severe punishments on this calculation; for the retributivist because the more serious the crime, the more severe the punishment that the offender deserves); and both wish to explain why it is that punishment is reserved as a response to only certain kinds of actions (for the deterrence theorist, to those acts where punishment will serve as a deterrent; for retributivists, to those acts which reveal an evil or wicked determination to do wrong).

What separates the two positions, and separates them fundamentally, is how they go about explaining why punishment is legitimate. Desert theory or retributivism, whose most theoretically demanding justifications were provided by the Enlightenment thinkers Kant and Hegel, is founded on the intuitively attractive thought that a criminal deserves his punishment. The challenge forever faced by retributivists is that of articulating the notion of desert, in particular that a criminal deserves the infliction of 'hard treatment', from fines and community service orders to bodily pain, imprisonment, or death, in the face of the challenge that retribution is nothing more than philosophically dressed-up *revenge*, the irrational, emotional, and unjustifiably barabaric assuaging of hurt feelings and harm by inflicting hurt on their perpetrator.

Deterrence theory is one element of a generally 'consequentialist' approach to moral issues. Consequentialists, utilitarians being a prime example, hold that the moral rightness of actions turns on their consequences, in particular how such actions affect the lives of persons. Different consequentialists measure the value or disvalue of consequences in different ways. For example, Bentham's 'felicific' calculus was directed to whether an action caused pleasure or pain. (More precisely, the act to be morally preferred is that which causes the greatest excess of pleasure over pain, or results in less pain than any alternative action.) Perhaps the form of consequentialism which commands the most attention nowadays is one which frames 'the good' not in terms of a notion of 'pleasure over pain', but in terms of an individual's realisation in his life of a plurality of distinct values, such as health, friendship, participation in a community, aesthetic experience, and so on. A consequentialist approach to punishment is broader than a deterrence approach because punishment, or more broadly, dealing with offenders, can be an occasion for the realisation of more consequences than simply deterring people from committing crimes. The rehabilitation of the offender, his incapacitation (preventing him from committing further crimes), or the reparation of the victim (by, for example, requiring the offender to repair the damage the crime caused) are all possible goals which a comprehensive consequentialist approach to dealing with offenders may incorporate. A broad notion of 'reparation' underlies the 'restorative justice' approach to offending which will be considered in Part III. We focus here on deterrence theory because it is the element of the consequentialist approach which most sharply conflicts with desert theory, and because it has historically formed such a central element of the consequentialist approach.

While the roots of deterrence theory stretch back to Plato, and though it was first expounded in a thorough way in modern times by Beccaria, it was Jeremy Bentham who articulated a nuanced theory of deterrence which was linked to a general and well worked-out comprehensive moral theory, his utilitarianism, of course.

In *An Introduction to the Principles of Morals and Legislation* Bentham (1982) set out in his customary exacting detail the circumstances in which it was meet on utilitarian terms to inflict suffering, and the basic point was that punishment should be exacted only where, and only in such amounts, as would, by deterring wrongdoing, cause an amount of utility that would outweigh the disutility the punishment causes the offender. This cost/benefit analysis approach to the justification of punishment is at the same time the theory's greatest strength and its greatest weakness. It is the former because it is such an eminently sensible and intuitively compelling rationale. We punish in order to keep the levels of crime to a reasonable minimum. It is as simple as that. It is the latter, a great weakness, for on these terms the duty or right to punish an offender is straightforwardly contingent on how much good the punishment will do – on how the utilitarian 'felicific' calculus turns out. So we do not punish 'as of right' in response to offending, so to speak, but whenever punishing people will deter others. And it is easy to conjure up hypothetical cases in which, because of the way the facts are shaped, deterrence theory would require punishing the innocent, excessively punishing, and so on; some examples are elaborated by McCloskey in the first reading; the classic is the case of a sheriff in a racist southern county in the United States who can stop riots and the lynching of blacks following an alleged rape by a black man by hanging a black man whom he knows to be innocent. On the utilitarian calculus, the hanging appears to be justified, indeed required, for it will save the lives of other blacks who will otherwise be lynched. But how, queries the desert theorist, can the punishment, indeed the execution, of an innocent person be morally right? The typical response to these sorts of examples is given by Sprigge in the second reading, which is to blunt the force of these examples by pointing out the somewhat fantastic array of facts, and challenging whether the utilitarian calculation has been rightly undertaken. But this pair of readings shows how ultimately the persuasiveness of the deterrence theorist turns on whether we accept that in the vast majority of cases, the facts do work out in such a way that punishment provides a properly measured deterrent.

Deterrence theory was largely accepted as the only sound philosophical justification of punishment for much of this century, but its dominance began to become unstuck in the 1970s. Partly this had to do with a re-invigoration of non-utilitarian theories in moral and political philosophy generally (see the discussion of Rawl's revival of political philosophy in Chapter 15), but had also to do with a disenchantment with the deterrent and rehabilitative effects of punishment (not, as we have seen, the same thing, but often lumped together because in both cases the efficacy of punishment turned on its ability to achieve certain desired outcomes, ie was consequentialist in orientation), often characterised by the slogan 'nothing works'. At the same time, advocates of prisoners' rights and philosophers interested in moral rights began to attack the way in which deterrence theory treated the punished not as individuals with moral standing, but rather as part of the means of achieving social goals (See Duff 1996, 1–4). Since that time, deterrence theory in a pure form has been largely on the defensive, though broader consequentialist approaches to punishment have become vigorous contenders in the philosophical debate; the expressive, communicative and penitential theories of punishment discussed in Part II provide some examples. The first reading is a good example of a piece which formed part of the 'retributivist revival', and the second is a utilitarian reply.

McCloskey (1965, 249–63)

At first glance there are many obvious considerations which seem to suggest a utilitarian approach to punishment. Crime is an evil and what we want to do is not so much to cancel it out after it occurs as to prevent it. To punish crime when it occurs is, at best, an imperfect state of affairs. Further, punishment, invoking as it does evils such as floggings, imprisonment, and death, is something which does not commend itself to us without argument. An obvious way of attempting to justify such deliberately created evils would be in terms of their utility.

This is how crime and punishment impress on first sight. A society in which there was no crime and no punishment would be a much better society than one with crime and resulting punishments. And punishment, involving evils such as deliberately inflicting suffering and even death, and consequential evils such as the driving of some victims into despair and even insanity, etc, harming and even wrecking their subsequent lives, and often also the lives of their relatives and dependents, obviously needs justification. To argue that it is useful, that good results come from such punishment, is to offer a more plausible justification than many so-called retributive justifications. It is obviously more plausible to argue that punishment is justified if and because it is useful than to argue that punishment is justified because society has a right to express its indignation at the actions of the offender, or because punishment annuls and cancels out the crime, or because the criminal, being a human being, merits respect and hence has a right to his punishment. Such retributive type justifications have some point, but they are nonetheless implausible in a way that the utilitarian justification is not.

...

II HOW OUR COMMON MORAL CONSCIOUSNESS VIEWS PUNISHMENT

...

Punishment which we commonly consider to be just is punishment which is deserved. To be deserved, punishment must be of an offender who is guilty of an offence in the morally relevant sense of 'offence'. For instance, the punishing of a man known to be innocent of any crime shocks our moral consciousness and is seen as a grave injustice. Similarly, punishment of a person not responsible for his behaviour, e.g. a lunatic, is evidently unjust and shocking. Punishment for what is not an offence in the morally significant sense of 'offence' is equally unjust. To punish a man who has tried his hardest to secure a job during a period of acute and extensive unemployment for 'having insufficient means of support', or to punish a person under a retroactive law is similarly unjust. So too, if the offence for which the person punished is one against a secret law which it was impossible for him to know of, the punishment is gravely unjust. Similarly, punishment of other innocent people – e.g. as scapegoats – to deter others, is unjust and morally wrong. So too is collective punishment – killing all the members of a village or family for the offences of one member. Whether such punishments successfully deter seems irrelevant to the question of their justice. Similarly, certain punishments of persons who are offenders in the morally relevant sense of 'offence' also impress us as gravely unjust. We now consider to have been gravely unjust the very severe punishments meted out to those punished by hanging or transportation and penal servitude for petty thefts in the 18th century. Comparable punishments, e.g. hanging for shoplifting from a food market, would be condemned today as equally unjust. It is conceivable that such unjust punishments may, in extreme circumstances, become permissible, but this would only be so if a grave evil has to be perpetrated to achieve a very considerable good.

In brief, our moral consciousness suggests that punishment, to be just, must be merited by the committing of an offence. It follows from this that punishment, to be justly administered, must involve care in determining whether the offending person is really a responsible agent. And it implies that the punishment must not be excessive. It must not exceed what is appropriate to the crime. We must always be able to say of the person punished that he deserved to be punished as he was punished. It is not enough to say that good results were achieved by punishing him. It is logically possible to say that the punishment was useful but undeserved, and deserved but not useful. It is not possible to say that the punishment was just although undeserved.

These features of ordinary moral thinking about just punishment appear to be features of which any defensible theory of punishment needs to take note. Punishment of innocent people – through collective punishments, scapegoat punishment, as a result of inefficient trial procedures, corrupt police methods, mistaken tests of responsibility, etc, or by using criteria of what constitute offences which allow to be offences, offences under secret and retroactive laws – is unjust punishment, as is punishment which is disproportionate with the crime. Thus the punishment which we consider, after critical reflection, to be just punishment, is punishment which fits a retributive theory. It is to be noted that it is just punishment, not morally permissible punishment, of which this is being claimed. Sometimes it is morally permissible and obligatory to override the dictates of justice. The retributive theory is a theory about justice in punishment and tells only part of the whole story about the morality of punishment. It points to a very important consideration in determining the morality of punishment – namely, its justice – and explains what punishments are just and why they are just.

Before proceeding further, some comment should be made concerning these allusions to 'what our common moral consciousness regards as just or unjust'. Utilitarians frequently wish to dismiss such appeals to our moral consciousness as amounting to an uncritical acceptance of our emotional responses. Obviously they are not that. Our uncritical moral consciousness gives answers which we do not accept as defensible after critical reflection, and it is the judgements which we accept after critical reflection which are being appealed to here. In any case, before the utilitarian starts questioning this approach, he would do well to make sure that he himself is secure from similar criticism. It might well be argued that his appeal to the principle of utility itself rests upon an uncritical emotional acceptance of what prima facie appears to be a high-minded moral principle but which, on critical examination, seems to involve grave moral evils. Thus the problem of method, and of justifying the use of this method, is one which the utilitarian shares with the non-utilitarian.

...

III WHAT UTILITARIANISM APPEARS TO ENTAIL IN RESPECT OF PUNISHMENT

Is all useful punishment just punishment, and is all just punishment useful? Here it is necessary first to dispose of what might not unfairly be described as a 'red herring'. A lot of recent utilitarian writing is to the effect that punishment of the innocent is logically impossible, and hence that utilitarianism cannot be committed to punishment of the innocent. Their point is that the concept of punishment entails that the person being punished be an actual or supposed offender, for otherwise we do not call it punishment but injury, harm-infliction, social quarantining, etc. There are two good reasons for rejecting this argument as nothing but a red herring. Not all unjust punishment is punishment of the innocent. Much is punishment which is excessive. Thus even if punishment of the innocent were not logically possible, the problem of justice in punishment would remain in the form of showing that only punishments commensurate with the offence were useful. Secondly, the verbal point leaves the issue of substance untouched. The real quarrel between the retributionist and the utilitarian is whether a system of inflictions of suffering on people without reference to the gravity of their offences or even to whether they have committed offences, is just and morally permissible. It is immaterial whether we call such deliberate inflictions of sufferings punishment, social surgery, social quarantining, etc. In any case ... the claim is evidently false. We the observers and the innocent victims of such punishment call it punishment, unjust punishment. In so referring to it there is no straining of language.

To consider now whether all useful punishment is just punishment. When the problem of utilitarianism in punishment is put in this way, the appeal of the utilitarian approach somewhat diminishes. It appears to be useful to do lots of things which are unjust and undesirable. Whilst it is no doubt true that harsh punishment isn't necessarily the most useful punishment, and that punishment of the guilty person is usually the most useful punishment, it is nonetheless easy to call to mind cases of punishment of innocent people, of mentally deranged people, of excessive punishment, etc, inflicted because it was believed to be useful. Furthermore, the person imposing such punishment seems not always to be mistaken. Similarly, punishment which is just may be less useful than rewards. With some criminals, it may be more useful to reward them. As Ross observes:

> A utilitarian theory, whether of the hedonistic or of the 'ideal' kind, if it justifies punishment at all, is bound to justify it solely on the ground of the effects it produces ... In principle, then, the punishment of a guilty person is treated by utilitarians as not different in kind from the imposition of inconvenience, say by quarantine regulations, on innocent individuals for the good of the community.

What is shocking about this, and what most utilitarians now seek to avoid admitting to be an implication of utilitarianism, is the implication that grave injustices in the form of punishment of the innocent, of those not responsible for their acts, or harsh punishments of those guilty of trivial offences, are dictated by their theory. We may sometimes best deter others by punishing, by framing an innocent man who is generally believed to be guilty, or by adopting rough and ready trial procedures, as is done by army courts martial in the heat of battle in respect of deserters, etc; or we may severely punish a person not responsible for his actions, as so often happens with military punishments for cowardice, and in civil cases involving sex crimes where the legal definition of insanity may fail to cover the relevant cases of insanity. Sometimes we may deter others by imposing ruthless sentences for crimes which are widespread, as with car stealing and shoplifting in food markets. We may make people very thoughtful about their political commitments by having retroactive laws about their political affiliations; and we may, by secret laws, such as make to be major crimes what are believed simply to be anti-social practices and not crimes at all, usefully encourage a watchful, public-spirited behaviour. If the greatest good or the greatest happiness of the greatest number is the foundation of the morality and justice of punishment, there can be no guarantee that some such injustices may not be dictated by it. Indeed, one would expect that it would depend on the details of the situation and on the general features of the society, which punishments and institutions of punishment were most useful. In most practical affairs affecting human welfare, e.g. forms of government, laws, social institutions, etc, what is useful is relative to the society and situation. It would therefore be surprising if this were not also the case with punishment. We should reasonably expect to find that different punishments and systems of punishment were useful for different occasions, times, communities, peoples, and be such that some useful punishments involve grave and shocking injustices. Whether this is in fact the case is an empirical matter which is best settled by social and historical research, for there is evidence available which bears on which of the various types of punishments and institutions work best in the sense of promoting the greatest good. Although this is not a question for which the philosopher *qua* philosopher is well equipped to deal, I shall nonetheless later briefly look at a number of considerations which are relevant to it, but only because the utilitarian usually bases his defence of utilitarianism on his alleged knowledge of empirical matters of fact, upon his claim to know that the particular punishments and that system of punishment which we regard as most just, are most conducive to the general good. J. Bentham, and in our own day, J. J. C. Smart, are among the relatively few utilitarians who are prepared – in the case of Smart, albeit reluctantly – to accept that utilitarian punishment may be unjust by conventional standards, but morally right nonetheless.

Against the utilitarian who seeks to argue that utilitarianism does not involve unjust punishment, there is a very simple argument, namely, that whether or not unjust punishments are in fact useful, it is logically possible that they will at some time become useful, in which case utilitarians are committed to them. Utilitarianism involves the conclusion that if it is useful to punish lunatics, mentally deranged people, innocent people framed as being guilty, etc, it is obligatory to do so. It would be merely a contingent fact, if it were a fact at all, that the punishment which works is that which we consider to be morally just. In principle, the utilitarian is committed to saying that we should not ask 'Is the punishment deserved?' The notion of desert does not arise for him. The only relevant issue is whether the punishment produces greater good.

*IV WHAT UTILITARIANISM IN FACT ENTAILS IN THE LIGHT OF EMPIRICAL
CONSIDERATIONS*

What is the truth about the utility of the various types of punishments? As I have already
suggested, it would be astonishing if, in the sphere of punishment, only those punishments
and that institution of punishment we consider to be just, worked best. To look at
particular examples.

[Elsewhere I have] argued that a utilitarian would be committed to unjust punishment,
and used the example of a sheriff framing an innocent negro in order to stop a series of
lynchings which he knew would occur if the guilty person were not immediately found,
or believed to have been found. I suggested that if the sheriff were a utilitarian he would
frame an innocent man to save the lives of others. Against this example, it is suggested
that we cannot know with certainty what the consequences of framing the negro would
be, and that there may be other important consequences besides the prevention of
lynchings. Utilitarians point to the importance of people having confidence in the
impartiality and fairness of the legal system, a belief that lawful behaviour pays, etc.
However, as the example is set up, only the sheriff, the innocent victim and the guilty
man and not the general public, would know there had been a frame-up. Further, even
if a few others knew, this would not mean that everyone knew; and even if everyone
came to know, surely, if utilitarianism is thought to be the true moral theory, the general
body of citizens ought to be happier believing that their sheriff is promoting what is
right rather than promoting non-utilitarian standards of justice. Since complex factors
are involved, this example is not as decisive as is desirable. It can readily be modified so
as to avoid many of these complications and hence become more decisive. Suppose a
utilitarian were visiting an area in which there was racial strife, and that, during his visit,
a negro rapes a white woman, and that race riots occur as a result of the crime, white
mobs, with the connivance of the police, bashing and killing negroes, etc. Suppose too
that our utilitarian is in the area of the crime when it is committed such that his testimony
could bring about the conviction of a particular negro. If he knows that a quick arrest
will stop the riots and lynchings, surely, as a utilitarian, he must conclude that he has a
duty to bear false witness in order to bring about the punishment of an innocent person.
In such a situation, he has, on utilitarian theory, an evident duty to bring about the
punishment of an innocent man. What unpredictable consequences, etc, are present
here other than of a kind that are present in every moral situation? Clearly, the utilitarian
will not be corrupted by bearing false witness, for he will be doing what he believes to
be his duty. It is relevant that it is rare for any of us to be in a situation in which we can
usefully and tellingly bear false witness against others.

We may similarly give possible examples of useful punishments of other unjust kinds.
Scapegoat punishment need not be and typically is not of a framed person. It may be
useful. An occupying power which is experiencing trouble with the local population
may find it useful to punish, by killing, some of the best loved citizen leaders, each time
an act of rebellion occurs; but such punishments do not commend themselves to us as
just and right. Similarly, collective punishment is often useful – consider its use in schools.
There we consider it unjust but morally permissible because of its great utility. Collective
punishments of the kind employed by the Nazis in Czechoslovakia – destroying a village
and punishing its inhabitants for the acts of a few – are notorious as war crimes. Yet
they appear to have been useful in the sense of achieving Nazi objectives. It may be

objected that the Nazi sense of values was mistaken, that such punishment would not contribute towards realizing higher values and goods. But it is partly an accident of history that it was the Nazis who, in recent times, resorted to this method. If we had had to occupy a Nazi territory with inadequate troops, this might have been the only effective way of maintaining order. As with human affairs generally, it would depend on many factors, including the strength of our troops, the degree of hostility of the occupied people, their temper and likely reaction to this sort of collective punishment, etc. Punishment of relatives could also be useful. It would be an interesting social experiment in those modem democracies which are plagued by juvenile delinquency, for parents as well as the teenage delinquents to be punished. Such punishment would be unjust but it might well be useful. It would need a number of social experiments to see whether it is or is not useful. It is not a matter we can settle by intuitive insight. If it did prove useful, it is probable people would come to think of such punishment of parents as punishment for the offence of being a parent of a delinquent! This would obscure the awareness of the injustice of such punishment, but it would nonetheless be unjust punishment.

Similarly with punishment for offences under secret and retroactive laws. Such laws, it is true, would be useful only if used sparingly and for very good reasons but it is not hard to imagine cases where the use of a retroactive law might be useful in the long as well as in the short run. That a plausible case could have been made out for introducing retroactive laws in post-war Germany on utilitarian grounds as well as on the other sorts of grounds indicated by legal theorists, suggests that such cases do occur. They may be the most useful means, they may, in the German case, even have been morally permissible means and the means of achieving greater total justice; but they are nonetheless means which in themselves are unjust. Retroactive laws are really a kind of secret law. Their injustice consists in this; and secret laws, like them, seem useful if used sparingly and with discretion. The Nazis certainly believed them to be very useful but again it will no doubt be said that this was because their system of values was mistaken. However, unless the system of values includes respect for considerations of justice, such secret laws are possibly useful instruments for promoting good.

In our own community we define 'offence' in such a way, with various laws, that we condone unjust punishment because of its utility. The vagrancy law is a very useful law but what it declares to be an offence is hardly an offence in the morally relevant sense. And it is not difficult to imagine countries in which it would be useful to have a law making it an offence to arouse the suspicions of the government. Suppose there were a democratic revolution in Spain, or in Russia, which led to the perilous existence of a democratic government. Such a government might find that the only way in which it could safely continue in existence was by having such a law and similar laws involving unjust punishments. It would then have to consider which was morally more important – to avoid the unjust punishments which such a law involves, or to secure and make permanent a democratic form of government which achieved greater over-all justice. That is, it would face conflicting claims of justice.

In an ignorant community it might well be useful to punish as responsible moral agents 'criminals' who in fact were not responsible for their actions but who were generally believed to be responsible agents. The experts suggest that many sex offenders and others who commit the more shocking crimes, are of this type, but even in reasonably enlightened communities the general body of citizens do not always accept the judgements of the experts. Thus, in communities in which enlightened opinion generally prevails (and these are few) punishment of mentally deranged 'criminals' would have little if any deterrent value, whereas in most communities some mentally deranged people may usefully be punished, and in ignorant, backward communities very useful results may come from punishing those not responsible for their actions. Similarly, very undesirable results may come from not punishing individuals generally believed to be fully responsible moral agents. Yet, clearly, the morality of punishing such people does not depend on the degree of the enlightenment of the community. Utilitarian theory suggests that it does, that such punishment is right and just in ignorant, prejudiced communities, unjust in enlightened communities. The utility of such punishment varies in this way, but not its justice. The tests of responsible action are very difficult to determine, although this need not worry utilitarians who use the test of utility in this area as elsewhere. However, to make my point, we need not consider borderline cases. The more atrocious and abominable the crime, the more pointless its brutality is, the more likely it is that the criminal was not responsible and the more likely that the general public will believe him to be fully responsible and deserving of the severest punishment.

Utilitarians often admit that particular punishments may be useful but unjust and argue that utilitarianism becomes more plausible and indeed, acceptable, if it is advanced as a theory about the test of rules and institutions. These utilitarians argue that we should not test particular punishments by reference to their consequences; rather, we should test the whole institution of punishment in this way, by reference to the consequences of the whole institution.

This seems an incredible concession; yet rule-utilitarianism enjoys widespread support and is perhaps the dominant version of utilitarianism. It is argued that particular utilitarian punishments may be unjust but that useful systems of punishment are those which are just systems in the judgement of our reflective moral consciousness. This modification of utilitarianism involves a strange concession. After all, if the test of right and wrong rules and institutions lies in their utility, it is surely fantastic to suggest that this test should be confined to rules and institutions, unless it is useful so to confine its application. Clearly, when we judge the utility of particular actions, we should take note of the effects on the institution or rule, but surely, it is individual acts and their consequences which ultimately matter for the utilitarian.

...

To consider now the implications of rule-utilitarianism. As with act-utilitarianism, it would be surprising if what was useful was also at all times just, and that what was the most useful institution of punishment was the same under all conditions and for all times. For example, what we in Australia regard as useful and just, fair trial procedures – and these are an important part of justice in punishment – for example, rules about the burden of proof, strict limitation of newspaper comment before and during the trial, selection of the jury, provision of legal aid for the needy, etc., differ from those found useful in dictatorships. Also, obviously a country emerging from the instability of a great revolution cannot afford to take risks with criminals and counter-revolutionaries which a stable, secure, well established community can afford to take ... Thus not only particular punishments but also whole institutions of punishment may be useful but of a kind we consider to be gravely unjust. It is these difficulties of utilitarianism – of act- and rule- utilitarianism – and the facts which give rise to these difficulties which give to the retributive theory, that the vicious deserve to suffer, its initial plausibility.

V POSITIVE CONSIDERATIONS FOR A RETRIBUTIVE THEORY OF PUNISHMENT

There are many positive considerations in support of the retributive theory of punishment, if it is constructed as the theory that the vicious deserve to suffer. Firstly, it is a particular application of a general principle of justice, namely, that equals should be treated equally and unequals unequally. This is a principle which has won very general acceptance as a self-evident principle of justice ... It is in terms of such a principle that we think that political discrimination against women and peoples of special races is unjust, and that against children, just. Justice in these areas involves treating equals equally, unequals unequally ... So too with justice and punishment. The criminal is one who has made himself unequal in the relevant sense. Hence he merits unequal treatment. In this case, unequal treatment amounts to deliberate infliction of evils – suffering or death.

We need now to consider whether our retributive theory implies that there is a duty to punish with full, deserved punishment. Look at the other areas of justice, for example, wage justice. If it is just, say, to pay a labourer £20 a week, there is no breach of justice if the employer shows benevolence and pays £25, whereas there is a grave breach if he pays only £15. Similarly with retributive justice, but in a reverse way. We do not act unjustly if, moved by benevolence, we impose less than is demanded by justice, but there is a grave injustice if the deserved punishment is exceeded. If the deserved punishment is inflicted, all we need to do to justify it is to point out that the crime committed deserved and merited such punishment. Suppose that the just punishment for murder is imprisonment for 15 years. Suppose also that the judge knows that the murderer he is about to sentence will never be tempted to commit another murder, that he is deeply and genuinely remorseful, and that others will not be encouraged to commit murders if he is treated leniently. If the judge imposed a mild penalty we should probably applaud his humanity, but if he imposed the maximum penalty we should not be entitled to condemn him as unjust. What we say in cases like this is that the judge is a hard, even harsh, man, not that he is an unjust man.

Is only deserved punishment morally permissible? Obviously not. Here we might take an analogy with other parts of morality. It is wrong to lie, to break promises, or to steal. This is not to say that we are never obliged to lie, break promises, steal, etc. What it means is that we need to have another, conflicting, more stringent duty which overrides the duty to tell the truth, keep our promise, or not steal, if we are to be justified in lying, breaking our promise, or stealing. Similarly with justice in punishment. The fact that a punishment is just entitles the appropriate authority to inflict it, but that is not to say that it must be inflicted nor that more cannot properly be inflicted. Many considerations may weigh with the relevant authority and make it morally right to inflict more or less than is strictly just; and not all such considerations will be utilitarian considerations – some may be other considerations of justice. We determine what punishment ought to be inflicted by taking into account firstly what punishment is deserved, and then other considerations. Relevant here are considerations such as that the criminal's wife and children may be the real victims of the punishment, that the criminal would be unable to make restitution to the person whose property he has stolen; of benevolence, e.g. in not imposing the punishment because the criminal has already suffered greatly in blinding himself in attempting to blow a safe; of the general good, as in making an example of the criminal and inflicting more than the deserved punishment because of the grave consequences that will come about if this type of crime is not immediately checked, etc. Production of the greatest good is obviously a relevant consideration when determining which punishment may properly be inflicted, but the question as to which punishment is just is a much more basic and important consideration.

...

It is important here to note and dismiss a commonly made criticism of this retributive theory, namely, that there is no objective test of the gravity of a crime except in terms of the penalty attached to the crime. If the penalty is hanging, then, it is argued, the crime is a serious one; if the penalty is a £2 fine, it is a trivial offence. This criticism is often reinforced by the contention that if all the people in any given group were to make out lists of crimes in order of their gravity, they would give significantly different lists such that what appear as grave crimes on one list are minor crimes on other lists. Obviously, if this criticism were sound, it would mean that one very important element of the retributive theory would be nullified, for punishment could not be other than commensurate with the offence. However, this criticism is unsound and rests on a number of confusions.

It is true that we speak of a crime as serious if the penalty is hanging, but this is not to say that it is therefore a grave crime in the morally significant sense of 'grave crime'. The fact that hanging was the penalty for stealing a loaf of bread made that a serious offence in one sense but not in another, for we speak of the punishment as gravely disproportionate and as treating the offence as much more serious than it really is. It is on this basis that we can and do speak of penalties as being too light or too heavy, even where similar offences have similar penalties. It is unjust that the theft of a loaf of bread should meet with the same punishment as murder. Further, the fact that we reach different conclusions about the relative gravity of different crimes constitutes no difficulty for the retributive theory. Most of us would agree that murder is a very serious crime and that shoplifting a cake of soap is a considerably lesser offence. We should perhaps differ about such questions as to whether kidnapping is more or less serious than black-mail ... We do disagree, and most of us would have doubts about the right order of the gravity of crimes. This shows very little. We have the same doubts – and disagreements – in other areas of morality ... Similarly, utilitarians differ among themselves about goods such that if a group of utilitarians were asked to list goods in their order of goodness we could confidently expect different lists of different goods and of goods listed in different orders ... With the utilitarian theory, the uncertainty and doubts arise concerning the assessments of the value of the goods and the determination of which goods should be promoted by punishment. With the retributive theory the difficulties arise in determining the relative gravity of offences; and there, clearly, the appropriate method of seeking to resolve our doubts is neither to look at what punishments are in fact imposed, nor at what punishments will produce the greatest good, but rather to look at the nature of the offence itself.

Note that under McCloskey's version of retributivism, he restricts the application of retributive theory to the question of the *justice* of punishment, and considers that justice is not the only relevant consideration in punishing. This is significant, first because it assumes that courts of justice, while necessarily attentive to justice as their starting point, are entitled to consider other values (consider how this fits within different theories of law), and second, because it allows, perhaps, a strong consequentialist element to enter into the overall morality of punishment (which Sprigge takes up in his response to McCloskey in the next reading). Note in particular how Sprigge attempts to defuse the 'parade of horribles', ie the series of examples of the sorts of dreadfully unjust punishments which McCloskey supposes a utilitarian would, consonant with his theory, be required to endorse.

Sprigge (1965, 268–70, 274–84, 286–89)

McCloskey emphasizes the point that retributivism 'tells only part of the whole story about the morality of punishment. It points to a very important consideration in determining the morality of punishment – namely, its justice – and explains what punishments are just and why they are just'. But an unjust punishment may at times be morally permissible (or even obligatory?) for other reasons. This admission blunts the force of certain of McCloskey's arguments against utilitarianism. To show that the utilitarian must classify as obligatory or permissible certain punishments which the common moral consciousness calls unjust is not of itself enough to show that the utilitarian diverges from this common moral consciousness. For the utilitarian might admit that they were *unjust*.

He can indeed only do this if he admits that although the principle of utility gives the criteria for morally permissible or obligatory punishment, the criteria for just punishment cannot simply be identified with this. Perhaps this sounds like the admission of conflicting moral criteria, but that would be a misunderstanding.

The utilitarian may allow that there are certain goods the promotion or diminution of which is likely to be the main way in which actions of certain recognized classes promote or diminish the general good.

...

For the utilitarian consideration of the likely effects of an action will properly start with those effects most likely to be important. Life is normally too complicated for equal attention to be paid to the effects it may have in every field irrespective of any prior presumptions as to where effects of the greatest importance are to be found. This being so, what more sensible than a special term for an action of this class which increases rather than diminishes goods of this class, with an opposite term for the opposite case? Now I suggest that the utilitarian may find the words 'just' and 'unjust' ideally suited for such a role. To the extent that ordinary moral opinion and terminology is of a utilitarian character they seem to play this role already, but the utilitarian need not deny that they sometimes have a less utilitarian character in ordinary usage.

If this view is right, actions which come under the heading imposition or infliction of punishment are peculiarly calculated to increase or decrease goods (or evils) of a certain type, which we may call the goods (or evils) of justice, and usually their main effect on the common good (or ill) is determined by their effects on these goods (or evils) of justice. All such actions will be appropriately called 'just' or 'unjust' according as they increase or diminish the goods of justice. It will usually but not necessarily always be true that just actions are right or good from a utilitarian point of view, and unjust ones are bad or wrong.

...

So the utilitarian need not assimilate the question whether a punishment is just or unjust to the question whether it is useful or harmful. The former question concerns only one specific set of utilities.

...

IV ACTUAL AND FANCIFUL EXAMPLES

... Now McCloskey's main argument against a utilitarian theory of punishment lies in examples which he presents of moral judgements which he supposes would follow from utilitarian theory, and which clash with our common moral consciousness, even presumably when this has been altered to meet the demands of critical reflection. Such examples may be of two types. They may be moral judgements regarding situations of a kind which actually occur or they may regard situations of a kind which do not occur. ... Although McCloskey recognizes this distinction, he evidently does not think it of much importance. For he says: 'Against the utilitarian who seeks to argue that utilitarianism does not involve unjust punishment, there is a very simple argument, namely, that whether or not unjust punishments are in fact useful, it is logically possible that they will at some time become useful, in which case utilitarians are committed to them.'

...

Now if one considers some fantastic situations ... one does of course consider them as a person with certain moral sentiments, the strength of which in society as it is, is an important utilitarian good. These sentiments are offended. A utilitarian will see no point in trying to imagine oneself looking with approval on the imaginary situation, since this is likely to weaken the feelings while not serving as a preparation for any actual situation. If in fact punishing the innocent (say) always is and always will be harmful, it is likewise harmful to dwell on fanciful situations in which it would be beneficial, thus weakening one's aversion to such courses. Thus the utilitarian shares (quite consistently so) in the unease produced by these examples. Although he may admit that in such a situation punishment of the innocent would be right, he still regards favourably the distaste which is aroused at the idea of its being called right.

Certainly, if one imagines the world as other than it is, one may find oneself imagining a world in which utilitarianism implies moral judgements which shock our moral sentiments. But if these moral sentiments are quite appropriate to the only world there is, the real world, the utilitarian is glad that moral judgements in opposition to them seem repugnant. He sees no need for moral acrobatics relevant only to situations which in fact are quite out of the question.

...

Suppose one describes a case where punishment of an innocent man would yield a balance of good, and ensures that this is so simply by stipulating certain striking benefits which will derive from it, and explicitly eliminating all the harms one can think of. If one finds oneself still half-inclined to call such punishment wrong, it may well be because one does not really succeed in envisaging the situation just as described, but surrounds it with those circumstances of real life which would in fact create a greater probability of unhappiness in its consequences than happiness.

...

V MCCLOSKEY'S EXAMPLES

...

The sheriff is supposed to have framed an innocent negro to prevent a series of lynchings which he knows will occur if no one is 'punished' for the offence. It is urged that this is obviously the right course from a utilitarian point of view.

One line of objection to this conclusion appeals to the likelihood that the facts will become known. I may urge parenthetically that in the real world such a likelihood is likely (surely) to be pretty strong. The utilitarian may then insist on a variety of evils which would result from its becoming known, such as a loss of confidence in the impartiality and fairness of the legal system, of a belief that lawful behaviour pays, etc. Now McCloskey says that 'even if everyone came to know, surely, if utilitarianism is thought to be the true moral theory, the general body of citizens ought to be happier believing that their sheriff is promoting what is right rather than promoting non-utilitarian standards of justice' . This strikes me as absurd. Let us consider first the white citizenry. It is quite obvious that they are not utilitarians, or that even if by chance some are in theory, their feelings are not in fact governed by utilitarian theory. For if they were utilitarians they would not be charging around the country lynching people. For who could seriously believe that this was the best way of creating the greatest happiness of the greatest number? If they were utilitarians (in practice) the sheriff would not be in the situation he is in. As it is, he has to think about them as they are. How they would react to the fact that the sheriff framed the negro is a different matter, but for a utilitarian to expect their satisfaction because he has done the right thing from a utilitarian point of view would be absurd. You might as well suggest that a utilitarian penologist should urge that all prisons should be without bars, on the grounds that once it is explained to the offenders how useful it is for society that they should be punished they will see the wrongness of escaping. Let us now consider the negroes. There is not the same evidence within the very hypothesis that their actions and feelings are opposed to utilitarian precepts. But one may take it that whatever their ethical views, they are filled with bitterness at white behaviour. They are hardly going to be overjoyed at learning that a negro up for trial is likely to be framed in order to sate the fury of brutish whites. Will not their incentives to law-abidingness be decreased when they learn that someone else's crime may just as well get them punished as one of their own? Is racial harmony really going to be advanced by such an event?

But I shall now turn to the second supposedly more forceful example. Here a utilitarian visitor from outside the area bears incriminating false witness against a negro so that his being 'punished' for a rape will put an end to a series of riots and lynchings. One main point of thus changing the example presumably is to eliminate such harrns as might be supposed to ensue from a local figure, especially a legal authority, practising the deception.

Before commenting on this example in further detail I should like to ask the reader (or McCloskey himself) to stand back for a moment and consider the prima facie implausibility of what McCloskey tries to show. Forget for a moment all question of the rightness or wrongness of utilitarian theory, forget morality, and imagine simply that you are a reasonable being with one overriding aim, to create as much happiness as possible at the cost of as little unhappiness as possible. Does it really seem on the cards that in a situation where race riots are going on as a result of a rape, you will find no more effective way of forwarding your aim in this area than to bear false witness against some unfortunate negro, thus ensuring that at least one human being is thoroughly miserable? Does not a vague unanalysed sense of how the world really works inform one that this is not a type of action which increases human happiness? People who lack this common-sense grasp of how the world runs are dangerous whatever moral backing they may claim for their actions.

Let us now turn to details. Our utilitarian is said to know 'that a quick arrest will stop the riots and lynchings'. How does he know this? How does he know that they aren't going to die down soon anyway? Even if he has good reason to think that they will go on unless such an arrest is made, does he know how intense they will be, how many people are actually going to get lynched? One thing he does know is that if he bears false witness (successfully) an innocent man is going to get punished. We are not told what the punishment will be, but it is likely either to be death or a long term of imprisonment, which will mean the ruin of the man's life. Suppose he does not bear the false witness, that the riots go on as he expected, but that no deaths or permanent injuries take place. Isn't it likely that the suffering in this case is less than that of a man sentenced to execution (together with the sufferings of his family) or languishing for long years in prison?

Utilitarian judgement that the false witness would be right must be based on its foreseeable consequences. Now an event can be foreseen as a probable (or certain) consequence of a given action on two roughly distinguishable grounds. It may be a well confirmed generalization that actions of that broad type in that broad type of situation very often (or always) have such a consequence. But an action may (also) be characterized by features too unusual to figure in such generalizations. If these are to provide a basis for prediction it must be because of some hunch about the situation which will be no more rational than an indefinite number of other hunches. Reliance on such hunches is something which often leads people wildly wrong. (This is well confirmed, I suggest.) This suggests that a product (such as happiness) will be increased in the long run more by those who base their expectations on well confirmed generalizations than on hunches, and that therefore the utilitarian should stick to the former, especially where the amounts of happiness or unhappiness are large.

…

Now I suggest that the prediction of misery for the innocent man if he is successfully framed rests on well confirmed generalizations, but that the prediction that this will stop lynchings, etc., which would otherwise have occurred, will be based on a hunch about the character of the riots. In that case the sensible utilitarian will attach a predominating weight to the former prediction, and refrain from framing the man.

McCloskey may, however, insist that the utilitarian has the very firmest grounds for his beliefs about the duration and degree of the rioting if no punishment takes place, and concerning the preventability of all this by the means in question. I'm inclined to suggest then that a man with such a rich knowledge of the nature of these riots should devote himself fully to a documented study of them with a view to putting his knowledge before such organizations as can arrange by propaganda and other means to alleviate their causes. If he has something to hide concerning his own illicit means of checking them, he will not be at ease in drawing up a report on the situation and will therefore not do his work properly, work which will stop more riot-caused suffering in the end than this isolated act.

If these last remarks seem somewhat fanciful I should urge that the situation in which a man knows that the riots will go on unless he tells this lie is also fanciful … In an actual situation this would probably only be a hunch, of little weight besides the well supported belief that a successful frame-up will produce massive suffering for the innocent man and his family. There is also good reason for believing that facing a man and telling lies which will ruin his life will blunt one's sensibilities in a way which may well lead one to use such methods again with still less justification. I should suspect, moreover, that a utilitarian who persuaded himself that such an act was useful would be finding an outlet for harmful impulses which it would behove him not to indulge; for instance an urge to exert power in a secret God-like manner, and without scruple. It is dangerously easy for someone who wants to do something for motives of which he is ashamed to persuade himself that the general good would be served by it. This gives another reason for suspicion of 'hunches'.

None of this has appealed to any such principle as that the suffering of an innocent man is a worse thing in itself than that of a guilty one. What of this principle? The utilitarian cannot consistently say that one is worse in itself if the degree of suffering is the same. But if there is reason to believe that more suffering is involved in a given punishment for an innocent man than for a guilty man this is something of which the utilitarian should take account.

There does seem some reason to believe this. An innocent man is liable to suffer more shock at being thus punished. He will suffer from an indignant fury as the guilty man will not.

…

Of course McCloskey can deal with each specific point by imagining a situation in which it would not arise. Let the innocent man be without family and a natural pessimist always prepared for the worst. But what sort of investigation prior to his false witness is our wily utilitarian to make into these matters? It is hard to believe that a man of such tenacity will not find less costly ways of advancing racial harmony.

It seems to me, then, highly unlikely that in a situation at all like the one described by McCloskey a man guided by a cool assessment of probabilities rather than by wild surmises will see such bearing of false witness as the most felicific act. This applies even if we ignore the effects on the utilitarian's own character, still more if we take these into account. Still, I should not say it was absolutely *out of the question* that situations may arise where a sensible utilitarian would think it right to implicate an innocent man. As I have explained at length, he could still think the resultant punishment unjust, although his production of it was right or justified. In such a situation the good to be achieved by the punishment would presumably be predictable as near certain on well confirmed principles, and be great enough to outweigh harms of the sort we have described, and such other evils (especially evils of injustice) as might arise. It would also have to be unobtainable at less cost. I suspect that with such goods to be gained our utilitarian's action would be such as many plain men (not just official utilitarians) would condone or approve.

What plain men would feel, however, is an uneasiness at the situation, and a deep regret about it. Now sometimes one gets a picture of the utilitarian who can feel no regret at any overriding of conventional moral principles provided his sums come out all right. This is a travesty of the utilitarian outlook.

There is indeed a certain problematicness about regret on any ethical theory. Everyone must admit that on occasion the action which on balance one ought to do, has characteristics or consequences which considered in themselves suggest the wrongness of the act. A general fighting for a good cause may well regard the dead and injured on the field of battle with a terrible regret that he should have brought this about, and yet think he acted rightly – although he always knew there would be a sacrifice like this. Moreover his regret may in a sense be a moral regret, different in character from the regret one feels at the sacrifice of one's own interests for the sake of duty. An unimaginative moral philosopher might say that such regret was inapposite, if he had really done the right thing. Most of us do not feel this way and utilitarianism offers at least two justifications for our attitude. First, a man who was not sad at producing suffering would lack the basic sentiment which inspires the utility principle, namely a revulsion at the suffering and a delight in the happiness of any sentient being. Second, sentiments such as the love of justice, respect for human life and so on, are sentiments which utilitarian considerations bid us cherish in ourselves and others. When the promptings of these sentiments have to be set aside in the interests of a greater good, the man who feels no regret can have them little developed, and the man who checks all regret will blunt them. Regret in such situations is therefore a desirable state of mind according to utilitarianism.

...

VI FURTHER EXAMPLES

Among further examples which McCloskey gives of unjust but useful laws are scapegoat punishment and collective punishment. He does not make it very clear, however, what his own moral attitude to such punishments is, or what he takes to be that of the common moral consciousness. Certainly he thinks they are unjust even when useful – and that is something with which the utilitarian can agree – but does he think that they are sometimes justified nonetheless? He seems at least to leave it open that they may be, and in one case, collective punishment in schools, he goes further. Now to say that they are unjust but all the same morally right or justified is a position which the utilitarian who really believed they produced more good than evil would probably adopt.

Consider the type of scapegoat punishment he mentions. It is within the bounds of possibility that a commander whose chances of victory demanded some sort of co-operation from the local people, and who had good reason to believe that without this victory the common good of humanity would suffer, finding this method of securing the population's co-operation the only workable one, would rightly consider that it was justified. I say that it is within the bounds of possibility, but it is also perhaps more probable that such a method is not even the most efficient for his end, or at least not more efficient than other means less damaging to the goods of justice. But if the circumstances really were as described most people who condone war at all would probably think the act was right.

In saying that such an undesirable means to a desirable end might possibly on rare occasions be justified, one is not giving one's general approval to such methods of gaining one's ends. There is, however, always the danger that when once one has allowed the justifiability of such means on one occasion, one will be ready to use them again on other occasions where although immediately convenient the same justifying conditions do not hold. The fact that an act may be a bad example to oneself and others (even if supposing this fact left out of account it would be justified) may often finally tip the balance against the rightness of doing it. As an example, I should like to take the bombing of centres of civilian population in wartime. For many such raids the British may well have had acceptable justification. This was certainly the belief of quite decent people in Britain. The victory of the allies really was an overwhelming good for humanity and this may have been an unavoidable means to it. But once moral scruples against such bombings were set aside in the interests of a greater good the capacity for moral reflection on the matter seems to have become blunted, and we have the bombing of Dresden which it is widely agreed served no essential purpose. In the same kind of way injustices in the treatment of an occupied country are likely to escalate, and this consideration should probably tip the balance in any cases (if there are such) where it might otherwise have been justified from a utilitarian point of view.

Just about the same can be said regarding collective punishments as scapegoat punishments.

In both cases one doubts whether these acts really ever are justified from a utilitarian point of view. Anyone concerned to gain the co-operation of an occupied territory without making it a slave population will presumably be concerned to gain its good will, to which end these methods are hardly conducive. The purposes for which the occupation is undertaken are obviously relevant here. On the whole, the more immoral the purposes the more such methods will seem required.

Although I am not attempting in this reply any account of what constitutes the goods (and evils) of justice (and injustice), I should perhaps mention a good of this type which would be prevented by scapegoat and collective punishment. One of the great goods furthered by various legal and quasi-legal institutions when properly conducted is the increased chance they give to everyone to control their own futures (so far as these depend on human agency) within limits imposed by the common good. This can perhaps be called one of the goods of justice, when it is the result of such institutions. ... Now we may accept that punishment (like the sack) is necessary evil, but granted that, we should try to preserve institutions according to which a man can predict and control the circumstances in which he will suffer it. Acts which weaken such institutions will be so far unjust, and be so even on those rare occasions where they may effect a predominating good and so be right.

...

The possibility remains that these unjust punishments may on occasion be right and proper, because useful in some other way. This possibility seems, however, to be allowed by McCloskey.

...

VII RULE-UTILITARIANISM

I have sought to defend utilitarianism against McCloskey's attacks, and what I have had in mind throughout has been 'act-utilitarianism', not 'rule-utilitarianism'. I entirely agree with McCloskey, however, that if his attacks on this are accepted, changing to rule-utilitarianism can hardly offer an acceptable remedy. There is indeed something absurd about rule-utilitarianism *if* it is thought of as in conflict with act-utilitarianism. If a rule is good precisely because action in accordance with it usually advances the general good, and this is the only reason, it is very odd to think that any value should be attached to action according to the rule in those exceptional cases where it hinders rather than advances the general good. When I talk of its hindering rather than advancing the general good, I mean that it does so even when such goods as that of keeping the rule in general respect are taken into account. For if the rule-utilitarian is only drawing attention to the need for keeping this particular highly important type of good in mind when evaluating an individual action, he is urging the value of general rules by the criteria of act-utilitarianism and is therefore not putting forward a rival view to it. If the rule-utilitarian thinks that on occasion one should do an act which has a predominantly unfavourable hedonic effect, because it is an example of a kind of action which usually has a predominantly favourable hedonic effect, one wonders why he has suddenly lost the concern for the general happiness which made him favour the rule in the first place.

So I am at one with McCloskey in regarding rule-utilitarianism as absurd. However, the matter has another aspect, which suggests that the contrast between act-utilitarianism and rule-utilitarianism is somewhat confused conceptually.

Any intelligent utilitarianism will acknowledge that the rightness and wrongness of an act is determined by the consequences reasonably predictable beforehand rather than by the actual consequences. An example used by several writers to support this point is that of a doctor called in to save the life of a certain baby, which baby later became Adolf Hitler. His life-saving action one can be almost sure resulted in more suffering than happiness, when the later actions of Hitler are taken into account, as clearly they should be. But these were not among the reasonably predictable consequences of the act, and it would seem absurd for the utilitarian to call the action wrong or bad.

Now the reasonably predictable consequences of an act will normally be predictable as probable to a certain degree rather than as certain, and in any case this last can be treated as a special degree of probability. Moreover incompatible consequences can be predictable as each probable to complementary degrees. It is clear that the probability with which a consequence can be predicted affects the weight which a utilitarian ascribes to it, so that its weight in terms of the amount of pleasure it involves has to be multiplied by its probability represented as a fraction.

...

Once these points are acknowledged we see that the contrast between individual utilitarian judgement of each act and the application of general principles supposed to have a utilitarian basis is confused. To calculate the hedonic value of an act (before its performance or non-performance) is to make an inductive assessment of probabilities. Essentially it is to take general characteristics of the act, and consider what has usually followed upon acts of this sort in the past. The characteristics which would show an act as prohibited by a general principle accepted because such acts usually do more harm than good are just such characteristics as would be taken in a utilitarian consideration of this individual action as indicative of its being probably more harmful than beneficial, and therefore bad. This suggests that only one type of utilitarian evaluation of acts can be seriously proposed. One considers the sort of act an act is, and considers what usually ensues upon acts of this sort. Reasonable prediction of consequences is always based upon general principles. It makes little difference in the end whether the utilitarian calls his principles scientific statements about the tendencies for weal or woe of certain types of action which can be used in making reasonable predictions about the probable effects on happiness of individual actions, or moral principles as to the rightness or wrongness of certain types of action based on their usual consequences for weal or woe.

Let us imagine a case where rule-utilitarianism and act-utilitarianism seem to conflict. Suppose it is accepted that F actions generally produce more unhappiness than happiness. The rule-utilitarian therefore accepts the rule that F actions are wrong. Now we consider a particular F action. The act-utilitarian who knows no more about it than its F-ness will agree with the rule-utilitarian that it is wrong, since the only evidence he has indicates its probable harmfulness. However, he studies it further and decides (let us suppose reasonably) that this F action will probably do more good than harm. This can only be because he notes some other characteristic of it, say G, such that the principle that F and G actions usually do more good than harm is acceptable. Now in view of this last, the rule-utilitarian can substitute for his original rule, this: 'F actions are wrong, except when they are also G.' This rule concerns a class of actions, F and non-G ones, which are more often harmful than these, the F actions, denounced in the original rule. The rules conflict, and it would surely be odd to prefer the original principle. But if the latter principle is chosen there is no occasion here for any conflict between act-utilitarianism and rule-utilitarianism. The latter only diverges from the former, if it is insisted that the rules must concern classes of act distinguished by predicates of a certain simplicity, such as F may be, but not F and not-G. Apart from being vague, this would be strangely arbitrary.

So we come round to the same point that rule-utilitarianism can only be opposed to act-utilitarianism at the cost of making it absurd.

Does Sprigge's subtle defence of utilitarianism disarm McCloskey's attack? In particular, to what extent are you satisfied by Sprigge's characterisation of rule-utilitarianism and its place in the argument?

Before moving on, it is worthwhile mentioning two further complications for the deterrence theorist's attempt to provide a genuine standard of justice in punishment. While, as we have seen, retributivists typically tax utilitarians with hypothetical cases of the punishment of the innocent (eg scapegoat or collective punishment) or of unjustly excessive punishment, Primoratz (1987, 210–11) looks in the opposite direction with his Adolph Eichmann example: 'when considerations of deterrence do not apply, the guilty may not be punished. No matter how grave and morally reprehensible a crime is, if by punishing for it no deterrent results are to be attained, it ought to remain unpunished. This argument on *non-punishment of the guilty* seems to carry greatest weight in cases of the gravest crimes of all – those committed against humanity. Was it, for example, justified to punish Eichmann? ... provided that punishing him served the purpose of deterring potential Eichmanns from committing genocidal acts in the future. Now this does not seem to be a very satisfactory answer. For we can assume, for the sake of argument, that there are no potential Eichmanns left in the world or, alternatively, that those that remain, and those still to come, are beyond deterrence ... The death sentences meted out at Nuremberg, or the one given to Eichmann, did not deter mass murderers who came later, such as Idi Amin, Pol Pot or Enrique Macias or their henchmen.'

Secondly, the proportionality problem can be sharpened by an economic analysis of law, such as the one undertaken by Posner (see the reading from Posner 1998 in Chapter 17). For deterrence, as Posner correctly argues, is not merely a matter of the expected punishment, but the *probability* that one will suffer it. Therefore one of the costs which go into the calculation is the cost of discovering crimes and capturing and convicting criminals. Within limits, the same deterrent effect can be equally achieved by a low probability of severe punishment as by a high probability of less severe punishment. Thus, for example, one might seek to punish only 50 car thieves each year, but execute every one of them, and this might have a stronger deterrent effect than trying (ineffectively) to capture the lot but impose at most a six-month prison term. It would also be much cheaper. But, the desert theorist would argue, such a punishment would be grossly unjust.

In the next reading, Brudner considers whether the death penalty is just, and argues that only retributive theory can properly fit the notions of pardon and mercy into an overall account of punishing. The reading provides an introduction to Kant's and Hegel's retributivism, and the differences between their views, which are expressed in very abstract terms; it is perfectly sensible to question whether their ideas, and what Brudner makes of them, partake more of mystery than sound reasoning. On the other hand, this reading brings out the depth of the difficulty underlying the notion of 'desert' and the retributive rationale for punishment. While some notion of 'just deserts' seems an obvious element of punishment, it has required sustained efforts by the best minds in history to make it theoretically acceptable; whether they have succeeded in doing so remains an open question.

Brudner (1980, 345–355)

In contrast to utilitarianism, the retributive theory views punishment as a moral good rather than as an evil requiring justification in terms of extrinsic advantages. Whether or not punishment yields these advantages is irrelevant to its justification, because the principal end of punishment is neither to deter, nor to protect, nor to reform, but to annul wrong and thereby vindicate right. This is not to say that the retributivist is indifferent to these other goals or regards them as improper objects of policy. The criteria of reform, deterrence, and protection do have their place, but it is a very subordinate one. Specifically, they are relevant only to the secondary question of how we shall punish and not to the primary question of whether we have the right to punish. Furthermore, even within the limits of the secondary question (with which we are here concerned) they have relevance only after the moral issue has been settled and what remains is merely the choice, judicial or administrative, between various morally acceptable types and measures of punishment. For the retributivist the sole criterion of just punishment as well as of a just measure of punishment is whether it annuls the wrong.

But precisely how, we may ask, does punishment annul wrong? 'Can the shrieks of a wretch recall from time, which never reverses its course, deeds already accomplished?' thundered Beccaria. Obviously punishment cannot undo the deed, for the past is irrevocable. And yet by 'annulment' of the wrong retributivists must mean something more than mere restitution, for restitution is not punishment. According to Hegel, punishment annuls wrong by demonstrating the non-being of the criminal principle, which might otherwise have seemed to possess validity. The principle of crime is the claim to a right of the arbitrary and unrestrained freedom of the will. Seen in this way, crime is more than, as Plato thought, a sickness in the individual soul; it is a challenge to the natural moral order underpinning civilized society. This is because it denies the validity of natural law and gives this denial itself a show of validity. Punishment, then, is the denial of the denial and so the vindication or reaffirmation of natural law. It is, in other words, the objective demonstration that the criminal claim is without natural support or sanction, without reality.

Because it looks backward to a crime over and done with rather than forward to its social effects, retributive punishment has always seemed to utilitarians a relic of more barbarous times, a mere rationalization of the lust for revenge. In part this judgment reflects the utilitarian's rationalist suspicion of popular sentiment, in which he is wont to see only vulgar prejudice and blind emotionalism. Beccaria saw in the penal law of his time only 'the accumulated errors of centuries', and this attitude finds its modern counterpart in the demand to keep separate the questions, Why do men punish? and What justifies punishment? On the other hand, because of his commitment to natural law, the retributivist is more inclined to see in public opinion a dim perception of moral truth. And he is thus also inclined to see his task as one of providing a rational account of action already in itself moral rather than one of excogitating a criterion of morality to which society may be indifferent. To his utilitarian critic, therefore, the retributivist would reply that his punishment is not a form of revenge, but that revenge and punishment are both forms of natural retribution, punishment being alone the adequate form because emancipated from subjective interest. He would, moreover, counter with the charge that whereas utilitarianism plays havoc with our common-sense notions of penal justice, retributivism confirms them.

First of all, retributivism justifies punishment by reference to a good that is genuinely common. Punishment vindicates human rights. It thus affirms and makes objective the real rights of the criminal himself, who, in asserting a right to unlimited freedom, had undermined right as such, his own no less than others'. In receiving punishment, therefore, the criminal is subjected not to someone else's good, but to his own true good, hence to his own rational will. His autonomy and dignity are thus respected.

Secondly, retributivism accounts for the connection between punishment and desert. If punishment is the vindication of right against wrong or the denial of a denial, then it logically presupposes wrongdoing. Thus retributivism condemns punishment of the innocent. Furthermore, if what requires annulment is not the criminal deed itself but rather its claim to validity, then clearly intent or mens rea is saved as a determinant of wrongdoing and hence of criminal desert. Retributivism thus condemns strict liability.

Thirdly, retributivism saves the rule of proportionality respecting the relation between punishment and crime. The punishment must annul the wrong. This it does by demonstrating the self-contradictoriness – that is, the inherent nullity – of the criminal act. If I steal, I deny the existence of property even for me. My act recoils upon itself and so destroys itself. Now punishment simply brings home this contradiction, or is this contradiction objectively manifest. I assert a right to unbridled freedom; I thereby deny the existence of right, which denial punishment brings home to me by depriving me of mine. I am the author of my punishment, inasmuch as the latter is simply the inner consequence of my deed. 'The Eumenides sleep,' says Hegel, 'but crime awakens them, and hence it is the very act of crime itself which vindicates itself.' Now this account of punishment explains the demand that the punishment fit the crime. Punishment must be related to the gravity of the wrong because it must signify nothing but the recoiling of the criminal's own act against itself. Only as such is punishment natural retribution and not another act of violence. It is in this sense that Hegel speaks of the criminal's 'right' to punishment – that is to be subjected only to the consequences immanent in his act and never to the alien exigencies of society. To punish the offender in accordance with the principle laid down by his deed is to honour his human subjectivity, his essential self-determination, while to fix penalties according to the requirements of deterrence or correction is to degrade him to an object and a tool. Moreover, only if the measure of punishment is derived from the deed itself does the punishment logically annul the wrong. Were a fine the penalty for murder, we would feel that murder had not been sufficiently repaid, hence not decisively invalidated. The Biblical *lex talionis* as well as the common opinion that the criminal incurs a debt that can be discharged only by suffering the appropriate punishment are prephilosophic apprehensions of punishment as nemesis.

...

What guidance does the classic retributivist theory offer in the matter of capital punishment? It is usually assumed that retributivism logically entails retention of the death penalty for first-degree murder because of its apparent confirmation of the *lex talionis*. Certainly this connection was maintained by Kant, for whom fitness meant, quite simply, equality. The murderer must die, insists Kant, because 'there is no sameness of kind between death and remaining alive even under the most miserable conditions, and consequently there is also no equality between the crime and the retribution unless the criminal is judicially condemned and put to death'. Theorists of punishment have had little difficulty in demolishing this conception of justice, thinking in having done so to have dealt a deathblow to retributivism. If by equality is meant equality in kind, then we must repay theft with theft, adultery with adultery, forgery with forgery, and so on.

If equal value is meant, then we must punish mass murderers on a scale repugnant to our moral sense. Moreover, even if it were possible to compare qualitatively different injuries in terms of their painfulness according to an average preference scale, the commensurability of crimes and punishments would be destroyed as soon as we added considerations of mens rea to the balance. For although suffering can be compared with suffering, how can suffering be compared with wickedness? All these and other arguments are useful and valid against the *lex talionis*, but against retributivism itself they are quite harmless. For the demand that, as the criminal has done, so shall it be done to him is merely a sensuous representation or image of the inner identity of crime and its nemesis. The conceptual likeness is represented by the popular imagination as a qualitative (or quantitative) one, and, as in the allegory of the cave, the representation is taken for the thing represented. That retributive justice has nothing to do with crude conceptions of equality was emphasized by Hegel. While agreeing that equivalence is the criterion of justice in the distribution of punishment, he pointed out that 'in crime, as that which is characterized at bottom by the infinite aspect of the deed, the purely external, specific character vanishes'. In other words, the injury to be annulled by punishment is not the determinate injury done to the victim but the noumenal injury done to the moral order. Hence the measure of punishment is properly derived not from the qualitative or quantitative aspects of the crime (as in revenge) but from its moral significance. The seriousness of the criminal's infringement of Right must be matched by an infringement of his right of 'equal' weight. Since, however, the first of these variables eludes measurement in quantitative terms, 'equal weight' cannot mean more than 'proportionate severity'. That is to say, the principle of equivalence properly understood translates into the rather vague demand for a graded proportionality, whereby more serious crimes are punished with severer penalties. Thus retributivism does not specifically enjoin the death penalty for first-degree murder, but neither of course does it absolutely condemn it. This result is not as unenlightening as it may seem, for that capital punishment is neither a moral imperative nor a moral wrong is no trivial conclusion.

Can we, however, go further? Can retributivism offer any guide as to how to go about matching punishments to crimes? Let us immediately grant the argument that, given the impossibility of assigning values to degrees of 'seriousness' or 'wickedness', we cannot fit penalties to offences according to the principle of proportionality literally construed. We may regard murder as a more serious crime than robbery, but as we have no way of assigning a numerical ratio to this comparison, we cannot achieve proportional equality between the relative severity of punishments and the relative seriousness of crimes. But although there is no principle of fitness by which we could establish natural correspondences between specific penalties and specific crimes, we can at least seek considerations relevant to determining the overall severity of the punishment scale taken by itself. And I want now to suggest that such considerations may be supplied by the retributivist understanding of mercy.

The charge is often heard that retributivism leaves no room for mercy, that it establishes not only the right to punish but also the positive duty to do so, so that any waiving of the right appears, on this theory, to be itself an injustice. I shall argue, however, that it is not retributivism as such which leads to this conclusion so much as Kant's metaphysical assumptions, and that Hegel offers a metaphysical context for retributivism significantly different from Kant's, one that saves mercy. Furthermore, the difference between the two accounts of mercy will suggest a criterion for determining whether and for what crimes death is an appropriate punishment. Let us first notice what Kant says about the right to pardon. In *The Metaphysical Elements of Justice* he writes:

> The right to pardon a criminal ... is certainly the most slippery of all the rights of the sovereign. By exercising it he can demonstrate the splendour of his majesty and yet thereby wreak injustice to a high degree. With respect to a crime of one subject against another, he absolutely cannot exercise this right, for in such cases exemption from punishment constitutes the greatest injustice toward his subjects. Consequently he can make use of this right to pardon only in connection with an injury committed against himself.

Kant is clearly uneasy about the right to pardon; indeed, he is totally at a loss to account for it and would restrict its application to the crime of treason. This is precisely what one would expect from a philosopher who regards punishment as a categorical imperative, an unconditional duty to be performed for its own sake and irrespective of its consequences. Kant would have the whole human race perish rather than exempt a criminal from punishment, for 'if legal justice perishes, then it is no longer worthwhile for men to remain alive on this earth'.

Now consider what Hegel says about the right to pardon.

> The right to pardon criminals arises from the sovereignty of the monarch since it is this alone which is empowered to actualize Spirit's power of making undone what has been done and wiping out a crime by forgiving and forgetting it.

> Pardon is the remission of punishment, but it does not annul the law. On the contrary, the law stands and the pardoned man remains a criminal as before. This annulment of punishment may take place through religion, since something done may by Spirit be made undone in Spirit. But the power to accomplish this on earth resides in the king's majesty alone and must belong solely to his self-determined decision.

Here there is no uneasiness. The right of pardon exhibits the majesty, the supreme self-confidence of Spirit in its cosmic authority, and Hegel places no limitations on its exercise. How can we account for this difference within retributivism between the Kantian and Hegelian attitudes towards mercy?

The answer lies, I believe, in their different understandings of the basis of human dignity. For Kant, the individual's dignity, and thus his title to rights, rests on his sharing the common personality of the human species. This common personality – Kant's pure ego – is a human essence abstracted from the empirical personality, which is ruled by self-love and which remains as a fixed reality opposed to the rational self. Now the fixed reality or naturalness of the self-seeking person poses an ever-present challenge to the objective reality of human dignity. For Kant this dignity is inherently insecure, because it is nothing more than a subjective claim asserted over against a hostile nature, a claim that must therefore be continually vindicated through the external conquest of its antithesis. From this perspective, therefore, to grant mercy to a criminal would be to leave standing the claim of selfishness to validity and thus to leave justice unsatisfied.

For Hegel, by contrast, the basis of human dignity is not solely a human essence of personality. It is a transcendent or divine Personality of which human selfhood is a subordinate though essential element. And this divine Person is no mere abstraction which leaves evil as a fixed reality outside it. Rather it is a Spirit which itself submits to negation by evil in order that, by the annulment of evil's claim to positive reality, its sovereignty might be objectively manifest. Stated otherwise, the natural (self-centred) will is for Hegel not primary and absolute, but is rather posited within the divine ground as an appearance of something independent, in order that, by the demonstration of its independence as appearance, the divine ground of being might be vindicated as such. This means that the naturalness of egoism is inherently a show, a passing phase in the self-reintegration of Spirit. Punishment is just the practical demonstration that the right of egoism is a mere show, and this constitutes its justification. But now mercy is a more perfect demonstration of this truth. For Kant, mercy was opposed to justice because it meant leaving unrefuted the claim of egoism to reality. For Hegel, mercy is a form of justice because it is itself the refutation of that claim. The passage quoted above suggests a distinction as well as a relation between divine and human forgiveness. Divine forgiveness flows from the divine nature as that which incorporates as a constituent element of itself the individual's alienation from, and return to, the divine ground. From the divine standpoint, therefore, mercy is reconciled with justice because, far from leaving the natural will in its otherness, it is the very process of positing and conquering it. Human forgiveness flows from the recognition that divine mercy robs evil of its power of being and so establishes man's dignity beyond threat of subversion. Thus, not even from the human standpoint is mercy opposed to justice, for it too attests to the nullity of evil. Like punishment, mercy presupposes wrongdoing; but it affirms that the wrong is insignificant, that its claim to validity is a mock claim, that it is powerless to prevail against right. This, then, is how mercy can have a place within a retributive theory of punishment. Mercy, no less than punishment, 'wipes out' the wrong, not by repaying it but by forgetting it.

Now the relevance of all this to the death penalty is simply this. If the purpose of punishment is to vindicate human rights against the pretended validity of the criminal act, it seems consequent to suppose that the severity of punishment in any epoch will depend on the perceived magnitude of the threat that crime poses to the reality of human dignity. A claim of human worth resting on the supposed sovereignty of individual personhood finds its sole objective confirmation in outward possessions. It will therefore see in any offence against property an infinite challenge to itself and punish it accordingly. Since, moreover, the absolutization of the isolated person brings the state of nature into political society, the penal system will take upon itself the enforcement of the law of private revenge, centralizing without reconstituting it. Retribution will thus take the form of the qualitative and quantitative redress of personal injury, and torture, the giving back of pain for pain, will be the paradigmatic form of punishment. On the other hand, a claim of dignity resting, like Kant's, on the assumed sovereignty of a common humanity (and hence of law) will view this dignity as established independently of external things, though still challenged by a natural will now regarded as evil. Since the state of nature is here abrogated as a normative principle, the law of retaliation will be reinterpreted as the impersonal vengeance of the general will, and minutely differentiated corporal punishments will give way to the uniform abstraction of imprisonment, corresponding to the abstraction of crime as an offence against right in general. Moreover, since it is now the principle of the criminal will and not the criminal act itself which challenges the objective reality of human worth, punishments will be adjusted more subtly to the evil quality of the will, and, in particular, the death penalty will be reserved for the only crime which, by destroying the body, also destroys the person. Finally, a people confident that human dignity is no mere subjective claim pitted against an indifferent nature but an objective fact rooted in a divinely governed cosmos; a people confident, in short, that the human personality cannot be destroyed will be inclined to temper punishment with mercy. We may imagine, therefore, that there exists an ideal penal code corresponding to the highest strength of the human spirit and in which the death penalty perhaps plays no part. But like representative government, this simply best penal code is not suited to all peoples at all stages of their moral development. At any stage, the strength of the basis of self-definition will determine the scale of punishments needed to preserve and reinforce the positive morality (understood as a particular perception of natural morality) on which the social order is founded. And any attempt to impose a higher, less severe code on a people unprepared for it risks undermining the belief in a natural moral order on which depends the conviction of personal worth as well as the habit of self-restraint.

Somewhat surprisingly, therefore, retributivism issues in a counsel of pragmatism with respect to the use of the death penalty. It leads to the Montesquieuian conclusion that that penal code is best which suits the 'spirit' of a people, by which is here understood the system of life-organizing beliefs regarding the foundation of human value. Not to be confused with this result is the conclusion of Beccaria, who thought that the scale of punishments ought to be relative to the level of civility of a people, the more savage requiring stronger deterrents. The question legislators must ask is not how much punishment is needed to deter potential criminals in the present state of society, but how much is needed to reassure decent men in the present state of their self-knowledge. Obviously these questions lead to different oracles. The first directs us to data on differential crime rates, the second to public opinion.

Are you convinced by Brudner's 'Montesquieuian' theory of proportionality in punishment? How would such an approach to proportionality best be incorporated in the structure of a criminal justice system? For example, would broad principles of sentencing giving judges much leeway be appropriate? Should the legislature fix scales of punishment? Should juries be able to set sentences? Keep Brudner's approach in mind when you look at the last reading in this chapter, Gardner 1998. To achieve proportion in punishment obviously requires a way of assessing the seriousness of crimes. For a recent attempt to do so in terms of the way in which criminal acts harm the standard of life of victims, see von Hirsch and Jareborg 1991.

To conclude this section, we turn briefly to 'mixed' theories of punishment, mixed in that they draw on elements of both desert theory and deterrence theory. The *locus classicus* of the 'mixed' justification of punishment is Hart's (1968). His work here is a further example of Hart's methodological avoidance of overarching single perspectives on philosophical problems – here as elsewhere he seeks to knit together a fuller understanding by trying to give weight to conflicting intuitions, paying close attention to the terms in which we speak of punishment.

Hart (1968, 1–9)

PROLEGOMENON TO THE PRINCIPLES OF PUNISHMENT

I. INTRODUCTORY

...

General interest in the topic of punishment has never been greater than it is at present and I doubt if the public discussion of it has ever been more confused. The interest and the confusion are both in part due to relatively modern scepticism about two elements which have figured as essential parts of the traditionally opposed 'theories' of punishment. On the one hand, the old Benthamite confidence in fear of the penalties threatened by the law as a powerful deterrent, has waned with the growing realization that the part played by calculation of any sort in anti-social behaviour has been exaggerated. On the other hand a cloud of doubt has settled over the keystone of 'retributive' theory. Its advocates can no longer speak with the old confidence that statements of the form 'This man who has broken the law could have kept it' had a univocal or agreed meaning; or where scepticism does not attach to the meaning of this form of statement, it has shaken the confidence that we are generally able to distinguish the cases where a statement of this form is true from those where it is not.

Yet quite apart from the uncertainty engendered by these fundamental doubts, which seem to call in question the accounts given of the efficacy, and the morality of punishment by all the old competing theories, the public utterances of those who conceive themselves to be expounding, as plain men for other plain men, orthodox or common-sense principles (untouched by modern psychological doubts) are uneasy. Their words often sound as if the authors had not fully grasped their meaning or did not intend the words to be taken quite literally. A glance at the parliamentary debates or the Report of the Royal Commission on Capital Punishment shows that many are now troubled by the suspicion that the view that there is just one supreme value or objective (e.g. Deterrence, Retribution or Reform) in terms of which all questions about the justification of punishment are to be answered, is somehow wrong; yet, from what is said on such occasions no clear account of what the different values or objectives are, or how they fit together in the justification of punishment, can be extracted. No one expects judges or statesmen occupied in the business of sending people to the gallows or prison, or in making (or unmaking) laws which enable this to be done, to have much time for philosophical discussion of the principles which make it morally tolerable to do these things. A judicial bench is not and should not be a professorial chair. Yet what is said in public debates about punishment by those specially concerned with it as judges or legislators is important. Few are likely to be more circumspect, and if what they say seems, as it often does, unclear, one-sided and easily refutable by pointing to some aspect of things which they have overlooked, it is likely that in our inherited ways of talking or thinking about punishment there is some persistent drive towards an over-simplification of multiple issues which require separate consideration. To counter this drive what is most needed is not the simple admission that instead of a single value or aim (Deterrence, Retribution, Reform or any other) a plurality of different values and aims should be given as a conjunctive answer to some single question concerning the justification of punishment. What is needed is the realization that different principles (each of which may in a sense be called a 'justification') are relevant at different points in any morally acceptable account of punishment. What we should look for are answers to a number of different questions such as: What justifies the general practice of punishment? To whom may punishment be applied? How severely may we punish? In dealing with these and other questions concerning punishment we should bear in mind that in this, as in most other social institutions, the pursuit of one aim may be qualified by or provide an opportunity, not to be missed, for the pursuit of others. Till we have developed this sense of the complexity of punishment (and this prolegomenon aims only to do this) we shall be in no fit state to assess the extent to which the whole institution has been eroded by, or needs to be adapted to, new beliefs about the human mind.

2. JUSTIFYING AIMS AND PRINCIPLES OF DISTRIBUTION

There is, I think, an analogy worth considering between the concept of punishment and that of property. In both cases we have to do with a social institution of which the centrally important form is a structure of legal rules, even if it would be dogmatic to deny the names of punishment or property to the similar though more rudimentary rule-regulated practices within groups such as a family, or a school, or in customary societies whose customs may lack some of the standard or salient features of law (e.g. legislation, organized sanctions, courts). In both cases we are confronted by a complex institution presenting different inter-related features calling for separate explanation; or, if the morality of the institution is challenged, for separate justification. In both cases failure to distinguish separate questions or attempting to answer them all by reference to a single principle ends in confusion. Thus in the case of property we should distinguish between the question of the *definition* of property, the question why and in what circumstance it is a *good* institution to maintain, and the questions in what ways individuals may become *entitled* to acquire property and *how much* they should be allowed to acquire. These we may call questions of *Definition*, *General Justifying Aim*, and *Distribution* with the last subdivided into questions of *Title* and *Amount*. It is salutary to take some classical exposition of the idea of property, say Locke's chapter 'Of Property' in the *Second Treatise*, and to observe how much darkness is spread by the use of a single notion (in this case 'the labour of (a man's) body and the work of his hands') to answer all these different questions which press upon us when we reflect on the institution of property. In the case of punishment the beginning of wisdom (though by no means its end) is to distinguish similar questions and confront them separately.

(a) Definition

Here I shall simply draw upon the recent admirable work scattered through English philosophical journals and add to it only an admonition of my own against the abuse of definition in the philosophical discussion of punishment. So with Mr. Benn and Professor Flew I shall define the standard or central case of 'punishment' in terms of five elements: (i) It must involve pain or other consequences normally considered unpleasant. (ii) It must be for an offence against legal rules. (iii) It must be of an actual or supposed offender for his offence. (iv) It must be intentionally administered by human beings other than the offender. (v) It must be imposed and administered by an authority constituted by a legal system against which the offence is committed.

In calling this the standard or central case of punishment I shall relegate to the position of sub-standard or secondary cases the following among many other possibilities. (a) Punishments for breaches of legal rules imposed or administered otherwise than by officials (decentralised sanctions). (b) Punishments for breaches of non-legal rules or orders (punishments in a family or school). (c) Vicarious or collective punishment of some member of a social group for actions done by others without the former's authorization, encouragement, control or permission. (d) Punishment of persons (otherwise than under (c)) who neither are in fact nor supposed to be offenders.

The chief importance of listing these sub-standard cases is to prevent the use of what I shall call the 'definitional stop' in discussions of punishment. This is an abuse of definition especially tempting when use is made of conditions (ii) and (iii) of the standard case in arguing against the utilitarian claim that the practice of punishment is justified by the beneficial consequences resulting from the observance of the laws which it secures. Here the stock 'retributive' argument is: If *this* is the justification of punishment, why not apply it, when it pays to do so, to those innocent of any crime, chosen at random, or to the wife and children of the offender? And here the wrong reply is: *That*, by definition, would not be 'punishment' and it is the justification of punishment which is in issue. Not only will this definitional stop fail to satisfy the advocate of 'Retribution', it would prevent us from investigating the very thing which modern scepticism most calls in question: namely the rational and moral status of our preference for a system of punishment under which measures painful to individuals are to be taken against them only when they have committed an offence. Why do we prefer this to other forms of social hygiene which we might employ to prevent anti-social behaviour and which we do employ in special circumstances, sometimes with reluctance? No account of punishment can afford to dismiss this question with a definition.

(b) The nature of an offence

... Why are certain kinds of action forbidden by law and so made crimes or offences. The answer is: To announce to society that these actions are not to be done and to secure that fewer of them are done. These are the common immediate aims of making any conduct a criminal offence and until we have laws made with these primary aims we shall lack the notion of a 'crime' and so of a 'criminal'. Without recourse to the simple idea that the criminal law sets up, in its rules, standards of behaviour to encourage types of conduct and discourage others we cannot distinguish a punishment in the form of a fine from a tax on a course of conduct.

...

It is important however to stress the fact that in thus identifying the immediate aims of the criminal law we have not reached the stage of justification. There are indeed many forms of undesirable behaviour which it would be foolish (because ineffective or too costly) to attempt to inhibit by use of the law and some of these may be better left to educators, trades unions, churches, marriage guidance councils or other non-legal agencies. Conversely there are some forms of conduct which we believe cannot be effectively inhibited without use of the law. But it is only too plain that in fact the law may make activities criminal which it is morally important to promote and the suppression of these may be quite unjustifiable. Yet confusion between the simple immediate aim of any criminal legislation and the justification of punishment seems to he the most charitable explanation of the claim that punishment is justified as an 'emphatic denunciation by the community of a crime'. Lord Denning's dictum that this is the ultimate justification of punishments can be saved from ... criticism ... only if it is treated as a blurred statement of the truth that the aim not of punishment, but of criminal legislation is indeed to denounce certain types of conduct as something not to be practised. Conversely the immediate aim of criminal legislation cannot be any of the things which are usually mentioned as justifying punishment: for until it is settled what conduct is to be legally denounced and discouraged we have not settled from what we are to *deter* people, or who are to be considered *criminals* from whom we are to exact *retribution*, or on whom we are to wreak *vengeance*, or whom we are to *reform*.

...

(c) General Justifying Aim

I shall not here criticize the intelligibility or consistency or adequacy of those theories that are united in denying that the practice of a system of punishment is justified by its beneficial consequences and claim instead that the main justification of the practice lies in the fact that when breach of the law involves moral guilt the application to the offender of the pain of punishment is itself a thing of value. A great variety of claims of this character, designating 'Retribution' or 'Expiation' or 'Reprobation' as the justifying aim, fall in spite of differences under this rough general description ... Here I shall merely insist that it is one thing to use the word Retribution *at this point* in an account of the principle of punishment in order to designate the General Justifying Aim of the system, and quite another to use it to secure that to the question 'To whom may punishment be applied' (the question of Distribution), the answer given is 'Only to the offender for an offence'. ... We shall distinguish the latter from Retribution in General Aim as 'retribution in Distribution'. Much confusing shadow-fighting between utilitarians and their opponents may be avoided if it is recognised that it is perfectly consistent to assert *both* that the General Justifying Aim of the practice of punishment should be qualified or restricted out of deference to the principles of Distribution which require that punishment should only be of an offender for an offence. Conversely it does not in the least follow from the admission of the latter principle of retribution in Distribution that the General Justifying Aim of punishment is Retribution though of course Retribution in General Aim entails retribution in Distribution.

Hart's mixed theory, roughly that the general justifying aim of punishment is deterrence which however is constrained by retributive limits on whom may be punished (only those guilty of an offence) and in what amounts, has been subject to numerous criticisms (see, eg Lacey 1988, 46–53; Primoratz 1987), the most basic one being that retributive theory and deterrence theory are so fundamentally at odds that any combination of the two is unstable. Consider, for example, Hart's claim at the end of the reading that while retribution in general aim would *entail* retribution in distribution, he appears not to think that deterrence in general aim would *entail* a deterrent rationale for distribution. But why not? Why shouldn't deterrence in general aim govern the distributional question? Conversely, can one distinguish the question of general aim from the issue of distribution in the case of punishment? Here one might argue that Hart's analogy with the case of property is false; the right to property in law, what kind of right a property right is, compared say, with a personal right like a right under a contract, is clearly distinguishable from laws which seek to distribute or re-distribute property rights. But, in the case of punishment, the law doesn't set out rights (or duties) to punish, *and then* devise a system of distribution – it's not as if there is a certain amount of punishment to be administered, and then the question arises 'who gets it?' The rights or duties of punishment are inextricably linked to their distribution, for any particular instance of the right or duty of punishment only arises when there is a particular offence. We don't build prisons or scaffolds because we want so much imprisonment and so many hangings, and then decide who goes to prison or the scaffold. We do those things in the grim realisation that, despite our fondest wish never to 'distribute' these things at all, we will almost certainly find it necessary to punish by these means.

It is probably fair to say that, at the current time, most theorists of punishment believe that retributive or desert theory's principled case against deterrence theory makes any purely deterrent approach to punishment unsatisfactory. At the same time, however, a great deal of disquiet with the pure retributive case remains, if only because retributive theory, being oriented to the past, ie in treating punishment purely as a backward-looking response to an offense, offers no account of how punishment might be forward-looking or productive in any way. This has led some theorists to emphasise the 'expressive', 'communicative' or penitential aspects of punishment, to which we now turn.

II Expressive, Communicative, and Penitential Theories of Punishment

'Expressive', 'communicative', and 'penitential' theories of punishment form a class. They each hold that the primary point of punishment is for the community to express in no uncertain terms its morally just disapproval of the offender's action; expressive theories tend to emphasise the community's right to vent its disapproval, irrespective of how much the offender chooses to listen; recall Denning's statement, quoted in the Hart reading above, that punishment is the 'emphatic denunciation by the community of a crime'. Feinberg (1994, 77–80) emphasises the community's disowning of the criminal's act; consider the case of a pilot of nation A firing upon an airplane of nation B; nation A's punishing of its pilot constitutes an unequivocal expression that it disavows, and shows symbolically its non-acquiescence in, the pilot's act. In the domestic setting, the state's punishment of the criminal has the same expressive function for the victim – the community, via the state, shows emphatically that it sides with the victim and takes no part in the criminal's depradation. To fail to punish in either of these cases would express the opposite, that the community or state treats the act as a valid one, as one of its own by one of its own. Punishment is, therefore, the necessary expression of the community's or state's *partiality* to victims as against their predators.

Communicative and penitential theories, by contrast, tend to emphasise that punishment is a communication by the community, or its authoritative representative, the state, *with the criminal*, so as to bring home to him its disapproval, in hopes that he will reform himself and so become a full member of the community once again. These theories emphasise that the criminal is still a rights-bearer who must be treated as a full moral agent. Thus his punishment must be addressed to him in terms which convey in some acceptably *rational* way the grounds of the community's disapproval.

All such theories face a significant obstacle with respect to the question of 'hard treatment', ie the painful or unpleasant side of punishment – imprisonment, flogging, fines, execution, etc. A desert or deterrence theorist might well say, 'If all you wish to do is to express your disapproval, well then, express it. Shout it from the roof tops; enact it dramatically in the form of a ritual dance; write a haiku. But don't pretend that the infliction of pain or suffering counts as "expression"'. Expressivists such as Feinberg address this question directly, claiming that the use of hard treatment simply counts as our conventional means of expressing our disapproval of crime, and claiming that different conventional means of expression are imaginable. But is this a satisfactory reply? Don't we require an explanation why hard treatment *is* our 'conventional' means of expression, and why, given our common understanding that hard treatment obviously causes pain and suffering in ways that other forms of expression don't, we haven't altered our conventions?

Expressivist and Communicative punishment theorists have offered alternative views. In the passage below, von Hirsch supplements the primary role of censure in his account of punishment with a prudential role for hard treatment.

Von Hirsch (1993, 12–13)

The criminal law seems to have preventive features in its very design. When the State criminalizes conduct, it issues a legal threat: such conduct is proscribed, and violation will result in the imposition of specified sanctions. The threat appears to be explicitly aimed at discouraging the proscribed conduct. Criminal sanctions also seem too onerous to serve just to give credibility to the censure. Even were penalties substantially scaled down from what they are today, some of them still could involve significant deprivations of liberty or property. In the absence of a preventive purpose, it is hard to conceive of such intrusions as having the sole function of showing that the state's disapproval is seriously intended.

This reasoning led me to suggest [elsewhere] a bifurcated account of punishment. The penal law, I said, performs two interlocking functions. By threatening unpleasant consequences, it seeks to discourage criminal behaviour. Through the censure expressed by such sanctions, the law registers disapprobation of the behaviour. Citizens are thus provided with moral and not just prudential reasons for desistence.

However, the two elements in my account, reprobation and prevention, remained uneasily matched. Whereas the censuring element appeals to the person's moral agency, does not the preventive element play merely on his fear of unpleasant consequences? If the person is capable of being moved by moral appeal, why the threat? If not capable and thus in need of the threat, it appears that he is being treated like a tiger [i.e. as a dangerous animal who can be controlled only by the whip or cage]. A clarification of the preventive function – and its relation to the censuring function – is needed.

The preventive function of the sanction should be seen, I think, as supplying a prudential reason that is tied to, and supplements, the normative reason conveyed by penal censure.

The criminal law, through the censure embodied in its prescribed sanctions, conveys that the conduct is wrong, and a moral agent thus is given grounds for desistence. He may (given human fallibility) be tempted nevertheless. What the prudential disincentive can do is to provide him a further reason – a prudential one – for resisting the temptation. Indeed, an agent who has accepted the sanction's message that he ought not offend, and who recognizes his susceptibility to temptation, could favour the existence of such a prudential disincentive, as an aid to carrying out what he himself recognizes as the proper course of conduct.

A certain conception of human nature ... underlies this idea of the preventive function as a supplementary prudential disincentive. Persons are assumed to be moral agents, capable of taking seriously the message conveyed through the sanction, that the conduct is reprehensible. They are fallible, nevertheless, and thus face temptation. The function of the disincentive is to provide a prudential reason for resisting the temptation. The account would make no sense were human beings much better or worse: an angel would require no appeals to prudence, and a brute could not be appealed to through censure.

Is von Hirsh's integration of hard treatment into his 'censuring' account more than just ingenious? Is he in danger of risking the dangers of a 'mixed' theory like Hart's? (See also Bottoms 1998.)

In the next reading, Duff provides what is probably the most carefully constructed communicative theory of punishment. Notice how hard treatment is justified only in so far as it serves to communicate to the offender his wrong, such that the pain and suffering involved can be taken on by the offender as a penance.

Duff (1996, 45–54)

A strict consequentialist portrays punishment as an instrumental means to some independently identifiable end. (The contingency of the connection between punishment and its justifying goals provokes the objections ... that any moral constraints on the distribution of punishment or its modes (on who may be punished; on how severe, or intrusive or degrading their punishments may be) must either be merely contingent constraints, which are thus vulnerable to changing contingencies, or be based on nonconsequentialist demands of justice which are quite separate from the justifying goals of punishment; and that both pure and side-constrained consequentialists fail adequately to respect or do justice to the moral status of those who are punished or threatened with punishment.) By contrast, a strict retributivist justifies punishment purely as an appropriate, backward-looking response to a past crime, which has no purpose beyond itself. But, apart from the problem of explaining the supposedly justificatory relationship between past crime and present punishment (particularly when punishment takes the form of hard treatment), there remains for many people the feeling that a system of punishment (especially, again, one of hard treatment punishments) should have some forward-looking purpose. To insist in advance that any adequate justification of punishment must show that it achieves some (by implication consequential) good is of course to beg the question against the retributivist, who would say that it matters *in itself* that justice be done, or that criminals he deprived of their unfair advantages, or that the truth be told; and if we then say in less overtly consequentialist tones that a system of punishment must be justified by showing that it contributes something to the continuing life of the community, a retributivist might reply that on her account it does – it contributes justice or truth. Nonetheless, even among those persuaded by retributivist objections to consequentialism, there may remain the thought that there should be more to punishment than this: while punishment is, as retributivists insist, essentially a matter of responding appropriately to a past crime, that response should also look toward the future.

The accounts to be considered [here] can be seen as trying to meet this worry by giving punishment a purpose beyond itself: a purpose to which it is contingently connected in that it might not in fact achieve its purpose. That connection is not, however, purely contingent (this distinguishes these accounts from any strictly consequentialist theories), for two reasons. First, that purpose itself determines which means (what kinds of punishment) are appropriate to it: on these accounts, it requires that punishment be a mode of communication with a responsible moral agent, which respects her status as a rational agent, and is proportionate to the seriousness of her crime. To try to pursue punishment's proper purpose by other means, for instance, by deliberately punishing innocents or by the excessive or merely manipulative punishment of the guilty, would be not merely contingently inefficacious, or inconsistent with independent side constraints of justice, but incoherent. Second, though this purpose is a 'justifying aim' in that punishment must pursue this purpose if it is to be justified, that justification does not depend wholly on its efficacy in achieving this purpose: sometimes what matters will be the attempt to achieve that purpose, even if we are sure that the attempt is doomed to fail.

A. REPENTANCE, REFORM, AND RECONCILIATION

Some theorists have suggested that punishment should function as moral education. This idea might sound strange. We can 'educate' someone only if there is something she does not yet know or understand, which we aim to teach her. But unless we take an implausibly strict Socratic view of the connection between moral knowledge and action, which ascribes all wrongdoing to ignorance of the good, we must surely see that many criminals know full well that they are doing wrong: not just that it is illegal or contrary to the moral beliefs current in their community, but that it is morally wrong. Few thieves, for instance, would agree that it is morally permissible for others to steal from them, or claim some special moral privilege that makes it right for them to steal, but not for others to steal from them. We may sometimes ascribe a crime to the agent's failure to think through the likely consequences or the moral implications of his action. But this is likely to be true only of some less serious crimes (and not of all of them): to suggest that an armed robber does not know that armed robbery is wrong would be to attribute to him a kind of moral ignorance that raises serious doubts about his status as a responsible moral agent.

But yet, if a responsible moral agent, without excuse or justification, breaks a criminal law that is itself justified (and if she is to be justly punished the law she breaks must be one that she was genuinely obligated to obey), there must be *something* amiss with her moral condition. Perhaps she was weak-willed: she gave in to momentary temptation, or concealed from herself the true moral character of her action. Perhaps she did not care enough for the values that the law embodies, or for the interests it protects, caring more for her own profit. Furthermore, without subscribing to the 'character' conception of criminal liability that portrays the criminal action merely as evidence of some underlying defect of character, we must recognize that whatever moral defect her action manifested was a defect in her as a *continuing* moral agent: that is, it is a defect which remains with her.

Different moral and political theories give different accounts of the nature and implications of the 'defect' that culpably criminal action manifests. Our concern here is with accounts that portray it as a defect not merely *within* the agent, but in those relationships that constitute her moral identity, and her own good. Some talk of a defect in her relationship to 'correct values'; others of a defect in her relationship with her community or her fellow citizens (whose rights or interests she has violated, whose values she has flouted); others, appealing to a Platonic conception of the self and its good, of a defect in her relationship to the Good, and therefore in her relationship with herself and her own good. These ways of talking are not wholly distinct from each other. Those who take seriously the communitarian conception of the individual as existing, and finding her identity and her good, only within a community of shared values and moral relationships, might say that crime marks a defect not merely in the agent's relationship with her fellow citizens, or to the values of her community, but also in her relationship to her own good, which depends on those other relationships; Platonists will portray defects in the person's relationship to 'Correct values' or to the Good as also injurious to her – as damaging her relationship to her own good.

We should notice, however, that such accounts do not portray the defect in, or damage to, such relationships either as an underlying condition, for which the particular criminal act provides evidence (which is how a character conception of criminal liability portrays the role of criminal conduct), or as something contingently caused by criminal action. The culpable wrongdoing itself *constitutes* that defect: it *necessarily* damages those relationships, separating the agent from the Good, her fellow citizens, and her own true good.

This way of understanding the moral significance and implications of crime underpins the idea that the purpose of punishment should be to repair or restore that which the crime has damaged: to repair not just any material harm caused by the crime (though punishment might consist in part in such material reparation), but that damage to the criminal's relationships which was intrinsic to her crime. The crime created a moral breach between the criminal and her fellow citizens or her community, or between the criminal and the Good (and her own good). That breach can be repaired, thus reconciling her with those from whom her crime threatened to separate her, only if she herself is prepared to heal it by repenting and forswearing her crime, which necessarily also involves a resolve and attempt so to reform herself that she avoids such wrongdoing in the future; and punishment aims precisely to bring the criminal to recognize – more adequately than she may yet have recognized – the wrongness of her crime, to repent that crime, and to reform herself.

On this view, it is natural to say that punishment benefits the criminal herself, as well as others: it aims to repair relationships whose damage or destruction is injurious to her as well as to others. Although punishment is not an unqualified blessing (it is better to avoid both wrongdoing and punishment than to do wrong and be punished), if I do wrong it is better to be punished than not (see Plato's Gorgias): punishment is therefore a good, rather than an unqualified evil for the criminal, although he might not himself recognize it as such. By contrast, deterrent theorists, and retributivists who justify punishment as an evil that is justly inflicted on those who do evil, must portray punishment simply as an evil for the person punished.

Though theorists who advocate this kind of view do typically talk of punishment as aiming to benefit the wrongdoer, it might seem unnecessary to do so: why can we not rather say that punishment aims to benefit the community, by protecting its values and dissuading criminals from further crimes; that any benefit to the criminal is only a side effect, not the direct purpose, of such punishment? This would not open such theories to a charge of using the criminal 'merely as a means' to that social benefit (for the aim would still be rational persuasion rather than coercion or manipulation, and we do not use a person 'merely as a means' if we try to persuade him, rationally, to act as he ought to); while it might protect such theories from the liberal argument that it should not be the state's task to seek the wrongdoer's own moral good by such coercive methods. The answer is, I think, that what matters on such accounts is not just that the criminal be persuaded to refrain from future crime but that he be restored to full membership of the moral community by repenting his crime; it is hard to see why this should matter if we do not see that the loss of or damage to his membership of the moral community injures *him*.

It is crucial to note the difference between this kind of account of punishment as educative or reformative and those cruder kinds of purely consequentialist account of punishment as 'rehabilitative' or 'reformative' that were criticized as failing to respect the moral standing of those who are punished. Those consequentialist accounts saw 'rehabilitation' as a matter of bringing about some desirable change in an offender's attitudes, dispositions, and conduct, to which punishment is at best a contingent means – and may not be an efficacious means at all. The aim is to bring it about that the offender accepts and obeys the law or (more ambitiously) to bring it about that he can function 'normally' and law-abidingly in his society, and the task is then to find some instrumentally effective means of achieving this. The offender thus figures as the *object* of our coercive attentions, in or on whom we must cause this change. The purpose of reformative punishment as it is portrayed here, however, is not so much to reform the offender, as to persuade her to reform *herself*: to 'correct' her as a rational and responsible moral agent. Now if that is our aim, the means that we use must themselves be appropriate to, respectful of, her status as a moral agent; indeed, if we are to count as pursuing that aim at all (as distinct from the crude aim of causing some desirable change in her attitudes and conduct), we must throughout treat and address her as a rational moral agent. Analogously, the proper aim of philosophical persuasion is not simply to bring it about that my interlocutor accepts what I assert, but to persuade her as a rational thinker of its truth: to try to achieve that end by manipulation, intellectual bullying, or deceit is not simply ineffectual; it is incoherent.

It is also, of course, crucial to note that this kind of account of justified punishment does not purport to be true of or to justify our existing penal practices. It does not claim that in our existing societies and legal systems every criminal offense damages the criminal's relationship to the Good or to a moral community of which she is truly a member – only that that is (would be) the implication of a crime in a well-ordered community with a just system of law. It does not claim that the kinds of punishment to which we currently subject criminals could plausibly be seen as exercises in such moral reform – only that that is what punishment should be if it is to be properly justified. Nonetheless, the claim that a system of state punishment should (even ideally) aim to benefit the criminal by enabling him to repair the moral damage wrought by his crime will still strike many as bizarre. In particular, it must face three challenges. First, can we really believe that even in a well-ordered society crime is harmful to the criminal himself? Second, how can punishment (especially hard treatment punishment) serve the aims that this kind of account sets for it? Third, should it anyway be the state's task to try, by such coercive means, to secure the moral good of its criminal citizens? I cannot discuss the first question further here: it marks one central difference between a roughly liberal conception of the person, according to which individuals might find their good in certain kinds of social or communal relationship, but might also find it in activities that involve doing serious harms or wrongs to others; and a communitarian conception, according to which we can find our individual goods (and our very identities as persons) only as members of a community of shared values and mutual concerns. But by trying to answer the other two questions, I can bring out more clearly some of the central features of this kind of theory.

B. PUNISHMENT AS PENANCE

How could a system of hard treatment punishment (even if the hard treatment is different from that typically inflicted by our existing penal systems) serve the goals of moral persuasion and reform which, on these accounts, punishment should serve? The criminal law itself declares certain kinds of conduct to be wrong; a criminal conviction condemns or censures the offender for having wrongfully breached the law's justified demands. These are possible ways of trying to persuade citizens to accept and obey the law, and of trying to persuade an offender to repent her crime; and one could imagine a system of more formal condemnations, or of purely symbolic punishments, which might also further that aim by making it clear to the criminal that and why we take her conduct seriously as something wrong. We can also envisage procedures undertaken *during* an offender's punishment that have the same aim: while in prison she could be exposed to various kinds of preaching or discussion (and we would then need to ask whether imprisonment can be justified, in part, as providing the opportunity for such procedures). These accounts, however, claim that punishment itself, *as* punishment, can serve the aim of moral persuasion and reform, and we need to ask how this could be so.

Punishment must obviously, on such accounts, be communicative: it aims to bring the offender to understand and repent the wrong he has done. But what could hard treatment communicate that is not communicated by a formal conviction or a purely symbolic punishment?

One answer, resembling the suggestion that hard treatment is necessary to communicate censure adequately, is that it shows the criminal that there is a barrier, a limit, to her actions: by inflicting such hard treatment on her, we show her how seriously we take her action as something that she should not have done. But why (if not for the sake of prudential deterrence) should this be the appropriate way of communicating such a message? Is there not a serious danger that the criminal will receive the message, and perceive the limit, in purely prudential terms – that its moral meaning will be drowned out by its character as hard treatment?

Perhaps, however, hard treatment punishment can do more than mark a barrier: it can help direct the offender's attention onto what he has done and bring him to a more adequate moral grasp of its wrongfulness. Consider ... programs for domestically violent men that aim to 'directly challenge men's violence' and 'make men responsible for their violence' through 'confrontational group work' involving both reenactment and discussion. An offender required to take part in such a program is *punished* by it. It is a burden imposed on him because of his crime, as a response to that crime. It is designedly painful, in that it is intended to challenge him, to confront him forcefully with the nature of what he has done, and thus to induce in him the painful recognition of his wrongdoing. It can also be said to constitute hard treatment, in that it is burdensome or painful even for those who close their ears to its moral message. Such punishments are communicative: they aim to communicate not merely censure, but a better understanding of what the offender has done. They also, therefore, aim to elicit an appropriate moral response from him: for an adequate understanding of what he has done must be a *repentant* understanding, involving his recognition of its wrongfulness. Furthermore, insofar as they aim to persuade him to confront, to understand, and to repent what he has done, such punishments aim at his moral (self-)reform: for to understand the wrong I have done must also be to recognize a need to reform my conduct and attitudes for the future.

Punishments of this kind are obviously and directly communicative in their focus on and insistent discussion of the offender's crime. But other kinds of punishment, including those familiar in existing penal systems (community service, fines, probation, even imprisonment), can serve the same communicative purpose, *if* administered in the right spirit and the right context: they too can force the criminal's attention onto his crime, thus aiming to induce his repentant understanding of what he has done. Such punishments can also assist, as well as stimulate, the further process of self-reform and reconciliation.

I have argued elsewhere that punishment should ideally constitute a penance which, though initially imposed by others on the criminal, he should ideally come to accept and will for himself. A penance can serve both to induce and to express a wrong-doer's repentant recognition of what she has done: the outward burden or pain it involves expresses the inward pain of remorse, and her acceptance of the pain manifests the sincerity of her remorse. It can also strengthen what might otherwise be a shallow or incomplete repentance, by keeping her attention on her offense and providing a structure within which she can reinforce her understanding of that offense and her resolve to reform herself. It can also help reconcile her with those she has wronged: with her victim, with her fellow citizens, with her community. For it expresses her repentant acceptance of responsibility for her offense, her determined disavowal of that offense, and her desire to restore those relationships which her offense damaged.

Such an account does not, we should note, justify keeping on with increasingly harsh punishment until the offender repents. For, first, punishment must aim at rational moral persuasion, not coerced (and hence inauthentic) acceptance: thus it must always address the offender as a rational moral agent and is necessarily fallible – it is intrinsic to any such rational process that it might fail to persuade. Second, because punishment must communicate an appropriate judgment on the criminal's offense: some principle of proportionality is thus intrinsic to this account. This account does, however, justify punishing those who are already repentant: for some penance is still needed to reinforce that repentance and to manifest its sincerity to others. It also justifies punishing those who will, we are certain, remain unpersuaded and unrepentant: for we owe it to them not to regard them as beyond moral salvation, however empirically unlikely we think that salvation is. Finally, it can also justify punishing the moral rebel who rejects the community's basic values, *if* we can properly say to him that he should accept those values. It does not, however, justify punishing those to whom we cannot properly say that they have flouted the values and damaged the bonds of a community to which they genuinely belong, one within which they are themselves treated as full members: which might well mean that it cannot justify the punishment of many actual criminals in our actual societies.

In this reading Duff appears to claim that his communicative theory of punishment would appeal only to a communitarian, and not to those with more individualistic, or liberal moral views. (For the debate between liberals and communitarians, see Chapter 15.) Do you think communicative theories are *necessarily* associated with communitarian theories? Can you provide a liberal defence of a communicative theory of punishment? More recently Duff has developed a liberal-communitarian theory of political morality in part to address this issue (Duff 2001) which, as one might expect, is controversial (see Lacey 2002). Duff relies heavily on the notion of penance, the notion that an offender can accept his own suffering under hard treatment as a ground for his redemption into the community. Does this erase or overcome misgivings about hard treatment? Is it any less 'mysterious' a justification of punishment than the retributivist's 'he deserves it'? For cannot an opponent of hard treatment, or a defender of it on purely deterrent grounds, say that an individual's willingness to suffer is no more coherent or rational a justification for imposing suffering than is an authority's retributive duty to inflict it on him?

It is worthwhile here drawing a distinction between 'discipline' and 'punishment'. Both von Hirsch and Duff appear to consider the appropriate response to criminal behaviour in a disciplinary frame of mind. That is, they both regard the criminal as one who has failed to live up to community standards, and therefore must be disciplined, that is, dealt with in such a way as to bring his future behaviour up to the mark. For von Hirsch, the hard treatment serves as a kind of spur to good behaviour, and for Duff, the penance serves to expiate the wrong. For both the goal is bringing the offender back into line. It would seem clear, therefore, that certain kinds of punishments, like banishment or execution (which might be regarded as the ultimate banishment) cannot *count as* punishments on these theories, for such punishments cannot serve any disciplinary purpose (except via deterrence, which both von Hirsch and Duff regard as deeply flawed). But it would seem odd to say that banishment or execution do not count as punishments, even if it is true that they are unjustifiable punishments. It is possible to regard punishment as being quite distinct from discipline – what punishment 'expresses' is not that an offender is a fellow citizen who fallen below the mark, as 'discipline' would have it, but that by his own act the criminal has taken himself out of his society. Thus the hard treatment expresses his status as a 'non-citizen', the ultimate expression of which would be execution, but which is also conveyed by imprisonment, slavery, banishment, outlawry, or the temporary reduction to the state of animal irrationality in the case of actual infliction of pain, as with flogging. The 'vale of tears', the 'world of pain' society takes him to is the destination he himself chose by his own acts; society simply provides the fare (usually a return ticket). The point of raising these considerations is not to argue for the correctness of one over the other, but rather to point out that communicative accounts may subtly alter the issues under discussion, by shifting from accounts of punishment *per se* to accounts of something importantly different, ie discipline.

Finally, we can register a more basic objection to the idea of punishment as a form of communication. Though principally directed at the deterrent rationale for punishment with its idea that punishment sends out a signal to possible perpetrators, Mathiesen (1990) questions whether penal 'communication' in general has the same meaning for the addressors as it does for the addressees. Any penal 'communication' will be directed to a multiple audience; to the criminal, to those who are likely to commit offences, to the generally law-abiding, all of whom must be further differentiated by factors such as sex, race, and class. Can any communicative theory genuinely claim that punishment treats all those subject to it as equals, if the symbols and concepts of penitence and penance in which it conveys its message are likely to be interpreted in profoundly different ways by those punished?

III Anti-Punishment: Restorative Responses to Deviance

In this section we will examine the restorative justice movement's challenge to traditional attitudes to punishment. This movement seeks to move the issue of our responses to 'criminal' behaviour away from an arena where the state authority passes moral judgment upon the 'criminal' and punishes him for his 'crime'.

Why are 'crime' and 'criminal' place in inverted commas? The reason is that, as we have seen, one essential conceptual aspect of punishment is that it responds to wrongs which count as punishable, which are called 'crimes'. To punish is to respond to a particular kind of wrong, and to conceive of this sort of wrong is to require that it be punished. Advocates of restorative justice can be ambivalent about the concepts of 'crime' and 'criminal': the offender's act ought perhaps to be seen as part of the ongoing interactions he has with his community; a 'criminal' should never be addressed as a criminal only or purely; rather what is important is to see how specific acts he has committed breach his relations with individuals and with his community generally, and equally importantly, how his acts often *arise from* pre-existing breaches in relations between himself and others which are not 'his fault'. From this perspective, the criminal justice system seems a wholly deracinated environment in which the state asserts its control over communities by taking advantage of conflicts within it. On this non-judgmental view in an extreme form, appropriate linguistic hygiene indicates that if you take my car, you are not a 'thief', but someone 'in conflict with the law'. There is, therefore, for some proponents, a strong abolitionist streak in much restorative justice thought.

This sort of philosophy is also occasionally dubbed 'reparative justice', to emphasise that the goal of dealing with offenders is to repair their relations with their victims and their communities, and sometimes more ambitiously 'transformative justice', to indicate that in the process of responding to offences, the final outcome may not be simply a return to the relations between the parties and the community, to the *status quo ante,* but a transformation of their relations, which puts the social relations of all concerned on a better footing, a footing which should remove some of the grounds which might have led to the offending in the first place.

The roots of restorative justice are various, involving a general dissatisfaction with the efficacy of the 'convict and punish' model of dealing with anti-social behaviour, the victims' rights movement, and the rise of communitarian ideas in political philosophy generally. There can also be detected an 'anthropological' or 'multicultural' strand in some restorative justice writings, including in the first reading below; roughly, the idea here is that western industrialised society may learn much from the way in which anti-social behaviour is dealt with in less-developed societies. There is now a burgeoning literature on the topic, but Christie 1977 stands as one of the seminal points of departure.

Christie (1977, 1–12)

... Conflicts ought to be used, not only left in erosion. And they ought to be used, and become useful, for those originally involved in the conflict. Conflicts *might* hurt individuals as well as social systems. That is what we learn in school. That is why we have officials. Without them, private vengeance and vendettas will blossom. We have learned this so solidly that we have lost track of the other side of the coin: our industrialised large-scale society is not one with too many internal conflicts. It is one with too little. Conflicts might kill, but too little of them might paralyse.

...

ON HAPPENINGS AND NON-HAPPENINGS

Let us take our point of departure far away. Let us move to Tanzania. Let us approach our problem from the sunny hillside of the Arusha province. Here, inside a relatively large house in a very small village, a sort of happening took place. The house was overcrowded. Most grown-ups from the village and several from adjoining ones were there. It was a happy happening, fast talking, jokes, smiles, eager attention, not a sentence was to be lost. It was circus, it was drama. It was a court case.

The conflict this time was between a man and a woman. They had been engaged. He had invested a lot in the relationship through a long period, until she broke it off. Now he wanted it back. Gold and silver and money were easily decided on, but what about utilities already worn, and what about general expenses?

The outcome is of no interest in our context. But the framework for conflict solution is. Five elements ought to be particularly mentioned: 1. The parties, the former lovers, were in the centre of the room and in the centre of everyone's attention. They talked often and were eagerly listened to. 2. Close to them were relatives and friends who also took part. But they did not *take over*. 3. There was also participation from the general audience with short questions, information, or jokes. 4. The judges, three local party secretaries, were extremely inactive. They were obviously ignorant with regard to village matters. All the other people in the room were experts. They were experts on norms as well as actions. And they crystallised norms and clarified what had happened through participation in the procedure. 5. No reporters attended. They were all there.

My personal knowledge when it comes to British courts is limited indeed. I have some vague memories of juvenile courts where I counted some 15 or 20 persons present, mostly social workers using the room for preparatory work or small conferences. A child or a young person must have attended, but except for the judge, or maybe it was the clerk, nobody seemed to pay any particular attention. The child or young person was most probably utterly confused as to who was who and for what, a fact confirmed in a small study by Peter Scott ... Recently, Bottoms and McClean have added another important observation: 'There is one truth which is seldom revealed in the literature of the law or in studies of the administration of criminal justice. It is a truth which was made evident to all those involved in this research project as they sat through the cases which made up our sample. The truth is that, for the most part, the business of the criminal courts is dull, commonplace, ordinary and after a while downright tedious.'

...

But let me keep quiet about your system, and concentrate on my own ... Courts are not central elements in the daily life of [Scandinavians], but peripheral in four major ways:—

1. They are situated in the administrative centres of the towns, outside the territories of ordinary people.

2. Within these centres they are often centralised within one or two large buildings of considerable complexity. Lawyers often complain that they need months to find their way within these buildings. It does not demand much fantasy to imagine the situation of parties or public when they are trapped within these structures ... I feel it safe to say that both physical situation and architectural design are strong indicators that courts in Scandinavia belong to the administrators of law.

3. This impression is strengthened when you enter the courtroom itself – if you are lucky enough to find your way to it. Here again, the periphery of the parties is the striking observation. The parties are represented, and it is these representatives and the judge or judges who express the little activity that is activated within these rooms ... In the small cities, or in the countryside, the courts are more easily reached than in the larger towns. And at the very lowest end of the court system – the so-called arbitration boards – the parties are sometimes less heavily represented through experts in law. But the symbol of the whole system is the Supreme Court where the directly involved parties do not even attend their own court cases.

4. I have not yet made any distinction between civil and criminal conflicts. But it was not by chance that the Tanzania case was a civil one. Full participation in

your own conflict presupposes elements of civil law. The key element in a criminal proceeding is that the proceeding is converted from something between the concrete parties into a conflict between one of the parties and the state. So, in a modern criminal trial, two important thing have happened. First, the parties are being represented. Secondly, the one party that is represented by the state, namely the victim, is so thoroughly represented that she or he for most of the proceedings is pushed completely out of the arena, reduced to the triggerer-off of the whole thing. She or he is a sort of double loser; first, *vis-à-vis* the offender, but secondly and often in a more crippling manner by being denied rights to full participation in what might have been one of the more important ritual encounters in life. The victim has lost the case to the state.

PROFESSIONAL THIEVES

As we all know, there are many honourable as well as dishonourable reasons behind this development. The honourable ones have to do with the state's need for conflict reduction and certainly also its wishes for the protection of the victim. It is rather obvious. So is also the less honourable temptation for the state, or Emperor, or whoever is in power, to use the criminal case for personal gain. Offenders must pay for their sins. Authorities have in time past shown considerable willingness, in representing the victim, to act as receivers of the money or other property from the offender. Those days are gone; the crime control system is not run for profit. And yet they are not gone. There are, in all banality, many interests at stake here, most of them related to professionalisation.

Lawyers are particularly good at stealing conflicts. They are trained for it. They are trained to prevent and solve conflicts. They are socialised into a sub-culture with a surprisingly high agreement concerning interpretation of norms, and regarding what sort of information can be accepted as relevant in each case. Many among us have, as laymen, experienced the sad moments of truth when our lawyers tell us that our best arguments in our fight against our neighbour are without any legal relevance whatsoever and that we for God's sake ought to keep quiet about them in court. Instead they pick out arguments we might find irrelevant or even wrong to use.

...

Conflicts become the property of lawyers. But lawyers don't hide that it is conflicts they handle. And the organisational framework of the courts underlines this point. The opposing parties, the judge, the ban against privileged communication within the court system, the lack of encouragement for specialisation – specialists cannot be internally controlled – it all underlines that this is an organisation for the handling of conflicts. *Treatment personnel* are in another position. They are more interested in *converting the image of the case from one of conflict into one of non-conflict*. The basic model of healers is not one of opposing parties, but one where one party has to be helped in the direction of one generally accepted goal – the preservation or restoration of health. They are not trained into a system where it is important that parties can control each other. There is, in the ideal case, nothing to control, because there is only one goal. Specialisation is encouraged. It increases the amount of available knowledge, and the loss of internal control is of no relevance. A conflict perspective creates unpleasant doubts with regard to the healer's suitability for the job. A non-conflict perspective is a precondition for defining crime as a legitimate target for treatment.

One way of reducing attention to the conflict is reduced attention given to the victim. Another is concentrated attention given to those attributes in the criminal's background which the healer is particularly trained to handle. Biological defects are perfect. So also are personality defects when they are established far back in time – far away from the recent conflict. And so are also the whole row of explanatory variables that criminology might offer. We have, in criminology, to a large extent functioned as an auxiliary science for the professionals within the crime control system. We have focused on the offender, made her or him into an object for study, manipulation and control. We have added to all those forces that have reduced the victim to a nonentity and the offender to a thing … So, as a preliminary statement: Criminal conflicts have either become other people's property-primarily the property of lawyers – or it has been in other people's interests to *define conflicts away.*

STRUCTURAL THIEVES

But there is more to it than professional manipulation of conflicts. Changes in the basic social structure have worked in the same way.

What I particularly have in mind are *two types of segmentation* easily observed in highly industrialised societies. First, there is the question of segmentation *in space.* We function each day, as migrants moving between sets of people which do not need to have any link – except through the mover. Often, therefore, we know our work-mates only as work-mates, neighbours only as neighbours, fellow cross-country skiers only as fellow cross-country skiers. We get to know them as roles, not as total persons. This situation is accentuated by the extreme degree of division of labour we accept to live with. Only experts can evaluate each other according to individual – personal – competence … Through all this, we get limited possibilities for understanding other people's behaviour. Their behaviour will also get limited relevance for us. Role-players are more easily exchanged than persons.

The second type of segmentation has to do with what I would like to call our re-establishment of caste-society. I am not saying class-society, even though there are obvious tendencies also in that direction. In my framework, however, I find the elements of caste even more important. What I have in mind is the segregation based on biological attributes such as sex, colour, physical handicaps or the number of winters that have passed since birth. Age is particularly important. It is an attribute nearly perfectly synchronised to a modern complex industrialised society. It is a continuous variable where we can introduce as many intervals as we might need. We can split the population in two: children and adults. But we also can split it in ten: babies, preschool children, school-children, teenagers, older youth, adults, pre- pensioned, pensioned, old people, the senile. And most important: the cutting points can be moved up and down according to social needs.

Segmentation according to space and according to caste attributes has several consequences. First and foremost it leads into a *depersonalisation* of social life. Individuals are to a smaller extent linked to each other in close social networks where they are confronted with *all* the significant roles of the significant others. This creates a situation with limited amounts of information with regard to each other. We do know less about other people, and get limited possibilities both for understanding and for prediction of their behaviour. If a conflict is created, we are less able to cope with this situation. Not only are professionals there, able and willing to take the conflict away, but we are also more willing to give it away.

Secondly, segmentation leads to destruction of certain conflicts even before they get going. The depersonalisation and mobility within industrial society melt away some essential conditions for living conflicts; those between parties that mean a lot to each other. What I have particularly in mind is crime against other people's honour, libel or defamation of character. All the Scandinavian countries have had a dramatic decrease in this form of crime. In my interpretation, this is not because honour has become more respected, but because there is less honour to respect. The various forms of segmentation mean that human beings are inter-related in ways where they simply mean less to each other. When they are hurt, they are only hurt partially. And if they are troubled, they can easily move away. And after all, who cares? Nobody knows me. In my evaluation, the decrease in the crimes of infamy and libel is one of the most interesting and sad symptoms of dangerous developments within modern industrialised societies. The decrease here is clearly related to social conditions that lead to increase in other forms of crime brought to the attention of the authorities. It is an important goal for crime prevention to re-create social conditions which lead to an increase in the number of crimes against other people's honour.

A third consequence of segmentation according to space and age is that certain conflicts are made completely invisible, and thereby don't get any decent solution whatsoever. I have here in mind conflicts at the two extremes of a continuum. On the one extreme we have the over-privatised ones, those taking place against individuals captured within one of the segments. Wife beating or child battering represent examples. The more isolated a segment is, the more the weakest among parties is alone, open for abuse. Inghe and Riemer made the classical study many years ago of a related phenomenon in their book on incest. Their major point was that the social isolation of certain categories of proletarised Swedish farm-workers was the necessary condition for this type of crime. Poverty meant that the parties within the nuclear family became completely dependent on each other. Isolation meant that the weakest parties within the family had no external network where they could appeal for help. The physical strength of the husband got an undue importance. At the other extreme we have crimes done by large economic organisations against individuals too weak and ignorant to be able even to realise they have been victimised. In both cases the goal for crime prevention might be to re-create social conditions which make the conflicts visible and thereafter manageable.

CONFLICTS AS PROPERTY

Conflicts are taken away, given away, melt away, or are made invisible. Does it matter, does it really matter?

... In our types of society, conflicts are more scarce than property. And they are immensely more valuable.

They are valuable in several ways. Let me start at the societal level, since here I have already presented the necessary fragments of analysis that might allow us to see what the problem is. Highly industrialised societies face major problems in organising their members in ways such that a decent quota take part in any activity at all. Segmentation according to age and sex can be seen as shrewd methods for segregation. Participation is such a scarcity that insiders create monopolies against outsiders, particularly with regard to work. In this perspective, it will easily be seen that conflicts represent a *potential for activity, for participation*. Modern criminal control systems represent one of the many cases of lost opportunities for involving citizens in tasks that are of immediate importance to them. Ours is a society of task-monopolists.

The victim is a particularly heavy loser in this situation. Not only has he suffered, lost materially or become hurt, physically or otherwise. And not only does the state take the compensation. But above all he has lost participation in his own case. It is the Crown that comes into the spotlight, not the victim. It is the Crown that describes the losses, not the victim. It is the Crown that appears in the newspaper, very seldom the victim. It is the Crown that gets a chance to talk to the offender, and neither the Crown nor the offender are particularly interested in carrying on that conversation. The prosecutor is fed-up long since. The victim would not have been. He might have been scared to death, panic-stricken, or furious. But he would not have been uninvolved. It would have been one of the important days in his life. Something that belonged to him has been taken away from that victim.

But the big loser is us – to the extent that society is us. This loss is first and foremost a loss in *opportunities for norm-clarification*. It is a loss of pedagogical possibilities. It is a loss of opportunities for a continuous discussion of what represents the law of the land. How wrong was the thief, how right was the victim? Lawyers are, as we saw, trained into agreement on what is relevant in a case. But that means a trained incapacity in letting the parties decide what they think is relevant. It means that it is difficult to stage what we might call a political debate in the court. When the victim is small and the offender big – in size or power – how blameworthy then is the crime? And what about the opposite case, the small thief and the big house-owner? If the offender is well educated, ought he then to suffer more, or maybe less, for his sins? Or if he is black, or if he is young, or if the other party is an insurance company, or if his wife has just left him, or if his factory will break down if he has to go to jail, or if his daughter will lose her fiancé, or if he was drunk, or if he was sad, or if he was mad? There is no end to it. And maybe there ought to be none. Maybe Barotse law as described by Max Gluckman is a better instrument for norm-clarification, allowing the conflicting parities to bring in the whole chain of old complaints and arguments each time. Maybe decisions on relevance and on the weight of what is found relevant ought to be taken away from legal scholars, the chief ideologists of crime control systems, and brought back for free decisions in the court-rooms.

A further general loss – both for the victim and for society in general – has to do with anxiety-level and misconceptions. It is again the possibilities for personalised encounters I have in mind. The victim is so totally out of the case that he has no chance, ever, to come to know the offender. We leave him outside, angry, maybe humiliated through a cross-examination in court, without any human contact with the offender. He has no alternative. He will need all the classical stereotypes around 'the criminal' to get a grasp on the whole thing. He has a need for understanding, but is instead a non-person in a Kafka play. Of course, he will go away more frightened than ever, more in need than ever of an explanation of criminals as non-human.

The offender represents a more complicated case. Not much introspection is needed to see that direct victim-participation might be experienced as painful indeed. Most of us would shy away from a confrontation of this character. That is the first reaction. But the second one is slightly more positive. Human beings have reasons for their actions. If the situation is staged so that reasons can be given (reasons as the parties see them, not only the selection lawyers have decided to classify as relevant), in such a case maybe the situation would not be all that humiliating. And, particularly, if the situation was staged in such a manner that the central question was not meting out guilt, but a thorough discussion of what could be done to undo the deed, then the situation might change. And this is exactly what ought to happen when the victim is re-introduced in the case. Serious attention will centre on the victim's losses. That leads to a natural attention as to how they can be softened. It leads into a discussion of restitution. The offender gets a possibility to change his position from being a listener to a discussion – often a highly unintelligible one – of how much pain he ought to receive, into a participant in a discussion of how he could make it good again. The offender has lost the opportunity to explain himself to a person whose evaluation of him might have mattered. He has thereby also lost one of the most important possibilities for being forgiven. Compared to the humiliations in an ordinary court ... this is not obviously any bad deal for the criminal.

But let me add that I think we should do it quite independently of his wishes. It is not health-control we are discussing. It is crime control. If criminals are shocked by the initial thought of close confrontation with the victim, preferably a confrontation in the very local neighbourhood of one of the parties, what then? I know from recent conversations on these matters that most people sentenced are shocked. After all, they prefer distance from the victim, from neighbours, from listeners and maybe also from their own court case through the vocabulary and the behavioural science experts who might happen to be present. They are perfectly willing to give away their property right to the conflict. So the question is more: are we willing to let them give it away? Are we willing to give them this easy way out?

Let me be quite explicit on one point: I am not suggesting these ideas out of any particular interest in the treatment or improvement of criminals. I am not basing my reasoning on a belief that a more personalised meeting between offender and victim would lead to reduced recidivism. Maybe it would. I think it would. As it is now, the offender has lost the opportunity for participation in a personal confrontation of a very serious nature. He has lost the opportunity to receive a type of blame that it would be very difficult to neutralise. However, I would have suggested these arrangements even if it was absolutely certain they had no effects on recidivism, maybe even if they had a negative effect. I would have done that because of the other, more general gains. And let me also add – it is not much to lose. As we all know today, at least nearly all, we have not been able to invent any cure for crime. Except for execution, castration or incarceration for life, no measure has a proven minimum of efficiency compared to any other measure. We might as well react to crime according to what closely involved parties find is just and in accordance with general values in society.

...

A VICTIM-ORIENTED COURT

There is clearly a model of neighbourhood courts behind my reasoning. But it is one with some peculiar features, and it is only these I will discuss in what follows.

First and foremost; it is a victim-oriented organisation. Not in its initial stage, though. The first stage will be a traditional one where it is established whether it is true that the law has been broken, and whether it was this particular person who broke it.

Then comes the second stage, which in these courts would be of the utmost importance. That would be the stage where the victim's situation was considered, where every detail regarding what had happened – legally relevant or not – was brought to the court's attention. Particularly important here would he detailed consideration first and foremost by the offender, secondly by the local neighbourhood, thirdly by the state. Could the harm be compensated, the window repaired, the lock replaced, the wall painted, the loss of time because the car was stolen given back through garden work or washing of the car ten Sundays in a row? Or maybe, when this discussion started, the damage was not so important as it looked in documents written to impress insurance companies? Could physical suffering become slightly less painful by any action from the offender, during days, months or years? But, in addition, had the community exhausted all resources that might have offered help? Was it absolutely certain that the local hospital could not do anything? What about a helping hand from the janitor twice a day if the offender took over the cleaning of the basement every Saturday? None of these ideas is unknown or untried, particularly not in England. But we need an organisation for the systematic application of them.

Only after this stage was passed, and it ought to take hours, maybe days, to pass it, only then would come the time for an eventual decision on punishment. Punishment, then, becomes that suffering which the judge found necessary to apply *in addition to* those unintended constructive sufferings the offender would go through in his restitutive actions *vis-à-vis* the victim. Maybe nothing could be done or nothing would be done. But neighbourhoods might find it intolerable that nothing happened. Local courts out of tune with local values are not local courts. That is just the trouble with them, seen from the liberal reformer's point of view.

A fourth stage has to be added. That is the stage for service to the offender. His general social and personal situation is by now well-known to the court. The discussion of his possibilities for restoring the victim's situation cannot he carried out without at the same time giving information about the offender's situation. This might have exposed needs for social, educational, medical or religious action – not to prevent further crime, but because needs ought to be met. Courts are public arenas, needs are made visible. But it is important that this stage comes *after* sentencing. Otherwise we get a re-emergence of the whole array of so-called 'special measures' – compulsory treatments – very often only euphemisms for indeterminate imprisonment.

Through these four stages, these courts would represent a blend of elements from civil and criminal courts, but with a strong emphasis on the civil side.

A LAY-ORIENTED COURT

The second major peculiarity with the court model I have in mind is that it will be one with an extreme degree of lay-orientation. This is essential when conflicts are seen as property that ought to be shared. It is with conflicts as with so many good things: they are in no unlimited supply. Conflicts can be cared for, protected, nurtured. But there are limits. If some are given more access in the disposal of conflicts, others are getting less. It is as simple as that.

Specialisation in conflict solution is the major enemy; specialisation that in due – or undue – time leads to professionalisation. That is when the specialists get sufficient power to claim that they have acquired special gifts, mostly through education, gifts so powerful that it is obvious that they can only he handled by the certified craftsman.

With a clarification of the enemy, we are also able to specify the goal; let us reduce specialisation and particularly our dependence on the professionals within the crime control system to the utmost.

The ideal is clear; it ought to be a court of equals representing themselves. When they are able to find a solution between themselves, no judges are needed. When they are not, the judges ought also to be their equals.

… We have lay judges already, in principle. But that is a far cry from realities. What we have, both in England and in my own country, is a sort of specialised non-specialist. First, they are used *again and again*. Secondly, some are even trained, given special courses or sent on excursions to foreign countries to learn about how to behave as a lay judge. Thirdly, most of them do also represent an extremely *biased sample* of the population with regard to sex, age, education, income, class and personal experience as criminals. With real lay judges, I conceive of a system where nobody was given the right to take part in conflict solution more than a few times, and then had to wait until all other community members had had the same experience.

Should lawyers he admitted to court? We had an old law in Norway that forbids them to enter the rural districts. Maybe they should be admitted in stage one where it is decided if the man is guilty. I am not sure. Experts are a cancer to any lay body. It is exactly as Ivan Illich describes for the educational system in general. Each time you increase the length of compulsory education in a society, each time you also decrease the same population's trust in what they have learned and understood quite by themselves.

Behaviour experts represent the same dilemma. Is there a place for them in this model? Ought there to be any place? In stage 1, decisions on facts, certainly not. In stage 3, decisions on eventual punishment, certainly not. It is too obvious to waste words on.

…

The real problem has to do with the service function of behaviour experts. Social scientists can be perceived as functional answers to a segmented society. Most of us have lost the physical possibility to experience the totality, both on the social system level and on the personality level … Our theme is social conflict. Who is not at least made slightly uneasy in the handling of her or his own social conflicts if we get to know that there is an expert on this very matter at the same table? I have no clear answer, only strong feelings behind a vague conclusion: Let us have as few behaviour experts as we dare to. And if we have any, let us for God's sake not have any that specialise in crime and conflict resolution.

Since Christie's paper was written there have been both theoretical and practical developments. There is now a burgeoning literature on the nature of restorative justice and its compatibility with desert and deterrence theory (for a review see Zedner 1994), and it has clearly generated some ideas underlying communicative theories of punishment. And various more or less far-reaching 'restorative' elements have been introduced into criminal justice systems around the world, from granting courts the right to make compensation orders, to victim-offender mediation schemes, to structured removals of cases from the regular criminal justice system into community forums which resemble more or less closely Christie's victim-centred, lay-oriented courts (for a recent review of restorative justice activity, see Braithwaite 2002).

Most people are, at first glance at least, strongly attracted *in principle* to restorative justice, but tend also to be sceptical of whether it would work in practice, generally for the reasons that Christie himself acknowledges. Do you think the practical difficulties are as large as they seem? What aspects of society in Britain today would, you think, need to change for the criminal justice system to substantially embrace restorative justice methods? Bearing in mind the discussion at the end of section II concerning the difference between 'punishment' and 'discipline', how serious could be the crimes dealt with by restorative justice methods? Assault causing grievous bodily harm? Rape? Murder? Is there an implicit claim in the restorative justice philosophy that more minor offences should count only as civil matters, whereas the most serious offences are crimes *just because* the possibility of restorative justice in those cases runs out? In considering this however, consider some of the atrocious acts committed under apartheid dealt with by the post-apartheid South African Truth and Reconciliation Commission, which for some is a model of restorative justice practice (see Tutu 1999).

There are, however, more principled objections, which turn on the civilianisation of the process, that is, treating offences as solely or principally conflicts between the victim and the offender, despite general community involvement. This clearly opens the way for disparate treatment, for the outcome of any process will depend upon the personalities of the victim and the offender. Can it be just if one thief receives one response, because his victim is magnanimous, whereas another receives much harsher treatment (a more onerous reparative decision), because his victim is hard-hearted. Would one expect an itinerant thief, apprehended in a community not his own, to receive a similar treatment as the local lag who, though his behaviour is frowned upon, is generally regarded with affection? This leads to the more general consideration; does the civilianisation not amount to the 'privatisation' of social conflict? Does not the localisation of the administration of justice fracture the sense in which all are equal citizens? Has the state as the community's political representative no substantial interest in strenuously enforcing the fundamental sense that certain depredations are 'beyond the pale', and become matters of concern for the polity in general. Does not restorative justice, to the extent criminal justice is made civil justice, effectively *abolish* not only the punitive response but the very criminality of those offences with which it deals? This conclusion, one must stress, might be perfectly welcome to the restorative theorist; one might well be an abolitionist of crime and punishment in so far as it deals with offences which can be dealt with by reparation, and dispute the extent to which substantial social and political values are bound up with a retributive attitude to, say, theft, or property damage; one might argue that the idea that our sense of political community depends upon the vindication of the law in these cases is just fanciful.

There is a final consideration, brought out in Gardner 1998, which has to do with the displacement function of criminal law, ie that one of the essential reasons for the institution of criminal law and punishment (and one which largely accounts for the actual historical development of the criminal law) is to remove conflicts from the private sphere where, plausibly enough, vengeful attitudes are as likely to reign as merciful ones.

Gardner (1998, 48–52)

For some distance, courts and retaliators travel on the same path even though the former cannot, consistent with their mission, deliberately track the latter. But as I have also attempted to show, the two paths do diverge at certain obvious points. First, ... to preserve the legitimacy of the criminal law's monopolization of retaliation the courts must stop short of institutionalizing the excusable but unjustifiable retaliatory excesses of victims and their sympathizers. Second, ... the principle of due process means that the wrongful action at the heart of the offender's crime cannot always, in the eyes of the law, and notably for the purposes of sentencing, be the same wrongful action which inspires retaliation by or on behalf of victims. The need to restrict the trial to the substance of the charges with which it began may lead to some differences between the victim's perception and the law's rendition of what the offender has done, even when the victim is not driven to retaliatory excess. Finally, the requirement to adjust the sentence for the offender's blameworthiness may ... drive some extra wedges between the court's sense of proportionality and the victim's retaliatory inclinations, even where those inclinations are not excessive and there are no due process impediments to their reflection in law. The court, as an agent of the State, owes a duty of humanity to all which may often exceed the duty each of us owes to other people, and which therefore requires the court to affirm each offender's moral agency and moral responsibility more conscientiously than need be the case in many of our ordinary interpersonal transactions, including transactions with those who wrong us. These three factors add up to constitute what I will call the 'displacement gap' in criminal sentencing: the gap between what retaliators want and what the courts can, in good conscience, deliver.

Traditionally, this displacement gap has been filled by the law's own wealth of symbolic significances. What was confiscated from victims and their sympathizers in point of retaliatory force has traditionally been compensated by the ritual and majesty of the law, and by the message of public vindication which this ritual and majesty served to convey. At one time it was the ritual of the punishment itself which made the greatest contribution. The pillory, the stocks, the carting, the public execution, and various other modes of punishment involving public display allowed the State to close the displacement gap by exhibiting the offender in all his shame and humiliation, in all his remorse and regret, while the proceedings remained under some measure of official control to limit retaliatory excess. But of course a new penal age dawned in the nineteenth century which put the offender out of reach and out of sight in the prison, where measured punishment and control of retaliation could he more successfully combined, both with each other and with the new disciplinary ambitions of supervision and rehabilitation. From then on, the burden of providing ritual and majesty to fill the displacement gap was to a large extent shifted off the shoulders of the punishment system (which was now practically invisible to the general public except in the gloomy expanse of the prison walls) and onto the shoulders of the trial system instead. The courts themselves now had to offer the would-be retaliator the kind of public vindication which would once have been provided by the act of punishment, and the ritual and majesty of the courtroom had to substitute for the ritual and majesty of the recantation at the gallows. Of course the pressure to get this substitution exactly right was eased by the fact that the prison would to some extent protect the offender against the retaliator even if the displacement gap had not been successfully filled by the court. But it was still crucial that the trial itself should offer the victim and his sympathizers some symbolic significances which would divert them from taking the matter into their own hands e.g. if the offender was acquitted, or if a custodial sentence was not used, or once the custodial sentence had expired. For this purpose the court could only rely on continuing respect, indeed deference, for its own heavily ceremonial processes and practices. If the court's processes and practices were to fall into disrepute, if they came to be seen as just distracting frippery, then the vindicatory symbolism of the trial would be lost and the displacement gap would open wide for all to see. We would then face a major legitimation crisis in the system of criminal justice.

My view is that we now face this crisis in Britain, and for the very reason I have just given. During the 1980s and 1990s the steady creep of the ideology of consumerism has led people to regard the courts, along with many other key public institutions, as mere 'service providers' to be judged by their instrumental achievements. League tables, customer charters, satisfaction surveys, outcome audits, and efficiency scrutiny became the depressing norm. Respect for valuable public institutions declined at the same time as expectations of them increased. Even among those who took themselves to be anti-individualistic, the demand that institutions should become more 'transparent' and 'accountable' came to be regarded as orthodoxy, and euphemistic talk of 'cost-effectiveness' became acceptable. All this was, essentially, a corruption of a sound idea, ... the idea that modern government is the servant of its people. It was mistakenly assumed that since public bureaucracies existed to serve social functions, ultimately serving people, they ought to be judged by the purely instrumental contribution they could make to those social functions, and hence their instrumental value for people. But it was forgotten that many social functions were not purely instrumental functions, i.e. many institutions made an intrinsic or constitutive contribution to their own social functions. The mission of such institutions ... was partly integral to their function. The National Health Service and other organs of Beveridge's welfare State are the most familiar examples in Britain; people who regard themselves as collectivists should rue the day they ever tried to defend these in purely instrumental terms, which was the day they surrendered to the creeping individualism of the consumer society. But the criminal courts exemplify the point even more perfectly. Historically they filled the displacement gap in criminal justice by their own (to the public eye) bizarre and almost incomprehensible processes, their own special black magic if you like, which lent profound symbolic importance to their work. But armed with new consumerist ideas people came to see all these processes as mere frippery. They came to ask what the courts were achieving by their black magic, and whether it was giving them the product they wanted, whether this was the service they were looking for, and of course those questions quickly broke the spell. The courts could no longer fill the displacement gap from their own symbolic resources, since their own symbolic resources had been confiscated by the popular expectation of raw retaliatory results.

The consequence of this rapid social change is that the displacement gap is now an open and suppurating social wound, and the threat of retaliation by or on behalf of aggrieved victims of crime looms ever larger. The courts themselves sometimes feel the pressure and feel constrained to penetrate their own veil of ignorance, abandoning their mission to do justice where, as increasingly often, it parts company with their function to displace retaliation. That seriously violates their duty as courts, which is above all the duty of justice, and which positively requires them to stay 'out of touch with public opinion' on matters of sentencing policy. Meanwhile populist politicians pander to retaliatory instincts by threatening to publish names and addresses of ex-offenders, to force ex-offenders to reveal old criminal records, even to license vigilantes in the form of private security guards – all in order 'to hand justice back to the people'. What they do not appear to appreciate is that all of this makes the justification for the criminal law less stable, not more so. For if the criminal law cannot successfully displace retaliation against wrong-doers, but instead collaborates with it, then a central pillar of its justification has collapsed.

I do not mean to suggest that the courts' recent well-documented waking-up to the existence of victims is in every way a bad thing. There has been, for as long as anyone can remember, a tendency for criminal courts, with typical bureaucratic abandon, to pretend that nobody was concerned in their processes but themselves. Victims of crime, in particular, were kept badly informed and given no quarter at all in the operation of the system. Except insofar as they were witnesses, they were expected to find out for themselves where and when the trial would take place, to queue for the public gallery, to sit with the accused in the cafeteria, etc. In their capacity as witnesses, meanwhile, no concessions were made for the special difficulty of confronting those who had wronged them. Much of this amounted to a violation of the State's duty of humanity towards the victims of crime, and to the extent that it still goes on, it still does. The courts should remember that victims, as well as offenders, are thinking, feeling human beings. But this has absolutely no connection with the far more sinister contemporary campaigns to turn victims into parties to the criminal trial or administrators of criminal punishments, or in some other way to hand their grievances back to them. That victims do not try, convict, sentence, or punish criminal offenders, and have no official part in the trial, conviction, sentencing, and punishment of criminal offenders, is not an accident of procedural history. It is, on the contrary, one of the main objects of the whole exercise.

Further Reading

The classic retributivist accounts are those of Kant 1965 and Hegel 1942; the classical utilitarian deterrence account is, of course, Bentham 1982. For a good selection of readings on punishment from a variety of perspectives see Duff and Garland 1994. In a paper combining retributivist and Marxist analyses, Murphy 1973 claims that while retributivism provides the only sound theory of punishment, the conditions of modern capitalist society generally make the infliction of punishment by the state unjust; similar criticisms are made by Hudson 1993. Lacey 1988 argues for a close connection between the justification of punishment and the justice of the social and political arrangements of the society in which it is administered, emphasising both the importance of community bonds and the autonomy of individuals.

Questions

1. 'The debate between retributivists, deterrence theorists, and expressivists illuminates important insights into the justification of punishment, but none provides a rationale for the infliction of hard treatment on convicts that appropriately covers all relevant cases.' Discuss.

2. 'As between desert theory and deterrence theory, one is face with a choice between the devil and the deep blue sea. The former requires one to embrace a mystery, while the latter treats the offender as a contingent means of pursuing social goals.'

3. 'Desert and deterrence theories of punishment naturally align with liberal, individualist political views, while communicative theories and restorative justice naturally align with communitarian political views.' Discuss.

4. Does a philosophy of restorative justice undermine the justification of punishment, or does it merely hope to minimise the use of punishment in practice?

5. What is punishment? Is it ever justified?

6. 'While Hart's own mixed theory of the justice of punishment was flawed, his general orientation to the question looks sounder now than ever; for if one thing is abundantly clear, it is that punishment performs a number of equally important functions, recognises a number of equally compelling values, and responds to a number of equally valid concerns.' Discuss.

13 Hohfeld and the Analysis of Rights

Hamish Ross

Introduction

Analytical jurisprudence can be described as a branch of legal positivism. If legal positivism seeks, among other things, to maintain the possibility of analytically separating law 'as it is' from law 'as it ought to be' then some set of analytical techniques has to be formulated to enable the analyst to say minimally and with confidence: this is the law 'as it is'. Analytical jurisprudence thus continually strives towards more rigorous, complete and perfect descriptions of law. It undertakes the analysis of legal concepts and the structure of laws and systems of laws. It also examines areas such as legal validity and the efficacy of laws and explores the nature of legal reasoning and legal interpretation. You have experienced some of this in your encounter with H L A Hart (Chapter 4) who criticised Austin's analysis of law as commands because, inter alia, it failed to recognise different kinds of rules: power conferring (secondary)/duty imposing (primary). Such analysis, which can run along more and different axes than the two provided by Hart, is the subject of much analytical jurisprudence.

Wesley Newcomb Hohfeld is perhaps one of the most celebrated exponents of the analytical method in jurisprudence. In this chapter we will examine Hohfeld's most important work – his eponymous 'analysis' – treating it primarily as an exercise in analytical jurisprudence. Underlying the Hohfeldian approach to legal concepts, however, is the more fundamental idea that the legal *relationship*, rather than the legal norm, should be seen as the basic conceptual unit of legal thinking: a kind of building block of the legal world. So, instead of examining how standards operate to measure or influence human behaviour, Hohfeld focused on the relationships that law creates between actors – legal or jural relations. His analysis purports to tackle much of the confusion and ambiguity contained within bald claims like 'I have a right to X'. Such claims can be interrogated: 'What sort of legal relationship do you claim to have, and with whom do you claim to have it?' This process of refinement offers a powerful tool in the analysis of law and legal terminology.

The idea of the legal relationship as the basic conceptual unit of legal thinking would be – and indeed, historically, *has* been – sufficient in itself to carve a quite significant role for Hohfeldian analysis within analytical jurisprudence. (Hohfeld refers to the eight fundamental conceptions in his table of jural relations as the 'lowest common denominators of the law'.) But it is also possible to see Hohfeldian analysis as sitting in tandem with a comparable seam of analysis running through *social* theory in terms of which the social world is seen to be made up of a network of *social* relationships. Although that possibility will only be touched upon lightly at various places in this chapter (for a fuller analysis see Ross 2001b), it points to a theoretical environment for Hohfeldian analysis that is of potentially greater explanatory power than analytical jurisprudence taken in isolation.

Hohfeld's Analysis

Hohfeld occupied a unique and unusual place in twentieth century jurisprudence. He was a jurist, and could legitimately be called a legal theorist, who paradoxically lacked any ambition to 'theorise' about law. He described *Some Fundamental Legal Conceptions as Applied in Judicial Reasoning* – his most influential piece of writing, commonly known as 'Hohfeld's Analysis' (which is how it will be referred to here) – as merely an attempt to clarify some 'oft-neglected' legal terminology, for example, 'claim-right', 'power', 'privilege', 'immunity'. His modest stated purpose was to aid students 'in the understanding and in the solution of practical, everyday problems of the law'. To add to the paradox, most actual 'theorising' in the Hohfeldian vein has been *post*-Hohfeldian. For instance, Albert Kocourek's now neglected treatise *Jural Relations* (1928) was one of the most systematic, if abstruse, attempts at Hohfeld-inspired theorising.

Yet the special significance of Hohfeld's contribution to jurisprudence is widely acknowledged. The secondary literature on Hohfeld, for instance, is vast. Hohfeld established perhaps the *basis* of a theoretical approach to the analysis of fundamental legal conceptions whilst leaving much of the most significant and often contentious work of refining and improving his analysis to his successors. The unresolved dilemma of Hohfeldian analysis, however, has been its enduring disengagement from any theoretical tradition that could today be described as 'mainstream': for instance Hartian theory, Kelsenian theory, (Weberian) social theory, sociology of law, and so on. Although Hohfeld's Analysis can be positioned within the broad tradition of legal positivism – specifically analytical jurisprudence – its lack of a more fundamental theoretical context has left it languishing somewhat at the edge of 'serious' theory. In consequence it has tended to be looked upon as part of 'something else' – a technical exercise in juristic analysis, perhaps: in classifying and defining key legal concepts – rather than as a viable theoretical enterprise in its own right.

It is important, at the outset, not to confuse Hohfeld's Analysis with *Hohfeldian analysis*. Hohfeld's Analysis could be described as the work of a skilled academic 'lawyer's lawyer' schooled in the pedagogical ethos of the common law and its traditions of legal debate and practical argumentation. Much Hohfeldian analysis – the work of post-Hohfeldian commentators – can be technical and highly sophisticated exercises in conceptual analysis. Undoubtedly, some of this brand of analysis has been inspired by H L A Hart's ordinary language methodology. But it is useful, and revealing, to get an initial flavour of the 'real Hohfeld': the Hohfeld whose writings are peppered with references to Coke, Blackstone, Pollock and Maitland, Holmes, Holland and numerous opinions of leading common law judges. This is a Hohfeld unencumbered by the excesses of many post-Hohfeldian theoreticians. Indeed, taking a step or two back, it now seems curious that the impetus for Hohfeld's hugely influential analysis appears to have been the inadequacy (as Hohfeld perceived it) of writings available in the early twentieth century on the subject of common law trusts and other equitable interests. Yet as Hohfeld is quick to point out, the analysis that he announces is to follow has a much wider reach and a quite fundamental import.

Hohfeld 1923, 25–26

It is believed that all of the discussions and analyses referred to are inadequate. Perhaps, however, it would have to be admitted that even the great intrinsic interest of the subject itself and the noteworthy divergence of opinion existing among thoughtful lawyers of all times would fail to afford more than a comparatively slight excuse for any further discussion considered as a mere end in itself. But, quite apart from the presumably practical consideration of endeavoring to 'think straight' in relation to all legal problems, it is apparent that the true analysis of trusts and other equitable interests is a matter that should appeal to even the most extreme pragmatists of the law. It may well be that one's view as to the correct analysis of such interests would control the decision of a number of specific questions. This is obviously true as regards the solution of many difficult and delicate problems in constitutional law and in the conflict of laws. So, too, in certain questions in the law of perpetuities, the intrinsic nature of equitable interests is of great significance, as attested by the well-known *Gomm* case and others more or less similar. The same thing is apt to be true of a number of special questions relating to the subject of *bona fide* purchase for value. So on indefinitely.

But all this may seem like misplaced emphasis; for the suggestions last made are not peculiarly applicable to equitable interests: the same points and the same examples seem valid in relation to all possible kinds of jural interests, legal as well as equitable, – and that too, whether we are concerned with 'property', 'contracts', 'torts', or any other title of the law. Special reference has therefore been made to the subject of trusts and other equitable interests only for the reason that the striking divergence of opinion relating thereto conspicuously exemplifies the need for dealing somewhat more intensively and systematically than is usual with the nature and analysis of all types of jural interests. Indeed, it would be virtually impossible to consider the subject of trusts at all adequately without, at the very threshold, analyzing and discriminating the various fundamental conceptions that are involved in practically every legal problem. In this connection the suggestion may be ventured that the usual discussions of trusts and other jural interests seem inadequate (and at times misleading) for the very reason that they are not founded on a sufficiently comprehensive and discriminating analysis of jural relations in general. Putting the matter in another way, the tendency – and the fallacy – has been to treat the specific problem as if it were far less complex than it really is; and this commendable effort to treat as simple that which is really complex has, it is believed, furnished a serious obstacle to the clear understanding, the orderly statement, and the correct solution of legal problems. In short it is submitted that the right kind of simplicity can result only from more searching and more discriminating analysis.

It is notable that the reason *Hart* gave for pursuing a mode of enquiry that culminated in the introduction to jurisprudence of the linguistic analytical method was in some ways not dissimilar to that offered by Hohfeld. For Hart the starting point was, again, a failure to 'think straight': 'Shadows often obscure our knowledge, which not only vary in intensity but are cast by different obstacles to light'. The confusion attending the analysis of legal concepts lay in the *mistaken* belief that there are 'certain fundamental concepts that the lawyer cannot hope to elucidate without entering a forbidding jungle of philosophical argument'. Hart took the view, instead, that legal notions, however fundamental, could be elucidated by a method – the ordinary language method – properly adapted to their special character. A sharpened awareness of words was the key to a sharpened perception of phenomena. For his part, Hohfeld makes resonantly 'Hartian' observations about the imprecise and ambiguous nature of legal terminology and about the analytical befuddlement often attending the use of such terminology. Yet for Hohfeld, as we saw in the previous extract, the solution lay in providing a more 'comprehensive and discriminating analysis of jural relations in general'. The key to banishing analytical confusion lay in an analysis of *jural relations*. But, as the next extract from Hohfeld demonstrates, confusion has always infiltrated the use of legal terminology. And the very nature of that terminology itself – its ambiguity and looseness – is partly to blame.

Hohfeld 1923, 27–31

At the very outset it seems necessary to emphasize the importance of differentiating purely legal relations from the physical and mental facts that call such relations into being. Obvious as this initial suggestion may seem to be, the arguments that one may hear in court almost any day, and likewise a considerable number of judicial opinions, afford ample evidence of the inveterate and unfortunate tendency to confuse and blend the legal and the non-legal quantities in a given problem. There are at least two special reasons for this.

For one thing, the association of ideas involved in the two sets of relations – the physical and the mental on the one hand, and the purely legal on the other – is, in the very nature of the case, extremely close. This fact has necessarily had a marked influence upon the general doctrines and the specific rules of early systems of law. Thus, we are told by Pollock and Maitland:

> 'Ancient German law, like ancient Roman law, sees great difficulties in the way of an assignment of a debt or other benefit of a contract ... men do not see how there can be a transfer of a right unless that right is embodied in some corporeal thing. The history of the incorporeal things has shown us this; they are not completely transferred until the transferee has obtained seisin, has turned his beasts onto the pasture, presented a clerk to the church or hanged a thief upon

the gallows. A covenant or a warranty of title may be so bound up with land that the assignee of the land will be able to sue the covenantor or warrantor.'

In another connection, the same learned authors observe:

'The realm of mediaeval law is rich with incorporeal things. Any permanent right which is of a transferable nature, at all events if it has what we may call a territorial ambit, is thought of as a thing that is very like a piece of land. Just because it is a thing it is transferable. This is no fiction invented by the speculative jurists. For the popular mind these things are things. The lawyer's business is not to make them things but to point out that they are incorporeal. The layman who wishes to convey the advowson of a church will say that he conveys the church; it is for Bracton to explain to him that what he means to transfer is not that structure of wood and stone which belongs to God and the saints, but a thing incorporeal, as incorporeal as his own soul or the *anima mundi*.'

A second reason for the tendency to confuse or blend non-legal and legal conceptions consists in the ambiguity and looseness of our legal terminology. The word 'property' furnishes a striking example. Both with lawyers and with laymen this term has no definite or stable connotation. Sometimes it is employed to indicate the physical object to which various legal rights, privileges, etc., relate; then again – with far greater discrimination and accuracy – the word is used to denote the legal interest (or aggregate of legal relations) appertaining to such physical object. Frequently there is rapid and fallacious shift from the one meaning to the other. At times, also, the term is used in such a 'blended' sense as to convey no definite meaning whatever.

For the purpose of exemplifying the looser usage just referred to, we may quote from *Wilson v. Ward Lumber Co.*:

'The term "property", as commonly used, denotes any external object over which the right of property is exercised. In this sense it is a very wide term, and includes every class of acquisitions which a man can own or have an interest in.'

Perhaps the ablest statement to exemplify the opposite and more accurate usage is that of Professor Jeremiah Smith (then Mr. Justice Smith) in the leading case of *Eaton v. B.C. & M.R.R. Co.*:

'In a strict legal sense, land is not "property", but the subject of property. The term "property", although in common parlance frequently applied to a tract of land or a chattel, in its legal signification "means only the rights of the owner in relation to it". "It denotes a right over a determinate thing." "Property is the right of any person to possess, use, enjoy, and dispose of a thing".'

...

Much of the difficulty, as regards legal terminology, arises from the fact that many of our words were originally applicable only to physical things; so that their use in connection with legal relations is, strictly speaking, figurative or fictional. The term 'transfer' is a good example. If X says that he has transferred his watch to Y, he may conceivably mean, quite literally, that he has physically handed over the watch to Y; or, more likely, that he has 'transferred' his *legal interest*, without any delivery of possession, – the latter, of course, being a relatively figurative use of the term … As another instance of this essentially metaphorical use of a term borrowed from the physical world, the word 'power' may be mentioned. In legal discourse, as in daily life, it may frequently be used in the sense of physical or mental capacity to do a thing; but, more usually and aptly, it is used to indicate a '*legal* power', the connotation of which latter term is fundamentally different. The same observations apply, *mutatis mutandis*, to the term 'liberty'.

Jural Relations

Hohfeld argues that the primary solution to problems of legal conceptual analysis – quite apart from difficulties peculiar to legal terminology – lies in a careful analysis of 'jural relations'. As we saw from the first extract:

> '… [T]he suggestion may be ventured that the usual discussions of trusts and other jural interests seem inadequate … for the very reason that they are not founded on *a sufficiently comprehensive and discriminating analysis of jural relations in general.*'

Hohfeld's confidence in the possibility of a more 'discriminating' (and thus revealing) approach to legal conceptual analysis is clear from the italicised part of this passage. Yet one would have expected such confidence to go hand in hand with a transparent concept of the jural relation itself: a concept potentially no less problematic than those Hohfeld seeks to explain. Hohfeld, however, treats the whole idea of legal relationships – specifically 'jural relations' (Hohfeld's unique terminology) – as read; as not, in other words, standing in need of clarification or elucidation. This point is touched upon in the next extract.

Ross (2001b, 48–49)

The conceptual apparatus of the jural relation by no means originated in the juristic writings of Hohfeld and Kocourek, although the expression 'jural relation' appears to have done. While those writers were certainly the principal *twentieth century* 'relational jurists' the essential idea of the jural relation probably had its historical origin at least as early as the Roman law concept of the legal bond (*juris vinculum*) which Justinian applied in the *Corpus Iuris Civilis*. Hohfeld did not attempt to define 'jural relation', reinforcing the view that his dissertation was essentially a practical one. Kocourek, on the other hand, whose approach was somehow more scientistic – though not necessarily more illuminating – undertook a critical assessment of a number of possible definitions drawn mainly from the work of nineteenth century jurists. According to Kocourek the jurist Puntschart recognised that Savigny had 'vaguely apprehended' the *juris vinculum* element of the jural relation. Through the application of legal norms legal bonds were created 'by which persons were gyved to persons and persons to things for definite purposes within the purview of the law'. Puntschart had also shown how the 'bond' idea runs through the whole system of Roman legal conceptions. As Kocourek observes:

> Puntschart … interposes a new mechanical element, the 'juris vinculum', as a kind of distributing center through which legal advantages are apportioned among

the members of a legal society as the purpose of the law directs. The norm creates the legal bond and from the legal bond are derived such claims and duties as are appropriate.

According to J.A.C. Thomas, the developed Roman law idea of a legal bond contained no other subjection than that of the duty to perform or pay damages. The language used by Justinian, however, had associations with bondage and this more literal connotation reflected something of the true nature of obligation as conceived in early Roman law. It might be argued that it required only a step rather than a great intellectual leap to move from the notion of physical bonds or fetters to that of *conceptual* bonds. Here the conceptual linkage which gyved persons to persons and persons to things, to use Kocourek's phrase, was more important than the physical linkage. Puntschart's clarification of the Roman law idea of *juris vinculum* of course stresses the conceptual element of the jural bond or *Rechtsverband*, as Puntschart terms it. The idea of jural relation as conceptual linkage finds its expression in Hohfeld's arrangement of relations in the form of a scheme of correlatives and opposites, in which jural correlatives represent each side of one jural relation, viewed from the respective points of view of each party to the relation. John Austin anticipated this correlativity when he defined legal right as '... the creature of a positive law: and it answers to a relative duty imposed by that positive law, and incumbent on a person or persons other than the person or persons in whom the right resides'. Austin was in no doubt concerning the relationality of law and to that extent was quite 'Hohfeldian': '... [A]ll rights reside in persons, and are rights to acts or forbearances on the part of *other* persons. Considered as corresponding to duties, or as being rights to *acts* or *forbearances*, rights may be said to avail *against* persons'.

Hohfeld's failure to offer even a working definition of the concept of the jural relation is perhaps in keeping with the dominant style of *Fundamental Legal Conceptions* as basically an exercise in common law case analysis and – judged from the standpoint of contemporary writing – a somewhat dated one at that. It takes the edge off Hohfeld's criticisms of other writers whose perceived analytical shortcomings were the stimulus, and a target, for Hohfeld's critique. What the Hohfeldian jural relation is, in the final analysis, is the sum total of the characteristics Hohfeld attributes to it. These include the pivotal ideas of *correlativity* and *opposition*. To understand the Hohfeldian jural relation is to understand how the mechanics of 'jural correlativity' and 'jural opposition' (as Hohfeld describes these) interact and coexist within his matrix of legal relationships. The significance of Hohfeld's Analysis does not, I believe, lie in the rigour or depth of his analytical insight but rather in, firstly, the originality and usefulness of his table of correlatives and opposites and, secondly, the undoubted wisdom of focusing on the legal relationship (instead of, for example, the legal rule or norm) as a basic building block or conceptual unit of legal thinking.

A first look at Hohfeld's scheme of rights is provided in the box below, which is followed by a reading which introduces Hohfeld's Analysis in a more precise form, by presenting Hohfeld's table of 'jural correlatives' and 'jural opposites'; the table is a variant of Hohfeld's table, preferred by later writers, according to which correlatives and opposites are arranged not as correlatives and opposites as such but around the fundamental distinction between legal rights in the 'strict sense' and legal powers.

Hohfeld – The Basics

Hohfeld's Analysis basically consists of four sets of correlative legal relationships that cover, or at least purport to cover, the most fundamental legal concepts that can be encompassed within the idea of (a legal) 'right':

1. the **right *stricto sensu*↔duty** relationship (arguably the most fundamental relationship)

2. the **liberty (not)↔no-right** relationship

3. the **power↔liability** relationship

4. the **immunity↔disability** relationship

Relationships 1 and 2 are opposites or negatives of one another, as are 3 and 4. The relationships are 'correlative' in the sense that where one party to the relationship (whom we might call the 'party of inherence') occupies one side of the relationship, *another* party (whom we might call the 'party of incidence') occupies the other side of the relationship. Thus a right-holder, as party of inherence, may have a right that a duty-bearer, as party of incidence, should perform some act.

The best way to illustrate these four sets of relationships is by two simple examples. (Some further examples are provided in the next section of this chapter.)

Example 1

The right *stricto sensu*↔duty relationship and its jural opposite

Wesley takes out an insurance policy on his brand spanking new car with The Hohfeld Insurance Corporation (THIC) and in so doing creates a set of brand spanking new (Hohfeldian) legally enforceable contractual relationships between himself and THIC.

Under the policy – a turgid, unreadable document which Wesley doesn't read – THIC undertakes to indemnify Wesley on the occurrence of certain contingencies. Someone suitably immersed in Hohfeldian terminology would say that the insurance policy only kicks in on the occurrence of certain defined 'operative facts'. The policy provides for an 'insurance excess' of £100. In other words, Wesley must pay the first £100 of any claim.

The day after he buys the car a tree falls on it damaging it beyond economic repair. Wesley makes a claim against THIC. THIC offers Wesley £13,900 in full and final settlement of the claim. This represents the market value of the car (£14,000) less the policy excess of £100.

Scenario 1 – The right stricto sensu↔duty relationship

So far as THIC is concerned (and its position is legally accurate):

- Wesley has a legal right *stricto sensu* (relative to THIC) that THIC shall pay Wesley £13,900

- THIC has a legal duty (relative to Wesley) to pay Wesley £13,900

So far so good.

Scenario 2 – The liberty (not)↔no-right relationship

Wesley, needless to say, is quite piqued at this 'derisory' offer. He bought the car for £14,000 and wants £14,000 from THIC.

'Haven't you read the policy?' says Miss Prism of THIC. (THIC isn't thick.) 'It provides for an excess of £100! *You* have to pay the first £100 of any claim!'

Wesley who – despite not having read the policy in the first place – isn't thick either becomes quite Hohfeldian at this point. 'You mean', he says, 'I have *no right* to claim that £100 from THIC?'

'Precisely,' replies Miss Prism, vying with Wesley's Hohfeldianism. 'In fact,' she stresses, 'so far as THIC is concerned:

- You have no legal right (relative to THIC) that THIC shall pay you £100

- THIC is at liberty – indeed it has a 'legal liberty' – relative to you *not* to pay you £100. Put another way, Mr Newcomb, THIC has *no duty* to pay you that £100!'

Wesley realises for the first time that the £100 insurance excess is the opposite or negation of his wider legal right to claim the market value of the new car from THIC. It constitutes an exception to, or exclusion from, that right and leaves THIC in a position where it has no legal duty (or 'liability' in the *non*-Hohfeldian sense!) to make the payment to Wesley. The absence of a duty to pay Wesley the £100 excess portion of the claim gives THIC the equivalent of a Hohfeldian 'legal liberty' not to pay Wesley.

Example 2

The power↔liability relationship and its jural opposite

Constable Newcomb, Wesley's brother, has just joined the police. In a brand spanking new uniform, and armed with all kinds of impressive legal powers, he sets off on the beat one evening charged with the task of rounding up malefactors and miscreants. He soon spots one crashing a brick through a car window and grabbing a mobile phone off the front seat of the car.

'Stop in the name of the law!' yells Constable Newcomb running after the miscreant. 'I have the power to arrest you!' he adds, somewhat implausibly.

'Am I liable to be arrested?' thinks the malefactor as he races from the scene of the crime. 'I don't think so!'

Constable Newcomb soon brings the miscreant to the ground with a rugby tackle and snaps on a pair of handcuffs. He cautions and charges the malefactor and runs through all the normal procedures preliminary to an arrest. The Hohfeld Professor of Jurisprudence at LSE – Professor Jura Drury – happens to be observing these events from a safe vantage point and in his mind runs through a Hohfeld-like checklist.

Scenario I – The power↔liability relationship

'Okay,' muses the professor. 'The crime of theft was committed back there. So that's our 'operative facts' dealt with. Now to be candid with myself, I've always struggled with the whole idea of relational Hohfeldian legal powers, but in principle I would concede that:

• The Constable has a legal power (relative to that miscreant) to arrest the miscreant

• The miscreant is under a legal liability (relative to the Constable) to be arrested by the Constable.'

Scenario 2 – The immunity↔disability relationship

To the surprise of Constable Newcomb *and* Professor Drury a curious, rather triumphant, smile begins to spread across the face of the miscreant.

'You can't do this! You *can't* arrest me! You don't have the power', laughs the miscreant, to the utter amazement of Constable Newcomb.

'Goglomov', says the miscreant sneeringly. 'I'm a senior diplomat, working at the Goglomov Embassy near Kensington Palace.'

'Good heavens! *Diplomatic immunity*', thinks Professor Drury.

'Diplomatic immunity?' exclaims Constable Newcomb, looking crestfallen. 'You, you mean …?'

'Been there, done that', smiles The Diplomat mischievously. 'In fact I have been attending law night-classes at the London …'

'Be blowed!' interrupts Constable Newcomb.

'Right', says The Diplomat. 'Let me explain:

• I have a legal immunity (relative to you) from arrest by you

• You are under a legal disability (relative to me) to place me under arrest. QED. Simple! Bye bye!'

Constable Newcomb quickly checks The Diplomat's credentials and releases him (leaving the matter of the stolen phone unresolved). He realises that the existence of diplomatic immunity negated his power of arrest over The Diplomat leaving him 'powerless'. He was, in short, legally disabled from carrying out the arrest.

Professor Drury walks away from the scene shaking his head slowly. 'I can't believe it. That bounder really knew his stuff. He explained that better than I could ever have done!'

Ross (2001b, 49–51)

Hohfeld's Table of Jural Relations

In *Fundamental Legal Conceptions*, Hohfeld arranges jural relations in one table organised around the dichotomy between jural opposition and jural correlativity. Subsequent writers have preferred to show jural correlativity and jural opposition (or jural 'contradiction') subsisting together in two tables, one pertaining to the right *stricto sensu* family of jural relations, and the other to the power family of jural relations. The following tables are based on those appearing in the eleventh edition of *Salmond on Jurisprudence*. It should be noted that Glanville Williams, the editor, argued that Hohfeld's 'privilege' was best conceived of as a 'liberty (not)' and Salmond himself preferred to substitute 'subjection' for Hohfeld's 'liability'. The two tables are arranged within rectangles, yet there is no necessary relationship between the rectangles for, as Salmond comments: '[T]he four concepts within each rectangle are intimately related to each other, whereas there is not the same relationship between the concepts in the one rectangle and the concepts in the other rectangle'.

In the tables, correlativity resides in *vertical* lines, while opposition or contradiction resides in *diagonal* lines.

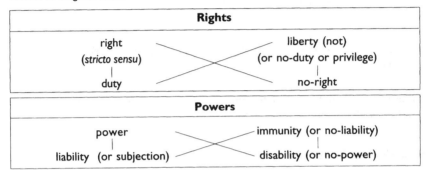

The derivative Hohfeldian arrangement shown in these tables is substantially in line with what has become a characteristically twentieth century analytical position in which a principled distinction is drawn between on one hand rights in the 'strict sense' (and duties) and on the other hand powers (and 'liabilities'). H.L.A. Hart, of course, brought this distinction to the forefront of more recent jurisprudential writing. In 1964 Lon Fuller noted the 'coincidence' of Hohfeld's analysis and Hart's distinction between duty-imposing and power-conferring rules:

> The Hohfeldian analysis discerns four basic legal relations: right-duty, no-right-privilege, power-liability, and disability-immunity. Of these, however, the second and fourth are simply the negations of the first and third. Accordingly the basic distinction on which the whole system is built is that between right-duty and power-liability; this distinction coincides exactly with that taken by Hart.

Fuller's assertion of an *exact* coincidence between the Hohfeldian and Hartian analyses of legal powers is overstated, however. A close examination of *The Concept of Law* shows that Hart's power-conferring rules are on any ordinary language account certainly power-conferring rules of a kind, but not of a rigorously Hohfeldian kind. Hart's distinction between power-conferring and duty-imposing rules centres upon perceived differences in the social functions which the respective rules perform. Hart's category of power-conferring or facilitative laws is distinguishable in terms of *social function* from certain duty-imposing laws and is probably wider than Hohfeld's abstract category of power↔liability legal relationships. As Hart points out '[l]egal rules defining the ways in which valid contracts or wills or marriages are made do not require persons to act in certain ways whether they wish to or not. Such laws do not impose duties or obligations. Instead, they provide individuals with *facilities* for realizing their wishes, by conferring legal powers upon them to create, by certain specified procedures and subject to certain conditions, structures of rights and duties within the coercive framework of the law'. The point here is that Hart's power-conferring rules are not in any strict sense *relational* power-conferring rules in the sense that Hohfeld envisages. Indeed, Hart virtually ignores Hohfeld's analysis in *The Concept of Law*: without doubt to the book's detriment. There are also very pronounced *analytical* differences between Hohfeldian legal rights *stricto sensu* and legal powers which Hart does not begin to address in *The Concept of Law*. Hart was undoubtedly aware of this, however, because in *Essays on Bentham* he referred to his 'previous inadequate approach' to the subject of legal powers in *The Concept of Law*, Hart comments that he (Hart) made no attempt in *The Concept of Law* to analyse closely either the notion of a power or the structure of the rules by which powers are conferred (1982, 196).

Elements of Jural Relations: Jural Correlativity and Jural Opposition

In the next extract the two key notions underpinning Hohfeld's Analysis – jural correlativity and jural opposition are briefly examined.

Ross (2001b, 51–53)

Arguably the key notion underlying Hohfeld's analysis – echoing, as I will later suggest, *sociological* analyses of legal relationships in terms of social power – is that of correlativity. The correlativity of jural relations entails that one term of the relation (e.g. the right) implies the other term (the duty) and *vice versa*. The notion of jural *opposition* (or contradiction) is also important to Hohfeld. He uses the expression 'jural opposite' to denote a term that is the negative of another term. This yields two jural correlatives: the negative jural relation of no-right↔privilege (i.e. the jural opposite in the right *stricto sensu* family of relations) and the negative jural relation of disability↔immunity (i.e. the jural opposite in the power family of relations). But jural correlativity is perhaps the more fundamental concept, underpinning as it does the relational nature of legal phenomena. The concept of jural opposition features only as a mode of classifying *types* of legal relationship.

Focusing, then, on correlativity, in the eleventh edition of *Salmond on Jurisprudence* Glanville Williams observes that the question whether rights and duties are necessarily correlative has resolved itself into two schools of thought according to one of which there can be no right without a corresponding duty, or duty without a corresponding right 'any more than there can be a husband without a wife, or a father without a child'. The other school of thought does not deny the correlativity of many rights or duties, or types of right or duty, but distinguishes between correlative rights or duties described as 'relative', and rights and duties described as 'absolute'. Absolute rights in this sense have no duties corresponding to them, and absolute duties similarly have no rights corresponding to them. Joel Feinberg, for instance, gives consideration to three classes of such duties: duties of status, duties of obedience and duties of compelling appropriateness. Similarly Neil MacCormick has argued that there are some rights – legal rights, no less – which, being logically prior to any correlative duties, are therefore 'dutiless' rights.

According to Williams the dispute between the two schools is merely a 'verbal controversy' devoid of practical consequences. It may be that the dispute turns more upon how the words 'right' or 'duty' are used or defined in a particular context than upon the existence of any principled difference between relative rights (duties) and absolute rights (duties). The difficulty faced by the 'absolutist' school, however, is to confront the underlying reality of norm-governed social action. It is difficult, in other words, to visualise a right or duty that does not in some sense avail against some other person or is at least in existence because the world of human beings is a *social* world. It may be that arguments favouring a concept of absolute rights or duties turn less on the denial of the possibility that such rights and duties avail against 'others' than on the determinacy (or indeterminacy) of the 'others' against whom they avail. For instance even if there is no-one in particular against whom (say) Max might assert a right 'to life' such an assertion would be meaningless were it not for the existence of 'others' – multitudes of indeterminate 'others' – who are, minimally, rational and intelligent beings more or less capable of understanding, and respecting, Max's assertion. The fact of making such an assertion involves at least a tacit assumption that those other beings have a 'social nature'. It may be the lack of determinacy of 'others' against whom absolute rights or duties avail that lends support to the 'absolutist' school. It cannot be maintained, however, that lack of determinacy of such 'others' – in the sense of difficulty of ascertainment of the specific individual or class against whom a right or duty avails – means *no-one at all*. In some cases the problem of identifying a party who 'correlates with' the holder of an absolute legal right or bearer of an absolute legal duty may derive from a failure to visualise the right or duty in question in its 'crystallised' form: that is, on the occurrence of relevant (Hohfeldian) 'operative facts'. In such a case, an 'uncrystallised' right or duty merely exists as an indeterminate hypothesis.

Correlativity also entails that the *content* of someone's right is precisely equivalent to the content of someone else's duty in terms of the subject matter of the prescribed act or forbearance. Similarly, in such a case, the content of someone's duty is precisely equivalent to the content of someone else's right. Mere contentual equivalence, however, does not entail that a right *is* a duty or a duty *is* a right. That is the error which Max Radin commits:

> A's demand-right and B's duty in I are not correlatives because they are not separate, however closely connected, things at all. They are not even two aspects of the same thing. They are two absolutely equivalent statements of the same thing. B's duty does not follow from A's right, nor is it caused by it. B's duty *is* A's right. The two terms are as identical in what they seek to describe as the active and passive form of indicating an act; 'A was murdered by B'; or 'B murdered A'. The fact that A and B are wholly distinct and separate persons must not be allowed to obscure the fact that a relation between them is one relation and no more. (1938, 1150)

Radin compounds his error by asserting that the fact that A and B are distinct persons may *obscure* the fact that the relationship between them is one relationship. It is precisely *because* the parties to whom such a relationship is ascribed are different that each side of the relationship requires a different term to describe it. Although A's right that B should φ is in terms of content (i.e. the prescribed act of φing) equivalent to B's duty to φ, if the right were truly *identical* to the duty the relationship would be unintelligible.

The point is that although there is identity with respect to the content of the prescribed act there is non-identity with respect to other important aspects of the relationship. For example if A has a right that B should φ A's position might be understood at least partly in terms of an expectation on A's part that B should φ but not in terms of any duty or compulsion to φ. In contrast B's position may be understandable in terms of a duty or compulsion on B's part to φ in fulfilment of A's assumed expectation. Nevertheless Radin usefully makes clear the identity of subject matter that characterises a jural relation: highlighting in particular that the act or forbearance that is the subject of the duty is also the subject of the right. Depending on the particular state of knowledge of the parties other 'identities' that may be highlighted here include: (1) that a specified act (φ) is to be performed by the *same* person (the duty-bearer), (2) that each party's 'opposite number' is identifiable (by each party) and (3) that the norms governing the relevant conduct are the same. [For another example of the argument that the identical content of the right and duty makes one of these relationships redundant, see Hart below.]

If each term of a jural relation, whether it be right or duty, implies the other term – i.e. A's right implies B's duty and *vice versa* – it follows that in order to understand either term properly it is necessary to have regard to the correlative term. In the context of Hohfeldian jural relations each term is inherently relational in that the expression 'a right' in a sense *contains* the notion of 'a duty' owed by another party. In his analysis of the underlying social power dimension of legal relationships – for example, in his sociological concept of legal right – Weber arguably lays the groundwork for, and demonstrates the relevance of, engaging in Hohfeldian-type legal conceptual analysis. Tellingly, both Hohfeld and Weber accentuate correlativity: for instance in the sense that the right of one may be regarded as the duty of another. In the legal world, social actors – and juridical entities such as corporations – are ideatively connected in a manner analogous to forms of social interaction or social relationships. Natural and juridical persons are, in other words, linked together in a legal nexus that echoes or replicates the social nexus.

Some Practical Implications of Hohfeld's Analysis

Jurists including, as we will see below, Neil MacCormick, have questioned whether legal rights and duties are necessarily correlative. Some have criticised as flawed the proneness of Hohfeld's Analysis (or indeed of Hohfeldian analysis) to rest an account of legal rights solely on the idea that they exist whenever a legal duty is imposed by law. That, among other things, arbitrarily narrows the use of the expression 'right' and fails to account for quite legitimate uses of the term 'right' where the idea of a correlative duty is simply untenable. There is nevertheless compelling support for the idea that – however much we may be forced to constrain the application of the correlativity thesis contained within Hohfeld's Analysis – there are, and it is overwhelmingly evident that there are, legal rights that correlate with legal duties, and that this class of cases is sufficiently important to merit the very serious attention of legal analysts.

In its simplest and most elemental form, Hohfeld's correlativity thesis, when applied to rights in the 'strict sense', involves a situation where a minimum of two individuals or legal persons are linked in a special way. For example, take the situation where Bob owes Amanda £10. In Hohfeldian terms this can be expressed as a correlative thus:

Amanda has a legal right (relative to Bob) that Bob shall pay £10 to Amanda

Bob has a legal duty (relative to Amanda) to pay £10 to Amanda.

If there is a contract between Bob and Amanda such that Bob must pay Amanda £10 in exchange for Amanda's coffee grinder, a further layer may be added to the scheme thus:

Bob has a legal right (relative to Amanda) that Amanda shall hand her coffee grinder over to Bob [in exchange for £10]

Amanda has a legal duty (relative to Bob) to hand her coffee grinder over to Bob [in exchange for £10].

The simplicity of this Hohfeldian scenario belies the fundamentality of the relational dynamic embedded within it: a dynamic that draws much of its significance from the possibility of *infinite repetition*. Hohfeld's correlative right↔duty schema is, in short, a blueprint for patterned human behaviour manifested in every aspect of day-to-day social and economic life in nearly every corner of the globe. Law creates relational behavioural regularity on an incalculably vast scale. Take the situation, for instance, where I spend the entire day shut in a room tapping away at my computer trying desperately to meet a publisher's deadline for an article. Apart from the legal (contractual) duty to meet the deadline that I may have in a question with the publisher there is not, perhaps, very much in that scenario to engage the interest of a perfervid Hohfeldian. In short, Hohfeld and hermits don't mix. But what if I get up from my desk and head into the city – to Oxford Street, for example? Certainly, I can go and buy a coffee and a croissant. My brief encounter with Starbucks in principle should differ little from the Hohfeldian scenario outlined above involving Bob and Amanda. Yet we can imagine other – perhaps slightly less obvious – Hohfeldian relationships, actual or potential. I am under a legal duty not to punch the good people of Oxford Street on the nose. Or kick them in the shins, or hit them with my umbrella, or smack them across the ear. (I probably wouldn't last very long if I tried that, anyway.) But in fact I am under a *specific* legal duty not to strike, among many others, that old lady standing outside the Oxford Circus tube station – the lady in the light blue coat wearing the ultramarine brooch. Thus:

The old lady in the light blue coat has a legal right (relative to me) that I shall refrain from assaulting her

I have a legal duty (relative to the old lady in the light blue coat) to refrain from assaulting her.

I have a similar duty to the twenty-something woman with the red-streaked hair. And the man in the beige sweater entering Marks & Spencer. And the little boy clutching the soft furry monster. Indeed, so far as the little boy is concerned, the toy monster is his property, not mine. So I am under a legal duty to the boy not to grab the monster out of his hands, stick it in my pocket and dash off down Regent Street.

But for their part, too, the good people of Oxford Street – for instance, the teenager at the street corner wearing the gold chain – must respect my right or liberty (freedom from legal restriction) to make unhindered progress between John Lewis and Selfridges. And if I want to walk all the way to Marble Arch and back to Charing Cross Road then so be it. But consider for a moment the actual or potential Hohfeldian relationships (of the variety I have just described) that obtain if I am taken to represent just *one* centre of such relationships as I meander up and down Oxford Street. There are at least as many sets of actual or potential relationships as there are people that I see. And people are constantly coming and going: entering and leaving shops, jumping on and off buses, joining and leaving the throng. The relationships are qualitatively different, too, and of great variety. As we saw, some can be described in terms of refraining from assault, respecting property interests, giving people an unhindered right of passage, entering into and complying with the terms of contracts, and so on.

Now if, in a shift of viewpoint, *everyone* in or around Oxford Street is treated as a centre of actual or potential Hohfeldian relationships the 'numbers' involved become mind-boggling. There are many thousands of contracts being entered into during the course of the day; millions of potential instances of people refraining from doing nasty things to each other, and so on. (It should be said that for most people it wouldn't even enter their head to do anything 'nasty'. But that is beside the point. It is a theoretical possibility.) Multiply the situation in Oxford Street across the length and breadth of the United Kingdom (because hitherto we have been thinking only of one very busy London street); then replicate this in France, Germany, the United States, China, Australia (just for starters). Billions and billions and billions of Hohfeld-like relationships underlie and underpin our day-to-day social existence. And that is merely the relationships that can be said to be defined in some way by *laws* – by legal rules – whose structure lends itself to correlative relationships of the right↔duty variety. There are other important types of legal rules: those that confer powers, for instance: about which, I have more to say below. And what of those relationships that may not be so readily expressed in terms of 'right' and 'duty' but which are highly valued and arguably give rise to a similar kind of 'Hohfeldian correlativity'. A practising Roman Catholic, for instance, may be morally bound according to the moral precepts of the Church to ensure that her son is educated in the teaching of the Church and introduced to the Sacraments at an appropriate age. The mother may thus consider herself duty-bound to the son (or to God, or to both). Whether the son has any kind of 'right' in the same sense that a legal right is capable of assertion and enforcement against another individual is questionable. But the moral precepts in question nevertheless serve to define correlative relationships between mother and son that may be thought no less important and binding as those defined by legal rules.

Without venturing too far upon the possible sociological implications of 'Hohfeldian correlativity' it is worth noting in passing that the social world has been described as being *made up of* social relationships: relationships between and among human actors. And, as we have just seen, many of these can be regarded as being of the 'Hohfeldian' right↔duty kind: that is, correlative relationships by virtue of which one person ought or ought not to do something relative to one or more other persons. As a leading American sociologist, Talcott Parsons, has commented:

> Since a social system is a system of processes of interaction between actors, it is the structure of the *relations* between the actors as involved in the interactive process which is essentially the structure of the social system. The system is a network of such relationships. (1951, 25)

The Hohfeldian right↔duty relationship, involving legal rights in the 'strict sense', can be readily and straightforwardly imagined *as* a relationship. A has a right that B should ϕ. B has a duty to ϕ relative to A. The relational nexus between A and B is very clear when seen in these terms. Hohfeld emphasises that a number of the fundamental concepts that he investigates can be, or have customarily been, called 'rights'; and these include concepts such as 'immunity', 'power' and legal 'liberty' (or 'privilege' as Hohfeld calls it)'. Diplomatic immunity, for instance, is an example of an 'immunity right'. It is a legal state or situation in which, for example, criminal prosecution authorities may be disempowered: divested, in other words, of their power to pursue criminal proceedings against a defined class of persons. But it is clear that the category of rights in the 'strict sense' – reflecting the right↔duty nexus – comes closest to the paradigm Hohfeldian correlative relationship linking one individual or legal person with one or more others. For their part, legal *powers* can be regarded as 'rights' in some sense and play a central role in Hohfeld's scheme of jural relations. It can be said that an individual or body vested with a legal power – for instance the power of a public authority to promulgate secondary legislation such as bye-laws – has a 'right' to bring the relevant legislation into existence. Yet the Hohfeldian power↔liability relationship is much more difficult to imagine *as* a relationship than the right↔duty relationship. Does A have a power that B should ϕ? And if so, is B under a liability to ϕ relative to A? The difficulty here is that legal powers do not 'behave' in the same way as legal rights in the 'strict sense'. Legal powers are a more complex species of legal concept with a more varied and elaborate structure. 'Hohfeldian correlativity' does not sit especially easily with the concept of the legal power, though it *can be maintained*, subject to a number of conceptual refinements, in certain important classes of cases. Arguably it is the lack of a sound definitional underpinning to Hohfeld's Analysis that problematises the analysis so acutely in the case of legal powers, an omission that impacts less adversely in the case of legal rights in the 'strict sense'.

Hohfeld's definition of legal power is not particularly helpful. Fortunately Roscoe Pound comes to the rescue. According to Pound:

> A power is a legally recognized or conferred capacity of creating, divesting, or altering rights, powers and privileges and so of creating duties and liabilities. It has been called a capacity of altering the sphere of rights or jural relations of persons, using these terms to mean rights in the broader sense. (1959, 93)

Aspects of Pound's definition are reflected in the definition of power suggested in *Salmond on Jurisprudence*. Here power is defined as an 'ability conferred upon a person by the law to alter, by his own will directed to that end, the rights, duties, liabilities or other legal relations, either of himself or of other persons.' (Williams 1957, 274)

What is clear at any rate is that a legal power is a capability of some kind that enables 'alteration' or change to be effected by some means by the person upon whom the power has been conferred. Unpacking the two definitions given above enables at least three situations of 'change' to be identified:

1. the *alteration*, by virtue of the power, of the incidence, scope, application or effect of existing legal rights or legal powers

2. the *extinction*, by virtue of the power, of existing legal rights or legal powers

3. the *creation*, by virtue of the power, of entirely new legal rights or legal powers.

To make the discussion more concrete let us imagine that Edith, an antiques dealer, is the proud owner of an elegant townhouse in Bath. It is the year 2030 and Britain has just declared war on the Central Republic of Goglomov. Edith has property rights in the cast-iron railings outside her townhouse, which rights include the right to prevent anyone from unlawfully interfering with the railings. Under the Wartime Powers Act 2030 the Minister of War has a legal power to expropriate iron railings 'wheresoever situate within the realm' for use in armaments production. If the Minister exercises the power vis-à-vis Edith's railings, a wide range of Hohfeldian scenarios emerge that are consistent with Pound's definition of power.

For instance, the Minister now has a legal right in the 'strict sense' specifically *to* Edith's iron railings. Thus, a legal (claim) right availing against Edith has been *created*. He may order the removal of the railings and in so doing he acquires legal title to them. He may then have them melted down and used for whatever purposes the Wartime Powers Act specifies.

In the meantime, until the railings are removed, Edith retains a legal right to the railings relative to everyone *other than* the Minister and those lawfully executing the directions of the Minister. So, on one hand, Edith's property rights remain unaffected or unaltered by the power. However, in a question with the Minister and those despatched to remove the railings Edith's property rights are either *extinguished* altogether (certainly after removal they are) or at least curtailed so as to prevent Edith from interfering with the railings prior to their lawful expropriation. Thus, Edith's property rights are at least restrictively *altered*.

Furthermore, Edith has 'no-power' in the sense that she is legally disabled (ie she is under a 'Hohfeldian disability') from preventing the Minister or his workmen from sawing away, blowtorching or ripping out the railings when they arrive at the Georgian terrace in Bath where the unfortunate railings are situated. For their part the Minister's workmen are legally immune (they are under a 'Hohfeldian immunity') from being prevented by Edith – for instance by way of civil action or criminal proceedings – from removing the railings.

If not to labour the point, Edith also has a duty not to interfere with the Minister's workmen. Indeed she probably has a 'Hohfeldian no-right' in relation to the Minister's workmen. For, the Minister has a legal liberty (or 'Hohfeldian privilege') – in the sense that there is no legal restriction on him – to remove the railings. He is, in other words, under no duty not to lay waste the railings and carry them off for his bellicose purposes.

Two things, above all perhaps, emerge from this orgy of Hohfeldian discourse. In the first place it is quite clear that the legal power can ride a double-decker bus through any existing, settled legal arrangements or legal state. It can thus be said of legal powers that they have the potential to modify the whole gamut of legal states and entire range of legal relationships obtaining at any given time in relation to a particular person or class of persons and specific subject matter. In the second place, and less obviously, it is a peculiarity of the legal power that no legally recognised 'change' of any significance can occur unless the power is *exercised*. The exercise of the power is what induces a change in the legal situation of persons, as we saw in the case of Edith. An unexercised legal power is merely a potential legal competence but it is of limited legal significance in so far as it remains unexercised.

The recognition that an unexercised legal power consists only in a potentiality to bring about legal change is possibly reflected in Hohfeld's Analysis in terms of which 'liability' is correlated with 'power'. 'Liability' in the specific context of legal powers perhaps has connotations of 'susceptibility': the susceptibility of being subjected to an *exercise* of legal power. (Hohfeld lists 'subjection' among his synonyms for legal power, though he unsurprisingly fails to engage with the notion of 'susceptibility'.) The susceptibility dimension of a legal power becomes an actuality at the moment of exercise of the power for this is, in a sense, the moment of 'crystallisation' of the power. As previously indicated, this does present a problem for Hohfeld's implicit assumption that legal powers and liabilities are straightforwardly, and correlatively, relational in the same sense as are legal duties and legal rights in the 'strict sense'. For we have seen that in Hohfeld's scheme of things to say that one term, of a jural relation (eg a right) is correlative to another term (eg a duty) means that one implies the other and *vice versa*. This fact in a sense 'locks' the two terms together in much the same way as – recalling our earlier discussion – the word 'husband' implies 'wife' and the word 'mother' implies 'child'. That much is definitionally true. So when Hohfeld maintains, for example, that a legal right in the 'strict sense' is correlative to a legal duty he means that one person has the relevant right and *another* person has the relevant duty. The problem with legal powers, however, is that someone who is potentially under a 'legal liability' to a power-holder prior to the exercise of a legal power usually enters into *a different legal state* on the exercise of the power. So, for instance, a police officer possessed of the power to arrest a criminal, on the exercise of the power among other things specifically places a suspect under a *legal duty* to submit to, and not to resist, arrest. And undoubtedly the police officer has a correlative legal right in the 'strict sense' to carry out the arrest. So, beyond the theoretical possibility of being made the subject of an exercise of a legal power, it is difficult to state with precision what is entailed in the notion of being under a 'legal liability' that is 'correlative' to a legal power. If a legal power is merely a potentiality it has no specific legal consequences of any significance prior to its exercise. Yet ironically, *following its exercise* the transforming nature of the legal power is such that often, though not in every case, it creates a Hohfeldian state of affairs, indeed a *correlativity*, that may be better and more accurately described in terms of legal duty and legal right in the 'strict sense' than legal power and legal liability.

'Multital' and 'Paucital' Jural Relations

The law of property provides an obvious difficulty and source of challenge to an analysis that seeks to describe law in terms of jural relations between persons. Property, or rights *in rem*, seems to lawyers and lay persons alike as a relationship between a property owner and some form of property, or at a more abstract level, between a person and a thing. How can such relationships be satisfactorily re-conceived in terms of jural relationships between persons?

A distinctive feature of Hohfeld's Analysis is the famous coining of the terms 'multital' and 'paucital' arising in the context of Hohfeld's discussion of rights *in personam* contrasted with rights *in rem*. Hohfeld argues that the distinctive feature of the right *in rem* is that unlike the right *in personam* it is not an isolated right availing against one determinate individual but a bundle of essentially similar rights availing respectively against each of a large and indefinite class of individuals. The relative fewness or paucity of those individuals bound by the right *in personam* leads Hohfeld to describe such rights as 'paucital'. By contrast the multiplicity of individuals bound by a right *in rem* inspired Hohfeld to attach the tag 'multital' to those rights. As we see from the next extract Hohfeld's 'numerical' test is rejected by A M Honoré who argues in effect that the number of persons subject to a legal duty corresponding to a right *in rem* is irrelevant to the essential character of the right. According to Honoré there is in theory no limit – although there may well be practical limitations – on the number of persons with whom (eg) Amanda could individually contract in order to ensure, for example, that the parties subject to the contractual duty did not walk across, or build upon, Amanda's land. Honoré also cites the converse case where a right may be *in rem* though few are bound by corresponding duties: '[a] landowner's right is *in rem* though he happens to live in a jurisdiction of which there are few subjects'.

Honoré (1960, 453–456)

The accounts of the distinction between rights *in rem* and *in personam* given by Anglo-American writers are very similar to the accounts of continental writers of the distinction between 'absolute' and 'relative' rights.

Hohfeld's well-known description serves as an example of the former. 'A paucital right or claim (right *in personam*) is either a unique right residing in a person (or group of persons) and availing against a single person (or single group of persons) or else it is one of a few fundamentally similar, yet separate, rights availing against a few definite persons.' And 'a multital right or claim (right *in rem*) is always one of a large class of fundamentally similar yet separate rights, actual and potential, residing in a single person (or single group of persons) but availing respectively against persons constituting a very large and indefinite class of people'. To this Kocourek added the twist that a right *in rem* ('unpolarised right') 'is one of which the essential investitive facts do not serve directly to identify the person who owes the incident duty' whereas a right *in personam* ('polarised right') is one for which 'the essential investitive facts serve directly to identify the person who owes the incident duty'. More recently it has been suggested that the distinguishing characteristic of a right *in rem* is that no rule of law limits the number of persons who may be subject to the corresponding duty.

Of the continental jurists Windscheid says that absolute rights are those which avail against everyone, relative rights those which avail only against a single person or a limited number of persons. Of more modern writers Palandt makes the same distinction and adds that the holder of an absolute right can exclude its infringement by third persons; such a right remains operative in preference to concurrent claims of third parties. Colin-Capitant-Julliot de la Morandìere explain that the absolute right 'can be opposed to all'. Such rights include real rights, family rights, political rights, public rights and those inherent in personality, such as the right of working.

The suggested criteria may be reduced to (i) the numerical: rights *in rem* bind all or very many, rights *in personam* few; (ii) the criterion of determinacy or identifiability: in the case of a right *in rem*, the persons bound cannot be determined or identified in advance, whereas in the case of a right *in personam* they can; or in a more precise version (Kocourek's) the duty owers can or cannot respectively be identified from the investitive facts creating the right; (iii) the criterion of legal limitation on the number of duty owers.

In considering these criteria we should bear in mind that a typical example of a right *in personam* is supposed to be the claim of A that B owes him a thousand dollars, viz. a contractual claim. Typical examples of rights *in rem* are the rights of an owner of property to or over it.

Obviously the numerical test is inadequate. It rests on a confusion of rules of law with facts. I may enter into a contract with a very large number of persons. I may contract with all the members of an unincorporated association, such as a trade union. The association may contain all the members of a given society except myself. It just happens that usually the parties to a contract are few. Whatever their numbers, my right under the contract is said to be *in personam*, or *in personas* (it is true that a contract may additionally give rise to rights *in rem*, as with the Anglo-American contract for the sale of specific goods).

Conversely, a right may be *in rem*, though few are bound by a corresponding duty. A landowner's right is *in rem* though he happens to live in a jurisdiction of which there are few subjects; he would still have it, though he had licensed all of them to roam and picnic on his land as they wished: licenses may be revoked or terminated and the landowner retains a right against all those not licensed, though at a given moment there may be no one subject to the legal system who is not so licensed. The character of the right does not turn on the numbers in fact bound to respect it.

The test of determinateness or identifiability is hardly more helpful. Given an adequate census and a record of visitors to the jurisdiction we can at any moment say exactly who is bound, by the rules of a given system, to respect a landowner's property. The duty owers are 'determinate' or 'identifiable', though it would be boring actually to list them. It seems at first sight more promising to say, with Kocourek, that the facts investing the right serve to identify the duty ower only when the right is *in personam*. Here again, unfortunately, there is a confusion between the description by which the legal rule in question defines the persons subject to the duty and the way in which it is in practice possible to identify those persons (if any) who satisfy the description. By the rules of contract, the persons bound must have made a promise or be deemed to have done so; to discover who has in fact done this, an empirical inquiry is needed.

The truth is that some duties or restrictions are imposed by the law on everyone subject to a given legal system except those who have an exemption or privilege. An example is the prohibition of trespass on a landowner's land. Other duties the law imposes not on all persons but on persons satisfying particular criteria (having made a valid promise, being parents, keeping dangerous animals). It is a mistake to think, with Kocourek, that there is a difference in the facts 'investing the right' in the two classes of case. In the one we know that all persons subject to the legal system, with exceptions, are prohibited from acting in a certain way. In the other we know that all those who own dangerous animals or who have contracted with the right-holder owe a duty. In each case the defining characteristics of the persons owing the duty are known; but in each there may be a practical difficulty in ascertaining which persons satisfy the definition, e.g., who are the members of an association which has made a contract.

Furthermore, if (as I shall argue) 'rights', as ordinarily understood by lawyers, and duties are not strictly correlative, the 'facts investing the right' are not a safe guide to the identity of the persons owing the duty. The fact investing a man's right to bodily security, the title of his right, is the fact of being born or conceived. The title of the duty owed him by the keeper of a dangerous animal is the fact of keeping a dangerous animal. It just so happens that in the case of contracts the title to the rights of one party and the duties of the other consists in the fact that each has assented to a certain agreement. This identity of title should not be treated as a feature of all duties arising by particular titles.

The suggestion that the distinguishing feature of claim-rights *in rem* is that no rule of law restricts the number of persons bound seems also inadequate. No rule of law restricts the number of possible cocontractors or keepers of dangerous animals. A better method is to distinguish, provisionally, between those claims which correspond to duties prima facie imposed on all subjects, (though there may be exemptions and privileges) and those claims corresponding to duties prima facie not imposed on all. If we designate as 'particular' any title other than the mere fact of being subject to a system, the duties corresponding to claims *in personam* are created by particular titles, as are exemptions from duties corresponding to claims *in rem*, but the duties corresponding to claims *in rem* are created by a general title – the fact of being subject to a given legal system.

Honoré's rejection of Hohfeld's determinacy thesis perhaps stands in need of some further clarification and discussion. As Honoré points out, the apparent lack of determinacy (in the sense of individual identity) of persons bound by a right *in rem* led Albert Kocourek (1928) to identify *polarity* as the root of the distinction. In other words, Kocourek held that rights *in rem* were unpolarised rights and rights *in personam* were polarised rights. According to this view a right *in rem* is an unpolarised right since there is no determinate or identifiable person in whom any correlative duties reside. This, of course, tends to undermine the relational notion of correlativity. Kocourek argued that a right *in personam* was to be seen as a polarised right since there *is*, generally speaking, a determinate or identifiable person in whom correlative duties reside. Honoré is unconvinced, pointing out that the problem of indeterminacy would disappear if, from a purely practical point of view, an adequate census and a record of visitors to the jurisdiction were put in hand. In this way it would be possible to identify each and every individual subject to the relevant duty. But Honoré's argument, ingenious as it is, ought not to displace a more careful examination of the problem of indeterminacy. A different account of the distinction between rights *in rem* and rights *in personam* is offered, for instance, by A H Campbell who examines the competing accounts put forward by Hohfeld and Kocourek. Campbell argues that the class of persons against whom a right *in rem* avails *is* in fact readily identifiable without recourse to something as labour-intensive as a census:

> Hohfeld appears to have overlooked an important point. Even if we agree that it is better to speak of several rights correlative to several duties, what we call a right *in rem* is not just one which *happens* to coincide with many other rights of similar content against other persons. A right *in rem* is presumed to exist against 'all the world', and therefore against any particular defendant unless he can prove the contrary; a right *in personam* has to be proved to exist against the particular defendant. (1941, 212)

At first sight Campbell appears to be of the view that the essential distinction lies in evidential (adjective) legal rules determining what must be *proved* in order to defeat – and if not, to set up – a right *in rem*. But Campbell's more telling point is that the right *in rem* is supported by a *legal presumption* that it avails against 'all the world'. More precisely, at a substantive level the right *in rem* is presumed to avail against the 'universe' of legal persons both natural and juridical excepting, of course, the right-holder and any others specifically excluded or exempted. The persons bearing the incident duties are more than adequately identified when this criterion is applied. It might, of course, be a pointless exercise or indeed boring, as Honoré suggests, to list them all individually, but that is at least a theoretical possibility if otherwise fundamentally impracticable.

Yet even the presumption of universal incidence does not in itself provide an adequate account of the nature of rights *in rem*. The Hohfeldian notion of 'multitality' which is imprecise and that of indeterminacy, which is untenable, may perhaps be laid to rest. Furthermore the apparent need to analyse the *distinction* between rights *in personam* and rights *in rem* (in order to approach a clearer understanding of the latter) is less pressing as the right *in rem* takes on the appearance of a 'right in its own right'. That is not to say that nothing is to be gained from drawing the traditional comparison between the two kinds of rights. But the presumption of universal incidence provides an incomplete explanation of rights *in rem* for it is clear that other rights – such as the right not to be physically assaulted by others – carry a similar presumption. To call those rights 'rights *in rem*' may not accord with conventional usage. In fact the concept of the right *in rem* has long been associated with the law of property both in continental and common law jurisdictions. According to William Gordon (1987) the distinction in Roman law between two types of *action* – the action *in rem* and the action *in personam* – is the key. (Honoré also alludes to this in the next extract.) Gordon points out that it was not necessary in the statement of claim in the relevant Roman form of action to name a *person* as the party defending the action where the existence of a property right was at issue because the party pursuing the action simply asserted a right *over the thing* in question. Gordon suggests that the action asserted a relationship between the pursuing party and the thing which was the object of the claim. Such an action furthermore differed from the action *in personam* in which it *was* necessary to name a specific defending party in the statement of claim. In that situation an action lay against the defending party arising from (for example) a specific contractual obligation between the parties or from an alleged wrong committed by the defending party.

Gordon's position not only leaves intact the presumption of universal incidence, but reinforces the suggestion that relationships recognised by law between persons and *things*, not merely those between persons and persons, accord with the entirely natural tendency to identify something as 'belonging' to oneself. That does not in any way diminish the importance of inter-*personal* legal relationships or the correlativity which a relational analysis, such as Hohfeld's, entails. The social underpinning of legal relationships arguably remains indispensable to the proper characterisation of key legal concepts such as right, duty and so on and the notion of correlativity is the clearest analytical expression of this social relationality.

Developing Hohfeld

In the next section we look at Honoré again, and then at J E Penner. Both of these writers develop new oppositions for understanding legal relations, most particularly in the context of property, out of their criticisms of Hohfeld. Honoré formulates a theory of *rights in rem*, and specifically of legal interests in property, based around two axes: rights of exclusion, and immunities against divesting. Penner bases his analysis on concepts of use and exclusion. Both (Honoré's and Penner's) theories use Hohfeld's Analysis as a point of departure and as a focus of critical discussion. Both writers comment on limitations in the possibility of applying Hohfeld's Analysis to (among other kinds of rights) property rights and engage in the entirely conventional academic pursuits of 'opposing' and 'discarding' (or 'rejecting'). In this case it is important aspects of Hohfeld's work which suffer that fate. Yet this very process – that of evolving new theories from the 'ashes' of old – neatly illustrates how a work of such analytical seminality as Hohfeld's can be dealt a myriad of near-fatal, if not surely decisively-fatal, blows yet still endure as a source of inspiration to scholars through successive generations.

Honoré (1960, 458–467)

Rights of Exclusion

Supposing we have elucidated the distinction between rights *in rem* and *in personam*, what is its application and significance? A first point to notice is that the rights classified as *in rem* (absolute, multital, etc.) are protected by claims to abstentions, not to performances on the part of persons generally. Thus, in Hohfeld's list of 'multital claims' some relating to tangible property, some to persons and some to neither, all are claims to exclude others and prevent others from doing acts. The lists of 'absolute' rights given by some continental jurists do not at first sight conform to this principle. Thus, Colin-Capitant-Julliot de la Morandière list among 'absolute' rights real rights, family rights, political rights, public rights and those inherent in personality, such as the right of working. Some of these at least are primarily claims to performances, e.g., family rights of support and the political right to vote, or are liberties e.g., the right to work. But this at least is true, that the protection of these rights against persons generally consists in a general prohibition of interference, not in a general command to perform something, and that there appears to be no instance, either in the Anglo-American or continental lists, of a right protected by a claim that persons generally should perform something.

We may put on one side rights vested in the state against its citizens, such as the right of the state that citizens should perform military service or render tax returns. It is not to be expected that a classification of private rights will apply without modification to the state. In any case, these rights do not altogether fit the notion of a right *in rem*, since the corresponding duties fall prima facie not on all persons but on those having a certain age or income; the possession of the age or income is the particular title on the fulfilment of which the duty arises.

Hence it seems safe to assert that the class of rights which jurisprudential writers seek to characterize under the heading 'rights *in rem*' or by similar phrases is that of rights protected by claims to exclude all persons who have not an exemption resting on a particular title.

...

In some cases a right is protected *primarily* by claims to exclude others generally, as in the case of the ownership of property and of the rights to bodily safety, reputation, etc. There may also, as we have seen, be supplementary claims protecting the right, which avail only against persons defined by a particular title, such as a contract or the ownership of a savage dog. Such rights are *in rem*. Other rights are primarily protected by or consist in claims against persons determined by a particular title (contract, will, marriage, parenthood) and are only secondarily reinforced by claims to noninterference against all persons who are not, by some particular title, exempt or privileged, (e.g., privileged to induce a breach of the contract). These rights are *in personam*. The contrast remains, but its black and white character dissolves.

Furthermore, it becomes clear that the terminology traditionally used to express the distinction is misleading. This applies both to the *in rem-in personam* and to the absolute-relative terminology. The objection to the former is that it is at most appropriate to those rights to exclude persons generally which relate to material objects. As regards those which relate to other things, it falsely suggests that lurking in the background in other cases are material objects of a complex or elusive sort, that, for instance, copyright somehow protects a specific group of books or manuscripts. The objection to the absolute-relative contrast is that the terms in question are unspecific and obscure the important distinction between primary and secondary protection. What needs to be said is that there is a classification of rights of exclusion into those which are primarily general and those primarily particular, but there is no such classification to be made of rights to performances, which, in legal systems as we know them, are all primarily particular. Let us speak, then, of rights (to exclude) primarily general and primarily particular, rather than *in rem* and *in personam*. The clumsier expression is in this case the clearer.

...

It is usually said that interests in property, or real rights to things, *dingliche Rechte,* form a species of the genus rights *in rem* or absolute rights. Historically, it is clear enough why this has come to be said. Actions *in rem* originally protected, *inter alia*, interests in tangible property. It came to be said that actions *in rem* were devised for the protection of rights *in rem* (or *in re*); so that legally protected interests in property were termed rights *in rem*. Those other interests which seemed to share with interests in property the characteristic of being protected against persons generally were then said to amount to rights *in rem* also, or absolute rights.

Once it is seen, however, that contractual rights are nowadays also protected against interference by persons generally, it becomes obvious that the distinction between interests in property and mere personal rights relating to property (e.g., between easements or servitudes and licenses or *precaria*) is not thus simply explained. Nor will it do to say that interests in property are protected by claims of exclusion primarily general, personal rights by claims primarily particular. This might seem to fit the contrast between, say, a right of way and a mere license to cross land, but it will not cater for all interests in property.

Thus, a positive servitude or easement is certainly an interest in property, but it is not primarily an exclusionary right; it is, in the first place, a claim that an adjoining landowner should maintain a fence, support a wall, etc. The person subject to the duty is identified by a particular title – the ownership of the servient land.

Again, a mortgage is an interest in property, but it is protected primarily by the mortgagee's claims that, in certain events, the property be sold and a debt satisfied from the proceeds. These claims correspond to duties imposed on the servient owner and on public officials – persons ascertained by particular titles; there is, of course, also a secondary protection against interference by third persons.

It seems that we must abandon the attempt to elucidate the distinction between interests in property and personal rights either in terms of the type of claim by which these interests are primarily protected or in terms of the degree of protection given by the law against third party interference.

Rights to Things

According to a view, popular on the continent, which makes an immediate appeal to common sense, the mark of an interest in property is that it gives the holder an immediate and independent right to the thing, not merely a right against a person or persons. In this context 'immediate' means 'exercisable without the co-operation of others'. The holder of an interest in property does not need the assistance of the owner of the burdened property to exercise his rights. 'Independent' means 'not affected by changes in the ownership of the burdened property'.

If noninterference counts as co-operation, the co-operation of others is always required for the exercise of a right. Even if it does not, positive servitudes and easements at least are interests in property which require positive acts from the servient owner for their realization. Hence it cannot be a defining characteristic of interests in property that they give the holder an 'immediate' right.

The notion of an 'independent' right applies to subordinate interests in property but not to ownership itself. Hence some say that ownership is not a real right or *dingliches Recht*. We shall see, however, that it is possible to find common characteristics of ownership and lesser interests in property: the label 'independent' is not mistaken but merely imprecise.

The most important argument of the main group of continental lawyers is that interests in property should be considered as giving rise to rights to things, not rights against persons. There can, obviously, be relations between persons and things, not merely between persons and persons. To argue that legal relations can only subsist between persons is either arbitrarily to restrict the definition of 'legal relation' or obscurely to reflect the truism that legal claims can only be enforced by proceedings brought against persons. When a person has a right to exclude others generally from tangible property or from interfering with the exercise of a right over tangible property he stands, legally, in a special relation to the property. It is entirely natural and unobjectionable to call his right a right *to* the thing or *to the use* of a thing or *over* a thing. Yet we would not say a person had a right to a thing unless he was protected by claims excluding persons generally from interfering with it. A right to a thing or its use or over a thing is *protected by* claims against persons but is not to be identified with them. When we think of the purpose for which the right is given, we think of the holder's relation to the thing. When we think of the mode of protection, we think of his relations to other persons. The two are complementary.

So much must be conceded to the continental point of view. But this view will not serve to delimit interests in property from merely personal rights over it. A contractual license, for example, being protected against certain forms of third-party interference (inducement of breach of the terms of the license) may properly be said to give a right to the use of or a right over the licensor's property: yet it is a merely personal right.

Immunities Against Divesting

A more promising idea is to return to the notion of an 'independent' right. One of the most obvious features of easements, servitudes and mortgages is that they persist despite changes of ownership in the property burdened. The survival of these rights is secured until their economic purpose is completed. The survival of merely personal rights is not so secured.

To appreciate the legal technique involved we must once again distinguish between rights and claims. The holder of a right of way and the holder of a mere license have each a right to go on the adjoining land. Both rights are secured by claims against the adjoining landowner to permit the exercise of the right. In both cases the landowner has a corresponding duty. The landowner's powers and the right-holder's 'liabilities' are, however, different in the two cases. In the case of the easement, the servient owner has a power, by alienating the property, to divest himself of his duty to the dominant owner, thereby divesting the dominant owner's claim against the *present* servient owner but not his right to go on the servient land, which is now protected by a new claim against the new owner. In the case of the owner of land subject to a contractual license the converse is true. The owner has no power to divest himself of the duty to allow the licensee to go on the land (unless there is a term of the license to that effect). Hence he has no power to divest the licensee of his claim against himself (the licensor) but he has power, by alienating the property, to divest the licensee of his right to go on the adjoining land, since the former licensee would then have no claim against the adjoining landowner to secure this right.

If, then, we adopt the terminology which, following ordinary legal usage, distinguishes between rights and claims, and speak of rights to certain things, or over certain things, or rights to do certain actions, as protected by claims against persons, we can distinguish simply between real rights or interests in property and personal or merely contractual rights. The distinction is that, in the case of the former, the right over the property, or the right to do something or have something done in relation to the property, is not liable to be divested, whilst in the latter case, though the claim against the present owner is not thus liable to be divested, the right over the property, etc. may be divested by alienation.

...

To describe an interest in property as a right to or over the property, not liable to be divested upon the alienation of the property by the duty-ower, is to say something more fundamental than to describe it as a right binding on the particular successors of the present owner of the property. The technique by which the duty securing the right is transferred to particular successors is only the most obvious and commonest technique for securing the right in question against divesting. An alternative technique is to make the property inalienable without the right-holder's consent. In South African land law, this is the technique by which the duly registered rights of mortgagees and fideicommissaries are secured. The Deeds Registries Act provides, not that the transfer of mortgaged land takes place subject to the mortgage, but that mortgaged land may not be transferred (with certain exceptions) unless the bond is paid off or the land released from the mortgage. The expectancy of a fideicommissary is preserved by the rule that his consent is necessary for any alienation of the land subject to the fideicommissum.

Again, the immunity of the holder of an interest in property or a real right against divesting is more fundamental than his preference over holders of personal rights, which some writers have sought to treat as the chief mark of a real right. The notion of a preference is a notion of a right necessarily relative to the claims of other creditors. A preferent right to be paid from the proceeds of sale of a given asset is simply a right to that effect not subject to divesting by the exercise of any power by the owner of the property or his creditors. Such creditors, whether in execution or in insolvency, are simply one class of particular successors; so that the nondivestible character of certain real rights of preference, such as mortgages, shows not that the fundamental mark of an interest in property is to give a preference, but that among other nondivestable interests in property legal systems recognize preferent rights of security over things.

...

It is now possible to see the justification for classing ownership with lesser interests in property as a 'real right' or 'interest'. The owner's rights are, in general, immune from divesting without his consent. Certainly most systems of law acknowledge some exceptions to this principle. Sometimes sale in market overt, or sale by a factor or sale by a bailee divests ownership. Immunity remains the general rule, but it is substantially an immunity against divesting by *purported* alienation of the property, while the immunity of holders of lesser interests is an immunity against divesting by actual alienation.

Penner (1997b, 166–169, 171–173)

Property as the right of exclusive use

'Property' is a legal term of art which describes an institutionalised practice, the practice of the way we deal with things. It takes some doing to elaborate what counts as a 'thing', why our labour is not a thing as far as the practice of property is concerned but land or a sandwich is, but for the purposes of this paper we must live in faith that such an elaboration is possible. The practice is framed principally in terms of what I have called 'the right of exclusive use'. If we describe that right properly, and elaborate what it entails in particular legal contexts, I have contended, one is able to make sense of the idea that property really is about the right to things, that is, a single, definable right to things, and thus is not to be understood as a bundle of rights to a thing. Here, two features of framing property in terms of the 'right to exclusive use of a thing' are pertinent.

First, 'use' has to be elaborated. The right protects not just 'use', but also the owner's determination of the way that his property may be used. It is quite clear that we would generally balk at the idea that property ownership gave us the right to the use of a thing, but not the right to decide which use that was. A simple point, perhaps, yet one I think which is often subconsciously glossed to ill effect. Concentration on 'use' *per se*, rather than on the determination of use, leads one to emphasise the tangible contact an owner has with his property at the expense of his intentions about disposing of the property in a way that may serve his interests, in particular his shared use of the property with others, or his licence or transfer of the property to others. The use of others is not a matter of the owner himself engaging the property and using it. Yet it is fully within the owner's determination of the use of the property and is equally protected by the right to property. The right of exclusive use I describe comprises this broader notion of use and would be better framed in terms of a phrase like 'the right exclusively to determine the disposition of the property' if that were not so long.

Secondly, our interest in the use of things (in this expanded sense) is the reason which grounds the institution of property, and thus the right of exclusive use. I hold the view that in order to make sense of norms, such as rights, duties, powers and so on, we must take into account the interest or interests which they serve or protect. The interest we have in things is using them in various ways, which is why the right is framed in terms of use. Rights, however, correlate with duties, so when we look to understand the nature of any particular right we must always remember that it is a right-duty relation which is in question. Thus any right has in reality two sides: the right side and the duty side. Right-duty relationships protect interests of the right-holder, which is why naming a right often equally names the interest at stake, as the right to freedom of assembly does. But the protection of the interest is afforded through the imposition of duties on others. My right to my property correlates with the duty on others not to interfere with it. In this sense, the duties are the legal means by which the protection of the interest is legally institutionalised. But the law does not impose duties willy nilly. The imposition of duties is a measured response to the legal recognition of the (significant) interest at stake. The duties are crafted taking into account a number of factors, such as the importance of the interest, the relationship of the right-holders to the duty-owers, the knowledge a duty-ower may be expected to have, and principles like the harm principle, which, roughly speaking, rules out the imposition of duties to act morally unless such a duty is required to prevent harm to others. Thus the right-duty relationship manifests not only the interest of the right-holder, which justifies its institution, but to the particular means, the particular duties, the law sees fit to impose to protect it. Property protects our use of things in a very particular way, that is by prohibiting the interference of others. Thus the right of exclusive use does not serve or protect our interest in using things by *enabling* the owner to use his property in the way he wants – owning a piano does not entitle one to piano lessons – but only by providing him a realm of liberty, or freedom from constraint, in which he may determine its use without interference. Property is neither simply a right to exclude nor simply a right to use, but a right framed in terms of exclusion whose purpose is to serve and protect the interest in use. Therefore on my view anyone who takes one of either 'use' or 'exclusion' to be the essence of property misses the mark. In formal, practical terms, the right to property is a right of exclusion. But in justificatory terms, i.e. in terms of what interest property is there to serve and protect, i.e. what the right to property is a right *to*, property is a right to use.

Difficulties with applying Hohfeld's scheme to property

Liberties and claim-rights

For Hohfeld, A's claim right, or right 'properly so called' correlates with a duty upon someone else, B, that B act or not act in some way. One cannot have a claim right to do (or not do) something oneself. In contrast, a liberty-right is a right to do (or not do) something oneself, but it does not correlate with a duty on any other person; it may only correlate with the no-right that someone else has. If I have a liberty to harvest clams vis-à-vis some other person, that person has 'no right' that I don't harvest them. These requirements concerning the description of rights and liberties makes the scheme fiendishly hard to apply, since it is so at odds with our normal practice of thinking about and describing rights. Thus, on the Hohfeldian scheme, since one cannot have the claim-right to do something oneself, one cannot have a right 'properly so-called' to vote, or marry, or express oneself. Rights only refer to the duties others have to do or not do things. 'Rights' to do things oneself only fit into the category of 'liberties', which correlate to 'no-rights'. I have a liberty to express myself if no one else has a right in regard to my expressing myself (if, in other words, I have no correlative duty in regard to my expressing myself). Thus rights to do things are framed in terms of the absence of legal norms. For this reason we are going to run into trouble describing use-rights in property as they are normally understood, since we normally think of these rights as rights to do something which correlate with duties on others. If I own a packet of cigarettes, my (use-)right to smoke them is normally regarded as correlating with a duty on others not to interfere with my smoking them. On the Hohfeldian scheme, there are no use-rights of this kind *per se*. Such a situation can only be described with two rights: my liberty to smoke my cigarettes (a right I have to do something) correlating with other's no-rights *and* my claim-right that you not interfere with my doing so.

Hart and Raz explain rights without similar counter-intuitive requirements. Their basic position is that the notion of right applies broadly to protect any kind of legally-recognised interest, including the right-holder's interest in doing or not doing something himself. Thus one can have a right to a liberty, for example, a right to freedom of expression, which correlates with a duty on others not to interfere with one's expression. As Raz has stated, whenever we claim a right we claim the existence of a duty on another (or others) of some kind. On this view the liberty-'no-right' correlation is simply false as a description of legal relations. The liberty-no right correlation is a description of the absence of any legal norm, not of the institution of one.

The Hohfeldian description of claim-rights and liberties has a pernicious consequence. If Hohfeldian liberties are regarded as legal relations, as rights freed from any necessary correlation to duties, then any freedom from constraint counts as a right, i.e. a liberty right. Some of these liberties, of course, will be paired with claim-rights, as is, for example, my liberty/claim-right to smoke the cigarettes I own, but not all. The ones that are not, however, are no less liberty rights for all that. We thus vastly expand the category of legal rights to include 'rights' which the law could not care less about and in respect of which the law has never instituted any norms. Furthermore the scheme does not distinguish between bare liberties of this kind and liberties which the law is not concerned to protect, but which, as Hart points out, benefit as a matter of fact from legal protection, like the liberty to scratch one's head. That liberty is protected because everyone has a duty not to assault other people. Just because many such freedoms from constraint are the result of legal duties does not mean that these freedoms are the legally recognised interests which underlie and therefore shape or define the duty or duties. By contrast, true legal rights precisely reflect their correlative duty or duties, and the correct statement of the right is framed in terms of the interest or interests which justifies the imposition of those duties. The law does not create any duties in order to allow a person to scratch his head, for the law, in this case at least, is not interested in securing trivial benefits. As I have said, to understand the nature of any right-duty relationship which the law institutes we must pay attention to the purposes for which it was instituted. Not every benefit falls within the purpose. This vital distinction is nothing more than the distinction between intended effects and side-effects.

...

Use-rights

There would seem to be no more secure proposition about the right to property than that it encompasses, or protects, or simply is, a right to use. As I have said, this is roughly, but only roughly, correct. The liberty to determine how things are to be used without the interference of others is the interest underlying the right to property, and the right to property is only explicable if we take that interest into account, since that interests justifies its legal institution and therefore shapes the contours of the right. Nevertheless, if we only consider our interests in treating some things as property we will fail to characterise it properly. There are many ways of serving that interest, in the same way that there are many ways of skinning a cat. The particular means of protecting this interest that concerns us here is the practice of property, and to describe this particular means we must have reference to the actual duties correlating to the right to property that the law imposes. Thus it is not difficult to point out problems which will arise when we try to define property in terms of use-rights.

Defining property in terms of use-rights clearly carries the imprint of Hohfeld's analysis. Failing to distinguish between mere liberties and liberties which are actually protected by rights, does not allow us to distinguish an appropriate level of analysis which would generate a definitive use-right (a liberty to use), or a definitive bundle of them. The trivial and essential have equal standing when a correlation to a 'no-rights' is the test of membership. Secondly, the definition of use-right itself in this way i.e. as a *liberty* to use, obscures the essential reference to the correlative duty that is part and parcel of any right. So, in the Hohfeldian mindset, treating use-rights as a defining feature of property disengages the interests protected by property from its legal, institutionalised, means of protection.

While the determination of the use of things is the interest underlying the right to property, no particular uses are favoured by law, and so none are individuable out of the right to property. Furthermore, and partly in consequence of this, the right to property does not *enable* use; rather, the right to property correlates with a duty on all but the owner of a thing not to interfere with it. Thus, the use of a thing by an owner is not enabled, rather the disabling of an owner's use is inhibited, because interferences are prohibited. Nor is the use of property positively required: in general we have no obligation to actively use our property in order for it to remain ours.

In view of this, there is simply no basis in the legal institution of property rights to individuate or identify particular use-rights as legally recognised elements of the bundle. The picture that emerges is one we would expect from framing property in terms of the right of exclusive use, not a bundle of use-rights: the use of a thing guaranteed by property is co-extensive with the duty of non-interference imposed on others, not co-extensive with some (as yet un-produced) canonical itemisation of particular use-rights. Property does not endow an owner with a right to any particular set of uses of a thing (try thinking of any particular use or set of uses which would realistically reflect the ownership of all items of property, from a copyright to a piece of land), but rather protects his pre-existing non-legal powers to determine the use of a thing according to his own intelligence, talents, and magnanimity, whether extensive or paltry. What is essential to grasp here is that property endows an owner with no powers or capacities to use a thing whatsoever. It only protects what he otherwise already had, but was subject in the case of his control over things to the interference of others.

At first glance this will seem contentious, because it is clear that owners do have the legal power to licence the use of their property and transfer it to others, and so change the existing pattern of legal norms: licensees and transferees have rights they did not have before, and they arise through the exercise of an owner's legal powers. But these powers merely recognise pre-existing 'social' powers a possessor of a thing already has regardless of whether there is a legal practice of property. No one is going to say that my ability to build a house on a patch of the earth arises because a legal practice affords protection to my doing so. Yet neither does my capability to share a bottle of wine, or give my guest a lamb chop for dinner; that social capability exists because I live in a society that understands what it is to share and give – the law did not create that understanding, though of course legal norms may shape it. The reason why the law must institute this recognition of pre-existing social capabilities in the form of legal powers, whereas the law need not do so in the case of my protected ability to build a house, i.e. by recognising a specific use-right, is explicable in terms of the general duty of non-interference. Because I am not necessarily connected to any of my property, it might as well be someone else's, anyone else's. Thus the duty on others, to be effective, must apply to everyone; this is the only appropriate 'default' position. In order, however, to allow me the full use of my property, which includes my use of it with others, I must have the power to release those with whom I want to share the property or to whom I want to give it from their duty to exclude themselves from it in this instance. A legal power, the power to alter the normative landscape in this way, is the only means of doing so. The interest underlying this power is the same interest underlying the general right of exclusive use, the determination of the use of one's property. The institution of this power is merely a legal recognition of the fact that anyone who would determine the use of a thing may wish do so in a social context. That legal recognition does not, however, turn such social uses into the objects of particular reified use-rights which can take their place in a defined bundle, any more than the protection of a liberty to build a house on one's land does so; while I have the power to licence others to use my land just as much as I have the right to use it myself, I do not have a use-power or a use-right to throw a party that forms an elemental right in the bundle any more than I have a right to play solitaire. The power to share and give extends the ambit of my use, but it does not identify any one use or any series of uses which can be isolated and framed as individual rights.

Hohfeld's Analysis and Divergent Theories of Rights

Hohfeld's analysis is only one way of analysing rights. Other theories of rights may conveniently be divided into two kinds. First, there are theories, like those of Dworkin, that examine how rights operate within law to organise packages of legal relationships. Talk of a 'right to free speech' may not, as Hohfeld's analysis would suggest, represent a confusing agglomeration of claim rights, liberties, no rights, etc. Instead, rights may operate to organise and unify disparate individuated legal relationships. You have experienced some of this in Chapter 8, with Dworkin's theory of institutional rights as consistent individuated political aims. Below there is a short extract from Honoré, who makes a similar argument about the role of rights as an organising category for packages of legal relationships.

Honoré (1960, 456–458)

Rights and Claims

I have so far assumed that the object of our inquiry was to characterize certain claim-rights or, alternatively, certain duties which are correlative to them. This assumes the truth of two disputable axioms adopted by Hohfeld. The first is that a 'right' means either a claim (its usual sense) or a 'liberty, power or immunity'. No word is available in his terminology for a collection or aggregate of claims, powers, etc., still less for a variable collection of such claims, etc. The second is that a 'right', so defined, is strictly correlative with a duty, or with a disability, immunity, etc. What Hohfeld does not notice or does not mind is that these axioms render impossible many of the uses of 'a right' to which lawyers and laymen are accustomed.

Ordinary legal usage certainly does treat a right as something different from a claim, power, liberty, etc. or even some aggregate of these. A lawyer would naturally speak of a 'right of way over Blackacre', a 'right to £100 under the contract', and the 'right to, or of, bodily security'. Sometimes it may seem that a right actually consists in a claim together with certain powers and liberties. Thus, the 'right to £100 under the contract' might seem to be identical with a claim for £100 against the debtor. But even this is plausible only as a description of the momentary position of the right-holder. Since there are rules of law by which duties under contracts are transferred on death or insolvency to persons other than the debtor, we shall sometimes be compelled to say that the right to £100 under the contract remains but that the claim securing it is not now against the debtor but against his trustee in insolvency or executor. This way of speaking, Hohfeld's axioms exclude. If a right *is* a claim then it cannot persist when the claim changes, and the claim must change when the duty changes. Nor will it do to say that the right consists in an aggregate of claims against the debtor, his executor and his trustee, for these are successive, not simultaneous claims, and Hohfeld nowhere caters for the possibility of a right consisting in many claims.

The third example enables us to press the argument further. It is natural to say that the right of bodily security is protected by the actions for assault and false imprisonment, by the law of negligence, by the *scienter* action against the owners of dangerous animals or, in a civilian system, by the Aquilian action, the actions for *injuria*, *pauperies*, etc. These actions arise when duties are broken some of which fall on all persons not exempt or privileged, but others of which fall on persons determined by a particular title (owners of dangerous animals). Corresponding to these duties are claims some of which must be classified in the Hohfeld view as *in rem* (multital), such as the claim not to be assaulted, others as *in personam* (paucital), such as the 'claim' not to be bitten by a dangerous dog. If the right of bodily security is the aggregate of these and other claims, it cannot be characterized as either *in rem* or *in personam*, but only as both. Yet lawyers feel, justifiably, that there is something to be said of the right itself as opposed to the particular claims by which it may happen to be protected. The right unifies the claims and, very often, outlives them. It existed before some of the claims presently recognized were evolved; it will continue to be the same right, in an intelligible sense, when new modes of protection are evolved. There would be no right without some claim securing it, but the right to bodily security is no more identifiable with the claims now directed to securing people's bodies than my right to £100 under a contract is identifiable with my present claim against the debtor for £100.

It seems preferable, therefore, to reject Hohfeld's axioms. Is anything gained by abandoning the ordinary sense of 'right' in which rights (such as the right to bodily security or the rights of an owner of property) are *protected by* certain claims and *give rise to* certain liberties. To admit that 'right' is often used in this way is not to deny that there may be some cases in which the right actually *consists* in a claim or liberty: it is merely to reject a definition which identifies a right with a claim or liberty, or even with an aggregate of claims or liberties, and, by prizing off the right from the claims which at a given moment protect or constitute it, or form a component of it, to restore the word 'right' to its ordinary use. We may then say that a right protected by claims against all except those exempt or privileged is *in rem*, even though the right is also protected by claims *in personam*. A right not so protected is *in personam*.

If we say then, that rights *in rem* are protected by claims against all except those exempt or privileged (hereafter called 'persons generally') we meet one objection which a continental lawyer might raise. But he might also object to use of 'claim' to describe the protection afforded by the law of delict and the law relating to dispossession. Delictual 'claims' are often extremely vague: a person has a 'claim' that his body or property shall not be harmed by the negligent conduct of others and, corresponding to this, there is imposed on persons generally a prohibition of negligent conduct. The fact that it is often difficult, indeed impossible, to specify in advance what would count as an infringement of the plaintiff's 'claim' makes it awkward to think of it as a claim, a *Forderungsrecht*. Despite this artificiality, there is perhaps enough common ground between claims to a specific act or abstention and these vague and general 'claims' to justify the use of the same word. In both cases the duty ower is legally bound to do or abstain from something and the 'claimant' is legally competent to release him from his duty.

Another form of critique shares the Hohfeldian project of seeking to identify rights as a particular form of legal relationship, but insists on the need to supplement the correlativity identified by Hohfeld. To put this in simple terms, even if rights are the correlative relationship of duties, this is not in itself enough to identify what constitutes a legal right. There are two highly influential, but divergent theories of this kind – theory based on will or choice and theory based on benefit or interest. As MacCormick puts it:

> Legal theorists have traditionally divided into two camps on the issue of the proper explanation of rights. One line of thought, which may be called the 'will theory', asserts that an individual's having a right of some kind depends upon the legal (or, *mutatis mutandis*, moral) recognition of his will, his choice, as being preeminent over that of others in relation to a given subject matter and within a given relationship. The 'interest theory', by contrast, contends that what is essential to the constitution of a right is the legal (or moral) protection or promotion of one person's interests as against some other person or the world at large, by the imposition on the latter of duties, disabilities or liabilities in respect of the party favoured. (1977, 192)

Arguments in support, or in the refutation, of each of these theories have partly turned on the core issue of the Hohfeldian correlativity of rights with duties.

H L A Hart, in the following extract, demonstrates among other things how the Hohfeldian correlativity thesis plays a quite pivotal role within the interest theory of rights (which Hart calls the 'benefit theory') and uses this as the main plank of an attack on that theory *towards support of* the theory to which he ultimately subscribes: the will theory. For Hart, weaknesses in the correlativity thesis lead him to reject the interest or benefit theory in favour of the will theory. For his part, MacCormick attacks the will theory on its own terms whilst acknowledging essential weaknesses in the correlativity thesis. In the final extract following that from Hart, MacCormick defends the interest theory – that being the theory to which *he* ultimately subscribes – on grounds that do not, and do not need to, rely on the strength of the correlativity thesis for its validity.

The first part of the extract from Hart – which is indebted to the work of Jeremy Bentham – can be regarded as a quite revealing analysis of legal concepts in its own right. Hart discusses key legal concepts left largely undefined and woefully under-analysed in Hohfeld's Analysis: for example, liberty-rights and powers.

Hart (1982c, 162, 164–170, 174–175, 181–186, 188–192)

Most English students of jurisprudence learn to take the first steps towards the analysis of the notion of a legal right from Hohfeld's *Fundamental Legal Conceptions*. In my view Bentham is a more thought-provoking guide than Hohfeld, and indeed than any other writer on the subject, though unfortunately his doctrine has to be collected from observations scattered through his voluminous and not always very readable works. Bentham certainly anticipated much of Hohfeld's work and he has moreover much to say about important aspects of the subject on which Hohfeld did not touch. But his account of legal rights is by no means free from objections; for at some important points his utilitarianism gets in the way of his analytical vision. Bentham's doctrine has however the supreme merit of confronting problems ignored by other theories, even where as in the case of 'interest-theories' of rights, they are similar to or even derived from his own.

...

Bentham distinguishes three principal kinds of right which correspond roughly to Hohfeld's 'claim-right', 'liberty' or 'privilege', and 'power', though he does not include an element corresponding to Hohfeld's 'immunity'. In spite of this rough correspondence there are many differences of which perhaps the most important is that unlike Bentham, Hohfeld considers that the very common use of the expression of a right to cover all the four cases which he distinguishes to be a 'loose' and even 'nebulous' usage: the 'proper meaning' of the term according to Hohfeld is to designate the element which he terms a claim-right, and the broad or loose use is described as 'unfortunate' because it leads to confusion of thought. Notwithstanding these strictures Hohfeld recognizes that the use of the term to cover claim-right, liberty, power, and immunity is a use of the term in a 'generic' sense and hints that the characteristic common to the genus is 'any sort of legal advantage' though he does not explain this idea further. Bentham does not express any similar misgivings concerning the wide extension of the term in ordinary usage, and though in the cases of other terms he is prepared to distinguish what is 'strictly and properly so called' from what is not, he does not do so in the case of rights.

Bentham starts by making what he says is a fundamental distinction between two sorts of rights distinguished by different relationships to the idea of obligation or duty. The first sort of rights owe their existence to (or as he says 'result from') the absence of legal obligation: the second sort result from obligations imposed by law. Rights of the first sort are rights to do or abstain from some action, and rights of the second sort are rights to what Bentham calls the 'services', i.e. the actions or forbearance, of others. Corresponding to these two different sorts of rights are two different sorts of law or states of the law. Rights resulting from obligation are conferred by (or as Bentham puts it, 'have as their base') coercive laws; rights resulting from the absence of obligation have as their base discoercive or permissive laws. In this last phrase Bentham includes three different cases. These are (i) *active* permission or countermand: where the law permits some action, previously legally prohibited or obligatory, to be done or not done; (ii) *inactive* or original permission: where the law simply declares that some action not previously prohibited or obligatory may be done or not done; (iii) the case where the law is silent. Such permissive laws or legal silence leave the individual who is the right-holder free or at liberty to do or not to do some action; I shall use the expression 'liberty-right' instead of Bentham's more explicit though clumsy circumlocution for this sort of right, and I shall use instead of Bentham's expression 'right resulting from obligation' the more familiar 'right correlative to obligation' for his second sort of right, which arises when the law imposes a duty not on the right-holder, but on another and thus restricts the other's freedom to act as he chooses.

...

The bilateral character of liberty-rights

In England and in most other countries a man has a right to look over his garden fence at his neighbour; he is under no obligation not to look at him and under no obligation to look at him. In this example the liberty is therefore bilateral; both the obligation not to look and the obligation to look are in Bentham's phrase 'absent'. Most of Bentham's examples of a liberty-right and his general account of them represents them as bilateral; they are, he says, such rights as men have in the state of nature where there are no obligations. But he occasionally speaks as if a unilateral liberty, that is the absence of *either* an obligation not to do something *or* an obligation to do it, were enough to constitute a right of this kind. On that footing a right to do an action would merely exclude an obligation not to do it, and men always have a right to do what they have an obligation to do. Hohfeld's 'liberty' or 'privilege' is by his definition a unilateral liberty, and, in some special contexts, to treat unilateral liberties as rights accords with a common and intelligible usage for which I offer an explanation below. But I shall treat Bentham as committed to regarding bilateral liberties as the standard type of liberty-right.

Liberty-rights and correlative obligations not to interfere

The fact that a man has a right to look at his neighbour over the garden fence does not entail that the neighbour has a correlative obligation to let himself be looked at or not to interfere with the exercise of this specific liberty-right. So he could, for example, erect a screen on his side of the fence to block the view. But though a neighbour may do this if he wishes, and so has himself a liberty-right or bilateral liberty to erect or not to erect such a fence, there are other things that, in most countries, he cannot legally do to prevent his tormentor looking at him. For he has certain legal obligations or duties, civil or criminal, or both, which preclude some, though not all forms of interference, and these in practice more or less adequately protect the exercise of the liberty-right. Thus he cannot enter the next-door garden and beat up his tormentor, for this would be a breach of certain duties not indeed correlative to his tormentor's liberty-right to look at him, but correlative at least in the case of civil duties to certain other rights, which his tormentor has and which are not mere liberties. These are the tormentor's rights not to be assaulted and his right that others should not enter on his land without his consent. These are rights correlative to obligations and to Bentham's account of these I now turn.

B. Rights correlative to obligations

The right not to be assaulted and the right of an owner or occupier of land that others should not enter on it without his consent are rights to what Bentham terms a negative service, that is to the abstention from 'hurtful action'; in other cases of rights correlative to obligations, where the obligation is to *do* something rather than abstain from action the right is to an 'affirmative' or 'positive' service, or, as Bentham paraphrases it, to 'a useful action'. All rights correlative to obligations are rights to services which consist in the performance of their correlative obligation and with two exceptions all legal obligations or duties have correlative rights. One exception is the case of 'self-regarding duties' where the duty is imposed by law solely for the benefit of the agent on whom they are imposed. Bentham's examples of self-regarding duties include duties to abstain from suicide, from 'indecency not in public', incest, idleness, gaming, and 'other species of prodigality'. The other more important exception to the principle that all legal obligations have correlative rights is where the legislator has disregarded entirely the dictates of utility and created obligations by which no one at all benefits. Such obligation Bentham terms 'ascetic', 'pure', or 'barren', or 'useful to no one', and he thought they had been all too numerous in the history of human law. But apart from these two cases, whenever the law creates civil or criminal obligations, it always thereby creates what Bentham terms 'an enforced service' negative or positive, for the benefit of others; and to have a right correlative to an obligation is to be the person or persons intended to benefit from the performance of the obligation. But not only individuals have rights; the public and also distinct classes included in it have, according to Bentham, rights in those cases where the persons intended to benefit are what he terms 'unassignable individuals'.

Accordingly, with the two exceptions mentioned, every offence, crime or civil wrong, is a violation of some right and a case of 'wrongful withholding of services' so that 'there is no law whatsoever that does not confer on some person or other a right'. I shall call this identification of a right-holder by reference to the person or persons intended to benefit by the performance of an obligation 'the benefit theory' of rights; and when I come to criticize it I shall try to make precise the sense not only of benefit but of a person intended to benefit and to clarify the distinction which Bentham makes between assignable and unassignable individuals.

C. Powers

Legal powers are for Bentham a species of right and his works contain a most elaborate taxonomy of the different kinds of legal powers together with a sophisticated analysis of the idea of a legal power and of the legal provisions by which powers are conferred on individuals. The simplest kind of power is that which a man has when he is allowed by law to interfere with or physically control things or the bodies of persons or animals. Bentham subsumes such interference (which of course may take a great variety of forms such as touching, holding, moving, confining) under the general notion of handling and he calls such powers 'powers of contrectation': examples are an owner's power to make physical use of his property or a policeman's power of arrest. Such powers are in fact liberty-rights differing from other liberty-rights in two respects: first the action which, in such cases, there is liberty to do is restricted to actions physically affecting things or bodies; secondly in such cases the liberty is exclusive or exceptional in the sense that it is a liberty to do something that others are generally under an obligation not to do. Such powers are conferred by permissive laws, but like other liberty-rights they may be protected or 'corroborated' by duties imposed on others not to obstruct, or even requiring them to assist, their exercise. If they are not so corroborated, they exist as 'bare' liberties: and then like other liberty-rights their existence does not entail the existence of any correlative obligations.

More important for our present purpose is the kind of power which Bentham calls 'investitive' and 'divestitive'. These are the powers which a man has when he is enabled by law to change the legal position of others, or of himself and others as he does for example when he alienates property or makes a will or contract. In entering into such legal transactions he does an act (usually the writing or saying of certain words according to more or less strictly prescribed forms) which manifest certain intentions as to future rights and duties of himself and others. Such acts, or acts in the law, are not only *permitted* by the law but are *recognized* by the law as having certain legal consequences: given certain circumstances, a duly executed conveyance of land is 'valid', i.e. legally effective in divesting the transferor of certain rights and duties and in investing the transferee with similar ones. Bentham's elaborate account of the legal provisions by which such investitive and divestitive powers are conferred is designed to reconcile their existence with his general 'imperative' theory of law according to which all laws either impose duties or grant permissions. There is not according to Bentham a further special kind of laws which confer powers; but powers are conferred when laws imposing duties or granting permissions are 'imperfect mandates', i.e. incomplete in some respects and so contain 'blanks' left to 'power-holders' to 'fill up', and when they do this they thereby determine or vary the incidence of existing 'imperfect' laws.

...

B. The benefit theory of rights correlative to obligation

The most striking feature of Bentham's analysis of legal rights is his benefit theory of rights correlative to obligation: the view that with the exception of 'barren' and 'self-regarding' obligation *all* obligations, civil or criminal, have correlative rights held by those intended to benefit by their performance. In considering this doctrine certain features of Bentham's elaborate classification of offences must be kept in mind, since, according to him, every offence, i.e. every breach of obligation with the two exceptions mentioned, violates a right. Bentham distinguishes between offences which are primarily or in the first instance detrimental to 'assignable persons' (which he terms 'offences against individuals' or 'private offences') and offences detrimental only to unassignable individuals. Of the latter there are two kinds, viz. public offences against a whole community or state, or semi-public offences against classes of persons within the community distinguished either by some class characteristic or by residence in a particular area. Offences of the first kind violate individual rights: examples of them are murder, assault, theft, and breach of contract: offences of the second kind violate the rights of the public or a class, and examples of them are failure to pay taxes or desertion from the army (public offences) and violation of health regulations imposed for the protection of a particular neighbourhood (semi-public offences).

...

Absolute and relative duties

The principal advocates of benefit or 'interest' theories of rights correlative to obligations have shown themselves sensitive to the criticism that, if to say that an individual has such a right means no more than that he is the intended beneficiary of a duty, then 'a right' in this sense may be an unnecessary, and perhaps confusing, term in the description of the law; since all that can be said in a terminology of such rights can be and indeed is best said in the indispensable terminology of duty. So the benefit theory appears to make nothing more of rights than an alternative formulation of duties: yet nothing seems to be gained in significance or clarity by translating, e.g. the statement that men are under a legal duty not to murder, assault, or steal from others into the statement that individuals have a right not to be murdered, assaulted, or stolen from, or by saying, when a man has been murdered, that his right not to be killed has been violated.

Ihering as I have said was visited by just such doubts. Bentham confronted them in his codification proposals in the form of an inquiry whether the law should be expounded at length in a list of rights or a list of obligations. The test which he proposed was 'Present the entire law to that one of the parties that has most need to be instructed' and he thought that the law should generally be expounded at length in terms of obligations but need 'only be mentioned' in a list of rights; his principal reason for this was that, because of the penalties imposed, the party on whom the law imposed the obligation had most need for instruction.

(a) *Criminal* versus *civil law.* The most cogent criticisms of the benefit theory are those that on the one hand press home the charge of redundancy or uselessness to a lawyer of the concept of right correlative to obligation defined simply in terms of the intended beneficiary of the obligation, and on the other hand constructively presents an alternative selective account of those obligations which are for legal purposes illuminatingly regarded as having correlative rights. This latter task amounts to a redrawing of the lines between 'absolute' and relative duties which for Bentham merely separated 'barren' and self-regarding duties from duties 'useful to others'. This has been done sometimes in too sweeping a fashion as a distinction precisely coinciding with that between the criminal and civil law, and on the assumption, which seems dogmatic, if not plainly mistaken, that the purpose of the criminal law is not to secure the separate interests of individuals but 'security and order', and that all its duties are really duties not to behave in certain ways which are prejudicial to the 'general interests of society'.

None the less a line may be drawn between most duties of the criminal law and those of the civil law which does not depend on this assumption, but would, on principles quite distinct from those of the benefit theory, reserve the notion of relative duties and correlative rights mainly for the obligations of the civil law, such as those which arise under contracts or under the law of tort, and other civil wrongs. For what is distinctive about these obligations is not their content which sometimes overlaps with the criminal law, since there are some actions, e.g. assault, which are both a crime and a civil wrong; nor is the only distinction of importance the familiar one that crime has as its characteristic consequence liability to punishment, and civil wrong liability to pay compensation for harm done. The crucial distinction, according to this view of relative duties, is the special manner in which the civil law as distinct from the criminal law provides for individuals: it recognizes or gives them a place or *locus standi* in relation to the law quite different from that given by the criminal law. Instead of utilitarian notions of benefit or intended benefit we need, if we are to reproduce this distinctive concern for the individual, a different idea. The idea is that of one individual being given by the law exclusive control, more or less extensive, over another person's duty so that in the area of conduct covered by that duty the individual who has the right is a small-scale sovereign to whom the duty is owed. The fullest measure of control comprises three distinguishable elements: (i) the right holder may waive or extinguish the duty or leave it in existence; (ii) after breach or threatened breach of a duty he may leave it 'unenforced' or may 'enforce' it by suing for compensation or, in certain cases, for an injunction or mandatory order to restrain the continued or further breach of duty; and (iii) he may waive or extinguish the obligation to pay compensation to which the breach gives rise. It is obvious that not all who benefit or are intended to benefit by another's legal obligation are in this unique sovereign position in relation to the duty. A person protected only by the criminal law has no power to release anyone from its duties, and though, as in England, he may in theory be entitled to prosecute along with any other member of the public he has no unique power to determine whether the duties of the criminal law should be enforced or not.

These legal powers (for such they are) over a correlative obligation are of great importance to lawyers: both laymen and lawyers will need, in Bentham's phrase, 'to be instructed' about them; and their exercise calls for the specific skills of the lawyer. They are therefore a natural focus of legal attention, and there are I think many signs of the centrality of those powers to the conception of a legal right. Thus it is hard to think of rights except as capable of *exercise* and this conception of rights correlative to obligations as containing legal powers accommodates this feature. Moreover, we speak of a breach of duty in the civil law, whether arising in contract or in tort, not only as wrong, or detrimental to the person who has the correlative right, but as *a wrong to* him and a breach of an obligation *owed* to him; we also speak of the person who has the correlative right as *possessing* it or even *owning* it. The conception suggested by these phrases is that duties with correlative rights are a species of normative property belonging to the right holder, and this figure becomes intelligible by reference to the special form of control over a correlative duty which a person with such a right is given by the law. Whenever an individual has this special control, as he has in most cases in the civil law but not over the duties of the criminal law, there is a contrast of importance to be marked and many jurists have done so by distinguishing the duties of the criminal law as 'absolute duties' from the 'relative' duties of the civil law.

It is an incidental, though substantial merit of this approach that it provides an intelligible explanation of the fact that animals, even though directly protected by the duties of the criminal law prohibiting cruelty to them, are not spoken or thought of as having rights. However it is to be observed that if the distinction between absolute and relative duties is drawn as above suggested, this does not entail that only duties of the civil law have correlative rights. For there are cases made prominent by the extension of the welfare functions of the state where officials of public bodies are under a legal duty to provide individuals if they satisfy certain conditions, with benefits which may take the form of money payments (e.g. public assistance, unemployment relief, farming subsidies) or supply of goods or services, e.g. medical care. In such cases it is perfectly common and natural to speak of individuals who have satisfied the prescribed conditions as being legally entitled to and having a right to such benefits. Yet it is commonly not the case that they have the kind of control over the official's duties which, according to the view suggested above, is a defining feature of legal rights correlative to obligations. For though such obligations are not always supported by criminal sanctions they cannot be extinguished or waived by beneficiaries, nor does their breach necessarily give rise to any secondary obligation to make compensation which the beneficiaries can enforce, leave unenforced or extinguish. None the less there are in most of such cases two features which link them to the paradigm cases of rights correlative to obligations as these appear in the civil law. In most cases where such public duties are thought of as having correlative rights, the duty to supply the benefits are conditional upon their being demanded and the beneficiary of the duty is free to demand it or not. Hence, though he has no power to waive or extinguish the duty he has a power by presenting a demand to substitute for a conditional duty not requiring present performance an unconditional duty which does, and so has a choice. Secondly, though breach of such duties may not give rise to any secondary duties of compensation, there are in many such cases steps which the beneficiary if he has suffered some peculiar damage may take to secure its performance, and in regard to which he has a special *locus standi* so that on his application a court may make a peremptory or mandatory order or injunction directing the official body to carry out the duty or restraining its breach. These two features of the case differentiate the beneficiary of such public duties from that of the ordinary duties of the criminal law. This explains why, though it is generally enough to describe the criminal law only in terms of duties, so to describe the law creating these public welfare duties would obscure important features. For the necessity that such beneficiaries, if they wish the duty to be performed must present demands, and the availability to them of means of enforcement, make their position under the law a focus for legal attention needing separate description from that of the duties beneficial to them.

...

The analysis of a right correlative to obligation which is suggested by the foregoing criticisms of the benefit theory is that for such a right to exist it is neither sufficient nor necessary for the person who had the right to be the beneficiary of the obligation; what is sufficient and necessary is that he should have at least some measure of the control, described above, over the correlative obligation.

...

If the arguments of the last section are accepted and if we substitute for the utilitarian idea of benefit, as a defining feature of a right correlative to obligation, the individual's legal powers of control, full or partial, over that obligation, a generalization may be made concerning all three kinds of right distinguished by Bentham. This is attractive because it imposes a pattern of order on a wide range of apparently disparate legal phenomena. Thus in all three kinds of right the idea of a bilateral liberty is present and the difference between the kinds of right lies only in the kind of act which there is liberty to do. In the case of liberty-rights such as a man's right to look at his neighbour, his act may be called a natural act in the sense that it is not endowed by the law with a special legal significance or legal effect. On the other hand in the case of rights which are powers, such as the right to alienate property, the act which there is a bilateral liberty to do is an act-in-the-law, just in the sense that it is specifically recognized by the law as having legal effects in varying the legal position of various parties. The case of a right correlative to obligation then emerges as only a special case of legal power in which the right-holder is at liberty to waive or extinguish or to enforce or leave unenforced another's obligation. It would follow from these considerations that in each of these three types of case one who has a right has a choice respected by the law. On this view there would be only one sense of legal right – a legally respected choice – though it would be one with different exemplifications, depending on the kind of act or act-in-the-law which there is liberty to do.

The merits of this analysis are therefore threefold. First, it coincides with a very wide area of common and legal usage. Secondly it explains why liberty-rights, powers, and rights correlative to obligations are all described as rights and does so by identifying as common to three superficially diverse types of case, an element which, on any theory of law or morals, is of great importance; namely an individual choice respected by the law. Thirdly, the concept which it defines is well adapted to a lawyer's purpose; for it will lead him to talk in terms of rights only where there is something of importance to the lawyer to talk about which cannot be equally well said in terms of obligation or duty, and this is pre-eminently so in the case of the civil law.

However, in spite of its attractions, this theory, centred on the notion of a legally respected individual choice, cannot be taken as exhausting the notion of a legal right: the notion of individual benefit must be brought in, though *not* as the benefit theory brings it in, to supplement the notion of individual choice. Unless this is done no adequate account can be given of the deployment of the language of rights, in two main contexts, when certain freedoms and benefits are regarded as essential for the maintenance of the life, the security, the development, and the dignity of the individual. Such freedoms and benefits are recognized as rights in the constitutional law of many countries by Bills of Rights, which afford to the individual protection even against the processes of legislation. In countries such as our own, where the doctrine of legislative sovereignty is held to preclude limiting the powers of the legislature by Bills of Rights, they are, though given only the lesser measure of legal protection in the form of duties of the criminal law, thought and spoken of as legal rights by social theorists or critics of the law who are accustomed to view the law in a wider perspective than the lawyer concerned only with its day-to-day working.

Immunity Rights

Both the benefit theory of rights and the alternative theory of a right as a legally respected choice are designed primarily as accounts of the rights of citizen against citizen; that is of rights under the 'ordinary' law. From that point of view the benefit theory was criticized above (*inter alia*) for offering no more than a redundant translation of duties of the criminal law into a terminology of rights, e.g. not be murdered or assaulted. But this accusation of redundancy is no longer pertinent when what is to be considered are not rights under the ordinary law, but fundamental rights which may be said to be against the legislature, limiting its powers to make (or unmake) the ordinary law, where so to do would deny to individuals certain freedoms and benefits now regarded as essentials of human well-being, such as freedom of speech and of association, freedom from arbitrary arrest, security of life and person, education, and equality of treatment in certain respects.

The various elements which the benefit theory uses to analyse rights correlative to obligations and those which the rival 'choice' theory uses to analyse these and other kinds of right (that is: duty, absence of duty, benefit, act, and act-in-the-law) are not sufficient to provide an analysis of such constitutionally guaranteed individual rights. These require for their analysis the notion of an immunity. Bentham, unlike Hohfeld, did not isolate this notion in distinguishing different kinds or meanings of legal right, and indeed his attention was never seriously given to the analysis of fundamental legal rights. This was, no doubt, because, although, unlike Austin, he did not think that there were logical or conceptual objections to the notion of legal limitations of a sovereign legislature he viewed with extreme suspicion any legal arrangements which would prevent the legislature enacting whatever measures appeared from time to time to be required by the dictates of general utility; and suspicion became contempt at the suggestion that such arrangements should be used to give legal form to doctrines of natural or fundamental individual rights. Hohfeld, who identified among the various 'loose' uses of the expression 'a right' its use to refer to an immunity, defined an immunity as the correlative of 'disability' or 'no power'; so that to say that a man, X, had a certain immunity meant that someone else lacked legal power to alter X's legal position in some respect. But, plainly, even in the loosest usage, the expression 'a right' is not used to refer to the fact that a man is thus immune from an *advantageous* change; the facts that the City Council cannot legally, i.e. has 'no power', to award me a pension, and my neighbour has no power to exempt me from my duty to pay my income-tax, do not constitute any legal rights for me. An individual's immunity from legal change at the hands of others is spoken and thought of as a right only when the change in question is *adverse*, that is, would deprive him of legal rights of other kinds (liberty-rights, powers, rights correlative to obligations) or benefits secured to him by law.

The chief, though not the only employment of this notion of an immunity from adverse legal change which we may call an 'immunity right' is to characterize distinctively the position of individuals protected from such adverse change by constitutional limitations or, as Hohfeld would say, by disabilities of the legislature. Such immunity rights are obviously of extreme importance to individuals and may usually be asserted in the form of justiciable claims that some purported enactment is invalid because it infringes them. There is here an illuminating contrast with the redundancy of rights as defined by the beneficiary theory; for whereas, as I have urged above, nothing is to be gained for the lawyer, either in clarity or the focusing of legal attention, by expounding, say, the law of murder or assault in terms of rights, the case is altered if a constitutional Bill of Rights precludes the legislature from depriving individuals of the protections of the criminal law. For then there is every reason why lawyers and others should have picked out for them, as rights to life or security of the person, legal immunities the assertion of which on behalf of the individual calls for their advice and skill. That is why I said above that though certain legally secured individual benefits would have to be brought in to any adequate account of legal rights, they would not be brought in as the benefit theory brings them in.

. . .

The central issue for Hart, then – the key to having a legal right – was *not* the utilitarian idea that the right-holder should be regarded as a beneficiary of the legal obligation to be performed by the duty-bearer: a recipient, in other words, of the *benefit* provided by such performance. What was required was that the right-holder should have control over, or some *choice* in the matter of, the performance of the legal obligation from the duty-bearer. As Hart puts it in the previous extract:

> The analysis of a right correlative to obligation which is suggested by the foregoing criticisms of the benefit theory is that for such a right to exist it is neither sufficient nor necessary for the person who had the right to be the beneficiary of the obligation; what is sufficient and necessary is that he should have at least some measure of the control, described above, over the correlative obligation.

In his essay 'Rights in Legislation' Neil MacCormick initially argues against Hart's commitment to a libertarian will- or choice-based theory, basing his opposition to the idea of 'choice' on (among other things) the fact that *in certain cases* the performance of legal obligations is beyond the control of the right-holder to waive and is not, therefore, a matter of choice at all. MacCormick cites the instance of an unqualified person carrying out a surgical operation. (The bogus surgeon has a legal duty not to carry out the operation which the right-holding 'patient' cannot by law waive.) According to MacCormick 'the law denies us the power to consent to these graver interferences with our physical security'. But if the power of waiver – the control or 'choice' element that, per Hart, is necessary and sufficient for the *existence* of a right – is denied by the law then *ipso facto* the right has no existence. It cannot, by definition, *be* a right which, of course, is an absurdity. MacCormick also observes that it must follow from the Hartian account of the will theory that the more 'inalienable' rights are said to be, 'the less they are rights'. MacCormick is thus driven to seek an alternative, more plausible, theory based on interest or benefit in terms of which rules which confer legal rights 'have as a specific aim the protection or advancement of individual interests or goods'.

MacCormick begins his defence of an interest-based theory with a discussion of Hart's 'reproach of redundancy': the idea, which Hart attributes to advocates of benefit theories of rights, that if to have a legal right means *no more than* to have the benefit of performance of a legal duty from someone other than the right-holder then the language of rights – and indeed the very idea of a right – is rendered redundant. Why use the expression legal 'right' at all when there could always be substituted a statement about legal 'duty' which would be more fundamental and would say just the same thing as the rights statement? Hart's answer – the salvation from the 'reproach of redundancy' – is the idea of control or choice. A theory of rights based on choice does not suffer from the 'reproach of redundancy' because the element of choice – the control that the right-holder is said to have over and above the mere benefit of performance of the legal obligation by the duty-bearer – goes *beyond* the idea (implied by the Hohfeldian correlativity thesis) that the content of a legal right is precisely equivalent to, and no more than, the content of a legal duty. But, as we will find in the next extract, MacCormick shows that it is possible to have an interest-based theory of rights that is entirely independent of, and in effect immune from, the 'reproach of redundancy'. He argues, ultimately, that the terminology of rights *is* indispensable even in the simplest case where the content of a legal right appears to be precisely and without remainder equivalent to the content of a legal duty. The law, as MacCormick demonstrates, is never that simple. The correlativity thesis does not give grounds for, and cannot precipitate, the abandonment of the expression 'right': and neither, for that matter, can *either* the benefit theory or the interest theory.

MacCormick (1977, 199–208)

'The principal advocates of benefit or "interest" theories of rights correlative to obligations have shown themselves sensitive to the criticism that, if to say that an individual has such a right means no more than that he is the intended beneficiary of a duty, then "a right" in this sense may be an unnecessary, and perhaps confusing, term in the description of the law; since all that can be said in a terminology of such rights can be and indeed is, best said in the indispensable terminology of duty.'

In that statement we find one of the principal grounds of Hart's case in favour of this [will- or choice-based] theory, and against any version of interest theory. By introducing 'the idea ... of one individual being given by the law exclusive control, more or less extensive, over another person's duty so that in the area of conduct covered by that duty the individual who has the right is a small-scale sovereign to whom the duty is owed', Hart claims to have shown us an idea by reference to which the 'terminology of ... rights' can be used without redundancy to say things which cannot be said in the 'indispensable terminology of duty' by itself.

This argument of Hart's perhaps has a certain force as against Bentham's account of rights – even in the brilliantly polished version of it expounded by Hart in his essay thereon. To rest an account of claim rights *solely* on the notion that they exist whenever a legal duty is imposed by a law intended to benefit assignable individuals (in which case all the beneficiaries of the law have rights as against all the duty bearers) is to treat rights as being simply the 'reflex' of logically prior duties. Accordingly, for any statement about rights there could always be substituted a statement about duties which would be at a more fundamental level analytically and which yet would say just the same as the 'rights statement'.

It is however no part of my intention here to advance a theory according to which even 'claim rights' are conceived as being merely the reflex of duties, as though the latter must always be understood as being in every way prior to rights. Here I return to the importance of my introductory point, that legal rights are conferred by laws, and that scrutiny of those laws which confer rights must therefore be profitable, not to say essential, for understanding rights. In relation to the point in hand, let me refer again to section 2(1) of the Succession (Scotland) Act 1964: '(a) Where an intestate is survived by children, they shall have right to the whole of the intestate estate.'

It is worth taking a few moments (and repeating a point which I have made elsewhere) in explaining the context and effects of that provision. Under it, whenever a person domiciled in Scotland dies intestate leaving children, there automatically vests in those children a right to the whole of that part of his estate statutorily entitled 'the intestate estate' (i.e. the residue after certain statutorily established prior claims have been satisfied). At the moment at which the right vests, it is not a 'real right' involving ownership of the estate or any particular assets included in it. Rather, each child's right is a right to receive in due course an equal share in the assets remaining in the executor's hands after satisfaction of prior claims. So it seems that we have a normal right-duty relationship, which could as well have been stated in the 'indispensable terminology of duty' as in the terminology which commended itself to the draftsman.

The problem, however, is that whereas the right vests at the moment of the intestate's death, there is not at that moment an executor to bear a correlative duty. Vesting of the right is temporally prior to the vesting in any other individual of the correlative duty, which can occur only when an executor has in due course been judicially confirmed or appointed. The executor dative has then the duty to wind up the estate and to transfer appropriate shares in the intestate estate to those having right thereto. What is more, when the question of confirmation of an executor dative is raised before the relevant court, a person who has beneficial rights in the estate is normally *on that ground* to be preferred to other parties, at least if the estate appears to be solvent. So one of the intestate's children may, *because of this right conferred on him by the Act,* have a resultant preferential right to be confirmed as executor. His confirmation as such will in turn result in his incurring the duties of executor, including the duty of distributing the intestate estate to those (including himself) who have right thereto under section 2(1)(a) of the 1964 Act.

In this case, therefore, it is not only the case that the vesting of a given right is temporally prior to the vesting of the correlative duty, but it is also the case that the vesting of the right in a given individual is a ground for confirming him in that office to which is attached the duty correlative to the like rights of his brothers and sisters; so that in this context right is logically prior to duty as well. Here then we have a concrete instance of a 'right of recipience' which correlates with 'duty' indeed, but in a much more interesting way than as being a mere 'reflex' of a duty which the legislator might have as readily imposed in simpler and more straightforward terms. An 'interest theory' of rights which can take account of such subtleties as this may well avoid the reproach of redundancy, as well as escaping the paradoxes in which (as the last section showed) the will theory is inevitably drawn.

In drafting a law to deal with intestate succession, a legislator might indeed be very likely to regard the crucial and primary question, as being who is to take the benefit of the estate left by the intestate, and to treat as secondary the means (appointment of executors or administrators, and imposition of appropriate duties upon them) of securing that the benefit in view should actually reach the hands of the intended beneficiary. It is the end which makes sense of the means, not vice versa. This is as obvious in relation to section 46 of the (English) Administration of Estates Act 1925, which likewise confers rights of succession on intestacy though without saying so expressly, as in relation to Section 2 of the Succession (Scotland) Act 1964.

In such a case, given that the legal system recognizes and establishes a system of private property, there is necessarily a vacant 'estate' whenever somebody dies possessed of property. The system must make *some* provision as to the destination of that estate. Whoever gets it, to him will be owed all the duties which are owed to property owners, and to him will ensue also the various liberties, powers, and immunities which accrue to property owners, but *that* person gets all that only because – only if – the law has already vested in him the right of ownership of the property in question. And the step before that is the conferment on some generically identified type of person(s) of the right to have ownership of some part of or share of the property comprising the estate invested in him. What is essentially at stake is, who is to get the more or less substantial advantage of inheriting what share of what part of the estate. It is a quite secondary question to settle by what precise means (imposition of duties and disabilities on *whom?*) that advantage shall be secured to him.

It seems obviously – even trivially – true that at least one function, and that a prominent one, of such laws as those concerning succession, is that they are concerned with the conferment and securing of advantages to individuals; or, rather, to members of given classes severally. To explain the idea of 'members of given classes severally': section 2(1)(a) of the Succession (Scotland) Act protects and promotes the interests of a certain class, the class of children of a parent who has died intestate but possessed of some property. But the protection is not of the interests of the class indiscriminately, taking them all together as a group – as, perhaps, aircraft-noise-control legislation indiscriminately protects everybody living or working or doing anything else in the near vicinity of airports. The protection, in the succession case, is rather of each and every individual who is within that class each in respect of some separate share of an identified estate.

It is not necessarily the case that each individual acquiring a right under the law should experience it as a benefit, an advantage, an advancement or protection of his interests. Perhaps there are some people who have been more harmed than benefited by an inheritance. Perhaps in some cases property inherited – e.g. slum properties subject to statutory tenancies at controlled rents – are literally more trouble than they are worth, and, besides, something of an embarrassment to their proprietor. None of that is in any way inconsistent with the proposition that the function of the law is to confer what is considered to be normally an advantage on a certain class by granting to each of its members a certain legal right.

The case of the mortgagor's entitlement (under s.96(1) of the Law of Property Act 1925) to inspect and make copies of title-deeds, also quoted as an example in the introductory section of the present paper, further indicates the way in which a legislator's concern with protecting what are conceived to be legitimate interests of the members of a given class of individuals leads naturally to the framing of legislation in terms of the rights or entitlements of the given class rather than in terms of the correlative obligations of the mortgagee. In just this sense, what is essential to a clear and comprehensible law relating to mortgages is that the relevant legislation should make clear the respective advantages, protections, and powers accruing to each of the parties to any mortgage. Judicial enforcement of the legislation may then proceed by elucidation and enforcement of duties etc. as necessarily consequential upon conferment of the relevant rights.

By contrast with this branch of the law, the criminal law is no doubt primarily concerned with duties, with laying down in clear and precise terms the prohibitions infraction of which may expose the citizen to prosecution and punishment. This of course follows from a respect for the right of individuals to freedom from interference by the state save for breach of clear rules of the criminal law. Thus, in so far as it is an important function of the criminal law to protect important individual rights – to freedom, to physical and mental security, and so on – it is nevertheless not surprising that the law is not expressly framed in terms of rights, but rather in terms of duties, or through the imposition of duties by the denomination of offences. Even at that, however, there is a large part of the criminal law which deals with crimes against property, and which therefore necessarily presupposes the existence of that elaborate and interlocking set of laws which define and regulate the institution of property and the many and various rights in relation thereto which the law confers. Rights of, and rights in relation to, property – e.g. a mortgagor's right to redeem, a child's right of intestate succession – are on the face of it much too complex to be dissoluble into a set of bare reflexes of correlative duties. But that is not an objection to the thesis that right-conferring laws are best understood in terms of a standard intention to confer some form of benefit or advantage or protection of interests upon the members of a class severally rather than collectively. There may indeed be simple cases in which some general duty – e.g. a duty not to assault – is imposed upon everyone at large with a view to protecting the physical security of each and every person in society, and where the 'right not to be assaulted' is simply the correlative of the duty not to assault; no doubt in such simple cases the 'terminology of rights' does not enable us to say very much more than can be said in the terminology of duty. But it may be well adapted even in this simple case to expressing a reason why people aggrieved by breaches of certain duties *should* be empowered to take various measures and actions at law to secure remedies therefor, and why they *should* be permitted, at least when there are no strong countervailing reasons of policy, to waive other people's duties in this respect. If I'm allowed to be the best judge of my own good, and if such laws (being right-conferring) are aimed at securing what's good for me, why should I not be allowed to have a say over their operation when only my own protection is at stake?

What is more, there are other, more complex, cases in which the legislative decision to confer certain benefits on individuals who satisfy certain generic qualifications ('institutive' or 'investitive' facts) is logically prior to the vesting or the enforcement of a correlative duty. Taken as a whole, there is no reason to suppose that an 'interest theory' so defines 'rights' as to make the term redundant.

In another context, I have expressed as follows the conclusion which follows from arguments such as the foregoing:

> 'To ascribe to all members of a class C a right to treatment T is to presuppose that T is, in all normal circumstances, a good for every member of C, and that T is a good of such importance that it would be wrong to deny it to or withhold it from any member of C. That as for moral rights; as for legal rights, I should say this: when a right to T is conferred by law on all members of C, the law is envisaged as advancing the interests of each and every member of C, and the law has the effect of making it legally wrongful to withhold T from any member of C.'

That is certainly not a perfect or watertight formulation, nor am I sure that I can at present make it so. But it does bring out the three features which must be included in any characterization of rules which confer rights.

First, they concern 'goods' (or 'advantages', or 'benefit', or 'interests', or however we may express the point). Whatever *x* may be, the idea of anyone's having a right to *x* would be absurd unless it were presupposed that *x* is normally a good for human beings, at any rate for those people who qualify as having the 'right' in question. That does not mean that in every case the *x* which is subject matter of a right need be beneficial to a particular potential right-holder, or be thought so by him. Some *hereditates* may be *damnosae,* but our general view of the law of succession as conceding '*rights*' of succession is founded on the firm supposition that most are not.

Secondly, they concern the enjoyment of goods by individuals separately, not simply as members of a collectivity enjoying a diffuse common benefit in which all participate in indistinguishable and unassignable shares. But since necessarily the qualifications and conditions which must be satisfied for the application of such a rule of law in favour of any given individual have to be expressible and expressed in generic terms, it is therefore correct to say that such rules of law must be concerned with classes of individuals, but the benefit secured is secured to each and every individual severally upon satisfaction of the 'institutive' or 'investitive' conditions.

Thirdly, benefits are secured to individuals in that the law provides normative protection for individuals in their enjoyment of them. No doubt it is too narrow to envisage such protection purely in terms of its being 'legally wrongful to withhold T from any member of C'. 'Normative protection' may be understood as involving any or all of the various modes identified by Hohfeld and others. Thus an individual A may in the relevant sense be 'protected' in his enjoyment of x if

(a) some or all other people are under a duty not to interfere with him in relation to *x* or his enjoyment of *x, or*

(b) he is himself not under any duty to abstain from enjoyment of, or avoid or desist from *x* (being therefore protected from any complaint as to alleged wrongful use, enjoyment, etc. of *x*), *or*

(c) some or all other individuals lack legal power to change the legal situation to the prejudice of *A*'s advantage in respect of *x* (the case of disability/immunity), *or*

(d) A himself is in some respect enabled by law to bring about changes in legal relations concerning *x* in pursuit of whatever he conceives to be his advantage.

Not every right entails protection at all these levels or in all these modes simultaneously, though more than one may be and all sometimes are (this being contrary to the Hohfeldian picture of rights as atomic relations between paired individuals). Consider section 5(1) of the Trade Union and Labour Relations Act 1974: '... [E]very worker shall have the right not to be – (a) excluded from membership (b) expelled from membership, of a trade union ... by way of arbitrary or unreasonable discrimination.' That confers protection of at least the first three kinds; it being presumed that membership of a union is beneficial to any worker in normal circumstances (a) people at large are put under a duty not to injure any worker by getting him excluded or expelled from a trade union, (b) every worker is in law free to apply for membership of a union of his choice, and (c) any act of purported expulsion of a worker from his union lacks legal effect if it is judged to be 'by way of arbitrary or unreasonable discrimination'. Consequentially, of course, A has various legal remedies which he may pursue for alleged infractions of the primary right conferred by the Act.

Thus using the terminology (in my view indispensable) of 'rights' the legislature can in short and simple words achieve complex legal protections for the several members of a given class. What is more, it can do so in a way which draws attention to the end in view, the protection of those people in relation to a supposedly advantageous condition of things. This serves better than would any alternative formulation the function of conveying to the population in general and to the judiciary in particular the intended aim and object of the measure.

The example most recently used can be used to show why we should not accept the Hohfeldian view of 'rights' as being reducible without residue to atomic relationships (belonging to one or other of his four types) between pairs of identified individuals; or even to sets of such relations. During the whole period when the 1974 Act was in force, any individual who was a worker had the right conferred by Section 5(1) of the Act. For any worker at any moment of time his having that right would have entailed a large set of Hohfeld-type atomic relationships with other individuals in a position to affect his membership (actual or projected) of some union. But although such individual atomic relationships are derivable from the existence of the right conferred by the Act, the converse is not true. The legislature can establish that vast myriad of atomic relationships by establishing the right to non-exclusion and non-expulsion. It could not establish the latter by establishing the former. (Of course, the legislature could establish a whole set of such 'atomic' relationships, but no particular set would be equivalent to the right actually established, which, depending on the circumstances which emerge, results in a variable set of claims, powers, etc.)

Rights, in short, may be more or less simple or complex and might be ranged on a scale of relative complexity. The more complex they are, the more it is necessary, at least for practical understanding, to envisage them as 'institutional' concepts, as I have elsewhere analysed that term. For any given right, e.g. a right of real security, it is (at least for practical comprehension) necessary to distinguish 'institutive' (*per* Bentham, 'investitive') provisions which establish the conditions upon which the right in question vests in qualified individuals; 'consequential' provisions establishing the various normative protections enjoyed by 'right-holders' as such; and 'terminative' or 'divestitive' provisions establishing the conditions in which the 'right' is 'lost' or 'transferred'. In the case of complex provisions of this kind, the concept of 'right' is for practical purposes indispensable. Even if it were theoretically the case that the whole set of rules comprising a developed legal system could be restated purely in terms of the imposition of duties and the conferment of powers, which I doubt, it would be of no advantage for the practical comprehension of the law were anyone to do so. (The difficulties can be gleaned from a scrutiny of Bentham's heroic attempt to show, by way of prolegomenon to a codification project, how it might in principle be done.)

Even in the case of very simple legal provisions expressed in the duty-imposing mode, the interpretation of such rules as also conferring rights is not wholly without point. First of all, if it be supposed that the law was made with a view to protecting the good of individuals severally, so that every qualified individual has a correlative right to the duty (a Hohfeldian 'claim right'), that would supply at least a prima facie reason for supposing that individuals adversely affected by anybody's breach of the duty imposed ought to be entitled to seek a private law remedy, 'Ubi ius, ibi remedium'; to interpret a law as right-conferring is to give a justifying reason why there should be a remedy at private law for its breach. Secondly, and by a similar line of argument, it would appear that when such a law is conceived as conferring individual rights, individuals ought normally to have the power of waiving the duty in particular cases affecting only themselves.

If it be accepted that the identifying feature of right-conferring laws is to secure certain goods to individuals, and if it be accepted (as liberals accept it) that people should have free choice as to the pursuit or not of their own good, that constitutes a reason why, when the law confers rights on people, they *ought* to have the kind of choice which the will theory conceives to be analytically entailed by the term 'right'. But surely it is better to conceive of such 'powers of waiver', like remedial powers, not as being essential to the definition of, but as being consequential on the recognition or conferment of, rights. Paternalistic legislation which seeks to protect people's rights by preventing them from waiving them may be objectionable, but that is for argument. Surely it cannot be the case that, by definition, it destroys as 'rights' the rights which it seeks better to protect? Freedom of choice is a good, but it is not necessarily the only good.

The more one considers the matter, and the more one looks at rights in legislation, the more implausible become the contentions of the 'will theory' as to the definition and elucidation of rights. Rights must be understood in terms of the type of 'interest theory' advanced in this essay. From that it may be seen that there are powerful reasons why people should be free to exercise or not exercise their rights. But these reasons are points of moral and political substance, not analytic truths about rights. What is more, the experience of the past century suggests that in contexts of economic inequality the value of freedom of choice (in its guise as freedom of contract) may justifiably be overridden by other values, at least sometimes. That gives a further reason for not erecting the liberal principle about freedom of choice into an analytic truth following from the definition of 'right'. To follow Hart's example by seeking to elucidate the character not of 'rights' directly, but of the laws that confer them, is to find grounds for rejecting his own theory of rights.

Further Reading

A highly accessible introduction to Hohfeld's Analysis is given in Simmonds 2002, Ch 8. See also Cook 1919 and Goble 1935.

For a philosophically sophisticated development of the interest theory of rights, which includes a critique of Hohfeld, see Raz 1988, Ch 7; for a critique of Raz's theory, see Penner 1997c.

For further examination of the social theory context in which Hohfeld's Analysis may be positioned, see Ross 2001a, especially Ch 7.

For a 'critical legal history', see Singer 1982.

Questions

1. To what extent is it possible to regard the fundamental legal conceptions identified in Hohfeld's analysis as the 'lowest common denominators of the law'?

2. 'Hohfeld's scheme of analysis offers a map of the relationships that make up law. Like all maps it is necessarily abstract and incomplete.' Discuss.

3. In what ways does Hohfeld's analysis lend support to the possibility of an interest (or benefit) theory of rights?

4. 'Talk of rights cannot simply be reduced to particular jural relationships between particular persons. Rights also operate to organise and generate such relationships.' Discuss.

14 Legal Reasoning

James Penner

The basic intellectual manoeuvres of what we call 'legal reasoning' are understood and practiced from a very early age. Anyone with experience of children knows that almost from the time they speak their first words, children will argue from precedent ('But you let us have sweets before dinner last night'), understand the application of rules (eg bedtime at 7.30), know that rules may not apply in certain circumstances (eg staying up later when guests are over), expect reasons for a decision which make sense to them, and place great weight on the principle that like cases must be decided alike ('You let *Madeleine* go out without boots on'). It is even the case that general justifying principles may be and are, on occasion, derived from a body of decisions, for example that the overarching guidance of the precedents is founded upon the general idea that one's parents ought to take care of one. Finally, it is also apparent that children employ concepts ('That's not *fair*') which to the tutored mind appear to be extremely abstract.

In light of this, one might conclude that we are all lawyers from toddlerhood, and that there is nothing special about the kind of reasoning lawyers engage in at all. This view attracts considerable further support from the experience of anyone who has ever been to law school. Neither you nor your fellow students had to *learn* how to apply rules to cases, or *learn* to argue that this case was relevantly similar to that one, or that certain reasons for a decision were better than others, and so on. You did of course have to learn what particular rules, similarities and reasons the law regards as valid ones, but the capacity to do those things was expected of you from the very outset, essentially from the first questions you were asked in class. Try to think how the process could even have got off the ground if this were not the case. It is doubtful that any of the skills, so effortlessly acquired by children and to so great an effect, *can* be 'taught', employing any sensible notion of teaching. Think of how one could possibly explain to someone who had no idea of relevant similarity what the notion of case A being relevantly similar to case B was? Note, not learning what *the law* counts as relevantly similar – of course you are taught that – but the idea of relevant similarity *per se*. Or imagine legal education had to begin by imbuing its students somehow with the very concept of a rule. What a wretched exercise that would be. Below we will consider how children acquire these skills and concepts in the first place, but for now it is probably enough to say that they are not *taught* them at all, but acquire them in much the same way as they acquire language, which they are not in any meaningful sense 'taught' by anyone either (see Pinker 1995). Saying this is not to say that learning to reason with legal rules, and appreciate what the law considers important, and making some sense of that is easy; not at all. But coming to grips with this exercise had nothing of the existential quality of say, learning differential calculus; learning to solve problems with differential calculus is a kind of intellectual achievement; it forms a sort of break with the mathematics one has studied up to that point, requiring a fairly radical new perspective in thought. Before Leibniz and Newton, no one had figured out how to think that way. Being led to address one's capacity to reason with rules, notions of similarity, and so forth, to cases in tort or contract does not demand a mind-shift of that kind.

So let us assume that we all arrive at law school as proto-lawyers, ready to reason from cases and so on. What then does it mean to 'think like a lawyer', to learn to engage in 'legal reasoning'? Of course, acquiring a knowledge of the law is essential, but in terms of legal reasoning *per se* that is an obvious and trivial requirement, no different from learning the particular rules of a particular game. In order to engage in legal reasoning, there must be some particular body of rules that one works with. In the same way, for a child to learn a natural language, it must be presented with Chinese or English or French, with some language or another. So if we are trying to identify the nature of legal reasoning, i.e. as some way of thinking which is common to lawyers in different legal systems, its distinguishing features must be largely 'doctrinal content-neutral' if the idea is to have more than the most parochial interest. Also to be put to one side here is the sort of tactical and strategic reason which may be of paramount importance in actually assisting clients, especially those facing litigation. This 'advocate's reasoning', while necessary to any practising lawyer, essentially involves an appreciation not only of the way legal procedure works, but with the general psychological, social, economic, and political influences which colour not only the conduct of litigation and negotiation, but shape the public perception of the lawyer's role, as a hired mouthpiece or the technical tactician or the power-broking negotiator or any other cliche which has currency. Our instant concern is with the sort of reasoning which is restricted to determining 'what the law is'.

How, then, do lawyers think differently from layman considering the same issues or situations?

Well, it might tell us something that lawyers have a reputation as cynical, or at least pessimistic, nit-pickers. Exposure to the body of law governing a substantive area of law, like property or contract, in particular exposure to the body of case law, has the salutary effect of making lawyers great believers in the principle that if something can go wrong, it will. In large measure the body of case law reveals the extent to which a simple-minded approach to justice is inadequate to the task of dealing with the practical issues that arise, and arise abundantly, in the course of human experience. A law student of any intelligence learns soon enough that overbroad statements of right or principle are easily up-ended by the next hypothetical case. Caution becomes a watchword, and fine, perhaps too fine, distinctions are constantly elaborated between cases which at first glance may appear essentially identical. In this way, lawyers are nit-pickers.

Secondly, and largely in consequence of this, in looking to the future, as for example when advising a client on a contract or a will, lawyers can easily give the appearance of cynicism or pessimism, and in a significant sense adopting that cheerless outlook is what lawyers are for. How many businessmen would, in the flush of having made what looks like a brilliant deal, wish to consider the issue of liquidated damages? How many people wishing to dispose of their fortune at their death consider, or wish to consider, what should happen if their children pre-decease them? Even more poignantly, consider the understandable reluctance of any emotionally normal human being to desire the full exploration of issues which ought to govern the making of a pre-marital agreement. Those exposed to the body of law in any significant sense soon appreciate that fortune is fickle and that truth is stranger than fiction, and for both reasons it is imperative for the lawyer giving advice to take into account the experience of the law, which is primarily addressed, of course, to situations where things have gone wrong. Hence the impression lawyers may give of cynicism about human nature and pessimism about the general course of human affairs. But the opposite side of the coin in this respect is that lawyers also often appear to be frustratingly tolerant about human behaviour, or give the impression of being indecisive, or at least inordinately cautious about rendering firm moral judgments, when compared to the layman. The lawyer's exposure to the wealth of case law reveals the intricacies of factual circumstances, and the various ways that facts may be turned to reveal morally significant features of all participants' behaviour; to put it in a cliché, things are rarely black and white. So lawyers tend to be both cynical and understanding at the same time.

If these are ways in which it appears that lawyers think differently from laymen, what does that tell us about legal reasoning? Essentially we take the reasoning skills of the layman and magnify them. Law is human practical reasoning with a vengeance, so to speak, or practical reasoning with what might appear to be an over-active imagination were it not, sometimes surprisingly, grounded in real-life cases. So let us begin our thinking about legal reasoning with the humble view that it doesn't differ in kind from what everyone does much of the time. We may find that there are some peculiarities of the way that lawyers reason that deserve our special attention, but let's start by placing the burden of proof upon those who would claim that legal reasoning is somehow special or mysterious.

Legal Reasoning is Practical Reasoning

A few sentences back I spoke of 'practical reasoning'. Practical reasoning is reasoning about what to do. How to act. How to react to something that happens or that someone else does. How to pursue goals, achieve projects. We distinguish practical reasoning from what I shall call 'knowledge' reasoning, for want of a better term. 'Knowledge' reasoning is reasoning about what to believe, rather than what to do. For example, we may have no interest in doing anything about the truth of whether Shakespeare really wrote all those famous plays himself, but we can look at the evidence, assess it, draw inferences and so on, to try to ascertain the truth. When we reason practically, we reason about getting what we want, fulfilling our desires or serving our interests. (Desires, interests, wants, etc are 'operative' or 'motivating' reasons, about which we will say more, below). Of course, knowing is generally a prelude to doing, indeed generally a condition on doing things successfully. If we're hungry, it is best to ascertain where the food is before acting to satisfy that desire. Similarly, knowing the facts of a situation generally suggests various things, prompting desires or revealing ways of serving our interests. But reasoning about the facts is clearly distinguishable from reasoning about our wants and how we might go about securing them, and we recognise the sorts of dangers that arise from mixing the two together, for example, the problem of 'wishful thinking'.

The simplest definition of legal reasoning is this: legal reasoning is practical reasoning where the rules, principles, and policies of the law must be taken as decisive. Legal reasoning is practical because it is reasoning about how the subjects of the law, or legal actors like judges, ought to act. And legal reasoning is legal because the practical directions the law insists be followed reflect values or interest or goals that the particular legal system has chosen. Therefore, we might explore these two facets of legal reasoning in turn.

We shall begin with practical reason in general, looking at the 'intellectual' tools of practical reason, specifically reasons, rules, and concepts. Then we will proceed to examine the nature of legal reasoning, in particular the reasoning of common law lawyers and judges, from two perspectives. First, we will examine Raz's positivist view of lawyer's reasoning, and consider criticisms of it. Then we will consider a conflict between two views of legal reasoning both of which relate legal reasoning to moral reasoning in a fairly direct way, the conflict between Dworkin's theory of legal reasoning, in which lawyers, in particular judges, are characterised as moral philosophers or theorists, and a what be called a 'moral wisdom' characterisation of legal reasoning.

I   The Tools of Practical Reason: Reasons, Rules, Concepts

1.   Reasons and Rules

When we act in a rational fashion we are able to give reasons for doing what we do. I go to the pub because I want a drink. Our reasons may not be very good ones, but to make any *sense* of our acting we either refer to reasons of some kind, or claim some kind of cognitive impairment – one was deluded, hallucinating, mad with rage, drunk, and so on. Sometimes our reason for acting in a certain way is that there is a rule that we must do so. I leave the pitch because I was bowled out; I keep looking for a parking place because I cannot park here on double-yellow lines. One of the most vexing questions that legal theorists have grappled with is exactly how rules operate as reasons, and how our handling rules fits into the way we consider all the other reasons that might bear upon an instance of deciding how to act. One of Raz's greatest achievements is the way he addresses this very issue in his account of practical reasoning, and so that account will be our focus. As a useful introduction to Raz's thought, we will first consider Raz's critique of Hart's theory of rules, which foundered for the very reason that he could not identify what made rules the particular sort of reason that they are.

RAZ'S CRITIQUE OF HART'S THEORY OF RULES

It was a lynchpin of Hart's theory that the nature of the law is revealed partly in the way that the law is *normative*. 'Normative' refers to the setting of a standard of behaviour, and the generic term for such standards is 'norms'. Morality is normative because morality sets standards, or norms, that you must follow if you are to behave morally. Not everything that is normative is morally normative, of course. The rules of chess establish the standards or norms by which we play chess, but those rules are not dictated by moral considerations. The rules of English grammar are normative, too, but a child doesn't violate morality in any way if it says 'I goed home'. One of Hart's most successful theses about the law was that, unlike 'the gunman situation writ large', the law generates norms to guide the behaviour of the subjects of the law. The norms that Hart focussed on, as we saw in Chapter 4, were rules. Hart then went on to try to explain how rules were normative, ie how they are treated by people as standards guiding their conduct. You will recall that Hart said, roughly, that standards of behaviour were regarded by people as norms governing their conduct when there was a practice of acting in a particular way, and when deviations from that practice were subject to the criticism of others. Unfortunately, this explanation of the nature of rules is hopeless. (NB: This does *not* entail that Hart's theory of law is wrong, much less hopeless. It only means that to make Hart's theory of law work, one needs to plug in a sound theory of how rules are normative.)

Raz (1999, 53–57)

The practice theory suffers from three fatal defects. It does not explain rules which are not practices; it fails to distinguish between social rules and widely accepted reasons; and it deprives rules of their normative character. Let us consider these points one by one.

Rules need not be practised in order to be rules. It may be true that certain types of rules must be practised. A legal rule is not a legal rule unless it is part of a legal system which is practised by a certain community. But this is necessary because it is a *legal* rule, and not because it is a rule. Likewise a rule is not a social rule unless it is practised by a certain community, but it may still be a rule. Moral rules are perhaps the clearest example of rules which are not practices. For example, many believe that it is a rule that promises ought to be kept. It may be true that this rule is practised in their communities, but what they believe when they believe that this is a rule is not that it is a practice. Nor is it a necessary condition for the correctness of their belief that the rule is practised. For one may believe that it is a rule that promises ought to be kept even if one is not, and has never been, a member of a community which practised the rule. Similarly, a person may believe in the validity of a rule that one ought to be a vegetarian even though he knows no other vegetarians.

A person may believe that a rule is valid even though he does not observe it. If so then on many occasions when a person believes in the validity of a moral rule the rule he believes in may not actually be his personal rule. Moreover, a man who follows a rule normally regards this fact as irrelevant to the correctness of his belief in the validity of the rule. We would not be surprised to hear him explain that he believes that it is a rule that such and such or that he believes that there is such a moral rule and therefore he has decided to try and follow it, or to make it his practice to follow it. Nor would we be surprised to hear him apologize and explain that despite his belief that there is such a moral rule he has never succeeded in behaving accordingly. We cannot refute him by saying that, since he is not actually following the rule, since it is not his personal rule, he must be wrong in thinking that it is a moral rule. Nor can we say that he is mistaken if it is neither his rule nor a social rule. He may admit to that and confess that neither he nor anybody he knows follows the rule, but regard this as proof of human imperfection and still believe in the validity of the moral rule.

...

These arguments do not, and are not designed to, prove that there are rules which are not practised. It may be that the person in my example is mistaken in believing that there are such rules, and he may be mistaken because the rules are not practised. He may be mistaken in thinking that there can be rules which are not practised. But even if he is wrong his belief is intelligible. He may be mistaken but he is not perverse or irrational or misusing language. This means that even if we believe that there can be a rule only if it is practised the word 'rule' does not mean 'a practice', and hence the explanation of what a rule is cannot be in terms of the practice theory. At best the practice theory is part of a substantive moral theory explaining when rules are valid or binding. It forms no part of the analysis of the concept of a rule.

The second major defect of the practice theory is its failure to distinguish between practised rules and accepted reasons. According to the practice theory, whenever a reason is believed in, followed and acted on by the relevant person or group, then they have a rule. If my first argument against the practice theory is sound, it follows that we can distinguish between a rule and a reason (which is not a rule) regardless of whether they are acted on and followed in practice. This suggests that there must be a distinction between the practice of acting on a general reason and that of following a rule. This distinction is in fact reflected in the way we interpret our practices. We do not regard every practice of acting on a general reason as acting on a rule. The practice theory fails to draw this distinction and it thereby fails to capture the essential feature of rules.

...

Consider a community in which almost everybody believes that babies should be breast-fed or that children should be encouraged to learn to read when they are three years of age. This is generally done and people tend to reproach mothers who do not breast-feed or parents who do not teach their three-year-old children to read. Yet people in the community do not regard these as rules. They merely think that they are good things to do. They do regard it as a rule, for example, that people should go to church on Sunday. Somehow they think differently of this, though the difference is not reflected in their practice (except that they would talk of a rule only in the latter case). Warnock in *The Object of Morality* makes the same point using the following example: 'Consider the situation of the spectator of a cricket match, ignorant of the game, and trying to work out what rules the players are following. He will find for instance that, when six balls have been bowled from one end, the players regularly move round and six balls are then bowled from the other end; deviations from this, he will observe, are adversely criticized. He will probably find also that, when a fast bowler is replaced by a slow one, some persons who were previously stationed quite close to the batsman are moved further away, some, probably, a lot further away; and he will find that, if this is not done, there is adverse criticism. But if he concludes that, in so acting, the players are following rules, he will of course be right in the first case, and wrong in the second. There is *no* rule that a slow bowler should not operate with exactly the same field setting as a fast one; this is indeed scarcely ever done, and it would nearly always be regarded as wrong to do it, but that is because, quite independently of any rules, it is something which there is nearly always good reason not to do' (pp 45–6). The practice theory is at fault for failing to recognize and explain this distinction.

The third major defect of the practice theory is that it deprives rules of their normative character. We have already mentioned that a rule is a reason for action. The fact that rules are normally stated by using normative terms (and in trying to refute the practice theory I am arguing, among other things, that it can only be stated in such terms) indicates that they are operative reasons. A practice as such is not necessarily a reason for action. It may be, provided that there is reason for all to behave as everyone does (to drive on the left, or follow the common rules of etiquette, etc.) or if a certain person has, generally or in particular circumstances, reason to conform to the practice (in order not to be rejected by his neighbours or not to lose his job, etc.). But the practice theory fails to account generally for the normative character of rules. At best it could claim to explain conventional rules, namely those social rules which are maintained because people believe that all have a reason to behave as everyone does. Ultimately it fails to explain even those.

The 'third major defect' Raz mentions needs to be elaborated. What Raz is pointing out here by referring to the normative character of rules is that rules are akin to 'oughts' in the sense that we are supposed *to do* what we ought to do, and likewise, if there is a rule, we are supposed *to follow it*. But just because there is a practice is not necessarily a reason to go along with the practice (even if everyone else does). So if rules were just practices, there would be no reason necessarily to follow them, but we understand rules as standards that we ought to follow; hence, the practice theory of rules fails to explain this 'ought'-characteristic of rules.

THE RAZIAN ANALYSIS OF PRACTICAL REASON AND NORMS

You have already come into contact with the Razian analysis when we considered his view of the authoritative nature of law in Chapter 10. Recall how he spoke about the deliberative and executive phases of practical reasoning. First we reason about how we should proceed, and come to a decision about that. Then we execute that decision. For Raz, rules, rights, duties and powers are *devices of practical reasoning which reflect decisions people have made as to how to act*. The law (in the form of legislatures or judges in individual cases) deliberates about what ought to be done, and renders its decisions in terms of rules, rights, duties, powers, etc and these decisions are what the subjects of the law must comply with. The core idea, which we will now look at, is the idea of an exclusionary reason.

Penner (1997d, 7–11)

A norm is a standard which guides behaviour. In the context of morality or law, norms are those standards which guide the behaviour of people in ways which have moral or legal consequence. Probably the most typical example of a legal or moral norm is a rule, for example the rule prohibiting murder. This rule sets a standard which governs our behaviour, by guiding us not to commit murder. Norms interact: … different rules interact with other rules, for example the way the rules of the law of theft interact with the rules of the law of property. Similarly, rights, duties, and powers are norms, and they interact as well. Together with rules they provide the elements of a normative system.

…

Raz famously introduced the notion of an exclusionary reason to explain how reasons for action operate at different levels. Normally, where one is not subject to any valid rules or other standards which bear directly on a decision, one simply decides what to do on the balance of reasons. If I am deciding what to do of an evening, different considerations will favour my staying at home to read, or going out to visit friends, or going to bed early. What I decide to do will depend on weighing the different reasons for each option. Exclusionary reasons are different. Their characteristic feature is that they are reasons for action that bear on the action of making the decision itself. They function as second-order reasons not to take into account other first-order reasons for acting when making a decision. Exclusionary reasons change the way we make decisions by guiding us not to decide on the balance of first-order reasons, or by altering the balance of first-order reasons in characteristic ways.

For example, having made a promise to buy A a drink is a reason not to take account of other reasons when deciding to act on the promise, such as the fact that one now doesn't feel much like having a drink with A, or that one now has a better use for the money. Having made the promise is like having made a previous binding decision. One is not allowed to re-open the discussion and weigh all the reasons for buying A a drink; all of these reasons have already been considered. The promise excludes our acting on the basis of these reasons; what we act on now is the promise. This example illustrates how exclusionary reasons are also typically first-order reasons for action. The promise stands as a first-order reason for action, since it is a reason for buying A a drink. But it is also a second order reason, because it operates on our decision to buy A a drink by excluding our acting on the basis of other reasons.

This feature of exclusionary reasons accounts for the categorical nature of norms in practical reasoning. The existence of a rule is like the existence of a binding general decision. Rules are not to be understood merely as particularly strong reasons for action – while there are important rules like the rule prohibiting murder, there are also trivial rules such as the more arcane rules of etiquette – but rather as a *kind* of reason which obliges one to exclude acting out of consideration of other reasons simply because of the *kind* of reason it is, i.e. an exclusionary reason the purpose of which is to settle the matter in one way or another. So we see how this distinction between first and second-order reasons elaborates how practical reason functions in many circumstances where we require a standard of action which is generally to be complied with: it works by shifting decision-making from a weighing of all the considerations to that of a straightforward compliance with an established standard. While this exclusionary function of second-order reasons is the most important one, one occasionally finds second-order reasons which are not exclusionary. An example would be the injunction to those adjudicating child custody cases that considerations of the child's welfare are paramount. This second-order reason influences the decision-making process by formally altering the way in which the normal balancing of reasons might otherwise occur. It works not to exclude reasons, but frames the consideration of reasons by making one kind of reason paramount, so that however the various factors are weighed up no decision will be taken in which the best interests of the child are significantly discounted.

We should not mistake the categorical nature of exclusionary reasons with the idea that the presence of an exclusionary reason is an absolute guide to behaviour, which covers all circumstances. Exclusionary reasons have scope. There is no reason to believe that exclusionary reasons must exclude all first-order reasons. A good example of this is one Raz gives himself, that of an order made by an officer to his inferior. An order is an exclusionary reason for the inferior: he should act on the basis of the order, ignoring the general balance of reasons which determines whether complying with the order is the right thing to do. But if the order was to commit an atrocity, the exclusionary reason would not exclude the first-order reason, that of the sanctity and dignity of human life, which counsels one never to commit an atrocity. That first-order reason does not fall within the exclusionary scope of the officer's order.

[This notion of the scope of a second-order reason is most clearly seen in that any decision might fail to consider all the appropriate first-order reasons. A decision does not normally have scope beyond the first-order reasons it has weighed and taken into account. We see this point taken in practice all the time. If we take our decisions seriously, we don't continually re-visit the decision-making process, re-weighing all the same reasons we considered before. But we may be prompted to do this if a new reason comes up (eg a new fact or evidence) which was not included in our previous decision. Such new first-order reasons cannot, obviously, have been accounted for in the decision-making process and therefore replaced by the second-order exclusionary reason that resulted. (Consider how this analysis applies to the law's treatment of new evidence in, for example, criminal cases.)]

The second major contribution that Raz makes to our understanding of practical reason is to show how this first-and second-order reasoning serves our interests. Interests are, along with values and desires, *operative* reasons for action. Operative reasons are things we believe that give us what Raz calls the 'practical critical attitude', the attitude that we ought to do something. In other words, our desires, interests, and values are reasons *for action*. If we desire food, then we have a reason for finding something to eat. Surveying our situation, other facts, such as whether there is a restaurant nearby, will, together with the fact of our desire, provide a complete reason for acting in a particular way, as in going to the restaurant for a meal. While interests and desires are both operative reasons for action, serving one's interests is not the same thing as satisfying one's desires.

The difference between the two is that we define our interests critically. If we have a desire, we just have a desire. When we speak of our interests, however, we manifest a critical attitude to the nature of our well-being, in which we regard some desires as more important, some as legitimate and others not, and so on. We can, of course, shape our own desires and those of others by various means, like education, and we usually participate or require the participation of others in practices like education as a result of deciding what is really in our interests. It is obviously a good thing if our desires conform with our interests. But our interests, unlike our desires, are necessarily related to a critical understanding of values, i.e. of those things which are truly of worth and those which are not. Underlying interests, then, is the existence of a critical practice which generates view's about what our interests are, though this does not mean that there is any consensus about the ultimate basis of those interests.

The particular operative reasons we shall be interested in here are our interests, as opposed to desires, [because] the law's legitimacy rests in part on whether it guides our behaviour critically, i.e. rationally. The law should not be regarded as there to serve our desires, but to serve our interests.

[But see Chapter 20 for the view that desire, properly formulated, and the law's expression and suppression of it, better characterises operative reason in law.]

Our interests are served by the way in which reasoning works at first-and second-order levels. The presence of a second-order level of reasoning in which exclusionary reasons do their work allows us better to *conform* to what is in our interests, better, that is, than we should do if we tried directly to *comply* with what is in our interests. This idea, while simple, has profound importance. In many cases, we will decide to do what we ought to do, that is, act in accordance with reason and serve our interests, not by weighing up all the reasons that bear on the decision, but by following an established standard which tells us what to do. Traffic rules confine our actions by requiring us not to make all our traffic manoeuvres on the basis of our own judgement about what is safe, but rather in accordance with the established standards. We do better by trying not to weigh up all the factors in each case about what is a safe or desirable manoeuvre, but rather by simply following the rule. Thus we *conform* better to what is in our interests by acting on the basis of an exclusionary reason like a rule, rather than trying directly to *comply* with the balance of reasons which would indicate what is best in the circumstances. Acting in accord with our interests is the ultimate aim of practical reason. We are not concerned, in the general case, that we do so *because* we have assessed the first-order reasons directly, but only that we achieve this result. Second-order reasons that bear on the reasoning process itself are one immensely powerful way of securing that achievement.

This achievement must often be measured in the long run. We cannot be sure that in every case complying with an exclusionary reason rather than directly balancing the first-order reasons will provide the better result. Consider the rule that promises must be honoured. We often regret particular promises, but we recognize that the peremptory force of promises protects the *practice* of promising. If promises were not binding, if instead people were to re-open their commitments to others and re-weigh all the factors bearing on performance whenever the promise started to bite, then a promise would not represent the kind of valuable commitment it is, and the practice would deteriorate. The rule serves our interests because the practice allows us to commit ourselves to others and to certain courses of action, and being able to make these commitments is valuable.

Note that Raz's explanation of rules as exclusionary reasons deals with the third defect he identifies in Hart's practice theory of rules, viz its failure to explain the normativity of rules. Because exclusionary reasons like rules are based on the first-order reasons which they reflect, they inherit the 'ought' or 'must do' quality of the interests, desires, or values found in the first-order reasons.

So far, the discussions have centred largely around rules. It is worthwhile, then, to briefly consider the normativity of rights, duties, and powers, or to put it another way, to consider how rights, duties, and powers are norms. The case of duties is the easiest. Duties guide your behaviour by telling you what to do or not to do. They are clearly norms, and are very close to rules, which is why, as Hart pointed out, so many theorists have tended to regard the law as made up only of duty-imposing rules. Rights are interestingly different. Rights reflect the interests of individuals or groups. We speak of one's right to life, one's right to assemble, and so on. How do rights guide the behaviour of people? They do so by requiring others to act appropriately in respect of your interests, if you have a right to those interests. Thus, if Fred has the right to life, others are required to meet a standard of behaviour which serves or protects Fred's interest in his life. In other words, rights can be formulated in terms of corresponding duties. (You might ask why, if rights can be formulated in terms of duties, we ever use the vocabulary of rights; the short answer is that *how* we express something, eg as a right to life rather than as a duty not to kill, is often important in how we appreciate the nature of a norm. For a longer answer, see Penner 1997c; Raz, 1984.) Powers are normative in still a different way. Powers guide your behaviour by providing you with a way of doing something so that it 'counts'. Legal powers provide you with a means of doing something so that it is effective as far as the law is concerned. So, for example, the legal power to write a will guides your behaviour by directing you to create legal rights in your property following your death, if that is, you wish to do so, by correctly following the procedure of making a will.

HOW DO WE FOLLOW RULES?

So far we have explored the way in which rules are kinds of reasons. But rules provoke a much deeper problem. What do we know when we know how to follow a rule correctly? This might seem a trivial or silly question. If I understand the rule, then I know what I must do in cases where it applies, and knowing that is to know how to follow it correctly. This short answer is perfectly correct, but it misses the point; the question is: what does understanding a rule consist in? Wittgenstein (1958) raised this question, and so let us consider an example which explains what worried him.

Consider a rule of arithmetic, the rule of addition. As children we were taught what it was to add two numbers together. If given two numbers, say 3 and 7, and told to add them, we would do our calculation and answer '10'. Now, you ask me to add two numbers which, assume for the sake of argument, I've never added before, say 123 and 456. I answer '5'. You say I've got it wrong but I object: I say I've given the right answer. Naturally, you would say that I'm not adding correctly, I'm not following the rule of addition; I'm not doing what 'addition' means. But I respond in this way: 'Of course I acknowledge that, in all the past cases where I was "adding", I agreed with you on the result; but as I understand addition, the sum of any two numbers where one of the numbers is 123 is 5.' What can you say to show that I'm wrong?

Consider another case. We have played chess together for years, but today when we play I exhibit what is, to your mind, strange behaviour. I move the queen as in the past I moved a knight, and move my pawns diagonally in any direction and as many spaces as I wish. You object. 'You're not following the rules of chess.' 'I am too,' I reply, 'these are the correct ways of moving the pieces according to the game of chess; they are to be moved this way whenever your opponent is over 25 years old, and you turned 25 last week.' Flabbergasted you might well be, but what are you to say?

The thrust of these examples is that I appear to be 'artificially' deviating from the established rules. I am treating a new case where the rule is to be applied as an opportunity to depart from the *real* rule by concocting some preposterous alternative rule that incorporated some 'hidden' exception or subrule all along, but which only now comes into play (in the novel case of the sum involving 123, or playing chess with you after you've turned 25). The question is how we vindicate our common sense understanding of addition or the rules of chess to rule such 'artificial' rules out.

There are two particular strategies that you might follow, which Wittgenstein considered and found wanting, which we will look at in turn.

You might say, 'it follows from all the past cases in which the rule was applied that you must go on in the way that I regard as correct; the pattern that results from applying the rule in past cases *logically dictates* what you must do in this case, and in acting the way you have, you are violating that pattern'. Unfortunately, as Wittgenstein made clear, this reply is hopeless. Answering 5 when asked to add 123 and 456 is to apply a *logically possible* rule, because the rule I apply covers all the past cases (where we agree) *and* accounts for this new case, 123 + 456, where we do not agree. There's nothing in our past behaviour which cannot be accounted for either by 'your' rule or 'my rule'. There's nothing in the pattern of our past behaviour you can point to which logically indicates that it was 'your' rule of addition that I was following rather than 'my' rule, because 'my' rule accounts for those past cases as well as yours does. We only discover now that we have been following different rules, and indeed I might argue that *you* have misunderstood the rule, and misunderstood the 'pattern' of the past cases because you don't see that 123 + 456 = 5. As this example shows, our past behaviour could be accounted for by an *infinite* number of rules, which would could lead us to act in new cases in radically different ways.

Note how corrosive this insight is for our belief that rules guide our behaviour: if we rely on the 'logical dictate' that is supposed to lie within patterns of past behaviour, not only can we not explain how we could possibly share rules with others, but it is not clear that we are ever required by a rule to act in one way rather than another, for 'complying with' patterns of past behaviour never requires us to do one thing rather than another.

We might then consider a different strategy. We admit that patterns lying in our past practice do not logically dictate how we should go in the next case, but perhaps the problem is that we haven't formulated or interpreted our rule, like the rule of addition, in a fashion explicit enough to rule out misunderstanding. Perhaps we can show that one way of acting is required by the rule once we spell out the rule in more concrete or explicit terms. Perhaps you could require me to get the sum 123 + 456 = 579 along these lines: to add one follows the formula: 'start with the first number, and count as many times as the second number'. So with 2 + 2, start at two, count twice (3, 4) and thus the answer is 4. Now do the same with 123 and 456 and you will get 579, the correct answer. Doesn't putting the rule this way *guarantee* that I will follow the rule properly? This strategy, while it looks promising, is unfortunately as hopeless as the 'logic in the pattern' strategy, though for a different reason. The problem here is that you implicitly depend in this strategy on our agreeing what all the terms of your new formulation mean. What do you mean by 'count'? Just as with the 'logic in the pattern' case, there doesn't seem to be anything in this formula which prevents me from understanding 'count' in my own way. I might agree with your formulation, but say that when we have the numbers 123 one counts 5...5...5...5... etc 456 times, with the result that the answer is 5. You may of course go on to define what 'counting' is, but I can in turn dispute what the terms of that definition mean. The point here is that the meanings of terms are themselves governed by the rule-governed use of those terms; 'count' means 'count' because we use that word in a particular way. In short, the meaning of words lies in the rules by which we use them. In just the same way that we might come into conflict when it comes to 'adding' 123 and 456, we can come into conflict in 'counting'. Providing a different formulation of a rule is providing an interpretation of it, but in the same way as we can misunderstand what a rule requires, we can misunderstand the interpretation or formulation of a rule. We can give further interpretations of our interpretations, one after another, but this just leads to an infinite regress; it doesn't solve the problem.

By this point, you may feel like a rule-sceptic, someone who doesn't believe that rules ever really require us to do one thing rather than another, that we can always get round the rules if we want (recall the rule-scepticism of the American realists and critical legal scholars, Chapter 7). But Wittgenstein was no rule-sceptic. What he showed with the preceding arguments was that if you looked to some kind of explicit 'logic of past cases' or to some ironclad, unmisinterpretable formulation to explain how rules worked, you would be unable to explain how they work. You would be looking in the wrong place.

Now, while everyone agrees with the points Wittgenstein made above, about the hopelessness of explaining rules by finding the logic of a pattern or by resorting to further and better formulations or interpretations of rules, Wittgenstein's own solution to the problem of rule-following he raised is controversial in two ways: first, the manner in which Wittgenstein expressed his thoughts has led to huge controversies concerning what Wittgenstein's own views were; secondly, it remains controversial whether the particular solution(s) one can arguably find in his writing really work, really are solutions. Be that as it may, I shall elaborate one textually well-supported and otherwise philosophically sophisticated solution to the problem.

In one sense, the solution is disarmingly simple, though it raises large issues about the nature of the human mind, of language, and more. For Wittgenstein, our ability to follow rules lies in our behavioural dispositions. We know how to go on in the same way, to act in a rule-governed fashion, because, in a sense, we are built that way. It is a facet of the kind of creatures we are. Humans are endowed with an ability to 'go on in the same way' which allows us both to act consistently, and to 'think' consistently, ie to use words in the same way from one conversation to the next, to calculate sums in a regular fashion, to treat a certain reason for acting (to boil the kettle when we want a cup of tea) as the same reason for acting on different occasions.

It is because of these dispositions that patterns of past behaviour figure in our understanding as instances of rule-following. Because we go on in a particular way, which we see as going on in the same way, we know what it is to add correctly and incorrectly. We created the pattern in our past behaviour by going on in the same way, and so we naturally point that pattern out to someone if they miscalculate. But we cannot explain the rule of addition by saying the pattern admits of only one logical explanation. If our interlocutor cannot see what going on in the same way amounts to, there is nothing logic can do for us or him. Similarly with providing re-formulations or interpretations of a rule. Because knowing how to follow a rule lies in our ability to act – to go on in the same way – understanding a rule does not amount to understanding a form of words. A formulation of a rule expresses the rule in language, and because our language expresses things more or less well, we are often able to explain rules to people with language. Statutes, of course, do this all the time. An expression of a rule in language is often all we need to allow someone to 'get' the rule, ie know how to act according to the rule. But a rule is not equivalent to the expression of a rule, just as the word 'dog' is not the same thing as a dog. If you didn't have the ability to see all the different examples of dogs as the same kind of thing, you could never learn the word 'dog', that is, you could never learn to use it correctly, applying it only to dogs. Similarly, if a person were not able to see what it was to go on in the same way in a particular case of rule-following, no expression or interpretation of the rule would overcome that inability.

One must be careful in putting it this way, but the central claim here is that in following rules, behaviour, not thinking, is fundamental, when by 'thinking' we mean it in the sense of 'reflecting' about what one must do. In this sense, one follows rules 'blindly' or automatically – to understand a rule is just to know how one must act; if one understands the rules of chess, one doesn't have to think about what you can and cannot do at each move. This is not to say that following rules may not involve thinking – for example, if one knows the rule of addition, one must still think in the sense of attending to one's calculations when one adds – it is however, to say, that the one thing one doesn't have to think about is what the rule is, what it requires one to do.

At first glance, all of this may seem rather technical and far from our concerns to explain the nature of legal reasoning. But if we reflect for a moment, we can see that this brief discussion of Wittgenstein's explanation of rule-following immediately yields two rather interesting results. First, of particular relevance to the common law, it is clear that no pattern of judgments in past judicial decisions 'logically' requires us to say that those decisions embody any one particular rule. Our understanding that a particular rule underlies a series of cases depends upon our seeing those cases in the same way. If, for example, different judges or lawyers find two different rules that explain a line of cases, and we can 'see' the force or plausibility of both as candidate rules underlying the decisions, then we are faced with a genuine choice between rules, or a genuine uncertainty as to which rule led to that series of decisions. But by the same token, a lawyer or judge cannot just propose any rule to explain the cases, proposing rules akin to the rule of 'addition' that would require $123 + 456 = 5$. While we cannot 'logically' rule out any preposterous rule, we are perfectly capable of judging rules of this kind to be 'non-starters'. And so we can see how Wittgenstein's analysis both makes sense of, and restricts, the scope of rule-scepticism in law. The thoroughgoing rule sceptic is not ruled out of order by any logical pattern in past cases; but by the same token, he cannot assume that in any legal case he can make what he wants of the past decisions. Our going-on-in-the-same-way sense or judgment allows us perfectly well to find that in many cases only one candidate rule plausibly underlies past decisions. In order to claim that a line of cases is uncertain, someone must do the work of proposing two or more candidate rules that really do plausibly account for the decisions. Scepticism must be earned, case by case, (or branch of law by branch of law if one wants to argue that legal doctrine incorporates fundamentally opposing principles, say in the law of contract), not assumed willy nilly. (You might wish to re-visit the Dworkin-Fish debate we considered in Chapter 9 with these points in mind.)

Secondly, our attention to the distinction between rule formulations or interpretations of rules, and the rules themselves, helps explain why the common law typically frowns upon treating particular statements in a case as 'canonical' rule statements, and why statutory interpretation is often a locus of legal argument. Rules lie in the behaviour they require, not in the way we might express them. When we read a case, we see judges trying to express what they mean with many different formulations; they try to put the point in different ways, so as not to give the impression that any one formulation is to be treated as a sacred statement. They thus wisely realise that the goal is for the reader of the judgment is to 'get' the rule, not to memorise some form of words, for no form of words uniquely captures the rule. In a later case, in a different context, the rule might better be formulated differently. Statutes present a constant problem in this respect. The point here is not to claim that rules cannot be expressed in language. The point is just that because a rule and its formulation are different things, the same formulation may be compatible with different rules. The famous jurisprudential hypothetical rule 'No vehicles in the park' provides a good example, as we will see below. But for just now, consider which possible rules expressed by this formulation would prohibit skateboarders, ambulances on emergency calls, or the placing of an army lorry on a pedestal in the park as a war memorial.

RULES AND 'HARD CASES'

Before leaving our exploration of the nature of rules, we will look at different ways in which there can be a conflict involving rules, what we might call 'hard cases'. There are many ways in which conflicts involving rules can occur, but if we can distinguish certain kinds of conflict from others, we can hope to avoid some of the confusions that, unfortunately, all too often occur in discussions of legal reasoning. We will look at five kinds of hard case here.

(1) *'Hard cases' that make 'bad law'*. Following Dworkin's use of the term 'hard cases', another meaning for 'hard case' has declined, though it has a traditional place in legal reasoning, which is captured in the phrase 'hard cases make bad law'. On this meaning of 'hard case', a hard case is one where the rules of law are clear, but the result they require is harsh or 'hard'. The classic example is the case of the widow and her seven hungry children facing eviction on Christmas Eve for rent or mortgage arrears. Here is another, real life, example, provided by Hutchinson (1988, 23):

> A year or so ago, a swimming meet took place at the University of Toronto. Most of the races proceeded as planned. But, at the end of one race, there was a challenge to the winner of the race. The appropriate group of officials convened. The deliberations were lengthy and tense. After much argument and poring over the rules, a decision was announced: the winner had been disqualified and the second swimmer was acclaimed the victor. The referee took the unusual course of offering a brief justification of the committee's decision – 'the rules were clear ('The winner is the first swimmer to touch the side of the pool with both hands') and, if this regrettable outcome is to be avoided in the future, it will be necessary to change the rules'. The winning swimmer had only one arm.

Sometimes these cases reveal a genuine conflict between law and morality, but in others, we just feel very sorry for the losing party – the result is not strictly-speaking unjust, but it is nevertheless a very sad turn of events. The phrase 'hard cases make bad law' is a warning. Judges are warned that trying to bend the rules, create *ad hoc* exceptions, and so forth, to get a more agreeable result, makes 'bad law', that is, unprincipled, confused, and uncertain law. The wish to get a pleasing result while sticking to one's principles is an age-old problem not just in law but in morality, and we must be very circumspect about dealing with such cases. Sometimes, one really must depart from the rules, sometimes by realising that the case really does provide the grounds for making a principled exception, and sometimes purely on the basis that, without framing a new exception or sub-rule, justice simply requires putting the rules to one side. The universal notion of 'equity' (not the one associated exclusively with the English Chancellor and the English Court of Equity) embraces this idea, that justice will require from time to time departure from established rules without purporting to alter the rules themselves. The essential point to take away from looking at this kind of hard case is that there is no uncertainty of the rules here, or difficulty in applying them – we are simply faced with unhappiness with the result if we do apply them.

A slightly different version of such a case occurs not where the result the rules dictate is harsh or hard, but just *unacceptable* to the mind of the judge. The recent Court of Appeal decision in *Regina (Quintavalle) v Secretary of State for Health* [2002] 2 All ER 625 provides an example. Under regulations made pursuant to the Human Fertilisation and Embryology Act 1990 the government licensed research using embryos created *in vitro.* Since the passing of the act a new method of creating such embryos was developed, embryos which could only be included in the statutory definition of embryos by, as the Court acknowledged, straining the statutory language (which was, if anything, an understatement). The prospect, however of leaving the creation and research of such embryos completely unregulated was so unappealing to the Court that they regarded a 'purposive' interpretation of the statute to be legitimate even though this would involve a gymnastic interpretive effort.

(2) *Rules requiring judgment in their application.* Sometimes rules require judgment in their application. This is a familiar problem in the case of many rules of the common law which rely upon more or less vague ideas, such as the rules requiring one to take 'reasonable care' in the law of negligence, or the rule governing 'remoteness of damage' in tort and contract law, or 'dishonesty' in the law of theft. Cases of this kind can be hard because it may be very difficult ultimately to decide whether, for example, a defendant took reasonable care (recall the case of *Bolton v Stone* [1951] AC 850, where the question was whether the defendant cricket club had failed to take reasonable care when it ignored the risk of a cricket ball leaving the ground and hitting a passer-by when only six balls had been hit out of the ground in thirty years). Positivists often assume that where a decision-maker must apply these sorts of rules, the judge, explicitly, and a jury, implicitly, must exercise discretion to devise a more concrete or specific rule to decide the case. In some instances this may be so, but it may not. There is a difference between (1) treating a direction to decide a case on a standard of 'reasonableness' as a direction to conceive a more concrete rule that falls within the general standard and decide on the basis of that, and (2) treating the direction to apply the general standard *per se* though doing so will require judgment, looking at the question from different perspectives, weighing different factors, and so on. Thus when judges and juries decide cases on the basis of standards of this kind, we cannot just conclude that they were exercising some kind of discretion to define the law as they thought best (within bounds), or that in applying such standards they were not deciding the case according to law. All it means is that rules may be difficult to apply. This doesn't detract from the Wittgensteinian point that rules are followed 'blindly'; if a judge or jury understands the rule they know what they must do – they must assess as best they can, must *judge* as best they can, whether the conduct was reasonable or the injury too remote. The Wittgensteinian point about following rules blindly does not mean that all rules are easy to follow. The distinction between (1) and (2) can be seen in the way past judicial decisions are treated. Sometimes, we regard a decision under a general standard as establishing new law, or settling the law in some specific way. But sometimes we just regard a decision as an example of applying the standard, an example which may give guidance for a later decision-maker in exercising his judgment, but not as laying down some specific rule; and we see this way of taking the cases when a textbook just lists a series of cases with a brief characterisation of the facts and the decision, rather than treating the cases as textual proof of some more concrete rule. (For a thorough discussion, see Stone 1995.)

(3) *Where the law is unsettled by reason of conflict between the rules.* This is a common occurrence in the law, and little needs to be said. Lines of cases sometimes conflict, as do different statutory rules. The law embraces a panoply of formal mechanisms which

resolves many of these conflicts – later statute 'beats' earlier statute, Court of Appeal decision 'beats' High Court decision, and so on – but of course not all. How we deal with this sort of hard case, or think judges do, whether we think of these cases as occasions for the exercise of judicial discretion or as occasions for Herculean efforts to discern a right answer is, of course, about the biggest controversy in jurisprudence, and no more need be said about that here, though we will return to it in Parts II and III.

(4) *Where the law is uncertain because of the ability to discern two or more plausible rules as underlying a series of cases or a statutory provision.* Here again, little need be said. This is a classic case and one famous (infamous?) hypothetical example will serve, Hart's example of the bye-law 'No vehicles in the park'. Some patriotic citizens wish to mount an old army lorry in the park as a memorial to war veterans. Does the bye-law prohibit this? Well, if the bye-law is there to regulate traffic, it does not. But if the bye-law was enacted to ensure a bucolic atmosphere in the park, to provide a haven from the mechanistic trappings of a technologically mad society, then it does. The case is clearly not a hard one if the bye-law was made pursuant to regulations found in some 'Vehicle Traffic Act', for then only the first rule would be a plausible candidate for the rule the bye-law expresses. But we can imagine circumstances in which there might be genuine uncertainty, for example where the Green party gained control of the local council and made it a policy to use all its powers to advance its environmental agenda. As with (3) above, how one regards decisions in cases where there genuinely are two plausible candidate rules will flow from one's positivistic or anti-positivistic views.

(5) *Where the law is uncertain due to the uncertain force of a rule formulation.* The law relies extensively upon language to express its rules, but as we now know from our discussion of rule-following, a formulation of a rule is not the rule itself, and for that reason many cases can arise where a rule statement is ambiguous between stating one rule or another (eg 'No vehicles in the park' in the last paragraph). But there is another problem with rule-formulations which deserves particular attention, for it arises commonly in the law: it is often difficult to determine whether a rule statement uses words in a way which requires us to treat those words as subject to 'special', restricted, or extended definitions or not. Here's a real life example. In *R v MacEwen* [1947] 2 DLR 62, a case from the Canadian province of Prince Edward Island, the accused had stolen bottles of liquor from a shop, and was in consequence charged with theft. However, the province's *Prohibition Act,* then in force, declared that no property right of any kind existed in liquors unlawfully kept at any place in the province, which this liquor was. Since the act of theft is constituted by the dishonest appropriation of *property*, the accused argued that he had committed no such offence. The question for the court was, obviously, whether the Prohibition Act's declaration was intended to deny the status of property to alcoholic beverages *for all purposes* in law, or just for its own provisions (the main thrust of which was to allow the province's officers to seize alcohol or require its destruction without being faced with the claim of expropriating private property.) Alternatively, one might put the question, should the alcohol that was taken be regarded as property for the purposes of the law of theft, irrespective of the statute. This sort of issue arises all the time in the law – should a word used in a rule formulation be interpreted to comply with what appears to be the obvious and intended thrust of a rule, to be interpreted 'locally' or 'contextually' given that we have a clear

understanding of the rule and regard the words of a formulation as a best effort to capture the rule, words to be more or less narrowly read to comply with that rule, or rather, are we to understand the words to be determinative in the sense that we should understand the rule to apply to cases that fall within the meaning of the words, giving those words their 'plain meaning' or their general legal meaning (as determined by reference to case law and statute). Definitions sections in statutes often provide special meanings for words, but these are notorious for causing as many problems as they solve. The essential point here is that we can treat our rule formulations as more or less determinative depending upon whether, when we use a particular word or phrase, we intend our understanding of that word or phrase (our rule-governed sense of what the word means) to be an essential reference point for our understanding of the rule that the formulation expresses, or whether, by contrast, we intend the whole formulation to capture the shape of a rule, so that we should not quibble about the particular words, seeing them as merely part of the attempt to do so. Consider again the 'swimmer' case in one above; it is at least arguable that the requirement to touch the end of the pool with 'both hands' properly understood according to the true nature of the rule really means 'all the hands the swimmer has', so that the one-armed swimmer would not be disqualified. But, given the technical nature of the rules of games, it is arguable that, on the contrary, the rule requires of any qualifying swimmer that he meets the condition of having two hands with which to touch the end of the pool, and so the plain meaning of 'both hands' accurately states the rule – on this view the joint competition of two-armed and one-armed swimmers was simply not contemplated and thus admitted as a form of competition under the rules.

2. Concepts

We have already looked at the nature of concepts in some detail already, in Chapter 10, and it is worth reviewing the first part of that chapter now.

The main points of that discussion which we must bear in mind here are (1) that there are different kinds of concept, and (2) that we distinguish concepts themselves from all our beliefs about them, ie we maintain a concept/conception distinction.

Recall that our concepts are different in terms of the different way we learn them and appreciate the nature of what they represent. Paradigm case concepts are learned on the basis of exposure to typical or paradigm cases of what a concept represents – we learn the word 'dog', acquire the concept of dog, by having typical dogs pointed out to us. We learn scientific or theoretical concepts by learning how they form part of a theoretical explanation of something, for example, learn the concept of proton in the course of understanding the nature of atoms. Dworkin, as we have seen, has developed a theory that certain kinds of concepts, prevalent in the law, are of a special kind, 'interpretive' concepts. In Part III of this chapter, we will also discuss a different distinction between different kinds of evaluative concepts, ie concepts that express values of some kind, like 'good', 'murder', 'courage' and so on, a distinction between 'thick' and 'thin' concepts. The distinction will be discussed in detail below, but the basic difference lies in noticing that some evaluative concepts, the thick ones, tend to be situation-specific and concrete, like 'courage' or 'theft', while others, the thin ones, tend to be much more general and abstract, like 'right' or 'good' or 'utility'. The essential point to take on board here is this: one's theory of law will heavily depend upon what sort of concepts you think legal concepts are. For example, as we saw in Chapter 10, Dworkin argues that positivists understand legal concepts to be 'paradigm case' concepts for the most part, which to his mind creates dire problems for positivism (though as we saw positivists do have resources to defend themselves). Dworkin, for his part, relies upon his characterisation of concepts as 'interpretive', for only on this basis is legal disagreement interpretive disagreement requiring the efforts of a Hercules, or rather judges and lawyers who model their legal reasoning behaviour on his. To consider an example we haven't discussed, but which is extensively covered in Chapter 17, an economic analysis of law relies upon treating legal concepts as theoretical concepts, the theoretical concepts of economics. Thus the legal concept of property is taken to coincide with the economic concept of property, a concept of property which is intimately related to the theoretical characterisation of efficient resource allocation. As we shall see in Part III, an explanation of legal reasoning as a kind of 'moral wisdom' relies extensively on the claim that most legal concepts are 'thick'.

The concept/belief or concept/conception distinction, you will recall, allows us to understand what Dworkin calls 'conceptual disagreement'. We can disagree about the nature of dogs or contracts or equality, safe in the knowledge that we are disagreeing about the same thing (not arguing at cross purposes as if you were making claims about river banks and I was making claims about merchant banks) because we can share the concept of dog or contract or equality though we have different beliefs about what those concepts represent. You may think dogs are friendly, and I don't; you may think contracts are mutual promises, and I don't; you may think equality is the fundamental political value, and I don't. We got all of that under our belts in Chapter 10, so why raise it again here? The reason is that it adds one more example of a hard case, a particularly important one, to our list.

(6) *Cases of Conceptual Disagreement.* Certain cases in law are hard cases because different lawyers can present different beliefs about the thing that a legal concept represents. Legal arguments can turn on whether a relationship really amounts to a trust, whether a particular transaction is really a contract in law, whether a certain type of sharp practice amounts to a fraud. Recall from Chapter 4 that Hart addressed himself to the debate about what a 'corporation' really is.

This sort of hard case is extremely important as a matter of jurisprudence. One of the main differences between Dworkin and his opponents is that Dworkin claims, and his opponents deny, that all significant hard cases in law can be treated as cases of conceptual disagreement. Dworkin would dispute our describing six different kinds of hard cases as separate cases in the way we have done. For Dworkin, they all can be reduced to, or interpreted as, cases of conceptual disagreement along the lines of case (6). For remember, according to Dworkin law is not a system of rules; rules are just more or less provisional standards whose status in legal reasoning turns upon their being correct characterisations of law according to the overall best theory or best interpretation of the law. Thus all hard cases ultimately turn on what we regard as the best conception of the fundamental concept of justice underlying the law (for Dworkin, roughly that the law justifies state coercion when it treats all subjects with equal concern and respect). The panoply of more specific legal concepts, from property to contract to theft to free speech are all ultimately linked to this foundation. There is, perhaps, no truer example of the way in which different legal theories turn upon what use they make of rules and what sorts of concepts they regard legal concepts as being. Positivist theories emphasise rules, and thus characterise hard cases as involving rules, as in hard cases (1) to (5), whereas Dworkin denies any determinative status to rules as such, emphasising legal concepts, and characterising legal concepts as interpretive concepts, to reveal that all hard cases manifest disputes over the true nature of what our legal concepts represent. A hard case does not reveal a conflict over rules in the law of contract or property or negligence, but is best seen as a conflict about what a contract, or property, or negligence, properly understood, really is.

Because this issue is of such vital importance, it is worthwhile pausing here before moving onto Part II, and drawing upon your experience as a student of the law, consider whether the various hard cases we have looked at are more or less independent, or rather are closely connected in some way, either in the way the Dworkin claims, or in some other way that occurs to you.

II Raz's Positivist Account of Legal Reasoning

In Chapters 8, 9, and 10 we looked at some of Raz's criticisms of Dworkin's account of legal reasoning; here we examine Raz's own, positivist account.

Raz (1979a, 180, 181–198, 200–209)

... This essay presents an outline of a positivist view of adjudication.

One distinction is fundamental: that between regulated and unregulated cases or disputes. Regulated cases are those which fall under a common law or statutory rule which does not require judicial discretion for the determination of the dispute (rules referring to what is reasonable or just, etc., do require, such discretion). A dispute is regulated if questions of the form: 'In this case should the court decide that *p*?' have a correct legal answer. It is unregulated if some of these questions do not have a correct legal answer, i.e. if there is a gap in the law applying to the case. Unregulated disputes, like regulated ones, are subject to laws applying to them and guiding the courts as to their solution. But since the law applying to unregulated disputes has gaps, no particular solution to the dispute is required by law, though the law may rule out several solutions as inappropriate and give some general guidance concerning the choice between some or all of the remaining possible solutions.

A regulated dispute may be governed by more than one rule, provided that in any case in which conflicting rules apply to a dispute, it is regulated only if a legally valid rule determines how the conflict is to be resolved. In short, a regulated dispute is one to which the law provides a solution. The judge can be seen here in his classical image: he identifies the law, determines the facts, and applies the law to the facts. There is nothing mechanical about this. Regulated cases can be complex and more difficult to decide than unregulated cases. The difficulty in solving a complex tax problem according to law may be much greater than that of solving a natural justice problem according to moral principles. The difference between a regulated and an unregulated dispute is not that only the second calls for the exercise of judgment by the court. Nor is it that in regulated disputes the courts use their legal judgment to apply the law whereas in unregulated disputes they use moral judgment to make law. The classical image mentioned above is misleading. The courts carry with them both their functions of applying pre-existing law and of making new ones into almost all cases (I do not mean they almost always make new laws, only that almost always they have to consider whether to do so). The difference between regulated and unregulated disputes is that because, by definition, in regulated disputes the law provides a solution to the case, the court cannot make new laws except by changing existing ones. Unregulated disputes are, as we shall see, partly regulated, hence the court has to apply existing law as well as to make new law. But since, by definition, in an unregulated dispute the law contains a gap, since it fails to provide a solution to the case, the court can make law without changing existing law. It makes law by filling in the gaps.

Here, then, is the problem this essay is about: To explain how the courts have both a law-applying and a law-creating role in regulated and unregulated disputes alike and how these respective functions differ in the different kinds of disputes. Finally, I shall show how the difference, though conceptually sharp, is gradual in application.

2. REGULATED DISPUTES – DISTINGUISHING

We may begin with a sketch of a simple case of following a binding rule. A reported decision, P, records that in that case where the facts were a, b, c, d, e, g, the decision was based on the rule that whenever A, B, C then X should be decided. (Lower-case letters stand for the particular circumstances of the case as recorded in the judgment – what is and what is not recorded will turn out to be important. Capital letters stand for general properties of facts so that a is an instance of A, etc.) The ruling in P, can be summarized as:

$$P: a, b, c, d, e, g/ A, B, C \rightarrow X.$$

The novel case, N, is a case of a1, b1, c1, e1 (i.e. not e1), f1 and is thus governed by P, which, it is assumed, is binding on the court. If the court decides to follow P its ruling will be:

$$N: a1, b1, c1, d1, e1, f1/A, B, C \rightarrow X$$

The normal interpretation of the doctrine of precedent is, of course, that it is not up to the court to decide whether to follow a precedent; it is bound to do so (we are after all considering regulated disputes, namely, those governed by binding precedent). Admittedly, this common interpretation has always been difficult to reconcile with the considerable freedom of action experienced and exercised by courts (especially the courts of appeal and the House of Lords) even in the face of a binding precedent. Consequently, most commentators on the doctrine of precedent try to resolve the difficulty by assuming that it is very difficult to discover the *ratio decidendi* of a case. Until fairly recently most of the writings on precedent in English Law (and related systems) were preoccupied with devising ever more sophisticated tests for identifying the ratio of a case, which were designed to reconcile the binding force of precedents with the wide discretion judges often have when faced with them. But there is something odd in the supposition that the identification of the *ratio* can be so difficult and mysterious. Essentially the *ratio* is the reason(s) by which the court justifies its decision ... In the main ... the identification of the *ratio* of a case is reasonably straightforward. This, however, merely leads back to the question of the compatibility of the well-known and extensive judicial flexibility with the doctrine of precedent.

The solution to the problem lies in the role of 'distinguishing' in the working of the doctrine of precedent. Like many other rules moulded and remoulded in the hands of judges in every age and over many years its boundaries are far from fixed. They undergo continual change. There is nevertheless value in a theoretical systematization. There is what I shall call 'the tame view' of distinguishing according to which to distinguish a binding precedent is simply to determine that its *ratio* does not apply to the instant case. The rule laid down in the precedent is that a certain decision is to be rendered if operative facts A, B, C obtain, but the instant case is a case of a2, b2, not-c2 and therefore the precedent does not apply. On this interpretation there is no special rule of distinguishing in the common law. A rule which does not apply to the case does not apply to it. To distinguish is simply to discover that the rule does not apply. As against this there is another view of distinguishing according to which one distinguishes a rule by changing it so that a rule which did apply to the present case no longer applies to it in its modified form. The rule laid down in P was when A, B, C then X. Since N is a case of a1, b1, c1, the rule applies to it. But the court has a power to distinguish. It can change the rule into A, B, C, E, then X. This modified rule does not apply to N, which is a case of not-e1. The rule in P was thus distinguished.

The English doctrine of precedent is that a precedent must be either followed or distinguished (though some courts also have power to overrule their own or other courts' decisions). It combines following precedent with considerable flexibility because it allows the courts, even those bound by precedent, to distinguish a previous decision rather than follow it. Since 'distinguishing' means changing the rule which is being distinguished, the power to distinguish is a power to develop the law even when deciding regulated cases and even by courts which have no power to overrule.

If distinguishing involves changing the rule distinguished how does it differ from overruling? Such a difference must exist for every court has the power to distinguish while only some have a power to overrule. Unless distinguishing differs from the general power to modify rules and to make new ones (as in overruling or in deciding unregulated disputes) my interpretation of distinguishing means, given the general power to distinguish, that precedents are never binding for the courts are always free to change them. Distinguishing, however, is a very restricted form of law-making. It is subject to two crucial conditions:

(1) The modified rule must be the rule laid down in the precedent restricted by the addition of a further condition for its application.

(2) The modified rule must be such as to justify the order made in the precedent.

The first condition means, first of all, that in distinguishing courts can only narrow down rules. They cannot extend them. (Their power to extend rules will be discussed in section 9 below.) This is a direct consequence of the very function of distinguishing, i.e.

modifying a rule to avoid its application to a case to which it does apply as it stands. This, in a precedent-based system, can only be done by restricting the application of the rule through adding to its conditions of application so that the modified rule no longer applies to the instant case. Furthermore, in distinguishing the court cannot replace the previous rule with any rule it may like even if it is narrower in application. The new rule must be based on the old one and contain all the conditions which the old one contains together with the new restricting condition. A, B, C then X is transformed into A, B, C, E then X. The previous conditions are preserved and become the foundation of the new rule.

The second condition restricts the power of the court still further. It limits its choice of the new restricting conditions. It must be such that the modified rule would be a possible alternative basis for the original decision. In our example the original decision was P: a, b, c, d, e, g/A, B, C→X. Given that the new case is one of a1, b1, c1, d1, e1, f1 the court will comply with the first condition of distinguishing equally by adopting A, B, C, not-D then X as by adopting A, B, C, E then X. Both are restrictive modifications of the rule in P. But only the second of these satisfies the second condition. A, B, C, not D then X would not in itself justify the order made in P, namely X. Note that the second condition is strong in that it does not merely require that the modified rule will be compatible with the earlier order. A, B, C, not D then X is compatible with the order of X in P, for it does not require a contrary decision. It merely fails to justify the order in P. But that it must do to meet the second condition.

In another respect the second condition is weak or at least ambiguous. Like other aspects of the doctrine of precedent it is concerned not with the actual facts of the case but with their public record. It seems to me that most of the time the doctrine is interpreted as allowing the court to distinguish P by adding the condition that not-F. The modified rule A, B, C, not-F then X may justify the order in P. There is no record whether it was a case of F or of not-F and the latter court is normally allowed the benefit of the doubt in such cases.

There is an indefinite number of different modifications of every rule conforming to the two conditions spelt out above. The court's obligation, however, is to adopt only that modification which will best improve the rule. Hence its real problem is usually limited to a judgment on the relative merits of but a few modifications. Often none will be accepted and the court will have to follow the rule. This will be the case not only when the court is perfectly happy with the rule but also when it would have preferred a different rule altogether but finds no improvement in the modifications it is allowed to make within the narrow boundaries of the rule of distinguishing.

A proper understanding of the substantial limitations the rule imposes on the court's creativity explains how it is possible and reasonable to allow a court that room for flexibility even when it is bound by a precedent. A modified rule can usually be justified only by reasoning very similar to that justifying the original rule. Not only will its justification show the reason for applying the ruling to a subclass of the cases to which it was originally applicable, it will also show the relevance of all the operative conditions set out by the original rule. The second condition above makes it tempting to say that the modified rule was really the rule the original court had in mind but which it failed to articulate clearly. Often enough this may indeed be the case. It may be that the court in P was influenced by the fact that the case was one of E but somehow perhaps they took this feature too much for granted, they failed to specify its existence among the operative conditions of their *ratio*. Yet this is not always so and often there is no evidence either way. Nevertheless this feature may hold the key to our understanding of the rationale of giving the court the power to distinguish: courts may be and often are a little careless in formulating rules. They approach the question through the example of one case (or several cases recorded in the law reports) and they do not enjoy the research and drafting facilities generally available to legislators. As a result it is unreasonable to attribute great weight to the actual formulation of the rule in the hands of the court. Statutory interpretation turns sometimes on the employment of one word rather than another. Not so the interpretation of precedent. Another result is that it is reasonable to read the rule in its context (i.e. the facts of the case as recorded) rather than in the abstract as one does a statute or a regulation. The power to distinguish reflects this dependence on context. The *ratio is* binding in its basic rationale and as applying to its original context. Courts can, however, modify its application to different contexts so long as they preserve its fundamental rationale.

…

This view of the doctrine of precedent enables one to adopt a simple and straightforward view of the identification of the *ratio*, but it presupposes a 'strong' interpretation of distinguishing, regarding it as a limited form of law-making.

3. REGULATED DISPUTES – OVERRULING

Like distinguishing, overruling is changing a common law rule established by precedent. Unlike the power to distinguish which is vested in all courts and which is frequently used, the power to overrule is more selectively distributed and is used more sparingly. On the other hand, its use is free of the restrictions attached to distinguishing. A court with the appropriate power can overrule a previous decision root and branch and substitute a completely different rule, even a diametrically conflicting one, in its place.

…

In a system based on precedent the power to overrule is necessarily limited. If every court is entitled to overrule any decision of any other court which applies to the case before it whenever it thinks it best to do so, then the legal system does not recognize the binding force of precedents. Precedents are binding only when the courts are not free to overrule them whenever they wish. The restrictions on the power of the courts to deviate from previous decisions are of three kinds: (1) Restrictions on the kind of rule they may substitute for the existing one; (2) Conditions which must obtain for them to have the power to introduce a new rule; (3) Conditions which must obtain before they may use their power to make a new rule. In the previous section I argued that restrictions of the first kind (and the first kind only) characterize the rule about distinguishing. No such restrictions apply to the power to introduce new rules when the court has power to overrule. Any new rule which will form the *ratio* of the case will become legally binding. In this respect overruling is like a decision in an unregulated dispute and unlike distinguishing. But the courts' right to overrule is limited by conditions of the remaining two kinds.

The precise nature of many restrictions is difficult to determine. On occasion it is undetermined in English Law today. For example, it seems that a decision of the court of appeal purporting to lay down a rule which overrules a rule by the House of Lords is not legally binding. The court has no power to overrule. But is the same true of a decision by the court of appeal overruling itself? Or does the latter decision bind despite the fact that the court should not have reached it? (*Davis v. Johnson* [1978] 1 All E.R. 1132 is ambiguous on this point.) A restriction which definitely belongs to the third kind is that a court should not overrule unless it is certain that the new rule is an improvement compared with the old. Here it is clear that if a court overrules because it thinks it likely (though it is not certain) that the new rule is an improvement, its decision is binding despite the fact that it acted improperly ... [T]here is a general reason for courts to observe such a restraint of caution in almost all their law-creating activities. It applies with particular force to overruling, for it (unlike decisions in unregulated disputes) upsets established legal rules and (unlike distinguishing) substitutes a rule which differs substantially from the old one ... This at least seems to me the best interpretation of the repeated judicial self-exhortations to exercise the power to overrule with great caution (particularly when the House of Lords intends to overrule its own decisions). It is unreasonable to regard these as implying that a rule should not be replaced by a new one unless the substitution will be a great improvement. Why not bring about small improvements? The exhortations obviously do mean that the court should be very careful to take notice of the possible bad effects of the very process of changing the law on the social and economic activities dependent on it. But beyond that the exhortations seem to reflect an awareness of the disadvantages under which the courts labour in trying to assess the different social and economic consequences of different legal arrangements ...

Distinguishing and overruling are the two kinds of powers to change existing common law rules which the courts have. They also have a more limited power to change statutory law. This power also will not be examined here. To do so will take one deep into the doctrines of statutory interpretation. Suffice to say that the power is exercised to 'update' old statutes and adjust their application to contemporary conditions and also to narrow down the application of a statutory rule where this is desirable and the case is one of open texture. In both situations the power is very limited, even more than in distinguishing, though the limitations are different.

4. REGULATED DISPUTES – CLOSURE RULES

One special case of law-making in regulated disputes should be briefly mentioned ... [A] dispute may be a regulated one not in virtue of a law governing its solution but because in the absence of any law applying to it a closure rule comes into operation. For example, since one of the disputants claims a right to a service from the other and since no law gives him such a right, he does not have it and the dispute should be settled in favour of the other party ... It is sometimes assumed that all courts have complete freedom to change the law when it rests on nothing more than silence, i.e. absence of sources. But this is a mistake. After all silence may speak louder than words, and a change in the law is a change in the law, regardless of the way the legal situation came to be. People rely on the law when it is based on silence as much as on the common law. The limitations of the courts' ability to improve the law are not much affected by the basis of the law they are trying to improve. Thus it is now generally accepted that the courts have no power or only a very limited power to create new criminal offences (to do so is often to change the law in cases now governed by the closure rule that what is not prohibited is permitted).

5. UNREGULATED DISPUTES

All unregulated disputes are due to intended or unintended indeterminacy of language and intention. The most simple kind comprises all the cases which fall within the vague borderlines of various descriptive concepts. Such are cases where it is unclear whether the instrument in question is an electrical appliance for the purpose of VAT, whether a person is domiciled in England, or whether a building is used for dwelling. In these cases the indeterminacy arises because of the vagueness in the criterion for the application of the concept or because the several criteria for its application yield, in the case under consideration, conflicting indications. Not all cases which fall within the borderline area of a legally relevant concept are unregulated. They may fall under a different rule as well and it may resolve the indeterminacy. But many cases are indeterminate for these reasons and appeal to legislative intention is often of no avail, for that intention, even when ascertained, is often itself indeterminate.

Slightly different is the indeterminacy of the cases falling under two conflicting rules, which is due to the absence of an appropriate conflict-resolving rule in the system. Here the verdict of each rule on the case is clear, but the system does not determine which rule is to be followed. It may lack an appropriate conflict-resolving rule altogether or it may include one which is indeterminate in its application to the present case.

It is true that the existence of unregulated disputes is an inevitable result of the indeterminacy of language and intention. Yet not all the existing unregulated disputes are inevitable. Very often legislators and courts when making laws prefer to use less rather than more determinate expressions in their formulation. They prefer to leave unregulated cases whose fate will be determined by the courts in due course, using their discretion within the limits allowed by the law. In such cases the law determines the general legal framework, leaving it to the courts to fill in the gaps which exist in all but the clearest of cases. Rules referring to 'reasonable care', 'good behaviour', 'just cause', 'material change in the use of the premises', 'offensive or abusive behaviour', 'obscene language', 'behaviour likely to lead to breach of the peace', or 'likely to offend religious feelings' are all examples of such deliberately underdetermined rules.

The common law divides such cases into two categories: those in which the gap in each case is filled by the judge, whose opinion becomes a precedent (so that in a sense the gaps narrow with every decision in an unregulated case), and those in which the decision is left to the jury, whose decisions are not explained and therefore not binding precedents. The distinction is tied up with the technical legal distinctions between law and fact and between terms used in a special legal signification to be explained by the court and terms used in their plain, ordinary meaning which the court may not explain but must leave it to the jury to apply. But in substance the decision in each case is a combination of two issues of legal principle. First, whether to regard the underdetermined law as a framework for further legal development filling in the gaps and charting out more and more detailed legal guidelines, or whether to hold that the law should remain underdetermined, the decision being left to the court to take afresh in every case. Second, whether to entrust the decision to judge or jury. The common law holds that generally when it is best to develop the law progressively the job is best done by judges, whereas where it is best to let full discretion reign in each new case the matter is to be entrusted to the jury to inform its decision with the shifting views and attitudes prevailing in society.

6. JUDICIAL LAW-MAKING AND LEGISLATION

In the previous sections the powers of the courts to make law both in regulated disputes (through distinguishing, overruling, and changing law governed by closure rules) and in unregulated ones (underdetermined by law, where the decision is assigned to a judge whose ruling creates a precedent) were described. The description intimated how extensive these law-making powers are. There is hardly a case of importance in which they cannot be used and often they are used. At the same time the description indicates the degree to which the use of these powers is limited and regulated by law. There are no pure law-creating cases. In every case in which the court makes law it also applies laws restricting and guiding its law-creating activities. Unregulated cases are partly, not wholly, unregulated, and distinguishing and overruling are circumscribed and hedged by legal limitations.

These limitations go a long way towards explaining the difference between judicial lawmaking and legislation. Yet the main conceptual difference is in the constant possibility of distinguishing judge-made law. This means that judge-made law has a different status from legislated law. Strictly speaking judge-made law is binding and valid, just as much as enacted law. But judge-made law is unique in the ample powers the courts have to change it by overruling and distinguishing. The importance of the point is not merely the existence of more numerous repeal powers, but rather in the occasion for their exercise. Judge-made law is constantly subject to potential (though modest) revision on all occasions on which its application is litigated (and it can be litigated in almost all cases to which the law applies). In this respect it can be metaphorically said that judge-made law is less 'binding' than enacted law.

This special revisability of judge-made law is of crucial importance in understanding the difference between enacted law and the common law and also the difference between the law-making function of courts and legislators. It accounts for the sense of organic growth which is so characteristic of the common law. It is typical of common law rules to be moulded and remoulded in the hands of successive courts using explicitly or unconsciously their powers of reformulating and modifying the rules concerned. Hence the reason for the judicial habit of citing the most recent important authorities dealing with a rule in addition to, or even instead of, those cases where the rule was first laid down.

Several further features of the doctrine of precedent help to explain the appropriateness of applying metaphors of organic growth to the common law. Judicial law-making tends to be by way of piecemeal reform. The ability of the courts radically to reshape a substantial area of the law by a single decision is very limited. This is partly due to the power to distinguish itself. It has the result that the wider the principle enunciated by a court the easier it is to distinguish it, to whittle it down. Consequently, judges often avoid pronouncing new general principles and prefer to trim their rulings to fit closely the case at hand. Needless to say, the fact that the bulk of judicial law- making is by way of filling in gaps in unregulated disputes and of distinguishing in regulated ones does in itself limit the opportunities for laying down radically new broad principles. Finally, there is the basic rule that only the *ratio* of the case is binding. Courts can never promulgate a code governing a whole area of law. They are basically limited to laying down single rules or principles. If they pronounce a view in favour of a whole set of principles this view is *obiter* except in so far as it concerns the principle on which the actual decision in the cases rests.

These explanations of the piecemeal progress of the common law are not meant to deny that over the years the common law may undergo radical transformation. Nor do they diminish the important contributions of single judgments by great judges to such developments. The very knowledge that one's pronouncements from the Bench can later be revised and moderated, while acting to restrain many judges from departing too far from existing doctrine, does on occasion encourage bold spirits to experiment. A judge may voice far-reaching innovative ideas hoping that they will bear fruits while enjoying the assurance that if they fall on unreceptive ground, or prove to be barren, the way of retreat is always open. This too is an important feature of the common law, but it exists against the more usual background of a succession of small-scale accumulating changes.

It is easy to see that this major difference between judicial law-making and legislation is not without justification. It is just what one would expect given the lack of special qualification in the Bench to carry out major law-reform. The judges' training and practice familiarize them with the detailed problems arising from the application of existing legal doctrines. It reveals to them opportunities and needs to extend or to attenuate the operation of those doctrines or to resolve conflicts or anomalies in their. application. But nothing prepares them to rethink radically the fundamental assumptions on which the law is based. Similar observations apply to the submissions before the courts by the attorneys of the litigants.

7. CONSERVATIVE RESTRAINTS

The previous section explains the difference between judicial law-making and legislation in terms of the more limited powers (in cases of distinguishing and of filling in gaps) and effects of the former ... Yet essentially it is true that in the exercise of their law-making power the courts should – within the legally imposed restrictions – act as one expects Parliament to act, i.e. by adopting the best rules they can find.

This last statement has often been criticized. Much of the criticism is confused. It is sometimes said that courts do not have lawmaking powers for they are not democratically elected. Quite apart from the fact that, given the supremacy or Parliament, judge-made law is no more undemocratic than much delegated legislation, the objection is at best a criticism of the existence of judicial law-making powers. It provides no evidence that they do not exist. The same is true of the objection that such powers mean that judge-made law is retroactively applied (to the instant case and all cases litigated after the precedent was laid down but where the cause of action occurred before it). It may be worth noting that the objection to retroactive law-making is based on the frustration of justified expectations. Such an objection to judicial law-making has no force at all when unregulated disputes or any hard and controversial legal case is concerned since no justifiable expectations can arise in such cases. The force of the retroactivity objection is confined to clear instances of distinguishing and is particularly acute in cases of overruling, where it accounts for the courts' great reluctance to overrule on any but the clearest grounds.

...

Most law-making decisions are concerned with extending existing doctrines, successively adjusting them to gradually changing technological, economic, or social conditions and introducing small alterations to avoid the undesirable and unintended consequences of applying rules to circumstances which were not foreseen when those rules were laid down. Such maintenance, repair, and conservation are the function of much legislated law as well. In this respect there is no substantial difference between precedent and legislation. But there is here already a difference in the public image of the institutions. In thinking of legislation one tends to think more of its innovative, reforming role than of its conserving role, which is more prominent in our image of the courts' law-making role. The real morally relevant difference lies in the conditions for introducing far-reaching reforms. The law affects social and economic conditions through the complex interaction of many legal provisions with various social and economic conditions which are usually at least partly unknown and invariably complex. It is a well-known truism that changes in the law do not always achieve their 'obvious' effects: the legally imposed duty to equalize women's pay may lead to women's unemployment, etc. A major reform in property law may necessitate changes in torts, criminal law, family law, and planning law to make sure that its objectives are achieved. For all the reasons explained above it is usually impossible for the courts to introduce in one decision all the changes necessary for the effective implementation of a radical reform in any aspect of the law. The choice a court will face is one between taking a first step towards reform in the hope that with time the work will be completed by other decisions (or by legislation) or to remain faithful to existing doctrines. Such a choice is often very hard since partial measures not only fall short of producing the good which a complete reform may bring, but they often have bad consequences. Partial reform introduces a new discordant element into an existing doctrine. It means that the law will now include provisions reflecting and pursuing different and inconsistent social goals. It incorporates pragmatically conflicting provisions. Normative conflict exists when two valid requirements cannot both be complied with. Pragmatic conflict is a wider concept. Laws conflict pragmatically if one is designed to promote or sustain a state of affairs which cannot coexist with that which the other is designed to promote or sustain. A law sustains or promotes a state of affairs not only through compliance with its requirements but also through actions using rights, powers, or permissions it grants and through the social and economic consequences of such behaviour. Partial reform does not involve normative conflict but it invariably introduces pragmatic conflict into the law.

Parliament does not normally have to choose between partial reform and conservatism. It can opt for radical reform (though for a variety of reasons this is not always a practical option). The courts are invariably presented with this choice.

8. ANALOGICAL REASONING

A court relies on analogy whenever it draws on similarities or dissimilarities between the present case and previous cases which are not binding precedents applying to the present case.

...

What are the conditions which a successful argument by analogy must meet? One talks of argument by analogy whenever the court relies on the existence of similarities with previous decisions, but naturally not all such reliance is justified. How is one to judge? Two major difficulties hinder a clear analysis of analogical argument. The first is the difficulty of providing a general test for relevance of similarities. The second difficulty, which compounds the first, is the problem of explaining how analogical arguments can be forceful and non-binding at the same time.

...

[I]n *D v. NSPCC* [1977] I All E.R. 589 the House of Lords had to decide whether the NSPCC is entitled to refuse to disclose the identity of one of their informers despite the fact that his identity is relevant to an action for negligence against the NSPCC. Existing rules compel the NSPCC to produce the information. There is, however, a rule allowing departments of the government to withhold relevant evidence when its production will harm the public interest in the proper and efficient functioning of the government. This rule does not cover the NSPCC, which is not a government department. The Lords, however, found sufficient similarity between cases governed by this rule and the present case to justify changing the law and extending the rule to protect the anonymity of NSPCC informers. The similarity is in the statutory functions which the NSPCC fulfils and those of various government agencies (police, social services, etc.). This similarity is sufficient because the purpose of the original rule is to secure the efficient exercise of powers of a certain character. One way of doing this is by providing protection to government departments. But the same purpose equally justifies extending the protection to other bodies fulfilling similar functions.

This is a brief and crude summary of a long and subtle judgment. The case itself is simple since the analogy drawn is just between one rule and the new case. Often analogies to a number of rules are invoked. But the case illustrates the general technique of analogical arguments – reliance on partial similarities to extend a rule ... or to create another rule leading to the same result ... when such a change in the law is justified by the same purpose or value which justifies the original rule on which the analogy is based.

...

This then is the answer to the first difficulty: the test of relevance for similarities is the underlying justification of the rule which forms the basis of the analogy. Argument by analogy is essentially an argument to the effect that if a certain reason is good enough to justify one rule then it is equally good to justify another which similarly follows from it.

These remarks implicitly contain the solution to the second difficulty in the explanation of analogical argument: if analogical argument has any force at all how can it fail to be absolutely binding? Why is it only one guide for the courts' exercise of their law-making discretion? The first thing to note is that argument by analogy does not in itself justify the new rule supposedly based on it. All it shows is that if the old rule is justified so is the new one. But then, it may be contended, analogical arguments are themselves without any force: if the old rule is a bad one and its supposed justification is faulty then it should not be relied on to generate a new rule. If, on the other hand, the justification is valid and good it can be relied upon to generate a new rule regardless of whether or not it is also the justification of an existing rule. Either way there is no force in the analogy as such. There is some truth in this argument, but ultimately it fails through overlooking the predicament of partial reform as described in the previous section. That predicament stems from the objection to partial reform based on its alleged bad by-products resulting from the introduction of pragmatic conflicts into the law. Argument by analogy shows that the new rule is a conservative one, that it does not introduce new discordant and conflicting purposes or value into the law, that its purpose and the values it promotes are already served by existing rules.

This is the force of the analogical argument, but this is also its limitation. As was noted in the previous section, though there is reason to avoid pragmatic conflicts, that reason is overridden if the conflict is likely to be short-lived or if, for any other reason, its undesirable consequences are less undesirable than the consequences of perpetuating and extending the scope of bad legal rules and doctrines. This is why analogical arguments have some force but are not conclusive. They establish coherence of purpose with certain parts of the law. This is a relevant consideration but there are others.

...

9. THE CONTINUITY OF APPLYING AND MAKING LAW

The analysis of judicial reasoning in this essay is inevitably simplified and one-sided. It is simplified for it attempts to isolate the elementary steps in judicial reasoning. Decisions in important cases involve reference to many rules of law, some of which are followed, some distinguished, while others provide the basis for various analogies. This complexity is not represented in the analysis here presented. The analysis provides, however, the means for understanding complex judicial arguments. The discussion above was also one-sided. It concentrated on the relations between law and value in judicial reasoning and neglected other questions. The judicial method of restricting previous rules by distinguishing them was analysed at length, but little was said, for example, about ways of extending the scope of rules. The reason is simple. There are no formal legal rules about how courts may extend rules. (Nor are all the cases of restricting rules governed by the rule of distinguishing. Whenever a court overrules it may narrow the scope of the overturned rule.) Sometimes one extends one rule by distinguishing and thus narrowing the scope of another rule which creates an exception to the first. Sometimes various separate rules are united into a new and wider doctrine which in effect extends the scope of the old rules. Analogical arguments are often used to support the case for new and independent rules by showing that they serve the same broad aims as existing ones. Equally often they are used to support the case for replacing a narrow rule by a more comprehensive one which, by stipulating that the legal result which the original rule provided for should apply to the original and to other circumstances, extends the scope of the old rule. These and other facets of judicial reasoning remain to be explored. Their exploration would be based on the foundations laid in the analysis above.

One remaining problem should be confronted now. The view defended above is that the courts make law in unregulated disputes. They do so regardless of whether they are aware of the fact that they do. This makes for an important conceptual difference between legislative and judicial law-making. A legislative action is an action intentionally changing the law. Judicial law-making need not be intentional. A judge may make a new rule in a decision which he thinks is a purely law-applying decision. Nowadays judges are for the most part fully aware of their law-making powers. Yet this conceptual distinction has not lost its importance. Even though judges know that they often make law, they do not always judge correctly whether a particular point made in a judgment is innovative or applicative. It is naturally of crucial importance to the proper functioning of the administration of justice that judicial decisions are valid regardless of whether the court correctly identified their character as innovative or applicative.

Notwithstanding all these facts it may be surprising that the courts do not take more trouble to identify the exact borderline between the parts of their judgments concerned with applying and creating law. Since the two are radically different one would have expected – it is sometimes said – that the courts will divide their judgment into clearly defined parts employing radically different reasons to justify their law-applying and law-creating conclusions. This, of course, does not happen. Though the courts often indicate their awareness that different kinds of arguments are appropriate when they consider using law-making powers, they often also move imperceptibly from one function to the other. Nor will anyone who accepts the analysis offered in this article be surprised by the existence of strong continuity between law-applying and law-making.

The continuity is not uniform in all types of cases. Overruling is normally clearly identified and moral, economic, etc, arguments are on the whole freely used. By and large this is also true of distinguishing, though here the confusion over what counts as *ratio* and the limited scope for reform often tend to blur the border between following and distinguishing a precedent. In cases of indeterminacy there is often no clear divide between application and innovation. Whether or not a case falls within the vague, indeterminate borderline area of a descriptive concept is often itself an indeterminate issue. In such decisions the continuity is complete.

The really important point to bear in mind, however, is that on most occasions the reasoning justifying law-making decisions is similar to and continuous with decisions interpreting and applying law. This is so in all cases of small-scale or conservative judicial law-making. Argument by analogy, used in law-making, involves interpreting the purpose and rationale of existing legal rules; these are equally essential for a correct interpretation and application of the law. Analogy is used in law-making to show harmony of purpose between existing laws and a new one. It is also used in interpretation through the assumption that the law-maker wished to preserve harmony of objectives and his Acts should be interpreted as designed to pursue goals compatible with those of related rules. The use of analogy both for law-making and for interpretation is merely an example of the fact that in general the same or very similar types of argument are relevant for both purposes. In most cases of interpreting relatively modern law it can he assumed, other things being equal, that the intention and purpose of the law-maker was to promote reasonable goals. Thus indirectly interpretation no less than law-making, involves evaluating different goals.

The fact that the same kind of arguments are used in applying and creating laws does not show that there is no difference between the two activities. The arguments are used under different assumptions and are assigned different roles and weights. But the occurrence of the same type of arguments in both kinds of judicial reasoning explains why the courts often do not bother to define explicitly which function they are fulfilling at any given stage in their reasoning. As we saw, for the most part such continuity of argument exists where it is inevitable, namely, in unregulated disputes where the indeterminacy does not allow sharp distinctions between applying and making law. It is not by chance that in such cases in particular very similar arguments are normally appropriate for either activity. It is perhaps apt to end on the theme of continuity of argument between law-applying and law-making for it has been the main objective of this article to demonstrate the intricate interconnection between these two judicial activities while maintaining that despite this intricacy the two are conceptually distinct and mutually present in the working of the English courts.

One aspect of Raz's account is fundamental: even though the distinction may be hard to discern in practice, there is a basic distinction between (1) applying existing law and (2) creating or devising new law. It is only in light of this distinction that Raz's produces his perhaps surprising characterisation of distinguishing, whereby he argues that judges in common law countries have a general law-making power to narrow the rules arising from previous court decisions. This view has been subject to criticism, especially by Simmonds, who doubts both Raz's explanation of distinguishing, and secondly, the extent to which the common law can even be conceived as a body of rules.

Simmonds (1984, 112–118)

DISTINGUISHING

The process whereby a court 'distinguishes' one case from another plays a central part in case-law reasoning, and must be accommodated by any theoretical account of case-law. The most sophisticated analysis of the issues involved here has been offered by Joseph Raz, and his account will merit some attention.

Raz distinguishes two views of distinguishing: a 'tame' view, and a 'strong' view that he himself advocates. According to the tame view, distinguishing is simply a matter of determining that the *ratio decidendi* of the earlier case does not apply to the later case. One distinguishes an earlier case (on the tame view) by holding that the rule laid down in that case does not extend to cases like the present one. On the strong view, however, the process of distinguishing represents a limited form of law-making. The court's power to distinguish earlier cases is, on this view, a power to modify the rule established in the earlier case, subject to two constraints:

1. The modified rule must be the rule laid down in the precedent restricted by the addition of a further condition for its application.

2. The modified rule must be such as to justify the decision made in the precedent.

The problem with the tame view is that it is difficult to reconcile with the apparent degree of freedom and creativity enjoyed by the courts, and with the fact that case-law reasoning just does not look like a business of applying rules and deciding whether cases fall within or without them. The traditional way of responding to this difficulty is by arguing that the task of ascertaining the *ratio decidendi* of a case is a very difficult one. The *ratio decidendi* is not identical with the general rule stated in a case, because that rule may fail to take account of facts that were material to the court's decision. When a later court 'distinguishes' a precedent it is holding that the general rule stated in that case does not represent the precedent's true *ratio*. On some views, the true *ratio* depends on what was considered to be material by the precedent court though they failed to take account of this in their general statement of the rule. On other views, the *ratio decidendi* depends not on what facts the precedent court considered material, but on what facts the later court considers material (such theories depart altogether from the notion of case-law as a body of rules, and are closer to the position argued for later in this chapter).

The strong view of distinguishing, by contrast, regards the ascertainment of the *ratio* of a case as unproblematic, but insists that in distinguishing an earlier case the later court is actually altering the law as laid down in that case. There are problems with the strong view that should not escape our notice, though they pass unmentioned by Raz. We have seen that Raz treats distinguishing as a law-making power subject to the two conditions described above. But why should this power be subject to precisely those conditions? Surely an account of case-law should reflect the intuition that these conditions are more than an arbitrary restriction on legislative power: they are somehow central to the whole nature of case-law. Raz's only attempt to explain the point of the two conditions is as follows. Courts approach law-making through the example of one case and they lack the research facilities available to legislatures. They are accordingly somewhat careless in the drafting of general rules. This makes it unreasonable to attach great weight to the precise verbal formulation of the rule issued by the court, and makes a power of modifying that rule (by distinguishing) seem reasonable. But it is necessary to read the rule in the context of the facts of the case as recorded. 'The *ratio*', Raz says, 'is binding in its basic rationale and as applying to its original context. Courts can, however, modify its application to different contexts *so long as they preserve its fundamental rationale*' (my italics).

Thus, in order to explain the point of the restrictions on judicial law-making, Raz ends up with something resembling the 'tame' view that he originally rejected. Courts, we are told, have power to modify *the ratio* of a case and that is what they are doing when they distinguish. But they must not alter the 'basic rationale': *that* must be preserved. We are all set to replace the game of 'hunt the *ratio decidendi*' with the game of 'hunt the basic rationale'. Raz has offered us not a new theory but a new label.

But let us suppose that Raz's 'strong' view was stronger than it really is. Let us suppose that he had said nothing about the 'basic rationale' and had simply claimed that the process of distinguishing earlier cases is a matter of modifying the law as established in those cases.

The distinction between making new law and applying existing law is one that runs throughout Raz's book. He relates it to a distinction between the 'different kinds of desirable characteristics judges should possess'. 'We value their knowledge of the law and their skills in interpreting laws and in arguing in ways showing their legal experience and expertise. We also value their wisdom and understanding of human nature, their moral sensibility, their enlightened approach, etc.' The first set of characteristics is associated with the proper application of the law, and the latter set is associated with the wise alteration of the law. If distinguishing cases is a matter of altering the law rather than applying it, it must involve the latter qualities rather than the former. A judge who is good at distinguishing cases must be one who exhibits understanding of human nature, moral sensibility, and so forth. A skilful and knowledgeable lawyer, on the other hand, might be an utter flop at distinguishing. But this clearly conflicts with our ordinary assumptions. We think of the business of distinguishing cases as one of the major professional skills that we want law students to acquire and practitioners to exercise. A student who thought it was possible to distinguish cases anywhere and for any reason would be exhibiting, not moral insensibility, but a failure to grasp the point of legal reasoning. A barrister who devises a neat line of argument through a body of seemingly adverse cases displays legal skill, not moral virtue (the moral arguments may all be on the other side); and a judge who merely stated the rules formulated in earlier cases without any attempt to distinguish them or ask whether they were distinguishable would be treated as deficient in his grasp of the law, not in his knowledge of human nature.

RULES

Propositions of law frequently take a rule-like form. We say that, as a matter of law, an occupier of land ought to take certain precautions to avoid injuring those who enter on his land, or that a motorist ought to give way to pedestrians. But why should these propositions be treated as reporting the content of rules? Why not simply say that they are propositions about legal rights and duties that are true by virtue of the existence of certain legislative or judicial decisions? This may not be a tempting approach in relation to statutes, but case-law is another matter. Why not treat case-law as a body of decisions rather than a body of rules?

It would be wrong to think that case-law *must* be a matter of rules in so far as it is prescriptive. For law is prescriptive in so far as it offers reasons for action, and there can be other reasons for action besides rules. The fact that a court has decided something may itself be a reason for action. So why should we interpose *rules* between judicial decisions and propositions of law?

Raz has raised a similar issue by asking why we should interpose 'laws' between sources and statements. He offers two reasons:

(1)   To speak of 'laws' in this way serves to distinguish law-creating facts from other facts relevant to the truth of propositions of law. Both the occurrence of a judicial decision and the occurrence of a delictual act may be relevant to the truth of a particular proposition of law: but they are clearly relevant in different ways.

(2)   Speaking of laws also enables us 'to refer to the content of the law without referring to the circumstances of its creation, the details of which are irrelevant for most practical purposes'.

Notice that Raz's second argument is much more obviously true of statute than of case-law. For the circumstances of the creation of case-law (the *facts* of the precedent case) are not 'irrelevant for most practical purposes'. Indeed, Raz himself notes that this is so, and that one must read 'rules' of case-law in context 'rather than in the abstract as one does a statute or regulation'.

Raz's first argument is based on a sound insight. But it is by no means clear that the difference (in 'law-making' effect) between a judicial decision and a contract or a delictual act should lead us to treat decided cases as laying down 'rules'. When we wish to speak of a rule of case-law in the abstract it is very rarely a rule established in an individual case. Rather, our 'rule' is a summary of the cumulative effect of several decisions (perhaps a great many: more, indeed, than we could trace or name). Even with such rules as the 'rule in *Rylands v. Fletcher*' this is so. As Honore has observed,

> The legal adviser, advocate, or writer who sets out the 'rule in *Rylands v. Fletcher*' does not copy it exactly from the case of *Rylands v. Fletcher*. He takes account of subsequent decisions, of the traditional formulation in textbooks and in general of professional tradition to add and subtract touches from the raw rule. Indeed, he may go further and extract from the raw material a law which is implicit in it but has not been enunciated, for example, that an interest in property of a certain type exists.

The rules and principles of case-law are formulated after the event in the reconstruction of an ordered body of law. They are not 'laid down' in cases, though it is of course true that judicial judgments are an important medium for ordered exposition. At least in relation to case-law, propositions of law should not be thought of as reporting posited rules, but as expressing elements of a general structure of rules and principles that may be treated as implicit in the decided cases as a whole.

To appreciate this point more fully we must return to the question of distinguishing cases and the nature of the *ratio decidendi*. Raz's analysis begins, as we have seen, with a contrast between the 'tame' and the 'strong' views of distinguishing. The tame view in effect holds that decided cases establish rules but in an obscure way; ascertaining *the ratio decidendi* is a problematic business. The strong view holds that individual cases establish more or less clear rules, but later courts have power to modify those rules, within certain constraints. But it is possible to offer a third view of distinguishing, wherein it is a mistake to think of cases as positing rules at all.

Suppose that, in an earlier case, it was held that a creditor should not be allowed to recover his debt when, in return for the debtor paying part of what he owed, the creditor had promised not to enforce his claim to the remainder. We are now faced with a case in which precisely that situation is present: the creditor accepted part payment and, in return, promised not to claim the residue. Are we bound to apply the earlier case or not?

The first point to notice is that we cannot answer the question until we are given the *facts* of the cases. This point is familiar to lawyers, but should be disturbing for legal theorists who see cases as laying down rules. A rule states that *if* certain conditions are satisfied *then* something ought to be done. If we know the rule and we know that our case satisfies the conditions, why should it be necessary for us to have any more detailed information?

By a familiar process of reasoning we could (depending on the facts) refuse to follow the earlier case. We might 'distinguish' it in various ways, e.g.:

(1) We might discover that in the earlier case the debtor had acted in reliance on the creditor's promise, and that in so acting he had put himself in a position where it would be unduly detrimental to him to insist on full payment now. If no such circumstances exist in the present case, we might say that the cases were distinguishable. This is so even if the court in the earlier case

did not appear to regard detrimental reliance as a material element of the case (but it may be otherwise if they expressly said that it was not material – see below).

(2) We might hold that, in the present case, the debtor has put pressure on the creditor to accept part payment in discharge of the debt by taking advantage of the creditor's pressing financial circumstances. This element of unfair duress, we might discover, was *not* present in the earlier case, and it constitutes a materially relevant difference between the two.

To attempt to fit these features of case-law reasoning into the idea of a search for the *ratio decidendi* of a case is a mistake. In each case the court is in effect asking 'Are there materially relevant grounds to justify differential treatment? Are there any facts which so distinguish this case from the precedent case that they justify and require different decisions in the two cases?' These are questions that can only be answered by knowing the facts of the cases. They are quite obviously not questions about the application of pre-existing rules.

But if, as I have suggested, 'materially relevant' does not mean 'considered relevant by the court in the precedent case', what *does* it mean? The question of what differences justify differential treatment in deciding litigated cases is a question of justice. Whether or not we consider this or that difference to be 'relevant' will clearly depend upon the conception of justice that we invoke. In deciding cases according to law we must rely on the law's conception of justice.

It is by reference to that conception that we distinguish one case from another. An exposition of an area of case-law is an exposition of the rules and principles composing the conception of justice on which that area of law is best regarded as being founded.

Does this entail that one can ignore what the judges say, and offer *any* theory that would justify their various decisions, as if that theory were the law? No, of course not. Judicial judgments are themselves attempts to expound the conception of justice that underlies the decision in question. As such they are entitled to great respect. That respect is in part entrenched by formal institutional rules. But even such institutionalised respect should not be confused with legislative power. Judges make law in so far as their *decisions* must be followed or distinguished, but the same is not true of their *opinions*, or the propositions of law that they formulate.

The form of legal reasoning that I have just described *assumes* that the law is based on some conception of justice. But if the argument of this book is correct, the law is increasingly seen as an instrument of shifting and changing social policies. The extent to which the law is still thought of as based on some coherent notion of justice is doubtful. It is therefore reasonable to expect an attempt to reinterpret the traditional forms of case-law reasoning so as to free them of their dependence on the assumed basis of justice. Such reinterpretation inevitably throws up difficulties in explaining such notions as 'distinguishing'; but the general strategy is to present the body of case-law as a matter of posited rules.

These developments in legal theory reflect the emerging features of a regulatory state that has a real presence at the level of institutional change (and institutional change cannot, in any case, be separated from changes in the theories that orient practices and institutions). Thus the doctrine of precedent becomes formalised as legislation becomes the dominant model for all law-making. Doctrinal argument comes to be less common than explicit policy decision in those areas of law most obviously shaped by instrumental considerations. It becomes hard to say whether legal positivism is true or false. The message of this book is, in a sense, that it is neither: legal positivism is an attempt to reinterpret traditional institutions and patterns of reasoning along lines consistent with a changed and changing situation. Whether or not that reinterpretation should be resisted is another question.

Simmonds faults Raz for failing to show why a particular similarity or difference between cases is a legally *relevant* one. Simmonds claims that this relevance will depend upon the law's conception of justice. Can you think of another basis upon which a difference or similarity might be regarded by the law as relevant? If Simmonds is right to claim that the law no longer evinces a coherent conception of justice, does that mean that the legal technique of distinguishing has become irrational? Unjust? Both? Do you think Simmonds is right to say 'Judges make law in so far as their *decisions* must be followed or distinguished, but the same is not true of their *opinions,* or the propositions of law that they formulate.'? Simmonds has more recently added a further twist to his critique of Raz's characterisation of distinguishing, arguing that judges do not necessarily 'add a further condition' to 'narrow' a rule when they distinguish it – rather, they often adopt an 'intellectual framework' or perspective on the facts of a case which is different from the one taken in the case in which the rule in question was laid down, and in so doing they avoid applying (i.e. distinguish) the rule; see Simmonds 1992.

One of the difficulties of assessing Simmonds's views lies in something he seems, at times at least, to think about rules, ie that for a rule to exist, one must be able to state it in some formulaic way. So, for example, because there is no standard way of stating the rule in *Rylands v Fletcher* (though isn't what I have just done to do that?) the 'rule' in that case is not really a rule at all, in contrast to a rule in a statute which is stated in language. But as we have seen from our consideration of the nature of rules above, a rule is not the same as its formulation, or statement, or presentation, whether in language or hand signals or picture signals like a no smoking sign composed of a red circle around a drawing of a cigarette. Though the way in which common law judges present their decisions may have great importance for our understanding of the common law, it does not follow that because they don't provide canonical formulations of rules that the common law is not a system of rules, ie that the common law does not provide standards of behaviour for its subjects which they can understand how to comply with. In view of this, is the force of Simmonds's critique diminished?

III 'Theory' versus 'Wisdom' in Legal Reasoning

In the introduction to this chapter, I suggested that lawyers's reasoning was practical reasoning with a vengeance, a sort of magnified version of the way we all reason practically. In this Part we consider two ways in which that 'magnification' might occur. Lawyers might enhance or magnify their reasoning skills by testing their arguments against philosophical theories concerning what they are reasoning about. Lawyers might examine their arguments in a contract case to see whether they comply with one or more theories of contract, for example Fried's theory that contracts are promises (Fried 1981), or Atiyah's theory that (roughly) contracts protect reliance (Atiyah 1978), or even more general and abstract theories about the nature of law, for example Dworkin's characterisation of legal reasoning.

From Chapters 8, 9, and 10 we have already become familiar with Dworkin's allegiance to the view that legal reasoning is a kind of philosophical or theoretical reasoning, indeed that legal reasoning is continuous with jurisprudence. To recapitulate the general idea: a judge tests propositions of law by determining how well they accord within a theory of political morality which justifies the use of state coercion, a theory which responds both to the historical legal tradition of the judge's jurisdiction and to ultimate moral values which are universal, ultimate moral values the exploration of which is the bread and butter work of moral and political philosophy. Hercules is, for Dworkin, the idealised model of the judge so conceived, and the account is both sophisticated and attractive. But is it true? Recently, Sunstein has argued that legal reasoning appears to be 'incompletely theorised', ie does not appear to involve recourse to the sorts of abstract philosophical arguments that Dworkin's theory would suggest it would.

Sunstein (1996, 35–46)

Incompletely theorized agreements play a pervasive role in law and society. It is quite rare for a person or group completely to theorize any subject, that is, to accept both a general theory and a series of steps connecting that theory to concrete conclusions. Thus we often have in law an *incompletely theorized agreement on a general principle* – incompletely theorized in the sense that people who accept the principle need not agree on what it entails in particular cases.

This is the sense emphasized by Justice Oliver Wendell Holmes in his great aphorism, 'General principles do not decide concrete cases.' Thus, for example, we know that murder is wrong, but disagree about whether abortion is wrong. We favor racial equality, but are divided on affirmative action. We believe in liberty, but disagree about increases in the minimum wage. Hence the pervasive legal and political phenomenon of an agreement on a general principle alongside disagreement about particular cases. The agreement is incompletely theorized in the sense that it is *incompletely specified*. Much of the key work must be done by others, often through casuistical judgments at the point of application.

Often constitution-making becomes possible through this form of incompletely theorized agreement. Many constitutions contain incompletely specified standards and avoid rules, at least when it comes to the description of basic rights. Consider the cases of Eastern Europe and South Africa, where constitutional provisions include many abstract provisions on whose concrete specification there has been sharp dispute. Abstract provisions protect 'freedom of speech', 'religious liberty', and 'equality under the law', and citizens agree on those abstractions in the midst of sharp dispute about what these provisions really entail.

Much lawmaking becomes possible only because of this phenomenon. Consider the fact that the creation of large regulatory agencies has often been feasible only because of incompletely specified agreements. In dealing with air and water pollution, occupational safety and health, or regulation of broadcasting, legislators converge on general, incompletely specified requirements – that regulation be 'reasonable', or that it provide 'a margin of safety'. If the legislature attempted to specify these requirements – to decide what counts as reasonable regulation – there would be a predictably high level of dispute and conflict, and perhaps the relevant laws could not be enacted at all.

Incompletely specified agreements thus have important social uses. Many of their advantages are practical. They allow people to develop frameworks for decision and judgment despite large-scale disagreements. At the same time, they help produce a degree of social solidarity and shared commitment. People who are able to agree on political abstractions – freedom of speech, freedom from unreasonable searches and seizures – can also agree that they are embarking on shared projects. These forms of agreement help constitute a democratic culture. It is for this reason that they are so important to constitution-making. Incompletely specified agreements also have the advantage of allowing people to show one another a high degree of mutual respect. By refusing to settle concrete cases that raise fundamental issues of conscience, they permit citizens to announce to one another that society shall not take sides on such issues until it is required to do so.

So much for incompletely specified provisions. Let us run to a second phenomenon. Sometimes people agree on a mid-level principle but disagree about both general theory and particular cases. These sorts of agreements are also incompletely theorized, but in a different way. Judges may believe, for example, that government cannot discriminate on the basis of race, without having a large-scale theory of equality, and also without agreeing whether government may enact affirmative action programs or segregate prisons when racial tensions are severe. Judges may think that government may not regulate speech unless it can show a clear and present danger – but disagree about whether this principle is founded in utilitarian or Kantian considerations, and disagree too about whether the principle allows government to regulate a particular speech by members of the Ku Klux Klan.

My particular interest here is in a third kind of phenomenon, of special interest for law: incompletely theorized agreements on particular outcomes, accompanied by agreements on the narrow or low-level principles that account for them. These terms contain some ambiguities. There is no algorithm by which to distinguish between a high-level theory and one that operates at an intermediate or lower level. We might consider, as conspicuous examples of high-level theories, Kantianism and utilitarianism, and see legal illustrations in the many distinguished (academic) efforts to understand such areas as tort law, contract law, free speech, and the law of equality as undergirded by highly abstract theories of the right or the good. By contrast, we might think of low-level principles as including most of the ordinary material of legal 'doctrine' – the general class of principles and justifications that are not said to derive from any large theories of the right or the good, that have ambiguous relations to large theories, and that are compatible with more than one such theory.

By the term 'particular outcome', I mean the judgment about who wins and who loses a case. By the term 'low-level principles', I refer to something relative, not absolute; I mean to do the same thing by the terms 'theories' and 'abstractions' (which I use interchangeably). In this setting, the notions 'low-level', 'high', and 'abstract' are best understood in comparative terms, like the terms 'big', 'old', and 'unusual'. The 'clear and present danger' standard is a relative abstraction when compared with the claim that members of the Nazi Party may march in Skokie, Illinois. But the 'clear and present danger' idea is relatively particular when compared with the claim that nations should adopt the constitutional abstraction 'freedom of speech'. The term 'freedom of speech' is a relative abstraction when measured against the claim that campaign finance laws are acceptable, but the same term is less abstract than the grounds that justify free speech, as in, for example, the principle of personal autonomy.

What I am emphasizing here is that when people diverge on some (relatively) high-level proposition, they might be able to agree when they lower the level of abstraction. Incompletely theorized judgments on particular cases are the ordinary material of law. And in law, the point of agreement is often highly particularized – absolutely as well as relatively particularized – in the sense that it involves a specific outcome and a set of reasons that do not venture far from the case at hand. High-level theories are rarely reflected explicitly in law.

Perhaps the participants in law endorse no such theory, or perhaps they believe that they have none, or perhaps they cannot, on a multimember court, reach agreement on a theory. Perhaps they find theoretical disputes confusing or annoying. What is critical is that they agree on how a case must come out. The argument very much applies to rules, which are, much of the time, incompletely theorized; indeed, this is one of the major advantages of rules. People may agree that a 60-mile-per-hour speed limit makes sense, and that it applies to defendant Jones, without having much of a theory about criminal punishment. They may agree that to receive social security benefits, people must show that they earn less than a certain sum of money, without having anything like a theory about who deserves what. Thus a key social function of rules is to allow people to agree on the meaning, authority, and even the soundness of a governing provision in the face of disagreements about much else.

…

My principal concern is the question of how judges on a multimember body should justify their opinions in public; the argument therefore has a great deal to do with the problem of collective choice. But some of the relevant points bear on other issues as well. They have implications for the question of how an individual judge not faced with the problem of producing a majority opinion – a judge, on a trial court, for example – might write; they bear on the question of how a single judge, whether or not a member of a collective body, might think in private; and they relate to appropriate methods of both thought and justification wholly outside of adjudication and even outside of law.

MULTIMEMBER INSTITUTIONS

Begin with the special problem of public justification on a multimember body. The first and most obvious point is that incompletely theorized agreements are well-suited to a world – and especially a legal world – containing social dissensus on large-scale issues. By definition, such agreements have the large advantage of allowing a convergence on particular outcomes by people unable to reach an accord on general principles. This advantage is associated not only with the simple need to decide cases, but also with social stability, which could not exist if fundamental disagreements broke out in every case of public or private dispute.

Second, incompletely theorized agreements can promote two goals of a liberal democracy and a liberal legal system: to enable people to live together and to permit them to show each other a measure of reciprocity and mutual respect. The use of low-level principles or rules generally allows judges on multimember bodies and hence citizens to find commonality and thus a common way of life without producing unnecessary antagonism. Both rules and low-level principles make it unnecessary to reach areas in which disagreement is fundamental.

Perhaps even more important, incompletely theorized agreements allow people to show each other a high degree of mutual respect, civility, or reciprocity. Frequently ordinary people disagree in some deep way on an issue – the Middle East, pornography, homosexual marriages – and sometimes they agree not to discuss that issue much, as a way of deferring to each other's strong convictions and showing a measure of reciprocity and respect (even if they do not at all respect the particular conviction that is at stake). If reciprocity and mutual respect are desirable, it follows that judges, perhaps even more than ordinary people, should not challenge a litigant's or another person's deepest and most defining commitments, at least if those commitments are reasonable and if there is no need for them to do so. Thus, for example, it would be better if judges intending to reaffirm *Roe v. Wade* could do so without challenging the judgment that the fetus is a human being.

To be sure, some fundamental commitments might appropriately be challenged in the legal system or within other multimember bodies. Some commitments are ruled off-limits by the authoritative legal materials. Many provisions involving basic rights have this purpose. Of course it is not always disrespectful to disagree with someone in a fundamental way; on the contrary, such disagreements may sometimes reflect profound respect. When defining commitments are based on demonstrable errors of fact or logic, it is appropriate to contest them. So too when those commitments are rooted in a rejection of the basic dignity of all human beings, or when it is necessary to undertake the challenge to resolve a genuine problem. But many cases can be resolved in an incompletely theorized way, and that is all I am suggesting here.

Institutional arguments in law – especially those involving judicial restraint – are typically designed to bracket fundamental questions and to say that however those questions might be resolved in principle, courts should stand to one side. The allocation of certain roles has an important function of allowing outcomes to be reached without forcing courts to make decisions on fundamental issues. Those issues are resolved by reference to institutional competence, not on their merits.

In particular, the principle of stare decisis, which instructs courts to respect precedent, helps produce incompletely theorized agreements, and it helps to avoid constant struggle over basic principle. It serves this function precisely because it prevents people from having to build the world again, and together, every time a dispute arises. People can agree to follow precedent when they disagree on almost everything else. As a prominent example, consider the United States Supreme Court's refusal to overrule *Roe v. Wade*, where the justices emphasized the difficulties that would be produced by revisiting so large-scale a social controversy. Members of the Court can accept the rule of precedent from diverse foundations and despite their many disagreements. Thus the justifications of the rule of precedent are diverse – involving predictability, efficiency, fairness, constraints on official discretion – and people who disagree on those justifications can agree on the practice, at least as a general rule.

MULTIMEMBER INSTITUTIONS AND INDIVIDUAL JUDGES

Turn now to reasons that call for incompletely theorized agreements whether or not we are dealing with a multimember body. The first consideration here is that incompletely theorized agreements have the crucial function of reducing the political cost of enduring disagreements. If judges disavow, large-scale theories, then losers in particular cases lose much less. They lose a decision, but not the world. They may win on another occasion. Their own theory has not been rejected or ruled inadmissible. When the authoritative rationale for the result is disconnected from abstract theories of the good or the right, the losers can submit to legal obligations, even if reluctantly, without being forced to renounce their largest ideals. I have said that some theories should be rejected or ruled inadmissible. But it is an advantage, from the standpoint of freedom and stability, for a legal system to be able to tell most losers – many of whom are operating from foundations that have something to offer or that cannot be ruled out a priori – that their own deepest convictions may play a role elsewhere in the law.

The second point is that incompletely theorized agreements are valuable when we seek moral evolution over time. Consider the area of constitutional equality, where considerable change has occurred in the past and will inevitably occur in the future. A completely theorized judgment would be unable to accommodate changes in facts or values. If the legal culture really did attain a theoretical end-state, it would become too rigid and calcified; we would know what we thought about everything. This would disserve posterity.

Incompletely theorized agreements are a key to debates over constitutional equality, with issues being raised about whether gender, sexual orientation, age, disability, and others are analogous to race; such agreements have the important advantage of allowing a large degree of openness to new facts and perspectives. At one point, we might think that homosexual relations are akin to incest; at another point, we might find the analogy bizarre. Of course a completely theorized judgment would have many virtues if it is correct. But at any particular moment in time, this is an unlikely prospect for human beings, not excluding judges.

A particular concern here is the effect of changing understandings of both facts and values. Consider ordinary life. At a certain time, you may well refuse to make decisions that seem foundational in character – for example, whether to get married within the next year, whether to have two, three, or four children, or whether to live in San Francisco or New York. Part of the reason for this refusal is knowledge that your understandings of both facts and values may well change. Indeed, your identity may itself change in important and relevant ways and for this reason a set of commitments in advance – something like a fully theorized conception of your life course – would make no sense.

Legal systems and nations are not so very different. If the Supreme Court is asked to offer a fully theorized conception of equality – in areas involving, for example, the rights of disabled people, children, and homosexuals – it may well respond that its job is to decide cases rather than to offer fully theorized accounts, partly because society should learn over time and partly because society's understandings of facts and values, in a sense its very identity, may well shift in unpredictable ways. This point bears on many legal issues. It helps support the case for incompletely theorized agreements.

The third point is practical. Incompletely theorized agreements may be the best approach that is available for people of limited time and capacities. Full theorization may be far too much to ask. A single judge faces this problem as much as a member of a multimember panel. Here too the rule of precedent is crucial; attention to precedent is liberating, not merely confining, since it frees busy people to deal with a restricted range of problems. Incompletely theorized agreements have the related advantage, for ordinary lawyers and judges, of humility and modesty. To engage in analogical reasoning, for example, one ordinarily need not take a stand on large, contested issues of social life, some of which can be resolved only on what will seem to many a sectarian basis.

…

Fourth, incompletely theorized agreements are well-adapted to a system that should or must take precedents as fixed points. This is a large advantage over more ambitious methods, since ambitious thinkers, in order to reach horizontal and vertical coherence, will probably be forced to disregard many decided cases. In light of the sheer number of decided cases and adjudicative officials, law cannot speak with one voice; full coherence in principle is unlikely in the extreme.

It is notable in this connection that for some judges and lawyers (lower court judges, for example), precedents truly are fixed (short of civil disobedience), whereas for others, including Supreme Court Justices, they are revisable, but only in extraordinary circumstances. If a judge or a lawyer were to attempt to reach full theorization, precedents would have at most the status of considered judgments about particular cases, and these might be revised when they run into conflict with something else that he believes and that is general or particular. This would cause many problems. Participants in a legal system aspiring to stability should not be so immodest as to reject judgments reached by others whenever those judgments could not be made part of reflective equilibrium for those particular participants. Thus the area of contract law is unlikely fully to cohere with the field of tort law or property; contract law is itself likely to contain multiple and sometimes inconsistent strands.

We can find many analogies in ordinary life. A parent's practices with his children may not fully cohere. Precedents with respect to bedtime, eating, homework, and much else are unlikely to be susceptible to systematization under a single principle. Of course, parents do not seek to be inconsistent. A child may feel justly aggrieved if a sibling is permitted to watch more hours of television for no apparent reason; but full coherence would be a lot to ask. The problem of reaching full consistency is all the more severe in law, where so many people have decided so many things and where disagreements on large principles lurk in the background.

There is a more abstract point here. Human morality recognizes irreducibly diverse goods, which cannot be subsumed under a single 'master' value. The same is true for the moral values reflected in the law. Any simple, general, and monistic or single-valued theory of a large area of the law – free speech, contracts, property – is likely to be too crude to fit with our best understandings of the multiple values that are at stake in that area. It would be absurd to try to organize legal judgments through a single conception of value.

What can be said about law as a whole can be said about many particular areas of law. Monistic theories of free speech or property rights, for example, will fail to accommodate the range of values that speech and property implicate. Free speech promotes not simply democracy, but personal autonomy, economic progress, self-development, and other goals as well. Property rights are important not only for economic prosperity, but for democracy and autonomy too. We are unlikely to be able to appreciate the diverse values at stake, and to describe them with the specificity they deserve, unless we investigate the details of particular disputes.

This is not a decisive objection to general theories; a 'top down' approach might reject monism and point to plural values. Perhaps participants in democracy or law can describe a range of diverse values, each of them at a high level of abstraction; acknowledge that these values do not fall under a single master value; and use these values for assessing law. But even if correct, any such approach would run into difficulty because of an important practical fact. social disagreements about how best to describe or specify the relevant values. Moreover, any such approach is likely to owe its genesis and its proof – its point or points – to a range of particular cases on which it can build. Of course full theorization of an area of law would be acceptable, or even an occasion for great celebration, if it accounted for the plural values at issue. But this would be a most complex task, one that requires identification of a wide range of actual and likely cases. At least we can say that incompletely theorized judgments are well-suited to a moral universe that is diverse and pluralistic, not only in the sense that people disagree, but also in the sense that each of us is attuned to pluralism when we are thinking well about any area of law.

None of these points suggests that incompletely theorized agreements always deserve celebration. The virtues of such agreements are partial. Some incompletely theorized agreements are unjust. If an agreement is more fully theorized, it will provide greater notice to affected parties. Moreover, fuller theorization – in the form of wider and deeper inquiry into the grounds for judgment – may be valuable or even necessary to prevent inconsistency, bias, or self-interest. If judges on a panel have actually agreed on a general theory, and if they are really committed to it, they should say so. Judges and the general community will learn much more if they are able to discuss the true motivating grounds for outcomes. All these are valid considerations, and nothing I am saying here denies their importance.

JUDGES, THEORY, AND THE RULE OF LAW

There is a close association between the effort to attain incompletely theorized agreements and the rule of law ideal. Insofar as a legal system involves rule by law rather than rule by individual human beings, it tries to constrain judgments in advance. Some people think that the rule of law, properly understood, is a law of rules; this claim will be discussed in later chapters. For the moment we can understand the rule of law more modestly. It is opposed to rule by individual human beings, who should not be permitted to govern as they wish through making law entirely of their choice in the context of actual disputes. Insofar as the rule of law prevents this from happening, it tries to prevent people in particular cases from invoking their own theories of the right or the good so as to make decisions according to their own most fundamental judgments.

Indeed, a prime purpose of the rule of law is to rule off-limits certain deep ideas of the right or the good, on the view that those ideas ought not to be invoked, most of the time, by judges and officials occupying particular social roles. Among the forbidden or presumptively forbidden ideas are, often, high-level views that are taken as too hubristic or sectarian precisely because they are so high-level. The presumption against high-level theories is an aspect of the ideal of the rule of law to the extent that it is an effort to limit the exercise of discretion at the point of application.

In this way we might make distinctions between the role of high theory within the courtroom and the role of high theory in the political branches of government. To be sure, incompletely theorized agreements play a role in democratic arenas; consider laws protecting endangered species or granting unions a right to organize. But in democratic arenas, there is no taboo, presumptive or otherwise, on invoking high-level theories of the good or the right. On the contrary, such theories have played a key role in many social movements with defining effects on American constitutionalism, including the Civil War, the New Deal, the women's movement, and the environmental movement. Abstract, high-level ideas are an important part of democratic discussion, and sometimes they are ratified publicly and placed in a constitution.

By contrast, development of large-scale theories by ordinary courts is problematic and usually understood as such within the judiciary. The skepticism about large-scale theories is partly a result of the fact that such theories may require large-scale social reforms, and courts have enormous difficulties in implementing such reforms. When courts invoke a large-scale theory as a reason for social change, they may well fail simply because they lack the tools to bring about change on their own. An important reason for judicial incapacity is that courts must decide on the legitimacy of rules that are aspects of complex systems. In invalidating or changing a single rule, courts may not do what they seek to do. They may produce unfortunate systemic effects, with unanticipated bad consequences that are not visible to them at the time of decision, and that may be impossible for them to correct thereafter. Legislatures are in a much better position on this score. Consider, for example, an effort to reform landlord-tenant law. Judges may require landlords to provide decent housing for poor tenants, but the result may be to require landlords to raise rents, with detrimental effects on the poor. To say this is not to say that judge-initiated changes are always bad. But it is to say that the piecemeal quality of such changes is a reason for caution. The claim that courts are ineffective in producing large-scale reform is a generalization, and it has the limits of all generalizations. The point does not count decisively against more ambitious judicial rulings when those rulings have a powerful legal and moral foundation. An ambitious ruling might announce an uncontestable high-level principle, and the announcement of the principle might be right even if courts lack implementing tools. What seems clear is that the difficulties of judge-led social reform provide a basis for judicial modesty ...

More fundamentally, it is in the absence of a democratic pedigree that the system of precedent, analogy, and incompletely theorized agreement has such an important place. The need to discipline judicial judgment arises from the courts' complex and modest place in any well-functioning constitutional system. To be sure, judges have, in some societies, a duty to interpret the Constitution, and sometimes that duty authorizes them to invoke relatively large-scale principles, seen as part and parcel of the Constitution as democratically ratified. Many people think that judicial activity is best characterized by reference to use of such principles. Certainly there are occasions on which this practice is legitimate and even glorious.

To identify those occasions it would be necessary to develop a full theory of legal interpretation. For present purposes we can say something more modest. Most of judicial activity does not involve constitutional interpretation, and the ordinary work of common law decision and statutory interpretation calls for low-level principles on which agreements are possible. Indeed, constitutional argument itself is based largely on low-level principles, not on high theory, except on those rare occasions when more ambitious thinking becomes necessary to resolve a case or when the case for the ambitious theory is so insistent that a range of judges converge on it. And there are good reasons for the presumption in favor of low-level principles – having to do with the limited capacities of judges, the need to develop principles over time, the failure of monistic theories of the law, and the other considerations traced above.

Sunstein attributes the law's reticence to engage in abstract theory to a number of factors, but two related ones are of particular importance:

(1) *Incomplete theorisation reduces the political cost of individual judicial decisions for, in not denying the losing party's fundamental values or perspective, the losing party can submit to the decision without being forced to renounce their largest ideals.*

(2) *Incomplete theorisation allows lawyers, judges, and the subjects of the law to reach a consensus on particular legal outcomes, ie the decisions in actual cases or the implementation of certain rules, without requiring a consensus of abstract political/philosophical perspectives, such as utilitarianism or Kantianism. Incomplete theorisation engenders stability, for not every issue then raises the most fundamental disagreements over values or the right way to see the world. Furthermore, to the extent that there is a plurality of values, finding a consensus amongst individuals at the level of fundamental values is made doubly difficult.*

But do these factors explain 'incomplete theorisation in law'?

As to (1), it is an empirical question whether and to what extent the exclusion of certain large ideals from legal discourse would engender political instability or a decline in 'democratic culture'. But more to the point, it is not clear that Sunstein is right to identify people's largest ideals, if that is meant to indicate their most sincere moral commitments, commitments which if excluded from political consideration are likely to drive them to the barricades, with abstract theoretical positions people hold. For example, a person's opposition to abortion or capital punishment, or another's belief that a woman has the right to choose abortion or that the state has a duty to take the lives of certain criminals, tend to express attitudes of great importance to them – having to subject themselves to the opposing position would seem very much like renouncing a large ideal – but strong proponents of these views need not have allied themselves to any particularly abstract theoretical positions to hold them as strongly as they do. For many the issue is decided by a deep sense or intuition that abortion or capital punishment is just fundamentally wrong somehow, or by contrast, that allowing abortion or capital punishment in some circumstances is justifiable or even morally required. So, while we might worry about a legal system requiring the renunciation of an individuals largest ideals, it is not the case that this worry can serve as one which particularly justifies incomplete theorisation in the law.

(2) seems very much to be the crux of the matter. It is certainly true that people may disagree about the correct abstract perspective to take on moral and political issues while at the same time agreeing upon the disposition of particular cases. In a similar fashion, individuals may disagree about what ought fundamentally to be valued, and whether there is a plurality of basic values, while agreeing as to the disposition of particular cases. In view of this, it does appear to make good 'political' or practical sense for lawyers and judges (both in their law-applying and law-making roles) to avoid grounding their arguments and rulings, respectively, on abstract theories of justice. Their decisions will give rise to disagreements less often simply because there will not usually be a large theoretical issue to chew on, and further, the scope of disagreement will be narrower because the scope of a less abstract decision will be. If it is regarded as a value within the liberal constitution that the courts be the least contentious branch, out of a concern to provide individual legal subjects with a measure of certainty as to their rights and efficiency in the application of the law, for example, or out of a concern for democratic legitimacy, then a judicial practice that law is applied and created on the basis of low level principles may serve such a value, providing one contour of the institutional competence of the judiciary. We must, however, be very careful here. If it were the case that deep fundamental belief, drawn from whatever source, religion, Marxism or what have you, was identical to adherence to abstract theory, then Sunstein would appear to be on solid ground. He is clearly right to point out how disastrous it would be in a pluralist society if lawyers could ground their arguments, and judges their decisions, in the fundamental tenets of one religion or another, or in political theories like Marxism or Libertarianism. But as was pointed out in considering point (1), 'incomplete theorisation' expresses exactly what it denotes: an absence of reliance on theory, not an absence of reliance on religion or contentious political allegiances. It is simply wrong to equate abstraction, as in the abstraction that the various rights protected in a bill of rights serve the value of autonomy, or in the abstraction that all elements of the law of contract can be explained in terms of a philosophically precise concept of promise, with this kind of commitment. If a judge held, in reviewing the academic contract literature that, in his opinion, Charles Fried has got contract right, and therefore he would decide the case before him applying the most up to date philosophical literature on the nature of promises, he would not be expressing an allegiance of a kind which raises any danger for a pluralist society, or at least no greater danger than he would by adopting the views of a black letter authority like Treitel. All he would be saying was that he found that Fried, rather than Atiyah or Posner, had the better of the philosophical argument, in the same way as he might justifiably prefer the view of Treitel to Cheshire and Fifoot. Thus the practical or political considerations Sunstein raises seem to fail to explain incomplete theorisation in the law.

We turn now consider an alternative characterisation of legal reasoning, by the chapter's author, which like Sunstein's, denies that legal reasoning is theoretical in the way that Dworkin would claim. First, however, we will look at a subtle critique of modern Anglo-American moral philosophy, upon which this alternative characterisation draws. The reading from Williams's *Ethics and the Limits of Philosophy*, below, begins with Williams's criticism of the 'reductionist' tendency in moral philosophising, ie the idea that the goal of a good moral theory is to find some single fundamental, essential, consideration, such as utility in utilitarianism, which properly understood gives rise to a theory which spelt out or applied explains all aspects of morality. In contrast, Williams emphasises the diversity of our moral considerations and the plurality of our ethical dispositions, and how we bring different ethical concepts to bear in different situations.

Williams (1985, 15–18, 47–48, 94–99, 128–131)

Philosophy has traditionally tried to reduce [the diversity of ethical and non-ethical considerations it takes into account in offering explanations of human behaviour]. It has tended, first of all, to see all non-ethical considerations as reducible to egoism, the narrowest form of self-interest. Indeed some philosophers have wanted to reduce that to one special kind of egoistic concern, the pursuit of pleasure. Kant, in particular, believed that every action not done from moral principle was done for the agent's pleasure.

...

The desire to reduce all non-ethical considerations to one type is less strong in philosophy now than it was when moral philosophy chiefly concentrated not so much on questions of what is the right thing to do and what is the good life (the answers to such questions were thought to be obvious), but rather on how one was to be motivated to pursue those things, against the motivations of selfishness and pleasure. The desire to reduce all *ethical* considerations to one pattern is, on the other hand, as strong as ever, and various theories try to show that one type or another type of ethical consideration is basic, with other types to be explained in terms of it. Some take as basic a notion of obligation or duty, and the fact that we count it as an ethical consideration, for instance, that a certain act will probably lead to the best consequences is explained in terms of our having one duty, among others, to bring about the best consequences. Theories of this kind are called 'deontological'.

...

Contrasted with these are theories that take as primary the idea of producing the best possible state of affairs. Theories of this kind are often called 'teleological'. The most important example is that which identifies the goodness of outcomes in terms of people's happiness or their getting what they want or prefer ... [I]f theories of this kind are offered descriptively, as accounts of what we take to be equivalent, they are all equally misguided. We use a variety of different ethical considerations, which are genuinely different from one another, and this is what one would expect to find, if only because we are heirs to a long and complex ethical tradition with many different religious and other social strands.

As an enterprise that intends to be descriptive, like anthropology, the reductive undertaking is merely wrongheaded. It may have other aims, however. It may, at some deeper level, seek to give us a theory of the subject matter of ethics. But it is not clear why that aim, either, must encourage us to reduce our basic ethical conceptions. If there is such a thing as the truth about the subject matter of ethics – the truth, we might say, about the ethical – why is there any expectation that it should be simple? In particular, why should it be conceptually simple, using only one or two ethical concepts such as *duty* or *good state of affairs*, rather than many? Perhaps we need as many concepts to describe it as we find we need, and no fewer.

The point of trying to reduce our ethical concepts must be found in a different aim of ethical theory, which is not just to describe how we think about the ethical but to tell us how we should think about it. Later I shall argue that philosophy should not try to reproduce ethical theory, though this does not mean that philosophy cannot offer any critique of ethical beliefs and ideas. I shall claim that in ethics the reductive enterprise has no justification and should disappear. My point here, however, is merely to stress that the enterprise needs justifying. A good deal of moral philosophy engages unblinkingly in this activity, for no obvious reason except that it has been going on for a long time.

There is one motive for reductivism that does not operate simply on the ethical, or on the nonethical, but tends to reduce every consideration to one basic kind. This rests on an assumption about rationality, to the effect that two considerations cannot be rationally weighed against each other unless there is a common consideration in terms of which they can be compared. This assumption is at once very powerful and utterly baseless. Quite apart from the ethical, aesthetic considerations can be weighed against economic ones (for instance) without being an application of them, and without their both being an example of a third kind of consideration. Politicians know that political considerations are not all made out of the same material as considerations against which they are weighed; even different political considerations can be made out of different material. If one compares one job, holiday, or companion with another, judgment does not need a particular set of weights.

This is not merely a matter of intellectual error. If it were that, it could not survive the fact that people's experience contradicts it, that they regularly arrive at conclusions they regard as rational, or at least as reasonable, without using one currency of comparison. The drive toward a *rationalistic conception of rationality* comes instead from social features of the modern world, which impose on personal deliberation and on the idea of practical reason itself a model drawn from a particular understanding of public rationality. This understanding requires in principle every decision to be based on grounds that can be discursively explained. The requirement is not in fact met, and it probably does little for the aim that authority should be genuinely answerable. But it is an influential ideal and, by a reversal of the order of causes, it can look as if it were the result of applying to the public world an independent ideal of rationality.

...

The formation of ethical dispositions is a natural process in human beings. This does not mean that it is spontaneous and needs no education or upbringing: in that sense, virtually nothing in human beings is 'natural', including the use of language – for while the capacity to learn a language is itself innate, and very probably specific, no child will learn any language unless exposed to a particular language, which is itself, of course, a cultural product. Nor does it mean that the ethical life does not involve convention: it is natural to human beings to live by convention. There is no sense in which it is *more* natural, as Thrasymachus supposed, to live outside ethical considerations. Moreover, we ourselves (most of us) are identified with some ethical considerations and have a conception of human well-being that gives a place to such considerations. We wish, consequently, to bring up children to share some of these ethical, as of other cultural, conceptions, and we see the process as good not just for us but for our children, both because it is part of our conception of their well-being and also because, even by more limited conceptions of happiness or contentment, we have little reason to believe that they will be happier if excluded from the ethical institutions of society. Even if we know that there are some people who are happier, by the minimal criteria, outside those institutions, we also know that they rarely become so by being educated as outlaws. As a result of all that, we have much reason for, and little reason against, bringing up children within the ethical world we inhabit, and if we succeed they themselves will see the world from the same perspective.

...

[I]ntuitions ... are very much part of the subject [of ethics]. These are spontaneous convictions, moderately reflective but not yet theorized, about the answer to some ethical question, usually hypothetical and couched in general terms. They are often questions about what to do. 'What should you do if you could, by switching the points, divert a runaway trolley from one line, where it would certainly kill three old men, to another line on which it would certainly kill one child and a gifted violinist?' This example is not much more fantastic than some that have been offered. But intuitions do not have to be expressed in answers to questions about what to do. Some may be found in our willingness to apply to some imagined situation one of those more substantive ethical concepts, such as those picking out virtues or types of action.

...

There is an analogy that has encouraged the revival of the term 'intuition' in these connections. This is its use in linguistics and the philosophy of language to refer to a speaker's spontaneous grasp of what can and cannot be said in his language, or of what can be correctly said in a particular kind of situation. A competent English speaker has the intuition that it is not correct – that is, it is not English – to say (as I once heard an emigre philosopher of language say), 'In English we are not using the present continuous to signify a custom or practice.' Such intuitions are the raw material of a theory of a natural language. We have good reason to believe that it should be possible to form such a theory, giving an account of the rules that have been internalized by the speaker, just because the speaker can unhesitatingly recognize as correct or incorrect in his language sentences he has never heard before. As Noam Chomsky has emphasized, we do this all the time. Moreover, some theorists, notably Chomsky, believe that since any human being can learn as a child any human language, there are grounds for expecting there to be a theory of rules underlying all natural languages, a universal grammar.

How does this linguistic conception of an intuition apply to ethics? There is one kind of intuition relevant to ethics that certainly fits the model, since it is merely an application of it. In the case of the substantive terms for virtues and kinds of action, there is room for linguistic intuitions about the situations they apply to, just because they are general terms in the language with complex conditions of application … With terms of this kind there will be disputes about their application at the margin, and these may carry serious practical consequences. They are disputes of the kind familiar in the law, where the issue may be whether a given act constituted theft, for instance. Legal theorists disagree about the exact nature of disputes of that kind and how they are properly decided, so-called legal realists allowing a larger and more explicit role for policy considerations in the decision of hard cases – but all are agreed that there has to be a shared understanding of some core or central cases to make these disputes about hard cases possible. To some extent this must be equally so within the less formal structures of the ethical discussions that involve these substantive terms.

In some traditions great weight is laid on this legalistic strain in ethical thought. It is encouraging to objectivist views of ethics, since the core cases are given in an understanding of these ethical terms, and their application to hard cases, though it is a contentious and ethically fraught matter, is constrained by rational criteria of what is and what is not an adequate similarity to the core cases. There can be rational discussion whether a given extension of the term properly bears the spirit or underlying principle of its application to the core cases. Arguments in this style are, in the Catholic tradition, known as arguments of casuistry (the unfriendly use of that term was a deserved reaction to devious uses made of the technique). The trouble with casuistry, if it is seen as the basic process of ethical thought, is not so much its misuse as the obvious fact that the repertory of substantive ethical concepts differs between cultures, changes over time, and is open to criticism. If casuistry, applied to a given local set of concepts, is to be the central process of ethical thought, it needs more explanation. It has to claim that there are preferred ethical categories that are not purely local. They may be said to come from a theory of human nature; … They may be said to be given by divine command or revelation; in this form, if it is not combined with the grounding in human nature, the explanation will not lead us anywhere except into what Spinoza called 'the asylum of ignorance.' An exponent of the casuistical method could perhaps fall back simply on the idea that the categories we prefer are the ones we have inherited. This has the merit of facing an important truth, but it will not be able to face it in truth unless more is said about ways in which those categories might be criticized.

When we turn away from the use of substantial ethical terms and merely consider such things as people's answers to question about the ethically right thing to do in certain situations, the analogy seems much slighter between, on the one hand, the ability to give 'intuitive' (assured and unprompted) answers to these questions and on the other hand, linguistic competence. The ability to give ethical answers does indeed require some explanation. The presented cases are not exactly like previous cases, and the respondent must have internalized something that enables him or her to respond to the new cases. But it is not obvious what that may be. In particular, it is not obvious that it must be a principle, in the sense of a summary and discursively stateable description that does not rely too much on vague references to degree ('too much', 'balances out', 'does not pay enough attention to …') … In the ethical case, inasmuch as the problem is seen as the explanatory problem of representing people's ability to make judgments about new cases, we do not need to suppose that there is some clear discursive rule underlying that capacity. Aristotle supposed that there was no such rule and that a kind of inexplicit judgment was essentially involved, an ability that a group of people similarly brought up would share of seeing certain cases as like certain others.

This is what followers of Wittgenstein are disposed to believe about all human learning. At some eventual level they must be right: understanding a summary discursive rule would itself involve a shared appreciation of similarities. But this conception of the ability to arrive at shared ethical judgments (and the same thing is going to apply to other kinds of practical judgment as well) goes further than that. It is not merely that the ability to use language requires a shared capacity to see similarities, but that the capacity to see ethical similarities goes beyond anything that can adequately be expressed in language. This is surely true, and it is what Wittgensteinians would predict. It does not mean, however (Wittgensteinians themselves are not always very clear about this) that there is no explanation, at any level, of these human dispositions. All it means is that the explanation does not lie in postulating a stateable rule, which the respondent has internalized and unconsciously consults. Inasmuch as we are concerned at an explanatory level with the ability to respond to new cases, we should not necessarily expect to elicit a rule underlying that ability.

The analogy between ethical and linguistic intuitions seems very weak if one considers the conflict of intuitions. When in the linguistic case there is a conflict between the intuitions of two different people, we recognize that there are two different (if only trivially different) dialects; if one person has conflicting intuitions, this represents an uncertainty that may arise because the answer about what to say in the given case is underdetermined by the language, or perhaps because the speaker has been trained in two dialects. In none of these cases is the theory of the language required to *resolve* the conflict. Linguistic theory will resolve some conflicts, for its own purposes. Indeed, it resolves some conflicts in arriving even at the idealized notion of an intuition, since observation of performance, of how people actually speak, reveals many incoherences due to the conditions of speech, and these are smoothed out in the conception of an intuition as a reflective answer to a question about the language. (Linguistic theorists disagree about the extent to which this is legitimate.) Moreover, it is certainly appropriate for a theory, having formed a principle on the strength of some intuitions, to discount other and conflicting intuitions. To discount them is to regard them as anomalies of performance, for instance, or, again, as yielding a fact about the language that has to be entered into the lexicon as a singularity, without being connected to any general principle. These notions are themselves theoretical devices for dealing with such conflicts.

It is not like this with ethical intuitions. A lot turns on what outlook is to be adopted, and an ethically idiosyncratic outlook will not simply be left alone inasmuch as it touches on any matters of importance or on the interests of others. Here the aim of theory is not simply, or even primarily, to understand conflict. We have other ways, historical and sociological, of understanding it. The aim of theory is rather to resolve it, in the more radical sense that it should give some compelling reason to accept one intuition rather than another. The question we have to consider is: How can any ethical theory have the authority to do that?

...

Theorists have particularly tended to favor the most general expressions used in ethical discussion – *good, right, ought,* and the rest. Our use of these words is of course not confined to ethical thought. That fact in itself would not necessarily wreck the inquiry, but, for two reasons at least, this concentration has helped to do so. One reason lies in the motive for choosing those words, which was the reductionist belief that those notions were contained in more specific ethical conceptions. This conceals the real nature of those conceptions and has helped to hide a truth that a purely linguistic inquiry is unlikely to bring to light in any case: a society that relies on very general ethical expressions is a different sort of society from one that puts greater weight on more specific ones ... A second reason why the concentration on these general terms has done no good to the linguistic philosophy of ethics is that the theorist, in trying to sort out the relevant uses of them, brings to the inquiry presuppositions that are not only already theoretical but already ethical. The results are usually bad philosophy of language.

They are certainly bad philosophy of ethics. There are genuine ethical, and ultimately metaphysical, concerns underlying the worries about *ought* and *is* and the naturalistic fallacy. At the heart of them is an idea that our values are not 'in the world', that a properly untendentious description of the world would not mention any values, that our values are in some sense imposed or projected on to our surroundings. This discovery, if that is what it is, can be met with despair, as can the loss of a telelogically significant world. But it can also be seen as a liberation and a radical form of freedom may be found in the fact that we cannot be forced by the world to accept one set of values rather than another.

This set of conceptions does constitute a belief in a distinction, some distinction, between fact and value. Whether some such distinction is sound is certainly a very serious issue ... The point that needs to be made now is a preliminary one, but important. It shows why the linguistic turn is likely to be unhelpful. If there is some fundamental distinction of fact and value, it is certainly not a universal feat of humanity to have recognized it – it is instead a discovery, an achievement of enlightenment. But then there is no reason to suppose that our ethical language, insofar as there is any such well-defined thing, *already* presents the distinction to us. It may be that it does not present anything of the sort, either suggestive of such a distinction or concealing it; it may be a mistake to think that language can embody distinctively metaphysical beliefs. But if it does have the capacity to convey anything on such a question, it must be at least as likely to convey an illusion as it is to convey the truth, and indeed more likely to do so, in view of the extent in space and time of the illusion and the recent arrival of enlightenment. If human values are projected from human concerns, and are not a feature of 'the world', it does not follow that there is to hand a description of the world – or rather, of enough of the world that is value-free. (Perhaps there could not be such a thing; but if not, then we should begin to wonder what the talk of projection is really saying. What is the screen?)

This may seem a rather paradoxical way of criticizing the linguistic enterprise. Those who have engaged in it have usually emphasised a fact-value distinction; the distinction between *ought* and *is* has been used to reveal it. So it seems, either language does not disguise the fact-value distinction, or else the linguistic theorist has managed to penetrate the disguise. But neither of these options is correct. What has happened is that the theorists have brought the fact-value distinction to language rather than finding it revealed there. What they have found are a lot of those 'thicker' or more specific ethical notions ... such as *treachery* and *promise* and *brutality* and *courage*, which seem to express a union of fact and value. The way these notions are applied is determined by what the world is like (for instance, by how someone has behaved), and yet, at the same time, their application usually involves a certain valuation of the situation, of persons or actions. Moreover, they usually (though not necessarily directly) provide reasons for action. Terms of this kind certainly do not lay bare the fact-value distinction. Rather, the theorist who wants to defend the distinction has to interpret the workings of these terms, and he does so by treating them as a conjunction of a factual and an evaluative element, which can in principle be separated from one another. The clearest account, as so often, is given by Hare: a term of this kind involves a descriptive complex to which a prescription has been attached, expressive of the values of the individual or of the society. A statement using one of these terms can be analyzed into something like 'this act has such-and-such a character, and acts of that character one ought not to do'. It is essential to this account that the specific or 'thick' character of these terms is given in the descriptive element. The value part is expressed, under analysis, by the all-purpose prescriptive term *ought*.

...

The prescriptivist account claims that the value part of these thick terms is entirely carried by the prescriptive function, which can be analyzed in terms of *ought*. It claims that everything we want to say or think in the ethical domain (and indeed in evaluative areas beyond it) could be said or thought in terms of that very general term. Other theorists say similar things about other general terms: some general, abstract term could do all the work. Indeed, since the thicker ethical terms are only compounds involving this term, it is already doing the work. If this kind of analysis proves to be a mistake, and more generally the impulse to reduce ethical language to such abstract terms is misguided, then they are not doing all the work, and this will leave room for an idea I have already suggested, that a society in which ethical life is understood and conducted in such general terms is socially different from one in which it is not, and the differences require social understanding. If that is a fact, the linguistic approach certainly does not help us to recognize it. It encourages us to neglect it even as a possibility.

It is an obvious enough idea that if we are going to understand how ethical concepts work, and how they change, we have to have some insight into the forms of social organization within which they work. The linguistic approach does not, at some detached level, deny this, but it does not ask any questions that help us to gain that insight or to do anything with it in philosophy if we have gained it. Its concentration on questions of logical analysis have helped to conceal the point, and so has its pure conception of philosophy itself, which indeed emphasizes that language is a social activity but at the same time, oddly enough, rejects from philosophy any concrete interests in societies. But it is at least potentially closer to some understanding of the social and historical dimensions of ethical thought than some other approaches, which see it entirely in terms of an autonomous and unchanging subject matter. To draw attention to our ethical language can at least hold out the prospect of our coming to think about it, and about the ethical life expressed in it, as social practices that can change. The linguistic turn could have helped us, even if it has not actually done so, to recognize that ethical understanding needs a dimension of social explanation.

Penner (2002)

I want now to suggest that expertise in academic or philosophical political morality is the wrong sort of moral expertise for judges to have, which goes a long way to explaining why judges do not typically reason like moral philosophers. In doing so, I hope to provide a rough sketch of the sort of moral expertise it might be more plausible to ascribe to them. Rather than offering a 'political' explanation of incomplete theorisation in common law legal reasoning, I want to offer what might be called a 'cognitive' one. The central claim of this explanation is that the kind of expertise judges and lawyers have is the expertise that comes from having acquired a great deal of moral knowledge and having to make sense of that knowledge, not in terms of aiming at theories which explain the fundamental or ultimate character of morality, but in terms of attending to moral concepts and moral beliefs so as to maintain their practical ability to judge the moral implications of a situation more or less successfully.

Once again, the starting point is the work of Raz. Without doing violence to the subtlety of Raz's work on the nature of morality and moral reasoning, the following perhaps captures the essential features of his position that are relevant to my purposes here. Humans are valuing creatures, which is to say that human beings respond to features of the world so as to value or disvalue them. A well-lived life is one in which values are realised and disvalues avoided, so it is in the interest of humans to realise values and avoid disvalues. There is an irreducible plurality of values. There are many distinct aspects of the world which can be valued or disvalued by humans, and no individual human can realise all values in a single life, though a well-lived life will be one in which a variety of values has been realised. Therefore values and disvalues, or the realising or avoiding of them, respectively, constitute reasons for action, and roughly speaking, reasoning in respect of values constitutes the core of practical reasoning, and where the values and disvalues are of primary importance, this practical reasoning can be regarded as moral reasoning. Moreover, reasoning in respect of values and disvalues in this way is rational, which is to say that we reason in terms of our understanding of the nature of these values and disvalues. It therefore follows that we can conceptualise these values and disvalues, ie. can have concepts of them, for it is only in virtue of having a concept of something that one can think about it, reason about it, form beliefs about it, and so on. In this respect our concepts of values and disvalues are no different than our concepts of anything else. Having a concept of dogs allows us to entertain thoughts about dogs, acquire beliefs about dogs, and so on. But in other respects our concepts of value, or perhaps the aspects of the world that we conceive as values, may have special characteristics. It is important therefore, in understanding moral reasoning and practical reasoning in general, to appreciate any special characteristics of value concepts (aka 'evaluative' concepts) or the aspects of the world these concepts are concepts of.

Raz has recently written about this. He examines the extent to which our moral reasoning depends upon 'parochial' concepts and 'thick' concepts. As to the former, Raz states:

> 'Parochial concepts' are concepts which cannot be mastered by all, not even by everyone capable of knowledge. 'Non-parochial' concepts can be mastered by anyone capable of knowing anything at all.

The acquisition of certain parochial concepts will depend upon having certain perceptual capabilities (i.e. the ability to see to acquire colour concepts), but our chief concern here are parochial evaluative concepts, and the way in which access to certain evaluative concepts may depend upon one's living in cultural circumstances which create, sustain, or provide access to certain values. To the extent that one's exposure to these values is contingent in the sense that they depend upon one's being in or sufficiently related to a particular culture, the concepts of those values are parochial.

Thick evaluative concepts are related, but distinct. 'Thick' evaluative concepts are concepts which cannot be analysed into descriptive and evaluative elements so as to preserve their normative sense. According to Williams:

> What has happened is that the theorists have brought the fact-value distinction to language rather than finding it revealed there. What they have found are a lot of those 'thicker' or more specific ethical notions … such as *treachery* and *promise* and *brutality* and *courage*, which seem to express a union of fact and value. The way these notions are applied is determined by what the world is like (for instance, by how someone behaved), and yet, at the same time, their application usually involves a certain valuation of the situation, of persons or actions. Moreover, they usually (though not necessarily directly) provide reasons for action.

Now the point about the thickness of these concepts is not that they cannot be analysed into parts, so to speak, to give a description which differentiates factual and evaluative elements. That is easy: consider this analysis of courage: courage is personally dangerous risk-taking for worthwhile purposes (personally dangerous risk-taking which is, for the agent, 'valuable'), whereas the failure to undertake a personally dangerous risk when it is worthwhile to do so is cowardice, and undertaking personally dangerous risks for low-value or trivial purposes is foolhardiness. The same can be done for murder: murder is killing that is evil, wicked, or otherwise 'bad'. These analyses are unacceptably vague, of course, but vagueness is always a problem and no doubt these definitions could be sharpened, yet what these thumbnail demonstrations show is that nothing in principle would appear to make such analyses impossible. And if that is right, then on what basis does Williams assert that theorists have 'brought' the fact-value distinction to these concepts, rather than its inherently being part of them? The mere existence of such 'thick' concepts in our thinking, which have both factual and evaluative criteria for their proper application, and corresponding words in our natural language to express them, cannot decide the issue. For in acquiring these concepts we may simply have acquired them on the basis of our attention being drawn to both the factual and evaluative criteria. That we now apply such concepts 'unreflectively', that is, when we identify an event as a murder we don't consciously reflect to ourselves 'killing' and 'evil' and then infer 'murder' is neither here nor there, for we apply all kinds of concepts on the basis of multiple criteria unreflectively. For example, assume that one workable set of criteria for the application of 'chair' is 'portable', 'seat', 'for one'. No one would insist that I reflect to myself on these separate criteria when I invite you to 'Take a chair'.

The crucial factor is the *abstract character* of the evaluative terms that are employed in the analysis. We see this when we look closely at the thumbnail analyses, or any others that people come up with: the evaluative criteria are all 'thin', that is, the most general, abstract terms of approbation or disapprobation, 'ought', 'good', 'right', 'praiseworthy', 'bad', 'wrong', 'wicked' and so on. All the thickness, the specific character of the concept, is deposited in the factual criteria. 'It is essential to this account that the specific or "thick" character of these terms is given in the descriptive element. The value part is expressed, under analysis, by the all-purpose prescriptive term *ought*'. So undertaking these analyses *itself* appears to 'reflect' an unspoken theoretical perspective, for these thin terms are, of course, the sort of abstract theoretical terms the investigation of which is the very essence of modern moral philosophising. From this perspective there is no courage-specific evaluative dimension in the statement that 'Paul displayed courage', no value, specifically, in or of 'courage' *per se*. Courage is merely the instantiation of the good or the right or what one ought to do where circumstances provide for personally dangerous risk-taking. The somewhat disconcerting message of the fact-value distinction as applied here, which at first glance seems so innocuous, is that there are no particular, specific, non-abstract ethical evaluations, so no specific ethical concepts to represent them, so no such particular, specific, non-abstract ethical thoughts or reasons – when we treat of the ethical or moral, it's abstract all the way down, so to speak. The application of the fact/value analysis drains most of the significance or meaning from ethical judgements employing these terms.

Given the prevalence of thick evaluative concepts in everyday practical judgment, it is worthwhile considering whether they rather than thin concepts are the basic foundation of normative or evaluative judgment, including moral judgment. If they are, then we might plausibly be able to construct a picture of common law lawyerly and judicial expertise which is not equivalent to expertise in abstract moral philosophical reasoning. Instead, perhaps, common law lawyers and judges may have some kind of superior knowledge of, i.e. expertise in dealing with, thick ethical concepts. Such an expertise, if it exists, would presumably be manifest or reflected in a legal discourse which is incompletely theorised from the perspective of moral and political philosophy.

THICK AND PAROCHIAL CONCEPTS AND THE TRANSPARENCY AND UNIVERSALITY, OR UNIVERSALISABILITY, OF MORAL REASONING

There does, however, appear to be a problem in this perspective, concerning the transparency and universality of the values which thick evaluative concepts represent. The problem can be stated in this way: according to Raz and Williams, thick ethical concepts are parochial concepts; they are 'thick' because they represent values which are created, sustained, or accessible only because of complex cultural or social practices of particular groups. Therefore they are neither 'transparent' nor 'universal' in the way we expect moral concepts to be. Moral concepts should be transparent in the sense that if we have them, we should have a grasp of their intelligibility which explains why they apply in specific circumstances. Thin ethical concepts offer this promise, in that the generality of the evaluations they permit us to make applies across specific thick ethical judgements. Thus the concept 'right' applies to and makes intelligible any number of different ethical circumstances, as do the concepts of 'duty', or 'freedom' or 'autonomy'. Thin ethical concepts also offer, if not the established reality of an appreciation of universal moral values, at least the means to achieve that appreciation. Thin ethical concepts, so the argument goes, are not parochial. Their very function lies in the fact that they make intelligible more specific or thick moral judgments, allowing us to see contradictions in our moral reasoning.

Raz examines the basis of this sort of argument, and concludes that both thick and thin ethical concepts have a role in our moral understanding. The analysis is rich and detailed, but I can, I think, present the general outline. According to Raz's account, thick ethical concepts and thin ethical concepts have different roles to play in our moral understanding. Roughly, the acquisition of thick ethical concepts by individuals goes hand in hand with the fact that the plurality of values which we are able to realise is context dependent. In the case of some values, access to them is dependent upon cultural conditions. In the case of others, they exist only where they are created and sustained by cultural or social practices. This cultural dependence is reflected in our possession of parochial, thick concepts of the values in question. The value of chess, for example, is dependent upon being familiar with the specific character of chess-playing, and the value of mastering the game so as to play it to some level of success. Roughly then, to realise the value of say, chess, is to have a concept of its value which is thick. On the other hand, our evaluative judgments are, more or less, intelligible to us. To act in response to values just is to act for reasons, and if that is right and we are rational, then we must have some appreciation of the character of all values *as* values, i.e. as possible instantiations of value. This intelligibility is provided by thin evaluative concepts. If thick evaluative concepts serve to represent the plurality of values in all their specificity, it is only by being able to subsume such thick evaluative concepts under thin evaluative ones which allows us to recognise them as intelligibly being examples of value. To quote Raz at some length:

> Evolving practices give rise to new values. Commonly their emergence is recognised by subsuming them under familiar values. Thus existing values make possible the recognition of new values when encountered, but they do not allow either the prescribing or designing them, in the sense of saying 'these are the values one should have in these cultural conditions', nor do existing values provide a base for predicting which new values would evolve. New values emerge with evolving social practices and cultural developments. Once new subsumed values emerge reflection on them leads to a reinterpretation and a change of understanding of the more universal value concepts under which they were subsumed, thus leading to the emergence of new abstract value concepts to cover both new and old concrete values. In this way the intelligibility and the social dependence of values are reconciled. They are reconciled through the fact that intelligibility does not mean a permanent frame of reference ... [I]n general it seems that the emergence of abstract value concepts merely improves the understanding of previously existing values ... [I]f there is a right not to be tortured that right predates the concept of a right. The emergence of the concept merely enables us to understand that the right exists. The same goes for other abstract value concepts, such as the value of self-expression or autonomy. The reason is that in these cases, the value can be enjoyed by people who do not have the abstract concept. They cannot enjoy it without some concepts, but it is enough for them to have more concrete concepts, which are appropriately related to the right against torture, or to the state of expressing oneself, or of being autonomous ... The thin and thick concepts are interdependent. Thick concepts have to be explained by reference to thinner ones in order to satisfy the requirement of intelligibility. The thin concepts, on the other hand, while

explained by reference to thicker ones, also have an open-ended aspect: new thick concepts subject to them can always emerge. This makes them relatively independent of the thick concepts currently subsumed under them.

This is an attractive and plausible picture, and can be taken as one perspective on the possibility that common law judges and lawyers have a kind of moral expertise endowing them with authority. Legal development in the common law occurs on the occasion that disputes are presented to courts. In order to understand the moral character of these disputes, one must understand their facts, and properly appreciate what values and disvalues, in all their cultural contingency, are instantiated. It follows from that that lawyers and judges would have to be familiar with the culturally thick ethical concepts which represent those values and disvalues. Furthermore, lawyers and judges are, in the common law tradition, supposed to explain their appreciation of the facts and reasons for their decisions. They must show the intelligibility of their reasoning. Thus one would expect them also to make use of thin ethical concepts for this very reason, perhaps in particular to show that their instant decision is not inconsistent with other relevant past decisions, or that no factors of importance (which possession of the more general, thin concept, prompts one to consider) have been left out of their reasoning or argument. This picture, besides being, I think, attractive, seems to represent the character of legal discourse with some fidelity. It occupies a median level of abstraction. And it also seems to permit the claim that judges and lawyers can have (not always, nor necessarily) the moral expertise which would entitle them to make law. This would lie in both their familiarity in applying thick ethical concepts to often puzzling or complex sets of facts, and in their learned facility in giving voice to the intelligibility of these thick ethical concepts and their application in particular cases by reference to thin ethical concepts, in particular thin ethical concepts which have made their appearance in law as much as moral and political philosophy, thin ethical concepts as 'right' and 'just'. Thus in addition to what I called his 'political' explanation for the law's being incompletely theorised from the perspective of academic moral and political philosophy, I think we can glean from Raz's recent writing a 'cognitive' explanation, i.e. one that arises from the nature of the concepts with which lawyers and judges must work. This latter explanation also provides some reason to believe that common law lawyers and judges might also be able to claim some legitimacy for their authority to make law: it lies in their ability, acquired through experience and study, to use this conceptual apparatus with greater facility than most of the subjects of the law. In short, in areas like the common law where the legal concepts at work are very closely related, if not identical to, moral concepts treating of the same factual situations, their legal expertise is, because of this facility, a kind of moral expertise.

Despite the attractiveness of this picture, it seems to me to embrace a mistaken assumption, viz. the assumption that thick evaluative concepts are parochial concepts, and that in comparison to thick evaluative concepts, thin evaluative concepts are less parochial in virtue of the fact that they, being more general and less context-dependent, can subsume thick ethical ones. What I am going to argue for (though unfortunately not nearly sufficiently to establish the truth of it) is the claim that the universality of ethical judgement is secured by the universality of certain thick ethical concepts, and that our claim to the intelligibility of these concepts and our application of them, while undoubtedly assisted by more abstract arguments making use of thin ethical concepts, lies more in acquiring true beliefs about what thick ethical concepts represent and systematising that knowledge for use in our practical reasoning.

The general drift of the argument to follow turns on treating evaluative concepts in the same way one would treat non-evaluative concepts to examine their role in our reasoning and understanding. The 'ontological' status of values may be puzzling to us, but if we accept (which is true) that we are valuing creatures, i.e. creatures which have access to and realise values, just as we are creatures with certain perceptual capacities able to access perceptual properties, there seems no reason to believe that our concepts of values should be puzzling *qua* concepts. That is, if the nature of values is mysterious to us, then that will make it difficult to form true beliefs about values. But it seems to be a necessary premise for a discussion of evaluative reasoning that there are values, and that we have enough acquaintance with them to be able to distinguish values from dis-values and one kind of value from another. If so, then we must have concepts of values and dis-values in sufficient working order to do for us what other concepts do, i.e. allow us to consider, form beliefs about, and otherwise deal with features of the world.

If this is roughly right, then just as it is the case that our access to different features of the world and our ability to form concepts of those features of the world may be underpinned in different ways, so may our access to values and concepts of values. We have already noted the distinction Raz draws between values which are dependent upon culture in the sense that they are created by culture, and dependent upon culture in the sense that access to them is mediated by cultural practices. The question I want to pursue is whether there is reason to believe that there are any universal *thick* evaluative concepts, in particular any universal thick *ethical* concepts, and if so, what their relation is to evaluative concepts which show this sort of cultural dependency. If there are universal thick ethical concepts, then the transparency and universality we associate with (or demand from) moral concepts may be secured, not because we have thin ethical concepts under which values can be intelligibly subsumed, but because we have universal access to certain thick values more or less as a matter of being human. It seems to me that there obviously are universal thick ethical concepts.

Williams identifies his thick ethical concepts as being the most *culturally specific* ethical concepts, and as far as I can tell, Raz assumes the same thing. However a scan back over the examples Williams gives suggests that, if anything, these concepts will have the most universal instantiation. What human culture, for example, would not have acquaintance with and formed a concept of courage, or could not think about brutality or promises or greed? As far as I can tell, Williams gives no reason for regarding these concepts as culturally specific beyond the fact that they are 'traditional', or 'hyper-traditional' as he puts it. But because a battery of concepts has existed as a long-standing feature of a traditional culture does not entail that the concepts are specific to that traditional culture, but only that even members of traditional cultures can acquire them, i.e., these concepts are not restricted to moderns. Neither, however, are moderns excluded from acquiring them (which Williams seems clearly to imply, since by presenting them to modern readers in our language without quotation marks around them, he would seem to indicate he believes that we have the concepts of courage, brutality, and so on). It may well be the case that in a very real way having access to the values and dis-values these concepts are concepts of, and therefore having the ability to acquire these concepts, does depend in a significant way on cultural or societal practices. It is, I think, easy to imagine the circumstances of someone who might not acquire such concepts. Consider a child raised in conditions of unrelenting abuse, perhaps one raised in a gulag or concentration camp. It seems right to suggest that there is a minimum standard of cultural practice, a recognisable level of basic human cultural 'success', for want of a better term, against which the plurality of values such as courage, or generosity, or dis-values such as malice or lying would be distinguishable. However I take it that concerns about cultural relativity are not primarily concerned with these sorts of possibility. The present point is that it seems right to think that in the vast range of human societies with their specific cultures of which we have knowledge, it seems much more plausible to believe that all of them would instantiate values like courage or generosity and disvalues like malice, and that people would acquire concepts of them, than that no instantiations of these values would occur, and that no concepts of them would be acquired. This, of course, is not to deny by any means the existence of those values whose creation or access to which has been shown to depend upon cultural practices which are far from universal. But the truth of that is not incompatible with there being universally instantiated values and dis-values, and universally acquired concepts of them.

'But', you may say, 'while we are able to perceive courage, malice, and so on in every culture, and can acquire the concepts "courage", "malice" etc., it does not follow that the members of those cultures have the *same* concepts of "courage" and "malice" we do, even if they have concepts which in some way or another represent those values. Therefore what has been said in no way proves the universality of these concepts.' This objection is roughly expressed, but I put it in these rough terms so as to reproduce a possible ambiguity in the sort of objection I am describing. The objection might be simply that people in different cultures, although they have a concept of courage or whatever, have different beliefs about courage than do we, and attribute different significance to it. If that is all that is meant, the claim is true, but does not undercut the claim of universality. Something Raz says is helpful in showing why not:

> Consider the sort of normative considerations advanced as universal and timeless. For example: it is always wrong to murder an innocent person. If we can judge people to have acted wrongly in having committed murder we must assume that it is possible for them to know that they should not perform the actions which are the murder of innocent people. But we need not assume that they must have been able to understand the concept 'murder', 'person', 'innocent', 'intention', and 'killing', which we use to articulate and explain this rule. Arguably, even before these concepts were available to people they had other ways of categorising mental states, other ways of marking transgressions, other ways of marking animals we now know belong to the species *Homo sapiens*. Their concepts and generalisations may have been based on false beliefs, and we may find them inadequate in many ways. But they may have enabled them to know that the acts which in fact constitute murder of innocent people are wrong. That is enough to establish that they had the access to the norm which is a pre-condition of being able to blame them for its violation. If people at all times had access to the norms, in one form or another, then we have here an example of a consideration, to which there is universal access, though that access is culturally determined.

Here Raz is directing his attention to the ability to appreciate a norm, and conceive of it, rather than appreciate a value, and have a concept of it, but I think the lesson is the same. As Raz points out, if all that this sort of objection is claiming is that the person from the other culture, though having the norm, has as well different concepts and beliefs which form part of his (to our minds, insufficient or flawed) overall understanding of the norm, that, while important, does not undercut the claim about universality. The same lesson must be applied to distinguish between having a concept and having particular beliefs about whatever the concept is a concept of. I think it plausible to say that I and Aristotle had the concept 'food', though I have beliefs about food which Aristotle did not, and indeed could not have. I, for example, believe, and indeed know, that many foods contain saturated fats. Aristotle didn't. Simply having different beliefs about the thing that a concept is a concept of does not entail that two people have a different concept of it. As a rough and ready guide, if two persons' concepts both distinguish paradigm cases of the thing a concept is a concept of, then they have the same concept. The beliefs one has about the thing may, and often do, lead different persons to disagree about whether a non-paradigmatic case falls under the concept or not. But this happens between different people in the same culture. The claim about the universality of the concept of 'courage' is that it is difficult to imagine any more or less functioning human culture in which cases we would regard as paradigm examples of the value of courage would not be accessible, whether courage in battle, or in facing wild animals, or in facing other hazardous physical dangers, and equally difficult to imagine that these paradigm examples would not be paradigm examples of courage in those cultures as well. It doesn't turn on different culture's particular beliefs about courage, for example that courage is a gift of the gods, or that one instils courage through physical privation, or anything else. Concepts are not to be individuated in terms of every belief that a person has in which that concept figures ... But one must be judicious about this. When we speak of concepts, we do sometimes wish to speak of more than people's ability to distinguish paradigm cases; rather, we wish to consider the broader constellation of beliefs which more or less make up a department of their thought. Here it is perfectly right to say that there was a different 'concept' or 'conception' of, say, 'courage' in Rome than most people have nowadays. This is a perfectly valid point to make: the point is that for some purposes, we should individuate concepts not on a belief-independent basis, but in terms of some more or less essential constellation of beliefs that a person has in respect of the feature of the world that the concept represents. But again, this does not count against the universality point. It only requires us to distinguish between different notions of a concept. For my purposes, the universality point is secured if restricted to individuating concepts on the basis that a person has a concept when able to identify paradigm cases of the value the concept represents, for the point is that the value the concept represents is a value which will be instantiated in any society and to which any individual will have access. Indeed, it would not only undercut the universality point to adopt the 'complex of beliefs' formulation of concept, it would obscure an important aspect of the universality claim.

The claim is precisely not that universal access to these values guarantees a universal set of beliefs in which the concept of the value figures, or a universal complex of beliefs about the nature of the concept. That would be a preposterous claim to make even within one's own culture in respect of the concepts people acquire and the beliefs they form. It is crucial to understand that having a concept does not make one an immediate know-it-all about whatever the concept is a concept of. Having the concept courage does not tell us everything important or significant about courage. Indeed, it may be the case that concepts (in the 'grasp of paradigms' sense) come cheap, in that one acquires concepts fairly easily either by direct exposure to the values or dis-values in question, or by being informed about those values or dis-values in various ways by others, but that knowledge of the things they are concepts of is hard won – knowledge requires investigation and thought. Think of it this way: acquiring a concept is like opening a file on a research project. Getting the concept of 'dog' so that one can distinguish dogs may not require much more than having dogs pointed out to one a couple of times; children seem to learn to pick out dogs very easily. But getting that under one's belt does not guarantee one much in the way of knowledge. There is a lot to learn about dogs, and indeed, having the concept of dog (having opened that file) is a pre-condition of learning new things about dogs, for only by having the concept 'dog' is one able to acquire new beliefs *about dogs*, about dogs *qua* dogs, about dogs as such.

There seems no reason to believe that evaluative concepts are any different in this regard. There is a lot to learn about the actual nature of murder, about its particular dis-value (how important is the mental state attending it, how are different cases of murder worse than others), about its relation to other dis-values (whether, and in what respects, it is like and different from, worse or less bad than, say, rape or treason), and about its limits (is euthanasia murder?). Forming new, true, beliefs about the nature of murder will require investigation into actual instances of it, and thought.

If this is right, then we have a picture of ethical evaluation which looks something like this: on the basis of our grasp of universal, thick ethical concepts, *and* whatever knowledge about what those concepts represent that we've managed to assemble and remember (knowledge that will turn very largely on the conditions of one's culture, for example, whether there are institutions in which this knowledge is developed or preserved, for example), we apply those concepts to particular cases to determine what appears to us to be the morally correct response.

But how, one may ask, do universal thick ethical concepts interact with thin ones? Recall that according to Raz, thinner concepts, those more abstract and general concepts, function in part to render intelligible the evaluative nature of thick evaluative concepts. Raz also makes the point that thin evaluative concepts are parochial. He says:

> But the same [parochial character] is true of our abstract normative concepts such as those designated by the terms 'duty', 'obligation', 'a right', 'valuable', 'good', 'beautiful', 'person', 'happiness', 'pleasure'. The history of these terms shows how their meaning mutated over time, and how different languages differ in their abstract normative vocabulary.

This point can be strengthened. To the extent that thin evaluative concepts are theoretical or philosophical, that is, derive (much of) their meaning from their situation within explicit philosophical theories, they depend upon (not necessarily academic) social practices in which theories or philosophies are formulated, considered, and criticised; it follows that these terms must be parochial, perhaps very parochial, for these practices are far from universal, and different cultures show very different practices of this kind.

If I am right about the universal, i.e. non-parochial character of (certain) thick ethical concepts and about the parochial character of thin ethical concepts, then the general relationship of thin to thick evaluative concepts advanced by Raz and discussed above is reversed. In particular, it does not seem clear from this new perspective quite how thin ethical concepts are necessary for our appreciating the intelligibility of thick ethical concepts. It would seem that thick evaluative concepts must provide intelligible access to value, or they would not be concepts of the values they must be. On the other hand, one could have access to these values without having the abstract theoretical concept 'value'. One would, of course, be less knowledgeable about the nature of the world than one who had such a concept, where, however, it is important to emphasise, that thin concept was supported by an intellectual practice which ensured that this thin ethical concept was in some sort of order, ie answered some sensible questions or organised the realm of values in some useful way. Presumably one would appreciate a range of values, and be able to respond more or less rationally to them − what one would be incapable of would be certain more sophisticated thoughts about these values, in particular thoughts which allowed one to treat the plurality of values as being of a kind. Furthermore, without these thinner terms, one would presumably be unable to discern certain aspects about the nature of values, which higher order theories provide one access to. 'Right', as in individual's possessing rights like the right to life, is an example. This term is clearly parochial, appearing in the West only from about the beginning of the 17th century. Having this concept of right allows us to organise what morality and law requires by reference to the interests of persons. And to say this is not to treat 'rights' as merely an 'interpretive' term in a theoretical framework, but to acknowledge that rights may be as real as any other thing of which we may have an evaluative concept. Acquiring the concept 'proton' depends on the access provided by theories in physics, but protons are real just the same, and there is no a priori reason that the same theory-dependent access to the normative realm can not be provided. (Again, it is worthwhile stressing that any truths being made available by these concepts depends upon these concepts being in 'working order', that is underpinned by practices, scientific or intellectual or otherwise which sharpen rather than obscure our grasp of reality.)

Thus, although the parochial/non-parochial polarity between thick and thin terms is reversed on the account I have offered, the role of thin concepts, in particular thin 'theoretical' or 'philosophical' concepts appears to be much the same. But rather than framing their function as subsuming thick terms to *provide* them with intelligibility or *make* them intelligible, they rather *advance* our understanding of the evaluative realm by providing access to aspects of that realm which are not captured by thick terms. To isolate one line previously quoted from Raz:

> … [I]n general it seems that the emergence of abstract value concepts merely improves the understanding of previously existing values.

In doing so, thin ethical concepts should also point out, or lead us to consider or examine, possible aspects of the nature of the values and dis-values that thick ethical concepts are concepts of.

V COMMON LAW MORAL EXPERTISE

I can now outline two claims about the nature of common law legal reasoning and the possibility of common law lawyers' judges having a kind of moral expertise. The first is that, despite a long history of the law's looking at the values and dis-values these concepts are concepts of, much of our knowledge remains in terms of a collection of relevant cases in which the facts have led us to apply one or more of our thick ethical concepts, a collection which is maintained by us through various methods of memory and recording. Not only does the past consideration and memorising of actual cases engender a facility of applying thick ethical concepts, but continuing exposure to actual cases of moral relevance allows us to refine our beliefs about those concepts. If this is right, then a casuistic approach to moral reasoning might better reflect what we most know about the values and disvalues our concepts represent, reflect it better, by and large, that is, than more abstract theoretical statements about what morality requires. And this casuistic approach is typical of common law reasoning. The law 'exists' in the cases because it is the cases which re-trigger our thick ethical concepts, and their interactions with each other in actual cases prompt further beliefs about the nature of what those concepts represent and the ways in which they interact. The short way of putting this is that *continuing* acquaintance in different contexts with the things our concepts of which are learned by acquaintance is probably the best trigger of our more or less untheorised catalogue of knowledge about the values and disvalues our thick ethical concepts represent, *and* the best ground of new knowledge about those values and dis-values. Beliefs newly acquired in the course of this exercise are then articulated and fitted within the catalogue of pre-existing belief, but generally 'locally', i.e. in specific areas of our body of knowledge, to refine and explain only a relatively small portion of the body of knowledge, and at a suitably low level of abstraction.

The second claim is that, despite the fact that I have emphasised the universal character of certain thick ethical concepts, any set of moral norms organised into a system which is to apply to persons within a society generally will be conventional to a large extent. This contention rests upon what might be called our 'paradigmatic' or 'stereotypical' access to concepts. This is simply the idea that, whilst our concepts are about more than paradigmatic or stereotypical instances of what they are concepts of – unstereotypical dogs are still dogs – our ability to apply our concepts is more difficult where non-stereotypical instances of the thing a concept represents are instantiated. Now, one obvious thought that arises from this is that in any system of norms where our concepts have uncertain boundaries in this way it will be imperative to stipulate (reasonable) boundaries for the application of these terms in order to provide some measure of certainty. This, recall, is one way in which the authority of law-makers can be justified, as providing conventions to ensure more or less certain boundaries, to ensure a more effective compliance with moral norms. But I think a different claim about the common law's conventionality can be made, having to do with what Raz calls the path-dependence of epistemic justification, and therefore of knowledge. If our understanding of the different values our thick concepts represent depends upon our experience in dealing with actual cases to which they apply, then it is obvious that different cultures or societies might come to more knowledge about, and therefore rely more upon, certain of these thick ethical concepts than others, simply because for various reasons they have acquired greater knowledge of some of the values and dis-values these concepts represent than others. Having the paradigmatic instances under one's belt is one thing; having a sophisticated knowledge of the value a concept represents so that one can identify the value's instantiation in atypical circumstances is quite another. Furthermore, here is a point where the influence of thin, parochial concepts, may have a great influence. A society's success in developing thin abstract concepts that illuminate and advance the intelligibility of the battery of universal thick ethical concepts will vary from one concept to another. Their appreciation of certain values and dis-values, and hence their interest in acquiring greater knowledge of these values and dis-values, will also be influenced by other factors, such as religion, economic conditions, and so forth. In consequence of these different cultural factors, different societies will have differing levels of interest and differing levels of knowledge about the values and dis-values represented by universal thick ethical concepts, and so will tend to rely upon some more than others in making sense of what is morally good, morally required, morally prohibited, and so on. Our thick ethical concepts interact, and different concepts may be instantiated in the same circumstances. An act may be courageous, generous, but also disloyal. A sale of goods reflects concepts both of agreement and property. In making sense of the moral significance of particular cases, different ethical concepts may be emphasised over others. As a result of this, different cultures will give rise to different moral systems of norms, even if they all begin with an identical battery of thick ethical concepts.

By making these remarks, I do not mean to suggest that all systems of norms represent morality in an equally sophisticated or equally valid way. But I do think that we must allow for the possibility that there is more than one way to skin a cat, morally speaking. It may be the case that given the plurality of even universally accessible values, success in generating a basic system of norms for the governing of behaviour may depend upon emphasising certain values over others – which is not to say that any value may be denied outright. The particular emphases of a culture in this respect will reflect something of its character. And it follows that the particular emphases a culture places on certain values must be preserved in its moral reasoning if basic desiderata such as certainty in norms, treating like cases alike, and so on, are to be achieved. In this way a culture of moral discourse, in particular an institutionalised culture of moral discourse, might make what appear from the outside to be purely arbitrary 'selections' of values to emphasise. My point is that given the state of knowledge, it might be not only perfectly sensible but morally praiseworthy to do so.

Much more needs to be said to flesh this very rough sketch out. But to give an indication of the kind of 'selection' I am talking about, consider the institution of the trust in English law. The norms governing the law of trusts reflect a number of thick ethical concepts, of which I would cite 'property', 'agreement', and 'loyalty' as being three examples. But this particular combination of norms is absent in civilian jurisdictions, though there are similar sorts of legal devices. Having made the selection to analyse cases in these terms, that is, as cases of trusts, will direct common law judges and lawyers to appreciate different aspects of fact situations than civilians will, and as importantly, will require them differently to explain their practical reasoning, making sense of their decisions in different ways, even if, as often seems to be the case, different legal systems achieve the same 'functional equivalent'.

In short, an institution of moral discourse which emphasises past assimilation of cases in which thick ethical concepts have been applied, continuing exposure to new cases as a source of knowledge, and a commitment to past 'selections' of particular values and the concepts that represent them as ones which are to serve more foundational roles in the discourse of practical reasoning, may count as a genuine case of institutionalised moral expertise. Besides its authority to solve co-ordination problems, then, the common law may be right to claim, and individual judges and lawyers learned in the common law may be right to claim, that it or he or she is experienced in the application of moral norms in a way which endows it or he or she with moral wisdom. 'Wisdom' here refers to a kind of expertise which exists at a lower level of abstraction than abstract theory, and which depends on the acquisition of correct beliefs about the nature of universal ethical values through long experience with dealing with them, and as well with the particular conventional selections of emphasis which colour but underpin a systematic and sophisticated discourse of practical reasoning.

Further Reading

For an extremely thorough criticism of the positivist's characterisation of legal reasoning drawing heavily upon the historical development of the common law, see Simpson 1987. For a recent statement by Dworkin of his commitment to the role of theory in legal reasoning, which includes his own response to Sunstein, see Dworkin 1997. For Raz's most recent views on moral and legal reasoning, see Raz 1999b, and for an alternative discussion of rules and reasons, see Schauer 1991. For those interested in pursuing Wittgenstein's arguments on rule following, Wittgenstein 1958, paras 1–242 and McDowell 1984 provide a place to start.

Questions

1. Critically assess whether Raz's 'exclusionary reason' thesis explains the force of legal norms, and further, whether it provides an important underpinning to his explanation of legal reasoning.

2. What is a rule? Is the law made up of rules?

3. 'Any theory of legal reasoning will largely be shaped by its answers to two questions: (1) What status does it give to rules in the law? and (2) How does it characterise legal concepts?' Discuss.

4. Explain Sunstein's claim that the law is 'incompletely theorised', and consider whether his explanations in support of the claim are persuasive.

5. 'In trying to characterise legal reasoning, a fundamental conflict emerges between those who believe that providing sound reasons for a legal decision is always ultimately dependent upon a "justificatory" ascent to more abstract theoretical principles, and those who accept the legal reasoning is essentially casuistic, a matter of drawing distinctions and recognising similarities which are not, and cannot be, grounded in abstract theory, but whose correctness rather depends upon both the common human nature of the subjects of the law and their shared historical and cultural experience.' Discuss.

6. What are 'thick' ethical concepts and what are 'parochial' ethical concepts; how, if at all, does making reference to these types of concepts help to explain the nature of legal reasoning?

15 Justice

Robert Reiner

Introduction

So much jurisprudence and legal practice assumes that one can talk meaningfully about justice. Indeed, 'justice' is often seen as virtually coterminous with law: we speak of the criminal or civil *justice* systems, of 'bringing people to *justice*', and so on. Justice has been an ideal since ancient times – the Bible, for example, urges us 'justice, justice, you shall pursue' (Deuteronomy 16:20). But defining and analysing the 'justice' to be pursued has been a thorny and vexed issue for philosophy since its earliest days, constituting the central question for Plato's *Republic*, Aristotle's *Ethics*, and other classical works. Justice is a paradigmatic example of an 'essentially contested concept', combining issues of analysis and evaluation in such complexly intertwined ways that no amount of debate is likely to achieve a final resolution (Gallie 1955–56). This chapter principally explores contemporary versions of this contested concept. Such an exercise is a very large task, but that is no reason to avoid tackling it.

A fundamental distinction in discussions of justice must be made between *procedural* and *substantive* conceptions. Procedural or formal approaches are concerned with the criteria for fair decision-making processes. The concept of procedural justice is roughly equivalent to ideas of 'due process' or the 'rule of law'. The promulgation, enforcement and administration of laws or other rules is just only if standards such as are spelled out in Lon Fuller's analysis in *The Morality of Law* (see Chapter 2) are complied with, for example that legal requirements are clearly articulated in advance. Or, in other theories, that at least, all citizens are treated equally by the law.

Substantive questions of justice refer to the *content* of law, policies, or social organisations, not only the formal procedures by which they are developed and applied. Is the impact of legal, political and social processes 'just' in terms of their substantive effect on people's life-chances? By what criteria can they be judged? In this sense, debates about substantive justice concern questions about the basic framework of social and political organisation.

John Rawls' magisterial *A Theory of Justice* has undoubtedly been the pivotal reference-point for debates about justice since its publication in 1972. Indeed it has rightly been credited with a revival of substantive political philosophy in the last thirty years, following its eclipse in the middle of the twentieth century when the dominance in philosophy in general of logical positivism and linguistic analysis cast doubt on the meaningfulness of normative theories. For all its influence, Rawls' work has generated a library of critical debate. In the 1970s the main thrust of attack came from the libertarian right, notably Robert Nozick's 1974 book *Anarchy, State and Utopia*. During the 1980s both Rawls and Nozick came under attack by what is usually referred to as the communitarian critique. In response to these arguments Rawls modified and developed his views in a series of papers during the 1980s and 90s, culminating in his 1993 book *Political Liberalism*.

The focus of this chapter will be on Rawls' *Theory of Justice*, and the debates it has engendered. However, before looking at Rawls' seminal work in detail, we will consider some earlier modern analyses of justice, notably utilitarianism, the background against which Rawls honed his own contribution.

Modern Theories of Justice Before Rawls

The theories discussed in this chapter are referred to as 'modern' because they share certain very fundamental features – despite all the impassioned disputes between them – that mark them off from ancient and medieval perspectives. They are all 'modern' in the very extended temporal sense that they have developed since the Renaissance and Reformation. More importantly they implicitly share some basic assumptions that contrast with classical approaches.

The most fundamental of these tacit assumptions is methodological agnosticism. This stance is shared with most modern philosophy, and has been aptly referred to as 'Cartesian anxiety' (Bernstein 1983). It is taken for granted implicitly that there are no absolutely indubitable starting points capable of providing an Archimedean lever for arguments. Even if writers do feel certain about particular propositions or values, they are aware that they operate in a world where there are radically conflicting perspectives held by others. This was made clear by such features of the early modern world as the voyages of discovery revealing the existence of many fundamentally different cultures, and the wars of religion and then revolution that divided Europe, and the New World, after the fifteenth century. Thus all modern theories assume that little if anything can be taken for granted in philosophical argument, certainly not in such an essentially contested area as the meaning of justice.

A related broad feature of modern theories of justice is their *humanism*. Implicitly the standpoint for assessing the justice of social arrangements is some conception of human well being, rather than any abstract value in itself, or some collective good unless it is a means of achieving greater individual welfare. Furthermore, even theories that are far from egalitarian nonetheless do not claim any fundamental differences in importance or value between categories of people, unlike classical perspectives such as Aristotle's which explicitly treat women or slaves as qualitatively less meritorious. Modern perspectives on justice accord all people 'equal concern and respect' (in Dworkin's phrase) at some point in the argument, even if this is seen as compatible with quite unequal outcomes (Dworkin 2000).

1. Early Modern Theories of Justice

In the seventeenth and eighteenth centuries two broad approaches to theorising justice can be distinguished, both with roots in earlier thought, and continuing to influence later discussions too: social contract theories and natural rights theories. These are not mutually incompatible and most writers clearly combined elements of both approaches.

The notion of a 'social contract' is most famously associated with the work of such leading early modern political philosophers as Thomas Hobbes (1588–1679), John Locke (1632–1704) and Jean Jacques Rousseau (1712–1778), although all these writers used the concept in quite different ways. The basic shared argument is that social arrangements can be regarded as just to the extent that they genuinely have the *consent* of those involved. The justice of a particular society derives from the members of it having entered into a contract agreeing to its rules and patterns, or at any rate being presumed to have done so. (Whereas earlier theories tend not to be explicit about whether the social contract they postulate actually occurred or is a hypothetical 'as if' device for assessing social arrangements, John Rawls' contemporary revival of the contractarian approach clearly only uses the notion as a thought experiment, as will be shown below.)

Contractarian theories were usually combined with the idea of 'natural rights' that defined boundaries for the legitimacy of states established by (actual or hypothetical) social contracts. The justice of a society and its laws is assessed by whether it respects or infringes people's natural rights. In so far as these natural rights are grounded either in a theological framework, or in a view of human nature and its demands, there is clearly an affinity with the natural law perspectives (discussed in Chapter 2).

In Hobbes' perspective the 'social contract' is essentially the lesser of several evils, representing a kind of rough but necessary justice. Without regulation, in a 'state of nature', people would compete with each other to such an extent that they would inevitably infringe each others' interests, with the result that life would be 'nasty, brutish and short'. The only way out of this 'war of all against all' is for people to agree to a social contract establishing a sovereign with the power to control conflict and restrain strife. Whether or not actually existing sovereigns did in fact emerge by such a contract is immaterial. Even if they acquired their power by force, it would be rational to deem people to have transferred power to the sovereign in return for protection by a putative contract, as the only feasible alternative to mutual destruction.

Locke's perspective incorporates assumptions about natural rights into his conception of the state of nature. People are seen as naturally enjoying rights to life, liberty, and estate (property). With this more benign view of the state of nature, the legitimacy of the state derived from it is correspondingly more conditional. People can acquire property justly, either by just primary acquisition of what one has mixed with one's labour, or by uncoerced exchange. To Locke the problem with an unregulated state of nature is that some might try to gain property by trespass, not by just acquisition. In order to protect against this, people are deemed to have established civil society by entering into a contract of mutual protection by a state. But as civil society and the state exist in order to protect natural rights, the state remains subject to these rights. If the state and its laws infringe natural rights, this can justify rebellion.

Rousseau viewed the social contract as representing the 'general will', realising the social aspect of people's natures, not just a prudent surrender of individual autonomy for the sake of self-preservation. People have dual characteristics: they have the potential both for egoistic striving and for communal sociability. Thus civil society and the state are not only necessary impositions restraining inter-personal conflict, but they are also the realisation of potentials within human nature. If the state is to be the expression of sociability rather than a tyrannical imposition it must accord citizens liberty according to their natural rights. Otherwise, consent to it could be revoked by the general will, and it could legitimately be overthrown and replaced by another regime.

In sum, early modern theories of justice rested on two basic notions, combined in various ways in the work of particular writers. Social arrangements and laws could be seen as just in that they ultimately derived from a putative contract, embodying people's enlightened self-interest. Whilst this underlay the basic legitimacy of states and the laws they promulgated and enforced, in many perspectives boundaries of legitimacy were defined by a notion of 'natural rights' the infringement of which justified the withdrawal of consent. Both these aspects were criticised by utilitarianism, which became the dominant political theory of the nineteenth and twentieth centuries, and the primary negative reference point for Rawls and subsequent debates.

2. Utilitarianism

Pioneered by Jeremy Bentham (1748–1832), and brought to its most sophisticated formulation by John Stuart Mill (1806–1873), utilitarianism remains in many ways the taken-for-granted 'common-sense' framework for most political debate today, despite being subject to nearly two centuries of philosophical critique. It was built upon a withering dismissal of earlier perspectives. Bentham rejected social contract theories as based on a fiction, and memorably dismissed natural rights theories as 'nonsense on stilts'. Where could such supposed rights come from, he argued, except through some ungrounded metaphysical speculations about God or an intrinsic human nature? Instead he proposed a deceptively simple test for the justice or merit of laws and social policies, based on his psychological analysis that human beings were motivated by the pursuit of 'utility' ie the maximum difference of pleasure over pain. Thus the test for judging any social arrangements was whether they maximised utility, the 'greatest happiness of the greatest number' – the so-called 'felicific calculus'.

Utilitarianism had many elements that made it immediately and widely appealing. First, it offered an apparently simple test for assessing what policies should be pursued in any situation. Second, it had an aura of benevolence at its core: concern for human happiness. Third, it had an egalitarian foundation: the calculus was based on equal consideration of every person's utility. With its egalitarian and humanist assumptions utilitarianism was the quintessential modern political philosophy, sweeping all before it and still exercising a powerful hold. Dennett's analysis of Darwinism as 'universal acid' can in many ways be applied to utilitarianism (Dennett 1995). Once formulated it eats its way through all alternatives. It is hard to imagine how it can be argued against fundamentally: policies that produce the greatest *unhappiness* of the greatest number are hardly attractive! Nonetheless utilitarianism immediately attracted much criticism, and has been reformulated or rejected many times by philosophers in the last two centuries.

Criticism has been levelled at many aspects of utilitarianism. To what kinds of decisions should the felicific calculus apply? What counts as utility, and how is it to be counted? Does utilitarianism really treat all people fairly? In response to such problems utilitarianism has become increasingly complex in its formulations, which of course detracts from the initial appeal of its apparent simplicity.

WHAT DECISIONS DOES UTILITARIANISM APPLY TO?

The main problem in relation to the scope of utilitarianism is whether it is applied to each and every single act, or to broad rules and patterns of behaviour. Act utilitarians argue most straightforwardly that there can be no reason in principle for adopting utilitarianism as the principle for deciding what rules should be promulgated and enforced but not applying this also to individual acts. However, many problems arise with act utilitarianism, above all the complex relationship between the consequences of single actions and wider patterns of behaviour. For example, there might well be occasions when an act of lying could plausibly be regarded as minimising the pain of all immediately involved parties – 'white' lying – and hence to satisfy the felicific calculus. But it is also plausible that as a rule the condemnation of lying is a better basis for general trust and consequently the maximisation of happiness. To restrict the scope of utilitarianism to rules not acts, however, is hard to justify in principle, and leaves us without a benchmark for evaluating individual acts. This tension between act- and rule-utilitarianism remains a vexed issue. (A related problem is the means/ends or 'dirty hands' issue. Can actions that clearly cause a net balance of pain in their immediate consequences, and hence are wrong in utilitarian (and many other) terms (say, torturing a captured terrorist) be justified by their wider beneficial consequences (for example if the terrorist reveals the location of a bomb)?)

HOW IS UTILITY TO BE COUNTED?

The Benthamite notion of a felicific calculus is a metaphor that dissolves as soon as it is probed. Is 'happiness' a purely subjective state of affairs, or is it to be assessed by some objective standard of satisfaction of wants? If it is the latter than who judges which are the wants to be satisfied, and by what criteria? How can a tyrannical imposition of the evaluator's conceptions on others be avoided, when one person's meat is another's poison? But if utility is to be regarded subjectively, other problems arise. We have no happiness detector for assessing people's subjective experiences of pleasure or pain.

Economics long ago resolved to deal with this issue by substituting the notion of revealed preference for utility: what people really, really, really want is what they demand in practice (see Chapter 17). Whilst this allowed economics to develop as a discipline, it does not really solve the philosophical issues of how we can judge whether particular states of affairs maximise happiness or not. Revealed preferences may in many obvious ways inaccurately reflect what makes for the happiness of a person. What if the power of advertising and consumer culture shape people's expressed desires in ways that lead away from their own deeper interests? Or if there are psychological complexities in people's wants, for example addictions or ambivalences? Does satisfying an alcoholic's revealed preference for whisky over water maximise happiness? Does satisfying my desire to turn off the alarm clock maximise my happiness if I have a train to catch (or a chapter on theories of justice to write)? Clearly, assessing what achieves utility maximisation is far from a precise simple metric, and leaves much scope for differences of viewpoint.

WHAT COUNTS AS UTILITY?

Utilitarianism has an initial appeal because of its apparently thoroughgoing egalitarianism and liberalism. Everyone's utility is weighed in the balance to find what achieves the greatest happiness of the greatest number. There is no 'judgementalism' exercised between people or their tastes. Pushpin ranks with poetry, in Bentham's phrase. Such a complete lack of discrimination between different desires immediately rankled with many critics. Indeed the implication that utilitarianism threatens to erode all values to a lowest common denominator remains one of the most common ways of attacking it. Utilitarian has indeed become a virtual synonym for crude materialism. John Stuart Mill wrestled with this problem, and sought to distance utilitarianism from a complete assimilation of all values to a single dimension. 'Better Socrates dissatisfied than a pig satisfied', he claimed. Nonetheless he was unable to resolve the problem of distinguishing between the value of different kinds of happiness in a non-subjective, non-rhetorical way.

A more specific aspect of the issue of what satisfactions to count in the felicific balance is what Ronald Dworkin has called the 'external preferences' problem: where A has clear preferences about what B does. How do we deal with anti-utilitarian or illiberal values? Does a sadist's pleasure count equally with the victim's pain? Does the homophobe's dislike of homosexual activity count in the balance alongside the gay person's happiness? Should the racist's unhappiness at encountering other ethnic groups be calculated in the same way as the desire of all people to be able to move freely and be equally eligible for all life-chances? Is the anti-pornographer's discomfort at seeing 'adult' bookshops weighed in the same way as the voyeur's pleasure in shopping there?

Dworkin argues that allowing such values into the reckoning is to 'double-count' the preferences of the illiberal: it is to take into account both their own taste for a puritanical life-style and the 'external' distaste they experience at the contemplation of activities they disapprove of. It is not clear, however, that this provides a non-evaluative way out of the problem. Many critics of pornography, for example, would not accept that their case rests only upon an 'external' revulsion at the activities of others. Rather they would argue that pornography involves a number of wider harms. The notion of 'external preferences' is clearly related to the idea of a separable sphere of 'private' activities that are 'not the law's business' which was the pivot of the celebrated Hart/Devlin debate in the 1960s (Hart 1963a; Devlin 1965). It is far from clear that 'external preferences' can provide an objective yardstick for excluding particular tastes from consideration, without making a moral evaluation of them.

Is utilitarianism fair?

One of the appeals of utilitarianism is its apparent egalitarianism. In the felicific calculus everyone's happiness counts equally, there are no favourites. However, the problem is that people are treated equally as interchangeable bearers of utility, not as particular individuals. As Rawls put it, there is no 'respect for persons'.

The initial equal consideration of all individuals in the utilitarian balance is compatible with highly unequal or unfair outcomes if this achieves the greatest happiness of the greatest number. Say that the population as a whole could be made happier by enslaving a minority to serve their needs. If the pleasure of the majority was enhanced to a greater degree than the abject misery of the slaves there could be no objection on the basis of the straightforward greatest happiness formula. Similarly if the population as a whole could be protected against crime by the deterrent effect of the public torture of a few supposed 'criminals', even if they were in fact randomly selected innocents, the felicific calculus could be satisfied despite the extreme injustice involved.

John Stuart Mill called this the 'tyranny of the majority' problem. He argued that it could be resolved only by building into utilitarianism a platform of minimum concern for every person's welfare below which they would not be allowed to fall, even though this might be incompatible with the greatest happiness of the greatest number. General utility cannot be a justification, he claimed, for denying some people 'the essentials of human well-being'. But how do we identify what these essentials are? Is this a way back in for the notion of natural rights that Bentham had dismissed as nonsense?

The issues discussed are clearly not knock-down reasons for rejecting utilitarianism. John Stuart Mill incorporated them into his more sophisticated version in his 1863 *Utilitarianism*, and the perspective has continued to be developed and debated (Smart and Williams 1973). This has been at the expense of the bold simplicity of Bentham's original formula, as refinements and qualifications have sought to grapple with the difficulties pointed out by critics. Many have felt that this indicates utilitarianism is fatally flawed. They have attempted to develop alternative modern theories of justice that retain utilitarianism's fundamental humanism and egalitarianism whilst rejecting what are seen as irredeemable defects, such as the failure to respect persons who are treated merely as vehicles for the greater good. The most notable of these has undoubtedly been the work of John Rawls, and the debate it has inspired.

Rawls' Theory of Justice

John Rawls' 1971 book *A Theory of Justice* is generally credited with reviving normative political philosophy. It has become a landmark in academic debate, generating a huge literature of exposition, critique and debate. In many ways it can be seen as the most coherent defence of the welfare state consensus that had dominated all liberal democracies since the Second World War. Yet paradoxically its publication came as the welfare state was beginning to be eroded by the rise of neo-liberal governments. Thus Rawls' huge academic influence has been in stark contrast to his lack of impact on policy. Some have sought to appropriate him as a potential guru of the 'third way' politics of the 1990s, but this almost certainly grossly underestimates the radical thrust of Rawls' analysis.

1. Justice As Fairness

Although *A Theory of Justice* is a vast and complex work of nearly 800 pages its essential thesis is very simple, and most of the volume is taken up with a detailed derivation and defence of it. Rawls' fundamental claim is that 'justice as fairness' can be defined by two basic principles. What is meant by 'justice as fairness', Rawls' major premise? Fairness to Rawls means neutrality, deciding what is just independently of any vested interests, bias or partiality. In the language of his later reformulation in his 1993 book *Political Liberalism*, principles of justice must be 'publicly reasonable', ie arguable from a diversity of particular social stakes or values. The core of this idea can be illustrated by a homely example that will be familiar to parents. Distributing pieces of birthday cake at a childrens' party is fraught with hazards, including the prospects of squabbles about whose slice is bigger. One device for minimising this tension is to separate the slicing and the choosing. If one child cuts the cake, and another distributes them, the slicer has every incentive to make each piece as close to equal as possible, as she does not know which one will be chosen as hers. Rawls' theory uses this device as its basis: principles agreed to in a position where nobody knows what their particular share is (behind a 'veil of ignorance') are 'fair' in the sense that they are not the result of vested interest.

2. Rawls' Methodology

Rawls' derivation of his two principles of justice uses two distinct methods of argument: the device of a hypothetical contract, and the idea of 'reflective equilibrium'.

The Contract

Rawls' resuscitates the old notion of the social contract, although quite explicitly as a hypothetical 'as if' rhetorical device. Rawls envisages an 'original position' (OP) in which people can negotiate and agree to the principles that are to govern their society fairly, stripped of the influence of vested interests and partisanship. The contract device has two functions. The first is *exposition* – it conveniently sums up the conditions under which a fair agreement can be reached. The second is *justification*: if the exposition of the OP is accepted then the principles agreed to in it can be regarded as fairly arrived at and hence as principles of justice. The OP is specifically constituted so that reasoning within it is impartial: all people are treated as worthy of equal consideration through abstracting from the influence of the particular wants, interests, tastes and values they have in their actual positions in life.

Reflective Equilibrium

Much of Rawls' book is taken up by a detailed comparison of rival theories of justice, especially utilitarianism, and arguments supporting his two principles. This largely rests on the method he calls 'reflective equilibrium'. The implications of the two principles, and of rival theories, are contrasted with reference to 'our considered judgements' about specific issues (say that slavery is wrong). If the implications of a general theory of justice contradict these 'considered judgements' there are two alternatives. We must reject and reformulate either the considered judgement or the general theory, for example by modifying the specifications of the OP, and then compare with the considered judgements again. After such shuttling back and forth between general theory and concrete judgements, and readjustments at both ends, 'reflective equilibrium' emerges. This is defined as coherence between a general theory of justice (say the two principles) and 'our considered judgements' on specific issues.

Since the conditions of the OP are tested and adjusted by the reflective equilibrium process, the contract argument really is a rhetorical device for exposition, rather than a proof of the two principles. The core value in Rawls' argument seems to be coherence: there must be consistency between one's theory of what is justice and one's particular views about the justice of specific arrangements. But neither is derived from the other: they are rendered compatible by the reflective equilibrium process – shuttle diplomacy in which both may be compromised.

3. The Original Position

Rawls uses the term 'original position' (OP) to refer to a hypothetical situation in which people are able to choose general principles for the organisation of their society in conditions of fairness, giving equal weight to each individual. Although analytically they can be regarded as agreeing to 'principles of justice', from their point of view the parties in the OP are negotiating a contract to protect and advance their own self-interests. They are seeking to achieve the best for themselves in the contract, with no assumptions of altruism or concern for justice.

Discussion in the OP takes place behind a 'veil of ignorance'. The participants do not know the particular tastes, abilities, conceptions of the good or positions in life that they will hold in the society. It is this that makes the outcome of their negotiations fair in the sense of unbiased by partisan interests and commitments. However, they are deemed to have certain information about social organisation and human motivation in general, which animates their bargaining. They know that irrespective of particular interests and tastes people might have there are some 'primary basic goods' that help anyone to fulfil their plans for life, irrespective of their specific content. People in the OP will thus seek to negotiate a contract that gives them the most satisfactory possible arrangement of such social primary basic goods as rights and liberties, opportunities, powers, self-respect, income and wealth. In this negotiation Rawls postulates that people operate with certain assumptions about human motivation in general (not knowing the specific personalities they will actually have). People are assumed not to be altruistic: they are concerned to look after their own self-interest, not others. However, they are not envious (if envy was assumed equality is the only distributional pattern people in the OP would accept). Nonetheless, since self-respect is seen as one of the primary basic goods, excessive inequality would be rejected as threatening this. Whilst people are assumed not to be altruistic in general, they are taken to have some 'family-feeling', being concerned about the welfare of those closely related to them. This makes them willing to plan fairly for future generations.

Rawls (1973, 3–22)

CHAPTER I. JUSTICE AS FAIRNESS

In this introductory chapter I sketch some of the main ideas of the theory of justice I wish to develop. The exposition is informal and intended to prepare the way for the more detailed arguments that follow. Unavoidably there is some overlap between this and later discussions. I begin by describing the role of justice in social cooperation and with a brief account of the primary subject of justice, the basic structure of society. I then present the main idea of justice as fairness, a theory of justice that generalizes and carries to a higher level of abstraction the traditional conception of the social contract. The compact of society is replaced by an initial situation that incorporates certain procedural constraints on arguments designed to lead to an original agreement on principles of justice. I also take up, for purposes of clarification and contrast, the classical utilitarian and intuitionist conceptions of justice and consider some of the differences between these views and justice as fairness. My guiding aim is to work out a theory of justice that is a viable alternative to these doctrines which have long dominated our philosophical tradition.

1. THE ROLE OF JUSTICE

Justice is the first virtue of social institutions, as truth is of systems of thought. A theory however elegant and economical must be rejected or revised if it is untrue; likewise laws and institutions no matter how efficient and well-arranged must be reformed or abolished if they are unjust. Each person possesses an inviolability founded on justice that even the welfare of society as a whole cannot override. For this reason justice denies that the loss of freedom for some is made right by a greater good shared by others. It does not allow that the sacrifices imposed on a few are outweighed by the larger sum of advantages enjoyed by many. Therefore in a just society the liberties of equal citizenship are taken as settled; the rights secured by justice are not subject to political bargaining or to the calculus of social interests. The only thing that permits us to acquiesce in an erroneous theory is the lack of a better one; analogously, an injustice is tolerable only when it is necessary to avoid an even greater injustice. Being first virtues of human activities, truth and justice are uncompromising.

These propositions seem to express our intuitive conviction of the primacy of justice. No doubt they are expressed too strongly. In any event I wish to inquire whether these contentions or others similar to them are sound, and if so how they can be accounted for. To this end it is necessary to work out a theory of justice in the light of which these assertions can be interpreted and assessed. I shall begin by considering the role of the principles of justice. Let us assume, to fix ideas, that a society is a more or less self-sufficient association of persons who in their relations to one another recognize certain rules of conduct as binding and who for the most part act in accordance with them. Suppose further that these rules specify a system of co-operation designed to advance the good of those taking part in it. Then, although a society is a cooperative venture for mutual advantage, it is typically marked by a conflict as well as by an identity of interests. There is an identity of interests since social cooperation makes possible a better life for all than any would have if each were to live solely by his own efforts. There is a conflict of interests since persons are not indifferent as to how the greater benefits produced by their collaboration are distributed, for in order to pursue their ends they each prefer a larger to a lesser share. A set of principles is required for choosing among the various social arrangements which determine this division of advantages and for underwriting an agreement on the proper distributive shares. These principles are the principles of social justice: they provide a way of assigning rights and duties in the basic institutions of society and they define the appropriate distribution of the benefits and burdens of social co-operation.

Now let us say that a society is well-ordered when it is not only designed to advance the good of its members but when it is also effectively regulated by a public conception of justice. That is, it is a society in which (1) everyone accepts and knows that the others accept the same principles of justice, and (2) the basic social institutions generally satisfy and are generally known to satisfy these principles. In this case while men may put forth excessive demands on one another, they nevertheless acknowledge a common point of view from which their claims may be adjudicated. If men's inclination to self-interest makes their vigilance against one another necessary, their public sense of justice makes their secure association together possible. Among individuals with disparate aims and purposes a shared conception of justice establishes the bonds of civic friendship; the general desire for justice limits the pursuit of other ends. One may think of a public conception of justice as constituting the fundamental charter of a well-ordered human association.

Existing societies are of course seldom well-ordered in this sense, for what is just and unjust is usually in dispute. Men disagree about which principles should define the basic terms of their association. Yet we may still say, despite this disagreement, that they each have a conception of justice. That is, they understand the need for, and they are prepared to affirm, a characteristic bed of principles for assigning basic rights and duties and for determining what they take to be the proper distribution of the benefits and burdens of social cooperation. Thus it seems natural to think of the concept of justice as distinct from the various conceptions of justice and as being specified by the role which these different sets of principles, these different conceptions, have in common. Those who hold different conceptions of justice can, then, still agree that institutions are just when no arbitrary distinctions are made between persons in the assigning of basic rights and duties and when the rules determine a proper balance between competing claims to the advantages of social life. Men can agree to this description of just institutions since the notions of an arbitrary distinction and of a proper balance, which are included in the concept of justice, are left open for each to interpret according to the principles of justice that he accepts. These principles single out which similarities and differences among persons are relevant in determining rights and duties and they specify which division of advantages is appropriate. Clearly this distinction between the concept and the various conceptions of justice settles no important questions. It simply helps to identify the role of the principles of social justice.

Some measure of agreement in conceptions of justice is, however, not the only prerequisite for a viable human community. There are other fundamental social problems, in particular those of coordination, efficiency, and stability. Thus the plans of individuals need to be fitted together so that their activities are compatible with one another and they can all be carried through without anyone's legitimate expectations being severely disappointed. Moreover, the execution of these plans should lead to the achievement of social ends in ways that are efficient and consistent with justice. And finally, the scheme of social cooperation must be stable: it must be more or less regularly complied with and its basic rules willingly acted upon; and when infractions occur, stabilizing forces should exist that prevent further violations and tend to restore the arrangement. Now it is evident that these three problems are connected with that of justice. In the absence of a certain measure of agreement on what is just and unjust, it is clearly more difficult for individuals to coordinate their plans efficiently in order to insure that mutually beneficial arrangements are maintained. Distrust and resentment corrode the ties of civility, and suspicion and hostility tempt men to act in ways they would otherwise avoid. So while the distinctive role of conceptions of justice is to specify basic rights and duties and to determine the appropriate distributive shares, the way in which a conception does this is bound to affect the problems of efficiency, coordination, and stability. We cannot, in general, assess a conception of justice by its distributive role alone, however useful this role may be in identifying the concept of justice. We must take into account its wider connections; for even though justice has a certain priority, being the most important virtue of institutions, it is still true that, other things equal, one conception of justice is preferable to another when its broader consequences are more desirable.

2. THE SUBJECT OF JUSTICE

Many different kinds of things are said to be just and unjust: not only laws, institutions, and social systems, but also particular actions of many kinds, including decisions, judgments, and imputations. We also call the attitudes and dispositions of persons, and persons themselves, just and unjust. Our topic, however, is that of social justice. For us the primary subject of justice is the basic structure of society, or more exactly, the way in which the major social institutions distribute fundamental rights and duties and determine the division of advantages from social cooperation. By major institutions I understand the political constitution and the principal economic and social arrangements.

Thus the legal protection of freedom of thought and liberty of conscience, competitive markets, private property in the means of production, and the monogamous family are examples of major social institutions. Taken together as one scheme, the major institutions define men's rights and duties and influence their life- prospects, what they can expect to be and how well they can hope to do. The basic structure is the primary subject of justice because its effects are so profound and present from the start. The intuitive notion here is that this structure contains various social positions and that men born into different positions have different expectations of life determined, in part, by the political system as well as by economic and social circumstances. In this way the institutions of society favor certain starting places over others. These are especially deep inequalities. Not only are they pervasive, but they affect men's initial chances in life; yet they cannot possibly be justified by an appeal to the notions of merit or desert. It is these inequalities, presumably inevitable in the basic structure of any society, to which the principles of social justice must in the first instance apply. These principles, then, regulate the choice of a political constitution and the main elements of the economic and social system. The justice of a social scheme depends essentially on how fundamental rights and duties are assigned and on the economic opportunities and social conditions in the various sectors of society.

The scope of our inquiry is limited in two ways. First of all, I am concerned with a special case of the problem of justice. I shall not consider the justice of institutions and social practices generally, nor except in passing the justice of the law of nations and of relations between states. Therefore, if one supposes that the concept of justice applies whenever there is an allotment of something rationally regarded as advantageous or disadvantageous, then we are interested in only one instance of its application. There is no reason to suppose ahead of time that the principles satisfactory for the basic structure hold for all cases. These principles may not work for the rules and practices of private associations or for those of less comprehensive social groups. They may be irrelevant for the various informal conventions and customs of everyday life; they may not elucidate the justice, or perhaps better, the fairness of voluntary cooperative arrangements or procedures for making contractual agreements. The conditions for the law of nations may require different principles arrived at in a somewhat different way. I shall be satisfied if it is possible to formulate a reasonable conception of justice for the basic structure of society conceived for the time being as a closed system isolated from other societies. The significance of this special case is obvious and needs no explanation. It is natural to conjecture that once we have a sound theory for this case, the remaining problems of justice will prove more tractable in the light of it. With suitable modifications such a theory should provide the key for some of these other questions.

The other limitation on our discussion is that for the most part I examine the principles of justice that would regulate a well-ordered society. Everyone is presumed to act justly and to do his part in upholding just institutions. Though justice may be, as Hume remarked, the cautious, jealous virtue, we can still ask what a perfectly just society would be like. Thus I consider primarily what I call strict compliance as opposed to partial compliance theory. The latter studies the principles that govern how we are to deal with injustice. It comprises such topics as the theory of punishment, the doctrine of just war, and the justification of the various ways of opposing unjust regimes, ranging from civil disobedience and militant resistance to revolution and rebellion. Also included here are questions of compensatory justice and of weighing one form of institutional injustice against another. Obviously the problems of partial compliance theory are the pressing and urgent matters. These are the things that we are faced with in everyday life. The reason for beginning with ideal theory is that it provides, I believe, the only basis for the systematic grasp of these more pressing problems. The discussion of civil disobedience, for example, depends upon it. At least, I shall assume that a deeper understanding can be gained in no other way, and that the nature and aims of a perfectly just society is the fundamental part of the theory of justice.

Now admittedly the concept of the basic structure is somewhat vague. It is not always clear which institutions or features thereof should be included. But it would be premature to worry about this matter here. I shall proceed by discussing principles which do apply to what is certainly a part of the basic structure as intuitively understood; I shall then try to extend the application of these principles so that they cover what would appear to be the main elements of this structure. Perhaps these principles will turn out to be perfectly general, although this is unlikely. It is sufficient that they apply to the most important cases of social justice. The point to keep in mind is that a conception of justice for the basic structure is worth having for its own sake. It should not be dismissed because its principles are not everywhere satisfactory.

A conception of social justice, then, is to be regarded as providing in the first instance a standard whereby the distributive aspects of the basic structure of society are to be assessed. This standard, however, is not to be confused with the principles defining the other virtues, for the basic structure, and social arrangements generally, may be efficient or inefficient, liberal or illiberal, and many other things, as well as just or unjust. A complete conception defining principles for all the virtues of the basic structure, together with their respective weights when they conflict, is more than a conception of justice; it is a social ideal. The principles of justice are but a part, although perhaps the most important part, of such a conception. A social ideal in turn is connected with a conception of society, a vision of the way in which the aims and purposes of social cooperation are to be understood. The various conceptions of justice are the outgrowth of different notions of society against the background of opposing views of the natural necessities and opportunities of human life. Fully to understand a conception of justice we must make explicit the conception of social cooperation from which it derives. But in doing this we should not lose sight of the special role of the principles of justice or of the primary subject to which they apply.

...

3. THE MAIN IDEA OF THE THEORY OF JUSTICE

My aim is to present a conception of justice which generalizes and carries to a higher level of abstraction the familiar theory of the social contract as found, say, in Locke, Rousseau, and Kant. In order to do this we are not to think of the original contract as one to enter a particular society or to set up a particular form of government. Rather, the guiding idea is that the principles of justice for the basic structure of society are the object of the original agreement. They are the principles that free and rational persons concerned to further their own interests would accept in an initial position of equality as defining the fundamental terms of their association. These principles are to regulate all further agreements; they specify the kinds of social cooperation that can be entered into and the forms of government that can be established. This way of regarding the principles of justice I shall call justice as fairness.

Thus we are to imagine that those who engage in social cooperation choose together, in one joint act, the principles which are to assign basic rights and duties and to determine the division of social benefits. Men are to decide in advance how they are to regulate their claims against one another and what is to be the foundation charter of their society. Just as each person must decide by rational reflection what constitutes his good, that is, the system of ends which it is rational for him to pursue, so a group of persons must decide once and for all what is to count among them as just and unjust. The choice which rational men would make in this hypothetical situation of equal liberty, assuming for the present that this choice problem has a solution, determines the principles of justice.

In justice as fairness the original position of equality corresponds to the state of nature in the traditional theory of the social contract. This original position is not, of course, thought of as an actual historical state of affairs, much less as a primitive condition of culture. It is understood as a purely hypothetical situation characterized so as to lead to a certain conception of justice. Among the essential features of this situation is that no one knows his place in society, his class position or social status, nor does any one know his fortune in the distribution of natural assets and abilities, his intelligence, strength, and the like. I shall even assume that the parties do not know their conceptions of the good or their special psychological propensities. The principles of justice are chosen behind a veil of ignorance. This ensures that no one is advantaged or disadvantaged in the choice of principles by the outcome of natural chance or the contingency of social circumstances. Since all are similarly situated and no one is able to design principles to favor his particular condition, the principles of justice are the result of a fair agreement or bargain. For given the circumstances of the original position, the symmetry of everyone's relations to each other, this initial situation is fair between individuals as moral persons, that is, as rational beings with their own ends and capable, I shall assume, of a sense of justice. The original position is, one might say, the appropriate initial status quo, and thus the fundamental agreements reached in it are fair. This explains the propriety of the name 'justice as fairness': it conveys the idea that the principles of justice are agreed to in an initial situation that is fair. The name does not mean that the concepts of justice and fairness are the same, any more than the phrase 'poetry as metaphor' means that the concepts of poetry and metaphor are the same.

Justice as fairness begins, as I have said, with one of the most general of all choices which persons might make together, namely, with the choice of the first principles of a conception of justice which is to regulate all subsequent criticism and reform of institutions. Then, having chosen a conception of justice, we can suppose that they are to choose a constitution and a legislature to enact laws, and so on, all in accordance with the principles of justice initially agreed upon. Our social situation is just if it is such that by this sequence of hypothetical agreements we would have contracted into the general system of rules which defines it. Moreover, assuming that the original position does determine a set of principles (that is, that a particular conception of justice would be chosen), it will then be true that whenever social institutions satisfy these principles those engaged in them can say to one another that they are cooperating on terms to which they would agree if they were free and equal persons whose relations with respect to one another were fair. They could all view their arrangements as meeting the stipulations which they would acknowledge in an initial situation that embodies widely accepted and reasonable constraints on the choice of principles. The general recognition of this fact would provide the basis for a public acceptance of the corresponding principles of justice. No society can, of course, be a scheme of cooperation which men enter voluntarily in a literal sense; each person finds himself placed at birth in some particular position in some particular society, and the nature of this position materially affects his life prospects. Yet a society satisfying the principles of justice as fairness comes as close as a society can to being a voluntary scheme, for it meets the principles which free and equal persons would assent to under circumstances that are fair. In this sense its members are autonomous and the obligations they recognize self-imposed.

One feature of justice as fairness is to think of the parties in the initial situation as rational and mutually disinterested. This does not mean that the parties are egoists, that is, individuals with only certain kinds of interests, say in wealth, prestige, and domination. But they are conceived as not taking an interest in one another's interests. They are to presume that even their spiritual aims may be opposed, in the way that the aims of those of different religions may be opposed. Moreover, the concept of rationality must be interpreted as far as possible in the narrow sense, standard in economic theory, of taking the most effective means to given ends. I shall modify this concept to some extent, as explained later, but one must try to avoid introducing into it any controversial ethical elements. The initial situation must be characterized by stipulations that are widely accepted.

In working out the conception of justice as fairness one main task clearly is to determine which principles of justice would be chosen in the original position. To do this we must describe this situation in some detail and formulate with care the problem of choice which it presents. These matters I shall take up in the immediately succeeding chapters. It may be observed, however, that once the principles of justice are thought of as arising from an original agreement in a situation of equality, it is an open question whether the principle of utility would be acknowledged. Offhand it hardly seems likely that persons who view themselves as equals, entitled to press their claims upon one another, would agree to a principle which may require lesser life prospects for some simply for the sake of a greater sum of advantages enjoyed by others. Since each desires to protect his interests, his capacity to advance his conception of the good, no one has a reason to acquiesce in an enduring loss for himself in order to bring about a greater net balance of satisfaction. In the absence of strong and lasting benevolent impulses, a rational man would not accept a basic structure merely because it maximized the algebraic sum of advantages irrespective of its permanent effects on his own basic rights and interests. Thus it seems that the principle of utility is incompatible with the conception of social cooperation among equals for mutual advantage. It appears to be inconsistent with the idea of reciprocity implicit in the notion of a well-ordered society. Or, at any rate, so I shall argue.

I shall maintain instead that the persons in the initial situation would choose two rather different principles: the first requires equality in the assignment of basic rights and duties, while the second holds that social and economic inequalities, for example inequalities of wealth and authority, are just only if they result in compensating benefits for everyone, and in particular for the least advantaged members of society. These principles rule out justifying institutions on the grounds that the hardships of some are offset by a greater good in the aggregate. It may be expedient but it is not just that some should have less in order that others may prosper. But there is no injustice in the greater benefits earned by a few provided that the situation of persons not so fortunate is thereby improved. The intuitive idea is that since everyone's well-being depends upon a scheme of cooperation without which no one could have a satisfactory life, the division of advantages should be such as to draw forth the willing cooperation of everyone taking part in it, including those less well situated. Yet this can be expected only if reasonable terms are proposed. The two principles mentioned seem to be a fair agreement on the basis of which those better endowed, or more fortunate in their social position, neither of which we can be said to deserve, could expect the willing cooperation of others when some workable scheme is a necessary condition of the welfare of all. Once we decide to look for a conception of justice that nullifies the accidents of natural endowment and the contingencies of social circumstance as counters in quest for political and economic advantage, we are led to these principles. They express the result of leaving aside those aspects of the social world that seem arbitrary from a moral point of view.

The problem of the choice of principles, however, is extremely difficult. I do not expect the answer I shall suggest to be convincing to everyone. It is, therefore, worth noting from the outset that justice as fairness, like other contract views, consists of two parts: (1) an interpretation of the initial situation and of the problem of choice posed there, and (2) a set of principles which, it is argued, would be agreed to. One may accept the first part of the theory (or some variant thereof), but not the other, and conversely. The concept of the initial contractual situation may seem reasonable although the particular principles proposed are rejected. To be sure, I want to maintain that the most appropriate conception of this situation does lead to principles of justice contrary to utilitarianism and perfectionism and therefore that the contract doctrine provides an alternative to these views. Still, one may dispute this contention even though one grants that the contractarian method is a useful way of studying ethical theories and of setting forth their underlying assumptions.

Justice as fairness is an example of what I have called a contract theory. Now there may be an objection to the term 'contract' and related expressions, but I think it will serve reasonably well. Many words have misleading connotations which at first are likely to confuse. The terms 'utility' and 'utilitarianism' are surely no exception. They too have unfortunate suggestions which hostile critics have been willing to exploit; yet they are clear enough for those prepared to study utilitarian doctrine. The same should be true of the term 'contract' applied to moral theories. As I have mentioned, to understand it one has to keep in mind that it implies a certain level of abstraction. In particular, the content of the relevant agreement is not to enter a given society or to adopt a given form of government, but to accept certain moral principles. Moreover, the undertakings referred to are purely hypothetical: a contract view holds that certain principles would be accepted in a well-defined initial situation.

The merit of the contract terminology is that it conveys the idea that principles of justice may be conceived as principles that would be chosen by rational persons, and that in this way conceptions of justice may be explained and justified. The theory of justice is a part, perhaps the most significant part, of the theory of rational choice. Furthermore, principles of justice deal with conflicting claims upon the advantages won by social cooperation; they apply to the relations among several persons or groups. The word 'contract' suggests this plurality as well as the condition that the appropriate division of advantages must be in accordance with principles acceptable to all parties. The condition of publicity for principles of justice is also connoted by the contract phraseology. Thus, if these principles are the outcome of an agreement, citizens have a knowledge of the principles that others follow. It is characteristic of contract theories to stress the public nature of political principles. Finally there is the long tradition of the contract doctrine. Expressing the tie with this line of thought helps to define ideas and accords with natural piety. There are then several advantages in the use of the term 'contract'. With due precautions taken, it should not be misleading.

A final remark. Justice as fairness is not a complete contract theory. For it is clear that the contractarian idea can be extended to the choice of more or less an entire ethical system, that is, to a system including principles for all the virtues and not only for justice. Now for the most part I shall consider only principles of justice and others closely related to them; I make no attempt to discuss the virtues in a systematic way. Obviously if justice as fairness succeeds reasonably well, a next step would be to study the more general view suggested by the name 'rightness as fairness'. But even this wider theory fails to embrace all moral relationships, since it would seem to include only our relations with other persons and to leave out of account how we are to conduct ourselves toward animals and the rest of nature. I do not contend that the contract notion offers a way to approach these questions which are certainly of the first importance; and I shall have to put them aside. We must recognize the limited scope of justice as fairness and of the general type of view that it exemplifies. How far its conclusions must be revised once these other matters are understood cannot be decided in advance.

4. THE ORIGINAL POSITION AND JUSTIFICATION

I have said that the original position is the appropriate initial status quo which insures that the fundamental agreements reached in it are fair. This fact yields the name 'justice as fairness'. It is clear, then, that I want to say that one conception of justice is more reasonable than another, or justifiable with respect to it, if rational persons in the initial situation would choose its principles over those of the other for the role of justice. Conceptions of justice are to be ranked by their acceptability to persons so circumstanced. Understood in this way the question of justification is settled by working out a problem of deliberation: we have to ascertain which principles it would be rational to adopt given the contractual situation. This connects the theory of justice with the theory of rational choice.

If this view of the problem of justification is to succeed, we must, of course, describe in some detail the nature of this choice problem. A problem of rational decision has a definite answer only if we know the beliefs and interests of the parties, their relations with respect to one another, the alternatives between which they are to choose, the procedure whereby they make up their minds, and so on. As the circumstances are presented in different ways, correspondingly different principles are accepted. The concept of the original position, as I shall refer to it, is that of the most philosophically favored interpretation of this initial choice situation for the purposes of a theory of justice.

But how are we to decide what is the most favored interpretation? I assume, for one thing. that there is a broad measure of agreement that principles of justice should be chosen under certain conditions. To justify a particular description of the initial situation one shows that it incorporates these commonly shared presumptions. One argues from widely accepted but weak premises to more specific conclusions. Each of the presumptions should by itself be natural and plausible; some of them may seem innocuous or even trivial. The aim of the contract approach is to establish that taken together they impose significant bounds on acceptable principles of justice. The ideal outcome would be that these conditions determine a unique set of principles; but I shall be satisfied if they suffice to rank the main traditional conceptions of social justice.

One should not be misled, then, by the somewhat unusual conditions which characterize the original position. The idea here is simply to make vivid to ourselves the restrictions that it seems reasonable to impose on arguments for principles of justice, and therefore on these principles themselves. Thus it seems reasonable and generally acceptable that no one should be advantaged or disadvantaged by natural fortune or social circumstances in the choice of principles. It also seems widely agreed that it should be impossible to tailor principles to the circumstances one's own case. We should insure further that particular inclinations and aspirations, and persons' conceptions of their good do not affect the principles adopted. The aim is to rule out those principles that it would be rational to propose for acceptance, however little the chance of success, only if one knew certain things that are irrelevant from the standpoint of justice. For example, if a man knew that he was wealthy, he might find it rational to advance the principle that various taxes for welfare measures be counted unjust; if he knew that he was poor, he would most likely propose the contrary principle. To represent the desired restrictions one imagines a situation in which everyone is deprived of this sort of information. One excludes the knowledge of those contingencies which sets men at odds and allows them to be guided by their prejudices. In this manner the veil of ignorance is arrived at in a natural way. This concept should cause no difficulty if we keep in mind the constraints on arguments that it is meant to express. At any time we can enter the original position, so to speak, simply by following a certain procedure, namely, by arguing for principles of justice in accordance with these restrictions.

It seems reasonable to suppose that the parties in the original position are equal. That is, all have the same rights in the procedure for choosing principles; each can make proposals, submit reasons for their acceptance, and so on. Obviously the purpose of these conditions is to represent equality between human beings as moral persons, as creatures having a conception of their good and capable of a sense of justice. The basis of equality is taken to be similarity in these two respects. Systems of ends are not ranked in value; and each man is presumed to have the requisite ability to understand and to act upon whatever principles are adopted. Together with the veil of ignorance, these conditions define the principles of justice as those which rational persons concerned to advance their interests would consent to as equals when none are known to be advantaged or disadvantaged by social and natural contingencies.

There is, however, another side to justifying a particular description of the original position. This is to see if the principles which would be chosen match our considered convictions of justice or extend them in an acceptable way. We can note whether applying these principles would lead us to make the same judgments about the basic structure of society which we now make intuitively and in which we have the greatest confidence;

or whether, in cases where our present judgments are in doubt and given with hesitation, these principles offer a resolution which we can affirm on reflection. There are questions which we feel sure must be answered in a certain way. For example, we are confident that religious intolerance and racial discrimination are unjust. We think that we have examined these things with care and have reached what we believe is an impartial judgment not likely to be distorted by an excessive attention to our own interests. These convictions are provisional fixed points which we presume any conception of justice must fit. But we have much less assurance as to what is the correct distribution of wealth and authority. Here we may be looking for a way to remove our doubts. We can check an interpretation of the initial situation, then, by the capacity of its principles to accommodate our firmest convictions and to provide guidance where guidance is needed.

In searching for the most favored description of this situation we work from both ends. We begin by describing it so that it represents generally shared and preferably weak conditions. We then see if these conditions are strong enough to yield a significant set of principles. If not, we look for further premises equally reasonable. But if so, and these principles match our considered convictions of justice, then so far well and good. But presumably there will be discrepancies. In this case we have a choice. We can either modify the account of the initial situation or we can revise our existing judgments, for even the judgments we take provisionally as fixed points are liable to revision. By going back and forth, sometimes altering the conditions of the contractual circumstances, at others withdrawing our judgments and conforming them to principle, I assume that eventually we shall find a description of the initial situation that both expresses reasonable conditions and yields principles which match our considered judgments duly pruned and adjusted. This state of affairs I refer to as reflective equilibrium. It is an equilibrium because at last our principles and judgments coincide; and it is reflective since we know to what principles our judgments conform and the premises of their derivation. At the moment everything is in order. But this equilibrium is not necessarily stable. It is liable to be upset by further examination of the conditions which should be imposed on the contractual situation and by particular cases which may lead us to revise our judgments. Yet for the time being we have done what we can to render coherent and to justify our convictions of social justice. We have reached a conception of the original position.

I shall not, of course, actually work through this process. Still, we may think of the interpretation of the original position that I shall present as the result of such a hypothetical course of reflection. It represents the attempt to accommodate within one scheme both reasonable philosophical conditions on principles as well as our considered judgments of justice. In arriving at the favored interpretation of the initial situation there is no point at which an appeal is made to self-evidence in the traditional sense either of general conceptions or particular convictions. I do not claim for the principles of justice proposed that they are necessary truths or derivable from such truths. A conception of justice cannot be deduced from self-evident premises or conditions on principles; instead, its justification is a matter of the mutual support of many considerations, of everything fitting together into one coherent view.

A final comment. We shall want to say that certain principles of justice are justified because they would be agreed to in an initial situation of equality. I have emphasized that this original position is purely hypothetical. It is natural to ask why, if this agreement is never actually entered into, we should take any interest in these principles, moral or otherwise. The answer is that the conditions embodied in the description of the original position are ones that we do in fact accept. Or if we do not, then perhaps we can be persuaded to do so by philosophical reflection. Each aspect of the contractual situation can be given supporting grounds. Thus what we shall do is to collect together into one conception a number of conditions on principles that we are ready upon due consideration to recognize as reasonable. These constraints express what we are prepared to regard as limits on fair terms of social cooperation. One way to look at the idea of the original position, therefore, is to see it as an expository device which sums up the meaning of these conditions and helps us to extract their consequences. On the other hand, this conception is also an intuitive notion that suggests its own elaboration, so that led on by it we are drawn to define more clearly the standpoint from which we can best interpret moral relationships. We need a conception that enables us to envision our objective from afar: the intuitive notion of the original position is to do this for us.

4. The Two Principles of Justice

At the heart of Rawls' theory are the two principles of justice that he argues would be agreed to by people in the OP, ie in conditions that ensure fair deliberation and negotiation. The first is said to be *lexically prior* to the second, by which Rawls means that it must be fully satisfied before the second principle is applied. The first principle concerns the distribution of liberty, the second – the 'difference' principle – refers to the distribution of social and economic welfare. The difference principle itself is divided into two parts, relating to the distribution of *outcomes* and *opportunities*.

The principles are as follows:

1. Each person has an equal right to the most extensive system of equal basic liberties, compatible with a similar system for all.

2. Social and economic inequalities are arranged so that
    a. They benefit the least advantaged as much as possible, subject to a just savings principle, and
    b. Inequalities are attached only to statuses open to everyone under conditions of fair equality of opportunity.

In short, there must be as much liberty for each person as is compatible with similar liberty for everyone else. Departures from equal distribution of welfare are justified only if they are necessary to make the least advantaged as well off as they possibly could be, allow fairly for future generations, and are achieved on the basis of equal opportunities. The equal liberty principle is lexically prior to the difference principle: equal liberties cannot be abridged for the sake of material welfare.

Rawls (1973, 54–65)

10. INSTITUTIONS AND FORMAL JUSTICE

The primary subject of the principles of social justice is the basic structure of society, the arrangement of major social institutions into one scheme of cooperation. We have seen that these principles are to govern the assignment of rights and duties in these institutions and they are to determine the appropriate distribution of the benefits and burdens of social life. The principles of justice for institutions must not be confused with the principles which apply to individuals and their actions in particular circumstances. These two kinds of principles apply to different subjects and must be discussed separately.

Now by an institution I shall understand a public system of rules which defines offices and positions with their rights and duties, powers and immunities, and the like. These rules specify certain forms of action as permissible, others as forbidden; and they provide for certain penalties and defenses, and so on, when violations occur. As examples of institutions, or more generally social practices, we may think of games and rituals, trials and parliaments, markets and systems of property. An institution may be thought of in two ways: first as an abstract object, that is, as a possible form of conduct expressed by a system of rules; and second, as the realization in the thought and conduct of certain persons at a certain time and place of the actions specified by these rules. There is an ambiguity, then, as to which is just or unjust, the institution as realized or the institution as an abstract object. It seems best to say that it is the institution as realized and effectively and impartially administered which is just or unjust. The institution as an abstract object is just or unjust in the sense that any realization of it would be just or unjust.

An institution exists at a certain time and place when the actions specified by it are regularly carried out in accordance with a public understanding that the system of rules defining the institution is to be followed. Thus parliamentary institutions are defined by a certain system of rules (or family of such systems to allow for variations). These rules enumerate certain forms of action ranging from holding a session of parliament to taking a vote on a bill to raising a point of order. Various kinds of general norms are organized into a coherent scheme. A parliamentary institution exists at a certain time and place when certain people perform the appropriate actions, engage in these activities in the required way, with a reciprocal recognition of one another's understanding that their conduct accords with the rules they are to comply with.

In saying that an institution, and therefore the basic structure of society, is a public system of rules, I mean then that everyone engaged in it knows what he would know if these rules and his participation in the activity they define were the result of an agreement. A person taking part in an institution knows what the rules demand of him and of the others. He also knows that the others know this and that they know that he knows this, and so on. To be sure, this condition is not always fulfilled in the case of actual institutions, but it is a reasonable simplifying assumption. The principles of justice are to apply to social arrangements understood to be public in this sense. Where the rules of a certain subpart of an institution are known only to those belonging to it, we may assume that there is an understanding that those in this part can make rules for themselves as long as these rules are designed to achieve ends generally accepted and others are not adversely affected. The publicity of the rules of an institution insures that those engaged in it know what limitations on conduct to expect of one another and what kinds of actions are permissible. There is a common basis for determining mutual expectations. Moreover, in a well-ordered society, one effectively regulated by a shared conception of justice, there is also a public understanding as to what is just and unjust. Later I assume that the principles of justice are chosen subject to the knowledge that they are to be public. This condition is a natural one in a contractarian theory.

It is necessary to note the distinction between the constitutive rules of an institution which establish its various rights and duties, and so on, and strategies and maxims for how best to take advantage of the institution for particular purposes. Rational strategies and maxims are based upon an analysis of which permissible actions individuals and groups will decide upon in view of their interests, beliefs, and conjectures about one another's plans. These strategies and maxims are not themselves part of the institution. Rather they belong to the theory of it, for example, to the theory of parliamentary politics. Normally the theory of an institution, just as that of a game, takes the constitutive rules as given and analyses the way in which power is distributed and explains how those engaged in it are likely to avail themselves of its opportunities. In designing and reforming social arrangements one must, of course, examine the schemes and tactics it allows and the forms of behavior which it tends to encourage. Ideally the rules should be set up so that men are led by their predominant interests to act in ways which further socially desirable ends. The conduct of individuals guided by their rational plans should be coordinated as far as possible to achieve results which although not intended or perhaps even foreseen by them are nevertheless the best ones from the standpoint of social justice. Bentham thinks of this coordination as the artificial identification of interests, Adam Smith as the work of the invisible hand. It is the aim of the ideal legislator in enacting laws and of the moralist in urging their reform. Still, the strategies and tactics followed by individuals, while essential to the assessment of institutions, are not part of the public systems of rules which define them.

We may also distinguish between a single rule (or group of rules), an institution (or a major part thereof), and the basic structure of the social system as a whole. The reason for doing this is that one or several rules of an arrangement may be unjust without the institution itself being so. Similarly, an institution may be unjust although the social system as a whole is not. There is the possibility not only that single rules and institutions are not by themselves sufficiently important but that within the structure of an institution or social system one apparent injustice compensates for another. The whole is less unjust than it would be if it contained but one of the unjust parts. Further, it is conceivable that a social system may be unjust even though none of its institutions are unjust taken separately: the injustice is a consequence of how they are combined together into a single system. One institution may encourage and appear to justify expectations which are denied or ignored by another. These distinctions are obvious enough. They simply reflect the fact that in appraising institutions we may view them in a wider or a narrower context.

...

11. TWO PRINCIPLES OF JUSTICE

I shall now state in a provisional form the two principles of justice that I believe would be chosen in the original position. In this section I wish to make only the most general comments, and therefore the first formulation of these principles is tentative. As we go on I shall run through several formulations and approximate step by step the final statement to be given much later. I believe that doing this allows the exposition to proceed in a natural way.

The first statement of the two principles reads as follows.

First: each person is to have an equal right to the most extensive basic liberty compatible with a similar liberty for others.

Second: social and economic inequalities are to be arranged so that they are both (a) reasonably expected to be to everyone's advantage, and (b) attached to positions and offices open to all.

...

By way of general comment, these principles primarily apply, as I have said, to the basic structure of society. They are to govern the assignment of rights and duties and to regulate the distribution of social and economic advantages. As their formulation suggests, these principles presuppose that the social structure can be divided into two more or less distinct parts, the first principle applying to the one, the second to the other. They distinguish between those aspects of the social system that define and secure the equal liberties of citizenship and those that specify and establish social and economic inequalities. The basic liberties of citizens are, roughly speaking, political liberty (the right to vote and to be eligible for public office) together with freedom of speech and assembly; liberty of conscience and freedom of thought; freedom of the person along with the right to hold (personal) property; and freedom from arbitrary arrest and seizure as defined by the concept of the rule of law. These liberties are all required to be equal by the first principle, since citizens of a just society are to have the same basic rights.

The second principle applies, in the first approximation, to the distribution of income and wealth and to the design of organizations that make use of differences in authority and responsibility, or chains of command. While the distribution of wealth and income need not be equal, it must be to everyone's advantage, and at the same time, positions of authority and offices of command must be accessible to all. One applies the second principle by holding positions open, and then, subject to this constraint, arranges social and economic inequalities so that everyone benefits.

These principles are to be arranged in a serial order with the first principle prior to the second. This ordering means that a departure from the institutions of equal liberty required by the first principle cannot be justified by, or compensated for, by greater social and economic advantages. The distribution of wealth and income, and the hierarchies of authority, must be consistent with both the liberties of equal citizenship and equality of opportunity.

It is clear that these principles are rather specific in their content, and their acceptance rests on certain assumptions that I must eventually try to explain and justify. A theory of justice depends upon a theory of society in ways that will become evident as we proceed. For the present, it should be observed that the two principles (and this holds for all formulations) are a special case of a more general conception of justice that can he expressed as follows.

All social values – liberty and opportunity, income and wealth, and the bases of self-respect – are to be distributed equally unless an unequal distribution of any, or all, of these values is to everyone's advantage.

Injustice, then, is simply inequalities that are not to the benefit of all. Of course, this conception is extremely vague and requires interpretation.

As a first step, suppose that the basic structure of society distributes certain primary goods, that is, things that every rational man is presumed to want. These goods normally have a use whatever a person's rational plan of life. For simplicity, assume that the chief primary goods at the disposition of society are rights and liberties, powers and opportunities, income and wealth. (Later on in Part Three the primary good of self-respect has a central place.) These are the social primary goods. Other primary goods such as health and vigor, intelligence and imagination, are natural goods; although their possession is influenced by the basic structure, they are not so directly under its control. Imagine, then, a hypothetical initial arrangement in which all the social primary goods are equally distributed: everyone has similar rights and duties, and income and wealth are evenly shared. This state of affairs provides a benchmark for judging improvements. If certain inequalities of wealth and organizational powers would make everyone better off than in this hypothetical starting situation, then they accord with the general conception.

Now it is possible, at least theoretically, that by giving up some of their fundamental liberties men are sufficiently compensated by the resulting social and economic gains. The general conception of justice imposes no restrictions on what sort of inequalities are permissible; it only requires that everyone's position be improved. We need not suppose anything so drastic as consenting to a condition of slavery. Imagine instead that men forego certain political rights when the economic returns are significant and their capacity to influence the course of policy by the exercise of these rights would be marginal in any case. It is this kind of exchange which the two principles as stated rule out; being arranged in serial order they do not permit exchanges between basic liberties and economic and social gains. The serial ordering of principles expresses an underlying preference among primary social goods. When this preference is rational so likewise is the choice of these principles in this order.

In developing justice as fairness I shall, for the most part, leave aside the general conception of justice and examine instead the special case of the two principles in serial order. The advantage of this procedure is that from the first the matter of priorities is recognized and an effort made to find principles to deal with it. One is led to attend throughout to the conditions under which the acknowledgment of the absolute weight of liberty with respect to social and economic advantages, as defined by the lexical order of the two principles, would be reasonable. Offhand, this ranking appears extreme and too special a case to be of much interest; but there is more justification for it than would appear at first sight. Or at any rate, so I shall maintain. Furthermore, the distinction between fundamental rights and liberties and economic and social benefits marks a difference among primary social goods that one should try to exploit. It suggests an important division in the social system. Of course, the distinctions drawn and the ordering proposed are bound to be at best only approximations. There are surely circumstances in which they fail. But it is essential to depict clearly the main lines of a reasonable conception of justice; and under many conditions anyway, the two principles in serial order may serve well enough. When necessary we can fall back on the more general conception.

The fact that the two principles apply to institutions has certain consequences. Several points illustrate this. First of all, the rights and liberties referred to by these principles are those which are defined by the public rules of the basic structure. Whether men are free is determined by the rights and duties established by the major institutions of society. Liberty is a certain pattern of social forms. The first principle simply requires that certain sorts of rules, those defining basic liberties, apply to everyone equally and that they allow the most extensive liberty compatible with a like liberty for all. The only reason for circumscribing the rights defining liberty and making men's freedom less extensive than it might otherwise be is that these equal rights as institutionally defined would interfere with one another.

Another thing to bear in mind is that when principles mention persons, or require that everyone gain from an inequality, the reference is to representative persons holding the various social positions, or offices, or whatever, established by the basic structure. Thus in applying the second principle I assume that it is possible to assign an expectation of well-being to representative individuals holding these positions. This expectation indicates their life prospects as viewed from their social station. In general, the expectations of representative persons depend upon the distribution of rights and duties throughout the basic structure. When this changes, expectations change. I assume, then, that expectations are connected: by raising the prospects of the representative man in one position we presumably increase or decrease the prospects of representative men in other positions. Since it applies to institutional forms, the second principle (or rather the first part of it) refers to the expectations of representative individuals. As I shall discuss below, neither principle applies to distributions of particular goods to particular individuals who may be identified by their proper names. The situation where someone is considering how to allocate certain commodities to needy persons who are known to him is not within the scope of the principles. They are meant to regulate basic institutional arrangements. We must not assume that there is much similarity from the standpoint of justice between an administrative allotment of goods to specific persons and the appropriate design of society. Our common sense intuitions for the former may be a poor guide to the latter.

Now the second principle insists that each person benefit from permissible inequalities in the basic structure. This means that it must be reasonable for each relevant representative man defined by this structure, when he views it as a going concern, to prefer his prospects with the inequality to his prospects without it. One is not allowed to justify differences in income or organizational powers on the ground that the disadvantages of those in one position are outweighed by the greater advantages of those in another. Much less can infringements of liberty be counterbalanced in this way. Applied to the basic structure, the principle of utility would have us maximize the sum of expectations of representative men (weighted by the number of persons they represent, on the classical view); and this would permit us to compensate for the losses of some by the gains of others. Instead, the two principles require that everyone benefit from economic and social inequalities.

...

5. Derivation of the Two Principles

Why does Rawls argue that these are the principles that would be agreed to by people in the OP? As discussed earlier, Rawls attributes people in the OP with some minimal presumed knowledge of human nature and social organisation (the value of primary basic goods, the absence of either envy or altruism as inevitable tendencies, and family feeling).

Rawls (1973, 141–142)

Now the reasons for the veil of ignorance go beyond mere simplicity. We want to define the original position so that we get the desired solution. If a knowledge of particulars is allowed, then the outcome is biased by arbitrary contingencies. As already observed, to each according to his threat advantage is not a principle of justice. If the original position is to yield agreements that are just, the parties must be fairly situated and treated equally as moral persons. The arbitrariness of the world must be corrected for by adjusting the circumstances of the initial contractual situation. Moreover, if in choosing principles we required unanimity even when there is full information, only a few rather obvious cases could be decided. A conception of justice based on unanimity in these circumstances would indeed be weak and trivial. But once knowledge is excluded, the requirement of unanimity is not out of place and the fact that it can be satisfied is of great importance. It enables us to say of the preferred conception of justice that it represents a genuine reconciliation of interests.

A final comment. For the most part I shall suppose that the parties possess all general information. No general facts are closed to them. I do this mainly to avoid complications. Nevertheless a conception of justice is to be the public basis of the terms of social cooperation. Since common understanding necessitates certain bounds on the complexity of principles, there may likewise be limits on the use of theoretical knowledge in the original position. Now clearly it would be very difficult to classify and to grade for complexity the various sorts of general facts. I shall make no attempt to do this. We do however recognize an intricate theoretical construction when we meet one. Thus it seems reasonable to say that other things equal one conception of justice is to be preferred to another when it is founded upon markedly simpler general facts, and its choice does not depend upon elaborate calculations in the light of a vast array of theoretically defined possibilities. It is desirable that the grounds for a public conception of justice should be evident to everyone when circumstances permit. This consideration favors, I believe, the two principles of justice over the criterion of utility.

25. THE RATIONALITY OF THE PARTIES

I have assumed throughout that the persons in the original position are rational. In choosing between principles each tries as best he can to advance his interests. But I have also assumed that the parties do not know their conception of the good. This means that while they know that they have some rational plan of life, they do not know the details of this plan, the particular ends and interests which it is calculated to promote. How, then, can they decide which conceptions of justice are most to their advantage? Or must we suppose that they are reduced to mere guessing? To meet this difficulty, I postulate that they accept the account of the good touched upon in the preceding chapter:

they assume that they would prefer more primary social goods rather than less. Of course, it may turn out, once the veil of ignorance is removed, that some of them for religious or other reasons may not, in fact, want more of these goods.

In addition, Rawls postulates two minimal motivational assumptions that animate negotiations in the OP, even behind the people's veil of ignorance about their particular social interests, tastes and values. These are:

1. Social co-operation: People are willing to be organised socially despite the lack of direct concern for the welfare of others, because they are aware that this helps their own plans of life to succeed. They may argue with others about the distribution of the fruits of co-operation, but are willing to work with them to increase the amount of goods available for division.

2. Risk aversion: In the OP people do not know what positions in society they will occupy. Rawls argues that in this condition of uncertainty people will be most concerned to minimise the risk of ending up in the worst possible situations – they will be risk averse, and use a maximin criterion for decision-making. This underlies the two principles, most obviously the difference principle's prioritisation of the plight of the worst off. The premise is that people don't like gambles, at any rate with their total life chances.

The two principles flow from these assumptions about motivation. The liberty principle, and its lexical priority, are the consequences of maximin decision-making behind a veil of ignorance about one's tastes, values and preferences for life. If people do not know what their religion, sexual orientation, political and cultural preferences will be, they will want a form of social organisation that preserves the maximum freedom for their choices whatever they may be.

How would people in the OP derive their principles for the best distribution of basic social goods? Not knowing what their position will be, they will probably first consider complete equality. If they were envious they would stick with this, because inequality per se would cause psychic pain to the less well off. But Rawls assumes that as long as inequalities are not sharp enough to threaten the self-respect of the disadvantaged, people are not envious of others but are primarily focussed on the maximisation of their own well-being. In the OP people might envisage that under some circumstances inequalities could increase the overall size of the cake, so that even the poorest were better off than they would be with equality – say if incentives are necessary to motivate people to undertake more demanding tasks. If we assume non-enviousness then they would agree to inequalities justified by the enhancement of the position of the least well off – the first leg of Rawls' difference principle. On the assumption of risk aversion people will be most concerned with the plight of the worst off in any distribution – in case they end up in that position – and not by average or total wealth. However, equality of opportunity is a precondition for any unequal distribution of goods to be seen as fair by everyone, even if it does make the poorest better off. If there are unfair starting advantages attached to any positions then the losers will not regard their lot as acceptable. Thus a necessary condition for accepting any inequalities is that they result from an equal distribution of opportunities. The assumption of family feeling, however, adds a further consideration. People will want to have a distribution of goods that is fair to future generations, hence the 'just savings' proviso in the difference principle.

Thus Rawls sees the two principles as flowing from the specified circumstances of the OP: the veil of ignorance, non-altruism but the absence of envy, family feeling, and maximin decision-making. These generate the difference principle presuming equality in the distribution of goods with exceptions only for inequalities that maximise the position of the least well off, subject to the preconditions of equal opportunity and just savings. However, people would not accept an abridgement of equal liberties under any circumstances, in case what turns out to be their preferred life-style was curtailed.

6. The Comparative Advantages of the Two Principles

Rawls devotes a large part of *A Theory of Justice* comparing the two principles to other possible theories seeking to establish their superiority. The alternative perspectives considered include:

(1) *Perfectionism.* By this Rawls means a view that society should be organised so as to achieve a specific 'ideal' state of affairs as closely as possible, say a particular political or theological conception of the good life. Rawls argues that no perfectionist model could be chosen in the OP, because behind the veil of ignorance people do not know what their own theory of the good will turn out to be. Any particular perfectionist model may turn out to be anathema to them. Thus in the OP people will opt for his first principle, preserving the maximum freedom for different conceptions of the good to be pursued, subject only to similar freedom for others. This argument would rule out any non-tolerant conceptions in favour of the priority of liberty, Rawls' first principle.

(2) *Average utility maximisation.* Maximising utility would not be chosen in the OP argues Rawls because it is compatible with extremely bad conditions for minorities, and nobody would want to risk ending up in those circumstances. Thus they would opt for the 'difference' principle to ensure the best possible position for the least well off.

(3) *Utility maximisation with a social minimum.* John Stuart Mill and many other utilitarians have argued that the problem of oppression of minorities can be dealt with by combining average utility maximisation with a floor of minimum welfare below which no-one would be allowed to fall. Rawls' problem with this is the difficulty of specifying the social minimum in any principled, non-arbitrary way, as indicated by the vexed debates about how to measure poverty. His argument is that the difference principle does give a principled specification of the social minimum (even though it remains almost impossible to measure): the level at which the worst off are as well off as they would be under any other alternative distribution. In this sense, Rawls' second principle is a more specific variant of utility maximisation subject to a social minimum, rather than fundamentally different from it.

7. Social psychological advantages of the two principles

Rawls claims that his two principles are likely to produce a more stable social order than any theory. This is because there is less 'strain of commitment' than with alternative conceptions of justice. It does the maximum possible to preserve the interests and values of all persons, irrespective of what their preferences might be. Because in the OP people are seen as negotiators seeking to protect themselves by reaching the best contract terms they can, not as legislators laying down principles of justice, Rawls argues no-one is required to sacrifice their interests for others or for some ideal of the greater good. The two principles represent the best bargain for everyone, and thus the strain of commitment to it is minimised. The least well off know that they are at least as well off as they would be under any alternative dispensation. High flyers receive whatever differential rewards are necessary for them to produce the best possible output for the two principles to work. They do not, however, receive any rent for being more talented. Rawls argues that the distribution of natural abilities is morally arbitrary, and there is no principled justification for rewarding superior talent per se, unless it is demanded by the difference principle, in order to produce the best possible conditions for the least advantaged. However, since in the OP the more talented would not know their abilities, they would agree to the difference principle prioritising the position of the least well off, in case they were in this category, rather than rewarding the winners in the lottery of natural abilities.

Perfectionists would also have less strain of commitment with the first principle, maximum basic liberties, even if it hampers achievement of their goal of organising the world according to their true beliefs. Since in the OP nobody knows their eventual preferences, everyone would agree to the maximum liberty for all, subject to not abridging the same liberty for others. This is the equivalent of accepting the rules of debate whereby the price of being given the opportunity to argue for your beliefs is being compelled to hear opposing views being championed, however nonsensical or odious they may be felt to be.

8. Criticisms of Rawls

Criticisms of Rawls can be divided into four broad groups. There are: a) extensions and developments of the perspective by those fundamentally sympathetic to it; b) alternative perspectives within liberalism, notably the neo-liberal attack on Rawls spearheaded by Nozick; c) criticisms of the liberal approach itself, such as communitarianism; d) critiques of the liberal-communitarian debate, from feminists, socialists and conservatives. These are not hermetically sealed groupings of course, and most particular authors would straddle these categories. In the last two sections of this chapter particular attention will be given to the neo-libertarian and the communitarian critiques, which have generated most of the critical literature on Rawls. The various critiques pick up on what are some fairly evident issues within Rawls' exposition of his own position.

1.   What liberties are basic? The first principle refers to a list of basic liberties that are to be protected equally. But how can such a list be generated in a non-arbitrary,

principled way? Does Rawls' own list include too much or too little? Why does it include property rights, for example, but exclude liberty of sexual preference?

2. Equality of what? One of the most extensive debates generated within the literature fundamentally sympathetic to Rawls concerns the issue of which 'goods' are to be equalised subject to the difference principle. If it is some measure of concrete things, then this may lead to different levels of 'welfare' derived by people from the same stock of goods, given their varying needs and tastes, as Sen has argued. But if we aim for equality of welfare allowing for such differences, this would mean that people would get more because they had cultivated what Dworkin calls 'champagne' tastes. Dworkin suggests we distinguish differences in people's needs that are *chosen* from those that are the product of ill fortune. In effect we would then be seeking to equalise people's life *chances*, not their life *conditions*, to shield them from bad luck but not to protect them from the bad consequences of their mistakes.

3. Can equality of opportunity be distinguished from equality of outcome? Rawls' second principle makes equality of opportunity a precondition of any equalities in condition being justifiable. But can equality of opportunity be achieved if there are substantive inequalities, which the better off are likely to pass on to their offspring? This is the problem that bedevils any attempt to champion meritocracy but not equality of outcomes (as New Labour does).

4. Why is the first principle lexically prior? Rawls argues that people in the OP would not countenance any abridgement of the liberty principle at all. It is not clear, however, that they might not agree to partial abridgements, even on Rawls' psychological assumptions. Say, for example, they thought that a five year plan for economic growth under Stakhanovite forced labour conditions could deliver on its promises, making the value of their liberties and welfare considerably greater thereafter – might they not agree to a temporary dictatorship?

5. Rawls' Methodology. The most serious issues concern Rawls' methods for deriving the principles. These issues range widely, deriving mainly from debates about particular assumptions he relies on in his basic epistemology.
   i. Is it plausible that people are completely risk averse? Empirical research on decision-making in conditions of uncertainty – and the history of the last thirty years – suggest that at least many people prefer risk-taking to security if the stakes are enticing enough.
   ii. Can we assume that people are only concerned about their own and their family's absolute well-being, and not their position relative to others? Can envy really be ignored?
   iii. Isn't there an issue about the distribution of liberties and goods *within* families? (This would be part of a feminist critique.)
   iv. Does allowing that inequalities may be necessary to boost the position of the least well off assume a capitalist ethos? It concedes the need for special incentives for the owners of special productive resources, in effect allowing them to hold society to ransom (as Cohen 2000, Ch 8 has argued).
   v. Why should people accept the implications of an abstract argument about

what they would have agreed to in a hypothetical OP in order to give up advantageous positions they enjoy through no illegal or immoral actions of their own? (This is the germ of Nozick's neo-liberal critique, set out later.)

vi.　Is it meaningful to conceive of decision-makers in the abstract, without any of the specific aspects of selfhood that are acquired through socialisation into specific cultural identities and group membership? (This is the core of the communitarian critique, see out later.)

vii.　Is the fundamental approach of postulating a set of rational decision-makers contemplating only their own well-being in the abstract a reflection of a mode of thinking that is specifically masculine? (Some feminist critics have argued this cf. the discussion in Fraser and Lacey 1993.)

viii.　Is the reference point of 'our' settled beliefs which is the basis of reflective equilibrium a sort of perfectionism, the world-view of liberal, middle-aged, middle-income males? (Aspects of Rawls' auto-critique in *Political Liberalism* 1993 imply this.)

These issues will be considered further through an examination of some alternative recent perspectives on justice.

Nozick and neo-liberalism

Robert Nozick's 1974 book *Anarchy, State and Utopia*, represents the quintessential statement of the neo-liberal critique of Rawls. *A Theory of Justice* can be seen as a clear philosophical defence of the kind of mixed economy, welfare state, Keynesian consensus that dominated all Western polities after the Second World War. By the early 1970s this consensus was increasingly under attack. Country after country voted into office governments committed to dismantling the welfare state and returning to free market, monetarist economic policies. Nozick's book was immediately lauded as the philosophical expression of this neo-liberalism.

Nozick's fundamental presumption is the primacy of certain natural rights, including the right to acquire property legitimately. Injustice results from the violation of a person's rights without their consent. Rights are 'side constraints' defining legitimate action.

A state can be justified only if it is arrived at from a 'state of nature' without infringing the rights of any non-consenting persons. Nozick claims that the only state that could satisfy this condition is a minimal 'night watchman' state, offering protection against violence, theft, and the breach of agreements. A more extensive state, especially one using its power in order to redistribute wealth through taxation, cannot be justified. Taxation amounts to forced labour.

Property can only be acquired legitimately in one of three ways:

1.　Just initial acquisition. In rare circumstances (primarily in a 'state of nature') a person can acquire property not yet belonging to anyone else. Following Locke, Nozick holds that this can be appropriated justly, provided a remainder is left for others.

2. Legitimate transfer. Most goods now do not exist unencumbered by existing rights of ownership. They can only be acquired justly through a voluntary transfer from the owner, for example by gift, exchange or sale.

3. Rectification of past injustice. If a person acquires property unjustly, for example by force, fraud or theft, then it can legitimately be taken away and restored to the proper owner.

Rights, including property rights, can only be violated or abridged legitimately if the person enjoying them consents. The separateness and individuality of persons must be respected. They may not be treated as means to an end, for some supposed greater good (a Kantian argument that Rawls himself levelled against utilitarianism). This leads Nozick to reject the legitimacy of what he calls *pattern* theories of justice (like Rawls' difference principle). By this Nozick means perspectives that assess the justice of social arrangements with reference to whether they match a specific goal or pattern. Pattern theories require the rights of some individuals to be sacrificed in order to achieve the desired end-state. Nozick proposes instead a *historical entitlement* theory of justice. A situation is assessed as just not against the benchmark of a particular pattern, but in terms of the historical process by which it came about. If it is the result of a series of legitimate interactions in which nobody's rights have been infringed then it is just, even if for example people are very unequal in their conditions of life. Trying to restructure the result of a series of just transfers in order to enhance the position of the least well off, or to achieve any other ideal pattern, is to unjustly violate the rights of the better off.

1. The minimal state

Nozick argues that a 'night watchman' state could emerge from a state of nature without harming anyone's rights. He constructs a hypothetical history of an 'invisible hand' process whereby the night watchman state could have evolved through a series of stages, without overall conscious design but with full consent at each step. Initially people might form voluntary mutual protection agencies to pool their resources against attack. In each area, one of these agencies gradually becomes dominant. In time it could prohibit the other protective agencies from acting independently. Although this itself is a curtailment of their rights, it could occur with their consent, for example if they are compensated or accept that the dominant agency offers more effective security. As the dominant agency achieves a monopoly of legitimate force it acquires the lineaments of the state (in Max Weber's classic definition). Thus the night watchman state can be reconciled with a just historical entitlement narrative.

Modern welfare states cannot be justified in this way, according to Nozick. The taxation that finances their public spending and redistribution of welfare is fundamentally unjust because it is involuntary (unlike charitable support of welfare services). It is analogous to slavery, claims Nozick, in that people are forced to work part of the time to generate their tax payments in order to benefit others. Nozick illustrates his argument with the celebrated example of Wilt Chamberlain, the basketball player. Suppose we start from any favoured pattern of justice, say Rawls' difference principle. Suppose further that a million fans are eager to pay $1 each to see Wilt Chamberlain play. He will end the season a multi-millionaire as the result of entirely voluntary transfers. Nozick claims that it would be unjust to force him to give up any of this money as taxation in order to restore the initial pattern. It would render Wilt Chamberlain a slave, compelled to work (play!) in part to support the least well off. Thus only the minimal night watchman state can be reconciled with a historical entitlement view of justice, concludes Nozick.

Nozick (1974, 149–164, 167–173, 228–231 (edited))

CHAPTER 7. DISTRIBUTIVE JUSTICE.

The minimal state is the most extensive state that can be justified. Any state more extensive violates people's rights. Yet many persons have put forth reasons purporting to justify a more extensive state … In this chapter we consider the claim that a more extensive state is justified, because necessary (or the best instrument) to achieve distributive justice.

…

The term 'distributive justice' is not a neutral one. Hearing the term 'distribution', most people presume that some thing or mechanism uses some principle or criterion to give out a supply of things. Into this process of distributing shares some error may have crept. So it is an open question, at least, whether redistribution should take place; whether we should do again what has already been done once, though poorly. However, we are not in the position of children who have been given portions of pie by someone who now makes last minute adjustments to rectify careless cutting. There is no *central* distribution, no person or group entitled to control all the resources, jointly deciding how they are to be doled out. What each person gets, he gets from others who give to him in exchange for something, or as a gift. In a free society, diverse persons control different resources, and new holdings arise out of the voluntary exchanges and actions of persons. There is no more a distributing or distribution of shares than there is a distributing of mates in a society in which persons choose whom they shall marry. The total result is the product of many individual decisions which the different individuals involved are entitled to make. Some uses of the term 'distribution', it is true, do not imply a previous distributing appropriately judged by some criterion (for example, 'probability distribution'); nevertheless, despite the title of this chapter, it would be best to use a terminology that clearly is neutral. We shall speak of people's holdings; a principle of justice in holdings describes (part of) what justice tells us (requires) about holdings. I shall state first what I take to be the correct view about justice in holdings, and then turn to the discussion of alternate views.

SECTION I

The entitlement theory

The subject of justice in holdings consists of three major topics. The first is the *original acquisition of holdings*, the appropriation of unheld things. This includes the issues of how unheld things may come to he held, the process, or processes, by which unheld things may come to be held, the things that may come to be held by these processes, the extent of what comes to be held by a particular process, and so on. We shall refer to the complicated truth about this topic, which we shall not formulate here, as the principle justice in acquisition. The second topic concerns the *transfer holdings* from one person to another. By what processes may a person transfer holdings to another? How may a person acquire a holding from another who holds it? Under this topic come descriptions of voluntary exchange, and gift and (on the other hand) fraud, as well as reference to particular conventional details fixed upon in a given society. The complicated truth about this subject (with placeholders for conventional details) we shall call principle of justice in transfer. (And we shall suppose it also includes principles governing how a person may divest himself of a holding, passing it into an unheld state.)

If the world were wholly just, the following inductive definition would exhaustively cover the subject of justice in holdings.

1. A person who acquires a holding in accordance with the principle of justice in acquisition is entitled to that holding.

2. A person who acquires a holding in accordance with the principle of justice in transfer, from someone else entitled to the holding, is entitled to the holding.

3. No one is entitled to a holding except by (repeated) applications of 1 and 2.

The complete principle of distributive justice would say simply that a distribution is just if everyone is entitled to the holdings they possess under the distribution.

A distribution is just if it arises from another just distribution by legitimate means. The legitimate means of moving from one distribution to another are specified by the principle of justice in transfer. The legitimate first 'moves' are specified by the principle of justice in acquisition. Whatever arises from a just situation by just steps is itself just. The means of change specified by the principle of justice in transfer preserve justice. As correct rules of inference are truth-preserving, and any conclusion deduced via repeated application of such rules from only true premises is itself true, so the means of transition from one situation to another specified by the principle of justice in transfer are justice-preserving, and any situation actually arising from repeated transitions in accordance with the principle from a just situation is itself just. The parallel between justice-preserving transformations and truth-preserving transformations illuminates where it fails as well as where it holds. That a conclusion could have been deduced by truth-preserving means from premises that are true suffices to show its truth. That from a just situation a situation *could* have arisen via justice-preserving means does *not* suffice to show its justice. The fact that a thief's victims voluntarily *could* have presented him with gifts does not entitle the thief to his ill-gotten gains. Justice in holdings is historical; it depends upon what actually has happened. We shall return to this point later.

Not all actual situations are generated in accordance with the two principles of justice in holdings. The principle of justice in acquisition and the principle of justice in transfer. Some people steal from others, or defraud them, or enslave them, seizing their product and preventing them from living as they choose, or forcibly exclude others from competing in exchanges. None of these are permissible modes of transition from one situation to another. And some persons acquire holdings by means not sanctioned by the principle of justice in acquisition. The existence of past injustice (previous violations of the first two principles of justice in holdings) raises the third major topic under justice in holdings: the rectification of injustice in holdings. If past injustice has shaped present holdings in various ways, some identifiable and some not, what now, if anything, ought to be done to rectify these injustices? What obligations do the performers of injustice have toward those whose position is worse than it would have been had the injustice not been done? Or, than it would have been had compensation been paid promptly? How, if at all, do things change if the beneficiaries and those made worse off are not the direct parties in the act of injustice, but, for example, their descendants? Is an injustice done to someone whose holding was itself based upon an unrectified injustice? How far back must one go in wiping clean the historical slate of injustices? What may victims of injustice permissibly do in order to rectify the injustices being done to them, including the many injustices done by persons acting through their government? I do not know of a thorough or theoretically sophisticated treatment of such issues. Idealizing greatly, let us suppose theoretical investigation will produce a principle of rectification. This principle uses historical information about previous situations and injustices done in them (as defined by the first two principles of justice and rights against interference), and information about the actual course of events that flowed from these injustices, until the present, and it yields a description (or descriptions) of holdings in the society. The principle of rectification presumably will make use of its best estimate of subjunctive information about what would have occurred (or a probability distribution over what might have occurred, using the expected value) if the injustice had not taken place. If the actual description of holdings turns out not to he one of the descriptions yielded by the principle, then one of the descriptions yielded must be realized.

The general outlines of the theory of justice in holdings are that the holdings of a person are just if he is entitled to them by the principles of justice in acquisition and transfer, or by the principle of rectification of injustice (as specified by the first two principles). If each person's holdings are just, then the total set (distribution) of holdings is just. To turn these general outlines into a specific theory we would have to specify the details of each of the three principles of justice in holdings: the principle of acquisition of holdings, the principle of transfer of holdings, and the principle of rectification of violations of the first two principles.

...

Historical principles and end-result principles

The general outlines of the entitlement theory illuminate the nature and defects of other conceptions of distributive justice. The entitlement theory of justice in distribution is *historical,* whether a distribution is just depends upon how it came about. In contrast, *current time-slice principles* of justice hold that the justice of a distribution is determined by how things are distributed (who has what) as judged by some *structural* principle(s) of just distribution. A utilitarian who judges between any two distributions by seeing which has the greater sum of utility and, if the sums tie, applies some fixed equality criterion to choose the more equal distribution, would hold a current time-slice principle of justice. As would someone who had a fixed schedule of trade-offs between the sum of happiness and equality. According to a current time-slice principle, all that needs to be looked at, in judging the justice of a distribution, is who ends up with what;

in comparing any two distributions one need look only at the matrix presenting the distributions. No further information need be fed into a principle of justice. It is a consequence of such principles of justice that any two structurally identical distributions are equally just. (Two distributions are structurally identical if they present the same profile, but perhaps have different persons occupying the particular slots. My having ten and your having five, and my having five and your having ten are structurally identical distributions.) Welfare economics is the theory of current time-slice principles of justice. The subject is conceived as operating on matrices representing only current information about distribution. This, as well as some of the usual conditions (for example, the choice of distribution is invariant under relabelling of columns), guarantees that welfare economics will be a current time-slice theory, with all of its inadequacies.

Most persons do not accept current time-slice principles as constituting the whole story about distributive shares. They think it relevant in assessing the justice of a situation to consider not only the distribution it embodies, but also how that distribution came about. If some persons are in prison for murder or war crimes, we do not say that to assess the justice of the distribution in the society we must look only at what this person has, and that person has, and that person has ... at the current time. We think it relevant to ask whether someone did something so that he *deserved* to be punished, deserved to have a lower share. Most will agree to the relevance of further information with regard to punishments and penalties. Consider also desired things. One traditional socialist view is that workers are entitled to the product and full fruits of their labor; they have earned it; a distribution is unjust if it does not give the workers what they are entitled to. Such entitlements are based upon some past history. No socialist holding this view would find it comforting to be told that because the actual distribution *A* happens to coincide structurally with the one he desires *D*, *A* therefore is no less just than *D*; it differs only in that the 'parasitic' owners of capital receive under *A*, what the workers are entitled to under *D*, and the workers receive under *A* what the owners are entitled to under *D*, namely very little. This socialist rightly, in my view, holds onto the notions of earning, producing, entitlement, desert, and so forth, and he rejects current time-slice principles that look only to the structure of the resulting set of holdings. (The set of holdings resulting from what? Isn't it implausible that how holdings are produced and come to exist has no effect at all on who should hold what?) His mistake lies in his view of what entitlements arise out of what sorts of productive processes.

We construe the position we discuss too narrowly by speaking *of current* time-slice principles. Nothing is changed if structural principles operate upon a time sequence of current time-slice profiles and, for example, give someone more now to counterbalance the less he has had earlier. A utilitarian or an egalitarian or any mixture of the two over time will inherit the difficulties of his more myopic comrades. He is not helped by the fact that *some of* the information others consider relevant in assessing a distribution is reflected, unrecoverably, in past matrices. Henceforth, we shall refer to such unhistorical principle's of distributive justice, including the current time-slice principles, as *end-result principles or end-state principles.*

In contrast to end-result principles of justice, *historical principles* of justice hold that past circumstances or actions of people can create differential entitlements or differential deserts to things. An injustice can be worked by moving from one distribution to another structurally identical one, for the second, in profile the same, may violate people's entitlements or deserts; it may not fit the actual history.

Patterning

The entitlement principles of justice in holdings that we have sketched are historical principles of justice. To better understand their precise character, we shall distinguish them from another subclass of the historical principles. Consider, as an example, the principle of distribution according to moral merit. This principle requires that total distributive shares vary directly with moral merit; no person should have a greater share than anyone whose moral merit is greater. (If moral merit could be not merely ordered but measured on an interval or ratio scale, stronger principles could be formulated.) Or consider the principle that results by substituting 'usefulness to society' for 'moral merit' in the previous principle. Or instead of 'distribute according to moral merit', or 'distribute according to usefulness to society', we might consider 'distribute according to the weighted sum of moral merit, usefulness to society, and need', with the weights of the different dimensions equal. Let us call a principle of distribution *patterned* if it specifies that a distribution is to vary along with some natural dimension, weighted sum of natural dimensions, or lexicographic ordering of natural dimensions. And let us say a distribution is patterned if it accords with some patterned principle. (I speak of natural dimensions, admittedly without a general criterion for them, because for any set of holdings some artificial dimensions can be gimmicked up to vary along with the distribution of the set.) The principle of distribution in accordance with moral merit is a patterned historical principle, which specifies a patterned distribution. 'Distribute according to I.Q.' is a patterned principle that looks to information not contained in distributional matrices. It is not historical, however, in that it does not look to any past actions creating differential entitlements to evaluate a distribution; it requires only distributional matrices whose columns are labelled by I.Q. scores. The distribution in a society, however, may be composed of such simple patterned distributions, without itself being simply patterned. Different sectors may operate different patterns, or some combination of patterns may operate in different proportions across a society. A distribution composed in this manner, from a small number of patterned distributions, we also shall term 'patterned'. And we extend the use of 'pattern' to include the overall designs put forth by combinations of end-state principles.

Almost every suggested principle of distributive justice is patterned: to each according to his moral merit, or needs, or marginal product, or how hard he tries, or the weighted sum of the foregoing, and so on. The principle of entitlement we have sketched is *not* patterned. There is no one natural dimension or weighted sum or combination of a small number of natural dimensions that yields the distributions generated in accordance with the principle of entitlement. The set of holdings that results when some persons receive their marginal products, others win at gambling, others receive a share of their mate's income, others receive gifts from foundations, others receive interest on loans, others receive gifts from admirers, others receive returns on investment, others make for themselves much of what they have, others find things, and so on, will not be patterned. Heavy strands of patterns will run through it; significant portions of the variance in holdings will be accounted for by pattern-variables. If most people most of the time choose to transfer some of their entitlements to others only in exchange for something from them, then a large part of what many people hold will vary with what they held that others wanted. More details are provided by the theory of marginal productivity. But gifts to relatives, charitable donations, bequests to children, and the like, are not best conceived, in the first instance, in this manner. Ignoring the strands of pattern, let us suppose for the moment that a distribution actually arrived at by the operation of the principle of entitlement is random with respect to any pattern. Though the resulting set of holdings will be unpatterned, it will not be incomprehensible, for it can be seen as arising from the operation of a small number of principles. These principles specify how an initial distribution may arise (the principle of acquisition of holdings) and how distributions may he transformed into others (the principle of transfer of holdings). The process whereby the set of holdings is generated will be intelligible, though the set of holdings itself that results from this process will be unpatterned.

...

How liberty upsets patterns

It is not clear how those holding alternative conceptions of distributive justice can reject the entitlement conception of justice in holdings. For suppose a distribution favored by one of these non-entitlement conceptions is realized. Let us suppose it is your favorite one and let us call this distribution *D* 1; perhaps everyone has an equal share, perhaps shares vary in accordance with some dimension you treasure. Now suppose that Wilt Chamberlain is greatly in demand by basketball teams, being a great gate attraction. (Also suppose contracts run only for a year, with players being free agents.) He signs the following sort of contract with a team: In each home game, twenty-five cents from the price of each ticket of admission goes to him ... Wilt Chamberlain winds up with $250,000, a much larger sum than the average income and larger even than anyone else has. Is he entitled to this income? Is this new distribution *D* 2, unjust? If so, why? There is no question about whether each of the people was entitled to the control over the resources they held in *D* 1; because that was the distribution (your favorite) that (for the purposes of argument) we assumed was acceptable. Each of these persons *chose* to give twenty-five cents of their money to Chamberlain. They could have spent it on going to the movies, or on candy bars, or on copies of *Dissent* magazine, or of *Monthly Review*. But they all, at least one million of them, converged on giving it to Wilt Chamberlain in exchange for watching him play basketball. If *D* 1 was a just distribution, and people voluntarily moved from it to *D* 2, transferring parts of their shares they were given under *D* 1 (what was it for if not to do something with?), isn't *D* 2 also just? If the people were entitled to dispose of the resources to which they were entitled (under *D* 1), didn't this include their being entitled to give it to, or exchange it with, Wilt Chamberlain? Can anyone else complain on grounds of justice? Each other person already has his legitimate share under *D* 1. Under *D* 1, there is nothing that anyone has that anyone else has a claim of justice against. After someone transfers something to Wilt Chamberlain, third parties *still* have their legitimate shares; *their* shares are not changed. By what process could such a transfer among two persons give rise to a legitimate claim of distributive justice on a portion of what was transferred, by a third party who had no claim of justice on any holding of the others *before* the transfer?

...

The general point illustrated by the Wilt Chamberlain example and the example of the entrepreneur in a socialist society is that no end-state principle or distributional patterned principle of justice can be continuously realized without continuous interference with people's lives. Any favored pattern would be transformed into one unfavored by the principle, by people choosing to act in various ways; for example, by people exchanging goods and services with other people, or giving things to other people, things the transferrers are entitled to under the favored distributional pattern. To maintain a pattern one must either continually interfere to stop people from transferring resources as they wish to, or continually (or periodically) interfere to take from some persons resources that others for some reason chose to transfer to them. (But if some time limit is to be set on how long people may keep resources others voluntarily transfer to them, why let them keep these resources for *any* period of time? Why not have immediate confiscation?) It might be objected that all persons voluntarily will choose to refrain from actions which would upset the pattern. This presupposes unrealistically (1) that all will most want to maintain the pattern (are those who don't, to be 'reeducated' or forced to undergo 'self-criticism'?), (2) that each can gather enough information about his own actions and the ongoing activities of others to discover which of his actions will upset the pattern, and (3) that diverse and far-flung persons can coordinate their actions to dovetail into the pattern. Compare the manner in which the market is neutral among persons' desires, as it reflects and transmits widely scattered information via prices, and coordinates persons' activities.

It puts things perhaps a bit too strongly to say that every patterned (or end-state) principle is liable to be thwarted by the voluntary actions of the individual parties transferring some of their shares they receive under the principle. For perhaps some *very* weak patterns are not so thwarted. Any distributional pattern with any egalitarian component is overturnable by the voluntary actions of individual persons over time; as is every patterned condition with sufficient content so as actually to have been proposed as presenting the central core of distributive justice. Still, given the possibility that some weak conditions or patterns may not be unstable in this way, it would be better to formulate an explicit description of the kind of interesting and contentful patterns under discussion, and to prove a theorem about their instability. Since the weaker the patterning, the more likely it is that the entitlement system itself satisfies it, a plausible conjecture is that any patterning either is unstable or is satisfied by the entitlement system.

Redistribution and property rights

...

Patterned principles of distributive justice necessitate redistributive activities. The likelihood is small that any actual freely-arrived-at set of holdings fits a given pattern; and the likelihood is nil that it will continue to fit the pattern as people exchange and give. From the point of view of an entitlement theory, redistribution is a serious matter indeed, involving, as it does, the violation of people's rights. (An exception is those takings that under the principle of the rectification of injustices.) From other points of view, also, it is serious.

Taxation of earnings from labor is on a par with forced labor. Some persons find this claim obviously true: taking the earnings of n hours labor is like taking n hours from the person; it is like forcing the person to work *n* hours for another's purpose. Others find the claim absurd. But even these, if they object to forced labor, would oppose forcing unemployed hippies to work for the benefit of the needy. And they would also object to forcing each person to work five extra hours each week for the benefit of the needy. But a system that takes five hours' wages in taxes does not seem to them like one that forces someone to work five hours, since it offers the person forced a wider range of choice in activities than does taxation in kind with the particular labor specified. (But we can imagine a gradation of systems of forced labor, from one that specifies a particular activity, to one that gives a choice among two activities, to … ; and so on up.) Furthermore, people envisage a system with something like a proportional tax on everything above the amount necessary for basic needs. Some think this does not force someone to work extra hours, since there is no fixed number of extra hours he is forced to work, and since he can avoid the tax entirely by earning only enough to cover his basic needs. This is a very uncharacteristic view of forcing for those who *also* think people are forced to do something *whenever* the alternatives they face are considerably worse. However, *neither* view is correct. The fact that others intentionally intervene, in violation of a side constraint against aggression, to threaten force to limit the alternatives, in this case to paying taxes or (presumably the worse alternative) bare subsistence, makes the taxation system one of forced labor and distinguishes it from other cases of limited choices which are not forcings.

The man who chooses to work longer to gain an income more than sufficient for his basic needs prefers some extra goods or services to the leisure and activities he could perform during the possible nonworking hours; whereas the man who chooses not to work the extra time prefers the leisure activities to the extra goods or services he could acquire by working more. Given this, if it would be illegitimate for a tax system to seize some of a man's leisure (forced labor) for the purpose of serving the needy, how can it be legitimate for a tax system to seize some of a man's goods for that purpose? Why should we treat the man whose happiness requires certain material goods or services differently from the man whose preferences and desires make such goods unnecessary for his happiness? Why should the man who prefers seeing a movie (and who has to earn money for a ticket) be open to the required call to aid the needy, while the person who prefers looking at a sunset (and hence need earn no extra money) is not? Indeed, isn't it surprising that redistributionists choose to ignore the man whose pleasures are so easily attainable without extra labor, while adding yet another burden to the poor unfortunate who must work for his pleasures? If anything, one would have expected the reverse. Why is the person with the nonmaterial or nonconsumption desire allowed to proceed unimpeded to his most favored feasible alternative, whereas the man whose pleasures or desires involve material things and who must work for extra money (thereby serving whomever considers his activities valuable enough to pay him) is constrained in what he can realize? Perhaps there is no difference in principle. And perhaps some think the answer concerns merely administrative convenience. (These questions and issues will not disturb those who think that forced labor to serve the needy or to realize some favored end-state pattern is acceptable.) In a discussion we would have (and want) to extend our argument include interest, entrepreneurial profits, and so on. Those who doubt that this extension can be carried through, and who draw the line here at taxation of income from labor, will have to state rather complicated patterned *historical* principles of distributive justice, since end-state principles would not distinguish *sources* of income in any way. It is enough for now to get away from end-state principles and to make clear how various patterned principles are dependent upon particular views about the sources or the illegitimacy or the lesser legitimacy of profits, interest, and so on; which particular views may well be mistaken.

What sort of right over others does a legally institutionalized end-state pattern give one? The central core of the notion of a property right in X, relative to which other parts of the notion are to be explained, is the right to determine what shall be done with X; the right to choose which of the constrained set of options concerning X shall be realized or attempted. The constraints are set by other principles or laws operating in the society; in our theory, by the Lockean rights people possess (under the minimal state). My property rights in my knife allow me to leave it where I will, but not in your chest. I may choose which of the acceptable options involving the knife is to be realized. This notion of property helps us to understand why earlier theorists spoke of people as having property in themselves and their labor. They viewed each person as having a right to decide what would become of himself and what he would do, and as having a right to reap the benefits of what he did.

This right of selecting the alternative to be realized from the constrained set of alternatives may be held by an *individual* or by a *group* with some procedure for reaching a joint decision; or the right may be passed back and forth, so that one year I decide what's to become of X, and the next year you do (with the alternative of destruction, perhaps, being excluded). Or, during the same time period, some types of decisions about X may be made by me, and others by you. And so on. We lack an adequate, fruitful, analytical apparatus for classifying the *types* of constraints on the set of options among which choices are to be made, and the *types* of ways decision powers can be held, divided, and amalgamated. A *theory* of property would, among other things, contain such a classification of constraints and decision modes, and from a small number of principles would follow a host of interesting statements about *the consequences* and effects of certain combinations of constraints and modes of decision.

When end-result principles of distributive justice are built into the legal structure of a society, they (as do most patterned principles) give each citizen an enforceable claim to some portion of the total social product; that is, to some portion of the sum total of the individually and jointly made products. This total product is produced by individuals laboring, using means of production others have saved to bring into existence, by people organizing production or creating means to produce new things or things in a new way. It is on this hatch of individual activities that patterned distributional principles give each individual an enforceable claim. Each person has a claim to the activities and the products of other persons, independently of whether the other persons enter into particular relationships that give rise to these claims, and independently of whether they voluntarily take these claims upon themselves, in charity or in exchange for something.

Whether it is done through taxation on wages or on wages over a certain amount, or through seizure of profits, or through there being a big *social pot* so that it's not clear what's coming from where and what's going where, patterned principles of distributive justice involve appropriating the actions of other persons. Seizing the results of someone's labor is equivalent to seizing hours from him and directing him to carry on various activities. If people force you to do certain work, or unrewarded work, for a certain period of time, they decide what you are to do and what purposes your work is to serve apart from your decisions. This process whereby they take this decision from you makes them a *part-owner* of you; it gives them a property right in you, just as having such partial control and power of decision, by right, over an animal or inanimate object would be to have a property right in it.

End-state and most patterned principles of distributive justice institute (partial) ownership by others of people and their actions and labor. These principles involve a shift from the classical liberals' notion of self-ownership to a notion of (partial) property rights in *other* people.

Considerations such as these confront end-state and other patterned conceptions of justice with the question of whether the actions necessary to achieve the selected pattern don't themselves violate moral side constraints ... Since deviation from the first two principles of justice (in acquisition and transfer) will involve other persons' direct and aggressive intervention to violate rights, and since moral constraints will not exclude defensive or retributive action in such cases, the entitlement theorist's problem rarely will be pressing. And whatever difficulties he has in applying the principle of rectification to persons who did not themselves violate the first two principles are difficulties in balancing the conflicting considerations so as correctly to formulate the complex principle of rectification itself; he will not violate moral side constraints by applying the principle. Proponents of patterned conceptions of justice, however, often will face head-on clashes (and poignant ones if they cherish each party to the clash) between moral side constraints on how individuals may be treated and their patterned conception of justice that presents an end state or other pattern that *must* be realized.

Collective assets

Rawls' view seems to be that everyone has some entitlement or claim on the totality of natural assets (viewed as a pool), with no one having differential claims. The distribution of natural abilities is viewed as a 'collective asset'.

...

We have used our entitlement conception of justice in holdings to probe Rawls' theory, sharpening our understanding of what the entitlement conception involves by bringing it to bear upon an alternative conception of distributive justice, one that is deep and elegant. Also, I believe, we have probed deep-lying inadequacies in Rawls' theory.

...

We began this chapter's investigation of distributive justice in order to consider the claim that a state more extensive than the minimal state could be justified on the grounds that it was necessary, or the most appropriate instrument, to achieve distributive justice. According to the entitlement conception of justice in holdings that we have presented, there is no argument based upon the first two principles of distributive justice, the principles of acquisition and of transfer, for such a more extensive state. If the set of holdings is properly generated, there is no argument for a more extensive state based upon distributive justice ... If, however, these principles are violated, the principle of rectification comes into play. Perhaps it is best to view some patterned principles of distributive justice as rough rules of thumb meant to approximate the general results of applying the principle of rectification of injustice. For example, lacking much historical information, and assuming (1) that victims of injustice generally do worse than they otherwise would and (2) that those from the least well-off group in the society have the highest probabilities of being the (descendants of) victims of the most serious injustice who are owed compensation by those who benefited from the injustices (assumed to be those better off, though sometimes the perpetrators will be others in the worst-off group), then a *rough* rule of thumb for rectifying injustices might seem to be the following: organize society so as to maximize the position of whatever group ends up least well-off in the society. This particular example may well be implausible, but an important question for each society will be the following: given *its* particular history, what operable rule of thumb best approximates the results of a detailed application in that society of the principle of rectification? These issues are very complex and are best left to a full treatment of the principle of rectification. In the absence of such a treatment applied to a particular society, one *cannot* use the analysis and theory presented here to condemn any particular scheme of transfer payments, unless it is clear that no considerations of rectification of injustice could apply to justify it. Although to introduce socialism as the punishment for our sins would be to go too far, past injustices might be so great as to make necessary in the short run a more extensive state in order to rectify them.

2. Critique of Nozick

The extensive critical literature on Nozick has raised many issues, ranging from relatively specific points of detail, to his fundamental methodology. Only a few will be indicated here.

1. Like any account of supposed rights in a state of nature, there are problems about how Nozick derives and defines them. Why is there a right to property, but not to welfare, or to concern from others? Should the moral landscape be limited to rights? What about duties?

2. The night watchman state arises through the suppression of competing protective agencies. If the others consent to this by being bought out, this makes the state a Chicago mobster style protection racket writ large. If consent to it is based on some notion that people would accept the rationality of one organisation having a monopoly of legitimate violence, then why would they not accept the rationality of having a more extensive protection from other insecurities, a more extensive welfare state?

3. Nozick's night watchman state arguably includes a measure of redistribution from the more to the less powerful. The strong only need to fear each other, so if they were purely self-interested they could include only themselves in the protective association. Why support a more extensive state offering general protection against violence? The logic of this has been developed *de facto* since Nozick's book appeared, as better off sections of society increasingly rely on private security for their protection. More extreme libertarians than Nozick have advocated the complete privatisation of policing, and even our New Labour government has presided over an extensive privatisation of areas of criminal justice. Perhaps Nozick's night watchman state is not as minimal as he thought in 1974.

4. There is a tension between justifying inequality through the historical entitlement argument, and the Wilt Chamberlain example, which sees it as the reward for the contribution of the talented to the happiness of the population generally. Wilt Chamberlain may have become rich by pleasing the crowds. But if he passes this

on to his heirs, what have they done to merit their wealth? Yet they have clearly acquired their inheritance through a voluntary transfer satisfying the historical entitlement test.

5. How extensive a degree of redistribution is envisaged on the rectification of past injustice argument? Nozick seems to have in mind the kind of compensation for specific wrongs involved in legal judgements for damages. But how is this to be demarcated in principle from wider and longer-term recompense for concrete injustices? Restitution to Holocaust survivors is widely seen as justified as many perpetrators and victims are still alive. But compensating Afro-Americans for the wrongs of slavery has proved acutely controversial, as has the use of affirmative action to overcome the continuing consequences of centuries of oppression and discrimination. How are the lines to be drawn?

6. Most fundamentally, Nozick criticises more egalitarian arguments such as Rawls' (or Dworkin's) for starting from a hypothetical initial position of equality and placing the burden of proof on those who seek to justify inequality (a burden which in Rawls' theory is satisfied by the difference principle). But doesn't Nozick's analysis simply invert the starting point and the onus of proof? The initial presumption is the right to property, and that the existing distribution is based on just acquisition. The onus of proof is on those who wish to change this, for example by establishing specific historical wrongs that deserve to be rectified. The Wilt Chamberlain parable starts from the assumption that he deserves his talent for basketball. But isn't there some plausibility in Rawls' argument that the distribution of natural talents is a morally arbitrary lottery, so there is no principled reason for rewarding its exercise per se? Can we escape from concluding that either starting point favours some interests over others? Perhaps Rawls' device of the OP as a way of deliberating fairly is the only way out after all?

As representatives of a liberal approach to justice, the theories of both Nozick and Rawls have been subject to criticism from communitarians, feminists, socialists, and conservatives for the individualistic slant of his arguments. We turn to the communitarian version of this claim next. Before doing so however, it is important to note that one of the consequences of the abstract character of both Rawl's 'difference principle' and Nozick's 'historical' theory of just entitlements is that the actual political arrangements they yield in practice overwhelmingly depends upon what further factual assumptions one makes, or what other theories one subscribes to. With respect to the difference principle, many neo-conservatives would be happy to accept it as a principle of justice but then go on to argue that the worst off will do best under laissez-faire capitalism, despite any inequalities it would generate; thus the principle will not necessarily dictate egalitarian economic policies, but perhaps the very opposite. Likewise it is a mistake to think that Nozick's principles of just acquisition, just transfer, and rectification are inherently 'right-wing'. First of all, the principle of rectification, broadly understood, would upset most of the holdings of land and goods presently enjoyed by people in the developed world, for it defies belief in light of human history to think that these were originally acquired justly, rather than by force, coercion and so on, and any subsequent holding (however just the transfers that led to it) will be compromised by any injustice in original acquisition. But the radical import of Nozick's theory doesn't stop there. For a holding to be just, any transfers leading to it must be just, and what the standards on just transfer amount to in practice is an extremely contentious issue. For example, if one thinks that just exchanges only occur in perfectly competitive, or nearly perfectly competitive, markets, then next to no real life contractual exchanges are just – the principle of just transfers might dictate the most extensive intervention in the economy, because without that intervention no transfer could be regarded as just. In short, the so-called minimal state could, in practice, be a more invasive or interventionist state than any developed country has yet seen.

The Communitarian Critique

During the 1980s a number of different writers advanced criticisms of the individualistic assumptions that are shared by liberals like Rawls and Nozick (despite the acute differences between them). This critique came to be labelled 'communitarianism', although it must be emphasised that the differences between these writers are profound, and in no sense do they constitute a united movement. (The leading works that have been referred to in this way are MacIntyre 1981; Sandel 1982; Walzer 1985; Taylor 1989. The most useful reviews of the liberal-communitarian debate are Frazer and Lacey 1993; Mulhall and Swift 1996. Avineri and de-Shalit 1992 is an invaluable collection of key sources. In the late 1980s communitarianism became a political movement in the United States and Britain (and elsewhere), seeking to find a way between the rugged individualism of the neo-liberals then in government, and the traditional socialism that seemed to have lost its social and political base (Etzioni 1993). It thus anticipated some aspects of what in the 1990s came to be espoused by a new clutch of centre-left governments as the 'third way'. There is only a tenuous reflection at best in this movement of the more fundamental and rigorous liberal v communitarian philosophical debate stimulated by Rawls' theory.) That communitarianism does not constitute a united movement is particularly evident if we consider what they seem to regard as desirable rather than what they reject in individualistic liberalism. Thus whilst some (notably Alasdair Macintyre) are *counter-modern* in harking back to the lost virtues of the ancient or medieval past, others seem post-modern or post-liberal in their pragmatic or principled acceptance of a variety of alternative spheres of justice that cannot be reduced to any single set of principles.

Two inter-related dimensions of the communitarian critique may be distinguished (Avineri and de-Shalit 1992, 2): methodological and normative. The *methodological* aspect of the critique questions the coherence and plausibility of the radically individualistic concept of the self that underpins liberal theories of justice. As made most explicit in Rawls' construction of the OP, liberalism appears to conceive the self as an abstracted capacity to choose, autonomous of any particular loyalties, values, tastes, commitments, history or identity. Sandel has memorably called this conception the 'unencumbered self' (Sandel 1984). All the attributes that characterise individuals are defined out of the OP, including even their distinctive abilities. Against this Sandel argues that people are not selves first, who then acquire a personality and group memberships: they are born already socially situated and constituted by their particular experiences. In MacIntyre's formulation of the point, a person can only have a sense of self in terms of a particular history and 'narrative' that forms a particular personal identity: 'I am born with a past' (MacIntyre 1981, 221). Our values in particular derive from our membership in specific cultures, and are not contingently but necessarily related to distinct practices and ways of life without reference to which it is impossible to make meaningful judgements of virtue. Justice cannot be universal or absolute, but is embedded in specific 'spheres' of activity with their own criteria of evaluation (Walzer 1985). Thus constructing a theory of justice on a concept of the 'unencumbered self' is not merely unappealing to communitarians but incoherent.

Sandel (1984, 81–96)

Political philosophy seems often to reside at a distance from the world. Principles are one thing, politics another, and even our best efforts to 'live up' to our ideals typically founder on the gap between theory and practice.

But if political philosophy is unrealizable in one sense, it is unavoidable in another. This is the sense in which philosophy inhabits the world from the start; our practices and institutions are embodiments of theory. To engage in a political practice is already to stand in relation to theory. For all our uncertainties about ultimate questions of political philosophy – of justice and value and the nature of the good life – the one thing we know is that we live *some* answer all the time.

In this essay I will try to explore the answer we live now ... What is the political philosophy implicit in our practices and institutions? How does it stand, as philosophy? And how do tensions in the philosophy find expression in our present political condition?

It may he objected that it is a mistake to look for a single philosophy, that we live no 'answer', only answers. But a plurality of answers is itself a kind of answer. And the political theory that affirms this pluralitv is the theory I propose to I explore.

THE RIGHT AND THE GOOD

We might begin by considering a certain moral and political vision. It is a liberal vision, and like most liberal visions gives pride of place to justice, fairness, and individual rights. Its core thesis is this: a just society seeks not to promote any particular ends, but enables its citizens to pursue their own ends, consistent with a similar liberty for all; it therefore must govern by principles that do not presuppose any particular conception of the good. What justifies these regulative principles above is not that they maximize the general welfare, or cultivate virtue, or otherwise promote the good, but rather that they conform to the concept of *right*, a moral category given prior to the good, and independent of it.

This liberalism says, in other words, that what makes the just society just is not the *telos* or purpose or end at which it aims, but precisely its refusal to choose in advance among competing purposes and ends. In its constitution and its laws, the just society seeks to provide a framework within which its citizens can pursue their own values and ends, consistent with a similar liberty for others.

The ideal I've described might be summed up in the claim that the right is prior to the good, and in two senses: the priority of the right means, first, that individual rights cannot be sacrificed for the sake of the general good (in this it opposes utilitarianism), and, second, that the principles of justice that specify these rights cannot be premissed on any particular vision of the good life. (In this it opposes teleological conceptions in general.)

This is the liberalism of much contemporary moral and political philosophy, most fully elaborated by Rawls, and indebted to Kant for its, philosophical foundations. But I am concerned here less with the lineage of this vision than with what seem to me three striking facts about it.

First, it has a deep and powerful philosophical appeal. Second, despite its philosophical force, the claim for the priority of the right over the good ultimately fails. And, third, despite its philosophical failure, this liberal vision is the one by which we live. ...

But before taking up these three claims, it is worth pointing out a central theme that connects them. And that is a certain conception of the person, of what it is to be a moral agent. Like all political theories, the liberal theory I have described is something more than a set of regulative principles. It is also a view about the way the world is, and the way we move within it. At the heart of this ethic lies a vision of the person that both inspires and undoes it. As I will try to argue now, what makes this ethic so compelling, but also, finally, vulnerable, are the promise and the failure of the unencumbered self.

KANTIAN FOUNDATIONS

The liberal ethic asserts the priority of right, and seeks principles of justice that do not presuppose any particular conception of the good. This is what Kant means by the supremacy of the moral law, and what Rawls means when he writes that 'justice is the first virtue of social institutions'. Justice is more than just another value. It provides the framework that *regulates* the play of competing values and ends; it must therefore have a sanction independent of those ends. But it is not obvious where such a sanction could be found.

Theories of justice, and, for that matter, ethics, have typically founded their claims on one or another conception of human purposes and ends. Thus Aristotle said the measure of a *polis is* the good at which it aims, and even J. S. Mill, who in the nineteenth century called 'justice the chief part, and incomparably the most binding part of all morality', made justice an instrument of utilitarian ends.

This is the solution Kant's ethic rejects. Different persons typically have different desires and ends, and so any principle derived from them can only be contingent. But the moral law needs a *categorical* foundation, not a contingent one. Even so universal a desire as happiness will not do. People still differ in what happiness consists of, and to install any particular conception as regulative would impose on some the conceptions of others, and so deny at least to some the freedom to choose their *own* conceptions. In any case, to govern ourselves in conformity with desires and inclinations, given as they are by nature or circumstance, is not really to be self-governing at all. It is rather a refusal of freedom, a capitulation to determinations given outside us.

According to Kant, the right is 'derived entirely from the concept of freedom in the external relationships of human beings, and has nothing to do with the end which all men have by nature [ie the aim of achieving happiness] or with the recognized means of attaining this end'. As such, it must have a basis prior to all empirical ends. Only when I am governed by principles that do not presuppose any particular ends am I free to pursue my own ends consistent with a similar freedom for all.

But this still leaves the question of what the basis of the right could possibly be. If it must be a basis prior to all purposes and ends, unconditioned even by what Kant calls 'the special circumstances of human nature', where could such a basis conceivably be found? Given the stringent demands of the Kantian ethic, the moral law would seem almost to require a foundation in nothing, for any empirical precondition would undermine its priority. 'Duty!' asks Kant at his most lyrical, 'What origin is there worthy of thee, and where is to be found the root of thy noble descent which proudly rejects all kinship with the inclinations?'

His answer is that the basis of the moral law is to be found in the *subject*, not the object of practical reason, a subject capable of an autonomous will. No empirical end, but rather 'a subject of ends, namely a rational being himself, must be made the ground for all maxims of action'. Nothing other than what Kant calls 'the subject of all possible ends himself' can give rise to the right, for only this subject is also the subject of an autonomous will. Only this subject could be that 'something which elevates man above himself as part of the world of sense' and enables him to participate in an ideal, unconditioned realm wholly independent of our social and psychological inclinations. And only this thoroughgoing independence can afford us the detachment we need if we are ever freely to choose for ourselves, unconditioned by the vagaries of circumstance.

Who or what exactly is this subject? – It is, in a certain sense, *us*. The moral law, after all, is a law we give *ourselves*; we don't *find* it, we *will* it. That is how it (and we) escape the reign of nature and circumstance and merely empirical ends. But what is important to see is that the 'we' who do the willing are not 'we' *qua* particular persons, you and me, each for ourselves – the moral law is not up to us as individuals – but 'we' *qua* participants in what Kant calls 'pure practical reason', 'we' *qua* participants in a transcendental subject.

Now what is to guarantee that I *am* a subject of this kind, capable of exercising pure practical reason? Well, strictly speaking, there *is* no guarantee; the transcendental subject is only a possibility. But it is a possibility I must *presuppose* if I am to think of myself as a free moral agent. Were I wholly an empirical being, I would not be capable of freedom, for every exercise of will would be conditioned by the desire for some object. All choice would be heteronomous choice, governed by the pursuit of some end. My will could never be a first cause, only the effect of some prior cause, the instrument of one or another impulse or inclination. 'When we think of ourselves as free,' writes Kant, 'we transfer ourselves into the intelligible world as members and recognize the autonomy of the will'. And so the notion of a subject prior to and independent of experience, such as the Kantian ethic requires, appears not only possible but indispensable, a necessary presupposition of the possibility of freedom.

How does all of this come back to politics? As the subject is prior to its ends, so the right is prior to the good. Society is best arranged when it is governed by principles that do not presuppose any particular conception of the good, for any other arrangement would fail to respect persons as being capable of choice; it would treat them as objects rather than subjects, as means rather than ends in themselves.

We can see in this way how Kant's notion of the subject is bound up with the claim for the priority of right. But for those in the Anglo-American tradition, the transcendental subject will seem a strange foundation for a familiar ethic. Surely, one may think, we can take rights seriously and affirm the primacy of justice without embracing the *Critique of pure Reason*. This, in any case, is the project of Rawls.

He wants to save the priority of right from the obscurity of the transcendental subject. Kant's idealist metaphysic, for all its moral and political advantage, cedes too much to the transcendent, and wins for justice its primacy only by denying it its human situation. 'To develop a viable Kantian conception of justice,' Rawls writes, 'the force and content of Kant's doctrine must be detached from its background in transcendental idealism' and recast within the 'canons of a reasonable empiricism'. And so Rawls's project is to preserve Kant's moral and political teaching by replacing Germanic obscurities with a domesticated metaphysic more congenial to the Anglo-American temper. This is the role of the original position.

FROM TRANSCENDENTAL SUBJECT TO UNENCUMBERED SELF

The original position tries to provide what Kant's transcendental argument cannot – a foundation for the right that is prior to the good, but still situated in the world. Sparing all but essentials, the original position works like this: It invites us to imagine the principles we would choose to govern our society if we were to choose them in advance, before we knew the particular persons we would be – whether rich or poor, strong or weak, lucky or unlucky – before we knew even our interests or aims or conceptions of the good. These principles – the ones we would choose in that imaginary situation – are the principles of justice. What is more, if it works, they are principles that do not presuppose any particular ends.

What they do presuppose is a certain picture of the person, of the way we must be if we are beings for whom justice is the first virtue. This is the picture of the unencumbered self, a self understood as prior to and independent of purposes and ends.

Now the unencumbered self describes first of all the way we stand towards the things we have, or want, or seek. It means there is always a distinction between the values I *have* and the person I am. To identify any characteristics as my aims, ambitions, desires, and so on, is always to imply some subject 'me' standing behind them, at a certain distance, and the shape of this 'me' must be given prior to any of the aims or attributes I bear. One consequence of this distance is to put the self *itself* beyond the reach of its experience, to secure its identity once and for all. Or to put the point another way, it rules out the possibility of what we might call *constitutive* ends. No role or commitment could define me so completely that I could not understand myself without it. No project could be so essential that turning away from it would call into question the person I am. For the unencumbered self, what matters above all, what is most essential to our personhood, are not the ends we choose but our capacity to choose them. The original position sums up this central claim about us. 'It is not our aims that primarily reveal our nature,' writes Rawls, 'but rather the principles that we would acknowledge to govern the background conditions under which these aims are to be formed ... We should therefore reverse the relation between the right and the good proposed by teleological doctrines and view the right as prior.'

Only if the self is prior to its ends can the right be prior to the good. Only if my identity is never tied to the aims and interests I may have at any moment can I think of myself as a free and independent agent, capable of choice.

This notion of independence carries consequences for the kind of community of which we are capable. Understood as unencumbered selves, we are of course free to join in voluntary association with others, and so are capable of community in the co-operative sense. What is denied to the unencumbered self is the possibility of membership in any community bound by moral ties antecedent to choice; he cannot belong to any community where the self *itself* could be at stake. Such a community – call it constructive as against merely co-operative – would engage the identity as well as the interests of the participants, and so implicate its members in a citizenship more thorough-going than the unencumbered self can know.

For justice to be primary, then, we must be creatures of a certain kind, related to human circumstance in a certain way. We must stand to our circumstance always at a certain distance, whether as transcendental subject in the case of Kant, or as unencumbered selves in the case of Rawls. Only in this way can we view ourselves as subjects as well as objects of experience, as agents and not just instruments of the purposes we pursue.

The unencumbered self and the ethic it inspires, taken together, hold out a liberating vision. Freed from the dictates of nature and the sanction of social roles, the human subject is installed as sovereign, cast as the author of the only moral meanings there are. As participants in pure practical reason, or as parties to the original position, we are free to construct principles of justice unconstrained by an order of value antecedently given. And as actual, individual selves, we are free to choose our purposes and ends unbound by such an order, or by custom or tradition or inherited status. So long as they are not unjust, our conceptions of the good carry weight, whatever they are, simply in virtue of our having chosen them. We are, in Rawls's words, 'self-originating sources of valid claims'.

This is an exhilarating promise, and the liberalism it animates is perhaps the fullest expression of the Enlightenment's quest for the self-defining subject. But is it true? Can we make sense of our moral and political life by the light of the self-image it requires? I do not think we can, and I will try to show why not by arguing first within the liberal project, then beyond it.

JUSTICE AND COMMUNITY

We have focused so far on the foundations of the liberal vision, on the way it derives the principles it defends. Let us turn briefly now to the substance of those principles, using Rawls as our example. Sparing all but essentials once again, Rawls's two principles of justice are these: first, equal basic liberties for all, and, second, only those social and economic inequalities that benefit the least-advantaged members of society (the difference principle).

In arguing for these principles, Rawls argues against two familiar alternatives – utilitarianism and libertarianism. He argues against utilitarianism that it fails to take seriously the distinction between persons. In seeking to maximize the general welfare, the utilitarian treats society as a whole as if it were a single person; it conflates our many, diverse desires into a single system of desires, and tries to maximize. It is indifferent to the distribution of satisfactions among persons, except in so far as this may affect the overall sum. But this fails to respect our plurality and distinctness. It uses some as means to the happiness of all, and so fails to respect each as an end in himself. While utilitarians may sometimes defend individual rights, their defence must rest on the calculation that respecting those rights will serve utility in the long run. But this calculation is contingent and uncertain. So long as utility is what Mill said it is, 'the ultimate appeal on all ethical questions', individual rights can never be secure. To avoid the danger that their life prospects might one day be sacrificed for the greater good of others, the parties to the original position therefore insist on certain basic liberties for all, and make those liberties prior.

If utilitarians fail to take seriously the distinctness of persons, libertarians go wrong by failing to acknowledge the arbitrariness of fortune. They define as just whatever distribution results from an efficient market economy, and oppose all redistribution on the grounds that people are entitled to whatever they get, so long as they do not cheat or steal or otherwise violate someone's rights in getting it. Rawls opposes this principle on the ground that the distribution of talents and assets and even efforts by which some get more and others get less is arbitrary from a moral point of view, a matter of good luck. To distribute the good things in life on the basis of these differences is not to do justice, but simply to carry over into human arrangements the arbitrariness of social and natural contingency. We deserve, as individuals, neither the talents our good fortune may have brought, nor the benefits that flow from them. We should therefore regard these talents as common assets, and regard one another as common beneficiaries of the rewards they bring. 'Those who have been favored by nature, whoever they are, may gain from their good fortune only on terms that improve the situation of those who have lost out ... Injustice as fairness, men agree to share one another's fate'.

This is the reasoning that leads to the difference principle. Notice how it reveals, in yet another guise, the logic of the unencumbered self. I cannot be said to deserve the benefits that flow from, say, my fine physique and good looks, because they are only accidental, not essential facts about me. They describe attributes I *have*, not the person I am, and so cannot give rise to a claim of desert. Being an unencumbered self, this is true of *everything* about me. And so I cannot, as an individual, deserve anything at all.

However jarring to our ordinary understandings this argument may be, the picture so far remains intact; the priority of right, the denial of desert, and the unencumbered self all hang impressively together.

But the difference principle requires more, and it is here that the argument comes undone. The difference principle begins with the thought, congenial to the unencumbered self, that the assets I have are only accidentally mine. But it ends by assuming that these assets are therefore common assets and that society has a prior claim on the fruits of their exercise. But this assumption is without warrant. Simply because I, as an individual, do not have a privileged claim on the assets accidentally residing 'here', it does not follow that everyone in the world collectively does. For there is no reason to think that their location in society's province, or, for that matter, within the province of humankind, is any *less* arbitrary from a moral point of view. And if their arbitrariness within me makes them ineligible to serve *my* ends, there seems no obvious reason why their arbitrariness within any particular society should not make them ineligible to serve that society's ends as well.

To put the point another way, the difference principle, like utilitarianism, is a principle of sharing. As such, it must presuppose some prior moral tie among those whose assets it would deploy and whose efforts it would enlist in a common endeavour. Otherwise, it is simply a formula for using some as means to others' ends, a formula this liberalism is committed to reject.

But on the co-operative vision of community alone, it is unclear what the moral basis for this sharing could be. Short of the constitutive conception, deploying an individual's assets for the sake of the common good would seem an offence against the 'plurality and distinctness' of individuals this liberalism seeks above all to secure.

If those whose fate I am required to share really are, morally speaking, *others*, rather than fellow participants in a way of life with which my identity is bound, the difference principle falls prey to the same objections as utilitarianism. Its claim on me is not the claim of a constitutive community whose attachments I acknowledge, but rather the claim of a concatenated collectivity whose entanglements I confront.

What the difference principle requires, but cannot provide, is some way of identifying those *among* whom the assets I bear are properly regarded as common, some way of seeing ourselves as mutually indebted and morally engaged to begin with. But as we have seen, the constitutive aims and attachments that would save and situate the difference principle are precisely the ones denied to the liberal self; the moral encumbrances and antecedent obligations they imply would undercut the priority of right.

What, then, of those encumbrances? The point so far is that we cannot be persons for whom justice is primary, and also be persons for whom the difference principle is a principle of justice. But which must give way? Can we view ourselves as independent selves, independent in the sense that our identity is never tied to our aims and attachments?

I do not think we can, at least not without cost to those loyalties and convictions whose moral force consists partly in the fact that living by them is inseparable from understanding ourselves as the particular persons we are – as members of this family or community or nation or people, as bearers of that history, as citizens of this republic. Allegiances such as these are more than values I happen to have, and to hold, at a certain distance. They go beyond the obligations I voluntarily incur and the 'natural duties' I owe to human beings as such. They allow that to some I owe more than justice requires or even permits, not by reason of agreements I have made but instead in virtue of those more or less enduring attachments and commitments that, taken together, partly define the person I am.

To imagine a person incapable of constitutive attachments such as these is not to conceive an ideally free and rational agent, but to imagine a person wholly without character, without moral depth. For to have character is to know that I move in a history I neither summon nor command, which carries consequences none the less for my choices and conduct. It draws me closer to some and more distant from others; it makes some aims more appropriate, others less so. As a self-interpreting being, I am able to reflect on my history and in this sense to distance myself from it, but the distance is always precarious and provisional, the point of reflection never finally secured outside the history itself. But the liberal ethic puts the self beyond the reach of its experience, beyond deliberation and reflection. Denied the expansive self-understandings that could shape a common life, the liberal self is left to lurch between detachment on the one hand, and entanglement on the other. Such is the fate of the unencumbered self, and its liberating promise.

THE PROCEDURAL REPUBLIC

But before my case can be complete, I need to consider one powerful reply. While it comes from a liberal direction, its spirit is more practical than philosophical. It says, in short, that I am asking too much. It is one thing to seek constitutive attachments in our private lives; among families and friends, and certain tightly knit groups, there may be found a common good that makes justice and rights less pressing. But with public life – at least today, and probably always – it is different. So long as the nation state is the primary form of political association, talk of constitutive community too easily suggests a darker politics rather than a brighter one; amid echoes of the moral majority, the priority of right, for all its philosophical faults, still seems the safer hope.

This is a challenging rejoinder, and no account of political community in the twentieth century can fail to take it seriously. It is challenging not least because it calls into question the status of political philosophy and its relation to the world. For if my argument is correct, if the liberal vision we have considered is not morally self-sufficient but parasitic on a notion of community it officially rejects, then we should expect to find that the political practice that embodies this vision is not *practically* self-sufficient either – that it must draw on a sense of community it cannot supply and may even undermine. But is that so far from the circumstance we face today? Could it be that through the original position darkly, on the far side of the veil of ignorance, we may glimpse an intimation of our predicament, a refracted vision of ourselves?

How does the liberal vision – and its failure – help us make sense of our public life and its predicament? Consider, to begin, the following paradox in the citizen's relation to the modern welfare state. In many ways, we in the 1980s stand near the completion of a liberal project ... But notwithstanding the extension of the franchise and the expansion on individual rights and entitlements in recent decades, there is a widespread sense that, individually and collectively, our control over the forces that govern our lives is receding rather than increasing. This sense is deepened by what appear simultaneously as the power and the powerlessness of the nation state. On the one hand, increasing numbers of citizens view the state as an overly intrusive presence, more likely to frustrate their purposes than advance them. And yet, despite its unprecedented role in the economy and society, the modern state seems itself disempowered, unable effectively to control the domestic economy, to respond to persisting social ills.

...

This is a paradox that has fed the appeals of recent politicians ... even as it has frustrated their attempts to govern. To sort it out, we need to identify the public philosophy implicit in our political practice, and to reconstruct its arrival. We need to trace the advent of the procedural republic, by which I mean a public life animated by the liberal vision and self-image we've considered.

The story of the procedural republic goes back ... to unfold around the turn of the century. As national markets and large-scale enterprise displaced a decentralized economy, the decentralized political forms of the early republic became out-moded as well. If democracy was to survive, the concentration of economic power would have to be met by a similar concentration of political power. But the Progressives understood, or some of them did, that the success of democracy required more than the centralization of government; it also required the nationalization of politics. The primary form of political community had to be a recast on a national scale.

...

What matters for our purpose is that, in the twentieth century, liberalism made its peace with concentrated power. But it was understood at the start that the terms of this peace required a strong sense of national community, morally and politically to underwrite the extended involvements of a modern industrial order. If a virtuous republic of small-scale, democratic communities was no longer a possibility, a national republic seemed democracy's next best hope. This was still, in principle at least, a politics of the common good. It looked to the nation, not as a neutral framework for the play of competing interests, but rather as a formative community, concerned to shape a common life suited to the scale of modern social and economic forms.

But this project failed. By the mid-or late twentieth century the national republic had run its course. Except for extraordinary moments, such as war, the nation proved too vast a scale across which to cultivate the shared self-understandings necessary to community in the formative, or constitutive sense. And so the gradual shift, in our practices and institutions, from a public philosophy of common purposes to one of fair procedures, from a politics of good to a politics of right, from the national republic to the procedural republic.

OUR PRESENT PREDICAMENT

A full account of this transition would take a detailed look at the changing shape of political institutions, constitutional interpretation, and the terms of political discourse in the broadest sense. But I suspect we would find in the *practice* of the procedural republic two broad tendencies foreshadowed by its philosophy: first, a tendency to crowd out democratic possibilities; second, a tendency to undercut the kind of community on which it none the less depends.

Where liberty in the early republic was understood as a function of democratic institutions and dispersed power, liberty in the procedural republic is defined, in opposition to democracy, as an individual's guarantee against what the majority might will. I am free in so far as I am the bearer of rights, where rights are trumps. Unlike the liberty of the early republic, the modern version permits – in fact even requires – concentrated power. This has to do with the universalizing logic of rights. In so far as I have a right, whether to free speech or a minimum income, its provision cannot be left to the vagaries of local preferences but must be assured at the most comprehensive level of political association ... As rights and entitlements expand, politics is therefore displaced from smaller forms of association and relocated at the most universal form – in our case, the nation. And even as politics flows to the nation, power shifts away from democratic institutions (such as legislatures and political parties) and towards institutions designed to be insulated from democratic pressures, and hence better equipped to dispense and defend individual rights (notably the judiciary and bureaucracy).

These institutional developments may begin to account for the sense of powerlessness that the welfare state fails to address and in some ways doubtless deepens. But it seems to me a further clue to our condition recalls even more directly the predicament of the unencumbered self – lurching, as we left it, between detachment on the one hand, the entanglement on the other. For it is a striking feature of the welfare state that it offers a powerful promise of individual rights, and also demands of its citizens a high measure of mutual engagement. But the self-image that attends the rights cannot sustain the engagement.

As bearers of rights, where rights are trumps, we think of ourselves as freely choosing, individual selves, unbound by obligations antecedent to rights, or to the agreements we make. And yet, as citizens of the procedural republic that secures these rights, we find ourselves implicated willy-nilly in a formidable array of dependencies and expectations we did not choose and increasingly reject.

In our public life, we are more entangled, but less attached, than ever before. It is as though the unencumbered self presupposed by the liberal ethic had begun to come true – less liberated than disempowered, entangled in a network of obligations and involvements unassociated with any act of will, and yet unmediated by those common identifications or expansive self-definitions that would make them tolerable. As the scale of social and political organization has become more comprehensive, the terms of our collective identity have become more fragmented, and the forms of political life have outrun the common purpose needed to sustain them.

… I hope I have said at least enough to suggest the shape a fuller story might take. And I hope in any case to have conveyed a certain view about politics and philosophy and the relation between them – that our practices and institutions are themselves embodiments of theory, and to unravel their predicament is, at least in part, to seek after the self-image of the age.

The *normative* aspect of the communitarian critique argues that individualistic liberalism fails to acknowledge any value in community and relationships per se. However, there are virtues, allegiances, and ethical commitments that are not universal and rule-based but particularistic. They arise from those self-constituting attachments that liberalism seeks to abstract the self from. Loyalty and fidelity to family, community, nation – even leading to virtuous self-sacrifice on occasion – are obligations that cannot plausibly be derived from the choices of an unencumbered self. Any resulting conception of justice derived from so atomistic a view of the self is merely formal and procedural, and hence impoverished and uninspiring, without moral depth.

The methodological and normative aspects of the communitarian critique are partly interdependent. In particular it has been tellingly argued against Rawls that a tacit normative communitarianism is smuggled into his derivation of the difference principle.

Even if we grant Rawls' premise that the distribution of natural talents is morally arbitrary and thus does not justify special rewards to the individual who has them, it does not follow that their fruits should be regarded as common assets and hence available for redistribution to the least well off. To make this further step is 'to presuppose some prior moral tie' between people (Sandel 1984, 90), which Rawls' conception of the OP explicitly denies. Thus the fundamentally egalitarian principles of justice formulated by Rawls cannot be supported without some hidden communitarian assumption of normative obligations between people. (Some liberal theories of justice do explicitly start from a fundamental premise of equality in order to avoid this problem cf Dworkin 2000.)

That these points are telling is indicated above all by the fact that Rawls himself has clearly developed his theory to take account of them, as shown by his restatement in *Political Liberalism* (1993). However, communitarianism has also been subject to effective methodological and normative critique. Methodologically it must grapple with the issue of how to accommodate individual autonomy and difference within an account stressing the social structuring of the self. It is necessary to develop a dialectical, interactive conception of the self, transcending the either/or of the 'unencumbered' and the 'over-socialised' models of simple liberalism and communitarianism (Frazer and Lacey 1993, Ch 6). Normatively communitarianism suffers from the spectre of ethical relativism that it indeed largely embraces. Is there any way of criticising practices accepted within particular communities and cultures as unacceptable without reference to the rejected notions of universal rationality and principles attributed to liberalism? All the communitarian philosophers seek some way out of this impasse, and indeed the political values espoused by them range from conservative to radical, but this necessitates some dilution of the notion of values as entirely embedded within distinctive and non-commensurate spheres of justice.

Political Liberalism

Rawls has devoted the three decades since the initial publication of *A Theory of Justice* to developing and reformulating it in the light of subsequent debate and criticism. His 1993 book *Political Liberalism* (the introduction to the paperback edition sets out the leading ideas) is the major attempt to do this, although Rawls has continued to elaborate his perspective since then (Rawls 2001). *Political Liberalism* restates the theory of justice as fairness in the face of the communitarian critique.

Rawls' project in this long and complex work is to take into account fully the implications of a world of culture wars, of radically diverse, conflicting views of the good, none of which can trounce the other on principled grounds. A theory of justice must be seen as purely *political*, that is restricted to the 'basic structure of society, its main political, social, and economic institutions as a unified scheme of social co-operation', and be formulated 'independently of any wider comprehensive religious or philosophical doctrine' (Rawls 1993, 223). Rawls explicitly rejects any claim that justice as fairness can be seen as a comprehensive philosophical doctrine based on a particular view of the self or society. Rather it is defended as the theory of justice that can satisfy the requirements of a political democracy. It presumes as a fact that in liberal democracies people regard each other as 'free and equal' (Rawls 1993, 19). They are committed both to particular conceptions of the good, rooted in comprehensive religious or philosophical doctrines, and to a conception of fairness about their relationship to other people with different conceptions.

The basic issue facing political liberalism in contemporary democratic societies is the 'fact of reasonable pluralism' (Rawls 1993, 36). There is an inevitable 'diversity of reasonable comprehensive religious, philosophical, and moral doctrines found in modern democratic societies' (Rawls 1993, 36). This can be suppressed only through the use of oppression, because it will never be possible through argument or reason alone to show that only one doctrine is correct. Not all doctrines are 'reasonable': those which oppose liberal democracy are 'unreasonable', for example, if they seek to distribute advantages according to race or gender, or to establish the political dominance of a particular theological or hierarchical scheme. Such views which deny the democratic assumption of the basic freedom and equality of all persons have to be 'contained' somehow (Rawls 1993, xvii). But there is inevitably going to be a pluralism of reasonable doctrines.

Citizens of a democracy have to operate therefore with some form of public/private distinction, whereby they accept co-operation with adherents of doctrines that they believe are wrong but reasonable. A democracy can only be stable given the fact of reasonable pluralism if there is an *overlapping consensus* about a basic view of political justice. This is not merely a modus vivendi based on a balance of power between competing ideologies. Such a position is always vulnerable to one view becoming dominant and suppressing the others. Overlapping consensus means that within each reasonable comprehensive doctrine there is a common 'module' which is the political conception of justice. People accept the diversity of reasonable positions not just as a compromise but because within their own world-view there is a conception of justice that sees this as right. This common module is Rawls claims the theory of justice as fairness, the two principles argued for in his earlier work. All general policy debates in a democracy are couched in terms of a 'public reason', arguments that hold good independently of particular world-views even if the adherents of each doctrine may have further particular reasons for their beliefs. For example, socialists might personally believe in redistribution to the least well off because they identify with the plight of the poor, but they would have to argue for it in the public arena in terms of the difference principle. Thus justice as fairness provides the public discourse of a democratic society, the overlapping consensus in the face of diversity.

Conclusion

Political Liberalism explicitly acknowledges what is apparent from the long history of attempts to characterise justice. There is no foundational, transcendent, knock-down argument that can convince everyone to agree on what is just. Justice as fairness may be embraced by the diversity of 'reasonable' doctrines as an overlapping consensus. But in the contemporary world there is a proliferation even in liberal democracies of many 'unreasonable' forms of fundamentalism denying the tenet of the freedom and equality of all citizens. There is much to be 'contained', in Rawls' terminology, and no Archimedean point of leverage for arguments capable of convincing the 'unreasonable'. Rawls' theory nonetheless offers the powerful argument that all denials of justice as fairness presuppose some vested interest or dogmatic viewpoint that is simply taken for granted as paramount. Against this he derives principles that could command the assent of all reasonable people if they were to deliberate without bias. In the words of one of his severest critics this remains an 'exhilarating promise' (Sandel 1984, 20).

Further Reading

S Mulhall and A Swift 1996 is a lucid and comprehensive account of the major perspectives considered in this chapter.

S Avineri and de-Shalit 1992 is an extremely useful selection of readings from the major participants in the debate.

Two important recent contributions to the discussion of justice are Dworkin 2000 and Cohen 2000.

Fraser and Lacey 1993 is a stimulating critique of the debate from a feminist perspective.

Portrait: John Rawls by Ben Rogers 1999 is a fascinating short account of Rawls' life and its relationship to his work, that brings his theory to life.

Questions

1. 'The original position is a complicated metaphor for a simple thought experiment; what would be just if I were you?' Discuss.

2. 'Abstracting from our personal circumstances stands as much chance of creating injustice as creating justice. This is the essence of the communitarian critique.' Discuss.

3. 'Justice is not a matter of what you have, but how you got it.' Discuss.

4. 'Views about what is just can never be anything more than reflections of self-interest or political preference.' Discuss.

16 Introducing Feminist Legal Theory

Emily Jackson and Nicola Lacey

Why Study Feminist Legal Theory?

For students familiar with the law's much prized neutrality and objectivity, the concept of feminist legal theory may initially seem rather puzzling. Even if some feminist writers have been encountered while studying other subjects on the law curriculum, their focus will usually have been on legal issues that quite obviously have a particular impact upon women, such as rape or sex discrimination. Outside of sex-specific laws like these, gender is – at least in theory – irrelevant. Since feminist legal theory will rarely be taught in the first week of a jurisprudence course, students' previous encounters with legal theorists will have reinforced this idea that the critical analysis of law is an essentially gender-neutral endeavour. Why then does feminist legal theory occupy such a lengthy chapter within this book?

At its most basic, feminist legal theory offers a thoroughgoing critique of law's claim to be impartial and objective. While students may have come across this sort of criticism before in particular contexts where the law has historically treated men and women differently from each other, the claim that the very fabric of law itself is gendered is both bold and thought-provoking. Studying feminist jurisprudence should equip law students with the theoretical tools necessary to question certain fundamental assumptions about law – for example, its capacity for neutrality – tools that might also be put to effective use in relation to other vectors of inequality such as age, disability, class or race. And when returning to some of the other subjects which students may be studying simultaneously, a certain amount of cross-fertilisation should become possible. Having thought in a general way about the law's role in the construction of sexual difference, students might be able to think of examples from, amongst others, criminal justice, family, medical or labour law. So rather than imagining that there is a series of isolated instances of gender bias within the British legal system, students may find that they can identify patterns or trends that both illuminate their understanding of feminist jurisprudence and enrich their studies in other courses.

The History of Feminist Thought about Law

1. Early feminism in legal and political thought

Reading many contemporary feminist texts on law, one could be forgiven for thinking that legal feminism is the creation of the late twentieth century. This, however, would be a mistake, for feminist thought about law stretches back for many centuries, encompassing a variety of genres, notably including early modern arguments for women's rights and equal legal and political status resoundingly articulated by Mary Wollstonecraft and Olympe de Gouges, and, of course, the suffragists of the nineteenth and early twentieth centuries. Though it is true that liberal and Enlightenment thinking has been associated with an intensification of feminist analysis, and notwithstanding the variety of feminist issues, perspectives and analyses, there is therefore a strong case for thinking of the feminist tradition as distinctive and important in its own right. On the other hand, a useful way of thinking about feminist critique of modern law is undoubtedly its status as an immanent critique of the promise of liberalism: as part of the conscience of a liberal order which has been slow to deliver the universalism which it promised.

It cannot be doubted, of course, that the second wave women's movement of the late 1960s and 1970s gave a fresh impetus to feminist thought, and in particular stimulated the gradual entry of feminist ideas into the academy. Perhaps the most receptive disciplines, originally, were sociology and literary studies; however, the capacity of feminist analysis to cross the boundaries of established disciplines led relatively quickly to the establishment of specific programmes and even departments of women's or gender studies – a disciplinary innovation that was arguably bought at the cost of keeping feminist issues relatively contained, not to say marginalised, in the academy. Nonetheless, the intellectual work done in this era of the women's movement affected not only popular consciousness and culture but put on the intellectual agenda a range of issues formerly ignored: questions about sexual violence; the gendered division of labour; questions of pay equity and discrimination, to name only the most obvious.

2. Women and law scholarship

These developments were, however, rather slow to reach British law schools. On the face of it, this is surprising: many of the political and analytic issues raised by the women's movement had, after all, centrally to do with women's legal and civic status. On the other hand, law departments at this time were still strongly vocational in orientation, with even jurisprudence, let alone socio-legal studies, occupying the margins of the curriculum and only slowly finding their way onto the research agenda. The gradual intellectualisation of law schools in the United Kingdom, along with an increased openness to interdisciplinary study, itself in part an offshoot of the expansion of universities in the 1970s, are an important part of the history of feminist issues finding their way into the law school. In the United States, this process had started rather earlier, which may account for the dominance of American academics within feminist legal studies.

Perhaps not surprisingly given the relatively atheoretical nature of much legal scholarship at the time, the earliest feminist legal scholarship – often known as 'women and law' work – can be not entirely unfairly summed up as the strategy of 'adding women and stirring'. The absence of women and women's issues from the agenda of legal study was deplored; questions such as domestic and sexual violence began to find their way into family and criminal law courses and texts; women's position in the economy and the division of labour within the family began to be acknowledged in labour law and social welfare law courses; and sex discrimination law – a central part of civil rights law since the passage of the Sex Discrimination Act and the implementation of the Equal Pay Act in 1975 – found a curiously tentative position in legal education, hovering somewhere between labour law and civil liberties, though all too often falling into the yawning gap between the two. Significantly, this initial move to include in the curriculum issues where women or gender questions were particularly visible soon led on to more searching work which identified gender issues in a far wider range of legal arrangements, with property laws, medical law and pensions law becoming a focus for analysis of 'indirect discrimination' broadly understood: ie the existence of arrangements which, though facially neutral, in fact served to exclude or disadvantage a disproportionate number of women (Atkins and Hoggett, 1984). And this in turn led to a more radical set of theoretical arguments, with the feminists of the Oslo school, led by the late Tove Stang Dahl, setting up a department of women's law and reorganising the very conceptualisation of subjects around women's lives – birth law, money law, housewives' law.

Central to these early feminist approaches was a rather sharp distinction between sex and gender, with sex understood as the bodily or biological category, and gender as the socially constructed meaning of sex. Though this distinction, as we shall see, rather soon came under intense critical scrutiny, it had an important (and controversial) effect in shifting the political and intellectual focus gradually towards an exploration of the role of law in constituting social meanings of gender. In this context, Katherine O'Donovan's 1985 book, *Sexual Divisions in Law*, part of the influential 'Law in Context' series then published by Weidenfeld and Nicolson, represented a watershed in British feminist legal scholarship. For while 'women and law' work tended to leave both categories intact, and appeared to assume that a particular 'women's perspective' could be identified, the approach adopted by O'Donovan presented the framework of gender divisions as a general category for critical legal analysis, and opened up the possibility that law's contribution to the gendering of its subjects might interact with other social forces. It assumed a powerful, dynamic role for law in the constitution of gender, and, hence, a wide-ranging and potentially radical law reform agenda. By moving away from analysis of 'women's issues', the emphasis on gender opened up the possibility of incorporating sexual orientation in the critical analysis of law's constitution of gender, and of analysing the social construction of masculinity.

As we have mentioned, however, the move from women and law to law and gender was not without its critics. A pervasive objection was that the shift threatened to make women, and issues of particular concern to women, disappear again just as they had seemed to be gaining a foothold. Furthermore, there was some concern about whether the analytic frame of gender analysis would submerge or displace feminisms' traditional political and ethical concerns in favour of a scientistic approach. And finally, the question had to be asked whether the shift to gender could really make the problem of sex disappear: granted that gender roles are socially constructed (which is not to say easy to change), why had they happened to be ascribed to men and to women in the way they had?

These concerns about the move to 'law and gender' prompted what can be identified as a third phase in the development of feminist legal scholarship, which might be called the move to feminist legal theory. In this phase, which is still in the course of development, the concern has been to reprioritise the political commitments of feminist scholarship, emphasising the combination of analytic and normative/ethical concerns on which feminist work is founded. Within this framework, feminist legal theory has come of age, and has begun to interact with other theoretical and political-academic movements such as critical race theory, post-structuralism, postmodernism and psychoanalysis. Perhaps the defining feature of this phase of intellectual development is its theoretical ambition to produce a feminist jurisprudence – a general feminist account of legal method and the substantive development of modern legal orders.

Mary Wollstonecraft (*A Vindication of the Rights of Woman* (1792))

From the tyranny of man, I firmly believe, the greater number of female follies proceed; and the cunning, which I allow makes at present a part of their character, I likewise have repeatedly endeavoured to prove, is produced by oppression..... Asserting the rights which women in common with men ought to contend for, I have not attempted to extenuate their faults; but to prove them to be the natural consequence of their education and station in society. If so, it is reasonable to suppose that they will change their character, and correct their vices and follies, when they are allowed to be free in a physical, moral and civil sense....Let woman share the rights and she will emulate the virtues of man; for she must grow more perfect when emancipated.

John Stuart Mill (*The Subjection of Women* (1869))

Hardly any slave...is a slave at all hours and all minutes...But it cannot be so with the wife. Above all, a female slave has (in Christian countries) an admitted right, and is considered under a moral obligation, to refuse to her master the last familiarity. Not so the wife: however brutal a tyrant she may unfortunately be chained to – though she may know that he hates her, though it may be his daily pleasure to torture her, and though she may feel it impossible not to loathe him – he can claim from her and enforce the lowest degradation of a human being, that of being made the instrument of an animal function contrary to her inclinations.

...

Think what it is to be a boy, to grow up to manhood in the belief that without any merit or any exertion of his own, though he may be the most frivolous and empty or the most frivolous and stolid of mankind, by the mere fact of being born a male he is by right the superior of all and every one of an entire half of the human race: including probably some whose real superiority to himself he has daily or hourly occasion to feel... Is it imagined that all this does not pervert the whole manner of existence of the man, both as an individual and as a social being? It is an exact parallel to the feeling of a hereditary king that he is excellent above others by being born a king, or a noble by being born a noble. The relation between husband and wife is very like that between lord and vassal, except that the wife is held to more unlimited obedience than the vassal was.

Editorial (*The Academy*, vol 74, 27 June 1908, 926–7)

The women of England desire the vote with no more desire than they desire that their faces should be embellished with whiskers. If a plebiscite of the women of the country could be taken tomorrow the Suffragists would find themselves in a hopeless and preposterous minority. The instinct of intelligent women is entirely against the whole business….The tap-root of the whole trouble lies in the vanity and the rebellion of certain ill-balanced women. The broad basis of their argument is that they can no longer 'trust' mankind. Though their liberties and rights are much more generously recognised in England than in any other country in the world, they pretend that they are ground down and treated improperly, and that the only way in which their dreadful state can be ameliorated is that the franchise be extended to them.

The working-class women of England see the falsity of all this, and so do the upper-class women. It is the middle-class women from whose ranks the agitators are, for the most part, recruited. There are reasons for this, the chief of them being that it is the middle-class woman who has brought herself most generally into conscious competition with salary-earning men, and it is the middle-class woman who is filled with the soaring ambition to conduct her life on an unfeminine basis. Her position is often a bitter one because she is only too frequently over-educated, and she can never make sure of getting married. Hence she is discontented, peevish, and prone to imagine that the world is wrongly made. There is an incompleteness about her life which is pitiful. It is natural that she should look round for something which will alleviate her condition, and she has got it into her head that 'the vote' will do this for her. Greater or more woeful mistake was never made. The political assuagement of a spiritual trouble is an impossibility. The wrongs of woman are certainly not political wrongs. Her private wrongs may be many and various.

...

Politics, like prize-fighting and war, is a man's job

O'Donovan (1985, 79–80)

Sex-neutral language is one tool for the reduction of inequality between the sexes. It is not sufficient in itself; without other changes in cultural beliefs, and in legal and social institutions, it may serve to mask continued discrimination. Family law, has been changed to functional classification with reciprocal duties being placed on spouses and on parents. This has not prevented the judiciary in family cases from interpreting neutral language, or other discretionary provisions, in the light of their beliefs about gender roles. Thus the 'loving and unselfish wife' is entitled to recognition of her good behaviour by the courts when awarding maintenance. In child-custody cases 'all things being equal, the best place for any small child is with its mother'; although 'one must remember that to be a good mother involves not only looking after the children, but making and keeping a home for them with their father ... in so far as she herself by her conduct broke up that home she is not a good mother'. A household in which there is some woman at home to look after the children is preferable to one where parents are out at work. Although spouses come neutrally and equally before the divorce court, there is ready prescription of their gender roles.

The object of providing these examples is to show how cultural views are embodied in institutional forms. As Sherry Ortner points out: 'efforts directed solely at changing the social institutions cannot have far-reaching effects if cultural language and imagery continue to purvey a relatively devalued view of women. But at the same time efforts directed solely at changing cultural assumptions ... cannot be successful unless the institutional base of the society is changed to support and reinforce the changed cultural view'. Law plays an active part in transmitting cultural views and in constructing social institutions. Functional classification may challenge cultural assumptions but further measures are required. It is the acceptance of a split between private and public spheres, and what happens in private, that provide the conditions for sex discrimination.

Cornell (1995, 6)

Feminists have relentlessly struggled to have gender accorded proper recognition in political philosophy and in law. Unfortunately, this insistence on 'gender' as if it were the category of legal analysis rather than 'sex' has been conserving of the category at the expense of putting gays and lesbians outside the reach of discrimination law. Making gender the 'single axis' of discrimination law has also failed to provide an analysis of the unique focus of discrimination endured by women of color as women of color.

In spite of the analytic shortcomings of the current legal analysis of gender equality for women, 'sex', even if understood exclusively as gender hierarchy and the subordination of women, has been accorded a place in some political philosophy. Even so, this 'place' is often reduced to a secondary category, or squeezed into schemes of equality tailored for some other subject such as class. I am arguing, on the contrary, that sex cannot be analogized to some other category. Sex and sexuality are unique and formative to human personality and should be treated as such. Thus, in order to have an adequate feminist theory of legal equality we must explicitly recognize the sexuate bases of each one of us as a human creature. At the very heart of the struggle to work through imposed and assumed personae is the matter of sex and sexuality.

Defining Feminist Legal Theory

Contemporary feminist legal theory is constructed out of a combination of analytic and political-ethical claims. Analytically, the claim is that sex/gender is one important social structure or discourse, or axis of social differentiation, and is hence likely to characterise and influence the shape of law. Politically and ethically, feminist theory starts out from the assumption that the ways in which sex/gender has shaped the world, including through law, have been politically and ethically problematic: ie it consists not just in differentiation but in domination or oppression or discrimination. Legal sex differentiation, in short, on the whole disadvantages women. This political and ethical stance is often combined with an incipient utopianism in legal feminism: its social constructionist methodology, which seeks to identify the historical bases of discrimination in social action rather than biological or social determinism implies a contingency which opens up radical possibilities for political and social change, notwithstanding the fact that what has been socially constructed as real – sex-role expectations for example – are sometimes harder to change than the biological or natural features such as the possession of certain sexed bodily characteristics.

Another important feature of feminist legal theory has to do with its distinctive methodology. Most legal theories adopt either an internal or an external theoretical approach. An internal analysis seeks to rationalise and explicate the nature of law and legal method from the point of view of legal reasoning or legal practice itself. An example might be the work of H L A Hart, considered in Chapter 4. In contrast, adopting an external approach means self-consciously standing outside legal practices, and reflecting on the extent to which they meet certain basic normative political objectives. Critical legal theory, the subject of Chapter 7, would be a good example of an essentially external critique of law. Much feminist theory instead occupies a third perspective, which might be called interpretive. In other words, feminist legal theories do not merely seek to rationalise legal practices; nor, conversely, do they typically engage in entirely external critique and prescription. Rather, feminist legal theory aspires to produce a critical interpretation of legal practices: an account which at once takes seriously the legal point of view yet which subjects that point of view to critical scrutiny on the basis of both its own professed values and a range of other ethical and political commitments. For this reason among others (notably the political antecedents of the feminist movements), feminist legal scholarship is characterised by a particularly intimate linkage between theory and practice: with both a rejection of any strong division between the two (which sometimes in fact implies a certain scepticism about theory), and an impulse to have effects beyond the academy. Hence feminist theory is grounded in particular legal issues far more than, say, positivist theory or even, for example, Derrida's deconstructive essay 'Force of Law'.

Naffine (1990, 33–4)

In Australian law schools, the curriculum is, in the main, traditional. Following the English model, its principal concern is the standard categories of law, such as torts, contract and property, subjects which are seen to be of immediate use to the legal practitioner. Emphasis is placed upon the study of the workings of specific, discrete laws. Critical discussion of legal theory and social policy is considered, in many law schools, to be peripheral to the central task of the lawyer.

Wherever this traditional style of legal training is offered, social problems tend to be reduced to a series of disconnected disputes between anonymous and interchangeable individuals. Hypothetical cases are manufactured for students who are expected to isolate the 'facts' and then apply the relevant law. The student's task is to arrive at the legally 'correct' solution by reasoning in an intelligent and objective manner. Social conflict and social inequalities are therefore reduced to an impersonal sort of algebra.

Injured and injuring parties become A and B; Cs and Ds enter the story to complicate the legal problem. Its resolution is in terms of the degree of fit between the situation of the parties and the given law. Legal technicalities, not the moral rights or wrongs of the case, determine the availability of a remedy. Whether the problem has a larger social cause or solution is simply not the point.

To invoke another metaphor, law is often delivered to the student as a jigsaw puzzle. For much of the time, the required task is skilfully to piece together small sections of the puzzle, without ever having to appreciate the entire composite legal picture and its implications for society. Thus is maintained the impression of a fair, dispassionate and objective treatment of all parties who come before the law. All As will be treated like other As, and Bs like Bs, generally without regard to the social implications of their class, colour, creed or sex, unless of course these factors are deemed to be legally relevant. Indeed ... law's much-prized neutrality resides in its refusal to look beyond the immediate facts in its resolution of each new dispute.

Naffine (2002, 73–6)

Perhaps the broadest intention of feminism within the legal academy has been to make sense of law and its institutions as 'a form of life' and to show how, where and why it has failed women. Ludwig Wittgenstein employed the term 'form of life' to refer to the community in which our language, and hence our world view, is embedded. This term is used in several of his works, but never with extended definition. In *Philosophical Investigations*, he said that 'to imagine a language is to imagine a form of life'. Thus , social practices were inextricably bound up with the use of language, which he regarded as a socially-determined and rule-governed activity much like a game. Wittgenstein coined the term 'language game', with a view to accentuating this idea that language is an organised conventional activity: to know how to play it, you must know and observe its rules, you must partake of the community in which its conventions are given meaning. It is through learning a language (its concepts, its rules and conventions), that is necessarily embedded in a particular community of language users, that we come to see and think as we do and also come to see our worldview as only right and natural. In order to appreciate the particularity of the manner in which we, ourselves, make sense of the world, we must therefore step outside of our community and acquire exposure to another group of language users.

The close relationship between life form, language and social power is now implicitly accepted within contemporary feminist theory, which has developed a strong interest in the uses and effects of language as a social and political practice. However, legal (and other) feminists have insisted that there are inevitably rival linguistic practices, not only between communities, but also within any given community, including the legal community. In other words, we participate in a world of competing socio-linguistic practices, some of them more powerful than others. These practices require explication and reconciliation if we are to lead lives that make sense to us: if we are to find our feet in that society.

An important contribution of the legal feminist project therefore has been to reveal the precise ways in which socio-economic and legal power (which intertwine) determine what can be said, persuasively and intelligibly, and by whom, within these multiple and overlapping communities of legal meaning. Feminists have also drawn to our attention the intellectual investment of analytic jurists in the exclusion or denial of these political considerations. As Nicola Lacey observes of the jurisprudence of Ronald Dworkin, 'questions of membership and power are quite simply not on the theoretical agenda' for the very reason that they might undermine the idea of the integrity of legal principle, upon which his theory of law relies. The raising of such questions would case doubt on the idea of 'a single interpretive community' from which law is said to derive its common, agreed-upon meaning and hence its legitimacy.

This is precisely the disruptive intent of legal feminists who insist on the political nature of the attribution of legal meaning: the way in which power determines the very plausibility of legal norms and their deployment. The impression we gain that there is broad agreement between users of legal language, they say, is often the result of the suppression of different and less powerful linguistic practices. It is a function of the unwillingness of the more powerful members of the dominant legal community to step outside of their own narrow, but influential, community of meaning. Feminists have also been alert to the possibilities of one community of language users influencing another by way of a vigorous sustained engagement about linguistic meaning. Indeed, they have put to good effect the naming and renaming of injuries to women, and thus theory and practice have been closely linked in feminist scholarship.

The introduction of terms such as 'date rape', 'domestic violence' and 'sexual harassment', for example, might seem rather simple and obvious linguistic ploys, but in some ways they have been remarkably effective. Their invocation entailed an implicit recognition that language is an instrument, a tool of communities of language users, and that it is possible to put these tools to a variety of uses, often in a highly political fashion. Not only have these new terms put a name to existing, but dimly perceived, wrongs to women, but they have also brought them into the broader public consciousness. That is, the terms have effectively brought the named phenomena into being for those parts of the community for which they were either invisible or unthinkable.

...

The term 'domestic violence' is now part of the vernacular and no longer surprises, it is a common place term. And yet the expression is highly subversive in that it comprises a juxtaposition of words that would once have been regarded as very odd. After all, the domestic sphere has traditionally been regarded as a refuge and a haven, not the site of violence. The broad acceptance of the term means that it is no longer a given that women are safe at home. Rather, this is the place where they are most likely to be hit and to be killed. We are now able to talk more openly of this phenomenon. Thus thinking has shifted as new concepts and new, implicitly politicised, understandings of old concepts have infiltrated the dominant vocabulary. This is also true of the term 'sexual harassment'. With the entry of this expression into common discourse, there is now a way of naming the more sinister dimensions of sexual approaches in the workplace which can reduce working life to a misery and drive women from their jobs. Unwanted sexual advances and even sexual assaults at the office are no longer just the stuff of office humour.

The Varieties of Feminist Legal Theory

So far, we have been speaking – albeit provisionally – as if feminist legal theory constituted a relatively unitary genre of jurisprudence. This is at one level both a necessary and a useful device: we need to generalise among feminist theories if we are going to characterise the genre. However, this convenient technique of generalisation should not mislead us about the true variety of feminist legal theories. Though debates between feminists are often interpreted as a sign of political strife or intellectual weakness, we should resist the idea that theoretical consensus among feminist scholars is any more to be expected, or indeed welcomed, than among positivists, natural lawyers or legal realists.

The existence of differences between feminist analyses of law could be interpreted in a variety of ways. Catharine MacKinnon, for example, has claimed that one particular branch of feminism, namely radical feminism, is in fact the only truly feminist theory. In fleshing out her own particular brand of feminism, MacKinnon is both critical and dismissive of other feminist approaches. A different sort of interpretation of the disagreements that clearly exist between feminists might be that it no longer makes any sense to talk about feminist legal theory as a distinctive genre. If feminists share little common ground, does the whole point of feminist legal theory collapse? The authors of this chapter would account for the plurality of modern feminism in a third and more inclusive way. We believe that gender does continue to be a significant axis of social organisation, while recognising that it is not the only, or even necessarily the most important way in which people are differentiated from each other. The effects of structural sexual difference are never experienced in isolation, rather they are interwoven with other constituent elements of a person's identity, such as their race, age, class or disability. It is therefore wholly unsurprising that feminists' other political or theoretical preoccupations inform their analysis of the ways in which the law has helped to construct the multiple social meanings of sexual difference.

Axes of differentiation

It is, however, particularly important, given the tendency to lump together all radical or critical legal theories, to be clear about identifying the main axes of differentiation between feminist legal theorists. In this section, we therefore distinguish four main theoretical points of distinction between feminist theorists, before going on to identify a number of important and distinctive genres of feminist scholarship.

A first – striking though often insufficiently analysed – difference between feminist writers on law has to do with a mixture of *methodology and written style*. If we take five of the writers represented in the extracts reproduced below, we can immediately see some significant differences. Catharine MacKinnon's written style is terse and polemical: her arguments are advanced by striking elisions and rhetorical tropes which are interspersed with more detailed analysis of particular legal institutions. In Patricia Williams, we also find a genre of rhetoric, but this time delivered in terms of narratives – often intensely personal – which deliver a political point obliquely and indirectly. Both of these styles contrast sharply with, for example, the more classic, analytic style of Ngaire Naffine, whose writing deploys the techniques of analytical legal scholarship and political theory. Moving on, Luce Irigaray writes in a seamlessly metaphorical style, weaving social critique with utopian visions and elliptical, poetic meditations: while Drucilla Cornell moves between each of the techniques of the other four.

These differences, we would argue, are not just a matter of style. They also reflect the idea that the very conceptual framework of legal scholarship makes it impossible to say certain kinds of things. Dominant theoretical paradigms are not, on this view, neutral communicative tools. Rather, the way in which particular intellectual disciplines and concepts have developed makes it difficult to conceptualise certain types of harm or wrong; or to reveal certain kinds of interest or subject position. To take a well-known example, the concept of harassment was developed (by MacKinnon) to identify a form of abuse of power which fell between a number of existing legal concepts such as rape, assault and sex discrimination.

A second important axis of differentiation among feminist legal theories has to do with their *underlying theories of sexual difference*. In Catharine MacKinnon's work, for example, we find a structural, material theory of women's oppression analogous to the theory of class difference to be found in Marxism. As MacKinnon herself puts it, sexuality is to feminism what work is to Marxism: 'that which is most one's own, that which most makes one the being the theory addresses, [and] that which is most taken away by what the theory criticizes' (MacKinnon 1987, 48). MacKinnon's view of sex difference is unitary and monolothic and, in contrast to Marxism, not especially historical. In MacKinnon's analysis, since the origins and maintenance of sex difference lie in domination grounded in the abuse of sexual power and the exercise of sexual violence, the kinds of issues which feminist legal theory should focus on are distinctively sexual: pornography, sexual violence, abortion, sexual harassment. An emphasis on the sexual origins of women's powerlessness contrasts with the more pluralistic and eclectic approach of, for example, Carol Smart, who emphasises not only these issues but also the economic position of women; the construction of women and femininity in legal discourse; and the impact of legal arrangements on family structure. To take a different example, Drucilla Cornell's approach is more eclectic than MacKinnon's in terms of subject matter, but is unified within a psychoanalytic account of the acquisition of sexual identity. Another variation would be Robin West's emphasis upon the biological differences between men and women. Yet other feminists would deny the need for any theory of the originating cause of women's oppression.

A third axis of differentiation between feminist theories has to do with the degree to which they exhibit *substantive or methodological continuities with other legal and social theories*. On one view (to which the authors of this chapter are sympathetic), feminist legal theory is not so much a discrete theoretical or methodological approach but rather a genre which places distinctive substantive issues on the agenda of legal scholarship and legal theory, using analytic and critical methods shared with, for example, the sociology of law, marxism or critical legal theory to illuminate sex/gender issues. Law is then seen as both a force within and a product of the social construction of reality. Feminist legal theory – on this view – is conceptualised as an interpretive approach which seeks to get beyond the surface level of legal doctrine and legal discourse, and which sees traditional jurisprudence as ideological – and hence as an apologia for the status quo. Radical feminists, however, would be more inclined to insist upon the autonomy of feminist theory at the level of method.

Williams (1991, 17–19)

The original vehicle for my interest in the intersection of commerce and the Constitution was my family history. A few years ago, I came into the possession of what may have been the contract of sale for my great-great-grandmother. It is a very simple but lawyerly document, describing her as 'one female' and revealing her age as eleven; no price is specified, merely 'value exchanged'. My sister also found a county census record taken two years later; on a list of one Austin Miller's personal assets she appears again, as 'slave, female' – thirteen years old now with an eight-month infant.

Since then I have tried to piece together what it must have been like to be my great-great-grandmother. She was purchased, according to matrilineal recounting, by a man who was extremely temperamental and quite wealthy. I try to imagine what it would have been like to have a discontented white man buy me, after a fight with his mother about prolonged bachelorhood. I wonder what it would have been like to have a thirty-five-year-old man own the secrets of my puberty, which he bought to prove himself sexually as well as to increase his livestock of slaves. I imagine trying to please, with the yearning of adolescence, a man who truly did not know I was human, whose entire belief system resolutely defined me as animal, chattel, talking cow. I wonder what it would have been like to have his child, pale-faced but also animal, before I turned thirteen. I try to envision being casually threatened with sale from time to time, teeth and buttocks bared to interested visitors.

... Her children were the exclusive property of their father (though that's not what they called him). They grew up in his house, taken from her as she had been taken from her mother. They became haughty, favored, frightened house servants who were raised playing with, caring for, and envying this now-married man's legitimate children, their half brothers and sister. Her children grew up reverent of and obedient to this white man – my great-great-grandfather – and his other children, to whom they were taught they owed the debt of their survival. It was a mistake from which the Emancipation Proclamation never fully freed any of them.

Her children must have been something of an ultimate betrayal; it could not have been easy to see in them the hope of her own survival. Freed from slavery by the Civil War, they went on to establish respected black Episcopal churches and to learn to play the piano. They grew up clever and well-bred. They grew up to marry other frightened, refined, master-blooded animals; they grew up good people, but alien.

Austin Miller, one of Tennessee's finest lawyers according to other records, went on to become a judge; and the sons by his wife went on to become lawyers as well. There is no surviving record of what happened to my great-great-grandmother, no account of how or when she died.

This story is what inspired my interest in the interplay of notions of public and private, of family and market; of male and female, of molestation and the law. I track meticulously the dimension of meaning in my great-great-grandmother as chattel: the meaning of money; the power of consumerist world view, the deaths of those we label the unassertive and the inefficient. I try to imagine where and who she would be today. I am engaged in a long-term project of tracking his words – through his letters and opinions – and those of his sons who were also lawyers and judges, of finding the shape described by her absence in all this.

I see her shape and his hand in the vast networking of our society, and in the evils and oversights that plague our lives and laws. The control he had over her body. The force he was in her life, in the shape of my life today The power he exercised in the choice to breed her or not. The choice to breed slaves in his image, to choose her mate and be that mate. In his attempt to own what no man can own, the habit of his power and the absence of her choice.

I look for her shape and his hand.

MacKinnon (1983, 638–40, 644–5)

Feminism does not begin with the premise that it is unpremised. It does not aspire to persuade an unpremised audience because there is no such audience. Its project is to uncover and claim as valid the experience of women, the major content of which is the devalidation of women's experience.

This defines our task not only because male dominance is perhaps the most pervasive and tenacious system of power in history, but because it is metaphysically nearly perfect. Its point of view is the standard for point-of-viewlessness, its particularity the meaning of universality. Its force is exercised as consent, its authority as participation, its supremacy as the paradigm of order, its control as the definition of legitimacy. Feminism claims the voice of women's silence, the sexuality of our eroticized desexualization, the fullness of 'lack', the centrality of our marginality and exclusion, the public nature of privacy, the presence of our absence. This approach is more complex than transgression, more transformative than transvaluation, deeper than mirror-imaged resistance, more affirmative than the negation of our negativity. It is neither materialist nor idealist; it is feminist. Neither the transcendence of liberalism nor the determination of materialism works for us. Idealism is too unreal; women's inequality is enforced, so it cannot simply be thought out of existence, certainly not by us. Materialism is too real; women's inequality has never not existed, so women's equality never has. That is, the equality of women to men will not be scientifically provable until it is no longer necessary to do so. Women's situation offers no outside to stand on or gaze at, no inside to escape to, too much urgency to wait, no place else to go, and nothing to use but the twisted tools that have been shoved down our throats. If feminism is revolutionary, this is why.

Feminism has been widely thought to contain tendencies of liberal feminism, radical feminism, and socialist feminism. But just as socialist feminism has often amounted to marxism applied to women, liberal feminism has often amounted to liberalism applied to women. Radical feminism is feminism. Radical feminism – after this, feminism unmodified – is methodologically post-marxist. It moves to resolve the marxist-feminist problematic on the level of method. Because its method emerges from the concrete conditions of all women as sex, it dissolves the individualist, naturalist, idealist, moralist structure of liberalism, the politics of which science is the epistemology. Where liberal feminism sees sexism primarily as an illusion or myth to be dispelled, an inaccuracy to be corrected, true feminism sees the male point of view as fundamental to the male power to create the world in its own image, the image of its desires, not just as its delusory end product. Feminism distinctively as such comprehends that what counts as truth is produced in the interest of those with power to shape reality, and that this process is as persuasive as it is necessary as it is changeable.

As a beginning, I propose that the state is male in the feminist sense. The law sees and treats women the way men see and treat women. The liberal state coercively and authoritatively constitutes the social order in the interest of men as a gender, through its legitimising norms, relation to society, and substantive policies. It achieves this through embodying and ensuring male control over women's sexuality at every level, occasionally cushioning, qualifying, or de jure prohibiting its excesses when necessary to its normalization. Substantively, the way the male point of view frames an experience is the way it is framed by state policy. To the extent possession is the point of sex, rape is sex with a woman who is not yours, unless the act is so as to make it yours. If part of the kick of pornography involves eroticising the putatively prohibited, obscenity law will putatively prohibit pornography enough to maintain its desirability without ever making it unavailable or truly illegitimate. The same with prostitution. As male is the implicit reference for human, maleness will be the measure of equality in sex discrimination law. To the extent that the point of abortion is to control the reproductive sequelae of intercourse, so as to facilitate male sexual access to women, access to abortion will be controlled by 'a man or The Man'. Gender, elaborated and sustained by behavioural patterns of application and administration, is maintained as a division of power.

Formally, the state is male in that objectivity is its norm. Objectivity is liberal legalism's conception of itself. It legitimises itself by reflecting its view of existing society, a society it made and makes by so seeing it, and calling that view, and that relation, practical rationality. If rationality is measured by point-of-viewlessness, what counts as reason will be that which corresponds to the way things are.

Naffine (2002, 98–100)

Still a further reason why feminists have failed to precipitate a jurisprudential crisis is that law has managed, at least partially, to accommodate women in its concept of person. It has therefore bent to the demands of feminism, not broken. This artful accommodation of women has perhaps been insufficiently recognised by feminists who have tended to characterise the legal subject as male and as singular. … Legal positivists have a legitimate point when they say that law's person should not be hypostatised as a natural being and (by necessary implication) that law's person is neither male nor female. Instead it is a legal device, an abstraction, with a multiplicity of purposes, and women have been able to avail themselves of many of those purposes.

…

The positivist argument continues that, as a purely formal device, legal personality simply entails the possession of a legally recognised right and even a small number of rights will make someone a legal person, as personality simply means the legal ability to bear a legal right ... The rights and duties which make someone or something a legal person arise out of a multiplicity of legal relations between persons; they are not necessarily a function of the positive attributes of the human beings in question (such as their sex).

...

From this it follows that law recognises a variety of legal identities, even in the one person, and it recognises these identities in both women and men. And the way it does this is by effectively reconstituting the person within each legal relation they enter. This chameleon nature of legal identity has important implications for feminists. It means that law has always been able to accommodate women, in a variety of legal relations, and that orthodox lawyers can point to this accommodation in their defence of law's commitment to sexual neutrality ... It remains incumbent of feminists to respond to these positivist claims about the complexity and the formal neutrality of personality, because they are persuasive and potentially damaging to the feminist case ... If we reflect seriously on the positivist explanation of personality, we must concede that the legal subject is in fact not a straightjacket. Rather, it is a highly flexible legal concept which may even be of considerable use to feminists given its shifting relational character.

...

But what the positivist case neglects (and where feminists can gain their intellectual purchase) is that there is a distinct patterning to the legal distribution of rights (conceived as shifting relationships) and that there are social and political reasons for this distribution. Women are recognised in fewer legal relations which constitute them as effective legal actors precisely because they are women. Extra-legal understandings of what it is to be a proper person (individuated, not-pregnant and so on) clearly do play their part in legal determinations about who should have rights and what form they should take. It is this benchmarking of the legal person against a (male) template of humanity which is, of course, implicitly denied by legal positivists, precisely because it entails an admission that law strays outside formal law to obtain its conception of a person.

QUESTION

How would you account for this variety in the written styles of feminist legal theorists?

The final and certainly the most obvious axis of differentiation among feminist theories is, however, their *political orientation*. We therefore now move on to sketch four different political versions of feminist theory. Again, it is important to realise that these are models rather than detailed taxonomies: some writers fall between several of the classifications, but the categories are useful both in understanding the development of feminist thought and in seeing how different political orientations have led feminists to take up very different questions about law and legal theory.

Liberal feminism

1. The modern ideal of (formal) equality

Liberal feminism finds its roots in the emergence of liberal political thought with the Enlightenment. Liberalism has become the dominant political expression of progressive thought in the modern age, but is itself very various. Most would agree that liberalism centres on core ideas of universal, equal citizenship and democracy – but exactly what these ideas amount to has varied over the decades, and early liberals were far from endorsing the priniciples of universal suffrage, property and other civil and political rights which are now taken to be intrinsic to liberalism. One way of looking at the development of liberal thought is that its universalist ideals have provided the basis for an immanent critique of its own forms: the liberal promise has come later for some groups than for others, and for some is still far from being a reality. Liberal feminism is simply the idea that those liberal ideals of equality and rights or liberties apply to women: in this sense it is not so much a distinctively feminist theory as liberalism applied to women. Liberal feminism has been particularly associated with the ideas of formal equality and of equality of opportunity, although contemporary liberal theories such as that of Ronald Dworkin also subscribe to stronger principles of equality such as equality of resources or equality of concern and respect.

Liberalism has often been associated with the birth of feminism, but although it is indeed a strong association, this is historically inaccurate: some early feminists, like Mary Astell, were conservative in their general political views, and took a much more distinctively feminist or woman-oriented stance than is implied in the idea of liberal feminism. And even early feminists (such as Mary Wollstonecraft) who were more sympathetic to developments such as the declarations of universal human rights which followed the French and American revolutions were quick to point out that women were all too often implicitly or explicitly excluded from the definition 'human' in the delineation and interpretation of those rights.

2. Limitations of liberal feminism

Since the 1980s, a recurring theme within much feminist writing has been the limitations immanent within liberal feminism. Four key criticisms might be identified.

The first limitation of liberalism from a feminist point of view is its trenchant *individualism*. Though this has become a mantra of contemporary feminist critique, it is extremely important to distinguish at least three different kinds of feminist objection to unmodified liberal individualism:

The first two objections are to the implicit individualism of the liberal legal subject. In the first place, the liberal focus on the interests, rights and entitlements of individuals obscures our vision of the systematic patterns of exclusion and disadvantage which characterise women's subordination. Differently patterned outcomes – for example, women's under-representation in various occupations and spheres of life – can be explained away as the product of autonomous individual choices and hence legitimated within a liberal world-view. Secondly, it is argued that liberal theory tends to operate with a pre-social conception of the individual: liberal rights and limits on governmental power are derived from an *a priori* idea of the nature of the human being which underplays the extent to which social and political institutions shape individual preferences, attitudes and dispositions. The screen brought in by liberal assumptions about human nature obscures the assumptions being made about women and about sexual difference which feminism wants to reveal and criticise.

A somewhat different criticism of liberal individualism has to do with its conception of political value. Here it is argued that liberalism's focus on the individual has realised itself in terms of a primary concern with individual entitlements at the expense of a proper appreciation of the importance of collective and public goods: once again, feminists have argued that these may be of particular importance to women.

A second general criticism of the limits of liberalism focuses on *liberal conceptions of freedom*. Liberal political frameworks operate with a basically negative conception of freedom: in other words, freedom is understood as consisting in being free from outside interference, particularly by the state. As a result, the capacity people actually have (or do not have) to exercise freedom or rights – which may require the positive provision of goods or resources – is underplayed in liberalism. This has important implications for feminist political arguments, which often advocate *entitlements* to empowering and facilitating resources. To take an example, MacKinnon's and Andrea Dworkin's argument about the threat which pornography poses to women's civil rights depends on the idea that a centrally important question about freedom of speech is just how much this freedom is worth to different social groups. Negative freedom of speech may be of little value to those whose capacity to speak or to be heard is systematically undermined by the exercise of others' freedom to speak.

A third general feminist criticism of liberal theory has to do with the reliance which it places on a distinction between *public and private spheres*. Typically, liberal political thought assumes the world to be divided into public and private spaces and issues. Governmental action, and hence liberal principles, apply primarily to the public world, while private lives and private spheres are properly subject to the regime of individual autonomy and negative freedom. This division has been criticised on both analytic and historical grounds. Analytically, it has been doubted whether a clear public/private boundary can be delineated; for example, most liberals would see the home and the family as quintessentially private spheres, but would hesitate about the implications of the classification when confronted with questions such as child abuse or domestic violence. Furthermore, it seems evident that disadvantages within the allegedly private sphere – unequal divisions of domestic labour for example – spill over into entitlements and opportunities in the public world. Historically and empirically, it has been argued that the received view of public and private tends to consign women's lives and concerns to the private sphere, thus defining them as outwith the scope of political intervention, and even rendering them invisible as political issues. This, it has been argued, explains the tardy reception of issues such as domestic violence, marital rape, domestic work and child abuse onto the political agenda.

At the root of some feminist criticisms of the public/private dichotomy was the contention that the law's reluctance to intrude into the private sphere in practice simply reinforced men's *de facto* power within familial and sexual relationships. The absence of effective legal control over domestic arrangements, according to this line of argument, served male interests by leaving (male) heads of households free to exploit their dominant position within the family. But while examples such as the marital rape exemption and police reluctance to prosecute domestic violence may have supported this critique of the public/private distinction, other feminists began to acknowledge that in other respects the claim that the domestic relationships are comparatively unregulated was empirically untrue, and thus represented a shaky basis for an effective critique of law. Adopting a broader conception of regulation, it becomes clear that the private sphere is in fact intensely regulated. Under social security and immigration rules, for example, eligibility for welfare benefits or a right of entry will generally depend upon the prior legal recognition or non-recognition of different familial relationships.

Thus the simplistic argument that political and legal disinterest in the private sphere gave men a free licence to exploit their greater physical and economic power to their own ends was gradually replaced by a more subtle feminist critique which instead deconstructed the web of assumptions about family life that underpin the regulation of domestic relationships. In relation to immigration, for example, the 'one year rule' stipulates that a woman who acquires British citizenship through marriage loses her right to remain in the United Kingdom should her marriage break down within one year. Although directed towards deterring marriages of convenience, the threat of deportation and its associated shame in practice force many women to stay with violent husbands. These women are not disadvantaged by an *absence* of regulation. On the contrary, through the 'one year rule', immigration regulations themselves have been instrumental in maintaining the relative powerlessness of first generation female immigrants.

Finally, though perhaps most radically of all, feminists have questioned both the political advisability and the analytic integrity of liberalism's commitment to *gender-neutrality* in law and legal analysis. In a world in which sex/gender is indeed a basic axis of social differentiation – albeit mediated through other axes such as class, race, age, ethnicity, geography and so on – can legal subjects generally be constructed as gender-neutral? And can this alchemy be effected by the mere palliative of gender-neutral language? Catharine MacKinnon famously quipped that she tended to talk not about persons but about women and men because she didn't see many persons around. This point will be taken up further in our analysis of 'difference feminism' below.

Nedelsky (1989, 2–3)

The notion of autonomy goes to the heart of liberalism and of the powerful, yet ambivalent, feminist rejection of liberalism. The now familiar critique by feminists and communitarians is that liberalism takes atomistic individuals as the basic units of political and legal theory and thus fails to recognize the inherently social nature of human beings. Part of the critique is directed at the liberal vision of human beings as self-made and self-making men (my choice of noun is, of course, deliberate). The critics rightly insist that, of course, people are not self-made. We come into being in a social context that is literally constitutive of us. Some of our most essential characteristics, such as our capacity for language and the conceptual framework through which we see the world, are not made by us, but given to us (or developed in us) through our interactions with others.

The image of humans as self-determining creatures nevertheless remains one of the most powerful dimensions of liberal thought. For all of us raised in liberal societies, our deep attachment to freedom takes its meaning and value from the presupposition of our self-determining, self-making nature: that is what freedom is for, the exercise of that capacity. No one among the feminists or communitarians is prepared to abandon freedom as a value, nor, therefore, can any of us completely abandon the notion of a human capacity for making one's own life and self.

Indeed, feminists are centrally concerned with freeing women to shape our own lives, to define who we (each) are, rather than accepting the definition given to us by others (men and male-dominated society, in particular). Feminists therefore need a language of freedom with which to express the value underlying this concern. But that language must also be true to the equally important feminist precept that any good theorizing will start with people in their social contexts. And the notion of social context must take seriously its constitutive quality; social context cannot simply mean that individuals will, of course, encounter one another. It means, rather, that there are no human beings in the absence of relations with others. We take our being in part from those relations.

The problem, of course, is how to combine the claim of the constitutiveness of social relations with the value of self-determination. The problem is common to all communitarians but is particularly acute for feminists because of women's relations to the traditions of theory and of society. It is worth restating the problem in terms of these complex and ambivalent relations. Feminists angrily reject the tradition of liberal theory that has felt so alien, so lacking in language and ability to comprehend our reality, and that has been so successful in defining what the relevant questions and appropriate answers are. Anyone who has listened closely to academic feminists will have heard this undercurrent of rage at all things liberal. Yet liberalism has been the source of our language of freedom and self-determination. The values we cherish have come to us embedded in a theory that denies the reality we know: the centrality of relationships in constituting the self.

That knowledge has its own ironies: women know this centrality through experience, but the experience has been an oppressive one. One of the oldest feminist arguments is that women are not seen and defined as themselves, but in their relations to others. The argument is posed at the philosophical level of de Beauvoir's claim that men always experience women as 'Other' (a perverse, impersonal form of 'relationship') and in the mundane, but no less important, form of objections to being defined as someone's wife or mother. We need a language of self-determination that avoids the blind literalness of the liberal concept. We need concepts that incorporate our experience of embeddedness in relations, both the inherent, underlying reality of such embeddedness and the oppressiveness of its current social forms. I think the best path to this end is to work towards a reconception of the term 'autonomy'.

Okin (1991, 92–5, 100–102) [see Chapter 15 for a description of John Rawls' *Theory of Justice*]

Rawls says that it is not necessary to think of the parties [in the original position] as heads of families, but that he will generally do so. The reason he does this, he explains, is to ensure that each person in the original position cares about the well-being of some persons in the next generation … The head of a family need not necessarily, of course, be a man. Certainly in the United States, at least, there has been a striking growth in the proportion of female-headed households during the last several decades. But the very fact that, in common usage, the term 'female-headed household' is used only in reference to households without resident adult males implies the assumption that any present male takes precedence over a female as the household or family head. Rawls does nothing to contest this impression when he says of those in the original position that 'imagining themselves to be fathers, say, they are to ascertain how much they should set aside for their sons by noting what they would believe themselves entitled to claim of their fathers'. He makes the 'heads of families' assumption only in order to address the problem of justice between generations, and presumably does not intend it to be a sexist assumption. Nevertheless, he is thereby effectively trapped into the public/domestic dichotomy and, with it, the conventional mode of thinking that life within the family and relations between the sexes are not properly regarded as part of the subject matter of a theory of social justice … Throughout all these discussions, the issue of whether the monogamous family, in either its traditional or any other form, is a just social institution, is never raised.

The central tenet of the theory … is that justice as fairness characterizes institutions whose members could hypothetically have agreed to their structure and rules from a position in which they did not know which place in the structure they were to occupy … [Rawls'] argument is designed to show that the two principles of justice are those that individuals in such a hypothetical situation would agree upon. But since those in the original position are the heads or representatives of families, they are not in a position to determine questions of justice within families. As Jane English has pointed out, 'By making the parties in the original position heads of families rather than individuals, Rawls makes the family opaque to claims of justice'.

…

The significance of Rawls's central, brilliant idea, the original position, is that it forces one to question and consider traditions, customs, and institutions from all points of view, and ensures that the principles of justice will be acceptable to everyone, regardless of what position 'he' ends up in. The critical force of the original position becomes evident when one considers that some of the most creative critiques of Rawls's theory have resulted from more radical or broad interpretations of the original position than his own. The theory, in principle, avoids both the problem of domination that is inherent in theories of justice based on traditions or shared understandings and the partiality of libertarian theory to those who are talented or fortunate. For feminist readers, however, the problem of the theory as stated by Rawls himself is encapsulated in that ambiguous 'he' … [Rawls] fails entirely to address the justice of the gender system, which, with its roots in the sex roles of the family and its branches extending into virtually every corner of our lives, is one of the fundamental structures of our society.

If, however, we read Rawls in such a way as to take seriously both the notion that those behind the veil of ignorance do not know what sex they are and the requirement that the family and the gender system, as basic social institutions. are to be subject to scrutiny, constructive feminist criticism of these contemporary institutions follows.

Lacey (1993, 95–8)

First, let us examine the descriptive version of the public/private dichotomy. To what extent is it sensible to see our social world as divided into spheres corresponding to state/civil society, market/family? Obviously, these categories have a certain degree of institutional validity. But, at the level of political and sociological analysis, taking these categories as a starting-point would be very crude. 'The' state consists of many interlocking institutions and practices, as does 'the' market; 'families' can be defined in different ways and come in a variety of forms. Nor does this three-tier institutional characterization seem an adequate starting-point for social theory. For modern capitalist societies also develop a 'public sphere' or set of 'publics' which constitute not only the state or state institutions but also non-state fora for public, political debate – social movements, trades unions, pressure groups and so on. Here, too, politics, in the broad sense of 'the critical act of raising issues and deciding how institutional and social relations should be organized', goes on.

What of the specific attempt to understand social institutions as public or private in the sense of their being (at least predominantly) regulated or unregulated by state power? Historically, it could fairly be said that in, for example, mid-nineteenth century Britain the operation of the market and contractual relations were relatively unregulated by the state, or that in mid-twentieth-century Britain legal regulation was not applied to some significant aspects of family life and relations. But we are talking here of *relativities* rather than clear divisions. Indeed, the very institution of contract law always, in some sense, regulates market transactions, even though the degree to which the state controls the terms on which parties may contract with each other has steadily increased. Similarly, in spite of a great deal of rhetoric about privacy in the family sphere, a moment's thought reveals that many aspects of life are hedged around with legal regulation – marriage, divorce, child custody, social welfare rules, to name but the most obviously relevant areas of law. Moreover, it would be wrong to see direct *legal* regulation as the touchstone for state involvement. In all sorts of indirect ways – economic, administrative, and political – state institutions have a crucial and often deliberate impact on the conduct of family life. Indeed, it might be argued that in late twentieth century Britain we have seen an increasing willingness to regulate the family whilst *laissez-faire* attitudes to the market (not always realized in practice as opposed to rhetoric) have experienced a revival. As for the non-state 'publics' referred to above, the question of regulation or non-regulation seems inappropriate, yet their importance to the conduct of social life further blurs any supposed division between public and private spheres. We may be able to make relative judgements, and draw crude distinctions between family, market, and state at an institutional level. But the search for the public/private division in terms of the presence or absence of state-directed or state-sponsored regulation is as hopeless as the analysis of society merely in terms of state, market, and family is inadequate.

This conclusion becomes even clearer when we take into account the difficulty in attaching any general significance to a distinction between regulation and non-regulation, or between intervention and abstention. In any given case it can be unclear analytically whether to characterize the state's position as one of regulation or non-regulation. For example, the exemption of married men from charges of rape of their wives which persists in many jurisdictions is generally seen in terms of non-regulation. Yet it discloses a certain view of the marriage relationship which is positively inscribed in law. In such cases, abstention amounts to a form of regulation. And even where a regulation/non-regulation distinction can be drawn analytically, its significance is called into question by the fact that decisions *not* to regulate made by state or other institutions with the power to do so are every bit as much political decisions as are decisions to regulate. Clearly, both within and beyond liberal theory, the shape of arguments for regulation and non-regulation cannot be taken to be identical. But the strong liberal presumption in favour of non-regulation which proceeds from the commitment of some of the most influential versions of modern liberalism to a *negative* conception of freedom – freedom as the absence of constraint – has obscured the way in which state decisions not to regulate are themselves political and call for justification.

Another problematic feature of the characterization of family or civil society as private in the sense of unregulated has to do with what such a characterization presupposes about the regulator. This is generally conceived in simple terms as 'the state'. But, as I have already observed, the state is not monolithic; it is rather a set of diverse institutions. This gives rise to further complexities in identifying regulation or non-regulation. What are we to say of issues such as wife-battering – always 'regulated' in the sense of being within the purview of criminal law, but frequently 'unregulated' because of the decisions of law enforcement agencies? ... Finally, the descriptive association of women with 'the private sphere', particularly in the sense of the family, is itself problematic. For whilst it is both true and highly significant that women still bear a disproportionate responsibility for domestic labour, the converse suggestion that women have lived their lives exclusively or even mainly in the private sphere of the family is quite unsustainable. Working-class women in particular have worked outside the home to a far greater degree than the public/private critique has tended to acknowledge. At a descriptive level, the idea of a private, unregulated family simply collapses when subjected to scrutiny.

Now let us move from the descriptive to the normative. The idea that the state's use of coercive force to curtail citizens' behaviour calls for special justification lies at the heart of liberal political philosophy. In Mill's famous formulation, the only justification for state intervention to curtail individual freedom lies in the prevention of harm to others. Individual freedom is the paramount liberal value. State power threatens that freedom in a peculiarly dangerous way, and must be strictly limited. Leaving aside for the moment Mill's unitary conception of state power, the implications of his argument depend on how freedom is conceived. To the extent that we recognize that genuine freedom depends not only on being left alone – not interfered with, regulated, or scrutinized – but also on being provided with certain positive goods and facilities, we will be alert to the freedom-enhancing as well as the freedom-threatening potential of state or state-sponsored action. This, certainly, was a position to which Mill was sympathetic, and it has come to be known as the idea *of positive freedom*. However, in modern debates about the proper limits of state action, the tendency has been to focus on *negative freedom* – freedom as being left in peace. On this view, a conceptually neat and rhetorically powerful way of realizing the argument for human freedom is in terms of the delineation of a 'private sphere' – famously described in the Wolfenden Report as that which is 'in brief and crude terms, not the law's business'. The central thrust of feminist critique has borne upon this normative interpretation, of liberal theory. For, it has been argued, the practical consequence of non-regulation is the consolidation of the *status quo*: the *de facto* support of pre-existing power relations and distributions of goods within the 'private' sphere. In effect, if not explicitly, much of the feminist critique espouses a positive conception of freedom. It exposes the way in which the ideology of the public/private dichotomy allows government to clean its hands of any *responsibility* for the state of the 'private' world and *depoliticizes* the disadvantages which inevitably spill over the alleged divide by affecting the position of the 'privately' disadvantaged in the 'public' world.

The feminist critique, then, is a direct attack on the idea of public and private spheres, which it sees as a politically and ethically inadequate realization of liberal arguments about individual freedom and the proper role of the state. The attack consists in both a normative argument about positive freedom and an analytical argument about the interdependence of regulated and unregulated spheres. Liberal theory which depends on the public/private distinction is self-defeating in that the guarantees of justice and equality held out to citizens in the 'public' sphere are worth systematically less to those who are pre-politically disadvantaged. The limits of the scope of politics and justice asserted by liberals such as Rawls, in other words, are inconsistent with the realization of the general values which they claim to espouse. Also notable from a critical point of view is a tendency to couch the normative argument in superficially descriptive terms, in a way which is at once intellectually indefensible and rhetorically powerful. As we saw above, the project of delineating public and private spheres at a descriptive level is fraught with difficulty. Yet the substantively normative argument often proceeds by simply announcing a particular issue to fall 'within the private sphere' and 'hence' to be inappropriate for regulation. The statement of the Wolfenden Committee quoted above is an excellent example: the labels 'public' and 'private' are used in question-begging ways which *suppress* the normative arguments which they actually presuppose so that the debate sounds common-sensical rather than politically controversial. One of the main successes of feminist critique has been to expose the *politics* – the 'power-laden' character of 'privatization' of this kind. It ought to go without saying that this repoliticization of attributions of 'privacy' is quite different from an argument for the propriety let alone the efficacy of state regulation: to say that what has been thought of as private is within the scope of political *critique* is not to say that it must necessarily be *regulated.*

QUESTION

Is there anything distinctively feminist about liberal feminism?

Radical Feminism

Radical feminism can perhaps claim to be the most autonomous and distinctive conception of feminism, in that it claims to be an exclusively feminist theory. Having said that, beyond identifying actual feminists who have claimed the label, it is more difficult to set out any unifying features of radical feminism. At the risk of stereotyping, we could say that radical feminists see sexual difference as having a certain priority in social life: they see sex difference as more radical or basic than, say, class difference or racial or ethnic difference: to radical feminists, sex difference is structural in just the way class difference is structural to marxism. Radical feminists have tended to stay within the analytic framework of sex rather than moving to that of gender: some radical feminists explicitly embrace the idea of an essential sex difference (an anathema to most other feminisms) and seek to explore and effect the re-evaluation of repressed aspects of women's culture, women's values and so on. There is also an ecological branch of radical feminism, sometime known as 'cultural feminism'. This genre of feminism argues that women's natural nurturing role in bearing and rearing children gives them a distinctive empathy with others, and even with the planet. Institutionally, radical feminists have been more inclined to pursue separatist and oppositional politics. Ideologically, radical feminism has also had a strongly utopian strand.

One useful way of illustrating the differences between radical and liberal feminism is provided by Frances Olsen's paper 'Feminism and Critical Legal Theory' (1990). Olsen starts out by noting the power of a number of binary divisions in western thought: male and female; subject and object; public and private; form and substance; mind and body; active and passive; reason and emotion. Feminists in general have asserted that these dichotomies are both hierarchised and sexualised: man is associated with the first half of each pair, and that half has been valued over and above the other. But strategic responses to this analysis differ as between radical and liberal feminists: radical feminists accept the sexualisation of the divisions, but seek to reverse the valuation, arguing for the greater social recognition of the emotive, the affective, the feminine in social practice. Liberals, by contrast, often accept the hierarchical ordering, but seek to reverse the sexualisation of the dichotomies, arguing that women are every bit as capable of reason, as entitled to inhabit the public sphere, as capable of activity and intellectual power and objectivity, as are men.

Radical feminist legal theory has been associated with the claim that the law in general, and legal theory in particular, are both male. Unlike liberal feminists whose focus tended to be on individual laws that disadvantaged women, and women's exclusion from the legal profession, radical feminists argue that legal reasoning itself reinforces men's power over women. In short, law's commitment to 'Rule of Law' values such as neutrality and formal equality works to disguise its own partiality. Because the sexes are not (and have never been) equally powerful, formal equality before the law 'equates substantive powerlessness with substantive power, and calls treating these the same "equality"' (MacKinnon 1987, 165). According to radical feminism, objectivity privileges a perspective which – under conditions of pervasive male power – will inevitably embody the dominant and therefore male point of view. If speaking objectively means speaking from the viewpoint of the powerful, domination is disguised and legitimated: the system of power 'is metaphysically nearly perfect' (MacKinnon 1989, 116). Since women do not occupy this position of power, they cannot speak from its objective viewpoint, and anything they say will automatically be marginalized by its lack of objective rigour. If, as radical feminists believe, men have exclusive access to objective truth, the power imbalance that is implicit in *all* of their assumptions about women will be obscured, and its overthrow obstructed. If men see women as sex objects, for example, this becomes simply the way things are. Since no neutral ground exists, even the language with which we describe the world will tend to reinforce men's (sexual) power over women. In one of MacKinnon's most memorable phrases: 'man fucks woman: subject verb object' (MacKinnon 1987, 124).

Olsen (1990, 199–201)

LIBERAL DUALISMS

Since the rise of classical liberal thought, and perhaps since the time of Plato, most of us have structured our thinking around a complex series of dualisms, or opposing pairs: rational/irrational; active/passive; thought/feeling; reason/emotion; culture/nature; power/sensitivity; objective/subjective; abstract/contextualized; principled/personalized. These dualistic pairs divide things into contrasting spheres or polar opposites.

This system of dualisms has three characteristics that are important to this discussion. First, the dualisms are sexualized. One half of each dualism is considered masculine, the other half feminine. Second, the terms of the dualism are not equal, but are thought to constitute a hierarchy. In each pair, the term identified as 'masculine' is privileged as superior, while the other is considered negative, corrupt, or inferior. And third, law is identified with the 'male' side of the dualisms.

SEXUALIZATION

The division between male and female has been crucial to this dualistic system of thought. Men have identified themselves with one side of the dualisms and have projected the other side upon women. I have listed each dualism in the same order, with the term associated with men on the left: rational, active, thought, reason, culture, power, objective, abstract, principled. The terms associated with women are on the right side: irrational, passive, feeling, emotion, nature, sensitivity, subjective, contextualized, personalized.

rational/irrational

active/passive

thought/feeling

reason/emotion

culture/nature

power/sensitivity

objective/subjective

abstract/contextualized

principled/personalized

HIERARCHIZATION

The system of dualisms is hierarchized. The dualisms do not just divide the world between two terms; the two terms are arranged in a hierarchical order. Just as men dominate and define women, one side of the dualism dominates and defines the other. Irrational is the absence of rational; passive is the failure of active; thought is more important than feeling; reason takes precedence over emotion.

This hierarchy has been somewhat obscured by a complex and often insincere glorification of women and the feminine. While men have oppressed and exploited women in the real world, they have also placed women on a pedestal and treasured them in a fantasy world. And just as men simultaneously exalt and degrade women, so, too, do they simultaneously exalt and degrade the concepts on the 'feminine' side of the dualisms. Nature, for example, is glorified as something awesome, a worthy subject of conquest by male heroes, while it is simultaneously degraded as inert matter to be exploited and shaped to men's purpose. Irrational subjectivity and sensitivity are similarly treasured and denigrated at the same time. However much they might romanticize the womanly virtues, most men still believe that rational is better than irrational, objectivity is better than subjectivity, and being abstract and principled is better than being contextualized and personalized. It is more complicated than this, however, because no one would really want to *eliminate* irrational, passive, etc. from the world altogether. But men usually want to *distance themselves* from these traits; they want women to be irrational, passive, and so forth. To women, this glorification of the 'feminine' side of the dualisms seems insincere.

LAW AS MALE

Law is identified with the hierarchically superior, 'masculine' sides of the dualisms. 'Justice' may be depicted as a woman, but, according to the dominant ideology, law is male, not female. Law is supposed to be rational, objective, abstract and principled, like men; it is not supposed to be irrational, subjective, contextualized or personalized, like women.

The social, political and intellectual practices that constitute 'law' were for many years carried on almost exclusively by men. Given that women were long excluded from the practice of law, it is not surprising that the traits associated with women are not greatly valued in law. Moreover, in a kind of vicious cycle, this presumed 'maleness' of law is used to provide justification for excluding women from practicing law. While the number of women in law has been rapidly increasing, the field continues to be heavily male-dominated. In a similar vicious cycle, law is considered rational and objective in part because it is highly valued, and it is highly valued in part because it is considered rational and objective.

West (1988, 1–4, 29, 35)

What is a human being? Legal theorists must, perforce, answer this question: jurisprudence, after all, is about human beings. The task has not proven to be divisive. In fact, virtually all modern American legal theorists, like most modern moral and political philosophers, either explicitly or implicitly embrace what I will call the 'separation thesis' about what it means to be a human being: a 'human being', whatever else he is, is physically separate from all other human beings. I am one human being and you are another, and that distinction between you and me is central to the meaning of the phrase 'human being'.

...

The first purpose of this essay is to put forward the global and critical claim that by virtue of their shared embrace of the separation thesis, all of our modern legal theory – by which I mean 'liberal legalism' and 'critical legal theory' collectively – is essentially and irretrievably masculine.

...

The claim that the word 'individual' has an uncontested biological meaning, namely that we are each physically individuated from every other, the claim that we are individuals 'first', – while 'trivially true' of men, are patently untrue of women. Women are not essentially, necessarily, inevitably, invariably, always, and forever separate from other human beings: women, distinctively, are quite clearly 'connected' to another human life when pregnant. In fact, women are in some sense 'connected' to life and to other human beings during at least four recurrent and critical material experiences: the experience of pregnancy itself; the invasive and 'connecting' experience of heterosexual penetration, which may lead to pregnancy; the monthly experience of menstruation, which represents the potential for pregnancy; and the post-pregnancy experience of breast-feeding. Indeed, perhaps the central insight of feminist theory of the last decade has been that woman are 'essentially connected', not 'essentially separate', from the rest of human life, both materially, through pregnancy, intercourse, and breast-feeding, and existentially, through the moral and practical life. If by 'human beings' legal theorists mean women as well as men, then the 'separation thesis' is clearly false. If, alternatively, by 'human beings' they mean those for whom the separation thesis is true, then women are not human beings. It's not hard to guess which is meant....

[T]he gap between legal theory's descriptions of human nature and women's true nature also presents a conceptual obstacle to the development of feminist jurisprudence: jurisprudence must be about the relationship of human beings to law, and feminist jurisprudence must be about women. Women, though, are not human beings. Until that philosophical fact changes, the phrase 'feminist jurisprudence' is a conceptual anomaly.

...

According to radical feminism, women's connection to others is the source of women's misery, not a source of value worth celebrating. For cultural feminists, women's connectedness to the other (whether material or cultural) is the source, the heart, the root and the cause of women's different morality, different voice, different 'ways of knowing', different genius, different capacity for care, and different ability to nurture. For radical feminists, that same potential for connection – experienced materially in intercourse and pregnancy, but experienced existentially in all spheres of life – is the source of women's debasement, powerlessness, subjugation and misery. It is the cause of our pain, and the reason for our stunted lives. Invasion and intrusion, rather than intimacy, nurturance and care, is the 'unofficial' story of women's subjective experience of connection.

...

[W]hile unwanted heterosexual intercourse is disastrous, even wanted heterosexual intercourse is intrusive. The penis occupies the body and 'divides the woman' internally, to use Andrea Dworkin's language, in consensual intercourse no less than in rape. It preempts, challenges, negates, and renders impossible the maintenance of physical integrity and the formation of a unified self. The deepest unofficial story of radical feminism may be that intimacy – the official value of cultural feminism – is itself oppressive.

MacKinnon 1983, 646–54

Feminists have reconceived rape as central to women's condition in two ways. Some see rape as an act of violence, not sexuality, the threat of which intimidates all women. Others see rape, including its violence as an expression of male sexuality, the social imperatives of which define all women ... The point of defining rape as 'violence not sex' or 'violence against women' has been to separate sexuality from gender in order to affirm sex (heterosexuality) while rejecting violence (rape). The problem remains what it has always been: telling the difference. The convergence of sexuality with violence, long used at law to deny the reality of women's violation, is recognized by rape survivors, with a difference: where the legal system has seen the intercourse in rape, victims see the rape in intercourse. The uncoerced context for sexual expression becomes as elusive as the physical acts come to feel indistinguishable. Instead of asking, what is the violation of rape, what if we ask, what is the nonviolation of intercourse? To tell what is wrong with rape, explain what is right about sex. If this, in turn, is difficult, the difficulty is as instructive as the difficulty men have in telling the difference when women see one. Perhaps the wrong of rape has proven so difficult to articulate because the unquestionable starting point has been that rape is definable as distinct from intercourse, when for women it is difficult to distinguish them under conditions of male dominance.

Like heterosexuality, the crime of rape centers on penetration ... Women do resent forced penetration. But penile invasion of the vagina may be less pivotal to women's sexuality, pleasure or violation, than it is to male sexuality. This definitive element of rape centers upon a male-defined loss, not coincidentally also upon the way men define loss of exclusive access. In this light, rape, as legally defined, appears more a crime against female monogamy than against female sexuality.

...

Men believe that it is less awful to be raped by someone one is close to ... But women feel as much, if not more, traumatized by being raped by someone we have known or trusted, someone we have shared at least an illusion of mutuality with, than by some stranger. In whose interest is it to believe that it is not so bad to be raped by someone who has fucked you before as by someone who has not?

...

Having defined rape in male sexual terms, the law's problem, which becomes the victim's problem, is distinguishing rape from sex in specific cases. The law does this by adjudicating the level of acceptable force starting just above the level set by what is seen as normal male sexual behavior, rather than at the victim's, or women's, point of

Introduction to Jurisprudence and Legal Theory

Corrigendum

The editors and publishers apologise for the late removal of pages 807-810, which contained a reading from the work of Catharine MacKinnon; the anticipated permission to reprint this text was refused by Professor MacKinnon in view of the authors' commentary on her work. The following should be read as continuing from the end of page 806 to the beginning of page 811.

violation. Rape cases finding insufficient force reveal that acceptable sex, in the legal perspective can entail a lot of force. This is not only because of the way specific facts are perceived and interpreted, but because of the way the injury itself is defined as illegal. Rape is a sex crime that is not a crime when it looks like sex. To seek to define rape as violent, not sexual, is understandable in this context, and often seems strategic. But assault that is consented to is still assault; rape consented to is intercourse. ...

The line between rape and intercourse commonly centers on some measure of the woman's 'will' ... Women are socialized to passive receptivity; may have or perceive no alternative to acquiescence; may prefer it to the escalated risk of injury and the humiliation of a lost fight; submit to survive. Some eroticize dominance and submission; it beats feeling forced. Sexual intercourse may be deeply unwanted – the woman would never have initiated it – yet no force may be present. Too, force may be used, yet the woman may want the sex – to avoid more force or because she, too, eroticizes dominance ... If sex is normally something men do to women, the issue is less whether there was force and more whether consent is a meaningful concept. ...

Here the victim's perspective grasps what liberalism applied to women denies: that forced sex as sexuality is not exceptional in relations between the sexes but constitutes the social meaning of gender ... To be rap*able*, a position which is social, not biological, defines what a woman is.

The law distinguishes rape from intercourse by the woman's lack of consent coupled with a man's (usually) knowing disregard of it. A feminist distinction between rape and intercourse, to hazard a beginning approach, lies instead in the *meaning* of the act from women's point of view ... The problem is this: the injury of rape lies in the meaning of the act to its victims, but the standard for its criminality lies in the meaning of the same act to the assailants. Rape is only an injury from women's point of view. It is only a crime from the male point of view, explicitly that of the accused. ...

What this means doctrinally is that the man's perceptions of the woman's desires often determine whether she is deemed violated ... Many women are raped by men who know the meaning of their acts to women and proceed anyway. But women are also violated every day by men who have no idea of the meaning of their acts to women. To them, it is sex. Therefore, to the law, it is sex. That is the single reality of what happened. When a rape prosecution is lost on a consent defense, the woman has not only failed to prove lack of consent, she is not considered to have been injured at all. Hermeneutically unpacked, read: because he did not perceive she did not want him, she was not violated. She had sex. Sex itself cannot be an injury. Women consent to sex every day. Sex makes a woman a woman. Sex is what women are *for*. ...

Men's pervasive belief that women fabricate rape charges after consenting to sex makes sense in this light. To them, the accusations *are* false because, to them, the facts describe sex. To interpret such events as rapes distorts their experience. Since they seldom consider that their experience of the real is anything other than reality, they can only explain the woman's version as maliciously invented. ...

From whose standpoint, and in whose interest is a law that allows one person's conditioned unconsciousness to contraindicate another's experienced violation? This aspect of the rape law reflects the sex inequality of the society not only in conceiving a cognizable injury from the viewpoint of the reasonable rapist, but in affirmatively rewarding men with acquittals for not comprehending women's point of view on sexual encounters.

[T]he deeper problem is the rape law's assumption that a single objective state of affairs existed, one which merely needs to be determined by evidence, when many (maybe even most) rapes involve honest men and violated women. When the reality is split – a woman is raped but not by a rapist? – the law tends to conclude that a rape *did not happen.*

Readers who would like to get a sense for themselves of the distinctive features of MacKinnon's theory of sexual difference discussed in our commentary should consult MacKinnon 1989 in general and the essay on 'Pornography', pp 138-45, 247 in particular. This essay elaborates MacKinnnon's argument about the nature of men's sexual dominance over women and the central role of pornography in sustaining it.

Limitations of Radical feminism

Radical feminism has been an influential and intellectually powerful strand in contemporary feminist legal scholarship. Like liberal feminism, however, it has been subject to a persuasive critique. The main criticisms of radical feminism focus on four features. First, critics have noted the dangers of its actual or apparent *essentialism.* This is a term which seems to be used with increasing frequency by feminists, although it is important to acknowledge that its meaning may have shifted somewhat in recent years. Biological essentialism used to be synonymous with biological *determinism.* This is the idea that gender inequality has its origins in the basic biological differences between women's and men's bodies. So to be essentialist was to see biology as the originating cause of women's oppression. And, of course, if gender inequality results from the natural differences between the sexes, it is in some sense presocial and arguably resistant to political change. More recently, essentialism has tended to refer to the accusation that certain feminists have tended to privilege or reify gender discrimination at the expense of a nuanced account of the interaction between multiple vectors of inequality, such as race, disability and class. Women's experiences of their gender, it is now contended, vary dramatically, and so a single account of the origins and effects of sex inequality cannot accommodate the fragmented, fluid and variable reality of gender difference. Radical feminism, with its tendency to find the origin of patriarchy in sexual difference, and its concentration upon sex inequality in isolation, has been accused of both types of essentialism. It is, however, important to remember that not all forms of radical feminism have embraced essentialism in this way. Rather, some have based their assertion of the primacy of sex difference on historical or psychoanalytic arguments which are, in principle, constructionist.

A second point of criticism has been the relatively *limited substantive focus* of radical feminism. Most radical feminist lawyers focus on a very particular set of issues – ie those around sex, sexuality, reproduction and ecology. Typically and as a direct result of their analysis of sex as the root of women's oppression, they show less interest in economic and political questions. While undeniably important, law's role in regulating rape, abortion and pornography is analysed at the expense of other significant legal issues, such as public or labour law.

A third object of critique has been the status of radical feminism as so-called *grand theory*: more eclectic or pluralistic feminists have objected to radical feminism's monolithic theory of patriarchy which is insensitive to comparative social differences around axes such as ethnicity and class, and again courts essentialism.

Finally, it has been argued that radical feminism's typically separatist stance risks *blunting the potential for possible political alliances* and continuities around issues of class, ethnicity and so on.

Cornell (1993, 132)

I can summarize my disagreement with MacKinnon as follows: For MacKinnon, feminism must involve the repudiation of the feminine; for me, feminism *demands* the affirmation of the feminine within sexual difference, and the challenge to women's shame of their 'sex' which flows inevitably from the repudiation of the feminine. Without this challenge, we are left with the politics of revenge and lives of desolation, which make a mockery of the very concept of freedom. But to understand how we can make this challenge without simply replicating the pattern of gender hierarchy, we must first give a different account of why a gender hierarchy cannot completely capture feminine sexual difference.

MacKinnon's own analysis of femininity does not turn on a naturalist account of anatomy as destiny or on appeal to natural libidinal drives as the basis of male desire and domination. She moves within accepted 'postmodern' insight by recognizing that femininity as imposed sexuality is a social construction. But, social construction or not, the constitution of the world through the male gaze as reinforced by male power totalizes itself as our social reality. Thus, if MacKinnon clearly rejects naturalism, she nevertheless remains a specific kind of essentialist. Under this patriarchal social reality, women's imposed 'sex' is women's 'essence', her only 'being'.

QUESTIONS

1. Why have radical feminists focused upon sexuality, rather than, say, economic or political issues?

2. Is there a meaningful distinction between sexual intercourse and rape?

Marxist and socialist feminism: socio-economic structure and women's oppression

Like liberalism, we might see marxist and socialist feminism as not so much a distinctively feminist position as an immanent critique of marxism which subtly transforms marxist arguments by pointing out the implications of traditional marxism once women are incorporated specifically into the analysis. The relevant aspect of the traditional marxist position is that the fundamental social division as based on class, and sex or other (for example, racial) subordination is epi-phenomenal – in other words is a side effect of class difference. Feminists have pointed out that this analysis is incapable of accommodating the sense in which all men – even poor men – benefit from the exploitation of women. Nonetheless, marxist and other materialist feminists have sought to extend and modify the marxist position by constructing an imaginative 'dual systems' argument which twins exploitation in the system of economic production with exploitation in the process of human reproduction: ie women's reproductive labour is exploited by men in just the same way as the working class's productive labour is exploited by capitalists.

Like liberal and radical feminism, marxist feminism however suffers some important weaknesses, particularly as applied to law. Of these, perhaps the most important is *its class reductionism:* can all exploitation of women be accommodated within the model of reproductive exploitation? There is a real problem here, because women suffer disadvantage and discrimination – for example in the labour market – which is neither exclusively based on assumptions about their reproductive lives nor a form of class exploitation. Furthermore, marxist feminism suffers from all the *general problems of marxist theory*: a unitary analysis of oppression as based on economic relations: obscurity in its analysis of the actual processes whereby the ownership of the means of production realises itself in particular relations of production and in particular in distinctive ideological, superstructural formations such as law; and (especially at the start of the twenty first century) the implausibility of the marxist theory of history.

Smart (1989, 163–5)

There have always been two components to feminism's engagement with law. One has been to resist legal changes which appear detrimental to women, the other has been to use law to promote women's interests. The latter increases legislative provisions and empowers law, the former withstands damaging changes but only maintains the status quo. In terms of practical politics these strategies have often been reactive and *ad hoc* and they do not appear to reflect any coherent feminist analysis of law.

It is therefore important to develop a clearer vision of law. [Previously] I have argued against the idea of a theory of law and the development of a totalizing theory such as that to be found in early Marxist analysis of law or some feminist analyses. The problem which then arises is whether, without such a general theory, it is ever possible to develop anything other than *ad hoc* tactics. Yet this is really a false problem. General theories never provide clear tactics, they are always open to interpretation precisely because the general theory operates at a level of considerable abstraction. So it is just as valuable to consider in detail how law operates in different fields and to analyse it in its specificity rather than generality. In consequence the vision of law I have outlined is not one that is unified but *refracted.* That is to say that law does not have one single appearance, it is different according to whether one refers to statute law, judge-made law, administrative law, the enforcement of law, and so on. It is also refracted in that it is frequently contradictory even at the level of statute. Hence legislation to preserve foetal life coexists with legislation which provides therapeutic abortions. Different legislation may have, therefore, quite differing goals; it cannot be said to have a unified aim. The law is also refracted in the sense that it has different applications according to who attempts to use it. For example, migrant families using the 'right to family life' against repressive governments which prevent such families from living together indicates the progressive potential of law. For individual men to use the 'right to family life' against individual women in order to defeat women's autonomy is quite a different matter. Finally law may have quite different effects depending on who is the subject of the law. Hence abortion laws may have different meanings for black or native women on whom abortions are pressed, than for white women who feel they can exercise 'choice'. So if law does not stand in one place, have one direction, or have one consequence, it follows that we cannot develop one strategy or one policy in relation to it.

It also follows that we cannot predict the outcome of any individual law reform. Indeed the main dilemma for any feminist engagement with law is the certain knowledge that, once enacted, legislation is in the hands of individuals and agencies far removed from the values and politics of the women's movement. So does this lead to the conclusion that law should be left unchallenged? This is not the position to which I believe my analysis inevitably leads. My conclusion is that feminism needs to engage with law for purposes other than law reform and with a clear insight into the problems of legitimating a mode of social regulation which is deeply antithetical to the myriad concerns and interests of women.

Precisely because law is powerful and is, arguably, able to continue to extend its influence, it cannot go unchallenged. However, it is law's power to define and disqualify which should become the focus of feminist strategy rather than law reform as such. It is in its ability to redefine the truth of events that feminism offers political gains. Hence feminism can redefine harmless flirtation into sexual harassment, misplaced paternal affection into child sexual abuse, enthusiastic seduction into rape, foetal rights into enforced reproduction, and so on. Moreover the legal forum provides an excellent place to engage this process of redefinition. At the point at which law asserts its definition, feminism can assert its alternative. Law cannot be ignored precisely because of its power to define, but feminism's strategy should be focused on this power rather than on constructing legal policies which only legitimate the legal forum and the form of law. This strategy does not preclude other forms of direct action or policy formation. For example, it is important to sustain an emphasis on non-legal strategies and local struggles. However, it is important to resist the temptation that law offers, namely the promise of a solution. It is equally important to challenge the power of law and to insist on the legitimacy of feminist knowledge and feminism's ability to redefine the wrongs of women which law too often confines to insignificance.

Difference Feminism and the critique of liberal legal feminism

These telling criticisms of the main genres of political feminism have led to the gradual emergence of a somewhat different set of models for feminist legal theory which can conveniently be grouped together under the label 'difference feminism'. These 'difference feminisms' have in common a certain engagement both with theoretical preoccuptions of *postmodernism* and the sociological category of *postmodernity*. Like postmodernism, they typically engage in a philosophical rejection of meta-theories and grand narratives; while their concern with multiple identities and subjectivities is also informed by sociological analysis of a stage in the development of late modern societies, in which social and geographical mobility, the fragmentation of values, identities and traditional institutions, and consequent feelings of anxiety and insecurity have become key objects of social analysis.

Beyond gender-neutrality?

Difference feminism moves beyond standard 'Rule of Law' values such as neutrality and formal equality. It criticises liberal feminism as being limited by its essentially comparative standard, the underlying strategy of which is said to be assimilation of women to a standard set by and for men: wherever a woman can make herself look sufficiently like a man, can conform her life to male patterns or standards, she will be treated equally. Within this liberal model, it is argued, it is impossible to recognise or accommodate differences between the lives of women and men without reinforcing views of woman which should be challenged. Liberalism accords no space for the revaluation of the feminine envisaged by radical feminism, and courts the constant danger of subtler disadvantage and discrimination being hidden behind the veil of neutrality.

Difference feminism is therefore associated with a shift of emphasis towards a questioning of the very idea of gender neutrality, as both ideal and as possibility; and towards a new focus not only on law's reflection of pre-legal sexual difference, but also on law's dynamic role in constructing, underpinning and maintaining sexual difference. Difference feminism is a more complex and a more radical legal critique than was liberal feminism, and it is now the dominant approach within feminist legal theory.

At a schematic level, we may characterise difference feminism in terms of the following themes.

1. The substance of law as reflecting, implicitly, a male point of view

The theoretical move here is beyond explicit exclusion to implicit discrimination: digging under the surface of the law to look at its unstated assumptions. The law of rape is a rare case where law contains sexual differentiation on its surface; yet even though rape law might be taken as specifically concerned with women's interests, the way it works in practice reflects both the defendant's interpretation of the sexual encounter (a view encapsulated in the legal position that a subjective mistake as to consent negatives culpability: *R v Morgan* [1976] AC 183) and a masculine view of the nature of female sexuality (for example in rules of evidence which construe the sexual history of the victim as potentially relevant to her credibility in alleging rape, and in the longevity of the marital rape exemption in many jurisdictions). Other examples would include facially neutral immediacy requirements in criminal defences such as self defence and provocation, which may serve to exclude the defences from people in vulnerable positions, of whom, in turn, women may make up a disproportionate number. Once again, the issue here can be identified in terms of a critique of neutrality: in moving to a model based on the reasonable person rather than the reasonable man, have women's perspectives and interests really entered the law, or have they rather been yet more effectively buried from view?

In tort law, the supposed neutrality embodied by the 'reasonable man' standard has also been challenged by feminists who are concerned that replacing him with a gender neutral 'reasonable person' test would simply disguise and legitimise tort law's structural masculine bias. The reasonable man, for example, will seldom be expected to act altruistically. When learning about the distinction between tort and contract, students are taught that positive duties to assist other people are owed only when they have been in some sense paid for. Duties to prevent harm to others are exceptional in tort law, and must generally be preceded by a voluntary assumption of responsibility. The reasonable man is therefore principally a self-interested creature whose conduct must be judged against what might reasonably be expected of other essentially atomistic individuals. Defendants will be exonerated if they behaved as reasonable *men*. The reasonable man is, for instance, entitled to assume that other citizens are sufficiently robust to withstand a certain amount of trauma without suffering psychiatric damage. In *Bourhill v Young* [1943] AC 92, a heavily pregnant fishwife whose baby was stillborn as a result of the severe nervous shock she suffered after witnessing an accident caused by a speeding motorcylist failed to establish that she was owed a duty of care because, as Lord Porter explained:

> The driver of a car or vehicle, even though careless, is entitled to assume that the ordinary frequenter of the streets has sufficient fortitude to endure such incidents as may from time to time be expected to occur in them, including the noise of a collision and the sight of injury to others, and is not to be considered negligent towards one who does not possess the customary phlegm. (at 117)

A further example of structural gender bias within tort law is that damages are most readily awarded for injuries sustained in the workplace or on the road, locations where the claimant is more likely to be male.

2. The constitution of the legal subject as male

An important statement of this argument is to be found in Ngaire Naffine's *Law and the Sexes*. Naffine's is a complex argument which, like Olsen's, sets out from the power of binary, sexualised and hierarchical oppositions such as male/female, subject/object and public/private in western thought. To the extent that law's construction of its subjects is in terms of the characteristics of the first members of the pairs – in other words, as a rational individual, in control of its cognitive capacities, inhabiting the public sphere – the legal subject is implicitly a man, and women will find themselves subtly excluded and silenced.

We could draw an analogy here with the Enlightenment move in political and legal thinking from a world based on status to one based on contract. Naffine argues that the legal subject is quintessentially a contracting subject, a rational individual abstracted from his affective ties and emotional and bodily dependencies: yet this subject is a fiction because whilst these characteristics are culturally marked as masculine, they do not express the whole of men's lives: men have bodies, ties, emotions, private lives, but these can be hidden from legal view because they are being sustained by women in the private sphere. Hence Naffine speaks of woman as sustaining the 'impossible paradox of the man of law'. Good examples of the features Naffine is identifying here would be the decontextualised construction of the subject in criminal law and the circumscription of rules of evidence discussed in the following extract.

Lacey (1998, 200–202)

A central aspect of the argument in both difference feminism and critical criminal law is a strategy of what we might call recontextualisation as critique. In [Alan] Norrie's account, subjects of criminalisation are recontextualised within a political and socio-economic world whose conditions help to explain the substantially different chances which differently situated subjects have to keep within the norms of criminal law as interpreted by enforcement agencies. This argument is used in turn to undermine the supposed legitimacy of liberal systems of criminal law, and to reveal the ideological operations within doctrine which sustain that image of legitimacy. Feminist theory also recontextualises the subject – for example the woman who has killed her husband within the long term context of his violence towards her, or within more general gendered imbalances of power. And this is used as a discursive strategy to reveal the substantive sexual injustice of the application of the criminal law's usually circumscribed focus. By seeing how criminal law excludes certain features of context which are extra-legally crucial to the shape of women's lives, we can reveal how women (and indeed non-'normally' situated men) are silenced. For they are made to tell their stories within a framework which, by assuming a particular image of 'normal' subjecthood, systematically excludes certain features of experience and keeps difficult political issues about imbalances of power out of the court room. This is an argument which of course reveals law's method not so much as a decontextualisation but rather as itself a specific and politically problematic contextualisation: abstraction is an ideology as much as a fact, and what matters is what gets abstracted and how.

CONTEXUALISATION AS FEMINIST STRATEGY

In some of its forms, however, the feminist argument builds on its critical recontextualisation to make a further and significantly different set of normative and strategic points. It asserts that the recognition and realisation of intersubjectivity and connection – what we might call the relational aspect of subjectivity – has itself been of greater importance in women's than in men's lives. Furthermore, it has been marked as feminine in our culture and correspondingly disvalued. One important source of this kind of argument is Carol Gilligan's book *In a Different Voice* [discussed more fully below], which drew a distinction between an individualistic, rights or justice-based mode of constructing moral questions and a holistic, responsibility-based, relational or caring model. Debate has raged about how we should understand Gilligan's association of the caring voice with women: whether this is a replay of damaging gender essentialism; whether the caring voice is, rather than something to be valued and celebrated, in fact the voice of the oppressed; and what Gilligan's argument implies for the critique and reconstruction of law and legal method. Here I merely want to point out the way in which arguments like Gilligan's have sometimes been taken to provide an ethical mandate for a set of institutional strategies which seek to relocate the legal subject within a broader bodily, psychological and relational context. This has taken the well known shape, for example, of arguments for specific defences such as that based on pre-menstrual syndrome or battered women's syndrome, or, perhaps less problematically, the reconstruction of existing defences such as provocation, diminished responsibility or self-defence in terms which take account of broader features of a woman's situation which are relevant to the behaviour in question. I want to consider this feminist leaning towards strategies of contextualisation, which I think entails certain confusions and complexities which have sometimes gone unnoticed.

What are we to make of the idea that a legal method which contextualised subjects more broadly – attending to their bodies, their relationships and responsibilities – would in itself be favourable to women? Clearly, the question of how we recognise and accommodate all subjects' interdependence, how we recognise the relational, embodied and affective aspects of lived experience within institutions whose method is to judge, fix, categorise (indeed whether these features of legal method could go unreconstructed) is crucially important. But the notion that we could make any progress to its solution by an introduction of increased 'contextualisation' of the conceptual framework of legal subjecthood strikes me as somewhat naive. For the idea that contextualisation within a broader set of relationships could in itself be progressive seems to depend on the idea that the broader social relationships within which we might locate a reconceptualised legal subject (for example by modifying rules of evidence to encompass the subject's location within the practices of the family, of the labour market, of the political sphere) and the non-legal discourses of femininity and masculinity which might thereby be invoked, can be assumed, on average, to be less excluding of women, less limiting and less strongly marked by stereotyped assumptions about sex difference than are legal discourse and legal practice. It assumes, in other words, that these other social practices are less implicated in the cultural production of a particular masculinity and femininity than is law.

Law's emphasis on the transactions of rational, self-interested, contracting (male) subjects has meant that, within legal terminology, other sorts of connections or relationships become anomalous or problematic. A particularly stark example is the relationship between the pregnant woman and the foetus she carries, which has proved exceptionally difficult to categorise using existing legal norms. In *Turley v Allders Stores Ltd Store* (1980) IRLR 4, the Employment Appeal Tribunal found that:

> [w]hen a woman is pregnant, she is no longer just a woman. She is a woman, as the authorized version of the Bible puts it, with child, and there is no masculine equivalent. (at 5)

In working out what obligations a pregnant woman might owe towards her foetus, the judiciary have wrestled with the problem that while not a person, the foetus is clearly 'not nothing'. Yet while the judiciary agonises over the uniqueness of pregnancy, its essential *ordinariness* is easily forgotten. The connection between a pregnant woman and a foetus may be quite unlike the sort of contractual or tortious relationships which are more familiar territory for legal argument, but it is also, in statistical terms, exceptionally common: after all, we were all foetuses once. To judge pregnancy irredeemably peculiar (or, as in sex discrimination law, as a form of illness: *Hayes v Malleable Working Men's Club* EAT 188/84) may therefore reflect the law's instrinsic blindness to connections that do not easily fit within conventional and masculine legal norms.

We could also draw an analogy here with psychoanalytic arguments explored in Chapter 19, especially those about the impossibility of women constituting full speaking subjects to be found in the work of both Drucilla Cornell and Luce Irigaray. The basic argument is that the conditions of identity formation are structured around sexual difference in such a way that the power to construct meaning – language – is always marked and masculine and is inaccessible to woman.

3. Legal methods as masculine

Building on the above argument about the legal subject, difference feminists have developed the idea that the very methods of law – its reasoning processes – are gendered, and are gendered to the disadvantage of women. Prime targets here are the competitive system of arriving at/constructing truth in adversarial legal orders in which legal processes are essentially a competition between individuals assumed to be equal, and abstracted from their social contexts and sexed bodies. There is an important link here with the influential and controversial work of psychologist Carol Gilligan.

Gilligan (1982, 25–31, 172–3)

The shift in imagery that creates the problem in interpreting women's development is elucidated by the moral judgments of two eleven-year-old children, a boy and a girl, who see, in the same dilemma, two very different moral problems. While current theory brightly illuminates the line and the logic of the boy's thought, it casts scant light on that of the girl.

The two children in question, Amy and Jake, were both bright and articulate and, at least in their eleven-year-old aspirations, resisted easy categories of sex-role stereotyping, since Amy aspired to become a scientist while Jake preferred English to math. Yet their moral judgments seem initially to confirm familiar notions about differences between the sexes, suggesting that the edge girls have on moral development during the early school years gives way at puberty with the ascendance of formal logical thought in boys.

The dilemma that these eleven-year-olds were asked to resolve was one in the series devised by Kohlberg to measure moral development in adolescence by presenting a conflict between moral norms and exploring the logic of its resolution. In this particular dilemma, a man named Heinz considers whether or not to steal a drug which he cannot afford to buy in order to save the life of his wife. In the standard format of Kohlberg's interviewing procedure, the description of the dilemma itself – Heinz's predicament, the wife's disease, the druggist's refusal to lower his price – is followed by the question, 'Should Heinz steal the drug?' The reasons for and against stealing are then explored through a series of questions that vary and extend the parameters of the dilemma in a way designed to reveal the underlying structure of moral thought.

Jake, at eleven, is clear from the outset that Heinz should steal the drug. Constructing the dilemma, as Kohlberg did, as a conflict between the values of property and life, he discerns the logical priority of life and uses that logic to justify his choice ... his ability to bring deductive logic to bear on the solution of moral dilemmas, to differentiate morality from law, and to see how laws can be considered to have mistakes points toward the principled conception of justice that Kohlberg equates with moral maturity.

In contrast, Amy's response to the dilemma conveys a very different impression, an image of development stunted by a failure of logic, an inability to think for herself ... Asked why he should not steal the drug, she considers neither property nor law but rather the effect that theft could have on the relationship between Heinz and his wife: ... Since Amy's moral judgment is grounded in the belief that, 'if somebody has something that would keep somebody alive, then it's not right not to give it to them', she considers the problem in the dilemma to arise not from the druggist's assertion of rights but from his failure of response. ... [S]eeing a world comprised of relationships rather than of people standing alone, a world that coheres through human connection rather than through systems of rules, she finds the puzzle in the dilemma to lie in the failure of the druggist to respond to the wife.....she assumes that if the druggist were to see the consequences of his refusal to lower his price, he would realize that 'he should just give it to the wife and then have the husband pay back the money later'. Thus she considers the solution to the dilemma to lie in making the wife's condition more salient to the druggist or, that failing, in appealing to others who are in a position to help.

Just as Jake is confident the judge would agree that stealing is the right thing for Heinz to do, so Amy is confident that, 'if Heinz and the druggist had talked it out long enough, they could reach something besides stealing' ... Just as he relies on the conventions of logic to deduce the solution to this dilemma, assuming these conventions to be shared, so she relies on a process of communication, assuming connection and believing that her voice will be heard ... When considered in the light of Kohlberg's definition of the stages and sequence of moral development, her moral judgments appear to be a full stage lower in maturity than those of the boy ... Yet the world she knows is a different world from that refracted by Kohlberg's construction of Heinz's dilemma. Her world is a world of relationships and psychological truths where an awareness of the connection between people gives rise to a recognition of responsibility for one another, a perception of the need for response. Seen in this light, her understanding of morality as arising from the recognition of relationship, her belief in communication as the mode of conflict resolution, and her conviction that the solution to the dilemma will follow from its compelling representation seem far from naive or cognitively immature. Instead, Amy's judgments contain the insights central to an ethic of care, just as Jake's judgments reflect the logic of the justice approach ... Thus in Heinz's dilemma these two children see two very different moral problems – Jake a conflict between life and property that can be resolved by logical deduction, Amy a fracture of human relationship that must be mended with its own thread.

Since the reality of connection is experienced by women as given rather than as freely contracted, they arrive at an understanding of life that reflects the limits of autonomy and control. As a result, women's development delineates the path not only to a less violent life but also to a maturity realized through interdependence and taking care.

As we have listened for centuries to the voices of men and the theories of development that their experience informs, so we have come more recently to notice not only the silence of women but the difficulty in hearing what they say when they speak. Yet in the different voice of women lies the truth of an ethic of care, the tie between relationship and responsibility, and the origins of aggression in the failure of connection. The failure to see the different reality of women's lives and to hear the differences in their voices stems in part from the assumption that there is a single mode of social experience and interpretation. By positing instead two different modes, we arrive at a more complex rendition of human experience which sees the truth of separation and attachment in the lives of women and men and recognizes how these truths are carried by different modes of language and thought.

Bottomley, Gibson and Meteyard (1987, 55)

It has always been implicit in feminism that its critique of existing theory is based upon the disjuncture of women's lived experience of reality and men's representations of it. In this sense, then, feminism is an attack of the specific (women's knowledge) upon the universal (that is what is represented as knowledge writ large). The point about male theorising is that if it has originated from men's lived experience this has never been explicitly acknowledged, so that specific theory becomes universal, in much the same way that 'man' has come to mean both man in particular and man and woman in universal. Gilligan's useful critique of theory building in the male mode contains some splendid examples of this kind of androcentric theorising, and demonstrates its pernicious effect upon the way in which judgment is constructed. Instancing, for example, a series of studies by Kohlberg on the development of moral judgment, Gilligan points out that the research group upon which Kohlberg's initial 'findings' were based comprised eighty-four boys. In a theory outlining a six stage sequence derived from his observations of this group, a mature woman's judgment generally exemplified stage three, a point at which 'morality is conceived in interpersonal terms and goodness is equated with helping and pleasing others'. Gilligan suggests, however, that Kohlberg's scale, based upon a study of *men's* maturation 'reflects the importance of individuation in *their* development' (our emphasis). She further suggests that had the pilot study been based upon a group of women, the 'moral problem' would be identified as arising:

> ... from conflicting responsibilities rather than from competing rights and would require for its resolution a mode of thinking that is contextual and narrative rather than formal and abstract. This conception of morality as concerned with the activity of care, centres moral development around the understanding of relationships, just as the conception of morality as fairness ties moral development to the understanding of rights and rules.

Lacey (1998, 5–6)

A central tenet of both positivist scholarship and the liberal ideal of the rule of law is that laws set up standards which are applied in a neutral manner to formally equal parties. The questions of inequality and power which may affect the capacity of those parties to engage effectively in legal reasoning have featured little in either mainstream legal theory or legal education. These questions have, on the other hand, been central to critical legal theory, and they find an important place within feminist legal thought. In particular, the work of social psychologist Carol Gilligan on varying ways of constructing moral problems, and the relationship of these variations to gender, has opened up a striking argument about the possible 'masculinity' of the very process of legal reasoning.

As is widely known, Gilligan's research was motivated by the finding of psychological research that men reach, on average, a 'higher' level of moral development than do women. Gilligan set out to investigate the neutrality of the tests being applied: she also engaged in empirical research designed to illuminate the ways in which different people construct moral problems. Her research elicited two main approaches to moral reasoning. The first, which Gilligan calls the ethic of rights, proceeds in an essentially legalistic way: it formulates rules structuring the values at issue in a hierarchical way, and then applies those rules to the facts. The second, which Gilligan calls the ethic of care or responsibility, takes a more holistic approach to moral problems, exploring the context and relationships, as well as the values, involved, and producing a more complex, but less conclusive, analysis. The tests on which assessments of moral development have conventionally been made by psychologists were based on the ethic of rights: analyses proceeding from the ethic of care were hence adjudged morally under-developed. It was therefore significant that Gilligan's fieldwork suggested that these two types were gender-related, in that girls tended to adopt the care perspective, whilst boys more often adopted the rights approach.

Gilligan's assertion of the relationship between the two models and gender is a controversial one. Nonetheless, her analytical distinction between the two ethics is of great potential significance for feminist legal theory. The idea that the distinctive structure of legal reasoning may systematically silence the voices of those who speak the language of relationships is a potentially important one for all critical legal theory. The rights model is ... reminiscent of law: it works from a clear hierarchy of sources which are reasoned through in a formally logical way. The more contextual, care or relationship-oriented model would, by contrast, be harder to capture by legal frameworks, within which holistic or relationally-oriented reasoning tends to sound 'woolly' or legally incompetent, or to be rendered legally irrelevant by substantive and evidential rules. Most law students will be familiar with the way in which intuitive judgements are marginalised or disqualified in legal education, which proceeds precisely by imbuing the student with a sense of the exclusive relevance of formal legal sources and technical modes of reasoning.

While Gilligan's articulation of a distinctively feminine ethic of care undoubtedly has considerable intuitive appeal, it should be noted that her research is controversial for a number of reasons. Gilligan herself has acknowledged the partiality of her research sample, and other psychologists have found that her results are not easily replicated. Critics have also pointed out that, at the level of practice, an ethic of care does not necessarily help us decide what we should do when faced with difficult moral choices. Invoking an ethic of care will not, for example, provide very much guidance when we are deciding how to allocate scarce medical resources. The gender-specificity of an ethic of care has also been disputed. According to Immanuel Kant, every one should 'endeavour, so far as in him lies, to further the ends of others', leading philosopher RM Hare to comment: 'if this is not caring, I do not know what is'. What would Gilligan have to say of the existence of widespread duties of care in the modern common law? In addition, different interpretations of Gilligan's conclusions are possible. Mary Joe Frug suggests two contrasting readings of *In a Different Voice*. Frug favours a progressive reading which would emphasise the fluidity rather than the fixity of gender differences. A conservative reading, Frug warns, 'sentimentalises and romanticizes self-sacrifice, and inadequately acknowledges the costs and problems of this attitude'.

Mary Joe Frug (1992, 38–49)

For conservative readers, the sex differences Gilligan discusses in the book validate gender differences. Pursuant to this reading of Gilligan, her book constitutes evidence that women are contextually focused, relationship-oriented and care-giving, whereas men are abstract, individualistic, and dominating. Gilligan's sympathetic presentation of women and her generalizations about the sexes are important to the conservative conclusion that, although Gilligan draws the cluster of sex-linked traits she discusses from the discourse of moral choice, these traits are universal characteristics of the sexes.

...

In contrast to the conservative position, a progressive reading would interpret Gilligan's use of sex differences as a methodology for challenging gender, as an example of how contingently-formed gender differences can be strategically deployed to unsettle existing inequalities between the sexes. Sex differences, pursuant to a progressive reading, are context-bound. They are associated with language, more than individual identity, so that to the extent language can be changed, gender identity can also be transformed. Progressive readers ground the sex differences Gilligan identifies in the context of the moral development theory she sought to change, overlooking the many instances where Gilligan seems to speak of sex differences as if they are universal.

4.   *The images of men and women, masculinity and femininity in legal discourse*

Difference feminists have also been concerned to emphasise the dynamic role of law in the positive construction of sexual difference, and of sexed social identities. When we look not just at legal doctrine but also at legal discourse – the structured language in which doctrine is formulated and discussed by judges – we find powerful and often prejudicial images of 'normal' men and women, of male and female sexuality, of femininity and masculinity. A spectacular example here is the English law of incest, which explicitly construes the masculine sexual role as active and the feminine as passive. The Sexual Offences Act 1956, s 10, provides that:

(1) It is an offence for a man to have sexual intercourse with a woman whom he knows to be his grand-daughter, daughter, sister or mother.

While s 11 provides that:

(1) It is an offence for a woman of the age of sixteen or over to permit a man whom she knows to be her grandfather, father, brother or son to have sexual intercourse with her by consent.

This can be compared with judicial discourse in sentencing of incest cases, in which stereotypes of wilful, seductive femininity have abounded:

Re Attorney-General's Reference (No 1 of 1989) [1989] 3 All ER 571

At one end of the scale is incest committed by a father with a daughter in her late teens or older who is a willing participant and indeed may be the instigator of the offences. In such a case, the court usually need do little more than mark the fact that there has been a breach of the law and little if anything is required in the way of punishment.

(See further Lacey and Wells 1998, Chapter 4, III, iv.) The focus here is the subtle and dynamic role which law has not just in regulating/empowering women and men who arrive at the legal forum, but also in constituting us as sexed subjects.

In its contribution to the construction of dominant images of female sexuality the law distinguishes between different sorts of women. We encounter this differentiation again later in this chapter when we consider the characterisation of black women as either sexless matriarchs or insatiable jezebels. A further example might be the judiciary's apparent inability to comprehend the sexuality of mentally disabled women and girls. When sanctioning their sterilisation, judges often appear to assume that mental disability is inevitably synonymous with the permanent and irrevocable absence of the capacity for both maternity and sexuality. Despite modern psychiatry's rejection of the rather simplistic analogy between normal stages of child development and mental health problems, the judiciary continue to describe mentally disabled women in terms of their 'mental age'. If a mature adult woman is equated with a five-year-old child, unsurprisingly it may be difficult to believe that she might be capable of either sexual expression or motherhood. In *In re F*, a 35-year-old woman was described as having 'the general mental capacity of around a four-or-five-year-old' (*In re F (Mental Patient: Sterilisation)* [1990] 2 AC 1 per Lord Brandon at 53). Notice also Lord Hailsham's description of a mature 17-year-old girl in *In re B (A Minor)* [1987] 2 WLR 1213:

The ward in the present case is of the mental age of five or six ... She has no maternal instincts and is not likely to develop any. (at 1215)

Lord Hailsham went on dismiss the suggestion that B's involuntary sterilization might interfere with her right to reproduce:

To talk of the 'basic right' to reproduce of an individual who is not capable of knowing the causal connection between intercourse and childbirth, the nature of pregnancy,

> what is involved in delivery, unable to form maternal instincts or to care for a child appears to me wholly to part company with reality. (at 1216)

By infantilising mentally handicapped women, the law contributes to the prevailing assumption that they are innately and irrevocably sexless.

One of the most obvious ways in which the law helps to define sexual difference is through some of its background assumptions about reproductive roles. In a nineteenth century case which decided that women should not be allowed to practice law in the state of Illinois, Bradley J claimed that '[t]he paramount destiny and mission of woman are to fulfil the noble and benign offices of wife and mother. This is the law of the Creator'. (*Bradwell v Illinois* 83 US (16 Wall) 130 (1872) at 141). A recurring theme has been the judiciary's tendency to assume that all women have an instinctive and boundless capacity for maternal self-sacrifice. The 'normal' pregnant woman, for example, is assumed to be prepared to go to extraordinary lengths to safeguard her baby's health. Women who would put foetal life at risk by, for example, taking drugs during pregnancy or refusing to consent to an emergency caesarean section are treated with a mixture of dismay and horror. Judge LJ said of one pregnant woman's persistent failure to follow medical advice: 'no normal mother-to-be could think like that' (*St. George's Healthcare NHS Trust v S* [1998] 3 WLR 936, at 957). In the United States, pregnant drug users have been imprisoned for minor offences, such as cheque forgery, which would not otherwise attract a custodial sentence. Note, for example, the comments of Peter Wolf J in *United States v Vaughn* 117 Daily Washington Law Reporter 441 DC Sup Ct (1988): 'I'm going to keep her locked up until the baby is born ... I'll be darned if I'm going to have a baby born that way.' As Iris Marion Young has put it, 'the mother who would harm her child is not merely a criminal; she is a monster' (Young 1997, 77).

It would, however, be a mistake to conclude that the law's construction of sexual difference is monolithic or immovable. While examples of sexual stereotyping are clearly evident in legal discourse, much feminist critique is founded upon the conviction that caricatured gender roles can be rewritten. An example of this sort of shift occurring comes from the so-called 'wrongful birth' cases in tort law. These are cases in which the negligence of a health authority leads, often as the result of a failed sterilisation operation, to the birth of a child. We quote here from Jupp J in the 1983 case *Udale v Bloomsbury Area Health Authority* [1983] 1 WLR 1098, and Hale LJ (the second woman to be appointed to the Court of Appeal) in the 2001 case *Parkinson v St James and Seacroft University NHS Trust* [2001] 3 WLR 376. Notice how the representation of motherhood has changed, from Jupp J's assumptions about the 'proper' mother's sense of fulfilment and joy, to Hale LJ's description of the invasion of pregnancy and the sheer hard work involved in being a mother.

In describing Mrs Udale, Jupp J said:

> Now, the plaintiff is a motherly sort of woman, nice-looking but rather over-weight ... she is not only an experienced mother but, so far as I am able to judge, a good mother, who has all the proper maternal instincts which make her work long and hard to look after her offspring. (at 1103)

Later Jupp J found himself 'inevitably reminded of the gospel':

> A woman when in travail hath sorrow because her hour is come; but as soon as she is delivered of the child she remembereth no more the anguish, for joy that a man is born into the world. (at 1104)

Finally, one of the reasons he gave for ultimately rejecting Mrs Udale's claim was that:

> A plaintiff such as Mrs Udale would get little or no damages because her love and care for her child and her joy, ultimately, at his birth, would be set off against and might cancel out the inconvenience and financial disadvantages which naturally accompany parenthood. By contrast, a plaintiff who nurtures bitterness in her heart and refuses to let her maternal instincts take over would be entitled to large damages. In short virtue would go unrewarded; unnatural rejection of womanhood and motherhood would be generously compensated. This, in my judgment, cannot be just. (at 1109)

Contrast Hale LJ, eighteen years later, who said that it was 'worthwhile spelling out the more obvious features' of 'the invasion of bodily integrity caused by conception, pregnancy and child birth' which, she says, are 'none the less an invasion because they are the result of natural processes'. In contrast to Jupp J's assumption that the pain of childbirth is transient and its effects short-lived, Hale LJ stresses its permanent consequences for a woman's life: 'Whatever the outcome, happy or sad, a woman never gets over it'. (at 394)

After discussing some of the risks of pregnancy, Hale LJ went on to say that:

> Along with these physical and psychological consequences goes a severe curtailment of personal autonomy. Literally, one's life is no longer just one's own but also someone else's ... Continuing the pregnancy brings a host of lesser infringements of autonomy related to the physical changes in the body or responsibility towards the growing child ... The process of giving birth is rightly termed 'labour'. It is hard work, often painful and sometimes dangerous. It brings the pregnancy to an end but it does not bring to an end the changes brought about by the pregnancy. It takes some time for the body to return to its pre-pregnancy state, if it ever does ... There are well-known psychiatric illnesses associated with child-birth ... Quite clearly, however, the invasion of the mother's personal autonomy does not stop once her body and mind have returned to their pre-pregnancy state ... The labour does not stop when the child is born. Bringing up children is hard work ... The obligation to provide or make acceptable and safe arrangements for the child's care and supervision lasts for 24 hours a day, 7 days a week, all year round, until the child becomes old enough to take care of himself. (at 394–5)

QUESTION

Is the stark difference between the language used to describe pregnancy and motherhood in these two cases evidence of a shift in the law's attitude towards childbearing between 1983 and 2001? Do you think that the gender of the judge is relevant, and, if so, why?

5. The conceptual framework of legal reasoning

The focus here is not so much on legal rules as on some of the conceptual building blocks out of which they are, often implicitly, constructed; for example the binaries or dualisms already discussed. Difference feminism is concerned with the moral and political assumptions which are concealed by broad structures of legal regulation or non-regulation in particular areas. Key examples would include the implicit role of the public/private distinction in underpinning the difficulty of getting domestic violence or sexual harassment taken seriously as legal issues. Once again, we can see a link with the negative conception of freedom: the basis of the public/private distinction is a liberal argument about the threat which state power poses to individual freedom, understood negatively; yet as MacKinnon has argued in relation to pornography, the US First Amendment's blanket protection of speech leaves no space to ask whose speech or what kind of speech is effectively protected, nor to raise questions about whether certain positive conditions are needed to guarantee access to speech for certain groups on certain issues. MacKinnon's argument is that pornography silences and changes the meaning of women's speech by trapping them within a degraded and objectified image; but because of its commitment to a predominantly negative conception of freedom, this inequality cannot be comprehended by American law.

6. The enforcement of laws

Like other feminists, difference feminists insist that the key focus of legal scholarship should be not only legal doctrine and discourse but also how law is interpreted and enforced by both legal and non-legal actors. Examples such as domestic violence, prosecution policy on marital rape and non-enforcement of laws against racial hatred are deployed to illustrate the political disadvantages and intellectual indefensibility of a purely doctrinal approach.

To summarise, in the first phase of feminist work on law, feminist scholarship focused on the liberal ideal of gender neutrality and equality before the law; the focus was instrumental: law was seen as a tool of liberal feminism and the impact of law as a basis for immanent critique of liberal legal arrangements. The second phase, now dominated by difference feminism, has been characterised by greater scepticism about the possibility of neutrality; by an implicit commitment to a more complex idea of equality which accommodates and values, whilst not fixing, women's specificity as women; and by a focus on the symbolic and dynamic aspects of law and not just on its instrumental effects.

Conaghan (2000, 377–9, 381–2)

[M]uch of the discomfort with the normative or prescriptive dimensions to the feminist project can be also attributed to the 'fall-out' generated by the critique of essentialism

... After all, if sexual categories are discursively created rather than grounded in any fixed or essential nature, in what sense can 'women' be *oppressed* by 'men' and on whose behalf are emancipatory norms invoked? Relatedly, if the individual is a product of discourse rather than an autonomous rational choosing agent, how do we give weight to her views, including the norms and principles she espouses and upon which she seeks to act? How do we decide *whose* values should prevail if all values are discursively derived?

Feminist theory precludes easy recourse to notions of objectivity or truth here. Feminists have long been sceptical of claims to objectivity, too often coming upon the pervasive partiality and bias which lurk beneath such assertions. Indeed, a primary focus of feminist theory has been the problematization of objectivity, both as a descriptive claim and as a normative ideal, as feminists scholars have gradually moved from assertions that *particular* claims to objectivity cannot be sustained to challenging the *possibility of* objectivity itself, at least as it is traditionally understood. Rejecting the idea of the theorist as an impartial observer deploying his analytical skills without reference to his particular views and uninformed by his own experiences, feminists relocate her as a participant, as someone who is *always situated* and thus can only ever offer a partial understanding of things. It follows that there are no 'Universal Truths' which feminists can invoke to justify their normative positions. Once it is understood that knowledge is a social product, contextually and temporally bounded and inseparable from the conditions within which it is produced, truth must be viewed as contingent and the possibility of one true *universal* representation of reality eschewed. Appeals to objectivity and truth are revealed as products of discursive understandings of how knowledge is legitimated, while norms and principles become simply preferences which are ideologically rather than epistemically endowed. So viewed, normativity, far from being a fine expression of a universal human yearning for unassailable standards, emerges as a 'regulative ideal which can operate coercively'. Moreover, it may be implicated in the kinds of repressive discursive effects which are the focus of postmodern feminist critique. Thus, Pierre Schlag, critiquing normativity in American legal thought, argues that it 'participates ... in the ideology of the individualist humanist self':

> On the one hand, such work may help achieve some desirable social end; on the other, the very performance of such work reproduces precisely the form of thought, the very rhetoric by which bureaucratic institutional practices represent, organize, and reproduce their own operations, their performances as the choices of autonomous rational agents. Accordingly, the participation of normative legal thought in this liberal humanist ideology has become, in terms of the very best values liberal humanism has to offer, morally ambivalent, if not immoral.

It begins to look as if feminists have been sleeping with the enemy.

'THERE'S NO SUCH PLACE AS NOWHERE'

The current reticence marking the relationship between feminists and their normative aspirations seems then to be a product of a number of overlapping concerns. There is clearly an epistemological concern with how knowledge is legitimated given its socially constituted and discursive derivation – this yields uncertainty about the status of norms in the absence of foundational (universalized, pre-discursive) justifications. It also raises questions of agency in what sense can we be said to be 'free' to pursue 'our' normative aspirations if 'we' are not unified, rational, self-present subjects but products of discourse? Finally, there is a concern with the regulatory and ideological effects of normativity, particularly in its foundationalist mode, the way in which it delimits the parameters of reasoned debate and shields from enquiry positions and assumptions which are deemed to be 'pre-given', incontrovertible, norms. The epistemological concern – the question of how we evaluate knowledge – provides a route back to the problems of woman-centredness and to uncertainties within feminism as to the validity and viability of 'standpoint' theoretical approaches. How can the experiences of women ground theoretical knowledge, and, among other things, provide feminism with its norms and aspirations, in the absence of validating standards such as objectivity or truth?

Nancy Fraser argues that the fact that subjects are culturally formed does not mean that they are without critical capacities; what it does mean, however, is that critique can only be *socially situated*, precluding the possibility of foundationalist or universal knowledge but not the possibility of critical and self-reflexive knowledge which advances understanding and, therefore, emancipatory ideals. Recognizing the possibility of socially situated criticism by the culturally formed subject does not require participation in the rhetoric of liberal humanism – indeed, is posited in opposition to it – and can, therefore, facilitate normative engagement and practices without incurring the political costs identified by Schlag, although it does demand an approach to knowledge and its evaluation which is tentative, revisionist, and relentlessly self-critical.

This means that feminist efforts to articulate and pursue normative aspirations – to ground their work in values or principles which are likely to further the goal of transformation – are problematized but not precluded by the postmodern deconstruction of the subject. Nevertheless, feminist legal scholars may be tempted to take the easy route of deploying immanent critique, that is, of invoking the norms of *law* – equality, justice, freedom, autonomy – to critique legal and social arrangements by showing how law fails to live up to its own standards. This allows feminist legal scholars to take a normative stance without asserting its status as a fundamental truth. However, although as an intellectual ploy, the application of immanent critique has the merit of preserving one's theoretical integrity intact, as a transformative strategy, it is seriously and unacceptably limiting, in most cases doing little more than facilitating women's access to 'a world already constituted'. Even at best, its deployment is likely to produce the dissolution of the very concepts being invoked – this is, for example, precisely what has occurred as feminists have probed the depths of the equality principle – in which case the feminist reconstruction of positions and values which facilitate the articulation and realization of women's needs and aspirations becomes the inevitable next step.

Cornell (1993, 141–2)

I believe my own program of equivalent rights can develop a different theory of equality and overcome the deficiency in MacKinnon's analysis. We need a theory of equality which does not end by reinforcing the privileging of the masculine as the norm. MacKinnon has correctly and profoundly challenged the 'sameness' ideology that informs so much of the law of sex discrimination. She explains that if we can show that women are like men, then we can show that we have been discriminated against if and when we are in fact like them, but are treated differently. As women we must continually analogize our experience to men's if we want it to be legally recognized as unequal treatment.

For MacKinnon, 'sameness' and 'likeness' analysis is itself a reflection of discrimination because it demands that women meet the male norm without questioning why the masculine was identified as the norm in the first place. My argument insists further that unless we recognize the value of the feminine within sexual difference we cannot adequately challenge the acceptance of the male as the human, and, therefore, we cannot ultimately challenge gender hierarchy. In other words, we need the affirmation of feminine sexual difference if we are to challenge the likeness analysis without reducing our insistence on women's rights to an appeal for special privilege.

A program of equivalent rights is the legal expression of the affirmation and valuation of sexual difference. 'Equivalence' means of equal value, but not of equal value *because of likeness*. Equivalence does not demand that the basis of equality be likeness to men. Such a view would once again deny that we are sexuate beings. Hopefully, this will continue to change as we challenge the reality of rigid gender identity. The human species is of two genres, not one species without differentiation. Equivalent rights can then be distinguished from the dominant analysis of sex discrimination that has been reflected in recent federal-court and United States Supreme Court opinions. Moreover, equivalent rights recognize the irreducibility of sexual difference to some universal conception of the asexual person. As Luce Irigaray has explained,

> I know that some men imagine that the great day of the good-for-everyone universal has dawned. But what universal? What new imperialism is hiding behind this? And who pays the price for it? There is no universal valid for all women and all men outside the natural economy. Any other universal is a partial construct and, therefore, authoritarian and unjust. The first universal to be established would be that of a legislation valid for both sexes as a basic element in human culture. That does not mean forced sexual choices. But we are living beings, which means sexuate beings, and our identity cannot be constructed without a vertical and horizontal horizon that respects difference.

The 'legislation valid for both sexes as a basic element in human culture' to which Irigaray refers must include equivalent rights as rights, and not as privileges needed to correct the imposed inequality of women. Equivalent rights are not merely a means to help women become more like men in order to promote one species undivided by sexual difference. Equivalent rights do not have as their sole or even main goal the allowance of entry into a male world from which we have previously been shut out. Rather, they are designed to enable women to value the choices we make about our lives and work without shame of our 'sex', even if such choices do not fit into the pre-established social world. Such rights, then, demand the restructuring of, not just accommodation to, the current world of work. MacKinnon has criticized the patriarchal culture which imposes 'forced sexual choices'. Yet she fails to see that one of these forced sexual choices is the very repudiation of the feminine within sexual difference.

Irigaray (1994, 59–63)

ELEMENTS OF A CIVIL LAW FOR WOMEN

The written law is a law established for a society of men – amongst – themselves. The trend for women to work outside the home and family, their entry into the world of work and public relationships, is raising questions about the current legal system, especially as far as human rights are concerned. The pretext of the neutral individual does not pass the reality test: women get pregnant, not men; women and little girls are raped, boys very rarely; the bodies of women and girls are used for involuntary prostitution and pornography, those of men infinitely less; and so on. And the exceptions to the rule or custom are not valid objections as long as society is for the most part run by men, as long as men are the ones who enact and enforce the laws.

The argument of the plurality of citizens is not valid, either. Society is made up of two sexes, not of 'men': youth, workers, the disabled, immigrants, the unemployed, women, etc. The urgency and simplicity of the legal problem today in terms of human rights causes politicians and jurists to sink into a virtually religious pathos of compassion for sexually neutralized individuals. All other differences are valid except the one that defines a society: sexual difference!

I shall therefore propose, in a style close to that of the legal code, several points of a legal system adapted to women individuals, starting with this aspect of liberation.

(1)   The right to human dignity, thus:

  –   an end to commercial use of their bodies or images – legitimate representations of themselves in actions, words and pictures in all public places

  –   an end to exploitation of a functional part of themselves by civil and religious powers, e.g. motherhood.

(2)   The right to a human identity, that is:

  –   the enshrining in law of virginity as a component of female identity that cannot be reduced to money, cannot in any way be converted into cash by the patriarchal family, state, or religion. This component of female identity gives girls a civil status and the right to keep their virginity (for their own relationship to the divine, too) as long as they like, and to bring charges against anyone inside or outside the family who violates it.

      ...

  –   the right to motherhood as a component of female identity. If the body is a legal issue, and it is, the female body must be identified civilly as both virgin and potential mother. This means that it is a woman's civil right to choose to be pregnant, and how many times. She or her legal representative will undertake the civil registration of the child's birth.

(3)   Mutual mother-child duties will be defined in the code, so that a mother can protect her children and be assisted by them under the law. This will allow her to bring charges of behalf of civil society when children, especially girls, are raped, battered, or kidnapped. The respective duties of the mother and the father will be covered by another provision of the law.

(4)   Women will have the civil right to defend their lives and those of their children, their homes, their traditions and their religion against any unilateral decision based on men's law.

(5) In strictly financial matters:

– Single people will not be penalized by the tax system or in any other way financially.

– If the state wishes to provide family allowances, they will be the same for each child.

– Women pay the same taxes as men for media such as television, so half of all media coverage will be specially aimed at women.

(6) Systems of exchange, languages, for example, will be restructured to ensure that women and men have a right of equivalent exchange.

(7) Women will be represented equally everywhere civil or religious decisions are made, since religion, too, is a civil power.

These are a few examples of priority rights to be written into the law to define women's civil identity. Naturally, this will also entail a redefinition of the rights and responsibilities of male citizens. The delusion of neutral, more or less equal individuals can no longer be perpetuated today, especially after the teachings of Marxism and Freudianism, the women's liberation movements, sexual liberation movements, and social and religious liberation movements, as well as with the blending of cultures we are now seeing, whose essential components deserve serious reflection.

Davies (1994, 175–6)

With the present emphasis on elaborating the ways in which different oppressive systems intersect, and the recognition that variations according to the cultural and political context are crucial, it is clear that some of the larger theoretical movements of feminists are tending towards a more detailed cultural critique.

This tendency in recent feminism reflects what Jean-Francois Lyotard called 'the postmodern condition', which is, briefly, a general movement away from large theoretical explanations, to the examination of more localised 'discourses'. Thus, rather than attempt to develop grand theories which factor in race, class, sexuality, and so on, current feminism is attempting to focus upon the specific ways in which systems of oppression relate in various contexts. However, it is not only the insensitivity of grand theory to 'intersecting' oppressions which has led to the breakdown of feminist categories. Many writers have recently begun to question the possibility of making anything but provisional and strategically useful classifications. For instance, many feminists have pointed out that while in many circumstances it may be politically appropriate to identify with a certain group (such as being a lesbian, a woman, or of a certain race), the identity of such groups is not (cannot and should not be) fixed. Indeed the fixing of such identities by a dominant ideology has always been one of the ways in which oppression is institutionalised. Women have been defined and stereotyped as a group: femininity has come to mean certain things which disempower and silence women, and which further marginalise women who do not conform. It is therefore necessary to question and re-formulate the meaning of 'the feminine' as a category, but to be aware at the same time that simply re-fixing the boundaries may be counter-productive. Modern feminism is also looking beyond the traditional political questions to issues inspired by the linguistic thought which has been so crucial to postmodernism: for instance the ways in which cultural meanings are produced, how they operate, and how they can be altered, have all been seen as increasingly significant matters.

THE OBJECT OF FEMINIST KNOWLEDGE

The other important thing to consider ... relates to how we view whatever it is that we think we know. This is a matter which has been given a great deal of attention by radical and postmodern feminism, especially insofar as the relationship between power and knowledge has been brought into the picture. Traditionally knowledge has been seen as power: to have knowledge is potentially to have access to a form of power. Those who know can use their knowledge to their own ends. More recent thought on this matter, including that of the radical feminists and postmodernists of all varieties, suggests that the inverse is also the case: that the conditions of what counts as 'knowledge' are in fact determined by relations of power. The structures and institutions which control society determine what is 'true', and what is not. What feminists have pointed out, often in conjunction with detailed explanations of the forms of male power and the ways in which the (male) culture defines women, is that the definitions we occupy are socially (not biologically) male, and that this is related to the empirical fact that men have power over women. It is men who traditionally have taken the position of 'knowers', and one of the things men have 'known' is women. The point was made very clearly by Catharine MacKinnon in *Feminism Unmodified*:

> Objectivity is a stance only a subject can take ... It is only a subject who gets to take the objective standpoint, the stance which is transparent to its object, the stance that is no stance. A subject is a self. An object is other to that self. Anyone who is the least bit attentive to gender since reading Simone de Beauvoir knows that it is men socially who are subjects, women socially who are other, objects. Thus the one who has the social access to being that self which takes the stance that is allowed to be objective, that objective person who is a subject, is socially male. When I spoke with David Kennedy about this earlier, he said that the objective subject didn't *have to be* male, so he didn't see how it was gendered. It *could be* any way at all, he said. Well, yes; but my point is that it *isn't* any way at all; it *is* gendered, in fact in the world. If, in order to be gendered, something has to be [that is, is of necessity] gendered, those of us in the social change business could pack up and go ... where? We would give up on changing gender, anyway. Of course it could be any way at all. That it could be and isn't, should be and isn't, is what makes it a political problem.

Young (1990, 163–6)

Those promoting a politics of difference doubt that a society without group differences is either possible or desirable. Contrary to the assumption of modernization theory, increased urbanization and the extension of equal formal rights to all groups has not led to a decline in particularised affiliations. If anything, the urban concentration and interactions among groups that modernizing social processes introduce tend to reinforce group solidarity and differentiation. Attachment to specific traditions, practices, language, and other culturally specific forms is a crucial aspect of social existence. People do not usually give up their social group identifications, even when they are oppressed.

Whether eliminating social group difference is possible or desirable in the long run, however, is an academic issue. Today and for the foreseeable future societies are certainly structured by groups, and some are privileged while others are oppressed.

Though in many respects the law is now blind to group differences, some groups continue to be marked as deviant, as the Other. In everyday interactions, images, and decisions, assumptions about women, Blacks, Hispanics, gay men and lesbians, old people, and other marked groups continue to justify exclusion, avoidance, paternalism, and authoritarian treatment. Continued racist, sexist, homophobic, ageist, and ableist institutions and behavior create particular circumstances for these groups, usually disadvantaging them in their opportunity to develop their capacities. Finally, in part because they have been segregated from one another, and in part because they have particular histories and traditions, there are cultural differences among social groups – differences in language, style of living, body comportment and gestures, values, and perspectives on society.

Today in American society, as in many other societies, there is widespread agreement that no person should be excluded from political and economic activities because of ascribed characteristics. Group differences nevertheless continue to exist, and certain groups continue to be privileged. Under these circumstances, insisting that equality and liberation entail ignoring difference has oppressive consequences in three respects.

First, blindness to difference disadvantages groups whose experience, culture, and socialized capacities differ from those of privileged groups. The strategy of assimilation aims to bring formerly excluded groups into the mainstream. So assimilation always implies coming into the game after it is already begun, after the rules and standards have already been set, and having to prove oneself according to those rules and standards. In the assimilationist strategy, the privileged groups implicitly define the standards according to which all will be measured. Because their privilege involves not recognizing these standards as culturally and experientially specific, the ideal of a common humanity in which all can participate without regard to race, gender, religion, or sexuality poses as neutral and universal. The real differences between oppressed groups and the dominant norm, however, tend to put them at a disadvantage in measuring up to these standards, and for that reason assimilationist policies perpetuate their disadvantage ... Second, the ideal of a universal humanity without social group differences allows privileged groups to ignore their own group specificity. Blindness to difference perpetuates cultural imperialism by allowing norms expressing the point of view and experience of privileged groups to appear neutral and universal. The assimilationist ideal presumes that there is a humanity in general, an unsituated group-neutral human capacity for self-making that left to itself would make individuality flower, thus guaranteeing that each individual will be different ... [B]ecause there is no such unsituated group-neutral point of view, the situation and experience of dominant groups tend to define the norms of such a humanity in general. Against such a supposedly neutral humanist ideal, only the oppressed groups come to be marked with particularity; they, and not the privileged groups, are marked, objectified as the Others.

Thus, third, this denigration of groups that deviate from an allegedly neutral standard often produces an internalized devaluation by members of those groups themselves. When there is an ideal of general human standards according to which everyone should be evaluated equally, then Puerto Ricans or Chinese Americans are ashamed of their accents or their parents, Black children despise the female-dominated kith and kin networks of their neighborboods, and feminists seek to root out their tendency to cry, or to feel compassion for a frustrated stranger. The aspiration to assimilate helps produce the self-loathing and double consciousness characteristic of oppression. The goal of assimilation holds up to people a demand that they 'fit', be like the mainstream, in behavior, values, and goals. At the same time, as long as group differences exist, group members will be marked as different – as Black, Jewish, gay – and thus as unable simply to fit. When participation is taken to imply assimilation the oppressed person is caught in an irresolvable dilemma: to participate means to accept and adopt an identity one is not, and to try to participate means to he reminded by oneself and others of the identity one is.

...

Under these circumstances, a politics that asserts the positivity of group difference is liberating and empowering. In the act of reclaiming the identity the dominant culture has taught them to despise, and affirming it as an identity to celebrate, the oppressed remove double consciousness. I am just what they say I am – a Jewboy, a colored girl, a fag, a dyke, or a hag – and proud of it. No longer does one have the impossible project of trying to become something one is not under circumstances where the very trying reminds one of who one is. This politics asserts that oppressed groups have distinct cultures, experiences, and perspectives on social life with humanly positive meaning, some of which may even be superior to the culture and perspectives of mainstream society.

...

In a political struggle where oppressed groups insist on the positive value of their specific culture and experience, it becomes increasingly difficult for dominant groups to parade their norms as neutral and universal, and to construct the values and behavior of the oppressed as deviant, perverted, or inferior. By puncturing the universalist claim to unity that expels some groups and turns them into the Other, the assertion of positive group specificity introduces the possibility of understanding the relation between groups as merely difference, instead of exclusion, opposition, or dominance.

QUESTION

By abandoning gender-neutrality, both as an ideal and as a possibility, is difference feminism in danger of fetishising characteristics that patriarchal culture has tended to associate with women?

Critical Race Theory and the Colour of Feminism

The open and pluralistic approach of what we have characterised in the previous section as difference feminism has opened up a new and important set of legal issues about the interaction between different axes of social differentiation in the constitution of legal subjects and the operations of legal power. Key among these interactions has been that between the social constitution of gender difference and that of racial or ethnic differences. While the tendency of 'feminism' to be associated with white, middle class women's issues remains a sensitive question in contemporary feminist thought, the development over the last decade of a productive exchange between feminist, anti-racist and post-colonial theory is incontrovertible.

Of these various points of intellectual exchange, perhaps the most interesting for feminist legal theory is that between feminist scholarship and a movement known in the United States as 'critical race theory'. Like feminist legal theory, critical race theory is a diverse genre, and some writers associated with it are even reluctant to adopt the label, pointing out that the plurality of racist and ethnic stereotypes, as much as the interaction between gender and ethnicity as sites of social disadvantage, render the constitution of critical interventions in terms of a unitary genre of theory unhelpful. For the purposes of our analysis, however, it will be useful to first offer a broad characterisation of critical race theory, before tracing its continuities with and influence upon feminist legal theory.

1. Critical Race Theory and the American Academy

The intellectual and political links between critical race theory and feminism, like those between feminism and critical legal studies, form an interesting but uneasy alliance. Like feminism, critical race theory finds its roots in a long history of political consciousness and activism, and in a critique of legal practice and legal theory (including white feminist legal theory) which is structurally similar to that mounted by feminism and critical legal studies against the mainstream academy. While in the United States the history of black consciousness had key legal targets in the forms of institutions such as slavery and segregation, and a key legal framework in the constitution and the Civil Rights Act which was the ultimate success of the civil rights movement of the 1950s and 1960s, in Britain, notwithstanding the enactment of race relations legislation from the 1960s on (itself, from 1976, modelled on American concepts), critical race theory has been slower to infuse the academy. Over the last thirty years, however, the cultural analyses of writers like Stuart Hall and Paul Gilroy – whose memorable claim that 'There Ain't No Black in the Union Jack' became a powerful symbol for the false race universality of British culture – have been influential. Such ideas have had a noticeable effect on the more interpretive aspects of the social sciences, history and literary studies. They have generated interest in post-colonialism and law both in Britain and in formerly colonised countries like India; while in countries such as Canada and Australia, the continuing effort to come to terms with the post-colonial state's implication in the racist and expropriating policies of its colonial predecessors has generated not only a powerful genre of identity-based legal theory but a significant wave of litigation over issues such as aboriginal land rights.

At the outset then, it is important to remember that much of the literature that falls loosely under the label 'critical race theory' has come from the United States, where the history of slavery and of the civil rights movement has inevitably shaped its political preoccupations. In contrast, the question of race within the United Kingdom has been influenced by the history of Empire, and the subsequent patterns of migration from Commonwealth countries. United States anti-discrimination legislation, too, is different from that of the United Kingdom. Nevertheless, despite clear cultural and legal differences between the United Kingdom and the United States, three central points of contact between critical race theory and feminist legal theory are of interest. First, there are a number of revealing similarities between the project of uncovering the gender of law and attempts to expose its colour. Second, black women have argued that neither feminism (with its exclusive focus on gender), nor critical race theory (with its exclusive focus on race) is able to accommodate the distinctive experience of falling into both 'minority' camps simultaneously. Third, critical race theorists have offered a thoroughgoing critique of feminism's tendency to universalise white women's experiences.

2.   Critical Race Theory and Feminist Legal Theory: Tracing the Analogies

It is not difficult to identify some important points of methodological and political contact between feminist and critical race theory in the legal sphere.

LITERARY STYLE

In the work, for example, of Patricia Williams, we find a style of elliptical argument, drawing on stories, poetic images and autobiography, which seeks to find a place for what has been repressed in institutional speech, breaking out of conceptual frameworks which have rendered some speech inaudible even when spoken; and some meanings entirely inexpressible.

EXPOSING HIDDEN VIEWPOINTS

Feminists argue that law's and legal practice's viewpoints are implicitly male: critical race theorists argue that they (and those of feminism) are implicitly white, yet invisibly so: in other words, they typically express a privileged white male's view of the world. Moreover critical race theorists argue that black people's, and especially black women's, voices continue to be marginalised in a process which resonates with the history of formal exclusion and slavery. In this sense, the critical race theorist's project could be described as the uncovering the hidden colour of law, just as the feminist's project has been to expose the hidden sex of law.

CRITIQUE OF LEGAL SUBJECTHOOD

Furthermore, just as feminists argue that the implicit subject of law is male, critical race theorists argue that the legal subject is implicitly white: black people's history and experience – their civic position, their employment and family patterns – are distorted by the version of individualism which characterises the legal subject.

CRITIQUE OF CONCEPTUAL FRAMEWORK

Critical race theory's critique of the legal subject represents one instance of a broader critique of the conceptual framework of legal practice which is structurally similar to that articulated within feminism. For example, the individualism of most anti-discrimination legislation, with its reliance on individual proof of discrimination and damage, its comparative standard which appeals implicitly to a white norm, and the consequent invisibility of group-based disadvantage has a number of drawbacks, not least in rendering affirmative action ethically suspect. Liberal-individualist anti-discrimination law implicitly adopts what has been dubbed a 'perpetrator perspective' – an individual, isolated and blameworthy act is what is made unlawful, and this constructs racism as abnormal rather than the norm in western social orders. Similarly, the structure of family or social welfare law is premised on a model of the family which fails to fit many families and which is particularly inapposite for certain ethnic groups. A key example here would be the statistical predominance of female-headed households in Afro-Caribbean communities. As a result, the diagnosis of single motherhood as a sign of deviance or disorder is particularly stigmatising to these groups. It might even be argued that single motherhood is condemned precisely because it is more common within particular racial groups.

DECONSTRUCTION OF PRETENSIONS TO OBJECTIVITY, NEUTRALITY AND AUTONOMY

Again, resonating with the feminist arguments already canvassed, critical race theorists argue that law's pretensions to objectivity and neutrality are really the privileging of a white male perspective. Law has an implicitly disciplinary function through which paradigms and norms of bodily comportment, attitude, lifestyle, employment history and family structure are coercively enforced. These paradigms, it is pointed out, have been constructed to reflect the lives of the privileged majority, and thus to stigmatize minority practices.

3.   The intersection of race and gender

A key argument which has been advanced by women exponents of critical race theory is that a combination of the monolithically sex-oriented and colour-blind stance of feminist theory and the monolithically race-oriented and sex-blind stance of critical race theory has meant that the distinctive position of black women has been obscured even within the intellectual discourses designed to reveal it. To put it crudely, it has been implicitly assumed that 'all the blacks are men and all the women are white'. In a number of articles, Kimberle Crenshaw has developed an analysis of the 'intersection of race and gender' which sets out from a powerful critique of the implications of a failure to recognise intersectionality in anti-discrimination law. She points out that legal regimes proscribing, separately, sex and race discrimination provide no protection for discrimination specifically against black women. Yet, ironically, they sometimes allow for recognition of black women's special position in a way which destroys solidarity by refusing to allow black women to represent the recognised group of either women or black people.

Crenshaw's analysis deserves careful examination. A useful starting point is her discussion of two American discrimination cases which illustrate the dynamics of intersectionality. In the first case, a group of black part time women workers hired after the passage of the Civil Rights Act 1964 (and hence of a non-discrimination norm in employment) were all dismissed in an economic recession. Their claim of indirect discrimination failed as it had to be established as *either* sex discrimination *or* race discrimination. In fact, neither claim could be made out statistically. For the group of those dismissed included a disproportionately high number of neither women nor black people relative to the total workforce The socially obvious, but legally inaudible fact was they had been disadvantaged neither as black people nor as women but specifically as black women. In the second case, a black woman sought to bring a discrimination claim as the representative of all black employees. Here, the law recognised her special position as both black and female – and used it to deny that she could occupy such a representative position. In the one case, the black woman's true social position was legally invisible; in the second, it was recognised, but used divisively as a basis for undermining her position within the ethnic group with which she belonged. Crenshaw's point – as simple in conceptual form as it is radical in institutional implications – is that until the intersection between social structures of race/ethnicity and sex/gender is legally recognised, nothing approaching equality or justice can be delivered to minority women in the legal order.

MULTICULTURALISM AND 'CULTURAL' DEFENCES IN CRIMINAL LAW

A further genre of intesectionality, in the rather different legal context of criminal law, has been identified by Leti Volpp. In the United States, criminal courts have in recent years begun to entertain excusing and justificatory arguments based on cultural difference: in other words, they have begun to entertain the idea that defendants should, at least within certain limits, be judged in terms of norms specific to her or his cultural group. For example, in judging what a reasonable person would have foreseen in certain circumstances, or how a reasonable defendant would have reacted to a certain provocation or threat, it is appropriate to contextualise the particular defendant within her or his own cultural experience, values and environment. This argument brings to the core of criminal law doctrine issues about racial (and sexual) neutrality and justice.

On the face of it, the idea of cultural defence appears consistent with a commitment to respecting cultural and sexual difference. Volpp's argument, however, pinpoints the serious political difficulties raised both generally and in particular by the intersection of multiple forms of difference and disadvantage. Her analysis takes off from two cases in which Asian Americans sought to claim cultural defence to homicide. The first concerned a man who killed his wife after she admitted to having another lover. At his trial, a cultural anthropologist was called to give evidence about Chinese codes of honour, shame and humiliation. The anthropologist extrapolated from this evidence to draw conclusions about the distinctive stress which the defendant felt when his wife admitted her other relationship, and drew on this extrapolation to question the prosecution's claim that he could have formed the mens rea for the crime. This evidence was accepted. Conversely, no argument or evidence was led in relation to the gender aspects of the case, and the dead woman's context and experience were simply obliterated. The defendant was convicted of a lesser offence than that with which he had been charged, and his jail sentence mitigated to a sentence of probation. Volpp contrasts this case with a second case concerning a Chinese-American woman who killed her nine-year-old son. The defendant had recently married a man who had been promising to marry her for several years: on returning to the United States to join him she found that he had taken another lover and that he had been mistreating their son, who had been left in his care. The defendant planned to return Macau, but before acting on the plan she killed her son and tried to kill herself. She was sentenced to a 15 year term for murder. Volpp argues that her attempt to invoke a cultural defence failed in part because of her gender: because of her relatively independent life style, and her recent trip abroad – leaving her child in his father's care – she was unable to meet the cultural stereotypes applying to Chinese women as submissive, and as good mothers.

These cases illustrate both the limits and the dangers of cultural defences: the problems posed by intersectionality; the risk of stereotypes being perpetuated rather than challenged, and the idea that only certain groups (ie not whites) have 'culture'. Cultural defences tend to fix identities within a particular group, and introduce essentialist assumptions about the group into the courtroom. As a result well-intentioned attempts to accommodate different cultural practices may in practice help to conceal coercive practices that institutionalise women's subordination. Community leaders – who will more usually be male – often articulate a partial and conservative account of their cultural traditions, giving a false impression of unity to a culture that is itself fluid and internally contested.

We might add that the cultural defence raises interesting (and intractable) questions about the notion of 'culture' and its relation to feminism: do feminists in any sense want to argue for respect for a feminine cultural identity? What, if anything, is valuable about culture? Is a man accused of rape who testifies that he genuinely believed the woman to be consenting because he was brought up to believe that women mean yes when they say no pleading a cultural defence? If so, should it prevail? Because of these sorts of difficulties, Volpp suggests that cultural defences should only be used in cases where they can be conducive to challenging stereotypes and dismantling oppression – a 'strategic essentialism' which tries to resolve the conundrum of 'difference politics'. Differences may be real though constructed; and justice may require us both to struggle to dismantle them yet to recognise their power. Can we do the latter without confirming them?

The question of multicultural accommodation and its relation to feminism is not confined to the criminal law. More generally, in fields as diverse as marriage and education, there will often be some tension between the feminist commitment to equality and the accommodation of minority religious or cultural groups. Because, as Susan Moller Okin has pointed out 'virtually all cultures are to some degree patriarchal' (Okin 2002, 209), respect for minority cultural practices may involve turning a blind eye to patterns of behaviour that systematically disadvantage women, such as early marriage, continual childbearing and restrictions on women's access to education. Okin therefore concludes that the state 'should not only not give special rights or exemptions to cultural groups that discriminate against or oppress women. It should also enforce individual rights against such groups when the opportunity arises and encourage all groups within its borders to cease such practices'. Not to do so, according to Okin, 'is to let toleration for diversity run amok'. (Okin 2002, 229–30)

4. Critical Race Theorists' Critique of Feminism

THE (INVISIBLE) COLOUR OF FEMINIST LEGAL THEORY

We hope to have said enough to illustrate both continuities between feminist and critical race analysis and the importance of focussing on the interaction of race and gender in the constitution of social institutions. But we have not yet addressed critical race theory's analysis of the limits of the feminist perspective. Structurally, this analysis echoes feminist arguments about mainstream legal theory, and brings with it the distinctive substantive agenda of critical race theory. As Angela Harris has put it, critical race theory accuses feminism of a certain essentialism about women. Feminist legal theory has, in short, been blind to the differences that exist between women. Let us flesh out this claim by considering some examples of feminism's tendency to ignore the distinctive perspectives of women of colour.

THE PUBLIC-PRIVATE DIVIDE AND IMAGES OF FEMININITY

Critical race theorists have pointed out that the public-private critique takes off from an analysis of the lives of white women: on both class and race bases it is wildly inaccurate, since poor black women have long worked outside the home in countries like Britain and the United States, often in the homes of white families. Moreover, the feminist image of women as passive or vulnerable is specific to white Europeans, and is inappropriate within certain cultural groups – for example to African Americans, who generally see women as strong and powerful. In short, critical race theory reveals a diversity of femininities in the course of its analysis of the whiteness of feminism. This, it is argued, gives positive resources for critique and utopian social reimagination.

RAPE

Critical race theorists have argued that the white feminist emphasis on rape as a key political issue has been insensitive to the role of rape in American racism, and to different constructions of sexuality in black American culture. The historical connection between rape accusations and lynching, and the role of false accusations of black men within the disciplinary apparatus of slavery means that rape is still, to put it mildly, a complex issue in the African-American community. In this context, the style of the white-dominated anti-rape 'Reclaim the Night' marches of the 1970s women's movement, with their candlelit processions which evoked the style of the Ku Klux Klan, were thought to be at best, insensitive, and at worst, racist. Conversely, the 'unrapeability' of black women – the way in which their status as property, and stereotypes about their voracious sexuality (reflected in the pornographic image of women as close to nature, and of black women as particularly so, to the extent of being animalised and dehumanised) rendered their lack of consent irrelevant or inaudible – gives rape a particular meaning to black feminists. Note, for example, the comments of a Florida court in 1918:

Dallas v State 79 So 690 (Fla 1918) at 691:

What has been said by some of our courts about an unchaste female in our country being a comparatively rare exception is no doubt true where the population is composed largely of the Caucasian race, but we would be blind ourselves to actual conditions if we adopted this rule where another race that is largely unmoral constitutes an appreciable part of the population.

5. The Distinctive Project of Critical Race Theory

ANTI-ESSENTIALISM

At root, therefore, critical race theory diagnoses essentialism within feminism; a priority for sex difference which represses diversity. By contrast, critical race theory is radically anti-essentialist and tends to both recognise and, positively, to use diversity as a resource for affirmation and reconstruction.

MULTIPLE SUBJECTIVITIES

Its engagement with the intersection of race and gender places black feminist critical race theory in a unique position to appreciate both the fragmentation of personal identities and the conflicting political alliances characteristically foregrounded in postmodernist thought. It also issues an invitation to a certain (in our view welcome) pragmatism and eclecticism in theory-construction. But black feminist thought has been much more cautious than has white feminism about giving up conceptions of agency and subjectivity (as well as legal rights). Its tone tends to be more optimistic, and it asserts that recognising the ways in which our identities are fragmented, and in which we move across different subjectivities, helps to avoid becoming trapped in the identities which, for political reasons, we have put on the agenda. In particular – as in the work of Ratna Kapur – critical race and postcolonial theory has been concerned to avoid constructing a passive, victimized image of the subject – an image which has often been seen as an unfortunate implication of radical feminism in relation to women.

RECONSTRUCTION AND THE ROLE OF BLACK WOMEN'S SUPPRESSED CULTURES AS AN IMAGINATIVE RESOURCE

This distinctive optimism and utopianism are widely reflected in black feminist thought. For example, in the work of Patricia Hill Collins, different models of dialogue and discussion in black culture are explored as a basis for political and institutional reconstruction. Collins' examples include the call and response mode in black churches; and polyrhythms and multiple harmonies in black music. Both of these cultural manifestations are argued to represent a politically welcome commitment to dialogue and deliberation rather than to the hierarchical assertion of unique meaning; a preference for debate and compromise rather than for the adversarial and competitive methods of constructing meaning, truth and right characteristic of law. In this kind of work, black culture is used not as a blueprint or as a source of valued identity but rather – in a style reminiscent of the more open-ended interpretations of Gilligan's 'ethic of care' – as an imaginative resource for social reconstruction.

Crenshaw (1989, 145, 154, 156–60)

Discrimination against a white female is ... the standard sex discrimination claim; claims that diverge from this standard appear to present some sort of hybrid claim. More significantly, because Black females' claims are seen as hybrid, they sometimes cannot represent those who may have 'pure' claims of sex discrimination. The effect of this approach is that even though a challenged policy or practice may clearly discriminate against all females, the fact that it has particularly harsh consequences for Black females places Black female plaintiffs at odds with white females.

The value of feminist theory to Black women is diminished because it evolves from a white racial context that is seldom acknowledged. Not only are women of color in fact overlooked, but their exclusion is reinforced when white women speak for and as women. The authoritative universal voice – usually white male subjectivity masquerading as non-racial, non-gendered objectivity – is merely transferred to those who, but for gender, share many of the same cultural, economic and social characteristics. When feminist theory attempts to describe women's experiences through analyzing patriarchy, sexuality, or separate spheres ideology, it often overlooks the role of race. Feminists thus ignore how their own race functions to mitigate some aspects of sexism and, moreover, how it often privileges them over and contributes to the domination of other women. Consequently, feminist theory remains *white,* and its potential to broaden and deepen its analysis by addressing non-privileged women remains unrealized.

Because ideological and descriptive definitions of patriarchy are usually premised upon white female experiences, feminists and others informed by feminist literature may make the mistake of assuming that since the role of Black women in the family and in other Black institutions does not always resemble the familiar manifestations of patriarchy in the white community, Black women are somehow exempt from patriarchal norms. For example, Black women have traditionally worked outside the home in numbers far exceeding the labor participation rate of white women. An analysis of patriarchy that highlights the history of white women's exclusion from the workplace might permit the inference that Black women have not been burdened by this particular gender-based expectation. Yet the very fact that Black women must work conflicts with norms that women should not, often creating personal, emotional and relationship problems in Black women's lives. Thus, Black women are burdened not only because they often have to take on responsibilities that are not traditionally feminine but, moreover, their assumption of these roles is sometimes interpreted within the Black community as either Black women's failure to live up to such norms or as another manifestation of racism's scourge upon the Black community. This is one of the many aspects of intersectionality that cannot be understood through an analysis of patriarchy rooted in white experience.

Another example of how theory emanating from a white context obscures the multidimensionality of Black women's lives is found in feminist discourse on rape. A central political issue on the feminist agenda has been the pervasive problem of rape. Part of the intellectual and political effort to mobilize around this issue has involved the development of a historical critique of the role that law has played in establishing the bounds of normative sexuality and in regulating female sexual behavior. Early carnal knowledge statutes and rape laws are understood within this discourse to illustrate that the objective of rape statutes traditionally has not been to protect women from coercive intimacy but to protect and maintain a property-like interest in female chastity. Although feminists quite rightly criticize these objectives, to characterize rape law as reflecting male control over female sexuality is for Black women an oversimplified account and an ultimately inadequate account.

Rape statutes generally do not reflect *male* control over *female* sexuality, but *white* male regulation of white female sexuality. Historically, there has been absolutely no institutional effort to regulate Black female chastity. Courts in some states had gone so far as to instruct juries that, unlike white women, Black women were not presumed to be chaste. Also, while it was true that the attempt to regulate the sexuality of white women placed unchaste women outside the law's protection, racism restored a fallen white woman's chastity where the alleged assailant was a Black man. No such restoration was available to Black women.

The singular focus on rape as a manifestation of male power over female sexuality tends to eclipse the use of rape as a weapon of racial terror. When Black women were raped by white males, they were being raped not as women generally, but as Black women specifically: Their femaleness made them sexually vulnerable to racist domination, while their Blackness effectively denied them any protection. This white male power was reinforced by a judicial system in which the successful conviction of a white man for raping a Black woman was virtually unthinkable.

In sum, sexist expectations of chastity and racist assumptions of sexual promiscuity combined to create a distinct set of issues confronting Black women. These issues have seldom been explored in feminist literature nor are they prominent in antiracist politics. The lynching of Black males, the institutional practice that was legitimized by the regulation of white women's sexuality, has historically and contemporaneously occupied the Black agenda on sexuality and violence. Consequently, Black women are caught between a Black community that, perhaps understandably, views with suspicion attempts to litigate questions of sexual violence, and a feminist community that reinforces those suspicions by focusing on white female sexuality. The suspicion is compounded by the historical fact that the protection of white female sexuality was often the pretext for terrorizing the Black community. Even today some fear that antirape agendas may undermine antiracist objectives. This is the paradigmatic political and theoretical dilemma created by the intersection of race and gender: Black women are caught between ideological and political currents that combine first to create and then to bury Black women's experiences.

Collins (1991, 77–8)

The image of the welfare mother provides ideological justifications for interlocking systems of race, gender, and class oppression. African-Americans can be racially stereotyped as being lazy by blaming Black welfare mothers for failing to pass on the work ethic. Moreover, the welfare mother has no male authority figure to assist her. Typically portrayed as an unwed mother, she violates one cardinal tenet of Eurocentric masculinist thought: she is a woman alone. As a result, her treatment reinforces the dominant gender ideology positing that a woman's true worth and financial security should occur through heterosexual marriage. Finally, in the post-World War II political economy, one of every three African-American families is officially classified as poor. With such high levels of Black poverty, welfare state policies supporting poor Black mothers and their children have become increasingly expensive. Creating the controlling image of the welfare mother and stigmatizing her as the cause of her own poverty and that of African-American communities shifts the angle of vision away from structural sources of poverty and blames the victims themselves. The image of the welfare mother thus provides ideological justification for the dominant group's interest in limiting the fertility of Black mothers who are seen as producing too many economically unproductive children.

[Another] controlling image – the Jezebel, whore, or sexually aggressive woman – is central in this nexus of elite white male images of Black womanhood because efforts to control Black women's sexuality lie at the heart of Black women's oppression. The image of Jezebel originated under slavery when Black women were portrayed as being, to use Jewelle Gomez's words, 'sexually aggressive, wet nurses'. Jezebel's function was to relegate all Black women to the category of sexually aggressive women, thus providing a powerful rationale for the widespread sexual assaults by white men typically reported by Black slave women. Yet Jezebel served another function. If Black slave women could be portrayed as having excessive sexual appetites, then increased fertility should be the expected outcome. By suppressing the nurturing that African-American women might give their own children which would strengthen Black family networks, and by forcing Black women to work in the field or 'wet nurse' white children, slaveowners effectively tied the controlling images of Jezebel and Mammy to the economic exploitation inherent in the institution of slavery.

[This] image of the sexually denigrated Black woman is the foundation underlying elite white male conceptualizations of the mammy, matriarch, and welfare mother. Connecting all three is the common theme of Black women's sexuality. Each image transmits clear messages about the proper links among female sexuality, fertility, and Black women's roles in the political economy. For example, the mammy, the only somewhat positive figure, is a desexed individual. The mammy is typically portrayed as overweight, dark, and with characteristically African features – in brief, as an unsuitable sexual partner for white men. She is asexual and therefore is free to become a surrogate mother to the children she acquired not through her own sexuality. The mammy represents the clearest example of the split between sexuality and motherhood present in Eurocentric masculinist thought. In contrast, both the matriarch and the welfare mother are sexual beings. But their sexuality is linked to their fertility, and this link forms one fundamental reason they are negative images. The matriarch represents the sexually aggressive woman, one who emasculates Black men because she will not permit them to assume roles as Black patriarchs. She refuses to be passive and thus is stigmatized. Similarly, the welfare mother represents a woman of low morals and uncontrolled sexuality, factors identified as the cause of her impoverished state. In both cases Black female control over sexuality and fertility is conceptualized as antithetical to elite white male interests.

Taken together, these ... prevailing interpretations of Black womanhood form a nexus of elite white male interpretations of Black female sexuality and fertility. Moreover, by meshing smoothly with systems of race, class, and gender oppression, they provide effective ideological justifications for racial oppression, the politics of gender subordination, and the economic exploitation inherent in capitalist economies.

Kapur (1999, 357–8)

Stories about sex have been tethered to an essentialist understanding of culture ... Sexuality and culture have been sutured together as a result of the 19th century colonial encounter and nationalist resistance ... Women and the private sphere of family and home were recast as a space of pure Indian culture uncontaminated by the colonial encounter. Issues such as *Sati* [the immolation of widows on the funeral pyres of their husbands], widow remarriage, or the age of consent to marriage were cast as cultural issues beyond any legitimate political intervention by the colonial state.

...

This 19th century suturing of sexuality and culture continues to haunt us today. The assertion of sexuality as a pure space of Indian culture is resurfacing in the contemporary moment as sexuality again is becoming a site of intense political contestation. And the idea of 'culture', of 'Indian cultural values', is being invoked by all sides in the legal domain to legitimate or de-legitimate sexual speech, sexual conduct and sexual identity ... Cultural nationalists are asserting that western cultural contaminants are metastasizing throughout Indian homes via satellite broadcasting. Programmes such as *Baywatch*, *The Bold and the Beautiful* and the MTV music channel, are being condemned for denigrating women and displacing them from the position of respect and honour they enjoyed in some long lost, ancient Hindu past. In addition, the increasing visibility of sexual subalterns such as sex workers, gays and lesbians, is alleged to be threatening to destroy the fantasy of the Indian joint family and the ancient cultural values and traditions that have cemented it together.

The language of Indian cultural values is deployed in two different ways in the sexuality debates. It is deployed by those in positions of power and dominance to legitimate dominant sexual norms in and through a stagnant, fetishised and exclusive understanding of culture. It is being used to weave a cultural tale based on a notion of oneness, of one culture that is fixed and timeless. The longing for a strong cultural identity has been an important desire and symptom of postcolonialism in the contemporary Indian context. In the hands of dominant conservative groups, it is based on the idea of a substantive or real essentialism, and becomes reactionary. It becomes an exclusionary discourse – a tale shaped in the image of intolerance and disapproval of difference. In India, the reactionary potential of substantive or real cultural essentialism can be found in the Hindu Right's efforts to construct a history of Indian culture based on the idea of one god, Ram, one temple, in Ayodhya, and one people, the Hindus.

Indian cultural values are also being used by disempowered and marginalised groups to counter the idea of the 'authentic subject' that informs dominant cultural essentialism and problematise the opposition between the 'western' and 'Indian' subject. They are challenging the search for a real originary culture as a narrow essentialist telling of the story of Indian culture in relation to sexuality. And they are promoting the idea that culture is never stagnant and fixed but is constantly shifting and fluid – that it is hybrid … Cultural hybridity represents the postcolonial moment, which Stuart Hall describes as the point of recognition that a return to a set of uncontaminated values is impossible. Revealing that culture, that Indian cultural values, is and continues to be in a process of construction, creates space for the possibility of alternative sexual practices and behaviour, that both challenge and subvert dominant sexual norms.

There is, however, still the concern that in engaging with Indian cultural values, cultural hybridity runs the risk of also essentialising Indian cultural values. There is a need to ensure that the cultural move, which is used to challenge master narratives about Indian cultural values, does not in turn become its own unifying, essentialist and exclusionary discourse.

Harris (1999, 313–6)

As a literature, critical race theory is flourishing … Yet critical race theory as a community seems ready to fall apart at the seams … First, I think that the fact that critical race theorists have largely failed to pay consistent conscious attention to our community building reflects in part a failure to pay attention to the lessons of feminism. In intellectual circles, community building is an area that consciously or unconsciously gets treated as 'women's work': it is considered not to be an area of intellectual or strategic interest; it is approached in an ad hoc way; it is considered 'touchy feely' and less important than the extremely important business of telling people about our ideas; and it is often left to women to do, along with related interpersonal caretaking activities. Feminism is [in] part the project of taking women, and the work that they are relegated to do, seriously. Moreover, one of the slogans of the second wave of the women's movement in the United States was 'the personal is political'. One of the many meanings of this slogan is the notion that justice must be sought in both the public and private spheres. A commitment to feminism, then, properly understood, requires serious attention to the issues we would otherwise treat as trivial, private or 'touchy feely'.

My second point should be a familiar one: if identity politics is to be anything more than another means of dominating people, identity claims must be scrutinized for their connection with social relations of injustice. I have argued before that failure to pay critical attention to issues of group constitution provides room for traditional status hierarchies to enter unannounced. Within critical race theory, the failure to pay adequate attention to, or to take charge of, how our community was growing and maintaining itself meant that a 'race-first' principle of racial solidarity took over a group that at least on paper was committed to recognising the 'intersectionality' or 'multidimensionality' of oppression. The 'race-first' principle, in turn, slid into a patriarchal conception of family. The result, not surprisingly, was a failure to adequately critique the group's internalized homophobia.

The third and last point I want to make is more grandiose, though I touch upon it only lightly … Critical race theory's troubles are a miniature version of the practical problem facing identity politicians all around the world: how to organise around the notion of a shared identity and yet fully acknowledge and include the multiple identity claims of group members, at the risk of (or perhaps with the purpose of) de-centering or obliterating the very sense of collectivity that brought the group together in the first place. Terry Eagleton describes this as the problem of the 'double optic'. Judith Butler describes it as the 'necessary error' of identity. It is not at all clear that such a self-transcendent community can exist; but to paraphrase an old civil rights saying: if not us, who? If not now, when?

(See also extract from Williams 1991 above.)

QUESTIONS

1. Why does discrimination law's separate treatment of race and sex discrimination disadvantage black women?

2. Does the idea of the 'cultural defence' allow sensitivity to cultural difference to take priority over the rights or needs of women?

3. Is feminism white? What is meant by this claim?

The Future of Feminist Legal Theory

At the beginning of the twenty first century, the future of feminist legal theory seems uncertain. It would be hard to overstate the impact of the 'essentialism' critique upon feminist jurisprudence during the 1990s. While postmodern scepticism about appeals to universality may initially have appeared to offer a healthy corrective to some of the unreflective 'grand theorising' of the 1970s and 1980s, the fear of 'essentialising' women's lives has led to a political reticence which many feminists now find troubling. Perhaps in part as a backlash to this rather introspective anxiety about the legitimacy of speaking for women as a group, some feminist lawyers are advocating a return to normative political engagement. For a number of feminists, this has meant renewed interest in rights, particularly within the international context, where sexual exploitation and other violations of women's most basic human rights often continue to be invisible. In the world's poorest and most populous countries, illiteracy rates for women are still significantly higher than for men (often by as much as 200%). But of course, these campaigns for women's equal access to the rights possessed by the individual subject of law have a great deal in common with the agenda pursued by liberal feminists. We seem, therefore, to be witnessing a revaluation of liberalism within feminist legal theory. Yet, despite the understandable frustration that many feminist lawyers feel with the normative stasis that has appeared to follow from postmodernism's rejection of 'grand theory', it is far from clear that the solution is simply to embrace liberalism.

Barron (2000, 276, 278–9)

A number of undesirable consequences have, in my view, flowed from the ascendancy of this postmodernist negativity in feminist thinking. Its most obvious manifestation is a palpable reluctance on the part of feminists now to formulate political programmes or proposals for legal reform that purport to articulate the interests and needs of women in general for fear of 'essentialising' the feminine in the process of doing so. Clearly, there are good reasons for building the feminist movement on as broad a base as possible, and for eschewing a narrow or exclusionary characterization of the 'Woman' at its centre that would privilege the needs and aspirations of white, bourgeois, heterosexual, 'able-bodied' women at the expense of others. But these ethical and strategic concerns could not account for the utter paralysis of political reflection that the spectre of essentialism appears to have induced in many feminist theorists at the present time, and it seems to me, rather, that this new quietism is in large part attributable to the theoretical frameworks that postmodernism's hegemony within the academy has driven feminists to adopt.

...

The modes of political struggle that emerge into view under this postmodernist-feminist gaze appear, moreover, frustratingly tiny and inconsequential to the eye of one interested in large-scale social and political change ... No mass movement of women can be envisaged from this perspective for that would invoke the dreaded essence it has become so fashionable to denounce. Even more obviously, no programme of sustained feminist engagement with the institutions of state is conceivable from this point of view. To advance political demands would necessarily require a relatively stable conception of the woman in whose name those demands were being made.

...

[F]or feminist legal theory, this loss of focus is particularly problematic ... [Law's] legitimacy resides in the conformity of its prescriptions to a conception of justice which is necessarily – given that law prescribes for all of us – universalistic. To register in law at all ..., a claim must be both determinate enough to be clothed in the form of a right that can be enforced and observed, and amenable to universalisation by reference to some conception of justice.

Nussbaum (1999, 9–11)

The Liberal tradition in political philosophy has frequently been thought to be inadequate for the goals of feminism. One central purpose of [this book] is to answer that charge, defending a form of liberalism ... that can answer the feminist charges that are legitimate and show why other charges are not legitimate. The version of liberalism here begins from the idea of the equal worth of human beings as such, in virtue of their basic human capacities for choice and reasoning. All, in virtue of those human capacities, are worthy of equal concern and respect. Thus, the view is at its core antifeudal, opposed to the political ascendancy of hierarchies of rank, caste and birth. The crucial addition liberal feminism makes to the tradition is to add sex to that list of morally irrelevant characteristics. It should have been there all along, for no liberal thinker ever presented a cogent argument to justify the subordination of women to men while opposing feudalism and monarchy. Subordination by sex was simply seen as natural, and the entire topic was basically ignored in theories of political justice. This was a profound inconsistency in the liberal tradition, as JS Mill powerfully showed already in 1869, but we have had to wait until the present decade for serious and sustained work on the justice of family arrangements that is beginning to make the promise of liberalism real for the world's women.

The basic argument I make, then, is that the liberal tradition of equal concern and respect should, and in all consistency must, be extended to women and to the relations between women and men in the family. In the process, we should not be quick to dismiss the often-criticized individualism of the liberal tradition. I argue that liberal individualism does not entail egoism or a preference for the type of person who has no deep need of others. Many liberal thinkers have made compassion, care, and love an essential part of their normative program. What does distinguish liberalism from other political traditions is its insistence on the separateness of one life from another, and the equal importance of each life, seen on its own terms rather than as part of a larger organic or corporate whole. Each human being should be regarded as an end rather than as a means to the ends of others. The liberal insists that the goal of politics should be the amelioration of lives taken one by one and seen as separate ends, rather than the amelioration of the organic whole or the totality. I argue that this is a very good position for women to embrace, seeing that women have all too often been regarded not as ends but as means to the ends of others, not as sources of agency and worth in their own right but as reproducers and caregivers.

The form of liberalism endorsed here is fully compatible with ascribing great importance to care and love. But it suggests a way in which the commitment to care should be qualified. Emotions of love and care, like other emotions, have in part a social origin, but this means that they are only as reliable as the social norms that give rise to them. The common propensity of women to subordinate themselves to others and to sacrifice their well-being for that of a larger unit may in many cases be taken for granted. Such dispositions have been formed, often, in unjust conditions and may simply reflect the low worth society itself has placed on women's wellbeing. My view urges that all such emotions be valued with the constraints of a life organized by critical reasoning. The same, I argue, is true of sexual desire and emotion: insofar as these are shaped by unjust social conditions, they should not be relied on as unproblematic guides to a flourishing life. The norm, here as elsewhere, should be the idea of being treated as an end rather than a means, a person rather than an object.

Liberalism concerns itself with freedom and with spheres of choice. As I conceive it, this does not mean maximising the sheer numbers of choices people get to make for themselves. The idea of liberty should be understood in close conjunction with the idea of equal worth and respect: the choices that liberal politics should protect are those that are deemed of central importance to the development and expression of personhood. In this sense, liberalism has to take a stand about what is good for people, and I argue that it needs a somewhat more extensive conception of the basic human functions and capacities than many liberal thinkers have used if it is to provide sufficient remedies for entrenched injustice and hierarchy. But the goal should always be to put people into a position of agency and choice, not to push them into functioning in ways deemed desirable. I argue that this is no mere parochial Western ideology but the expression of a sense of agency that has deep roots all over the world; it expresses the joy most people have in using their own bodies and minds.

Jackson (2001, 3–8)

The problem with the conventional feminist critique of autonomy is that it sets up a binary opposition between interdependence and autonomy, as if the two were inevitably mutually exclusive. Thus it assumes we can only give priority to the autonomous choosing self if we completely disregard the web of connections that have moulded her identity, and conversely, that the project of respecting an individual's choices necessarily disintegrates if we acknowledge human beings' social embeddedness. Yet is this perceived tension between autonomy and interdependence simply the ways things are? Do alienation and self-determination always come as an indissoluble package?

That an association has commonly been drawn between self-sufficiency and self-determination does not, in itself, establish their inseparability ... Certainly many mainstream liberal philosophers acknowledge that it is impossible to think about ourselves without acknowledging the web of obligations that we acquire by virtue of our multiple connections with others. Bernard Williams, for example, has argued that commitments, duties and relationships are precisely what give our lives meaning and character ... In fact few liberals believe that the capacity for autonomous choice is an innate attribute of humanness, rather most would argue that it emerges from the set of cultural traditions within which individuals learn to interact with each other, and to develop their sense of self.

Within conventional liberal accounts of the self, it is not simply the existence of freedom of choice that matters, rather their habitual concern has been with the conditions and resources that may be necessary precursors of the capacity for autonomy. It is therefore axiomatic that without socialisation within a strong network of relationships, an individual's right to self-determination would be both meaningless and irrelevant.

Possessing freedom of choice does not, without more, guarantee that an individual's life will be enriched by choosing between the options that are available to them. The space within which autonomy may be exercised will always perhaps be comparatively small, but I would argue that possessing *some* control over the direction of one's life is a necessary constituent part of a 'good' or agreeable existence. A commitment to autonomy may therefore emerge precisely from the recognition that many people's capacity to lead a self-authored life is profoundly limited.

Liberal theory does not necessarily presuppose that every individual *already has* the freedom to choose between a set of genuine and valuable alternatives, rather this may be a principal *goal* of theories of redistributive justice. In order to treat individuals with dignity and respect, we should therefore give them both the freedom to exercise meaningful choice, *and a set of realistic and valuable opportunities* from which to choose. Here Joseph Raz's formulation of autonomy is useful:

> To be autonomous a person must not only be given a choice but he must also be given an adequate range of choices

Thus, my point is not to argue that our choices exist and can be satisfied in a social vacuum, instead I suggest that a community should be concerned to foster an environment in which the exercise of choice is both possible *and valuable.*

In order to establish its target's excessive and objectionable individualism, the conventional feminist critique of autonomy may therefore be relying upon a distorted and exaggerated version of the liberal conception of the self. The liberal tradition is a broad and varied one, and while there may be some liberals who believe that the self is intrinsically insular, there are others for whom a commitment to autonomy is synonymous with a rich and nuanced account of our inevitable interdependence.

In recent years there has been revived feminist interest in reworking the concept of autonomy so that the part relationships and community play in its realisation are properly acknowledged. This feminist analysis has rejected the 'pathological conception of autonomy as boundaries against others', in order to understand that relationships and interdependence may be necessary preconditions for the productive exercise of meaningful choice ... Thus our preoccupation should not be with the essentially uncontentious insight that we are not self-sufficient, atomistic individuals relentlessly pursuing our own purely self-interested ends, but rather we should be thinking about what sort of laws, institutions and services might allow us to maximise our capacity to exercise control over our lives given the network of social constraints that will always tend to limit our options.

A crucial initial step might be the recognition that autonomy is not something that an individual either has or does not have. It is not a static or innate quality, rather a person's capacity to make meaningful choices about their lives may fluctuate according to a complex matrix of social, economic and psychological factors. Autonomy is, as Jennifer Nedelsky has explained

> ... a capacity that requires ongoing relationships that help it flourish; it can wither or thrive throughout one's adult life.

Autonomy, then, is not just the right to pursue ends that one already has, but also to live in an environment which enables one to form one's own value system and to have it treated with respect.

Acknowledging that our preferences do not spring unbidden from the inner depths of our self-constituting minds need not lead to the refusal to respect those preferences on the grounds that they are inevitably socially constructed. It is true that none of us chooses some of the crucial determinants of our values and beliefs, such as our parents, nationality, education, religion etc ... But the fact that we cannot choose *who we are* does not necessarily mean that we should not be allowed to choose *what we do.* Our choices are, of course, shaped by multiple external influences, but they are the only choices we have, and they are therefore of critical importance to our sense of self. Even if we recognise that social forces may shape and constrain our choices, our sense of being the author of our own actions is profoundly valuable to us. We cannot believe that all of our preferences are irredeemably 'not ours' without our sense of self effectively collapsing.

Human beings are not self-constituting subjects, with a set of pre-social desires, but neither do they entirely lack the capacity for agency and self-direction, otherwise it would be impossible to account for the different choices made by similarly situated people. We may be able to explain many of our beliefs with reference to our circumstances, but our socially constructed value system does not effectively predetermine *all* of the decisions that we take about the course of our lives. Replacing the caricatured version of the autonomous self's endless capacity for unmediated, self-interested decision making with a theoretical paradigm that leaves no room for an individual to make unexpected or unorthodox choices is, I argue, equally unsatisfactory. Equivalent respect for both surprising and predictable decisions is one of the most important features of a commitment to autonomy.

...

Moreover, proper respect for autonomy cannot be limited to removing external constraints from an individual's capacity to follow preferences that are *already* fully formed and clearly articulated. Instead there may be times when the positive provision of resources and services may be necessary in order to assist people both to work out their own priorities and to realise them.

QUESTIONS

1.   What future is there for feminist legal theory?

2.   Why is feminist legal theory returning to the values and principles of liberalism? What might be lost in such a move?

Further Reading

For a more detailed account of the themes that we have considered in this chapter, we would recommend Lacey 1998, especially the Introduction and Ch 7 and Smart 1989, Chs 1, 7 and 8.

MacKinnon 1983 is an uncompromising account of radical feminism, it is a ground-breaking piece of work, and is worth reading in its entirety. It is reproduced in full in Olsen, 1995. MacKinnon 1989, Ch 13 provides a useful summary of MacKinnon's feminist jurisprudence.

Drucilla Cornell's argument for *equivalent* rather than equal rights is a good example of what we have called 'difference feminism'. See, in particular, Cornell 1995, Ch 1.

Naffine 2002 offers a clear and compelling analysis of the current state of feminist legal theory.

Questions

1.   'Feminists who wish to introduce legal reforms must understand the implications of different feminist theories of law. Liberal feminist theory requires law to live up

to its own rhetoric of equality and rights. Other forms of feminism see not just laws, but law itself, as a major part of the problem.' Discuss.

2.   'No feminist theory of law can entirely acquit itself of the charge of essentialism.' Discuss.

3.   'The ideal of gender-neutrality in law should be replaced by a commitment to the accommodation of difference.' Discuss.

4.   To what extent does law deny the reality of 'woman'?

17 Economic Analysis of Law

Richard Nobles

Economic analysis of law does not address the question of what it means to claim that a legal system exists, or why a particular law is valid. As such, it is not a theory of law, like those of Natural Law, Legal Positivism or Realism. It is, instead, a theory about law, a theory that purports to allow laws to be assessed and evaluated. Your understanding of Natural Law theories should have awakened you to the difficulties of establishing an objective basis for talking about justice. And examining theories about distributive justice in Chapter 15 will have enhanced your understanding of these problems. These difficulties should alert you to the attractions of a theory that appears to offer its adherents an objective basis from which to criticise and evaluate the usual objects of legal study: legislation, adjudication and doctrine.

The Law and Economics movement

The use of economics to criticise laws is as old as the discipline of economics, if not older. Adam Smith, commonly regarded as the 'father' of modern economics, criticised laws that impeded trade in his book *The Wealth of Nations*. Karl Marx, in *Capital* (Ch 10, 'The working day'), offered a critique of factory legislation, particularly laws relating to the length of the working day, in terms of his theories of the nature of capitalist production. But the beginning of sustained application of economic theory to legal topics dates from the 1960s, and occurred in the United States of America, where today it is probably the dominant form of legal critique. Prior to this period, the use of economics within United States law schools was limited to subjects like anti-trust (anti-monopoly) law (see Veljanovski 1982, Chs 1 and 2). Legislation aimed at controlling monopolies could obviously be better understood using economics, since the definition of monopolies, and the rationale for their regulation, both come from economic theory. The use of economics to study such avowedly 'economic' laws, contrasts with the use of economic theory in law schools today, where it is used not only to study commercial subjects, which are closely linked to the operation of markets, but even such *apparently* non-market activities as family law, criminal law, tort and constitutional law. Indeed part of the attraction of economic theory to its proponents, and a major source of concern to its critics, is the belief that such activities as marriage, rape, accidents and voting can be usefully conceptualised as markets.

The beginnings of law and economics as a movement can conveniently be traced to the writings of Ronald Coase, a Nobel Prize winning economist who in 1960 wrote a seminal work on the interaction of the market and the distribution of legal rights (Coase 1960). This work provides a model for the analysis of legal rights, often referred to as 'Coase's theorem', which forms the basis for much scholarship in this area (described below and in the extract from Polinsky). The particular problem that he addressed was known to economists as the problem of social cost, the idea that an activity can generate costs on other persons which are not charged to those carrying out that activity (externalities). The failure to charge (internalise) these costs may lead to that activity being carried out to a greater extent than otherwise, which may be a source of inefficiency. Coase's first insight was to challenge the idea that any one activity generates such external costs and imposes them on others. Rather, such costs are a consequence of competition between activities for scarce resources. So, instead of saying that a smoking factory chimney damages the washing of neighbouring residents, one has to see the competing demand for the supply of clean air between two activities: smoke (as part of manufacturing) and clean washing. The economic approach to this question is not to ask which party is at fault (answered by reference to such matters as who is the more active party, or who came to the area first), but to establish the appropriate trade off between the two activities. What level of respectively smoke, and clean washing, represents the most efficient use of the resource, clean air? Coase's second insight was to provide a model which could be used to analyse the manner in which legal rights and markets might interact to answer this question (see below).

The combination of these two insights offers a potentially unrestricted scope for the application of economics to law. Every legal right can be examined from the perspective of its contribution to the efficient co-ordination of activities that compete for the same resources. Even basic rights to autonomy can be analysed in this way. A rapist can be seen as a person who has a different use for your body than you have, and the law of rape can be analysed to see whether the use of bodies, as between rapers and rapees, is efficient. (This is not to say that it is appropriate to analyse rape in this way). Coase's theorem is not essential for the economic analysis of law. In 1957 Gary Becker used economics to analyse anti-discrimination laws (Becker 1957), and in 1961 Calabresi wrote an article (Calabresi 1961, later a book, 1970) on the role of the law of tort as a tool for establishing the optimum level of accidents. But Coase's theorem provided an approach and methodology that allowed every type of legal right to be analysed for its contribution to efficiency. In 1970, Richard Posner gave the movement a huge impetus by publishing *Economic Analysis of Law*, a student text which applied economics in a manner comprehensible to law students. This book, which eschewed the impenetrable mathematical formulae often found in this genre, combined a predictive use of the theory (as a guide to what people will do in response to legal rules), a normative use (arguing for rules and policies which facilitated trading or directly maximised social wealth) and a descriptive theory of the common law (a claim that most common law rules are, in fact, efficient). The book, and his articles on the subject, provoked a debate on the nature of economic analysis, with many writers anxious to expose the assumptions that underlie economic theory, and its limitations as a tool for legal analysis. Posner, now a judge, has continued to write on law and economics, both at the level of particular legal topics, and as a general methodology, and his writings have continued to generate debate. His role as an advocate for the application of economics to the study of law should not lead one to the conclusion that all proponents of the application of economics to legal questions share his commitment to the value of this approach. While he acts as a useful source of writings for those who wish to debate with the law and economics movement, many of those who apply economics to law are both aware of its limitations as a form of analysis, and anxious to distance themselves from Posner's more extreme claims (see, for example Polinsky 1974 and 1982).

In the space of forty years the study of law from an economic perspective has grown to the point where it has been said that 'no approach to law has been more influential in recent decades than economic analysis of law ...' (Bix 1999, 177). Indeed, there is a sense in which economics has replaced justice as the dominant basis for the critique of law, offering a common methodology and set of terms which justice, at this point in the beginning of the twenty first century, so self-consciously lacks. Quantifying the success of a particular approach to legal and political scholarship has its own problems (how does one measure such things?). But the real point is to stress that this approach, in the United States, has an importance far beyond that found in the United Kingdom. In the United States, debates on political and legal reform are typically couched in terms of a proposal's likely contribution to efficiency and the generation of wealth, a fact which forces even those opposed to these values to engage in economic analysis. A perusal of United States law journals will find enormous numbers of articles that refer to economic concepts, as well as a number of specialist journals devoted entirely to the economic analysis of law. Economic analysis of law has also generated offshoots such as games theory and public choice theory which, although not strictly economic in their approach, use some of the assumptions and methodology of economic analysis to analyse individual behaviour and address important questions of regulation and constitutional law. The particular strand of economics which dominates economic analysis of law is called neo-classical economics. The focus of this economics is the behaviour of individuals entering into transactions in a market place, and the assumptions that make the behaviour of such individuals, in the aggregate, predictable. There are other approaches, most notably institutional economics. One version of institutional economics builds on the observation that individuals do not operate as individuals in markets, but in associations (firms, clubs, etc), and seeks to identify and model the kinds of rationality that allow such collective entities to function (see Veljanovski 1982, 54–63). Many of the criticisms levied at the dominant neo-classical form of economic analysis of law do not apply to institutional analysis.

This chapter on economic analysis of law as a form of jurisprudence will not attempt to identify the social conditions that have led to the spread and success of this form of analysis. Rather, it will concentrate on the substance of the debate that it has generated. What is it that economic analysis of law purports to offer to the study of law? This question can be addressed without claiming that academia operates as a meritocracy, whereby only the most inherently valuable ideas gain widespread acceptance. Instead, we can look at the analysis to see how it changes our view of the legal world, and what values are served by looking at law from this perspective.

Economic analysis and liberalism – the ethical attraction of efficiency

Much of the attraction of this approach lies in its relationship to liberal political theory. Liberalism respects the individual. In particular, it respects the individual as a person who should be, as far as possible, free to choose how to live. Thus, for example, liberalism does not embrace one religious belief as superior to another. It is simply a matter of choice. From a starting point of respect for the individual and the celebration of freedom to choose, liberal theories debate the appropriate basis on which to reconcile the choices of different individuals, and how to conduct those aspects of social life which require a collective response. One of the most influential liberal theories is that of utilitarianism. Within this theory, the preferences of all individuals weigh equally. Adding up the preferences of all individuals to see which approach maximises their achievement ('the greatest good for the greatest number') can identify the common good. Here the common good becomes the greatest amount of individuals' satisfaction. There are numerous criticisms of this theory, including liberal ones; what if the majority of the population want to see one person tortured – where is the respect for the individual in that? (Other criticisms of utilitarianism have been set out in Chapter 15.) But the particular weakness in the theory to which economic analysis responds is the problem of measurement. Utilitarianism relies on our ability to aggregate individuals' satisfactions. But how do you know what preferences people have, and how strongly they feel them? There are obvious dangers in judging such things by reference to how loudly people demand something, or how much they protest if it is taken away.

Like utilitarianism, economics purports to value peoples' preferences subjectively, by the value that they themselves place upon them. However, the economist's measure of value is how much an individual is willing to give up or forgo in order to have a particular outcome. Value is measured according to the individual's willingness to pay, or be paid. Economists understand this measure in its widest possible terms: all the things (time, possessions, opportunities, etc) that an individual would be willing to forgo to acquire something, or all the things they could do instead if they did not have it. The technical term for this willingness to pay is 'opportunity cost' (only reducible to money to the extent that all these other opportunities can be bought or sold). To the extent that we can establish the willingness of individuals to pay for what they prefer, economics appears to offer the respect for individual preferences characteristic of utilitarianism, but with an objective basis for weighing and comparing such preferences.

Alongside economists' concept of value, we find their concepts of efficiency. Efficient outcomes increase individuals' satisfaction, as measured by their willingness to pay. Within economic analysis of law, a number of concepts of efficiency operate. These are often confused. The first is Pareto superiority. This provides the most ethically attractive basis for economic analysis. A Pareto superior change occurs when at least one person is made better off, and no one is made worse off. The better off person is in a situation that he values more in terms of his willingness to pay, and no one is in a position which they value less in terms of their willingness to pay. Alongside Pareto superiority, we have the concept of Pareto optimality. This is simply a position in which no one can be made better off without someone else being made worse off. Within Pareto analysis, this is a state of efficiency. There is no Pareto superior move that can be made. A move from this position will not, in Pareto terms, be efficient.

When one combines the Pareto definition of efficiency with one of the central assumptions of economic theory (that the individual is a rational preference maximiser) then a Pareto superior move is an improvement in value that can be expected to occur by consensus, ie without coercion. To put all this in the form of a question which presents efficiency as an expression of liberalism: 'If two people can make a change, without coercion, which leaves at least one of them feeling better off, without the other (or any other person) feeling any worse off, why should the change be prevented?' (The formal statement of Pareto superiority makes no reference to consent. It occurs when the value of one individual's position is increased without decreasing any others. But if such changes occur through coercion, we lack the evidence of value represented by consensual changes. In practice, we return to the problem of measurement found in utilitarianism.) Pareto analysis thus represents a substantial challenge to any form of paternalism. If prostitutes and their clients are made happier through prostitution, why is it illegal? While there may be any number of answers to this question, Pareto analysis challenges those based on the claim that illegality is an attempt to coerce prostitutes or their clients, or those who would otherwise choose to become prostitutes or their clients, for their own good.

While Pareto efficiency has ethical appeal as a liberal theory, it has limited practical value. There are very few changes in the real world that can be made without someone being worse off, and this includes many changes that are dear to the hearts of economists. Does one replace a system of state rationing with a market? Not without upsetting many state bureaucrats. Does one repeal the law against prostitution? Not without upsetting those who find prostitution by others unappealing. Much, if not most, of any status quo **is** a Pareto optimal situation.

Alongside Pareto concepts of efficiency one finds those of maximum social wealth. This is a state in which every resource is, so far as is possible, held by the person who values it the most in terms of their willingness to pay. This version of efficiency can transcend many status quos in a much more dynamic fashion than Pareto analysis. There are radical changes, which leave some people worse off, but still move resources to persons who value them more. The introduction of markets is one such change. By introducing markets we create conditions in which persons who value the things which they have less than the things they could have instead are likely to conduct exchanges. The market is an obvious way of triggering a fresh set of Pareto superior moves, but its introduction is not itself a Pareto superior move. And if we pursue maximum social wealth, and the introduction of a market is not possible or prohibitively expensive, then a goal of maximum social wealth might lead one to make changes without reference to markets or other examples of consensual exchange. If we know that goods are valued more by one person (in terms of their willingness to pay) than another, why not just make an order that the resource be transferred?

Maximising social wealth can be achieved through the pursuit of a form of efficiency known as Kaldor-Hicks efficiency. A change is Kaldor-Hicks efficient whenever the increase in value to those who gain outweighs the losses to those who lose (both measured in terms of willingness to pay). Both Kaldor-Hicks and Pareto superior moves increase social wealth, but you can continue making Kaldor-Hicks moves in situations where it is too costly, (or just too inconvenient) to compensate the losers. While Pareto superiority is the most attractive version of efficiency, the concept of efficiency that informs most economic analysis of law is maximising social wealth. If one's goal is maximum social wealth, the presence of markets, exchanges, even freedom, are not things that are values in themselves. These things only help to overcome the difficulty of knowing who actually values a resource more.

Knowing exactly what needs to go to who in order to maximise social wealth is simply an unrealisable thought. Indeed, it is actually incoherent since, without having some initial wealth, we have no way of placing a value on anything. (What we own affects what we are willing to pay, and what we need to receive, before buying or selling a resource. How can you know what you are willing to pay, without something to pay with?) In practice therefore, assessments of what will maximise social wealth are usually made by reference to peoples' current entitlements. And while economists can theorise about an end state where social wealth has been achieved (a general equilibrium), practical applications of the theory require us to consider whether a particular change will *increase* social wealth, ie whether it is Kaldor-Hicks efficient.

Economic Models: Perfect Competition and Zero Transaction Costs

The model used by neo-classical economists to analyse efficiency is the concept of perfect competition. This is a market in which there are too many sellers and buyers to influence price (no one is a monopolist or monopsonist) and there is perfect information about prices and goods. (A fuller statement is set out in the extract by Polinsky.) Within such markets, the goods in question will end up in the hands of those who value them most in terms of their willingness to pay. If all markets are perfect, then all goods will end up with the consumer who values them the most, and all resources (capital, labour and land) with the entrepreneur who produces the greatest amount of valuable goods using them. This model is largely an exercise in logic. Given its assumptions, maximum social wealth is its outcome, **and** this outcome is produced through Pareto superior moves (exchanges and trades which produce a general equilibrium). Economists who subscribe to this model don't claim that it reflects life. However, they use it to analyse real life situations. Obstacles to markets which share these characteristics may be classified as market 'failures', and causes of inefficiency.

Perfect competition is a model that is often difficult to utilise within legal analysis. One can use economics in market situations to devise laws that assist to make that market more efficient (more like a perfect market). For example, one might seek to justify doctrines of implied terms in contract on the basis that these overcome some of the difficulties of imperfect information between buyers and sellers. One can also use economic analysis to challenge attempts to regulate markets by reference to ideas of justice such as 'unconscionable contracts'. (If a market is nearly perfect, how can one purchaser be said to have coerced a seller into accepting standard terms – no one purchaser can dictate terms – see Trebilcock extract below). But while the application of law to existing markets is fairly easily analysed in terms of perfecting the market, other areas of law seem quite removed from the market model. How is crime, tort, and family law to be analysed in terms of markets?

The obstacle to such analysis can be overcome if one thinks of legal rights as entitlements which can be traded. How much will you pay me to give up my right not to be polluted by your factory's smoke? From this perspective, any legal right could generate a market. And if a trade of legal rights created a situation whereby at least one person was better off, and nobody worse off (a Pareto superior move) why should it be prohibited? This observation forms part of Coase's theorem. Coase showed that, if transactions were costless (an assumption of zero transaction costs) any allocation of legal rights would be traded until they ended up in the hands of those who value them the most. If one's only goal were efficiency (whether as Pareto superiority or maximum social wealth) it would not matter to whom one allocated legal rights under conditions of zero transaction costs. They would always be traded to end up with the party who valued them the most in terms of their willingness to pay.

If few markets come close to the perfect market (and social wealth is only guaranteed to be maximised by markets if **all** markets are perfect), the assumption of zero transaction costs is even more utopian. If trading took no time, and no resources, we could simultaneously bargain with everybody at the same time, and through consensual trades, maximise social wealth. But the paradigm is still informative. Where there are low transaction costs, (eg people are already in contact with each other, and can use the opportunity to trade) they can be expected to trade legal entitlements for other things which they value more. And, if they wish to do so, why should we object? This leads to a form of analysis, which is similar to that described above in connection with perfect markets: how law can be used to lower transaction costs, and encourage the trading of legal entitlements.

Alongside the use of these models to argue for changes which facilitate trading, one finds them used to argue for the **results** which would be achieved through trading: the allocation of legal entitlements to those who value them the most in terms of their willingness to pay. This approach is often described as 'mimicking' the market.

Wealth effects and the effects of wealth

The model of zero transaction costs is a situation in which the initial allocation of legal rights will not prevent their eventual distribution from being efficient. It would be quite wrong to conclude from this that initial distributions do not matter. Transaction costs may prevent or impede trading altogether, or make it less likely if there is one allocation rather than another (see Polinsky 1989, extract set out below). In addition to this, one can show that the allocation of legal rights will alter outcomes in important ways, even under conditions of zero transaction costs. An initial allocation of entitlements affects what people have to trade, and what trades need to occur for efficiency to result. To use the smoke and washing example again. If it is more valuable to allow the smoke than to keep the washing clean then the smoke will always occur (given zero transaction costs). But if the residents are given a legal right to clean washing the factory owner will buy up those rights in order to continue to produce smoke, whereas if the factory owner is given a right to produce the smoke no purchases need take place. Both outcomes are efficient, but in the first scenario the residents receive payments (and are thereby wealthier) whereas in the second they receive nothing. The difference in outcome, which depends on initial allocation, is a wealth transfer.

Whilst one needs to be aware of changes in wealth that result from the allocation of particular legal entitlements, one needs to be even more aware of the general effects of wealth on decisions as to what is efficient. Differences in wealth raise important questions regarding the ethical implications of the economist's measure of human preferences: willingness to pay. An individual's willingness to pay is inevitably linked to their ability to pay. This is most obvious when one thinks about the ability of poor people to purchase things: the most they can be willing to pay for anything is all that they have. There may be many goods, even necessities such as food and medicine, that they cannot afford to purchase. It seems odd, if not immoral, to describe this situation as one where the poor are unwilling (or less willing than the rich) to pay for such things. Should one give even more resources to the rich because of the fact that rich people, due to their increased ability to pay, apparently value such resources more? One can improve this situation somewhat by assessing efficiency not by reference to what people are willing to pay to receive a resource, but what they would have to be paid to give it up. For example, instead of assessing the value which poor people place on medicine by reference to how much they will pay to acquire it, we can look instead on what they must be paid to give it up. But one is still left in doubt that willingness to pay is an objective basis from which to measure the relative strength of the preferences of the rich and poor. If we find that poor people sell their medicines to the rich in order to buy alcohol on the basis that they value the relief from misery provided by the latter more than the longer life promised by the former, does this really tell us that poor people value medicines less than the rich? Would a transfer of medicines from the poor to the rich, even if efficient in both social wealth and Pareto terms, really represent an increase in human welfare? (Insisting that the poor don't exchange their medicines for drink, while doing nothing about the misery which leads to such choices, forces the poor to endure an even lower level of preference satisfaction than they would choose for themselves. Preventing such choices, while doing nothing to remedy the inequalities which lead to them, is a suspect form of paternalism.)

At the most macro level, our allocation of wealth alters the kind of 'efficient' world that results. A society made up of one small class of very rich persons with the rest in dire poverty will have a different 'efficient' allocation of resources than one where the wealth of individuals is relatively equal. The former might be a world with a few Rolls Royces but lots of prostitutes, while the latter has only bicycles and no prostitutes. They could both be efficient (every resource is with the person who values it the most in terms of their willingness to pay), but they are very different worlds. Similar changes to outcomes occur at more specific levels, and may even be the result of wealth transfers. If residents own, and then sell, the right to stop smoke, they will use their increased wealth to generate demand for other goods. The goods purchased by these residents after selling their right to stop smoke may be different from those which would be purchased by the factory owner if he did not have to purchase the right to make smoke from the residents.

Positive, normative, and descriptive uses of economics

Economics offers a model of human behaviour which can be used both to predict what the consequences of any particular scenario might be, and to indicate what ought to be done about it. The model 'homo-economicus' is formed through the assumptions which are made about individuals: that they are rational utility maximisers. The assumption of rationality does not imply that all humans have acute critical faculties. It is an assumption linked to the idea of utility maximising. The theory assumes that individuals have desires, that they will act to satisfy those desires, that those desires have an order (the individual has preferences), that the order of preferences does not change radically in the short term and that, all other things being equal, they prefer more of what they desire to less. There is no requirement that an individual should be self-consciously aware of his desires and their ranking.

In order to use this model as a predictive tool we have to know something about the existing preferences of individuals. This points immediately to a number of limitations. As well as the possibility that particular individuals fail even this limited requirement of rationality (their preferences change from moment to moment, making it impossible to predict their behaviour) the predictive use of the theory requires knowledge of the very thing which gave economics a superiority over utilitarianism: knowledge of the subjective preferences of individuals. That said, the model has certain strengths. In particular, it stresses the dynamic nature of individual action. People are not viewed as robotic creatures of habit, but as individuals who respond to changes in the relative cost of satisfying their preferences. If you change the cost to individuals of satisfying their desires, you can expect a change in their behaviour. If you make a single good they desire less expensive in terms of the resources which they have to give up to acquire it, they will want more of it, and conversely if you make it more expensive (the so-called law of demand). Similar observations apply when individuals are viewed as producers (profit-maximisers). A rise in the amount paid for particular goods, or a fall in the cost of supplying them, can be expected to lead to an increase in their supply, as producers seek the increased profits (the so-called law of supply).

This is not a particularly sophisticated model of human behaviour. At the level of specific individuals, we cannot know what things they place a positive value upon (if I hate television, a drop in its price is not going to increase my demand for the product). But if we have the same kind of knowledge that we need to be utilitarians (we know what generally is desired, and what generally is disliked) we can begin to predict the consequences of making changes to the costs of different things. And if we can acquire reliable and relevant information on the value which groups of individuals place upon things they desire (in terms of their willingness to pay) and/or on the level of profits required for particular producers to stay in business, we may be able to predict the consequences of particular scenarios, including legal reforms. For example, if a health and safety measure will increase the price of milk by 20p a bottle, we may be able to predict the size of a fall in demand, and the likely contraction in the size of the farming industry. And while improvements in health and safety may be a 'good' thing, the likely consequences of such improvements (the consumption of less milk and more coca cola, and the rise of unemployment in rural areas) may involve other values whose attainment we might not wish to diminish, or at least not without an awareness of the choices implicit in the changes we introduce.

The use of economics to predict the consequences of legal reforms has become a central part of policy analysis, not only in the United States and the United Kingdom, but in most developed and developing nations. It is part of the legislative process. More controversial is the question of whether predictive economics should have a role in the adjudicative process. As a form of critique, predictive economics can remind us that judicial decisions have their own costs, and that any concept of justice that has regard to consequences needs to take these into account. As the extract from Leff illustrates, this can challenge some of our unconsidered ideas of just outcomes. But what follows from this? Should economic analysis be used by judges to assess the likely consequences of their decisions?

It is quite common for judges to be aware, or made aware by the parties, of the possible repercussions of their decisions. Consequential reasoning **does** enter into adjudication. And in thinking about consequences, economic man, or at least utilitarian man (who avoids pain and seeks pleasure) is likely to form part of this reasoning. If one suggests to a judge that a light sentence will encourage more crimes of the same sort, or that an interpretation of tax law that imposed higher costs on charities might result in less good works, one might perhaps be said to be making economics arguments. But at this level of sophistication, one is only really buying into a model of human action that allows one to think, in a fairly simple way, about the consequences of decisions. To argue against the use of economics at this basic level, is really to argue against consequentialism (rights and duties should be established without reference to the consequences of decisions, their nature and extent). If one wanted to use positive economics to assist adjudication, to rise much above this simple form of consequentialism, one would need to have regard to more sophisticated models of human behaviour, statistical evidence, and to find judges trained to make an informed judgement on the merits of the economic arguments and evidence presented to them. An awareness of the debates conducted between economists over the likely economic effects of quite mainstream economic variables (minimum wage, interest rates, etc) might lead you to conclude that while economic concepts may help one to think about consequences, clear answers on the size and distribution of consequences are much less likely to be forthcoming. The world is simply too complicated.

Positive economics is a tool to model human behaviour, to assist us to think about consequences. It does not tell us how to judge those consequences. By contrast, normative economics dictates that one should seek to bring about the consequences that are most efficient (on a Pareto or Kaldor-Hicks basis). The earlier sections of this chapter and the extracts which follow (particularly Dworkin) should give you some idea of the strengths and weaknesses of adopting efficiency as an ethical goal. Dworkin, in the extract, argues that, if one was to pursue a consequentialist form of ethics, then utilitarianism (the greatest happiness of the greatest number) would be superior to Posner's version of normative economics (maximising society's wealth).

As well as offering a defence of the application of both predictive and normative economics to law, Posner argues that economics can account for much of the substance of law, particularly common (judge made) law. While not claiming that judges have consciously sought to maximise social wealth when developing legal doctrines, he believes that a judge who was seeking to achieve maximum social wealth would have developed most of the existing doctrines of the common law. Thus according to Posner the common law **is** efficient, which allows us to use normative economics to predict the manner in which it is likely to develop in future. It is important to realise what this claim involves. All the difficulties of positive economics alert one to the difficulties of saying that a particular change will produce a certain outcome and, in the absence of such knowledge, how can one say that the change will increase social wealth? If the use of positive economics is little more than consequential reasoning using the idea of homo-economicus (which is all most judges can muster) the claim is even more suspect. But Posner's claim that the common law is efficient is not based on a vast empirical survey of the contribution of common law rules to the production of wealth. Indeed, his enterprise is not an empirical one. His claim that the common law is economic is a claim that he can produce sound economic justifications for common law rules: that common law rules will influence human behaviour in ways that economists would expect to result in an increase in social wealth. Thus Posner's claim that the common law is efficient is not a claim about the actual consequences of legal rules, but a claim that there is considerable congruency between legal rules and justifications derived from normative economics. (Although mostly at the level of general economic concepts: 'few principles such as cost benefit analysis, the prevention of free riding, decisions under uncertainty, risk aversion and the promotion of mutually beneficial exchanges can explain most doctrines and decisions'. (Posner 1990, 361))

The difficulties of reasoning from moral values to ethical behaviour (belief in the value of God, Socialism, etc does not prevent one facing acute ethical dilemmas) should alert you to the difficulties of reasoning from the goal of efficiency to identify the structure of legal rules that are likely to further this goal. While there are some clear cases (economists value markets, and prefer those markets to be as perfect as possible), arguing that legal rules contribute to efficiency is, for much of the common law, just that: an argument. While an economist can recognise an argument/justification of this kind as economic in the sense that he can understand the nature of the claimed link to efficiency, this does not mean that he must accept that efficiency will in fact result. He can come up with counter-arguments, also recognised as valid by economists, why the rule in question might not contribute to efficiency. Posner does not deny these criticisms, but argues that they do not justify rejecting the thesis that the common law doctrines can be explained (and improved) by reference to their congruence to economic theory. He regards the use of economic analysis to explain common law doctrines as an example of 'weak' science (see the extract from Posner).

Posner's claim that the common law is efficient has produced a number of responses. Dworkin argues that judges are unlikely to develop the common law to achieve efficient outcomes because maximum social wealth is such a poor ethical goal. (This argument relies on a model of judicial behaviour that assumes judges decide hard cases by reference to the relative superiority of moral arguments, in keeping with Dworkin's theory of adjudication, as described in Chapters 8 and 9). Another possible response, and one that adds considerable fuel to the economics and law movement, is to come up with further and different economic reasons for why existing legal rules, or changes to them, might increase efficiency. The ability to generate such arguments might be thought to undermine any bald claim that the common law could simply **be** efficient, and eliminate any expectation that normative economics could provide an objective basis for deciding hard cases. The fact that it does not, points to the fact that economic analysis of law attracts its adherents not because it provides clear objective answers in place of the indeterminacy of ethics and (depending on your legal theory) law, but despite the fact that it does not. The consensus within economic analysis of law is not at the level of merits of particular laws, but on the language, concepts and argumentation which qualify as 'economic'. ('Kaldor-Hicks provides a rhetoric within which liberals debate conservatives, rather than a [determinate] analytic ...' Kennedy 1998, 465)

This brings me back to the question I do not intend to answer: what are the social conditions that have led to the success of the law and economics movement? The debate between the proponents of economic analysis of law and its critics centres around the question of whether it is an objective, valuable, or practical basis for assessing laws. While the theory has ethical aspects and practical applications, it has come in for quite sustained criticism. In contemplating its success, despite these weaknesses, one is forced to move from considering economic analysis of law in isolation, as a theory with strengths and weaknesses that can be explored through the application of practical reason. Instead, one must consider the connection between economics as a knowledge and discipline and different areas of social life. For example, if lawyers wish to participate in policy analysis they have to understand the concepts used in forums for policy formation, and if these are conducted predominantly through economic discourse then, despite the weaknesses and contradictions we have explored here, economics will continue to be used by academic lawyers who wish to contribute to these policy debates.

Some comments on the extracts

The first, by Leff, provides an amusing example of one of the great strengths of economic analysis, in that it requires us to focus on the consequences (often unintended) of our decisions, before concluding that we have been just. The second and third, by Polinsky, introduce the models and assumptions of economic analysis of law. The fourth, by Trebilcock, illustrates the potential for economic analysis to inform judicial reasoning, at least in areas of law most concerned with markets. The fifth extract is taken from a chapter from Posner's book, on the criminal law. This provides an opportunity for you to see the legal world from an economic perspective. In place of often taken for granted ideas of the function of criminal law, such as the punishment of 'wrongs', or the protection of particular values, we find the criminal law explained by reference to the need to protect markets. Theft is not an inherent wrong, but a transaction that is less likely to result in Kaldor-Hicks efficiency than consensual trading in a situation of low transaction costs. The next extract, from an article by Dworkin, seeks to challenge Posner's normative use of economics by asking whether maximising social wealth is a value worth pursuing. The article also seeks to question Posner's claim that common law rules promote efficiency, and that economic reasoning accounts for much, if not most, of the common law. The final extract, by Posner again, concedes many of the points made by critics of the approach, but nevertheless argues for its merits (at least in light of the alternatives) as both a descriptive and normative theory.

Leff (1974, 460–461)

[I]n addition to its value as a way to continue to ignore our otherwise desperate intellectual straits, [economics] frequently serves intelligently to inform actual legal choices. For the central tenet and most important operative principle of economic analysis is to ask, of every move (1) how much it will cost; (2) who pays; and (3) who ought to decide both questions.

That might seem obvious. In fact, it is not. It is a most common experience in law schools to have someone say, of some action or state of events, 'how awful', with the clear implication that reversing it will de-awfulize the world to the full extent of the initial awfulness. But the true situation, of course, is that eliminating the 'bad' state of affairs will not lead to the opposite of that bad state, but to a third state, neither the bad one nor its opposite. That is, before agreeing with any 'how awful' critic, one must always ask him the really nasty question, 'compared to what?' Moreover, it should be, but often is not, apparent to everyone that the process of moving the world from one state to another is itself costly. If one were not doing *that* with those resources (money, energy, attention), one could be doing something else, perhaps righting a few different wrongs, a separate pile of 'how ghastly's'.

One can illustrate this basic kind of economic analysis by working with quite simple fact situations. There is this old widow, see, with six children. It is December and the weather is rotten. She defaults on the mortgage on her (and her babies') family home. The mortgagee, twirling his black moustache, takes the requisite legal steps to foreclose the mortgage and throw them all out into the cold. She pleads her total poverty to the judge. Rising behind the bench, the judge points her and her brood out into the swirling blizzard. 'Go', he says 'Your plight moves me not'. 'How awful', you say?

'Nonsense', says the economic analyst. 'If the old lady and kids slip out into the storm, they most likely won't die. There are people a large part of whose satisfactions come from relieving the distress of others, who have, that is, high utilities for beneficence and gratitude. So the costs to the widow are unlikely to be infinite. Moreover, look at the other side of the (you should pardon the expression) coin. What would happen if the judge let the old lady stay on just because she was out of money? First of all, lenders would in the future be loathe to lend to old widows with children. I don't say that they wouldn't lend at all; they'd just be more careful about marginal cases, and raise the price of credit for the less marginal cases. The aggregate cost to the class of old ladies with homesteads would most likely rise much more than the cost imposed on this particular widow. That is, the aggregate value of all their homes (also known as their wealth) would fall, and they'd all be worse off.

'More than that, look at what such a decision would do to the motivation of old widows. Knowing that their failure to pay their debts would not be visited with swift retribution, they would have less incentive to prevent defaults. They might start giving an occasional piece of chicken to the kids, or even work up to a fragment of beef from time to time. Profligacy like that would lead to even less credit-worthiness as their default rates climbed. More and more of them would be priced out of the money market until no widow could ever *decide for herself* to mortgage her house to get the capital necessary to start a seamstress business to pull herself (and her infants) out of poverty. What do you mean, 'awful'? What have you got against widows and orphans?'

Now, I have with malice aforethought tendentiously chosen and written this particular example sharply to highlight an otherwise unexpected possibility: the economic analyst may well be right. He is not necessarily 'right' in the sense that one ought to throw out this particular old lady (for the analysis is too sketchy and data-free to decide that). But he is certainly 'right' in this sense: the effect of not throwing her out is not a net gain, to society in general, or even to others in her 'class', equal to what she personally is saved by staying in possession. Choosing to favor her is not cost free, *even to others like her.*

Polinsky (1989, Ch 3)

THE COASE THEOREM

One of the central ideas in the economic analysis of law was developed in an article by Ronald H. Coase in 1960. This idea, which has since been named the *Coase Theorem,* is most easily described by an example. Consider a factory whose smoke causes damage to the laundry hung outdoors by five nearby residents. In the absence of any corrective action each resident would suffer $75 in damages, a total of $375. The smoke damage can be eliminated by either of two ways: A smokescreen can be installed on the factory's chimney, at a cost of $150, or each resident can be provided an electric dryer, at a cost of $50 per resident. The efficient solution is clearly to install the smokescreen because it eliminates total damages of $375 for an outlay of only $150, and it is cheaper than purchasing five dryers for $250.

ZERO TRANSACTION COSTS

The question asked by Coase was whether the efficient outcome would result if the right to clean air is assigned to the residents or if the right to pollute is given to the factory. If there is a right to clean air, then the factory has three choices: pollute and pay $375 in damages, install a smokescreen for $150, or purchase five dryers for the residents at a total cost of $250. Clearly, the factory would install the smokescreen, the efficient solution. If there is a right to pollute, then the residents face three choices: suffer their collective damages of $375; purchase five dryers for $250, or buy a smokescreen for the factory for $150. The residents also would purchase the smokescreen. In other words, the efficient outcome will be achieved regardless of the assignment of the legal right.

It was implicitly assumed in this example that the residents could costlessly get together and negotiate with the factory. In Coase's language, this is referred to as the assumption of *zero transaction costs*. In general, transaction costs include the costs of identifying the parties with whom one has to bargain, the costs of getting together with them, the costs of the bargaining process and the costs of enforcing any bargain reached. With this general definition of transaction costs in mind, we can now state the simple version of the Coase Theorem: If there are zero transaction costs, the efficient outcome will occur regardless of the choice of legal rule.

Note that, although the choice of the legal rule does not affect the attainment of the efficient solution when there are zero transaction costs, it does affect the distribution of income. If the residents have the right to clean air, the factory pays $150 for the smokescreen, whereas if the factory has the right to pollute, the residents pay for the smokescreen. Thus, the choice of the legal rule redistributes income by the amount of the least-cost solution to the conflict. Because it is assumed for now that the income can be costlessly redistributed, this distributional effect is of no consequence – if it is not desired, it can be easily corrected.

POSITIVE TRANSACTION COSTS

The assumption of zero transaction costs obviously is unrealistic in many conflict situations. At the very least, the disputing parties usually would have to spend time and/ or money to get together to discuss the dispute. To see the consequences of positive transaction costs, suppose in the example that it costs each resident $60 to get together with the others (due, say, to transportation costs and the value attached to time). If the residents have a right to clean air, the factory again faces the choice of paying damages, buying a smoke-screen, or buying five dryers. The factory again would purchase the smokescreen, the efficient solution. If the factory has a right to pollute, each resident now has to decide whether to bear the losses of $75, buy a dryer for $50, or get together with the other residents for $60 to collectively buy a smoke-screen for $150. Clearly, each resident will choose to purchase a dryer, an inefficient outcome. Thus given the transaction costs described, the right to clean air is efficient, but the right to pollute is not.

Note that in the example the preferred legal rule minimized the effects of transaction costs in the following sense. Under the right to clean air, the factory had to decide whether to pay damages, install a smokescreen, or buy five dryers. Because it was not necessary for the factory to get together with the residents to decide what to do, the transaction costs – the costs of the residents to get together – did not have any effect. Under the right to pollute, the residents had to decide what to do. Because the residents were induced to choose an inefficient solution in order to avoid the cost of getting together, the transaction costs did have an effect. Thus, even though no transaction costs were actually incurred under the right to pollute because the residents did not get together, the effects of transaction costs were greater under that rule.

We can now state the more complicated version of the Coase Theorem: If there are positive transaction costs, the efficient outcome may not occur under every legal rule. In these circumstances the preferred legal rule is the rule that minimizes the effects of transaction costs. These effects include actually incurring transaction costs as well as the inefficient choices induced by a desire to avoid transaction costs.

The distributional consequences of legal rules are somewhat more complicated when there are transaction costs. It is no longer true, as it was, when there were zero transaction costs, that the choice of the rule redistributes income by the amount of the least-cost solution. In the example, if the residents have the right to clean air, the factory pays $150 for the smokescreen, whereas if the factory has the right to pollute, the residents pay $250 for five dryers.

Although the simple version of the Coase Theorem makes an unrealistic assumption about transaction costs, it provides a useful way to begin thinking about legal problems because it suggests the kinds of transactions that would have to occur under each legal rule in order for that rule to be efficient. Once these required transactions are identified, it may be apparent that, given more realistic assumptions about transaction costs, one rule clearly is preferable to another on efficiency grounds. The more complicated version of the Coase Theorem provides a guide to choosing legal rules in this situation ... nuisance law, breach of contract, automobile accidents, law enforcement, pollution control, products liability, and litigation – can be approached in this way, although some fit more naturally into the Coasian framework than others.

Here are some questions to get you thinking about the Coase theorem, and its implications for legal doctrine.

1.   What are transaction costs?

2.   If transaction costs are zero, the outcome will be efficient, whatever party is given the legal right, but how will the wealth of the parties be affected?

3.   From an economic perspective, is a court which decides a case under conditions of zero transaction costs, or low transaction costs (where the parties can easily bargain with each other to correct any inefficiency in the original allocation of entitlements) really adjudicating on the relative merits of the parties' actions, or just giving one or other party a legal entitlement which they may sell if they should so choose?

4.   Is justice in such situations simply a matter of getting wealth to the party who deserves it?

5.   If transaction costs are significant, adjudication will not simply have a wealth effect, but may alter the respective level of conflicting activities, resulting in more of one, and less of another, than the parties would 'bargain for'. Should a court in this situation attempt to achieve the same outcome as would result under zero transaction costs, or should the knowledge that the decision cannot be easily undone through market transactions encourage it to have regard to considerations other than wealth and efficiency?

6.   If there were no legal entitlements (no ownership of anything, including money) could the Coase theorem operate? How could resources be allocated to those who value them the most, in terms of their willingness (which includes ability) to pay, if no one owns anything? Does this mean that legal entitlements have to be constructed, and allocated, without reference to willingness to pay before economic analysis can operate?

7.   If economics requires the allocation of legal entitlements prior to any assessment of willingness to pay, what scope is there for judges to adjudicate on disputes over those entitlements using economics? Does your answer depend on whether the judge is exercising discretion, as opposed to following precedent?

The next extract describes the competitive market paradigm and relates it to efficiency and the distribution of income.

Polinsky (1974, 1666–81)

A simple model of competitive behavior provides a comprehensible view of the interactions between consumers and producers within an economic system. Each consumer has a set of preferences, or tastes, which relates his level of 'utility' to his consumption of various commodities. In addition, each consumer possesses an *initial factor endowment,* which is what he owns initially that is of value to producers – such as land, labor, and capital. The consumer obtains income by selling his factor endowment, and uses the income to purchase various commodities. He chooses that combination of commodities which provides him with the greatest 'utility', but is limited to choosing a combination whose total price does not exceed his income. There are many consumers, each of whom controls a very small share of total resources in the society. Thus, each consumer takes the prices in the marketplace as given.

Producers transform factors of production into final commodities according to the existing technology. The producer acts rationally by selecting a level of output, and a mix of inputs sufficient to produce this output, which maximizes his profits. There are many producers of each commodity, each of whom supplies a very small fraction of output. Thus, each producer has virtually no market power and takes commodity and factor prices as given.

The economy is in equilibrium when supply equals demand for each factor of production (where consumers are the suppliers and producers are the demanders) and each final commodity (where producers are the suppliers and consumers are the demanders). The prices at which supply equals demand in all markets are the competitive market prices, and given these prices, no consumer or producer will desire to alter his behavior in any way. However, if tastes, technology, or the distribution of initial factor endowments (i.e., income) were to change, the economy would readjust to a new equilibrium in which prices and the levels of final outputs differed. Thus, for each given set of tastes and technology there are an infinite number of competitive equilibria, each corresponding to some initial distribution of income.

Will a competitive equilibrium exist (i.e., is there a set of prices which will clear all markets?), and if so, will the resulting configuration be Pareto efficient and socially optimal? Three further sets of assumptions will be useful in order to answer these questions. These are not the only assumptions required, but they are the ones most likely to be invalid in the real world, so they will be considered explicitly. One of these is the *zero transaction costs assumption.* For purposes of this assumption transaction costs are all the costs which inhibit competitive markets from working. It implies, for example, that consumers and producers are able to obtain perfect information about market prices and product quality at no cost, and that the process of exchange is itself costless. The second of these assumptions is the *convexity assumption*. It limits the structure of the consumer's preferences and of the producer's technology. For example, it rules out the following possibility for a consumer's preferences. Suppose that a consumer prefers to swim in a clean river, but, after pollution exceeds a certain level he prefers to take up another form of recreation. Once he quits swimming in the river he no longer cares how dirty the river becomes. The last of the assumptions is the *zero redistribution cost assumption*. It states that the process of redistributing initial factor endowments (income), among consumers is not costly in the sense that it does not distort behaviour, or involve administrative cost. It precludes the use of any form of redistribution which affects consumer behaviour in any way except by increasing or decreasing the consumer's budget. For example, all income tax is inconsistent with this assumption because it artificially lowers the price of leisure relative to the price of all other commodities.

Three important theorems of modern economics may now be summarized. First, if the convexity assumption is satisfied, then a competitive equilibrium will exist. Second, if a competitive equilibrium exists and if the zero transaction cost assumption is satisfied, then it is Pareto efficient. Third, if all three assumptions are satisfied, then any Pareto efficient allocation of resources can be achieved as a competitive equilibrium with all appropriate initial distribution of income (factor endowments).

These results provide a powerful case for the separation of efficiency goals from equity goals, and for the reliance on competitive markets to achieve efficiency. Within the paradigm, the attainment of the *socially optimal* organization of society can be thought of as a two-stage process: first, redistributing income until the most desirable distribution is achieved and then allowing competitive markets to determine the Pareto efficient allocation of resources for this distribution. Thus the paradigm reduces questions of public policy to the determination of the most desirable distribution of income. The decision involves a value judgment about whether one person's welfare should be increased at the expense of another's, a judgment outside the scope of the economist's professional expertise.

The next extract is part of an article which uses economic analysis (the model of perfect competition) to criticise a House of Lords decision that struck down a standard term from a record production contract on the basis that there had been substantial inequality of bargaining power and that the contract itself, being one-sided in its terms, was unfair. The article relies on the nature of perfect (or near perfect) markets as described by Polinsky: where there are a large number of buyers and sellers and a fairly homogenous service being sold (record promotion) the market will tend to offer standardised terms. No producer or consumer has any market power. Each takes their terms from the market. Under these conditions, what does it mean to assert that one of two contracting parties took advantage of their unequal bargaining power?

Trebilcock (1976, 359–85)

In what is likely to become a landmark case, the English House of Lords in *Macaulay v Schroeder Publishing Co Ltd* appears to have espoused explicitly a general doctrine of inequality of bargaining power as a bar to contract enforcement. This article explores, from an essentially economic perspective, the ramifications of such a doctrine.

...

The central facts in the case were these. An unknown 21-year-old popular-songwriter (hereinafter the plaintiff) entered into a contract in 1966 with a firm of music publishers (hereinafter the defendants). Under this contract (in standard form) the plaintiff assigned the copyrights to all his songwriting output for the term of the contract to the defendants in return for agreed royalties (generally 50 per cent of the net royalties received by the defendants) in the event of songs being published. The term was for five years, renewable automatically for a further five years if the plaintiffs royalties during the first term exceeded £5000. The defendants could terminate the agreement at any time on one month's notice, and were entitled to assign it, and any copyright held under it, without the consent of the plaintiff. The plaintiff had no right to terminate and could only assign the agreement with the consent of the defendants. The plaintiff received a payment of £50 against future royalties on the signing of the agreement. A unanimous court ... held that the contract so far as unperformed was unenforceable.

...

(Their Lordships considered that the one-sided nature of this contract (the record company had numerous and valuable rights, but no certain obligation beyond the payment of £50) was evidence of inequality of bargaining power and substantive unfairness. Trebilcock takes issue with both claims.)

First, the proposition that the use of consumer standard-form contracts is the result of the concentration of market power is entirely without factual foundation. The reason why such contracts are used is exactly the same as for their use in the commercial context, that is to 'facilitate the conduct of trade', or in economic terms, to reduce transaction costs. If an agreement had to be negotiated and drafted from scratch every time a relatively standard transaction was entered into, the costs of transacting for all parties involved would escalate dramatically. Moreover, it is a matter of common observation that standard forms are used (for this reason) in countless contexts where no significant degree of market concentration exists. Dry-cleaners have standard form dry-cleaning agreements, hotels standard registration forms, credit-grantors standard financing agreements, insurance companies standard life, fire, and automobile insurance policies, real estate agents standard sale and purchase agreements, landlords standard leases, restaurants set menu and price lists, and, for that matter, department and grocery stores set product ranges and price terms. The fact that in these cases a supplier's products are offered on a take-it-or-leave-it basis is evidence not of market power but of a recognition that neither producer-nor-consumer-interests in aggregate are served by incurring the costs involved in negotiating separately every transaction. The use of standard forms is a totally spurious proxy for the existence of market power. The real measure of market power is not whether a supplier presents his terms on a take-it-or-leave-it basis but whether the consumer, if he decides to 'leave it', has available to him a workably competitive range of alternative sources of supply. Whether this is or is not so simply cannot be derived intuitively from the fact that a particular supplier is offering non-negotiable standard-form terms. It is a matter for independent inquiry. If the market is workably competitive, any supplier offering uncompetitive standard-form terms will have to reformulate his total package of price and non-price terms to prevent consumers (at least consumers at the margin, which are the decisive consideration in such a market) from switching their business to other competitors.

It is, of course, true that general use of common standard-form contracts throughout an industry may, on occasion, be evidence of cartelization. But here one must be discriminating. If a reasonable choice of different packages of price and non-price terms is available in the market, albeit all through the medium of different standard-form contracts, then obviously the allegation of a 'fix' will not stand up. Even where all contracts are the same, in perfectly competitive markets where the product is homogeneous, commonality of terms is what one would expect to find (for example, the wheat market). Every supplier simply, 'takes' his price and probably other terms from the market and is powerless to vary them. In a perfectly competitive market, with many sellers and many buyers each supplying or demanding too insignificant a share of total market output to influence terms, all participants, sellers and buyers, are necessarily confronted with a take-it-or-leave-it proposition. Thus uniformity of terms, standing alone, is ambiguous as between the presence or absence of competition.

It is clear that the music publishing industry does not conform to all the criteria of a perfectly competitive market, given that the products (that is, the service packages) offered by different suppliers to composers are presumably widely differentiated. Because each package may possess a degree of uniqueness, each supplier may have a small measure of ability to adjust price and output combinations in relation to his differentiated product. But, provided that a substantial measure of substitutability is possible between one supplier's product and those of others, the market is as workably competitive as most real-world markets are likely to be. Moreover, as experience in the anti-trust context has demonstrated, an industry whose products are widely differentiated will almost never be able to sustain a stable cartel, as the possibilities for cheating on agreed price and output restrictions are extensive and largely unpoliceable. This difficulty, in the way of effective cartelization is, of course, compounded if the industry comprises many firms and entry barriers are low, both features of the music publishing industry, as we shall see.

The suggestion by Lord Diplock, that consumer standard-form contracts are explicable only on the basis that they are dictated by a party whose bargaining power, either exercised alone (monopolization) or in conjunction with others (cartelization), enables him to adopt the position that these are the only terms on which the product is obtainable, simply does not stand up as a matter of a priori analysis. This is not to suggest that monopolization or cartelization may not in fact have been present in *Macaulay*. But not a shred of relevant evidence was adduced on this issue.

This use of economic analysis puts considerable strain upon a commitment, central to the rule of law, to 'treat like cases alike'. (Music producers deserve the same respect for their contracts as other contracting parties). If Trebilcock can show that courts were wrong to conclude that a one-sided contract was evidence of some inequality of power between the parties, then he can demonstrate that the decision was arbitrary, or erroneous. But what is the solution? Must law inevitably fail to see facts as other discourses would? (See Chapter 18.) Or should judges learn economics and statistics to avoid such errors?

While the last piece pointed to the advantages of having an economically informed judiciary deciding cases arising from market activities, the next extract points to a more troubling application of economic analysis: its use in areas of the law that are not obviously markets. Posner offers an economic rationale for the nature and function of the criminal law. The principal 'wrongs' to be prevented are coerced transfers: transfers of wealth (which includes ownership of one's body as well as one's possessions) without consent. Coerced transfers are to be discouraged, at least where transaction costs are low, in order to provide incentives for people to obtain what they desire through non-coercive transactions. To put this simply: the criminal law forces individuals to get what they want through markets. The benefits of this approach are that markets provide good evidence that resources end up with persons who value them most in terms of their willingness to pay (whilst a thief might take something worth £100 to you and sell it for £10); and coerced transfers cause people to purchase things they only need because they are being coerced (like security grills and alarms). The latter expenditures are a social cost (in the absence of the coercion you would buy something else).

Note that 'willingness to pay' means willingness to give up resources that other people want. It does not mean willingness to suffer things that they do not want. The fact that a criminal will take a risk of imprisonment that you would not does not mean that he values your possessions more than you do. The value of his imprisonment to you is zero – you would not pay him to go to prison. As he is not offering you anything you value, one cannot say that he values your possessions more than you do.

This extract provides a good opportunity to see how much the world changes when viewed through economic spectacles. Conventional ideas of desert are replaced by the goal of efficiency, the advantages of market transactions as a means to achieve efficiency, and the need to deter potential (insolvent) offenders from bypassing the market.

Posner (*Criminal Law* Ch 7, 1998)

THE ECONOMIC NATURE AND FUNCTION OF CRIMINAL LAW

There are five principal types of wrongful conduct made criminal in our legal system.

1. Intentional torts, examined in the last chapter, that represent a pure coercive transfer either of wealth or utility from victim to wrongdoer: Murder, robbery, burglary, larceny, rape, assault and battery, mayhem, theft by false pretenses, and most other common law crimes (i.e. crimes punishable under the English common law) correspond to such intentional torts as assault, battery, trespass, and conversion, although we shall see that the state-of-mind and injury requirements sometimes differ for the criminal counterpart of the intentional tort. Here, however, are some more problematic examples of crime-as-pure-coercive-transfer:

(1) Counterfeiting. This can be viewed as a form of theft by false pretenses, the pretense being that the payor is paying with legal tender. If the counterfeiting is discovered, the victim is whoever ends up holding the worthless currency. If it is not discovered, the loss is more widely diffused. Since the amount of money in circulation is now larger than it was before the counterfeiting relative to the total stock of goods in society, everyone's money is worth less (inflation); everyone but the counterfeiter is a loser. (What about debtors?) In addition to this coerced transfer, counterfeiting imposes the usual deadweight costs (such as?).

(2) Rape. Rape bypasses the market in sexual relations (marital and otherwise) in the same way that theft bypasses markets in ordinary goods and services, and therefore should be forbidden. But some rapists derive extra pleasure from the fact that the woman has not consented. For these rapists, there is no market substitute – market transaction costs are prohibitive – and it could be argued therefore that, for them, rape is not a pure coercive transfer and should not be punished if the sum of satisfactions to the rapist (as measured by what he would be willing to pay – though not to the victim – for the right to rape) exceeds the victim's pain and distress. There are practical objections, such as that these rapists are hard to distinguish empirically from mere thieves of sex and that giving them free rein would induce women to invest heavily in self-protection which would in turn incite heavy spending by rapists to overcome that investment; but the fact that any sort of rape license is even thinkable within the framework of the wealth-maximization theory that guides so much of the analysis in this book is a limitation on the usefulness of that theory.

...

Now back to our typology.

2. Other coerced transfers. such as price fixing ... and tax evasion ... the wrongfulness of which may not have been recognized at common law.

3. Voluntary, and therefore presumptively value maximizing, exchanges incidental to activities that the state has outlawed. Examples of such exchanges are prostitution, selling pornography, selling babies for adoption, selling regulated transportation services at prices not listed in the carrier's published tariffs, and trafficking in narcotics.

4. Certain menacing but nontortious preparatory acts, such as unsuccessfully attempting or conspiring to murder someone where the victim is not injured and the elements of a tortious attempt are not present (as they would not be if, for example, the victim did not know of the attempt at the time it was made).

5. Conduct that if allowed would complicate other forms of common law regulation. Examples are leaving the scene of an accident and fraudulently concealing assets from a judgment creditor.

Why, though, cannot all five categories be left to the tort law? An answer leaps to mind for categories 3 and 4: No one is hurt. But this is a superficial answer; we could allow whomever the law was intended to protect to sue for punitive damages. A better answer, but incomplete, is that detection is difficult when there is no victim to report the wrongdoing and testify against the wrongdoer. Punitive damages can be adjusted upward to take account of the difficulty of detection; in principle this device could take care of category 5 crimes as well. We shall see, however, that the higher the optimal level of punitive damages, the less likely they are to be a feasible sanction. Another question about categories 3 and 4 is, why punish acts that don't hurt anybody? For category 3 the answer lies outside of economics; it is difficult for an economist to understand why, if a crime is truly 'victimless', the criminal should be punished. (Of course, ostensibly victimless crimes may, like other contractual exchanges, have third-party effects; the sale of liquor to a drunk driver is an example.) For category 4 the answer is bound up with the question – to which we can now turn – why tort law is not adequate to deal with categories 1 and 2 (coerced transfers in violation of common law or statutory principles).

We know from the last chapter that the proper sanction for a pure coercive transfer such as theft is something greater than the law's estimate of the victim's loss – the extra something being designed to confine transfers to the market whenever market transaction costs are not prohibitive. Damages equal to market value would thus be inadequate even if the owner valued the good in question at its market price. He might well value it at a higher price (remember that the market price is the value to the marginal, not the average purchaser). The law cannot readily measure subjective values, so this is an argument for adding a very hefty bonus to damages based on market value – an argument for heavy punitive damages in a case of theft.

In the case of crimes that cause death or even just a substantial risk of death, optimal damages will often be astronomical ... If A will accept $1 in compensation for a .0001 chance of being accidentally killed by B, it does not follow that he will demand only $10,000 to let B murder him. Of course dead is dead; but whereas the risk of being killed by accident is more or less randomly distributed throughout the population, the risk of being murdered is concentrated on the relatively small number of people who constitute obstacles to the goals of persons willing to murder –and for those people (the potential murder victims) the probability of death, in the absence of sanctions, would be much higher than the probability of an accidental death, and so the optimal damages would exceed those in an ordinary (that is, negligent) wrongful death.

...

Once the damages in the pure coercive transfer case are adjusted upward to discourage efforts to bypass the market, to recognize the nonlinear relationship between risk of death and compensation for bearing the risk, and to correct for concealment, it becomes apparent that the optimal damages will often be very great – greater than the tortfeasor's ability to pay. Three responses are possible, all of which society uses. One is to impose disutility in nonmonetary forms, such as imprisonment or death. Another is to reduce the probability of concealment by maintaining a police force to investigate crimes. A third, which involves both the maintenance of a police force and the punishment of preparatory acts (category 4), is to prevent criminal activity before it occurs.

When tort remedies are an adequate deterrent because optimal tort damages, including any punitive damages, are within the ability to pay of the potential defendant, there is no need to invoke criminal penalties (which, as explained below, are costlier than civil penalties even when just a fine is imposed). The criminal (= tortious) conduct probably will be deterred; and if it is not, even though the tort remedy is set at the correct level of severity and there is no solvency problem to interfere with it, there still is no social gain from using the criminal sanction (why not?). Although in some cases, notably antitrust and securities cases, affluent defendants are both prosecuted criminally and sued civilly, criminal sanctions generally are reserved, as theory predicts, for cases where the tort remedy bumps up against a solvency limitation. The 'double punishment' (tort and criminal) of the affluent makes sense. Their wealth enables them to hire good lawyers, reducing the probability of conviction (even if guilty) and the deterrent effect of the threat of criminal punishment.

The argument that the criminal law system is primarily (though not exclusively) designed for the nonaffluent is not refuted by the use of fines as a criminal penalty. They are generally much lower than the corresponding tort damages and even then are often forgiven because of the defendant's indigence.

...

We saw earlier that the criminal sanction ought to be so contrived that the criminal is made worse off by committing the act. But now a series of qualifications has to be introduced. Suppose I lose my way in the woods and, as an alternative to starving, enter an unoccupied cabin and steal a trivial amount of food which I find there. Do we really want to make the punishment for this theft death, on the theory that the crime saved my life, and therefore no lesser penalty would deter? Of course not. The problem is that while the law of theft generally punishes takings in settings of low transaction costs, in this example the costs of transacting with the absent owner of the cabin are prohibitive. One approach would be to define theft so as to exclude such examples; and in fact the criminal law contains a defense of necessity that probably could be invoked successfully in this example.

...

But change the example slightly: I am starving and beg a crust of bread from a wealthy gourmand, who turns me down. If I go ahead and snatch the bread from his hand, I am guilty of theft and cannot interpose a defense of necessity. The economic rationale for this hard-hearted result is that since transaction costs are low, my inability to negotiate a successful purchase of the bread shows that the bread is really worth more to the gourmand. Transaction costs were prohibitive in our earlier example of stealing food from a cabin in the woods, so that is a better case for the defense.

QUESTIONS

1. Why does Posner conclude that the criminal law is primarily for the non-affluent?

Note the difficulties that Posner has with rape. The rapist who wants non-consensual sex cannot find market substitutes. His punishment is therefore not as obviously within the functions of the criminal law as say, a burglar, who could as easily offer to purchase your possessions as steal them (if they are worth more to him in terms of his willingness to pay you).

Note the rationale for the limited interpretation of the defence of necessity. The need of the starving beggar and the starving person in the wilderness is the same, but in the latter case there are high transaction costs.

2. Why has Posner no 'economic' explanation for criminalizing activities where there is no victim (ie where no one is coerced)?

These issues beg a number of questions, many of which are addressed in the next extract, Dworkin's criticism of 'economic analysis of law'.

Dworkin (1980, 191–226 (edited))

In this essay I consider and reject a political theory about law often called the economic analysis of law.

...

The concept of wealth maximization is at the center of both the descriptive and normative aspects of the theory. But it is a concept that is easily misunderstood, and it has been misunderstood, in a certain way, by its critics. 'Wealth maximization' is a term of art within the theory, and is not intended to describe the same thing as 'Pareto efficiency'. In this introductory section, I shall try to explain each of these terms, to show why it misunderstands the economic analysis of law to suppose, as critics have, that the lawyer's definition of the former is a botched attempt to capture the meaning of the latter.

Wealth maximization, as defined, is achieved when goods and other resources are in the hands of those who value them most, and someone values a good more only if he is both willing and able to pay more in money (or in the equivalent of money) to have it. An individual maximizes his own wealth when he increases the value of the resources he owns; whenever he is able, for example, to purchase something he values for any sum less than the most he would be willing to pay for it. Its value to him is measured by the money he would pay if necessary; if he is able to pay, say \$4, for what he would pay 5 to have if necessary, his wealth has been increased by \$1. Society maximizes its wealth when all the resources of that society are so distributed that the sum of all such individual valuations is as high as possible.

...

For most people there is a difference between the sum they would be willing to pay for something that they do not have and the sum they would take in exchange for it if they already had it.

...

Neither Posner nor other proponents of economic analysis of law seem much bothered by either possibility ... It will do no harm, however, to tighten their definitions. We may say that the goal of wealth maximization is served by a particular transfer or distribution only when that transfer would increase social wealth measured by what the person into whose hands the good falls would pay if necessary to acquire it, and *also* by what he would take to part with it. In cases where the two tests disagree, the standard of social wealth maximization is indeterminate. Indeterminacy in some cases is no great objection to any standard for social improvement, provided, of course, that such cases are not disagreeably numerous.

The familiar economist's concept of Pareto efficiency (or Pareto optimality) is a very different matter. A distribution of resources is Pareto efficient if no change in that distribution can be made that leaves no one worse off and at least one person better off. It has often been pointed out that almost any widespread distribution of resources meets that test. Even willing trades that improve the position of both parties may adversely affect some third party by, for example, changing prices. It would be absurd to say that judges should make no decision save those that move society from a Pareto-inefficient to a Pareto-efficient state. That constraint is too strong, because there are few Pareto-inefficient states, but it is also too weak because, if a Pareto-inefficient situation does exist, any number of different changes would reach a Pareto-efficient situation and the constraint would not choose among these.

...

So the theory of wealth maximization is both different from the theory of Pareto efficiency and more practical.

But now comes the nerve of the problem. Economic analysis holds, on its normative side, that social wealth maximization is a worthy goal so that judicial decisions should try to maximize social wealth, for example, by assigning rights to those who would purchase them but for transaction costs. But it is unclear why social wealth is a worthy goal.

...

If economic analysis argues that law suits should be decided to increase social wealth, defined in the particular way described, then it must show why a society with more wealth is, for that reason alone, better or better off than a society with less. I have distinguished, and now propose to consider, one form of answer: social wealth is in itself a component of value. That answer states a theory of value. It holds that if society changes so that there is more wealth then that change is in itself, at least *pro tanto*, an improvement in value even if there is no other change that is also an improvement in value, and even if the change is in other ways a fall in value. The present question is not whether a society that follows the economic analysis of law will produce changes that are improvements in wealth with nothing else to recommend them. The question is whether such a change would be an improvement in value. That is a question of moral philosophy, in its broadest sense, not of how economic analysis works in practice. If the answer to my question is no – a bare improvement in social wealth is not an improvement in value – the claim that social wealth is a component of value fails, and the normative claim of economic analysis needs other support.

Consider this hypothetical example. Derek has a book Amartya wants. Derek would sell the book to Amartya for $2 and Amartya would pay $3 for it. T (the tyrant in charge) takes the book from Derek and gives it to Amartya with less waste in money or its equivalent than would be consumed in transaction costs if the two were to haggle over the distribution of the $1 surplus value. The forced transfer from Derek to Amartya produces a gain in social wealth even though Derek has lost something he values with no compensation. Let us call the situation before the forced transfer takes place 'Society 1' and the situation after it takes place 'Society 2'. Is Society 2 *in any respect* superior to Society 1? I do not mean whether the gain in wealth is overridden by the cost in justice, or in equal treatment, or in anything else, but whether the gain in wealth is, considered in itself, any gain at all. I should say, and I think most people would agree, that Society 2 is not better in any respect.

It may be objected that in practice social wealth would be maximized by rules of law that forbid theft and insist on a market exchange, when it is feasible, as it is in my imaginary case. It is true that Posner and others recommend market transactions except in cases in which the transaction costs (the costs of the parties identifying each other and concluding an agreement) are high. But it is crucial that they recommend market transactions for their evidentiary value. If two parties conclude a bargain at a certain price we can be sure that wealth has been increased (setting aside problems of externalities) because each has something he would rather have than what he gave up. If transaction costs are 'high' or a transaction is, in the nature of the case, impossible, Posner and others recommend what they call 'mimicking' the market, which means imposing the result they believe a market would have reached. They concede, therefore, or rather insist, that information about what parties would have done in a market transaction can be obtained in the absence of the transaction, and that such information can be sufficiently reliable to act on.

I assume, therefore, that we have that information in the book case. We know that there will be a gain in social wealth if we transfer the book from Derek to Amartya. We know there will be less gain (because of what either or both might otherwise produce) if we allow them to 'waste' time haggling. We know there can be no more gain in social wealth if we force Amartya to pay anything to Derek in compensation. (Each would pay the same in money for money.) If we think that Society 2 is in no respect superior to Society 1, we cannot think that social wealth is a component of value.

It may now be objected, however, that wealth maximization is best served by a legal system that assigns rights to particular people, and then insists that no one lose what he has a right to have except through a voluntary transaction. Or (if his property has been damaged) in return for appropriate compensation ideally measured by what he would have taken for it in such a transaction. That explains why someone who believes that wealth maximization is a component of value may nevertheless deny that Society 2 is in any way better than Society 1. If we assume that Derek has a right to the book under a system of rights calculated to maximize wealth, then it offends, rather than serves, wealth maximization to take the book with no compensation.

I shall discuss later the theory of rights that is supposedly derived from the goal of maximizing wealth. We must notice now, however, that the goal justifies only instrumentally rights like Derek's right to the book. The institution of rights, and particular allocations of rights, are justified only insofar as they promote social wealth more effectively than other institutions or allocations. The argument for these rights is formally similar to the familiar rule-utilitarian account of rights. Sometimes an act that violates what most people think are rights – such as taking Derek's book for Amartya – improves total utility. Some rule utilitarians argue that such rights should nevertheless be respected, as a strategy to gain long-term utility, even though utility is lost in any isolated case considered by itself.

This form of argument is not to the point here. I did not ask whether it is a wise strategy, from the standpoint of maximizing social wealth in the long run, to allow tyrants to take things that belong to one person and give them to others. I asked whether, in the story of Amartya and Derek, Society 2 is in any respect superior to Society 1. The utilitarian, assuming that Amartya would get more utility than Derek would lose, might reply that it is. He might say that, if we confine our attention only to this case, Society 2 is in every way better because there is more happiness, or less suffering, or whatever. He would add, however, that we should nevertheless impose on the tyrant a rule forbidding the transfer because, although the act makes the immediate situation better, its consequences will make the situation in the future much worse. This distinction is important, because a utilitarian who takes this line must concede that, if the tyrant's act would not have the long-term adverse utility consequences he supposes (because the act could be kept secret, or because a suitably limited exception to the general rule he endorses could be carved out and maintained), then the tyrant *should* so act. Even if the utilitarian insists that a rule forbidding the transfer in all cases will improve long-term utility, he still concedes that something of value is lost through the rule, namely the utility that would have been gained but for the rule.

The wealth maximizer's answer to my question about Amartya and Derek – that economic analysis would not recommend a set of legal rules permitting the tyrant to transfer the book without compensation – is simply an evasion. Like the reply that market exchanges provide the most reliable information about value, it misunderstands the force of my story. I still ask whether the situation is in any respect better if the transfer is made. If Society 2 is not in any way superior to Society 1 – considered in themselves – then social wealth is not even one among several components of social value.

I have assumed so far, however, that you will agree with me that Society 2 is not superior. Perhaps I am wrong. You may wish to say that a situation is better, *pro tanto,* if goods are in the hands of those who would pay more to have them. If you do, I suspect it is because you are making a further assumption, which is this: if Derek would take only $2 for the book and Amartya would pay $3, then the book will provide more satisfaction to Amartya than it does to Derek. You assume, that is, that the transfer will increase overall utility as well as wealth. But Posner, at least, is now explicit that wealth is conceptually independent of utility. He now allows that interpersonal comparisons of utility make sense and holds that increases in wealth may produce decreases in utility and vice versa.

I must thus make my example more specific. Derek is poor and sick and miserable, and the book is one of his few comforts. He is willing to sell it for $2 only because he needs medicine. Amartya is rich and content. He is willing to spend $3 for the book, which is a very small part of his wealth, on the odd chance that he might someday read it, although he knows that he probably will not. If the tyrant makes the transfer with no compensation, total utility will sharply fall. But wealth, as specifically defined, will improve. I do not ask whether you would approve the tyrant's act. I ask whether, if the tyrant acts, the situation will be in any way an improvement. I believe it will not. In such circumstances, that goods are in the hands of those who would pay more to have them is as morally irrelevant as the book's being in the hands of the alphabetically prior party.

Once social wealth is divorced from utility, at least, it loses all plausibility as a component of value.

...

It is false that even an individual is necessarily better off if he has more wealth, once having more wealth is taken to be independent of utility information. Posner concedes that improvements in wealth do not necessarily lead to improvements in happiness. He should also concede that they sometimes lead to a loss in happiness because, as he says, people want things other than wealth, and these further preferences may be jeopardized by more wealth. That is, after all, a staple claim of sentimental fiction and quite unsentimental fairy tales. Suppose, therefore, that an individual faces a choice between a life that will make him happier (or more fulfilled, or more successful in his own lights, or whatever) and a life that will make him wealthier in money or the equivalent of money. It would be irrational of him to choose the latter. Nor – and this is the crux – does he lose or sacrifice anything of value in choosing the former. It is not that he should, on balance, prefer the former, recognizing that in the choice he sacrifices something of value in the latter. Money or its equivalent is useful so far as it enables someone to lead a more valuable, successful, happier, or more moral life. Anyone who counts it for more than that is a fetishist of little green paper.

...

Posner suggests that wealth maximization is a value because a society that takes wealth maximization to be its central standard for political decisions will develop other attractive features. In particular, it will honor individual rights, encourage and reward a variety of 'Protestant' virtues, and give point and effect to the impulses of people to create benefits for each other. Posner believes that it will do better in promoting these attractive traits and consequences than a society that takes, as its central standard for political decisions, either utilitarianism or some 'Kantian' position.

...

We may begin with the claim that wealth maximization will encourage respect for individual rights. A society that sets out to maximize social wealth will require, of course, some assignment of rights to property, labor, and so forth. That is a conceptual requirement, because wealth is measured by what people are willing to pay, in money or its equivalent, but no one can pay what he does not own, or borrow if he has nothing to pledge or if others have nothing to lend. Society bent on maximizing wealth must specify what rights people have to money, labor, or other property so that it can be determined what is theirs to spend and, in this way, where wealth is improved. A society is, however, not a better society just because it specifies that certain people are entitled to certain things. Witness South Africa. Everything depends on which rights society recognizes, and on whether those rights should be recognized according to some independent test. It cannot, that is, provide an instrumental claim for wealth maximization that it leads to the recognition of certain individual rights, if all that can be said, in favor of the moral value of these rights, is that these are the rights that a system of wealth maximization would recognize.

There is, however, a danger that Posner's argument will become circular in that way. According to the economic analysis of law, rights *should be* assigned instrumentally, in such a way that the assignment of rights will advance wealth maximization. That is, indeed, the principal use of the standard of wealth maximization in the judicial context.

...

Economic analysis ... claims that the right answer is right only because the answer increases social wealth.

Nor does Posner limit the scope of that argument – that assignments of rights must be made instrumentally – to what might be called less important rights, like the right to an injunction in nuisance or to damages in negligence. On the contrary, he is explicit that the same test must be used in determining the most fundamental human rights of citizens, including their right to life and to control their own labor rather than be slaves to others. He counts it an important virtue of wealth maximization that it explains why people have those rights. But if wealth maximization is only to be an instrumental value – and that is the hypothesis now being considered – then there must be some independent moral claim for the rights that wealth maximization recommends. These rights cannot have a moral claim on us simply because recognizing those rights advances wealth.

...

In order to test the claim – that wealth maximization would (determinately) assign the right to labor to the 'natural owner' – we suppose that the right to the labor of a certain easily distinguished group of people (say those with IQs over 120) is taken from them (perhaps by some anti-emancipation proclamation) and assigned to others. The present wealth of those who have lost these rights (as well as the present wealth of those who have gained them) is not otherwise disturbed. Can we say that at least most of those who have lost their rights would now repurchase them or would but for transaction costs?

We must remind ourselves that willingness to purchase these rights supposes ability to purchase them – the ability to pay what those who have the rights would ask in the market. It may be – indeed it would be for most people today – impossible to repurchase the right to their labor, because the value of that labor represents more than half of their present wealth. Could they borrow, in the money market, the necessary funds? Posner speaks to this possibility. He says, 'No doubt the inherent difficulties of borrowing against human capital would defeat some efforts by the natural owner to buy back the right of his labor ... even from someone who did not really value it more highly than he did – but that is simply a further reason for initially vesting the right in the natural owner'.

...

So let us assume that the 'inherent difficulties' can be overcome so that someone who has lost the right to his labor can borrow against the discounted value of his future labor. Will he thereby gain enough capital so that we can be confident that he (or most people in his position) will be able to purchase the right to his labor back from someone else? Almost certainly not, because the monetary value of his future labor is unlikely to be worth more to him, for this purpose, than it is to someone else.

Suppose someone called Agatha who is poor but who can write detective stories so brilliantly that the public will relish and pay for as many books as she can possibly write. Suppose the right to Agatha's labor is assigned to Sir George. That means that Sir George can direct the way Agatha's labor is to be used: she is his slave. Sir George will, of course, be an enlightened slave owner, in the sense that he will not work Agatha so hard that the total value of what she produces declines. But he will work her just short of that point. Suppose that Agatha, if she had the right to her own labor, would work as an interior designer, at which work she would make much less money but find her life more satisfying. Or suppose that she would write many fewer detective stories than she could, sacrificing the additional income to spend time at her garden. At *some* point she would rather stop writing to enjoy what she has made, rather than make marginally more money, but have no time to enjoy anything. She may, perhaps, work somewhat more effectively while she works if she is her own master – but she will probably work at a less lucrative job, and almost certainly will work less.

If she tells the bank manager that she intends to design interiors, or to work at her garden, she will not be able to borrow anywhere near the funds necessary to buy the right to her own labor from Sir George. If she does not, but leads her life that way anyway, she will soon be in default on debt service. She can borrow enough money, even to make Sir George indifferent about selling her the right to her labor, only by undertaking to lead a life as distasteful to her as the life she would have led under Sir George. She will have to perform almost exactly the labors that he, as a master of enlightened self-interest, would prescribe. She will cease to be his slave only by becoming the slave of the First National Bank (of Chicago, of course).

Indeed, her situation is even worse than that, because I have ignored the interest the bank will take. (The rate may be high if others are at the same time trying to find capital to buy back the right to their labor.) So her ability to borrow enough to make Sir George indifferent will depend upon his other investment opportunities, and (if he is confident about her abilities) his risk aversion. Nor is it by any means plain that, if she could borrow enough, she would. She gains very little actual control over the conduct of her life, as we have seen, and she loses a considerable degree of security. The main value of freedom is the value of choice and self-direction, and if she starts her career a slave she will never be able to recapture more than a token amount to these. We cannot be confident (to understate) that a thorough analysis would justify the conclusion that Agatha either could or would buy back the right to her labor. We therefore cannot claim that economic analysis supports giving her that right in the first place.

Readers will no doubt think that I have gone mad some time ago. They will think that the character of the arguments I have been making demeans the case against the normative aspect of the economic analysis of law. Many will think it more important to say that a theory that makes the moral value of slavery depend on transaction costs is grotesque. They are right. But my present point is not that wealth maximization, taken seriously, may lead to grotesque results. It is the more limited point that this particular effort to show that wealth maximization has strong instrumental value wholly fails.

...

Economic analysis of law is a descriptive and a normative theory. Does the failure of the normative limb impair the descriptive limb? The latter offers an explanation of one aspect of human behavior, namely the decisions of common law judges in the cases economic analysis purports to explain. There are several modes (or, as some would say, levels) of explanation of human behavior. Some of these are nonmotivational. These include genetic or chemical or neurological accounts of either reflex or reflective behavior. The motivational modes of explanation may also be of different forms. The most straightforward is explanation from the agent's point of view, an explanation that cites the agent's goals or intentions and his belief about appropriate means. But there are more complex forms of motivational explanation. Invisible hand explanations, for example, suppose that people act out of certain motives, and explain why, that being so, they collectively achieve something different from what they aim at individually. One class of Freudian explanations also assumes that people act out of motives, but holds that these motives are unconscious. These Freudian explanations are, nevertheless, motivational because their explanatory power hinges on the claim that people whose behavior is so explained are acting in a way best expressed by analogy to the behavior of people who hold such motives consciously. The theory is therefore dependent on an understanding of that straightforward motivational claim.

The argument of economic analysis, that judges decide hard cases so as to maximize social wealth, is not a genetic, chemical, neurological, or any other form of nonmotivational explanation. Nor is it an invisible hand explanation. It is true that something like an invisible hand explanation of why common law decisions promote social wealth has been offered, but this is not part of the claims of Posner, Calabresi, or other proponents of economic analysis. To my knowledge economic analysis has never been presented as a Freudian analysis. But even if it had, that analysis would presuppose the sense of a straightforward claim. So economic analysis, in its descriptive limb, seems to rest on the sense and the truth of a straightforward motivational claim, which is that judges decide cases with the intention of maximizing social wealth.

But my arguments against the normative limb of economic analysis also call any such motivational claim into question. I did not argue that maximizing social wealth is only one among a number of plausible social goals, or is a mean, unattractive, or unpopular social goal. I argued that it makes no sense as a social goal, even as one among others. It is preposterous to suppose that social wealth is a component of social value, and implausible that social wealth is strongly instrumental towards a social goal because it promotes utility or some other component of social value better than would a weak instrumental theory. It is, therefore, bizarre to assign judges the motive either of maximizing social wealth for its own sake or pursuing social wealth as a false target for some other value. But a straightforward motivational explanation makes no sense unless it makes sense to attribute the motive in question to the agents whose behavior is being explained.

It follows that the descriptive claims of economic analysis as they have so far been presented, are radically incomplete. If they are to have descriptive power, they must be recast. They might be recast, for example, in some way appropriate to a weak instrumental claim. The arguments must then become more discriminating. They must pick out particular classes of judicial decisions and explain why it was plausible for judges to suppose that a rule improving social wealth was likely, for that reason, to advance some independent social goal these judges valued – utility, maximin, the relief of poverty, the economic power of the country in foreign affairs, or some other goal. That becomes a claim of great complexity, for it involves, not only a detailed causal account, but detailed intellectual history or sociology. Did judges who developed the fault system in negligence or the system of strict liability suppose that their decisions would advance average total utility? Were these judges uniformly utilitarians, who would therefore count that an advantage? Does this explanation hold good only for a certain group of cases at a particular point in the development of the common law? Is it plausible to suppose that judges throughout some extended period held the same theory of social value? Is it plausible to suppose, for example, that they were utilitarians indifferently before, during, and after the academic popularity of that theory of social justice? That only scratches the surface of the kind of account that would be needed to give a weak instrumental explanation of judicial behavior along wealth maximization lines, but it is enough, perhaps, to suggest how far short the present literature falls. It has not achieved the beginning of a beginning.

It may now be objected, however, that I am asking for far too much, and unfairly discounting what has been done already. Suppose that the economic analysts have established an important correlation between the decisions that common law judges have reached in some particular area – say nuisance or negligence or contract damages – and the decisions that would have been taken by judges explicitly seeking to maximize social wealth. Suppose that, although not every decision actually made is the decision such a judge would reach, the great majority are. (I know this putative correlation is contested, and I assume it, in this section, *arguendo*.) It seems silly, not to say churlish, to turn our backs on all this information. We may hold the following attitude. No doubt it would be better still if an intellectual historical account could explain why actual judges acted in this way, either by showing that they took wealth maximization itself to be a component of value, or because they held a strong instrumental theory of wealth maximization, or a weak instrumental theory that had the consequences discovered. But the correlation, in and of itself, advances our understanding of the legal process to an important degree.

I think this attitude is wrong. It is wrong because a correlation of this sort has no explanatory power unless it is backed by some motivational hypothesis that makes independent sense. Suppose the following exercise. Let us construct a binary alphabetical priority sequence for all cases ever decided by the highest court in Illinois. (We take 1 if the winning party's name is alphabetically prior to the loser's; 0 otherwise. Forget complications or ties). Call the sequence Arthur. We would not say that Arthur explains the judicial decisions in these cases, although Arthur is, in fact, a perfect correlation. Arthur has indefinitely many projections into the future. Suppose each academic lawyer in the United States were to project Arthur to a further 100 places at random. We would then have a very large variety of further sequences (Arthur Posner, Arthur Michelman, Arturo Calabresi, etc.) one of which would predict the results of the next, say, 100 decisions of the Illinois court better than any other, and, quite likely, very well indeed. But we would not say that, for example, Arthur Michelman had great predictive power or was a better theory of judicial decision making in Illinois on that account.

The point is both evident and important. Our standards for the explanation of human behavior require, in order for some account even to be a candidate for an explanation, that it bring to bear either a biological or a motivational account. If a correlation, however secure, cannot promise even the prospect of such a connection – if these connections cannot sensibly be taken even as mysteries waiting to be solved – then it becomes coincidence only. The claims for astrological and other occult explanations of behavior are problematical in this way. It strikes many people that both a motivational and a biological account are excluded by positive conclusions of physics that are beyond reexamination; but it strikes others that Hamlet's warning to Horatio is sound and pertinent.

We have three choices. We may disregard the putative correlation, between actual and wealth-maximizing decisions, as coincidental, and attempt to construct theories of adjudication that ignore it. That seems wasteful and perverse, for the correlation, if it exists, is different from the correlation between Arthur and the cases from which Arthur was constructed in one important respect. In the case of Arthur the method of construction guarantees that the correlation is coincidental rather than explanatory. In the case of economic analysis, coincidence is one hypothesis only.

Second, we may pursue the enterprise I suggested earlier in this section. We may try to construct a weak instrumental theory of wealth maximization showing why, in just the areas of law where the correlation holds, the weak instrumental theory, harnessed to some conventional idea of social value like utility, would recommend the wealth-maximizing strategy as a good means, and why it is plausible that judges realized this, in at least a rough and inarticulate way. That enterprise would carry economic analysis into layers of detail, of both political theory and intellectual history, it has not yet even begun to reach. But the enterprise cannot be dismissed in advance. There is a third choice. We may try to embed the correlation in a radically different sort of analysis and explanation. We may try to show that the decisions that seem to maximize wealth are required, not as instrumental decisions seeking to produce a certain state of affairs, of social wealth, utility, or any other goal of policy, but rather as decisions of principle enforcing a plausible conception of fairness. We might aim, that is, at an explanation of principle, instead of an explanation of policy. I have, on various occasions, tried to show why an account of judicial decisions on grounds of principle should always be preferred to one on grounds of policy, for normative and positive reasons. I have also illustrated a strategy for a principled account of judicial decisions that look to consequences, including third-party consequences. This strategy of principle seems to me much more promising than the weak instrumental program of policy just described. But I have not yet provided any compelling reasons why you should join me in that confidence.

In the final extract, a defence of economic analysis of law, Posner concedes many of the points made by its critics (the claim that the common law is efficient is unprovable, and that making maximum social wealth an aim for all law would conflict with utilitarianism, egalitarianism, and fundamental rights and freedoms). He seeks to defend the positive and normative branches of the approach on the basis that maximum social wealth is a relatively uncontroversial aim for judges to pursue when developing the common law (that it is the best aim for them to adopt when the conflict with fundamental rights or justice is not obvious).

Posner (*The Economic Analysis of Law* Ch 12 (edited), 1990)

THE ECONOMIC APPROACH TO LAW

What drives judges to decide common law cases in accordance with the dictates of wealth maximization. Prosperity, however, which wealth maximization measures more sensitively than purely monetary measures such as GNP, is a relatively uncontroversial policy, and most judges try to steer clear of controversy: their age, method of compensation, and relative weakness vis-a-vis the other branches of government make the avoidance of controversy attractive. It probably is no accident, therefore, that many common law doctrines assumed their modern form in the nineteenth century, when laissez-faire ideology, which resembles wealth maximization, had a strong hold on the Anglo-American judicial imagination.

...

It may be objected that in assigning ideology as a cause of judicial behavior, the economist strays outside the boundaries of his discipline; but he need not rest on ideology. The economic analysis of legislation implies that fields of law left to the judges to elaborate, such as the common law fields, must be the ones in which interest-group pressures are too weak to deflect the legislature from pursuing goals that are in the general interest. Prosperity is one of these goals, and one that judges are especially well equipped to promote. The rules of the common law that they promulgate attach prices to socially undesirable conduct, whether free riding or imposing social costs without corresponding benefits. By doing this the rules create incentives to avoid such conduct, and these incentives foster prosperity. In contrast, judges can, despite appearances, do little to redistribute wealth. A rule that makes it easy for poor tenants to break leases with rich landlords, for example, will induce landlords to raise rents in order to offset the costs that such a rule imposes, and tenants will bear the brunt of these higher costs. Indeed, the principal redistribution accomplished by such a rule may be from the prudent, responsible tenant, who may derive little or no benefit from having additional legal rights to use against landlords – rights that enable a tenant to avoid or postpone eviction for nonpayment of rental – to the feckless tenant. That is a capricious redistribution. Legislatures, however, have by virtue of their taxing and spending powers powerful tools for redistributing wealth. So an efficient division of labor between the legislative and judicial branches has the legislative branch concentrate on catering to interest-group demands for wealth distribution and the judicial branch on meeting the broad-based social demand for efficient rules governing safety, property, and transactions. Although there are other possible goals of judicial action besides efficiency and redistribution, many of these (various conceptions of 'fairness' and 'justice') are labels for wealth maximization or for redistribution in favor of powerful interest groups; or else they are too controversial in a heterogeneous society, too ad hoc, or insufficiently developed to provide judges who desire a reputation for objectivity and disinterest with adequate grounds for their decisions.

...

CRITICISMS OF THE POSITIVE THEORY

Stated as boldly, as provocatively, as I have stated it, the economic thesis invites attack from a variety of quarters ... It will be convenient to divide the attackers into two camps: those who attack the positive aspect of the economic theory of law (law can best be understood in wealth-maximizing and rent-seeking terms, the former being the domain of common law, the latter of statute law), and those who attack the normative aspect (law should be made to conform as closely as possible to the dictates of wealth maximization). Of course often the same people attack on both fronts.

Two criticisms of the positive theory are fundamental. The first is that the economic model of human behavior is wrong, and economic science phony. The second is that the proper study of economics is markets rather than nonmarket activity, the latter being the category that includes crime, adjudication, and other characteristic concerns of the legal system.

Economists pride themselves on being engaged in a scientific endeavor. From the basic premise that people are rational maximizers of their satisfactions the economist deduces a variety of hypotheses, of which the best known is the 'law of demand' – a rise in the relative price of a product will, other things held constant, cause a reduction in the quantity of the product demanded. These hypotheses are confirmed or refuted by studies of actual economic behavior. Usually the studies are statistical in nature, though much of the evidence that actually persuades people that there is 'something to' economics is of a more casual sort – for example, observing that nonprice rationing leads to queuing. Although many positive economists are followers of Karl Popper and therefore believe that falsifiability is the defining characteristic of a scientific theory, empirical economists in practice place far greater emphasis on confirmation than on falsification. In part this is because economic theory has become so rich, so complex, that almost any hypothesis, even one that appeared to deny a fundamental implication of the theory such as the law of demand, could be made to conform to the theory. For example, a finding that the demand for a product had risen in response to an increase in its price could be rationalized by arguing either that the product was a Giffen good or that consumers had been fooled by the price increase into thinking that the quality of the product had improved; consumers often take prices as an index of quality and often are warranted in doing so. In fact, the law of demand seems robust; but it is distressingly easy to explain away empirical findings that appear to conflict with the basic theoretical assumptions and propositions of economics.

Falsifiability is placed still farther beyond the economist's reach by the infeasibility in most areas of economic inquiry of performing controlled experiments. The normal method of seeking to confirm or falsify all economic hypothesis is by conducting a 'natural' experiment: an economic model is used to predict a relationship between statistical variables (for example, between price data and quantity data) and the reliability of the prediction is evaluated by applying tests of statistical significance. The problems with this methodology include the tedium, expense, and sometimes impossibility of obtaining the data that the model implies are relevant, and as a result of these obstacles the low ratio of empirical to theoretical work; the absence of professional rewards for negative findings, or, what amounts to the same thing, career pressures to come up with positive results by hook or by crook; the large, sometimes indefinite number of omitted independent variables that may be correlated with the independent variables the researcher is trying to test for; the typically very low percentage of the variance in the observations that is explained by the model, suggesting either that the data are poor or that the economic model is able to capture only a small part of the social phenomenon being investigated; the case of explaining away poor results as being due to problems with data; and the fact that the results being predicted are known in advance, which creates both pressure and opportunity to tinker with the model in order to make it conform better to the data – and the complexity of economic theory makes such tinkering easy to do. The last two points may explain why negative findings are likely to be ascribed to lack of imagination on the part of the researcher.

A theory that is not effectively falsifiable, but only confirmable, is tenuously grounded. One can never be certain whether observations that confirm (that is, are consistent with) theory A are not really confirming theory B instead, which overlaps with or includes A. The low percentage of variance explained by most econometric studies makes this a lively possibility.

...

These points suggest that economics is weak in comparison with the natural sciences, although it is the strongest of the human sciences. But the discussion has not shown, and it would be a mistake to believe, that it is a false science, like astrology, or an ideology, like Marxism.

...

The economics of law may well be a weak field, partaking of the general weakness of economics and of additional weaknesses specific to itself. But is the psychology of law strong? The sociology of law? Legal anthropology? Jurisprudence as a positive theory of law? These fields of interdisciplinary legal studies, and others that could be named, are older than economic analysis of law yet are weaker candidates for a leading role in fashioning a positive theory of law.

...

A number of specific objections are made to the positive side of the economic theory of law. The first is that the theory cannot really be tested (and is therefore pseudo-scientific), because the data required to form a judgment on whether a particular legal doctrine is wealth maximizing are, as a practical matter, unobtainable. This criticism, which is frequently and inconsistently joined to the criticism that particular doctrines believed by economic analysts of law to be efficient can be shown to be inefficient, is overstated. The data required to test the positive theory – in the case of tort doctrines, data on number of accidents, number and cost of lawsuits, levels of liability insurance and accident insurance premiums, and variations in legal doctrine, both statutory and common law – are obtainable, and are no more scanty or refractory than the data that are required for testing many other economic theories. What is true, however, is that few statistical tests have been performed on the positive economic theory of law and that instead analysts have been largely content to make a qualitative assessment of the wealth-maximizing properties of the legal rules, doctrines, and decisions being studied. It would be error to think that rules cannot be data for science; several branches of linguistics that study language rules are scientific. But characterizing legal rules as efficient or inefficient, in circumstances where the measurement of costs and benefits is infeasible or simply not attempted, is fraught with subjectivity and makes it difficult to evaluate claims that the theory has been confirmed or falsified by being confronted with the actual rules of law or outcomes of cases. The looseness of economic theory does not help.

...

Next is the objection that no adequate explanation has been offered for why judges would shape common law doctrine in the direction indicated by the norm of wealth maximization.

...

Yet, poorly understood as judicial incentives are, it is at least plausible that they push judges toward common law rule making that promotes the diffuse but powerful social policy of making markets work. For this may be the only social policy that the tools of the judicial process enable judges to promote in a consistent and reasonably uncontroversial fashion; if so, wealth maximization offers judges a comfortable as well as socially useful guidepost. Against this it can be argued that the articulation of legal rules in judicial opinions is a self-conscious, expressive activity, unlike a consumer's response to a change in relative prices; so that if wealth maximization were really the life blood of the common law we could expect to find the judges using the vocabulary of economics – especially now that economic analysts have extended that vocabulary to embrace legal doctrine. The vocabulary of economics, however, is designed for the use of specialists in economics. We should be no more surprised that judges talk in different terms while doing economics than that businessmen equate marginal cost to marginal revenue without using the terms and often without knowing what they mean.

...

The last important criticism of the positive economic theory of law, and the bridge to the criticisms of the normative theory, is that wealth maximization is so incoherent and repulsive a social norm that it is inconceivable that judges would embrace it.

...

CRITICISMS OF THE NORMATIVE THEORY

...

The normative theory has been highly contentious in its own right. Most contributors to the debate over it conclude that it is a bad theory, and although many of the criticisms can be answered, several cannot be, and it is those I shall focus on.

The first is that wealth maximization is inherently incomplete as a guide to social action because it has nothing to say about the distribution of rights – or at least nothing we want to hear. Given the distribution of rights (whatever it is), wealth maximization can be used to derive the policies that will maximize the value of those rights. But this does not go far enough, because naturally we are curious about whether it would be just to start off with a society in which, say, one member owned all the others. If wealth maximization is indifferent to the initial distribution of rights, it is a truncated concept of justice.

...

Suppose it were the case – it almost surely is the case – that some people in modern American society would be more productive as slaves than as free persons.

...

It is no answer that it would be inefficient to enslave such people unless they consented to be enslaved, that is, unless the would-be slavemaster met the asking price for their freedom. The term 'their freedom' assumes they have the property right in their persons, and the assumption is arbitrary.

...

This example points to a deeper criticism of wealth maximization as a norm or value: like utilitarianism, which it closely resembles, or nationalism, or Social Darwinism, or racialism, or organic theories of the state, it treats people as if they were the cells of a single organism; the welfare of the cell is important only insofar as it promotes the welfare of the organism. Wealth maximization implies that if the prosperity of the society can be promoted by enslaving its least productive citizens, the sacrifice of their freedom is worthwhile.

...

But at least in the present relatively comfortable conditions of our society, the regard for individual freedom appears to transcend instrumental considerations; freedom appears to be valued for itself rather than just for its contribution to prosperity – or at least to be valued for reasons that escape the economic calculus. Is society really better off in a utilitarian or wealth-maximizing sense as a result of the extra ordinarily elaborate procedural safeguards that the Bill of Rights gives criminal defendants? ... The main reasons these institutions are valued seem not to be utilitarian or even instrumental in character. What those reasons are is far from clear; indeed, 'noninstrumental reason' is almost an oxymoron. And as I have suggested, we surely are not willing to pay an infinite price, perhaps not even a very high price, for freedom.

...

Still, hypocritical and incoherent as our political ethics may frequently be, we do not permit degrading invasions of individual autonomy merely on a judgment that, on balance, the invasion would make a net addition to the social wealth. And whatever the philosophical grounding of this sentiment, it is too deeply entrenched in our society at present for wealth maximization to be given a free rein.

...

I have said nothing about the conflict between wealth maximization and equality of wealth, because I am less sure of the extent of egalitarian sentiment in our society than that of individualistic sentiment (by 'individualism' I mean simply the rivals to aggregative philosophies, such as utilitarianism and wealth maximization). Conflict there is, however, and it points to another important criticism of wealth maximization even if the critic is not an egalitarian. Imagine that a limited supply of growth hormone, privately manufactured and sold, must be allocated. A wealthy parent wants the hormone so that his child of average height will grow tall; a poor parent wants the hormone so that his child of dwarfish height call grow to normal height. In a system of wealth maximization the wealthy parent might outbid the poor parent and get the hormone.

...

What seems impossible to maintain convincingly in the present ethical climate is that the wealthy parent has the right to the hormone by virtue of being willing to pay the supplier more than the poor parent can; more broadly, that consumers have a right to purchase in free markets. These propositions cannot be derived from wealth maximization.

...

The strongest argument for wealth maximization is not moral, but pragmatic ... We look around the world and see that in general people who live in societies in which markets are allowed to function more or less freely not only are wealthier than people in other societies but have more political rights, more liberty and dignity, are more content (as evidenced, for example, by their being less prone to emigrate) – so that wealth maximization may be the most direct route to a variety of moral ends.

...

It may be impossible to lay solid philosophical foundations under wealth maximization, just as it may be impossible to lay solid philosophical foundations under the natural sciences, but this would be a poor reason for abandoning wealth maximization, just as the existence of intractable problems in the philosophy of science would be a poor reason for abandoning science. We have reason to believe that markets work – that capitalism delivers the goods, if not the Good – and it would be a mistake to allow philosophy to deflect us from the implications.

...

A sensible pragmatism does not ignore theory. The mounting evidence that capitalism is more efficient than socialism gives us an additional reason for believing economic theory (not every application of it, to be sure). The theory in turn gives us greater confidence in the evidence. Theory and evidence are mutually supporting.

...

The fact that wealth maximization, pragmatically construed, is instrumental rather than foundational is not an objection to its use in guiding law and public policy. It may be the right principle for that purpose even though it is right only in virtue of ends that are not solely economic. At least it may be the right default principle, placing on the proponent of departures from wealth maximization the burden of demonstrating their desirability.

...

COMMON LAW REVISITED

The case for using wealth maximization as a guiding principle in common law adjudication is particularly strong. The common law judge operates within a framework established by the Constitution, which, by virtue of a number of the amendments, not only rules out of bounds the ethically most questionable applications of wealth maximization but largely eliminates the problems of incompleteness and indeterminacy that result from the uncertain relationship between wealth maximization and the initial distribution of rights. That initial distribution is more or less a given for the common law judge. A related point is that such a judge operates in a domain where distributive or egalitarian considerations can play at best only a small role. The judge whose business is enforcing tort, contract, and property law lacks effective tools for bringing about all equitable distribution of wealth, even if he thinks he knows what such a distribution would be.

...

If it could be shown or if it is conceded that common law decision making is indeed not an apt field for efforts to redistribute wealth, then it may be possible to ground wealth maximization (as used to guide such decision making) in a more powerful normative principle of economics, the Pareto principle.

...

The ethical appeal of the Pareto principle is similar to that of unanimity. If everyone affected by a transaction is better off, how can the transaction be socially or ethically bad? There are answers to this question, yet a Pareto-superior transaction makes a powerful claim for ethical respect because it draws on intuitions that are fundamental to both utilitarianism and Kantian individualism – respect for preferences, and for persons, respectively.

...

No doubt most judges (and lawyers) think that the guiding light for common law decision making should be either an intuitive sense of justice or reasonableness, or a casual utilitarianism. But these may all be the same thing, and if pressed such a judge would probably have to admit that what he called utilitarianism was what I am calling wealth maximization. Consider whether a thief should be permitted to defend himself at trial on the ground that he derived greater pleasure from the stolen item than the pain suffered by the owner. The answer obviously is no, but it is offered more confidently by the wealth maximizer than by the pure utilitarian. The former can point out that the thief is bypassing the market system of exchange and that the pleasure he derives from the good he has stolen has no social standing because his desire for the good is not backed by willingness to pay. These are separate points. The thief might be willing to pay if he had to – that is, he might value the good more than its owner – yet prefer theft because it is a cheaper way for him to acquire the good. So theft might be utility maximizing, although this is unlikely because a practice of theft would result in enormous, utility-reducing expenditures on protection of property.

Since utility is more difficult to estimate than wealth, a system of wealth maximization may seem a proxy for a utilitarian system, but it is more; its spirit is different. Wealth maximization is an ethic of productivity and social cooperation – to have a claim on society's goods and services you must be able to offer something that other people value – while utilitarianism is a hedonistic, unsocial ethic, as the last example showed. And an ethic of productivity and cooperation is more congruent with the values of the dominant groups in our society than the pure utilitarian ethic would be. Unfortunately, wealth maximization is not a pure ethic of productivity and cooperation, not only because even lawful efforts at maximizing wealth often make some other people worse off, but more fundamentally because luck plays a big role in the returns to market activities. What is worse, it is always possible to argue that the distribution of productivity among a population is itself the luck of the genetic draw, or of upbringing, or of where one happens to have been born, and that these forms of luck have no ethical charge. There are counterarguments, of course, but they are not decisive. So, once again, the foundations of an overarching principle for resolving legal disputes are rotten, and one is driven back to the pragmatic ramparts.

Further Reading

For a fuller statement of the matters dealt with in this chapter, as well as a guide to further readings, see Veljanovski 1982.

A useful source book for all aspects of law and economics is Newman (ed) 1998. This 3 volume work contains, in particular, 20 short introductory essays.

For a short but clear analysis of the different meanings given to the concept of efficiency within economic theory, see Coleman 1982.

The article from which the extract by Leff 1974 was taken provides a very good and extremely accessible general critique of economic analysis of law.

Recent developments in economic analysis of law have sought to develop the theory in response to more realistic assumptions about human behaviour and the efficiency of markets. On this see Williamson 1985, Chs 1–3; Jolls, Sunstein and Thayer 1998, Posner 2001, Ch 8.

Questions

1. 'Economic analysis of law is based upon the erroneous assumption that all legal doctrine can be reduced to calculations of cost, and that these calculations are objective.' Discuss.

2. 'While efficiency is never synonymous with justice, maximum social wealth is more unjust than Pareto efficiency.' Discuss.

3. 'Efficiency does not provide a practical basis for deciding easy or hard cases.' Discuss.

4. 'Economic analysis of law can challenge some of our naïve assumptions about the effectiveness and justice of laws, but the dangers of its use outweigh these benefits.' Discuss.

18 The Autonomy of Law: An Introduction to Legal Autopoiesis

Gunther Teubner, Richard Nobles, David Schiff

Preamble: Explaining and developing the theory

Autopoiesis is a theory that requires some introduction, especially to those who are coming across it for the first time in a jurisprudence course. It is quite hard to understand some of the writings on this theory without knowing something about the debate which proponents of the theory are having with other theorists, and other kinds of theory. (Chapter 6, on law and social theory, offers a beginning to understanding this debate.)

Autopoiesis presents new insights for many of the big questions of social theory. The biggest of these questions is how society has changed – and how it is likely to change in future – and how we can understand what is taking place at the moment. This is one of the central questions of sociology. Modern society is complex, and fragmented. There is increasing specialisation. How is it all kept together? Theories like those of Marx, which seek to reduce society to a few variables – the class struggle between the bourgoisie and the proletariat – don't seem to do justice to the complexity of modern life. At the most general level, it may be correct to say that we belong to different classes, but there is nothing as simple as the 'relations of production'. We are doctors, managers, lawyers, politicians, clerics, teachers, skilled workers, unskilled workers, electricians, scientists, horticulturists etc. On top of this, we are of different races, cultures, gender etc. But if Marxism offers a reductive analysis, which fails to do justice to the complexity of modern society, what is the alternative? Another social theorist, Durkheim, sought to account for the solidarity of modern society by reference to its complexity. For him, modern societies were actually more integrated than older ones because of their complexity. Modern societies involve a division of labour – specialism increases productivity – but it also increases interdependence. This interdependence leads to stronger links between persons in a modern society than in a primitive one. Durkheim's theory may celebrate complexity, but it does not really explain how this complexity leads to solidarity. There is an assumption that an increase in interdependence will lead spontaneously to greater co-operation. But will it? Each person is dependent for their welfare on an infinite number of persons – farmers, train drivers, policemen, bureaucrats, engineers, doctors etc. What makes the doctor turn up and act as a doctor, the farmer continue as such etc? What keeps it all in place? How can so many different people be co-ordinated? This is all too big for any one person, or group of persons, to control. It is impersonal. Can material rewards, and self-interested individualism (the law of the market) really account for the incredible degree of specialisation and co-ordination required?

This sociological question spills over into questions of knowledge, language and, at the basic level, meaning. Autopoiesis, as set out in the writings of Luhmann (extracts of whose writings are found in this chapter), gives an explanation of social order (and knowledge and meaning) which focuses on the differentiated (specialised) nature of social communication. Co-ordination is made possible, according to this theory, by the use of common reductive terms, self-referential communication, and (at the level of self-observation) widely shared values. While we have fragmentation of experience, we also have systems of communication which give rise to 'objective meanings' which limit the possibilities of what may happen, and thus facilitate co-ordination.

To put this in simpler terms, what occurs within modern society is the growth of specialist languages. This is a system of differentiation. But the differentiation is not at the level of role or function (law is a dispute resolution system, politics is a decision making system etc), but in language. Different systems of communication encode the world in different ways. The legal system encodes the world into what is legal and illegal. Medicine encodes the world into what is healthy and unhealthy. Science encodes the world into what is true or false. Accountancy constructs the world into debits and credits. The Economy perceives the world in terms of profits and losses.

What are the implications of all this? It is functional for society to develop in this manner – but, by functional, Luhmann does not mean that systems operate in a positive way for the good of society: this is not another idea of progress. And functionality does not mean that each system carries out a particular task. He does not mean that it is the function of the health system to keep society healthy, or the function of the education system to produce knowledge. Or the function of the legal system to resolve disputes. Each system may communicate about itself, or be communicated about in other systems, by reference to such ideals, but it is not the pursuit of these separate ideals that maintains each of these systems, and keeps each separate from the other. The differences between systems of communication lie not in the task that they carry out, or the ideal that they appear to strive towards, but in the fact that they communicate about events using different codes.

The functionality of these different systems of communication – sub-systems of language and social communication – is that they increase the number of ways in which we can adapt. Society has more possibilities – it can become more complex. It can become more complex because while differentiation creates different languages, or jargons, and the notion of a universal language appropriate to all situations becomes less and less possible or real, the range of meanings that can be generated within any system of communication is limited by that particular system of communication.

Let us apply all this to some questions in jurisprudence. How, in a fractured society, where there is no agreement on the common good, can we have something which is peculiarly legal? How can we have law separate from other systems, and what if anything is the basis of any certainty in the law? Many legal sociologists will look to politics (see the analysis of the Critical Legal Studies movement in Chapter 7). They will see the certainty if any, in law, not in the rules, or kinds of legal reasoning, but in the politics of those who decide. Know the politics of your judges, police etc, and you will know what to expect from the law. This is often called law in action – to distinguish it from those, like Kelsen, who might expect to find objective legal meanings in books, or statutes, or case reports. From this law in action perspective, there is little that is peculiarly legal – law is an extension of politics. But what does it mean to say that law is just politics. Politicians find themselves in the courts. Pressure groups sometimes give up on politicians and bring legal cases. Is this just a case of seeking to bring politics to bear on a different group of persons, judges instead of ministers? An autopoietic answer to this question is to claim that law is not politics, in the very real sense that an attempt to talk 'politics' in a court room simply does not work. To speak in a court room, one has to speak law. Whatever political cause one wishes to advance has to be pleaded, as a cause of action. A claim for resources for doctors, has to become an action for breach of contract, or a judicial review, or an action for damages. To turn politics into law, one has to stop speaking politics and start speaking law. One cannot advance a claim in law by arguing about the interest groups affected, or the votes that can be gained, as one might in politics. To make a political dispute into a legal one, one has to reconstitute it within existing legal communications, in order for the law to recognise the political claim. And of course it works the other way. Those politicians who are dissatisfied with legal decisions, don't have to speak about case reports, pleadings, orders etc. They can talk about a legal decision in political terms – public interest, votes lost, economic losses etc.

The origins of autopoietic theory lie in biology, in particular, in theories of evolution that concentrate on the nature of cells. Systems of communication, if autopoietic, are like cells. The fact that cells can operate alongside each other to form complex physical beings – plants, animals, human societies – does not make each cell a part of the next. They are separate entities. The outcome of their developing complex relationships with each other is a complex being. But this is not a mechanical relationship, with one cell being the input to another cell. Each cell is a separate entity which reproduces itself from itself: from its own DNA and its own cell wall. Understanding the processes by which cells reproduce themselves in this way, the internal processes (which determine what is feasible for a cell to become) provide a basis for understanding living organisms. This is a different, and perhaps more sophisticated understanding of the nature of life, from simply identifying inputs (such as nutrients, oxygen and drugs) and observing how changes in these inputs affect the ability of cells to survive. This biological theory has been adapted by Luhmann, who argues that it is appropriate for the study of social processes. Instead of cells and biological processes, the focus is on systems of communication and social processes, and in particular, how we communicate and produce meaning. Legal systems, political systems etc are analysed like cells. They are seen as separate entities, each of which can have proximate relationships with the other without actually becoming part of the other. Communication within each system is, like the genetic material of cells, fashioned out of what already exists within the system. (To make a legal communication one has to link to existing legal communications.)

At the level of social communication as a whole, the analogy with cells works. We cannot communicate with each other except by drawing upon existing forms of communication, although we may use communications in novel ways. The more controversial, and potentially more illuminating claim, is that sub-systems of communication are (or can be usefully studied as if they were) autopoietic. Legal autopoiesis treats the legal system as a closed system of communication that can only make further legal communications out of existing ones. But how could law be like a living cell? How can law be said to reproduce itself from its own elements? Let's look back at the circularity found within some legal theories – take, for example, legal positivism. Within positivist legal theories, one finds attempts to explain law by reference to a hierarchical source, which establishes what is to count as law. But closer examination of these theories suggests not a source, or hierarchy, but circularity. Take Hart. The source of law is the rule of recognition that establishes what can count as a rule of a particular legal system. The rule of recognition is the rule used by officials to identify what is to count as law. But who the officials are is established by law – constitutional law. So the law identifies the law. Take Kelsen. The law is the norms authorised by the historically first constitution. The law is authorised by the law. The logical impossibility of this is acknowledged by Kelsen, who says that we presuppose a source for legal authority – above the constitution – called the grundnorm. And is this source hierarchical? Well yes and no. For we are told that law must be effective to explain the actions of officials. There must be some convergence between primary norms, and the actions of officials, for the point of legal knowledge is to give us the normative meaning of official action. To put this another way – if the constitution we have identified does not explain what the officials are doing, then we have identified the wrong constitution. So, does the legal meaning of official action come from the constitution, or does the legal meaning of the constitution come from the officials. Or is it both – is it not really hierarchical, but circular?

Autopoiesis is a social theory which makes sense of the circularity of legal authority – that it is law that decides what is to count as law. Autopoiesis tells us not to worry unduly about this, for it is a feature not only of law, but of all autopoietic sub-systems of social communication. Education, politics, law, the economy – these entities exist not as things which one can touch or feel, but as circulating systems of communication. A legal communication is a link in a system of communications. It refers back to earlier legal communications, and it can in turn trigger further legal communications. Let us try a specific example. What makes a fine something 'legal'. The positivist theories make us look for a source of some kind: a hierarchical chain of commands, rules or norms. With autopoiesis we have something similar. The communication of a notice of a fine will be linked to an order of a court, which will be linked to a judgement, which will be linked to a summons, which will be linked to an arrest, which will be linked to a police officer's power, and to a statute etc. Note that this is not a simple tracing upwards of a hierarchy of sources – upwards to a constitution or its equivalent. What makes the meaning of a fine 'legal' is the system which generates the notice of the fine. Now, and this may be difficult to understand, the notice of a fine is still 'legal' even if it has been issued under some mistake, or if the judgment was wrong, or the arrest was ultra vires. A fine is a legal communication because it is part of the system of legal communications – it is not only legal when that system operates in some manner which is regarded as 'correct'. To use the biological metaphor – a cancerous cell is still a cell, and a cell that has been made from its own elements – the fact that those elements have combined in unusual ways does not make it cease to be a cell. To return to the fine – a valid fine is as legal as an invalid fine – a valid communication by an official is as legal as an invalid communication. Any communication generated by a legal system is legal. In that case, you might ask, what is **legal** about a legal **system's communications?** The answer to that is the code which law applies. Legal communications apply the code legal/illegal. Implicit or explicit in all legal communications is this labelling of events into this opposition. The statement 'this is legal' is a legal communication. The statement, 'this is illegal' is a legal communication. A notice of a fine, is a coding of events as illegal.

But what, you may ask, of the hierarchies within legal systems? How do we compare a ruling by the House of Lords with a mistaken imposition of a fine? In the language of the theory, systems develop second order observations of themselves. What this means is that communications develop which observe (and communicate those observations) on the communications circulating within the system. In the theory of H L A Hart a similar role is played by secondary rules: rules which identify, change and enforce primary rules. Within this theory, communications about legal communications develop within the legal system. Concepts of mistake, constitutionalism, precedent, reflect the system's communications to itself, about itself. Such communications cannot (as Hart attempts) be reduced to master rules. For they are not rules. The communications are 'moves in the game': communications which have complex, contingent and contestable relationships to the communications from which they draw their meaning. Their success as communications (established moves, false moves etc) depends on their role in later communications. (Try reading the difficulties in describing the meaning of precedent, as set out in Chapter 14, with this paragraph in mind.)

So what does this theory add to all the others you have looked at in this book? First, it takes a positivist view of law – law is not morality. Second, it takes a realist view of law – law is something that happens in the real world. Third, although realist, it does not support the idea that there is an opposition between law in the books and law in action. The reality of law is not found in its ability to control actual events, but simply in the continued circulation of legal communications. If we think of law like the cell, then we can take a radically different view of the sort of things that are ordinarily taken to influence or determine law – class, politics, money, interests groups, power, race, gender etc. To understand how law reacts to the things in its environment, we should not assume that it simply takes them into itself in some simple way. It does not, it re-organises itself. To make this concrete, think of the complaint of so many of those who have experienced litigation, that the experience had nothing to do with what they were seeking to achieve. This is not simply an experience of private individuals. Businessmen complain that law does not reflect their need to do business, teachers say law cannot capture what they mean by education, doctors speak of the difficulty of fitting good medicine into legal rights. The fact that business influences law, that education influences law, that the medical establishment influence law, or even that such groups dominate their particular areas of law, does not explain such complaints. The distortion lies in the need for law to make things legal, to include things into itself by communicating about them through legal communications, that link to earlier, past legal communications, and forward to future ones. When events outside of law generate communications within this chain or system, they are transformed in a way that their authors would not recognise. This is due to the necessity for those events to generate legal communications, which link to other legal communications. The need for legal communications to link in this way is what allows law (like any system of communication involving different individuals with different backgrounds, experiences etc) to have congruent meanings, and an existence which cannot be simply be reduced to the materials (money, power etc) which sustain it.

The anti-formalist revolution in law

The view that law is an autopoietic system has been met with some suspicion. Any notion of autonomy and closure of law can appear located in the past, a return to the outdated and narrow 'conceptualist' view of law that sees law as essentially private law (most notably property and contract), and the primary function of law as the guarantee of private arrangements (including guaranteeing freedom from state interference). While liberal legal theories still stress the importance of law in private ordering (think of Hart's emphasis on power conferring rules) such an understanding of law's autonomy cannot survive the evolution of a welfare state, which not only leads to a vast increase in the amount of legislation and regulation compared to private law, but to the colonisation of law by political forms of discourse, such as arguments of policy and consequential reasoning.

The autonomy of private law was based on formalism and non-intervention. For example, judges dealt with private contracts on the basis of a highly developed and complex artificial formal language that often had little obvious connection to the real-world issues as seen by the people involved in the dispute. Formalism was tied to non-intervention. Judges generally left it to the freedom of the private parties to decide what was actually to be done. With the rise of positive social rights, as part of a move from liberal states to states organised to promote their subjects welfare (hence 'welfare states') private law changes. It becomes politicised. Instead of appearing as the formal expression of private intentions it becomes an inextricable mixture of legal, political, economic and other social elements. For example, contract law became more political as judges actively intervened more directly in contractual affairs and the power conflicts between contractual actors. Judges often corrected and rewrote contracts in order to translate the policy goals of legislation into contracts. Adjudication became an opportunity for contracts to be regulated, rather than simply enforced.

If law, even private law, is now political, economic, social etc. how can it be seen as autonomous? And how can autopoeisis, which seeks to describe law as a system constantly regenerating itself from its own elements, improve our understanding of law? Are we trying to pretend something that quite obviously is not the case: that law can exist separately from politics etc? Autopoietic systems theory in the tradition of Luhmann (1987; 1992a; 1992b), however, opposes this apolitical perspective and provides an alternative approach to understanding how the nature of modern society is determined by the highly intensive mixture of law, politics, economics and other social domains. This perspective uses an analysis of the closed, autopoietic forces within the legal system to illuminate the complex processes involved in the open, transformational relations between law and other social systems.

Maturana defines an autopoietic system according to its inward-looking characteristics of self-reproduction, self-reference, and closure (Maturana and Varela 1980; 1988). Law is a network of elementary legal acts that reproduces itself. On the other hand, law is a system that is significantly open to its turbulent external environment. In order to understand the openness, and the transformations of law under the influence of society, it is necessary first to analyse the mechanisms of autopoietic operational closure, which underpin the legal system. This apparent paradox is encapsulated by Edgar Morin (1977): L'ouvert s'appuye le fermé – 'the open rests on the closed'.

Luhmann (*Law as a Social System* 136–144 (1989))

In the classical division of labor between jurisprudence and sociology, jurisprudence is concerned with norms, and sociology, in contrast, with facts. The jurist's task is to interpret norms and apply them. The sociologist may concern himself only with the existing context of the law, with its social conditions and consequences. But this classical view was already out of date, if not anachronistic, even at the time when Hans Kelsen gave it its most precise formulation.

...

The resulting dissolution of the sharp demarcation between jurisprudence and sociology has given rise, since the beginning of this century, to the hope that sociology will be able to make a contribution to the administration of justice. From the perspective of the law, however, sociology's function remains more that of an auxiliary science. Aside from a few exceptions (the concept of an institution, for example), sociology has had no influence on legal theory and scarcely any impact on legal doctrine. Nor is it clear whether a special discipline called 'legal sociology' can provide the law with information, or whether all branches of sociology would be available to do so. And there is still no adequate sociology of legal doctrine or legal theory.

There has not been much movement on any of these questions in the last two decades. It is clear, however, that the quite optimistic expectations for a sociological contribution to the administration of justice have diminished and become more realistic. At present, moves toward a radical alteration in the way these questions are posed can be expected neither from jurisprudence nor from sociology. To the surprise of scholars of both disciplines, they are coming from elsewhere – from research that is attracting more and more attention under such names as general systems theory, cybernetics (of the third or fourth generation), multivalent logic, theory of automata, information theory, and, recently, as a general theory of self-referential 'autopoietic' systems, with which we shall be concerned here.

This detour by way of general autopoietic theory is currently producing more confusion than clarity and more problems and open questions than answers. The confusion is closely related to the fact that the offerings of existing theories have their origins in mathematics, biology, or neurophysiology, and do not take matters of psychic or social fact into consideration. As yet there has been no place in this discussion for systems that conduct their operations with the aid of the medium of 'meaning'. The new discovery is that biological systems, if not physical systems in general, are characterized by a circular, recursive, self-referential mode of operation. The mode of analysis that has emerged from this discovery has dethroned the 'subject' in its claim to be unique in its self-referentiality. This does not have to mean that psychic and social systems are now to be interpreted in terms of the model of biological systems. A mere analogy between them would miss the mark, as would a merely metaphorical transfer of biological terms to sociology. The challenge is rather to construct a general theory of autopoietic systems that can be related to a variety of bases in reality and can register and deal with experiences deriving from such diverse domains as life, consciousness, and social communication. Current uncertainty is due primarily to the fact that a general theory of this kind does not exist, and consequently one is frequently working too directly with concepts borrowed from mathematics or biology, without adequate concern for the appropriateness of the transposition.

In the application of the theory of autopoietic systems to the specific case of the law, there is an additional problem of coordination among multiple levels. One can conceive of law as a social system only if one takes into consideration the fact that this system is a subsystem of society, and that there are other subsystems as well. To conceive of society as itself a differentiated social system presupposes a general theory of social systems that can deal not only with the comprehensive system of society as a whole but also with other social systems, such as face-to-face interaction, or organizations. Theoretical decisions must therefore be distributed across several levels and must be checked to see whether what is asserted of the law does not hold for society as a whole, or even for every social system or every autopoietic system as well.

The following reflections focus on the legal system and must therefore largely disregard these problems of coordination among multiple levels. In the treatment of a relatively concrete subject, this omission will produce the appearance of excessive abstraction. The reader should not let this intimidate him; nor should he see it as proof, in and of itself, of the scientific character of the treatment. In fact, it is only in this way that one can confront general theories with the realities of concrete areas of investigation to see whether the theories are functional and what modifications they might need.

I.

There are two innovations that especially lend themselves to use in a theoretically grounded sociology of law: (1) the theory of system differentiation, inspired by general systems theory, which conceives of differentiation as the establishment of system-environment relationships in systems; and (2) the assumption that such differentiation is possible only through the establishment of a self-referential closedness in the systems becoming differentiated. Without such closure, the systems would have no way of distinguishing their own operations from those of the environment. With the aid of these two concepts we can achieve an understanding of the social character of law and, at the same time, the legal system's own reflective accomplishments. In other words, doctrine or legal theory can be better understood as one formulation of the legal system's self-referentiality. This understanding does require, however, a much more precise mode of presentation than has tended to be customary, a presentation that is consistent with systems theory.

Formulations such as the statement that there are 'connections between' law and society (which presupposes that law is something outside of society) especially must be avoided. The legal system is a differentiated functional system *within* society. Thus in its own operations, the legal system is continually engaged in carrying out the self-reproduction (autopoiesis) of the overall social system as well as its own. In doing so, it uses forms of communication that, for all their esoteric quality, can never be so abstract as to be completely removed from normal, comprehensible meaning. This means not only that the legal system fulfills a function for society – that it 'serves' society – but also that the legal system participates in society's construction of reality, so that in the law, as everywhere in society, the ordinary meanings of words (of names, numbers, designations for objects and actions, etc.) can, and must, be presupposed. In the legal system, then, Mr. Miller is still Mr. Miller. If he is only claiming to be Mr. Miller, and this question must be examined within the legal system, then a language that is generally comprehensible is indispensable for resolution of that question as well.

The legal system, however, is distinct in many ways from law's environment within society (and of course from its extra-societal environment as well). The law is not politics and not the economy, not religion and not education; it produces no works of art, cures no illnesses, and disseminates no news, although it could not exist if all of this did not go on too. Thus, like every autopoietic system, it is and remains to a high degree dependent on its environment, and the artificiality of the functional differentiation of the social system as a whole only increases this dependency. And yet, as a closed system, the law is completely autonomous at the level of its own operations. Only the law can say what is lawful and what is unlawful, and in deciding this question it must always refer to the results of its own operations and to the consequences for the system's future operations. In each of its own operations it has to reproduce its own operational capacity. It achieves its structural stability through this recursivity and not, as one might suppose, through favorable input or worthy output.

In this conceptualization both the dependence and the independence of the law are more strongly emphasized than in the customary expression 'relative autonomy'. When sociological theory is used to formulate a theory of the legal system, it reveals many more aspects of dependence and many more aspects of independence than one tends to notice in the normal activity of the law, and consequently theory has to abandon the amorphous formulation 'relative autonomy'. Differentiation gives rise to an escalating relationship in which aspects of dependence and aspects of independence both increase, because differentiation leads to greater complexity in relationships between the system and the environment. For this reason, the concept of the autonomy of the legal system cannot be formulated on the level of (causal) relationships of dependence and independence. Rather, the concept of autonomy refers only to the system's operative closedness, as a condition for its openness.

A theory of this kind, however, is convincing only if it succeeds in precisely defining the elements of the closed character of the system and how those elements determine the system's openness. This can be done by describing more precisely the components of the particular elementary operations peculiar to the law (those which occur nowhere else but in law) and how they are reproduced through reference to one another.

In a way that no other system does, the law processes normative expectations that are capable of maintaining themselves in situations of conflict. The law cannot guarantee, of course, that these expectations will not be disappointed. But it can guarantee that they can be maintained, as expectations, even in case of disappointment, and that one can know this and communicate it in advance. From the sociological point of view, then, normativity is nothing but counterfactual stability. To formulate this differently: in that it protects expectations, the law frees us from the demand that we learn from disappointments and adjust to them. It thereby holds out the prospect of resolving conflicts (and at the same time makes it possible to seek out and withstand conflicts), for it contains a preliminary decision (however unclear it may be in the individual case) about who has to learn from disappointment and who does not.

Processing these expectations requires a binary code that contains a positive value (justice) and a negative value (injustice), and that artificially excludes both contradictions (justice is injustice, injustice is justice) and other values (utility, political expediency, and so forth). This coding is of decisive significance for the differentiation of the legal system, as it provides the system with its own internally constituted form of contingency. Everything that enters the law's sphere of relevance can be either lawful or unlawful, and anything that does not fit into this code is of legal significance only if it is important as a preliminary question in decisions about justice and injustice.

One could show through more detailed analysis that this coding fulfills a dual function. The first function of the code serves to differentiate the system for the specific task of the law. It simulates the problem of the disappointment of expectations by providing that either the expectation or the conduct that disappoints the expectation will elicit either the positive or the negative evaluation. To this extent, the coding is tied to the law's function. At the same time, however, the coding also serves the system's ongoing process of checking for consistency, that is, the actualizing of its memory. For memory is nothing but checking for consistency, and to this end it presupposes, presumably even on the neurophysiological level, a binary coding that can ascertain both consistencies and inconsistencies and can link them to further operations. Thus, the second function serves the autopoietic reproduction of the system – the closure of the system's reproduction complex. It makes it possible to examine all processing of normative expectations in terms of the key question whether or not the processing is compatible with previous processing.

Once this dual function, and with it the law's autopoiesis, has been assured, the system can develop reflexive processes and, ultimately, self-reflection. It can regulate its own regulation, and thereby also regulate, legally, alterations in the law. Further, it can evaluate the system as a whole from its own perspectives (e.g., in terms of the idea of justice).

II.

The next sections of this essay will deal with some of the consequences of this theoretical point of departure. Especially important here are aspects in which this theory leads to views that are new or that differ from ones previously accepted.

A.

An especially important implication of this theory of the law's autopoietic character is that the boundaries of the system must be drawn differently than has been customary (even in the way sociologically oriented systems theory has dealt with law). Up to now the law has been treated either from the perspective of jurisprudence, as a complex of norms, or as a system of knowledge, in abstraction from real social behavior. Jurists saw the legal system as a macro-text. Or, as is customary in sociology, the focus was shifted to institutions that are concerned with law on a full-time basis, whether those institutions were organizations (primarily the courts), or the legal profession. This perspective permitted empirical treatment of such problems as 'access to the law'. Yet distinguishing between the legal system and the state as the basis for organizations and the source of power was difficult. Political influence on the law was conceived as a kind of input (of the law into the law). Alternatively, the legal system as a whole was even conceived from the standpoint of the political system, as an 'implementation' of politics. For all its ambivalence, this perspective has left a definite mark on jurists' attitudes toward the relationship between law and politics.

Assuming that the system has a self-referential, closed character leads to completely different notions about the boundaries of the system. They are defined not at the institutional but at the operative level. And, as is evident to the sociological observer, the system's boundaries are defined by the legal system itself, with the aid of a recursive referral of operations to the results of (or the prospects for) operations by the same system. In these terms, every communication that makes a legal assertion or raises a defense against such an assertion is an internal operation of the legal system, even if it is occasioned by a dispute among neighbors, a traffic accident, a police action, or any other event. It is sufficient that the communication be assigned a place within the system, and that has already occurred with the use of the code lawful/unlawful. Of course, the law can also be observed from the outside, as in a news report in the press. And within the educational system there is also a didactic treatment of law that only simulates legal cases and thus does not aim at a decision. Consequently not every reference to the law is an operation internal to the legal system. But whenever a communication occurs in the context of the administration of justice, the context of providing for conflicts within the law, or the context of an alteration of the law – that is, in the processing of normative legal expectations – we are dealing with an operation internal to the legal system, and this operation simultaneously defines the boundaries between the legal system and the everyday life context that occasions the posing of a legal question.

These system boundaries are a good place to study the filtering effect of the legal system. One sees clearly, for example, how difficult it can be in ongoing life relationships (marriages, work relationships, relationships between neighbors) to resort to the law to give force to one's own views. The rigidity of the binary code makes the reasons for this difficulty clear: asserting one's own legal position is tied to designating opposing views as unlawful. A look at the legal cultures of the Far East also shows that recourse to the law can be interpreted as an intention to engage in conflict, and consequently it is institutionally discouraged.

Clearly there is a connection between the complexity of the law, its resulting opaqueness, and how high this threshold of discouragement is. Corruption, which a look at various civilizations will show to be a normal phenomenon, has an equally discouraging effect on potential users of the legal system. Corruption in law is a normal phenomenon: it is only realistic to assume that the law accommodates dominant interests; it could not conduct itself otherwise and still be accepted. (This does not mean, however, that corruption is a part of official legal policy or that it is consciously cultivated.) Rather, what is amazing is the degree to which the law can be purged of corruption in spite of this. With a decrease in corruption, the threshold of discouragement is thereby lowered; people have confidence in a judge who is impartial. Yet, this relief itself leads to an increase in the complexity of the law. With less corruption to filter people out of the legal system, the number and diversity of cases increases, and as a result there is increased need for regulation. With this increase in complexity, the threshold of discouragement shifts its location from corruption to complexity. It thereby acquires a form against which the legal system itself is powerless and which is the subject of recurrent complaints throughout the history of law.

If one adopts a self-referential autopoietic theory, it no longer makes sense to assume that the structures of the legal system, which themselves regulate the production of its operations, can be specified as input and output. The specification of structures always presupposes operations of the system itself. This does not contradict the assumption of a normal complicity with dominant interests on the part of the law. Nor does it exclude the possibility that an outside observer could describe the legal system with the aid of an input-transformation output model. But such a description would be compelled to give the transformation function the form of a 'Mack box', and to take into consideration the fact that the law adjusts its reactions to its condition at any given time, that it can change even if external interests do not change, and that it thus does not function as a 'trivial machine'. To the degree to which these factors are taken into consideration, however, it makes sense to move from an input-output model to the theory of self-referential systems. It is better suited to the existing state of affairs.

B.

The most important advantage of this theory of a closed self-referential legal system may lie in its close resemblance to the notions of legal doctrine and legal theory, a closeness which by virtue of its alienation effect proves surprising and irritating at the same time.

...

Our starting point is the thesis that a self-referential system can link its operations together and reproduce them only through concurrent self-observation and self-description. To put it very simply, one needs 'reasons' in order to be able to deal selectively with the multitude of possible internal connections, and to check for consistency and inconsistency. Consequently, all processing of expectations is always accompanied by a supervisory observation through which the way the world is observed is itself observed – that is, the way one communicates correctly or incorrectly within the system is itself the subject of communication.

...

Basic principles of legal autopoiesis

How does legal autopoiesis deal with the battle between the formalism associated with much traditional jurisprudence and anti-formalism of much realist jurisprudence. The theory of law as an autopoietic system is not concerned with the insulation of 'the legal' from 'the economic' and 'the political'. The special contribution of autopoiesis to legal theory, as opposed to other 'realist' theories of the materialisation of law, lies in what it says about the conditions, mechanisms and consequences of mutual interference between law and other systems. Its central thesis is as follows:

1. Modern law is highly politicised through an intense structural coupling of law and politics, and law and the economy (the prime example of which is legislation);

2. Political-legal intervention in the economy is pervasive and necessary because of the closely interwoven mix of these areas.

This central thesis builds on two main concepts (Teubner 1993):

1. The law is defined as an autonomous system whose legal operations form a closed network. This idea of an autopoietic operational closure is different from the inadequate concept of relative autonomy (eg Lempert 1987), which regards law as being more or less dependent on society and the main question is to determine empirically the precise balance between its internal and external causation.

2. Heteronomy (law's interrelationship with other social domains) is treated as 'structural coupling'. This view, expounded by Maturana, involves the multiple membership of legal communications in other autonomous domains.

A clear distinction is made in legal autopoiesis between the mechanisms responsible for the autonomisation of law (its self-reference) and those responsible for its heteronomisation (its reference to other social systems). The autonomy of law is concerned solely with operational closure and the way legal operations form a closed network in which units of communication self-reproduce. This does not involve causal, informational or environmental closure. It acknowledges that law cannot be insulated from politics or the economy. But it moves the focus of analysis of heteronomy from the causal influences of outside forces to the complex ways in which, say, a legislative event also participates in political, economic and other 'worlds', each (as law has) with its own special language, logic and dynamics.

Such autonomy does not focus only on issues like the institutionalisation of the courts and legal concepts, and their independence from politics. Rather, it has to do with the constitution of elementary legal acts, which are different from any other kinds of communication. Law's autonomy and its heteronomy can vary from each other greatly. They are not in some kind of zero-sum game. At present there is probably a mutual increase in both making modern law simultaneously highly autonomous, and in making it highly heterogeneous (both highly specialised and technical, and at the same time closely connected to other areas of social life).

Social and legal autopoiesis

A legal system is constituted whenever legal acts emerge as a set of operations that go back recursively to earlier acts of their own kind, in order to produce new legal acts of the same kind. The legal system is a network of legal acts, which confer validity on normative expectations (giving meaning to what ought to occur even in the face of factual divergence) which are expressed through the 'legal/illegal' binary code.

A fully-fledged legal order is produced by the institutionalised distinctions between normative/cognitive, legal/illegal and valid/invalid. Legal acts driving the dynamics of this network include the making of a judgement in a court, the passing of a law by parliament or the concluding of a contractual agreement by the parties to it. These are defining 'magic moments', when validity is conferred on a new norm or rule. Thus, the important thing about the closure or autonomy of law is not institutionalised separation of powers, or the invention of rules and concepts, but the emergence of specific communications which distinguish themselves from other kinds of communication and are recursively connected to each other in a self-propelling network.

This process is not stable and self-maintaining. It is a network of fast-moving change through micro-variations generated in the second-by-second performance of legal acts that alter the inner content of the legal order. Each act creates new structures and the new structures create new acts in a continuous cycle. This closed communication network conforms to Maturana's definition of biological autopoiesis. It is not a subclass of it, but is a different manifestation of self-reproduction.

Social autopoiesis offers a broad view of the legal system, which encompasses private contracts and lay acts and not just state-centred legal operations. However, there is a special class of communications within the legal system which carry authority in making a statement about the validity of certain legal rules. This would include a pronouncement on the law by a legal authority, for example the judge, the legislator or the law professor, but not other general comments by that professor or other observers, such as journalists.

Autonomy in legal autopoiesis

Some theories on the autonomy of rule systems (eg Hart 1961) can be seen as predecessors of legal autopoiesis. But they are different because they emphasise the structures of the legal system, such as its rules, their hierarchies, delegation and the creation of new spaces of legal autonomy. Autopoiesis finds such a structural orientation too narrow because it fails to recognise the dynamism and recursiveness of legal acts in which the rules are essentially a by-product. We can understand this point if we use Hart's own example of chess. Most people consider the constitutive rules of chess as the game's defining feature. (Remember how Hart develops this analysis to understand rules.) But chess did not emerge fully developed, and then remain static. Chess, like any form of social communication, emerged (and continues to emerge) through moves (through playing if you like). The process of play establishes legitimate and illegitimate moves, which in turn form rules. Challenges continue, and the game continues to develop from itself. The degree to which chess has stabilised itself, leads us to see it as an institution whose meaning lies in its rules, rather than its moves, and the relation between them. Social autopoiesis, however, explains chess as a 'living' social system based on a dynamic chain of events. From this system, a new autonomous unit of communication – the move – emerges, which is recursively linked to other moves. The move is the emergent element of the chess game, with the rules only a secondary phenomenon. The dynamics of chess are concerned essentially with the 'emergence of something new that is not contained already in the lower strata', to use Maturana's language of autopoietic emergence. Chess is an example of the way a very artificial type of communication specialises itself and begins to operate recursively on different types of its own kind, thereby beginning the development of a chain of distinctions that propels itself into the future. The dynamic game consists of recursively linked moves in a web of expectations, moves and rules. Law as an autopoietic system emerges from general communications in society in a similar way. (Once you see even chess in this dynamic way, the ability to use traditional games as a metaphor for what is stable in a system as dynamic as law becomes quite suspect.)

Autopoietic autonomy is also different from the notion of a self-regulating system. Usually this is understood as self-organisation of systems which govern themselves by creating their own rules. Autopoiesis goes a step further than other theories of self-organisation by saying that the process produces the basic operations, in addition to self-reproducing the rules.

Another distinction needs to be highlighted between autopoietic autonomy and ideas of 'causal independence', like relative autonomy (Lempert1987), the 'last instance' of Marx and Engels, or political intervention. Causal closure would be a very different type of closure, with the system insulated from all outside interference (bar one, in Marxist writing, this being the material base and relations of production, society's economic infrastructure). Autopoeitic theory does not assert that systems of communication such as law are closed to, and unaffected by, other systems of communication. (How is statutory interpretation to occur without parliamentary proceedings?). Nevertheless, the fact that systems create or induce effects in each others operations, should not lead to the conclusion that one system's operations are the 'cause' of another system's operations in any simple sense. The operational closure of social autopoiesis recognises the system's openness to an array of external influences. It also, importantly, emphasises the way operational closure enables the system to have a decisive influence on the way the external causes are able to act on the system through an internal, circular causal process which is influenced by the outside world.

Autonomy has also been defined in terms of the creation of independent, self-contained worlds of social meaning (Lempert 1987). Autopoietic operational closure creates a 'meaning world' of its own that does not exclude outside influences. It recognises the steady stream of external influences on the communication systems and world-views of lawyers, which are so important in the creation of a legal system. However, the important factor in this autopoietic process is 'reconstruction'. Reconstruction translates and re-signifies social meaning in the legal world. For instance, the current economic analysis approach to law prevalent in the United States (see Chapter 17) may seem to transform law into being a part of economics by reducing justice to notions of efficiency. (See the final extract from Teubner at the end of this chapter.) On closer inspection, however, it can be seen that strange things happen to economic constructs when they travel into a legal context. Take the concept of an 'enterprise'. In economics, the enterprise represents the basis of a theory from which hypotheses are derived and challenged by empirical results. In law, enterprise is transformed into a normative concept as part of legal doctrine.

Each autopoietic system could be seen as a unique ongoing dynamic that cannot be controlled from elsewhere. Such systems cannot participate directly in each other's worlds, yet an ongoing process of structural coupling between worlds creates zones of contact between them (for a detailed discussion, see Teubner 1993).

A new perspective on contract

Luhmann's concept of 'functional differentiation' is a vital correlate to social autopoietics. It describes society as being differentiated into a number of autonomous systems, such as the law, the economy, science and politics. Autopoietic theory sees society as an ensemble of differentiated autonomous discourses or systems, which have evolved via processes in which distinctive characteristics become more and more prominent through their recursive operations.

Functional differentiation can be understood as the emergence of a series of autonomous systems based on operations of their own, like legal or economic or scientific or political acts. Each autonomous system has its own binary code and reproduces itself through a highly specialised language and ruthless logic of its own. That analysis offers a new twist to ideas from earlier social theorists like Durkheim (1933), Parsons (1971) and Weber (1978) – see Chapter 6.

Under conditions of extreme functional differentiation, the social world becomes fragmented into different dynamics of rationality. This means that a contract can no longer be regarded as a simple exchange between two actors and their resources, which actors have certain goals in mind. In autopoiesis, the contract reappears as different projects in at least three different social worlds: legal, economic and productive. There are many distinct productive worlds, including ones for science, engineering, health, the arts, education, distribution, manufacturing, tourism, sport and communication media. However much these worlds may be coupled with economic communications, they cannot be reduced to them. Doctors may work within budgets, but health is not the same thing as balanced expenditure. Even in commerce, the product is an expression of something (art, design etc) which is not reducible to the revenue that it may generate. With a contract we see communications about production, communications about budgets, costs and prices, and communications about legality. None of these can be reduced to each other. Individual legal words, or even sentences, cannot be made to stand for economic ones, which in turn equal legal ones. This applies even if the same word ('contract') is being used in all three systems of communication. In production, a contract may be a communication about opportunities to produce. In economics it forms part of a calculation about committed expenditure and expected income. In law, it exists in a circulation of communications about contract formation, contract interpretation, contract enforcement etc, all of which are linked to each other through processes of linkage and differentiation. (Textbooks which separate contract formation, interpretation and enforcement for heuristic purposes, make sense of a system of communications in which all of these exist at the same time – what contracts require and how they will be enforced is also part of what it means to create legal relations).

A contract in modern society is therefore essentially a compatibility relation between separate, differentiated social systems and their ongoing distinct dynamics of rationality. Provided this relation is effective in each system, the contract will be reconstructed in terms of three types of projects:

1. A productive agreement for a project in one or more of the autonomous autopoietic productive worlds, operating according to the way people work within the social dynamics of that system;

2. An economic transaction for a profit-seeking entrepreneurial project obeying the logic of the market;

3. A legal project in the world of law, based on time-binding promises and rule-producing obligations.

These three projects are not just different aspects of one contractual relation viewed from different analytical dimensions. They are empirical observations about three independent projects that participate in separate worlds of meaning. These worlds are operationally closed to each other and are on autonomous path-dependent evolutionary trajectories that propel them along very different routes. The unity of the modern contract lies in the precarious and provisional relations of compatibility between these fragmented discursive projects. A 3D image might help here. Consider the contract as the tangential intersection of three circles. Start by imagining two spinning circles alongside each other, with contact limited to a single point. Add a third circle, spinning on a different plane and touching the other two at the same point. Then consider this: the meaning generated in the different circulating systems of communication cannot become one single meaning for all three systems even if there is a common moment when the word contract is used in all three systems. The meaning of a communication about a contract within legal communications is connected to all the other kinds of communications that can be made in legal discourse about contracts. Any communication fits into a wider network of such communications. Similar connections determine the meaning of a contract within the other systems.

Functional differentiation also leaves its mark on contracts in the way an agreement reappears in different worlds. This means 'enslavement', in the language of self-organisation. An agreement in the economic world, say, is 'enslaved' to obeying all the conditions for the realisation of an economic transaction. Similar forces affect all the other worlds into which the agreement is transformed. Highly gifted entrepreneurs can observe the different highly specialised social dynamics simultaneously and then spot the opportunity to maximise autopoietic operation in each domain, creating highly effective contracts. Nevertheless, routinely effective contracts, where the legal, economic and productive meanings operate alongside each other without causing undue disturbance or 'perturbation' are quite normal (a relationship not limited to contracts, and described in the theory as 'structural coupling').

The 'self' that emerges from contractual discourses

Social autopoiesis argues for the modern contract to be seen as being primarily about inter-discursivity, not the inter-personal relations between two actors with their own goals and resources. This means giving up the idea of the dominance of actors and their subjective meanings and individual resources. Of course, a contract always needs an agreement between at least two actors, whether they are real people or fictitious entities, like an enterprise acting as a 'legal person'. But the unmediated relation of such contractual inter-subjectivity has been supplanted today by the greater complexities of inter-textuality between several functionally differentiated worlds of meaning.

The participants in this process can be considered as 'social homunculi of modernity', in that they are artificial personae arising purely from social discourse. The contract can then be seen as being not between physical beings but between highly artificial structures, whose interactions form an autopoietic system of contract that has a logic and dynamic of its own. The interests that people think they are realising or exchanging through a contract are therefore not their personal interests, but are social or discursive products. This analysis illuminates contracts formed between artificial persons such as corporations, whose intention cannot refer to an inner psychic state. More controversially, individuals as contracting parties are identified as creations of discourse. A human being is not a 'contracting party' except as a construct of a legal discourse. As a contracting party, the manner in which an individual signifies assent to terms, her/his intention to form legal relations, and the meaning of the normative expectations generated by the contract, are all products of legal discourse.

This analysis reveals the contract as an inter-discursive relation between its temporal states at the moment it is struck and at the transformations of the contract through its fulfilment stages. This inter-discursivity has its own socially-constructed goals that are different from the interests of its individual human actors. One could even go as far as talking about the 'self' or 'identity' of a contract. If one thinks of long-term contracts like a franchising-chain with its own corporate identity, this idea becomes plausible.

The contract binds the ongoing actions of the socially-constructed interests of the contractual partners. This social binding exists only as semantic artefacts, like texts and other products of discourse, which become the bearers of obligation in the contract. The source of the social dynamics of contract can then be understood as its binding of the actions of a social system towards achieving the contractual purpose.

Creative misunderstanding and surplus value

The trick in creating successful contractual autopoiesis (close structural coupling) across functionally differentiated worlds lies in unlocking a hidden agenda toward compatibility between different worlds. A contract makes possible translations between specialised autonomous worlds which can lead to exploitation through processes of 'creative misunderstanding' that take place during the translation of a contractual agreement into the languages of other related specialised worlds.

For example, the economic language of profit reappears in the productive world as the personal resources available to a project. The economic expectation of market prices is transformed into legal payment obligations. Law's creation of rules and expectations reappears as a factor that reduces or increases costs in the economic world, or as kind of moral bindingness within the productive discourse. What is deemed valid in one world might be invalid according to the logic of another, such as a contract that is acceptable from an economic perspective being rejected as an invalid/illegal (immoral, contrary to public policy) agreement.

Creative misunderstandings introduced by these compatibility activities offer an escape from the impossibility of ever being able to translate accurately the language of one world into another domain's communication system. One discourse uses the meaning materials of another as a provocative stimulus to reformulate something new in its own internal context. Since a real translation is impossible, something is invented. This inventiveness creates the surplus value of a contract, which is added to the autopoietic dynamics within and between systems. The ability of systems to create internal versions of the communications of other systems overcomes what otherwise would constitute an enormous impoverishment of opportunities resulting from the specialist systems of communication. Conversely, increasing numbers of functionally differentiated systems of communication increase what meanings (and thus opportunities for co-ordinated action) are possible. An example, using other materials in this book, may assist. Consider the enterprise known as economic analysis of law (Chapter 17). If all legal terms are reduced to an economic model, so that all entitlements are simply offered to the person who bids most for them at an imaginary auction, the very idea of entitlement (as understood by lawyers) disappears. But so too does the ability to do the calculation required by the economic model. One cannot know what can be paid for an entitlement, without having already allocated lots of entitlements (rights to property and contracts) on an non-economic basis. Thus the complete reduction of one system of communication to another is counter-productive for both systems. They need to maintain their differentiation. On the other hand, total closure of each system to another is also counter-productive. Take another example from the same chapter. Laws against monopolies are hardly likely to have much purchase on market activity if law is incapable of making any kind of economic communications. Law has to re-package economic calculations inside itself: to find forms of communications about markets that it can link with communications within the existing legal network. Economics has similarly to re-package legal communications to link them with communications within the existing network of economic communications. This process, which is not the simple reduction of one set of communications to another, or their translation into a common simpler meta-language, is productive. This does not, however, mean that every coupling between systems of communication involves major re-combinations within each respective system. Productive couplings can be routine and simplistic. A contract can be productively understood within the economic system without an awareness of the circumstances in which contracts may be declared invalid or frustrated. The ability to re-work the communications from one system in order to fine tune its coupling with another offers one kind of opportunity, the routine failure to invest resources in such endeavours offers another.

Luhmann's revolution in autopoiesis theory – the individual in autopoiesis

The above example from contract reflects the very different manner in which individuals are understood within the theory. The social system creates products of meaning which do not represent an aggregation of what has gone on in individuals' minds and is different from the thoughts and memories of each individual. Unlike Maturana, who reserves the concept of autopoiesis for human individuals, Luhmann sees both the individual **and** society as autopoietic systems.

The idea that meaning is located within systems of communication, and that subjects are just as much constructs of those systems when they are individuals as when they are corporations or institutions, threatens to deny that individuals have a separate existence despite their obvious separate physical identity. This threatens to lead to a theory which, like some variants of Marxism, makes the individual human subject simply an object, the bearer of dispositions imposed by outside structures, in the case of Marxism, class relations. (For a fuller account of this see the introductory paragraphs to Chapter 19.) Luhmann's revolutionary idea is to distinguish between psychic autopoiesis and social autopoiesis which create worlds of meaning in their own rights. The individual operates as an autopoietic system. Our own internal communications (thoughts) are related to other operations in our heads. Indeed, it is only by constantly connecting thoughts together and constructing relationships of consistency (memories) that we can have a sense of an ordered world, or environment. The relationship between communications within the individual psyche are not rigidly separated into the separate social systems in which the individual may participate. They have their own dynamic internal relationships. The fact that individuals can organise such dynamic relationships between their internal communications is one reason why their subjectivity, the meanings unique to each individual, cannot form part of the everyday objective meanings that circulate (or rather are produced in and through circulation) in social systems. However, the deep meanings of an individual's psychic world are not therefore lost within the social, as they have been in theories that seek to socialise the individual or language-centred views that deconstruct the subject. Luhmann essentially identifies two autonomous worlds of meaning based on different operations. These are interrelated in very indirect and complicated ways. Systems can construct individuals as subjects in ways that recognise their separate autopoietic existence whilst at the same time, and inevitably, failing to give full effect to it.

The individual thus re-emerges in Luhmann's theory as an autopoietic system of its own. But this subject now has a new competitor in the social system, which has the ability to cognise through communication. This is different to all other approaches to thinking about the relationship between the individual and society, from individualist psychological reductionism to socialisation and language reductionism and the undifferentiated mix of inter-subjectivity in between.

The concepts of individual and social autopoiesis reflect the split in modernity that distinguishes between personae as social 'masks' and the inner subjective thoughts and feelings to which the personae refers, but can never be a part of. These metaphors of personae and masks help to understand the role of actors in social worlds consisting only of communications. Actors as personae are secondary phenomena, given that it is the communication act which creates structures which do not have an independent existence outside the system. Every communication invokes its structures explicitly or implicitly only through this ongoing process of invocation. All the language cues and other identifying characteristics of an actual person form a particularly rich structure, but its meaning continually changes through invocation in different ongoing communication acts. Other structures could be roles or principles or rules.

The way personae operate can be seen when an expert participates in a different arena. Evidence given in court by, say, a medical doctor could be treated as a valid contribution to the legal process. However, that evidence might not be recognised as a valid scientific statement within the specialist medical system, where the perception of that expert in subsequent medical discourses could be altered. One of the best examples of this is the insanity plea in criminal law. The M'Naughten rules require that the accused 'at the time of committing the act ... was labouring under such a defect of reason, from disease of the mind, as not to know the nature and quality of the act he was doing; or, if he did know it, that he did not know he was doing what was wrong'. A 'disease of the mind' is not the same thing as mental illness, even though psychiatrists are the most likely persons to be called to testify on an individual's state of awareness at the date of the crime. It is said to be a 'legal' question, albeit one 'informed' by medical evidence. Doctors have to provide evidence of the likely consequences of illnesses not on the brain, but on the 'ordinary sense of mental faculties of reason, memory and understanding'. (*Sullivan* [1984] AC 156 at 172) This division between cognitive openness to medical facts, and normative closure in defining what facts are legally relevant, can produce complex results.

The really creative communication acts are those which can survive the difficult test of belonging successfully to different discourses. A successful contract is one that finds the creative words to enable it to participate effectively in legal, economic and productive worlds.

Despite the part played in the theory by individual autopoiesis, an uncomfortable, but necessary consequence of autopoiesis is its anti-individualistic view of many forms of action. Consider again contract making. Despite much rhetoric about the revival of an individual's autonomy in modern private law, an understanding of contract as an autopoietic system demonstrates that the individual subject is not the master of the contractual relation. Autopoiesis fragments the subjective actor's rich social fullness into diverse semantic artefacts. The rational economic persona thus created maximises efficiencies and utilities; the rule-bound legal subject fulfils contractual obligations; and the productive actor produces or consumes goods and services. None of these personae expresses the desires of the full human subject.

It would be wrong to interpret social autopoiesis as in some way giving meaning to the actors within the process. Instead, autopoiesis suggests that ongoing communication acts produce their own meanings in the form of semantic artefacts. Within the overall stream of talk in society, specialised languages emerge for each of the functionally differentiated systems. Each of these creates its own artificial 'homunculi' actors, such as the 'legal person' or the 'homo economicus'.

It is also often not clear who the actor actually is. For instance, according to some economic theories the corporate actor is the corporation itself. Other theories identify the resource bearing employees of the enterprise. Most contracts are based on the same actors participating in all relevant worlds, although in many cases the contractual partner is different in different worlds, as when the 'legal person' appears in different productive or economic worlds as a manager, worker or the organisational entity itself.

Socio-Animism[1]: the collectivist danger of autopoiesis

Durkheim's concept of the 'collective consciousness' refers to the parts of our psychic lives, which integrate into a social consciousness, that is more than just individual motives and actions (see Chapter 6). In autopoiesis, however, meaning emerges in the social sphere as a way of processing information and putting it into a multitude of different contexts, then moving from one actualisation to another. This can be regarded as a form of 'socio-animism'.

When a lawyer or economist or poet creates a work of meaning, the important thing in an autopoietic system is not what that work means to its author's individual psyche, but the way the work gains in meaning when it moves through different worlds. This is similar to the way in which the legal world interprets a contract in terms of its observable meaning, rather than according to the subjective motivations of individual actors.

To some extent, autopoiesis thus reifies collectivities and deconstructs the reality of the actor through socio-animism. This process has implications for what it means to observe. It multiplies the number of observational perspectives as the observer is not identified just with the mind of an individual agent but with a 'chain of distinctions', which could be a human actor or an ongoing process of communication involving people. Rather than see observers as persons who stand outside of the social activity, which they observe and reflect on, observation and criticism is located in systems of communication. What is commonly conceived of as individuals commenting on social life, is reconceived in autopoiesis as the ability of systems of communication to communicate about events, and even to develop communications about themselves. Thus for example, lawyers don't simply comment on law as impartial observers, they utilise communications (including ideals) developed within law in order to communicate about law. Economists can criticise law, but they utilise the communications of economics to produce an observation and critique. There is no possibility of abstract observation and critique as a human being, but only observation and critique within systems of communication. Once this is accepted, there is a danger of concluding that there is really no human subjectivity separate from systems, and that it makes as much sense to speak of law observing itself (Teubner 1989), as lawyers criticising law.

1   A social version of animism, which is the belief that animals and natural phenomena have souls or spirits as well as a material existence.

However, social autopoiesis based on Luhmann's principles creates a distance between real people and their engagement in social processes, which also makes clear we are dealing with profound and infinite dynamics that never intersect with each other. Autopoietic systems theory recognises consciousness as psychic autopoeisis, but sees it as parallel to – and in competition with – several autonomous 'language games'. Theories which can too easily conjure up a merging of the individual with the social (such as Marxism) can be very dangerous in certain political arenas (consider the experience of Soviet Russia, and Nazi Germany). Individual or psychic autopoiesis can, hopefully, provide some resistance to this temptation to dissolve the individual into the social.

Intervention and innovation in social autopoiesis

The clear boundaries between functionally differentiated autopoietic worlds and the resultant impossibility of direct influence of each internal world across those boundaries means autopoietic influence can occur only through internal reconstruction. This has profound implications for concepts of political, legal and other intervention. Any attempt at intervention must now recognise the internal dynamics of autopoietic systems, which direct any external force away from the paths and goals sought by the external influencers. This has implications for issues such as juridification (the ever increasing proliferation of legal rules in modern societies) and regulatory failure (the failure of vast amounts of such rules to influence behaviour in the manner desired, or often, their failure to have any influence at all on conduct).

Autopoietic insights allow fresh attempts to be made to find more indirect forms of influence that accept they will be subjected to the changes brought about by internal meaning worlds. The central problem becomes that of the degree to which external guidance or regulation can lead to innovation. In autopoietic systems, innovation is not caused by outside change as such (law telling others what to do) but depends on the degree to which a system is able to construct novelties that may be triggered by perturbations in the outside world (law, or any other system, inducing reconfigurations of the communications within the other system). Metaphors can be used here. The contacts between a system and the environment caused by these perturbations are reduced to external 'hammering' – perturbations having no meaning until their informational 'noise' has been interpreted internally by the system. Some attempts at intervention elicit no response – an example of deafness. Some attempts produce new configurations (order from noise). At its extreme, this leads to intervention in which the external intervener perturbs the internal world exposing its limitations. The most extreme of these limitations can be described as 'paradoxes'. One example (relevant to most of Part I of this book) is that law, which codes what is legal and illegal, has no ultimate basis for deciding what should be legal as opposed to illegal. It is just an endless process of communicating the distinction. (This 'paradox' may demystify much of the Positivist-Dworkin debate on the division between applying law and making law). 'It is legal, because it is legal' is the ultimate paradox of law. Suggestions that it might be legal because it is 'just' collapse when it is realised that Law's recognition of what is just, in its operations, is limited to what it recognises as legal. Law is quite vulnerable to any demand for the basis of the legal/illegal distinction to be located in some fundamental fact or value. A constitutional crisis can be viewed as a situation which exposes this paradox (would anything you have read in Part I equip you to respond to demands in the media or politics for the fundamental basis of legality to be explained and justified?).

Another variant of this same paradox, and an example of the kind of changes produced by perturbation, is the meaning of miscarriage of justice within criminal justice. Not everything which occurs in law is considered just. Law generates critiques of its own earlier communications, and is capable of declaring them to be mistakes (a feature of the development of doctrine as well as the identification of miscarriages of justice). Not only does the basis for such criticism and judgements have no ultimate justification outside of the linguistic practices of the participants, but the ability of law to recognise earlier communications (convictions) as mistakes will not correspond to what other systems of communication identify as Law's mistakes. The sustained media campaign on miscarriages of justice toward the end of the last century (Guildford Four, Birmingham Six etc) exposed Law's inability, given its practices for identifying miscarriages of justice, to respond to dense media and political communications about the innocence of many persons serving life sentences for murder. Eventually Law responded. The reforms of law (the most important of which went to changes in the rights of appeal) will not prevent such perturbations occurring again, as Law's communications about miscarriages continue to differ from those made in the media and politics. Nevertheless, the pressure of media and political communications on Law and its failings did produce change (Nobles and Schiff 2000).

The potential for being stubbornly unchanging or highly adaptive depends on the extent to which a system can break, or deconstruct, its internal chain of distinction in order to react to its environment. Systems with higher internal sensitivity to the opportunities created by perturbations will be more creative and adaptable. If the system does not have the potential to create internal variety, innovation will not take place. Such stability might even be a good survival strategy in a very turbulent world. But it should be recognised that social communication in itself can be highly innovative through the autopoietic process of creative misunderstanding.

Social autopoiesis is particularly appropriate as a tool for analysing the highly fragmented nature of modern society. It is less valuable in looking at societies where there is tight integration of legal, religious and political aspects in communication. At a global level, the unpredictable dynamics of autopoiesis argues against the unrealistic view of those who believe that it is possible to move world society in a desired direction via a deliberative global democratic process. An autopoeitic understanding reveals such enterprises as necessarily utopian. Autopoiesis is closer to the 'new polytheism' of Weber which suggests different rationalities have developed their own systems and that people are exposed to these ongoing rationalising process without being able to create a super-process to control those systems.

This approach should result in a modest attitude to how far organised political processes can cope with chaotic, uncontrollable autopoietic forces. It leaves the only feasible strategy as one which seek goals like containment and reduction of conflict, not the creation of a benign omnipotent controlling process.

Luhmann (*Law as a Social System* 144–150 (1989))

Every complex system must balance variety, that is, the number and diversity of its basic elements, against redundancy. In a complex environment it is not possible to operate in a completely rigid fashion, without surprises. Rather, the system must be open to irritations that disrupt the usual practice. If the law, however, is to provide security, this openness cannot be carried too far. There must be a provision for redundancy so that knowledge of one or more elements (knowledge of important court decisions, for example, or knowledge of decisions about laws) can be relied upon to permit inferences about how the system will behave in concrete instances.

This issue of the relative degrees of variety and redundancy is closely connected to the system's relationships with its environment. One can proceed on the assumption that in interactions between elastic and rigid systems the elastic systems will adapt to the rigid ones, just as sand conforms to stone but stone does not conform to sand. A legal culture of argumentation that produces a high degree of variety, that emphasizes the individual nature of each case and is content with vague general formulas like 'proportionality' or 'balancing interests', will tend to open the legal system to adaptation to rigid environmental systems such as large-scale organizations whose form is set by technology or capital investment. Whereas a rigid, highly redundant legal system will be able to maintain itself, whatever the social consequences may be, in the face of the more elastic systems of its environment and to turn such highly elastic communications media as money or political power to its own ends.

This is only one of many examples of the way sociological analysis produces an 'alienation effect' through its special understanding of the way systems observe and describe themselves. Reconstructing argumentation as the management of redundancy does not grasp argumentation the way it is intended; it understands argumentation not as a search for convincing rational grounds but as a way of mastering contingency and as a condensation of the systemic context. The sociological description of the system's own self-description could not be accommodated within that self-description (although there is more to be said on that point). For that reason, in observing the legal system, sociological description always uses the schema manifest/latent as well, and with the help of this schema it also sees that the system does not see that it does not see what it doesn't see.

But in contrast to the aims of a critique of ideology, no unmasking or enlightening effect is intended here. Rather, this way of seeing things follows logically from the assumption that every autopoietic system differentiates its own operations with the aid of its own distinctions, and thus, if it wants to preserve this differentiation it is prevented from distinguishing itself in turn from these distinctions.

How far into legal doctrine this impossibility extends shall remain an open question here. Certainly it applies to the code itself. To deal with the question whether the distinction between justice and injustice is being used justly or unjustly would lead the system into paradoxes and block at least the operations based on this question. Observation and description of the legal system in terms of legal theory must presuppose the acceptability of the code. It may proceed neither on the basis of a tautology (justice is what is just) nor on the basis of a paradox (what is just is what is unjust). It has to 'tune out' this possibility of defining the unity of the system within the system itself; it has to de-tautologize and de-paradoxicalize the description of the system and at the same time make the operations through which this is done invisible.

If it is important to him to do so, the sociologist can observe, with the aid of the schema manifest/latent, legal theory's efforts to de-tautologize and de-paradoxicalize the system; he locates the latent functions of the manifest intention of the legal discourse, which will be directed elsewhere. In doing so, he can make use of general systems theory's distinction between natural and artificial necessities. The operations that serve to de-tautologize and de-paradoxicalize the system will seem to the system to be naturally necessary. An observer, in contrast, can recognize the function of these semantic efforts and speculate about other, functionally equivalent possibilities; to him, every specific semantic solution to this problem appears historically determined and contingent, dependent on the supply of plausibility in the specific sociohistorical circumstances.

C.

Finally, with the help of a general theory of self-referential autopoietic systems it is possible to connect systems theory to a theory of evolution more adequately than before. What results is a weakening of the concept of 'adaptation' to the environment, a concept that cannot adequately explain either the high degree of form constancy in natural evolution nor the accompanying tempo of innovations. This is true for the theory of the evolution of living systems, but even more true for the theory of social evolution.

Special evolutionary paths become possible when the differentiation of particular autopoietic systems is successful; for as soon as this occurs a system can vary its structures, insofar as this is compatible with its continued self-reproduction. In constructing and altering structures, autopoietic systems can make use of contingent impulses from the environment that occur and disappear again, as well as of errors in the reproduction of their own operations. The possibilities are often restricted more by the demands of internal consistency than by problems of survival in the environment. In other words, very often a system fails to make full use of the degrees of freedom the environment permits it and restricts its own evolution to a greater degree than would be ecologically necessary. Even with this modification to the theoretical apparatus of classical Darwinism, however, it is still correct to characterize evolution as an unplanned (not coordinated and in this sense making use of 'accidents') differentiation in variation, selection, and restabilization.

Accordingly, a theory of the evolution of law has to clarify two primary questions: (1) what problem leads to the differentiation of a particular evolution of law within a general social evolution, and (2) what is the nature of the autopoiesis of law that allows it to be maintained even when structural alterations take place? The answer to these questions must start from the principle of variation, for a specific selection mechanism can be formed only if the pertinent variation manifests specific peculiarities.

The problem that gives rise to a special evolution of the law must lie in uncertainty about whether expectations, and which expectations, can be maintained, or at least be proven to be counterfactually justified, in the case of conflict. This problem becomes relevant, if it was not so from the outset, because a segmentary social structure establishes who is to be on what side, who is to confirm claims, to take oaths, and if necessary, to fight. The evolution of law then begins with the loosening of the structures of segmentary societies, and especially with the introduction of a sufficient measure of uncertainty into social conflicts. For it then becomes a question of how this uncertainty is to be resolved, and selection criteria can be developed for that. A certain independence of religious or tribal political roles from preexisting ties of kinship or proximity was probably decisive for this development. In any case, whether or not an evolution of the law is set in motion does not depend on the prior institutionalization of the competence to make legally binding ('judicial') decisions. Such an arrangement is still inconceivable in fairly well developed late archaic societies, and presumably even for Mycenean culture. It presupposes a critical mass of already existing, already evolved legal rules that make it possible to think of this judicial competence as connected with law. Thus, in theoretical terms, the autopoiesis of law, the production of law by law, must already be possible for the central institution of a court that makes binding decisions, the institution that in turn makes possible the autopoiesis of law, to be possible. Evolution does not work directly; it works epigenetically. Only in this way can innovations that presuppose themselves arise. This is why contemporary observers give a mythic or religious interpretation to the paradox of the asymmetry in the origin of this circle: The Areopagus, for example, is instituted through divine intervention. Or, God puts the law under the bush. Or later, and in more civilized form, law is created by God in the form of human nature.

Only when adequate differentiation in variation and selection has been established, and when every legal claim is no longer both lawful and unlawful at the same time, depending on the person involved, can criteria for selection among selection criteria be developed. A long period of practicing law and observing its transformations over time is required before possibilities for distinguishing between selection and restabilization arise. The legal system that has already evolved develops possibilities for reflection, puts its own 'justice' into question, and has recourse to moral ideas in order to protect a subsistence economy (limiting tax levies and debt collection, for instance, as in the reforms of the lawgiver Solon in classical Athens). Religion and morality place limits on the structure of argumentative justification in the law, and thereby also limit the possibility of giving law the stability of tradition. In addition, due to peculiarities of its organizational practice, the law can become so complex that legal knowledge can no longer be taken for granted as part of the normal knowledge of the aristocracy. Thus there arises a need for special educational arrangements. We are familiar with the result of this process in the concept of an institution (which originally meant 'teaching'). The function of stabilizing the law is transferred to processes of doctrinalization and systematization, which then in turn outlast changes in society by virtue of their own potential for innovation, which is inherent in their concepts.

When the peculiarities of modern positive law are considered against this background, it becomes obvious that in many respects this kind of evolution no longer functions. Perhaps it is too slow for our circumstances. At any rate, the impetus to variation no longer lies in anticipating conflicts that can be expected; instead, the law regulates modes of behavior that are themselves provided with the capacity for conflict. The law itself creates the conflicts that it needs for its own evolution, and thereby perfects its own autopoiesis. It ordains, for example, that only a limited amount of wine is eligible for subsidy, and in doing so it gives rise to problems that can in turn be fed into the legal system as legal problems. As a consequence, the law evolves – there is no question of planning here – so rapidly that traditional means of stabilization no longer come into play. The law evades the control of doctrine. Nor can it any longer properly be described as a system of norms, to say nothing of a system of 'knowledge'. At this point it can only be described as a social system defined by its own code. Stabilization now lies only in the positive character of legal validity – in the fact that specific norms are given force by decisions (whether it is the decision of the legislator, the judge, or the current opinion of the commentators), and *have not yet been changed.* For this reason the stability of the law must be understood as something completely temporal, and objective questions come into the picture only from the standpoint of complexity. They make alterations difficult, and as a result, the law, despite its accelerated tempo of change, remains by and large the same.

...

III.

Legal theory has found it difficult (and perhaps it always will) to grasp this positive quality of the law in the absence of any conception of an external (especially a moral) justification. The 19th century's attempt to understand law as a guarantee of freedom (and that means freedom for irrational and immoral conduct) and thereby to accommodate it to the disintegration of the traditional unity of reason and morality, did not succeed. Even Kelsen still needs a fundamental norm, even if it is one with the ambivalent status of an epistemological hypothesis. And for the normal jurist, the idea that even good, pertinent arguments lead only to the confirmation of argumentation itself – to the strengthening of its redundancy – must still be completely unacceptable. In this situation the theory of autopoietic systems offers at least the possibility of an adequate description. Whether this description can be introduced into the legal system itself (i.e., used as its self-description) must be left an open question (which means, left to evolution). In this situation the theory of autopoietic systems can only make use of its own autopoiesis as clearly as possible.

At this point the question of the basis and the justification for legal validity leads us to assume an escalating relationship between closedness and openness in a system. Only as a self-referential closed system can the legal system develop 'responsiveness' to social interests. Viewed in this way, evolution selects (on the level of organisms as well as on the level of social systems) forms that permit greater complexity in combining closedness and openness. But that certainly does not mean better adaptation to the powers that be; it does not mean more efficient corruption.

A second, related point concerns the creative character of paradoxes. The term 'paradox' signifies here a phenomenon of observation or description – that accepting a description has as its consequence the acceptance of the opposite description. The observation of paradoxes, something which occurs, for example, in the application of the code to itself, blocks the system's observation and description, even though at the same time the observer must concede that the system's own autopoiesis is not blocked by the paradox. In other words, the system can simultaneously both be observed and not be observed as a paradoxical system. The observer must then transform this self-paradoxicalization into a quality of his object by asking how the system de-paradoxicalizes itself.

These reflections hold both for outside observation and for self-observation. Consequently, they state the problem in such a way that sociology and legal theory could collaborate on it. That would presuppose, of course, that legal theory reconceived things it had previously taken for granted and saw them now as functions of de-paradoxicalization, thus making the transition from natural to artificial necessities. And such reconceptualization will probably become possible only when sociology can offer a good deal more theoretical certainty for this step into the unknown, this illumination of what has been latent, than it has hitherto been able to do.

Coda: The creative element in social autopoiesis

The fact that autopoiesis can illuminate such issues as regulatory failure should not lead one to conclude that autopoiesis is mainly concerned with ameliorating failures of old techniques for manipulating society, say through developing new approaches to auditing and the instrumentalisation of knowledge. On the contrary, the central message of the theory comes from its understanding of the non-instrumental character of knowledge and meaning. It emphasises a creative, almost playful and artistic development of different knowledge fields. (See the extract from Luhmann below, on the creative use of paradox throughout legal history and legal theory.) This has nothing to do with the instrumental manipulation of actors or systems. There is something in legal culture which cannot be reduced to the narrow view of law as a manipulative political and economic instrument. This follows from the inability of systems to completely incorporate each other, and the lack of any common meta-language into which they can all be translated. While communications within law and politics take the form which philosophy calls 'practical reason', the communications of neither system can be reduced to this. It may be true that the internal models of certain worlds might take a more instrumentalist view of social autopoiesis (for example, politics and law may use autopoietic insights to develop indirect forms of intervention into other areas of social life). Nevertheless, social autopoiesis is essentially an aesthetic theory whose main importance is in its analysis of the way new and unexpected worlds of meaning emerge by processes which create their own realities. Any patterns of communication are only provisional. (Remember, even the game of chess continues to develop as it is played). As an example of such emerging worlds of meaning see the final extract in this chapter from Teubner.

Luhmann (*The Third Question: The Creative Use of Paradoxes in Law and Legal History* 1988, 153–165])

A recent book of Henri Atlan with the suggestive title *A tort et a raison* (wrong *and* right) begins by telling a famous story, allegedly of talmudic origin. A teacher was asked about his judgement on a question disputed by some of his students. The first student explained his point of view. After a long reflection the teacher answered 'You are right'. Then the second student, who had not been heard so far, protested and gave his reasons. And the teacher answered again, 'You are right'. Now, other students butted in, objecting that he could not accept both opinions if they contradicted each other. And the teacher, after a long reflection, once more said 'You are right'. The third question, too, received a friendly answer.

This feeling had been shared, it seems, by Tristram Shandy's father. 'Tis a pity', he said, 'that truth can only be on one side, brother Toby – considering what ingenuity these learned men have all shown in their solution.' Hence, in spite of binary coding there seem to be good reasons to give both sides their due and to accept the binary code of truth as well.

In one sense, this is harmless, innocent self-reference. The teacher presents himself as willing to see the best in every cause. In social affairs, this is the easiest way not to get mixed up with the quarrels of others. A therapist probably would react in a similar way. The therapist, too, would start by agreeing and then, remembering her or his professional obligations, would add 'but you could see it also in a different way'.

But a judge? A judge, of course, cannot be permitted to avoid taking sides. A judge has to decide. The daily problem for a judge is: who is right and who is wrong? And a judge has sufficient knowledge of the books and of life to decide the issue. But remember the third question! On one hand, the judge is not allowed to take the stance of the teacher and accept the right on both sides. But on the other hand, there might be deeper reasons to accept controversies with their right on both sides, and if this is so, what or who justifies the judge in eschewing these reasons as if they were not valid?

The judge has to pay for it, to be sure. There is nothing for nothing under the sun. The price is acceptance of the paradox of a binary code applied to itself. What, then, about the right or the wrong to decide about right and wrong? How is it that somebody has the right to say that a position or an opinion is wrong? Is there any right to invent the wrong, to create the wrong, or in more recent terms, to 'construct' the wrong?

In a famous essay Walter Benjamin made the point that there is no such right above right and wrong, no such superright. There is simply *Gewalt.* The whole Frankfurt School of 'critical theory' would join him, because, for them, critique would mean exposure of the contradictions which exist in reality, for instance the contradictions between assumed right and assumed wrong. But then we find ourselves transferred to the same issue in epistemology: how to prove with a noncontradictory logic that the reality is contradictory?

There are paradoxes everywhere, wherever we look for foundations. The founding problem of law, then, is not to find and identify the ultimate ground or reason which justifies its existence. The problem is how to suppress or to attenuate the paradox which an observer with logical inclinations or with a sufficient degree of dissatisfaction could see and articulate at any time. It remains possible to ask the third question: can we accept contradictory opinions as being both right and wrong? Or eventually: how can we rightly or wrongly differentiate the right and the wrong? At least under modern conditions we cannot avoid the issue. But it is also possible to unask the question and to transform the paradox into a less troubling issue. By some sort of *Gestalt* switch there may be ways of transforming the question which make it possible to give an answer. Or there may be answers which make it possible to ask the question.

For this lecture my proposal is to use the invisible hand of the legal paradox as a guideline for an investigation of the history of legal thought. If the assumption holds that there is always a primary necessity to avoid the paradox, there may be different ways to do so. In many ways the forms of deparadoxifying the paradox depend on conditions of social acceptability, and these conditions change with the transformations of the social system of the society. They depend on social structures and are therefore historical conditions.

The background assumption of the paradoxical foundation of the legal system (and, for that matter, of all systems working under a binary code) offers the possibility to connect logical and historical reflection and to see correlations between changes in social structures and changes in legal semantics. We have to remain at a rather detached level – at the level of the third question and at the level of observing observers. But concepts and theories developed for this level have been influential in practical matters, and I shall touch on some of these issue during the course of my lecture.

II.

First of all, we have to limit the case. There are many paradoxes in law connected with specific problems. Normally, they pass unobserved. But as soon as legal theory develops an interest in consistent reasoning and decision-making, paradoxes surface. A recent essay by George Fletcher discusses some of them; for example, the paradoxes connected with paying attention within the law to ignorance of law or to error concerning legal questions, or the paradoxes of the changing interpretation of law which has to, but cannot, refer to itself as some kind of legislation. Other paradoxes are connected with taking into account subjective self-consciousness, reflecting mitigating circumstances in breaking the law. And, again, others have to do with the so-called economic theory of law, calculating the consequences of divergent legal solutions, including the consequences of the decisions themselves for future behaviour, and then using the consequences as a criterion for the decision itself.

Fletcher shows that legal theory copes with such paradoxes by conceptual innovations. He observes two ways of handling such problems: either by abstaining from the legal practice that leads into the contradiction and by limiting the scope of attention for reasons and interests; or by finding or constructing a distinction that dissolves the paradox. Only the second technique is creative and leads to the advances in legal thought. Then, Fletcher proceeds to distinguish the innovative distinctions. There are those which have already been found or constructed and are today incorporated in the established body of legal thought; they are already law, so to speak. And there are others as yet unknown. They have to be found or constructed and remain, for the time being, a matter of further legal thought.

We may share this optimistic outlook and accompany the development of legal theory with our best wishes. But one question remains, and this is, in a different guise, again the third question. Are we sure that we can replace all emerging legal paradoxes by appropriate distinctions? What about the paradoxes implied in using distinctions, the paradoxes of the same that is treated as different? And above all, what about the paradox of defining the law by the distinction of legal and illegal?

This question leads back to my topic. I want to reformulate the third question in the following way: how can a society enforce a binary code? How can one ever be sure that the true is not untrue and the right is not wrong – given experiences which are reported in Greek tragedies or South American novels? And in addition, what happens within the legal system when the society enforces its code?

III.

The main body of my lecture will abstain from further theoretical arguments and replace them with a historical survey, comparing different types of society with respect to the ways in which they handle – within given structural and semantical limitations – this problem of binary coding.

Larger societies of the past were organised by two kinds of differences – social strata and centre/periphery. They described themselves as hierarchical order of castes or estates and were at the same time what we would call 'urban societies' or 'peasant societies', depending on the distinction between urban centres and rural periphery. Putting the emphasis on one form or the other, they could observe their unity by looking at the top or by looking at the centre. There was no problem of representing the unity of the system within the system. These societies could see their order as natural order and could therefore characterise alternatives as disorder. Ambiguities came up, and particularly so in the Middle Ages, when both forms disintegrated – that is, when the aristocracy was no longer urban aristocracy, and also when the top groups were split according to religious and political functions without clear primacy (or with a semantic primacy of religion and a real primacy of estate-based politics). But even then the system was described as a natural order, and the concept of nature had normative connotations because its antonym was disorder - and not, for example, civilisation.

These societies could easily describe law as natural law. Within old mythical traditions the genesis of order was conceived as emanation. The one (which in Greek arithmetic was not a number) generated the numbers, that is, the difference between odd and even numbers. All multiplicity came out of unity. The unmoving mover created the difference between moving and static entities. In this sense it was easy to conceive the law in the fundamental sense of eternal or divine law creating the distinction of natural and positive law and the distinction of legal and illegal behaviour as well.

By now you may see that this is a way of handling the paradox. The paradox remained invisible and became replaced with a narrative telling the genesis of distinctions. However, this semantic strategy did not succeed completely. Paradoxes have a fatal inclination to reappear. Necessities came up – or at least the urgent necessity to decide at particular occasions against the valid law, the famous *excessum iuris communis propter bonum commune.* For this purpose, new characterisations were invented which provided for new antonyms. The law was characterised as *strict and formal* – and *equity* was invented to justify its neglect in cases where it would be hard to follow the law. This distinction of cruelty and leniency *(crudelitas/clementia)* served to reject the legal code of right and wrong and to re-incorporate the law into the human society. After centuries of decision-making this distinction re-enters the law and we find a casuistry which remembers the cases in which the law itself allows for lenient, attenuating considerations. The distinction which first articulated the paradox of rejectable law is finally transformed into a device for creative social learning within the legal system.

Something similar happened with another distinction, likewise used to present a paradox and to suggest creative ways of solving it. In this case the law was characterised as *normal* – and the institution of *derogation* was invented to justify a violation of the law in view of higher necessities or utilities (and the social order left no doubt about who was and who was not able to do that). The paradox reappeared in long debates about whether derogation is an institution of natural law, permitting the violation of natural law, or whether it can and has to be justified as positive law only in view of postlapsarian conditions. The first opinion could refer to Cicero's dictum *communis utilitas derelicto contra naturam est*. The second requires a psychological brake. It has to be practised *a regret et en soupirant* as Gabriel Naude recommends.

However, the paradox not only reappeared, it also revanished. As soon as equity and derogation evolve into a system of definitions and rules – and what else could a jurist do with them – the paradox makes an evasive move, being unprepared to accept regulations. As Wittgenstein asked, 'What use is a rule to us here? Could we not (in turn) go wrong in applying it?'

[As with 'rules of equity', think of how to formulate rules for emergencies when the order that law relies on is threatened. Can one write rules for disorder? Attempts to do so, elucidating on 'states of emergency' can never be complete even though they might appear to be; the paradox can always reappear.]

IV.

During the seventeenth and eighteenth centuries a remarkable change occurred. The third question looks for new answers. The paradox of law looks for new places to hide away. It appears in new disguises, more appropriate to changing social conditions. The law of nature contracts and becomes the law of reasonable arguments, supposing that reason at least is the nature of human beings. This gives more freedom from theological supervision and more hope for progress by refining and improving the self-control of human affairs. Reason appeals to reason as the last court which is supposed to be able to judge its own affairs. Hence, the paradox is maintained as tautology – as a distinction which is supposed to be none: as reasonable reason. (For affairs not suitable for the jurisdiction of reason, we find at roughly the same time parallel concepts of self-authentification, that is, taste for art and love for intimate relations.)

And again, the paradox reappears, being more sophisticated than reason itself. In practical affairs of acquisition and use of property, reason argues with equal voice for equality and inequality. The desire for property and its accumulation is clearly wrong, violating the natural (and the created!) equality of human beings. And the demand for equality is clearly wrong, violating the law of property. How, then, to drive the paradox back into its invisible retreat?

One easy solution consists in using a double concept of nature. Natural reason may demand to surpass nature. 'Men are born naked, but they are clearly better off in clothes'. But then we have to face the question whether nature teaches us that we are better off with an unequal distribution of property.

For more than one century, the question of property becomes the problem in terms of which the foundations of the society are discussed. 'Le partage des biens est la première loi de la société, et le tronc, pour ainsi dire, de toutes les autres lois', wrote the Marquis de Mirabeau. Jurists tend to recognise a contract, albeit an implicit contract, because the acquisition and use of property implies the recognition of the property of others. Also, until the second half of the eighteenth century, the society itself is thought to have been based on contract with roughly the same kind of argument. Thus, there is no place for separating state and society; the deparadoxification has to take place within the context of reflections about political society or civil society, and the arguments have to lead back to its *origin*.

In this sense, the authors of the seventeenth and eighteenth centuries used thoughts of Greek and Roman origin to reformulate the paradox. The form was again a quasi-mythical narration. At the beginning there was communal property in the state of nature. But then, the multiplication of people and the invention of arts and sciences made it advisable to separate the goods and to give the chance to augment her or his property to each individual. For a certain time, the selections of Roman materials under the heading of 'about acquiring property' played a decisive role in legitimating the law as such. During a long discussion, distinctions became refined. Pufendorf, basing himself on Grotius, introduced the famous distinction of negative and positive community of property – the negative being in a sense property *avant la lettre* (property before the law), the positive being private property with more than one owner. John Locke added the idea that the real reason for the distinction of state of nature and civilisation was the necessity of organising labour, and that the situation became problematic only by the invention of money taking away any limits of acquiring and preserving property.

I cannot go into details here, but have to mention two points. The first is that, in this account, the origin of property has to be a mythical one, not simply a historical state. Hence, the whole structure of deparadoxification became vulnerable to historical and comparative research. This happened in the middle of the eighteenth century, particularly in the writings and lectures of David Hume and Adam Smith. Secondly, if we decipher the structure of the thought looking through its mythical form, we find the idea of natural rights. Natural rights are rights whose recognition does not depend on complementary obligations. They are rights in the sense of Thomas Hobbes or Jeremy Taylor, that is, rights before the law, rights not depending on the recognition of others (for example, the right to preserve and to move one's own body, the old *potestas in se ipsum*) – that is, rights before the distinction of right and wrong. You may recognise it: it is a paradoxical right, a right answering the third question.

But this is a concept of the seventeenth century. The eighteenth century, preoccupied with morality and reason, found what seemed to be good arguments against this concept and insisted that there could not be rights without complementary obligations. Of course not! The paradox has to remain invisible. But then, where does it hide now?

V.

In the course of the eighteenth century, the strategy of deparadoxification became reversed. The tradition had started with the idea of an innocent beginning. Once there had been a golden age. Once, in the state of nature, human beings could live according to their needs in a state of communal peace. Then, deterioration set in and mechanisms to compensate needs. Already in the seventeenth century doubts were raised about this version, as in Hobbes, but the countermodel could not really be constructed. There was the dispute of the ancients and the moderns and there was the idea that, on the whole, we might be better off in modern times. But only in the second half of the eighteenth century do we find the complete reversion. Only then do we find the idea that the beginning was wrong, that the beginning was violence, or that it consisted in the enclosure of property and the co-operation of people stupid enough to believe that this was just. Therefore, it was felt that only the process of civilisation would take us into a better future and justify the past in retrospect. The hidden message of the paradise lost was no longer sin (which presupposes the law) but the violence of God, expelling Adam and Eve from the garden of Eden and preventing their return by his armed troops.

We find this new look with authors who rejected the idea of a contractual foundation of the law – an idea which is evidently tautological (that is, paradoxical) in founding the law on the presupposition of the law. We find this rejection and the corresponding foundation of law on violence in Linguet, one of those writers of the French post-enlightenment who were particularly fond of frivolous paradoxes. And we find it, better known, but also less intriguing, in Kant.

At the beginning was violence. Forget it. Things are much better by now and we can embark on further improvements, for instance by designing a constitution . But then, are we to know the unknown, the future? And do we, in rejecting the past, reject the story of the Tower of Babel as well?

At any rate, the paradox, like the sun, passes underground and reappears in the future. The attempts to domesticate it by reasonable elaboration fail, of course. The Kantian inflation of hopes regarding the foundations of law failed to impress professional men in law, in religion, and in pedagogy as well. The famous names are Gustav Hugo and Anselm, Feuerbach, but a whole school of thought developed which criticised the inexact and superficial ways in which Kantianism had been transferred into jurisprudence. At that time, a science of the positive law was in demand, and the options seemed to be whether the positive law should be designed by conceptual constructions, taking the historical experiences of generations of lawyers into account, or whether, on the base of the constitutional state, legislation should be the preferred road into the future.

The paradox now disguises itself as the splendid future of divine mankind, the future of freedom and equality, the future of emancipation and democratic constitutions, or the future of the greatest happiness of the greatest number of people, and finally as the future of the communist society as the new state of nature, the state after the state, after property, after all divisions and distinctions. The paradox prevents observations and descriptions, the future being unobservable by itself anyway. The future becomes the grand excuse for all the misdeeds of the new industrial society, the grand excuse for applying the law which the society itself produces according to a calculus of interest and, increasingly, as a reaction to its own self-created problems.

And again, as always, we find more technical forms of deparadoxification. One of them is the distinction between legislation and administration of justice. Statutes have to be general, court decisions have to apply the law to the concrete case. The production of law has to proceed without paying attention to particular cases, and it finds its justification, if not its innocence, in its general form. Court decisions have to distribute the symbols 'right and wrong' to particular circumstances, taking the validity of the law as given. In many senses, this is not the final answer. There remain the well-known problems of self-referring laws and the problem of circular loops between legislation and adjudication. But these are theoretical concerns. In practice, the institutional role differentiation works sufficiently well, and remaining problems can be collected under the heading of 'legitimacy', understood as the popularity of governments, exposed to periodic elections. Moreover, it is now easy to solve a very old paradox, that is the paradox of the right to change the law. The legal system may recognise political motives as sufficient for changing the law – but only at the level of legislation and not at the level of adjudication.

This, too, is a way to replace the paradox by a distinction. Moreover, its distinctive feature is avoiding any reference to natural law or morality, having recourse to positive law only. This makes it meaningful to replace the distinction of right and wrong with the distinction of legal and illegal and thereby in addition attenuate the problem. What had been a morally upsetting paradox can now be seen as a simple contradiction between morality and legality – for example, a morally-required disobedience to the law.

The other modern device is the result-oriented practice on both levels, in legislation and in court decisions. What counts is not a principle, nor a logical deduction, nor the elegant conceptual construction, but the difference a decision effectuates either in social reality or in the legal system itself. Are legal effects therefore the criterion of law? This is certainly not a convincing theory but it is the usual practice and the distinguishing mark of the good lawyer. It is something like cutting the future into small chunks that can be handled in the situations of daily life. But again and nevertheless, the future remains unobservable. The legal decisions claim to be right (and not wrong) immediately and remain so, whether their intended results come about or not at a later time.

Logically then, the validity of a programme depends on its own execution. The execution of the programme becomes the condition of the execution of the programme. Hang the man if – and only if – you hang him. This instruction, of course, would make issues undecidable. You really need the future – that is, your present opinions about the future – to discriminate decisions and to deparadoxify a self-conditioned conditional programme. But then you have the question: whose guesses about the future are valid guesses, which is the question: who is in power?

When this form of deparadoxification becomes institutionalised we can expect a need for compensating mechanisms, in particular for self-correcting devices. When the results do not show up, the law has to be changed accordingly. The future remains the future, the problems change their shape, the situations can be handled in one sense or another. The legal system grows by what can be called, using a linguistic term, hypercorrection. The machine ends by being constantly in repair. The promoting paradox remains invisible.

VI.

We could make a dream out of this, perhaps a nightmare – the crumbling tower of Babel without the hope for the celestial Jerusalem. We could also decide to risk another look at the paradox or to ask the third question again.

An answer to the third question is a way to put a basement under the building, a basement in which the secrets of the system can be preserved, or, as some would rather suppose, the corpses. We need this basement as the rule without exception, that is, as the exception to the rule that there are no rules without exception. We need it as the paradox.

It may not be obvious that we need a paradoxical foundation at all. To be sure, the language of law permits the construction of sentences which are inconsistent. This is true for all language specialised on cognition, and so much more for normative languages. But why do we not simply avoid these pitfalls, why not steer clear of certain questions and certain constructions and, with this precaution, use the language of law without the embarrassment of looking into the Gorgonian face of the paradox? Even logicians and philosophers try, in constructing formal systems, to design exclusion-devices or to simply put an embargo on what otherwise would seem to be a possible move. We know that this does not work, except *ad hoc*. But what prevents us from doing it nevertheless? It could be sufficient to say that there are rules with exceptions and rules without exceptions. Or that there be right claims and wrong claims. But then, what is indicated by the 'and' and what is excluded by the 'and'? Nothing. The 'and' serves as the joker replacing within the system the unity of the system. Like the end of the system the 'and' of the systems operates as symbol for the unity of the system within the process of reproducing the system — here and now. It is not a sufficient description of the unity of the system. It is again a hiding-place of the paradox.

The unity of the system is not something outside of the system. It is not something inside the system. How and where, then, can we observe the unity? The system is the multiplicity of its operations. It never acts as this multiplicity, it never acts as the network of its operations — for example, as the network of all the legal decisions. It is nothing but the constraints produced by one decision for others of the same system. These constraints exclude other possibilities of the same system. But then, how do we justify these exclusions — for example, of women from certain clubs, of non-owners from property, of prisoners from freedom? The system itself contains these excluded possibilities. If you have clubs, you have members and non-members. If you have prisons you have people inside and outside prison. For every owner of a house there are by now five billion non-owners of this house. How to cope with these atrocities? Technically speaking, exclusion-devices may work sufficiently well. The law can forbid or make it simply invalid to ask the third question. It may prescribe the expulsion from office of a judge who behaves like a wise person. And indeed, we all know that there is a law which forbids the defiance of justice. This makes it possible to ignore the problem. It does not eliminate it.

From a systems point of view we can, following Talcott Parsons, make a distinction between this technical level of the execution of social functions and an institutional level at which a system has to reflect its integration into the encompassing system of the total society. More recent theories make a distinction between 'natural' and 'artificial' devices for handling the paradoxes of self-reference or between internal and external observation. These differences in conceptual style reflect advances in systems theory which we can leave aside at the moment. My final question is, rather, are there structural reasons in modern society which make it appropriate to enforce this two-level thinking on the legal system and to provide for higher levels of description, be it internal or external, which go beyond merely technical advice? And my proposal will be that in modern society this is not simply a question of legitimation in the sense of taking into account symbolically shared values in communicating the intentions which guide your actions. Indeed, this is too easy to do. The problem is, rather, to improve on the transparency of the internal workings of functionally differentiated systems for themselves and for others. But if paradoxes are the crucial obstacles for observing systems, and if the ways in which systems treat their paradoxes produce transparencies and intransparencies as two sides of the same coin, then this issue has to replace the rather trivial topic of legitimation. And the distinction between the two levels of operative theories and of reflective theories, of technical advice in legal problem solving and of reflection upon the ways in which a system becomes understandable for itself and for others, may become not the solution of the problem and certainly not a new technique of self-legitimation, but at least an adequately differentiated way to produce descriptions.

Now, all this may seem to be a highly theoretical problem without any impact on practical affairs. Lawyers who are programmed for decisions are likely to find this sort of problem uninspiring. My intention has been to show that this is not the case. The historical survey teaches that there is one general technique of avoiding the third question, namely replacing it by a distinction. The code of the legal system, the distinction between right and wrong or, for modern conditions, between legal and illegal acts, is itself a first scheme to articulate the paradox, to found the possibility of self-reference. But then, further distinctions are needed to solve the resulting problems, distinctions like rigid justice and equity, or rules and exceptions, or the distinctions of property, or the differentiation between statutes and court decisions, or between decisions with more or less preferred consequences for legitimate interests. On this level of secondary distinctions the law adapts to social evolution and, in particular, to its own increasing differentiation. These distinctions have a technical side. They are undisputed assumptions in the reasonings of lawyers as persons of practical competence. But they have also an institutional side mediating between the decisions and the unity of the system. 'Saving distinction' – this is the recipe for solving the paradox, and 'saving' should be taken in the double sense of saving the system in spite of the paradox by using a distinction and saving the distinction itself by the operation that makes use of them.

The prevailing opinion in legal and social science describes the unity of the system as a value, representing the social and cultural autonomy of its task. The legal system then has to implement justice. This comes close to being tautological. In my opinion, the unity of a system is realised by its guiding *distinction*. The legal system then has to implement the distinction of legality and illegality. This comes close to being paradoxical, seeing unity as the unity of a difference.

These are clearly competing theories. We will have to choose between beginning and ending with unity or with difference. And there is no other final answer to the third question.

Teubner (*Altera pars audiatur: Law in the Collision of Discourses* 1997, 149–176)

POLYTHEISM AND (POST-)MODERNITY

It is like the days of old when the world was full of many gods and demons, only different; it is like when the Greeks made sacrifices, one time to Aphrodite, another time to Apollo and above all to the gods of their home towns, only today the magical and mythical is missing from existent conduct. It is fate that reigns supreme over all the gods and their struggles, and definitely not knowledge. (Max Weber)

Today the only god left to whom law is supposed to make sacrifices is called rational choice. Over the past thirty years, a quasi-religious academic movement has spread through all the law schools of North America with a particular zeal. After its high priest, Richard Posner announced 'the demise of law as an autonomous discipline', economic rationality is supposed to represent the new universality of law. Theory of transaction costs, theory of property rights, public choice and economic analysis of law are different currents in the broad stream of a movement which is intent on replacing the emaciated concept of justice with the ideal of the economic efficiency of law. This new monotheism speaks with the pathos of natural law in the name of both 'nature' and 'reason'. The internal laws of the market and of organisation are in the nature of modern society and law has to reflect them. The philosophy of 'rational choice' elaborates on the principles of reason in this new order and they apply to law as well.

Law and economics claims to be the new victorious paradigm which eliminates older moral-political orientations of law, and it does not tolerate the co-existence of any other paradigms alongside it. 'Thou shalt have no other gods but me'. Law and economics justifies its exclusivity with its historic victory in modern societies, with the society-wide, and today almost worldwide institutionalisation of economic rationality. Its strength lies here, without doubt, for who can reject the argument that modern society is economic society and that modern law has to provide market-adequate, economy-adequate legal forms?

At the same time, this is exactly the great weakness of the law and economics movement. Economic rationality does not have the privilege of society-wide institutionalisation all to itself. There has, indeed, been a paradigm shift. However, it is heading in a different direction. It is not the case of eliminating moral-political monotheism in favour of economic monotheism which law needs only to reflect. Rather, it is the case of a change from monotheism to polytheism, from the monotheism of modern rationality to a polytheism of the many discourses. There is a paradigm shift to the particularistic rationalities of the many gods to which law has to respond in other ways than by just adopting a new god.

Apart from economics, it is, above all, politics, science and technology, the health sector, the media, the law and possibly also the morality of lifeworlds which have all individually developed their own self-centred rationalities. They all expose a strange contradiction. On the one hand, they are all clearly particularistic rationalities. On the other hand, they are all institutionalised, in effect, society-wide and they all demand universal acceptance. In this way, the cost-benefit calculus of economic rationality is only institutionalised in economic transactions; however, economisation takes hold of the whole society and rational choice makes its claims in all social contexts. Accordingly, rational choice also demands law's obedience. Efficiency instead of justice. The same is true for political rationality. Democratic legitimation of power is typically only institutionalised in the political context. Nevertheless the ideal of democracy demands society –wide acceptance and, accordingly, realisation in law. Democratic legitimacy today is seen as the only valid foundation of law. Again, the core of scientific rationality

– uncompromising search for intersubjective truth – is essentially only institutionalised in teaching and research. However, scientification is a society-wide process which forces even the law to take a scientific approach in its regulatory aspirations. Finally, moral criteria develop typically only through concrete small-scale interactions as evidence of mutual esteem. Nevertheless morals, especially in their academic forms of philosophical ethics systems, want to regulate all social, today especially ecological issues and request a hearing on legal issues as well.

If all these belief-systems were only airy-fairy theoretical constructs, mere philosophical abstractions, law could easily reject their claims for universality as merely academic. However, the many new gods do not just create faint theologies. They exercise their firm power grip in concrete world-regimes. Max Weber's 'iron cages' or, as one would say today, 'computer networks of a new domination' have their foundations in social practices themselves. These universal regimes of particularism have five characteristics of social effectiveness which render their influence on law well nigh irresistible.

First, their material base consists of manifest *social practices*, on which the distinctions of the various universalities have been inscribed. Markets and business organisations, elections and political associations, government and opposition, research practices and technologies, information systems of the media and the agencies of health and social security systems all demand from law specific regulatory measures which have to reflect the universal principles of particularism which each of these entities has institutionalised separately. The modern plurality of gods is not a matter of individual belief but is a hard social reality which is forced inexorably upon law. To the detriment of its effectiveness, law has to abandon the simple model of threatening (dis)obedient subjects with sanctions and must reformulate its norms in order to 'match' specific constraints in the economic, political and scientific-technological domains.

Secondly, neither are these social practices mere conventions, brought about by the typical economic, political, scientific, or ethical motives of actors. Rather, the many gods have created many theologies, elaborate social abstractions in the form of self-concepts and *reflexive theories* which in turn control and rationalise the practices. As we said, they are bold enough not to respect their own boundaries. Each of these partial reflexive theories claims to be accepted as the one and only one universal rationality. Economic theory has long since crossed the borders of its specific domain of the economy and claims to be the valid theory of society which interprets society as a giant network of cost benefit calculations. The same applies to political theory which in its turn reduces society into conflicts of interest and power between groups and political aggregates. As both these reflexive theories are not restricted to cognitive issues only, serious consequences emerge for law. Both theories develop, each by itself, mutually exclusive normative concepts about a just society which compete, as political justice or economic justice, with a specific legal justice. Beyond economics and politics, sensitive observers have discovered other 'spheres of justice' in many social domains which present their own autonomous concepts of a non-legal justice.

Thirdly, the many gods have even taken residence in the inner sanctum of law, in *legal theory and jurisprudence*. Of course, 'political theories of law' are not new; there is a long tradition of providing concepts of law from the perspective of political sovereignty. Today, however, political theories of law have experienced an extraordinary radicalisation, ranging from old German *Freirecht* and American legal realism, the international movement of law and society, and the more recent critical legal studies movement to feminist jurisprudence and critical race theories. In their way of destructing the legal in law, they are only surpassed by recent economic theories of law. 'Law is politics' is the war cry of critical legal studies, but is now drowned out by the war cry 'law is economics'. As if that were not enough, we can hear today a crescendo of aesthetical-antirational theories of law announcing the ultimate deconstruction of the legal proprium.

Fourthly, legal practice itself has not been spared the plurality of gods either. Politicisation, moralisation, scientification and economisation of legal practice itself have profoundly changed methods of judicial decision-making and their use of *legal doctrine*. Although the results are strikingly different, the new method is always the same: law plays society. Legal decision-making is invited to play-act. Legal reasoning is supposed to simulate the practices of other social subsystems in order to produce socially adequate norms, that is norms which do reflect the inner logic of law's social environments. Balancing interests as a judicial method is a typical simulation of the political process. The predominant purpose-orientation in legal practice and the regulatory spirit of modern law necessitate simulations of scientific-technical behaviour. The appeal to community values asks for a simulation of moral universalisation. The model of a hypothetical contract situation simulates economic behaviour, law mimics the market.

Fifthly, the most powerful weapon yet of the new polytheism may be the creation of an array of various independent machineries of *social norm production* which produce legal norms directly from outside the law, from the various subsystems of society. With the help of these machineries, heterogeneous particularistic rationalities and their normative claims massively infiltrate the law which has little control over them. The most productive extra-legal rule-making machines which are driven by the inner logics of one specialized social domain are installed in various formal organisations and processes of standardization which are competing today with the legislative machinery and the contracting mechanism. In the light of their massive operations, the question as to whether or not law should remain 'pure' as against the contaminations of particularistic rationalities of society has long since been decided. It is no longer a question as to whether or not, but only as to how!

FROM POLYTHEISM TO POLYCONTEXTURALITY

This scenario may sound very much like the patchwork of post-modernity, but it by no means refutes the modernity of law. On the contrary, the pluralisation of discourses to which law is subject today is the typical modern experience which only is stylized anew in the post-modernist gesture. This is why we find the fundamental analysis of the new polytheism not with the contemporary theoreticians of discourse plurality but back with Max Weber, the grand old man of modern social and legal theory. Late modern and post-modern authors are refining and elaborating Max Weber's analyses. At the same time, however, they radicalize his ideas on the new polytheism. What can we gain from this debate stretching from Max Weber to Francois Lyotard as to the position of law in the plurality of discourses?

Max Weber analysed modernity as the era of absolute polytheism. Parallel historical processes of rationalising different value spheres have led to insoluble conflicts between the many gods of modernity, between depersonalised powers of belief which cannot be resolved or removed through reference to the One Reason. These conflicts, Max Weber submitted, have to be endured, have to be suffered subjectively and individually. We have to live through these conflicts in a chain of ultimate decisions.

Max Weber articulated the collision of discourses only vaguely and metaphorically as 'the struggle of the gods', that is, as a conflict of the spheres of ideal values. In the later discussion, this problem has been redefined sociologically as a real phenomenon of society and analyzed more precisely by linguistics as a collision of different 'grammars'. Weber took his metaphor from the sociology of religion where the old polytheism of the Greeks appeared to be replaced temporarily by the Judaeo-Christian monotheism, only to resurface in modern times as the struggle between depersonalised powers of belief, between spheres of secularised values. The crucial aspect of the collision according to Weber is the insoluble contradiction between knowledge and values, on the one hand, and the antagonism between the different spiritual spheres, the good, the holy, and the beautiful, on the other hand.

Wittgenstein's plurality of language games gives the collision of values a linguistic turn which deprives it of its transcendental motives articulated by Weber and which, as it were, naturalises it. 'Language games' collide because of their idiosyncratic structures of rules which can be referred neither to principles of reason nor to abstract values, but only to the practice of real 'forms of life' in society: 'One could say that what is given and what has to be accepted are forms of life'.

The contemporary discussion elaborates in more detail the grammars of language games, analyses more accurately the social practices at their roots and assumes the incommensurability of discourses and the lack of any meta-discourse. Today, at the provisional conclusion of the debate, we find Francois Lyotard's distinction between *litige and differend* of the discourses, Niklas Luhmann's plurality of closed self-referential systems and Jurgen Habermas's normative propositions as to how to resolve discourse collisions. From these perspectives, the conflicts to which law is subject today, do not result from colliding ideal values but from colliding real social practices with their own logic and with an enormous potential for self-inflicted damage. Law is not called upon to decide the eternal conflicts between the holy, the good, the utilitarian, the true, the just and the beautiful. Law is exposed to potentially destructive conflicts between concretely conducted discourses in society, between self-reproductive concatenations of *enonces* which are conditioned by an internal grammar and by binary codes and programmes, which reproduce their internal logic with hermetic closure.

Recent theorizing has produced more than mere refinements and greater detail. Contributions from, above all, systems theory and deconstructivism have radicalised Max Weber's proposition of a new polytheism in all its three elements – plurality, god, and conflict.

First, the diagnosis of plurality – the assumption of a social poly-centrism – is too harmless as it is, for instance, proposed by Schluchter in his interpretation of Weber's work. Polycentricity still maintains the comforting assumption of an ultimate unity of context in which various centres of action co-exist – as it were, the Olympus of the gods. It is replaced today by a more threatening 'polycontexturality', that is, a plurality of mutually exclusive perspectives which are constituted by system/environment operations and which are not compatible with one another.

Second, Max Weber's many gods who, even after secularisation, still represent basic authorities in the sphere of values are replaced today by strange paradoxes lurking at the foundation of social discourses and threatening to paralyze the observer. Quasi-religious value as the basis of a discourse has given in to paradox, the new 'fondement mystique de l'autorite'.

Third, the severity of the conflict between the gods appears to have dramatically increased. This is no longer a competition between different value systems; in the contemporary view of discourse collisions the 'warring gods' have assumed almost self-destructive proportions. According to Lyotard discourses are so hermetically closed that they deny each other the right to be heard and only do 'violence', 'tort', 'injustice' to one another. According to Luhmann and Habermas, social systems have developed such powerful and uncontrollable internal dynamics that they not only overburden individuals and harm the ecology, but also have disintegrating effects upon one another. Truly, the struggle between the new powers of belief produces a tortious society, if not a tortured society.

A NEW CONFLICT OF LAWS

The recent debate has not only changed the perspective on the phenomena of collision but also questioned Weber's 'solution' of the collision problem – subjectivisation. Weber identified the individual subject as the true victim of the struggle of the gods and he celebrated the tragedy of individuals in their inevitably guilt-ridden decisions about conflicts and coping with them. Today attention has moved away from individuals to discourses. Not only individuals but also discourses, and among them law, are exposed to the conflicts which they have created for themselves. Society does harm to itself in its different discourses. Weber could still believe that the spheres of values could be kept out of the problems of collision successfully by the sophistication of their formal rationality. This explains his celebration of the formal rationality of law. This explains also why he was so suspicious about substantive rationality, why he dismissed and marginalised all the moralisation, politicisation and economisation of law.

Nonetheless, Weber got it wrong. Formalisation did not protect the law against infiltration through extra-legal rationalities. Above, we have already inspected the Trojan horses which today successfully lead the extra-legal normativities into the empire of law. We found: (1) norms produced outside the legal system which compete with the norms produced in courts; (2) extra-legal references in doctrinal analysis and legal method which materialise the formal law; and (3) non-legal theories of law which destroy the unity of jurisprudential reflections of law.

Law cannot be kept immune against the collision of different rationalities by formalisation. Of course, formalisation changes the quality of the collisions because the universality of law is protected against immediate competition from other universalities by formal coding. The legal code of law/not law rejects the codes of other discourses, such as true/false, moral/immoral, have/have not, government/opposition. However, this is only a matter of replacement. The other discourses which have been defeated at the level of codes return even more vigorously at the level of legal programmes and wreak havoc on law from that point. The arguments which are used in legal argumentation, reasons of policy, cost-benefit calculations and moral grounds will always defer to the legal code of legal/illegal but will nevertheless rule as the successful criteria which control the distribution of the values of legal and illegal. Law cannot get rid of the threatening polycontexturality of society by, first, contributing to it in producing its own rationality and, second, by observing the pluralism of the other social rationalities through the looking-glass of its own rationality. No, the repressed fragmentation of society is returning in the inner workings of formalised law as a fragmentation of law itself, even if modified by the specific legal perspective.

Therefore, we are faced with legal pluralism in a more radical sense than how the term is used in current legal sociology. It does not just refer to a plurality of local laws, of ethnic and religious rule-systems or of institutions and organisations. Rather, it refers to a plurality of incompatible rationalities, all with a claim to universality within a modern legal system. Different social particularistic rationalities have formed bridgeheads within the law from which they operate in the designing of mutually incompatible legal concepts, to represent alternative doctrinal arguments and methods, and to project norms which contradict each other. Given this situation, there may be a temptation in the Law's Empire to give in and to hand over the unity of law to one of those bridgeheads. If it is impossible to constitute the unity of law through its own closure, formalisation and positivity, such a unity has to be constituted by extra-legal means. Such colonialist claims come today from an economic theory of law, a political theory of law, and from a moral theory of law. Their fatal attraction is that they can provide, within one approach, a framework of legal theory, doctrinal arguments and methodological instruments. However, the question still remains: how can the law decide between them, if each one of them is legitimately institutionalised in social practice and if each one of them can demonstrate a universal rationality? Or to put it more strongly: is it possible for society to protect itself against self-destructive tendencies of the colliding discourses by giving preference to one of them? Is it not, on the contrary, plausible that these self-destructive tendencies are increased by a preferential treatment of one of the discourses?

A counter-position would be to refuse such a momentary decision of faith and the *sacrificium intellectus* connected with it, and to accept the controversial plurality within the law and to see it as an opportunity rather than as a sign of decay. The question, then, is whether such a plurality of legal 'ontologies', juridical concepts, and legal models has to be avoided, or whether one can cope with it. Does the pluralisation of the rationalities of law necessarily lead to relativism and nihilism? Or can it not be turned around constructively? One would accept the permanent conflict between ontologies within the legal system as such and without the possibility of ever deciding it. The idea would be to transform law into a discourse that maintains conflict or even increases conflict, not reduces it. This is not anything-goes-relativism but a position that argues for an increase of 'agonistic aspects of society'. Is there not a case for finding ways and means to increase the plurality by 'civilising' the conflict of discourses and to use its rich tapestry of conflicts productively? Here we can see new life in Max Weber's suggestion as to how to deal with modern polytheism; but we have to shift the accent away from the individual onto legal discourse:

> ... to lead one's life consciously, if it is not to pass by like a natural event, means to know about those contradictions, and it means to see that each singular

important act, and even more so, life as a whole, are a chain of final decisions through which the soul, as seen by Plato, chooses its own fate, that is, the meaning of its actions and its existence.

Can the legal discourse cope with the struggle of the gods and can it choose its own fate through a chain of decisions?

As far as current German legal theory is concerned, there are above all two authors who confess candidly to the new polytheism, Rudolf Wietholter and Karl-Heinz Ladeur. Wietholter's work concentrates on the question as to how law can deal with the collision between different grand theories, that is, economic theory, systems theory and critical theory. In spite of personal sympathies for the most critical among them, he avoids bias which would impoverish the discussion and puts his bets on mutual enlightenment – and on the capacity of law to syphon off productive norms from these learning processes. Ladeur's work represents the turning of jurisprudence to post-modern legal theory. In analysing the plurality of discourses and the variety of systems, he concludes normatively that the law should not again favour a doubtful unity but should rather deliberately maintain its internal plurality and guarantee mutual transparency of the discourses against their tendencies to block each other. Is there scope for an elaboration of these approaches?

My suggestion is to work out the concept of a new law of conflicts. The issue here is the new situation of law having to decide between colliding rationalities of different discourses, not the classic collision between national regimes of law or between competing jurisdictions. The new areas of conflicts are defined by symbolic codes and programmes delineating discourses and are not made up by territorial borders. Is there something to be learnt from the historical experience with international conflicts between laws for dealing with the conflicts between discourses and systems? In the classic international law of conflicts there are many collisions which cannot be resolved by reference to hierarchy, there is an abundance of circular references, self-references and paradoxes, which all have to be coped with in one way or other. So there may be a case for fruitful analogies for a law of interdiscursive conflicts which is faced with similar challenges.

A starting point could be the equal authority of colliding discourses, just as conflicting national legal regimes have equal authority in the international law of conflicts. This position does not allow for a permanent solution. It facilitates, on the contrary, a never-ending routine of referring the one regime to the other and vice versa, and it arrives at decisions in the course of this routine, without, however, questioning overall the respective authorities of the conflicting regimes. Accordingly, a law of discourse conflicts can only be understood as an infinite 'chain of ultimate decisions' in the sense of Max Weber, in which the legal argument 'passes through' the different particularistic rationalities which are institutionalised in law, and arrives at decisions on this basis, without ever resolving the permanent conflict. This hardly satisfies the romantic desire to reconcile the divisions in society, but it increases variety considerably and may lead to more adequate and acceptable results. By 'ceaselessly contextualizing and relativizing law's knowledges' it may open 'possibilities for productive confrontations between discourses'. It reconstructs the different normative projections of the other particularistic rationalities and attains its norms through decisions on what cannot be decided.

This sounds paradoxical, and it is paradoxical. However, it only provides the situation of legal discourse in today's society with the name of the paradox of a *unitas multiplex* which is also reflected in its parts as a *unitas multiplex*. Such a *unitas multiplex* cannot be resolved by referring hierarchically to the whole, or to the centre, or to the top, but it can be 'deparadoxified' through the grand tour of references and references back.

The traditional international conflict of laws can thus be seen as a vast network of references to foreign law and references back to the domestic law. The relevant technical terms here are called choice of law, qualification, assimilation, *ordre public*, internal and external consistency of decisions, *renvoi* as the reference back to the local order and onward to third orders. These terms provide a legal form for oscillating between inside and outside, for blending the foreign with the familiar, and for the game of confusion of self-reference and hetero-reference. Here it is in particular the legal concept of the *renvoi* which, as the reference to a foreign legal order referring back to the local legal order, has always fascinated legal scholars in conflict of laws by the very nature of its paradoxical, circular structure? Should the *renvoi* be prohibited? Should the *renvoi* be aborted, or should one follow its lead? Or can it be made productive by introducing appropriate distinctions?

Is there in the collision of the discourses a similar game of confusions in form of the *renvoi,* that is, in the discursive references back and forth? Indeed, those other discourses refer to the law, when in conflict, and the law refers to other discourses, when in conflict. Are these only infinite reflections of symmetries, empty tautologies and vicious circles? There is a case to be made for observing if and how legal practice succeeds in shifting symmetries into asymmetries, in unfolding apparently empty tautologies, in turning the vicious circles of references and references back into virtuous circles.

Now, if legal theory could search into this direction, it could play an entirely different role in the game of references. It would definitely get away from merely endlessly pitting a political theory of law, a moral theory of law, and an economic theory of law against a legal (*sic!*) theory of law, and calling one of them the ultimate one. Instead of trying once more to declare one of the particularistic rationalities as the very deepest fundament of law and justice, jurisprudence should develop a theory of discourse collisions which calibrates law precisely to the plurality of social rationalities. Such a theory could delineate, in the never-ending game of references, how to arrive at the necessary asymmetries, substantiate tautologies, unfold paradoxes without reducing the plurality of the points of references, and it could perhaps contribute to its refinement.

So the specific mission of legal theory would be to reflect upon the infinite game of references played out between a plurality of observation posts and, upon its translation into a 'constitutional' form. Will such a constitutionalisation reformulate the classical compensatory task of law in a new context? Will a constitutional form for the conflict of discourses be able to curb self-destructive dynamics? Or at the very least will it counter them with some measure of compensation? In the old inter-personal conflicts, the classical task of law has been to guarantee the mutual acknowledgement of autonomy, to curb mutual infringement and to compensate for mutually inflicted harm. Is there a way to translate these classical concepts into today's interdiscursive conflicts?

Of course, there is one fundamental difficulty of such an interdiscursive law of conflicts. It must accept the conflicting particularistic rationalities on equally authoritative footing without being able to assume the rationality of the whole. However, exactly the same has always been the situation of the international conflict of laws which does not assume a hierarchical top of world-law that would have to decide on conflicts. Historically and by default, conflict of laws has used a strangely paradoxical technique of self-application. National laws have been judges in their own case. Conflict of laws has designed a multiplicity of national *fora* which decide international conflicts by recourse to one of the laws in conflict. This multiplicity of decentralised *fora*, deciding on conflicts, fills the void of one central international conflict forum. This is indeed the situation of conflicting discourses which, as is well-known, have lost their *meta-recit* in the course of the most recent history of the Western world. Discursive collision can only be decided decentrally, only within each discourse, and in each case afresh and differently.

This leads, as it does in the case of the national *fora* of the international law of conflicts, to the further question as to what the forum for the interdiscursive law of conflicts could be like. What is the appropriate forum on which the conflict of discourses can be treated? In principle, there are two venues: either it is the *forum internum*, situated in the legal system itself or it is the *forum externum*, situated in one of the other social subsystems. Either the collision is 'incorporated' in the operations of the internal forum of law, or it is 'externalised' into the operations of an external forum. Both scenarios are institutional reality today. They reveal, each for itself, quite different normative perspectives which indicate how law can respond reflexively to the collision of discourses if it translates the game of references into constitutional forms.

In the following, I shall concentrate on these two scenarios and what follows from their normative perspectives. In the first scenario, the case of 'incorporation', the elements of the colliding social discourses are reconstituted *ab initio* in the forum of law. This opens up perspectives on how legal argument can respond to the conflicts of discourses. My example here will be from the field of legal reasoning – the methods of legal consequentialism. Can we gain new results for the discourse conflicts through consequentialist argumentation? In the second scenario, the case of 'externalisation', discourse collisions are dealt with in the *fora* of social subsystems other than law. Here the perspectives for a translation of the game of references into legal constitutional forms are quite different. My example will be the institution of ethics committees, a selection of social, non-legal *fora* for the treatment of social conflicts. My chosen perspective leads here to the question: is it possible to counteract the imperialism of one particularistic rationality by counterinstitutions in the fabric of social discourses?

DISCOURSE COLLISIONS BEFORE THE FORUM INTERNUM

Jurgen Habermas, in his work *Faktizitdt und Geltung* has dealt exhaustively with the first scenario, the case of the incorporation of conflicts and the battle of autonomous social discourses before the forum of law. He pursues the question as to how different discourses find their way into the law, and how law can decide between them. He draws a distinction between moral discourses which aim for universality, ethical discourses which target individual or collective identities, pragmatic discourses which establish relations between ends and means and rank the priorities for certain collective goals, and finally forms of bargaining which constitute a culture of fair compromise. They all turn into an internal conflict for law in the moment that these autonomous forms of discourse are 'translated' – to use Habermas's word – by the legal discourse which represents an autonomous form of discourse in its own right, guided by the criterion of legal coherence.

According to Habermas, law solves conflicts of discourses by adhering to a 'processual model'. Pragmatic, ethical, moral and interest-oriented arguments are freely exchanged in legislative process, as Habermas sees it, until they reach the filter of legal argumentation at the end. Here the legislative programmes resulting from discourse are subjected to a test of norm coherence, especially constitutionality, in order to find out whether they fit the relevant legal system. According to Habermas, the situation of judicial decision-making in applying norms is quite similar. Here too, Habermas identifies a number of pragmatic, ethical, and interest-oriented arguments which are at the end controlled by the measure of legal coherence. Coherence appears in both cases as a kind of filtering device which excludes as non-consistent some of the solutions which result from the free play of discourses in the forum of law.

In my view, Habermas has found a sensitive concept for the problem of collision with this approach. However, he simultaneously overestimates and underestimates the role of law in resolving this problem. On the one hand, Habermas overestimates the communicative rationality which is actually provided by legal procedure; on the other hand, he underestimates the single-mindedness of legal dynamics which does far more than just filtering out arguments. The overestimation of law leads Habermas to believe that the procedural rationality which is incorporated in law does not only produce substantial norms discursively but can even assist in clarifying argumentatively the meta-question of the collision of different discourses. This will surely be well received by some legal scholars in their professional self-aggrandizement who celebrate, in particular, constitutional law as the place where the social divisions are healed. In fantasies of omnipotence entertained by a 'New Republicanism', constitutional law emerges as the locus of a social super-discourse of a fictitious civil society which takes over the tasks of integration of fragmented society.

It is certainly asking too much of law to achieve this, for where are the cognitive and procedural resources of the legal process which could empower it to decide between economic, political and moral rationality and claim to be binding for all society? If science which, after all, is stacked with shining intellectual riches for problem-solving cannot succeed here, how much less likely is it that law can succeed with its comparatively impoverished intellectual equipment? Instead of taking the normative projections of constitutional law scholars too seriously, one should observe legal practice itself more accurately. In doing so, it is easy to see that legal practice indeed reconstructs the arguments of the other autonomous discourses but that it, at the same time, 'deconstructs' these external universalities in a particular fashion. Law turns their universal rationality into local rationality. It produces precisely the contrary of what a super-discourse would produce in terms of substantial rules and what a meta-discourse would produce in terms of collision rules. It does not solve the conflict at the highest level of universal justice, that of the super- and meta-norms but, in fact, chooses the lowest level, that of local justice. It does not perceive the different discourses as a conflict of universalities but only through the looking glass of a local conflict and resolves it at this level, only locally, without ever coming close to universal perspectives.

It is here that Habermas, on the other hand, underestimates the specific contribution which law can make towards coping with discourse collisions. The legal arguments which are applied locally have a greater effect than that of a mere filtering device which excludes some of a number of discursively established results as inconsistent with the past legal practices. Rather, the concrete question of applying the law, that is, the local practice of equal or unequal treatment is the crucially productive mechanism which also copes with the collision problem. To treat what is equal equally and what is unequal unequally is not only a fundamental legal norm but also a dynamic process of law-making which triggers off a self-propelling series of distinctions. It is not only a question as to the test of normative coherence, as implied by Habermas, it is above all the question as to a generative mechanism, a 'historical machine' or a 'non-trivial machine' as Forster would call it. In this context, concepts like precedent, *stare decisis, and* treating the equal equally are not what is interesting. Rather, it is the deviation from the precedent, the 'distinguishing' and 'overruling', the unequal treatment of what is not equal, which provokes the search for new legal norms and produce arguments on which to ground them. Legal inequality provides the conceptual framework for the never-ending search for alternative norms and facts, principles and values. It provokes innovations which, in turn, introduce a new round of questions of 'equal or unequal?' in the chain of distinctions.

Law also uses this local rationality to treat the collision of discourses. 'Equal or unequal?' – that is the question with which new constellations are absorbed by law by subsuming them under a local rule. In order to answer that question, law incorporates incrementally, *ad hoc* and eclectically some of the arguments provided by other discourses. Here it is crucial that law does not accept, as a whole, the method of universality from morality, the issue of identity from ethics, the goals – means relation from pragmatics, the cost-benefit logic of economy, and the policy method of politics. Rather, law collects from these conceptual edifices individual pieces *ad hoc* which are then fitted in its own constructs according to the blueprint of equal treatment. Constantly on the relentless search for criteria for the distinction of equal versus unequal, legal discourse is scanning its discursive environments, borrows ideas, rules and principles where it can, and exploits moral, ethical, pragmatic and strategic arguments. However, it transforms them all into legal criteria for the assessment of the issue as to whether the new constellation has to be decided differently according to norms which have yet to be found. Contrary to Habermas's conclusions, we do not see here a free play of discourses in the forum of law but find that external rationalities are literally 'enslaved' for the purposes of the legal system. Francois Lyotard introduced the distinction of '*litige*' *and* '*differend*' in order to define that slavery. Discourses are closed off from each other because of their different internal grammars in such a way that, in the case of a conflict between them, no '*litige*' is possible, and that means no fair trial in which both parties can make their cases authentically and in which a just decision can be made. Nonetheless discourses can 'meet' in spite of their hermetical closedness, but only by way of '*differend*', that is, a confrontation, in which one discourse perpetrates structural violence on the other and commits injustice.

A more accurate way to analyse the slavery perpetrated by the '*differend*' is to look how the 'history machine' of an equal/unequal treatment of cases treats arguments which are foreign to law. This machine forces the strict discipline of a legal procedure on them which decides, on the basis of the current law, which arguments are admissible, which aspects of the foreign argument are legally relevant and which are not, how priorities are set and how conflicting perspectives are treated. Indeed, the current law as the historical product of the operatively closed legal system decides how unequal cases are currently decided. To have disposition over inequality is the privilege of law and this includes the legally authorised use of arguments which are foreign to law.

Just as a domestic court does not apply foreign law authentically in the international law of conflicts, legal discourse does not all of a sudden act in an authentic manner morally, ethically, scientifically, economically or politically when it uses non-legal arguments. In both situations, foreign concepts are radically reconstructed. National law of conflicts constructs, in cases which touch upon foreign law, a mixture of domestic and foreign rules from the perspective of the local forum, that is, a hybrid body of rules which is significantly different from the rules which a foreign court would apply. Ago has captured this 'constructivist' method in conflict of laws aptly:

> Necessarily, the legal order is always exclusive in the sense that it excludes a legal aspect of everything which does not re-enter that order as legal.

Indeed, re-entry – in the terminology of Spencer-Brown – is the term which captures the remarkable transformation of foreign concepts into legal conflicts. An original concatenation of distinctions separates, through their operations, the legal system from its environment; what is legal from what is not legal. Legal operations, by their very operative closure and, as a matter of principle, cannot reach out into the domains of non-law. As a result, law can only reconstruct its environment internally through closed, self-referential operations. This internal reconstruction of the external world is never identical with the events as they happen in the external world. Even if their substance appears to be identical, they are different because they are recontextualized. For instance, at the very moment that law reconstructs moral arguments internally, they lose their relation to the criterion of universality and to the moral code. They are now subjected to the mechanics of the equal/unequal treatment, pressed into the programmes of law (rules, principles, doctrines) and ultimately linked to the binary legal code of legal/illegal. Calculations of costs and calculations of power, policy arguments and scientific constructs, they are all treated by the law in the same way. They all become strange hybrids which are now, however, the sole responsibility of the legal discourse.

The most important effect of enslaving as far as discourse collisions are concerned, is that what could not be compared before can be compared now. Or what could not be decided before can be decided now. However, and this cannot be stressed strongly enough, this effect works only within the symbolic territory of law. Law does not assume the role of the super umpire of the grand society game. It can only compare discourses within the legal game, and that only in the aforementioned local way. Discourses remain incompatible outside the world of law. The re-entry to the internal side of law has the effect of making incomparable universalities appear all of a sudden as comparable entities inside law by reproducing the external world internally.

Precisely this, making slaves and comparing what was incomparable, is what happens through the re-entry of foreign meaning into law. All these concepts lose their original meaning and appear as items for decision-making in the history machine of law. Moral maxims, ethical identities, pragmatic recommendations, economic cost considerations, policy strategies all undergo a remarkable process of transubstantiation; after their re-entry they appear as mere components of the legal discourse: as legal values, legal principles, norm purposes, interests and ambits for decision-making. Consequently, this is not a case of the moralising, politicising, economising of law but it is, on the contrary, the case of the legalising of moral, economic, political phenomena with the effect that their discursive differences become neutralised. In this way, perspectives of efficiency, effects of policies and moral principles can be offset one against the other in each case – but to repeat: only in so far as the internal realm of legal discourse is concerned.

It seems as if, with this approach, legal practice is quite in touch with most recent developments. Indeed, legal practice seems to fulfil the extravagant demands of a post-modern plurality of discourses. Law does not need the *meta-racit* of a societal central agency in order to treat the conflicts between different social rationalities; nor does law itself become such a *meta-racit*; nor must law give in to an economic, political or any other particularistic rationality. Rather, the re-entry of particularistic rationalities into the realm of law makes them now reappear as comparable components of legal discourse, and can so be offset against one another on the basis of legal argument in each individual case and in a form which resolves the conflict between the particularistic rationalities.

CONSEQUENTIALIST REASONING AND POLYCONTEXTURALITY

An ingenious solution, indeed! Of course, legal practice invented it and not legal theory. But there is a price to pay for it. This is not only the trivialisation of 'high-cultural' achievements which become legal petty cash. Far worse is a loss of reality which comes along with making social particularistic rationalities the slaves of law. Law seems to lose contact with social reality by enslaving it, precisely by making contact with the social reality through the incorporation of its concepts. Enslavement takes care of the conflict, at least in the single case, in the small world of law. However, what does that imply for the acceptance of the decision in the large world of society? Seen in the perspective of the international law of conflicts, law has solved, with the re-entry, the problem of its 'internal consistency', that is, the problem of the coherence of its own order, satisfactorily. However, what about the 'external consistency', the acceptance in the external order? The ingenious solution is not reflected in the environment of law; it may even result in environmental damage as far as the other discourses are concerned.

A similar effect can be seen particularly clearly in the parallel case of economic calculations: just like the legal discourse the economic discourse also enslaves the world in its entirety – including events which are clearly far away from economics like love, religion or the law – in assessing them all as cost factors and submitting them, even if under the mute protest of the enslaved rationalities, as now comparable items to the economic calculus. However, this way of calculation has no base in the social context and it creates harmful effects on the ecology. As a consequence, the ecologisation of the economic discourse, that is, the 'external consistency' of economic calculation, is a burning political issue.

Perhaps, then, the ecologisation of the law of discursive conflicts is the point where legal theory can inform legal practice? For theory can show that the law has created an asymmetry in the form of the 're-entry' which enables society to refer to law. But at the same time, this has seriously prevented law from referring back to society completely, and has at the same time denied law a sensibility as far as society is concerned. Is there not a case to be made that law should develop conceptual sensors as to whether or not its treatment of collisions has harmful effects on its social environment? Should the law not be concerned as to whether or not its well-meaning conflict decisions are inflicting damage on its social environment? Should one not here once more introduce the circular reference of the maligned *renvoi* in order to give law a base in society?

I would like to examine this general argument using an example from legal methodology – consequentialist reasoning in law. I shall suggest a particular form of teleological orientation to legal practice which would be not to adopt teleological orientation in general but which is tailored to the problem of the ecologisation of legal discourse.

Today lawyers make, as a matter of routine, decisions contingent on their actual outcomes. They do so even though they know, or at least could know, that this cannot work. However, lawyers have hoped that concrete empirical findings on the causal consequences of legal decisions will lead to general models which will warrant predictions as to judicial or legislative actions. These predictions, in turn, could then be translated into legal argument for or against a concrete legal decision.

However, there are new doubts in sociology as to the prognostic capacity of social sciences which undermine a consequentialist orientation in law. These doubts are not only related to the temporary backwardness of the social sciences when compared with the more successful natural sciences, a backwardness which may soon level out. These doubts extend to the fundamental principles of scientific methodology. There are now theories in the natural sciences which categorically deny predictability in certain constellations, even if events are fully determined and all laws governing them are well known. Furthermore, the chaos character of social processes is cited as a reason why predictions are impossible in principle or only possible within extremely narrow margins.

A second problem for legal consequentialism is that causal chains are infinite. According to Luhmann, a form for legal consequentialism has to be found which does not increase the 'variety' of law to such an unbearable degree that the functioning of law is put at risk. The challenge is to find new 'redundancies' in law mitigating uncertainty in decision-making which has been increased by consequentialist reasoning.

Here Dworkin made the widely recognised suggestion that rights be rendered indispensable and be excluded altogether from consequentialist considerations. The interesting point about this suggestion is that it shifts the relation between variety and redundancy clearly in favour of redundancy by excluding whole bands of objectives for teleological considerations and thus from creating variety. However, in view of the density of interdependent social actions such a clean dissection of spheres of subjective rights will not be possible without considering the consequences of actions which are covered by law.

Therefore, the suggestion by MacCormick to limit the array of the outcomes which have to be considered rather than the band of objectives for consequentialist considerations, appears to be more realistic. MacCormick permits legal consequentialism only when general rules are at stake and excludes it in relation to individual decisions. He refers such a 'rule consequentialism' to the concept of universal applicability in law. 'Rule consequentialism', in contrast to 'act consequentialism', would clearly increase redundancy and decrease variety.

A suggestion by Mengoni takes a similar direction. He perceives the problem of consequentialism as caused by the, in principle, indeterminacy of infinite concatenations of consequences and wants to distinguish between long-term outcomes and short-term outcomes. Judges are advised to consider exclusively the first links in the chain. In this way, the number of external variables can be drastically reduced.

Grimm, finally, counts on a more normatively defined limitation of relevant consequences. He holds that it is primarily a problem for legal doctrine to develop criteria which allow a selection from the infinite number of consequences. He hopes that a systematic development of the concept of purpose in law will lead to further impulses for legal doctrine.

We have to follow these leads, in my opinion, but must also move with our abstraction in a different direction. The relevant consequences of modern law are today no longer experienced in the diffuse lifeworlds of the subjects of law with their infinite causal chains but in the other specialised social subsystems where decisions of the legal discourse are translated, through a new form of re-entry. Only after such a translation has taken place, can it be detected in law whether a legal decision can be tolerated in the other discourse or whether it inflicts negative, disintegrative or even destructive effects. *Altera pars audiatur.* This means that not only must the other party involved in each individual case be heard before a legal conclusion but also that the other discourse involved has to be heard before the law can make a decision on the collision of discourses. With the help of a 'back translation', law should be made capable of receiving the specific linguistic form of such 'translations' and their possible damaging effects. Law should make good use of the sociological insight that, in social discourse, legal norms are not just read as expectations of the law addressed to them and demanding obedience. Rather, legal norms are reconstituted economically, politically and pedagogically in a 'second reading' by respective discourses. Rules are 'translated' as cost factors, power positions and as instruments of education. A legal observation of the consequences of decisions should now, by way of a 'third reading', limit the relevance of the, in principle, infinite consequences to the few but decisive consequences which have a negative impact on the law's discursive environment.

'Translations' matter, not causal chains! How is the legal norm translated into the other concrete discourse? How is the re-entry of the legal decision into society worked out? What does the 'second reading' of legal norms look like in other discourses? Does the legal norm have negative, disintegrative, destructive effects? And further: how can the legal discourse respond, in a 'third reading', with new norms which take its social environment into account? This should be, in my opinion, the search and find formula of a realistically defined consequentialist orientation.

This orientation is limited, as it were, to the destructive effects of discourse collisions. At the very least, this orientation could make up, in parts, for the lost contact with the social environment which came about because law legalised the conflict between colliding discourses, enslaving it and reducing it to trivial routine. Now the question could be examined as to whether or not the legal decision would have negative effects on the discursive environments of law. In essence, this means limiting the analysis to one and only one consequence of legal decision-making: how do the actors in the relevant social system really read the legal decision? As a factor in a costs-benefits analysis? As a change of the concrete power relations? As a change to an educational programme? Does the translation have negative effects on the everyday life in that social sphere? This one consequence of decision-making has to be translated back again: what are the reactions which law can muster to respond to the negative consequences of its social transformations? There would be no need to rely on the impossible prediction as to how the actors in the respective social context would react to their second reading of legal norms. On the other hand, law would clearly gain in realism if it registered, in each case, only the one consequence, namely, whether the legal decision had a damaging effect in the second reading of the relevant social context, and whether it adjusted to these perceived effects by issuing norms which are less damaging.

Recent trends of 'contractualization' illustrate how consequentialist reasoning may be fitted to this iterative translation of discourses. Hugh Collins analyses how social discourses reread the norms of contract law and reconstruct their worlds of meaning after their 'contractualization'. Assessing their damaging effects on social relations (bilateralism, specificity, externalities, power relations) he proposes new ways of how contract law could respond to its own negative consequences.

Of course, one should not overestimate the anticipatory capabilities of law. If it is correct that the prognostic potential of the social sciences is far more limited than previously thought, the only solution which is left must be to strip legal consequentialism as far as possible of predictions of possible future consequences and to focus on the observation of environmental damage which has actually materialised. Retrospective observation of consequences is what is needed, not prospective predictions of consequences. In essence, we are no longer concerned with the ambitious project of applying sociological models for the prognosis of future behaviour in a response to legal change, but we are concerned, more modestly, with collecting factual information about the environmental damage which has resulted from the concrete second reading in the other discourses after they have reconstructed the legal decision on their own terms. The legal forum which has to decide on the collision of discourses would accept a greater responsibility if it exposed itself to the consequences of the decision, that is, if it tried to find out whether the decision had disintegrative effects in the other discourses and if it tried to draw conclusions from that.

However, the question remains as to whether we have found the sought-after antidote to law's tautologies, symmetries and paradoxes if it only returns the conflict between discourses as a legal conflict loaded, as has been discussed, with arguments about consequences back to the discourses. Is that not only pushing conflicts back and forth between different domains? The difference is made by the real changes which result from this process of translations and back translations. 'Re-entry' does not mean that external meaning is mirrored accurately internally, it means that external meaning is reconstructed internally and that new decisions are made on this basis. Ultimately, we can observe here a series of multiple transforming re-entries. First, the conflict between discourses enters the law and is decided there in the specific 'local' form. Second, the legal decision is reconstructed in the other discourse and leads to a reaction which is specific for this discourse. Third, the reaction is brought back to law and appears, legally reconstructed, on the screen for inspection, providing a new basis for decision-making.

As the discourses are operatively closed, they can only misunderstand each other in this recursive process of reconstruction. At the same time, such misunderstandings are not mere fiction because they are, in fact, an internal reaction to an external irritation. They build on the 'tacit knowledge' of the other discourse. This added value is given by, as it were, a series of productive misunderstandings.

Are we only projecting an ideal world of law which is supposed to translate conflicts between discourses into law, decide on them and control the consequences argumentatively? I do not think so. Here, we can refer once more to the current practice of legal economics, this time in order to show that such a game of references is already played out in an advanced version between law and another discourse. First, law reconstructs here economic transactions on legal terms with the help of economic analysis; secondly, it adjusts legal argumentation to anticipated and possibly already materialised economically damaging consequences; and thirdly, it reformulates legal norms on the basis of these transformations. Nevertheless one has to be on one's guard as to the imperialism, or even totalitarianism of economic theory. If the law opens up to the claims of universality of economics in this way, it must be open to the other discourses as well. The task here is to generalise this game of *renvoi* as practised by legal economics and to apply it to the multiplicity of discourses in society.

DISCOURSE COLLISIONS BEFORE THE FORUM EXTERNUM

Of course, law's cognitive resources are considerably strained, if not to say overburdened, in this intricate game of *renvoi* by internalisation of collisions and observation of their consequences. Unquestionably it is somewhat demanding to ask down-to-earth lawyers who are trained in case analysis to demonstrate multilingual attitudes which help them to reconstruct the language game of economics, politics and ethics within the language game of law. Then it is even more important to focus attention on other forums in society outside the law, in which conflicts between discourses are taking place. What can law contribute to this external treatment of the collision of discourses?

Here our attention is drawn to autonomous social fields of rule-making in which different social universalities are directly expressed in legal form. As we mentioned before, following the historical example of legislation and contract, a number of other plural sources of law have been developed, especially rule-making in formal organisation, technical-professional standardisation and other forms of private justice. The trick is always the same: transactions which are specific for one discourse-economic exchanges, political acts, management decisions within organisations and acts of standardisation – are misunderstood as legal actions and perceived in law as contracts, statutes, associational laws and technical or professional standards. Thus, without going into the details of a demanding economic, political or technical analysis, law attains 'implicit' knowledge about the particularistic rationality of the social sector involved, if it is only sensitive enough to assimilate carefully the concrete social process and its rule-formation.

However, in this ongoing practice of social rule-making, law is prepared to make sacrifices to one god only, and is therefore at risk of losing its polytheistic virtues. Joining forces in this way with only one of the other particularistic rationalities, law may inflict damage on other social sectors. Seen in this light, constitutional review of legislation and, to a lesser degree, judicial review of contracts and standard terms of business can be called a service for polytheism. In this sense, constitutional civil rights and general clauses in private law can be understood as collision rules in the law of conflicts, in which the particularistic universality of politics or economics is changed by the incorporation of polycontextural elements. In comparison with judicial review of statutes and contracts the judicial review of the internal laws of organisations and of technical-professional standards is clearly lagging behind.

Even more exciting is the question as to how discourse collisions arise in arenas of legal pluralism itself. This exports, as it were, the collision from law to other discourses themselves. According to Wietholter, this creates a situation in which 'autonomy' understood as self-determination of social discourses needs to be respected by the law and, at the same time, control by law is not exercised as outer-directed but as a possible help in the situation of impossible self-help, a maeuetic situation, not unlike counselling and mediation arrangements outside of law.

Can this subtle game of autonomy and heteronomy be institutionalised? Again, I have chosen an example, in order to illustrate the abstract perspective. 'Ethics committees' in the broadest sense are currently one of the politically most exciting experiments. This is perhaps less so for the national top level ethics committees which work out general rules and is more so for the small local ethics committees in hospitals, business firms and universities which review problematic decisions. In the polycontextural perspective, they are problematic because they are highly specialised, particularistic unidimensional transactions that are in potential conflict with the inner logic of other discourses. The primary task of ethics committees would be to search for discourse collisions: can these decisions be justified in the light of different universalities in order to do 'local justice'? These questions should not be decided by the law, rather they provide law with a new task: to constitutionalize alternative institutions which infuse a polycontextural orientation into highly specialised discourses in society.

One aspect of this new task for law is particularly important. In order to cope with collisions, law would have to switch over from the current pluralism of interest groups to a pluralism of discourses, a pluralism of language games. Law should not attempt a micropolitical imitation of interest group pluralism as it is practised in a larger political arena with changing corporate participants. To structure ethics committees with a concept of group pluralism in mind would be a mistaken method of their 'politicisation'. The decisive question is whether or not in a rule-making process which is dominated by only one type of discourse it is possible to institutionalise competing rationalities via participation rights, demands for information, evidential procedures and decision-making procedures. *Altera pars audiatur.* This would mean here that ethics committees would not just listen to different group interests but make sure that the dominant economic or medical discourse would not inflict damage on the internal life of other social areas, on the conditions for their proper functioning and on their guiding principles.

JUSTICE FOR THE HETEROGENEOUS

Here, then, are our principles for the conflict of discourses under law. The infinite game of *renvoi* reappears now in a double way. If discourse collisions are internalized and brought before the *forum internum* of law, legal reasoning should take on a consequentialist orientation which focuses on negative effects of those collisions. If the collisions are externalised and disputed before non-legal *fora* the law should be brought in to transform those uni-dimensional extra-legal rule-making processes into polycontextural institutions.

However, in both cases we should be resigned to the fact that there are no general and substantive legal principles, no super-norms, no meta-norms which could ultimately resolve the collision of universalities. Rather, in both cases the role of law is limited to simply participating in the infinite game of *renvoi* played out by closed discourses. Law only influences this game in a particular way, constitutes it in legal forms and infuses it with elements of juridical rationality, at best, contributes to minimising destructive tendencies in the collision of discourses. Emile Durkheim could still hold that the threatening centrifugal tendencies of the modern division of labour will be countered with integration through organic solidarity, restitutive law and professional-corporative ethics. However, today in a world of radicalized polycontexturality, an 'integrative' role of law is definitely ruled out, if it means that the law signifies governing values, principles and norms as valid. Rather, law's role is externally to impose internal limits on the unfettered dynamics of a specialized discourse in the interest of other discourses. The current task of law cannot be to reconstitute the lost unity of society but to designate borders of plural identities, protect them against domination by other discourses and limit damage from the fallout of discourse collisions.

The central concept is 'justice for the heterogeneous'. Lyotard says about a justice of multiplicity:

> Justice would be this: acknowledging that the plurality of the interwoven language games cannot be translated into each other, and that they have their own autonomy, their own specificity which cannot be reduced to one.

One would extend the old *altera pars audiatur* from an individual to a social perspective that sees the plurality of discourses as the central problem of society today. No longer can these conflicts be decided by a central authority; rather, central authorities are in an intractable conflict with one another. If we insist on such a position 'beyond hierarchy', justice could be conceived as a relative term which would not be applicable in one location only, say, law or politics, but which would have currency in all discourses. So justice would denote the deeply problematic relation between discursive identity and discursive otherness, not however from a superior third party perspective but from the unique perspective of one singular discourse in relation to the meaning worlds of other discourses. Justice, then, would not be anything specifically legal, something which under current circumstances would still justify a privileged role of law. Rather, justice is a provocation for each discourse. A legal system would respond to the challenge of justice in a double way. It would not only attempt to achieve the internal consistency of law but, at the same time, would attempt to reconstruct internally the rationality of the other discourse which is involved in the conflict. Justice seen in this way would put modern law under a demand which is two-fold. The question is no longer only: is law treating what is equal equally and what is unequal unequally, but the question is now also: does the law do justice to other discourses on their own terms?

Without doubt, such a justice for discourses has to live, from its inception, with the certainty of its failure. Principally, this justice cannot rule out that discourses violate one another. It cannot reverse the fall from grace in the form of a profound social divide, functional differentiation and fragmentation of discourses with all their self-destructive tendencies. 'Compensatory' as this justice is, it can only insist less ambitiously on an *ad hoc* limitation, reduction and compensation of the harm which is inflicted by the collision of discourses.

Further Reading

For an accessible introduction, see King 1993.

For a more substantial elaboration of the theory, see Teubner 1993.

For useful collections of essays, including critical essays (especially that by Lempert) see Teubner (ed) 1987c and Teubner and Febbrajo (eds) 1992.

For application of the theory see Nobles and Schiff 2000, especially Chs 1 and 4.

For a selection of criticisms, albeit with a somewhat robust rebuttal, see King 2001.

Questions

1. 'Systems can never be each other's inputs and outputs. They can only productively misread each other.' Discuss.

2. 'In order to use law instrumentally, one must grasp the paradox that it is not an instrument. Only by being closed, can it be open to its environment.' Discuss.

3. 'The meaning of law cannot be found in concepts, definitions, or politics, it exists solely in self-referential communications.' Discuss.

4. 'Law is Politics. Law is Economics.' Does legal autopoiesis deal adequately with these claims of critical legal studies and economic analysis of law?

19 Foucault and Law

Anne Barron

The purpose of this chapter is to provide a critical introduction to Michel Foucault's writings on the operation of power in modern societies, and in particular to explore the implications of these writings for legal theory. It begins with three caveats. First, Foucault's *oeuvre* covers a vast canvas and is so varied in its themes as to resist any attempt at a neat summary. Second, it defies explanation in terms of the familiar categories of academic discourse: Foucault's vocabulary, preoccupations and methods of analysis, though clearly informed by (amongst others) the disciplines of philosophy, history, and sociology, systematically flout the scholarly conventions governing these disciplines and constantly transgress the boundaries between them. Third, whatever label might be devised for Foucault, that of 'legal theorist' is singularly inappropriate, for he was not a legal theorist in any conventional sense of the term. This is partly because Foucault would have denied that he was producing a 'theory' of any kind in any of his works; partly because law was in any case not one of the major preoccupations of his work, even of his work on power. All of this makes Michel Foucault an unusually difficult thinker to 'cover' in the manner required for an introductory course or text on jurisprudence.

Perhaps the most useful way in to Foucault's reflections on power is by way of the subject matter of Chapter 6 of Part I of this volume, for Foucault's work unquestionably has more in common with Marxist theory than with mainstream jurisprudential approaches to law. In a general sense, what it shares with Marxism is a tendency to de-centre the consciousness of the individual as the origin of all human knowledge and action. To understand Foucault, then, no less than Marx, is above all to grasp the radical inversion he perpetrates on our comfortingly 'self-centred' way of seeing the world and our place within it. In modern liberal culture generally, the sovereignty of the individual – the choosing, initiating, responsible human will – is simply taken for granted as both the foundation and the *raison d'être* of all social, cultural and political institutions. This assumption is generally regarded as being so self-evident that it requires no special attention or justification. It is deeply embedded as the unarticulated premise of our daily practices and routines, and it is implicitly appealed to in the way we attribute and evaluate human achievements in the arts and sciences, as well as in the way we engage with the legal and political systems. The language of rights, after all, is the language through which liberal law and politics is conducted, and this discourse assumes the individual to be the bearer of rights claimed in court and lobbied for in Parliament. It is not surprising, then, that the priority of the individual is also fundamental to liberal legal theory. This is particularly evident in the early work of Ronald Dworkin (see Chapters 8 and 9), where the category of the autonomous individual plays a central role in explaining and justifying the legal system: here, law is represented as constituted by principles which are themselves founded on the right of the individual to equal concern and respect for his or her choices. And although Dworkin distinguishes his position very deliberately from the economic analysis of law, the same basic commitment to the sovereignty of the choosing individual can also be seen in the work of theorists such as Posner and Coase (see Chapter 17), where law is conceived of as an instrument for ensuring efficiency, and efficiency consists in the satisfaction of individual preferences as revealed through actual or projected purchasing decisions.

By contrast, Marxism professes all forms of consciousness, including the modern consciousness of the self as a sovereign individual, to be *effects of*, rather than *prior to*, social practices: specifically, production (labour) practices. As production practices change over time, so forms of consciousness also change, and the form of consciousness that generates in each of us a sense of ourselves as a sovereign individual is the historically specific effect of capitalist production practices. Of course, to speak of 'capitalist' production practices implies that one can interpret these as having a certain shape or structure that enables them to be identified and analysed. Indeed it is fundamental to the Marxist approach to history to see production practices as organised into patterns of relations – power relations – that change over time in response to a particular dynamic of evolution. For the Marxist, capitalist production is organised around a hierarchy between capitalists and workers: capitalists own the means of production; workers own nothing but their labour, and must sell this labour to the capitalist class in order to survive. Because this mode of production requires as its model of subjectivity an agent for whom a particular kind of choice – the choice to sell one's labour – can be regarded as natural, capitalist ideology actually generates the figure of the sovereign individual, yet represents this figure as preceding and enabling capitalist relations of production and exchange. It is this bourgeois subject which becomes institutionalised in law as the universal legal subject, characterised by an abstract freedom of (and responsibility for) decision and action. The inequalities that characterise real social relations between people in capitalist societies are masked by the purely formal equality of persons considered as legal subjects.

Like Marx's materialist account of the bourgeois individual, Foucault's 'genealogies' of the modern subject also purport to reveal the practices which produce that subject's experience of autonomy and self-determination. Foucault also sees these practices as held together by power, and regards the rule of law ideal, and the image of social relations it presupposes – a series of free exchanges between equal citizens – as disguising the inequalities and forms of domination that are bound up with them. Further, Foucault joins Marx in questioning a particular narrative of historical change: that history (including legal history) can be explained as the progressive undoing of all constraints on the sovereignty of the autonomous individual, and that the *telos* of history is the emancipation of this individual from everything that gets in the way of its self-determination. Yet despite these parallels, Foucault's understanding of 'practices', 'power', and the relation between this 'power' and law is quite different from anything that could be characterised as Marxist; and Foucault's own conception of history departs radically from that of Marx in many fundamental respects. Each of these themes – practice, power, law and history – will now be considered in turn.

I. Practice

What exactly does Foucault have in mind when he refers to 'practices'? This is a difficult question to answer, but it is worth engaging with it briefly because otherwise the import of Foucault's larger themes, as well as the basis of his method in exploring them, is likely to be misunderstood.

It is useful to begin with ordinary dictionary definitions of the word 'practice'. A practice can be understood on the one hand as a habitual routine or ritual: simply, that which is commonly done. On the other hand, *to* practice is to train, often with a view to turning something that doesn't come naturally (writing or typing, for example) into something that one can do with ease, without thinking, such that its very artificiality – the fact that it has been learned – is forgotten or repressed. Practices, considered both as routines and as effects of training, are simultaneously the most and the least visible of phenomena. They are the most visible because they are more or less pervasive, and because they precede and enable the supposedly more profound and important manifestations of culture. (Without being able to read and write, for example, how would it be possible to contribute to a book on legal theory?) They are the least visible because they tend to be regarded as neutral, technical, mundane accompaniments to our more important actions and decisions. Part (though not all) of what Foucault means by the notion of practice is captured by these common definitions. Very broadly, it can be said that Foucault's concern in much of his work on power is to pay close attention to apparently inconsequential practices: to reveal how these take shape and take root, how they interact with each other, and how they underpin the grander phenomena upon which 'serious' social analysis usually focuses to the exclusion of everything else. The variety of the practices that in Foucault's view would merit this kind of attention appears (at least) to be infinite, and it is immediately obvious that Foucault is interested in a much broader range of phenomena than production practices in the Marxian sense. So broad is it, indeed, that it could be questioned whether the notion of practice has any analytic purchase at all in Foucault's work. At times the reader may get the impression that what is on offer here is simply a kind of hyper-positivism: the relentless recording of endless small details culled from a wide array of settings, with no attempt to draw these particularities into a larger structure (such as the Marxian 'mode of production'), much less attribute the structure to a single determining cause. Each of these impressions needs to be explored a little further.

I.A. Regimes of Practices?

In an essay entitled 'Questions of Method', Foucault offers this explanation of the nature of his research:

It is a question of analysing a regime of practices – practices being understood here as places where what is said and what is done, rules imposed and reasons given, the planned and the taken for granted meet and interconnect. To analyse 'regimes of practices' means to analyse programmes of conduct which have both prescriptive effects regarding what is to be done (effects of 'jurisdiction') and codifying effects regarding what is to be known (effects of 'veridiction'). (Foucault 1991b, 75 – hereafter all references to Foucault's writings will be abbreviated to F.)

From this it is clear that Foucault is indeed interested in the forces – or 'regimes' – that connect up and give a pattern to the small details of everyday life in modern society. What is not clear, however, is how he conceives of these connections and patterns. The difficulty is compounded by the fact that Foucault was never particularly interested in providing definitions that would govern the reader's interpretations of his texts: many of his explanations of problematic issues such as this one are elliptical and metaphorical. The above quote is fairly typical of his fondness for gnomic aphorisms, and patient exegesis is required to illuminate what Foucault might mean by it. The concept of 'place', first of all, refers in this context not to a physical location, but to a cluster of procedures, routines, institutions and forms of knowledge: a network of practices. Yet the statement quoted above is more specific: Foucault characterises the elements comprising a 'place' as including 'what is said and what is done, rules imposed and reasons given, the planned and the taken for granted'. Three further points should be made in connection with this. First, Foucault seems here to be emphasising the equal importance of 'what is said and what is done' – discourse and action – in giving shape to 'places'. Second, he indicates that 'rules imposed and reasons given' – prescriptive codes and scientific knowledge – are somehow mutually involved in the constitution of these 'places'. Third, he appears to be suggesting that the notion of place accommodates both 'the planned and the taken for granted': both programmes – explicit schemes – of action, and those apparently neutral and technical mechanisms which are the indispensable but 'taken for granted' means for making these schemes workable.

Foucault's method of analysis will be further explored in Section II below. For the moment, however, one conclusion can be drawn: to attend to 'places' in the Foucaultian sense is to recognise that although the tiniest of mechanisms may indeed be interesting and significant, they must be located in relation to other elements with which they form larger networks in order that analysis of them may yield insights of any value. It is precisely because Foucault is interested in these larger networks that to label him a mere chronicler of detail and particularity would be misguided. There is in fact a double move within his work, and Foucault's study of the birth of the prison, *Discipline and Punish* (F 1977) illustrates it well. On the one hand, Foucault aims in this book thoroughly to dissect the prison, to break it down into the smallest of its constituent parts, so that we no longer see it as a unified 'thing' but rather as a complex assemblage of heterogeneous practices. The point of this move is to undo any sense of the given-ness of the prison: to expose the cracks in the edifice, as it were, and to induce a new sensitivity to the sheer contingency of the intersections that enable its many parts to appear as forming a quasi-natural whole. The second move, however, is to rebuild the prison, that is, to make sense of it in a new way, and this second move is at least as important to Foucault's project in *Discipline and Punish* as the first: 'the further one breaks down the processes under analysis, the more one is enabled and indeed obliged to construct their external relations of intelligibility' (F 1991b, 77). Foucault, in other words, is simultaneously concerned to undo the received explanations for existing phenomena like imprisonment, and to build up new grids of analysis for them which could enable their intelligibility to be appreciated differently.

In Foucault's view, then, practices do indeed have a kind of logic; the social order does, as a result, have a degree of coherence and patterning, though not in the manner, or for the reasons, that we commonly imagine: his hypothesis is that practices 'possess up to a point their own specific regularities, logic, strategy, self-evidence and "reason". It is a question of analysing a "regime of practices" ...' (F 1991b, 75). So, as shall be explained further in Section II below, he argues that the advent of imprisonment in the early nineteenth century is intelligible in relation to the spread of what was then a new form of power – a new 'political technology of the body' – which he calls disciplinary power. Foucault's new grid of analysis reveals a cluster of practices to be constitutive of this 'technology': processes of partitioning space and time, processes of subjecting individuals to graduated exercises with a view to building their capacities, and processes of synchronising these capacities with those of others. All of this, he says, is enforced by a combination of 'hierarchical observation' and 'normalising judgement'; and is oriented towards the ordering of 'dangerous masses' of people and the production of individuals who are both more obedient and more useful. Jeremy Bentham's design for a 'panoptic' prison – a circular cell block with a tower in the middle, from which the inhabitant of each and every cell could at all times be seen – is, for Foucault, the 'architectural figure' (F 1977, 200) of disciplinary power. Even though no prison was ever built to this design, Foucault's view is that it should not be dismissed as a 'bizarre little utopia' (F 1977, 225), nor its significance limited to the realm of penal policy alone. The Panopticon expressed a logic and condensed a set of techniques that emerged, albeit in a scattered form, in other social locales from around the same time and were hugely effective in transforming the means of population control and behaviour management in a whole range of contexts: it is 'the diagram of a mechanism of power reduced to its ideal form' (F 1977, 205). As such, it could be detached from any specific use and applied to many purposes: 'Whenever one is dealing with a multiplicity of individuals on whom a task or a particular form of behaviour must be imposed, the panoptic schema may be used' (F 1977, 205).

As we shall see, Foucault's new grid of analysis brings to light – and groups together into a 'regime' – practices that would be ignored or kept separate within other, more orthodox, versions of history: 'humble modalities, minor procedures, ... simple instruments ...' (F 1977, 170). The result is a unique and undeniably suggestive account of the functioning of a distinctively modern modality of power.

I.B. Practices and Causality

The question of what, if anything, *grounds* a regime of practices such as the prison, or discipline in general, raises difficult philosophical issues that can only be touched on here. It suffices for the moment to note that Foucault's preoccupations all relate to the 'how', rather than the 'why', of practices, and that he systematically refuses to pinpoint a single determining cause of the 'regimes' that he claims to uncover. Foucault, that is to say, is primarily interested in the logic of how practices work as an ensemble. This logic, he suggests, is internal to the practices themselves: it is not given by ideologies, determined by material circumstances, or derived from the needs of institutions (such as the state) or interest groups (such as the capitalist class). Although the new kind of intelligibility that Foucault claims to uncover is variously described as rationality, system, and – most provocatively – 'strategy', his method does not presuppose an agency to which this intelligibility is attributable: strategies are endogenous (rather than exogenous) to the practices that form them, and are said to be 'without strategists'. They emerge out of the supports that practices find in each other, and the result is what Foucault calls a *dispositif* (apparatus), a structure of flexible and contingent but nonetheless relatively stable relationships between practices. It is this structure that Foucault wants to decipher, taking account both of the contingency of these relationships, and their relative stability and durability.

But if practices have no ultimate ground, are we to assume that they are themselves a ground, or, to use Marxian terminology, a 'base'? Caution must be exercised here, because although Foucault characterises practice as a complex interplay of action and knowledge, he ultimately refuses the base(activity)/superstructure(ideas) metaphor that organises Marxist thinking. Action, as we have seen, is for Foucault thoroughly entwined with 'what is said', with 'discourse'. Now discourse is roughly analogous to the Marxian concept of ideology, in the specific sense that, like ideologies, discourses systematically form the objects of which they speak (Foucault, 1972): they construct the 'realities' that they are supposed merely to reflect and describe. Crucially, however, Foucault would deny that discourse is directly or indirectly generated by productive action, or indeed by action in general: he would simply reject any rigid distinction of the base/superstructure variety. Far from being located at different 'levels', the one prior to the other, action and discourse are inextricable. This is not only because action on a particular object requires knowledge of that object, but also because discourse is itself practical (in the ordinary sense of that word), and not simply speculative. Foucault is interested in what discourse *does*, not simply in what it *says*: how it *forms* 'the objects of which it speaks'. This leads him to pay as much, if not more, attention to the procedures for producing and recording knowledge – 'methods of observation, techniques of registration, procedures for investigation and research, apparatuses of control' (F 1980, 102) – as to the contents of that knowledge (eg theories of delinquency, its signs and causes) once produced. Hence he particularly emphasises the techniques for demarcating, measuring, observing, and interpreting 'objects' that precede and enable the content of any discourse about them; and the modes of writing and recording that constrain the material forms that discourse may take.

One plausible interpretation of Foucault's action/discourse complexes, however, would be that they – that is to say, the structures or apparatuses that they form through their mutual interconnectedness – are foundational in relation to the modern social order as a whole. The notion of 'strategy' is again significant here. It has already been suggested that Foucault resorts to this notion in accounting for how the multiplicity of elements that comprise an action/discourse complex combine to form a more or less coherent network of relations. Yet he also suggests that, having thus emerged from the mutual reinforcements that these elements find in each other, strategies achieve an 'institutional crystallisation [which] is embodied in the state apparatus, in the formulation of the law and in the various social hegemonies' (F 1979, 93). This could be taken as implying that it is on the basis of such strategies that modernity (which for Foucault includes, but is not defined by, the modern capitalist economy, the modern state, and bourgeois ideology) has taken shape. The strategies immanent to social practices, Foucault seems to be suggesting, are the indispensable props on which the larger structures characteristic of modernity stand. From this perspective, even the Marxian 'base' begins to look 'superstructural', and indeed Foucault openly contrasts his approach with what he calls a 'descending type of analysis', according to which a development such as the birth of the prison is explained by deduction from the premise that 'the bourgeoisie has, since the sixteenth or seventeenth century, been the dominant class' (F 1980, 99). Foucault is clearly referring here to a broadly Marxist approach to social explanation, which would account for every feature of modernity, including the emergence of imprisonment as the dominant form of punishment in the early nineteenth century, by reference to the requirements of capitalist production. A simple deduction from the Marxian premise, for example, might be that prisons emerged at this time because they were sites where a criminal underclass – potentially a pool of labour resources – could be rehabilitated for the world of work and so rendered economically useful. While not denying that the birth of the prison was connected with the birth of the factory, Foucault's argument about the nature of this connection is subtly different: the disciplinary 'strategy' refined in the prison – and in other closed institutions like the school, the hospital and the military barracks – had its own specific trajectory, and its emergence was if anything a precondition, rather than an effect, of the growth of the capitalist economy and the modern state. 'The bourgeoisie could not care less about delinquents, about their punishment and rehabilitation, which economically have little importance, but it is concerned about the *complex of mechanisms* with which delinquency is controlled, pursued, punished and reformed ...' At some point around the end of the eighteenth century, this complex of mechanisms began 'to reveal their political usefulness and to lend themselves to economic profit, and ... as a natural consequence, all of a sudden, they came to be colonised and maintained by global mechanisms and the entire State system'. From the smallest of beginnings, that is to say, these mechanisms, and the rationality encoded within them, gradually took root in every corner of modern society. 'It is only if we grasp these techniques ... and demonstrate the economic advantages or political utility that derives from them in a given context for specific reasons, that we can understand how these mechanisms come to be effectively incorporated into the social whole' (F 1980, 101).

The process by which 'mechanisms' become formed into 'complexes', which in turn become 'colonised' by 'ever more general mechanisms' (F 1980, 99) that organise the 'social whole' is one aspect of what Foucault names 'power'. It is to that large theme that we now turn.

II. Power

[T]he word power is apt to lead to a number of misunderstandings – misunderstandings with respect to its nature, its form, and its unity. By power, I do not mean 'Power' as a group of institutions and mechanisms that ensure the subservience of the citizens of a given state. By power, I do not mean, either, a mode of subjugation which, in contrast to violence, has the form of the rule. Finally, I do not have in mind a general system of domination exerted by one group over another, a system whose effects, through successive derivations, pervade the entire social body … It seems to me that power must be understood in the first instance as the multiplicity of force relations immanent in the sphere in which they operate and which constitute their own organisation; as the process which, through ceaseless struggles and confrontations, transforms, strengthens, or reverses them; as the support which these force relations find in each other, thus forming a chain or system, or on the contrary, the disjunctions and contradictions which isolate them from one another; and lastly, as the strategies in which they take effect, whose general design or institutional crystallisation is embodied in the state apparatus, in the formulation of the law, in the various social hegemonies. Power's condition of possibility, or in any case the viewpoint which permits one to understand its exercise, even in its more 'peripheral' effects, and which also makes it possible to use its mechanisms as a grid of intelligibility of the social order, must not be sought in the primary existence of a central point, in a unique source of sovereignty from which secondary and descendant forms would emanate; it is the moving substrate of force relations which, by virtue of their inequality, constantly engender states of power, but the latter are always local and unstable. The omnipresence of power: not because it has the privilege of consolidating everything under its invincible unity, but because it is produced from one moment to the next, at every point, or rather in every relation from one point to another. Power is everywhere, not because it embraces everything, but because it comes from everywhere. And 'Power', insofar as it is permanent, repetitious, inert and self-reproducing, is simply the overall effect that emerges from all these mobilities, the concatenation that rests on each of them and seeks in turn to arrest their movement. One needs to be nominalistic, no doubt: power is not an institution, and not a structure; neither is it a certain strength we are endowed with; it is the name that one attributes to a complex strategical situation in a particular society. (F 1979, 92–3)

Thus far, we have considered the significance to Foucault's work of practices (intersections of action and discourse); systems of practices; strategies immanent to systems; and the larger social arrangements and institutions into which strategies become incorporated. What the passage just quoted suggests, however, is that each of these phenomena reveals a different dimension of Foucault's primary focus of study, which is 'power'. More precisely, each occupies a different level in the 'ascending analysis of power' (F 1980, 99) that Foucault is chiefly interested in carrying out. It is power that effects the intersection of knowledge and action that is characteristic of practice; power that organises practices into 'chains or systems'; and power that directs these systems into the interstices of state, economy and society. It is power, in short, that makes social order effective and intelligible.

This is a large claim, and what makes it even more contentious is Foucault's insistence that power can do all of this, and yet have none of the characteristics that are normally attributed to it by social and political theorists. Power is not that which is concentrated in the State or any other 'unique source of sovereignty' such as the dominant class: 'let us not look for the headquarters that presides over its rationality; neither the caste which governs, nor the groups which control the state apparatus, nor those who make the most important economic decisions direct the entire network of power that functions in a society (and makes it function) ...' (F 1979, 95). Power is not something acquired or possessed: it is neither a 'thing' nor a 'lever'. Power is not violence, and neither is it a form of regulation that is effectuated solely through law. Foucault contests any account of power that sees it as enlisting physical force to crush or subdue the bodies of individuals; or as deploying ideological means to constrain the consciousness of individuals, thus imposing limits on their capacity to perceive and pursue their true interests; or as involving the repression of authentic desire, thus banishing true subjectivity to the realm of the unconscious. Power, for Foucault, is neither repressive nor prohibitive. Power is not even opposed to freedom: on the contrary, '[p]ower is exercised only over free subjects, and only insofar as they are free' (F 1983, 221). It follows that power is not opposed to truth, either. Traditionally, the relationship between power and truth has been conceived of as one in which power excludes truth and truth, power: the two are entirely antithetical to one another. Marxism, for example, proceeds from this supposition: the idea that false consciousness is generated in and through capitalist domination of the working class exemplifies this way of thinking about power. But this view, Foucault argues, depends precisely upon the representation of power as repression. Power-as-repression suppresses desire, fosters false consciousness, promotes ignorance: in short, it is an instrument which prevents or at least distorts the formation of true knowledge. For Foucault, on the contrary, power and truth directly imply one another: truth is an effect of power and in turn reproduces power.

It follows from all of this, then, that when Foucault refers to 'power', he does not mean 'Power' 'as a group of institutions and mechanisms that ensure the subservience of the citizens of a given state'. But given that this is so, what positive conception of power remains in the wake of all of these denials and refutations? To what end is this power directed, if not that of 'ensuring subservience'? And how does it work, if not by means of violence, rules, ideology or repression? Foucault's method precludes a straightforward answer to these questions, and he was not generally given to reducing the results of his *analyses* of power to neat propositions that could form the basis of a 'Foucaultian' *theory* of power[1]. For this reason, Section II.A will begin to explore the Foucaultian conception of power by engaging with the analysis of disciplinary power presented in *Discipline and Punish*, Foucault's major work on the prison (an extract from *Discipline and Punish* is reproduced as the first reading at the end of this chapter).

1   In the essay entitled 'The Subject and Power' (F 1983) – in a section headed 'Why Study Power?' – Foucault denies that a 'theory' of power is analytically useful, and warns against interpreting the ideas expressed in this essay as representing either a theory or a methodology. Though he concedes that 'analytical work cannot proceed without an ongoing conceptualization' of power (F 1983, 209), he insists that this is one which is endlessly revisable, requiring 'constant checking' (F 1983, 209). Accordingly, Foucault's conceptualization, together with its assertions about the ends towards which power in modern society is directed, undergoes a number of transformations between 1975 (the year in which *Discipline and Punish* was published in France) and Foucault's death in 1984. During this period, the focus of Foucault's research shifts from a preoccupation with the production of 'docile bodies' as mute objects through the functioning of disciplinary technologies, to the activation of the inner consciousness of the speaking subject through the operation of confessional technologies, to the regulation of whole populations through 'governmentality', and ultimately to the interaction of all of these forms (see text of this chapter for elucidation).

Scattered about his writings of the later 1970s and early 1980s, however, are a few texts in which Foucault shows a willingness to reflect at a more abstract level about the picture of power that emerges from his studies and the methodological procedures that are needed to uncover it. One of these texts – an untitled lecture delivered in 1976 – is reproduced as the second reading below under the title 'Power/Knowledge', and Section II.B aims to summarise the generalisations that emerge from all of them. It must be borne in mind, however, that even Foucault's own comments in these texts need to be treated with caution, because they run the risk, as Foucault himself warned, of reducing complex ideas to a few simplistic aphorisms. As has already been noted, Foucault generally tended to steer clear of anything that could serve as a definition of the kind of power he was interested in analysing, preferring instead to illustrate its operations through highly detailed 'genealogies' of exemplary sites such as the prison (see Section IV below for a brief explanation of the meaning of 'genealogy' in this context).

II.A. Disciplinary Power

Once again, practices are the starting point for Foucault's analyses of discipline, characterised in *Discipline and Punish* as a 'political technology of the body'. This characterisation arguably captures the key features of Foucault's conception of power, and the main concern of this section will be to explore what is meant by it. There is no substitute for a close reading of Foucault's own words on this subject, and what follows is only a brief overview of the themes discussed in Part Three – the central part, for our purposes – of *Discipline and Punish*, in which Foucault explains what disciplinary technology is and how it works (all quotations, unless otherwise indicated, are from that work).

Foucault begins the first of these chapters, tellingly entitled 'Docile Bodies', with the observation that the eighteenth century saw a great increase in attention paid to the body 'as object and target of power' (136): as an instrument that could be trained and manipulated, whose forces could be extracted and increased. Books on the anatomy of the human body proliferated at the same time as new instructions and methods emerged for controlling the operations of the bodies of soldiers, schoolchildren, workers – all those, in short, whose activities required to be closely coordinated with the activities of large numbers of others. Throughout this period, Foucault argues, the question of the intelligibility of the body was linked to the question of how it could be made both more compliant and more useful. The notion of 'docility' is invoked by Foucault to express these connections: this term 'joins the analysable body to the manipulable body' (136). The production of docile bodies, Foucault suggests, was the goal of a whole range of social projects and experiments that combined a knowledge of the human body's limits and capacities with techniques for intervening in and improving its functioning. And the docile body, in turn, was one constituted in such a way that as it functioned more efficiently, so also it became more obedient, and *vice versa*. What was new about these 'projects of docility' (136) compared with earlier regimes of bodily regulation (eg slavery, vassalage, and service) was the scale, object and modality of the controls that they imposed. Their focus was minute: the body was now seen not as an undifferentiated unity but as a complex mechanism comprised of a multiplicity of components and processes, each of which – individually and in its relationships to others – became the object of continuous and unrelenting supervision. 'These methods, which made possible the meticulous control of the operations of the body, which assured the constant subjection of its forces and imposed upon them a relation of docility-utility, might be called "disciplines"' (137). Disciplinary power 'increases the forces of the body (in economic terms of utility) and diminishes those same forces (in political terms of obedience)' (138). Its emergence was gradual, and it took different forms in different institutional locations, but wherever it appeared discipline was characterised by certain essential techniques which 'defined a certain mode of detailed political investment of the body, a "new microphysics" of power' (139). All of these techniques involved a process of partitioning – of space; of time; and of the movements or gestures of the body relative to each other, to external objects, and to the movements and gestures of other persons. In what follows, the elements of discipline will be described partly in the present tense, because although it first took shape in the eighteenth century, discipline remains, for Foucault, a characteristic form of power in modern societies.

'In the first instance, discipline proceeds from the distribution of individuals in space' (141). This sometimes, but not necessarily, involves the enclosure of particular spaces – schools, barracks, hospitals, factories – but the partitioning of space is of more fundamental importance. 'Disciplinary space tends to be divided into as many sections as there are bodies or elements to be distributed' (143). Here the ancient architectural model of the monastic cell found a new application – 'disciplinary space is always, necessarily, cellular' (143) – but was adapted to serve a variety of overlapping, secular, purposes. One of these was the control of dangerous masses of people: 'One must eliminate the effects of imprecise distributions, the uncontrolled disappearance of individuals, their diffuse circulation, their unusable and dangerous coagulation; it was a tactic of anti-desertion, anti-vagabondage, anti-concentration' (143). But there was more to partitioning than simply social control. 'Particular places were defined to correspond not only to the need to supervise, to break dangerous communications, but also to create a useful space' (143–4), where what was considered useful depended on the functions the place was designed to serve. In factories, for example, '[i]t was a question of distributing individuals in a space in which one might isolate and map them; but also of articulating this distribution on a production machinery that had its own requirements' (144). A factory for the production of printed fabrics, built in 1791, contained two rows of tables along its length with workers positioned alongside and racks of finished products at the end of each row. This, for Foucault, was an exemplary 'disciplinary space', because it was one in which productive functions were efficiently performed, while simultaneously a mass of people was effectively managed, by tactics of disaggregation; individualisation; and the confinement of each individual within the mass to his or her 'cell':

> By walking up and down the central aisle of the workshop, it was possible to carry out a supervision that was both general and individual: to observe the worker's presence and application, the quality of his work, to compare workers with each other, to classify them according to skill and speed, to follow the successive stages of the production process ... At the emergence of large-scale industry, one finds, beneath the division of the production process, the individualising fragmentation of labour power; the distributions of the disciplinary space often assured both. (145)

The possibility of ranking individuals relative to each other was therefore inherent in the process of partitioning space. Discipline 'individualises bodies by a location that does not give them a fixed position, but distributes them and circulates them in a network of relations' (146). It is in this connection that Foucault singles out the procedure of drawing up tables, or classificatory schemes, as 'the first of the great operations of discipline' (148). Tables 'transform the confused, useless or dangerous multitudes into ordered multiplicities' (148). So in schools, for example, the traditional organisation of educational space – whereby pupils of all ages and abilities sat together under the eye of one master – began to be replaced in the eighteenth century by the 'class', which gathered pupils of similar ages and abilities in a single room and ranked them in relation to each other. The homogeneous classroom, and the rankings expressed in its spatial arrangement, is a kind of three-dimensional 'table'. It made possible a more efficient system of teaching than had prevailed before (each pupil working for only a few minutes at a time with the master while the rest of the group remained idle and unattended), by permitting a precise and continuous evaluation of each pupil relative to others. Thus it too was a disciplinary space: 'It made the educational space function like a learning machine, but also as a machine for supervising, hierarchizing, rewarding' (147).

Closely related to the disciplinary partitioning of space is the partitioning of time. The chief mechanism here was and remains the timetable. This, like the cell, was of monastic origin – it clearly derived from the regular division of the monk's day into set tasks and a set rhythm of activities – but the disciplines refined it considerably. Consider, for example, this extract from the rules drawn up for inmates of a Paris reformatory of the 1830s:

> At the first drum roll, the prisoners must rise and dress in silence, as the supervisor opens the cell doors. At the second drum roll, they must be dressed and make up their bed. At the third, they must line up and proceed to chapel for morning prayer. There is a five-minute interval between each drum roll. (6)

What we see here, first, is a much more detailed partitioning of time than had ever been attempted in the medieval monasteries: 'one began to count in quarter hours, in minutes, in seconds' (150). Second, time measured out in this way must be spent with the maximum efficiency: it is with the emergence of the disciplines, Foucault implies, that the notion of 'quality time' – time well spent on the precise purpose to which it has been allotted – is born. Discipline posits that time itself can be expanded by being divided up into ever more minute parcels, and it requires that the best possible use is made of these parcels: 'it is a question of extracting, from time, ever more available moments and, from each moment, ever more useful forces' (154). Third, the disciplines applied temporal imperatives not only to the individual's general activities, but beyond these to the most minute movements and gestures of the body. Bodily movements are dissected into individual acts and organised into chronological stages in the achievement of particular tasks:

> A sort of anatomo-chronological schema of behaviour is defined. The act is broken down into its elements; the position of the body, limbs, articulation is defined; to each movement is assigned a direction, an aptitude, a duration; their order of succession is

prescribed. Time penetrates the body and with it all the meticulous controls of power (152).

The prescribed 'order of succession', moreover, is always calculated to ensure that series of gestures performed will be the most efficient relative to the task or act to be carried out. In this connection Foucault refers to La Salle's lengthy description of exactly what position each part of a pupil's body should assume in relation to every other part at every stage in the achievement of good handwriting (152). Now the process of handwriting as La Salle described it involves a complex series of movements which involve relations not only between parts of the human body (fingers, wrists, elbows etc), but between the body and external objects (pens, surfaces, desks, chairs etc). Similarly, eighteenth century military manuals tended to break down the apparently simple action of loading a rifle into a series of minute acts performed on various parts of the rifle by various parts of the body. Thus a fourth characteristic of the disciplinary partitioning of time is what Foucault terms 'the instrumental coding of the body':

> [This] consists of a breakdown of the total gesture into two parallel series: that of the parts of the body to be used (right hand, left hand, different fingers of the hand, knee, eye, elbow etc.) and that of the parts of the object manipulated (barrel, notch, hammer, screw etc.); then the two sets of parts are correlated together according to a number of simple gestures (rest, bend); lastly, it fixes the canonical succession in which each of these correlations occupies a particular place. This obligatory syntax is what the military theoreticians of the eighteenth century called 'manoeuvre' ... Over the whole surface of contact between the body and the object it handles, power is introduced, fastening them to one another. It constitutes a body-weapon, body-tool, body-machine complex. (153)

If the partitioning of space is achieved by means of the table, and the partitioning of time by the manoeuvre, then a third procedure – the exercise – is instrumental to what Foucault calls 'the "seriation" of successive activities' (160), which in turn is a third component of disciplinary power. 'Exercise is that technique by which one imposes on the body tasks that are both repetitive and different, but always graduated.' (161) The notion of progress or evolution is integral to the technique of exercise, which links a series of increasingly difficult assignments into a programme of individual improvement oriented towards a determinate goal. Like the partitioning of space and time, the exercise had a long history, particularly amongst religious communities where it appeared in the guise of an increasingly rigorous sequence of devotional practices undertaken with the aim of ultimately purifying oneself spiritually and so finding salvation. Foucault cites 'an educational 'programme' that would follow the child to the end of his schooling and which would involve from year to year, from month to month, exercises of increasing complexity' (161) as an example of its modern, and specifically disciplinary, form.

Fourthly, discipline required a means of synchronising the movements of each individual subjected to these spatial fragmentations, manoeuvres and exercises with the movements of other such individuals. Discipline composes individuals' activities into an efficient 'machine': a force superior to the sum of the elements comprising it.

The shift in the organisation of the military at the end of the seventeenth century – from the army as a mass of troops, undifferentiated except by reference to individual soldiers' qualities of courage or honour, to the army as a mechanical arrangement of units (regiments, battalions, sections) – is exemplary here: the new model army is a 'geometry of divisible segments whose basic unity was the mobile soldier with his rifle; and, no doubt, below the soldier himself, the minimal gestures, the elementary stages of actions, the fragments of space occupied or traversed' (163). Pursuing the military analogy, Foucault applies the term 'tactics' to this process of arranging combinations of forces: 'tactics', after all, is commonly defined as the art of directing the detailed movement of forces in battle to achieve an aim. If it is to work effectively in any context, the tactical deployment of forces requires a precise, economical system of command, not dissimilar to the system of dressage by which horses are trained to perform movements automatically in response to their riders' signals. In the army, for example, a kind of human dressage can be observed in the way soldiers are trained to respond promptly and blindly to verbal orders issued by senior officers.

Discipline, then, comprises four types of practice, corresponding to four types of effect on those individuals who are subjected to discipline:

> To sum up, it might be said that discipline creates out of the bodies it controls four types of individuality, or rather an individuality that is endowed with four characteristics: it is cellular (by the play of spatial distribution), it is organic (by the coding of activities), it is genetic (by the accumulation of time), it is combinatory (by the composition of forces). And in doing so, it operates four great techniques: it draws up tables; it prescribes movements; it imposes exercises; lastly, in order to obtain the combination of forces, it arranges 'tactics'. Tactics, the art of constructing, with located bodies, coded activities and trained aptitudes, mechanisms in which the product of the various forces is increased by their calculated combination are no doubt the highest form of disciplinary practice. (167)

Through the deployment of these four techniques, localised on the body, individuals could be coaxed into routinised modes of conduct that were both predictable and useful. In addition, however, the successful functioning of discipline required procedures through which this conduct could be evaluated and where necessary improved. This was achieved, according to Foucault, by practices of 'hierarchical observation' and 'normalising judgement', as combined in the form of yet a further technique: the examination. With regard to observation, first, Foucault notes that the eighteenth century heralds the rise of a form of power that functions by seeing (everything, in immense detail), rather than by being seen: 'Disciplinary power ... is exercised through its invisibility; at the same time it imposes on those whom it subjects a principle of compulsory visibility' (187) This new kind of relation between power and visibility is most clearly evidenced by the emergence of new architectural forms. Palaces and the other great buildings of state had long served to enthral, terrify or inspire the subjects who looked at them with their size and ostentation. The disciplinary spaces that began to emerge in the early eighteenth century, by contrast, turned a meticulous gaze on those arranged *inside*: they were instruments of an intense and continuous surveillance that, though hierarchically organised, could in principle issue from bottom to top and from side to side as well as from top to bottom. As we shall see presently, Jeremy Bentham's design for a 'panoptic' prison – a circular cell block with a tower in the middle, from which each and every cell could at all times be seen – is, for Foucault, the 'perfect disciplinary apparatus' because it 'make[s] it possible for a single gaze to see everything constantly' (173).

Normalising judgement, on the other hand, is the specific form of disciplinary punishment. A number of features distinguish it from the kind of punishment meted out by the state through the criminal justice system. First, its scale and regularity: Foucault terms disciplinary punishment a 'micro-' or 'infra-penality' that operates continuously in the gaps left by the criminal law to regulate trifling infractions (such as lateness for work, inattentiveness during lessons, or untidy uniforms) by a variety of 'minor deprivations and petty humiliations' (178). This is a form of punishment, then, that is continuous and microscopic rather than occasional and spectacular. Second, what might be called its governing logic: a 'juridico-natural' logic involving the enforcement of an order constituted of both rules and norms. The difference between rules and norms is difficult to grasp – not having been particularly clearly explained by Foucault himself – and is made more difficult by the fact that both of these terms have been defined in completely incompatible ways by other theorists, including legal theorists (see for example Kelsen on norms, Chapter 5; Hart on rules, Chapter 4). Foucault's own usage must be seen in relation to his conception of the relation between power and knowledge, which is explained further below. 'Norm' in the Foucaultian sense (contrast Kelsen's interpretation) refers to a standard representing an average. Norms necessarily, therefore, invoke a knowledge of 'natural' facts – about people's 'normal' capacities and limits, for example – in the very process of their formulation. Hence when viewed in relation to the norm, behaviour is not so much obedience (or not) to the norm as that which is widely distributed around it: compliance is always relative; a matter or more or less rather than yes or no. Rules, on the other hand, are artificially posited (made rather than discovered); they are prescriptive rather than descriptive; and their application can produce only two possible outcomes: observance or non-observance. When Foucault remarks that '[i]n a disciplinary regime punishment involves a double juridico-natural reference' (179), he may be referring to the reciprocal dependence of rules and norms in such regimes. On the one hand, the content of rules (eg mandatory educational programmes; school regulations) is derived from norms (eg of ability and behaviour in children of different ages). On the other hand, the process of quantifying and averaging out infractions and observances of rules to produce a model of the normally obedient individual turns rule-following behaviour into just another source of norms: 'by the play of this quantification, this circulation of awards and debits, thanks to the continuous calculation of plus and minus points, the disciplinary apparatuses hierarchized the 'good' and the 'bad' subjects in relation to one another'. (181).

The 'juridico-natural' regimes of discipline thus place the individual who is subjected to them under an *obligation to be normal*, or at least not to be abnormally 'bad': the rule is 'made to function … as *an average to be respected* or as *an optimum towards which one must move*' (183, emphasis added). In this way, discipline acknowledges differences between people while imposing homogeneity. Having described the grading system (very good, good, mediocre, bad and shameful) used at a French military school during the eighteenth century, Foucault concludes as follows:

> This hierarchizing penality had, therefore, a double effect: it distributed pupils according to their aptitudes and their conduct, that is, according to the use that could be made of them when they left the school; it exercised over them a constant pressure to conform to the same model, so that they might all be subjected to 'subordination, docility, attention to studies and exercises, and to the correct practice of duties and all the parts of discipline'. So that they might all be like one another. (182)

It follows, thirdly, that the purpose of disciplinary punishment is the correction of deviant individuals, whereas that of the criminal justice system is the condemnation of forbidden acts:

> It [ie normalising judgement] is opposed ... to a judicial penalty whose essential function is to refer, not to a set of observable phenomena, but to a corpus of laws and texts that must be remembered; that operates not by differentiating individuals, but by specifying acts according to a number of general categories; not by hierarchizing but quite simply by bringing into play the binary opposition of the permitted and the forbidden; not by homogenizing, but by operating the division, acquired once and for all, of condemnation. (183)

What then of the 'examination'? What role does it play in disciplinary power? Examination is a process of comparing individuals, deriving a norm on the basis of that comparison, judging those same individuals on the basis of the norm as derived, and intervening to enforce the norm in relation to those who depart from it. Disciplinary power is characterised by an ongoing examination: continuous surveillance coupled with a constant process of judging.

> The examination combines the techniques of an observing hierarchy with those of a normalizing judgement. It is a normalizing gaze, a surveillance that makes it possible to qualify, to classify and to punish. It establishes over individuals a visibility through which one differentiates and judges them. (184)

Finally, writing is thoroughly bound up with disciplinary power. 'The examination that places individuals in a field of surveillance also situates them in a network of writing; it engages then in a whole mass of documents that capture and fix them' (189). A vast documentary archive, a mountain of files and dossiers containing the most minute observations, constitute individuals as 'cases': describable, analysable objects of a possible normalization (190). Discipline thus marks out those on whom it is exercised as particular individuals – by fixing individual differences in a recorded form – and in so doing it reverses the traditional relationship between individualisation and power. In feudal societies, the closer one is to the sovereign or the feudal lord – the traditional loci of power – the more one is singled out as an individual by written and pictorial representations of one's deeds, status and wealth. In disciplinary regimes, by contrast, it is the marginal and the lowly who become the focus of attention: 'the child is more individualised than the adult, the patient more than the healthy man, the madman and the delinquent more than the normal and the non-delinquent' (193). At the same time, power is dis-individualised: it is embodied a set of practices, not in the person of a king or other figurehead. Both of these aspects of disciplinary power emerge particularly clearly in Foucault's account of the 'panoptic' prison ('Panopticism', reproduced as the first reading below). Consider the fate of the prisoners arranged in the circular cell block around the prison's central tower:

> By the effect of backlighting, one can observe from the tower, standing out precisely against the light, the small captive shadows in the cells of the periphery. They are like so many cages, so many small theatres, in which each actor is alone, perfectly individualized and constantly visible ... Each individual, in his place, is securely confined to a cell from which he is seen from the front by the supervisor; but the side walls prevent him from coming into contact with his companions. He is seen, but he does not see; he is the object of information, never a subject in communication ... The crowd, a compact mass, a locus of multiple exchanges, individualities merging together, a collective effect, is abolished and replaced by a collection of separated individualities. From the point of view of the guardian, it is replaced by a multiplicity that can be numbered and supervised; from the point of view of the inmates, by a sequestered and observed solitude. (200–201)

At the same time, the power that acts on the delinquent individual is perfectly anonymous. Anyone – not only the prison governor but their friends, family or employees – can switch on the panoptic machine by standing in the central tower and spying on the prisoners in the surrounding cells. No one – not even the prison governor – is immune from examination: even the supervisor is subject to supervision. A prison inspector, for example, would be able to judge at a glance how the establishment as a whole was functioning, and so determine the competence of the governor, by standing in the tower and surveying the scene. But crucially, the machine does not even require a human operator in order to achieve its effects. Bentham's design was calculated to ensure that no prisoner would ever be able to tell for sure whether or not anyone was in the tower observing them, and thus that every prisoner would behave at all times as if they were being observed. The paradoxical result, according to Foucault, is that these objectified individuals, who are seen but do not see, internalise the 'gaze' of the supervisor and begin to supervise themselves:

> He who is subject to the field of visibility and who knows it, assumes responsibility for the constraints of power; he makes them play spontaneously upon himself; he inscribes in himself the power relation in which he simultaneously plays both roles; he becomes the principle of his own subjection. (202–3)

It follows that 'it is not necessary to use force to constrain the convict to good behaviour' (202). Anyone caught within the Panopticon's disciplinary apparatus, Foucault suggests, will develop the capacity to reflect on and correct their own behaviour. This, indeed, is probably the single most significant feature of disciplinary power: the way it eschews the use of force and instead insinuates itself into the bodies and minds of individuals, forming the very aptitudes that are supposed to be innate to the individual – physical capacities; the capacity for conscience and self-reflection – and working with, rather than against, these to produce subjects who are at the same time 'objects and instruments of its exercise' (170). The double meaning of the term 'subject' should be noted here, linked as it is both with subjection and with agency or freedom. For Foucault, the subject of conscience who freely chooses to reform himself or herself is always already an artefact of discipline.

This is perhaps an appropriate point at which to summarise Foucault's main conclusions about the nature and effects of discipline. Discipline, first, is a 'technology': 'it is a type of power, a modality for its exercise, comprising a whole set of instruments, techniques, procedures, levels of application, targets; it is a "physics" or an "anatomy" of power, a technology' (215). We have identified the main instruments that comprise it, and their respective targets and levels of application. But why describe discipline as a 'technology' at all? In ordinary parlance, technology is 'the appliance of science': a practical application of scientific knowledge, usually in the form of a mechanism that is capable of intervening in some object or process to produce some end. Foucault's choice of this term to characterise discipline is therefore probably calculated to draw attention to the entwinement of knowledge and power – or investigation and intervention – within the techniques that make it up. The acts of seeing and supervising; notating and normalising; classifying and correcting are thoroughly bound together in the practices described above: practices of partitioning space and time, linking movements to objects and to other movements, designing exercises to mould individual conduct towards particular ends, and so on. Foucault identifies the early eighteenth century as a crucial moment in the formation of a distinct technology out of these practices, many of which had existed before in different forms. It was at this time that they converged to 'produce the blueprint of a general method' (138) that remains active in contemporary society, which Foucault often refers to as a 'disciplinary society' or a 'society of normalisation'. These power/knowledge complexes continue to envelop individuals in a dense mesh of 'continuous and uninterrupted processes' (97) that train and optimise our capacities and aptitudes, govern our gestures, and organise our responses by reference to the norms identified by a relentlessly vigilant 'gaze'. The modern individual, then, *precisely in his or her individuality*, is a normalised, docile object, actively constituted as such through the workings of discipline.

It is because discipline *is* a technology, Foucault argues, that it has proved to be so adaptable and enduring. As we have seen, Foucault detects it at work in many locations from the beginning of the eighteenth century: not only prisons, but schools, factories, hospitals, insane asylums, workhouses and army barracks. It spread through these institutions for the same reason that any new technology becomes widely used: it worked better than what was there before. 'The panoptic schema makes any apparatus of power more intense: it assures its economy (in material, in personnel, in time); it assures its efficacy by its preventative character, its continuous functioning and its automatic mechanisms' (206). The panoptic schema also ensures that this growth in the efficiency of power's 'mechanisms' enhances the output of the institutions (educational, military, industrial or medical) in which it is installed. The emergence of a disciplinary society, however, involved much more than the spread of the disciplinary mechanism within and amongst enclosed institutions: it was enabled by the 'escape' of the technology from the confines of these institutions and its free circulation throughout society at large. The conduits for this were initially charitable organisations and private philanthropists, such as those who set off into the urban slums thrown up by the Industrial Revolution on expeditions that were calculated both to explore and improve the lives and morals of the 'labouring classes'. Subsequently, however, it was the role assumed by the state in relation to disciplinary technology that ensured the latter's capacity to penetrate every corner of society. We will return to this important theme in Section III below.

II.B. Power, in General

Having looked in some detail at the components and *modus operandi* of disciplinary power as Foucault perceives it, it is now time to reflect more generally on the method he uses to analyse power, to clarify his terminology, to consider the peculiarities of his approach relative to the perspectives on power traditionally presupposed by legal theory, and to identify some of its obvious difficulties. Perhaps the most striking feature of Foucault's method is his choice of initial starting point. In analysing the emergence of the form of power in which he is interested, Foucault does not begin, as most political theorists would, with processes of state formation or great constitutional upheavals such as the bourgeois revolutions of the eighteenth and nineteenth centuries or the rise of social democracy in the twentieth. Although he sees power manifesting itself at many levels – from the architectural arrangements of particular buildings to the constitutional arrangements of particular states – in his view it is best approached 'at the point where it is in direct and immediate relationship with ... its object, its target, its field of application, there ... where it installs itself and produces its real effects' (F 1980, 97). The primary unit of analysis for the study of power from a Foucaultian perspective, then, is practice and the relations between practices, many of which appear to be infinitesimally small and insignificant. Thus for Foucault, tiny changes in the way soldiers were instructed to hold their rifles in the early eighteenth century are at least as interesting as, and in an important sense paved the way for, the massive economic, cultural and political transformations associated with the French Revolution. This yields our first 'Foucaultian' proposition: *power is embedded in, and is made effective through, micro-practices and the relations between them.*

'Technologies' of power emerge from these relations, and technologies are complexes of discourse and action; knowledge and the forms of intervention that knowledge makes available. It has already been noted that Foucault is also interested in 'regimes' of practices, which occupy a higher stratum in his 'ascending analysis of power'. But here again, 'to analyse regimes of practices means to analyse programmes of conduct which have both prescriptive effects regarding what is to be done (effects of 'jurisdiction') and codifying effects regarding what is to be known (effects of 'veridiction')' (F 1991b, 75). For Foucault, then, *power and knowledge are inextricably intertwined at every level at which power manifests itself.* Further, *these power/ knowledge apparatuses are regulatory in their effects.* 'Technologies' are the actual mechanisms through which the conduct, thoughts, decisions and aspirations of persons are shaped and moulded towards some particular end. 'Regimes' are arguably the ensembles that technologies form both with each other, and with other elements – such as philosophical propositions, moral codes, and rules of positive law – which are less directly oriented towards intervention in individual conduct, but which nonetheless help to organise domains for action and render certain ways of acting upon them thinkable. To return again to the example of the prison, disciplinary technology manifests itself here as a set of power/knowledge practices focused on the behaviour of the prison inmate and oriented towards his or her rehabilitation. 'The prison' itself, however, is the effect of a regime of practices comprising this technology as one of its elements: others would include the humanitarian discourse of the Enlightenment and translations of these ideas into criminological theories; utilitarian arguments for penal reform; and legal rules affecting punishment.

Relations between individuals and groups, as well as relations between practices, are clearly indispensable to the effectiveness of power: power targets individuals and groups, and is mobilised through the actions of individuals and groups (F 1983, 217). Hence the prison cannot function as a prison without prison authorities which 'exercise power' over inmates. But for Foucault, these human actions are not the essence of power so much as elements within the repertoire of means by which power produces its effects: as Foucault continually emphasises, 'power is not something that is acquired, seized or shared, something that one holds onto or allows to slip away ...' (F 1979, 94). This distinction between *exercising* power and being an instrument *for* its exercise is a difficult one to comprehend, and some would say that it exposes a serious problem with Foucault's analysis: a tendency to dispense with human agency only to install 'Power' as a new, non-human and deeply mysterious, super-agent. We have already seen evidence of this tendency in the notion that 'strategies without strategists' co-ordinate micropractices, and the networks they form in combination with each other, into larger systems. Foucault would seem to be suggesting that the emergence of these systems, and the relationships between them, are attributable to power, not to people. He continually reiterates this controversial idea, as here:

> Power relations are both intentional and nonsubjective. If in fact they are intelligible, this is not because they are the effect of another instance that 'explains' them, but rather because they are imbued, through and through, with calculation: there is no power that is exercised without a series of aims and objectives. But this does not mean that it results from the choice or decision of an individual subject ... [T]he rationality of power is characterised by tactics that are often quite explicit at the restricted level where they are inscribed (the local cynicism of power), tactics which, becoming connected to one another, attracting and propagating one another, but finding their base of support and their condition elsewhere, end by forming comprehensive systems: the logic is perfectly clear, the aims decipherable, and yet it is often the case that no one is there to have invented them, and few who can be said to have formulated them: an implicit characteristic of the great anonymous, almost unspoken strategies which coordinate the loquacious tactics whose 'inventors' or decisionmakers are often without hypocrisy. (F 1979, 95)

True, the kinds of metaphors to which Foucault resorts when drawing attention to power's priority relative to people do not 'personify' power so much as represent it to be a kind of machine: power is described as achieving its effects through 'mechanisms', 'techniques' or 'technologies'. And considered as a means or medium for power's exercise, the individual is represented as a machine part: 'it' is described as a 'vehicle', 'instrument' or 'relay' of power, or as 'the element of [power's] articulation'. Yet this still leaves us with a picture of power as a kind of thinking machine, and individuals as that machine's cogs, and even, as we are about to discover, its artefacts.

Power is productive, both in the sense that it maximises the capabilities of individuals, and in the deeper sense that it constitutes human beings as individuals ('subjects') in the first place. As Foucault puts it, in a much-quoted passage:

> The individual is not to be conceived of as a sort of elementary nucleus, a primitive atom, a multiple and inert material on which power comes to fasten or against which it happens to strike, and in so doing subdues or crushes individuals. In fact, it is already one of the prime effects of power that certain bodies, certain gestures, certain discourses, certain desires, come to be identified and constituted as individuals. The individual, that is, is not the vis-à-vis of power; it is, I believe, one of its prime effects. (F 1980, 98)

A related point which has already been noted is that 'the individual which power has constituted is at the same time its [ie power's] vehicle' (F 1980, 98). Individuals are constituted as active participants in the network of relations that forms them: they function as relays within the network, linking its elements together and so ensuring its continued efficacy. Thus, individuals 'are always in the position of simultaneously undergoing and exercising this power. They are not only its inert or consenting target; they are always also the elements of its articulation' (F 1980, 98). Yet despite being produced by, endlessly in the grip of, and necessarily functional for, power, individuals are also free: in fact *freedom is the condition for the exercise of power*. This is one of the most baffling of Foucault's claims, and it appears in the context of the following important passage:

> [W]hat defines a relationship of power is that it is a mode of action which does not act directly and immediately on others. Instead, it acts upon their actions ... [The exercise of power] is a total structure of actions brought to bear upon possible actions; it incites, it induces, it seduces, it makes easier or more difficult; in the extreme it constrains or forbids absolutely; it is nevertheless always a way of acting upon an acting subject or acting subjects by virtue of their acting or being capable of action. A set of actions upon other actions.

> Perhaps the equivocal nature of the term conduct is one of the best aids for coming to terms with the specificity of power relations. For to 'conduct' is at the same time to 'lead' others (according to mechanisms of coercion which are, to varying degrees, strict) and a way of behaving within a more or less open field of possibilities. The exercise of power consists in guiding the possibility of conduct and putting in order the possible outcome.

> ...

> When one defines the exercise of power as a mode of action upon the actions of others ... one includes an important element: freedom. By this we mean individual or collective

subjects who are faced with a field of possibilities in which several ways of behaving, several reactions and diverse comportments may be realized. Where the determining factors saturate the whole there is no relationship of power; slavery is not a power relationship where man is in chains. (In this case it is a question of a physical relationship of constraint.) Consequently there is no face to face confrontation of power and freedom which is mutually exclusive (freedom disappears everywhere power is exercised), but a much more complicated interplay. In this game, freedom may well appear as the condition for the exercise of power (at the same time its precondition, since freedom must exist for power to be exerted, and also its permanent support, since without the possibility of recalcitrance, power would be equivalent to a physical determination) (F 1983, 220–221).

What this suggests, first, is that *the end of power is the production of a kind of regulated freedom*: a form of individuality that, precisely in its freedom, is also useful; that through its experience of autonomy is neatly integrated into the social order. Power 'makes society function', that is to say, by maximising the capacities and aptitudes of 'free' individuals, while at the same time acting upon these capacities and aptitudes so that they are exercised consistently with the demands of social coordination. It does this *by means of mechanisms that are local, material, continuous, and exhaustive, and that combine scientific observation and assessment of persons with precisely targeted interventions in their behaviours and attitudes*. Hence, the analysis of power should be concerned with 'power at its extremities, in its ultimate destinations, with those points where it becomes capillary, that is, in its more local and regional institutions' (F 1980, 96), and the key question for this kind of analysis is 'how things work at the level of ongoing subjugation, at the level of those continuous and uninterrupted processes which subject our bodies, govern our gestures, dictate our behaviours etc … We should try to grasp subjection in its material instance as a constitution of subjects' (F 1980, 96–97).

But second, the success of this 'government of individualisation' (F 1983, 210) can never be guaranteed, because *the possibility of recalcitrance is integral to power's exercise*. This brings us to yet another of Foucault's assertions about power which at first glance appears somewhat counterintuitive: 'Where there is power, there is resistance, and yet, or rather consequently, this resistance is never in a position of exteriority in relation to power' (F 1979, 95). If, as Foucault insists, '[a]t the very heart of the power relationship are the recalcitrance of the will and the intransigence of freedom' (F 1983, 221–222), then it follows that resistance must be inscribed as an 'irreducible opposite' (F 1979, 96) in every power relationship. And if power is indeed produced from one moment to the next, at every one of the 'innumerable points' from which it is exercised; if power relations form a 'moving substrate of force relations' (F 1979, 93), then the same can surely be said of the resistances that power incites:

> Hence they too are distributed in irregular fashion: the points, knots, or focuses of resistance are spread over time and space at varying densities, at times mobilizing groups or individuals in a definitive way … producing cleavages in a society that shift about, fracturing unities and effecting regroupings, furrowing across individuals themselves, cutting them up and remoulding them … Just as the network of power relations ends

by forming a dense web that passes through apparatuses and institutions, without being exactly localized in them, so too the swarm of points of resistance traverses social stratifications and individual unities. (F 1979, 96)

Yet this kind of rhetoric, compelling though it may be, seems to expose a serious contradiction at the heart of Foucault's thinking. Here he gives us a view of the social order as precisely an anti-order – a teeming mass of powers and counter-powers, endlessly in tension – whereas elsewhere, as we have seen, Foucault represents social practices as congealed into 'comprehensive systems' (F 1979, 95) which function – through power's 'strategising' – like well-oiled machines. To which view does Foucault wish to commit himself? The answer is: both, simultaneously. Certainly, power 'must be analysed as something which circulates ... never localised here or there, never in anybody's hands ... employed and exercised through a net-like organisation' (F 1980, 98). On the other hand, Foucault also wants to account for the relative durability and stability of our social arrangements – the fact that these are clearly not in a state of endless flux, but are relatively patterned and predictable. He acknowledges that there are locations in which struggle seems to have been brought to a halt, and where 'stable mechanisms' (F 1983, 225) – and, resting upon these, systems of domination – have taken root and arrested 'the free play of antagonistic reactions' (F 1983, 225):

> When I say that power establishes a network through which it freely circulates, this is true only up to a certain point ... I do not believe that one should conclude from this that that power is the best distributed thing in the world, although in some sense that is indeed so ... (F 1980, 99)

Foucault's point is that there is no necessity to this experience of fixity and stability, and he offers a dualistic way of interpreting social relations which, while taking seriously this experience, is also capable of showing how it could yet be undone:

> At every moment the relationship of power may become a confrontation between two adversaries. Equally, the relationship between adversaries in society may, at every moment, give place to the putting into operation of mechanisms of power. The consequence of this instability is the ability to decipher the same events and the same transformations either from inside the history of struggle or from the standpoint of the power relationships. The interpretations which result will not consist of the same elements of meaning or the same links or the same type of intelligibility, although they refer to the same historical fabric and each of the two analyses must have reference to the other. In fact it is precisely the disparities between the two readings which make visible those fundamental phenomena of 'domination' which are present in a large number of human societies. (F 1983, 226)

It follows, finally, that the form of power in which Foucault is interested will indeed appear to be 'invisible' to the extent that it is embedded in what we are conditioned to see as innocuous, commonplace aspects of social life. Foucault's argument, however, is that this conditioning and this invisibility have to be understood, not as signs of power's absence, but rather of its efficacy. '*[S]ecrecy is not in the nature of an abuse [of power]; it is indispensable to its operation*' (F 1979, 86). Hence the analysis of power is inevitably a process of 'deciphering' its operations in what may seem, at first sight, unlikely processes and places.

It would appear, then, that a radical political agenda underlies Foucault's investigations: to bring 'domination' to light by finding conflict (or 'struggle') where there appears to be only consensus and stability, and by showing how domination is perpetuated precisely through the production of the *appearance* of consensus and stability. Foucault's rejection of orthodox accounts of the character of power and domination in modern societies assumes a new significance when viewed in this light. As we shall explore further in Section III.C below, Foucault does not simply regard these accounts as inadequate and incomplete. More fundamentally, he sees their inadequacy and incompleteness as functioning to mask the forms that domination takes and so as *enabling* domination. Liberal political theory, for example, which characterises power as centralised in the state – and reconciles us to it by distinguishing between its legitimate and illegitimate exercise (the rule of law versus arbitrary state coercion) – is, for Foucault, itself simply one element within the much more extensive and complex power/knowledge regimes that he is interested in analysing. It follows that liberal political theory, far from being a helpful guide to understanding power in modern societies, misrepresents power; disguises it; and thus facilitates its operations.

Once again, however, difficulties arise here: this time from Foucault's refusal to engage directly with the normative questions – the 'ought' questions – that emerge from his investigations of how power works. These have been cogently addressed by Nancy Fraser in an important early critique of this aspect of Foucault's work (Fraser, 1981). Fraser argues that in diagnosing the role played by liberal political theory – with its categories of right, limit, sovereignty, contract and oppression – in facilitating the spread of the kind of power in which he is interested, Foucault 'brackets' or suspends the problem of power's justification: the problem, that is, of distinguishing between its legitimate and illegitimate exercise. Yet when he adverts to the existence of 'domination', and particularly when he refers approvingly to 'resistance' and 'struggle', he necessarily brings normative standards back into his analysis, though without articulating what exactly these are:

> Why is struggle preferable to submission? Why ought domination to be resisted? Only with the introduction of normative notions of some kind could Foucault begin to answer such questions. Only with the introduction of normative notions could he begin to tell us what is wrong with the modern power/knowledge regime and why we ought to oppose it. (Fraser 1981, 283)

In fact, Fraser argues, the normative force of the idea that domination should be resisted seems to depend upon an implicit invocation of the very liberal norms Foucault ostensibly suspends; hence his use of such terms seems to ensnare him in a contradiction, since Foucault wants to treat liberal norms merely as *instruments* of domination. This contradiction emerges particularly clearly, she suggests, in *Discipline and Punish*. The originality of Foucault's analysis of the prison in this work is that it breaks with the common-sense view that power is exercised over prisoners by depriving them of their dignity and autonomy. What Foucault claims to find exemplified in the modern prison, instead, is a form of power that is thoroughly consistent with (a certain kind of) autonomy and self-respect, and is oriented towards augmenting, rather than diminishing, the capacities of those in relation to whom it is exercised. It is this form of power which, he claims, has become generalised within the disciplinary society that we currently inhabit. Yet as Fraser points out,

> If one asks what exactly is wrong with that society ... one cannot help but appeal to such concepts as the violation of dignity and autonomy involved in the treating of persons solely as means to be causally manipulated. But ... these Kantian notions are clearly related to the liberal norms of legitimacy and illegitimacy defined in terms of limits and rights. (Fraser 1981, 284)

With this in mind, it is now time to examine the relationship, as Foucault sees it, between discipline and the liberal notions of 'limits and rights'. This will return us to the theme left hanging at the end of Section II.A above: the relation between discipline, the state, and law.

III. Law

One of the most striking tendencies of Foucault's work on discipline is that it continually draws sharp contrasts between disciplinary power and another, radically different, form of power that Foucault designates as sovereign power or juridical power. It is tempting, but wrong, to conclude from this that disciplinary power is necessarily always exercised beyond the state, using other than legal means. Foucault's writings confront us time and again with the suggestion that, in fact, the state has played a crucial role in the spread and consolidation of disciplinary mechanisms:

> [I]n contemporary societies the state is not simply one of the forms or specific situations of the exercise of power – even if it is the most important – but ... in a certain way all other forms of power relation must refer to it. But this is not because they are derived from it; it is because power relations have come more and more under state control ... power relations have become progressively ... elaborated, rationalised and centralised in the form of, or under the auspices of, state institutions. (F 1983, 224)

Further, this process has had important effects on the form and functions of law:

> I do not mean to say that the law fades into the background or that the institutions of justice tend to disappear, but rather that the law operates more and more as a norm, and that the judicial institution is increasingly incorporated into a continuum of apparatuses (medical, administrative, and so on) that are for the most part regulatory. (F 1979, 144)

Clearly, then, Foucault envisages a complicated set of relationships between disciplinary power, sovereign power, the state, and law: an antithetical relationship between disciplinary power and sovereign power, but a cooperative relationship between discipline and the state. How are we to make sense of this apparent contradiction? Before attempting any further engagement with Foucault's often confusing remarks on these themes, it may be useful to bear the following points in mind. Generally, the term 'state' refers to a particular set of institutions, personnel and activities, whereas 'sovereignty' is a concept that (when used in relation to the state) serves to define the nature and limits of these institutions' powers. The concept of legality, when used in relation to that of state sovereignty, refers to a sovereign power limited by law and/or acting through the legal form. *A* law, on the other hand, is simply a particular instrument of state action. Foucault himself does not always observe these distinctions: his use of the term 'law' is particularly loose, and tends to be invoked to refer simultaneously to the concept of legality, the legal system, and the set of particular legal measures enacted and enforced by the state apparatus. Because of this, much confusion reigns in the secondary 'Foucault and law' literature as to what exactly Foucault had to say to lawyers and legal theorists (see eg Hunt, 1993, Ch 12; Hunt and Wickham, 1994, Chs 2 and 3; Palmer and Pearce 1983; Tadros, 1998). Nonetheless, a plausible way of reading the contradiction noted above might be the following. On the one hand, disciplinary power is at odds with the *concepts* of sovereignty and legality, which in defining and seeking to justify 'power', adopt an extremely restricted understanding of what power is. On the other hand, the actual mechanisms of discipline are thoroughly compatible with the regulatory *practices* of the modern state. Section III.A will explore the first of these propositions; Section III.B the second; and Section III.C will consider the relation between them.

III.A.   Sovereignty, Right and Legality

The primary point of reference for any exploration of Foucault's use of the above terms is a lecture delivered on 14 January 1976 (F 1980, reproduced below under the title 'Power/ Knowledge'). Foucault opens this lecture with the statement that one aim of his work on power is to relate its mechanisms to 'the rules of right that provide [power's] formal delimitation' (F 1980, 93). The rules of right, he goes on, are those yielded by 'legal thought', which represents power as that which is wielded by a sovereign authority: they are, therefore, the rules that delimit sovereign power. Foucault's usage of the term 'sovereignty' in this lecture, in turn, suggests that it is an umbrella term simultaneously accommodating these rules of right, the power they define – 'juridical power' – and the political and legal theories that seek to explain why this power is legitimate. Foucault's comments on all of these themes are highly schematic, and it might be useful at this point to refer to Jürgen Habermas' brief history of modern forms of 'sovereignty' for some clarification of what is in issue here. Habermas identifies what he calls 'four epochal juridification processes' (Habermas 1985, 204) as having occurred since the start of the seventeenth century:

> The first thrust led to the *bourgeois state* which, in Western Europe, developed during the period of Absolutism in the form of the European state system. The second thrust led to the *constitutional state* which assumed an exemplary form in the monarchy of 19th century Germany. The third thrust led to the *democratic constitutional state* which spread in Europe and North America in the wake of the French revolution. The last stage (to date) culminates in the *social and democratic constitutional state*, which was achieved through the struggles of the European workers' movement in the course of the 20th century ... (Habermas 1985, 204–5)

To revert now to Foucault's terminology, the first three of these state forms could each be said to be underpinned by a different conception of the 'rules of sovereign right'; characterised by a different kind of 'juridical power'; and accompanied by a different political theory. In the bourgeois state, as Habermas puts it, 'public law authorises a sovereign state power with a monopoly on coercive force as the sole source of legal domination' (Habermas 1985, 205) and Thomas Hobbes' *Leviathan* provides the justificatory theory: political sovereignty is said to originate in a contract under which individuals in the state of nature, to ensure their own survival, agree to hand over their prerogatives to a single authority whose power would be absolute. The constitutional state, by contrast, is one whose powers are limited by legally actionable constitutional norms: citizens are given rights against the sovereign (rights to life, liberty and property); the sovereign is obliged to use its monopoly on coercive force in accordance with the rule of law; and this is justified by reference to the ideal of freedom from *arbitrary* state coercion (the idea of individual freedom is particularly associated with the philosophy of Immanuel Kant, considered in Chapter 20). With the rise of the democratic constitutional state, thirdly, citizens are provided with rights of political participation: the right to vote and the freedom to organise political parties. This carries with it a new set of qualifications on sovereign power: to be validly enacted, laws must express the general will (a notion extensively addressed in the philosophical writings of Jean Jacques Rousseau), and this is assured by 'a procedure which binds legislation to parliamentary will-formation and public discussion' (Habermas 1985, 207). Habermas' fourth phase of juridification is of less significance than the other three for our purposes here (although we will return to it in Section III.B below), because its effect is not so much to redefine 'sovereignty' as to extend its domain of operation. The social and democratic constitutional state juridifies relations of inequality in society – particularly economic relations – that had previously been regarded as private and thus not amenable to state interference. Examples would include the use of law to equalise the relationship between workers and employers by shortening working hours and introducing collective bargaining rights and rights to social security.

Whereas Habermas is clearly concerned to chart the changes in 'sovereignty' over time, Foucault is interested in what he regards as a more fundamental continuity – not only as between these modern forms of sovereignty, but between them and the constitutional arrangements and theories of pre-modern times. For Foucault, the model of power that is presupposed by all of these remains the kind of absolute centralised power that was wielded by the monarchies of the late medieval West:

> [I]n Western societies since medieval times it has been royal power that has provided the essential focus around which legal thought has been elaborated. It is in response to the demands of royal power ... that the juridical edifice of our own society has been developed ... And when this legal edifice escapes in later centuries from the control of the monarch, when, more accurately, it is turned against that control, it is always the limits of this sovereign power that are put in question. (F 1980, 94)

Even as liberal legal thought has become preoccupied with imposing limits on power in order to guarantee its legitimacy, the assumption remains that without these limits power *would* be absolute. The liberal vision of a legally limited and hence legitimate power –

ideally, a democratically elected parliament exercising authority on the basis of the rule of law – is, for this reason, lumped together by Foucault with attempts by earlier thinkers to justify the authoritarian, administrative and absolutist monarchies of pre- and early modernity (F 1980, 103). 'In political thought and analysis, we still have not cut off the head of the king' (F 1979, 89): the way we think about politics, and hence about power, is still dominated by the huge, threatening, spectacular, yet distant figure of the Leviathan, even if today's 'king' is a democratically elected government hemmed in by constitutional refinements of various kinds.

What did undeniably change with the rise of the bourgeois state, however – and Foucault does not contest this – was the method by which the 'king's' right was legitimated. The notion that kings derive their powers from God alone – the divine right of kings – dominated political theory in the West from the later Middle Ages until the seventeenth century; thereafter, the idea that the authority of governments is derived from the consent of the governed began to take root. Yet although this latter notion has undergone many changes since the seventeenth century, here again Foucault sees a fundamental continuity in the midst of change. Political theory since Hobbes answers the question 'by what right does the sovereign wield power?' by invoking some notion of a contract between sovereign and subjects, where the identity of the subject is conceived of in terms of a capacity to contract, ie a will. It is through the instrumentality of this contract that a single – universal – will is distilled from the particular wills of a multiplicity of individuals (F 1980, 97). The shift from Hobbes's 'bourgeois state' to the 'democratic constitutional state' simply brings with it a new and more complicated social contract and a different conception of how the universal will is to be formed. Hobbes' rather one-sided deal gives way to an arrangement under which sovereign authority may only be exercised in accordance with certain rules: rules that constitute the sovereign; rules about how the sovereign, once constituted, can legitimately exercise power – including rules about the kinds of activities it can require or proscribe, and the procedures which must be followed in the process (the rule of law) – and rules of citizenship which determine the membership of the community to which the sovereign's authority extends, and the rights and obligations of those designated in this way as citizens.

Foucault's main point is that all of these efforts to delimit and legitimate sovereign power are not only fundamentally at one in their assumptions about the essential nature of power, but endlessly replay a narrow repertoire of solutions to the problems presented by this power: contract, limits, freely willed government and legitimate obligation pitted against usurpation, absolutism, oppression and coerced obedience. What this produces is a highly restrictive array of permissible questions for anyone who sets out to analyse the nature of power in modern society through the lens of political theory: What are the legitimate rights of sovereignty? Under what circumstances do we have a legal obligation to obey the sovereign (F 1980, 95)? Until the seventeenth and eighteenth centuries, Foucault suggests (F 1980, 104), this equation of power with sovereignty was in fact no reduction at all, because it reflected the actual mode of power's exercise: actual power relations in society took the same form as that of the sovereign-subject relation. But at around this time, a new mechanism of power (which we have encountered above as disciplinary power) emerged, and this, in Foucault's view, was 'absolutely incompatible with the relations of sovereignty' (F 1980, 104). This incompatibility revealed itself in the different targets, methods and objectives of disciplinary power and sovereign power. Disciplinary power is exercised over human bodies and their operations, and is oriented towards 'generating forces, making them grow, and ordering them, rather than ... impeding them, making them submit, or destroying them' (F 1979, 136). Monarchical power, by contrast, was exercised over the earth and its products, over land and goods; and it was 'a power of deduction, a subtraction mechanism ... essentially a right of seizure – of things, time, bodies and ultimately life itself' (F 1979, 136). Disciplinary power is constantly exercised by means of surveillance rather than sporadically by means of specific and defined obligations, and it presupposes a tightly knit grid of regulation rather than the physical existence of a monarch. Further, its ideal deployment is measured in terms of quiet efficiency – the minimum expenditure for the maximum return – and not, like monarchical power, in terms of a spectacular excess of terrifying force.

For all of these reasons, disciplinary power is 'impossible to describe in the terminology of sovereignty' (F 1979, 106): it simply cannot be accounted for using the categories of universality, citizenship, legality, and the separation of a public sphere of state power from a private sphere of individual freedom. Discipline circulates everywhere throughout the social order rather than being centralised in a single unitary agency. The logic of its operation is that of the norm, not that of the 'juridical rule': '[t]he disciplines may well be the carriers of a discourse that speaks of a rule, but this is not the juridical rule deriving from sovereignty, but a natural rule, a norm' (F 1979, 106). Finally, and most importantly, it *constructs* the individuals over whom it is exercised, and so cannot be explained by a theory which takes as *given* the 'delegative status of each citizen' (F 1979, 106). Sovereignty, as it is theorised from Hobbes onwards, is deemed to derive from the status of the individual as an abstract subject of will, and the rules which delimit it are oriented towards maintaining a totalising politico-legal framework within which the activities of a conglomeration of these ready-made subjects can be organised consistently with the maintenance of their originary autonomy. Discipline, on the other hand, starts from the premise that each individual is an embodied, living creature, an inhabitant of a particular environment, with a unique set of needs, interests, abilities and aptitudes; it seeks to administer and normalise the conduct of these discrete and disparate persons with a view to ordering a multiplicity of persons and making each and all of them more useful. Far from being the 'given' of power, individual capacities are in this modality the effect of power; far from being universal, they are irreducibly particular and endlessly differentiated.

III.B. The Regulatory State

Towards the end of Section II.A above, mention was made of a process Foucault describes in *Discipline and Punish* as 'a generalization of the disciplines that became co-extensive with the state itself' (F 1977, 215). Writing in relation to France, Foucault attributes this phenomenon to the growth of a centralised 'police' apparatus there during the eighteenth century. It should be noted that he is not here referring to the 'police' in the contemporary sense of the term: the police as a crime prevention and detection agency. The term 'police' in the eighteenth century sense designated a massive and somewhat formless field of intervention, from building construction, to matters concerning health and cleanliness, to the behaviour and dress of the poor: everything, in other words, that was untouched by the sovereign's law (Pasquino 1991). 'With the police, one is in the indefinite world of a supervision that seeks ideally to reach the most elementary particle, the most passing phenomenon of the social body … the infinitely small of political power' (F 1977, 213–4). Although a centralised administrative machinery under the control of the king exercised the police power in France, it did so by means of mechanisms that were specific to it and quite distinct from the formal institutions of sovereignty: a vast network of spies and informers 'that transformed the whole social body into a field of perception', and an immense archive of documents recording tiny details of 'behaviour, attitudes, possibilities, suspicions' (F 1977, 214).

For Foucault, the consolidation of the police power in France at this time is bound up with what he will later describe as the emergence of 'governmentality', a concept that is perhaps best understood when rendered in the form: govern/mentality. (Foucault's most sustained consideration of this theme appears in an essay entitled 'Governmentality' (F 1991a), extracts from which are reproduced below as the third reading.) Like power/knowledge, the term is calculated to draw attention to an ensemble of practices in which ways of ordering or ruling human activities are inextricably bound up with ways of knowing them. To this extent, governmentality has an affinity with discipline, though it operates on a larger scale than discipline: its target is not the body of an individual or a defined group of individuals, but an entire population. Like discipline, Foucault argues, governmentality assumed its modern form in the eighteenth century, triggered in part by linked processes of demographic expansion and socio-economic change. Together, these developments helped to bring 'the population' into view for the first time as a general problem – particularly for state officials facing the possibility of large-scale civil and political unrest. The rapid growth of anonymous urban spaces, the mobility of persons within and between them, the disintegration of traditional loci of social authority and the dissolution of customary rights and obligations: all of this would have exposed the patrimonial form of rule that had been associated with feudalism – and that had sustained the remote sovereign's occasional and intermittent displays of power – as inadequate to control the new 'masses', or to co-ordinate the force they represented with the requirements of capitalist production. Against this background, Foucault implies, it became evident that the security and prosperity of the state could not be guaranteed merely by the existence of a formal legal duty on every citizen to obey the sovereign and its laws. Obedience itself had to be actively secured, and prosperity positively enabled, by precisely targeted interventions in the social 'body', and this involved supplementing the structures and institutions of sovereignty with knowledges and techniques of population management.

The gathering of statistics – on the birth and death rates of populations, on the incidence of disease, criminality, unemployment and migration within them, on the differences of wealth that divided them, on the customs and rituals that united them – accorded an objective reality to these phenomena of population, and in this way helped to pave the way for a series of interventions oriented towards maximising its internal forces while minimising the threats that it posed. The knowledge required for government, however, is more than a list of data: it demonstrates relations between these phenomena of population, and between them and all those processes that affect the population. (Hence Foucault identifies political economy as governmentality's 'principal form of knowledge' (F 1991a, 102).) In so doing, it enables 'a plurality of specific aims' to be formulated: 'for instance, government will have to ensure that the greatest possible quantity of wealth is produced, that the people are provided with sufficient means of subsistence, that the population is enabled to multiply, etc.' (F 1991a, 95). Aims are achieved, in turn, by means of 'a range of multiform tactics':

> [W]ith sovereignty the instrument that allowed it to achieve its aim – that is to say, obedience to the laws – was the law itself; law and sovereignty were absolutely inseparable. On the contrary, with government it is a question not of imposing law on men, but of disposing things: that is to say, of employing tactics rather than laws, and even of using laws themselves as tactics – to arrange things in such a way that, through a certain number of means, such and such ends may be achieved (F 1991a, 95).

Foucault did not write a great deal on the theme of governmentality, and what he did write is short on the kind of detail and definition that characterises his work on discipline. Consequently, his treatment of this theme invites many questions. Only two of these will be considered here. First, what is the relationship between governmentality and the generalisation of the disciplines, and what do either of these phenomena, or both in combination, have to do with the state? Second, how have these phenomena affected the form and functions of modern law?

POWER AND THE MODERN STATE

One passage in Volume One of *The History of Sexuality* (F 1979) – a work completed after *Discipline and Punish* but before 'Governmentality' – suggests that governmentality, like discipline, is a form of 'power over life':

> In concrete terms, starting in the seventeenth century, this power over life evolved in two basic forms which constituted two poles of development ... One of these poles – the first to be formed, it seems – centred on the body as a machine: its disciplining, the optimisation of its capabilities, the extortion of its forces, the parallel increase of its usefulness and its docility, its integration into systems of efficient and economic controls, all this was ensured by the procedures of power that characterised the disciplines. The second, formed somewhat later, focused on the species body, the body imbued with the mechanics of life and serving as the basis of the biological processes: propagation, births and mortality, the level of health, life expectancy and longevity, with all the conditions that can cause these to vary. Their supervision was effected through an entire series of interventions and regulatory controls: a bio-politics of the population. (F 1979, 139)

Let us assume, first, that this second form of power – 'biopower' – approximates to what Foucault will later describe as governmentality, and second, that the 'interventions and regulatory controls' through which this biopower has been effected include interventions by the state. Putting these points together with Foucault's earlier assertions about the state's role in the generalisation of discipline, we end up with a preliminary hypothesis about the position of the state in relation to both governmentality and discipline. The emergence of governmentality coincided with the beginning of a process in which the state gradually assumed more and more responsibility for ensuring the health and fecundity of the 'species-body': the rise of a 'welfare' state. (For example, the regulation of public hygiene, food quality and sanitation; efforts to combat famines and epidemics and generally reduce the incidence of disease; and building and environmental controls – all paradigmatically 'bio-political' interventions – eventually became centralised under the auspices of the state and remain important state activities.) The spread of discipline, meanwhile, was connected with the rise of the 'social' state: a state that not only assumed control over certain disciplinary functions (especially through its increased role in education), but also acknowledged a responsibility to provide 'social security'. The architecture of the contemporary social security apparatus, with its all-seeing, all-knowing bureaucracy of officials and professionals, is really, it might be argued, a kind of Panoptic prison, which functions by surrounding the recipient of benefits with an array of disciplinary practices oriented towards re-forming him or her as a responsible, active citizen. Once caught in the welfare 'safety' net, beneficiaries are subjected to the 'pervasive investigative vigilance of the state' (H Dean 1991, 62): they are classified, assessed and finally labelled as deserving or undeserving, responsible or irresponsible, genuinely needy or merely a scrounger. Foucault's account of the strategy behind the grading system at the eighteenth century military academy mentioned in Section II.A above could, with only minor adaptations, qualify as an apt description of what the social security system does to its beneficiaries:

> it exercise[s] over them a constant pressure to conform to the same model, so that they might all be subjected to 'subordination, docility, attention to [work] and [domestic responsibilities], and to the correct practice of duties ...'

The social state, in short, is pre-eminently a *disciplinary* state which 'isolates, individuates, observes and controls the behaviour of the poor' (H Dean 1991, 62). Add to this a diagnosis of the '*national* security state' – and particularly the forms of continuous technological surveillance (CCTV, email-monitoring techniques, phone-tapping and so forth) associated with it – as also dependent for its efficacy upon a takeover of disciplinary techniques, and we might conclude that for Foucault, modern politics simply revolves around the containment of various kinds of threat and danger, and that governmentality and discipline have become crucial in facilitating this.

There are, however, problems with this interpretation of the governmentality-discipline-state relation. First, the representation of governmentality as biopower arguably yields an excessively narrow conception of governmentality, which in turn leaves unexplained the range of other (non- or not directly 'biological') functions performed by the state. Indeed Foucault elsewhere seemed to adopt a wider conception of governmentality, suggesting that it was concerned with just about every aspect of collective 'life':

> men in their relations, their links, their imbrication with other things which are wealth, resources, means of subsistence, the territory with its specific qualities, climate,

irrigation, fertility, etc.; men in their relation to ... customs, habits, ways of acting and thinking etc.; lastly, men in their relation to ... accidents and misfortunes such as famine, epidemics, death, etc. (F 1991a, 93)

Second, the suggestion that the state education, social security and crime prevention systems are the pre-eminent loci of disciplinary power in modern society leaves us to infer that the private, non-state, domain is now somehow a power-free zone. Both propositions seem at odds with the Foucaultian emphasis on the utter pervasiveness of power, although due to his untimely death in 1983, Foucault never had the opportunity (or, perhaps, the inclination) to develop a definitive account of the role of the state in relation to the forms of power in which he was interested. This has not deterred other commentators from attempting to do just this, and a large literature – far too complex and dense to tackle in detail here – has taken shape around this general theme. It suffices for our purposes to make a few fairly brief points about some of the questions discussed in this literature.

Most importantly, it makes considerable use of Foucault's writings on 'techniques of the self'. These writings have not been mentioned thus far in this chapter, but they arguably emerge out of, and develop, a theme that was already apparent in *Discipline and Punish*. *Discipline and Punish* focuses on disciplinary practices that act on human bodies as objects. We saw, however, that these practices could lead to the formation of self-conscious 'subjects', as the objectified individual became the instrument and vehicle of power: here, subjection is linked with 'subjectification', or the making up of individuals with developed capacities of self-reflection and free will. At times throughout *Discipline and Punish*, Foucault seems to suggest that discipline is the only force of subjectification: that the self is completely determined by disciplinary relations of power. Subsequently, however, he concedes that there are other practices of self-formation which are not reducible to the workings of disciplinary power (although they may well complement it). He names these other practices techniques of the self, and argues that they coalesce in their turn into a distinct technology: that of 'confession'. The key to the success of confession as a technology of the self is the widely held belief that one can – with the help of a certain kind of expertise – discover and act on the truth about oneself. This belief – harboured within such widely invoked notions as 'finding true love', 'listening to your inner child', 'expressing the real you' – is central not only to modern therapy culture and the 'psych' sciences that support it, but also to the most ordinary affairs of everyday life, including dieting, exercising, and shopping. What characterises all of these practices is that they are mediated by some form of expertise – whether a science of nutrition, or the latest fitness fad, or fashion know-how – yet the 'naturalness' of absorbing and acting on such expertise is so uncontested that it seems unreasonable to posit that any of this could be bound up with power. For Foucault, however, techniques of the self are linked to a form of power that 'categorizes the individual, marks him by his own individuality, attaches him to his identity, imposes a law of truth on him which he must recognize and which others have to recognize in him. It is a form of power which makes individuals subjects' (F 1983, 212). It follows that discipline and confession are two sides of the same coin – or perhaps two heads of the same many-headed monster. Discipline is a set of micro-practices oriented towards the government of others as 'mute and docile bodies'; techniques of the self are oriented towards the government of oneself as a self-determining, desiring, expressive subject. Disciplinary power implies a knowledge of the body and a capacity to intervene in its operations; 'confessional' power implies a knowledge of the well-springs of inner desires, energies and aspirations and an ability to direct these in particular ways.

The potential of Foucault's insights concerning techniques of the self to offer a new perspective on contemporary politics in the West has not been lost on Foucault's interpreters. The work of sociologists Peter Miller and Nikolas Rose, for example, proceeds from the assumption that the prosperous, responsible, self-determining individual is just as much an artefact of practices of power/knowledge as is the reformed criminal or the welfare beneficiary – and just as liable to be functional for the state (Rose and Miller, 1992). Far from being 'natural', the capacities, identities and forms of conduct – choice; the free individual; the cultures of enterprise, self-help and self-realisation – which are held up as the valued antitheses of those linked with welfare-dependency require themselves to be artificially arranged or produced (Burchell 1993, 269–276; Rose 1994, 381–386). That the state does not itself *oversee* their production does not mean that it cannot *mobilise* their production, or exploit them once produced. The privatisation and deregulation policies that dominated politics in the West during the 1980s and 1990s, for example, stimulated the refinement and spread of techniques of management – of the self and of others – in a way that distanced the state from a private sphere of free choice, while at the same time moulding and shaping that sphere in particular directions. In the United Kingdom, the policy of selling local authority houses to tenants under the 'right to buy' legislation was calculated to cause residents to cultivate the habits and financial disciplines characteristic of homeowners, at the same time as it promised to relieve the sense of alienation that was thought to permeate public housing estates and relieve the local state of the cost of maintaining the stock of public housing. Again, recent reforms to education law have led parents of children attending state schools to adopt the attitudes and practices of discerning private consumers when choosing and monitoring the performance of schools, and this in turn has served the political imperative of pressurising schools to raise standards (Barron, 1996). Examples could be multiplied: the point is that the regulatory state has come to rely increasingly, if indirectly, upon techniques for building the *self*-regulatory capacities of 'private' individuals. To the extent that these techniques produce outcomes that mesh with the objectives of political authorities, they enable citizens to govern themselves while at the same time serving larger political priorities.

This approach to Foucault's project yields a new way of analysing the role of the state in relation to the forms of power in which he is interested: discipline, governmentality and 'confession'. Those who adopt this approach focus on how practices of self-government and the government of others have become utilised by the modern state towards the government of whole populations. Government is here defined very broadly: it designates a 'triple domain' (M Dean 1994, 176) of objectifying and subjectifying practices oriented towards 'the conduct of conduct' – that of other individuals, of oneself, and of populations. Though utilised by the state, government is not regarded as being reducible to state action: government designates neither a particular apparatus (the executive and its agencies), nor a particular set of political instruments (rules; administrative judgements), but a heterogeneous array of practices oriented towards the conduct of the conduct of a given population and each of its members. Further, the relation between government and the state is not understood as one in which the former derives from the latter: for Miller and Rose, 'the question is [not that] of accounting for government in terms of "the power of the state", but of ascertaining how, and to what extent, the state is articulated into the activity of government' (Rose and Miller 1992, 177).

However one judges the fidelity of these arguments to Foucault's somewhat sketchy remarks concerning the state, they proceed from a thesis that is, undeniably, Foucault's own: that power relations, in his sense of the term (be they based on disciplinary, confessional or governmental mechanisms), 'have come more and more under state control'. Hopefully, the above excursus will have drawn attention to some of the lines of inquiry that this thesis has opened up for sociologists seeking to understand the nature of the state's activities in modern society. But what of its implications for legal theory? Foucault tantalised his readers with suggestions that as the state has become more reliant upon mechanisms of power that have nothing to do with sovereignty, so law has become 'invaded' or 'colonised' by procedures of normalisation; or has become used as a governmental 'tactic'; or has become 'incorporated' into a 'continuum' of regulatory apparatuses. Foucault does not provide much in the way of a detailed elaboration of these metaphors, so a certain amount of imaginative rewriting is necessary if we are to pull them together into a coherent narrative about the relationship between power and modern law.

POWER AND MODERN LAW

In one sense, there is nothing particularly controversial, or even new, about the phenomenon that Foucault's metaphors attempt to invoke: it is the same phenomenon that elsewhere is this volume is described as 'the materialisation of formal law' (Teubner 1987b, on juridification), and has already been adverted to in this chapter as Jürgen Habermas' fourth 'wave' of juridification. All of these formulations contain a recognition that the form of law changed in fundamental ways with the rise of the social or welfare state, although they differ in the assumptions they make about the causes and implications of that shift.

The form of law that Teubner (following Max Weber) describes as 'formal' begins to take shape with the rise of the bourgeois state in the seventeenth century and persisted as the dominant form of law in the West until roughly the end of the nineteenth century (a period encompassing the first, second and third of Habermas's four juridification waves). Very schematically, the characteristic features of formal law as an 'ideal type' are the following: It tends to be framed in abstract and general (rather than concrete and particularistic) terms, and to be universally applicable to all subjects within a given jurisdiction; it thereby assumes that all legal persons are formally the same. The characteristics of the legal person, in turn, are a free, responsible will and a capacity to exercise that will by entering into contracts with others and acquiring and disposing of property. The predominant function of formal law is to provide for the coexistence of these persons: to describe the limits on the freedom of each, such that each has the maximum liberty to pursue their own ends consistently with the equal liberty of every other. To this end, it guarantees the life, liberty and property of individuals, and makes available procedures for entering into and enforcing contracts. These guarantees are positively instituted by a state apparatus that is recognised as the sole source of law-making authority throughout its territory. State power, in turn, is divided between the legislature, the courts, and the executive with its administrative arm, but the courts are the particular guardians of the generality and universality of law. On the one hand, they ensure that the legislative will is only universally binding when expressed in the form of duly enacted public general statutes; on the other hand, they ensure that executive power is exercised impartially under the authority given by statute. Adjudication, that is to say, subjects both legislation and administration to its own rationality. Further, in a legal order characterised by the quality of formality, adjudicative rationality is itself formal: decision-making proceeds through the deployment of a method characterised by abstract conceptual logic and deductive rigour, regard being had only to the general characteristics of each individual case.

The existence of a legal order broadly exhibiting the characteristics of formal rationality is now said to have corresponded to an earlier phase in the development of the modern state: as a systems theorist might put it, the *materialisation* of formal law appears to be the dominant trend in legal 'evolution' since the emergence of the welfare state and throughout the period of its expansion and consolidation. This trend is accompanied by a different set of assumptions concerning the nature of civil society and the state's role in relation to it. Far from being populated by a collection of abstract 'wills', each pursing their own independent ends in the exercise of a legally guaranteed autonomy, civil society is seen as a living, working, reproducing, social 'body' that sustains itself through the conflictual interdependence of a vast array of different 'interests', and that requires state intervention to 'balance' these interests. The state duly takes on the task of examining the social body, locating its imbalances, and prescribing the appropriate remedies. It formulates goals designed to manage a wide range of social processes, and enlists the legal system in the project of realising them. The effects upon the form of law 'range from a weakening of the idea of generality to changes in methods of interpretation' (Teubner 1987b, 15). Policies are designed to be achieved, if necessary by changing the behaviour of particular individuals. They are directed towards the realisation of concrete ends in a way that general, impersonal rules are intended not to be. Consequently, the interpretation of goal-oriented legislation requires a purposive rather than a deductive mode of reasoning, and this in itself appears to erode the distinction between the process of making laws and that of applying them: where adjudication becomes a matter of determining the purpose of a legislative provision, courts are driven to employ arguments of policy similar to those characteristic of the parliamentary arena. A further concomitant of purpose-orientation in law is the expansion of the state's administrative apparatus. The range of social interests is large and varied. They often conflict; their status is relative to time, place and context; and there are always more interests waiting to be discovered. The task of defining and weighing them is therefore a delicate one, beyond the resources and capacities of any legislature. Yet the realisation of legislative goals is typically dependent upon a careful balancing of diverse considerations: policies are often formulated as vague standards that require to be given a concrete meaning by those responsible for their execution.

Hence the need for administrative agencies to be given broad discretionary powers: the achievement of comprehensive regulation requires not only more administration, but wider discretion in administrative decision-making.

Three implications of these changes in the form of law in the social state merit particular mention, because they may throw some light on Foucault's remarks concerning the 'colonisation' of law by the procedures of normalisation (Barron 1990). First, whereas formal law belongs to the order of the 'as if' (Ewald 1987, 104) – it is not deduced from facts about the world – 'social' law relies heavily on a knowledge of the contexts in which it is to take effect: a knowledge of populations and their environments, resources, needs, problems and pathologies. The materialisation of formal law consists in the juridification of the facts and needs exposed (and in a sense constructed) by this knowledge – the most compelling of which at the end of the nineteenth century were the living and working conditions of the urban proletariat. 'It was the conflict between political demands for compensation for the results of industrialisation and the structures of classical formal law that triggered the crisis of formal law, to which the law has responded with materialisation tendencies' (Teubner 1987b, 18). Political demands have been translated into 'social rights' – for workers to protection from exploitation at work, for tenants to protection from arbitrary eviction, and so forth – and law has equipped the administrators of the social state with (discretionary) powers to 'compensate' those unable to find employment or housing in the first place. Second, whereas within a formal legal order the legal subject is an abstract entity, stripped of empirical determinations and thus formally equal to all other legal subjects, social law takes people as it finds them in the world and abandons the idea that the law ought to be the same for everyone (Ewald, 1988). 'The legal subject gives way to the wage-earner, the consumer, the professional ...' (Ewald 1987, 109) Third, whereas formal law is comprised of rules, social law achieves its effects by means of norms. The open-ended policies and vague standards it enunciates invite administrative agencies to consider a huge and constantly shifting range of facts and issues, in order then to make judgements about particular persons and situations. But 'judging in terms of balance means judging the value of an action or practice in its relationship to social normality, in terms of the customs or habits which at a given moment are those of a given group' (Ewald 1988, 68). The norm, by definition, supplies no universal criterion of judgement, because its content is always relative to its context. 'The norm raises the problem of a legal rationality whose categories are not definable *a priori*, but only *a posteriori*' (Ewald 1987, 109).

In Foucaultian terms, then, the existence of social law bears witness to the emergence of the not-legal – the government of the social – within legality itself. Its role in relation to civil society is not to delineate spheres of autonomous action, but to prescribe a route to the regulation of social behaviour. As such, administrative judgements must always refer to a knowledge of social behaviour: they are dependent upon the assessments and diagnoses of a coterie of technicians whose expertise extends across the full range of the social sciences – a field of knowledge co-extensive with the State's domain of intervention. The fate of regulatory law in general is to be 'redefined by knowledge' (F 1977, 22): to become sociologised. Administrative power – the power of 'government' in both the traditional and the Foucaultian sense – consists in the deployment of social scientific knowledge towards the micro-management of individual and collective 'life', a process that is not restrained, but rather encouraged, by the judicial as well as the legislative branch of the state. Attempts to subject administrative processes to adjudicative rationality either have no effect whatsoever on those processes, or else result in the invasion of judicial discourse by the particular rationality of the administrative institution concerned. Consider the following comment by a respected commentator on administrative law in Britain:

> The general principles of judicial review have become incapable of either influencing the exercise of powers or of placing controls upon them. Each area of administrative activity has its own goals, policies and institutions and there is little common ground from one context to another. On the other hand, where courts have tried to control discretionary power, their actions have been apparently unprincipled and particularistic ... (Galligan 1982, 258)

Judges end up engaging in the same ad hoc balancings of interest that preoccupy the bureaucrats whose actions they are concerned to control, employing the same modes of reasoning and deferring to the same expert knowledge of facts and issues.

It is possible, then, to make sense of Foucault's remarks concerning the implications for law of the rise of governmentality by interpreting them as referring to familiar phenomena such as the knowledge-dependence of modern law, the recognition of the lived experience of 'real' people (tenants, workers, consumers, women ...) as capable of influencing the definition of subjectivity in law, and the law's tendency to facilitate state activities of bureaucratic-administrative regulation. When Foucault's remarks *are* read in this way, some common criticisms of his stance in relation to law begin to appear misplaced. Alan Hunt, for example, has argued that Foucault adopts a reductive and ahistorical conception of law by wedding himself to a broadly Austinian model of law as command or prohibition (Hunt 1993, Ch 12). Foucault's failure to recognise the shift from the command to the regulation as the dominant form of modern law testifies, Hunt maintains, to a deeper failure to recognise that the form of law is subject to change and variation over time. Consequently, law is necessarily relegated within Foucault's framework to a position which is both radically separate from and irrelevant to the workings of power in modern society: the operation of the disciplines, after all, is not ensured by prohibition, but by processes of normalisation which tend to be productive rather than repressive in character. For Hunt, on the contrary, regulatory law 'has become a primary agency of the advance of the new modalities of power and provides one of the distinctive methods of operation of the new technologies of power' (Hunt 1993, 299), such that it is now the mediating mechanism through which contemporary mechanisms of normalisation are aggregated (Hunt 1993, 274), coordinated (Hunt 1993, 289) and supervised (Hunt 1993, 300). Far from being irrelevant to the operation of the new forms of power in modern society, law is entwined with them, and 'in some important sense, constitutive of [them]' (Hunt 1993, 279).

It should be clear from the foregoing that the first of these charges simply cannot stand: Foucault is undoubtedly sensitive to the emergence of regulatory law, and acutely aware of the importance of the latter in framing and institutionalising disciplinary and other 'technologies' of power. Hunt's argument would seem to be based upon a misinterpretation of Foucault's admittedly confusing use of the term 'law', in that it dissolves the distinction, noted above, between 'laws' as particular instruments of state action, and 'legality' as a juridical system of power. When Foucault writes, for example, that from the perspective of government(ality), 'law is not what is important' (F 1991a, 95), we must assume that what he really means is that *legality* is not what is important, albeit that governmentality may make use of regulatory *laws* (amongst other instruments) in achieving its objectives. Thus it is legality – a system for ensuring the legitimacy of power by requiring adherence to the rule of law ideal – and not laws as such, that Foucault presents as being radically other to the forms of power in which he is interested (discipline, confession and governmentality) and as we shall see in III.C below the tension between these two modalities of power (described in III.A above) remains, even with the emergence of the regulatory state and its characteristic instruments, regulatory laws. That power which is targeted and restrained by the rule of law ideal *is* prohibitive, in the specific (Kantian – see Chapter 20 of this volume) sense that it is premised on the notion that citizens form a community of rational actors who may choose to follow their desires and inclinations and act contrary to legitimate laws: for a citizen conceived of in this way, therefore, obedience to legitimate laws is both a 'categorical imperative' – a rational necessity – but also a prohibition, since it inevitably requires a repression of desires and inclinations. Discipline, confession and governmentality, on the other hand, focus precisely on moulding and managing desires and inclinations: they are forms of power that work with these experiences rather than opposing them outright.

Hunt's second charge is more serious, because his own analysis of the relationship between regulatory law and normalisation processes is clearly at odds with that of Foucault. Foucault attributes the changes in the form and functions of modern law to the increasing dependence of the legal system upon technologies of power that initially took shape *beyond and apart from* the state and its legal system: it is more a case of the modern state and its law being *constituted by* these technologies than the other way around. So where other commentators (including Hunt) would see a 'top-down' process of *étatisation* and juridification, Foucault sees a 'bottom-up' process by which the state becomes 'governmentalised' through its increasing reliance on techniques of population management, and the law becomes 'colonised' by a logic of normalisation already embedded in social relations.

III.C.   Sovereign People/Governable Population

We arrive at this point, then, in possession of two insights. First, the most significant forms of power in modern society cannot be explained or accommodated by the concepts and constitutional frameworks associated with the terms 'sovereignty' and 'legality'. But second, these same forms of power have been facilitated, and their grip has been intensified, by the practices and instruments of the modern state and its legal apparatus. We need now to explore the relationship between these two apparently contradictory propositions. The issue is this: what precisely is the relationship between juridical power on the one hand, and, on the other hand, the networks of disciplinary/confessional/ governmental power relations that actually function in society, underpinned as they may be the state's activities and institutionalised as they sometimes are by legal instruments?

At least two possible answers to this question emerge from Foucault's own writings. The first relies upon something akin to the Marxian base/superstructure metaphor, with juridical power represented as 'superstructural' relative to what we shall for convenience refer to as 'other' forms of power. Writing of discipline, for example, Foucault remarks as follows:

> The general juridical form that guaranteed a system of rights that were egalitarian in principle was supported by [the] tiny, everyday, physical mechanisms [of discipline], by all those systems of micro-power that are essentially non-egalitarian and asymmetrical that we call the disciplines. And although, in a formal way, the representative regime [of parliamentary sovereignty] makes it possible, directly or indirectly ... for the will of all to form the fundamental authority of sovereignty, the disciplines provide, at the base, a guarantee of the submission of forces and bodies. The real, corporal disciplines constituted the foundation of the formal, juridical liberties. (F 1977, 222)

In political theory and constitutional law, Foucault seems to be saying, each subject is equal before the law vis-à-vis all other subjects: equally in possession of a will; equally able, therefore, to participate in the contract that 'forms the fundamental authority of sovereignty'; equally able to vote; equally able to participate in those other kinds of contract which are contracts of employment, marriage and so forth. If these acts of will are to be practicable and workable, however, their subjects have to be actively produced through an ensemble of 'other' power relations as the bearers of particular capacities and orientations: for example, the capacity to lead a law-abiding life, observe schedules, achieve quotas, and perform the tasks contracted for. This is precisely the role of disciplinary and other technologies: they 'seem to extend the general forms defined by law [eg contracts] to the infinitesimal level of individual lives; or they appear as methods of training that enable individuals to become integrated into these general demands' (F 1977, 222). These other forms of power, moreover, proceed from and multiply *in*equalities. Thus although the formally egalitarian framework of the law is in reality epiphenomenal, it performs the useful task of 'concealing', 'effacing' or 'disguising' the actual procedures of power and the domination intrinsic to them by representing power to be other than what it is in fact. Foucault suggests that this framework, the theories that explain and justify it, and the representation of society that these theories presuppose – a society populated by free and equal citizens – conceal domination by representing power as capable, in principle, of being exercised legitimately: that is, in a way that produces obedience while respecting the fundamental freedom and equality of citizens. This 'juridicism' (F 1977, 223) places limits on sovereign power that in no way constrain other forms of power. All it can tell us about the behaviour produced by discipline is that this behaviour is freely willed. All it can tell us about the inequalities that discipline produces is that these are trivial and incidental.

This might be taken as suggesting that juridical power is for Foucault a mere form, an empty shell with no substance of its own beyond that given to it by mechanisms of power deriving from elsewhere, and with no role other than that of legitimating these other powers. Yet it should be noted that Foucault at times hints at a rather different conception of the relationship between juridical power and its 'other'. This second conception presents juridical power more as the 'necessary companion' (F 1980, 106) than the redundant servant of disciplinary/confessional/governmental power. The two are certainly heterogeneous – 'so heterogeneous that they cannot possibly be reduced to each other' (F 1980, 106) – but 'sovereignty and disciplinary [and other] mechanisms are two absolutely integral constituents of the general mechanism of power in our society' (F 1980, 108). The maintenance of order and the optimisation of collective life, Foucault implies, require instruments *both* of legal-political *and* of social integration. Discipline, confession and government are forms of power that deal in singularities: particular persons and populations, and specific elements and relations within and between these; particular aims; particular instruments of intervention. Juridical power, on the other hand, is a form of power that totalises, abstracts and generalises: its categories are the universal subject (the citizen); the universal will; the universal rule. Each form of power operates at the limit of the other. Juridical power has no grasp of particularities: it rules a totality of citizens, but cannot manage a population or guide individual existences. Disciplinary/confessional/governmental power can do all of this, but only by constituting 'society' as the incubator for a plurality of needs, interests and forms of life, and by fragmenting the social totality into a multiplicity of persons and groups who can claim these needs, interests and forms of life as their own and assert them in the political domain. This form of power, therefore, generates a permanent possibility of social conflict and instability. Recall Foucault's assertions, noted above, that power is productive and that the possibility of resistance is inscribed in every power relationship. Discipline/confession/government is indeed productive, and the resistance that it provokes is actually or potentially everywhere: that 'bio-power' which turns life and its mechanisms into objects to be manipulated for political ends, for example, has generated a wide variety of oppositional social movements that assert an array of particular 'rights' 'to life, to one's body, to health, to happiness, to the satisfaction of needs ... which the juridical system [is] utterly incapable of comprehending' (F 1979, 145). This form of power, then, requires to be accompanied by another modality of power that can contain resistance, filter the claims that accompany resistance by reference to a universal criterion of right, and represent a differentiated social order as underpinned by a more fundamental commonality around which we can all unite. This other modality of power is juridical power: the power that is exercised through law by a democratically elected parliament. Juridical power enforces obedience because its rules have been consented to by the citizenry; it recognises only those rights that are necessary to respect the autonomy and dignity of the citizen *qua* citizen; and it appeals to the abstract category of citizenship as the common identity that makes these responsibilities and rights both possible and desirable. The government of the population absolutely requires, even as it opposes itself to, the sovereignty of 'the people' and the rule of law.

It follows from this that the categories of 'citizenship' and 'right' cannot, for Foucault, be invoked to give political expression to resistance without neutralising that resistance by forcing it back inside the very apparatus that it seeks to escape. Writing of struggles against disciplinary power, for example, Foucault argues that because the notion of rights is inextricably bound up with the logic of sovereignty, appealing to rights (eg the right to 'rediscover what one is and all that once can be' (F 1979, 145)) as a way of counteracting discipline can only lead to a 'blind alley: it is not through recourse to sovereignty against discipline that the effects of disciplinary power can be limited' (F 1980, 108). And although Foucault adverts to 'a new form of right, one which must indeed be anti-disciplinarian, but at the same time liberated from the principle of sovereignty' (F 1980, 108) this idea is never developed in his writings. This returns us to Nancy Fraser's argument, noted above, about the normative contradictions embedded in Foucault's project. He approves of resistance, but sees the language of rights as thoroughly complicit with power, so cannot recommend using that language as a framework for expressing resistance. Yet when he tries to formulate an alternative language he either lapses back into a version of rights-discourse ('a new form of right') ... or says nothing at all.

IV. History

> Under no circumstances should one pay attention to those who tell one: 'Don't criticise, since you're not capable of carrying out a reform.' That's ministerial cabinet talk. Critique doesn't have to be premise of a deduction which concludes: this then is what needs to be done. It should be an instrument for those who fight, those who resist and refuse what is. Its use should be in processes of conflict and confrontation, essays in refusal. It doesn't have to lay down the law for the law ... It is a challenge directed to what is. (F 1991.b, 84)

The above statement could well be seen as Foucault's rejoinder to Fraser's reproach. Although admitting that he offers no normative theory from which a programme of law reform could be derived, Foucault nonetheless insists here that critique need not – ought not – take this form. Instead, it should consist of 'essays in refusal', or as he puts it elsewhere, 'problematisations' of 'what is'. Central to this variety of critique is the emphasis it places on the *history* of 'what is' – the history of the present – and the use it makes of a particular method for interpreting past events. Foucault's approach to history raises difficult philosophical questions, as does his conception of the relationship between doing history and engaging in 'critique'. These questions cannot be dealt with here, and it suffices for our purposes simply to describe both in this very brief final section. Following Nietzsche, Foucault calls his method 'genealogy' rather than history, as if to signify its distance from traditional historiography. 'The way [historians] work is by ascribing the object they analyse to the most unitary, necessary, inevitable and (ultimately) extra-historical mechanism or structure available' (F 1991b, 78), so making the emergence of the 'object' appear self-evident and indispensable. Foucault wants instead to emphasise the contingent status of historical events, to see these first and foremost *as* 'events', without presuming an inevitable process that gave rise to them. One aspect of genealogy, then, is what Foucault calls 'eventalization': 'making visible a *singularity* ... where there is a temptation to invoke a historical constant' (F 1991b, 76, emphasis in original). For Foucault, a genealogical investigation of, for example, the substitution of imprisonment for torture as the general means of punishment does not link this process to some 'law' of historical evolution such as the spread of humanistic ideals in the wake of the Enlightenment. On the contrary, it takes seriously the *dis*continuity which this event effected in penal practice. This attentiveness to discontinuity does not entail, however, that the genealogist views past events as utterly random and unconnected: the point is to complicate the notion of historical causality rather than rejecting it entirely. A second aspect of genealogy, then, involves *multiplying* the 'causes' of events: 'constructing around the singular event analysed as process a "polygon" or "polyhedron" of intelligibility, the number of whose faces is not given in advance and can never properly be taken as finite' (F 1991b, 77). This in turn leads the genealogist to accommodate elements that might well be rendered invisible within orthodox accounts of how things have come to be the way they are – either because they seem trivial, or because their relation with the event in question seems distant or non-existent – and to make sense of the event by linking these elements together, often in surprising ways. As regards the birth of the prison, for example, it is a matter of making visible 'not its arbitrariness, but its complex interconnection with a multiplicity of historical processes' (F 1991b, 75) including, as we have seen in *Discipline and Punish*, 'the history of pedagogical practices, the formation of professional armies, British empirical philosophy, techniques of use of firearms, new methods of division of labour' (F 1991b, 77).

What then is 'critical' about all of this? Here, in brief, is Foucault's answer: Genealogical investigation is always motivated and shaped by a question posed about some aspect of the present that the genealogist regards as a *problem*. Its aim is to engage with the present, not by providing a blueprint for change, but by asking 'how did we get here?' 'It's a matter of shaking [the] self-evidence, of demonstrating [the] precariousness' (F 1991b, 75) of current social arrangements by unsettling received understandings about the value and necessity of these arrangements, and pointing towards fault-lines within and between them that might permit them to be prized open and re-imagined.

Foucault (1977, 195–228)

3. PANOPTICISM

The following, according to an order published at the end of the seventeenth century, were the measures to be taken when the plague appeared in a town.

First, a strict spatial partitioning: the closing of the town and its outlying districts, a prohibition to leave the town on pain of death, the killing of all stray animals; the division of the town into distinct quarters, each governed by an intendant. Each street is placed under the authority of a syndic, who keeps it under surveillance; if he leaves the street, he will be condemned to death. On the appointed day, everyone is ordered to stay indoors. It is forbidden to leave on pain of death. The syndic himself comes to lock the door of each house from the outside; he takes the key with him and hands it over to the intendant of the quarter; the intendant keeps it until the end of the quarantine. Each family will have made its own provisions; but, for bread and wine, small wooden canals are set up between the street and the interior of the houses, thus allowing each person to receive his ration without communicating with the suppliers and other residents; meat, fish and herbs will be hoisted up into the houses with pulleys and baskets. If it is absolutely necessary to leave the house, it will be done in turn, avoiding any meeting.

Only the intendants, syndics and guards will move about the streets and also, between the infected houses, from one corpse to another, the 'crows', who can be left to die: these are 'people of little substance who carry the sick, bury the dead, clean and do many vile and abject offices'. It is a segmented, immobile, frozen space. Each individual is fixed in his place. And, if he moves, he does so at the risk of his life, contagion or punishment.

Inspection functions ceaselessly. The gaze is alert everywhere: 'A considerable body of militia, commanded by good officers and men of substance', guards at the gates, at the town hall and in every quarter to ensure the prompt obedience of the people and the most absolute authority of the magistrates, 'as also to observe all disorder, theft and extortion'. At each of the town gates there will be an observation post; at the end of each street sentinels. Every day, the intendant visits the quarter in his charge, inquires whether the syndics have carried out their tasks, whether the inhabitants have anything to complain of; they 'observe their actions'. Every day, too, the syndic goes into the street for which he is responsible; stops before each house, gets all the inhabitants to appear at the windows (those who live overlooking the courtyard will be allocated a window looking onto the street at which no one but they may show themselves); he calls each of them by name; informs himself as to the state of each and every one of them – 'in which respect the inhabitants will be compelled to speak the truth under pain of death'; if someone does not appear at the window, the syndic must ask why. 'In this way he will find out easily enough whether dead or sick are being concealed.' Everyone locked up in his cage, everyone at his window, answering to his name and showing himself when asked – it is the great review of the living and the dead.

This surveillance is based on a system of permanent registration: reports from the syndics to the intendants, from the intendants to the magistrates or mayor. At the beginning of the 'lock up', the role of each of the inhabitants present in the town is laid down, one by one; this document bears 'the name, age, sex of everyone, notwithstanding his condition': a copy is sent to the intendant of the quarter, another to the office of the town hall, another to enable the syndic to make his daily roll call. Everything that may be observed during the course of the visits – deaths, illnesses, complaints, irregularities – is noted down and transmitted to the intendants and magistrates. The magistrates have complete control over medical treatment; they have appointed a physician in charge; no other practitioner may treat, no apothecary prepare medicine, no confessor visit a sick person without having received from him a written note 'to prevent anyone from concealing and dealing with those sick of the contagion, unknown to the magistrates'. The registration of the pathological must be constantly centralized. The relation of each individual to his disease and to his death passes through the representatives of power, the registration they make of it, the decisions they take on it.

Five or six days after the beginning of the quarantine, the process of purifying the houses one by one is begun. All the inhabitants are made to leave; in each room 'the furniture and goods' are raised from the ground or suspended from the air; perfume is poured around the room; after carefully sealing the windows, doors and even the keyholes with wax, the perfume is set alight. Finally, the entire house is closed while the perfume is consumed; those who have carried out the work are searched, as they were on entry, 'in the presence of the residents of the house, to see that they did not have something on their persons as they left that they did not have on entering'. Four hours later, the residents are allowed to re-enter their homes.

This enclosed, segmented space, observed at every point, in which the individuals are inserted in a fixed place, in which the slightest movements are supervised, in which all events are recorded, in which an uninterrupted work of writing links the centre and periphery, in which power is exercised without division, according to a continuous hierarchical figure, in which each individual is constantly located, examined and distributed among the living beings, the sick and the dead – all this constitutes a compact model of the disciplinary mechanism. The plague is met by order; its function is to sort out every possible confusion: that of the disease, which is transmitted when bodies are mixed together; that of the evil, which is increased when fear and death overcome prohibitions. It lays down for each individual his place, his body, his disease and his death, his well-being, by means of an omnipresent and omniscient power that subdivides itself in a regular, uninterrupted way even to the ultimate determination of the individual, of what characterizes him, of what belongs to him, of what happens to him. Against the plague, which is a mixture, discipline brings into play its power, which is one of analysis. A whole literary fiction of the festival grew up around the plague: suspended laws, lifted prohibitions, the frenzy of passing time, bodies mingling together without respect, individuals unmasked, abandoning their statutory identity and the figure under which they had been recognized, allowing a quite different truth to appear. But there was also a political dream of the plague, which was exactly its reverse: not the collective festival, but strict divisions; not laws transgressed, but the penetration of regulation into even the smallest details of everyday life through the mediation of the complete hierarchy that assured the capillary functioning of power; not masks that were put on and taken off, but the assignment to each individual of his 'true' name, his 'true' place, his 'true' body, his 'true' disease. The plague as a form, at once real and imaginary, of disorder had as its medical and political correlative discipline. Behind the disciplinary mechanisms can be read the haunting memory of 'contagions', of the plague, of rebellions, crimes, vagabondage, desertions, people who appear and disappear, live and die in disorder.

If it is true that the leper gave rise to rituals of exclusion, which to a certain extent provided the model for and general form of the great Confinement, then the plague gave rise to disciplinary projects. Rather than the massive, binary division between one set of people and another, it called for multiple separations, individualizing distributions, an organization in depth of surveillance and control, an intensification and a ramification of power. The leper was caught up in a practice of rejection, of exile-enclosure; he was left to his doom in a mass among which it was useless to differentiate; those sick of the plague were caught up in a meticulous tactical partitioning in which individual differentiations were the constricting effects of a power that multiplied, articulated and subdivided itself, the great confinement on the one hand; the correct training on the other. The leper and his separation; the plague and its segmentations. The first is marked; the second analysed and distributed. The exile of the leper and the arrest of the plague do not bring with them the same political dream. The first is that of a pure community, the second that of a disciplined society. Two ways of exercising power over men, of controlling their relations, of separating out their dangerous mixtures. The plague-stricken town, traversed throughout with hierarchy, surveillance, observation, writing; the town immobilized by the functioning of an extensive power that bears in a distinct way over all individual bodies – this is the utopia of the perfectly governed city. The plague (envisaged as a possibility at least) is the trial in the course of which one may define ideally the exercise of disciplinary power. In order to make rights and laws function according to pure theory, the jurists place themselves in imagination in the state of nature; in order to see perfect disciplines functioning, rulers dreamt of the state of plague. Underlying disciplinary projects the image of the plague stands for all forms of confusion and disorder; just as the image of the leper, cut off from all human contact, underlies projects of exclusion.

They are different projects, then, but not incompatible ones. We see them coming slowly together, and it is the peculiarity of the nineteenth century that it applied to the space of exclusion of which the leper was the symbolic inhabitant (beggars, vagabonds, madmen and the disorderly formed the real population) the technique of power proper to disciplinary partitioning. Treat 'lepers' as 'plague victims', project the subtle segmentations of discipline onto the confused space of internment, combine it with the methods of analytical distribution proper to power, individualize the excluded, but use procedures of individualization to mark exclusion – this is what was operated regularly by disciplinary power from the beginning of the nineteenth century in the psychiatric asylum, the penitentiary, the reformatory, the approved school and, to some extent, the hospital. Generally speaking, all the authorities exercising individual control function according to a double mode; that of binary division and branding (mad/sane; dangerous/harmless; normal/abnormal); and that of coercive assignment, of differential distribution (who he is; where he must be; how he is to be characterized; how he is to be recognized; how a constant surveillance is to be exercised over him in an individual way, etc.). On the one hand, the lepers are treated as plague victims; the tactics of individualizing disciplines are imposed on the excluded; and, on the other hand, the universality of disciplinary controls makes it possible to brand the 'leper' and to bring into play against him the dualistic mechanisms of exclusion. The constant division between the normal and the abnormal, to which every individual is subjected, brings us back to our own time, by applying the binary branding and exile of the leper to quite different objects; the existence of a whole set of techniques and institutions for measuring, supervising and correcting the abnormal brings into play the disciplinary mechanisms to which the fear of the plague gave rise. All the mechanisms of power which, even today, are disposed around the abnormal individual, to brand him and to alter him, are composed of those two forms from which they distantly derive.

Bentham's *Panopticon* is the architectural figure of this composition. We know the principle on which it was based: at the periphery, an annular building; at the centre, a tower; this tower is pierced with wide windows that open onto the inner side of the ring; the peripheric building is divided into cells, each of which extends the whole width of the building; they have two windows, one on the inside, corresponding to the windows of the tower; the other, on the outside, allows the light to cross the cell from one end to the other. All that is needed, then, is to place a supervisor in a central tower and to shut up in each cell a madman, a patient, a condemned man, a worker or a schoolboy. By the effect of backlighting, one can observe from the tower, standing out precisely against the light, the small captive shadows in the cells of the periphery. They are like so many cages, so many small theatres, in which each actor is alone, perfectly individualized and constantly visible. The panoptic mechanism arranges spatial unities that make it possible to see constantly and to recognize immediately. In short, it reverses the principle of the dungeon; or rather of its three functions – to enclose, to deprive of light and to hide – it preserves only the first and eliminates the other two. Full lighting and the eye of a supervisor capture better than darkness, which ultimately protected. Visibility is a trap.

To begin with, this made it possible – as a negative effect – to avoid those compact, swarming, howling masses that were to be found in places of confinement, those painted by Goya or described by Howard. Each individual, in his place, is securely confined to a cell from which he is seen from the front by the supervisor; but the side walls prevent him from coming into contact with his companions. He is seen, but he does not see; he is the object of information, never a subject in communication. The arrangement of his room, opposite the central tower, imposes on him an axial visibility; but the divisions of the ring, those separated cells, imply a lateral invisibility. And this invisibility is a guarantee of order. If the inmates are convicts, there is no danger of a plot, an attempt at collective escape, the planning of new crimes for the future, bad reciprocal influences; if they are patients, there is no danger of contagion; if they are madmen there is no risk of their committing violence upon one another; if they are schoolchildren, there is no copying, no noise, no chatter, no waste of time; if they are workers, there are no disorders, no theft, no coalitions, none of those distractions that slow down the rate of work, make it less perfect or cause accidents. The crowd, a compact mass, a locus of multiple exchanges, individualities merging together, a collective effect, is abolished and replaced by a collection of separated individualities. From the point of view of the guardian, it is replaced by a multiplicity that can be numbered and supervised; from the point of view of the inmates, by a sequestered and observed solitude.

Hence the major effect of the Panopticon: to induce in the inmate a state of conscious and permanent visibility that assures the automatic functioning of power. So to arrange things that the surveillance is permanent in its effects, even if it is discontinuous in its action; that the perfection of power should tend to render its actual exercise unnecessary; that this architectural apparatus should be a machine for creating and sustaining a power relation independent of the person who exercises it; in short, that the inmates should be caught up in a power situation of which they are themselves the bearers. To achieve this, it is at once too much and too little that the prisoner should be constantly observed by an inspector: too little, for what matters is that he knows himself to be observed; too much, because he has no need in fact of being so. In view of this, Bentham laid down the principle that power should be visible and unverifiable. Visible: the inmate will constantly have before his eyes the tall outline of the central tower from which he is spied upon. Unverifiable: the inmate must never know whether he is being looked at at any one moment; but he must be sure that he may always be so. In order to make the presence or absence of the inspector unverifiable, so that the prisoners, in their cells, cannot even see a shadow, Bentham envisaged not only venetian blinds on the windows of the central observation hall, but, on the inside, partitions that intersected the hall at right angles and, in order to pass from one quarter to the other, not doors but zig-zag openings; for the slightest noise, a gleam of light, a brightness in a half-opened door would betray the presence of the guardian. The Panopticon is a machine for dissociating the see/being seen dyad: in the peripheric ring, one is totally seen, without ever seeing; in the central tower, one sees everything without ever being seen.

It is an important mechanism, for it automatizes and disindividualizes power. Power has its principle not so much in a person as in a certain concerted distribution of bodies, surfaces, lights, gazes; in an arrangement whose internal mechanisms produce the relation in which individuals are caught up. The ceremonies, the rituals, the marks by which the sovereign's surplus power was manifested are useless. There is a machinery that assures dissymmetry, disequilibrium, difference. Consequently, it does not matter who exercises power. Any individual, taken almost at random, can operate the machine: in the absence of the director, his family, his friends, his visitors, even his servants. Similarly, it does not matter what motive animates him: the curiosity of the indiscreet, the malice of a child, the thirst for knowledge of a philosopher who wishes to visit this museum of human nature, or the perversity of those who take pleasure in spying and punishing. The more numerous those anonymous and temporary observers are, the greater the risk for the inmate of being surprised and the greater his anxious awareness of being observed. The Panopticon is a marvellous machine which, whatever use one may wish to put it to, produces homogeneous effects of power.

A real subjection is born mechanically from a fictitious relation. So it is not necessary to use force to constrain the convict to good behaviour, the madman to calm, the worker to work, the schoolboy to application, the patient to the observation of the regulations. Bentham was surprised that panoptic institutions could be so light: there were no more bars, no more chains, no more heavy locks; all that was needed was that the separations should be clear and the openings well arranged. The heaviness of the old 'houses of security', with their fortress-like architecture, could be replaced by the simple, economic geometry of a 'house of certainty'. The efficiency of power, its constraining force have, in a sense, passed over to the other side – to the side of its surface of application. He who is subjected to a field of visibility, and who knows it, assumes responsibility for the constraints of power; he makes them play spontaneously upon himself; he inscribes in himself the power relation in which he simultaneously plays both roles; he becomes the principle of his own subjection. By this very fact, the external power may throw off its physical weight; it tends to the non-corporal; and, the more it approaches this limit, the more constant, profound and permanent are its effects: it is a perpetual victory that avoids any physical confrontation and which is always decided in advance.

Bentham does not say whether he was inspired, in his project, by Le Vaux's menagerie at Versailles: the first menagerie in which the different elements are not, as they traditionally were, distributed in a park. At the centre was an octagonal pavilion which, on the first floor, consisted of only a single room, the king's *salon*; on every side large windows looked out onto seven cages (the eighth side was reserved for the entrance), containing different species of animals. By Bentham's time, this menagerie had disappeared. But one finds in the programme of the Panopticon a similar concern with individualizing observation, with characterization and classification, with the analytical arrangement of space. The Panopticon is a royal menagerie; the animal is replaced by man, individual distribution by specific grouping and the king by the machinery of a furtive power. With this exception, the Panopticon also does the work of a naturalist. It makes it possible to draw up differences: among patients, to observe the symptoms of each individual, without the proximity of beds, the circulation of miasmas, the effects of contagion confusing the clinical tables; among school-children, it makes it possible to observe performances (without there being any irritation or copying), to map aptitudes, to assess characters, to draw up rigorous classifications and, in relation to normal development, to distinguish 'laziness and stubbornness' from 'incurable imbecility'; among workers, it makes it possible to note the aptitudes of each worker, compare the time he takes to perform a task, and if they are paid by the day, to calculate their wages.

So much for the question of observation. But the Panopticon was also a laboratory; it could be used as a machine to carry out experiments, to alter behaviour, to train or correct individuals. To experiment with medicines and monitor their effects. To try out different punishments on prisoners, according to their crimes and character, and to seek the most effective ones. To teach different techniques simultaneously to the workers, to decide which is the best. To try out pedagogical experiments ... [O]ne could bring up different children according to different systems of thought, making certain children believe that two and two do not make four or that the moon is a cheese, then put them together when they are twenty or twenty-five years old ... The Panopticon is a privileged place for experiments on men, and for analysing with complete certainty the transformations that may be obtained from them. The Panopticon may even provide an apparatus for supervising its own mechanisms. In this central tower, the director may spy on all the employees that he has under his orders: nurses, doctors, foremen, teachers, warders; he will be able to judge them continuously, alter their behaviour, impose upon them the methods he thinks best; and it will even be possible to observe the director himself. An inspector arriving unexpectedly at the centre of the Panopticon will be able to judge at a glance, without anything being concealed from him, how the entire establishment is functioning. And, in any case, enclosed as he is in the middle of this architectural mechanism, is not the director's own fate entirely bound up with it? The incompetent physician who has allowed contagion to spread, the incompetent prison governor or workshop manager will be the first victims of an epidemic or a revolt ... The Panopticon functions as a kind of laboratory of power. Thanks to its mechanisms of observation, it gains in efficiency and in the ability to penetrate into men's behaviour; knowledge follows the advances of power, discovering new objects of knowledge over all the surfaces on which power is exercised.

The plague-stricken town, the panoptic establishment – the differences are important. They mark, at a distance of a century and a half, the transformations of the disciplinary programme. In the first case, there is an exceptional situation: against an extraordinary evil, power is mobilized; it makes itself everywhere present and visible; it invents new mechanisms; it separates, it immobilizes, it partitions; it constructs for a time what is both a counter-city and the perfect society; it imposes an ideal functioning, but one that is reduced, in the final analysis, like the evil that it combats, to a simple dualism of life and death. that which moves brings death, and one kills that which moves. The Panopticon, on the other hand, must be understood as a generalizable model of functioning; a way of defining power relations in terms of the everyday life of men. No doubt Bentham presents it as a particular institution, closed in upon itself. Utopias, perfectly closed in upon themselves, are common enough. As opposed to the ruined prisons, littered with mechanisms of torture, to be seen in Piranese's engravings, the Panopticon presents a cruel, ingenious cage. The fact that it should have given rise, even in our own time, to so many variations, projected or realized, is evidence of the imaginary intensity that it has possessed for almost two hundred years. But the Panopticon must not be understood as a dream building: it is the diagram of a mechanism of power reduced to its ideal form; its functioning, abstracted from any obstacle, resistance or friction, must be represented as a pure architectural and optical system: it is in fact a figure of political technology that may and must be detached from any specific use.

It is polyvalent in its applications; it serves to reform prisoners, but also to treat patients, to instruct schoolchildren, to confine the insane, to supervise workers, to put beggars and idlers to work. It is a type of location of bodies in space, of distribution of individuals in relation to one another, of hierarchical organization, of disposition of centres and channels of power, of definition of the instruments and modes of intervention of power, which can be implemented in hospitals, workshops, schools, prisons. Whenever one is dealing with a multiplicity of individuals on whom a task or a particular form of behaviour must be imposed, the panoptic schema may be used.

...

In each of its applications, it makes it possible to perfect the exercise of power. It does this in several ways: because it can reduce the number of those who exercise it, while increasing the number of those on whom it is exercised. Because it is possible to intervene at any moment and because the constant pressure acts even before the offences, mistakes or crimes have been committed. Because, in these conditions, its strength is that it never intervenes, it is exercised spontaneously and without noise, it constitutes a mechanism whose effects follow from one another. Because, without any physical instrument other than architecture and geometry, it acts directly on individuals; it gives 'power of mind over mind'. The panoptic schema makes any apparatus of power more intense: it assures its economy (in material, in personnel, in time); it assures its efficacity by its preventative character, its continuous functioning and its automatic mechanisms.

...

It can in fact be integrated into any function (education, medical treatment, production, punishment); it can increase the effect of this function, by being linked closely with it; it can constitute a mixed mechanism in which relations of power (and of knowledge) may be precisely adjusted, in the smallest detail, to the processes that are to be supervised; it can establish a direct proportion between 'surplus power' and 'surplus production'. In short, it arranges things in such a way that the exercise of power is not added on from the outside, like a rigid, heavy constraint, to the functions it invests, but is so subtly present in them as to increase their efficiency by itself increasing its own points of contact. The panoptic mechanism is not simply a hinge, a point of exchange between a mechanism of power and a function; it is a way of making power relations function in a function, and of making a function function through these power relations.

...

The panoptic schema, without disappearing as such or losing any of its properties, was destined to spread throughout the social body; its vocation was to become a generalized function. The plague-stricken town provided an exceptional disciplinary model: perfect, but absolutely violent; to the disease that brought death, power opposed its perpetual threat of death; life inside it was reduced to its simplest expression; it was, against the power of death, the meticulous exercise of the right of the sword. The Panopticon, on the other hand, has a role of amplification; although it arranges power, although it is intended to make it more economic and more effective, it does so not for power itself, nor for the immediate salvation of a threatened society: its aim is to strengthen the social forces – to increase production, to develop the economy, spread education, raise the level of public morality; to increase and multiply.

How is power to be strengthened in such a way that, far from impeding progress, far from weighing upon it with its rules and regulations, it actually facilitates such progress? What intensificator of power will be able at the same time to be a multiplicator of production? How will power, by increasing its forces, be able to increase those of society instead of confiscating them or impeding them? The Panopticon's solution to this problem is that the productive increase of power can be assured only if, on the one hand, it can be exercised continuously in the very foundations of society, in the subtlest possible way, and if, on the other hand, it functions outside these sudden, violent, discontinuous forms that are bound up with the exercise of sovereignty. The body of the king, with its strange material and physical presence, with the force that he himself deploys or transmits to some few others, is at the opposite extreme of this new physics of power represented by panopticism; the domain of panopticism is, on the contrary, that whole lower region, that region of irregular bodies, with their details, their multiple movements, their heterogeneous forces, their spatial relations; what are required are mechanisms that analyse distributions, gaps, series, combinations, and which use instruments that render visible, record, differentiate and compare: a physics of a relational and multiple power, which has its maximum intensity not in the person of the king, but in the bodies that can be individualized by these relations. At the theoretical level, Bentham defines another way of analysing the social body and the power relations that traverse it; in terms of practice, he defines a procedure of subordination of bodies and forces that must increase the utility of power while dispensing with the need for the prince. Panopticism is the general principle of a new 'political anatomy' whose object and end are not the relations of sovereignty but the relations of discipline.

The celebrated, transparent, circular cage, with its high tower, powerful and knowing, may have been for Bentham a project of a perfect disciplinary institution; but he also set out to show how one may 'unlock' the disciplines and get them to function in a diffused, multiple, polyvalent way throughout the whole social body. These disciplines, which the classical age had elaborated in specific, relatively enclosed places – barracks, schools, workshops – and whose total implementation had been imagined only at the limited and temporary scale of a plague-stricken town, Bentham dreamt of transforming into a network of mechanisms that would be everywhere and always alert, running through society without interruption in space or in time. The panoptic arrangement provides the formula for this generalization. It programmes, at the level of an elementary and easily transferable mechanism, the basic functioning of a society penetrated through and through with disciplinary mechanisms.

There are two images, then, of discipline. At one extreme, the discipline-blockade, the enclosed institution, established on the edges of society, turned inwards towards negative functions: arresting evil, breaking communications, suspending time. At the other extreme, with panopticism, is the discipline-mechanism: a functional mechanism that must improve the exercise of power by making it lighter, more rapid, more effective, a design of subtle coercion for a society to come. The movement from one project to the other, from a schema of exceptional discipline to one of a generalized surveillance, rests on a historical transformation: the gradual extension of the mechanisms of discipline throughout the seventeenth and eighteenth centuries, their spread throughout the whole social body, the formation of what might be called in general the disciplinary society.

...

But this extension of the disciplinary institutions was no doubt only the most visible aspect of various, more profound processes.

1. *The functional inversion of the disciplines.* At first, they were expected to neutralize dangers, to fix useless or disturbed populations, to avoid the inconveniences of over-large assemblies; now they were being asked to play a positive role, for they were becoming able to do so, to increase the possible utility of individuals. Military discipline is no longer a mere means of preventing looting, desertion or failure to obey orders among the troops; it has become a basic technique to enable the army to exist, not as an assembled crowd, but as a unity that derives from this very unity an increase in its forces; discipline increases the skill of each individual, co-ordinates these skills, accelerates movements, increases fire power, broadens the fronts of attack without reducing their vigour, increases the capacity for resistance, etc. The discipline of the workshop, while remaining a way of enforcing respect for the regulations and authorities, of preventing thefts or losses, tends to increase aptitudes, speeds, output and therefore profits; it still exerts a moral influence over behaviour, but more and more it treats actions in terms of their results, introduces bodies into a machinery, forces into an economy ... The disciplines function increasingly as techniques for making useful individuals. Hence their emergence from a marginal position on the confines of society, and detachment from the forms of exclusion or expiation, confinement or retreat. Hence the slow loosening of their kinship with religious regularities and enclosures. Hence also their rooting in the most important, most central and most productive sectors of society. They become attached to some of the great essential functions: factory production, the transmission of knowledge, the diffusion of aptitudes and skills, the war-machine. Hence, too, the double tendency one sees developing throughout the eighteenth century to increase the number of disciplinary institutions and to discipline the existing apparatuses.

2. *The swarming of disciplinary mechanisms.* While, on the one hand, the disciplinary establishments increase, their mechanisms have a certain tendency to become 'de-institutionalized', to emerge from the closed fortresses in which they once functioned and to circulate in a 'free' state; the massive, compact disciplines are broken down into flexible methods of control, which may be transferred and adapted. Sometimes the closed apparatuses add to their internal and specific function a role of external surveillance, developing around themselves a whole margin of lateral controls. Thus the Christian School must not simply train docile children; it must also make it possible to supervise the parents, to gain information as to their way of life, their resources, their piety, their morals ... Similarly, the hospital is increasingly conceived of as a base for the medical observation of the population outside; after the burning down of the Hotel-Dieu in 1772, there were several demands that the large buildings, so heavy and so disordered, should be replaced by a series of smaller hospitals; their function would be to take in the sick of the quarter, but also to gather information, to be alert to any endemic or epidemic phenomena, to open dispensaries, to give advice to the inhabitants and to keep the authorities informed of the sanitary state of the regions.

One also sees the spread of disciplinary procedures, not in the form of enclosed institutions, but as centres of observation disseminated throughout society. Religious groups and charity organizations had long played this role of 'disciplining' the population. From the Counter-Reformation to the philanthropy of the July monarchy, initiatives of this type continued to increase; their aims were religious (conversion and moralization), economic (aid and encouragement to work) or political (the struggle against discontent or agitation).

...

3. *The state-control of the mechanisms of discipline.* In England, it was private religious groups that carried out, for a long time, the functions of social discipline; in France, although a part of this role remained in the hands of parish guilds or charity associations, another – and no doubt the most important part – was very soon taken over by the police apparatus.

The organization of a centralized police had long been regarded, even by contemporaries, as the most direct expression of royal absolutism; the sovereign had wished to have 'his own magistrate to whom he might directly entrust his orders, his commissions, intentions, and who was entrusted with the execution of orders and orders under the King's private seal'. In effect, in taking over a number of pre-existing functions – the search for criminals, urban surveillance, economic and political supervision – the police magistratures and the magistrature-general that presided over them in Paris transposed them into a single, strict, administrative machine.

...

But, although the police as an institution were certainly organized in the form of a state apparatus, and although this was certainly linked directly to the centre of political sovereignty, the type of power that it exercises, the mechanisms it operates and the elements to which it applies them are specific. It is an apparatus that must be coextensive with the entire social body and not only by the extreme limits that it embraces, but by the minuteness of the details it is concerned with. Police power must bear 'over everything': it is not however the totality of the state nor of the kingdom as visible and invisible body of the monarch; it is the dust of events, actions, behaviour, opinions – 'everything that happens'; the police are concerned with 'those things of every moment', those 'unimportant things', of which Catherine II spoke in her Great Instruction ... With the police, one is in the indefinite world of a supervision that seeks ideally to reach the most elementary particle, the most passing phenomenon of the social body: 'The ministry of the magistrates and police officers is of the greatest importance; the objects that it embraces are in a sense definite, one may perceive them only by a sufficiently detailed examination': the infinitely small of political power.

And, in order to be exercised, this power had to be given the instrument of permanent, exhaustive, omnipresent surveillance, capable of making all visible, as long as it could itself remain invisible. It had to be like a faceless gaze that transformed the whole social body into a field of perception: thousands of eyes posted everywhere, mobile attentions ever on the alert, a long, hierarchized net-work which, according to Le Maire, comprised for Paris the *forty-eight commissaires,* the twenty *inspecteurs,* then the 'observers', who were paid regularly, the '*basses mouches*', or secret agents, who were paid by the day, then the informers, paid according to the job done, and finally the prostitutes. And this unceasing observation had to be accumulated in a series of reports and registers; throughout the eighteenth century, an immense police text increasingly covered society by means of a complex documentary organization (on the police registers in the eighteenth century). And, unlike the methods of judicial or administrative writing, what was registered in this way were forms of behaviour, attitudes, possibilities, suspicions – a permanent account of individuals' behaviour.

Now, it should be noted that, although this police supervision was entirely 'in the hands of the king', it did not function in a single direction. It was in fact a double-entry system: it had to correspond, by manipulating the machinery of justice, to the immediate wishes of the king, but it was also capable of responding to solicitations from below; the celebrated *lettres de cachet,* or orders under the king's private seal, which were long the symbol of arbitrary royal rule and which brought detention into disrepute on political grounds, were in fact demanded by families, masters, local notables, neighbours, parish priests; and their function was to punish by confinement a whole infra-penality, that of disorder, agitation, disobedience, bad conduct; those things that Ledoux wanted to exclude from his architecturally perfect city and which he called 'offences of non-surveillance'. In short, the eighteenth-century police added a disciplinary function to its role as the auxiliary of justice in the pursuit of criminals and as an instrument for the political supervision of plots, opposition movements or revolts. It was a complex function since it linked the absolute power of the monarch to the lowest levels of power disseminated in society; since, between these different, enclosed institutions of discipline (workshops, armies, schools), it extended an intermediary network, acting where they could not intervene, disciplining the non-disciplinary spaces; but it filled in the gaps, linked them together, guaranteed with its armed force an interstitial discipline and a meta-discipline. 'By means of a wise police, the sovereign accustoms the people to order and obedience'.

The organization of the police apparatus in the eighteenth century sanctioned a generalization of the disciplines that became co-extensive with the state itself. Although it was linked in the most explicit way with everything in the royal power that exceeded the exercise of regular justice, it is understandable why the police offered such slight resistance to the rearrangement of the judicial power; and why it has not ceased to impose its prerogatives upon it, with ever-increasing weight, right up to the present day; this is no doubt because it is the secular arm of the judiciary; but it is also because, to a far greater degree than the judicial institution, it is identified, by reason of its extent and mechanisms, with a society of the disciplinary type. Yet it would be wrong to believe that the disciplinary functions were confiscated and absorbed once and for all by a state apparatus.

'Discipline' may be identified neither with an institution nor with an apparatus; it is a type of power, a modality for its exercise, comprising a whole set of instruments, techniques, procedures, levels of application, targets; it is a 'physics' or an 'anatomy' of power, a technology. And it may be taken over either by 'specialized' institutions (the penitentiaries or 'houses of correction' of the nineteenth century), or by institutions that use it as an essential instrument for a particular end (schools, hospitals), or by pre-existing authorities that find in it a means of reinforcing or reorganizing their internal mechanisms of power (one day we should show how intra-familial relations, essentially in the parents-children cell, have become 'disciplined', absorbing since the classical age external schemata, first educational and military, then medical, psychiatric, psychological, which have made the family the privileged locus of emergence for the disciplinary question of the normal and the abnormal); or by apparatuses that have made discipline their principle of internal functioning (the disciplinarization of the administrative apparatus from the Napoleonic period), or finally by state apparatuses whose major, if not exclusive, function is to assure that discipline reigns over society as a whole (the police).

On the whole, therefore, one can speak of the formation of a disciplinary society in this movement that stretches from the enclosed disciplines, a sort of social 'quarantine', to an indefinitely generalizable mechanism of 'panopticism'. Not because the disciplinary modality of power has replaced all the others; but because it has infiltrated the others, sometimes undermining them, but serving as an intermediary between them, linking them together, extending them and above all making it possible to bring the effects of power to the most minute and distant elements. It assures all infinitesimal distribution of the power relations.

... The formation of the disciplinary society is connected with a number of broad historical processes – economic, juridico-political and, lastly, scientific – of which it forms part.

1. Generally speaking, it might be said that the disciplines are techniques for assuring the ordering of human multiplicities. It is true that there is nothing exceptional or even characteristic in this: every system of power is presented with the same problem. But the peculiarity of the disciplines is that they try to define in relation to the multiplicities a tactics of power that fulfils three criteria: firstly, to obtain the exercise of power at the lowest possible cost (economically, by the low expenditure it involves; politically, by its discretion, its low exteriorization, its relative invisibility, the little resistance it arouses); secondly, to bring the effects of this social power to their maximum intensity and to extend them as far as possible, without either failure or interval; thirdly, to link this 'economic' growth of power with the output of the apparatuses (educational, military, industrial or medical) within which it is exercised; in short, to increase both the docility and the utility of all the elements of the system. This triple objective of the disciplines corresponds to a well-known historical conjuncture. One aspect of this conjuncture was the large demographic thrust of the eighteenth century; an increase in the floating population (one of the primary objects of discipline is to fix; it is an anti-nomadic technique); a change of quantitative scale in the groups to be supervised or manipulated (from the beginning of the seventeenth century to the eve of the French Revolution, the school population had been increasing rapidly, as had no doubt the hospital population; by the end of the eighteenth century, the peace-time army exceeded 200,000 men). The other aspect of the conjuncture was the growth in the apparatus of production, which was becoming more and more extended and complex; it was also becoming more costly and its profitability had to be increased. The development of the disciplinary methods corresponded to these two processes, or rather, no doubt, to the new need to adjust their correlation. Neither the residual forms of feudal power nor the structures of the administrative monarchy, nor the local mechanisms of supervision, nor the unstable, tangled mass they all formed together could carry out this role: they were hindered from doing so by the irregular and inadequate extension of their network, by their often conflicting functioning, but above all by the 'costly' nature of the power that was exercised in them. It was costly in several senses: because directly it cost a great deal to the Treasury; because the system of corrupt offices and farmed-out taxes weighed indirectly, but very heavily, on the population; because the resistance it encountered forced it into a cycle of perpetual reinforcement; because it

proceeded essentially by levying (levying on money or products by royal, seigniorial, ecclesiastical taxation; levying on men or time by *corvees* of press-ganging, by locking up or banishing vagabonds). The development of the disciplines marks the appearance of elementary techniques belonging to a quite different economy: mechanisms of power which, instead of proceeding by deduction, are integrated into the productive efficiency of the apparatuses from within, into the growth of this efficiency and into the use of what it produces. For the old principle of 'levying-violence', which governed the economy of power, the disciplines substitute the principle of 'mildness-production-profit'. These are the techniques that make it possible to adjust the multiplicity of men and the multiplication of the apparatuses of production (and this means not only 'production' in the strict sense, but also the production of knowledge and skills in the school, the production of health in the hospitals, the production of destructive force in the army).

In this task of adjustment, discipline had to solve a number of problems for which the old economy of power was not sufficiently equipped. It could reduce the inefficiency of mass phenomena: reduce what, in a multiplicity, makes it much less manageable than a unity; reduce what is opposed to the use of each of its elements and of their sum; reduce everything that may counter the advantages of number. That is why discipline fixes; it arrests or regulates movements; it clears up confusion; it dissipates compact groupings of individuals wandering about the country in unpredictable ways; it establishes calculated distributions. It must also master all the forces that are formed from the very constitution of an organized multiplicity; it must neutralize the effects of counter-power that spring from them and which form a resistance to the power that wishes to dominate it: agitations, revolts, spontaneous organizations, coalitions – anything that may establish horizontal conjunctions. Hence the fact that the disciplines use procedures of partitioning and verticality, that they introduce, between the different elements at the same level, as solid separations as possible, that they define compact hierarchical networks, in short, that they oppose to the intrinsic, adverse force of multiplicity the technique of the continuous, individualizing pyramid. They must also increase the particular utility of each element of the multiplicity, but by means that are the most rapid and the least costly, that is to say, by using the multiplicity itself as an instrument of this growth. Hence, in order to extract from bodies the maximum time and force, the use of those overall methods known as time-tables, collective training, exercises, total and detailed surveillance. Furthermore, the disciplines must increase the effect of utility proper to the multiplicities, so that each is made more useful than the simple sum of its elements: it is in order to increase the utilizable effects of the multiple that the disciplines define tactics of distribution, reciprocal adjustment of bodies, gestures and rhythms, differentiation of capacities, reciprocal co-ordination in relation to apparatuses or tasks. Lastly, the disciplines have to bring into play the power relations, not above but inside the very texture of the multiplicity, as discreetly as possible, as well articulated on the other functions of these multiplicities and also in the least expensive way possible: to this correspond anonymous instruments of power, coextensive with the multiplicity that they regiment, such as hierarchical surveillance, continuous registration, perpetual assessment and classification. In short, to substitute for a power that is manifested through the brilliance of those who exercise it, a power that insidiously objectifies those on whom it is applied; to form a body of knowledge about these individuals, rather than to deploy the ostentatious signs of sovereignty. In a word, the disciplines are the ensemble of minute technical inventions that made it possible to increase the useful size of multiplicities by decreasing the inconveniences of the power which, in order to make them useful, must control them. A multiplicity, whether in a workshop or a nation, an army or a school, reaches the threshold of a discipline when the relation of the one to the other becomes favourable.

If the economic take-off of the West began with the techniques that made possible the accumulation of capital, it might perhaps be said that the methods for administering the accumulation of men made possible a political take-off in relation to the traditional, ritual, costly, violent forms of power, which soon fell into disuse and were superseded by a subtle, calculated technology of subjection. In fact, the two processes – the accumulation of men and the accumulation of capital – cannot be separated; it would not have been possible to solve the problem of the accumulation of men without the growth of an apparatus of production capable of both sustaining them and using them; conversely, the techniques that made tile cumulative multiplicity of men useful accelerated the accumulation of capital. At a less general level, the technological mutations of the apparatus of production, the division of labour and the elaboration of the disciplinary techniques sustained an ensemble of very close relations. Each makes the other possible and necessary; each provides a model for the other. The disciplinary pyramid constituted the small cell of power within which the separation, coordination and supervision of tasks was imposed and made efficient; and analytical partitioning of time, gestures and bodily forces constituted an operational schema that could easily be transferred from the groups to be subjected to the mechanisms of production; the massive projection of military methods onto industrial organization was an example of this modelling of the division of labour following the model laid down by the schemata of power. But, on the other hand, the technical analysis of the process of production, its 'mechanical' breaking-down, were projected onto the labour force whose task it was to implement it: the constitution of those disciplinary machines in which the individual forces that they bring together are composed into a whole and therefore increased is the effect of this projection. Let us say that discipline is the unitary technique by which the body is reduced as a 'political' force at the least cost and maximized as a useful force. The growth of a capitalist economy gave rise to the specific modality of disciplinary power, whose general formulas, techniques of submitting forces and bodies, in short, 'political anatomy', could be operated in the most diverse political regimes, apparatuses or institutions.

2. The panoptic modality of power – at the elementary, technical, merely physical, level at which it is situated – is not under the immediate dependence or a direct extension of the great juridico-political structures of a society; it is nonetheless not absolutely independent. Historically, the process by which the bourgeoisie became in the course of the eighteenth century the politically dominant class was masked by the establishment of an explicit, coded and formally egalitarian juridical framework, made possible by the organization of a parliamentary, representative regime. But the development and generalization of disciplinary mechanisms constituted the other, dark side of these processes. The general juridical form that guaranteed a system of rights that were egalitarian in principle was supported by these tiny, everyday, physical mechanisms, by all those systems of micro-power that are essentially non-egalitarian and asymmetrical that we call the disciplines. And although, in a formal way, the representative regime makes it possible, directly or indirectly, with or without relays, for the will of all to

form the fundamental authority of sovereignty, the disciplines provide, at the base, a guarantee of the submission of forces and bodies. The real, corporal disciplines constituted the foundation of the formal, juridical liberties. The contract may have been regarded as the ideal foundation of law and political power; panopticism constituted the technique, universally widespread, of coercion. It continued to work in depth on the juridical structures of society, in order to make the effective mechanisms of power function in opposition to the formal framework that it had acquired. The 'Enlightenment', which discovered the liberties, also invented the disciplines.

In appearance, the disciplines constitute nothing more than an infra-law. They seem to extend the general forms defined by law to the infinitesimal level of individual lives; or they appear as methods of training that enable individuals to become integrated into these general demands. They seem to constitute the same type of law on a different scale, thereby making it more meticulous and more indulgent. The disciplines should be regarded as a sort of counter-law. They have the precise role of introducing insuperable asymmetries and excluding reciprocities. First, because discipline creates between individuals a 'private' link, which is a relation of constraints entirely different from contractual obligation; the acceptance of a discipline may be underwritten by contract; the way in which it is imposed, the mechanisms it brings into play, the non-reversible subordination of one group of people by another, the 'surplus' power that is always fixed on the same side, the inequality of position of the different 'partners' in relation to the common regulation, all these distinguish the disciplinary link from the contractual link, and make it possible to distort the contractual link systematically from the moment it has as its content a mechanism of discipline. We know, for example, how many real procedures undermine the legal fiction of the work contract: workshop discipline is not the least important. Moreover, whereas the juridical systems define juridical subjects according to universal norms, the disciplines characterize, classify, specialize; they distribute along a scale, around a norm, hierarchize individuals in relation to one another and, if necessary, disqualify and invalidate. In any case, in the space and during the time in which they exercise their control and bring into play the asymmetries of their power, they effect a suspension of the law that is never total, but is never annulled either. Regular and institutional as it may be, the discipline, in its mechanism, is a 'counter-law'. And, although the universal juridicism of modern society seems to fix limits on the exercise of power, its universally widespread panopticism enables it to operate, on the underside of the law, a machinery that is both immense and minute, which supports, reinforces, multiplies the asymmetry of power and undermines the limits that are traced around the law. The minute disciplines, the panopticisms of every day may well be below the level of emergence of the great apparatuses and the great political struggles. But, in the genealogy of modern society, they have been, with the class domination that traverses it, the political counterpart of the juridical norms according to which power was redistributed. Hence, no doubt, the importance that has been given for so long to the small techniques of discipline, to those apparently insignificant tricks that it has invented, and even to those 'sciences' that give it a respectable face; hence the fear of abandoning them if one cannot find any substitute; hence the affirmation that they are at the very foundation of society, and an element in its equilibrium, whereas they are a series of mechanisms for unbalancing power relations definitively and everywhere; hence the persistence in regarding them as the humble, but concrete form of every morality, whereas they are a set of physico-political techniques.

To return to the problem of legal punishments, the prison with all the corrective technology at its disposal is to be resituated at the point where the codified power to punish turns into a disciplinary power to observe; at the point where the universal punishments of the law are applied selectively to certain individuals and always the same ones; at the point where the redefinition of the juridical subject by the penalty becomes a useful training of the criminal; at the point where the law is inverted and passes outside itself, and where the counter-law becomes the effective and institutionalized content of the juridical forms. What generalizes the power to punish, then, is not the universal consciousness of the law in each juridical subject; it is the regular extension, the infinitely minute web of panoptic techniques.

3. Taken one by one, most of these techniques have a long history behind them. But what was new, in the eighteenth century, was that, by being combined and generalized, they attained a level at which the formation of knowledge and the increase of power regularly reinforce one another in a circular process. At this point, the disciplines crossed the 'technological' threshold. First the hospital, then the school, then, later, the workshop were not simply 'reordered' by the disciplines; they became, thanks to them, apparatuses such that any mechanism of objectification could be used in them as an instrument of subjection, and any growth of power could give rise in them to possible branches of knowledge; it was this link, proper to the technological systems, that made possible within the disciplinary element the formation of clinical medicine, psychiatry, child psychology, educational psychology, the rationalization of labour. It is a double process, then: an epistemological 'thaw' through a refinement of power relations; a multiplication of the effects of power through the formation and accumulation of new forms of knowledge.

...

Questions

1. In what sense is Foucault's account of the transition from the leper colony, to the plague town, to the panoptic prison a 'genealogical' account?

2. What methods were elaborated to deal with the threat of plague, and how did these differ from the strategy that had been used to deal with leprosy? What, in Foucault's view, was the point of adopting these methods? In what sense, and to what extent, is the panoptic prison the effect of a coming together of these 'different projects'?

3. How does the panoptic institution work? How does the power of the governor of such an institution differ, in Foucault's view, from the power of a political sovereign?

4. Is 'discipline' co-extensive with a particular institution such as the panoptic prison? If not, what is the relationship between discipline and its institutional manifestations?

5. How, if at all, was the spread of discipline linked (a) with the growth of the capitalist economy, and (b) with the emergence of the constitutional state?

6.   What might Foucault mean by the suggestion that discipline is both an 'infra-law' and a 'counter-law'?

Foucault (Power/Knowledge, Lecture Two, 92–108 (1980))

LECTURE TWO: 14 JANUARY 1976

The course of study I have been following until now – roughly since 1970/71 – has been concerned with the *how* of power. I have tried, that is, to relate its mechanisms to two points of reference, two limits: On the one hand, to the rules of right that provide a formal delimitation of power; on the other, to the effects of truth that this power produces and transmits, and which in their turn reproduce this power. Hence we have a triangle: power, right, truth.

Schematically, we can formulate the traditional question of political philosophy in the following terms: how is the discourse of truth, or quite simply, philosophy as that discourse which *par excellence* is concerned with truth, able to fix limits to the rights of power? That is the traditional question. The one I would prefer to pose is rather different. Compared to the traditional, noble and philosophic question it is much more down to earth and concrete. My problem is rather this: what rules of right are implemented by the relations of power in the production of 'discourses of truth'? Or alternatively, what type of power is susceptible of producing discourses of truth that in a society such as ours are endowed with such potent effects? What I mean is this: in a society such as ours, but basically in any society, there are manifold relations of power which permeate, characterise and constitute the social body, and these relations of power cannot themselves be established, consolidated nor implemented without the production, accumulation, circulation and functioning of a discourse. There can be no possible exercise of power without a certain economy of discourses of truth which operates through and on the basis of this association. We are subjected to the production of truth through power and we cannot exercise power except through the production of truth. This is the case for every society, but I believe that in ours the relationship between power, right and truth is organised in a highly specific fashion. If I were to characterise, not its mechanism itself, but its intensity and constancy, I would say that we are forced to produce the truth of power that our society demands, of which it has need, in order to function: we *must* speak the truth; we are constrained or condemned to confess or to discover the truth. Power never ceases its interrogation, its inquisition, its registration of truth: it institutionalises, professionalises and rewards its pursuit. In the last analysis, we must produce truth as we must produce wealth, indeed we must produce truth in order to produce wealth in the first place. In another way, we are also subjected to truth in the sense in which it is truth that makes the laws, trial produces the true discourse which, it least partially, decides, transmits and itself extends upon the effects of power. In the end, we are judged, condemned, classified, determined in our undertakings, destined to a certain mode of living or dying, as a function of the true discourses which are the bearers of the specific effects of power.

So, it is the rules of right, the mechanisms of power, the effects of truth or if you like, the rules of power and the powers of true discourses, that can be said more or less to have formed the general terrain of my concern, even if, as I know full well, I have traversed it only partially and in a very zig-zag fashion. I should like to speak briefly about this course of research, about what I have considered as being its guiding principle and about the methodological imperatives and precautions which I have sought to adopt. As regards the general principle involved in a study of the relations between right and power, it seems to me that in Western societies since Medieval times it has been royal power that has provided the essential focus around which legal thought has been elaborated. It is in response to the demands of royal power, for its profit and to serve as its instrument or justification, that the juridical edifice of our own society has been developed. Right in the West is the King's right. Naturally everyone is familiar with the famous, celebrated, repeatedly emphasised role of the jurists in the organisation of royal power. We must not forget that the re-vitalisation of Roman Law in the twelfth century was the major event around which, and on whose basis, the juridical edifice which had collapsed after the fall of the Roman Empire was reconstructed. This resurrection of Roman Law had in effect a technical and constitutive role to play in the establishment of the authoritarian, administrative, and, in the final analysis, absolute power of the monarchy. And when this legal edifice escapes in later centuries from the control of the monarch, when, more accurately, it is turned against that control, it is always the limits of this sovereign power that are put in question, its prerogatives that are challenged. In other words, I believe that the King remains the central personage in the whole legal edifice of the West. When it comes to the general organisation of the legal system in the West, it is essentially with the King, his rights, his power and its eventual limitations, that one is dealing. Whether the jurists were the King's henchmen or his adversaries, it is of royal power that we are speaking in every case when we speak of these grandiose edifices of legal thought and knowledge.

There are two ways in which we do so speak. Either we do so in order to show the nature of the juridical armoury that invested royal power, to reveal the monarch as the effective embodiment of sovereignty, to demonstrate that his power, for all that it was absolute, was exactly that which befitted his fundamental right. Or, by contrast. we do so in order to show the necessity of imposing limits upon this sovereign power, of submitting it to certain rules of right, within whose confines it had to be exercised in order for it to remain legitimate. The essential role of the theory of right, from medieval times onwards was to fix the legitimacy of power; that is the major problem around which the whole theory of right and sovereignty is organised.

When we say that sovereignty is the central problem of right in Western societies, what we mean basically is that the essential function of the discourse and techniques of right has been to efface the domination intrinsic to power in order to present the latter at the level of appearance under two different aspects: on the one hand, as the legitimate rights of sovereignty, and on the other, as the legal obligation to obey it. The system of right is centred entirely upon the King, and it is therefore designed to eliminate the fact of domination and its consequences.

My general project over the past few years has been, in essence, to reverse the mode of analysis followed by the entire discourse of right from the time of the Middle Ages. My aim, therefore, was to invert it, to give due weight, that is, to the fact of domination, to expose both its latent nature, and its brutality. I then wanted to show not only how right is, in a general way, the instrument of this domination – which scarcely needs saying – but also to show the extent to which, and the forms in which, right (not simply the laws but the whole complex of apparatuses, institutions and regulations responsible for their application) transmits and puts in motion relations that are not relations of sovereignty, but of domination. Moreover, in speaking of domination I do not have in mind that solid and global kind of domination that one person exercises over others, or one group over another, but the manifold forms of domination that can be exercised within society. Not the domination of the King in his central position, therefore, but that of his subjects in their mutual relations: not the uniform edifice of sovereignty, but the multiple forms of subjugation that have a place and function within the social organism.

The system of right, the domain of the law, are permanent agents of these relations of domination, these polymorphous techniques of subjugation. Right should be viewed, I believe, not in terms of a legitimacy to be established, but in terms of the methods of subjugation that it instigates.

The problem for me is how to avoid this question, central to the theme of right, regarding sovereignty and the obedience of individual subjects in order that I may substitute the problem of domination and subjugation for that of sovereignty and obedience. Given that this was to be the general line of my analysis, there were a certain number of methodological precautions that seemed requisite to its pursuit. In the very first place, it seemed important to accept that the analysis in question should not concern itself with the regulated and legitimate forms of power in their central locations, with the general mechanisms through which they operate, and the continual effects of these. On the contrary, it should be concerned with power at its extremities, in its ultimate destinations, with those points where it becomes capillary, that is, in its more regional and local forms and institutions. Its paramount concern, in fact, should be with the point where power surmounts the rules of right which organise and delimit it and extends itself beyond them, invests itself in institutions, becomes embodied in techniques, and equips itself with instruments and eventually even violent means of material intervention. To give an example: rather than try to discover where and how the right of punishment is founded on sovereignty, how it is presented in the theory of monarchical democratic right, I have tried to see in what ways punishment and the power of punishment are effectively embodied in a certain number of local, regional, material institutions, which are concerned with torture or imprisonment, and to place these in the climate – at once institutional and physical, regulated and violent – of the effective apparatuses of punishment. In other words, one should try to locate power at the extreme points of its exercise, where it is always less legal in character.

A second methodological precaution urged that the analysis should not concern itself with power at the level of conscious intention or decision; that it should not attempt to consider power from its internal point of view and that it should refrain from posing the labyrinthine and unanswerable question: 'Who then has the power and what has he in mind? What is the aim of someone who possesses power?' Instead, it is a case of studying power at the point where its intention, if it has one, is completely invested in its real and effective practices. What is needed is a study of power in its external visage, at the point where it is in direct and immediate relationship with that which we can provisionally call its object, its target, its field of application, there – that is to say – where it installs itself and produces its real effects.

Let us not, therefore, ask why certain people want to dominate, what they seek, what is their overall strategy. Let us ask, instead, how things work at the level of on-going subjugation, at the level of those continuous and uninterrupted processes which subject our bodies, govern our gestures, dictate our behaviours etc. In other words, rather than ask ourselves how the sovereign appears to us in his lofty isolation, we should try to discover how it is that subjects are gradually, progressively, really and materially constituted through a multiplicity of organisms, forces, energies, materials, desires, thoughts etc. We should try to grasp subjection in its material instance as a constitution of subjects. This would be the exact opposite of Hobbes' project in *Leviathan,* and of that, I believe, of all jurists for whom the problem is the distillation of a single will – or rather, the constitution of a unitary, singular body animated by the spirit of sovereignty – from the particular wills of a multiplicity of individuals. Think of the scheme of Leviathan: insofar as he is a fabricated man, Leviathan is no other than the amalgamation of a certain number of separate individualities, who find themselves reunited by the complex of elements that go to compose the State; but at the heart of the State, or rather, at its head, there exists something which constitutes it as such, and this is sovereignty, which Hobbes says is precisely the spirit of Leviathan. Well, rather than worry about the problem of the central spirit, I believe that we must attempt to study the myriad of bodies which are constituted as peripheral *subjects* as a result of the effects of power.

A third methodological precaution related to the fact that power is not to be taken to be a phenomenon of one individual's consolidation and homogenous domination over others, or that of one group or class over others. What, by contrast, should always be kept in mind is that power, if we do not take too distant a view of it, is not that which makes the difference between those who exclusively possess and retain it, and those who do not have it and submit to it. Power must by analysed as something which circulates, or, rather as something which only functions in the form of a chain. It is never localised here or there, never in anybody's hands, never appropriated as a commodity or piece of wealth. Power is employed and exercised through a net-like organisation. And not only do individuals circulate between its threads; they are always in the position of simultaneously undergoing and exercising this power. They are not only its inert or consenting target; they are always also the elements of its articulation. In other words, individuals are the vehicles of power, not its points of application.

The individual is not to be conceived as a sort of nucleus, a primitive atom, a multiple and inert material on which power comes to fasten or against which it happens to strike, and in so doing subdues or crushes individuals. In fact, it is already one of the prime effects of power that certain bodies, certain gestures, certain discourses, certain desires, come to be identified and constituted as individuals. The individual, that is, is not the *vis-à-vis* of power; it is, I believe, one of its prime effects. The individual is an effect of power, and at the same time, or precisely to the extent to which it is that effect, it is the element of its articulation. The individual which power has constituted is at the same time its vehicle.

There is a fourth methodological precaution that follows from this: when I say that power establishes a network through which it freely circulates, this is true only up to a certain point. In much the same fashion we could say that therefore we all have a fascism in our heads, or, more profoundly, we all have a power in our bodies. But I do not believe that one should conclude from that that power is the best distributed thing in the world, although in some sense that is indeed so. We are not dealing with a sort of democratic or anarchic distribution of power through bodies. That is to say, it seems to me – and this then would be the fourth methodological precaution – that the important thing is not to attempt some kind of deduction of power starting from its centre and aimed at the discovery of the extent to which it permeates into the base, of the degree to which it reproduces itself down to and including the most molecular elements of society. One must rather conduct an *ascending* analysis of power, starting that is, from its infinitesimal mechanisms, which each have their own trajectory, their own techniques and tactics, and then see how these mechanisms of power have been – and continue to be – invested, colonised, utilised, involuted, transformed, displaced, extended etc., by ever more general mechanisms and by forms of global domination. It is not that this global domination extends itself right to the base in a plurality of repercussions: I believe that the manner in which the phenomena, the techniques and the procedures of power enter into play at the most basic levels must be analysed, that the way in which these procedures are displaced, extended and altered must certainly be demonstrated; but above all what must be shown is the manner in which they are invested and annexed by more global phenomena and the subtle fashion in which more general powers or economic interests are able to engage with these technologies that are at once both relatively autonomous of power and act as its infinitesimal elements. In order to make this clearer, one might cite the example of madness. The descending type of analysis, the one of which I believe one ought to be wary, will say that the bourgeoisie has, since the sixteenth or seventeenth century, been the dominant class; from this premise, it will then set out to deduce the internment of the insane. One can always make this deduction, it is always easily done and that is precisely what I would hold against it. It is in fact a simple matter to show that since lunatics are precisely those persons who are useless to industrial production, one is obliged to dispense with them. One could argue similarly in regard to infantile sexuality – and several thinkers, including Willhelm Reich have indeed sought to do so up to a certain point. Given the domination of the bourgeois class, how can one understand the repression of infantile sexuality? Well, very simply – given that the human body had become essentially a force of production from the time of the seventeenth and eighteenth century, all the forms of its expenditure which did not lend themselves to the constitution of the productive forces – and were therefore exposed as redundant – were banned, excluded and repressed. These kinds of deduction are always possible. They are simultaneously correct and false. Above all they are too glib, because one can always do exactly the opposite and show, precisely by appeal to the principle of the dominance of the bourgeois class, that the forms of control of infantile sexuality could in no way have been predicted. On the contrary, it is equally plausible to suggest that what was needed was sexual training, the encouragement of a sexual precociousness, given that what was fundamentally at stake was the constitution of a labour force whose optimal state, as we well know, at least at the beginning of the nineteenth century, was to be infinite: the greater the labour force, the better able would the system of capitalist production have been to fulfil and improve its functions.

I believe that anything can be deduced from the general phenomenon of the domination of the bourgeois class. What needs to be done is something quite different. One needs to investigate historically, and beginning from the lowest level, how mechanisms of power have been able to function. In regard to the confinement of the insane, for example, or the repression and interdiction of sexuality, we need to see the manner in which, at the effective level of the family, of the immediate environment, of the cells and most basic units of society, these phenomena of repression or exclusion possessed their instruments and their logic, in response to a certain number of needs. We need to identify the agents responsible for them, their real agents (those which constituted the immediate social *entourage*, the family, parents, doctors etc.), and not be content to lump them under the formula of a generalised bourgeoisie. We need to see how these mechanisms of power, at a given moment, in a precise conjuncture and by means of a certain number of transformations, have begun to become economically advantageous and politically useful. I think that in this way one could easily manage to demonstrate that what the bourgeoisie needed, or that in which its system discovered its real interests, was not the exclusion of the mad or the surveillance and prohibition of infantile masturbation (for, to repeat, such a system can perfectly well tolerate quite opposite practices), but rather, the techniques and procedures themselves of such an exclusion. It is the mechanisms of that exclusion that are necessary, the apparatuses of surveillance, the medicalisation of sexuality, of madness, of delinquency, all the micro-mechanisms of power, that came, from a certain moment in time, to represent the interests of the bourgeoisie, Or even better, we could say that to the extent to which this view of the bourgeoisie and of its interests appears to lack content, at least in regard to the problems with which we are here concerned, it reflects that fact that it was not the bourgeoisie itself which thought that madness had to be excluded or infantile sexuality repressed. What in fact happened instead was that the mechanisms of the exclusion of madness, and of the surveillance of infantile sexuality, began from a particular point in time, and for reasons which need to be studied, to reveal their political usefulness and to lend themselves to economic profit, and that as a natural consequence, all of a sudden, they came to be colonised and maintained by global mechanisms and the entire State system. It is only if we grasp these techniques of power and demonstrate the economic advantages or political utility that derives from them in a given context for specific reasons, that we can understand how these mechanisms come to be effectively incorporated into the social whole.

To put this somewhat differently: the bourgeoisie has never had any use for the insane; but the procedures it has employed to exclude them have revealed and realised – from the nineteenth century onwards, and again on the basis of certain transformations – a political advantage, on occasion even a certain economic utility, which have consolidated the system and contributed to its overall functioning. The bourgeoisie is interested in power, not in madness, in the system of control of infantile sexuality, not in that phenomenon itself. The bourgeoisie could not care less about delinquents, about their punishment and rehabilitation, which economically have little importance, but it is concerned about the complex of mechanisms with which delinquency is controlled, pursued, punished and reformed etc.

As for our fifth methodological precaution: it is quite possible that the major mechanisms of power have been accompanied by ideological productions. There has, for example, probably been an ideology of education, an ideology of the monarchy, an ideology of parliamentary democracy etc.; but basically I do not believe that what has taken place can be said to be ideological. It is both much more and much less than ideology. It is the production of effective instruments for the formation and accumulation of knowledge-methods of observation, techniques of registration, procedures for investigation and research, apparatuses of control. All this means that power, when it is exercised through these subtle mechanisms, cannot but evolve, organise and put into circulation a knowledge, or rather apparatuses of knowledge, which are not ideological constructs.

By way of summarising these five methodological pre-cautions, I would say that we should direct our researches on the nature of power not towards the juridical edifice of sovereignty, the State apparatuses and the ideologies which accompany them, but towards domination and the material operators of power, towards forms of subjection and the inflections and utilisations of their localised systems, and towards strategic apparatuses. We must eschew the model of Leviathan in the study of power. We must escape from the limited field of juridical sovereignty and State institutions, and instead base our analysis of power on the study of techniques and tactics of domination.

This, in its general outline, is the methodological course that I believe must be followed, and which I have tried to pursue in the various researches that we have conducted over recent years on psychiatric power, on infantile sexuality, on political systems, etc. Now as one explores these fields of investigation, observing the methodological precautions I have mentioned, I believe that what then comes into view is a solid body of historical fact, which will ultimately bring us into confrontation with the problems of which I want to speak this year.

This solid, historical body of fact is the juridical-political theory of sovereignty of which I spoke a moment ago, a theory which has had four roles to play. In the first place, it has been used to refer to a mechanism of power that was effective under the feudal monarchy. In the second place, it has served as instrument and even as justification for the construction of the large scale administrative monarchies. Again, from the time of the sixteenth century and more than ever from the seventeenth century onwards, but already at time of the wars of religion, the theory of sovereignty has been a weapon which has circulated from one camp to another, which has been utilised in one sense or another, either to limit or else to reinforce royal power: we find it among Catholic monarchists and Protestant anti-monarchists, among Protestant and more-or-less liberal monarchists, but also among Catholic partisans of regicide or dynastic transformation. It functions both in the hands of aristocrats and in the hands of parliamentarians. It is found among the representatives of royal power and among the last feudatories. In short, it was the major instrument of political and theoretical struggle around systems of power of the sixteenth and seventeenth centuries. Finally, in the eighteenth century, it is again this same theory of sovereignty, re-activated through the doctrine of Roman Law, that we find in its essentials in Rousseau and his contemporaries, but now with a fourth role to play: now it is concerned with the construction, in opposition to the administrative, authoritarian and absolutist monarchies, of an alternative model, that of parliamentary democracy. And it is still this role that it plays at the moment of the Revolution.

Well, it seems to me that if we investigate these four roles there is a definite conclusion to be drawn: as long as a feudal type of society survived, the problems to which the theory of sovereignty was addressed were in effect confined to the general mechanisms of power, to the way in which its forms of existence at the higher level of society influenced its exercise at the lowest levels. In other words, the relationship of sovereignty, whether interpreted in a wider or a narrower sense, encompasses the totality of the social body. In effect, the mode in which power was exercised could be defined in its essentials in terms of the relationship sovereign-subject. But in the seventeenth and eighteenth centuries, we have the production of an important phenomenon, or rather the invention, of a new mechanism of power possessed of highly specific procedural techniques, completely novel instruments, quite different apparatuses, and which is also, I believe, absolutely incompatible with the relations of sovereignty.

This new mechanism of power is more dependent upon bodies and what they do than upon the Earth and its products. It is a mechanism of power which permits time and labour, rather than wealth and commodities, to be extracted from bodies. It is a type of power which is constantly exercised by means of surveillance rather than in a discontinuous manner by means of a system of levies or obligations distributed over time. It presupposes a tightly knit grid of material coercions rather than the physical existence of a sovereign. It is ultimately dependent upon the principle, which introduces a genuinely new economy of power, that one must be able simultaneously both to increase the subjected forces and to improve the force and efficacy of that which subjects them.

This type of power is in every aspect the antithesis of that mechanism of power which the theory of sovereignty described or sought to transcribe. The latter is linked to a form of power that is exercised over the Earth and its products, much more than over human bodies and their operations. The theory of sovereignty is something which refers to the displacement and appropriation on the part of power, not of time and labour, but of goods and wealth. It allows discontinuous obligations distributed over time to be given legal expression but it does not allow for the codification of a continuous surveillance. It enables power to be founded in the physical existence of the sovereign, but not in continuous and permanent systems of surveillance. The theory of sovereignty permits the foundation of an absolute power in the absolute expenditure of power. It does not allow for a calculation of power in terms of the minimum expenditure for the maximum return.

This new type of power, which can no longer be formulated in terms of sovereignty, is, I believe, one of the great inventions of bourgeois society. It has been a fundamental instrument in the constitution of industrial capitalism and of the type of society that is its accompaniment. This non-sovereign power, which lies outside the form of sovereignty, is disciplinary power. Impossible to describe in the terminology of the theory of sovereignty from which it differs so radically, this disciplinary power ought by rights to have led to the disappearance of the grand juridical edifice created by that theory. But in reality, the theory of sovereignty has continued not only to exist as an ideology of right, but also to provide the organising principle of the legal codes which Europe acquired in the nineteenth century, beginning with the Napoleonic Code.

Why has the theory of sovereignty persisted in this fashion as an ideology and an organising principle of these major legal codes? For two reasons, I believe. On the one hand, it has been, in the eighteenth and again in the nineteenth century, a permanent instrument of criticism of the monarchy and of all the obstacles that can thwart the development of disciplinary society. But at the same time, the theory of sovereignty, and the organisation of a legal code centred upon it have allowed a system of right to be superimposed upon the mechanisms of discipline in such a way as to conceal its actual procedures, the element of domination inherent in its techniques, and to guarantee to everyone, by virtue of the sovereignty of the State, the exercise of his proper sovereign rights. The juridical systems – and this applies both to their codification and to their theorisation – have enabled sovereignty to be democratised through the constitution of a public right articulated upon collective sovereignty, while at the same time this democratisation of sovereignty was fundamentally determined by and grounded in mechanisms of disciplinary coercion.

To put this in more rigorous terms, one might say that once it became necessary for disciplinary constraints to be exercised through mechanisms of domination and yet at the same time for their effective exercise of power to be disguised a theory of sovereignty was required to make an appearance at the level of the legal apparatus, and to re-emerge in its codes. Modern society, then, from the nineteenth century up to our own day, has been characterised on the one hand, by a legislation, a discourse, organisation based on public right, whose principle of articulation is the social body and the delegative status of each citizen; and, on the other hand, by it closely linked grid of disciplinary coercions whose purpose is in fact to assure the cohesion of this same social body. Though a theory of right is a necessary companion to this grid, it cannot in any event provide the terms of its endorsement. Hence these two limits, a right of sovereignty and a mechanism of discipline, which define, I believe, the arena in which power is exercised. But these two limits are so heterogeneous that they cannot possibly be reduced to each other. The powers of modern society are exercised through, on the basis of, and by virtue of, this very heterogeneity between a public right of sovereignty and a polymorphous disciplinary mechanism. This is not to suggest that there is on the one hand an explicit and scholarly system of right which is that of sovereignty, and, on the other hand, obscure and unspoken disciplines which carry out their shadowy operations in the depths, and thus constitute the bedrock of the great mechanism of power. In reality, the disciplines have their own discourse. They engender, for the reasons of which we spoke earlier, apparatuses of knowledge (*savoir*) and a multiplicity of new domains of understanding. They are extraordinarily inventive participants in the order of these knowledge-producing apparatuses. Disciplines are the bearers of a discourse, but this cannot be the discourse of right. The discourse of discipline has nothing in common with that of law, rule, or sovereign will. The disciplines may well be the carriers of a discourse that speaks of a rule, but this is not the juridical rule deriving from sovereignty, but a natural rule, a norm. The code they come to define is not that of law but that of normalisation. Their reference is to a theoretical horizon which of necessity has nothing in common with the edifice of right. It is human science which constitutes their domain, and clinical knowledge their jurisprudence.

In short, what I have wanted to demonstrate in the course of the last few years is not the manner in which at the advance front of the exact sciences the uncertain, recalcitrant, confused dominion of human behaviour has little by little been annexed to science: it is not through some advancement in the rationality of the exact sciences that the human sciences are gradually constituted. I believe that the process which has really rendered the discourse of the human sciences possible is the juxtaposition, the encounter between two lines of approach, two mechanisms, two absolutely heterogeneous types of discourse: on the one hand there is re-organisation of right that invests sovereignty, and on the other, the mechanics of the coercive forces whose exercise takes a disciplinary form. And I believe that in our own times power is exercised simultaneously through this right and these techniques and that these techniques and these discourses, to which the disciplines give rise invade the area of right so that the procedures of normalisation come to be ever more constantly engaged in the colonisation of those of law. I believe that all this can explain the global functioning of what I would call a *society of normalism*. I mean, more precisely, that disciplinary normalisations come into ever greater conflict with the juridical systems of sovereignty: their incompatibility with each other is ever more acutely felt and apparent; some kind of arbitrating discourse is made ever more necessary, a type of power and of knowledge that the sanctity of science would render neutral. It is precisely in the extension of medicine that we see, in some sense, not so much the linking perpetual exchange or encounter of mechanisms of discipline with the principle of right. The developments of medicine, the general medicalisation of behaviours, conducts, discourses, desires etc, take place at the point of intersection between the two heterogeneous levels of discipline and sovereignty. For this reason, against these usurpations by the disciplinary mechanisms, against this ascent of a power that is tied to scientific knowledge, we find that there is no solid recourse available to us today, such being our situation, except that which lies precisely in the return to a theory of right organised around sovereignty and articulated upon its ancient principle. When today one wants to object in some way to the disciplines and all the effects of power and knowledge that are linked to them, what is it that one does, concretely, in real life, what do the Magistrates Union or other similar institutions do, if not precisely appeal to this canon of right, this famous, formal right, that is said to be bourgeois, and which in reality is the right of sovereignty? But I believe that we find ourselves here in a kind of blind alley: it is not through recourse to sovereignty against discipline that the effects of disciplinary power can be limited, because sovereignty and disciplinary mechanisms are two absolutely integral constituents of the general mechanism of power in our society.

If one wants to look for a non-disciplinary form of power, or rather, to struggle against disciplines and disciplinary power, it is not towards the ancient right of sovereignty that one should turn, but towards the possibility of a new form of right, one which must indeed be anti-disciplinarian, but at the same time liberated from the principle of sovereignty. It is at this point that we once more come up against the notion of repression, whose use in this context I believe to be doubly unfortunate. On the one hand, it contains an obscure reference to a certain theory of sovereignty, the sovereignty of the sovereign rights of the individual, and on the other hand, its usage introduces a system of psychological reference points borrowed from the human sciences, that is to say, from discourses and practices that belong to the disciplinary realm. I believe that the notion of repression remains a juridical-disciplinary notion whatever the critical use one would make of it. To this extent the critical application of the notion of repression is found to be vitiated and nullified from the outset by the two-fold juridical and disciplinary reference it contains to sovereignty on the one hand and to normalisation on the other.

QUESTIONS

1. What does Foucault have in mind when he refers to 'the rules of right that provide a formal delimitation of power?

2. Why, for Foucault, is 'the system of right ... centred entirely on the King'? How

does this efface 'the fact of domination and its consequences'? In what ways is the system of right a 'permanent agent' of relations of domination?

3.   In what ways are sovereign power and disciplinary power 'heterogeneous'? Why is it impossible to reduce either of these forms of power to the other? Why is each a 'necessary companion' for the other?

4.   What would the 'new form of right' to which Foucault alludes – both anti-disciplinarian, but also 'liberated from the principle of sovereignty' – look like?

Michel Foucault (*Governmentality* 87–104 (1991a))

... Throughout the Middle Ages and classical antiquity, we find a multitude of treatises presented as 'advice to the prince', concerning his proper conduct, the exercise of power, the means of securing the acceptance and respect of his subjects, the love of God and obedience to him, the application of divine law to the cities of men, etc. But a more striking fact is that, from the middle of the sixteenth century to the end of the eighteenth, there develops and flourishes a notable series of political treatises that are no longer exactly 'advice to the prince', and not yet treatises of political science, but are instead presented as works on the 'art of government'. Government as a general problem seems to me to explode in the sixteenth century, posed by discussions of quite diverse questions. One has, for example, the question of the government of oneself, that ritualization of the problem of personal conduct which is characteristic of the sixteenth century Stoic revival. There is the problem too of the government of souls and lives, the entire theme of Catholic and Protestant pastoral doctrine. There is government of children and the great problematic of pedagogy which emerges and develops during the sixteenth century. And, perhaps only as the last of these questions to be taken up, there is the government of the state by the prince. How to govern oneself, how to be governed, how to govern others, by whom the people will accept being governed, how to become the best possible governor – all these problems, in their multiplicity and intensity, seem to me to be characteristic of the sixteenth century, which lies, to put it schematically, at the crossroads of two processes: the one which, shattering the structures of feudalism, leads to the establishment of the great territorial, administrative and colonial states; and that totally different movement which, with the Reformation and Counter-Reformation, raises the issue of how one must be spiritually ruled and led on this earth in order to achieve eternal salvation.

There is a double movement, then, of state centralization on the one hand and of dispersion and religious dissidence on the other: it is, I believe, at the intersection of these two tendencies that the problem comes to pose itself with this peculiar intensity, of how to be ruled, how strictly, by whom, to what end, by what methods, etc. There is a problematic of government in general.

Out of all this immense and monotonous literature on government which extends to the end of the eighteenth century, with the transformations which I will try to identify in a moment, I would like to underline some points that are worthy of notice because they relate to the actual definition of what is meant by the government of the state, of what we would today call the political form of government. The simplest way of doing this is to compare all of this literature with a single text which from the sixteenth to the eighteenth century never ceased to function as the object of explicit or implicit opposition and rejection, and relative to which the whole literature on government established its standpoint: Machiavelli's *The Prince*.

...

This politics of *The Prince* ... from which people sought to distance themselves, was characterized by one principle: for Machiavelli, it was alleged, the prince stood in a relation of singularity and externality, and thus of transcendence, to his principality. The prince acquires his principality by inheritance or conquest, but in any case he does not form part of it, he remains external to it. The link that binds him to his principality may have been established through violence, through family heritage or by treaty, with the complicity or the alliance of other princes; this makes no difference, the link in any event remains a purely synthetic one and there is no fundamental, essential, natural and juridical connection between the prince and his principality. As a corollary of this, given that this link is external, it will be fragile and continually under threat – from outside by the prince's enemies who seek to conquer or recapture his principality, and from within by subjects who have no *a priori* reason to accept his rule. Finally, this principle and its corollary lead to a conclusion, deduced as an imperative: that the objective of the exercise of power is to reinforce, strengthen and protect the principality, but with this last understood to mean not the objective ensemble of its subjects and the territory, but rather the prince's relation with what he owns, with the territory he has inherited or acquired, and with his subjects. This fragile link is what the art of governing or of being prince espoused by Machiavelli has as its object. As a consequence of this the mode of analysis of Machiavelli's text will be twofold: to identify dangers (where they come from, what they consist in, their severity: which are the greater, which the slighter), and, secondly, to develop the art of manipulating relations of force that will allow the prince to ensure the protection of his principality, understood as the link that binds him to his territory and his subjects.

Schematically, one can say that Machiavelli's *The Prince*, as profiled in all these implicitly or explicitly anti-Machiavellian treatises, is essentially a treatise about the prince's ability to keep his principality. And it is this *savoir-faire* that the anti-Machiavellian literature wants to replace by something else and new, namely the art of government. Having the ability to retain one's principality is not at all the same thing as possessing the art of governing. But what does this latter ability comprise?

... [First,] whereas the doctrine of the prince and the juridical theory of sovereignty are constantly attempting to draw the line between the power of the prince and any other form of power, because its task is to explain and justify this essential discontinuity between them, in the art of government the task is to establish a continuity, in both an upwards and a downwards direction.

Upwards continuity means that a person who wishes to govern the state well must first learn how to govern himself, his goods and his patrimony, after which he will be successful in governing the state ... It is the pedagogical formation of the prince ... that will ensure this upwards continuity. On the other hand, we also have a downwards continuity in the sense that, when a state is well run, the head of the family will know how to look after his family, his goods and his patrimony, which means that individuals will, in turn, behave as they should. This downwards line, which transmits to individual behaviour and the running of the family the same principles as the good government of the state, is just at this time beginning to he called *police*. The prince's pedagogical formation ensures the upwards continuity of the forms of government, and police the downwards one. The central term of this continuity is the government of the family, termed *economy*.

The art of government, as becomes apparent in this literature, is essentially concerned with answering the question of how to introduce economy – that is to say, the correct manner of managing individuals, goods and wealth within the family (which a good father is expected to do in relation to his wife, children and servants) and of making the family fortunes prosper – how to introduce this meticulous attention of the father towards his family into the management of the state.

This, I believe, is the essential issue in the establishment of the art of government: introduction of economy into political practice. And if this is the case in the sixteenth century, it remains so in the eighteenth.

...

The word 'economy', which in the sixteenth century signified a form of government, comes in the eighteenth century to designate a level of reality, a field of intervention, through a series of complex processes that I regard as absolutely fundamental to our history.

...

[Second,] [g]overnment is the right disposition of things. I would like to pause over this word 'things', because if we consider what characterizes the ensemble of objects of the prince's power in Machiavelli, we will see that for Machiavelli the object and, in a sense, the target of power are two things, on the one hand the territory, and on the other its inhabitants. In this respect, Machiavelli simply adapted to his particular aims a juridical principle which from the Middle Ages to the sixteenth century defined sovereignty in public law: sovereignty is not exercised on things, but above all on a territory and consequently on the subjects who inhabit it. In this sense we can say that the territory is the fundamental element both in Machiavellian principality and in juridical sovereignty as defined by the theoreticians and philosophers of right. Obviously enough, these territories can be fertile or not, the population dense or sparse, the inhabitants rich or poor, active or lazy, but all these elements are mere variables by comparison with territory itself, which is the very foundation of principality and sovereignty. On the contrary ... the definition of government in no way refers to territory. One governs things. But what does this mean? I do not think this is a matter of opposing things to men, but rather of showing that what government has to do with is not territory but rather a sort of complex composed of men and things. The things with which in this sense government is to be concerned are in fact men, but men in their relations, their links, their imbrication with those other things which are wealth, resources, means of subsistence, the territory with its specific qualities, climate, irrigation, fertility, etc.; men in their relation to that other kind of things, customs, habits, ways of acting and thinking, etc.; lastly, men in their relation to that other kind of things, accidents and misfortunes such as famine, epidemics, death, etc. The fact that government concerns things understood in this way, this imbrication of men and things, is I believe readily confirmed by the metaphor which is inevitably invoked in these treatises on government, namely that of the ship. What does it mean to govern a ship? It means clearly to take charge of the sailors, but also of the boat and its cargo; to take care of a ship means also to reckon with winds, rocks and storms; and it consists in that activity of establishing a relation between the sailors who are to be taken care of and the ship which is to be taken care of, and the cargo which is to be brought safely to port, and all those eventualities like winds, rocks, storms and so on; this is what characterizes the government of a ship. The same goes for the running of a household. Governing a household, a family, does not essentially mean safeguarding the family property; what concerns it is the individuals that compose the family, their wealth and prosperity. It means to reckon with all the possible events that may intervene, such as births and deaths, and with all the things that can be done, such as possible alliances with other families; it is this general form of management that is characteristic of government; by comparison, the question of landed property for the family, and the question of the acquisition of sovereignty over a territory for a prince, are only relatively secondary matters. What counts essentially is this complex of men and things; property and territory are merely one of its variables.

...

To govern, then, means to govern things. '[G]government is the right disposition of things, arranged so as to lead to a convenient end'. Government, that is to say, has a finality of its own, and in this respect again I believe it can be clearly distinguished from sovereignty. I do not of course mean that sovereignty is presented in philosophical and juridical texts as a pure and simple right; no jurist or, *a fortiori* theologian ever said that the legitimate sovereign is purely and simply entitled to exercise his power regardless of its ends, The sovereign must, always, if he is to be a good sovereign, have as his aim, 'the common welfare and the salvation of all'. Take for instance a late seventeenth-century author. Pufendorf says: 'Sovereign authority is conferred upon them [the rulers] only in order to allow them to use it to attain or conserve what is of public utility'. The ruler may not have consideration for anything advantageous for himself, unless it also be so for the state. What does this common good or general salvation consist of, which the jurists talk about as being the end of sovereignty? If we look closely at the real content that jurists and theologians give to it, we can see that 'the common good' refers to a state of affairs where all the subjects without exception obey the laws, accomplish the tasks expected of them, practise the trade to which they are assigned, and respect the established order so far as this order conforms to the laws imposed by God on nature and men: in other words, 'the common good' means essentially obedience to the law, either that of their earthly sovereign or that of God, the absolute sovereign. In every case, what characterizes the end of sovereignty, this common and general good, is in sum nothing other than submission to sovereignty. This means that the end of sovereignty is circular: the end of sovereignty is the exercise of sovereignty. The good is obedience to the law, hence the good for sovereignty is that people should obey it. This is an essential circularity which, whatever its theoretical structure, moral justification or practical effects, comes very close to what Machiavelli said when he stated that the primary aim of the prince was to retain his principality. We always come back to this self-referring circularity of sovereignty or principality.

... Government is defined as a right manner of disposing things so as to lead not to the form of the common good, as the jurists' texts would have said, but to an end which is 'convenient' for each of the things that are to be governed. This implies a plurality of specific aims: for instance, government will have to ensure that the greatest possible quantity of wealth is produced, that the people are provided with sufficient means of subsistence, that the population is enabled to multiply, etc. There is a whole series of specific finalities, then, which become the objective of government as such. In order to achieve these various finalities, things must be disposed – and this term, *dispose,* is important because with sovereignty the instrument that allowed it to achieve its aim – that is to say, obedience to the laws – was the law itself, law and sovereignty were absolutely inseparable. On the contrary, with government it is a question not of imposing law on men, but of disposing things: that is to say, of employing tactics rather than laws, and even of using laws themselves as tactics – to arrange things in such a way that, through a certain number of means, such and such ends may be achieved.

I believe we are at an important turning point here: whereas the end of sovereignty is internal to itself and possesses its own intrinsic instruments in the shape of its laws, the finality of government resides in the things it manages and in the pursuit of the perfection and intensification of the processes which it directs; and the instruments of government, instead of being laws, now come to be a range of multiform tactics. Within the perspective of government, law is not what is important: this is a frequent theme throughout the seventeenth century, and it is made explicit in the eighteenth-century texts of the Physiocrats which explain that it is not through law that the aims of government are to be reached.

Finally ... a good ruler must have patience, wisdom and diligence ... [T]he good governor does not have to have a sting – that is to say, a weapon of killing, a sword – in order to exercise his power; he must have patience rather than wrath, and it is not the right to kill, to employ force, that forms the essence of the figure of the governor. And what positive content accompanies this ...? Wisdom and diligence. Wisdom, understood no longer in the traditional sense as knowledge of divine and human laws, of justice and equality, but rather as the knowledge of things, of the objectives that can and should be attained, and the disposition of things required to reach them; it is this knowledge that is to constitute the wisdom of the sovereign. As for his diligence, this is the principle that a governor should only govern in such a way that he thinks and acts as though he were in the service of those who are governed ... We can see at once how far this characterization of government differs from the idea of the prince as found in or attributed to Machiavelli. To be sure, this notion of governing, for all its novelty, is still very crude here.

This schematic presentation of the notion and theory of the art of government did not remain a purely abstract question in the sixteenth century, and it was not of concern only to political theoreticians. I think we can identify its connections with political reality. The theory of the art of government was linked, from the sixteenth century, to the whole development of the administrative apparatus of the territorial monarchies, the emergence of government apparatuses; it was also connected to a set of analyses and forms of knowledge which began to develop in the late sixteenth century and grew in importance during the seventeenth, and which were essentially to do with knowledge of the state, in all its different elements, dimensions and factors of power, questions which were termed precisely 'statistics', meaning the science of the state; finally, as a third vector of connections, I do not think one can fail to relate this search for an art of government to mercantilism and the Cameralists' science of police.

...

The art of government could only spread and develop in subtlety in an age of expansion, free from the great military, political and economic tensions which afflicted the seventeenth century from beginning to end. Massive and elementary historical causes thus blocked the propagation of the art of government. I think also that the doctrine formulated during the sixteenth century was impeded in the seventeenth by a series of other factors which I might term, to use expressions which I do not much care for, mental and institutional structures. The pre-eminence of the problems of the exercise of sovereignty, both as a theoretical question and as a principle of political organization, was the fundamental factor here so long as sovereignty remained the central question. So long as the institutions of sovereignty were the basic political institutions and the exercise of power was conceived as an exercise of sovereignty, the art of government could not be developed in a specific and autonomous manner.

...

Thus, throughout the seventeenth century up to ... the beginning of the eighteenth, the art of government remained in a certain sense immobilized. It was trapped within the inordinately vast, abstract, rigid framework of the problem and institution of sovereignty. This art of government tried, so to speak, to reconcile itself with the theory of sovereignty by attempting to derive the ruling principles of an art of government from a renewed version of the theory of sovereignty – and this is where those seventeenth-century jurists come into the picture who formalize or ritualize the theory of the contract. Contract theory enables the founding contract, the mutual pledge of ruler and subjects, to function as a sort of theoretical matrix for deriving the general principles of an art of government. But although contract theory, with its reflection on the relationship between ruler and subjects, played a very important role in theories of public law, in practice, as is evidenced by the case of Hobbes (even though what Hobbes was aiming to discover was the ruling principles of an art of government), it remained at the stage of the formulation of general principles of public law.

On the one hand, there was this framework of sovereignty which was too large, too abstract and too rigid; and on the other, the theory of government suffered from its reliance on a model which was too thin, too weak and too insubstantial, that of the family: an economy of enrichment still based on a model of the family was unlikely to be able to respond adequately to the importance of territorial possessions and royal finance.

How then was the art of government able to outflank these obstacles? Here again a number of general processes played their part: the demographic expansion of the eighteenth century, connected with an increasing abundance of money, which in turn was linked to the expansion of agricultural production through a series of circular processes with which the historians are familiar. If this is the general picture, then we can say more precisely that the art of government found fresh outlets through the emergence of the problem of population; or let us say rather that there occurred a subtle process, which we must seek to reconstruct in its particulars, through which the science of government, the recentring of the theme of economy on a different plane from that of the family, and the problem of population are all interconnected.

It was through the development of the science of government that the notion of economy came to be recentred on to that different plane of reality which we characterize today as the economic, and it was also through this science that it became possible to identify problems specific to the population; but conversely we can say as well that it was thanks to the perception of the specific problems of the population, and thanks to the isolation of that area of reality that we call the economy, that the problem of government finally came to be thought, reflected and calculated outside of the juridical framework of sovereignty. And that 'statistics' which [previously] ... only ever worked within and for the benefit of a monarchical administration that functioned according to the form of sovereignty, now becomes the major technical factor, or one of the major technical factors, of this new technology.

In what way did the problem of population make possible the derestriction of the art of government? The perspective of population, the reality accorded to specific phenomena of population, render possible the final elimination of the model of the family and the recentring of the notion of economy. Whereas statistics had previously worked within the administrative frame and thus in terms of the functioning of sovereignty, it now gradually reveals that population has its own regularities, its own rate of deaths and diseases, its cycles of scarcity, etc.; statistics shows also that the domain of population involves a range of intrinsic, aggregate effects, phenomena that are irreducible to those of the family, such as epidemics, endemic levels of mortality, ascending spirals of labour and wealth; lastly it shows that, through its shifts, customs, activities, etc., population has specific economic effects: statistics, by making it possible to quantify these specific phenomena of population, also shows that this specificity is irreducible to the dimension of the family. The latter now disappears as the model of government, except for a certain number of residual themes of a religious or moral nature. What, on the other hand, now emerges into prominence is the family considered as an element internal to population, and as a fundamental instrument in its government.

In other words, prior to the emergence of population, it was impossible to conceive the art of government except on the model of the family, in terms of economy conceived as the management of a family; from the moment when, on the contrary, population appears absolutely irreducible to the family, the latter becomes of secondary importance compared to population, as an element internal to population: no longer, that is to say, a model, but a segment. Nevertheless it remains a privileged segment, because whenever information is required concerning the population (sexual behaviour, demography, consumption, etc.), it has to be obtained through the family. But the family becomes an instrument rather than a model: the privileged instrument for the government of the population and not the chimerical model of good government. This shift from the level of the model to that of an instrument is, I believe, absolutely fundamental, and it is from the middle of the eighteenth century that the family appears in this dimension of instrumentality relative to the population, with the institution of campaigns to reduce mortality, and to promote marriages, vaccinations, etc. Thus, what makes it possible for the theme of population to unblock the field of the art of government is this elimination of the family as model.

In the second place, population comes to appear above all else as the ultimate end of government. In contrast to sovereignty, government has as its purpose not the act of government itself, but the welfare of the population, the improvement of its condition, the increase of its wealth, longevity, health, etc.; and the means that the government uses to attain these ends are themselves all in some sense immanent to the population; it is the population itself on which government will act either directly through large-scale campaigns, or indirectly through techniques that will make possible, without the full awareness of the people, the stimulation of birth rates, the directing of the flow of population into certain regions or activities, etc. The population now represents more the end of government than the power of the sovereign; the population is the subject of needs, of aspirations, but it is also the object in the hands of the government, aware, vis-à-vis the government, of what it wants, but ignorant of what is being done to it. Interest at the level of the consciousness of each individual who goes to make up the population, and interest considered as the interest of the population regardless of what the particular interests and aspirations may be of the individuals who compose it, this is the new target and the fundamental instrument of the government of population: the birth of a new art, or at any rate of a range of absolutely new tactics and techniques.

Lastly, population is the point around which is organized what in sixteenth-century texts came to be called the patience of the sovereign, in the sense that the population is the object that government must take into account in all its observations and *savoir*, in order to be able to govern effectively in a rational and conscious manner. The constitution of a *savoir* of government is absolutely inseparable from that of a knowledge of all the processes related to population in its larger sense: that is to say, what we now call the economy ... The new science called political economy arises out of the perception of new networks of continuous and multiple relations between population, territory and wealth; and this is accompanied by the formation of a type of intervention characteristic of government, namely intervention in the field of economy and population. In other words, the transition which takes place in the eighteenth century from an art of government to a political science, from a regime dominated by structures of sovereignty to one ruled by techniques of government, turns on the theme of population and hence also on the birth of political economy.

This is not to say that sovereignty ceases to play a role from the moment when the art of government begins to become a political science; I would say that, on the contrary, the problem of sovereignty was never posed with greater force than at this time, because it no longer involved, as it did in the sixteenth and seventeenth centuries, an attempt to derive an art of government from a theory of sovereignty, but instead, given that such an art now existed and was spreading, involved an attempt to see what juridical and institutional form, what foundation in the law, could be given to the sovereignty that characterizes a state ... [In] *The Social Contract* ... [Rousseau] poses the problem of how it is possible, using concepts like nature, contract and general will, to provide a general principle of government which allows room both for a juridical principle of sovereignty and for the elements through which an art of government can be defined and characterized. Consequently, sovereignty is far from being eliminated by the emergence of a new art of government, even by one which has passed the threshold of political science; on the contrary, the problem of sovereignty is made more acute than ever.

As for discipline, this is not eliminated either; clearly its modes of organization, all the institutions within which it had developed in the seventeenth and eighteenth centuries

– schools, manufactories, armies, etc. – all this can only be understood on the basis of the development of the great administrative monarchies, but nevertheless, discipline was never more important or more valorized than at the moment when it became important to manage a population; the managing of a population not only concerns the collective mass of phenomena, the level of its aggregate effects, it also implies the management of population in its depths and its details. The notion of a government of population renders all the more acute the problem of the foundation of sovereignty (consider Rousseau) and all the more acute equally the necessity for the development of discipline (consider all the history of the disciplines, which I have attempted to analyze elsewhere).

Accordingly, we need to see things not in terms of the replacement of a society of sovereignty by a disciplinary society and the subsequent replacement of a disciplinary society by a society of government; in reality one has a triangle, sovereignty-disclipline-government, which has as its primary target the population and as its essential mechanism the apparatuses of security. In any case, I wanted to demonstrate the deep historical link between the movement that overturns the constants of sovereignty in consequence of the problem of choices of government, the movement that brings about the emergence of population as a datum, as a field of intervention and as an objective of governmental techniques, and the process which isolates the economy as a specific sector of reality, and political economy as the science and the technique of intervention of the government in that field of reality. Three movements: government, population, political economy, which constitute from the eighteenth century onwards a solid series, one which even today has assuredly not been dissolved.

...

[W]hat I would like to undertake is something which I would term a history of 'governmentality'. By this word I mean three things:

1. The ensemble formed by the institutions, procedures, analyses and reflections, the calculations and tactics that allow the exercise of this very specific albeit complex form of power, which has as its target population, as its principal form of knowledge political economy, and as its essential technical means apparatuses of security.

2. The tendency which, over a long period and throughout the West, has steadily led towards the pre-eminence over all other forms (sovereignty, discipline, etc.) of this type of power which may be termed government, resulting, on the one hand, in the formation of a whole series of specific governmental apparatuses, and, on the other, in the development of a whole complex of *savoirs*.

3. The process, or rather the result of the process, through which the state of justice of the Middle Ages, transformed into the administrative state during the fifteenth and sixteenth centuries, gradually becomes 'governmentalized'.

We all know the fascination which the love, or horror, of the state exercises today; we know how much attention is paid to the genesis of the state, its history, its advance, its power and abuses, etc. The excessive value attributed to the problem of the state is expressed, basically, in two ways: the one form, immediate, affective and tragic, is the lyricism of the *monstre froid* we see confronting us; but there is a second way of overvaluing the problem of the state, one which is paradoxical because apparently reductionist: it is the form of analysis that consists in reducing the state to a certain number of functions, such as the development of productive forces and the reproduction of relations of production, and yet this reductionist vision of the relative importance of the state's role nevertheless invariably renders it absolutely essential as a target needing to be attacked and a privileged position needing to be occupied. But the state, no more probably today than at any other time in its history, does not have this unity, this individuality, this rigorous functionality, nor, to speak frankly, this importance; maybe, after all, the state is no more than a composite reality and a mythicized abstraction, whose importance is a lot more limited than many of us think. Maybe what is really important for our modernity – that is, for our present – is not so much the *etatisation* of society, as the 'governmentalization' of the state.

We live in the era of a 'governmentality' first discovered in the eighteenth century. This governmentalization of the state is a singularly paradoxical phenomenon, since if in fact the problems of governmentality and the techniques of government have become the only political issue, the only real space for political struggle and contestation, this is because the governmentalization of the state is at the same time what has permitted the state to survive, and it is possible to suppose that if the state is what it is today, this is so precisely thanks to this governmentality, which is at once internal and external to the state, since it is the tactics of government which make possible the continual definition and redefinition of what is within the competence of the state and what is not, the public versus the private, and so on; thus the state can only be understood in its survival and its limits on the basis of the general tactics of governmentality.

...

Questions

1. 'What government has to do with is not territory but rather a sort of complex composed of men and things.' Explain.

2. How is government, in Foucault's sense of the term, distinguishable from sovereignty? What purposes, if any, do 'laws' serve as instruments of government? Give examples of the kinds of laws that might fit this description.

3. 'Within the perspective of government, law is not what is important.' Explain.

4. What accounted for the refinement and practical realisation of the art of government from the eighteenth century? How was this related to the consolidation and spread of disciplinary power? How was sovereignty re-theorised in the light of these developments?

5. What does Foucault have in mind when he refers to the 'governmentalization of the state'?

Further Reading

It is well worth reading the whole of *Discipline and Punish* (Foucault 1977). Fraser (1981) and Habermas (1987a, 266–293) have produced powerful critiques of the conception of power elaborated in this book. For an illuminating interview with Foucault, in which he addresses questions about his method and fields some criticisms of his work, see 'Questions of Method' (1991b), reprinted in Burchell et al (1991). For an interesting development of the notion of 'governmentality' and its relationship with the form of modern law and the modern state, see M Dean (1994), especially pp 152–162 and Chs 9 and 10. Finally, for a sophisticated but clear overview of Foucault's *oeuvre* as a whole, see Dreyfus and Rabinow (1983).

Questions

1. 'To understand power in modern society, one needs to get beyond the preoccupation with law and the sovereign and focus upon what Foucault has called "those continuous and uninterrupted processes which subject our bodies, govern our thoughts, dictate our behaviour ...".' Discuss.

2. 'Foucault's image of law is one of a mechanism that is ineffectual and generally epiphenomenal, confined mainly to providing legitimations for the disciplinary technologies and normalising practices established by other mechanisms.' Discuss.

3. 'Suggestive and novel though Foucault's analyses of disciplinary power may be, his conception of law remains entirely familiar and surprisingly ahistorical, for it is nothing other than Austin's imperative view of law as the commands of a sovereign backed by sanctions imposed on the transgressors.' Discuss.

20 (Legal) Reason and its 'Others': Recent Developments in Legal Theory

Anne Barron

I. Introduction

The 1990s saw the consolidation of a tendency within critical legal theory in the United Kingdom and the United States towards a direct engagement with contemporary themes in cultural theory and Continental philosophy. This chapter will attempt a selective introduction to these themes, as well as drawing attention to some of the routes by which they have entered legal theory. The developments that will be analysed here are complex, wide-ranging and extremely difficult for the uninitiated to grasp, and the readings accompanying this chapter may be experienced by the student reader as more than usually abstruse. The commentary that follows is intended only as a broad outline of a highly diverse field of intellectual inquiry.

It should be stressed at the outset that none of the territory to be covered here lends itself to easy or precise mapping. 'Cultural theory' is a particularly woolly label, because it names a still emerging field of interdisciplinary investigation characterised by its loosely defined boundaries, the vast and heterogeneous range of phenomena it takes to be worthy of serious theoretical attention, and the variety of concepts and methods it uses to make sense of these phenomena. Any summary of the field will necessarily be under-inclusive, but the following three points of departure are widely shared. First, the fundamental preoccupation of cultural theory is with 'signifying practices' and how these are organised or regulated in the form of 'discourses'. Although the exemplary form of signifying practice is the use of linguistic signs in speech and writing, cultural theorists tend to analogise culture *to* language, and so discern systems of signs at work everywhere: for example, in the design of built space and the visual environment in general, in the codes of dress, deportment and gesture that structure the routines of daily life, and in the codification of social relations through the categories of the law. Second, the central message of cultural theory is that discourses – which it holds to be social rather than individual in origin – produce rather than simply express meanings and therefore actively construct what we tend to think of as 'reality'; that everything that makes up this 'reality' is therefore a product of, rather than prior to, culture (ie that 'reality' is an *effect* of the myriad discourses that form the symbolic order of culture); that different discourses can produce different meanings for what seems to be the same aspect of 'reality'; that these differences cannot be resolved by invoking a true reality which is beyond discourse; that culture nonetheless gives shape to 'reality' by privileging some meanings over others (that is, treating some meanings as self-evidently true, while marginalising others as bogus or biased); but that these dominant meanings are inherently unstable and liable to be disrupted by alternative, suppressed, meanings. Third, in exploring these processes of the production and undoing of meaning, cultural theory today takes its methods and its arguments from a wide variety of sources – including semiotics (broadly understood as the study of signs, including but not limited to linguistic signs), literary theory and psychoanalysis – and authors, including such diverse figures as Roland Barthes (1915–1980), Jacques Derrida (1930–), Jacques Lacan (1901–1981), Julia Kristeva (1941–), Gilles Deleuze (1925–1995) and Michel Foucault (1926–1984).

Continental philosophy, on the other hand, is a little easier to identify, for it is partly bounded by the conventions – contested though these are – constituting the discipline of philosophy, and partly by the designation 'Continental', which confines its contents to the texts and arguments that have preoccupied modern European (primarily German and French) philosophers from Kant and Hegel through to more contemporary figures such as Theodor Adorno (1903–1969), Martin Heidegger (1889–1976), Derrida, Jean-Francois Lyotard (1924–1988) and Emmanuel Levinas (1906–1995). The writings of Immanuel Kant (1724–1804) can fairly be said to have inaugurated this philosophical tradition, although it is significant that the (predominantly Anglo-American) 'analytic' approach to philosophy also anchors itself, very differently, by reference to Kant's insights. Kant's most important legacy to both Continental and analytic philosophy has been his trilogy of 'Critiques' – the *Critique of Pure Reason* (1781), the *Critique of Practical Reason* (1788) and the *Critique of Judgement* (1790) – which, respectively, explored the conditions under which human knowledge could be objectively true, human action could be categorically right, and human feeling could be the basis for universally valid judgements (especially aesthetic judgements). Throughout the trilogy, Kant argued that these conditions could indeed be discovered through philosophical investigation, and his investigation revealed first, that they were located in the structure of the human subject's innate mental faculties rather than in the extrinsic structure of the world, and second, that they were incommensurable with each other: cognitive propositions, moral determinations and aesthetic judgements, he argued, proceed from different faculties within the subject, employ reason in different ways, and appeal to criteria of validity – truth, rightness and beauty – that are irreducible to each other.

Although viewed in very broad terms Kant's relentlessly 'subject-centred' philosophy simply continued a tradition of thought associated generally with the Enlightenment, he is widely acknowledged as having succeeded in resolving many of the tensions that had divided and debilitated that tradition (while generating new tensions in his turn) and in giving the tradition its most comprehensive and rigorous expression. (The philosophy of the Enlightenment was arguably inaugurated much earlier, by the seventeenth century French philosopher René Descartes (1596–1650), who declared the *cogito* (the self-consciousness of the thinking subject) to be *the* truth of human existence – 'I think, therefore I am' – and the only possible foundation for philosophical certainty: with Descartes, the world finally ceases to be seen as ordered according to the will of God; instead it comes to be regarded as an object, existing for a subject.) Kant is also widely credited with being the pre-eminent philosopher of modernity, because his trilogy gave philosophical expression to the institutionalisation – as autonomous and separate spheres of social practice – of the domains of science and technology, morality and law, and art, a division peculiarly associated with the onset of the modern era. There, however, agreement about the significance of Kant's Critical project ends, because whereas analytic philosophers broadly acknowledge that it achieved what it set out to do, and approve of its conclusions (if not every detail of its method in reaching them), Continental philosophers tend to probe and push at the contradictions within and between the three *Critiques*, uncovering what is negated in their privileging of the subject as the foundation of all knowledge, morality and aesthetic experience, and undoing the carefully elaborated distinctions on which the arguments of the *Critiques* depend, or showing how they undo themselves.

It is this approach to contradiction – one that sees contradiction as fundamental to human experience, and so actively seeks to give philosophical expression to it – that in general distinguishes Continental from analytic philosophy. The analytic style is to approach philosophical inquiry with clarity and rigour with a view to producing solutions to identifiable problems and resolving doubts and ambiguities. From this perspective, contradictions equate to confusions that must be resolved rather than entertained; and it follows that to omit to resolve them is a mark of intellectual failure, whereas to generate them is a sign of nothing other than sloppy thinking. Practitioners of the analytic approach accordingly tend to define their questions precisely and, some would say, narrowly: precise questions, after all, are manageable and more likely to be amenable to resolution. Along with this incremental method goes a deep suspicion of what might be called 'systematic' philosophy: the creation of overarching theoretical frameworks which purport to explain 'life, the universe and everything' on the basis of a few key concepts or insights. Many of the core texts of modern jurisprudence covered in Part I of this volume – notably Hart's *Concept of Law* – have been informed by the analytic method, which remains the dominant approach to academic philosophy in Britain and the United States. The Continental approach, by contrast, is to confront big questions – the nature of being and the relationship between being and the world, the bases of subjectivity and intersubjectivity, the limits of human knowledge and experience, and what, if anything, lies beyond those limits – head-on, and in so doing to activate philosophical uncertainty rather than close it down. It is fair to say that in general, cultural theorists and Continental philosophers share a suspicion that analytic philosophy's very much more cautious and 'bitty' approach to these questions is tantamount to avoiding them and the uncertainty that accompanies any attempt to ponder them; perceive the problems that analytic philosophy selects out for serious attention as tending to triviality relative to these questions; and criticise analytic philosophy for its apparent inability to address the presuppositions involved in identifying the problems it poses for itself as significant issues to begin with. It is little wonder, then, that legal theory's importation of insights drawn from cultural theory and Continental philosophy has earned it the label '*critical* legal theory', for these insights have certainly led it to be critical of the methods and preoccupations of mainstream jurisprudence.

As well as uniting around a suspicion of analytic philosophy, cultural theory and Continental philosophy share many of the same substantive concerns, albeit that they comprise different 'discourses' made up of different texts, which use different vocabularies organised in different ways. Generally, both cultural theory and Continental philosophy tend to share a suspicion of the heritage of the Enlightenment, and an ambivalent attitude to modernity and the forms of rationality that are associated with modernity. More specifically, cultural theory has been particularly influenced by the so-called 'linguistic turn' in Continental philosophy, which fore-grounded language as the foundation of any possible experience of, or action in, the world, and so de-centred the subject privileged by Kant. Neither the critique of Enlightenment rationality nor the linguistic turn can be understood without an appreciation of what preceded it, and so the next Section focuses on the following questions: First, what is Enlightenment? Second, what exactly does it mean to 'privilege' the subject? Answers will be sought through an engagement with the philosophy of Immanuel Kant – partly because his treatment of these questions is widely regarded as exemplary; but partly also because Kant's conceptual vocabulary can be viewed as forming a bridge between analytic philosophy on the one hand, and cultural theory and Continental philosophy on the other; between those perspectives that seek to continue the Enlightenment project and those that oppose this project; and between mainstream jurisprudence and its critics. All of these traditions of thought, that is to say, speak to (or against) some aspect of Kant's *oeuvre* and so necessarily engage with the problems he posed, even if they unequivocally reject his solutions to these problems. In order to clarify what is at issue between these traditions, then – and at the risk of over-simplifying the differences between them – Kant's vocabulary will be treated in subsequent Sections as a kind of lingua franca into which their disparate theoretical languages may be translated.

II. Kant, Enlightenment and Modern Reason

II.A. What is Enlightenment?

In an essay published in 1784 (Kant 1996b, 11–22), Kant responded to the question 'what is enlightenment?' by equating it with the individual's attainment of maturity through the use of reason: thinking and deciding for oneself rather than deferring to established authority or tradition. The original vocation and sacred right of mankind in general, he declared, is to emerge from its 'minority' (ie the state of being guided by instinct, custom, blind faith or any other force that displaces self-directing reason) and advance towards attaining a state of enlightenment. This project has political and legal implications. It requires a legally recognised right of free speech – a right to publicly express one's criticisms of the existing social order, including criticisms of legislation – and more generally a legal structure that facilitates the continued progress towards enlightenment of individuals and society as a whole. 'The touchstone of whatever can be decided upon as law for a people lies in the question: whether a people could impose such a law upon itself' (Kant 1996b, 20) and a people could never decide to violate its own sacred right to enlightenment. This right, on the other hand, does not entail a right to disobey the law, even if one disagrees with it. Rulers have a legitimate authority to enact whatever laws are necessary to ensure civil order, and they are entitled to say to their citizens: 'argue as much as you will and about what you will; only obey!' (Kant 1996b, 22).

Packed into this short essay is a cluster of ideas that together define the broad outlines of what the Enlightenment meant during the eighteenth century. First, it signified a fervent belief in the power of human reason: a power that was held to be innately present in all persons, albeit one that needed to be activated through appropriate educational means. Second, the Enlightenment stood for a commitment to the idea of progress in history, made possible by the exercise of this reason. Eighteenth century Enlightenment intellectuals celebrated contemporary (real and imagined) social transformations – the continued advance of Newtonian science; the overthrow of absolutist rule; the defeat of barbarism; the questioning of religious dogmas and the tempering of sectarian bigotry; the beginnings of industrialisation; population growth and urbanisation; the spread of literacy; the rise of commerce and, with it, a prosperous bourgeoisie with new and varied tastes and values; the emergence of a new 'public sphere' for the circulation of bourgeois opinion, facilitated by a relative freedom of the press and of association; the rise of a nascent individualism amid the constraints imposed by custom and kinship – as stages on an evolutionary path whose continuance was guaranteed as long as freedom in the use of reason was itself guaranteed. Third, however, these thinkers also concurred in the view that freedom, and hence progress, depended for its full realisation on appropriate legal arrangements and political institutions. Although individuals were certainly regarded as responsible for liberating their own reason by daring to think for themselves, the success of this project was understood to depend also on the removal of external constraints on independent thought, the acquisition of knowledge, and open public debate. The Enlightenment therefore also yielded a particular ideal for the conduct of politics: the promotion of laws and institutions that would respect individual autonomy while also guaranteeing civic peace. It followed, fourth, that proponents of Enlightenment were united in their antipathy to any belief, practice or institution that claimed immunity from the critical scrutiny of reason. The enemies of progress were thus taken to be tyrannical governments; theological dogmatism; censorship; any received wisdom or tradition that appealed to myth or mysticism, rather than reason, as the basis for the truths or norms that it advanced: anything, in short, that was born of intolerance, ignorance or superstition.

The Enlightenment as described above was primarily a Euro-American phenomenon, and it has, rightly or wrongly, become synonymous with the philosophical innovations of a canon of (British, French, and especially German) intellectual heavyweights – Descartes, Locke, Leibniz, Rousseau, Hume, Kant – somewhat to the neglect of the more prosaic changes in values, attitudes and behaviours that manifested themselves in eighteenth century streets and coffee-houses (Porter, 2000). Yet the philosophy of the Enlightenment was no haven of calm and homogeneity in a century of rapid social change: by Kant's time, certainly, deep tensions, and a degree of disillusionment with the claims of reason, had emerged between and within its key texts. The division that tends to be emphasised most in histories of Enlightenment philosophy is that between the rival traditions of 'rationalism' and 'empiricism', the latter dominant in Britain (where it was first systematically expounded by Locke (1632–1704) and subsequently developed by Hume (1711–1776)); and the former in Germany (where it was particularly associated with Leibniz (1646–1716) and his follower Wolff (1679–1750)). Empiricism showed its commitment to the Enlightenment through its suspicion of lofty but unverifiable assertions about what was true or what was good, its belief in human progress and improvability, and its attempt to lay solid foundations for the advancement of knowledge and virtue on the mundane bedrock of observable facts and measurable phenomena, common sense and reasonable public opinion. However, though driven by a faith in the power of critical reason, empiricists insisted that this reason must also be critical of itself, that it was limited in what it could do, and that it could only yield reliable insights when it anchored itself in the empirical world. The apparent paradox of a reason which was all-powerful yet radically limited was rendered unproblematic by the conviction that reason's capacities, though modest, were nonetheless sufficient for people's practical needs: that knowledge gathered through patient investigation of perceptible reality would be useful and cumulative, and that the cultivation of natural sentiments within a framework of tried and tested prudential rules would be adequate to maintain sociability and social order.

All of this marked empiricism's break from scholasticism, a marriage of Christian theology and Aristotelian philosophy that had dominated medieval thought in western Europe in the guise of Thomas Aquinas' hugely influential writings. By the early 1700s, however, empiricism's chief rival was another Enlightenment tradition, rationalism. This tradition of thought also celebrated human reason, but by contrast with empiricism it conceived of reason's powers as unbounded. Rationalists argued that reason could deduce reliable knowledge of reality from innate ideas about the world lodged in the human mind, rather than proceeding carefully by induction from empirical investigation of observable phenomena; and that it could soar beyond any possible experience of reality to make dogmatic assertions, posing as incontrovertible truths, about such imponderables as the nature of the cosmos, God and the soul. Clearly, then, the gap between empiricism and rationalism was a large one, and this debate was connected to other tensions within Enlightenment philosophy: between what the new science revealed about human beings and the demands of religion and morality, between scientific method and metaphysical speculation, and between the role of reason in human life and the role of feeling and the senses.

Kant's achievement was to negotiate his way through these tensions by redefining reason's nature and limits, and in so doing, to give Enlightenment philosophy its most complete and systematic expression. At a general level, Kant shared the Enlightenment's conception of reason as an innate human capacity to think and decide independently, but in analysing reason he adopted the method of separating this general intellectual capacity into distinct types of mental operation, and distinct 'faculties', whose characteristics and limits could then be investigated and compared. To this end, he reaffirmed and consolidated certain distinctions that were already recognised in the philosophical learning of the time. One of these was the distinction between the theoretical and the practical use of reason: theoretical reason is a cognitive faculty, implicated in the acquisition of knowledge; practical reason is the capacity to select the goals or 'ends' that we want to pursue, formulate rules of conduct that will dictate how we achieve them, and act on those rules. A further distinction that is crucial to (though also not invented by) Kant's philosophy is that between 'pure' and 'empirical' uses of reason. In general, pure reason is the capacity to transcend the experiences that we have through our senses: the transcendence of experience in thought (about what *is* the case) is the theoretical use of pure reason; its transcendence in moral reflection (about what *ought* to be done) is its practical use. An example of what counts as a pure theoretical proposition is 'every event has a cause'; an example of an empirical theoretical proposition is 'the walls of this room are blue'. The former is explicitly universalistic: it amounts to the claim that *every* past, present and future event has or will have some natural cause (as opposed to being generated by supernatural intervention). However this principle cannot be established by an appeal to the evidence of the senses, because causal relations between events (ie necessary connections between events as opposed to their regular occurrence in spatio-temporal succession) are not themselves observable, and even if they were, empirical investigation could only validate the principle of causality in respect of the relations between the *particular* events investigated, not *all* events. The second proposition, by contrast, emerges directly from sensory experience: my sense of sight tells me that the walls of this particular room are blue, and no further evidence or argument is required to establish my claim. An example of what counts as a pure practical proposition for Kant is 'I ought to respect human dignity'; an example of an empirical practical proposition is 'if I want to pass my exams, I ought to study'. The first proposition claims that it is unconditionally right to respect human dignity, regardless of the affection, aversion or indifference that experience leads us to feel towards other persons. The second is contingent on experience – or as Kant would have said, 'empirically conditioned' – because it is only from experience that we learn both that passing exams is one of our goals and that diligent study is the way to achieve that goal: this proposition is 'right' only insofar as it is effective as a guide for successfully achieving the goals we happen to have.

Kant acknowledged that propositions of the first – 'pure' or 'metaphysical' – variety were problematic because of the difficulty of finding grounds for them. In particular, he affirmed that some of the metaphysical assertions that philosophers before him (notably rationalists like Descartes) had confidently made – such as the claim that the soul is immortal, or that God exists – could not be shown to be true. However, he refused to conclude from this (as the empiricist, Hume, had concluded) that metaphysics was impossible, ie that no pure theoretical or pure practical claim could convincingly be made, because the consequences of this capitulation, in Kant's view, simply could not be tolerated. As regards what counted as knowledge, the complete repudiation of metaphysics would necessarily, Kant argued, invalidate many propositions that could not be grounded in sense experience yet were generally accepted to be true (he was particularly worried about the status of the 'laws' uncovered by Newtonian science and Euclidean geometry). As regards what constituted right action, salvaging metaphysics in some form was positively necessary, in Kant's view, if morality was not to collapse into 'prudence': the use of practical reason to determine the means for achieving ends that happened to be given to us empirically. This reduction would amount to an acknowledgement (with Hume) that practical reason is the slave of our contingent wants, or 'passions', and would declare the notion of a moral law binding on everyone, regardless of what they happened to want, to be illusory. For Kant, then, the problem of metaphysics raised the question of what pure reason was capable of, and its solution required the subjection of pure reason in both its theoretical and practical modes to a 'critique'.

'Critique', in the Kantian sense, does not mean evaluating the merits of something or condemning it outright, but rather *exploring its conditions of possibility and the limits of its legitimate use*. A critique of reason, then, is the subjection of reason to a kind of self-examination which reveals its proper jurisdiction: both its area of competence, and its boundaries. It follows that in the two of his three *Critiques* that deal directly with reason – the *Critique of Pure Reason* and the *Critique of Practical Reason* – Kant aimed not to dismiss all propositions of pure reason as groundless, but to determine when they were erroneous and when they could be regarded as objectively valid. With this dual strategy, Kant worked through the tensions that had dogged his rationalist and empiricist predecessors, and mounted a defence of reason that survives in a recognisable form to the present day. We begin in Section II.B below with the *Critique of Pure Reason* (which is really a critique of pure *theoretical* reason). Section II.C deals with the *Critique of Practical Reason* (which is really a critique of *pure* practical reason). Section II.D deals with the *Critique of Judgement*.

II.B. Reason and Knowledge

Despite its title, relatively little of the *Critique of Pure Reason* actually deals directly with *pure* reason: in much of the text Kant is preoccupied with exploring the conditions under which ordinary cognition (or knowledge) of objects of experience is possible. The details of Kant's account have been widely questioned in the centuries since its publication, but it is not necessary for our purposes to explore these in depth. What is more important is the radically new (for Kant's time) perspective that informs it, and the general outline of its method. The most fundamental innovation of the first *Critique* is the way in which it conceives of 'objects of experience': even now, Kant's explanation jars with most people's unreflective understandings of what these are and how we can come to have knowledge of them. There is, we are inclined to suppose, a real world composed of real things. These real things become objects for us – they 'appear' to us – because human beings somehow have an innate capacity to be affected by external reality and to form mental representations of real things that reveal the truth of what they are. There is a perfect match, in short, between real things and our mental pictures of them: the latter are completely adequate to the former. Kant subjects this common sense understanding to a radical questioning that he analogised to the Copernican revolution in astronomy. Copernicus had argued that the explanation of the observed motion of celestial bodies like the sun should be sought 'not in the celestial objects, but in the spectator' (Kant 1996a, 25): if the sun appears from an earthly perspective to move around our planet, it is not because the sun is really moving, but because the earth, and with it the observer, is moving around the sun. Kant goes even further along the path of substituting subjective for objective explanations for what we perceive, arguing that *all* objects we can know must conform to the mind of the knowing subject rather than having a knowable reality of their own that yields itself up to our passive minds. All our knowledge of 'reality', Kant insists, is radically dependent on the ways our mental faculties structure the objects and events that we experience. From the new perspective afforded by this revolutionary vantage point, 'philosophical concern focuses on the task of explicating the concept of an *object-for-us*, that is, defining the class of knowable objects' (Gardner 1999, 39[1]) rather than reflecting on the nature of an independent reality and the 'being' of real things. Otherwise put, the focus shifts to the *subject's* cognitive capacities, because it is to these capacities that objects have to conform if they are to 'appear' to us at all:

> To suppose that objects must conform to us is to reverse the customary direction of explanation of knowledge. In the realist [common sense] scheme, the arrow of explanation runs from the object to the subject: if a subject S knows object O, then the explanation for S's representing O lies ultimately in O's being the way it is; had O not existed or been otherwise, S would not have represented O or would have represented O differently. Kant reverses the arrow: the deepest, most abstract and encompassing explanation of representation lies in how S is. The constitution of objects is thus determined at the most fundamental level by the subject. And it is a corollary of this pattern of explanation that the subject is *active* in knowing objects.
>
> ...
>
> The general approach of Copernican philosophy in answering the question of how objects are possible for us, is therefore to say that, in a recondite philosophical sense, the subject *constitutes* its objects. It maintains, furthermore, that these subject-constituted objects compose the only kind of reality to which we have access: reality in the stronger sense of a realm of objects constituted independently of the subject may be admitted as something we can (perhaps, must) conceive, but knowledge of it is held to be impossible. (Gardner 1999, 41)

KNOWLEDGE AND THE SUBJECT

Kant's lengthy exploration of the subject's cognitive capacities in the *Critique of Pure Reason* reveals that five mental faculties – sensibility, imagination, understanding, judgement and reason (the term 'reason' here being used in a narrower sense than in the title, which shall be explained further below) – are involved in constituting, and thus experiencing, and thus knowing, objects. The two faculties with the most initial spade-work to do in this regard are sensibility and understanding, which Kant describes as the 'two stems' (Kant 1996a, 67) of human cognition. Sensibility, Kant argues, enables the subject to have 'intuitions' or sensations of (and so be immediately affected by) particular objects and events in the world; understanding is the faculty which yields concepts for organising or 'determining' intuited material so that knowledge of it is possible. Intuitions are in an immediate relation to particular, individual objects; concepts by contrast are inherently general because they indicate similarities across objects (a greyhound is only an instance of the type designated by the concept 'dog', for example, and a particular animal can be brought within the concept only by subsuming it, despite

---

1   Many of this chapter's formulations of Kant's arguments in the *Critique of Pure Reason* are indebted to Gardner's admirably lucid guide.

its particular features, under a more general classification). Both types of mental 'representation', and both faculties responsible for them, are necessarily implicated in the acquisition of knowledge: as Kant famously put it, concepts without intuitions are empty; intuitions without concepts are blind (Kant 1996a, 107), so neither can yield knowledge without the other. 'The understanding cannot intuit anything, and the senses cannot think anything. Only from their union can cognition arise' (Kant 1996a, 107). It should be noted that Kant also mentions two further faculties of imagination and judgement as figuring respectively in the roles of 'apprehending' the otherwise disordered 'manifold' of intuitions as a unity (Kant 1996a, 153–5; 167–8) and subsuming this unified manifold correctly under concepts supplied by the understanding: these two faculties receive relatively little attention in the first *Critique*, although they loom very large in Kant's later work on aesthetics, the *Critique of Judgement* (see Section II.D below).

Thus far, Kant's explanation of cognition accords with the common sense account of experience outlined above: things in the world affect us by means of sense impressions (a multiplicity of 'intuitions') impinging upon our sensory apparatus; we form these impressions into a coherent mental representation – of a surface extending vertically, for example – and we make sense of them by applying to them concepts formed by our intellect (the concept 'wall', for example). But Kant is really interested in getting behind these mundane cognitive activities and exploring what makes them possible at all: how we can have intuitions, how we can form concepts, and how we can put them together – the necessary operations involved in all cognition. To uncover these necessary operations is to reveal the mental structure in the subject that enables objects to appear to us, and so to deliver on Kant's 'Copernican' promises. Briefly (because its details are of no particular concern to us here, and have in any case been undermined by modern cognitive science), this structure comprises: the pure forms of intuition (space and time), the pure concepts of the understanding (twelve concepts in all, which Kant terms the 'categories' because they are basic concepts not derived from more general ones), and an *a priori* (or 'transcendental') synthesis. First, whatever objects we actually intuit, Kant argues, they necessarily appear to us as existing in space and time; space and time not being real entities but grids through which we humans, given the mental apparatus that we have, process our sensations of objects in the world: without these grids, the world would affect us only as a blur of which we could have no consciousness at all. Second, in order to conceptualise objects, we have to employ certain prior and enabling concepts: for example concepts of quantity (like the concepts of unity (one object) and plurality (more than one object)); and concepts of relation (like the concept of a relation between the substance of an object (a wall) and its accidental properties (blueness), or between an object's existence or properties and something else that has caused these). Third, in order that the objects we conceptualise match up with the objects we intuit, there must be a structure common to both thought and intuition that can enable the synthesis of the two: this is what Kant calls the transcendental unity of apperception, or a unified consciousness. (This unity has to be transcendental because it cannot be empirical: there can be no sensory impression of a unified self. It follows that the existence of the self cannot be proved: the 'I' in 'I think' has to be regarded as the necessary accompaniment to experience, but cannot – contrary to Descartes famous assertion that 'I think, *therefore* I am' – be regarded as a knowable entity). Taken together, these elements comprise the transcendental conditions of all possible experience.

The Possibility of Truth

Mention of the transcendental returns us to the problem of metaphysics referred to above. To repeat, the problem of metaphysics is that of finding a grounding for claims (knowledge claims, in this context) that cannot be established by appealing to the evidence of the senses alone. How can it be shown to be true, for example, that every event has a cause if it is impossible to prove this hypothesis empirically? The importance of Kant's Copernican revolution to this debate is that it enabled him to show not only that knowledge is possible *a posteriori* (ie based on the evidence of the senses), but also that certain knowledge claims must be true *a priori* (ie independently of sensory experience, and thus universally and necessarily: with no possibility of any exceptions). Kant's crucial insight was precisely that the ultimate foundation for knowledge lies not beyond, but prior to, experience: in the universal mental operations that necessarily precede and enable experience. This insight enabled Kant to remove from many metaphysical claims – such as the claim that every event has a cause – the shadow of sceptical doubt that empiricists like Hume had cast over them, and in so doing marked Kant's decisive break with empiricism. Although Kant concurred with Hume that only objects which are capable of being sensed can appear to and thus be known by us – as noted above, concepts of objects yield no knowledge without sense impressions ('intuitions') to which they can be applied – his uncovering of the transcendental conditions that make both concepts and intuitions possible at all enabled him to show that certain further knowledge claims, beyond *immediate* sensory experience, must also be true – and true *a priori* – *because they proceed from these conditions*. The claim that every event has a cause, he argued, falls into this category. Certainly, when we observe one occurrence succeeding another we are never furnished with a sense impression to which the concept of a necessary connection between these occurrences could be applied. Nonetheless, Kant argued, the claim that every event has a cause must be true of all the events we can possibly experience, because it invokes a concept – causality: one of the 'pure' or basic concepts of the understanding – which is indispensable for any experience at all. It is certainly a metaphysical claim, but it is one that relies, quite legitimately, on a metaphysics *of experience*.

Essence and Appearance

However, Kant also distanced himself from rationalists like Descartes, because for Kant, if a claim like this is true, it is not because it reflects the way the world is 'in itself', but because the world 'as it appears' to us reflects the way our mental operations proceed, and must proceed if we are to have any knowledge at all based on the evidence presented to our senses. What then of the world 'as it is in itself'? If reality as we experience and know it is only that which appears to us through the mind's operations, is there something 'out there' which is *not* co-extensive with what Kant called the 'sensible' or 'phenomenal' world of appearances? Perhaps surprisingly, Kant contended that this 'something' does indeed exist, and although subsequent interpreters have challenged the coherence of the notion that we can be sure of the existence of that which we cannot know, it has been argued that this contention is required by the nature of Kant's project in the *Critique of Pure Reason*. To say that the subject constitutes its objects is not to say that the subject *creates* its objects, because to say this would return us to a version of the realist common sense outlined above: that we can know an existent reality. 'The Copernican revolution – accounting for objects as appearances rather than as things in themselves – requires the data out of which our objects are constituted to be grounded on something transcendentally "other"' (Gardner 1999, 288). For Kant, then, appearances are *not* entirely dependent upon the mental faculties of the subject: the ground for their existence (as opposed to the forms that they take for us) lies outside the subject, although what exactly that ground is, or how precisely it relates to the appearances that stand in for it in the empirical world, is unknowable. But further, Kant insisted that it is in the nature of human reason to *think* about this transcendent reality that lies beyond our experience, even though it exceeds what is possible for us to *know*. The scope of our thought, that is to say, exceeds that of our knowledge, and it is thus possible for us to think of things as they are in themselves. Kant called this thinkable (but unknowable) reality the 'noumenal', 'supersensible' or 'intelligible' world.

REASON, TOTALITY AND PROGRESS

This kind of thinking is neither random nor incidental: it obeys a certain kind of logic and as such it plays a crucial role in our cognitive operations. For Kant, human beings are innately disposed to look for ultimate and complete explanations for appearances, and it is with the faculty of reason (as distinct from the understanding) that this vocation resides: in Kant's own vocabulary, it falls to reason to discover all the 'conditions' for all 'appearances'. Reason – here understood, not as the intellect in general, but more narrowly as the capacity to unify and systematise all of the individual fragments of knowledge generated by the understanding – cannot but refer to the totality of these conditions, which is tantamount to saying that it must refer to a totality of conditions which is itself unconditioned. To this end it produces concepts – which Kant calls 'transcendental ideas' or Ideas of reason – through which these 'unconditioned totalities' or 'absolute unities' can be thought. More specifically, reason is impelled to elaborate concepts of a unified thinking subject (in Descartes' terms, an indivisible soul), a unified object of knowledge (the world as a whole: the cosmos), and the unity of subject and object (in a supreme being: God).

For Kant, the elaboration of these concepts is inevitable given the nature of our reason (reasoning persons can and indeed must think of the objects to which they refer). Although they cannot be shown to correspond to knowable reality (we cannot claim any *knowledge* of these objects, or even that they exist), it does not follow that they have no role at all in the acquisition of knowledge. On the contrary, transcendental Ideas perform an important 'regulative' function in relation to our experience of the world of appearances, because they direct the humble, partial and particular determinations of the understanding towards a grander horizon. Whereas understanding shows us only fragments of reality, reason rightly seeks, by means of its Ideas of the unconditioned, to organise these fragments into a whole. This can be illustrated by examining how the Idea of the cosmos – the Idea that the totality of appearances forms a unity, combined according to necessary laws which themselves are organised by reference to a single principle – regulates the progress of science. According to Kant, this Idea guides or directs the process by which science gains knowledge of the empirical world, by setting up as the goal of science a complete grasp of the world as a whole. If this goal could be realised, science would be characterised by the broadest possible diversity and the greatest possible unity of its objects: it would have discovered every single empirical phenomenon, as well as the system of principles – and ultimately the first principle – that explains them all. But of course it cannot be realised, because the world as a whole cannot be known in itself: it will always be a target, and never an achievement, of science. The Idea of the unified totality remains, nonetheless, as a standard for empirical research that drives the (endless) quest to obtain comprehensive knowledge; as a reminder to science that all current knowledge remains incomplete; and as a promise that the world can come to light more and more (though never entirely) through investigation (ie that scientific progress is possible).

II.C. Reason, Morality and Justice

By the late eighteenth century, unbridled optimism about the capacity of science to explain the world would have been understandable: the great scientific advances of the sixteenth and seventeenth centuries – in astronomy, mechanics, mathematics and physics – seemed to have shown that nature was a kind of mechanism made up of material particles governed by a relatively few fundamental laws which could be represented in mathematical form. This mechanistic view of nature extended to human behaviour, and precursors of today's social and human sciences – psychology, sociology and economics – modelled on Newtonian natural science, took shape in the wake of the latter's success. Yet the dominance of the mathematico-mechanical view of the world, while affirming the power of science, exposed a problem for Enlightenment philosophy, which was how to account at the same time for the possibility of morality. The new science could not conceive of nature as having moral purposes embedded within it – it broke decisively with Aquinas's teleological conception of natural law – so to say that human behaviour was subject to merely *mechanical* 'natural laws' seemed to deny that human behaviour could be impelled by moral values. This was also a problem for Kant's philosophy to the extent that it defended a Newtonian conception of the natural order: we have seen that for Kant, in order to understand the world, and ourselves as part of it, we must presuppose that everything in it – including human behaviour – is governed by causal forces. The logic of Kant's own position, then, seemed to suggest that the only solution to the problem was to accept that human action is determined empirically, particularly by the inclinations that we experience, and to try to build some kind of moral theory on that basis: to argue, as Hume did, for example, that actual predilections and sentiments were both necessary and sufficient to motivate people to perform virtuous actions. Yet this solution was decisively rejected by Kant, who first in the *Groundwork of the Metaphysics of Morals* (1785; Kant 1996b, 37–108), and then in the *Critique of Practical Reason* (1788; Kant 1996b, 133–271), set out to present 'a pure moral philosophy completely cleansed of everything ... empirical'

(Kant 1996b, 44). The key to this radical new philosophy was once again to be the human subject, and the ground Kant would thereby establish for morality was to be the autonomy of this subject's will: the capacity of the will to legislate for itself. Yet as we shall see, this was to generate a tension between Kant's philosophy of knowledge and his moral philosophy, because the latter is based precisely on what the former had shown to be undemonstrable: namely, the transcendental freedom of the will.

Kant's double agent

In order to explicate this tension, and Kant's resolution of it, we first need to return to the distinction between moral reasoning and prudential reasoning that was briefly introduced in Section II.A above. Both are instances of practical reasoning in general, and this is simply the capacity to will: the capacity to say that x *ought to be* the case and to act accordingly. For Kant, the capacity to will is a uniquely human capacity, and it enables people to suspend (though not eliminate) the jurisdiction of nature's laws by conceiving of and acting in accordance with laws of their own making. Both of the rules mentioned above – the rule mandating respect for other persons and the rule requiring diligent study – are laws of practical reason in this general sense: because human beings have the capacity to formulate such laws for ourselves, we can determine our actions independently of such forces as instincts, impulses and inclinations whereas animals, for example, can act only according to the 'will' of nature. However, as was pointed out earlier, there is for Kant a crucial difference between pure practical reasoning and prudential reasoning. Although both involve the application of reason to action, prudential reasoning (reasoning of the form: 'If I want y, I ought to do x') remains in part 'empirically conditioned', or determined by wants that we actually experience. In Kant's view, this means that prudential reasoning can never give rise to properly moral 'oughts': moral laws that are universally and necessarily valid for everyone regardless of their social situation or actual desires. Rules of prudence such as 'I ought to study' certainly appear to us as imperatives, in that they constrain us to act in ways that may be contrary to our inclinations, but these can only ever be *hypothetical* imperatives. This is to say that their validity is limited by a presupposition that is contingent on our subjective preferences, interests, hopes, the possibilities afforded by the environment in which we are situated, and so on: this presupposition being that we actually do want 'y'. Universal, objective moral laws – *categorical* imperatives that are valid unconditionally – can only be generated by pure practical reason: practical reason uncontaminated by any dependence on the phenomenal, sensible world and the goals that we happen to have as a result of inhabiting that world. Here, clearly, Kant reverses the argument that animated his critique of pure theoretical reason: what we can know is dependent on experience, but what we ought to do – the moral law – is emphatically not.

Pure practical reason, then, is rational agency that is completely self-determining: a totally free will. It is important to be clear about the meaning of freedom in this context. Kant conceives of that freedom on which morality is founded as *autonomy*: persons are autonomous, not in the sense that we have a propensity to follow our actual desires wherever they lead us (this, indeed, is the opposite of autonomy: heteronomy), but in the sense that through our power of rational agency we can choose our own ends and give ourselves our own laws. We can do this because we are innately equipped with a will that can transcend subjective and contingent wants and decide what course of action is universally and categorically (ie absolutely) right, rather than merely prudent in a particular set of circumstances. For Kant, being equipped with a rational will in this sense – ie *pure* practical reason – is what makes a human being a moral person; that is, a person for whom moral action is possible. His conception of moral personality is therefore abstract, unconditioned by the 'mechanism of nature', and utterly *im*personal: it does not depend on any contingent facts about a person's life history or physical, psychological, environmental and cultural constraints, nor their actual decisions, accomplishments and so on; and it transcends empirical desires and inclinations. On this view, then, morality is only possible if human beings are transcendentally free: if they are entities whose wills are not determined by empirical causes.

The problem Kant faced in grounding morality on transcendental freedom, however, was that the *Critique of Pure Reason* had already shown that its existence in each of us could not be proved: all we can know for sure is that everything we can experience is governed by causal laws, and so it follows that we cannot be sure that we are really free (ie that we really are the agents of a causality which is itself uncaused). (We might *feel* free – we might have experiences of choosing and deciding for ourselves where we feel utterly unconstrained – but this as far as Kant is concerned proves nothing, because the feeling could be illusory.) Yet in making 'ought' judgements of any kind, Kant argues, we necessarily assume the existence of a causality, or 'necessity', that is not to be found in nature, because knowledge of nature can only ever tell us what *is* the case (here Kant's distance from Aquinas's natural law theorising is evident). This extra-natural causality – the capacity of our own power of rational agency to determine what ought to be – is thus a presupposition of *practical* reason. (Recall (Chapter 5) Kelsen's use of the term 'presupposition' to describe the role of the grundnorm in founding the normativity of law: it is partly for this reason that Kelsen's theory has been described as 'Kantian'.) Further, Kant takes it to be established by the existence of moral consciousness – the awareness within each of us of the existence of the moral law, and of that law's capacity to bind us even in the face of competing inclinations – that in the practical sphere at least rational agency can operate independently of all empirical determinants: everyone is aware, he opines, that lying is wrong, even when it is not in one's interests to tell the truth. Now it is here that an apparent contradiction arises within Kant's philosophical system, for practical reason clearly requires us to assume what theoretical reason cannot prove: that we can freely determine our own actions. Crucially, however, the *Critique of Pure Reason* does not *dis*prove the existence of transcendental freedom either: indeed it specifically leaves open the possibility that such freedom might exist. This follows from Kant's elaboration, described above, of the relation between appearances and things in themselves. As we have seen, Kant insists that appearances are not only conditioned by other appearances but may also be grounded in some way in things in themselves. This enables two views of that category of appearances which is human behaviour. On one level, the actions that we perform are undoubtedly effects of the self considered as an appearance (ie an empirically existing, flesh-and-blood human agent whose acts are themselves empirically determined). But on another level, they can be regarded as effects of the self considered as a thing in itself (ie as an autonomous rational will whose acts are unconditioned). Therefore, according to Kant, it is possible for natural causality and a causality of unconditioned freedom to co-exist, because they belong to different orders: not two worlds, but the same world considered from different viewpoints depending on whether one is reasoning for theoretical purposes (reflecting on the world as it is) or practical purposes (reflecting on the world as it ought to be).

THE CATEGORICAL IMPERATIVE

Having established that transcendental freedom can conceivably be posited in respect of every rational agent, Kant is able to identify an ultimate, *a priori* principle of action that holds universally for all such agents, regardless of their empirical make-up or situation: what Kant calls the categorical imperative. There is only one categorical (or moral) imperative, but Kant offers three alternative formulations of it. The primary formulation is this: 'never act except in such a way that you could also will that the maxim of your action should be a universal law' (by 'maxim' here Kant means the reason for one's action, expressed in a general and impersonal form as the rule governing that action). Or in other words: before one acts, one should first bring the anticipated action under a general maxim (ie propose a kind of moral constitution for oneself), and then consider whether any rational person could adopt the same maxim to govern their own conduct; if so, then it qualifies as a possible maxim for the ideal moral community, and an action based upon it is permissible. So stated, of course, the categorical imperative is empty of content, for it is not in itself a comprehensive moral code that tells us what ought to be done in any particular set of circumstances, still less a set of instructions as to how to apply any such code to the complex and varied circumstances in which we have to act. Instead, it sets out a procedure to be followed in elaborating a moral code in the first place. This procedure requires a universal perspective to be adopted by the decider: the categorical imperative is first and foremost, then, a principle of universality, and it is primarily negative in character, though it also has a positive dimension. Negatively, it operates to disqualify any maxim designed merely to enable us to satisfy our individual wants, because such would be a merely 'subjective' maxim that would hold only for one person and so involve a claim to special privileges or exemptions which would be inconsistent with the universalistic orientation of the categorical imperative. (Put differently, this means that we are permitted to pursue our wants as long as this pursuit is limited by the principle that what is permissible for one ought to be permissible for all.) Positively, it mandates the elaboration of rules of conduct to which any rational agent would consent as necessary to the maintenance of a community of such agents.

The first formulation of the categorical imperative assumes that what defines the rational moral will is its ability to legislate for itself and act in accordance with its self-created rules; its ability, in so doing, to transcend the empirical world; and its consistency (the specific actions of a rational agent will always ultimately be capable of being systematised under maxims; and such an agent will never adopt maxims that are self-contradictory, or that contradict other maxims the agent could adopt, or that conflict with other maxims other agents in the moral community – who by definition are the same, because equally rational – could adopt.) At the risk of over-emphasising this point, the idea it foregrounds is that the freedom, in the sense of autonomy, of this will is the very basis of morality. (Thus, to repeat, for Kant the opposite of freedom-as-autonomy is not constraint, but heteronomy: autonomous action is not lawless action, but action which is (self-) determined by laws freely prescribed by the actor and which, as such, accords with the actor's noumenal being as a rational agent who can transcend contingent empirical determinants; heteronomous action is action which is determined by empirical causes and which, as such, contradicts this idea of moral self-determination.) Autonomy also figures in Kant's second formulation of the categorical imperative, which requires respect for the autonomy inhering in every person: 'act so that you treat humanity, whether in your own person or in the person of any other, always as an end and never as a means only'. Kant calls this version of the categorical imperative the formula of autonomy or the 'formula of respect for the dignity of persons'.

The unity of the first and second formulations lies in the shared presupposition that every human being is a rational agent characterised by free will. As such, human beings – unlike things, animate or inanimate – have an objective worth, an intrinsic and absolute value or dignity simply because they exist: their value does not depend on whether they happen to be regarded as useful, admirable, likeable or important; instead, they are ends in themselves. This means that there is a condition limiting what we may do in pursuit of our ends: it is morally wrong to act in ways that violate or deny any person's autonomy or dignity, including our own. (Enslaving others is an obvious example of a practice that this formulation of the categorical imperative would expose as immoral, because it literally involves treating other individuals only as things: using them as means for the achievement of their 'owner's' purposes.) And since all rational persons have dignity, all have an equal and inalienable right to respect as the correlative of this duty of respect: hence the second formulation of the categorical imperative implicitly restates the universality principle embedded in the first. In the end, then, the second version also proceeds from a formal, abstract conception of the person, and what it is about the person that merits respect: respect is owed to persons as free, rational agents capable of what no other living creature is capable, namely, conducting ourselves on the basis of our own decisions and rules of our own making. Hence the feelings of indifference or disdain we may have towards particular individuals with particular characteristics, life histories, aspirations or achievements are morally irrelevant, and when these conflict with the duty to treat persons with respect, that duty clearly takes priority. Kant was careful to acknowledge that feelings of respect for oneself and for others *are* feelings, because he recognised the importance of feeling to human motivation, but he insisted that they are only morally significant to the extent that they proceed from a prior recognition of the moral significance of our duties to ourselves and others, and thus from a feeling of respect for the moral law itself.

The third formulation of the categorical imperative is the 'formula of legislation for a moral community': 'all maxims that proceed from our own making of law ought to harmonise with a possible kingdom of ends as a kingdom of nature'. The kingdom of ends is the ideal moral community, a community of autonomous rational persons in which the will of each member is determined in the manner specified by the first (or second, for it is the same) formulation of the categorical imperative. The kingdom of nature, on the other hand, is the phenomenal community of heteronomous human actors who are subject to empirical (or natural) determinants, including the force of our own inclinations. The formula of legislation for a moral community, then, sets out Kant's vision of our ultimate collective destiny as moral beings: it requires us to realise the ideal moral community in the phenomenal world – that is, to bridge the gulf between noumenal freedom and phenomenal nature – by acting in accordance with the categorical imperative. Actual human society, this formulation urges, *should* be – even if it is not yet – a community of persons all of whom at all times act autonomously, observe laws that are genuinely universal in that they reflect no one's special interests, and respect each other's innate dignity. Because, as autonomous beings, we are equipped to act in this way even when it goes against our inclinations to do so, Kant maintains that this kind of society could conceivably be accomplished through our actions. Hence although the idea of a kingdom of ends is only an Idea of (practical) reason, 'yet it is a practical idea that actually can and ought to have its influence on the world of sense, in order to bring this world as much as possible into accordance with the moral world' (Kant 1996a, 738). (This shows that for Kant it is in the sphere of morality that metaphysics, the deployment of pure reason, really comes into its own, because here Ideas of reason are not merely regulative, as they are of the process of acquiring knowledge of the empirical world as it is, but constitutive of that world *as it ought to be*. It is through our moral consciousness that the noumenal world – the 'beyond' of the world we experience – makes its existence felt and, through the moral law, that it makes its claims upon us).

Clearly, then, morality for Kant has an inescapable social dimension, which the third formulation of the categorical imperative is designed to emphasise. The kingdom of ends is the exemplary form of human community, and this has two implications that are relevant in this context: first, it defines the kind of ethical association that we should strive for in our personal relations with others; and second, it serves as a model for the political community, the state. The ideal of the moral community is more exacting in the first of these roles than in the second, because in the first role it reaches parts that in the second it cannot reach, namely, people's actual motivations and aims as well as their observable behaviour. The perfect moral community, for Kant, would be one whose members obeyed the moral law out of respect for the moral law: for the sake of duty alone, and from no other motive. This is because from a Kantian perspective the morality of a person's action does not depend simply on whether that action outwardly conforms with the moral law. Such conformity – what Kant calls the 'legality' or moral correctness of an action – is undoubtedly necessary, but the further question is always whether one does what is morally right *for no other reason* than that it is morally right: only then is one's will really the determining cause of the good action and only then, therefore, can the resulting action be regarded as *unconditionally* good. (Likewise, the moral worth of an action cannot depend on the success of the action, otherwise moral imperatives would again hold only conditionally.) The positive law of the state on the other hand, Kant insists, cannot force anyone's will to adopt the right intentions without itself violating the imperative to respect the autonomy of persons, so a just political order must confine itself to regulating only the observable behaviour of citizens. Yet although their remit is limited, just laws are nonetheless necessary, Kant argues, to guarantee the kind of the environment in which unconditional moral goodness can thrive. What then is the principle to which positive laws must adhere if they are indeed to be just?

THE UNIVERSAL PRINCIPLE OF JUSTICE

The analogue of the categorical imperative in the political sphere is what Kant calls the Universal Principle of Justice (or Right), and the important role Kant attributes to this principle follows from his rejection of empiricism in politics no less than in ethics: Kant grounds law and the state, as well as personal morality, on pure practical reason. That said, Kant's legal and political philosophy is widely acknowledged not to be as original or as comprehensive as his critiques of theoretical and moral reason: it shares many of the premises (and prejudices) of the mainstream thought of his day, and is particularly strongly influenced by the thought of Hobbes and Rousseau. Like Hobbes, Kant regards the state as the effect of a social contract motivated primarily by fear of others and a concern for self-preservation. Because of our empirical nature as phenomenal beings with desires and inclinations, individuals, in Kant's view, inevitably tend to see others either as instruments for or barriers to the satisfaction of our own wants. For such individuals, social interaction is always liable to descend into anarchy and violence, hence the establishment of a state with a monopoly on coercion is in everyone's interests, for it alone has the capacity to guarantee civil order and ensure the protection of life and property. Where Kant departs from Hobbes, however, is in his insistence that the state's authority must – if it is truly to qualify as legitimate authority rather than retain the character of raw coercive power – rest upon a principle of pure reason, for to base it on the self-interest of particular persons alone would be to deny that it could be unconditionally just and capable of commanding everyone's rational obedience. Hence for Kant the state cannot be justified by reference to empirical assumptions about what might have occurred in an actual 'state of nature'. An *a priori* idea of pure practical reason constitutes the standard for what the polity ought to be, precisely by making no reference to any historically existent polity.

This argumentative strategy will by now be familiar, for it is essentially the same strategy as that animating Kant's critique of practical reason, duly adjusted to account for the specific task that the institutions of law and the state perform: that of making possible an association of free persons. Because positive law, unlike the moral law, cannot concern itself with the citizen's 'inner' freedom (in the sense outlined above: the independence of his or her will from all empirical determinants) without violating that very freedom, and because what is essential to good public order is only correct behaviour, not the aims and motives that may accompany it, 'free persons' in this context are defined simply as acting subjects *who are able to act without coercive interference from others.* (Significantly, Kant also excludes all aspects of the 'external' social environment in which these persons might find themselves, and all features of their public selves apart from their capacity to originate their own actions, as irrelevant to the rational idea of their association.) The crucial question, in Kant's view, is this: under what conditions could acting subjects retain their freedom of action and still co-exist with each other in society? The answer: only when this freedom is regulated by law. At first glance this might seem paradoxical, for it is difficult to see how freedom can persist in a context of regulation. However, unqualified freedom would lead to the coercion of the wills of some by those of others, and so would be inconsistent with everyone's freedom. Hence some limitation on freedom is rationally necessary, and it is the role of the state to enforce it. Not just any restriction on freedom or any form of government is in accordance with reason, however. Government should represent the *general* will (here the influence of Rousseau on Kant's rendition of the social contract idea is evident), and its laws should be *universal* in nature. This, essentially, is the message of the *a priori* principle on which a just state and system of laws is founded: the universal principle of justice. Concisely put, the principle 'requires two things: that laws hold universally and impersonally, thereby avoiding partiality toward special interests; and that laws be such that every person could agree to their enactment after setting aside considerations of self-interest' (Sullivan 1994, 152). Hence the achievement of justice necessitates a legal structure that guarantees the equality of persons before the law (this is to say that the law should apply to everyone in the same way, with no legally privileged groups or individuals). Further, it requires that positive law protect the maximum freedom of all citizens to pursue their own welfare by limiting lawful actions to those to which all members of the polity could rationally consent, or in other words, by ensuring that the freedom allowed to each citizen is compatible with that allowed to everyone else. An association of persons regulated in accordance with this principle would be the ideal political community, for each person within it could be regarded as both its sovereign and its subject: only obligated by laws which they could themselves have willed. Each person's freedom, therefore, would be limited only in a manner consistent with that freedom.

The universal principle of justice implies that equality and freedom are human rights, that is, rights which inhere in persons considered from the perspective of practical political reason and which every human being has as such. These rights, then, are also Ideas of reason, and to this extent they can be called natural rights which are prior to any empirically existing government or actual legal initiative. This insight is undoubtedly Kant's most enduring contribution to political theory. Although he also had a great deal to say about how both public law and private law should translate the ideas of justice, freedom and equality into actual institutions and regimes of rules (pertaining, for example, to property, contract, and marriage and the family) (Kant 1996b, 353–603), many of his concrete proposals both lack the analytical rigour characteristic of his deduction of the universal principle itself, and clearly reflect the prejudices of his time. Perhaps most fundamentally, Kant saw no contradiction in stating on the one hand that all human beings are innately free and equal, and on the other that not all citizens need necessarily have equal rights as a matter of positive law. The most striking manifestation of this way of thinking is that Kant professes no particular preference for democracy, and specifically states that 'women and, in general, anyone whose preservation in existence (his being fed and protected) depends not on his management of his own business but on arrangements made by another [eg apprentices and domestic servants]' (Kant 1996b, 458) cannot vote in elections to the legislative authority, whatever the latter's constitutional position. Kant's attitude to these 'mere underlings of the commonwealth (Kant 1996b, 458) is difficult to square with his theoretical premises, but his perspective on democracy arguably follows from the fact that the general will – the identity of legislators and subjects – is for him an idea of pure reason, not the aggregate of citizens' actual preferences. For Kant, the question is 'not whether any proposed piece of legislation will agree with the popular will of the electorate, but whether it could arise rationally out of a contractual agreement with the people' (Sullivan, 1994, 19). Thus the crucial distinction is between arbitrary government and limited government (government limited by the obligation to respect equality and freedom), not between arbitrary government and democracy. That said, even a despotic government which violates freedom and equality, Kant insists (in another argument the logic of which is questionable), must be obeyed: there is no right of rebellion even against a tyrannical regime, because the existence of such a right would imply that every citizen could claim universal validity for their own opinion as to the legitimacy of the state and its laws, and this would simply continue the anarchy characteristic of the state of nature. Instead of a right to resist by violence or disobedience, Kant advocates public criticism of unjust rule and efforts to win reform by persuasive argument. To return to the essay with which Section II of this chapter opened, Kant's message is: 'argue as much as you will and about what you will, only obey!'

II.D. Feeling and Universality

Although Kant's third *Critique*, the *Critique of Judgement*, is probably the least understood of the three, no introduction to Kant's Critical project can afford to ignore it. It is an important work, and not only for what it has to say about art, genius and the special character of aesthetic experience. Certainly, it is best known for its treatment of these themes – which were central to the Romantic movement in art theory and practice in the early nineteenth century – and analytic philosophy still regards the significance of the *Critique of Judgement* as lying in its status as a foundational text in the philosophy of art. Continental philosophy, on the other hand, takes a broader view of the third *Critique*, placing more emphasis on the importance it gives to the encounter with particular objects and events as a condition for universal judgements about them; the weight it gives to consensus as the ground for the universalisability of these judgements; the recognition it accords to human feeling as the focus of this consensus; and the role it marks out for aesthetic experience as a bridge spanning the gulf (noted in Section II.C above) between the moral subject's transcendental freedom and the human being's phenomenal existence. Continental philosophers would argue that in pursuing these themes, Kant (whether wittingly or not) revisited questions that had been left unexplored, ignored or incompletely addressed in the first and second *Critiques* respectively. Accordingly, they would regard the third *Critique* as an interrogation of the lacunae, blindspots and contradictions that sustain Kant's theories of knowledge and morality, and as an attempt to recover what is repressed by a conception of reason as the negation or overcoming of the realm of feeling and experience. Continental philosophers thus regard the *Critique of Judgement* as an invaluable resource in the project of unravelling the very philosophical certainties that Kant had announced with such confidence in his earlier works, and that have proved foundational to Enlightenment thought (including modern jurisprudence) ever since.

Ostensibly, however, Kant's project in the *Critique of Judgement* was to establish the autonomy of the aesthetic domain relative to the realm of cognition and practical action, and in this way to stabilise, rather than to disrupt, the divisions between the three spheres. To this end, Kant brought together a range of older theoretical discourses pertaining to sensory perception (the original meaning of *aisthesis* as Aristotle understood it), beauty, and art or the arts; but surpassed all of these by offering a novel account of the nature of aesthetic experience that incorporated traces of these older discourses, but organised them in relation to his Critical agenda and vocabulary. Kant thus retained the Aristotelian notion that *aisthesis* is rooted in the first instance in encounters with particular sensory objects (objects of sight, hearing and so forth), but translated into the terms of his 'faculty' psychology, this means that the aesthetic in general is essentially connected with the faculty of sensibility, which enables the subject to have intuitions of (and so be affected by) particular events and objects of sensation. Kant added to this the notion that judgements of beauty could be occasioned by sensory perceptions, but argued that the kind of response that would support such a judgement was a particular kind of feeling that was not at all reducible to, although arising (at one remove) from, sensation. Though apparently subjective and personal, this feeling – a feeling of 'harmony' between the subject's faculties of imagination and understanding – could be described as a universal response that anyone encountering the same object or event could be expected to experience. Finally, although it would usually be occasioned by a natural object or event, it was possible for a creative genius to produce works of art that could engender the same kind of response in anyone who encountered them.

This, in a nutshell, is Kant's theory of beauty. The major problem that he faced in elaborating it was that of accounting for how a judgement of beauty could be universal in the sense outlined in the last paragraph. (Other related problems are also addressed in this text, but for ease of exposition we shall focus primarily on this one). The key question, in other words, was as follows: under what conditions would it be possible to state that a judgement of the form 'this is beautiful', made in relation to a particular object or event encountered by the senses, could hold for everyone who encountered that object or event? Philosophically speaking, this was a controversial question, because a proposition such as 'this (rose, for example) is beautiful' seems to be steeped in empirical contingency, and as such to be merely *subjective*: it rests, after all, on a particular individual's response to a particular object of sensation. Further, experience tells us that what one person holds to be beautiful another may find profoundly distasteful. Yet Kant was struck by the fact that, nonetheless, people routinely assume their judgements of an object's beauty to hold universally: here, 'the subject, merely on the basis of his *own* feeling of pleasure in an object ... judges this pleasure as one attaching to the presentation of the same object *in all other subjects*, and does so a priori, i.e., without being allowed to wait for other people's assent' (Kant 1987, 153). Kant's question in the third *Critique* was as follows: given the variety of opinions that exist in relation to aesthetic matters, how is it possible to claim universal validity for any of these opinions?

In seeking to answer this question, Kant rejected the empiricist position, according to which the claim of apriority that aesthetic judgements involve is a fallacy since aesthetic pleasure is always reducible to sensory gratification. Although Kant agreed that what he called 'aesthetic judgements of sense' (eg 'this makes me feel good') rest solely on 'the sensation that is produced directly by the empirical intuition of [an] object' (Kant 1987, 143), he insisted, against the empiricists, that not all aesthetic judgements fall into this category: some objects or events occasion a kind of response in the subject that is simply not reducible to sensory pleasure, and the judgement 'this is beautiful' records that response. However, against the rationalists, Kant refused to locate the source of this special kind of response solely in the object or event itself. Like his theories of knowledge and morality, Kant's aesthetic theory is resolutely subject-centred: if we are moved to say 'this rose is beautiful', what we are registering is not some quality inherent in the rose, but a pleasurable feeling of 'harmony' between our mental faculties that any subject, *qua* subject, ought equally to be able to feel. Thus, for Kant, what accounts for the universality and necessity of a judgement of beauty is the quality of the feeling upon which the judgement is based. In claiming of an object 'this is beautiful', he argues, one supposes that the subjectively felt pleasure occasioned by the object is by rights valid for everyone, and one claims that everyone ought to feel it. The project of (Part I of) the *Critique of Judgement* is to identify what *justifies* the claim to universality and necessity involved here by elucidating the conditions under which it is possible.

REFLECTIVE JUDGEMENT

In order to advance this project, Kant set about analysing the mental processes involved in forming judgements of beauty, a sub-category of what he called 'aesthetic judgements of reflection'. This latter characterisation was calculated to distinguish judgements of beauty not only from judgements of sense, but also from cognitive judgements (such as 'this is a rose') or practical judgements (such as 'this rose bush ought to be pruned'). Analysing what made aesthetic judgements of reflection different from cognitive and practical judgements in turn led Kant to a much closer examination of the faculty of judgement and the activity of judging than that offered in either the first or the second *Critiques*. 'Judgement in general', he announces in the Introduction to the third *Critique*, 'is the ability to think the particular as contained under the universal' (Kant 1987, 18). A cognitive judgement such as 'this is a rose', for example, involves the application of a 'universal' (the concept 'rose') to a particular object of sensation ('this'). The major faculties involved here, as was explained in Section II.B above, are sensibility, which enables the subject to have sensory impressions (received through the five senses) of objects in the world; and understanding, which supplies concepts for 'determining' objects (or in other words, for giving meaning to them). It has already been mentioned that Kant identified two further faculties of imagination and judgement as figuring respectively in the roles of 'unifying' the otherwise disordered 'manifold' of sensory impressions, and subsuming this unified manifold correctly under a concept. But judgement has little to do here except to link up a concept (given by the understanding) with an agglomeration of sensory perceptions (given by sensibility and imagination between them). Here, then, judgement is simply 'determinative': its role is to ensure that particular objects are correctly determined or 'subsumed' by universal concepts. Hence in explaining what makes knowledge possible, the *Critique of Pure Reason* presents judgement merely as subsumption, as nothing more than the application of concepts already supplied by the faculty of understanding. Likewise, the *Critique of Practical Reason* theorises practical action as governed by either hypothetical or categorical imperatives ('ought' propositions). Since Kant offered no theory of judgement here either, he arguably invited his readers to assume that rules could actually determine action and that judgement was therefore unproblematic (cf

Herman 1993). One of the main innovations of the third *Critique*, by contrast, is its suggestion that there is another way of 'thinking the particular in relation to the universal' – or in other words that there is another form of judgement which is not determinative, but 'reflective' – and that this second form of judgement is a complex function in its own right:

> If the universal (the rule, principle, law) is given, then judgement, which subsumes the particular under it, is *determinative* ... But if only the particular is given and judgement has to find the universal for it, then this power is merely *reflective*. (Kant 1987)

Both cognitive and practical judgements are determinative. Aesthetic judgements, by contrast, are reflective. In particular, they involve a process of *adjudicating between* the claims of the imagination and the understanding, a process which terminates in a kind of 'harmony' between these faculties.

The Harmony of the Faculties: The Basis of the Judgement of Beauty

The key to the difficult notion of the harmony of the faculties lies in Kant's characterisation of imagination in terms of 'freedom' and of understanding in terms of 'lawfulness' (Kant 1987, 151), and the easiest way to grasp their relationship in aesthetic experience is to compare Kant's account of what occurs in the mind when it responds aesthetically to an object, with what occurs when it simply identifies the object. When assisting in the performance of this ordinary cognitive operation, Kant argues, the imagination is not free: it submits to the law of the understanding by synthesising the manifold of sensory impressions generated by the object in accordance with concepts given by the understanding. Here, concepts operate like rules or laws, organising and curtailing the diversity and plenitude in the material intuited by the senses; and the imagination's unifying function *serves* the understanding's task of conceptualisation. Imagination operates freely, on the other hand, when it apprehends a unity in the manifold *without* this unity then being subsumed under a concept supplied by the understanding, and arguably also where it apprehends other possible forms of unity (Kant calls these 'images') beyond those presupposed by any concepts which may determine the object. The role of reflective, as opposed to determinative, judgement is to negotiate between understanding's lawfulness (its search for unity and closure) and imagination's freedom (its pursuit of diversity and indeterminacy). Henrich describes this activity as follows:

> [i]t is reflective judgement that holds the power of imagination (as it perceives and thus synthesises a manifold) up to the understanding. But that does not necessarily mean that it is engaged in a search for concepts that would actually apply to the perception in question [for that would amount to the subordination of imagination to understanding through the process of cognition]. *Rather, it compares the state of imagination with the conditions of a possible conceptualisation in general.* (Henrich 1992, 49, emphasis added)

Reflective judgement, then, performs the role of preserving the imagination's freedom, while at the same time checking this freedom by holding it accountable to the understanding's authority. Put in slightly more colloquial terms, reflective judgement seeks to generalise from a particular object of sensory perception (to say 'this is ...'), while at the same time suspending the urge to 'sum it up' once and for all by applying a concept to it (to say 'this is a rose'). A judgement of beauty ('this is *beautiful*') results in the following circumstances. On the one hand, the experience of trying to 'find a universal' for the particular object is accompanied by an awareness that the concepts that are available ('flower', 'red', 'fragrant' and so forth, as well as 'rose') to grasp the object are insufficient to pin down all the ways in which it strikes the imagination. On the other hand, the object does appear to be amenable to subsumption under a concept: it has the kind of coherence that is the usual condition for applying a concept to an object. It is this 'harmonic' combination of wildness and domestication – arising from an excess in the object that eludes the grasp of any concept, but that still tantalises our power to conceptualise by remaining within that power's jurisdiction – that is generally attributed to the object itself as its 'beauty'. But for Kant, predictably, the harmony in question is subjective, not objective: although occasioned by an object, it describes a harmony of the subject's faculties rather than of any properties intrinsic to the object. The basis of a judgement of beauty therefore lies, not in the object, but in the subjective feeling that results from the encounter with the object. This feeling, though pleasurable, is quite distinct from sensory pleasure: instead, it is experienced as '*a mental state ... that can be sensed*' (Kant 1987, 411).

Digressing briefly at this point, it is worth noting that Kant's account of the harmony of the faculties not only illustrates the close link between aesthetic and cognitive judgements – the same faculties, after all, are involved in both types of operation – but also seems to depart from the position set out in the *Critique of Pure Reason*. There Kant had argued that since an appearance exists only in cognition, an appearance which is not an object of cognition is 'nothing at all' (Kant 1996a, 167). From the *Critique of Judgement*, however, it seems that there can be a pre-conceptual (Henrich 1992, 36) or non-conceptual (Guyer 1997, 88–93) experience of an object apart from its actual cognition that manifests itself in a feeling: the feeling of pleasure. Further, the model of judgement presented here seems to challenge the paradigm of knowing as the subsumption of particulars under concepts, to the extent that it involves an acknowledgement that every act of cognition contains a reflective dimension. Another way of putting this is to say that every cognitive operation seems to present at least the opportunity for aesthetic contemplation, or for the de-familiarisation of the object through the recognition of a coherence (an alternative 'image') beyond the unities imposed by whatever concepts apply to it. This opportunity is passed over or suppressed when judgement proceeds directly to a determination of the object without pausing, as it were, to 'indulge' in a reflective moment.

Ambiguities also attend the definition of the pleasure that accompanies the harmony of the faculties. This pleasure is clearly not a sensation of agreeableness, but what exactly does it consist in, and why is it pleasurable? Kant himself described it as a 'feeling of life' or as a positive sense of our own mental powers, but his text is notoriously opaque and admits of a variety of interpretations. The differences between the analytic and Continental interpretations of this aspect of the third *Critique* are worth noting briefly, because they exemplify the divergent preoccupations of these two philosophical traditions. The main bone of contention between them is whether the true basis of aesthetic pleasure is the play (which could imply an uneasy and perpetual antagonism) between lawfulness and indeterminacy, or the harmony that brings an *end* to the play – on terms set by 'the power of concepts'. Analytic philosophy's leading contemporary interpreter of the third *Critique* emphasises the latter view. For Paul Guyer, Kant must be read as arguing that 'all pleasure is connected with the satisfaction of an aim or objective, and that universally valid pleasures must therefore be connected with the satisfaction of some universally valid objectives' (Guyer 1996, 9). The aesthetic pleasure which supports a judgement of beauty emerges from the subject's capacity to synthesise the 'manifold' of intuitions presented by an object so as to make possible its conceptualisation, albeit without actually determining it. Since it is the act of subsumption that usually achieves this synthesis, unification without a concept is a surprising, and therefore noticeably pleasurable, achievement (Guyer 1997, 70–88), and this pleasure is universally valid because 'finding unity in all our manifolds of intuition' (Guyer 1996, 10) is a universally valid human objective.

This interpretation privileges conceptualisation or lawful determination as the real *telos* (ie end or goal) of judgement: the pleasure one takes in an object of aesthetic contemplation is the pleasure of contingently foreseeing its possible subsumption under a concept and thus the satisfaction of an aim that every subject is presumed necessarily to share. In adopting this reading, Guyer seems concerned to defuse the capacity of the third *Critique* to destabilise the Critical project as a whole; to minimise the tension between cognitive concept and aesthetic feeling by arguing for the ultimate sovereignty of the former. Lyotard's 'Continental' interpretation, by contrast, represents these categories as absolutely opposed: Lyotard insists that what deserves emphasis in relation to the feeling of pleasure is not that it anticipates conceptualisation but that it is absolutely incompatible with conceptualisation, and must always remain so, since 'feeling isn't transcribed in the concept, it is suppressed, without "relief" ...' (Lyotard 1988b, 20–21). On this view then, aesthetic pleasure is not the complacent gratification that accompanies an achievement, but the 'miserable' delirium that attends the *postponement* of the closure that satisfaction brings with it: 'This feeling escapes being mastered by [the] concept ... It extends itself underneath and beyond [its] intrigues and [its] closure' (Lyotard 1988b, 22). And this in turn could be taken as suggesting that, bound up with every act of conceptualisation is a *resistance to* conceptualisation – registered in the subject as a 'feeling' – which is *internal* to the subject's own efforts to grasp objects and events in the world through its faculties of imagination and understanding. (This, it should be noted, is distinct from the feeling of 'negative pleasure' that accompanies the experience of the sublime (explained briefly below). The sublime feeling results from the subject's being affected by a particular object or event that subsists beyond the grasp of its faculties altogether, and it therefore registers the subject's relation to what is radically 'other' to it: that which eludes or exceeds it completely.)

THE UNIVERSALITY OF THE JUDGEMENT OF BEAUTY

Returning very briefly now to the central narrative of (Part I of) the third *Critique*: where there is a causal relationship between the harmony of the faculties and a feeling of pleasure – ie when a pleasure felt in the presence of an object can indeed be attributed to the harmony of the faculties and not, for example, to mere sensory gratification –

then a judgement of beauty founded upon it has universal and necessary validity. This is because this pleasure registers a 'common sense' (a *sensus communis*) which, as such, can indeed be 'presuppose[d] in everyone else' (Kant 1987, 54) and so assumed to be universally and necessarily communicable even if not in fact universally shared. The generalisability of the feeling of pleasure occasioned by an object in turn depends on whether two criteria – of disinterestedness and 'formal finality' – have been satisfied in the process of responding to it: it is the disinterested contemplation of an object solely in relation to its form and independent of any purpose it might serve which makes possible a universally valid judgement of beauty.

Here again, Continental philosophers have managed to find the resources for an immanent critique of Kant's own project, although it is primarily Kant's practical philosophy that is said to be challenged by the notion of universal validity developed in the third *Critique*. Hannah Arendt, for example, has identified an analogy between the differences of taste that prompted Kant's search for a criterion of universal aesthetic judgement, and the differences of opinion that characterise the public sphere of politics and generate the problem of political legitimacy. According to Arendt (Arendt, 1968a; 1968b; 1982), the conception of universality advanced in the third *Critique* hints at 'another' political philosophy, quite distinct from that expounded in the *Critique of Practical Reason*, which can fairly be attributed to Kant even if he never expressly claimed it as his own. This is a philosophy which proceeds from the recognition of the diversity of human experiences and opinions. Its universalism is not dependent on an absolute standard formulated from some Archimedean point beyond experience: it proposes that diversity be mediated by an appeal, not to pure reason, but to the possibility of a common sense that – being common – is irreducible to the aggregate of subjective preferences. This shared public experience is not given in advance: access to it is contingent on the encounter with a particular object or event; an undertaking to consider the latter from a disinterested point of view; and a commitment to persuading others of the generalisability of one's opinions. Hence judgement – rather than law – is central to this philosophy, and 'the power of judgement rests on a potential agreement with others' (Arendt 1968a, 220). Further, since one can never be sure that the ground of one's judgement is indeed a generalisable experience rather than a merely private whim, consensus about the status of a given judgement must be argued for rather than read off from some *a priori* principle. Whereas the moral law obligates absolutely and '*command[s]* that everyone approve' (Kant 1987, 126) an aesthetic judgement of reflection can only *claim* general assent.

Aesthetic Feeling and Morality

Though he himself emphasised the difference between the structure of moral rules and aesthetic reflective judgements, Kant was acutely concerned to forge a connection between morality and feeling, and it is worth considering this connection before finally concluding our analysis of his Critical philosophy. The issue is of major importance to the scheme of the Critical project as a whole, because the second *Critique* had neglected to explain how the supersensible moral law could give rise to moral action in a subject embedded in the phenomenal world: a subject inevitably moved to action by such motivations as desires, impulses and instincts. The moral person described in the

Critique of Practical Reason is bloodless, disinterested and dispassionate: hardly recognisable, in other words, as a real human being. To counteract this difficulty Kant's practical philosophy contained a recognition of the importance of feeling to human motivation, but only a limited recognition: the second *Critique* emphasised that a feeling of respect will be experienced as the *effect* of a prior acknowledgement of the binding force of the moral law. This feeling of respect is a feeling of admiration for the principle of the rational will's triumph over what Kant often describes in this context as the 'pathological' or 'cancerous' determinants of action – passions, affects, sensible inclinations – and it *proceeds from* the awareness of one's duty rather than *contributing to* this awareness. The significance of feeling shifts markedly, however in the passage from the second to the third *Critique*. One sign of this is that feeling, as we have seen, is made the very condition of universal judgements (of beauty) – though only to the extent that it is distinct from mere sensory pleasure. Another indicator of the new significance given to feeling (which follows from the foregoing), is that it is held up in the *Critique of Judgment* as offering a glimpse of freedom from the limits of sensibility and thus as bringing to life, as it were, the supersensible realm of reason in which the moral subject essentially resides. Kant argues, for example, that the experience of beauty inclines the subject to disinterested enjoyment in general and thus cultivates the capacity to disregard personal desire when morality so requires; and that aesthetic feeling enhances our receptivity to moral feeling, because the form of the one is analogous to that of the other. In these ways, aesthetic feeling positively contributes to the cultivation of the moral sense.

However, it is in relation to the sublime – not so far discussed in any detail here – that Kant's understanding of the link between aesthetics and morality becomes most explicit. Very briefly, the experience of the sublime, as Kant describes it, is occasioned by an exceedingly large natural object (such as a huge mountain range) which the imagination cannot grasp in one apprehension, or an overwhelmingly powerful natural phenomenon (such as a devastating volcano) that makes the human capacity to resist seem like an 'insignificant trifle' (Kant 1987, 120). These kinds of encounters, Kant argues, are also capable of giving rise to universalisable aesthetic judgements (of the sublime, not of beauty), grounded in their turn by a particular kind of feeling. Now this – described briefly above as a feeling of 'negative pleasure' – is also, like moral feeling, interpreted by Kant as one of admiration or respect. Significantly, however, this respect is not directed at the astonishing grandeur or awe-inspiring power of nature, which in Kant's account only provides the *occasion* for the sublime experience. On the contrary, the sublime feeling arises from an awareness of man's *superiority* to nature: the experience of such phenomena as boundless oceans and howling hurricanes, Kant argues (Kant 1987, 120–121), awakens the feeling that man alone possesses a supersensible faculty of reason which can think the totality in response to the suggestion of infinity in nature and can legislate for the will in response to the suggestion of irresistible might in nature. In particular:

we like to call these [phenomena] sublime because they ... allow us to discover in ourselves an ability to resist which is of a quite different kind ... [T]hough the irresistibility of nature's might makes us, considered as natural beings, recognise our physical impotence, it reveals in us at the same time an ability to judge ourselves independent of nature, and reveals in us a superiority over nature ... Hence sublimity is contained not in any thing of nature, but only in our mind, insofar as we can become conscious of our superiority to nature within us, and thereby also to nature outside us (as far as it influences us). (Kant 1987, 120–123)

This 'ability to resist' proceeds of course from the autonomous human will, which can rise above all empirical determinations, including the laws of nature, to conceive of and act in accordance with *moral* laws of its own making. For Kant, then, the sublime feeling arises from a palpable experience of this triumph of autonomous reason, and – since the latter is the very agency of moral action – is especially apt to dramatise the sovereignty of the will and so induce a respect for the moral law based upon it.

III. Contemporary Debates in Cultural Theory and Continental Philosophy: A Cook's Tour

Taken together, the first two of Kant's three *Critiques* yield the paradigmatically 'modern' philosophical ideas of truth, totality, progress, autonomy, justice and rights; and they explain all of these by reference to an overarching conception of the human subject. All of these ideas, as we shall see in this Section, have been challenged by cultural theory and Continental philosophy in the context of a thorough-going interrogation of modernity in general. The ultimate casualty of this critical onslaught has been Kant's conception of the subject: although cultural theory and Continental philosophy share Kant's predisposition to 'think big' about the conditions under which truth and justice could be (or appear to be) possible, they tend to reject any explanation that takes as given the sovereignty, unity and priority of the subject vis-à-vis the phenomenal world of appearances in which it finds itself. Instead, they tend to emphasise the priority of that world in relation to the subject, and sometimes also the priority of the 'beyond' of that world, or the unknowable – what Kant would have called the noumenal realm of 'things as they are in themselves' – in relation both to the subject and its lived 'reality'. Although, as has been suggested, some of these concerns had already been thematised in Kant's own writings, and particularly in the third *Critique* (though with markedly different emphases), the inflections given to them by cultural theory and contemporary Continental philosophy are generally attributed to the 'linguistic turn' mentioned briefly in Section I above. This is because the conviction that today underlies both traditions is that Kant's 'phenomenal world of appearances' is constituted, through and through, by language. From the perspective of cultural theory and Continental philosophy, then, the linguistic turn – a twentieth century development that was arguably completed by Ludwig Wittgenstein's *Philosophical Investigations* (1953) (Wittgenstein, 1958) – ranks as the contemporary equivalent of Kant's Copernican revolution. It is now time to consider this crucial development in a little more depth.

III.A. The 'Linguistic Turn'

It is worth noting in passing here that, just as Kant's *oeuvre* both unites and divides the analytic and Continental traditions in philosophy, so too does that of Ludwig Wittgenstein. Wittgenstein (1889–1951), who shared Kant's concern to characterise the limits of human knowledge, departed from Kant in finding its conditions of possibility in the enabling conventions of language. As far as many analytic philosophers are concerned, this departure sounded the death knell of the kind of systematic philosophy engaged in by Kant: it inspired 'modest' philosophical endeavours like J L Austin's 'ordinary language philosophy', for example (recall Hart's reliance on Austin, Chapter 4), and more generally it gave rise to the idea that the value of philosophy lies in sorting out the particular conceptual confusions that arise from the 'ungrammatical' use of language, rather than in providing ultimate explanations for the nature of reality, truth, morality and so forth. By contrast, for others (including Continental philosophers), Wittgenstein *can* be read as offering a grand theory: a theory about the role of shared symbolic practices (not simply spoken languages, but systems of signs generally) in constituting reality. From this perspective, the linguistic turn is significant because it contested Kant's subject-centred scheme only to replace it with another – equally ambitious – philosophical project. On the one hand, it undermined the notion that there could be direct access to a reality unmediated by language and so dismantled Kant's conception of truth: this was because Kant – though departing, as we have seen, from the notion that there could be direct access to reality – had re-located the possibility of truth in the universal subject's 'faculties' of perceiving, understanding and reasoning about the world. On the other hand, it offered to show how perceptions, understandings and thoughts of objects in the world – including oneself and other human beings – are 'always already' mediated by language.

From this perspective, language constitutes reality, and it does so by the play of relations between its elements rather than by anchoring itself to an independent world of objects existing self-sufficiently beyond language. For Wittgenstein, although the meanings generated by language nonetheless achieve a degree of stability through social use – language is implicated in 'forms of life' or 'language games' – this permits an accumulation of knowledge which can only be characterised as 'the truth about the world' insofar as it is a collection of linguistic propositions which through practice and convention have become what *counts* as the truth about the world. Following Wittgenstein, Jean-Francois Lyotard has argued that since there is a plurality of these language games, and since knowledge is constituted in and through them, there cannot be a universal truth: philosophy, he argues, must embrace the notion of local, plural and heterogeneous knowledges, and accept that these are not translatable into each other by reference to a 'meta-narrative' which accounts for and includes them all (Lyotard 1984). This vision of a non-totalisable universe of language games contrasts markedly with Kant's Idea of a unified totality as the horizon towards which all knowledge should tend, and it contests the ideology of relentless scientific progress that the Kantian framework implies. (As we have seen, Kant's *Critique of Pure Reason* builds into the knowing subject's faculty of reason an insatiable urge to understand the world in its entirety and as a unified whole, and from the perspective of such a subject, partial or local knowledges are valid only insofar as they fit, like pieces of a jigsaw, into this larger picture.)

Another contemporary French philosopher, Jacques Derrida, pays close attention to the procedures by which meanings are produced within language. Borrowing the terminology of Ferdinand de Saussure, the early twentieth century pioneer of semiotics,

Derrida takes it as axiomatic that language is a system of signs; that each sign is comprised of a 'signifier' (a sound-image, or its graphic equivalent), and a 'signified' (the concept to which the signifier is linked); and that meaning is generated by relations of difference between signifiers rather than by a necessary correspondence between signifiers and signifieds, or a necessary bond between signs and their 'referents' (the reality ostensibly denoted by language). Thus, for example, the meaning of the word 'tree' is not determined by that word's correspondence with a particular member of the plant kingdom, but by its difference from other words such as 'three', 'free' and so on. On this view, the concepts of which meaningful propositions are composed are effects of signifiers rather than prior to, and served by, signifiers. But Derrida radicalises Saussure's position by arguing that because meaning results from a play of differences between signifiers, it is also endlessly deferred: the meaning of one word, for example, requires reference to another word from which it differs, but that word can only be interpreted with the help of yet more words from which it in turn differs ... and so on along an infinite chain of these signifiers. ('Tree' means what it means because it is not 'three' or 'free', but also because it is not 'bush', 'bird', 'twig', and so on indefinitely.)

Rather than theorising meaning by assuming an identity of word with concept, and concept with object, Derrida introduces the notion of *différance* – which connotes both difference and deferral – to convey a sense of the slippage, supplementation and instability that is bound up with every appearance of meaning. Given that *différance* is indeed characteristic of language, however, the question arises of how appearances of stable meaning can be generated at all. This, for Derrida, involves the reduction of differences to one or other term within a series of hierarchically ordered binary oppositions (and Kant's own discourse is full of these oppositions, eg universality/particularity; autonomy/heteronomy; feeling/sensation): the apparent unity and self-sufficiency of a category is achieved only by constituting another category as subordinated and inferior. Nevertheless, this manoeuvre is never entirely successful, and Derrida's 'deconstructive' readings of these dichotomies aim to reveal their fragility: the suppression, devaluation and marginalisation of the second term can only be achieved through an acknowledgement of its persistence within the first. Deconstruction draws explicit attention to the dependence of the privileged term on that which has been banished as 'other' to it, and shows that identity is ineradicably dependent on difference. (Thus, for example, 'universality' acquires its meaning in Kant's discourse through its exclusion of 'particularity' (among other terms), but this other term, because it is actually constitutive of the meaning of 'universality', remains in some way traced through it. If Continental philosophers tend to find Kant's third *Critique* especially interesting, it may be because here Kant appears to acknowledge that the rigid hierarchies erected in the first two *Critiques* are unsustainable, and goes some way towards allowing the subordinate terms within his binaries to assert themselves within the dominant ones.)

Other philosophers working within the Continental tradition have concerned themselves with what exceeds or lies beyond language. Given that language constitutes reality, is it possible, they ask, to speak of a domain beyond this reality without invoking notions of immediacy which have been disqualified by the linguistic turn? Kant is once again an exemplary thinker here, for he too grappled with a similar question. Although insisting that reality as it 'appears' is constituted by the subject, Kant retained the notion that there is a world of things as they are 'in themselves' which is not identical to what appears. Theodor Adorno takes up this theme in the wake of the linguistic turn's decentring of Kant's subject, but inverts Kant's presentation of the relation between appearances and things in themselves: Adorno's 'materialist' philosophy testifies to the object's (ie the referent's) priority over both the subject, and the classifications through which language-as-correspondence seeks to grasp the object. Involved in this is the idea that language-as-correspondence inevitably reduces and impoverishes that which it purports to describe. Signifieds or concepts cannot fully correspond to real objects as these are in themselves, because the process of conceptualising objects is necessarily a process of generalising from their particularity: thinking different objects together and reducing them to unity under a single designation. (Even a procedure as innocent as applying the concept 'person' – or 'woman', for that matter – to a particular individual exemplifies this reduction: although ostensibly 'identified' by the concept, the individual's specificity is actually sacrificed in the process of being subsumed under the concept.) Not unlike Derrida, then, Adorno shows that the 'identity thinking' accompanying correspondence theories of language necessarily involves a denial or repression of difference, a difference Adorno names the 'non-identical'. Adorno refuses to liquidate the non-identical by theorising language and its concepts as 'all there is', and his writings constantly invoke the 'utopian' possibility of a reconciliation of identity and non-identity, language and its referents, culture and nature. Yet he insists that the excess in the object which eludes the concept cannot itself be positively identified; instead, it can only be illuminated by showing how conceptualisation continually *fails* in its identifications, a process Adorno calls 'negative dialectics' (Adorno, 1973). (It should be noted that even Kant was forced to acknowledge those uncontainable moments of excess when the subject's sovereignty over all it surveys is (momentarily) disrupted. This emerges particularly clearly in his treatment of the sublime experience (see Section II.D above), which both Adorno and Derrida interpret as 'the site where the claims of identity and presence are resisted; for both, sublimity is the figure of an alterity [an 'otherness'] that eludes conceptual capture' (Bernstein 1992, 235).)

Some of these innovations in Continental philosophy have filtered into cultural theory, albeit by circuitous routes: Derrida's ideas, for example, have been particularly influential, but have entered the field via literary theory and criticism, where deconstruction first established itself as a strategy for reading literary texts. Apart from Derridean deconstruction, however, the other two engines powering cultural theory's development over the past twenty years bear a peculiar relationship to Continental philosophy, taking up what appear to be similar themes – especially the question of the subject and its sovereignty – but refusing the label and conceptual vocabulary of 'philosophy', and for the most part repudiating the philosophical method of abstract conceptual analysis. One of these influences is the 'genealogical' work of Michel Foucault, which sets out to investigate the social practices/discourses of 'normalisation' that in Foucault's view have formed the rational subject celebrated by Enlightenment philosophy. The other major influence on cultural theory has been psychoanalysis – particularly the theoretical insights of the French psychoanalyst Jacques Lacan – which offers an account of the psycho-social processes of ego-formation. Foucault's project has been explored at length in Chapter 19 of this volume. Psychoanalytic theory is too complex to explore adequately in the space available here, but the importance of Lacan's insights to contemporary theoretical debates across all disciplines, including law, requires that some attempt be made to introduce its major themes. These will be explained very briefly here, and some aspects of their relevance to jurisprudence are explored in the first reading reproduced below. As we shall see, Lacan addresses many of the 'philosophical' questions that have informed the work of Kant, Adorno and Derrida, although in a terminology very much his own.

III.B. Psychoanalysis, Language and Subjectivity

Broadly, Lacan (Lacan 1977, 1979) takes up the Freudian insight that the human subject is radically divided or split (in Freudian terms, between the ego, the unconscious and the superego), and deploys this against all forms of thought – everyday discourse no less than Kantian philosophy – that insist on reducing subjectivity to the conscious ego. For Lacan, the ego is the precipitate of idealised images internalised during the period he names the 'mirror stage', which occurs between the sixth and the eighteenth month of the human infant's life. During this phase, the infant's experience of its body as fragmented and incomplete is overcome by its apprehension and affirmation of the image of its body in the mirror as a unified, self-contained whole. This overcoming is registered by the child's jubilant identification with the image – jubilant because the image is actually at odds with its lived experience of its body, and thus anticipates what has yet to be realised in fact – and the infant obtains its earliest sense of self through this identification. But since the image is indeed alien to the child's experience, this founding moment in the development of the ego is premised upon the existence of a gap between the human being and its imaginary representation, a gap which is denied in the process of identification. Even with the infant's maturation into adulthood, this gap is never dissolved, for the individual's life is punctuated by similarly narcissistic processes of identification in which the ego continually seeks to identify with something external to itself in order to bolster its identity. The otherness or 'alterity' of this external other both motivates the identification, and at the same time destabilises it. Thus what passes for subjectivity – the autonomous ego – is only apparently complete and self-contained, and this appearance is the effect of a denial of the alterity that propels it into being and on which it depends.

If the *ego* emerges within what Lacan calls the 'imaginary' order of 'specular' identifications, the *subject* is a product of what he calls the 'symbolic' order; but the production of this subject is again attended by its splitting. Lacan's account of the child's entry into the symbolic order upon its acquisition of language corresponds to what for Freud was the resolution of the Oedipus complex: it describes a renunciation (in Freudian terms, of the incestuous relation with the mother) and a form of submission (in Freudian terms, to the prohibition of incest and the law of the father) in exchange for social belonging or recognition; and it shows that a divided subject results from this process. However, Lacan's conception of the symbolic order reflects the influence not only of Freud, but also of Saussurian linguistics, and in this respect there are real affinities between Lacan's conception of the symbolic and Derrida's conception of language.

Like Derrida, Lacan prioritises the signifier over the signified, arguing that (the illusion of) stable meaning is produced by the play of signifiers, rather than by a set of correspondences between signifiers and signifieds or between signs and their external referents. Superimposed upon the relations between the signifier, the signified and the referent, however, is a schema that is peculiar to Lacan: a tripartite division of the dimensions of human experience into the symbolic, the imaginary and the real orders. In Kantian terms, the Lacanian *real* is the domain of things as they are 'in themselves', but this is the domain of 'the impossible': that which cannot be represented or, therefore, experienced (compare Adorno's 'utopia'). This impossibility, however, must somehow be covered over if meaning/experience is to assume any shape at all. The notion that signifieds are indeed anchored in the real is the necessary illusion that sustains meaning (it is crucial, as we have seen, to Kant's conception of the world of 'appearances'), and this illusion belongs to the *imaginary* order. Yet it is indeed an illusion, because it is the play of signifiers that produces the imaginary signified, and this play belongs to the *symbolic* order, the entire field of discursive representation that includes not only linguistic signs but political ideologies, social codes and so forth. Moreover, it is an illusion that is continually shattered, because signifiers form an endless web that encircles the signified but never actually reaches it: meaning therefore slides around rather than remaining fixed in one place.

To say that the subject is an effect of the symbolic order, then, is to say that it too is marked by a fundamental impossibility; that the apparent completeness of its identity is a mirage; and that it is the unstable effect of the play of signifiers. The 'I' that appears in language can never represent the real 'I', because this can never be symbolised: the representation of the subject in language presupposes the sacrifice of unmediated access to the real, singular (mythical) subject. The only identity that it is possible to experience, therefore – an identity mediated by language – is constituted on the basis of a fundamental alienation, loss and lack. Something is forever left behind with the entry into language, and the quest to recover this impossible real 'I' motivates all subsequent efforts to achieve identity through language. (Once again, 'language' in this context includes all those discourses that construct social 'reality' as we experience it.) Language, however, offers poor compensation for the subject's loss, because its appearance as a stable totality is, as we have seen, illusory. Language only *appears* to have an anchorage in the real, and so can never deliver what Lacan calls the *jouissance* (enjoyment) that would attend the subject's 'completion'. But to the extent that language invokes the fantasy of this anchorage, it is able to represent the impossible (the recovery of what the subject has lost) as the merely prohibited. Thus 'the prohibition of *jouissance* is exactly what permits the emergence of desire; a desire that is structured around the unending quest for the lost/impossible *jouissance*' (Stavrakakis 1999, 42). It is this desire that motivates the endless, and endlessly failing, identifications that characterise participation in the symbolic order.

Lacan thus reinterprets Freud's separation of the ego from the unconscious in terms of this split between the (imaginary) identity 'achieved' through language (what he calls the 'subject of the statement'), and the desiring subject (the 'subject of enunciation') that can never be satisfied with this identity and constantly operates to destabilise and exceed it. Like the unconscious, the desiring subject and the play of the signifier must be repressed if identity and meaning are to be stabilised at all, even temporarily. The only check on the flux of desire/signification is fantasy: the fantasy that desire will be satisfied by some privileged object, ie an object that would make *jouissance* possible within the symbolic order. In psychoanalytic terms, therefore, the sense that social reality is ordered and meaningful is necessarily sustained by the illusion that this object – what Lacan calls the *objet petit a* – is attainable. Every discourse that seeks to explain the sources of this order and meaning equally invokes a fantasy, although the characterisation of the privileged object at its centre varies between discourses. (Kant's vision of the moral universe as a 'noumenal' realm of transcendentally free subjects is fantastic in this sense, the privileged object around which it is organised being the capacity for rational agency, the pure will.) Fantasy, however, cannot satisfy desire, since the object around which it is organised cannot deliver the promised *jouissance*. Instead, and consequently, it can only sustain desire and the disruptions that accompany desire: hence the repressed continuously 'returns' within the dominant order and the narratives that sustain it.

IV. Cultural-Legal Theory

The deconstructive (Derridean), genealogical (Foucaultian) and psychoanalytic (Lacanian) approaches are methodologically very different, and indeed incompatible in certain important respects. Nonetheless, what in general links them to each other and to the post-Kantian philosophical tradition more broadly is that they yield an account of subjectivity not as a given essence – an origin – but as an *effect*: an effect, moreover (no less than the reality it perceives), of language or discourse, the stable order of cultural representations. But further, all three approaches stress that this order is both productive and prohibitive; and that the relation between the productive and prohibitive dimensions of discourse is somehow both constitutive of what we experience as reality and subjectivity, and at the same time the key to their instability (and for deconstruction and psychoanalysis, their insufficiency). The implications of all of this for the understanding of law have only recently begun to be addressed, but since the beginning of the 1990's the incorporation of the methods and themes of Continental philosophy and/or cultural theory into legal theory has gathered pace. For the sake of convenience, the body of work that has resulted will be referred to here as 'cultural-legal theory' to distinguish it both from traditional jurisprudence and from legal theory in general. (This term, though clumsy, is arguably preferable to others – such as 'postmodern jurisprudence' or 'postmodern legal theory' – that invoke an inaccurate, over-worked, and now rather jaded label to grasp a very disparate variety of theoretical approaches.)

In general, cultural-legal theory would suggest that law can be viewed both as an object *of* discourse, and as *itself* discourse; and this in turn draws attention to the ways in which meanings are constructed for law and through law, and how these meanings are supported by, and support, those that sustain the wider culture. To give a simple example, whenever law or the workings of the legal system are covered by the news media, or represented in film, law is made the object of discourse: here, the discourses of journalism or the cinema. These are of course different from jurisprudential discourse about law, but the cultural-legal theorist would regard them as equally worthy of serious attention. To regard law as itself a discourse, on the other hand, may seem counter-intuitive, since students of law are generally taught to regard law as a system of *regulation*, the fundamental constituents of which are rules, not signs. Yet the cultural-legal theorist would say that rules are invariably formulated in relation to some representation of the social relations (between persons, things, actions, domains) that they are meant to regulate, and the process of applying a rule is always a process of deciding whether a particular factual matrix matches that picture of the world. Cultural-legal theory recommends that careful attention be paid to these representations and to the interpretive strategies by which their dominance is secured in the process of applying rules.

Of course, mainstream jurisprudence is also preoccupied with legal interpretation, for it attempts to explain how 'right answers' – correct interpretations of law's official texts: legislative provisions and judicial utterances – are produced, and what accounts for their legitimacy. Drawing upon deconstruction and psychoanalytic theory, however, cultural-legal theory would aim to reveal the dependence of these rational 'right answers' – and the narratives that support them – on the seductive power of rhetoric and fantasy, and on the suppression of other narratives, claims and possible outcomes. But further, cultural-legal theory denies the official texts of the law the privileges that mainstream jurisprudence confers on them. From the perspective of cultural-legal theory, other non-written legal 'texts' – such as the rituals, procedures, architecture and symbolism of legal institutions – are in principle just as significant as statutes and cases, because they are just as liable to generate representations: in this instance, of the law's unique majesty and unquestionable legitimacy. And since written law depends for its authority precisely on the circulation and continuous reinforcement of signs of this authority, it is appropriate to pay as much attention to these signs as to the written codes themselves. Indeed the cultural-legal theorist would argue that if mainstream jurisprudence *can* only theorise law in terms of rules which are rationally formulated, applied and obeyed, this testifies to its own repression of law's dependence on non-rational factors – such as unconscious desire, or the experiences registered by the senses – for its efficacy. Cultural-legal theorists sometimes characterise these non-rational aspects of law's hold over the citizen as pertaining in some way to the realm of aesthetic experience, this being defined very broadly to include emotion and imagination as well as bodily/sensory experience (especially vision) and unconscious desire (see eg Goodrich 1991). This has the effect of linking – if only at the level of terminology (Barron 2000a; 2000b) – some of Kant's preoccupations in the *Critique of Judgement* (particularly his treatment of the relation between reason and feeling) with those of psychoanalysis and deconstruction.

In general, then, cultural-legal theory dwells on questions that simply cannot be posed in the idiom of traditional jurisprudence: How does law make sense of the world as it orders and regulates 'reality'? How does law establish the truth of its world picture, or bolster the truth claims of the other knowledges that it admits into itself? What 'fantasies' underpin these narratives? What other representations of reality, and other normative orders, are excluded or denied in this process? How do these excluded meanings and values 'return' to de-stabilise the legal text, or the other social 'texts' (ie discursive formations) that law helps to 'write'? In posing these questions, cultural-legal theorists have refused to engage with other, more familiar, questions such as 'what distinguishes legal rules from other social rules?' or 'why do legal rules generate obligations?' or 'what makes one interpretation of a legal rule better than another?' The move beyond these preoccupations is certainly to be welcomed, because it interrogates the presuppositions they contain: that law is fundamentally distinct from other social phenomena, because comprised of norms that emanate from a particular institutional source; that its norms are *ipso facto* legitimate; and that legal interpretation can in principle terminate in a just outcome. However, in ignoring the preoccupations of jurisprudence altogether, cultural-legal theory arguably adopts an opposed, but equally problematic, series of assumptions: that law is essentially the same as other social phenomena, i.e. just one system of representation among others, all of which generate culturally dominant ways of being and acting; that the order it helps to impose – just because it *is* an order – is necessarily repressive; and that legal interpretation inevitably terminates in injustice. Each of these assumptions, and their associated difficulties, merits a brief elaboration.

Law and/as 'Culture'

One way of accounting for the first assumption might be to say that cultural-legal theory simply lacks the conceptual resources to account for law's functional and discursive specificity. In other words, cultural-legal theory is unable to theorise what makes law *different* from other social 'codes': whether this difference is regarded as residing in law's institutional source, or its role as a dispute resolution mechanism, or the special kind of force (state coercion) that underpins it, or its normative character, or something else. Fundamentally, what cultural-legal theory tells us about law is that it is governed, in the last instance, by a universal and apparently transhistorical dialectic of identity and alterity, or the stabilisation and undoing of 'meaning'. But further, it tells us that this is the same dynamic that underpins culture as a whole, and so is not peculiar to law at all. Hence 'culture' also tends to be characterised in a rather reductive fashion by cultural-legal theory: the notion of 'meaning-making' serves as a catch-all for a wide variety of not obviously commensurable processes. It must be said that the influence of deconstruction and psychoanalysis on cultural-legal theory seems to have been largely responsible for these tendencies. Michel Foucault's genealogical explorations, by contrast, are designed to uncover the variety of discursive and material practices involved in the making and undoing of privileged meanings, and the social contexts, contours and contingencies of their operation. As Chapter 19 shows, Foucault is also reasonably attentive to the specificity of what he calls 'juridical' discourse.

Law and Disorder

What unites deconstruction, psychoanalysis and genealogy, however (and this goes to the second and third of the assumptions referred to above) is a lack of clarity about the normative commitments entailed by the use of these approaches, either individually or in combination. Again, deconstruction and psychoanalysis are particularly vulnerable to the charge of ethical relativism. To draw attention to the disruptions that *différance* or desire effect within the symbolic order is implicitly to celebrate the possibility that ossified social meanings could be destabilised and transformed. Yet *différance* and desire are normatively neutral: each refers to a pure force of subversion that indifferently confounds every 'text' constituting the symbolic order (and institutional arrangements, including arrangements of legal rights and obligations, are 'texts' in this sense). Further, there would seem to be no set of social arrangements, no reorganisation of the symbolic order, that could bring an end to the possibility of subversion: subversion, broadly speaking, is the 'return' of what is repressed within discourse – including legal discourse – but every attempt to accommodate what has been repressed will necessarily be repressive, in its turn, of something else. Interesting though it may be to chart the social manifestations of these dynamics of meaning-and-*différance* or repression-and-return, then, the perspectives afforded by deconstruction and psychoanalysis cannot generate the 'ought' propositions characteristic of normative thinking. While the adoption of one or other of these perspectives may lead to a belief in the *inevitability* of subversion, it cannot enable the theorist to prioritise particular social arrangements or institutions as especially *worthy* of being subverted, or give reasons for subversion in general. Arguably, the most that can be said is that deconstruction and psychoanalysis gesture towards the idea of all-out and permanent rebellion against order *per se*, a rebellion that is indifferent to all distinctions between the principles on which order is founded (eg the distinction between democracy and authoritarianism). This poses an obvious difficulty for theorists of law who profess a commitment to deconstruction or psychoanalysis. Law is necessarily oriented towards the achievement of order, and even when it registers conflict or effects change, it does so in a programmed and deliberate fashion that simply cannot be grasped by Derridean *différance* or Lacanian desire. Moreover, the discourse of law is inescapably normative, and the legitimacy of law's prescriptions resides in their conformity to some conception of justice. Arguably, a theory that cannot account for the specific nature of law's relation to social order, and can say nothing substantive about justice, cannot claim to be a theory of law at all.

Law and (In)justice

The significance of what is at stake here may become clearer in the light of a consideration of how mainstream jurisprudence understands the relationship between legality and justice. The dominant figure here is still Immanuel Kant, whose *Critique of Practical Reason* continues to cast a long – and for cultural-legal theory, malign – shadow. As we have seen, Kant places at the centre of his moral theory a conception of the moral subject as rational, autonomous, and ontologically prior to the contingencies of experience: prior, then, to 'language' in the complex sense outlined above. This moral subject, Kant argues, is universal, because every person has the innate capacity to abstract themselves from the empirical forces that condition their actions and act as if determined solely by the force of their own reason. To be self-determining in this way is, for Kant, to be free, and the capacity for freely willed action is precisely what makes morality possible: to act morally, in Kantian terms, is to elaborate and act upon a code of behaviour that complies with the dictates of a 'pure' moral reason, and this requires that one assume the position of the *universal* rational subject and treat others as if they too occupied that position. A code elaborated in this way can be said to be binding on everyone, and this ensures its status as an objective universal code, and thus a reliable guide to moral action. Kant's theory of justice is derived from his account of morality: the *Critique of Practical Reason* supplies the philosophical basis for the view that the law is just if it is, or could have been, prescribed by those who have to obey it; subjects, conceived of as members of a universal (but abstract) community of equally rational actors, are obligated by the law to the extent that it could have been legislated by their acts of will. (The Kantian underpinnings of Rawls's theory of justice, discussed in Chapter 15, are obvious.) This will only be the case if guarantees of respect for the equality and innate dignity (ie autonomy) of all persons are inscribed in the law, and so Kant can fairly be regarded as having originated the modern notion of human rights.

Within this framework, then – which still dominates both lay and academic thinking about justice, and is presupposed by the institutions of the liberal democratic state – justice consists in guaranteeing human rights through general laws which are impartially applied; what these 'rights' are can be read off from what it is to be 'human'; and what it is to be human is, essentially, always and everywhere the same: possession of a capacity for reason that permits us to a transcend the particular empirical circumstances and non-rational forces that influence us, in order to freely determine our actions. However, once subjectivity is seen as an effect of discourse (or in Lacanian terms, the symbolic order), this approach to justice begins to look not only implausible, but itself repressive. If there is no subject-position that is outside discourse, then the position of the Kantian moral subject is simply unavailable. But further, to the extent that it is argued to be both available and privileged, what we have here is a *representation* of moral subjectivity, which acquires its privileges only by excluding and repressing what is 'other' to it. Since from the Kantian perspective a person only deserves respect insofar as s/he can assume the position of the moral subject, and since the moral subject is premised upon a denial that human difference has any moral relevance (except as an impediment to moral action), Kantian respect comes to be seen as a kind of disrespect: a disrespect for the radical 'otherness', or 'alterity', or unique particularity, of persons. Kantian justice reduces the other to the same, and is inconceivable without this reduction.

In 'The Illusions of the "I"' (Barron 1993), an extract from which appears as the first reading below, Lacan's insights are brought to bear on the Kantian conception of justice. The argument here is that Kant's vision of the political community, and that of his contemporary interpreters such as Rawls and Dworkin, is a kind of fantasy which masks the impossibility of a totally harmonious, inclusive and unified polity. The fantasy represents a particular vision of community – open to all rational, autonomous citizens who can phrase their claims upon one another in the language of rights and mutual respect – as capable of satisfying the desire for this impossible harmony, but it is continually outflanked by that same desire:

> The symptoms of desire, in this context, manifest themselves in the eruption of political subjectivities that cannot be captured by the category of the citizen, and by forms of

> political and legal expression which exceed the logic of right ... [T]o eradicate the
> symptom is an impossibility, for it is an inevitable expression of the antagonism that
> constitutes, sustains and finally limits the discursive field of the political. Lacanian
> psychoanalysis demands a constant awareness of this surplus of the real over every
> attempt at symbolisation; it requires a coming to terms with what remains always beyond
> accommodation; and it serves as a reminder that every description of the just society
> bears witness to the unpresentable. Justice, in short, has no guarantee. It 'remains to
> be attained: it is ahead of us'. (Barron 1993, 97–98)

Other cultural-legal theorists have been prompted to reflect upon the *in*justice of law's
'justice'. As Douzinas and Warrington put it in *Justice Miscarried: Ethics, Aesthetics
and the Law* (Douzinas and Warrington 1994), an extract from which appears as the
second reading below:

> In the universal community of reason, which acts as the horizon for the realisation of
> the law, the other ... is turned into the same, the critical distance between self and
> other is reduced and the experience of value or moral conscience is grounded solely
> on the representation of the other by the knowing and willing ego. The alternative is
> the other's exclusion, banning or forgetting. But the other who approaches me is singular
> and unique; she cannot be reduced to being solely an instance of the universal concept
> of the ego nor can she be subsumed as a case or example under a general rule or norm.
> The law of modernity based on self's right and the subject's empire is strangely immoral
> as it tries either to assimilate or exclude the other. (Douzinas and Warrington 1994,
> 149–150)

The argument here is that justice is actually denied by the enforcement of abstract,
formal norms presupposing a universalistic conception of moral personality: positive
law purports to achieve justice by judging persons and situations in a way that is
inevitably reductive (of particular persons to abstract, rights-bearing legal subjects),
and there is something 'strangely immoral' about this. However, it is difficult to imagine
how this kind of 'immorality' could be avoided, for it would seem to follow from law's
very character as a regulatory system, and from the appeal to universality that is
embedded in every conception of justice according to law. Law performs its regulatory
function by supplying a framework of certain and predictable rules; and its legitimacy
rests upon the conformity of these rules to a conception of justice that is necessarily
– given that law prescribes for everyone – universalistic. It follows that to register in
law at all, a claim must be both determinate enough to be clothed in the form of a right
that can be enforced and observed, and justifiable by reference to some universal norm.
To institutionalise any claim as a legal right, then, is inevitably to subsume it under a
legal category (thus leaving an ungraspable 'excess' outside the category), and
necessarily to assimilate the claimant within the domain of rights-bearing legal subjects
(thus negating her 'otherness') – all in the name of justice. In short, the reduction of
alterity would seem to be an inescapable part of the legal process. This being so, it is
difficult to see how the condemnation of law's 'exclusion of the other' could have any
critical purchase; and equally difficult to understand how the assertion that justice
remains always 'ahead of us' could be of any practical assistance in determining what
ought to be done *now*. Thus although there is undoubtedly a critical impulse at work
in cultural-legal theory – to speak for the marginalised and oppressed by portraying

them as the 'excluded others' of legal discourse – adopting the perspective of the excluded other seems to render it impossible to subject legal initiatives to critique in the original sense of that word: that is, to examination, comparison and judgement.

ANOTHER JUSTICE?

To their considerable credit, Douzinas and Warrington have recognised that the challenge facing cultural-legal theory (or what they call 'postmodernist jurisprudence') is to 'articulate a theory of ethical action upon which a practice of justice can be built which itself would not reproduce the totalising tendencies that deconstruction so correctly challenged' (Douzinas and Warrington 1994, 17. See also Cornell et al, 1992). In this they share an assumption that is deeply embedded in the work of Continental philosophers like Derrida, Adorno and Lyotard: that the demonstration of modern reason's repressive tendencies renders the problem of injustice *more* urgent and important, not less. As Honneth puts it, in the third reading reproduced below:

> Whoever attempts to uncover the separated and the excluded in the thought systems of the philosophical tradition is driven finally with a certain necessity to ethical conclusions ... In such cases it appears justified to comprehend the element sacrificed to uniform thinking, that is, the unmistakable particularity of concrete persons or social groups, as the essential core of every theory of morality or justice. For this reason, the ethics of postmodernism today also proceeds theoretically from the idea of morally considering the particular, the heterogeneous. Not unlike Adorno's unwritten theory of morality, this ethics revolves around the idea that it is only in dealing appropriately with the nonidentical that the claim to human justice can be redeemed. (Honneth 1995, 290)

The concern here, then, is not simply to draw attention to law's blindness to otherness, but to search for an alternative, 'ethical', model of judgement that could somehow 'deal appropriately' with it. In the extract from their book that is reproduced below, Douzinas and Warrington sketch the outlines of such a model by entering into a direct engagement with Continental philosophy, especially the writings of Jacques Derrida (see in particular Derrida 1990), Emmanuel Levinas (Levinas 1969) and Jean Francois Lyotard (Lyotard 1985, 1988a, 1988b; Benjamin 1992). Very briefly, Levinas describes the relation between what he calls the Same (the Lacanian ego: Kant's knowing and willing subject) and the Other (absolute alterity: that which escapes this subject's cognitive and moral powers) as an *ethical* relation, which is to say a relation of *infinite openness and responsibility*. This alterity or 'exteriority' is named 'face' by Levinas, a term which is apt to draw attention to the radical contrast between the Levinasian Other and the Kantian moral person (Levinas 1969, 194–219; Levinas 1993, 116–125). (The Other faces me in his or her absolute singularity, places a unique demand upon me and seeks my response; the moral person appeals to what makes us both the same, presents a claim which is universally recognisable, and demands my respect as a fellow member of the moral community.) Once again language is crucial here, because language, for Levinas, enacts the ethical relation. However, in a manner reminiscent of Lacan's distinction between the subject of enunciation and the subject of the statement, Levinas distinguishes between the ethical form of language, the 'Saying' (the attempt at a response to the

Other that motivates every speech act) and the 'Said' (the legal or other statement that fixes, renders manageable and so truncates this response). For Douzinas and Warrington, a 'justice of alterity' would require a kind of creative antagonism between the Saying and the Said, such that the former could be openly accommodated within the latter as a kind of perpetual interruption of the invitation to complacency that it would otherwise contain. Legal judgement, they argue, must '[bring] together ... the limited calculability and determinacy of law with the infinite openness and contingency of alterity' (Douzinas and Warrington 1994, 179). The turn to Levinasian ethics is accompanied in Douzinas and Warrington's analysis by a return to Kant, though to Kant's aesthetic theory, not his moral philosophy: they read Kant's account of reflective aesthetic judgement as suggesting an 'ethical' (in the Levinasian sense) alternative *to* legal judgement as it is currently understood and practised. Without launching into detail here, what enables this analogy is Kant's argument that aesthetic (reflective) judgement proceeds from an encounter with a particular object or event that does not result in its subsumption under a concept: the object is appreciated for its own sake and grasped in its singularity, while also being recognised as amenable to a possible conceptualisation. Similarly, Douzinas and Warrington argue that 'legal phronesis [practical reason] must move between the norm and the event in the same way that reflective judgments find in each particular the mark of an undetermined universal' (Douzinas and Warrington 1994, 182). However, '[t]he action of justice requires an incessant movement between the general rule and the specific case that has no resting place and finds no point of equilibrium' (Douzinas and Warrington 1994, 184).

Ultimately, then, Douzinas and Warrington's analysis does not actually deliver the new model of legal judgement that it claims is suggested by these philosophical arguments. Further, its diagnosis of the problem that this new model would resolve reflects a blindness to its own 'other' – mainstream jurisprudence – for it tends to conflate two aspects of legal judgement that jurisprudents have come to regard as separate and distinct: the practice of deliberation and the rendering of a verdict. Crude legal positivism, admittedly, recognises no such distinction. From this perspective, law is a system of valid rules (the validity of a rule being demonstrable by reference to a test of its institutional source), and rules deliver verdicts with little in the way of deliberative effort: interpretation is unproblematic because words have 'plain meanings'. Yet whereas this model of legal judgement does appear to replicate the subsumptive procedure that so worries the theorists of 'alterity', it is now widely regarded as incapable of grasping the complexities and subtleties of adjudicative practice. The work of Ronald Dworkin, in particular, contests the notion that the process of assessing what positive law requires is reducible to the simple act of subsuming particular cases under given rules. Dworkin offers a model of adjudication as involving the use of indeterminate principles – themselves constructed out of a reflective movement between considerations of their legal 'fit' and intuitions about their political/moral 'value' – which are neither uncontroversial nor demonstrable and operate at most as reasons for deciding cases one way or another, not as all-or-nothing rules that necessitate particular outcomes.

True, Dworkin's understanding of reflective deliberation is one that ultimately subordinates indeterminacy to the imperative of the rightful determination: there is always, after all, a right answer. His contribution has, however, greatly refined the positivist understanding of adjudication, and cannot be ignored by any theorist of law wishing to engage in a critical rethinking of legal judgement. Far from engaging with Dworkin's model of judgement – much less offering a viable alternative to it – Douzinas and Warrington's commitment to an impossible 'justice of alterity' leads them to dismiss it out of hand. The interpretative (deliberative or reflective) moment of legal judgement as theorised by Dworkin is reduced to the (determinative) moment of decision or verdict; and the latter is condemned as nothing other than an act of violence, which is to say an act that negates the particularity and otherness of the claimant and the claim. 'Hermeneutically oriented legal theory assumes that the rightness, fairness or justice of the interpretative enterprise will bestow its blessing on the active component of judgement and justify its violence' (Douzinas and Warrington 1994, 213). Douzinas and Warrington simply reverse this assumption, arguing, in effect, that the legal decision projects its violence onto the interpretative procedure that precedes it. The active or performative component of legal judgement – the verdict – necessarily:

> abstracts the particular, generalises the event, calculates and assesses individuals and distributes them along normative and normal(ised) paths under a rule that subjects the different to the same and the other to the self ... Concrete individuals are turned into legal subjects, unique and changeable characteristics are subsumed under (ideal?) types and roles, singular and contingent events are metamorphosed into model 'facts' and scenes in impoverished narratives constructed according to the limited imagination of evidence and procedure. (Douzinas and Warrington 1994, 230–231)

For Douzinas and Warrington, '*[n]othing that happened earlier* – a reading of the law or a commitment to principle' (Douzinas and Warrington 1994, 239, emphasis added) can mitigate the reductive finality of the decision; indeed the more careful the deliberation, the more apt it is to disguise the brutality of the action that follows upon it. All of those aspects of the deliberative process – contingency, openness to the event, the encounter with the particular other, indeterminacy – which are the true guarantors of a 'justice of alterity' are necessarily extinguished at the moment of the legal decision, and this would appear to be fatal to any hope of achieving this 'justice' through law. Hence Douzinas and Warrington conclude that 'law's inescapable commitment to the rule means that injustice is the inescapable condition of all law' (Douzinas and Warrington 1994,183).

V. Redeeming Reason: Intersubjectivity and Discourse Ethics

Fundamentally, what this latter statement voices is an attitude of deep suspicion towards the heritage of ideals yielded by the Enlightenment – reason, universality, the unified sovereign subject, a conception of justice organised around this subject's abstract rights, and a conception of human history as tending towards the single goal of emancipating this subject's reason – that cultural-legal theory has absorbed from cultural theory and Continental philosophy. Foucault's genealogies of disciplinary power, for example, (examined in detail in Chapter 19) draw attention to the dark side of the Enlightenment's ideals of reason and freedom: the practical history of objectification and domination that has accompanied their elaboration. In an early work, *The Order of*

Things (Foucault 1970), Foucault explicitly links Kant's Copernican revolution in philosophy with the despotism that for him is bound up with the Enlightenment. Kant finds the condition of the possibility of knowledge in man's own finite limits – the limits of the human faculties – but what this amounts to in turn, as Foucault sees it, is that man claims total knowledge by virtue of his limitations, or infinite knowledge by virtue of his finitude: he affirms his finitude only to deny it. This 'produces a peculiar dynamic of a will to truth for which every frustration is only a new stimulus to an increased knowledge which then fails in its turn' (Habermas 1989, 177). The task of acquiring total knowledge of the world of objects, included in which is man himself, demands infinite power, and the terrain on which this power is exercised is 'occupied by the human sciences, in which Foucault sees an insidious disciplinary force at work' (Habermas 1989, 177). For Foucault, Enlightenment thus sanctions the unleashing of that form of reason (scientific-technical rationality) which is a mere tool of calculation, and the engendering of 'others' who fail its criteria of progress and responsible subject-hood: the transformation (in more ways than one) of revolution into terror. Kant's transcendental meaning-giving subject makes possible this insatiable will and its pathological implications – one of which is the objectification of that same subject in its guise as a living, empirical human being. And for Adorno, Derrida, Lacan and others (including the early Foucault), the only way out of this 'analytic of finitude' lies in that which refuses the objectifying structures of meaning: whatever it is – the non-identical, *différance*, desire, alterity, madness, corporeality – that resists or lies beyond reason and its representations.

Not all Continental philosophers would agree either with this bleak diagnosis, or with the proposed antidote to modernity's malaise. The contemporary German social theorist Jürgen Habermas has established himself as the leading contemporary defender of reason, the Enlightenment and what he calls the 'project' of modernity against their postmodernist (or as he would characterise them, anti-modernist) detractors. Indeed in one surprisingly vehement attack, Habermas has dismissed the theorists of difference, desire and alterity as decadent, anarchistic, antihistorical, irresponsible and conservative, their thought blighted by a wholly negative 'attitude' that 'in Manichaean fashion oppose[s] instrumental reason with a principle accessible only to evocation' (Habermas 1996a, 53). Although this characterisation is undoubtedly harsh, it testifies to a deeply felt concern on Habermas's part about the political positions and consequences with which these perspectives, albeit unintentionally, seem compatible. It also brings into focus what for Habermas is a crucial distinction between two kinds of philosophical gesture – 'critique' and 'negation' – only the first of which, in his view, is appropriate to the *project* of modernity. Critique in this context signifies something more exact than an evaluation of the merits of a practice or institution: it draws its meaning instead from the philosophical method used by Kant to investigate the human capacities for knowledge, willed action and judgement in his three *Critiques*. Kantian critique, as we have seen, is a form of reflection upon the intrinsic structure of a human faculty that both reveals its limits and demarcates its proper jurisdiction. Thus Kant's critiques of theoretical and practical reason comprise both a negative and a positive aspect: negatively, they mark out the boundaries beyond which reason must not stray if it is to avoid lapsing into error or illusion; positively, they entrench reason within the field of competence thereby defined. In their negative aspect, the limits revealed by Kant's critical project constituted a refutation of the dogmatic metaphysics of the rationalist tradition, which held that reason could generate truths about a transcendent reality: reason, Kant insisted, cannot deduce the fundamental properties of the universe; nor can it prove that God exists, that the will is truly free, or that beauty inheres in objects. In their recuperative aspect, however, Kant's limits described the conditions under which cognitive propositions, moral-practical determinations and aesthetic judgements *could* be possible *a priori*, and so they also invalidated the empiricist position that there can *no* basis for claims to truth, morality or beauty prior to experience. True, these conditions are lodged in the universal subject's faculties of knowing, willing and judging rather than in the objective structure of the world, but they are as foundational in their respective domains as they are irreducible to each other.

Habermas recognises that a by-product of the advance of modern reason, as Kant theorised it, has been the relentless spread of instrumental-technocratic consciousness: a consciousness oriented towards strategic action in, and manipulation of, the natural and social environment through the calculation of efficient means to achieve given ends. He also acknowledges that the freedom celebrated by Kant's Enlightenment has been shadowed by new forms of domination. This is because the very political and economic systems (the capitalist economy and the centralised state) that have secured some freedoms have also overseen the invasion of what Habermas calls the 'lifeworld' by these systems' media of money and bureaucratic-administrative power, with consequences that include alienation and atomisation (effects particularly associated with the market); and dependency and normalisation (effects particularly associated with the welfare state). Since the lifeworld (the realm of shared norms, understandings and identities) is constituted by processes requiring communication and solidarity for their survival (processes of cultural transmission, social integration and socialisation), this process of 'colonisation' is corrosive of the lifeworld, and compromises the possibilities it presents for collective self-determination. However, Habermas sees rationalisation occurring on two fronts in modernity: both at the systemic level, where instrumental rationality has become ever more sophisticated and effective, but also at the level of the lifeworld itself. Here, he argues, the grip of unquestioned tradition and hierarchy on 'communicative action' (generally, social interaction: communication conceived of as a way of acting co-operatively with others) has been progressively loosened in the modern era, with the result that communication has become increasingly capable of yielding a genuine consensus of free and equal participants. This evolution in communicative rationality is, Habermas argues, an aspect of the advance of modern reason that must not only be retrieved from the jaws of its technocratic counterpart (which threatens to swallow it), but maximised and expanded. And this in turn requires a form of Kantian critique: Habermas's aim is not to negate Enlightenment rationality, but to rework Kant's critical method to mark out reason's limits and possibilities, and to elaborate a standpoint from which to confront the pathological social and political implications of its unbalanced development – the one-sided progress of instrumental reason at the expense of the communicative structures of the lifeworld. In opposition to totalizing rejections of rationality *tout court*, Habermas offers a 'less dramatic' critique which sees the strategic calculations of an essentially monadic individual subject 'as a systematic foreshortening and distortion of a potential always already operative in the communicative practice of everyday life, but only selectively exploited' (Habermas 1987a, 311). For Habermas, to recognise and advance the rationality embedded in modern communicative practice would be to 'complete' the (critical) project of modernity as inaugurated by Kant.

That said, the relation between Habermas's theory of communicative action and Kant's conception of reason and its limits is marked by divergences as well as commonalities. Habermas's most fundamental departure from Kant consists in his substitution for the latter's purely subject-centred reason an *intersubjective* conception of rationality whose conditions of possibility are rooted in the social interactions constituting the lifeworld (Habermas 1987a, 294–326). The new focus on intersubjectivity follows from Habermas's identification of communication *between* subjects as the privileged site for the enactment of rationality, and is Habermas's own rendition of the 'linguistic turn'. His explanation of this form of reason proceeds from a consideration of the actual and ideal conditions under which communication occurs. Implicit in the practice of communicating, he argues, is an orientation towards consensus and mutual understanding, and this in turn commits interlocutors to 'redeeming' (fulfilling) certain 'validity claims' (ie standards that are claimed to hold trans-subjectively) regarding the comprehensibility, truth, normative rightness and sincerity of their statements:

> Acts of linguistic communication ... presuppose four validity claims: that what we say is comprehensible, that it is true, that it is right, i.e. that there is a normative basis for the utterance, and that it is a sincere expression of the speaker's feelings. The background consensus between speaker and hearer includes the fact that they implicitly make these claims and could if necessary justify them. Thus we can ask a speaker 'What do you mean?', 'Is what you say true?', 'Are you entitled to say that?' and 'Do you really mean it?' In other words, at the back of every act of communication is the implication that we could reach a consensus on the validity of these claims. (Outhwaite 1994, 40)

This account of communicative practice raises two points that merit particular emphasis in this context. First, that speakers *do* regard claims to truth, normative rightness and sincerity as distinct testifies, as far as Habermas is concerned, to their recognition of the differences between three worlds of discourse relating respectively to facts, values, and the realm of inner experience. But although these distinctions roughly correspond to the distinctions between knowledge, morality and feeling that underlie Kant's Critical project, Habermas sees them as presupposed by modern communicative practice rather than as residing in the mental faculties of the universal subject. Second, Habermas conceives of 'discourse' as the practice of giving and contesting *grounds* for factual, moral and expressive statements. Communicative rationality is thus bound up with a preparedness to convince others by argument that the grounds of one's claims are acceptable because of their capacity to withstand criticism. In making any kind of validity claim, 'one at once (a) opens one's claim to an objective evaluation and thereby to others' criticism, and (b) maintains that what is claimed can withstand such evaluation. In these features Habermas finds his notion of reason' (Rehg 1994, 28). Simone Chambers has pointed to a connection between this idea of rationality and the conception of public reason elaborated by Kant in his 1784 essay 'An Answer to the Question: What is Enlightenment?' (considered above in Section II.A):

> For [the] enlightenment [of a public] ... nothing is required but ... freedom to make public use of one's reason in all matters ... But by the public use of one's own reason

I understand that use which someone makes of it as a scholar before the entire world of the public of the world of readers ... A citizen cannot refuse to pay the taxes imposed upon him ... But the same citizen does not act against the duty of a citizen when, as a scholar, he publicly expresses his thoughts about the inappropriateness or even injustice of such decrees. (Kant 1996b, 18–19)

Kant thus saw the right to argue as a fundamental political right, although as we have seen he professed no commitment to democracy, and he assumed that argument about political matters would be confined to 'men of learning'. Nonetheless, beneath these outmoded prejudices lies a conviction that the legitimacy of a demand for compliance to a proposition (in this case, the sovereign's demand for compliance to a legal norm), depends on the availability of a space in which to seek and contest reasons for the proposition. As Chambers points out, Habermas can be read as radicalising and expanding that vision, and rooting it in the mutual suppositions made by those who engage in discourse rather than in the fundamental capacities of the rational citizen (Chambers 1995). It might be added that Habermas can also be read as building on Hannah Arendt's interpretation of Kant's third *Critique* (see Section II.D above).

Mention of law and politics brings us to the implications of Habermas's conception of communicative reason for questions of ethics, morality and justice. Here again, Habermas proclaims the continuity of his project with that of the Enlightenment, for as well as defending the primacy of (communicative) reason, he also affirms a conception of *practical* reason – a 'discourse ethics' – that is organised around the ideals of freedom and equality. To this end, Habermas elaborates a 'discourse principle' that retains some similarity to Kant's categorical imperative. (Both the contrasts and the similarities between Kant's moral theory and Habermas's discourse ethics are explored by Axel Honneth in the third reading reproduced below.) Returning to the different species of 'validity claim' mentioned above, the kind of claim involved in a moral statement is the claim to its normative rightness. If a claim of this kind were to be challenged, it could only be redeemed, Habermas argues, in a 'practical discourse' in which reasons or grounds for its rightness could be demanded and contested, and agreement could be reached on the appropriateness or otherwise of those grounds. Thus his discourse principle states that 'only those norms are valid to which all affected persons could agree as participants in a practical discourse'.

Habermas offers no substantive account of what grounds would suffice to merit consensus in such a discourse; instead, the discourse principle specifies a procedure to be followed in order to ensure that the outcome of the discussion could represent a genuine consensus. In this respect it is not unlike Kant's categorical imperative, which also requires a decision procedure to be adopted by the moral reasoner in order to ensure that norms invoked to justify actions have universal validity. However, as we have seen (in Section II.C above), Kant's universalisation test essentially involves a monological process of self-interrogation, the aim of which is to examine whether proposed 'maxims' of action are logically consistent with one another. (It is monological because subjects considered as moral persons are all equally reduced, from the Kantian perspective, to their capacity for rational agency, and so a Kantian 'dialogue' with other moral persons is really a conversation with oneself; it yields a test of logical consistency because of the character of the rationality (a rationality of non-contradiction) in which that sameness consists.) For Habermas, on the other hand, 'the test of successful universalization is no longer found in the question: Is a world regulated by my maxim logically consistent? From the discursive perspective, the question we ask ourselves is: Would everyone agree to be regulated by my maxim?' (Chambers 1995, 233). According to this test, a subject must consider whether the norm by which s/he proposes to act has universal validity by staging a *dialogue* among all those potentially affected by the proposed action. Further, this conversation must be a real process of debate, where all parties have the opportunity to articulate their different perspectives and interests. This embedding of practical discourse in actual communicative interactions contrasts sharply with Kant's siting of morality – pure practical reason – in a transcendental realm of noumenal subjectivity (Section II.C). However, Habermas also insists that practical discourse must aim to replicate the conditions prevailing in what he calls the 'ideal speech situation' – a situation of unconstrained discussion to which all speakers have equal access, where no one is coerced, and where only the force of the better argument prevails – because the practice of engaging in dialogue oriented towards a rational consensus unavoidably presupposes a commitment to this counterfactual model of debate. 'To that extent ... the possibility of making the validity of norms dependent on a procedure of discursive will formation is tied to the transcendental idea of a discourse free from domination' (Honneth 1995, 296).

The many aspects of the task of elaborating a discourse ethics have preoccupied Habermas for several years, but of most importance for our purposes here is his recent effort to develop a detailed model of democratic politics founded on the discourse principle, and more recently still, his exploration of the implications for law of the priority of this principle as a normative criterion of legitimacy. In an essay published in 1985, law is described as having two aspects, summed up by the phrase 'law as medium and law as institution' (Habermas 1985). 'Law as medium' refers to law's existence as a structure of formal general rules which operates 'as a means for organising [the] media-controlled subsystems' (Habermas 1985, 212) of state and economy. Administrative law and commercial law exemplify this link with the 'system'. Here 'the law is combined with the media of power and money in such a way that it takes on the role of a steering medium' (Habermas 1985, 212): directly constituting the political and economic 'domains of action'; ensuring a certain and predictable framework for strategic-rational action within these domains; and generally serving as an instrument of stability and social control. Further, '[l]aw used as a control mechanism is relieved of the problem of justification and is only connected through formally correct procedures with the body of law whose substance requires legitimation' (Habermas 1985, 213).

However, law is also rooted in the lifeworld of shared norms and understandings to the extent that it gives institutional expression to them: the basic principles of constitutional law and those parts of the criminal law that regulate 'offences close to morality' (Habermas 1985, 212) are exemplary here. By contrast with law in its role as medium, legal institutions 'need substantive justification, because they belong to the legitimate orders of the lifeworld itself and, together with the informal norms of conduct, form the background of communicative action' (Habermas 1985, 213). Thus,

legal institutions have no constitutive power, but only a regulative function. They are embedded in a broader political, cultural and social context; they stand in a continuum with moral norms and remould communicatively structured areas of action; they give the already informally constituted domains of action a binding form backed by sanctions. (Habermas 1985, 213)

Despite its acknowledgement of law's dual aspect in modern society, 'Law as Medium and Law as Institution' portrays modern law as having, at best, an ambivalent relationship to social emancipation. On the one hand, it suggests that the protections afforded by the legal system to the rights of individuals – certainly their rights against, and of participation in, concentrations of political and economic power – have been 'unambiguously freedom guaranteeing'. On the other hand, it argues that the latest 'juridification thrust' – exemplified in the emergence of social welfare law as a medium to regulate 'communicatively structured action areas' like the family and the school – is deeply implicated in the system's colonisation of the lifeworld. However, in *Between Facts and Norms* (which appeared in German in 1992, and in English in 1996), Habermas offers a more optimistic view of law's capacities and potential. At a time when traditional lifeworld institutions (shared beliefs, cultural assumptions, substantive values, collective identities) can no longer – in modern conditions of secularism, pluralism and social fragmentation – furnish a comprehensive backdrop for social interactions, discursively rational legal institutions, he argues, have emerged as the only available source of normative integration. And since law also speaks the language of the system, it can function as a bridge between lifeworld and system, and a vehicle for the former's defence and reinvigoration. In particular, law can serve as the 'transformer' that converts the 'communicative power' generated by discursive processes in the lifeworld into the 'administrative power' of the state. This leads Habermas to a revised version of the liberal ideal of a state limited by law: 'the administrative system, which is steered through the power code, [should] be tied to the law-creating communicative power and kept free of illegitimate interventions of social power (i.e. of the factual strength of privileged interests to assert themselves)' (Habermas 1996b, 150).

The key distinction in *Between Facts and Norms* is that between the 'facticity' of law – its social function as the coercive, regulatory instrument of state authority – and the 'validity' of law, its claim to normative legitimacy. It is precisely because law combines positivity with legitimacy that the role of 'hinge' between lifeworld and system is available to it. Law's legitimacy lies in its reflecting and remaining open to the communicative rationality of the lifeworld. Rejecting any version of legal positivism which would see the legitimacy of law as residing in the formal procedures of its making, Habermas argues that law's legitimacy turns on whether the deliberative process leading to its making satisfies the discourse principle, whose complement in the political context is the democratic principle: 'only those statutes may claim legitimacy that can meet with the assent of all citizens in a discursive process of legislation that in turn has been legally constituted' (Habermas 1996b, 110). This presupposes a system of basic citizen rights of participation and unconstrained communication, and so contradicts the notion that democracy and rights are fundamentally in tension. Insisting that both democracy and rights are built on the common intersubjective ground of communicative action, Habermas thus also rejects natural rights theories of law's legitimacy. Individual rights, far from existing in a prior state of nature, emerge only as by-products of individuals undertaking to regulate their common life through the legal form; and they give effect to relations of mutual recognition rather than equipping individuals with alienated liberties (see generally Baynes, 1995). It is the facticity of law that enables it to give a binding force to these relations and the norms emerging from them, and so foster solidarity and social integration at a time when the capacity of informal lifeworld institutions to do so has waned.

The legitimacy of state action in general, then, depends on whether the decision process leading up to it complies with the democratic principle and respects the basic rights of individuals. Despite the refinements mentioned above, it might appear that Habermas is offering little more here than a fairly orthodox liberal model of democracy and human rights as the institutional manifestation of his discourse ethics: certainly, his attitude towards liberal democracy has softened considerably over recent years. What equips his model with a more radical edge is the argument that the political and legal systems of the social democratic and constitutional state must be institutionally linked to communication processes in society at large for a fully deliberative politics to be possible. The full realisation of the discourse principle in the political arena thus depends on 'the interplay of institutionalised deliberative processes with informally developed public opinions' (Habermas 1996b, 298), ie with opinions emerging from the informally organised public sphere – extending from the pub to the press – beyond the formal arenas of political action. The judiciary's role is to adapt legal norms to particular cases in a 'dialogic' fashion that takes into account the perspectives of all affected parties. This openness will inevitably, Habermas acknowledges, be in tension with law's facticity, which demands the certainty of a determinate outcome. But unlike the 'postmodernist' legal theorists mentioned above, for whom law's tendency to closure via the 'violence of the verdict' makes justice impossible, Habermas takes the view that law's position as a 'hinge' between system and lifeworld enables it to play a crucial role in securing that outcomes are at least supported by grounds that could meet the requirement of public justification, and so are 'both compulsory and compelling' (Outhwaite 1994, 140). To sum up Habermas's position:

> the socially integrating force of solidarity, which can no longer be drawn solely from sources of communicative action, must develop through widely diversified and more or less autonomous public spheres, as well as through procedures of democratic opinion- and will-formation institutionalised within a constitutional framework. In addition, it should be able to hold its own, in the medium of law, against the two other mechanisms of social integration, money and administrative power. (Habermas 1996b, 299)

Postmodernist theorists in their turn would doubtless focus on the exclusionary operations that are bound up with articulating grounds and establishing their intersubjective validity, but for Habermas, this alone cannot undermine the necessity of defending moral or legal claims by reference to generalisable criteria. In particular, whereas for Habermas too the silencing of 'other' perspectives in the settling of normative disputes raises a problem of legitimacy, it remains necessary to show, by (discursively) rational argument, that this silencing is *itself* unjustified. Further, to take communicative action seriously as the paradigm of reason is to recognise the emergence, out of everyday language use, of specialised spheres of discourse oriented to the redemption of different kinds of validity claim. Postmodernist theorists, by contrast, tend to obliterate the distinctions between discourses through their totalising negation of reason in all its forms. In Habermasian terms, they regard the validity claims that accompany conceptual and normative statements as equally (and ineradicably) reductive and terroristic; and rely upon a discreditable version of aesthetic experience (alluded to by notions such as *différance* and desire) to articulate that 'excess' which is left out of account in the process of normative and conceptual 'calculation'. In this way they pit an undifferentiated and essentially pathological reason against an amorphous force of resistance, and posit the latter as offering the only way out of reason's iron cage. In Habermas's view, however, 'no emancipatory effect results' (Habermas 1996a, 49) from this strategy. His project is one of defending the differentiated process of cultural rationalisation that has produced the divided spheres of modernity, while at the same time seeking to re-integrate these spheres (without conflating them) and heal the rift between their expert cultures (including those associated with law and the formal political structure) and the informal discourses of the lifeworld. In elaborating this project, he has arguably provided the most powerful critique yet of the intellectual forces which have formed cultural-legal theory.

Barron (1993, 80–100 (edited))

This [essay] ... seeks to explore the processes of exclusion upon which the liberal subject of rights is founded and upon which it depends. [It argues that John] Rawls's conception of the 'moral person' ... embodies the features which liberal thought holds to be essential to political agency ... [and] achieves its identity as an autonomous being through separation from what it is not, a separation effected by the imposition of a barrier, the veil of ignorance [see Chapter 15 for an account of Rawl's *A Theory of Justice*]. For Rawls, the veil of ignorance symbolises that which distinguishes the subject appearing within the political domain from what cannot be signified politically: it is the very mechanism of exclusion. As such ... it recalls the repression which Freud identified as constituting the structure of the human ego, and suggests an analogy between this ego and the Rawlsian moral person. Yet the central insight of Freudian psychoanalysis is that the repression upon which the ego is founded also constitutes the unconscious as the locus of whatever is denied access to consciousness. Further, the unconscious cannot be seen as the effect of an absolute exclusion, for it constantly manages to evade the ego's censorship, speaking through and against the latter's 'rational' discourse. [What follows is an exploration of] ... the implications for political theory of this understanding of the subject as perpetually divided against itself, inhabited from within by what it negates. It will be argued that [Louis] Althusser's account of the 'interpellation' of the individual as a subject usefully appropriates Lacan's reading of Freud for a critique of liberalism, for it explicitly equates the liberal political subject with the ego of psychoanalytic theory. Althusser's work therefore invites an exploration of the repressed unconscious that shadows the political 'ego', (the citizen) and its forms of expression, and it would tend to expose the figure of the citizen as the effect of a rigorous policing of political identity and speech that, however vigilant, is never entirely successful. Nonetheless, in identifying the agency of interpellation as ideology – a unified and cohesive discourse – Althusser is driven to insist upon the univocity and stability of the subject as interpellated. He therefore defuses the significance of the unconscious and so leaves out that dimension of political identity which is, in Lacanian terms, 'beyond' interpellation. Ultimately, then, Althusser accepts the claim to integrity and coherence that Rawls and [Ronald] Dworkin make on behalf of the liberal political tradition and the subject that lies at its centre: his argument that the latter functions only as ideology in no way undermines its efficacy as an autonomous and unified agent. A recuperation of those aspects of Lacanian – and Freudian – psychoanalysis that Althusser ignores helps, on the contrary, to expose the precariousness of the liberal subject of rights, the fact that it is inhabited from the start, and threatened always with disruption, by its other.

...

ALTHUSSER AND PSYCHOANALYSIS: SUBJECTIVITY AS MISTAKEN IDENTITY

Marxist critiques of liberal political philosophy have long sought to demonstrate the impossibility of the [Kantian] ideal of autonomy. Within the Marxist tradition, subjectivity is regarded as a function of one's place within the social formation, and the 'bourgeois' individual as an effect, in the last instance, of capitalist relations of production. Hence, to suggest that the 'man' of liberal thought occupies a position from which the social totality can be apprehended and understood disguises the partiality of 'his' perspective: the perspective of the dominant class. As far as some variants of Marxism are concerned, it follows that the consciousness celebrated within liberalism is merely false, a myth woven by ideology, and that the latter in turn is a bourgeois illusion, an empty distortion of real social relations. Yet this position mirrors the assumptions of the liberalism that it sets out to refute, for it too refuses to renounce the possibility of a true consciousness, an entirely unmediated (non-ideological) perception of reality. For Althusser, on the contrary, the subject's relation to its real conditions of existence is never immediate, but is always necessarily an 'imaginary' relation, which is lived through the signifying practices by which societies sustain and reproduce themselves. Ideology therefore always precedes the subject: it is the process by which social meanings, and the forms of human identity that these require, are produced. It is not to be understood as a system of ideas interpreting or representing an existing and independent reality, for it is inscribed within material practices and has material effects. Through the process of 'interpellation', it equips the individual with an imaginary (but lived) self, one which makes choices, adopts beliefs, reflects, acts, initiates relationships with others, and which, in short, believes itself to be at the centre of its own world. It thus enables a recognition by the biological individual of itself as an autonomous subject. But at the same time, ideology hides from that self the conditions of its own emergence, the structures that have produced it. In particular, it disguises the biases that permeate those structures, and their tendency to yield only those subject positions which are appropriate to a particular social formation. Identities, ideas and values which appear to be freely chosen are in reality generated elsewhere – within institutions, rituals and practices that systematically validate and facilitate some possibilities while excluding others.

Law, as far as Althusser is concerned, is one set of institutions and practices through which ideology operates and in which it is concretised: it is an 'ideological state apparatus' which in a capitalist society plays a crucial role in reproducing capitalist relations of exploitation and consolidating the power of the dominant class. It achieves this in part by mobilising the forces of repression against the recalcitrant and the deviant. Yet, as an ideological practice, law must and does construct the figure of the free and responsible agent as a measure against which a refusal of the state's authority can be judged and found wanting. Far from being prior to law and the state, the sovereign will of the individual is generated in the process of law's functioning. It is required by the social relations of capitalism, relations which, because based upon ownership and exchange, depend upon a conception of the subject as one in possession of (as opposed to being identified with) a realm of objects, included in which is the body itself and its labour.

Althusser's deployment of the concept of the imaginary owes much to Lacan's account of the 'mirror stage' in the development of the individual. Indeed, in very general terms, Althusser and the interpreters of Freud unite around an insistence upon the *misrecognition* that is an inevitable part of the subject's perception of itself as autonomous. 'Just as in Althusser's thought the subject of ideology exists only through ignorance of its true conditions, so the paradox of Freud ... is that the subject comes into being only on the basis of a massive repression of its own unconscious determinants'. For Freud, the id produces – and threatens always to dethrone – the ego:

> Unconsciousness is a regular and inevitable phase in the processes constituting our psychical activity; every psychical act begins as an unconscious one, and it may either remain so or go on developing into consciousness, according as it meets with resistance or not.

Yet even 'wishful impulses' that have been repressed can generate effects that reach consciousness and destabilise the efforts of the rational mind to engage in autonomous moral reflection: conscious mental life is thus continually subverted by 'drives' which arise outside it and remain beyond its comprehension or control. The realm to which the ideational representations of these drives are banished – the id – 'knows no judgements of value: no good and evil, no morality'. True, the renunciation of instinctual satisfaction, and the elaboration of moral norms justifying this renunciation, is made possible through the operations of conscience: the 'higher, moral, supra-personal side of human nature'. Yet conscience, or the superego, is nothing more than the internalisation of parental (specifically, paternal) authority: 'As the child was once under a compulsion to obey its parents, so the ego submits to the categorical imperative of its super-ego'. For Freud, the moral voice is merely a trace – albeit a particularly powerful and lasting one – of the same processes that produce the ego: the introjection of the id's abandoned object choices, such that the latter are 'set up again inside the ego' and the ego itself becomes the object of libidinal investment. The superego, 'a special agency in the ego', is a residue of the id's earliest object cathexes – the child's parents. As such, it is the 'heir of the Oedipus complex, and thus it is also the expression of the most powerful impulses and the most important libidinal vicissitudes of the id ...'.

The recognition that desire and its repression, organised within a structure of identifications, is *internally* related to the development of a sense of moral autonomy casts doubts upon some of the central assumptions of liberal political thought. According to the Freudian interpretation of the categorical imperative, for instance, the argument that human beings can release themselves from the effects of socialisation and thereby realise the capacity for moral action refuses to acknowledge the very forces that enable moral action. It fails to recognise that this capacity develops; not despite, but because of the individual's entry into the social order: it is a precipitate of the individual's 'first and most important identification' with other human beings. To equate moral personality with the sovereignty of the ego is therefore to deny the *subjection* (to the cultural norms thereby introjected) that is an inescapable part of every act of moral choice. But further, it is to obscure the constitutive role played by desire in sustaining the structures of social power. In suggesting that desire motivates the identifications forming the superego, 'Freud's work powerfully undercuts traditional philosophical notions that posit the possibility of a transcendental law or rational authority'. Far from being 'higher' than the rational mind, the superego is sustained by the vicissitudes of desire: it 'reaches deep down into the id and for that reason is farther from consciousness than the ego is' (Freud). Moreover, not only does it find its roots in the id, but its efficacy is continually undermined by the latter's recalcitrance. The superego

> issues a command and does not ask whether it is possible for people to obey it. On the contrary, it assumes that a man's ego is psychologically capable of anything that is required of it, that his ego has unlimited mastery over his id. This is a mistake; and even in what are known as normal people the id cannot be controlled beyond certain limits.

If this is so at the level of the individual, then it may also have implications for the way in which the polity is understood, for a community's system of law and the political morality that underpins it can, Freud implies, be represented as the demands of a sort of cultural superego upon the members of that community. As such, it would seem always to be vulnerable to subversion and resistance from a cultural/political 'id', a collective unconscious which is never quite repressed by the association of sovereign subjects that constitutes the political realm. Nonetheless, the potential of orthodox Freudian psychoanalysis for a critique of liberal political morality is ultimately limited by the apparent biologism of Freud's account of the drives which structure the unconscious – for the effect of this is to naturalise the phenomenon of resistance – coupled with Freud's own conception of the proper aim of psychoanalysis: the conquest of the drives by the ego. And although Althusser recognises that potential in general terms, he too ultimately defuses the implications of the unconscious for such a critique. By giving the name 'ideology' to Freud's cultural superego, Althusser suggests that social processes beyond the nuclear family may be responsible for the production of the norms concretised within the structures of the liberal state, and this in turn enables an explanation of the latter as the object and effect of a range of social (as opposed to purely familial) struggles. Yet Althusser's (imaginary) subject submits readily and unproblematically to the demands of this superego: the possibility of rebellion by the unconscious is simply left out of Althusser's account. In this respect, Althusser's deployment of psychoanalytic theory obscures some of its most subversive implications for liberal political thought.

THE RETURN OF THE UNCONSCIOUS: LACANIAN PSYCHOANALYSIS

An assessment of these implications necessitates a closer look at Lacan's rereading of Freud than Althusser's treatment of it can afford. Lacan foregrounds what had remained only partially developed in Freud's work – the importance of narcissistic processes of identification to the formation of the ego – and in so doing reinterprets the Freudian theory of the ego in terms of the Hegelian dialectic of self and other: 'consciousness can grasp itself only through its reflection in and recognition by the other, yet ... an inherent aspiration towards autonomy repugns against the dependency which this relation implies'. In thus emphasising that self-identity is a fragile effect of processes of intersubjective negotiation, which in turn are propelled by a desire for recognition in/ by the other, Lacan rejects Freud's (actual or perceived) tendency to reduce ego development to a series of biologically determined stages, and desire to a derivative of instinctual stimuli. For Lacan, '[t]he social and linguistic orders function in place of the instinctual in human existence'.

Lacan's 'mirror stage' – that phase in the development of the human subject when the child begins to recognise its image in the mirror – inaugurates a process that recurs with every attempt by the subject to represent itself both to itself and to others. The reflection *anticipates*, in the realm of the imaginary, that which has yet to be realised in actuality: the infant's mastery of its body. Captivated by what it sees in the mirror – the body as a unified whole – the child jubilantly identifies with this image, although its own experience of its body is one of fragmentation and dependence. It is through an identification with this ideal-ego, Lacan argues, that the ego itself is constructed as unified and autonomous, the procedure being repeated subsequently through the individual's relationships with other persons. However, the ego thus formed is founded upon an imaginary representation of the subject, which in turn divides the subject against itself. The difference between experience and image is precisely what enables an identification to take effect – it explains the child's fascination with its mirror image – yet the otherness of the image is overlooked in the perception of sameness. Thus, the sense of identity and autonomy that the subject derives from its ego is the deceptive outcome of a persistent denial of the alterity that brings it into being and upon which it depends. The ego, in short, is constituted in and through this otherness, or difference, yet the imaginary is 'an order of representation which misrepresents difference as the image of identity'. Nevertheless, this process of dissimulation is never entirely successful. The unified ego itself 'is the means by which the individual retains an active memory of his earliest sense of physical disarray', and aggressiveness is the behavioural manifestation of this 'return' of the fragmented body in the form of fantasies of mutilation and disintegration.

If the imaginary order effects an alienation of the subject from itself, then a second 'splitting' of the subject occurs with its entry into the symbolic order through the acquisition of language. The subject of the statement, the 'I' which appears in language, purports to reflect the true subject, the subject of enunciation, the 'I' which makes use of language in order to represent itself. Yet (like the child's mirror image), it is never entirely adequate to the task. Language can only be said to represent the subject of enunciation if it is understood as a set of correspondences between signifiers (sound-images) and signifieds (concepts), the latter being prior to, and determining, the former. But for Lacan, language, on the contrary, is a system of differential relations between signifiers. As one commentator explains ...

> [a]nyone who goes in search of meaning at its source, or in its essential forms, has no choice but to travel by way of language, and at every moment on this journey variously connected signifiers extend to the horizon in all directions. When the signified seems finally to be within reach, it dissolves at the explorer's touch into yet more signifiers.

Recognition of the subject can only be achieved through language, yet a subject constituted through its combinatory 'play' can never be the self-identical entity presupposed by the imaginary order. The operations of language always leave an irreducible residue, something which is unpresentable; hence, whatever the subject is represented as being will be characterised by a lack, an absence. It is this very lack that constitutes the existence of the subject of enunciation as a desiring subject, and that motivates the continuing flux of the signifying process. The truth of the subject is therefore to be found not in the signified but in the spaces between signifiers, simultaneously fading and becoming through a paradoxical juncture of retroactivity and anticipation. 'There where it was just now, there where it was for a while, between an extinction that is still glowing and a birth that is retarded, "I" can come into being and disappear from what I say' (Lacan).

Lacan interprets the separation of the ego from the unconscious in terms of this split between the subject of the statement and the subject of enunciation. The unconscious, characterised, as Freud had demonstrated, by the primary processes of condensation and displacement, exhibits the same polysemy and the same sliding of meaning as the signifying function itself. However, the very existence of the subject depends upon its recognition as such by other subjects, and this in turn requires the assumption of a site of intentionality within language – language here being understood as a set of determinate meanings, existing for a subject who intends those meanings. Hence, the subject is forced into a separation from the movement of the primary processes: conscious thought (the secondary process characteristic of the ego) is the outcome of this separation. So too is the resolution of the Oedipus complex: the acquisition of a place within culture is the child's 'reward' for its acceptance of paternal authority and its renunciation of desire for the mother. However, in Lacan's account of the Oedipus complex, the child's submission is not to a real, biological father, but to the Other, the symbolic father, the author of the law governing the symbolic order: '[i]t is in the *name-of-the-father* that we must recognise the support of the symbolic function, which, from the dawn of history, has identified his person with the figure of the law'. In identifying with the position of this father, the child identifies with the possessor of the phallus, the signifier of that which satisfies desire, or, in Lacanian terms, of that which controls the signifying process itself. The superego is born through the internalisation of the symbolic father's authority, and it is through the superego that the infant's imaginary relation with the (m)other is disrupted: desire for the (m)other, or, in Lacanian terms, for the recognition that the (m)other can bestow, is repressed and displaced onto the phallus. The 'resolution' of the Oedipus complex thus consists in an acknowledgement of the phallus as the ultimate guarantee of meaning/identity/recognition, of the mother's (and the child's) lack of the phallus, of the father's possession of it, and of the prospect that through introjecting the father's authority the father's the child too will eventually gain access to it.

The subject of the signified/statement emerges at this point, yet the repression which brings it into being also establishes the unconscious as the subject of the signifier/ enunciation. It follows from Lacan's conception of the symbolic order that the Other 'does not exist': the position of the Other, and with it the phallus, is unattainable, which is to say that the desire for recognition, for a stable position within language, is insatiable. The unconscious is the locus of this desire. It is therefore the unconscious that guarantees the ceaseless motion of the signifying process, its discourse manifesting itself in the inevitably metaphoric and metonymic structure of conscious thought and speech through which repressed signifiers constantly interfere with, subvert, and evade the censorship of, the subject of the signified. In this sense, it 'provides the most rigorous criticism of the presupposition of a consistent, fully finished subject'. Yet in a manner anticipated precisely by the mirror stage, the ego denies the inevitability of the gap between the subject reflected in language and that which exceeds representation. Just as the mirror stage involves a misrecognition by the child of itself as autonomous in relation to its body, the acquisition of language permits the speaking subject to misrecognise itself as the author and master of its speech (possessor of the phallus), and speech itself as the transparent medium of its relations with others. For Lacan, psychoanalysis, far from seeking to strengthen the alienating and inert form of the ego, should aim at helping the analysand to accept his/ her desire, and the lack of which it is a manifestation, and relinquish the ultimately self-destructive commitment to plenitude and autonomy.

Beyond interpellation

It is precisely the operations of the unconscious that are obscured by Rawls's invocation of the original position in *A Theory of Justice*. Clearly, to the extent that the moral person describes an essential human nature, the original position signals Rawls's commitment to an ontology which refuses the possibility of the unconscious altogether, for the moral person is simply the ideal-ego, a (mirror) image of the ego, and the basis for the subject's perception of itself as a unified entity, determined solely by its capacity for rational and autonomous action. In Lacanian terms, the original position can only be the realm of the imaginary. Yet for the 'later' Rawls ... the original position is to be understood as reflecting a truth which is 'political, not metaphysical': it is not to be taken as representing the essential form of human agency as such but merely the vision of political agency, and of the public realm, that is immanent within 'the political institutions of a constitutional democratic regime and the public traditions of their interpretation'. The apparent shift in Rawls's position here, towards an acknowledgement that the identity of the political subject is an effect of political practices and the ideas concretised within them, is reminiscent of the progression of Lacan's work from a preoccupation with the formation of the ego in the register of the imaginary to a concern with language as constitutive of the subject. Rawls's later work clearly attests to the constitutive force of the 'symbols' through which the political domain is organised. Moreover, the condition of access to this domain is analogous to that described by Lacan in relation to the subject's entry into culture. For Rawls, the position of author (of the law), which is the original position, is occupied by the moral person, and the citizen is brought into being through an identification with this author, the bearer of the 'phallus' (the capacity for autonomous action). And since that identification in turn can only be achieved through submission to the restrictions imposed by the veil of ignorance, the latter effectively sets up the condition that must be fulfilled if the subject is to 'signify' within the normative order of institutionalised politics. The desire for (political) recognition, that is, propels the subject into an assumption of the identity of the citizen, and the person attains a place within the political order only to the extent that he or she can achieve this identification.

For Rawls, however, this process is inherently unproblematic. Unlike Lacan, for whom the perception of a stable and unified subject position within language is an effect of *méconnaissance,* sustained only by the operations of the ego, and continually interrupted by the playfulness of language (the discourse of the unconscious) itself, Rawls regards the signifying practices that constitute liberal political culture as capable of being 'organised' into a coherent whole. Hence, the acknowledgement that the political subject is discursively produced does not operate to shatter its imaginary unity: the agency of its production, the 'language' of public life, is itself unified. The 'fundamental intuitive idea' structuring these institutions and practices is that of the political community as an association of free and equal persons who are the architects of the norms by which they are governed. Therefore, as far as Rawls is concerned, the only conception of political agency that can be said to be true (i.e., publicly recognised as true) for a constitutional democratic regime is that of the citizen as author.

It is this notion that Althusser exposes as the imaginary effect of the process of interpellation, one which operates not to reveal but to obscure the true conditions of the individual's existence in a liberal capitalist society. For Althusser, what Rawls insists on describing as 'our public political culture ... the *shared* fund of implicitly recognised basic ideas and principles' is an ideological apparatus which disguises its true function – the reproduction of capitalist relations of production and of the dominance of the ruling class within capitalism – and enables the individual to misrecognise him/herself in its specular structure as the author of its laws and underlying norms. Nevertheless, although the influence of Lacanian psychoanalysis is evident here, Althusser's reading of Lacan's oeuvre as a whole is highly selective. For Lacan, there can be *no* position 'behind' language which would constitute its point of origination – the author, prior to difference, fixed, stable: that which can control the movement of the signifier. Yet, while Rawls reserves this position for the autonomous individual, Althusser seems to permit 'the ruling class' to occupy it in relation to ideology. Language is reduced to ideology, and the latter in turn is conceived of as a seamless web of coherent meanings: 'the ideology by which [the ISA's] function is always in fact unified, despite its diversity and its contradictions, *beneath the ruling ideology* which is the ideology of "the ruling class"'. Consequently, Althusser can recognise no split between the subject interpellated in ideology and that which exceeds interpellation, the unconscious: in place of a separation, he posits an absolute alienation of the subject in ideology. His silence with respect to the unconscious, in turn, is an effect of his dismissal of the Lacanian real, that 'kernel resisting symbolic integration-disolution' which is the object-cause of desire. Althusser focuses upon Lacan's account of the formation of an autonomous ego through the subject's identification with an imaginary representation of itself in the symbolic forms by which capitalist social relations are sustained. Yet he sees the subject interpellated in 'language' (ideology) as simply that which the imaginary represents it to be – unified, self-contained, and self-identical. In this respect, Althusser ultimately allies himself with none other than Rawls.

Althusser and Rawls concur in conceiving of the liberal political subject as one produced by, rather than being prior to, the institutions, practices and discourses of the liberal state; Dworkin performs a similar manoeuvre in relation to the subject inscribed within law. Indeed, like Althusser, Rawls acknowledges that there may be a split between the public identity which is allotted to the person in law and his/her lived experience: the veil of ignorance serves as a metaphor for the boundary separating the 'public' from the merely 'private'. But further, Althusser, Dworkin and Rawls all unite around a conception of that (public) subject as the stable, unified, non-contradictory effect of these processes of 'interpellation', and of the discourse of rights as a coherent and unitary medium in which it addresses its demands to an imaginary counterpart, an 'other' which is nothing more than a reflection of itself. To adapt Lacan's insights to an analysis of the political domain is, however, to recognise that the splitting that accompanies the construction of the subject of rights, the subject of the statement, at the same time produces the subject of enunciation, and the desire which exceeds the fulfilment of (political) demand. In other words, the very process by which the citizen is constituted and inscribed constantly generates something akin to a political 'unconscious', identities and voices which are repressed within, but nonetheless ineradicable from, the categories and structures of liberalism: the 'beyond of the demand' which is at the same time 'hollowed within' it (Lacan). In the words of Zizek,'[i]f the Name-of-the-Father functions as the agency of interpellation, ... desire ... marks a certain limit at which every interpellation necessarily fails'. The final section will sketch the terrain occupied by this 'other scene', and argue that its continuing significance lies in its disruption of the liberal citizen's capacity to exhaust the meaning of political identity and political expression.

The place of the other

Lacan's account of the denials upon which the ego is founded suggests an approach to the category of the citizen that asks *how* it achieves its unity and identity: what is excluded in the process of its construction? It draws attention to the negations upon which Rawls's vision of the political subject is founded, and which are structured by his insistence upon the autonomy of the rational will as the characteristic feature of the moral person. The citizen is autonomous, not heteronomous; unified, not plural; static, not shifting; individual, not collective; abstract, not material. Above all, however, Rawls's moral person is characterised by its will, rather than its bodily existence. The body here can be understood as a metaphor for everything that the Rawlsian subject is not: it signifies 'embodiment', that which situates the person in time and space, equips the person with a perspective on the world which is necessarily limited, though mobile, and differentiates the person from others. Bodily characteristics also link individuals with one another: it is by appealing to shared physical attributes such as gender, skin colour and age that people identify with others in the context of social groups. Finally, the body is the site of desire, impulse and sentiment: 'the passions', as Hobbes would have put it. The will, on the other hand, is disembodied and transcendent, and thus stands outside of and opposed to everything the body represents. Action originates with the will, which thus frees the person from the determinations of bodily existence. It reduces the heterogeneous needs, inclinations and perspectives of the body to the unity of a personality: the subject realises itself as a subject by conquering the body through its capacity for rational choice and responsibility. It is individual, yet possessed by everyone in the same way, and thus enables, while being prior to, relationships with others.

It is the existence of a barrier separating those attributes which are proper to the citizen from those which are not that constitutes citizenship as a mechanism, not of inclusion, but of closure. Given that it defines the characteristics that qualify the person for participation in public life, the category of citizenship marks out a boundary between that which properly belongs within the realm of politics and that which is eliminated from it: as Iris Young in particular has shown, it purports to determine who can be a political subject, and thereby guarantees that only those issues appropriate to that subject, as defined, can count as political issues. To attribute the status of citizenship to the individual rather than to the group, for instance, is to refuse the notion that identity is an achievement of intersubjective negotiation: it is to represent the individual as prior to any groups to which s/he belongs; the group as, at most, the result of an act of choice that leaves the self intact; and the needs that groups take to be definitive of their shared identity as nothing more than claims of right asserted by their individual members. Again, the identification of the individual in terms of the will rather than the body has the effect of disqualifying from the public realm those who are deemed incapable of rational thought and action because determined by the bodily and affective aspects of existence. Feminist analyses of the public/private distinction have explained the denial of political rights to women until relatively recently in the history of the liberal state as an effect of precisely this antinomy between reason and its other. More fundamentally, feminists have argued that the exclusion of women from citizenship persists, albeit not in formal legal terms, by the association of traits culturally defined as masculine with the capacities that privilege the citizen as a universal subject. Thus the public realm of citizens achieves its unity and universality only by defining the civil individual in opposition to that which is identified as feminine: everything which embraces the body.

It is as a rational person, as pure will, abstracted from the empirical conditions of lived experience, that one is 'capable ... of a sense of justice' (Rawls) and therefore entitled to a political voice. The freedom of the individual citizen, which is the project of liberal politics, is articulated in terms of liberation from external constraints, and the discourse of rights is the language in which this project is properly expressed. Yet Dworkin's account of the political subject as a subject of rights can be understood as calculated to censor rather than to enable the articulation of claims, in that it dispels those claims which are appropriate to a subject that falls on the wrong side of the divide separating the rational autonomous citizen from what it is supposed not to be: a subject of need or desire. Further, this censorship, since it is the very condition of the subject's political 'speech', cannot itself be signified within the idiom of liberal discourse. The perspective of the universal citizen is deemed to be equally available to all, and from that perspective, politics 'begins' only when the will of the individual is, coerced; when the capacity for rational action is interfered with in some determinate way. The processes that constitute both the rational citizen and its rejected others remain inaccessible to explicitly political intervention.

The free, rights-bearing individual functions in liberal political theory as the pre-eminent 'anchoring point' within the montage of signifiers that constitute the political domain. By means of this (phallic) category, 'the political institutions of a constitutional democratic regime and the public traditions of their interpretation' (Rawls) can be totalised into a coherent structure of meaning and equipped with a defining essence. Yet Lacan's conception of the symbolic order suggests that meaning cannot be regarded as immanent within a given discursive field, but is rather a retroactive effect of the relational interplay between signifiers, an effect, moreover, which is illusory in its consistency. The node around which these elements are articulated – the original position, the place of the Other/Author – is not the repository of truth, but another signifier, itself implicated in the play of differences: the embodiment of a fundamental lack. The fantasy of the veil of ignorance, through which the closure of the political realm can be achieved and the latter represented as coherent and complete, is the screen which masks this lack, represses everything that recalls it, and 'sutures' the insufficiency of the signifier by displacing the lack to another place. Yet the attempt to encircle the real place of the political reveals not a presence but a failure of representation, and it is through this failure that 'desire' makes itself known. The symptoms of desire, in this context, manifest themselves in the irruption of political subjectivities that cannot be captured by the category of the citizen, and by forms of political and legal expression which exceed the logic of right: the subversive power of the repressed other of liberalism consists precisely, then, in its 'refusal of a unitary construct of citizenship as exhaustive of the political tasks of the present'. The attempt to argue for the institutionalisation of a reworked notion of citizenship that could accommodate these identities and claims, and for mechanisms and structures within or linked with the state that might entertain them, now constitutes an identifiable trend within postliberal political theory. Yet to eradicate the symptom is an impossibility, for it is an inevitable expression of the antagonism that constitutes, sustains and finally limits the discursive field of the political. Lacanian psychoanalysis demands a constant awareness of this surplus of the real over every attempt at symbolisation; it requires a coming to terms with what remains always beyond accommodation; and it serves as a reminder that every description of the just society bears witness to the unpresentable. Justice, in short, has no guarantee. It 'remains to be attained: it is ahead of us' (Lyotard).

Douzinas and Warrington (1994, Chapter 4 (edited))

... If modernity is an era of a profound 'moral catastrophe', modern law, both as an institution and as the theoretical solution to the weakening of authority and of the social bond, has been the field where the abandonment of ethics has been carried out in its most radical form. Jurisprudence has based the specificity of the law in the programmatic exclusion of all considerations of value and substance from its domain. But at the same time, the law is proposed as the main substitute for the absent value consensus and the emptied normative realm. We are well aware of both the de-ethicalisation of law, of the banning of morality from legal operations and of the demand and expectation that law should become the public face of an absent morality. For the bulk of modern jurisprudence, the law is public and objective; its posited rules are structurally homologous to ascertainable 'facts' that can be found and verified in an 'objective' manner, free from the vagaries of individual preference, prejudice and ideology. Its procedures are technical and its personnel neutral. Any contamination of law by value will compromise its ability to turn social and political conflict into manageable technical disputes about the meaning and applicability of preexisting public rules. Morality as much as politics must be kept at a distance; indeed the main requirement of the rule of law in its contemporary version of legality is that all subjective and relative value should be excluded from the operation of the legal system. This insulation of law from ethico-political considerations allegedly makes the exercise of power impersonal and guarantees the equal subjection of citizens and state officials to the dispassionate requirements of the rule of rules as opposed to the rule of men. And as adjudication is presented in common law jurisdictions as the paradigm instance of law, the demand for justice is equated with the moral neutralisation of the judicial process. In formal terms, justice becomes identified with the administration of justice and the requirements and guarantees of legal procedure, and the 'interests of justice' are routinely interpreted as the interests of adjudication. In substantive terms, justice loses its critical character. The identification of justice with legality may have a long historical pedigree since the coming of modernity; this institutional-formal conception of justice, however, cannot act as critique but solely as critical apology for the extant legal system. Justice has changed from a utopian, even mystical tool of denunciation of personal and sociopolitical wickedness into the key legitimatory theme of modern law.

...

... The separation of law and morals means that, for the jurisprudence of orthodoxy, morality has vacated the normative universe, which is now exclusively inhabited by the prescriptions of the legislator and the decrees of the institution. Consequently, the main ethical concept and concern of law and jurisprudence, justice, is not directly involved with moral values.

... This predominantly positivistic attitude is taken a (sophisticated) step further in the writings of Dworkin. The law is no longer just about rules à la Hart, and certainly it is not the outcome of the unlimited will and power of the omnipotent legislator à la Austin. Law's empire includes principles and policies and its operation involves interpretative acts of judges who are invited to construct creatively the 'right answer' to legal problems; to do so judges must develop and apply political and moral theories that should present the law in the best possible light and create an image of the community as integrity. Morality (and moral philosophy) now enters the law and is properly recognised as an inescapable component of judicial hermeneutics. But its task is to legitimise judicial practice by showing the law to be the perfect narrative of a happy community. Morality is no longer a set of subjective and relative values nor is it a critical standard against which acts of legal and judicial power can be judged. The law is assumed to possess an internal integrity and coherence that allows the construction of public and quasi-objective principles of morality which can then be used as its underlying grammar and help resolve 'hard cases'.

Law's morality, as found by the judge with the help of moral philosophy, becomes the guarantee that the law never runs out. If a right answer exists, it can be discovered in every case through the mobilisation of the morality that law's internal criteria of coherence yield. Judges are never left to their own devices; the dreaded supplement of judicial discretion (in other words, the individual morality of the judge) that Hart had reluctantly admitted at the cost of endangering rational completeness, coherence and the closure of law is firmly kept outside. Dworkin seems prepared to reintroduce moral consideration to law. But his theory is the last step in the juridification of morality and in the assertion of the moral legitimacy of legalism, common symptoms of the process of de-ethicalisation of the law. The radical gap in the normative universe created by the strict separation between legality and morality and the reduction of ethics to the private and subjective is filled by the discourse of law, as the lighthouse on the way to universal and objective truth. But for those who want to challenge the dominant political theory; for those unrepresented, unrepresentable and excluded from the 'integrated' community; for those who experience the law not as rationality, rights and justifications but as victims of the exercise of power and as targets of legal force; for all those 'others', law's empire has no place.

... Against ... the complacency of orthodoxy ... postmodern jurisprudence insists that morality and justice are not identical with legality nor can they be simply reduced to the following of legal principle and procedures. Acts of power cannot be criticised solely according to other acts of power. Justice is either a critical concept or it is totally redundant if not positively harmful for jurisprudence by encouraging an unquestioning attitude to law. But is there a critical conception of justice and morality that can be used to arbitrate between the various conflicting versions of the good or of ethical action after the modern attack on the Good and the postmodern attack on the power of reason?

...

[Emmanuel] Levinas's ethics is a wholly different enterprise from that of traditional moral philosophy and jurisprudence. It calls for the re-ethicalisation of law, but the ethical substance to be reintroduced or reactivated in the body of law has nothing in common with the moralism of moral philosophy that exclusively builds collections of rules and principles.

Levinas argues that western philosophy and ethics share a common attitude towards the world which reduces the distance between self and other and returns the different to the same ... Respect for the other is the unconditioned bedrock of Kantian morality. But this respect is motivated by the fact that the other, too, obeys the law and thus becomes a facet of my own respect for the law. I perceive the other as a free subject to the extent that she is governed like myself by the moral law and I offer her my respect for her obedience which is also the best available evidence of the operation of the law.

...

The ethics of alterity ... always starts with the other and challenges the various ways in which the other has been reduced to the same ... The other comes first ... In the philosophy of alterity, the other can never be reduced to the self or the different to the same. Nor is the other an instance of otherness or of some general category.

...

The sign of another is the face. The face is unique ... In its uniqueness, the face gets hold of me with an ethical grip, I find myself beholden to, obligated to, in debt to, the other person, prior to any contracts or agreements about who owes what to whom ... In the face-to-face, I am fully, immediately and irrevocably responsible for the other who faces me ... The only possible answer to the ethical imperative is 'an immediate respect for the other himself ... because it does not pass through the neutral element of the universal, and through respect, in the Kantian sense for the law'.

...

The appeal of the other is direct, concrete and personal; it is addressed to me and I am the only one who can answer it. Against the claims of moral philosophy, this demand does not depend on universal reason or general law but on the concrete historical and empirical encounter with the other. It is this situated encounter and unrepeatable, unique demand which assigns me to morality and makes me a bound and ethical subject. Our relationship is necessarily non-symmetrical and non-reciprocal as her unique demand is addressed to me and me alone. Equity is not equality but absolute dissymmetry.

...

Let us summarise our argument. Modernity, in destroying any generally acceptable conception of value or virtue and in disassociating ethics from law, makes justice a central concern of political theory and the main area of contention of practical politics ... Justice becomes a key concern for social theory and secondarily for jurisprudence but it is no longer about ethics, either in the sense of the good or in the sense of 'boundedness' to the other. It is either the justice of the social contract, based on the claim that obligation is binding only if all subjects rationally agree to it; or, in law, it becomes a derivative of the morality of the Kantian imperative and combines self-legislation with the rational form of moral law ... [This] ends up in the blatant assertion that formal legality equals justice and identifies justice with the administration of justice. We need to reintroduce ethics in law but traditional moral philosophy has proved insufficient. At this turning-point, the ethics of Levinas can provide the initial inspiration for imagining an Other justice.

The ethics of alterity is a challenge to all attempts to reduce the other to self and the different to the same. The ethical arises in relation to a point of exteriority that cannot be included in any of the totalities and systematicities that philosophy and law build. Moral consciousness is not an experience of values but the anarchic (*an-arche*, without beginning or principle) access to a domain of responsibility and the obligated answer to the other's demand. Unlike moral philosophy and applied ethics, the ethics of alterity is not concerned to legislate moral codes or to discuss and apply norms of morality. Unlike jurisprudence, it does not attempt to legitimise the operations of the law but to justify the law, to bring it before the altar of justice. This is not the traditional moralistic ethics of deontologists or the consequential and calculative morality of utilitarians. Levinasian ethics ... is an origin before any origin, an ethics of ethics and the law of law; it is the opening upon which rises individual and community and which grounds the moral stimulus, the legality of laws and the politics of community.

Political philosophy and jurisprudence have based their theories on the assumption of the immorality of human nature. The law, too, as the secular successor of religion and jurisprudence, as the heir to theology, has insisted that pre-legal human nature is morally ignorant, inept or plainly evil while the law is the embodiment of morality. The ethics of alterity, on the other hand, starts from the opposite premise, namely that the ineradicably intersubjective nature of consciousness points in the direction of an innate human ethicity.

... It is not the existence or operation of rules that creates feelings of obligation, of 'ought' and 'ought not', nor is it the normative horizon that generates the 'internal aspect' of human behaviour. The good is not the outcome of the operation of the law but precedes all laws, norms and principles. In this sense, the good is the name for the radical ethical turning of human consciousness to the other which creates a feeling of duty before and beyond any rules and norms. It is this ethical attitude that establishes the possibility of all law and it is the relationship to the other that lies behind its – often unjust – crystallisation in rules. This attitude is characterised by unconditioned concern and care for the other which is not based on calculation of reward or fear of sanction. This disinterested concern resembles the Kantian respect for the law, but unlike the latter, it has the other as its exclusive target. It starts from the other's demand and finishes with its satisfaction. It does not follow the contours of traditional natural law; there is no claim that the world is organised in morally significant ways that allow us to learn our duty through our rational comprehension of its purposeful patterns. No law follows from the observation of nature and no law can be discovered exclusively through even the most elaborate rational deliberation. The concern for the other is innate, it needs no excuse or justification, it allows no choice and asks to be acted upon immediately.

... But how can we move from the ethics of responsibility to the law? What is the relevance of a discourse that claims pre-ontological and pre-rational status and emphasises the uniqueness of the face for a legality that has universalistic pretensions and bases its empire upon the rationality of judgment and the thematisation of people and circumstances? If the ethical response is based on the contingent appearance of a face in need, can there be a justice that moves beyond the ethicity of the contingent, thus helping the re-ethicalisaton of the law? Can the ethics of alterity be generalised and thus become the justice of the law? Does the justice of the law derive from the unabiding hostility of one for another and the need to restrain violence or does it derive from ethics and responsibility? These are the key questions that we have to answer.

The ethics of alterity is unequivocal; the sense of responsibility, the 'internal' point of view speaks to me and commands me, the 'should' and 'should not' that lie at the base of all law come from the proximity of one for another, from the fact that we are involved and implicated as we are faced and addressed by the other. In my proximity to the other, within the law or outside of it, I am preoccupied by the absolute asymmetry and I find myself in an irreplaceable and irreversible relation of substitution. The ethical critique of the law has as its main aim to alert law to its ethical significance ... The ethical critique of law is conducted in the name of another justice. To be sure, the law is about calculation and systematisation, it regulates and totalises the demands that are put before it. The law translates these requests in the universalisable language of rights, legal entitlements and procedural proprieties and synchronises them, makes them appear contemporaneous and comparable. Almost by definition and necessity the law seems to forget the difference of the different and the otherness of the other. To say, therefore, that the law begins as ethics, as the infinite, non-totalisable and non-regulated moment of the encounter with another, sounds counterfactual. And yet it is on the basis of ... the 'legal as ethical' that we can visualise a politics of law that disturbs the totalising tendency of the legal system. Such a politics would allow the other to reappear both as the point of exteriority and transcendence that precludes the closure of ontology and as the excluded and unrepresentable of political and legal theory.

We should start with critique. Law and jurisprudence share fully the cognitive and moral attitudes of modernity. Cognitively, the law knows the world to the extent that it subjects it to its regulative operations. For the jurisprudence of modernity, the law and the world are potentially coextensive. The legal system has all the necessary resources to translate non-legal phenomena into law's arcane discourse and thus exercise its regulative function ... In moral terms, on the other hand, the law is declared free of any ambition and is assigned to the technical administration of the world and of justice. But as we saw this moral indifference or impotence of law results in the central paradox of modern political theory and jurisprudence: ethics is absent from law but social theory becomes obsessed with justice. Ancient and medieval theories linked ethics and the good with the just organisation of the community and thus facilitated the mediation between individual ethical responses and the structures of social power. And as we now move from the certainties of modernity to the postmodern condition, the demand for an ethics becomes the most important theoretical and practical priority.

The second major criticism of law and jurisprudence concerns the form of personhood that the law makes central to its operations. In existential terms, the subject of legal and contractual rights and agreements stands at the centre of the universe and asks the law to enforce his entitlements without great concern for ethical considerations and without empathy for the other. If the legal person is an isolated and narcissistic subject who perceives the world as a hostile place to be either used or fended against through the medium of rights and contracts, (s)he is also disembodied, genderless, a strangely mutilated person. The other as legal subject is a rational being with rights, entitlements and duties like ourselves. We expect to be treated equally with the other and reciprocity of entitlement and obligation is placed at the base of the legal mentality. But this conception of justice as fairness must necessarily reduce the concreteness of the other, it must minimise the differences of need and desire and emphasise the similarities and homologies between the subjects. The moral worthiness of the other's demand is to be sought more in what self and other share than in those differences and specificities that make the other a concrete historical being.

The other of law is not dissimilar in its main characteristics from the Rawlsian moral agent. It would be useful to examine briefly Benhabib's important feminist critique of Rawlsian theory which is of great relevance for law too. The Rawlsian self in the original position is blindfolded, like many artistic representations of justice, by 'the veil of ignorance'. She does not know her class, her status, her fortune and ability or her intelligence and strength, nor does she have any conception of the good or a rational plan of life. Behind this absurd hypothesis lies the concern of moral philosophy for the interests of the other. The – temporary and heuristic – destruction of identity puts self in a position of reversibility with the others, thus enabling the agent to consider their interests while still acting as a rational egoist, since she cannot tell what her exact state in life is. Such a huge abstraction from what a real self is and from how moral argument operates is necessary to sustain the Kantian claim of universality of the moral law. The subject of concern of moral philosophy is a 'generalised other' with whom we relate through public and institutional norms of formal equality and reciprocity. The other is a representative of humankind and as such dignified and worthy of respect as much as self. But as Benhabib notes, while such individuals may have the capacity of agency, they are not human selves at all.

> Identity does not refer to my potential for choice alone, but to the actuality of my choices, namely to how I, as a finite, concrete, embodied individual, shape and fashion the circumstances of my birth and family, linguistic, cultural and gender identity into a coherent narrative that stands as my life's story.... The self is not a thing, substrate but the protagonist of a life's tale. The conception of selves that can be individuated prior to their moral ends is incoherent.

The proper moral standpoint of the 'concrete other', by contrast, is based on norms of 'equity and complementary reciprocity: each is entitled to expect and to assume from the other forms of behaviour through which the other feels recognised and confirmed as a concrete, individual being with specific needs, talents and capacities'. The veil of ignorance and all such generalising by obscuring the concreteness of the other, destroy her identity and, as they lack the necessary criteria for individuation, they cannot distinguish between self and other.

These criticisms are equally valid in law. Legal rules ensure equality before the law and guarantee the freedom of the parties. But this equality is only formal: it necessarily ignores the specific history, motive and need that the litigant brings to the law in order to administer the calculation of the rule and the application of the measure. Similarly with legal freedom: it is the freedom to accede to the available repertoire of legal forms and rights, the freedom to be what the law has ordained, accompanied by the threat that opting out is not permitted, that disobedience to a legal norm is disobedience to the rule of law *tout court* and that life outside the legal form ceases. We examined above how legal rules and their mentality are strangely amoral as they promise to replace ethical responsibility with the mechanical application of predetermined and morally neutral rules and justice with the administration of justice. But there is more: moral philosophy in its ontological imperialism needs and creates the generalised other. The law, on the other hand, sharing the preoccupation to abstract and universalise, turns concrete people into generalised legal subjects. But the legal subject, too, is a fiction and the natural (legal) subject is infinitely more fictitious than the corporate. The difference between the fictions of Rawls and those of the law is that the legal subject is a persona, a mask, veil or blindfold put on real people who, unlike the abstractions of moral philosophy, hurt, feel pain and suffer. It is doubly important in law and jurisprudence, therefore, to remove the mask from the face of the subject and the blindfold from the eyes of justice. But is there an ethical residue in the law behind the all-concealing veil of formal legality?

In *Otherwise than Being*, Levinas (1991) introduced the distinction between saying and said as the main metaphor for the opposing fields of ethics and ontology. The opposition is not between two aspects of the same phenomenon nor is it a totalisable dialectical relationship. The two are both connected and radically separate: every said proceeds from an act of saying radically turned and addressed to an other. But as soon as saying becomes said/heard, it takes the form of a constative or descriptive proposition or judgment in which a subject is assigned to a predicate (y is z). The constative proposition, Levinas's 'said', states truth, it is public, generalisable and objective; the said enters the language of ontology, which is concerned with the meaning of beings and thematises concepts and entities whose essence belong to the presence of Being. But ontological philosophy has forgotten that all speculation on Being and beings in verbal form is always addressed to other(s). For philosophy, the exclusive domain of intervention is the said or the text. The act of saying, of speaking/hearing, the performance which takes place diachronically and involves at least two in a face-to-face has not been of much concern. Indeed, structuralist linguistics examines the act of enunciation but only after it reduces it to a said, a description of a state of affairs that has lost its radical nature as a saying that happens here and now. The time of the said is synchronous, unified, its order is linear, an orderly succession of past, present and future points along a continuum ... [T]his is also the time of (legal) interpretation. The time of saying, on the other hand, is diachronic: a dispersed arrangement of unrepeatable moments, the authentic time of the event when it happens, in its discontinuous, unpredictable seriality. This is the time of ethics.

Levinas uses the auditory metaphor to emphasise the difference between an ethics of alterity and western ontology, which has used the all-seeing eye (*theorein, theories:* to see, the gaze) as its main symbol and organ. But the metaphor helps us identify a key area of law that seems still to acknowledge the importance of alterity. The law recognises within its own procedures and attempts to impose to a certain extent upon decision-makers and judges the principle of speaking/hearing: *audi alteram partem,* let the other speak, before judging another give her a hearing. This is the first principle of natural justice ... The injunction that the judge should hear the other speak can first be explained as a requirement of logic. If we look at criminal law and procedure, intention has been defined as a requirement of foreseeability, of prognosis and acceptance of one's acts. As in all other areas, here too, the law has eliminated aspects of value and the good by addressing all such matters as questions of capacity or by reducing them to the formal question of whether the defendant acted with the intention to bring about the consequences of his actions. The criminal subject autonomously calculates, wills and causes the acts for which he takes responsibility but has no moral existence that is relevant to the question of guilt. To the extent that law's theory of action distinguishes between intentional and unpredictable or unintended consequences, hearing the litigant is a main prerequisite for categorising his actions and determining responsibility. Legal procedure cannot operate with the litigant silent. This requirement may have now turned into a formality as the civil litigant in particular will be heard in person only rarely; yet the legitimacy of adjudication is largely based on the oral character of the procedure.

But, second, the *audi* rule shows the law concerned to hear the concrete person who comes before it, rather than to calculate and adjudicate the general qualities and characteristics of the abstracted legal person. Not to give the other a hearing is to deny her humanity, to treat her as someone without the basic qualities of moral worth and capacity. Even more, the demand to hear the concrete other undermines the persistent claim of the law that persons must be judged exclusively according to their classification in broad categories and be treated equally as instances of the application of general rules. The *audi* rule turns the ethical obligation to treat the other as a full and unique person into a logical prerequisite of all judgment.

...

But can the recognition of the ethical grounding of law help us approach the demand for justice in the contemporary legal institution? The ethical relationship concerns the encounter between self and other. The law, on the other hand, introduces the demands and expectations of the third party. When someone comes to the law, he is already involved in a situation of disagreement or conflict with at least one more person; the judge will often have to balance the conflicting requests of two others. Indeed, the judge himself, seen from the perspective of the litigants, is a third person, whose action removes the dispute from the domain of interpersonal hostility and places it within the confines of the institution. In all instances, the law appears to be concerned not just with 'I' and 'Thou', but with the public aspect of the intersubjective encounter which is mandated by the existence of the third ... Thus, my ethical response to the other who faces me is also and inevitably an address to the community. 'The other is from the first the brother of all the other men' (Levinas). But the co-existence of 'all the other men' places a limit on my infinite responsibility towards the other.

Because the third is always present in my encounter with the other, the law is implicated in every attempt to act morally and the need for justice arises....

For Levinas, 'law' refers to the Torah, and his Talmudic readings give a moving analysis of the unconditional acceptance Jews owe to the gift of law, an acceptance that precedes any examination and a commitment to action before any understanding or conscious adherence. This specific use of the term 'law' makes Levinas use the word 'justice' to describe the operations of the legal institution. It is justice in Levinas's terminology or the law in ours that limits the infinite responsibility for the other and introduces the element of calculation, representation, synchronisation and thematisation in the asymmetrical ethical encounter ... In a community of equals, I, too, am another like the others, and I, too, am a legitimate claimant and recipient of the other's care. Community, then, is double: first, it is an ethical community of unequal hostages to the other, a network of undetermined but immediate ethical relationships of asymmetry where I am responsible and duty-bound to respond to the other's demand. But community also implies the commonality of law, the calculation of equality, and the symmetry of rights. Here we approach a key contemporary aspect of the *aporia* of justice: to act justly you must treat the other both as equal and as entitled to the symmetrical treatment of norms and as a totally unique person who commands the response of ethical asymmetry.

While the ethical community lives in the synchrony of the here and now expressed in the active mode of saying, the community of law is that of the contemporaneity of the said.

...

But do we not betray our responsibility to the other by moving from the saying to the said and from ethics to justice and the law? Is justice possible? What would it mean for justice to be empirically possible? We have already seen that no ethical theory that describes ethical action is possible. Similarly, if we were to define justice as the ethical operation of the law, no theory of justice would be possible nor could we say in advance 'justice is x or y', because that would turn the injunction of ethics into an abstract theory and the command 'be just' to an empty judgmental statement. Justice is not about theories and truth; it does not derive from a true representation of just society. If the law calculates, if it thematises people by turning them into various types of legal subject endowed with rights and entitlements, ethics is a matter of an indeterminate judgment; a judgment without criteria. Justice is the bringing together of the limited calculability and determinacy of law with the infinite openness and contingency of alterity.

The idea of an indeterminate judgment refers us to two seemingly unrelated traditions, Aristotelian practical wisdom and Kantian reflective judgment. To be sure, Aristotelian ethics is criticised by the neo-Kantians for being undetermined by moral principle and therefore open to manipulation through the masquerading of unbridled decisionism as (non-existent) virtue. Similarly, the principle of reflective judgment has been restricted to aesthetic matters while practical judgment is presented as the determined action of the universal moral law. But the postmodern condition has increased our awareness of the aporia of justice: legal authorities proliferate in a pluralistic, under-regulated manner without the false solace of universal reason or principle that modernity promised, and this pluralism injects decisions with the sense and urgency of ethical responsibility. But at the same time the only principle capable of universalisation is that of personal freedom. In these conditions, the eclectic adoption by law of principles from the traditions of practical wisdom and of reflective aesthetic judgment is imperative.

… In Aristotle, *phronesis*, or practical wisdom, can become a coherent theory of judgment because it is inextricably linked with a clear teleology of persons and actions. The aim of ethics is the achievement of the good life, but similarly every practice, profession or engagement is unified through what Macintyre calls 'standards of excellence' which allow us to call an orator, or a politician or a carpenter good. The good life is always situated, it is good for us; it involves an ongoing dialogue and adjustment between our actions, aiming at the standards of excellence of the various practices we engage in, and our overall 'life plan', the more or less clear set of ideas, hopes, dreams and expectations that make us believe that our life, through its various episodes, joys and mishaps, is a fulfilled, good, successful one. Against this background, *phronesis* is the method of deliberation followed by the prudent in order to arrive at judgments that will help them achieve the standards of excellence of the various practices, as stations of the wider project of enjoying the good life.

Practical wisdom is, then, the virtue of praxis, the achievement of the good in practical matters under our control … Practical judgments, unlike theoretical statements, do not deal with essences or with necessary and immutable relations; they have a timely and circumstantial character and depend on a full and detailed understanding of the factual situation. The theoretical sciences examine general principles and the formal connections between phenomena, while practical knowledge deals with the changing and the variable, with 'ultimate particulars', and tries to grasp the situation in its singularity. Indeed, Aristotle goes as far as to compare the singularity of practical judgment to that of perception (*aisthesis*). Thus, while the evolving knowledge of the aims of good life forms the horizon of Aristotelian ethics, *phronesis* recognises that moral norms and values are just that, a horizon. And in his discussion of justice, Aristotle argues that equity (*epieikeia*) is the rectification of legal justice (*nomos*) insofar as the law is defective on account of its generalisations. While laws are universal, 'the raw material of human behaviour' is such that it is often impossible to pronounce about it in general terms … Justice and the variety of circumstances in which practical judgment is exercised require that the prudent go beyond the application of rules. Aristotle did not follow the casuistical route and did not compile lists and classifications of good and bad acts like his medieval followers. But the Aristotelian practical judgment is preoccupied with the specificity of the situation and with the perception, understanding and judging of the singular as singular.

For the Kantian morality of duty, on the other hand, practical judgments are determinant and their task is simply to subsume the particular under the universal law. In contrast to aesthetic judgments, practical judgments follow a *factum rationis*, the law given to practical reason as an a priori transcendental precondition. This formal law gives rise to duty, not to specific duties to do something or other, but to the feeling of duty in general and to the pain of feeling obliged, which must be concretised by the subject. But while the moral law, respect of which leads to the morally good, is 'supersensuous', moral actions belong to the phenomenal world and the senses. It has been repeatedly observed that the idea of moral law and universal freedom as a fact of reason cannot subsume or direct empirical behaviour. If it belongs to the suprasensible world, the law itself becomes an undetermined concept ... Thus, free will, to become moral, must be embodied in action as determined by the law but as soon as it becomes concretised, the law loses its pure character and stops being a fact of reason. This paradox of practical judgment alerts us to the relevance of the reflective judgment for ethics.

A reflective judgment starts from the particular object that confronts us and functions without preexisting general rules. Aesthetic judgments make a claim to universality, but their law is unknown, indeed non-existent; it is active in its application and yet always still to come and be formalised. The appeal to the universal makes a promise of community, of a *sensus communis,* and that appeal differentiates aesthetic judgments from contingent or idiosyncratic preferences and tastes. But the community remains virtual; aesthetic judgment alludes to its existence but this republic of taste can never become actual. These strict preconditions and qualities necessarily make the aesthetic a judgment of pure form, uncontaminated by considerations of need, interest, desire or use. While everyone should be able to experience the pleasure of the feeling of beauty in confronting the aesthetic object, the subject cannot formulate the concept or the law that her judgment implies and thus make it accessible to others. Aesthetic judgments are examples in search of their rule, subjective and individual yet in the service of the undetermined universal. As the universal law and the community they imply cannot he actualised, they are only an idea present in each judgment which carries 'the promise of its universalisation as a constitutive feature of its singularity' (Lyotard). The aesthetic community is in a continuous state of formation and dissolution; it is the precondition and horizon of judgment but each judgment passed marks the community's end.

This analysis can be of great importance for the revitalisation of justice and ethics in law. The Aristotelian *phronesis* insists on the importance of situation and context but is predicated upon a teleology that does not exist and cannot be recreated. The judge may be the person closest to the classical model of the *phronimos* in modernity but, in the absence of a shared universe of value, his ethical prudence is strictly circumscribed. We, therefore, must envision new ways of giving the other her due and of returning law to justice. Modern legal *phronesis* must move between the norm and the event in the same way that reflective judgments find in each particular the mark of an undetermined universal. The morality of legal duty and right produces inevitable and inescapable conflicts and injustices that the legal institution can address only if it returns to the initial intuition of ethics, that practical judgment only works in the context of the good (life). But this universal can no longer be the consensual virtue of the *polis* of classical teleology nor the abstract duty to follow the law of modern deontology. At the end of modernity, the good can only be defined according to the needs and demands of the other, the person in need, but also the self-defining autonomous person whose request asks for the reawakening of the sensitivity to singularity inherent in the sense of justice as *dike* [the social face of the ethics of intersubjectivity]. The demand that the other be heard as a full person, in other words the demand for ethics, introduces certain minimum communicative and moral requirements for legal procedure as to the type of hearing to be given to the person before the law and the nature of the interpretation and application of the relevant legal rules. The sense of justice returns the law to the other and the good. But we should repeat and conclude: law's inescapable commitment to the rule means that injustice is the inescapable condition of all law.

Laws and judgments are performatives. They perform on the world and they change it. Law's performance subjects people to the norm and makes them instances of a rule. It is predicated on predictability and the subsumption of facts to an authorised repertory of narrative patterns. Its normative formulation makes the law a cognitive field, an object of representation, interpretation and description. As we saw, the 'we' of the norm, the authority that attaches to the law, is based on the elimination, regulation or containment of differences, the thematisation of persons and the generalisation of situations. The law both becomes an object of representation and creates the legal subject, corporate and individual. But as representable and knowable, the legal system claims to have a referent and the injustice of the silencing of all those who are not representable is inevitable.

Justice, on the other hand, cannot be represented or be turned into a normative sentence. But although we cannot say what justice is, we can attempt to say what would be injustice. The first thing to emphasise is that while legal justice asks the judge to sit in judgment, 'justice is impossible without the one that renders it finding himself in proximity ... The judge is not outside the conflict, but the law is in the midst of proximity' (Levinas). The judge is always involved and implicated, called upon to respond to the ethical relationship when he judges. Justice is not a mere legality regulating the subjects or the subsumption of particular cases under general rules. He who judges must compare and calculate, but he remains responsible and always returns to the surplus of his duties over his rights. Injustice would be to forget that the law rises on the ground of responsibility for the other and that ethical proximity and asymmetry overflow the equality of rights. The law can never be the last word. Legal relations of equivalence, comparison and attribution are just only if they recognise 'the impossibility of passing by he who is proximate'.

This is another instance of the sense of justice which takes again the form of an aporia: to be just you must both be free and follow a rule or a prescription. A just and responsible decision must both conserve and destroy or suspend the law sufficiently in order to reinvent it and rejustify it in each case. Each case is different and requires a unique interpretation which no rule can guarantee absolutely. But at the same time, there is no just decision if the judge does not refer to law or rule, if he suspends his decision before the undecidable or leaves aside all rules. This is why we cannot say that a judgment is just. A decision may be recognised as lawful, in accordance with legal rules and conventions, but it cannot be declared just because justice is the dislocation of the said of the law by the – unrepresentable – saying of ethics. The incalculable justice demands of us to calculate and to make the relationship between calculation and the incalculable central to all judgment. Justice seeks the particular at the moment when the universal runs the risk of turning to its opposite, and as such it has the characteristics of a double bind. The action of justice requires an incessant movement between the general rule and the specific case that has no resting place and finds no point of equilibrium. There is a dislocation, a delay or deferral, between the ever-present time of the law and the always-to-come temporality of ethics. Justice inscribes itself on this imperceptible moment and mobilises an open, plural, opaque network of ethical relations which are non-totalisable ... If there are criteria of justice, they are only momentary, they arise at the point of their application, as the just decision must be both regulated and without regulation. These criteria are local, partial and concrete, they give justice body, gender, a place.

We can conclude that justice has the characteristics of a promissory statement. A promise states now something to be performed in the future. Being just is acting justly; it always lies in the future, it is a promise made to the future, a pledge to look into the event and the uniqueness of each situation and to respond to the absolute unrepeatability of the face that will make a demand on me. This promise, like all promises, does not have a present time, a time when you can say there it is, justice is this or that. Suspended between the law and the good in-the-face-of-the-other, justice is always still to come or always already performed. But as the ethical exposure to the other is inevitably and necessarily reduced to the simultaneity of the text, the law and the judge are unavoidably implicated in violence. There is violence in law: the violence of turning the other to an instance of interpretation but also the physical violence that follows every verdict and judgment. Postmodern jurisprudence has to keep disrupting the law in the name of justice and to keep reminding the law of its inescapable violence. A postmodern theory of justice allows otherness to survive and to become a critical space to criticise the operations of the same. The law is necessarily committed to the form of universality and abstract equality, but it must also respect the requests of the contingent, incarnate and concrete other, it must pass through the ethics of alterity in order to respond to its own embeddedness in ethics. In this unceasing movement between the most general and calculating and the most concrete and incalculable, or between the legality of form and subjecthood and the ethics of response to the concrete person, law answers the primordial sense of another justice.

Honneth (1995, 289–323)

> Injustice is the medium of real justice
>
> Theodor W. Adorno

If the philosophical movement of postmodernism was, in its beginnings, apparently strictly directed against every kind of normative theory, then this initial reticence has since given way to a dramatically changed attitude. Writers like Derrida and Lyotard, at first primarily concerned with a radical perpetuation of the critique of reason, turn today to questions of ethics and justice to such a degree that commentators are already speaking of an ethical turn. The field of moral theory, which until recently had constituted for all representatives of poststructuralism a particularly salient example of modernity's compulsive universalism, has now become the true medium for the further development of postmodern theories. The change of attitude accompanying such a reorientation can be understood in part as a reaction to a critique that had been harbored for some time among philosophers and political theorists. Quite early in its development, not only critics but also partisans of postmodernism raised the objection that if the program of philosophical critique is exhausted in the language-theoretic subversion of metaphysics, this will necessarily lead to an indeterminacy in respect of ethical-political matters; for it is both with an interest in the expansion of human freedom and with the objective of simply destroying established systems that it is possible to direct criticism and protest against the uniform ideas of the European intellectual tradition. Thus, in order to avoid the danger of ethical indifference, what is needed is the additional specification of the normative-political orientations according to which the critique of metaphysics is to be guided. But it is probably not just the attempt to invalidate objections of this kind that has recently occasioned the recurrence of ethical considerations in the philosophical movement of postmodernism. The very intention of criticizing metaphysics also carries with it certain normative-political consequences, as the example of Adorno's philosophy shows: Whoever attempts to uncover the separated and the excluded in the thought systems of the philosophical tradition is driven finally with a certain necessity to ethical conclusions, at least when, with regard to these 'others', it is a matter not of cognitive alternatives but of human subjects. In such cases it appears justified to comprehend the element sacrificed to uniform thinking, that is, the unmistakable particularity of concrete persons or social groups, as the essential core of every theory of morality or justice. For this reason, the ethics of postmodernism today also proceeds theoretically from the idea of morally considering the particular, the heterogeneous. Not unlike Adorno's unwritten theory of morality, this ethics revolves around the idea that it is only in dealing appropriately with the nonidentical that the claim to human justice can be redeemed.

Of course, nothing very much has been stated by merely referring to this central motif, since various forms of ethics can be developed from it. Everything depends upon how one determines both the meaning of the particular worthy of protection and the kind of moral protection to be provided. There immediately arises a whole spectrum of possible alternatives, each of which constitutes a different version of a postmodern ethics. The threatened element of particularity can be seen in the singularity of a social language game, in the irrevocable difference of all human beings, or in the individual human being's constitutive need of help; and the kind of consideration, which is to protect that element morally, can he comprehended as an extended form of socially equal treatment, as an intensification of ethical sensitivity, or as an asymmetrical obligation between people. My reconstruction of the various approaches will amount to the thesis that only the last of these three alternatives leads to a form of postmodern ethics that represents a real challenge for modern theories of morality in the Kantian tradition. While the ethical concerns of the first two alternatives can be justified more appropriately within the framework constituted by Habermasian discourse ethics, the third approach remains conceptually intractable for such an ethics. Here, as I would like to demonstrate, particularity is introduced as a moral reference point in such a way that its consideration is guaranteed not by an expansion of the justice perspective but by its other, human care. The moral point of view of equal treatment – as we shall see – requires continuous correction and supplementation by a viewpoint indebted to our concrete obligation to individual subjects in need of help. I would like to proceed by first ... presenting the reflections advanced by Jean-Francois Lyotard for justifying a postmodern ethics. One can show not only that this conception is compatible with discourse ethics but also that it can be articulated better within that framework, since its normative core is nothing but a radicalized idea of equal treatment ... Only in the reflections recently engaged in by Jacques Derrida, relying on the work of Emmanuel Levinas, do moral points of view emerge which go beyond the conceptual horizons of discourse ethics. His contribution to a postmodern ethics ... ties to moral responsibility for the concrete other a perspective that is not congruent with the idea of equal treatment, but rather conflicts with this idea. From this perspective, care or help can be elaborated – ... in critique of Habermas's ideas – as the moral point of view that forms as necessary a counterpoint to the justice perspective as the viewpoint of solidarity does on the other side.

Already at the end of his study on the 'postmodern condition' Lyotard made the first reference to a concept of justice that, in contrast to the tradition of moral universalism, is to guarantee the protection of the heterogeneous. These somewhat casual remarks were then followed – in a work whose title alludes to Kant: *The Differend: Phrases in Dispute* – by an argument that, though still cryptic, is, on the whole, easier to reconstruct. The departure point of the reflections forming the moral-philosophical core of both books is a specific version of the thesis that we are living under the conditions of postmetaphysical thinking today – and indeed, irreversibly so. Under the pressure of the historical experiences that have markedly shaped our century, any possibility of narratively legitimating the course of human history by referring to a supraindividual subject has vanished once and for all. For Lyotard, the end of the 'grand narratives', as exemplarily represented by the philosophies of history of Marxism and liberalism, is also accompanied by the dissolution of the universal claim to reason which the sciences could hitherto unassailably assert for themselves, for their precedence over other forms of knowledge was secure against objection only as long as they could parasitically utilize the circumstance that they were constantly ascribed the role of in emancipatory force in all reconstructions guided by a philosophy of history. If, therefore, with the overcoming of metaphysical thinking, the legitimating source of the sciences has also dried up, then it becomes evident for the first time that no form of knowledge is, by nature, equipped with a superior epistemological competence; rather, numerous linguistically articulated forms of knowledge confront one another in social reality, and it is not possible on the basis of reason to decide which of them can raise a legitimate claim to validity. Thus, like Rorty, Lyotard starts off with the premise that the truth of a linguistically articulated validity claim is measured by the degree to which it has attained social predominance.

From this first thesis, which of course has not gone uncontested, Lyotard proceeds in a second step to a detailed analysis of the characteristics that the field of linguistic utterances possesses. In his short study on the 'postmodern condition', an idea dominates that reminds us of Foucault's 'orders of discourse', even though it is introduced with reference to Wittgenstein. According to this idea, human language provides a potential for aesthetic possibilities of expression, and social groups compete permanently with one another for the appropriation of these possibilities. In *The Differend,* by contrast, a somewhat different model appears, one that is again explained by referring to Wittgenstein, although it now displays a certain proximity to cybernetics. Reaching understanding (*Verständigung*) in language is presented here as an anonymous process in which sentences are interlinked according to certain rules, enabling thereby an exchange between the sender and recipient. Now, in Lyotard's view, this process is characterized by the circumstance that a principle of strict incommensurability prevails between the various rule systems according to which the specific possibility of linking sentences is measured: Every rule system or, as *The Differend* states, every genre of discourse follows a logic of argumentation that, in a strict sense, is incompatible with that of every other genre of discourse. For this reason, there can be no rationally verifiable transitions between the various language games whose employment obeys such a particular genre of discourse; rather, the collision of two sentences belonging to different genres of discourse means a 'dispute' *(Widerstreit)* in the sense that a comparison (of whatever kind) between them is no longer possible. Lyotard now only needs to draw the conclusions from this argumentation to arrive at the striking thesis that every sentence can conjure away the preceding utterance without a trace; for if the two sentences belong to different genres of discourse, the validity claim of the first sentence is fully obliterated by the validity claim of the second one, since the former can be neither perceived nor articulated in the latter's logic.

Lyotard uses this last thesis as an argumentative bridge to the moral-philosophical conclusions of his reflections; however, the basic idea behind these conclusions is not as obscure as the theory of language sketched here could lead one to believe. First, Lyotard translates what he has hitherto described as a purely linguistic event into one with moral character: The morally neutral fact that the validity claim of a linguistic utterance is not met by an appropriate rejoinder now becomes the fact of an 'injustice' that the succeeding sentence perpetrates on the preceding one. Because the scarcely plausible assumption that linguistic entities enjoy rights (of whatever kind) would have to be associated with such a claim, Lyotard's next step consists in reimporting human subjects into his theoretical system of concepts. While they were first totally ostracized from the linguistic event *(Sprachgeschehen)* because of an objectivistic approach, they now unexpectedly reappear in it as the agents of linguistic utterances. This becomes apparent, for instance, in the examples introduced to prove historically the injustice of the untranslatability of one language game into another: the survivors of Nazi concentration camps, whose moral grievances are gradually being silenced, because they do not find an appropriate medium of articulation in the genre of discourse constituted by formal law; and the workers, whose protest against unacceptable working conditions ultimately ends in silent indignation, because it cannot find expression in the language of economic efficiency. If examples of this kind are systematically generalized, we come to the intuition that probably represents the moral-philosophical core of Lyotard's reflections: Because in our society certain genres of discourse, particularly those of positive law and economic rationality, have achieved an institutionally secured predominance, certain language games with a different kind of validity remain almost permanently excluded from societal articulation. To rescue this 'silent' dispute from the danger of being forgotten, a political-ethical orientation is necessary, one that can help the socially repressed, anomalous side find articulation.

At this point, Lyotard could choose between two alternatives in order to develop a model for philosophical ethics from his moral intuitions. He could reconcile himself to the social dominance of certain language games and assign to ethics the resigned task of again and again bearing 'witness' to the existence of inarticulate interests and needs. Moral protection of the particular would then mean the ceaseless, but practically ineffective attempt to preserve in memory, and in the medium of another language, societally repressed experiences of suffering. Or else Lyotard could envision a critique of the predominance of certain language games and turn to the justification of a philosophical ethics whose normative goal is to open societal communication to hitherto ostracized language games. Moral protection of the particular would then mean the politically effective attempt to provide all subjects with the equal chance to publicly articulate their interests and needs. So far, Lyotard has not really decided between these two models – if I read him correctly. Sufficient evidence can be found in his writings both for the idea of ethics merely bearing witness and for the notion of envisioning a new form of justice with the help of this ethics. The first model, which displays a faint resemblance to Adorno's thoughts, can hardly be satisfactory for Lyotard, because it would mean forgoing every practical implementation of justice. As long as he retains the intention of bringing about a new form of justice with his conception of 'postmodernism', he will have to choose the second model. However, working this out would require of Lyotard an argumentation that would point in the direction he has so far emphatically and consistently opposed; after all, Habermasian discourse ethics is also based on the idea – as its morally propelling motif – that every subject must get an equal chance to articulate his or her interests and needs.

When viewing our present world, Habermas, like Lyotard, assumes a constitutive pluralism of competing ideals of life and value orientations, and just like the latter, he reckons with a society in which institutional and language barriers are responsible for the fact that only some of these dispositions reach a level of public articulation. In contrast to Lyotard, however, Habermas has been convinced from the outset that a critique of these circumstances necessitates the development of a moral theory that must have normative character: For him, there is no doubt that restrictions on societal communication are to be described as 'injustice' only if they can be proven to be violations of justified claims raised by human beings. Habermas has attempted to provide such a moral justification with his draft of a discourse ethics. This ethics contains at its core that stock of universalist principles which Lyotard cannot completely forgo either, if he wishes to further develop his conception in the direction of a critique of the given relations of communication.

Habermas arrived at the basic assumptions of discourse ethics by taking as his starting point a premise that he shares with the entire Kantian tradition of moral theory: Under modern conditions, individual ideals of life diverge to such an extent that, in view of moral-practical conflicts, ethics cannot normatively recommend particular values anymore, but can only provide a specific procedure of conflict resolution; and in order for it in turn to be able to satisfy moral claims, this procedure must give expression to the substantive conviction that all human beings have to respect one another as free and equal persons. In contrast to tradition, however, Habermas defends the thesis that Kant draws false conclusions from his correct initial thesis when he goes on to determine the appropriate procedure. The formulation of the categorical imperative evokes the misleading impression that every subject has to fend for him – or herself in moral conflicts and is separated from all the others affected by an abyss of speechlessness. That is why Habermas, in cooperation with Karl-Otto Apel, gives Kant's proposed procedure a formulation that attempts to take the linguistic intersubjectivity of the subject into consideration; accordingly, the universalization test (with whose help Kant has the individual subject check whether moral validity can be ascribed to the practical norms of his or her action) must now be conceived of as a procedure that can find appropriate application only in a discussion among all those potentially affected. Therefore, a subject must now explore whether a disputed norm can redeem the claim to universal validity not just in the light of his or her own particular arguments, but also against the background of the arguments of all those also affected. But Habermas sees an additional argument connected to this reformulation of the categorical imperative, one that can already be understood as in indirect reference to the normative standard of a conception of justice: If a moral norm may be regarded as justified only on the condition that all those potentially affected have agreed to it, then we must be able to assume – in principle always – that each of them has equally had the chance to take (free of constraint) a position

(Stellungnahme) for or against it; for without such an assumption we would not be in a position to regard the agreement reached as an expression of the interests of all those involved. To that extent, however, the possibility of making the validity of norms dependent on a procedure of discursive will formation is tied to the transcendental idea of a discourse free from domination.

Of the many consequences accompanying this fundamental moral-theoretic idea, only those that can clarify the normative problems associated with the conception of dispute are of interest here. At various levels of his argumentation Lyotard is forced, against his own intentions, to employ moral ideas of the kind present in discourse ethics. Even the departure point of his analysis cannot be described at all appropriately without having recourse to the normative principle of discursive will formation. Only if we make the assumption that all those involved in a practical conflict have in fact been able to articulate their interests and views, can we establish in the first place whether there is a 'dispute' between different genres of discourse. If, on the other bind, it is the case that some of those involved have not been able to express their convictions unconstrainedly because they were prevented from doing so by institutional or language barriers, then discourse ethics intercedes at a second level. Now we can infer from it what normative standards we must presuppose in the critique of those communication blocks that are operative; for instance, in certain ostracizing mechanisms, in the political regulation of language, or in the psychological exercise of violence. When these two theoretical levels have been reached and a case of discursive will formation is on hand, then, finally, the possibility can arise that the parties involved might diverge from one another in their value convictions or interests so much so that a moral-practical consensus cannot be reached. Because discourse ethics does not assume any force (of whatever kind) necessary to reach an agreement, under such empirically infrequent conditions it accomplishes its task by describing the procedural rules according to which fair compromises can be reached in a 'dispute'. Taken together, all three levels show unambiguously that Lyotard simply cannot accept what he, with Rorty, seems to claim in some places: that only that language game or that belief system which has successfully asserted itself socially may raise a claim to truth. Instead, he ought to be convinced, and not without good reason, that the socially repressed, ostracized language games contain a truth claim that, unjustly, has not yet obtained recognition within societal communication. To be able to defend this conviction, Lyotard is dependent upon discourse ethics' idea that every subject must equally get the chance to articulate his or her interests unconstrainedly – and that means: free from domination. Without moral universalism, which is present here in Kant's sense, one cannot at all understand what having to defend the particularity of the suppressed language game against the dominant agreement is supposed to mean.

...

III

[O]ne can speak – in a normative sense – of impediments to achieving intersubjective understanding, of the necessity for an affective openness to the particularity of the other only if one first defends the universalist idea that every subject in his or her individuality should get the chance of an unconstrained articulation of his or her claims ... Lyotard [has not moved] beyond the thought horizons determined by this idea. Such a move, however, can be found in the approach to an ethics Jacques Derrida has developed in broad outlines over the last few years. Supported by Levinas's reflections, his recent writings ... counter the Kantian perspective of equal treatment with a second moral point of view.

If the transition to ethics in Lyotard is grounded – with a certain stringency – in the diagnosis of the times he had already developed, then the comparable form of internal motivation is completely absent in Derrida. True, it is not difficult indeed to recognize, in the early essay he wrote on the work of Emmanuel Levinas, references to moral motifs of an entirely unique kind; and, certainly, the deconstructivist interpretations, in which he has examined philosophical texts in terms of uncontrollable meaning references, can be grasped as indirect evidence not only for a new theory of meaning hut also for an ethics of correct understanding. But all this is not sufficient in order to explain appropriately the transition to a normative conception that Derrida has consummated in his recent writings. Instead of merely negatively explicating the indeterminacy of moral rules – as all his previously developed reflections would have suggested – one finds here the thoroughly positive outlines of an ethics that is entirely untouched by deconstructivist self-reservation. The categorical link that nevertheless maintains the connection to the earlier writings is represented, as in the other sketches of a postmodern ethics, by the concept of 'individual particularity'. Thus, Derrida too is concerned with the attempt to identify the point within moral philosophy where the uniqueness of the individual person must he awarded greater theoretical attention ... [He] does not see this critical point of intervention is being located at the place occupied by the moral perspective of justice in the philosophical tradition since Kant. Rather, his thesis is that only a moral perspective that is in a relation of productive opposition to the idea of equal treatment can come to terms with the individual subject in his or her difference to all others. It is this relation of tension that Derrida attempts to elaborate in his ethics; its theoretical core is formed by a phenomenology of moral experience, which has to carry the entire burden of justification.

For Derrida, the basic features of the relevant form of moral experience are apparent in the phenomenon of friendship. From Aristotle to Kant, this type of human interaction always enjoyed the special attention of practical philosophy, because in friendship, it was believed, one could study how two different attitudes to morality form a unity in a single social relationship. What was consistently viewed by the classical philosophers as the particular of friendship was the fact that affection and regard, sympathy and moral respect, flow together here without relinquishing much of their individual force. Derrida has this tradition in mind when, in his essay on 'The Politics of Friendship', he sets about broaching the phenomenon of the moral from the perspective of the experience of friendship. What interests him primarily is the question of how two intersubjective attitudes that refer to different kinds of human responsibility form a synthesis. In every relation of friendship, Derrida claims, there is first a dimension of the relationship to the other in which he or she appears in the role of the concrete, unrepresentable individual person. A principle of responsibility governs here, one that has asymmetrical features because I am obligated to respond to my friend's pressing request or entreaty without considering reciprocal duties. But if the relationship were determined solely by such a principle of asymmetrical, one-sided obligation, it would no longer be friendship but already love. Only in affection, which is untroubled by any other considerations, do I experience the other as a person to whom I am obligated unconditionally, that is, beyond every moral responsibility. That is why, for Derrida, a second dimension of intersubjectivity is a factor in friendship, a dimension in which the other person appears in the role of the generalized other. In this moment of generality those institutionally embodied moral principles emerge which regulate within a society the responsibility – according to symmetrically distributed rights and duties – I have for all other persons. Thus, in a relation of friendship I encounter my vis-à-vis in a double role in that he or she can appeal, on the one hand, at the affective level of sympathy and affection to my asymmetrical obligations, but simultaneously wants to be respected, on the other, as a moral person just like everyone else; and it is this irresolvable tension between two different forms of responsibility that establishes the bond of friendship in the first place. However, the chain of reasoning presented so far has only shown that there are two different ways of morally relating to human subjects. In a relation of loving concern, the other appears as the exclusive addressee of asymmetrical obligations, whereas from the standpoint of valid moral norms, he or she is the addressee of obligations shared in a symmetrical way with all other subjects. What has of course not been clarified by this is the question as to the extent to which these two patterns of recognition actually oppose each other on principle; an opposition, moreover, that supposedly determines, in the form of a tension, the entire experiential field of the moral. The philosophical deliberations Derrida undertakes in the remaining parts of his essay do not provide an answer to this. Essentially, they serve to justify the thesis that in the course of a friendship various sublevels are constantly being superimposed on one another, sublevels that result from maintaining one of the two responsibilities. Derrida's position does not become clear until his essay on modern law from a deconstructivist viewpoint [Derrida 1990]. Here he attempts to show what law – according to its innermost form – has to contribute to justice by analysing the productive opposition of the two types of moral responsibility.

Derrida does not spend much time in his text on an examination of the universalist content that the legal relation has received under the conditions of modernity. Indeed, there are points in it where one gets the impression that the circumstance that modern law is anchored in the moral principle of equal treatment is not sufficiently clear to him. What is of interest to us here is thus not so much the difficulties Derrida has with the moral justification of formal law in modernity, as it is the reflections in which he considers the application of law to concrete cases. According to him, the situation of application shares with the relation of friendship the characteristic that two different principles of human responsibility confront each other, and both embody equally legitimate moral points of view.

In order to justify this thesis, Derrida outlines, in a first step, how the normative founding conditions of the formal legal relation in modernity are constituted. Every modern system of positive rights is accompanied by the prescription to regulate possible conflicts of interest according to the notion that all subjects are entitled to equal chances to exercise their legally restricted liberties. The practical application of this principle of equality implies, as we know, the task of clarifying anew in each individual case of a concrete legal dispute that, and in what respect, is to be regarded as equal and what as unequal. Because there are interpretative problems associated with this which must be solved not once and for all but over and over again, the application of law has an open, hermeneutical, and procedural character. According to its structure, it is the nonterminable process of checking again and again in the case of every new conflict what, in consideration of all the relevant aspects, must be regarded as equal and what as unequal.

So far, Derrida's presentation is still largely in agreement with leading currents in recent legal philosophy. It is only in the second step of his presentation that he veers away from them. It is not the principle of equality which he regards as the principle by which the practice of applying law should ideally be oriented; rather it is the idea of a justice that considers the 'infinity' of the concrete other. What is meant by this in contrast to traditional views becomes tentatively clear when the consequences of the thesis are considered. The normative idea that should guide the practice-oriented interpretation of the equality prescription does not itself come from the moral foundations of the legal system, but approaches them from without in the form of a second moral principle. In the legal relation, just as in friendship, Derrida distinguishes two reference levels that are constituted by different, but reciprocally supplementing moral points of view. The demarcation line he suggests here runs 'between justice (infinite, incalculable, rebellious to rule and foreign to symmetry, heterogeneous and heterotropic) and the exercise of justice as law or right, legitimacy or legality, stabilizable and statutory, calculable, a system of regulated and coded prescriptions'. [Derrida]

Everything of course depends on what Derrida specifically means by that moral point of view from which justice is to be done, in consideration of the 'absolute difference' of the individual person, In the case of friendship, it is a matter of the perspective we adopt when we love another person and have a feeling of unconditional obligation to this person. But what corresponds to this pattern of recognition, namely, love, at the social level, where we are concerned with the modern system of formal rights? Here, a brief reference must he made to the basic ethical ideas Derrida takes from the work of the philosopher of religion, Emmanuel Levinas.

For Levinas, the ethical beliefs we have so far gotten to know as the late product of postmodernism's reflecting on its own foundations are already present at the start of the path into philosophy. The departure point of his theoretical work is the thesis that the intersubjective relationship to other persons possesses a normative content that the philosophical tradition has not been able to acknowledge because of its ontological premises. As with many Jewish philosophers of religion of his time, the religious tradition of the Bible represents for Levinas a theoretical source of the first order. That is why he takes from it, even before he turns systematically to philosophy, the normative models according to which communication between humans ought to be able to be determined ethically in concepts like goodness and empathy. In attempting to articulate these moral contents of experience in the conceptual frame provided by his teachers, Husserl and Heidegger, it was inevitable that he quickly ran into systematic difficulties: For all their differences, both of them determined the realm of being (*Seinde*) in the same way in terms of a context of given, finite circumstances, so that there could not be any place for that experience which occurs in the direct communication between human subjects. In encounters of this kind – and there was no doubt about it for Levinas – the other human being always faces me as a person in need of protection and concern to such a degree that I am overburdened in all my finite possibilities to act and thus concurrently become aware of a dimension of infinity. Levinas concludes from this reflection, however, something more than merely the necessity to extend traditional ontology (which continues up to Husserl and Heidegger) by the appropriate categories. Rather, he draws the far-reaching conclusion that the relation between ontology and ethics must in the first place be reversed in order to give expression to the existential priority of the interpersonal encounter over all realms of being. The categorial construction of reality must be comprehended in terms of the leitmotif provided by the ethical experience of interaction, because here there is the inner-worldly reference to a transcendence, one in comparison to which all other occurrences and events appear as merely secondary, derivative, or reified. Levinas found in this idea a theoretical basis on which he could further develop his religiously motivated ethics as the fundamental philosophical discipline.

The theoretical steps that were necessary to realize this program constitute today the various layers of Levinas's philosophical oeuvre. Its core must of course consist in a phenomenological demonstration of the fact that we, in encountering other persons, have precisely that moral experience which can be interpreted as the inner-worldly representative of a principle of infinity. For Levinas the starting point for such a description is the sentiment present in the visual perception of a human face. If this optical process is only described genuinely enough, then it should become evident that the experience of an ethical demand is also always given. At the sight of the 'face' (Ger: *Antlitz*; Fr: *visage*) of another person, we have no choice but to feel obligated to help this person immediately and to assist him or her in coping with existential problems. Levinas does not, however, clarify whether such a face refers only to the faces of those objectively in need of help, that is, 'the poor' and 'the strange', or to the faces of all other human subjects. Yet, the answer to this question would indicate to what degree we must regard as plausible the phenomenological claim that the cognitive reference to a moral obligation is also always included in the visually given meaning horizons of a face. If, therefore, the empirical core of Levinas's ethics remains somewhat obscure, then determining the necessary consequences of that perception is all the more evident: Because, at the sight of the face of another person, I am said to have no choice but to feel obligated to care for this person, I must be aware that I am restricted in my individual autonomy in the sense that my own interests are only of subordinate significance. In this situation of an unintended deprivation of liberty, there is what Levinas believes to be an inner-worldly experience of infinity: My vis-à-vis is a person who, in his or her unrepresentable individuality, is so incalculable that I am presented with the demand to render help infinitely. To that extent, the intersubjective encounter is, for Levinas, structurally bound up with the experience of a moral responsibility that contains the infinite task of doing justice to the particularity of the other person by caring everlastingly. Furthermore, only by accepting such a boundless obligation, through which the egocentrism of interest-oriented action is broken, can the individual mature into a moral person.

It is not difficult to recognize in this basic conception of Levinas's ethics Derrida's references to the idea of a justice that considers the particularity of each individual subject. Like Levinas, though without the phenomenological foundation in an analysis of the 'face to face', Derrida views as a central principle of morality the asymmetrical obligation to provide unlimited care and help for the human being in his or her individual need. But Levinas did not reduce the domain of the moral to a single perspective; rather he supplemented it at a second level with a further perspective that is supposed to be in permanent tension with the first. Here we again find a theoretical construction that anticipates one we have already come across in Derrida's recent writings. Levinas introduces into the process of interaction, which he has hitherto described in his phenomenological analysis, a second dimension, in that he expands this process by adding the role of a neutral observer. The latter's perspective constitutes an authority [*Instanz*] according to which, in the normal case of a conflict between a number of duties to care, I must decide how I have to act fairly. It is easy to see that this authority of a generalized 'third' represents the moral point of view which has always been designated as 'justice' in the tradition going back to Kant, and what is meant by this here is the perspective we adopt as soon as we direct our action according to the standard of the universalizability of normative claims. Like Derrida later, Levinas does not hesitate to fully equate this standpoint of impartial justice with that sphere in which the principles of modern law are anchored: Legal norms, insofar as they are a component of the legal order founded on equality, reflect at the level of state institutions the moral perspective that urges us to bring about a fair compromise between conflicting duties to care. Thus, by means of the system of formal rights, what was formerly the infinite and asymmetrical responsibility for the well-being of the individual is demoted to a reciprocal duty to treat everyone equally. But in this way there emerges for the individual subject, indeed even for the legal order as a whole, a tension that permeates all morally relevant conflicts; for we cannot locate a superordinate perspective that could help us to decide which of the two principles of responsibility should direct us in a concrete case: 'in reality, justice does not include me in the equilibrium of its universality; justice summons me to go beyond the straight line of justice, and henceforth nothing can mark the end of this march; behind the straight line of the law the land of goodness extends infinite and unexplored, necessitating all the resources of a singular presence'. [Levinas, 1990, 245]

The point of this line of reasoning consists of course in the fact that, in accordance with his starting point, Levinas distinguishes two different perspectives on the moral, both of which he designates, however, as attitudes of 'justice' in order to be able to formulate the surprising thesis that justice always pushes beyond justice itself. The moral orientation of goodness, which is concerned with boundless care for a single, unrepresentable individual, contains a viewpoint from which it becomes apparent that injustice is perpetuated on an individual whenever he or she is treated as an equal among equals within the framework of law's moral orientation. It is only from the perspective of this interim result that Levinas can reach, in the next step, that part of his philosophical work which is sketching to drafting a social ontology. This is assigned the task of deciphering the elementary constituents of social life in such a way that their emergence becomes clear as a process of violent abstraction from that primary experience which transpires in the intersubjective encounter with the other. We can, however, refrain here from presenting the ideas Levinas develops in this domain of his ethics because the theoretical point has already been reached from where we can further pursue our question. This is so because, for Derrida to be able to reach his own determination of the domain of the moral, he only had to radicalize one degree further what Levinas designated (in the line of reasoning cited above) as a tension between two moral orientations – that of 'law' and that of 'goodness'. For Derrida, the perspectives of equal treatment and of care represent two different sources of moral orientation, between which there is absolutely no possibility for the kind of continuum Levinas seems to assume. Rather, the application of law, that is, that normative sphere in which the idea of equal treatment is embodied, encounters again and again concrete cases whose 'just' resolution can be attained only if the viewpoint of individual well-being is abruptly adopted. The perspective change that occurs in such situations bears something violent insofar as it must transpire without any legitimation in a comprehensive idea of the moral.

As we shall presently see, a weakness of this thesis consists in its having been developed exclusively along the guidelines of modern legal relations; for it is here that there exists a series of special arrangements that see to it that, from within these legal relations themselves, the individual case is considered as comprehensively as possible and in a manner that Derrida can only imagine as the addition of a goodness or care perspective from without. For the moment, however, we need only point out that Derrida claims – revealingly – that a relation of violent and irresolvable, but at the same time productive, conflict obtains between the two moral viewpoints Levinas distinguishes in his ethics. This conflict is irresolvable because the idea of equal treatment necessitates a restriction of the moral perspective from where the other person in his or her particularity can become the recipient of my care; for my showing him or her boundless concern and providing unlimited help would mean tending to neglect the moral duties that follow from the reciprocal recognition of human beings as equals. And this conflict is productive because the viewpoint of care continually provides a moral ideal from which the practical attempt to gradually realize equal treatment can take its orientation – in a self-corrective manner; for it is only that kind of responsibility which is developed in loving concern for individual persons that brings about the moral sensorium which the possible suffering of all other human beings can also be perceived. But with this line of reasoning Derrida has already gone way beyond the limits drawn today in the tradition of justice going back to Kant, because now the attempt is being made to integrate the two different moral perspectives in a single frame of orientation.

IV

In the course of his elaborating discourse ethics, Habermas has had to confront the question of the relation between the modern idea of equal treatment and the moral principle of care. With the development of feminist moral theory in general and especially following Carol Gilligan's research, the criticism was soon voiced that the Kantian approach of discourse ethics neglects those moral attitudes in which, without considering reciprocal obligations, we attend to the concrete other and, of our own free will, provide help and support. If we reconstruct discourse ethics' program again up to that point at which it was a question of the significance of communicative virtues and capabilities, it will quickly become evident that this objection is justified in a trivial sense, without however initially having systematic relevance. Every person is indeed always included in a practical discourse only as an unrepresentable individual, but the presuppositions of symmetry obtaining in practical discourse necessitate that all particular bonds be disregarded and, accordingly, that viewpoints of care recede into the background. There is no problem in such an attitude as long as practical discourse is regarded as a procedure that serves the consensual resolution of intersubjective conflicts of interest. This is so because, in the case of conflicting interests, a just form of settlement can he reached only if all the persons involved show one another the same respect, without allowing feelings of sympathy and affection to come into play. To that extent, attitudes of asymmetrical responsibility, on which, for instance, care or benevolence is based, must remain excluded from the procedure of a practical discourse from the very beginning. This does not of course answer the question of how the moral perspective of discourse ethics is at all related to the principle invoked by feminist ethics today (and rightly so) under the heading 'care'. It can hardly be denied that our notion of the moral does not exhaust itself in the concept of equal treatment and reciprocal responsibility, but includes those modes of conduct that consist of asymmetrical acts of benevolence, helpfulness, and philanthropy. The theoretical conclusions that Derrida drew from his research on the application problem in law are not of any help here either, because they are in danger of locating the principle of benevolence at the wrong place. In a discourse ethics' view of law, it can easily he shown that there are now in law itself standpoints, such as that of 'equity', which allow justice to be done to the particularity of an extremely difficult situation without, in the process, invalidating the basic norm of equal treatment. Thus, for the question of how discourse ethics relates to the principle of 'care', the moral foundations of modern law do not provide the appropriate departure point. On the other hand, however, Derrida's thesis – according to which the principle of equal treatment is always in a state of both irresolvable and productive tension with the principle of benevolence – retains some of its penetrating force, even if it proves to be false with regard to law. For in the light of this thesis, it becomes apparent that Habermas's attempt to mediate between the two moral principles has the features of a precipitate and inappropriate reconciliation.

Even if discourse ethics did not necessarily get into immediate difficulties as a result of the challenge of feminist ethics, it is nevertheless necessary to provide an answer to the question of how it relates on the whole to the principle of care. For that reason, Habermas has attempted to develop his own proposal for a response in an essay devoted to the then recent work of Lawrence Kohlberg. His argument amounts to the notion that the communicative presuppositions of discourse do not indeed include the viewpoint of care, but they do encompass a related principle in which it is also a matter of the 'welfare of one's fellow man': Taking one's orientation from the moral perspective of 'solidarity' is built into every practical discourse because here the participants must recognize one another not only as equal persons but at the same time as unrepresentable individuals. This principle, which Habermas refers to as the 'other' of justice, is said to share with care the feature of a concern (*Anteilnahme*) for the existential fate of other human beings, a concern that extends into the affective. It is different from care in that individual concern applies to all human beings to the same degree, that is, free from any kind of privileging or asymmetry. For Habermas, solidarity is the other of justice because with it all subjects reciprocally attend to the welfare of the other, with whom they also share, as equal beings, the communicative form of human life.

What necessarily remains unclear in such a generalized form of concern is of course the particular motives and experiences that are said to be able to lead to its development in the first place. In this context Habermis speaks of a consciousness of one's 'membership in an ideal communication community', and this consciousness arises from the 'certainty of intimate relatedness in a shared life context'. However, such a feeling of social membership in a shared form of life can be formed in the first place only to the degree to which burdens, suffering, and tasks are experienced as something shared; and because such an experience of shared burdens and hardships can, for its part, develop only on the condition of collective goals, whose definition, however, is only possible in the light of commonly shared values, the development of a feeling of social membership remains necessarily bound to the presupposition of a value community. For this reason, solidarity – understood as the moral principle of reciprocal concern – cannot be conceived of without that element of particularism which is inherent in the development of every social community, insofar as its members understand themselves as being in agreement on particular, ethically defined goals and thereby share the experience of specific burdens. The fixed point of a solidary humanity can indeed be located on a normatively graded scale, but only on the extremely idealizing assumption that all human beings have, over and above their cultural differences, a shared goal. Hence, in contrast to the universalist idea of equal treatment, there is something abstractly utopian inherent in the notion of a solidarity encompassing humanity; but that is all the more reason for not being able to regard it as a universalist representative of that moral principle which, in the form of unilateral care and benevolence, has always constituted a transcending element of our social world.

What, following Levinas, Derrida referred to as a caring justice that considers the infinite particularity of the individual human being has, in contrast to both equal treatment and solidarity, the character of a completely unilateral, nonreciprocal concern. The obligation accompanying it will always tend to be so extensive that even one's own autonomy in action has to be restricted to a high degree. To that extent, it cannot be expected of all human beings that they assume such a form of responsibility in the same way as respect for the dignity of each individual is morally expected of them. Genetically speaking, however, the experience of this moral principle precedes the encounter with all other moral points of view because, under favorable circumstances, it stands at the beginning of the child's developmental process. Indeed, it may be the case that a sensorium for what can be called, in an unrestricted sense, equal treatment can only be developed in the first place if one's own person has had the experience of unlimited care at some time. Between the two principles, however, there is not only a relation of genetic primacy but also one of reciprocal exclusiveness: An obligation to care and to be benevolent can only exist where a person is in a state of such extreme need or hardship that the moral principle of equal treatment can no longer he applied to him or her in a balanced manner. Thus, human beings who are either physically or mentally unable to participate in practical discourses deserve at least the selfless care of those who are close to them via emotional ties. But, conversely, the moment the other person is recognized as an equal being among all others – in that he or she can participate in practical discourses – the unilateral relation of care must come to an end; an attitude of benevolence is not permissible toward subjects who are able to articulate their beliefs and views publicly.

Yet, in no way may we draw from all this the conclusion – as Levinas does – that care or benevolence be declared not only the genetic but also the logical foundation of all principles of the moral. What we, under modern conditions, understand as the 'moral point of view' is explained first and foremost by the universalist principle of equal treatment. But what has been said so far must also be accompanied by the conclusion that care be again awarded that place in the domain of the moral which it has all too frequently been denied in the tradition of moral philosophy going back to Kant: In the same way as solidarity constitutes a necessary counterpoint to the principle of justice, insofar as it furnishes it in a particularistic manner with the affective impulses of reciprocal recognition, care represents, on the other side, its equally necessary counterpoint because it supplements this principle of justice by a principle of unilateral, entirely disinterested help. The accomplishment of Derrida's recent writings is to have discovered the irresolvable but productive tension that prevails in the domain of the moral; ultimately, they reveal that postmodern ethics has indeed taken a small, but significant step beyond the normative horizons that, constituted by the idea of equal treatment, have hitherto been the determining factor for modernity.

Further Reading

Sebastian Gardner (Gardner 1999) and Roger Sullivan (Sullivan 1989 and 1994), provide excellent guides to Kant's theories of knowledge and morality respectively, though Kant's aesthetic theory is less well served by expository texts. For a concise overview of the Critical project as a whole, the best source is probably Höffe (1994). Stavrakakis (1999) offers a clear and insightful presentation of the implications of Lacanian psychoanalysis for the understanding of politics. Drucilla Cornell has arguably done more than any other legal scholar to introduce Lacanian (and Derridean, and Levinasian) concepts into legal theoretical analysis: one of her more accessible texts is *Transformations* (1993). Finally, Salter (1997) provides a very helpful review of Habermas's recent work on law and democracy.

Questions

1. What is meant by the notion that both the subject, and the reality experienced by the subject, are discursively constructed? Outline the implications of these insights for the understanding of law.

2. How, if at all, might the psychoanalytic concept of 'desire' be useful for legal theory?

3. 'Almost by definition and necessity the law seems to forget the difference of the different and the otherness of the other.' Explain.

4. 'By means of the formal system of legal rights, an infinite and asymmetrical responsibility for the particular other is demoted to a reciprocal duty to treat everyone equally. Therein lies the injustice of modern law.' Discuss.

5. How, if at all, might an 'ethics of alterity' be introduced into the practice of adjudication?

Appendix: A Note to Teachers

In writing this book we have focused on the need to make jurisprudence accessible to students. In so doing, we have been acutely aware of the dangers of dumbing down. This includes the dangers of over-simplifying that which is complicated or generating misunderstanding through simplification. However, we hope that our book reflects the difference between accessibility and simplicity. One does not need to talk down to students. Nor should one teach with low expectations of what they are capable of understanding. But in seeking to increase student understanding, to transmit meaning, one has to think seriously about the audience, and the need to facilitate their learning. One has to start at a place where they can be engaged, not at the place one wishes them to arrive. We offer this book, not as a final word on the subject of jurisprudence, or even a final word on how to start the journey. We expect that you will wish to take your students further, and to criticise our commentaries. If what we have written is accessible, if your students can engage with it, if they are ripe to be told more, and to have our views re-assessed in your classes, then we shall have succeeded.

Teachers will decide for themselves how to use this book. Nevertheless, it might be useful for you to know how the book supports the course at LSE. Here, Part I, made up of 10 chapters, represents 10 weeks' work in the first term. In our second term, five or six of the topics selected from Part II form the basis of lectures. The class teachers then choose three of the lecture topics to tackle in their class groups. This works out at about three lectures per topic, and three weeks of classes per topic. The change of organisation between the two terms reflects a belief that, once a sufficiently solid basis or orientation has been provided to students, one can move from coverage, or breadth, to tackling subjects in greater depth. You may wish to specialise to a greater degree than this, using a small number (perhaps only one) of our chapters as an introduction to a topic, supplemented by a large selection of further reading. Teachers should feel free to specialise on whatever topics, in whatever depth, they choose, and should not feel concerned that any topic, or topics, are not covered. Teachers (and students) may also find some topics more difficult than others, and will wish to spend more time working through them. They may also wish to tackle some subjects in particular years, and leave others to a later date. As an alternative, some teachers may wish to continue working through all of Part II chapters within the time available to them, allocating an equal amount of time to each of them. The fact that we do not adopt this approach at the LSE does not mean that it is inappropriate. The inescapable fact that by covering more topics you give students less time to reflect on each does not mean that the benefits of knowing more of these topics will not, for you and your students, prove more rewarding. This flexibility reflects one of our concerns in producing the book. While the principal aim of the book was to write an introductory text that was accessible to students, we also wanted to produce a book that was of practical assistance to jurisprudence teachers, recognising that they have different levels of resources available to them in terms of library acquisitions, staffing, experience and interests.

We commend this book to you, in the hope that these materials inspire those new or newish to the teaching of jurisprudence, and revive the enthusiasm of old hands whose interest may have flagged.

Bibliography

Adorno, T W (1973) *Negative Dialectics* (translated by E B Ashton) London, Routledge

Albrow, M (1975) 'Legal Positivism and Bourgeois Materialism: Max Weber's View of the Sociology of Law' 2 *British Journal of Law and Society* 14–31

Albrow, M (1990) *Max Weber's Construction of Social Theory* London, Macmillan

Aquinas (1959 edn) *Selected Political Writings* (translated by J G Dawson) Oxford, Blackwell

Aquinas (1993 edn) *Saint Thomas Aquinas: The Treatise on Law* (translated by R J Henle) Notre Dame, Indiana, Notre Dame Press

Arendt, H (1968a) 'The Crisis in Culture: its Social and Political Significance' in *Between Past and Future: Eight Exercises in Political Thought*, 197–226 New York, Penguin

Arendt, H (1968b) 'Truth in Politics' in *Between Past and Future: Eight Exercises in Political Thought*, 227–264 New York, Penguin

Arendt, H (1982) *Lectures on Kant's Political Philosophy* R Beiner ed, London, Harvester

Arkes, H (1992) 'That 'Nature Himself Has Placed in Our Ears a Power of Judging': Some Reflections on the 'Naturalism' of Cicero' in George 1992, Ch 9

Aristotle (1976 edn) *The Ethics of Artistotle: the Nicomachean Ethics* (translated by J A K Thomson) Harmondsworth, Penguin

Aristotle (1981 edn) *The Politics: Aristotle* (translated by T A Sinclair) Harmondsworth, Penguin

Atkins, S and Hoggett, B (1984) *Women and the Law* Oxford, Blackwell

Atiyah, P S (1978) 'Contracts, Promises, and the Law of Obligations' 94 *Law Quarterly Review* 193–223

Augustine (1984 edn) *Concerning the City of God Against the Pagans* (translated by H.Bettenson) London, Penguin

Austin, J (1955 edn) *The Province of Jurisprudence Determined and The Uses of the Study of Jurisprudence* (reprint of originals dated respectively 1832 and 1863) London, Weidenfeld and Nicolson

Avineri, S and de-Shalit, A (eds) (1992) *Communitarianism and Individualism* Oxford, Oxford University Press

Barnett, H (1995) 'The province of jurisprudence determined-again!' 15 Legal Studies 88–127

Barron, A (1990) 'Legal Discourse and the Colonisation of the Self in the Modern State' in A Carty (ed) *Post-Modern Law: Enlightenment, Revolution and the Death of Man*, 107–125 Edinburgh, Edinburgh University Press, 1990

Barron, A (1993) 'The Illusions of the 'I': Citizenship and the Politics of Identity' in A Norrie (ed) *Closure or Critique: New Directions in Legal Theory*, Ch 5 Edinburgh, Edinburgh University Press, 1993

Barron, A (1996) 'The Governance of Schooling' 15 *Studies in Law, Politics and Society* 167–204

Barron, A (2000a) 'Spectacular Jurisprudence' 20 *Oxford Journal of Legal Studies* 301–315

Barron, A (2000b) 'Feminism, Aestheticism and the Limits of Law' 8 *Feminist Legal Studies* 275–317

Baynes, K (1995) 'Democracy and the *Rechtstaat*: Habermas's *Faktizität und Geltung*' in S K White (ed) (1995) 201–232

Becker, G (1957) *The Economics of Discrimination* Chicago, University of Chicago Press

Bedau, H (ed) (1990) *Civil Disobedience in focus* London, Routledge

Benjamin, A (ed) (1992) *Judging Lyotard* London, Routledge

Benson, L (1978) *Proletarians and Parties* London, Tavistock

Bentham, J (1843) 'Anarchical Fallacies' in *The Works of Jeremy Bentham* (J Bowring, ed, vol 2) Edinburgh, W Tait

Bentham, J (1948 edn) *A Fragment on Government with An Introduction to the Principles of Morals and Legislation* (reprint of originals first published respectively in 1776 and 1789, W Harrison, ed) Oxford, Basil Blackwell

Bentham, Jeremy (1982 edn) *An Introduction the Principles of Morals and* Legislation (J H Burns and H L A Hart, eds) London, Methuen

Berman, H and Reid, C J (2000) 'Max Weber As Legal Historian' in S Turner (ed) (2000), Ch 11

Bernstein, J (1992) *The Fate of Art* Cambridge, Polity

Bernstein, RJ (1983) *Beyond Objectivism and Relativism* Oxford, Blackwell

Beyleveld, D and Brownsword, R (1986) *Law as a Moral Judgment* London, Sweet & Maxwell

Bix, B (1999) *Jurisprudence: Theory and Context* (2nd edn) London, Sweet & Maxwell

Blackstone, W (1979 edn) *Commentaries on the Laws of England* in 4 volumes, 1765–1769 Chicago, University of Chicago Press

Bottomley, A, Gibson, S and Meteyard, B (1987) 'Dworkin; Which Dworkin? Taking Feminism Seriously' 14 *Journal of Law and Society* 47–60

Bottomley, A and Conaghan, J (eds) (1993) *Feminist Theory and Legal Strategy* Oxford, Blackwell

Bottoms, A (1998) 'Five Puzzles in von Hirsch's Theory of Punishment' in A Ashworth and M Wasik (eds) *Fundamentals of Sentencing Theory*, 53–100 Oxford, Clarendon Press 1998

Braithwaite, J (2002) *Restorative Justice and Responsive Regulation* Oxford, Oxford University Press

Brudner, A (1980) 'Retribution and the Death Penalty' 30 *University of Toronto Law Journal* 337–355

Burchell, G (1991) 'Peculiar interests: civil society and governing "the system of natural liberty"' in G Burchell, C Gordon and P Miller (eds) (1991) 119–150

Burchell, G (1993) 'Liberal Government and Techniques of the Self' 22(3) *Economy and Society* 267–282

Burchell, G, Gordon, C and Miller, P (eds) (1991) *The Foucault Effect* London, Harvester

Burrows, P and Veljanovski, C G (eds) (1981) *The Economic Approach to Law* London, Butterworths

Cain, M (1974) 'The Main Themes of Marx and Engels' Sociology of Law' 1 *British Journal of Law and Society* 136–148

Cain, M and Hunt, A (1979) *Marx and Engels on Law* London, Academic Press

Calabresi, G (1961) 'Some Thoughts on Risk Distribution and the Law of Torts' 70 *Yale Law* Journal 499–553

Calabresi, G (1970) *The Cost of Accidents* New Haven, Yale University Press

Campbell, A H (1941) 'Some Footnotes on Salmond's Jurisprudence' 7 *Cambridge Law Journal* 206–223

Campbell, T (2001) 'Incorporation through Interpretation' in T Campbell et al (eds) *Sceptical Essays on Human Rights*, 79–101 Oxford, Oxford University Press, 2001

Chambers, S (1995) 'Discourse and Democratic Practices' in S K White (ed) (1995) 233–259

Christenson, R (1986) *Political Trials: Gordian Knots in the Law* New Brunswick, Transaction

Christie, N (1977) 'Conflicts as Property' 17 *British Journal of Criminology* 1–15

Christodoulidis, EA (1996) 'The Inertia of Institutional Imagination: A Rely to Roberto Unger' 59 *Modern Law Review* 377–397

Cicero (1999 edn) *On the Commonwealth and On the Laws* J E G Zetzel (ed) Cambridge, Cambridge University Press

Cleaver, E (1992 edn) *Soul on Ice* New York: Bantam Doubleday Dell, originally published 1968

Coase, R (1960) 'The Problem of Social Cost' 3 *Journal of Law and Economics* 1–44

Cohen, G A (2000) *If You're An Egalitarian, How Come You're So Rich?* Cambridge MA, Harvard University Press

Cole, D H (2001) '"An Unqualified Human Good": E.P. Thompson and the Rule of Law' 28 *Journal of Law and Society* 177–203

Coleman, J L (1982) 'The Normative Basis of Economic Analysis: A Critical Review of Richard Posner's *The Economics of Justice*' 34 *Stanford Law Review* 1105–1131

Coleman, J L (1998) 'Incorporationism, Conventionality, and the Practical Difference Thesis' 4 *Legal Theory* 381–425

Coleman, J L (2001) *The Practice of Principle: In Defence of a Pragmatist Approach to Legal Theory* Oxford, Oxford University Press

Coleman, J and Shapiro, S (eds) (2002) *The Oxford Handbook of Jurisprudence and Philosophy of Law* Oxford, Oxford University Press

Collins, H (1982) *Marxism and Law* Oxford, Clarendon Press

Collins, H (1987) 'The Decline of Privacy in Private Law' 14 *Journal of Law and Society* 91–103

Collins, P (1991) *Black Feminist Thought: Knowledge, Consciousness and the Politics of Empowerment* London, Routledge

Conaghan, J (2000) 'Reassessing the Feminist Theoretical Project in Law' 27 *Journal of Law and Society* 351–85

Cook, W W (1919) 'Hohfeld's Contribution to the Science of Law' 28 *Yale Law Journal* (1919) 721–738

Cook, W W (1924) 'The Logical and Legal Bases of the Conflict of Laws' 33 *Yale Law Journal* 457–488

Cornell, D, Rosenfeld, M, Carlson, DG (eds) (1992) *Deconstruction and the Possibility of Justice* London, Routledge

Cornell, D (1993) *Transformations: Recollective Imagination and Sexual Difference* London, Routledge

Cornell, D (1995) *The Imaginary Domain: Abortion, Pornography and Sexual Harassment* London, Routledge

Cotterrell, R (1989) *The Politics of Jurisprudence: A Critical Introduction to Philosophy of Law* London, Butterworths

Cotterrell, R (1992) *The Sociology of Law: An Introduction* (2nd edn) London, Butterworths

Cotterrell, R (1998) 'Why Must Legal Ideas Be Interpreted Sociologically?' 25 *Journal of Law and Society* 171–192

Cotterrell, R (1999) *Emile Durkheim: Law in a Moral Domain* Edinburgh, Edinburgh University Press

Cotterrell, R (2000) 'Pandora's box: jurisprudence in legal education' 7 *International Journal of the Legal Profession* 179–187

Crenshaw, K (1989) 'Demarginalizing the Intersection of Race and Sex: A Black Feminist Critique of Antidiscrimination Doctrine, Feminist Theory and Antiracist Politics' *The University of Chicago Legal Forum* 139–67

Culler, J (1981) *The Pursuit of Signs* London, Routledge

Dahl, T (1986) *Women's Law* Oslo, Norwegian University Press

Davies, M (1994) *Asking The Law Question* London, Sweet & Maxwell

Dean, H (1990) *Social Security and Social Control* London, Routledge

Dean, M (1994) *Critical and Effective Histories* London, Routledge

Dennett, D (1995) *Darwin's Dangerous Idea* London, Penguin

D'Entreves, A P (1970) *Natural Law: an introduction to legal philosophy* (2nd revised edn) London, Hutchinson

Derrida, J (1973) *Of Grammatology* Baltimore, Johns Hopkins

Derrida, J (1990) 'The Force of Law: the "Mystical Foundation of Authority"' 11 *Cardozo Law Review* 919–1046

Devlin, P (1965) *The Enforcement of Morals* London, Oxford University Press

Dias, R W M (1968) 'Legal Politics: Norms Behind the *Grundnorm*' 26 *Cambridge Law Journal* 233–259

Douzinas, C and Warrington, R (1994) *Justice Miscarried: Ethics, Aesthetics and the Law* London, Harvester 1995

Downes, D and Rock, P (1998) *Understanding Deviance* (3rd edn) Oxford, Oxford University Press

Dreyfus, H and Rabinow, P (eds) (1983) *Michel Foucault: Beyond Structuralism and Hermeneutics* Chicago, Chicago University Press

Duff, R A, and Garland, D (eds) (1994) *A Reader on Punishment* Oxford, Oxford University Press

Duff, R A (1996) 'Penal Communications: Recent Work in the Philosophy of Punishment' in M Tonry (ed) *Crime and Justice: A Review of Criminal Research*, vol 20, 1–97 Chicago, University of Chicago Press

Duff, R A (2001) *Punishment, Communication and Community* Oxford, Oxford University Press

Durkheim, E (1893/1964) *The Division of Labour in Society* Glencoe, Free Press

Duxbury, N (1995) *Patterns of American Jurisprudence* Oxford, Clarendon Press

Dworkin, R (1975) 'Hard Cases' 88 *Harvard Law Review* 1057–1109

Dworkin, R (1977) *Taking Rights Seriously* London, Duckworth

Dworkin, R (1980) 'Is Wealth a Value' 9 *Journal of Legal Studies* 191–226

Dworkin, R (1983) 'A Reply by Ronald Dworkin' in M Cohen (ed) *Ronald Dworkin and Contemporary Jurisprudence*, 247–300 London, Duckworth, 1983

Dworkin, R (1985) *A Matter of Principle* Cambridge, Mass, Harvard University Press

Dworkin, R (1986) *Law's Empire* London, Fontana

Dworkin, R (1996) 'Objectivity and Truth: You'd Better Believe It' 25 *Philosophy & Public Affairs* 87–139

Dworkin, R (1997) 'In Praise of Theory' [1997] *Arizona State Law Journal* 353–376

Dworkin, R (2000) *Sovereign Virtue* Cambridge, Mass, Harvard University Press

Dworkin (2002) 'Thirty Years On; A Review of Jules Coleman, *The Practice of Principle*' 115 *Harvard Law Review* 1655–1687

Edmundson, W A (ed) (1999) *The Duty to Obey the Law* Lanham, Maryland, Rowman & Littlefield

Eekelaar, J M (1973) 'Principles of Revolutionary Legality' in A W B Simpson (ed) *Oxford Essays in Jurisprudence*, Ch 2 (Second Series) Oxford, Oxford University Press, 1973

Ehrlich, E (1936) *Fundamental Principles of the Sociology of Law* (1912 edn translated by W L Moll) Cambridge, Mass, Harvard University Press

Eikema Hommes, H J van (1979) *Major Trends in the History of Legal Philosophy* Amsterdam, North Holland

Endicott, T A O (1998) 'Herbert Hart and the Semantic Sting' 4 *Legal Theory* 283–300

Etzioni, A (1993) *The Spirit of Community: rights, responsibilities, and the communitarian agenda* New York, Crown Publishers

Ewald, F (1987) 'Justice, equality, judgement: on social justice' in G Teubner (ed) (1987a) 91-110

Ewald, F (1988) 'A concept of social law' in G Teubner (ed) (1988) 40–75

Feinberg, J (1994) 'The Expressive Function of Punishment' in R A Duff and D Garland (eds) (1994), Ch 3

Fenton, S (ed) (1984) *Durkheim and Modern Sociology* Cambridge, Cambridge University Press

Fine, B (1984) *Democracy and the Rule of Law* London, Macmillan

Fine, B (1994) 'The Rule of Law and Muggletonian Marxism: The Perplexities of Edward Thompson' 21 *Journal of Law and Society* 193–213

Finnis, J (1980) *Natural Law and Natural Rights* Oxford, Clarendon Press

Finnis, J (1987a) 'On Reason and Authority in Law's Empire' 6 *Law and Philosophy* 357–80

Finnis, J (1987b) 'On "The Critical Legal Studies Movement"' in J Eekelaar and J Bell (eds), *Oxford Essays in Jurisprudence,* Ch 7 (Third Series) Oxford, Clarendon Press, 1987

Fischl, M (1992) 'The Question That Killed Critical Legal Studies' 17 *Law and Social Inquiry* 779–820

Fish, S (1982) 'Working on the Chain Gang: Interpretation in Law and Literature' 60 *Texas Law Review* 551–567

Fish, S (1989) *Doing What Comes Naturally* Oxford, Clarendon

Fitzpatrick, P (1992) *The Mythology of Modern Law* London, Routledge

Foucault, M (1970) *The Order of Things* London, Tavistock

Foucault, M (1972) *The Archaeology of Knowledge* (translated by A M Sheridan Smith) London, Tavistock

Foucault, M (1977) *Discipline and Punish* (translated by A Sheridan) London: Penguin

Foucault, M (1979) *The History of Sexuality: An Introduction* (translated by R Hurley) London, Penguin

Foucault, M (1980) 'Two Lectures' in *Power/Knowledge*, C Gordon (ed), 78–108 London, Harvester, 1980

Foucault, M (1983) 'The Subject and Power' in H Dreyfus and P Rabinow (eds) (1983), 208–226

Foucault, M (1991a) 'Governmentality' in G Burchell, C Gordon and P Miller (eds) (1991), 87–104

Foucault, M (1991b) 'Questions of method' in G Burchell, C Gordon and P Miller (eds) (1991), 73–86

Fraser, N (1981) 'Foucault on Modern Power: Empirical Insights and Normative Confusions' *Praxis International* 272–287

Frazer, E and Lacey, N (1993) *The Politics of Community: A Feminist Critique of the Liberal-Communitarian Debate* Hemel Hempstead, Harvester-Wheatsheaf

Fried, C (1981) *Contract as Promise* Cambridge, Mass, Harvard University Press

Friedrich, C J (1963) *The Philosophy of Law in Historical Perspective* (2nd edn) Chicago, University of Chicago Press

Frug, G E (1984) 'The Ideology of Bureaucracy in American Law' 97 *Harvard Law Review* 1276–1388

Frug, M J (1992) *Postmodern Legal Feminism* London, Routledge

Fuller, L L (1940) *The Law In Quest Of Itself* Boston, Beacon Press

Fuller, L L (1949) 'The Case of the Speluncean Explorers' 62 *Harvard Law Review* 616–645

Fuller, L L (1958) 'Positivism and Fidelity to Law – A Reply to Professor Hart' 71 *Harvard Law Review* 630–672

Fuller, L L (1969) *The Morality of Law* (revised edn) New Haven, Yale University Press

Gabel, P and Harris, P (1983) 'Building Power and Breaking Images: Critical Legal Theory and the Practice of Law' 11 *NYU Review of Law and Social Change* 369

Gallie, W B (1956) 'Essentially Contested Concepts' 56 *Proceedings of the Aristotelian* Society 167–198

Galligan, D J (1982) 'Judicial Review and the Textbook Writers' (1982) 2 Oxford Journal of Legal Studies, 25–276

Gardner, J (1998) 'Crime: in Proportion and in Perspective' in A Ashworth and M Wasik, M (eds) *Fundamentals of Sentencing Theory*, 31–52 Oxford, Clarendon Press, 1998

Gardner, S (1999) *Kant and the Critique of Pure Reason* London, Routledge

Garland, D (1990) *Punishment and Modern Society* Oxford, Oxford University Press

George, R P (ed) (1992) *Natural Law Theory: Contemporary Essays* Oxford, Clarendon Press

George, R P (1993) *Making Men Moral* New York, Oxford University Press

George, R P (1996) 'Natural Law and Positive Law' in RP George (ed) *The Autonomy of Law: Essays on Legal Positivism*, Ch 11 Oxford, Clarendon Press, 1996

George, R P (1999) *In Defence of Natural Law* Oxford, Clarendon Press

Gewirth, A (1970) 'Obligation: Political, Legal, Moral' in J Pennock and J Chapman (eds) 1970, Ch 4

Gilligan, C (1982) *In a Different Voice* Cambridge, Mass, Harvard University Press

Gilroy, P (1987) *There Ain't No Black in the Union Jack* London, Hutchinson

Goble, G W (1935) 'A Redefinition of Basic Legal Terms' 35 *Columbia Law Review* 535–547

Goodrich, P (1991) 'Specula Laws: Image, Aesthetic and Common Law' 2 Law and Critique 233

Gordon, R W (1984) 'Critical Legal Histories' 36 *Stanford Law Review* 57–125

Gordon, W M (1987) 'The Wrongs and Rights of Vesting' 32 *Journal of the Law Society of Scotland* 218

Greenawalt, K (1987) *Conflicts of Law and Morality* Oxford, Clarendon Press

Griffith, J (1997) *The Politics of the Judiciary* (5th edn) London, Fontana

Grigg-Spall, I and Ireland, P (1992) *The Critical Lawyers' Handbook* London, Pluto

Grotius, H (1925 edn) *De Jure Belli ac Pacis* (translated F W Kelsey) Oxford, Clarendon Press

Guest, S (1991) *Ronald Dworkin* (2nd edn, 1997) Edinburgh, Edinburgh University Press

Guest, S (ed) (1996) *Positivism Today* Aldershot, Dartmouth

Guyer, P (1996) *Kant and the Experience of Freedom* Cambridge, Cambridge University Press

Guyer, P (1997) *Kant and the Claims of Taste* Cambridge, Cambridge University Press

Habermas, J (1984) *The Theory of Communicative Action, Vol 1: Reason and the Rationalization of Society* Boston, Beacon

Habermas, J (1985) 'Law as Medium and Institution' in G Teubner (ed) *Dilemmas of Law in the Welfare State*, 203–220 Berlin, de Gruyter

Habermas, J (1987a) *The Philosophical Discourse of Modernity* Cambridge, Polity

Habermas, J (1987b) *The Theory of Communicative Action, Vol 2: Lifeworld and System - A Critique of Functional Reason* Boston, Beacon

Habermas, J (1989) 'Taking Aim at the Heart of the Present' in his *The New Conservatism: Cultural Criticism and the Historians' Debate*, Ch 7 Cambridge, Mass, MIT Press

Habermas, J (1996a) 'Modernity: an Unfinished Project' in M P d'Entreves and S Benhabib (eds) *Habermas and the Unfinished Project of Modernity*, 38–55 Cambridge, Polity

Habermas, J (1996b) *Between Facts and Norms: Contributions to a Discourse Theory of Law and Democracy* (translated by W Rehg) Oxford, Polity

Hacker, P M S and Raz, J (eds) (1997) *Law, Morality, and Society: Essays in Honour of H.L.A. Hart* Oxford, Clarendon Press

Harris, A (1990) 'Race and Essentialism in Feminist Legal Theory' 42 *Stanford Law Review* 581–616

Harris, A (1999) 'Building Theory, Building Community' 8 *Social and Legal Studies* 313–325

Harris, J W (1971) 'When and Why Does the Grundnorm Change?' 29 *Cambridge Law Journal* 103–133

Hart, H L A (1954) 'Definition and Theory in Jurisprudence' 70 *Law Quarterly Review* 37–60. (Also in Hart, H L A 1983, Essay 1)

Hart, H L A (1958) 'Positivism and the Separation of Law and Morals' 71 *Harvard Law Review* 593–629. (Also in Hart, H L A 1983, Essay 2)

Hart, H L A and Honoré, A M (1959) *Causation in the Law* Oxford, Clarendon Press

Hart, H L A (1961) *The Concept of Law* Oxford, Clarendon Press

Hart, H L A (1963a) *Law, Liberty and Morality* Oxford, Oxford University Press

Hart, H L A (1963b) 'Kelsen Visited' 10 *UCLA Law Review* 709–728. (Also in Hart, H L A 1983, Essay 14)

Hart, H L A (1964a) *The Morality of the Criminal Law* Jerusalem, Magnes Press

Hart, H L A (1964b) 'Bentham and Beccaria' in Hart, H L A 1982a, Ch II

Hart, H L A (1968) *Punishment and Responsibility: Essays in the Philosophy of Law* Oxford, Clarendon Press

Hart, H L A (1973) 'The Demystification of the Law' in Hart, H L A 1982a, Ch I

Hart, H L A (1982a) *Essays on Bentham: Jurisprudence and Political Theory* Oxford, Clarendon Press

Hart, H L A (1982b) 'Legal Duty and Obligation' in Hart, H L A 1982a, Ch VI

Hart, H L A (1982c) 'Legal Rights' in Hart, H L A 1982a, Ch VII. (Originally published as 'Bentham on Legal Rights' in A W B Simpson (ed) *Oxford Essays in Jurisprudence* Ch 7 (Second Series, Oxford, Oxford University Press, 1973))

Hart, H L A (1983) *Essays in Jurisprudence and Philosophy* Oxford, Clarendon Press

Hart, H L A (1994) *The Concept of Law* (2nd edn) Oxford, Clarendon Press

Hartney (1991) 'Introduction' to Kelsen 1991

Hegel, G W F (1942) *The Philosophy of Right* (translated by T M Knox) Oxford: Clarendon Press

Henrich, D (1992) 'Kant's Explanation of Aesthetic Judgement' in *Aesthetic Judgement and the Moral Image of the World* 29–56 Stanford, Stanford University Press

Herman, B (1993) *The Practice of Moral Judgement* Cambridge, Mass, Harvard University Press

Himma, E (2002) 'Inclusive Legal Positivism' in J Coleman and S Shapiro (eds) 125–165

Hirst, P (1994) 'The Concept of Punishment' in A Duff and D Garland (eds) 264–280

Hirst, P Q (1975) 'Marx and Engels on Law, Crime and Morality' in I Taylor, P Walton and J Young (eds) *Critical Criminology* London, Routledge

Hobbes, T (1651) *Leviathan* (reprint of original, M.Oakeshott edn, 1960) Oxford, Basil Blackwell

Höffe, O (1994) *Immanuel Kant* Albany, State University of New York

Hohfeld, W N (1923) *Fundamental Legal Conceptions: as applied in judicial reasoning* (ed W W Cook, New Haven, Yale University Press). (Originally published in (1913) 23 *Yale Law Journal* 16)

Honneth, A (1995) 'The Other of Justice: Jurgen Habermas and the Ethical Challenge of Postmodernism' in S K White (ed) Ch.6 (1995)

Honore, A M (1960) 'Rights of Exclusion and Immunities against Divesting' 34 *Tulane Law Review* 453–468

Horwitz, M (1977) *The Transformation of American Law, 1780–1860* Cambridge, Harvard University Press

Howarth, D (1992) 'Making Sense out of Nonsense' in H Gross and R Harrison (eds), *Jurisprudence: Cambridge Essays*, 29–53 Oxford, Clarendon Press

Hudson, B (1993) *Penal Policy and Social Justice* Basingstoke, MacMillan

Hudson, W D (ed) (1969) *The Is-Ought Question* London, MacMillan

Hudson, W D (1970) *Modern Moral Philosophy* London, MacMillan

Hume, D (1888) *A Treatise of Human Nature* Selby-Bigge edn, Oxford, Clarendon Press

Hunt, A (1978) *The Sociological Movement in Law* London, Macmillan

Hunt, A (ed) (1991) *Reading Dworkin Critically* New York, Oxford, Berg

Hunt, A (1993) *Explorations in Law and Society: Towards a Constitutive Theory of Law* London, Routledge

Hunt, A and Wickham, G (1994) *Foucault and Law* London, Pluto

Hutchinson, A C (1988) *Dwelling on the Threshold* Toronto, Carswell

Hutchinson, A C (ed) (1989) *Critical Legal Studies* New Jersey, Rowman & Littlefield

Irigaray, L (1994) *Thinking the Difference: For a Peaceful Revolution* (translated by Karin Montin London, Athlone Press

Jackson, E (2001) *Regulating Reproduction: Law, Technology and Autonomy* Oxford, Hart Publishing

Johnson, P E (1984) 'Do You Sincerely Want to Be Radical?' 36 *Stanford Law Review* 247–291

Jolls, C, Sunstein, C R and Thayer, R (1998) 'A Behavioral Approach to Law and Economics' 50 *Stanford Law Review* 1471–1550

Kairys, D (ed) (1990) *The Politics of Law: A Progressive Critique* New York, Pantheon

Kant, I (1788/1956) *Critique of Practical Reason and Other Writings in Moral Philosophy* (translated by L W Beck) New York, Macmillan

Kant, I (1787/1964) *The Critique of Pure Reason* (2nd edn translated by N K Smith) London, Macmillan

Kant, I (1965) *The Metaphysical Elements of Justice* (translated by J Ladd) London, Collier Macmillan

Kant, I (1987) *Critique of Judgement* (translated by W S Pluhar) Indianapolis, Hackett

Kant, I (1996a) Critique of Pure Reason (translated by W S Pluhar) Indianapolis, Hackett

Kant, I (1996b) *Practical Philosophy* (Mary J Gregor ed) Cambridge, Cambridge University Press

Kapur, R (1999) '"A Love Song to Our Mongrel Selves": Hybridity, Sexuality and the Law' 8 *Social and Legal Studies* 353–68

Kelly, J M (1992) *A Short History of Western Legal Theory* Oxford, Clarendon Press

Kelman, M (1981) 'Interpretive Construction in the Substantive Criminal Law' 33 *Stanford Law Review* 591–673

Kelman, M (1984) 'Trashing' 36 *Stanford Law Review* 293–348

Kelman, M (1987) *A Guide to Critical Legal Studies* Cambridge, Mass, Harvard University Press

Kelsen, H (1934/1992) *Introduction to the Problems of Legal Theory* (translated by B L and S L Paulson) New York, Oxford University Press

Kelsen, H (1945/1961) *General Theory of Law and State* (translated by A Wedberg) New York, Russell & Russell

Kelsen, H (1957a) *What is Justice? Collected Essays of Hans Kelsen* California, University of California Press

Kelsen, H (1957b) 'The Pure Theory of Law and Analytical Jurisprudence' in *What is Justice?* 226–287

Kelsen, H (1957c) 'A "Dynamic" Theory of Natural Law' in *What is Justice?* 174–197

Kelsen, H (1965) 'Professor Stone and the Pure Theory of Law' 17 *Stanford Law Review* 1128–1157

Kelsen, H (1966a) *General Principles of International Law* (2nd edn) New York, Holt, Rinehart and Winston

Kelsen, H (1966b) 'On the Pure Theory of Law' 1 *Israel Law Review* 1–7

Kelsen, H (1967) *Pure Theory of Law* (2nd edn, translated by M Knight) California, University of California Press

Kelsen, H (1991a) *General Theory of Norms* (translated by M Hartney) Oxford, Clarendon Press

Kelsen, H (1991b) 'Is and Ought in Kant's Philosophy' in Kelsen 1991a, Ch 18

Kelsen, H (1991c) 'Logical Problems about Grounding the Validity of Norms' in Kelsen 1991a, Ch59

Kennedy, D (1979) 'The Structure of Blackstone's Commentaries' 28 *Buffalo Law Review* 209–382

Kennedy, D (1981) 'Rebels from Principle: Changing the Corporate Law Firm From Within' 33 *Harvard Law School Bulletin* 36–40

Kennedy, D (1983) *Legal Education and the Reproduction of Hierarchy: A Polemic Against the System* Cambridge, Mass, Afar

Kennedy, D (1998) 'Law and Economics from the perspective of critical legal studies', in P Newman (ed) (1998) vol 2, 465–73

King, M (1993) 'The Truth about Autopoiesis' 20 *Journal of Law and Society* 218–236

King, M (2001) 'The Construction and Demolition of the Luhmann Heresy' in J Priban and D Nelken (eds), Ch 6 Aldershot, Ashgate/Dartmouth

Klare, K E (1978) 'Judicial Deradicalization of the Wagner Act and the Origins of Modern Legal Consciousness' 62 *Minnesota Law Review* 265–339

Kocourek, A (1928) *Jural Relations* (2nd edn) Indianapolis, Bobbs-Merrill

Kramer, M H (1988) 'The Rule of Misrecognition in the Hart of Jurisprudence' 8 *Oxford Journal of Legal Studies* 401–433

Kramer, M H (1999) *In Defense of Legal Positivism: Law Without Trimmings* Oxford, Oxford University Press

Kronman, A T (1983) *Max Weber* London, Arnold

Lacan, J (1977) *Écrits* (translated by A Sheridan) London, Routledge/Tavistock

Lacan, J (1979) *The Four Fundamental Concepts of Psychoanalysis* (translated by A Sheridan) London, Penguin

Lacey, N (1988) *State Punishment* London, Routledge

Lacey, N (1993) 'Theory into Practice: Pornography and the Public/Private Dichotomy' in A Bottomley and J Conaghan (eds) (1993), 93–113

Lacey, N (1998) *Unspeakable Subjects* Oxford, Hart Publishing

Lacey, N (2002) 'Review of Duff, *Punishment, Communication and Community*' 111 Mind 392–396

Lacey, N and Wells, C (1998) *Reconstructing Criminal Law* (2nd edn) London, Weidenfeld & Nicolson

Laski, H (1950) *A Grammar of Politics* (5th edn) London, Allen and Unwin

Leff, A (1974) 'Economic Analysis of Law: Some Realism about Nominalism' 60 *Virginia Law Review* 451–492

Lempert, R (1987) 'The Autonomy of Law: Two Visions Compared' in G Teubner (ed) 1987c, 152–190

Levinas, E (1969) *Totality and Infinity: An Essay on Exteriority* (translated by A Lingis) Pittsburgh, Duquesne University Press

Levinas, E (1993) *Outside the Subject* (translated by M B Smith) Stanford, Stanford University Press

Llewellyn, K (1930) *The Bramble Bush* New York, Oceana

Llewellyn, K (1931) 'Some Realism about Realism – Responding to Dean Pound' 44 *Harvard Law Review* 1222–1256, reprinted in K Llewellyn *Jurisprudence* (Chicago, University of Chicago Press, 1962) 42

Locke, J (1640) *The Second Treatise of Civil Government* (J W Gough edn 1948) Oxford, Basil Blackwell

Luhmann, N (1987) 'Closure and Openness: On Reality in the World of Law' in G Teubner (1987c), 335–348

Luhmann, N (1988) 'The Third Question: The Creative Use of Paradoxes in Law and Legal History' 15 *Journal of Law and Society* 153–165

Luhmann, N (1989) 'Law as a Social System' 83 *Northwestern University Law Review* 136–150

Luhmann, N (1992a) 'The Coding of the Legal System' in G Teubner and A Febbrajo (eds) (1992), 145–185

Luhmann, N (1992b) *Social Systems* Palo Alto, Ca, Stanford University Press

Lukes, S (1973) *Emile Durkheim* London, Penguin

Lukes, S and Scull, A (eds) (1983) *Durkheim and the Law* Oxford, Martin Robertson

Lyons, D (1984) *Ethics and the Rule of Law* Cambridge, Cambridge University Press

Lyotard, J F (1984) *The Postmodern Condition: A Report on Knowledge* Manchester, Manchester University Press

Lyotard, J F (1985) *Just Gaming* (translated by V Godzich) Manchester, Manchester University Press

Lyotard, J F (1988a) *The Differend: Phrases in Dispute* (translated by G Van den Abeele) Manchester, Manchester University Press

Lyotard, J F (1988b) 'Sensus Communis' 11 Paragraph 1–23

MacCormick, N (1977) 'Rights in Legislation' in P Hacker and J Raz (eds) (1977), Ch 11

MacCormick, N (1978) *Legal Reasoning and Legal Theory* Oxford, Clarendon Press

MacCormick, N (1981) *H.L.A.Hart* London, Edward Arnold

MacCormick, N (1999) *Questioning Sovereignty: law, state, and nation in the European Commonwealth* Oxford, Oxford University Press

MacIntyre, A (1981) *After Virtue: a study in moral theory* London, Duckworth

MacKinnon, C (1983) 'Feminism, Marxism, Method and the State: Towards Feminist Jurisprudence' 8 *Signs: Journal of Women in Culture and Society* 635–58

MacKinnon, C (1987) *Feminism Unmodifed* (Cambridge, Mass, Harvard University Press

MacKinnon, C (1989) *Toward a Feminist Theory of the State* Cambridge, Mass, Harvard University Press

McDowell, John (1984) 'Wittgenstein on Following a Rule' 58 *Synthese* 325–63

Magee, B (1982) *Men of Ideas* Oxford, Oxford University Press

Marcuse, H (1986 edn) *One-Dimensional Man. Studies in the Ideology of Advance Industrial Society* London, Ark, originally published 1964

Marmor, A (1992) *Interpretation and Legal Theory* Oxford, Clarendon Press

Marmor, A (ed) (1995) *Law and Interpretation* Oxford, Clarendon Press

Marmor, A (1998) 'Legal Conventionalism' 4 *Legal Theory* 509–531

Marmor, A (2002) 'Exclusive Legal Positivism' in J Coleman and S Shapiro (eds) (2002) 104–124

Marx, K (1970 edn) 'Preface to *A Contribution to the Critique of Political Economy*' in *Marx and Engels Selected Works* London, Lawrence and Wishart

Marx, K (1976 edn) *Capital* Vol 1 London, Penguin

Marx, K and Engels, F (1998 edn) *The Communist Manifesto* London, Verso

Mathiesen, T (1990) *Prison on Trial* London, Sage

Maturana, H R and Varela, F J (1980) *Autopoiesis and Cognition* Boston, Reidel

Maturana, H R and Varela, F J (1988) *Tree of Knowledge: Biological Roots of Human Understanding* Boston, Shambhala

McCloskey, H J (1965) 'A Non-Utilitarian Approach to Punishment' 8 *Inquiry* 249–63

McCoubrey, H (1997) *The Obligation to Obey in Legal Theory* Aldershot, Dartmouth

Menand, L (1986) 'Radicalism for Yuppies' *The New Republic* 17 March 1986

Miliband, R (1969) *The State in Capitalist Society* London, Weidenfeld

Mill, J S (1869) *The Subjection of Women* (in J Gray (edn) *On Liberty and Other Essays*) Oxford, Oxford University Press, 1998

Moles, R (1987) *Definition and Rule in Legal Theory: A Reassessment of H.L.A. Hart and the Positivist Tradition* Oxford, Basil Blackwell

Moore, G E (1903) *Principia Ethica* Cambridge, Cambridge University Press

Morin, E (1977) *La Méthode: la Nature de la Nature* Paris, Seuil

Morrison, W L (1958) 'Some Myths about Positivism' 68 *Yale Law Journal* 212–233

Morrison, W L (1982) *John Austin* London, Edward Arnold

Mulhall, S and Swift, A (1996) *Liberals and Communitarians* (2nd edn) Oxford, Blackwell

Murphy, J G (1973) 'Marxism and Retribution' 2 *Philosophy and Public Affairs* 217–243

Naffine, N (1990) *Law and the Sexes: Explorations in Feminist Jurisprudence* Allen and Unwin

Naffine, N (2002) 'In Praise of Legal Feminism' 22 *Legal Studies* 71–101

Nedelsky, J (1989) 'Reconceiving Autonomy: Sources, Thoughts and Possibilities' 1 *Yale Journal of Law and Feminism* 1–36

Nelken, D (1998) 'Blinding Insights? The Limits of a Reflexive Sociology of Law' 25 *Journal of Law and Society* 407–426

Newman, P (ed) (1998) *The New Palgrave Dictionary of Economics and the Law* London, MacMillan, in 3 volumes

Nobles, R and Schiff, D (2000) *Understanding Miscarriages of Justice: Law, the Media, and the Inevitability of Crisis* Oxford, Oxford University Press

Northrop, F C S (1959) *The Complexity of Legal and Ethical Experience* Boston, Little, Brown & Co

Nowell-Smith, P H (1954) *Ethics* Harmondsworth, Penguin

Nozick, R (1974) *Anarchy, State and Utopia* Oxford, Blackwell

Nussbaum, M (1999) *Sex and Social Justice* Oxford, Oxford University Press

O'Donovan, K (1985) *Sexual Divisions in Law* London, Weidenfeld and Nicholson

Okin, S M (1991) *Justice, Gender and the Family* New York, Basic Books

Okin, S M (2002) '"Mistresses of Their Own Destiny": Group Rights, Gender, and Realistic Rights of Exit' 112 *Ethics* 205–230

Olivecrona, K (1939) *Law as Fact* Copenhagen, Einar Munksgaard

Olivecrona, K (1953) 'Editor's Preface' to A Hagerstrom *Inquiries into the Nature of Law and Morals* Almqvist & Wiksells, Uppsala

Olsen, F (1990) 'Feminism and Critical Legal Theory: An American Perspective' 18 *International Journal of the Sociology of Law* 199–215

Olsen, F (ed) (1995) *Feminist Legal Theory I: Foundations and Outlooks* Aldershot, Dartmouth

Outhwaite, W (1994) *Habermas: A Critical Introduction* Oxford, Polity

Palmer, J and Pearce, F (1983) 'Legal discourse and state power: Foucault and the juridical relation' 11 *International Journal of the Sociology of Law* 361–383

Parekh, B (1973) *Bentham's Political Thought* London, Croom Helm

Parkin, F (1982) *Max Weber* London, Tavistock

Parsons, T (1951) *The Social System* New York, The Free Press

Parsons, T (1971) *The System of Modern Societies* Englewood Cliffs, NJ, Prentice-Hall

Pasquino, P (1991) 'Theatricum Politicum: The Genealogy of Capital – Police and the State of Prosperity' in G Burchell, C Gordon and P Miller (eds) (1991) 105–118

Paulson, S L (1992) 'The Neo-Kantian Dimension of Kelsen's Pure Theory of Law' 12 *Oxford Journal of Legal Studies* 311–332

Paulson, S L and Paulson, B L (eds) (1998) *Normativity and Norms: Critical Perspectives on Kelsenian Themes* Oxford, Clarendon Press

Penner, J E (1997a) 'Review of N. Stavropoulos, *Objectivity in Law*' 60 *Modern Law Review* 747–752

Penner, J E (1997b) 'Hohfeldian Use-Rights in Property' in J W Harris (ed) *Property Problems: From Genes to Pension Funds* 164–174 London, Kluwer

Penner, J E (1997c) 'The Analysis of Rights' 10 *Ratio Juris* 300–315

Penner J E (1997d) *The Idea of Property in Law* Oxford, Clarendon Press

Penner J E (2002) 'Legal Reasoning and the Authority of Law' in S Paulson, S Pogge, T and L Meyer (eds) *Rights, Culture, and the Law: Essays after Joseph Raz* Oxford, Oxford University Press, forthcoming 2002

Pennock, J R and Chapman, J W (eds) (1970) *Political and Legal Obligation* Nomos XII, New York, Atherton Press

Phillips, A (1999) *Which Equalities Matter?* Cambridge, Polity Press

Phillips, P (1980) *Marx and Engels on Law and Laws* Oxford, Martin Robertson

Pinker, S (1995) *The Language Instinct* London, Penguin

Plato (1959 edn) *The Last Days of Socrates* (translated by H Tredennick) Harmondsworth, Penguin

Plato (1970 edn) *The Laws of Plato* (translated by T J Saunders) Harmondsworth, Penguin

Polinsky, A (1974) 'Economic Analysis as a Potentially Defective Product: a Buyer's Guide to Posner's Economic Analysis of Law' 87 *Harvard Law Review* 1655–1681

Polinsky, A (1981) 'A Tentative Assessment' in Burrows and Veljanovski 1981, Ch 6

Polinsky, A (1989) *An Introduction to Law and Economics* (2nd edn) Boston, Little Brown

Porter, R (2000) *Enlightenment* London, Penguin

Posner, R (1986) *The Economic Analysis of Law* (3rd edn) Boston, Little Brown & Co

Posner, R (1990) *The Problems of Jurisprudence* Cambridge, Mass, Harvard University Press

Posner, R (1998) *Economic Analysis of Law* (5th edn) New York, Aspen

Posner, R (2001) *Frontiers of Legal Theory* Cambridge, Mass, Harvard University Press

Poulantzas, N (1978) *State, Power, Socialism* London, New Left Books

Pound, R (1954) *An Introduction to the Philosophy of Law* (Revised edn) New Haven, Yale University Press

Pound, R (1959) *Jurisprudence Vol.IV* St Paul, Minnesota, West Publishing

Primoratz, I (1987) 'The Middle Way in the Philosophy of Punishment' in R Gavison (ed) *Issues in Contemporary Legal Philosophy* 193–220 Oxford, Clarendon Press, 1987

Radin, M (1938) 'A Restatement of Hohfeld' 51 *Harvard Law Review* 1141–1164

Rawls, J (1973) *A Theory of Justice* (Oxford, Oxford University Press, first published 1971)

Rawls, J (1993) *Political Liberalism* New York, Columbia University Press

Rawls, J (2001) *Justice as Fairness: a restatement* (E Kelly ed) Cambridge, Mass, Harvard University Press

Raz, J (1972) 'Legal Principles and the Limits of Law' 81 *Yale Law Journal* 823–854

Raz, J (1975) *Practical Reasons and Norms* London, Hutchinson

Raz, J (1979a) *The Authority of Law: essays on law and morality* Oxford, Clarendon Press

Raz, J (1979b) 'Kelsen's Theory of the Basic Norm' in Raz (1979a), Ch 7

Raz, J (1980) *The Concept of a Legal System* (2nd edn) Oxford, Clarendon Press

Raz, J (1981) 'The Purity of the Pure Theory' 138 *Revue Internationale de Philosophie* 441 (Also in R Tur and W Twining (eds) (1986), Ch 3)

Raz, J (1984) 'On the Nature of Rights' 93 *Mind* 194–214

Raz, J (1986) 'Dworkin: A New Link in the Chain' 74 *California Law Review* 1103–1119

Raz, J (1988) *The Morality of Freedom* Oxford, Clarendon Press

Raz, J (1994) *Ethics in the Public Domain* Oxford, Clarendon Press

Raz, J (1998) 'Two Views of the Nature of the Theory of Law' 4 *Legal Theory* 249–282

Raz, J (1999a) *Practical Reason and Norms* Oxford, Oxford University Press

Raz, J (1999b) *Engaging Reason* Oxford, Oxford University Press

Rehg, W (1994) *Insight and Solidarity: A Study in the Discourse Ethics of Jurgen Habermas* Berkeley, University of California Press

Reiman, J H (1990) *Justice and Modern Moral Philosophy* New Haven, Yale University Press

Reiner, R (1984) 'Crime, law and deviance: The Durkheim Legacy' in S Fenton (ed) (1984), 175–201

Robinson, CD and Scaglion, R (1987) 'The Origin and Evolution of the Police Function in Society' 21 *Law and Society Review* 109–53

Rogers, B (1999) 'John Rawls' 42 *Prospect*, June, 50–55

Rose, N and Miller, P (1992) 'Political power beyond the state: problematics of government' 43(2) British Journal of Sociology 173–205

Rose, N (1994) 'Expertise and the Government of Conduct' 14 Studies in Law, Politics and Society 359–397

Ross, A (1974) *On Law and Justice* London, Stevens and Sons

Ross, H (2001a) *Law as a Social Institution* Oxford, Hart Publishing

Ross, H (2001b) 'Social Power and the Hohfeldian Relation' 10(1) *Nottingham Law Journal* 47–63

Rousseau, J J (1762) *The Social Contract* (translated by G D H Cole, 1973 edn) London, Campbell

Salter, M (1997) 'Habermas's new Contribution to Legal Scholarship' 24 *Journal of Law and Society* 285–305

Sandel, M (1982) *Liberalism and the Limits of Justice* Cambridge, Cambridge University Press

Sandel, M (1984) 'The Procedural Republic and the Unencumbered Self' 12 *Political Theory* 81–96

Schauer, F (1991) *Playing by the Rules* Oxford, Clarendon Press

Scheer, R (1969) *Eldridge Cleaver, Post Prison Writings and Speeches* London, Cape

Schwartz, R D and Miller, J C (1964) 'Legal Evolution and Societal Complexity' 20 *American Journal of Sociology* 159–169

Shiner, R (1992) *Norm and Nature* Oxford, Clarendon Press

Simmonds, N E (1984) *The Decline of Juridical Reason* Manchester, Manchester University Press

Simmonds, N E (1986) *Central Issues in Jurisprudence* London, Sweet & Maxwell

Simmonds, N E (1987) 'Imperial Visions and Mundane Practices' 46 *Cambridge Law Journal* 465–488

Simmonds, N E (1990) 'Why Conventionalism Does Not Collapse Into Pragmatism' 49 *Cambridge Law Journal* 63–79

Simmonds, N E (2002) *Central Issues in Jurisprudence* (2nd ed) London, Sweet & Maxwell

Simpson, A W B (1964) 'The Analysis of Legal Concepts' 80 *Law Quarterly Review* 535–558

Simpson, A W B (1987) 'The Common Law and Legal Theory' in A W B Simpson *Legal Theory and Legal History* 359–382 London, Hambledon

Singer, J W (1982) 'The Legal Rights Debate in Analytical Jurisprudence from Bentham to Hohfeld' Wisconsin Law Review 975–1059

Singer, J W (1988) 'The Reliance Interest in Property' 40 Stanford Law Review 614–751

Smart, C (1989) *Feminism and the Power of Law* London, Routledge

Smart, J J C and Williams, B (1973) *Utilitarianism – for and against* London, Cambridge University Press

Smith, Adam (1976) *An Enquiry into the Wealth of Nations* (Campbell and Skinner ed) Oxford, Oxford University Press

Smith, M B E (1973) 'Is There a Prima Facie Obligation to Obey the Law?' 82 *Yale Law Journal* 950–976

Spitzer, S (1975) 'Punishment and Social Organisation' 9 *Law and Society Review* 613–637

Sprigge, T L S (1965) 'A Utilitarian Reply to Dr. McCloskey' 8 *Inquiry* 264–291

Stavrakakis, Y (1999) *Lacan and the Political* London, Routledge

Stavropoulos, N (1996) *Objectivity in Law* Oxford, Clarendon Press

Stavropoulos, N (2001) 'Hart's Semantics' in Jules Coleman (ed) *Hart's Postscript* 59–98 Oxford, Oxford University Press

Stewart, I (1986) 'Kelsen and the Exegetical Tradition' in R Tur and W Twining (eds) (1986), Ch 6

Stokes, M (1986) 'Company Law and Legal Theory' in W Twining (ed) *Legal Theory and Common Law* 155–183 Oxford, Blackwell

Stone, J (1950) *The Province and Function of Law* Sydney, Maitland

Stone, J (1964) *Legal System and Lawyers' Reasonings* London, Stevens

Stone, M (1995) 'Focusing the Law' in A Marmor (ed) 31–96

Sullivan, R (1989) *Immanuel Kant's Moral Theory* Cambridge, Cambridge University Press

Sullivan, R (1994) *An Introduction to Kant's Ethics* Cambridge, Cambridge University Press

Summers, R S (1982) *Instrumentalism and American Legal Theory* Ithaca, Cornell University Press

Summers, R S (1984) *Lon L. Fuller* London, Edward Arnold

Sunstein, C R (1996) *Legal Reasoning and Political Conflict* New York, Oxford University Press

Tadros, V (1998) 'Between Governance and Discipline: The Law and Michel Foucault' 18 *Oxford Journal of Legal Studies* 75–103

Taylor, C (1989) *Sources of the Self: The Making of Modern Identity* Cambridge, Cambridge University Press

Taylor, I, Walton, P and Young, J (1973) *The New Criminology* London, Routledge

Teubner, G (ed) (1987a) *Juridification of Social Spheres* Berlin, de Gruyter

Teubner, G (1987b) 'Juridification – Concepts, Aspects, Limits, Solutions' in G Teubner, (ed) (1987a) 3–48

Teubner, G (ed) (1987c) *Autopoietic Law: A New Approach to Law and Society* Berlin, de Gruyter

Teubner, G (ed) (1988) *Dilemmas of Law in the Welfare State* Berlin, de Gruyter

Teubner, G (1989) 'How the Law Thinks: Toward a Constructivist Epistemology of Law' 23 *Law and Society Review* 727–757

Teubner, G and Febbrajo, A (eds) (1992) *State, Law, and Economy as Autopoietic Systems: Regulation and Autonomy in a New Perspective* European Yearbook in the Sociology of Law Milan, Giuffre

Teubner, G (1993) *Law as an Autopoietic System* Oxford, Blackwell

Teubner, G (1997) 'Altera pars audiatur: Law in the Collision of Discourses' in Rawlings, R (ed) *Law, Society and Economy* 149–176 Oxford, Oxford University Press

Thompson, E P (1975) *Whigs and Hunters* London, Penguin

Thoreau, H (1849) 'On the Duty of Civil Disobedience' (in H Bedau (ed) 1990, ch 2)

Trebilcock, M (1976) 'The doctrine of inequality of bargaining power: Post-Benthamite Economics in the House of Lords' 26 *University of Toronto Law Journal* 359–385

Trubek, D (1972) 'Max Weber on Law and the Rise of Capitalism' *Wisconsin Law Review* 720–753

Turner, B (1981) *For Weber* London, Routledge

Turner, S (ed) (2000) *The Cambridge Companion to Weber* Cambridge, Cambridge University Press

Turner, S P and Factor, R A (1994) *Max Weber: The Lawyer As Social Thinker* London, Routledge

Tur, R and Twining, W (eds) (1986) *Essays on Kelsen* Oxford, Clarendon Press

Tutu, D (1999) *No Future Without Forgiveness* London, Rider Books

Twining, W (1985) *Karl Llewellyn and the Realist Movement* London, Weidenfeld

Twining, W (1996) 'General and Particular Jurisprudence – Three Chapters in a Story' in S Guest (ed) Ch 8 (1996)

Unger, R M (1983) 'The Critical Legal Studies Movement' 96 Harvard Law Review 561–675

Unger, R M (1987) False Necessity: Anit-Necessitarian Social Theory in the Service of Radical Democracy Cambridge, Cambridge University Press

Unger, R M (1996) 'Legal Analysis as Institutional Imagination' 59 *Modern Law Review* 1–23

Veljanovski, C G (1982) *The New Law-and-Economics: a research review* Oxford, Centre for Socio-Legal Studies

Vincent, A (1993) 'Marx and Law' 20 *Journal of Law and Society* 371–397

Volpp, L (1994) '"(Mis)identifying Culture": Asian Women and the "Cultural Defence"' 17 *Harvard Women's Law Journal* 57–101

Von Hirsch, A (1993) *Censure and Sanctions* Oxford, Clarendon Press

Von Hirsch, A and Jareborg, N (1991) 'Guaging Criminal Harm: A Living-Standard Analysis' 11 *Oxford Journal of Legal Studies* 1–38

Walzer, M (1985) *Spheres of Justice: A defence of pluralism and equality* Oxford, Blackwell

Wasserstrom, R A (1963) 'The Obligation to Obey the Law' 10 *UCLA Law Review* 780–807

Weber, M (1976 edn) *The Protestant Ethic and the Spirit of Capitalism* London, Unwin

Weber, M (1978 edn) *Economy and Society*, Vol 1 Berkeley, University of California Press

Wechsler, H (1959) 'Toward Neutral Principles of Constitutional Law' 73 *Harvard Law Review* 1–35

West, R (1988) 'Jurisprudence and Gender' 55 *University of Chicago Law Review* 1. Also in K Bartlett and R Kennedy (eds) *Feminist Legal Theory: Readings in Law and Gender* 201–34 (Westview, 1991)

Wheen, F (1999) *Karl Marx* London, Fourth Estate

White, S K (ed) (1995) *The Cambridge Companion to Habermas* Cambridge, Cambridge University Press

Wiethölter, R (1989) 'Procedularization of the Category of Law' in Joerges, C and Trubek, D (eds) *Critical Legal Thought: An American-German Debate* Baden-Baden, Nomos 501

Williams, B (1985) *Ethics and the Limits of Philosophy* London, Fontana

Williams, G (ed) (1957) *Salmond on Jurisprudence* (11th ed) London, Sweet & Maxwell

Williams, P (1991) *The Alchemy of Race and Rights* Cambridge, Mass, Harvard UP

Williamson, O E (1985) *The Economic Institutions of Capitalism* New York, The Free Press

Wilson, A (1986) 'Is Kelsen Really a Kantian?' in R Tur and W Twining (eds) (1986) Ch 1

Wittgenstein, L (1958) *Philosophical Investigations* (translated by G E M Anscombe) Oxford, Blackwell

Wollstonecraft, M (1792) *A Vindication of the Rights of Woman* London, Penguin Classic, 1985

Woozley, A (1979) *Law and Obedience: the arguments of Plato's Crito* London, Duckworth

Young, I (1990) *Justice and the Politics of Difference* Princeton, NJ, Princeton University Press

Zedner, L (1994) 'Reparation and Retribution: Are They Reconcilable?' 57 *Modern Law Review* 228–250

Zinn, H (1968) *Democracy and Disobedience: Nine Fallacies on Law and Order* New York, Vintage Books

Zwieback, B (1975) *Civility and Disobedience* Cambridge, Cambridge University Press

Index